Advantage series

Microsoft® Office System 2003®

Glen J. **Coulthard**
Okanagan University College

Sarah Hutchinson **Clifford**

Ann **Miller**
Columbus State Community College

Pat R. **Graves**
Eastern Illinois University

McGraw Hill **Technology Education**

Boston   Burr Ridge, IL   Dubuque, IA   Madison, WI   New York   San Francisco   St. Louis
Bangkok   Bogotá   Caracas   Kuala Lumpur   Lisbon   London   Madrid   Mexico City
Milan   Montreal   New Delhi   Santiago   Seoul   Singapore   Sydney   Taipei   Toronto

The McGraw·Hill Companies

Technology Education

ADVANTAGE SERIES: MICROSOFT® OFFICE SYSTEM 2003

Published by McGraw-Hill Technology Education, an imprint of The McGraw-Hill Companies, Inc., 1221 Avenue of the Americas, New York, NY, 10020. Copyright © 2004, by The McGraw-Hill Companies, Inc. All rights reserved. No part of this publication may be reproduced or distributed in any form or by any means, or stored in a data base or retrieval system, without the prior written consent of The McGraw-Hill Companies, Inc., including, but not limited to, in any network or other electronic storage or transmission, or broadcast for distance learning.

Some ancillaries, including electronic and print components, may not be available to customers outside the United States.

 This book is printed on acid-free paper.

3 4 5 6 7 8 9 0 WEB/WEB 0 9 8 7 6 5

ISBN 0-07-283444-7

Editor-in-chief: Bob Woodbury
Publisher: Brandon Nordin
Sponsoring editor: Marc Chernoff
Developmental editor: Lisa Chin-Johnson
Senior marketing manager: Andy Bernier
Senior project manager: Lori Koetters
Production supervisor: Debra R. Sylvester
Producer, media technology: Mark Molsky
Designer: Adam Rooke
Senior supplement producer: Rose M. Range
Senior digital content specialist: Brian Nacik
Cover design: Andrew Curtis
Cover image: © 2003 Getty Images
Typeface: *10/12 Garamond*
Compositor: *GTS Graphics, Inc.*
Printer: *Webcrafters, Inc.*

Library of Congress Cataloging-in-Publication Data
Office system 2003 / Glen J. Coulthard ... [et al.].
　　p. cm.
　Includes index.
　ISBN 0-07-283444-7
　1. Microsoft Office. 2. Business—Computer programs. I. Coulthard, Glen J.

HF5548.4.M525O3346 2003
005.5—dc22　　　　　　　　　　　　　　　　　　　2003068622

www.mhhe.com/it

McGraw-Hill Technology Education

At **MCGRAW-HILL TECHNOLOGY EDUCATION,** we publish instructional materials for the technology education market, particularly computer instruction in post-secondary education—from introductory courses in traditional four-year universities to continuing education and proprietary schools. McGraw-Hill Technology Education presents a broad range of innovative products—texts, lab manuals, study guides, testing materials, and technology-based training and assessment tools.

We realize that technology has created and will continue to create new mediums for professors and students to use in managing resources and communicating information to one another. McGraw-Hill Technology Education provides the most flexible and complete teaching and learning tools available and offers solutions for the changing world of teaching and learning.

McGraw-Hill Technology Education is dedicated to providing today's instructors and students with the tools that will enable them to successfully navigate the world of Information Technology.

- **McGraw-Hill/Osborne**—This division of The McGraw-Hill Companies is known for its best-selling Internet titles Harley Hahn's *Internet & Web Yellow Pages* and the *Internet Complete Reference*. For more information, visit Osborne at www.osborne.com.

- **Digital Solutions**—Whether you want to teach a class on line or merely to post your "bricks-and-mortar" class syllabus, McGraw-Hill Technical Education is committed to digital publishing solutions. Taking your course on line does not have to be a solitary adventure, nor does it have to be a difficult one. We offer several solutions that will allow you to enjoy all the benefits of online course material.

- **Packaging Options**—For more information about our discount options, contact your McGraw-Hill sales representative at 1-800-338-3987 or visit our Web site at www.mhhe.com/it.

Preface

Goals/Philosophy

The Advantage Series presents the **What, Why,** and **How** of computer application skills to today's students. Each lab manual is based upon an efficient learning model that provides students and faculty with complete coverage of the most powerful software packages available today.

Approach

The Advantage Series builds upon an efficient learning model that provides students and faculty with complete coverage and enhances critical thinking skills. This "problem-solving" approach teaches the What, Why, and How of computer application skills. This approach was further strengthened last year when the lead author of *the Advantage Series,* Glen Coulthard, met with members of the Microsoft Office Team to ensure that all the pedagogical features of the book are compatible with the requirements and standards of Microsoft.

    The Advantage Series introduces the "**Feature-Method-Practice**" layered approach. The *Feature* describes the command and tells the importance of that command. The *Method* shows students how to perform the feature. The *Practice* allows students to apply the feature in a keystroke exercise.

About the Series *The Advantage Series* offers *three levels* of instruction. Each level builds upon the previous level. Following are the three levels of instructions:

> *Brief:* covers the basics of the application, contains four chapters, and is typically 120–190 pages long.

> *Introductory:* includes the Brief Lab manuals plus four additional chapters. The Introductory lab manuals are approximately 300 pages long and prepare students for the *Microsoft Office Specialist Core Exam.*

> *Complete:* includes the Introductory lab manuals plus an additional four chapters of advanced level content. The Complete lab manuals are approximately 600–800 pages in length and prepare students to take the *Microsoft Office Specialist Expert Exam.*

> *Office 2003:* includes the Brief lab manuals for Word, Excel, Access, and PowerPoint, plus three chapters of Integrating with Microsoft Office 2003.

Features of This Book

New and Improved Features:

- An attractive new design that makes it easy for students to follow and succeed with the material.

- An increased number of screenshots enhances visual appeal and helps students successfully complete the Hands-On Exercises.

- More vigorous end-of-chapter contents available on the Web site.

- Updated Case Studies and Hands-On Exercises.

- Better implementation of design elements and shading for "Feature, Method, Practice" areas.

- Chapter Prerequisites

Each lab manual features the following:

- *Learning Objectives:* At the beginning of each chapter, a list of action-oriented objectives is presented detailing what is expected of the students.

- *Prerequisites:* Each chapter begins with a list of prerequisites that identify the skills necessary to complete the modules in that chapter.

- *Chapters:* Each lab manual is divided into chapters.

- *Modules:* Each chapter contains three to five independent modules, requiring approximately 30–45 minutes each to complete. Although we recommend you complete an entire chapter before proceeding, you may skip or rearrange the order of these modules to best suit your learning needs.

- *Case Studies:* Each chapter ends with a Case Study. The student is introduced to a fictitious person or company and their immediate problem or opportunity. Throughout the chapter, students obtain the knowledge and skills necessary to meet the challenges presented in the Case Study. At the end of each chapter, students are asked to solve problems directly related to the Case Study.

- *Feature-Method-Practice:* Each chapter highlights our unique "**Feature-Method-Practice**" layered approach.

The *Feature* layer describes the command or technique and persuades you of its importance and relevance. The *Method* layer shows you how to perform the procedure, and the *Practice* layer lets you apply the feature in a hands-on step-by-step exercise.

- *Instructions:* The numbered step-by-step progression for all hands-on examples and exercises are clearly identified. Students will find it surprisingly easy to follow the logical sequence of keystrokes and mouse clicks and will no longer worry about missing a step.

- *In Addition Boxes:* These content boxes are placed strategically throughout the chapter and provide information on advanced topics that are beyond the scope of the current discussion.

- *Self-Check Question Boxes:* At the end of each module, a brief self-check question appears for students to test their comprehension of the material. Answers to these questions appear in the Appendix.

- *Chapter Review:* The *Command Summary* and *Key Terms* provide an excellent review of the chapter content and prepare students for the short answer, true/false and multiple choice questions at the end of each chapter.

- *Hands-On Exercises:* Each chapter concludes with hands-on exercises that are divided into *Step-by-Step* and *On Your Own* that reflect different levels of difficulty. In the *Step-by-Step* exercises, students are given step-by-step instructions and directions on how to complete a task. However, in the *On Your Own* exercises, students are provided with instructions that allow for greater opportunities to apply the software to a variety of creative problem-solving situations.

- *Appendix: Preparing to Use Microsoft Office.* Each lab manual contains an Appendix that teaches students the fundamentals of using a mouse and a keyboard, illustrates how to interact with a dialog box, and describes the fundamentals of how to use the Office 2003 Help System.

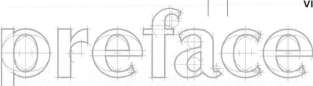

preface

Features of This Lab Manual

Instructions

The numbered step-by-step progressions for all hands-on examples and exercises are clearly identified. Students will find it easy to follow the logical sequence of keystrokes and mouse clicks and will no longer worry about missing a step.

In Addition Boxes

These content boxes are placed strategically throughout the chapter and provide information on topics that are beyond the scope of the current discussion.

Self-Check Question Boxes

At the end of each module, a brief self-check question appears for students to test their comprehension of the material. Answers to these questions appear in the Appendix.

Hands-On

exercises

step by step ▶

1. Creating and Using Range Names

In this exercise, you will practice working with named cell ranges in constructing formulas. To begin, you will use existing labels in the worksheet to define the range names automatically and then paste those names into the worksheet.

1. Open the data file named EX04HE01.

2. Save the workbook as "Departments" to your personal storage location.

3. To begin, name cell B8 "Total" using the Name Box in the Formula bar.

4. Use the existing worksheet labels in A2 through A7 to define range names for the data stored in cells B2 through B7. After choosing the Insert ➡ Name ➡ Create command, your screen should appear similar to the one shown in Figure 4.39.

Figure 4.39

Creating range names

In Addition MAKING EFFICIENT USE OF RANGE NAMES

Range names facilitate the entry of formulas and functions in a worksheet. By using range names in place of cell references, you are less likely to make data-entry errors when constructing complex formulas. For those cells on a worksheet to which you must refer frequently, consider naming the cell ranges immediately. You can always delete, rename, or redefine these range names at a later date.

---

depending on the result, perform one of two calculations. Because the IF function is used in more complex problems, it is covered in Chapter 6 of the Advantage Series' Introductory and Complete editions.

 SelfCheck **4.2** When might you use the Function Arguments dialog box or Insert Function dialog box to enter a function into the worksheet?

4.3 Creating an Embedded Chart

Since the earliest versions of spreadsheet software became available, users have been able to display their numerical data using graphs and charts. Although these graphics were acceptable for in-house business reports and school projects, they often lacked the depth and quality required by professional users. Until now! You can confidently use Excel 2003 to produce visually stunning worksheets and charts that are suitable for electronic business presentations, color print masters, published reports, and Web pages.

Many types of charts are available for presenting your worksheet data to engineers, statisticians, business professionals, and other audiences. Some popular business charts—line charts, column charts, pie

Features of This Lab Manual

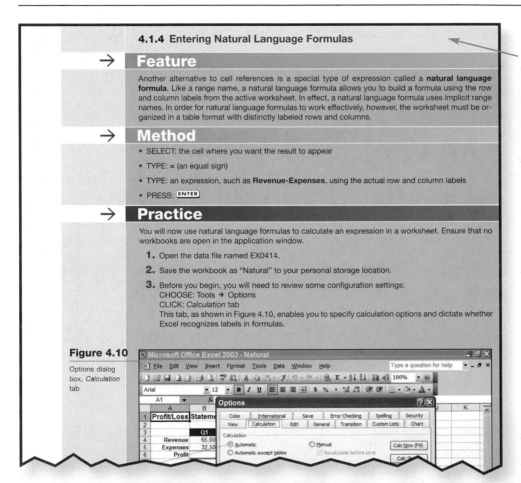

4.1.4 Entering Natural Language Formulas

→ **Feature**

Another alternative to cell references is a special type of expression called a **natural language formula**. Like a range name, a natural language formula allows you to build a formula using the row and column labels from the active worksheet. In effect, a natural language formula uses implicit range names. In order for natural language formulas to work effectively, however, the worksheet must be organized in a table format with distinctly labeled rows and columns.

→ **Method**

- SELECT: the cell where you want the result to appear
- TYPE: = (an equal sign)
- TYPE: an expression, such as **Revenue-Expenses**, using the actual row and column labels
- PRESS: ENTER

→ **Practice**

You will now use natural language formulas to calculate an expression in a worksheet. Ensure that no workbooks are open in the application window.

1. Open the data file named EX0414.

2. Save the workbook as "Natural" to your personal storage location.

3. Before you begin, you will need to review some configuration settings:
   CHOOSE: Tools → Options
   CLICK: *Calculation* tab
   This tab, as shown in Figure 4.10, enables you to specify calculation options and dictate whether Excel recognizes labels in formulas.

Figure 4.10

Options dialog box, *Calculation* tab

Feature-Method-Practice

Each chapter highlights our unique **"Feature-Method-Practice"** layered approach. The *Feature* layer describes the command or technique and persuades you of its importance and relevance. The *Method* layer shows you how to perform the procedure; while the *Practice* layer lets you apply the feature in a hands-on step-by-step exercise.

CaseStudy   INTERIOR FOOTBALL LEAGUE (IFL)

The Interior Football League consists of eight elite football teams in as many communities. The IFL is run by a small group of dedicated volunteers who handle everything from coaching to administration. An ex-player himself, Doug Allen has volunteered for the organization for the past four years. In addition to fundraising, Doug is responsible for keeping records and tracking results for all of the teams in the league.

Shortly after the end of each season, the IFL publishes a newsletter that provides various statistics and other pertinent information about the season. In the past, this newsletter required weeks of effort, followed by days of typing results into a word processor. After enrolling in an Excel 2003 course, Doug now realizes that worksheets and charts can help him to complete his upcoming tasks. Specifically, he

Case Studies

Each chapter ends with a Case Study. Throughout the chapter, students obtain the knowledge and skills necessary to meet the challenges presented in the Case Study. At the end of each chapter, students are asked to solve problems directly related to the Case Study.

Features of This Lab Manual

Chapters

Each lab manual is divided into chapters. Each chapter is composed of three to five modules. Each module is composed of one or more lessons.

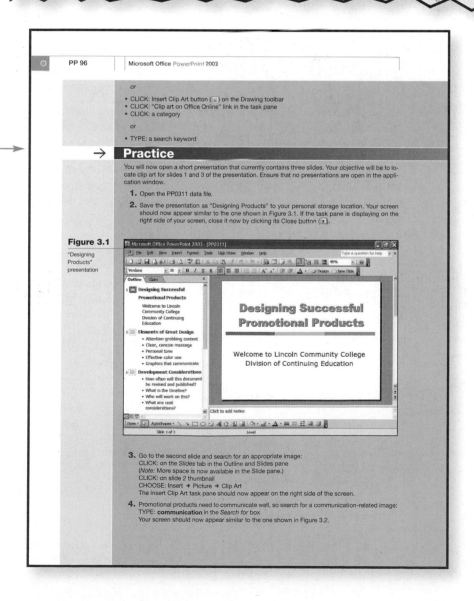

CHAPTER 4: Creating Tables, Charts, and Diagrams

4.1 Creating Tables

    4.1.1 Creating the Table Structure
    4.1.2 Navigating a Table and Entering Data
    4.1.3 Formatting Table Cells
    4.1.4 Sizing and Moving a Table

4.2 Creating Charts for Numeric

Chapter Summary

    Command Summary
    Key Terms

Chapter Quiz

    Short Answer
    True/False
    Multiple Choice

Hands-On Exercises

    Step-by-Step: Creating a Table

New Design

The new *Advantage Series* design offers a more vibrant colored environment overall, including a shaded area where the Feature-Method-Practice and numbered step-by-step instructions helps maintain the focus.

PP 96   Microsoft Office PowerPoint 2003

or

- CLICK: Insert Clip Art button (🖼) on the Drawing toolbar
- CLICK: "Clip art on Office Online" link in the task pane
- CLICK: a category

or

- TYPE: a search keyword

→ Practice

You will now open a short presentation that currently contains three slides. Your objective will be to locate clip art for slides 1 and 3 of the presentation. Ensure that no presentations are open in the application window.

1. Open the PP0311 data file.

2. Save the presentation as "Designing Products" to your personal storage location. Your screen should now appear similar to the one shown in Figure 3.1. If the task pane is displaying on the right side of your screen, close it now by clicking its Close button (✕).

Figure 3.1
"Designing Products" presentation

3. Go to the second slide and search for an appropriate image:
CLICK: on the *Slides* tab in the Outline and Slides pane
(Note: More space is now available in the Slide pane.)
CLICK: on slide 2 thumbnail
CHOOSE: Insert → Picture → Clip Art
The Insert Clip Art task pane should now appear on the right side of the screen.

4. Promotional products need to communicate well, so search for a communication-related image:
TYPE: **communication** in the Search for box
Your screen should now appear similar to the one shown in Figure 3.2.

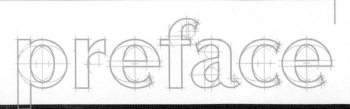

Teaching Resources

We understand that in today's teaching environment, offering a textbook alone is no longer sufficient to meet the needs of the many instructors who use our books. To teach effectively, instructors must have a full complement of supplemental resources to assist them in every facet of teaching from preparing for class, to conducting a lecture, to assessing students' comprehension. *The Advantage Series* offers a fully integrated supplements package and Web site, as described below.

Instructor's Resource Kit

- The **Instructor's Resource Kit** contains a computerized Test Bank, an Instructor's Manual, and PowerPoint Presentation Slides. Features of the Instructor's Resource Kit are described below.

- **Instructor's Manual:** The Instructor's Manual contains a chapter overview, lecture outlines, teaching tips, teaching strategies, pre-tests, post-tests, and additional case problems. Also included are answers to all end-of chapter material.

- **Computerized Test Bank:** The test bank contains more than 1,200 multiple choice, true/false, fill-in-the-blank, short answer, and essay questions. Each question will be accompanied by the correct answer, the level of learning difficulty, and corresponding page references. Our flexible Diploma software allows you to easily generate custom exams.

- **PowerPoint Presentation Slides:** The presentation slides include lecture outlines, text figures, and speaker's notes. Also included are bullets to illustrate key terms and FAQ's.

Online Learning Center/Web Site

Found at www.mhhe.com/cit/advantage2003, this site provides additional learning and instructional tools to enhance the comprehension of the text. The OLC/Web Site is divided into three areas:

> **Information Center:** Contains core information about the text, supplements, and authors.

> **Instructor Center:** Offers instructional materials, downloads, additional exercises, and other relevant links for professors.

> **Student Center:** Contains fifty percent more end-of-chapter questions, hands-on projects, matching exercises, Internet exercises, learning objectives, prerequisites, chapter outlines, and more!

Skills Assessment

SimNet is a simulated assessment and learning tool for either Microsoft® Office XP or Microsoft® Office 2003. SimNet allows students to study MS Office skills and computer concepts and allows professors to test and evaluate students' proficiency within MS Office applications and concepts. Students can practice and study their skills at home or in the school lab using SimNet, which does not require the purchase or installation of Office software.

SimNet includes:

Structured Computer-Based Learning: SimNet offers a complete computer-based learning side that presents each skill or topic in several different modes. *Teach Me* presents the skill or topic using text, graphics, and interactivity. *Show Me* presents the skill using an animation with audio narration to show how the skill is used or implemented. *Let Me Try* allows you to practice the skill in SimNet's robust simulated interface.

Computer Concepts Coverage: SimNet includes coverage of 60 computer concepts in both the Learning and the Assessment side.

The Basics and More: SimNet includes modules of content on:

Word	Windows 2000
Excel	Computer Concepts
Access	Windows XP Professional
PowerPoint	Internet Explorer 6
Office XP Integration	FrontPage
Outlook	

More Assessment Questions: SimNet includes more than 1,400 assessment questions.

Practice or Pre-Tests Questions: SimNet has a separate pool of more than 600 questions for Practice Tests or Pre-Tests.

Comprehensive Exercises: SimNet offers comprehensive exercises for each application. These exercises require the student to use multiple skills to solve one exercise in the simulated environment.

Simulated Interface: The simulated environment in SimNet has been substantially deepened to more realistically simulate the real applications. Students are no longer graded incorrectly just because they chose the wrong sub-menu or dialog box. The student is not graded until he or she does something that immediately invokes an action—as in the real applications!

Digital Solutions to Help You Manage Your Course

- *PageOut:* PageOut is our Course Web Site Development Center, which offers a syllabus page, URL, McGraw-Hill Online Learning Center content, online exercises and quizzes, a grade book, a discussion board, and an area for student Web pages.

Available free of charge with the purchase of any McGraw-Hill Technology Education product, PageOut requires no prior knowledge of HTML or long hours of coding and serves as a way for course coordinators and professors to provide a full-course Web site. PageOut offers a series of templates—simply fill them with your course information and click on one of 16 designs. The process takes under an hour and leaves you with a **professionally designed Web site.** We will even get you started with sample Web sites or will enter your syllabus for you. PageOut is so straightforward and intuitive; it's little wonder why more than 12,000 college professors are using it.

For more information, visit the PageOut web site at www.pageout.net.

- *Online Courses Available:* Online Learning Centers (OLCs) are the perfect solutions for your Internet-based content. Simply put, OLCs are "digital cartridges" that contain a book's pedagogy and supplements. As students read the book, they can go on line and take self-grading quizzes or work through interactive exercises. OLCs also provide students appropriate access to lecture materials and other key supplements.

OLCs can be delivered through any of these platforms:

- McGraw-Hill Learning Architecture (TopClass)
- Blackboard.com
- Ecollege.com (formally Real Education)
- WebCT (a product of Universal Learning Technology)

McGraw-Hill has partnerships with **WebCT** and **Blackboard** to make it even easier to take your course on line. Now you can have McGraw-Hill content delivered through the leading Internet-based learning tool for higher education.

Acknowledgments

The success of *the Advantage Series* software tutorials is confirmation of the effort, teamwork, and dedication of many people. We sincerely thank the instructors, students, reviewers, and editors who have shared their comments and suggestions with us over the years. Our authors take pride in their work, and your comments help us to publish relevant learning materials with a sound pedagogical approach. The product you hold in your hands is a culmination of our best practices in writing and development, classroom testing, and your personal feedback.

McGraw-Hill Higher Education and, specifically, the Technology Education publishing group are composed of caring and talented people. We are fortunate to have had Steve Schuetz manage the series into the new millennium. Marc Chernoff and Lisa Chin-Johnson, our current publishing team, deserve our sincere appreciation for their skillful handling of this edition. Special recognition also goes to the individuals mentioned in the credits on the copyright page.

Thanks to the Advantage Series Team

The following technical editors and supplements writers worked very hard to ensure the accuracy and integrity of every book in the series. Thank you for your efforts!

Maureen Ellis, Indiana University at Bloomington

Dominic Ligori, Seneca College, Canada

Wendy Hon Kam, Loyola University

Rajiv Malkan, Montgomery College

Randy Cullom, University of Northern Colorado

Jacob Phillips, Northern Virginia Community College

Jan Cady, Trinity Valley Community College

Ken Baker, Sinclair Community College

Ryan Murphy, Sinclair Community College

A special thank you goes to Ann Miller and Pat R. Graves for their invaluable contribution and commitment in getting the series published on time. Ann (co-author for Microsoft Word) and Pat (co-author for Microsoft PowerPoint) are extremely talented and conscientious writers. We are very fortunate to have them on *the Advantage Series* team. We are also very thankful to David Shank and other members of the Microsoft Office team for their valuable insight and contributions.

Pat R. Graves, author of *the Advantage Series* PowerPoint Brief: Many thanks go to Glen Coulthard for his guidance, the editors for their helpful suggestions, and to Lisa Chin-Johnson for managing the development process so effectively. I sincerely thank the many students who shared ideas and contributed resources, especially Kristen Goodman, Stephanie Nimmons, Mary Phelps, Ryan Gibson, and Jerry Rankin. Thanks also to William J. Gibbs for his technical assistance and to the management of Beaver Run Resort and EIU Booth Library for the resources shared. And to Brent Graves who has been continually supportive, I appreciate his encouragement.

Ann Miller, author of *the Advantage Series* Word Brief: Thanks to Glen Coulthard for allowing me to be a part of such a wonderful writing team. His professionalism and sense of humor have added to my enjoyment of this project. I would also like to thank my family for their support and faith in me, my colleagues at Columbus State Community College for 30 years of friendship and learning, and finally, the editorial staff at McGraw-Hill for all their help and the opportunity to complete this project.

Write to Us

We welcome your comments and suggestions for books in *the Advantage Series.* On behalf of *the Advantage Series* team, please contact the lead author for the series at:

Glen J. Coulthard

glen@coulthard.com

www.coulthard.com

www.advantageseries.com

Advantage series

Microsoft® Office Word®

2003

Brief edition

Contents Word

Advantage
series

Microsoft® Office Excel®

2003

Brief
edition

Contents Excel

Advantage series

Microsoft® Office PowerPoint® 2003

Brief edition

Contents PowerPoint

Microsoft® Office Access® 2003

Brief edition

Contents Access

Advantage
series

Microsoft® Office System 2003®

Contents Integrating

CHAPTER 3 **Extending Office 2003 to the Web**

3.1 Using Hyperlinks

3.2 Saving Documents to HTML and XML

3.3 Preparing Web Pages Using Office 2003

Chapter Review

Chapter Quiz

Hands-On Exercises

Contents End Matter

Microsoft® Office Word® 2003

CHAPTER 1

Creating a Document

PREREQUISITES

Although this chapter assumes no previous experience using Microsoft Word, you should be comfortable using a keyboard and mouse in the Microsoft Windows environment. You should be able to launch and exit programs and perform basic Windows file management operations, such as opening and closing documents.

LEARNING OBJECTIVES

After completing this chapter, you will be able to:

- Identify different components of the application window

- Select commands and options using the Menu bar and right-click menus

- Create, save, open, and print a document

- Correct mistakes

- View documents using various methods

1.1 Getting Started with Word

Microsoft Word is a sophisticated **word processing** application that helps you create and edit all types of business and personal documents, including letters, reports, memos, resumes, Web documents, and much more. In this module, you will learn how to start Word and become familiar with the Word interface, how to create and edit documents using basic editing techniques, and how to save and print files.

1.1.1 Loading and Exiting Word

→ # Feature

You launch Word from the Windows Start menu, accessed by clicking the Start button (start) on the taskbar. Your steps may vary slightly, depending on your setup. After you have finished your work in Word, you may want to exit the program in order to conserve system memory. You exit Word by clicking the Close button (X) appearing in the top right-hand corner of the Word application menu.

→ # Method

To load Word:

- CLICK: Start button (start)

- CHOOSE: Programs, Microsoft Word. (Your actual steps may vary slightly; check with your instructor.)

To exit Word:

- CLICK: Close button (X) appearing in the top right-hand corner, or

- CHOOSE: File, Exit from Word's Menu bar

→ # Practice

You will now launch Microsoft Word using the Windows Start menu.

1. Position the mouse pointer over the top of the Start button (start) and then click the left mouse button once. The Start pop-up menu appears.

2. Point to All Programs. Note that you do not need to click the left mouse button to display the list of programs in the fly-out or cascading menu.

3. Move the mouse pointer horizontally to the right until it highlights the option you want, in this case, Microsoft Word. Your screen should appear similar to the one shown in Figure 1.1.

Figure 1.1

The Programs menu

Task bar

4. Point to Microsoft Office, then click Microsoft Word from the cascading menu.

5. After a few more seconds, an Office Assistant character, such as "Clippit" (shown at the right), may appear. You will learn how to hide this character in lesson 1.1.2.

1.1.2 The Word Interface

→ **Feature**

The Word **application window** acts as a container for your documents. As you might expect, the Word application window contains a menu bar, toolbars, status bar, various icons, and a task bar. It also includes several tools that you will use when creating and editing documents including the *Ruler, Scroll bars,* and *View buttons*. Figure 1.2 identifies several of these components. The Word application window may also contain an Office Assistant.

→ **Practice**

In a guided tour, you will explore the features of Word's application window. Ensure that you have launched Word.

- Word's application window is best kept maximized to fill the entire screen, as shown in Figure 1.2. As with most Windows applications, you use the Title bar icons—Minimize (⬜), Maximize (⬜), Restore (⬜), and Close (✕)—to control the display of a window using the mouse. These same icons appear in almost all Windows applications and behave in the same manner. Familiarize yourself with the components labeled in Figure 1.2.

Figure 1.2

Word's application window

View Buttons

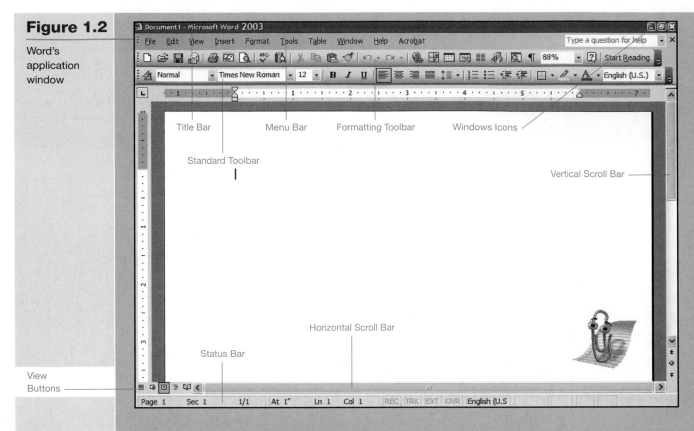

2. The Menu bar contains Word's menu commands. To execute a command, you click once on the Menu bar option and then click again on the desired command. Commands that appear dimmed are not available for selection. Commands that are followed by an ellipsis (. . .) will display a dialog box asking for additional information. Most commands also have a shortcut key assigned to them. Shortcut keys are keystroke combinations that allow you to use the keyboard instead of the mouse to access many of Word's commands. The shortcut key designation appears to the right of the menu command. As you become more familiar with Word, you may find it faster to use the shortcut commands rather than the Menu bar.

3. To practice working with the Word Menu bar:
CHOOSE: Help
This instruction tells you to click the left mouse button once on the Help option appearing in the Menu bar.

4. To display other pull-down menus, move the mouse to the left over other options in the Menu bar. As each option is highlighted, a pull-down menu appears with its associated commands. To select a command, you simply left-click on the command name.

5. Highlight the View pull-down menu.
The options in this menu let you customize the look of your document to your preferred way of working. Your screen should now appear similar to the one shown in Figure 1.3. (*Note:* Some options may be grayed out.)

Figure 1.3

Word's View
Menu

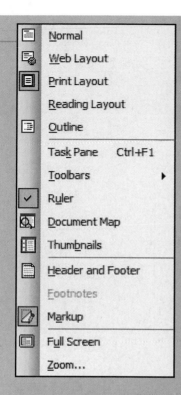

6. For now, do the following to ensure that your screen looks the same as in Figure 1.3:
CHOOSE: Print Layout from the View menu.
Print Layout allows you to work with your document and see it as it will be printed, including headers and footers and page numbers.

7. Word provides many context-sensitive *right-click menus* for quick access to menu commands. Rather than searching for the appropriate command in the Menu bar, you can position the mouse pointer on any object, such as a graphic or toolbar button, and right-click the mouse to display a list of commonly selected commands.

To display a document's right-click menu:
Open a blank document
RIGHT-CLICK: in the blank document area
The menu shown in Figure 1.4 should now appear.

Figure 1.4

Right-click menu

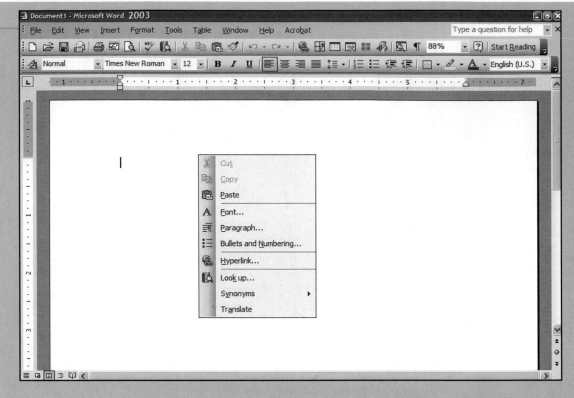

8. To remove the right-click menu from the screen:
   CLICK: in the blank document area

9. If an Office Assistant character currently appears on your screen, do the following to hide it from view:
   RIGHT-CLICK: *the character*
   CHOOSE: Hide

10. Continue to the next lesson.

1.1.3 Customizing Menus and Toolbars

→ **Feature**

Microsoft gives you great flexibility in customizing your work environment. For example, some people find **adaptive menus** distracting. Adaptive Menus display only the most commonly used commands, with other commands available by clicking on the chevron symbol (⊻) that appears at the bottom of each menu. You can also pause over a menu to display the entire menu. Additionally, you may not like the Standard and Formatting toolbars displayed side by side. The **Task pane,** which opens as a default when you start a Word document, may get in the way. Fortunately, you can customize all of these aspects of your working environment.

→ **Method**

To disable the adaptive menus feature and display the Standard and Formatting toolbars on separate rows:

- CHOOSE: Tools, Customize

- CLICK: *Options* tab

- SELECT: *Show Standard and Formatting toolbars on two rows* check box

- SELECT: *Always show full menus* check box
- CLICK: Close command button

To display or hide a toolbar:

- CHOOSE: View, Toolbars
- CHOOSE: a toolbar from the menu

To display and hide the task pane:

- CHOOSE: View, Task Pane

or

- CLICK: its Close button (✕)

→ Practice

In this lesson, you will disable the adaptive menus feature, display the Standard and Formatting toolbars on separate rows, and toggle the display of the task pane. Ensure that you have completed the previous lesson.

1. To begin, display the Tools menu.
CHOOSE: Tools
You should now see the Tools pull-down menu (Figure 1.5).

Figure 1.5

Tools pull-down menu

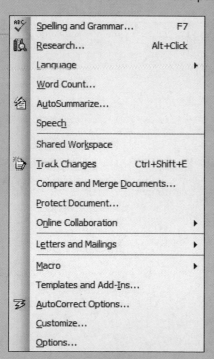

ᴬᴮꟲ	Spelling and Grammar...	F7
🔍	Research...	Alt+Click
	Language	▶
	Word Count...	
📄	AutoSummarize...	
	Speech	
	Shared Workspace	
🖉	Track Changes	Ctrl+Shift+E
	Compare and Merge Documents...	
	Protect Document...	
	Online Collaboration	▶
	Letters and Mailings	▶
	Macro	▶
	Templates and Add-Ins...	
ᴢ̄	AutoCorrect Options...	
	Customize...	
	Options...	

2. Let's turn off the adaptive menus feature and customize the Standard and Formatting toolbars. Do the following:
CHOOSE: Customize from the Tools pull-down menu
CLICK: *Options* tab
The Customize dialog box should now appear (Figure 1.6).

Figure 1.6

Customize dialog box: *Options* tab

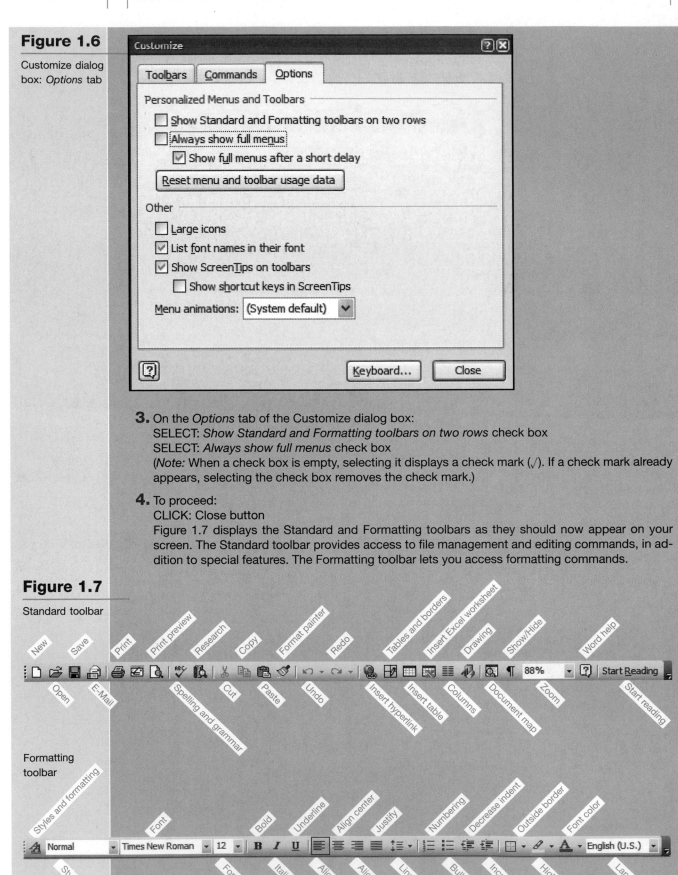

3. On the *Options* tab of the Customize dialog box:
SELECT: *Show Standard and Formatting toolbars on two rows* check box
SELECT: *Always show full menus* check box
(*Note:* When a check box is empty, selecting it displays a check mark (√). If a check mark already appears, selecting the check box removes the check mark.)

4. To proceed:
CLICK: Close button
Figure 1.7 displays the Standard and Formatting toolbars as they should now appear on your screen. The Standard toolbar provides access to file management and editing commands, in addition to special features. The Formatting toolbar lets you access formatting commands.

Figure 1.7

Standard toolbar

Formatting toolbar

5. To hide the task pane:
CHOOSE: View, Task Pane
(*Note:* When a toolbar or the task pane is displayed, a check mark appears beside the option in the pull-down menu.)

6. To display the task pane:
CHOOSE: View, Task Pane
Your screen should now appear similar to the one shown in Figure 1.8.

Important: For the remainder of this learning guide, we assume that the adaptive menus feature has been disabled and that the Standard and Formatting toolbars are positioned on separate rows.

Figure 1.8

Customizing the application window

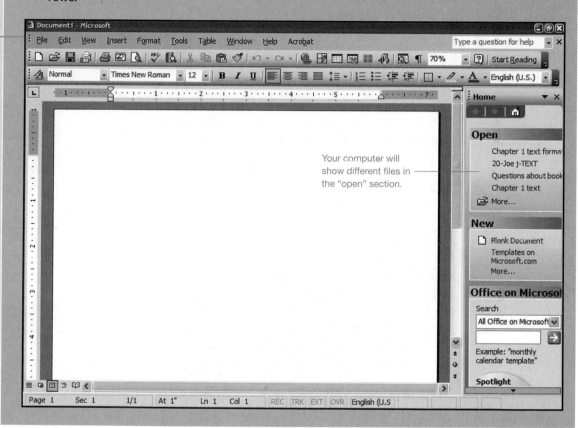

Your computer will show different files in the "open" section.

In Addition MOVING TOOLBARS

You can move toolbars around the Word application window using the mouse. A *docked toolbar* appears attached to one of the window's borders. An *undocked* or *floating toolbar* appears in its own window, complete with a Title bar and Close button. To float a docked toolbar, drag the Move bar (⫾) at the left-hand side toward the center of the window. To redock the toolbar, drag its Title bar toward a border until it attaches itself automatically.

 **1.1** How do you display standard and formatting toolbars on the different lines?

1.2 Creating Your First Document

Creating a document in Word is simple. You type information onto the screen, save the document to the disk and, if desired, send it to the printer. In the next few lessons, you will create the letter appearing in Figure 1.9.

Figure 1.9

Sample document

November 22, 2003

Dear Friends:

Hello! Bob and I are new to the neighborhood and would like to get to know our neighbors. Please stop by sometime on Sunday, August 24, 2003, between 1:00 p.m. and 5:00 p.m. to meet our family and enjoy refreshments in our home. There's no need to RSVP; just feel free to stop by.

We look forward to meeting all of you. Your children are welcome, also.

Sincerely,

Emily and Bob Watson
245 Liberty Road
Greenville, OH 43086

1.2.1 Inserting and Deleting Text

→ Feature

You create and edit documents by inserting and deleting text. As you type, Word employs five separate features to help you get your work done. Word's **AutoCorrect** feature works on your behalf to correct common capitalization, spelling, and grammatical errors. AutoCorrect also allows you to enter "abbreviations" for words, which Word replaces with the full text of the word or phrase. For example, AutoCorrect will automatically replace "teh" with "the," "firts" with "first," etc. By creating abbreviations, you can speed up data entry and reduce errors. For example, if your company's name was "Trattoria Products and Services, Inc.," you could create an abbreviation "tpsi" and have it replaced with the full company name each time you used the abbreviation.

AutoFormatAsYouType allows you to automatically replace straight quotes with curly quotes, create bulleted and numbered lists, capitalize the first letters of sentences, and correct the accidental use of CAPS LOCK.

AutoText allows you to insert frequently used text, such as "Sincerely" and "Thank You" as you type. You can create and add your own AutoText entries.

AutoFormat provides for built-in heading styles, automatic list numbering, and replacement of dashes with em or en dashes.

Smart Tags lets Word recognize certain types of data in your document. You can perform specific actions on the data, depending on the data type. For example, if you enter an address, a smart tag appears which allows you to add the name and address to your Outlook contacts list.

→ Method

- To insert text, begin typing. Insert spaces by pressing the Space Bar. Insert blank lines by pressing `ENTER`.

- To toggle between Insert and Overtype modes, double-click the OVR indicator in the Status bar or press the Ins key on the numeric keypad. (Make sure Num Lock is turned off.)

- Press DELETE to delete text to the right of the insertion point. Press BACKSPACE to delete text to the left of the insertion point.

Note: *Insert Mode means that when you type into a document, new text is inserted among any existing text, and existing text is moved to the right as you type. Overtype mode means that what you type will replace the existing text.*

→ ## Practice

You will now create a letter so that you can practice the basics of inserting and deleting text. You will also use Word's AutoText and AutoCorrect features. Ensure that you have completed the previous lesson and that a blank document appears.

1. We will begin this exercise by inserting the current date. Make sure you have a blank document open and your blinking insertion point is in the upper left-hand corner of the document. A blinking insertion point indicates the position where text will be inserted. Rather than entering the date manually, let's use Word's AutoText feature. Begin typing the current date.
TYPE: **Novem** (assuming the current date is November something)
Word now displays the complete month name in a yellow suggestion box, as shown in Figure 1.10.

Figure 1.10

An AutoText suggestion appears

AutoText suggestion

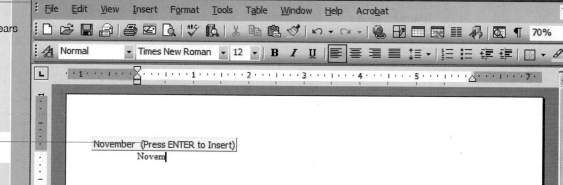

2. As indicated in the suggestion box, you must press ENTER to insert the current month in your document.
PRESS: ENTER
Word automatically inserts the rest of the characters in the current month.

3. To proceed with typing in the date:
PRESS: Space Bar
If November 22, 2003, were the actual current date, your screen would now look like Figure 1.11. Continue with step 4.

Figure 1.11

Current date inserted

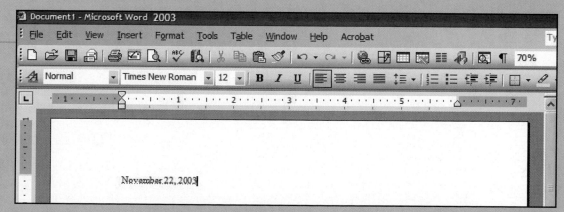

4. TYPE: **22**
TYPE: **,**
PRESS: Space Bar
TYPE: **2003**
The date of November 22, 2003, in its entirety, should now appear at the top of your document. The insertion point appears one character to the right of the date.

5. To move the insertion point back to the beginning of the date line:
PRESS: **HOME**
The insertion point should now appear to the left of the date (Figure 1.12). Note that purple dots now appear beneath the date. (*Note:* If the dots do not appear yet, they will in step 6, when you press the **ENTER** key.) These dots indicate that the date is a *smart tag*. When you move the mouse pointer over a smart tag, Word displays the Smart Tag Actions button (⊞). We describe smart tags in more detail in lesson 1.2.4. For now, ignore each smart tag in your document and its associated Smart Tag Actions button (⊞).

Figure 1.12

The date has been entered

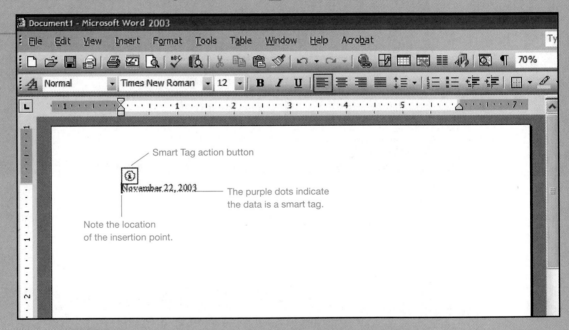

6. The **ENTER** key inserts blank lines into a document and signifies the end of a paragraph. To illustrate:
PRESS: **ENTER** three times
Note that the date moves down with the insertion point and blank lines are inserted into the document.

7. To get the date back to its original location, you must delete the blank lines. To move the insertion point to the top of the document:
PRESS: **CTRL** + **HOME**
This instruction tells you to press and hold down the **CTRL** key and tap **HOME** once. You then release both keys. The insertion point jumps to the left side of the first line in the document.

8. To delete the blank lines:
PRESS: **DELETE** three times

9. To move the insertion point down three lines without moving the date, you must first position the insertion point at the end of the line. To illustrate:
PRESS: **END** to move the insertion point to the end of the line
PRESS: **ENTER** three times
The insertion point is now in the correct position for you to type your salutation. (*Note:* A salutation is a greeting, such as "Dear Mr. Jones," that appears at the beginning of a letter.)

10. Type the following, exactly as it appears:
TYPE: **FRiends,**
Conveniently, Word's AutoCorrect feature corrected your capitalization error at the beginning of the word. Your document should now appear similar to the one shown in Figure 1.13.

Figure 1.13

AutoCorrect in action

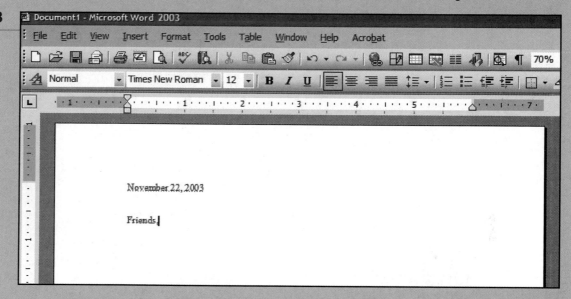

11. Note that the letters OVR in the Status bar appear dimmed. This tells you that Word's current mode is Insert Mode and not Overtype Mode. To move the insertion point back to the beginning of the line so you can insert the word "Dear," do the following:
PRESS: HOME
A hollow blue bar (═), the AutoCorrect Options button, should now appear beneath the "F" in "Friends." For now, ignore this button.

12. TYPE: **Dear**
PRESS: Space Bar
The Insert Mode lets you insert text and spaces at the current position by simply typing the characters and pressing the Space Bar. The existing information is pushed to the right.

13. Locate OVR, the abbreviation for Overtype mode, on the Status bar (Figure 1.14).
DOUBLE-CLICK: OVR
The letters OVR appear highlighted (not dimmed) in the Status bar.

14. TYPE: **My**
PRESS: Space Bar
The letters and following space overwrote the first three characters of "Friends." Your screen should now appear similar to the one shown in Figure 1.14.

Figure 1.14

Overtype mode

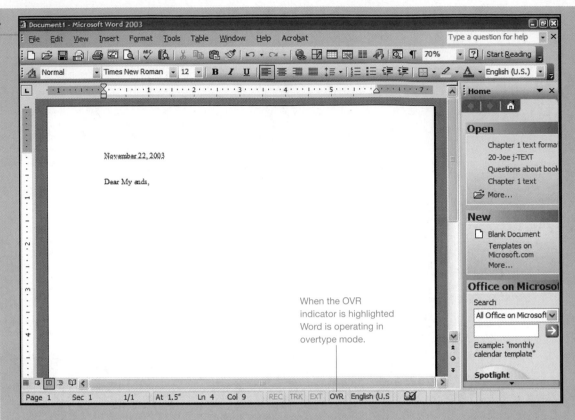

When the OVR indicator is highlighted Word is operating in overtype mode.

15. To toggle back to Insert Mode:
DOUBLE-CLICK: OVR in the Status bar
The letters OVR should now appear dimmed.

16. Let's complete the phrase:
TYPE: **Fri**

17. To illustrate the use of the **BACKSPACE** key, position the insertion point to the left of the word "Friends."

18. PRESS: **BACKSPACE** three times
The word "My" and the space are deleted. The text now reads "Dear Friends,".

19. To prepare for the next lesson, let's delete the date from the top of your document.
PRESS: **CTRL** + **HOME**
PRESS: **DELETE** until the month information is deleted

20. While being careful to not delete any blank lines:
PRESS: **DELETE** a few more times to delete the day and year information
The **insertion point** should now be positioned on a blank line at the top of your document (Figure 1.15).

Figure 1.15

The insertion point is positioned on a blank line at the top of the document

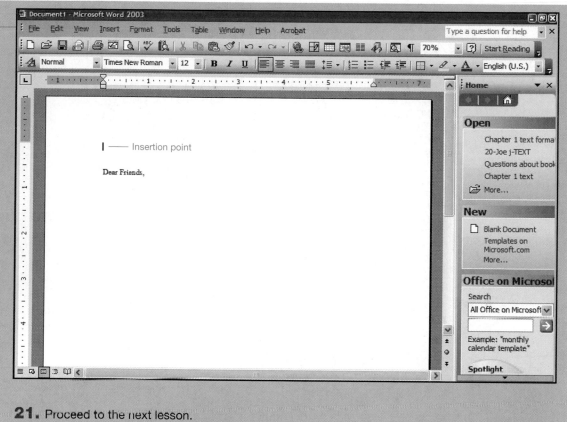

21. Proceed to the next lesson.

1.2.2 Inserting the Date and Time

→ **Feature**

In the last lesson, Word assisted you when typing the current date. You can also insert the current date in its entirety using a command from the Menu bar. Optionally, you can insert the current date as a field that causes Word to update the date whenever you open or print the document.

→ **Method**

- CHOOSE: Insert, Date and Time
- SELECT: a format in the *Available formats* list box
- CLICK: OK command button

→ **Practice**

You will now insert the current date at the top of your document. Ensure that you have completed the previous lesson. The insertion point should be positioned on a blank line at the top of your document, as shown in Figure 1.15.

1. CHOOSE: Insert, Date and Time
The Date and Time dialog box appears, as shown in Figure 1.16.

Figure 1.16

Date and Time
dialog box

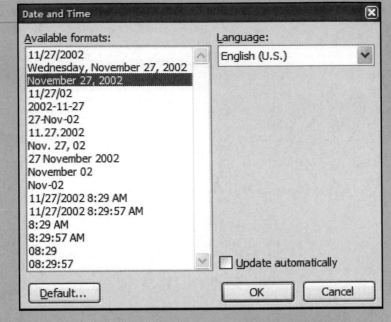

2. SELECT: the "Month ##, 200#" (as shown in Figure 1.16)
   CLICK: OK command button
   The date is inserted at the top of the document.

3. To position the insertion point in the correct position so you can begin typing your letter:
   PRESS: **CTRL** + **END** to move to the end of your document
   PRESS: **ENTER** twice

4. If the Office Assistant appears:
   RIGHT-CLICK: the Office Assistant character
   CHOOSE: Hide

5. Proceed to the next lesson.

1.2.3 Putting "Word Wrap" to Work

→ **Feature**

The **word wrap** feature of Word allows you to type continuously without having to press the **ENTER** key at the end of each line. This feature is designed to help you type faster.

→ **Method**

When typing a paragraph, do not press the **ENTER** key at the end of each line. The **ENTER** key is used only to end a paragraph or to insert a blank line in a document.

→ **Practice**

You will now complete the sample document. Ensure that you have completed the previous lesson. The insertion point should be positioned two lines below the salutation. Do not press **ENTER** unless we tell you to do so.

1. TYPE: **Hello! Bob and I are new to the neighborhood and would like to get to know our neighbors. Please stop by sometime on Sunday, August 24, 2003, between 1:00 p.m. and 5:00 p.m. to meet our family and enjoy refreshments in our home.**
   PRESS: **ENTER** twice

There's no need to RSVP; just feel free to stop by. We look forward to meeting all of you. Your children are welcome, also.
PRESS: [ENTER] twice

2. To complete the note:
TYPE: **Sincerely,**
PRESS: [ENTER]
TYPE: **Emily and Bob Watson**
PRESS: [ENTER]
TYPE: **245 Liberty Road**
PRESS: [ENTER]
TYPE: **Greenville, OH 43086**
PRESS: [ENTER]

3. Because the task pane may be obscuring a portion of your document, let's hide it from view.
CHOOSE: View, Task Pane
Your screen should now appear similar to the one shown in Figure 1.17. (*Note:* Depending on your screen's resolution, words may wrap differently than in the figure. This is not a problem.)

Figure 1.17

Sample document

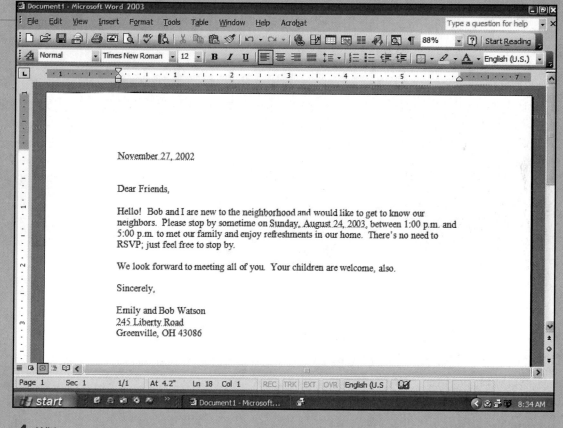

4. With your document still displaying, proceed to the next lesson.

1.2.4 Using Smart Tags

→ **Feature**

As you already know, Word includes many features that work in the background to save you time. For example, Word automatically corrects common capitalization, spelling, and grammatical errors. Word even tags some data, such as a person's name or the current date, so that you can more easily use the data elsewhere, such as in your address book or e-mail message. Once Word recognizes a piece of data, it labels it with a purple dotted underline. Information that has been marked in this way is called a **smart tag.** When you move the mouse pointer over a smart tag, a **Smart Tag Actions button** (⊡) appears. You can click this button to display a list of possible actions. Because smart tags will not appear in your printed documents it is also fine to ignore them.

→ Method

To perform an action on a smart tag:

- CLICK: Smart Tag Actions button (⊡)

- CHOOSE: an option from the menu

→ Practice

You will now see what actions you can perform on the three smart tags displaying in your sample document.

1. Position the mouse pointer over the current-date smart tag positioned at the top of the document. The Smart Tag Actions button (⊡) should now appear.

2. To see what actions you can perform on this smart tag:
CLICK: Smart Tag Actions button (⊡)
Your screen should now appear similar to the one shown in Figure 1.18. Note that Word identified the smart tag as a Date field, as indicated at the top of the smart tag menu.

Figure 1.18

Smart Tag
Actions menu

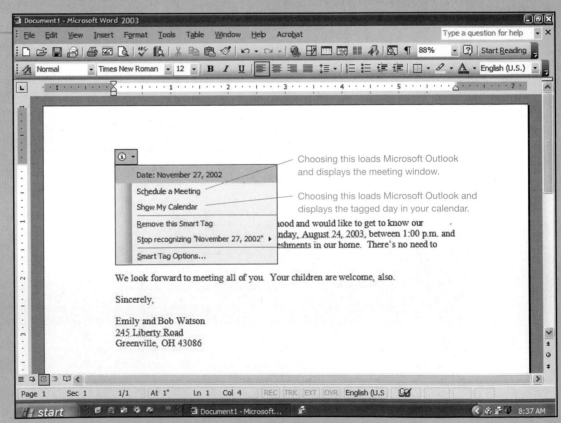

3. To remove the smart tag:
CHOOSE: Remove this Smart Tag
The date should no longer be marked as a smart tag.

4. In the body of your letter, "Sunday, August 24, 2003," may be marked as a smart tag. Emily and Bob's address should also be marked as a smart tag at the end of the letter. Move the mouse pointer over the address.
CLICK: Smart Tag Actions button (ⓘ) associated with your name.
The menu shown in Figure 1.19 should now appear. Note that the menu contains different options than before.

Figure 1.19

Smart Tag
Actions menu

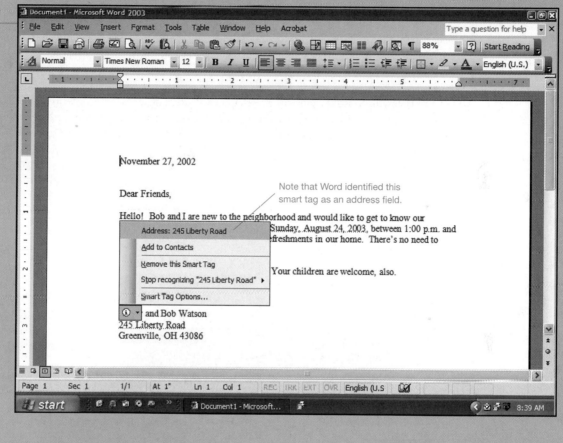

5. To ignore the displayed menu and return to your document:
CLICK: in the document area

6. To conclude this module, you will close the document without saving changes. From the Menu bar:
CHOOSE: File, Close

7. In the dialog box that appears:
CLICK: No command button
There should be no documents open in the application window.

1.2   How do you insert the current date into a document?

1.3 Managing Files

Managing your document files is an important skill. The document you create exists only in the computer's RAM (random access memory), which is highly volatile. In other words, if the power to your computer goes off, your document is lost. For safety and security, you need to save your document permanently to the local hard disk, a network drive, or a floppy diskette.

Saving your work to a named file on a disk is like placing it into a filing cabinet. Important documents (ones that you cannot risk losing) should be saved every 15 minutes, or whenever you are interrupted, to protect against an unexpected power outage or other catastrophe. When naming your document files, you can use up to 255 characters, including spaces, but it is wise to keep the length under 20 characters. Furthermore, you cannot use the following characters in naming your documents:

$$\backslash \quad / \quad : \quad ; \quad * \quad ? \quad " \quad < \quad > \quad |$$

In the following lessons, you will practice several file management procedures, including creating a new document, saving and closing documents, and opening existing documents.

*Important: In this guide, we refer to the files that have been created for you as the **student data files**. Depending on your computer or lab setup, these files may be located on a floppy diskette, in a folder on your hard disk, or on a network server. If necessary, ask your instructor or lab assistant where to find these data files. To download the Advantage Series' student data files from the Internet, visit the Advantage Series' Web site at:*

http://www.advantageseries.com

You will also need to identify a personal storage location, such as a removable disk or hard-drive subdirectory, for the files that you create, modify, and save.

1.3.1 Beginning a New Document

→ **Feature**

There are three ways to create a new document. First, you can start with a blank document and then create the document from scratch. Next, you can select a document **template** that provides preexisting data and design elements. Lastly, you can employ a **wizard** to lead you step-by-step through the creation of a particular type of document.

→ **Method**

- To display a new blank document:
  CLICK: New button (□)

- To begin a document using a template or wizard:
  CHOOSE: File, New

→ **Practice**

In this example, you will use one of Word's templates to create a résumé. Ensure that no documents are open in the application window.

1. A document template is a model that you can use to create new documents. By its very nature, a template is a time-saver that promotes consistency in both design and function. To view the templates that are available to you, do the following:
CHOOSE: File, New
The New Document task pane should now appear, as shown in Figure 1.20. Task panes contain textual links, called **hyperlinks,** for performing Word procedures. When you move the mouse pointer over a link, the mouse pointer changes to a hand (🖑). You select a link by clicking.

Figure 1.20

New Document
task pane

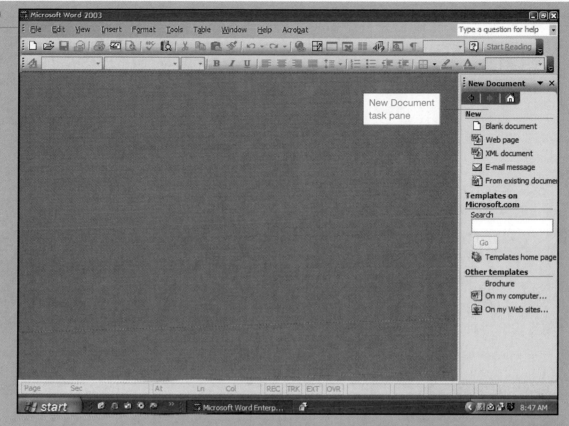

2. Move the mouse pointer over the "Blank document" hyperlink. Note that a hand (🖑) appears indicating that you are pointing to a hyperlink. To select the link:
   CLICK: "Blank document" link
   A blank document appears. The Task pane should no longer appear. You can also start a new blank document by clicking the New button (🗋) on the Standard toolbar.

3. Word includes many custom templates that simplify the process of starting common documents such as résumés and letters. For example, to display a selection of templates for creating résumés:
   CHOOSE: File, New
   CLICK: "On my computer . . ." link under "Other templates"
   CLICK: *Other Documents* tab
   The Templates dialog box should look like Figure 1.21. (*Note:* Different tabs may be displaying on your computer.)

Figure 1.21

Displaying
document
templates

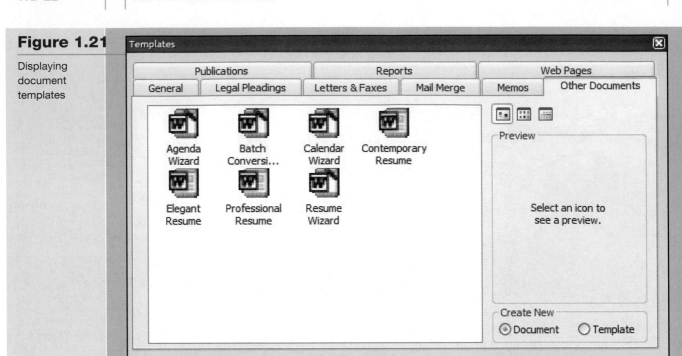

4. To create a new document based on the "Professional Resume" template:
DOUBLE-CLICK: Professional Resume template icon
(*Note*: If your lab administrator has not installed the document templates, skip to step 5.) You should now see the Professional Resume template, as shown in Figure 1.22. If you were creating your resume right now, you would proceed by editing this document to include your information.

Figure 1.22

New document
based on the
Professional
Resume template

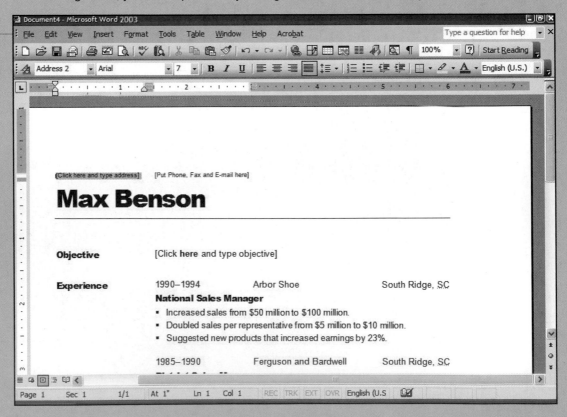

5. Rather than editing this document now, let's close the document and continue our discussion of file management.
CHOOSE: File, Close
CLICK: No command button, if asked to save the changes

6. The blank document should be displaying. Do the following:
TYPE: **Saving Files**
PRESS: ENTER twice
(*Note:* Depending on what settings are in effect on your computer, Word may have automatically formatted your title using a heading style.)

7. Again, let word wrap happen naturally. Don't press ENTER after each sentence.
TYPE: **Saving your work to a named file on a disk is like placing it into a filing cabinet. Important documents (ones that you cannot risk losing) should be saved every 15 minutes, or whenever you're interrupted, to protect against an unexpected power outage or other catastrophe.**
Your screen should now appear similar to the one shown in Figure 1.23. In the next lesson, you will learn how to save this document.

Figure 1.23

Current document

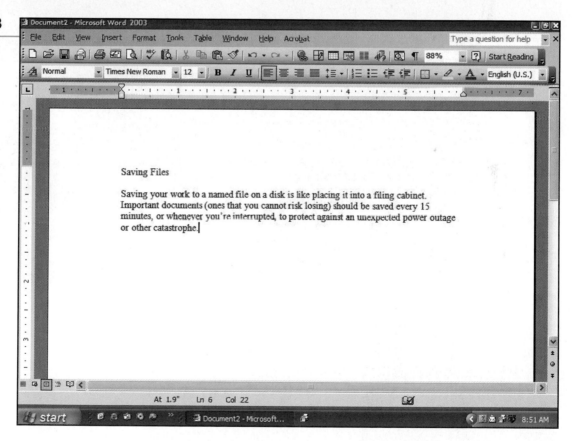

   **1.3**   What are three ways to create a new document?

1.3.2 Saving and Closing a Document

→ **Feature**

You can save the currently displayed document by updating an existing file on the disk, by creating a new file, or by selecting a new storage location. The File, Save command and the Save button () on the toolbar allow you to overwrite a disk file with the latest version of a document. The File, Save As command enables you to save a document to a new filename and/or storage location. When you are finished working with a document, ensure that you close the file to free up valuable RAM.

→ **Method**

To save a document:
- CLICK: Save button (🖫)
  or
- CHOOSE: File, Save
  or
- CHOOSE: File, Save As

To close a document:
- CHOOSE: File, Close

→ **Practice**

You now practice saving and closing a document. Ensure that you have completed the previous lesson. You also need to identify a storage location for your personal document files. If you want to use a diskette, place it into the diskette drive now. Remember always to write your name on the diskette label.

1. If you are working in a new document that has not yet been saved, Word displays the Save As dialog box (Figure 1.24), regardless of the method you choose to save the file. To demonstrate:
   CLICK: Save button (🖫)
   (*Note*: The filenames and directories that appear in your Save As dialog box may differ from those shown in Figure 1.24.) The **Places bar,** located along the left border of the dialog box, provides convenient access to commonly used storage locations.

Figure 1.24

Save As dialog box

Places bar

2. In the next few steps, you will practice navigating your computer's disks. To begin, let's view a list of the files that you have worked with recently:
CLICK: My Recent Documents button (🖳) in the Places bar
(*Note:* Although we do not want you to do this now, you can open listed files by double-clicking them.)

3. To browse the files in your "My Documents" folder:
CLICK: My Documents button (📁)

4. Let's browse the local hard disk:
CLICK: down arrow attached to the *Save in* drop-down list box
SELECT: 💾 Local Disk C:
(*Note:* Your hard drive may have a different name.) The list area displays the folders and files stored in the root directory of your local hard disk. The root directory is the directory that contains all other directories.

5. To drill down into one of the folders:
DOUBLE-CLICK: Program Files folder
(*Note:* If the Program Files folder is not located on your local hard disk, select an alternate folder to open.) This folder contains the program files for several applications.

6. Let's drill down one step further:
DOUBLE-CLICK: Microsoft Office folder
This folder contains the Microsoft Office program files. Your screen may now appear similar, but not identical, to the one shown in Figure 1.25.

Figure 1.25

Displaying the contents of the Microsoft Office folder

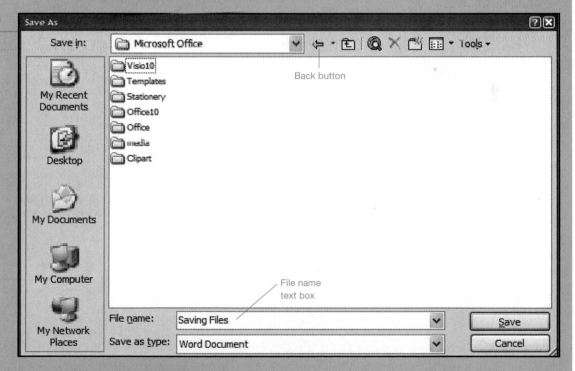

7. To return to the previous display:
CLICK: Back button (⬅) in the Save As dialog box
(*Note:* The button is renamed "Program Files," because that is where you will end up once the button is clicked.)

8. To return to the "My Documents" display:
CLICK: Back button (⬅) twice
(*Hint:* You could have also clicked the My Documents button in the Places bar.)

9. Now, using either the Places bar or the *Save in* drop-down list box:
SELECT: *a storage location for your data files*
(*Note:* In this guide, we save files to the Data Files folder, located in the My Documents folder. Check with your instructor for the appropriate location to save your files.)

10. Next, you need to give the document file a unique name. Let's stick with the name "Saving Files" that already appears in the *File name* text box.

11. To save your work:
CLICK: Save command button
Note that the document's name now appears in the Title bar (Figure 1.26).

Figure 1.26

The file name now appears in the Title bar

The document's name

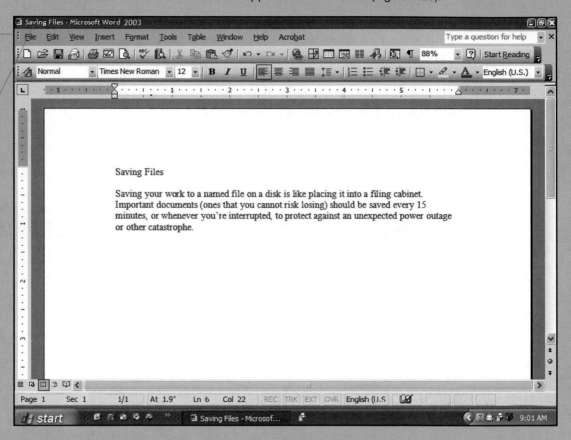

12. Move the insertion point to the bottom of the document.

13. To insert a blank line and then type your name:
PRESS: **ENTER**
TYPE: *your name (for example, Jeanne Patton)*

14. To save the updated document:
CLICK: Save button (⊟)
There are times when you may want to save an existing document under a different filename. For example, you may want to keep different versions of the same document on your disk. You may instead want to use one document as a template for future documents that are similar in style and format. To do this, save the document under a different name using the File, Save As command.

15. Let's save a copy of the "Saving Files" document to your personal storage location and name the copy "Backup Document."
CHOOSE: File, Save As
TYPE: **Backup Document** to replace the existing filename
CLICK: Save command button
The document was saved as "Backup Document" to your personal storage location.

16. To close the document:
CHOOSE: File, Close

1.3.3 Opening and Printing a Document

→ ## Feature

You use the Open dialog box to search for and retrieve existing documents that are stored on your local hard disk, a floppy diskette, a network server, or on the Web. To load Word and an existing document at the same time, you can use the Open Office Document command on the Start menu. If you have recently used the document, you can use the My Recent Documents command on the Start menu. This menu lists the 15 most recently used files. After you have opened a document, especially a long document that you have not worked with before, you may choose to send a copy of it to the printer and then review the printed copy.

→ ## Method

To open a document:
- CLICK: Open button (⬜)
  or
- CHOOSE: File, Open

To print a document:
- CLICK: Print button (⬜)

→ ## Practice

In this lesson, you will open and print a document that describes how to build a dog house. Ensure that you have completed the previous lesson. No documents should be displaying in the application window. You will also need to know the storage location for the Advantage data files.

1. To display the Open dialog box:

CLICK: Open button (⬜)

2. Using the Places bar or the *Look in* drop-down list box, display the contents of the folder containing the Advantage data files. These are the files we have provided. (*Note*: In this guide, we retrieve the student data files from a folder named "Data Files.")

3. To view additional information about each file:
CLICK: down arrow beside the Views button (see Figure 1.27)

Figure 1.27

Open dialog box

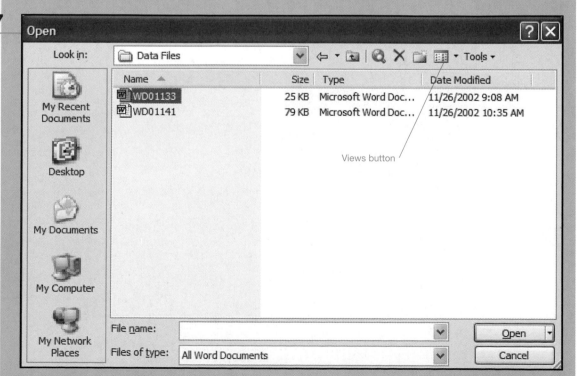

CHOOSE: Details
Each document is presented on a single line with additional file information, such as its size, type, and date it was last modified, as shown in Figure 1.27.

4. To alphabetically sort the list of files displayed in the Open dialog box:
CLICK: Name button in the column heading area

5. When you click the same column heading a second time, the order of the listing is reversed. To illustrate:
CLICK: Name button

6. To sort the list by size:
CLICK: Size button in the column heading area

7. To chronologically sort the file list by the date of modification:
CLICK: Date Modified button

8. To resort the list on order by the Name field and then return to a list format:
CLICK: Name button
CLICK: down arrow beside the Views button
CHOOSE: List

9. Let's open one of the documents in the list area:
DOUBLE-CLICK: WD01133
The dialog box disappears and the document is loaded into the application window. (*Note:* The "WD01133" filename reflects that this document is used in Chapter 1, lesson 1.3.3 of the Word learning guide.)

10. To print the current document:
CLICK: Print button (▣)
(*Note:* We describe printing in more detail in Chapter 4.)

11. Keep this file open for use in the next lesson.

1.3.4 Creating a New File Folder

→ **Feature**

As files accumulate on your computer, you may want to create folders to help you better organize your work. For example, you may have one folder for your faxes and memos and individual folders for each course you are taking at school. In Word, you create folders directly within the Open and Save As dialog boxes. Microsoft Word uses the Folder icon (▢) to identify folders.

→ **Method**

To create a new folder:

- In the Open or Save As dialog box, navigate to the disk or folder where you want to create the new folder.

- RIGHT-CLICK: *an empty part of the dialog box*

- CHOOSE: New, Folder from the right-click menu

- TYPE: **a folder name**

To delete a folder:

- In the Open or Save As dialog box:

  RIGHT-CLICK: a folder

- CHOOSE: Delete from the right-click menu

→ **Practice**

In this lesson, you create a folder named My Homework in the My Documents folder. You then save the open file into the new folder. As a final step, you delete the folder and file.

1. To display the Save As dialog box:
   CHOOSE: File, Save As

2. To open the My Documents folder:
   CLICK: My Documents button in the Places bar

3. To create a new folder called My Homework in the My Documents folder:
   RIGHT-CLICK: *an empty part of the window*
   CHOOSE: New from the right-click menu
   The New menu is shown in Figure 1.28. (*Note:* Your screen may differ slightly.)

Figure 1.28

Creating a new folder

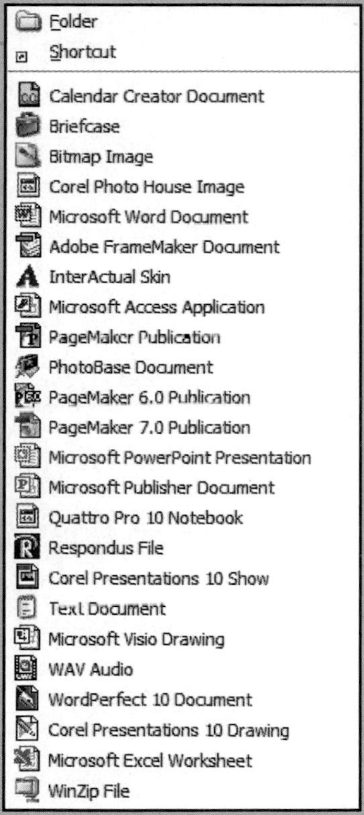

    ☐ Folder
    ☐ Shortcut
    ☐ Calendar Creator Document
    ☐ Briefcase
    ☐ Bitmap Image
    ☐ Corel Photo House Image
    ☐ Microsoft Word Document
    ☐ Adobe FrameMaker Document
    A InterActual Skin
    ☐ Microsoft Access Application
    ☐ PageMaker Publication
    ☐ PhotoBase Document
    ☐ PageMaker 6.0 Publication
    ☐ PageMaker 7.0 Publication
    ☐ Microsoft PowerPoint Presentation
    ☐ Microsoft Publisher Document
    ☐ Quattro Pro 10 Notebook
    ☐ Respondus File
    ☐ Corel Presentations 10 Show
    ☐ Text Document
    ☐ Microsoft Visio Drawing
    ☐ WAV Audio
    ☐ WordPerfect 10 Document
    ☐ Corel Presentations 10 Drawing
    ☐ Microsoft Excel Worksheet
    ☐ WinZip File

4. To proceed with creating the new folder:
   CHOOSE: Folder
   A folder entitled New Folder should appear, as shown below:

5. Since the folder's title is already highlighted, you can simply type over the name to name your new folder. Do the following:
   TYPE: **My Homework**
   PRESS: **ENTER**
   A new folder named My Homework should appear in the file listing. The Folder icon identifies the new item as a folder. If the folder name is not highlighted, right-click the folder and choose Rename from the shortcut menu.

6. To open the new folder:
   DOUBLE-CLICK: My Homework folder
   The Save As dialog box should now appear similar to the one shown in Figure 1.29. Note that the folder is empty.

Figure 1.29

"My Homework" folder

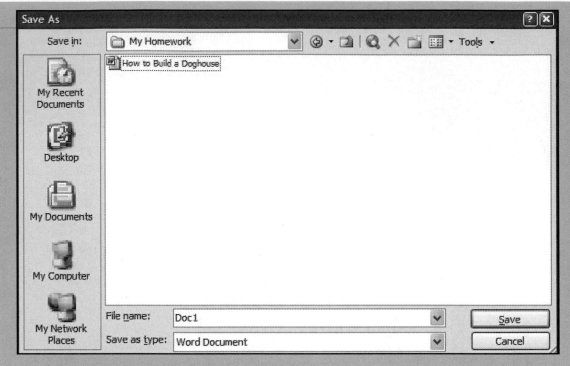

Figure 1.29

"My Homework" folder

7. To save the open file to the new folder, using a different filename:
   TYPE: **How to Build a Dog House**
   CLICK: Save command button
   This is a great way to keep your files organized!

8. As a final housekeeping task, let's delete the My Homework folder and its contents. Before you can delete a folder, you must close the folder and close any documents located with in it.
   CLICK: File, Close to close the open document

9. Before you can delete a folder you must display its name in your file list. To do this:
   CLICK: Open button (⬚)
   CLICK: My Documents button in the Places bar
   RIGHT-CLICK: the My Homework folder

10. To delete the folder:
    CHOOSE: Delete from the right-click menu
    CLICK: Yes command button to delete the folder and its contents
    The My Homework folder and its contents have been moved to the Recycle Bin.

11. To close the Open dialog box:
    CLICK: Cancel command button

12. Close any documents that remain open.

1.4 Customizing Your Work Area

Word provides four primary views for working with documents: Normal, Web Layout, Print Layout, and Outline. In addition, Word provides a Reading Layout view that displays your document with special formatting so that it is easy to read on screen. You do not actually work with your documents in Reading Layout view; it is used only for reading.

Although each view has its own advantages, all four together give you the best overall working environment. In addition, for optimal viewing Word lets you zoom in and out on a document, increasing and decreasing its display size.

1.4.1 Selecting a View

→ **Feature**

Your selection of a view depends on the type of work you are performing. You will want to perform most of your work in **Print Layout view**. In this view mode, your document displays with headers, footers, and columns. To view how your documents appear without graphics and formatting, use **Normal view**. **Web Layout view** enables you to see how a document will look in a Web browser and **Outline view** provides a convenient environment for organizing a document. **Reading Layout view** allows you to easily read your document on the screen.

→ **Method**

To change the display view of an open document:

- CHOOSE: View, Normal (or click 🔲)
- CHOOSE: View, Web Layout (or click 🔲)
- CHOOSE: View, Print Layout (or click 🔲)
- CHOOSE: View, Outline (or click 🔲)
- CHOOSE: View, Reading Layout (or click 🔲)

→ **Practice**

You will now practice switching views using a two-page newsletter. Ensure that no documents are open in the application window.

1. Open the WD01141 document file. If you completed the last module, the task pane should not be displaying. If it is showing, please close it.

2. Save a copy as "Newsletter" to your data files storage location. The "Newsletter" document should be displaying in Print Layout view (Figure 1.30). The blank space at the top of the document corresponds to the top margin.

Figure 1.30

Print Layout view

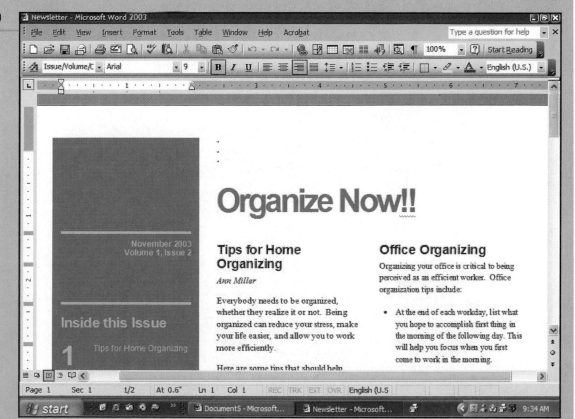

3. To switch to Normal view:
CHOOSE: View, Normal
(*Note:* You can also click the Normal view button (☰), located to the left of the horizontal scroll bar.) Your screen should now appear similar to the one shown in Figure 1.31. Note that Normal view does not display columns and other formatting in the newsletter.

Figure 1.31

Newsletter displayed in Normal view

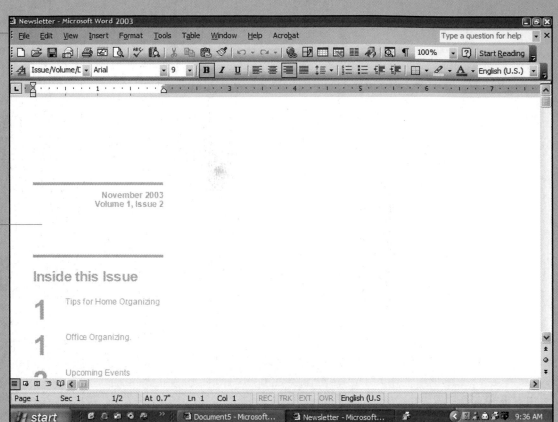

Note that the text is no longer in the columns

4. To switch to Web Layout view:
CHOOSE: View, Web Layout
In this mode, you see how your document will look when viewed in a Web browser.

5. Let's view the document in outline view.
CHOOSE: View, Outline
The Outlining toolbar is now positioned above the Formatting toolbar. Once again, most of the formatting is hidden.

6. To view just the main headings in the document:
CLICK: Show Level drop-down arrow (Show All Levels ▾)
CHOOSE: Show Level 1 from the drop-down list
Your screen should now appear similar to Figure 1.32. In this view mode, it is easy to organize the different parts of your document.

Figure 1.32

Outline view with
Level 1 headings
displayed

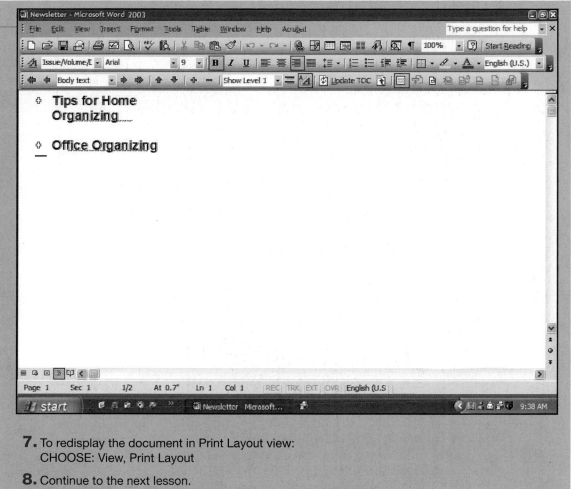

7. To redisplay the document in Print Layout view:
   CHOOSE: View, Print Layout

8. Continue to the next lesson.

1.4.2 Zooming the Display

→ **Feature**

Regardless of the view you select, Word lets you zoom in and out on a document, increasing and decreasing its display size. For example, you may want to enlarge Word's Normal view to 200% of its
original size when working with detailed graphics.

→ **Method**

• CLICK: Zoom drop-down arrow (125% ▾)

   or

• CHOOSE: View, Zoom

→ **Practice**

You will now practice zooming the display. Ensure that you have completed the previous lesson and
that the "Newsletter" document is displaying.

1. To zoom the document to 200% its original size:
   CLICK: Zoom drop-down arrow on the Standard toolbar

2. From the drop-down list:
   CHOOSE: 200%
   Your screen should now appear similar to the one shown in Figure 1.33. The document is imme-
   diately magnified to twice its original size.

Figure 1.33

Increasing the zoom factor to 200%

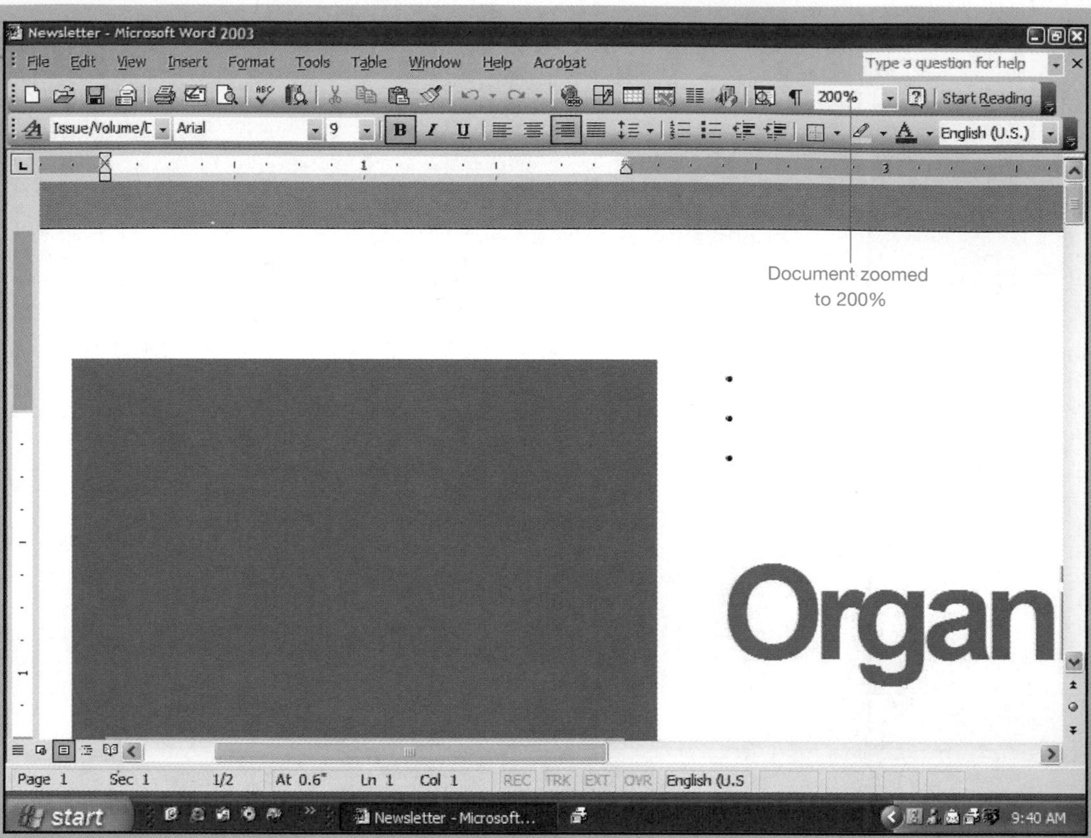

Document zoomed to 200%

3. To find the best-fit magnification:
CLICK: Zoom drop-down arrow
SELECT: Page Width from the drop-down list
The view is zoomed to the best fit for your screen's resolution.

In Addition USING CLICK AND TYPE

In Print Layout and Web Layout views, consider trying out Word's Click and Type feature. This feature enables you to insert text almost anywhere in your document. Simply double-click where you want to begin typing and the Click and Type feature will align the insertion point depending on where you clicked. If you double-click near the center of your page, Click and Type will center-align the insertion point. Likewise, if you double-click near the right side of your page, Click and Type will right-align the insertion point.

1.4.3 Using Reading Layout View

→ **Feature**

Reading Layout view allows you to temporarily view your document so that it is easily read on the screen with a minimum of scrolling. Typically, your document will display two pages at a time with an increased font size for easy viewing. To toggle between two-page view and one-page view, click the 2 Pages icon (🕒).

→ **Method**

- CLICK: View, Reading Layout
  or

- CLICK: the Start Reading icon (📖 Read) on the Standard toolbar

To return to the previous view

- CLICK: Close (📖 Close).

→ **Practice**

You will now practice reading the newsletter in Reading Layout view.

1. CLICK: Start Reading (📖 Read) on the Standard toolbar. Your screen should be similar to Figure 1.34.

Figure 1.34

Reading Layout view

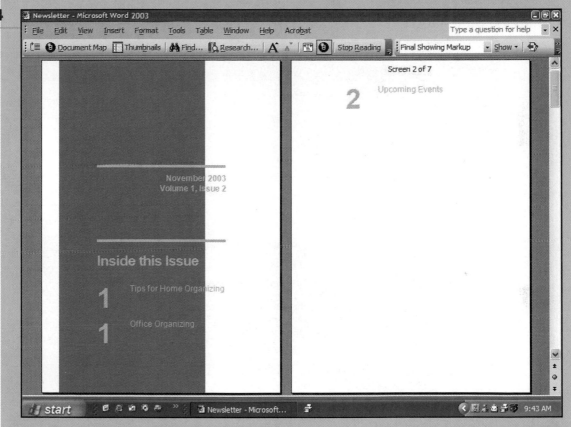

2. CLICK: 2 Pages icon (⊕) to toggle the view from two pages to one page.

3. CLICK: Next Page icon (⊡) to scroll through the newsletter.

4. CLICK: Stop Reading (📖 Close) to return the document to its previous view.

5. CHOOSE: File, Exit to close the document and exit Word. If prompted, do not save the changes.

 **SelfCheck**   **1.4** How do you change the document's zoom setting?

Chapter
summary

To create a basic document in Word, simply begin typing after loading the application. Keep in mind that when the end of the current line is reached, the feature called *word wrap* automatically moves the insertion point to the beginning of the next line. You can easily remove characters from a document using **DELETE** and **BACKSPACE**, and insert blank lines using **ENTER**. Word also employs the AutoText and AutoCorrect features to correct certain errors automatically. In addition to creating documents, it is important to know how to execute common file management procedures, including saving, opening, closing, and printing documents.

Command Summary
Many of the commands and procedures appearing in this chapter are summarized in the following table.

Skill Set	To Perform this Task...	Do the Following...
Starting and Exiting Word	Launch Microsoft Word	CLICK: Start button (<img> start </img>) CHOOSE: Programs, Microsoft Word
	Exit Microsoft Word	CLICK: its Close button (⊠), or CHOOSE: File, Exit
Inserting and Modifying Text	Insert the date and time	CHOOSE: Insert, Date and Time
	Insert blank lines	PRESS: **ENTER**
	Toggle between Insert and Overtype modes	DOUBLE-CLICK: OVR in the Status bar
	Delete text to the right of the insertion point	PRESS: **DELETE**
	Delete text to the left of the insertion point	PRESS: **BACKSPACE**
	Perform an action on a smart tag	CLICK: Smart Tag Actions button (⊡) CHOOSE: an option from the menu
Managing Documents	Browse through files	CLICK: buttons on the Places bar, located in the Save As or Open dialog boxes CLICK: *Save in* or *Look in* drop-down list and select a disk location CLICK: Back button (⬅) to return to the previous location
	Save a document with the same name	CLICK: Save button (🖫)
	Save a document with a different name	CHOOSE: File, Save As
	Close a document	CLICK: Close button (⊠) of the document window, or CHOOSE: File, Close
	Begin a new blank document	CLICK: New button (◱)
	Begin a new document from a wizard or template	CHOOSE: File, New
	Open a document	CLICK: Open button (⬚), or CHOOSE: File, Open

	Print a document	CLICK: Print button (▣), or CHOOSE: File, Print
	Create a new file folder	RIGHT-CLICK: an empty part of the Open or Save dialog box CHOOSE: File, New TYPE: a folder name
Customizing Your Work Area	Switching views	CHOOSE: View, Normal, or CHOOSE: View, Web Layout, or CHOOSE: View, Print Layout, or CHOOSE: View, Outline CHOOSE: View, Reading Layout
	Zooming the display	CLICK: Zoom drop-down arrow (125% ▾), or CHOOSE: View, Zoom

Key Terms

This section specifies page references for the key terms identified in this chapter. For a complete list of definitions, refer to the Glossary provided immediately after the Appendix in this learning guide.

adaptive menus, *p. WD6*

application window, *p. WD3*

AutoCorrect feature, *p. WD10*

AutoFormat feature, *p. WD10*

AutoText feature, *p. WD10*

hyperlinks, *p. WD20*

insertion point, *p. WD14*

Normal view, *p. WD31*

Outline view, *p. WD31*

Places bar, *p. WD24*

Print Layout view, *p. WD31*

Reading Layout view, *p. WD6*

Smart Tag, *p. WD10*

Smart Tag Actions button, *p. WD18*

Task pane, *p. WD6*

template, *p. WD20*

Web Layout view, *p. WD31*

wizard, *p. WD20*

word processing, *p. WD2*

word wrap, *p. WD16*

Chapter
quiz

Short Answer

1. What are the five views you can use when working with a document?

2. What is the difference between a wizard and a template?

3. What is the purpose of Smart Tags?

4. How do you turn off adaptive menus?

5. Within Word, how do you create a new folder on your disk?

6. When happens when you press (ENTER)?

7. What is the purpose of the Places bar?

8. How can you leave a menu without making a selection?

9. How can you leave a dialog box without making a selection?

10. What does the ellipsis mean after a menu selection?

True/False

1. _____ Print Layout view can be used to edit your documents.

2. _____ Web Layout view allows you to see how your document will look when printed.

3. _____ Using the Open dialog box, you can sort a file listing.

4. _____ To exit Word, you must choose File, Exit.

5. _____ To move to the top of the document, press (CTRL) + (HOME).

6. _____ Normal view describes in outline form how your document will appear in your Web browser.

7. _____ You can remove smart tags.

8. _____ To switch between Insert and Overtype modes, double-click the OVR indicator on the Standard toolbar.

9. _____ In Print Layout view, you see how your document will look when viewed in a Web browser.

10. _____ To delete the character to the left of the insertion point, press (DELETE).

Multiple Choice

1. To use a template, you:
   a. Click the New icon (▢)
   b. Click File, Template
   c. Click File, New, choose On My Computer . . ., then select a template
   d. Click the Template button on the Standard toolbar

2. Which of the following keys deletes the characters to the right of the insertion point?
   a. (BACKSPACE)
   b. (DELETE)
   c. (Ins)
   d. (PgUp)

3. This feature enables you to type continuously without having to press (ENTER) at the end of each line:
   a. AutoCorrect
   b. AutoText
   c. Smart Tags
   d. Word Wrap

4. In this view, you can see how text and graphics will appear on the printed page:
   a. Web Layout view
   b. Normal view
   c. Print Layout view
   d. Reading Layout view

5. When you create a new document, until you save it, it exists only in:
   a. ROM
   b. Cache
   c. RAM
   d. Clipboard

6. Right-click menus are also called:
   a. Formatting menus
   b. Context-sensitive menus
   c. Abbreviated toolbars
   d. Function menus

7. To save a document with the same name:
   a. Click 🖫 on the Standard toolbar
   b. Click File, Save
   c. Click File, Save As, keep the same name
   d. All of the above

8. The Insert Date and Time dialog box:
   a. Allows you to insert the current date
   b. Allows you to specify the date format
   c. If you specify, will update the date when the document is printed
   d. All of the above

9. This feature allows you to create abbreviations in your document which will be replaced by full text:

   a. AutoFormat
   b. AutoCorrect
   c. AutoFormatAsYouType
   d. Smart Tags

10. To leave a menu without making a selection, click:

   a. Any option in the menu
   b. Any area outside of the menu
   c. The Office Assistant
   d. None of the above

Hands-On
exercises

1. Creating a Document

In this exercise, you will create a simple letter. The final letter is shown in Figure 1.35.

Figure 1.35

"Invite" document

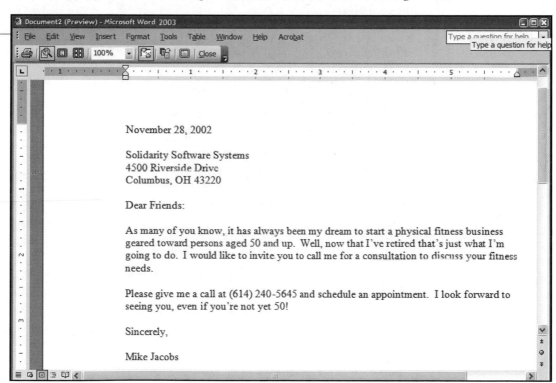

1. Start a new blank document.

2. To insert the date at the top of the blank document:
CHOOSE: Insert, Date and Time
SELECT: the appropriate format in the *Available formats* list box
CLICK: OK command button

3. To position the insertion point before typing the name and address information:
PRESS: (ENTER) three times

4. TYPE: **Solidarity Software Systems**
PRESS: (ENTER)
TYPE: **4500 Riverside Drive**
PRESS: (ENTER)
TYPE: **Columbus, OH 43220**

5. To position the insertion point before typing the salutation:
PRESS: (**ENTER**) twice
TYPE: **Dear Friends:**
PRESS: (**ENTER**) twice

6. If the Office Assistant character appears:
RIGHT-CLICK: the character
CHOOSE: Hide

7. TYPE: **As many of you know, it has always been my dream to start a physical fitness business geared toward persons aged 50 and up. Well, now that I've retired that's just what I'm going to do. I would like to invite you to call me for a consultation to discuss your fitness needs.**
PRESS: (**ENTER**) twice

8. TYPE: **Please give me a call at (614) 240-5645 and schedule an appointment. I look forward to seeing you, even if you're not yet 50!**
PRESS: (**ENTER**) twice

9. To complete the letter:
TYPE: **Sincerely,**
PRESS: (**ENTER**) twice
TYPE: **Mike Jacobs**

10. Using the Save As feature, save the letter as "Invite" to your personal storage location.

11. Print and then close the document. Your printout should look like the document in Figure 1.35.

step by step

2. Editing an Existing Document

In this exercise, you will edit the document you created in Exercise 1 above.

1. Open the "Invite" document you created in Exercise 1.

2. Save the document as "RevisedInvite" to your personal storage location.

3. Let's change the salutation. Begin by positioning your cursor after the word "Friends," but before the colon.

4. To add text:
PRESS: the spacebar once
TYPE: **and Co-Workers**

5. Let's add the following paragraph to the document. Before typing, position the insertion point at the end of the first paragraph.

6. PRESS: (**ENTER**) twice

7. TYPE: **This consultation will give us a chance to talk about your fitness goals and evaluate your current level of fitness. There is no obligation, and the consultation is free.**
Your document should appear similar to the one shown in Figure 1.36.

Figure 1.36

Completed "RevisedInvite" document

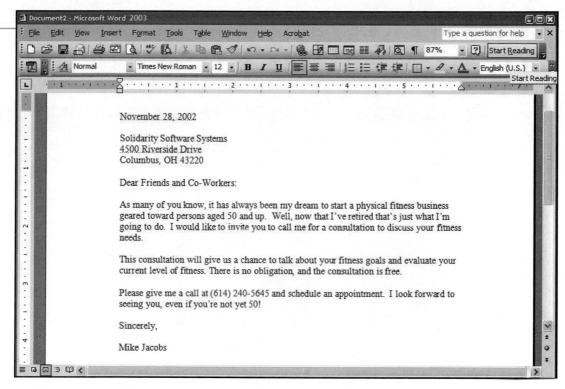

8. Print, save, and then close the document.

step by step

3. Creating a Fax from a Template

In this exercise, let's create a fax from a Word template.

1. To launch the template:
   CHOOSE: File, New
   CLICK: "On My Computer . . ." hyperlink in the Templates section of the task pane
   CLICK: *Letters & Faxes* tab
   DOUBLE-CLICK: Business Fax

2. Click in the upper-left corner of the document where it says "Company Name."

3. Type the following name and address:
   Precious Pets Day Care
   45 Longfellow Drive
   Indianapolis, IN 54132

4. Complete the fax by clicking in the appropriate areas so that it includes the details shown below:
   To: Joyce Willison
   Fax: (614) 235-7800
   From: Mary Insabella
   Fax: 614-287-2545
   Date: *Insert the current date here*
   Regarding: Charges for day care services
   Phone number for follow-up: (614) 240-5645

5. Delete the word "Comments" in the comments section. Double-click on the left edge of the Comments box to place the insertion point, and type this:
   Joyce, thank you for calling about our pet day care services. Our company takes a lot of pride in the exceptional care it provides to your beloved pets. Our fees are $25 per day,

which includes food, exercise, and boarding. For an additional $15, we will groom your pet before you pick it up. I hope this answers your questions. We are currently booked until the third week in August, so I suggest you call early to make reservations.

6. Using Save As, save the document as "Willison Fax" to your personal storage location. At this point, the fax document should appear similar to the one shown in Figure 1.37.

Figure 1.37

"Willison Fax" document

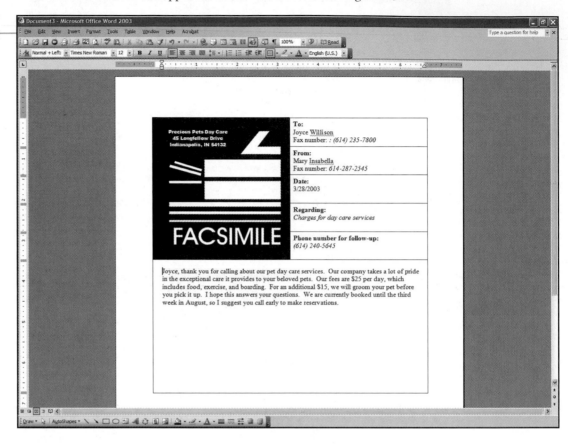

7. Print and then close the document.

on your own

4. Establishing a Document Filing System

In this exercise, you will create folders in which to store documents and then move documents into the new folders.

1. Make sure Word is loaded and no documents are open.

2. Open the "My Documents Folder."

3. Create a new folder and name it "Letters."

4. In the "My Documents Folder" create another new folder named "Faxes."

5. Open the "RevisedInvite" letter from your data files storage location.

6. Using Save As, save the letter to the "Letters" folder created in step 3. Close the file.

7. Open the "Willison Fax" document from your personal storage location.

8. Save the "Willison Fax" document to the "Faxes" folder created in step 4.

9. Close the file.

10. Delete the "RevisedInvite" document and the "Willison Fax" document from their original locations.

on your own

5. Writing a Letter to a Client

In this exercise, you will create the letter shown in Figure 1.38. Type the letter as shown, correcting any mistakes as you go. Press Enter twice after the date, again after the address, and again after the salutation. Press Enter twice to separate paragraphs. When finished, use Reading Layout view to review the letter. Print the document and save it as "Sears Letter" in the "Letters" folder you created in Exercise 4.

Figure 1.38

"Sears Letter" document

> November 28, 2002
>
> Ms. Debbie Sears
> 1432 Grove Avenue
> Gahanna, OH 43156
>
> Dear Debbie:
>
> Thank you for allowing us at *Fitness for Seniors* to help you meet your fitness goals. We hope you are satisfied with our services and will refer your family and friends.
>
> You did a wonderful job reaching your fitness goals. I know it was difficult, but the worst is over! To maintain your fitness level, I recommend you do the following: (1) walk at least 2 miles a day, at least three days a week; (2) drink at least 8 glasses of water each day; and (3) eat no more than 1500 calories per day. By following this regimen, you can maintain your current fitness level.
>
> The balance on your account is $435.00. Please remit this payment within 15 days of receipt of this letter. Don't hesitate to call me if you have any questions. Thanks again.
>
> Sincerely,
>
> Mike Jacobs

on your own

6. Searching the Internet, Creating and Modifying a Document, and Filing it in a New Folder

In this exercise, you will search the Internet for information on shark attacks. Using your Web browser, search for this information (find at least two sources). Summarize the information into a one-to-two page report. Title the document "*SharkAttackInfo.*" Proofread the document, ensuring that it is correct. Print the document. Save the document into a new folder called "WebResearch" in your personal storage location. Print the document and turn it in to your instructor.

CaseStudy   NATIONAL PAPER COMPANY

Meg has just been hired as an Office Associate at the National Paper Company. National Paper manufactures and distributes various paper supplies, such as bubble wrap, packing paper, paper towels, and plastic shopping bags. Her job is to assist the Director of Operations and the Sales Manager in communicating with customers and potential customers, as well as internal staff members.

In the following case problems, you'll assume the role of Meg as she performs some basic Word functions.

1. Meg has been asked to prepare a memo to company employees indicating that a 3% pay increase will be given to all employees, effective January 1, 2004. Meg will use Word to create a draft of the letter to show to her supervisor, Peggy. Because Meg does not yet know about Word's many formatting features, she will format it later.

(Insert Current Date here)

Dear Employees,

This is to inform you that all employees will be given a 3% pay increase effective January 1, 2004.

If you have any questions, please call Ms. Hemenway at ext. 302.

She then saves the letter as "PayRaiseNotice." Save the file to your data file storage location. The completed document is shown in Figure 1.39.

Figure 1.39

Completed
"PayRaiseNotice"
document

December 1, 2002

Dear Employees,

This is to inform you that all employees will be given a 3% pay increase effective January 1, 2004.

If you have any questions, please call Ms. Hemenway at ext. 302.

2. After showing the letter to her supervisor, Peggy has several changes and has asked Meg to revise the letter as shown below.

- In the Salutation, add "**Fellow**" after Dear.

- Add a sentence to the beginning of the first paragraph that reads:

  As you know, National Paper had record-breaking earnings this past year. We could not have accomplished this without the help of all employees.

- Press **ENTER** twice.

- Change last paragraph to read **If you have any questions, please contact me at ext. 302.**

- Press **ENTER** twice.

- Type:
  Peggy Hemenway
  Director of Operations
  National Paper

Save the letter with the same name.

The revised letter should look like Figure 1.40.

Figure 1.40

Revised
"PayRaiseNotice"
document

December 1, 2002

Dear Fellow Employees,

As you know, National Paper had record-breaking earnings this past year. We could not have accomplished this without the help of all employees.

This is to inform you that all employees will be given a 3% pay increase effective January 1, 2004.

If you have any questions, please call me at ext. 302.

Peggy Hemenway
Director of Operations
National Paper

3. National Paper intends to hold an annual golf outing at Muirfield Country Club. Many important members of the golfing community, as well as prominent business leaders, will be invited. Meg has been asked to write an announcement for the company bulletin board asking for employee volunteers. Meg writes the following announcement; the completed document appears in Figure 1.41.

(Insert Current Date here)

Call for Volunteers!

National Paper is hosting a golf outing on July 13–15, 2004, at the Muirfield Country Club. Many important community leaders will be invited as well as several well-known golf professionals.

We need volunteers for the following:

Greeters
Food and Beverage Servers
Caddies
Registration

If you are interested in volunteering your services, please call the Marketing Department at ext. 309 no later than June 15, 2004.

Save the notice as "Volunteers" to your personal data storage location. Print the document.

Figure 1.41

Completed "Volunteers" document

> Insert Current Date here
>
> Call for Volunteers!
>
> National Paper is hosting a golf outing on July 13-15, 2004, at the Muirfield Country Club. Many important community leaders will be invited as well as several well-known golf professionals.
>
> We need volunteers for the following:
>
> Greeters
> Food and Beverage Servers
> Caddies
> Registration

4. The Marketing Department needs to approve the "Volunteers" document before it is posted throughout the company. Meg decides to fax the "Volunteers" document to Marketing in order to speed things up. She creates a new fax document based on the "Contemporary Fax" template and modifies the template to reflect the information shown below.

National Paper Company
10245 Hilliard Rome Road
Hilliard, Ohio 53345

To: Jeff Hughes
From: Meg Zimmerman
Fax: (216) 349-0897
Re: Notice for Volunteers
Pages: 2
Cc: Peggy Hemenway

Attached is the draft notice requesting employee volunteers for the annual Muirfield Golf Outing. If this meets with your approval, please call me at the Hilliard office so that we can get this finalized and posted as soon as possible.

Thank you.

Meg now saves the document as "Volunteer Fax." Remove any smart tags in the document. Then she prints and closes the document. The completed document is shown in Figure 1.42.

Figure 1.42

Completed
"Volunteer Fax"
document

National Paper
10745 Hilliard Rome Road
Hilliard, OH 53345

facsimile transmittal

To:	Jeff Hughes	Fax:	(216) 349-0897
From:	Meg Zimmerman	Date:	12/1/2002
Re:	Notice for Volunteers	Pages:	2
CC:	Peggy Hemenway		

☐ Urgent   ☐ For Review   ☐ Please Comment   ☐ Please Reply   ☐ Please Recycle

Attached is the draft notice requesting employee volunteers for the annual Muirfield Golf Outing.
If this meets with your approval, please call me at the Hilliard office so that we can get this
finalized and posted as soon as possible.

Thank you.

Answers to Self-Check Questions

SelfCheck

1.1 To display the standard and formatting toolbars on different lines, click Tools, Customize, select the Options tab and check Show Standard and Formatting toolbars on two rows.

1.2 To insert the current date in a document choose Insert, Date and Time.

1.3 Three ways to create a new document are start with a blank document, select a document template, or use a wizard.

1.4 To change the document's zoom setting, click the Zoom drop-down arrow and choose a magnification. You can also choose View, Zoom and choose a setting.

Notes

Microsoft® Office**Word**®

2003

CHAPTER 2

Modifying a Document

PREREQUISITES

To successfully complete this chapter, you must be able to insert and delete text in Word. You will also be asked to open, save, and close documents and use Word's toolbars, Menu bar, and right-click menus. You should know how to create folders from within the Word Save and open dialog boxes.

LEARNING OBJECTIVES

After completing this chapter, you will be able to:

- Use fundamental editing procedures

- Search for and replace words and phrases

- Copy and move information within the same document and among documents

- Check for spelling and grammar errors

- Use the Research tool to polish your document

2.1 EDITING A DOCUMENT

What if you type a word into a document and then decide it needs to be changed? Both novices and experts alike make data-entry errors when creating documents. Fortunately, Word provides several features for editing information that has already been entered. One of Word's most popular commands is the **Undo command,** which lets you correct mistakes by undoing your most recent actions. Another popular feature is the spelling and grammar checker, which scans your documents for errors as you type. You also have at your disposal the Research Tool. This tool offers dictionary, encyclopedic, and translation services to help you find the perfect word! This module covers all three of these features.

You will find that many editing procedures require that you first position the insertion point in a certain location or select one or more characters of text. Word provides an invisible column in the extreme left margin of the document window called the **Selection bar.** When the mouse is moved into this area, the pointer changes from an I-beam to a right-pointing diagonal arrow (⦢). The Selection bar provides shortcut methods for using the mouse to select text, as summarized in Table 2.1 along with other selection methods.

Table 2.1

Selecting Text
Using the Mouse

To Select This ...	Do This ...
Single Letter	Position the I-beam pointer to the left of the letter you want to select. Press down and hold the left mouse button as you drag the mouse pointer to the right.
Single Word	Position the I-beam pointer on the word and double-click the left mouse button.
Single Sentence	Hold down `CTRL` and click once with the I-beam pointer positioned on any word in the sentence.
Block of Text	Move the insertion point to the beginning of the block of text and then position the I-beam pointer at the end of the block. Hold down `SHIFT` and click once.
Single Line	Move the mouse pointer into the Selection bar, beside the line to be selected. Wait until the pointer changes to a right-pointing arrow and then click once.
Single Paragraph	Move the mouse pointer into the Selection bar, beside the paragraph to be selected. Wait until the pointer changes to a right-pointing arrow and then double-click.
Entire Document	Move the mouse pointer into the Selection bar. Wait until the pointer changes to a right-pointing arrow and then hold down `CTRL` and click once. (*Note:* You can also press `CTRL` + **a** to select the entire document or triple click from the selection bar.)
Deselecting Text	Click anywhere outside of the selected text.

We describe each of these features in the following lessons.

2.1.1 Positioning the Insertion Point

→ **Feature**

As for many procedures in Word, the mouse provides the easiest method for moving through a document. To position the insertion point, you scroll the document window until the desired text appears
and then click the I-beam mouse pointer in the text. Contrary to what you might think, scrolling the
document window does not automatically move the insertion point. If you forget to click the mouse
and start typing or press an arrow key, Word takes you back to the original location of the insertion
point before you started scrolling.

→ **Method**

Some common methods for positioning the insertion point using the keyboard include:

- ⬆ or ⬇ to move up or down one line

- ⬅ or ➡ to move to the previous or next character

- END to move to the end of the current line

- HOME to move to the beginning of the current line

- PgUp or PgDn to move up or down one screen

- CTRL + HOME to move to the beginning of the document

- CTRL + END to move to the end of the document

To access the Go To dialog box:
CHOOSE: Edit, Go To or press CTRL + g

→ **Practice**

You will now open an existing six-page document and practice positioning the insertion point. Ensure
that you have loaded Word and that you have disabled the adaptive menus feature as described in
Chapter 1. Ensure also that the Standard and Formatting toolbars are positioned on separate rows.

1. Open the WD0210 data file. This document discusses physical fitness as advised by the President's Council on Physical Fitness and Sports.

2. If the task pane is displaying:
   CHOOSE: View, Task Pane to hide it from view

3. Save the file as "Fitness" to your personal storage location. (*Hint:* Choose File, Save As.) Your
   screen should now appear similar to the one shown in Figure 2.1. Note that the insertion point is
   positioned at the beginning of the document.

Word

Figure 2.1

"Fitness"
document

Insertion point

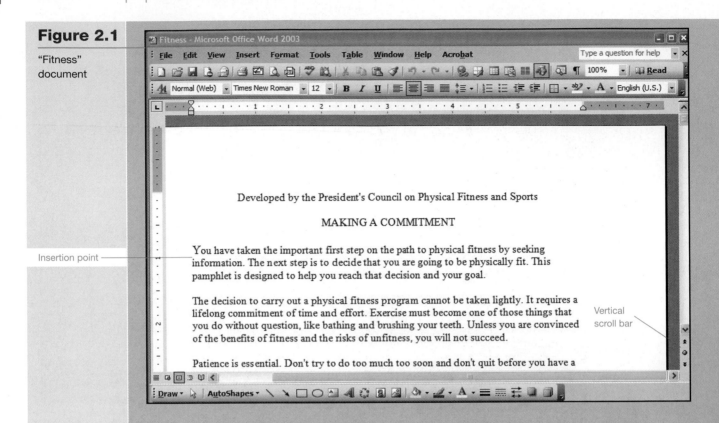

4. To move down through the document one screen at a time:
CLICK: below the vertical scroll box on the vertical scroll bar repeatedly

5. To move to the top of the document:
DRAG: the scroll box to the top of the vertical scroll bar
(*Note:* The term "drag" means to press and hold down the mouse button as you move the mouse pointer from one location to another.) As you drag the scroll box along the scroll bar, Word displays the current page number. You can also see the current page number in the bottom-left corner of the screen.

6. To move the insertion point directly to the bottom of the document using the keyboard:
PRESS: CTRL + END

7. To move back to the top of the document using the keyboard:
PRESS: CTRL + HOME

8. To move to the end of the current line:
PRESS: END

9. To move to the beginning of the current line:
PRESS: HOME

10. To move to the top of the second page in the document:
CLICK: Next Page button (⊽) on the vertical scroll bar
The insertion point automatically moves to the first line of page 2 (Figure 2.2).

Figure 2.2

The insertion point is on the top of page 2

Insertion point —

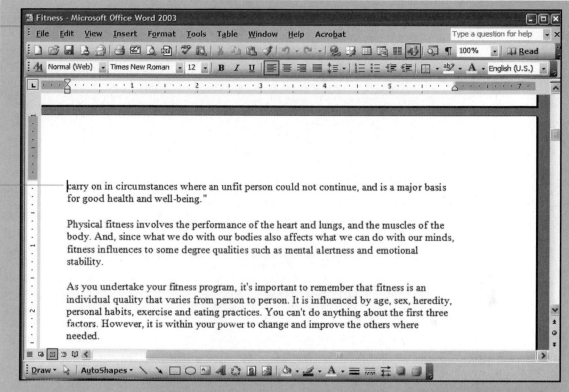

carry on in circumstances where an unfit person could not continue, and is a major basis for good health and well-being."

Physical fitness involves the performance of the heart and lungs, and the muscles of the body. And, since what we do with our bodies also affects what we can do with our minds, fitness influences to some degree qualities such as mental alertness and emotional stability.

As you undertake your fitness program, it's important to remember that fitness is an individual quality that varies from person to person. It is influenced by age, sex, heredity, personal habits, exercise and eating practices. You can't do anything about the first three factors. However, it is within your power to change and improve the others where needed.

11. To practice using the Go To dialog box:
CHOOSE: Edit, Go To or press **CTRL** + g
Other methods for displaying the Go To dialog box include double-clicking the page area—"Page 2"—in the Status bar or pressing **F5** . Your screen should now appear similar to the one shown in Figure 2.3.

Figure 2.3

The Find and Replace dialog box, Go to tab

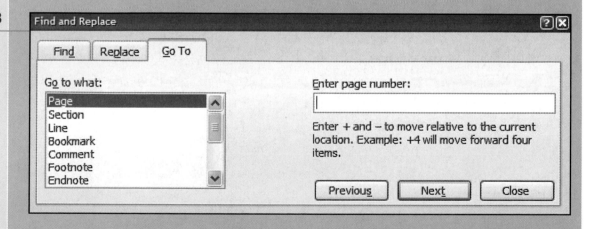

12. TYPE: **P2L16**
CLICK: Go To command button
The "P" tells Word that the following number is a page number, and the "L" tells Word that the next number is a line number. The letters can be typed in either uppercase or lowercase characters. In this step, the insertion point is moved to line 16 on page 2.
(*Note:* Word counts blank lines when positioning the insertion point in this manner, but it does not count header/footer text lines.)

13. In the Find and Replace dialog box:
CLICK: Close command button

14. To move to the top of the document:
PRESS: **CTRL** + **HOME**

15. Keep this document open for the next lesson.

2.1.2 Using Undo and Redo

→ **Feature**

The **Undo command** enables you to cancel the last several commands you performed in a document. The **Redo command** repeats the last action you performed in the document, such as inserting or deleting text or using a menu command.

→ **Method**

To undo the last action:

- CLICK: Undo button (⟲▾) on the Standard toolbar

or

- CHOOSE: Edit, Undo

or

- PRESS: **CTRL** + z

To undo the last several actions:

- CLICK: down arrow next to the Undo button (⟲▾)

- CLICK: an action in the drop-down list to execute that action and all the actions above

To repeat the last command:

- CHOOSE: Edit, Repeat

→ **Practice**

You will now practice using the Undo and Redo commands.

1. Make sure the "Fitness" document is open.

2. DELETE: The first heading on the first page (MAKING A COMMITMENT)

3. To undo the deletion you just performed:
CLICK: Undo button (⟲▾)
(*Caution:* Place the tip of the mouse pointer over the curved arrow on the left side of the button, as opposed to the downward pointing arrow, before clicking the left mouse button.)

4. In this step, you retype the title and perform several actions.
PLACE: the insertion point after the last "T" in COMMITMENT
PRESS: **ENTER** twice

TYPE: *your name*

Your document should now appear similar to that shown in Figure 2.4. Depending on the settings of your computer, Word may have applied automatic formatting to the text. Your text may also wrap differently. These differences are not a problem.

Figure 2.4

Using the Undo command

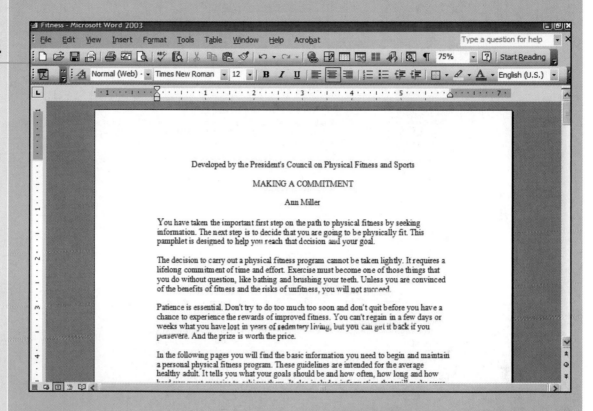

5. To view all the actions that you can undo:
CLICK: down arrow beside the Undo button (↩ ▾)
Your screen should now appear similar to the one shown in Figure 2.5. You may have different items in your Undo list. This difference is not a problem.

Figure 2.5

Using the Undo command

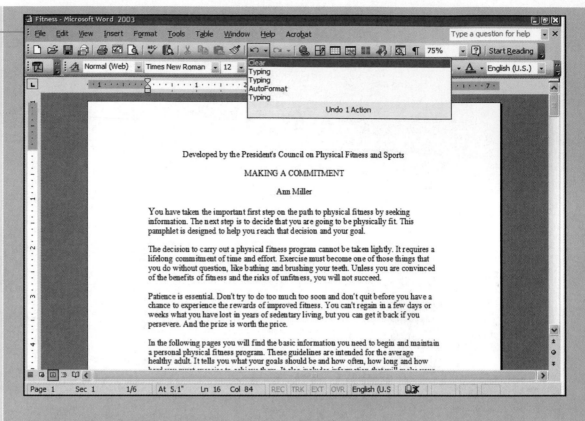

6. To exit the drop-down list without selecting an item:
   CLICK: in the Title bar

7. To illustrate the use of the **Repeat command**:
   CHOOSE: Edit, Repeat from the Menu bar. Because the last action you performed was to type your name, it is repeated.

8. To remove the duplicate name from the document:
   CLICK: Undo button (🔄)

9. Keep the document open for the next lesson.

 **SelfCheck**

2.1 How do you select a single sentence at one time?

2.1.3 Correcting Mistakes as You Go

→ ## Feature

By default, Word checks your documents for spelling and grammar errors as you type. Word marks spelling errors with a red wavy underline and grammar errors with a green wavy underline. You have the choice of accepting or ignoring Word's suggestions.

→ ## Method

To correct spelling and grammar errors:

- Point to a word with a wavy red or green underline and then right-click with the mouse.

- Choose Word's suggestion from the right-click menu, choose the Ignore All or Ignore Sentence command if no error has been made, or edit the error yourself.

→ ## Practice

You will now practice correcting a spelling error. Ensure that you have completed the previous lesson and the "Fitness" document is open.

1. In this step, force an intentional spelling error by deleting the "i" of "Council" in the title of the document on your screen.

2. To register the error with Word, you must move the insertion point.
PRESS: ⬇
Note that a red wavy underline appears beneath the misspelled word.

3. To correct the word, point to the word and then right-click using the mouse. Your screen should now appear similar to the one shown Figure 2.6.

Figure 2.6

The Spelling
right-click menu

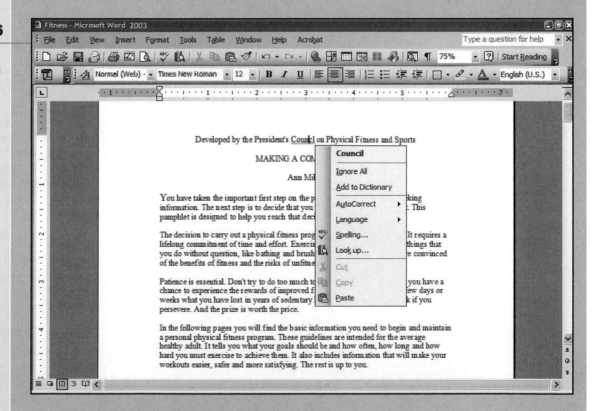

4. Using the mouse, choose the word "Council" in the menu. The word "Council" should have replaced "Councl" in the document.

5. To conclude this lesson, save changes to the document. From the Menu bar:

CHOOSE: File, Save or click (🖫)

6. Keep the file open for the next lesson.

2.1.4 Selecting and Changing Text

→ # Feature

A selection of text may include letters, words, lines, paragraphs, or even the entire document. Many Word procedures require that you begin by making a text selection.

→ # Method

The methods for selecting text are summarized in Table 2.1, shown earlier. To deselect text, click once in the text area or elsewhere in the document.

→ # Practice

You will now use the "Fitness" document with which you have been working to practice the various methods of selecting text.

1. Make sure the "Fitness" document is open and the insertion point is at the top of the document.

2. To select the word "Developed" in the title, first position the I-beam mouse pointer anywhere on the word.

3. DOUBLE-CLICK: Developed
The word should be highlighted in reverse video. Your screen should now appear similar to Figure 2.7. (*Note:* Unless a font color has been applied to text, selected text always appears in reverse video, with white text on a black background.)

Figure 2.7

Selecting a word

Selected word

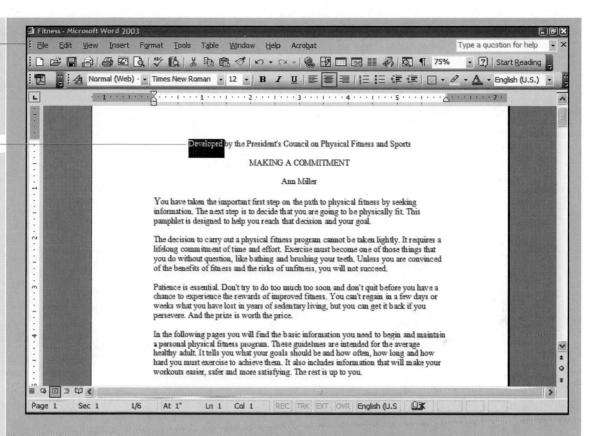

4. In the title, let's select the letters "President" in the word "President's." To do this, first position the I-beam pointer to the left of the "P" in "President's."

5. PRESS: left mouse button and hold it down
DRAG: I-beam to the right until "President" is highlighted

6. To select the first sentence in the first paragraph, first position the I-beam pointer over any word in the sentence.

7. PRESS: CTRL and hold it down.
CLICK: left mouse button once
The first sentence, including the period and following space, is highlighted (Figure 2.8).

Figure 2.8

Selecting a
sentence

Selected sentence

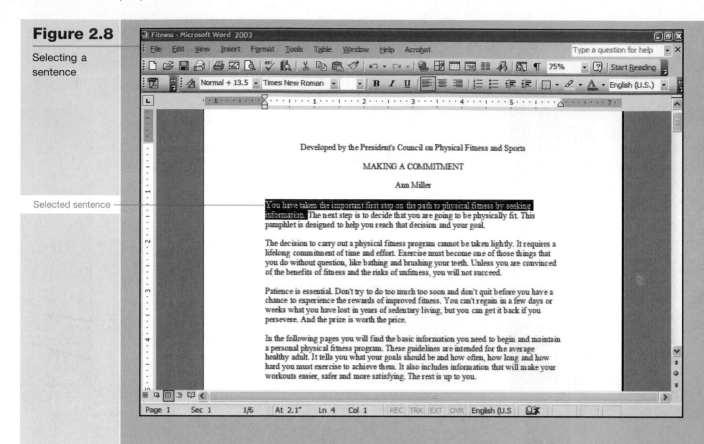

8. To select only the second line in the first paragraph, position the mouse pointer to the left of the line in the Selection bar. The mouse pointer should change from an I-beam to a right-pointing diagonal arrow.

9. CLICK: the Selection bar beside the first word in the second line

10. To select the entire first paragraph:
DOUBLE-CLICK: the Selection bar beside the first paragraph
(*Note*: You can also position the I-beam pointer on any word in the paragraph and triple-click the left mouse button to select the entire paragraph. Remember that Word considers a paragraph to be any line or lines of text that ends with your having pressed ENTER.) Your screen should now appear similar to the one shown in Figure 2.9.

Figure 2.9

Selecting a paragraph

Selected paragraph —

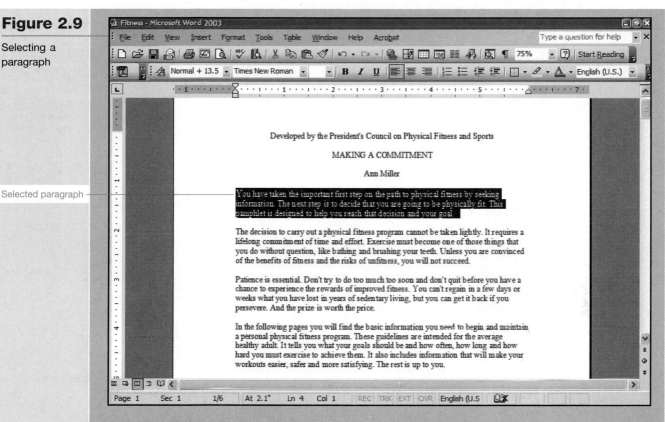

11. To delete the selected paragraph:
    PRESS: DELETE
    The entire paragraph is removed from the document.

12. To undo the previous action:
    CLICK: Undo button (↺ ▾)

13. To practice changing selected text, do the following:
    SELECT: the word "important" in the first sentence

14. TYPE: critical
    Note that your typed word replaced the current selection (Figure 2.10).

Figure 2.10

Selecting and
replacing a word

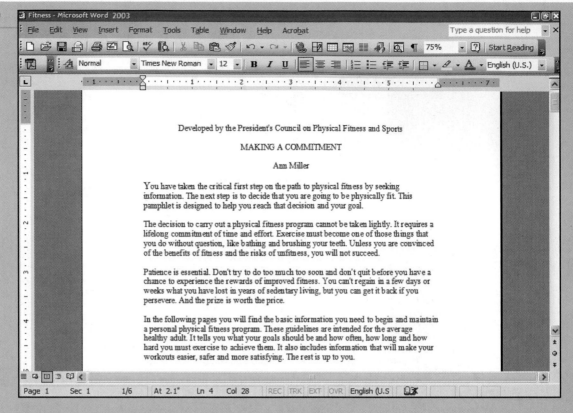

15. To select the entire document:
PRESS: **CTRL** and hold it down
CLICK: once anywhere in the Selection bar
(*Note:* You can also position the mouse pointer in the Selection bar and triple-click the left
mouse button to select the entire document.)

16. To remove highlighting from the text:
CLICK: once anywhere in the text area

17. Save and then close the document.

2.2   How does Word define a paragraph?

2.2 Finding and Replacing Text

Imagine that you have just written a history of your school that will be submitted to the local business leaders in anticipation of garnering their support and funding. You have run the spell checker on the document and found no errors. However, upon further reading, you realize that you used the word "technical" instead of "technician." Because these are both legitimate words, the spell checker did not catch the error. Therefore, you must use another of Word's editing features—the Find and Replace utility—to correct the mistake.

2.2.1 Finding Text

→ **Feature**

The Find command enables you to search for text (such as the word "hello"), nonprinting characters (such as the Paragraph ¶), and formatting characteristics (such as boldface). This tool is also useful for quickly finding your place in a document.

→ **Method**

To use the Find command:

- CHOOSE: Edit, Find
- TYPE: *the text you are looking for* in the *Find what:* text box
- CLICK: More button to refine your search (optional)
- SELECT: Find Next

→ **Practice**

You will now open a document that outlines the history of a small college and its subsequent growth. Ensure that Word is loaded and that the application window is maximized.

1. Open the WD0221 data file.

2. Save the file as "Mid-City" to your personal storage location.

3. To begin a search for a word or phrase in a document:
CHOOSE: Edit, Find
The Find and Replace dialog box should now appear (Figure 2.11). Your *Find what:* text box may not show the same text as Figure 2.11. That difference is not a problem.

4. CLICK: the Replace tab

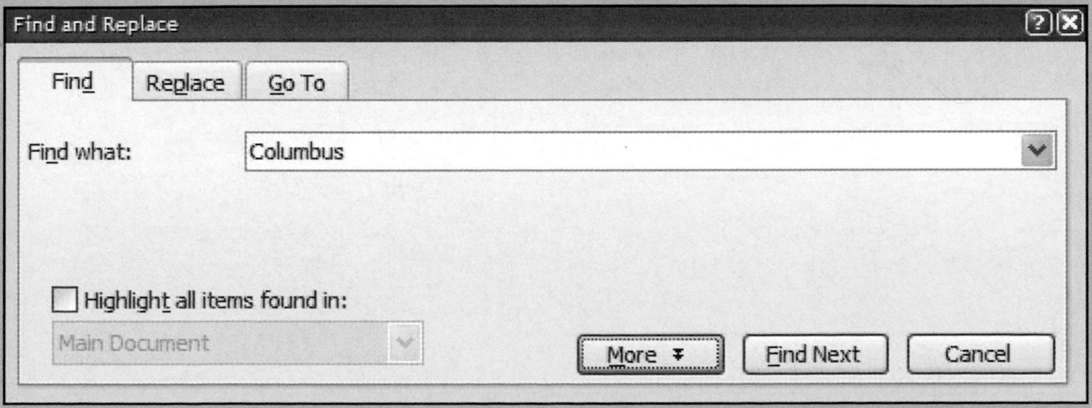

Figure 2.11

Find and Replace dialog box: *Find* tab

5. With the insertion point in the *Find what:* text box:
   TYPE: **technical**
   (*Note:* If there is text in the *Find what:* text box, delete it first.)

6. Let's see what options are available when you click the More button.
   CLICK: More command button in the Find and Replace dialog box.
   The Find and Replace dialog box should appear similar to the one shown in Figure 2.12. Note the *Find whole words only* option. This option is useful for bypassing those words that may appear as a part of another word.

Figure 2.12

Find and Replace dialog box: Displaying additional options

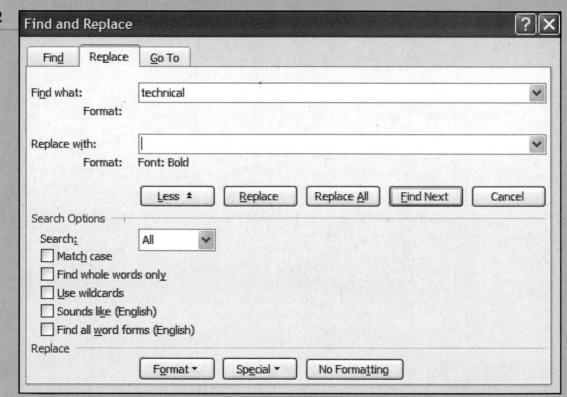

7. To display less information in the Find and Replace dialog box:
   CLICK: Less command button

8. To tell Word to begin the search:
   CLICK: Find Next command button

9. Word stops at the first occurrence of "technical." (*Note:* You may have to drag the dialog box downward or to the side to see that "technical" is now selected in your document.) To continue the search:
   CLICK: Find Next command button
   Word stops at the second occurrence of "technical."

10. To continue the search:
    CLICK: Find Next
    Your screen should be similar to the one shown in Figure 2.13.

Figure 2.13

The search is complete

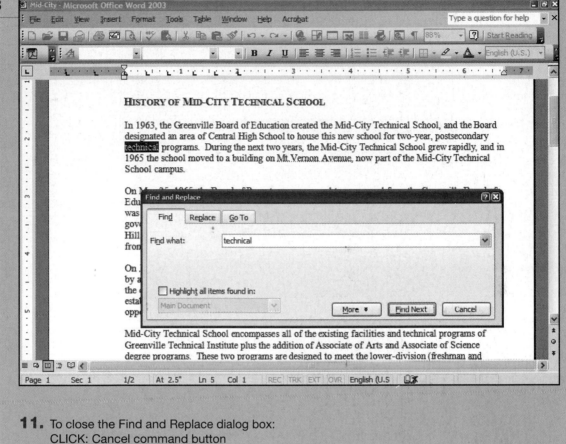

11. To close the Find and Replace dialog box:
    CLICK: Cancel command button

2.2.2 Replacing Text

→ **Feature**

The Replace command enables you to search for and replace text, nonprinting characters, and formatting characteristics. This command is extremely useful when you have made the same error repeatedly throughout a document.

→ **Method**

To initiate the Replace command:

- CHOOSE: Edit, Replace
- TYPE: *the text you are looking for* in the *Find what:* text box
- TYPE: *the replacement text* in the *Replace with:* text box
- CLICK: More button to refine your search (optional)
- SELECT: Replace, Replace All, or Find Next

→ **Practice**

You will now replace the word "technical" with "technician" throughout the "Mid-City" document. Ensure that the insertion point is positioned at the beginning of the document.

1. CHOOSE: Edit, Replace
Notice that the word "technical" already appears in the *Find what:* text box from the last time you performed the Edit, Find command.

2. To enter the replacement text, click the I-beam mouse pointer in the *Replace with:* text box to position the insertion point.

3. TYPE: **technician**
The Find and Replace dialog box should now appear similar to the one shown in Figure 2.14.

Figure 2.14

Find and Replace
dialog box:
Replace tab

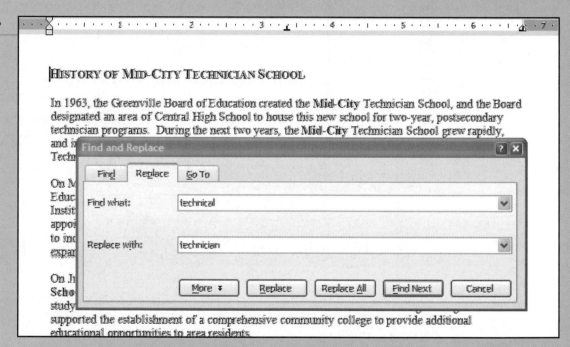

4. To execute the replacement throughout the document:
CLICK: Replace All command button
A dialog box appears informing you that 18 replacements were made in the document.

5. To close the dialog boxes:
CLICK: OK command button
CLICK: Close command button

6. Now let's make all occurrences of the word "Mid-City" appear in bold letters:
CHOOSE: Edit, Replace

7. In the *Find what:* text box:
TYPE: **Mid-City**

8. Position the insertion point in the *Replace with:* text box by clicking the I-beam mouse pointer in the text box.

9. TYPE: **Mid-City**
PRESS: CTRL + **b**
CTRL + **b** is a shortcut key for applying bold formatting. Notice that the text "Format: Font: Bold" appears below the text box (Figure 2.15). (*Note:* You learn to apply many types of formatting in Chapter 3.)

Figure 2.15

Using the Replace command to apply bold formatting

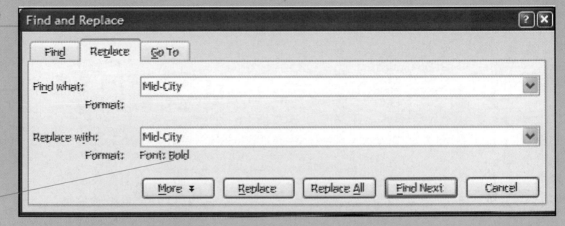

Bold formatting selected

10. To perform the replacement:
CLICK: Replace All command button
Similar to last time, 12 replacements were made in the document.

11. To close the dialog boxes:
CLICK: ☒ icon
If you browse through the document, you will notice that all occurrences of the word "Mid-City" are now bold.

12. Save and then close the "Mid-City" document.

 **SelfCheck**   **2.3** What is the difference between Find and Replace?

2.3 Copying and Moving Information

In Word, it is easy to copy and move information within the same document and among documents. Like all Microsoft Office System applications, Word provides several methods for copying and moving information. First, you can cut or copy a single piece of data from any application and store it on the **Windows Clipboard** and then paste the data into any other application. Second, you can use the **Office Clipboard** to collect up to 24 items and then paste the stored data singularly or as a group into any one of the Office applications. You can also use **drag and drop** to copy and move information using the mouse.

2.3.1 Using The Clipboard

→ ## Feature

You use the Windows and Office Clipboards to copy and move information within Word and among other applications. The Windows Clipboard can store a single item of data from any application, and the Office Clipboard can store up to 24 items. (*Note*: The last item that you cut or copy to the Office Clipboard will appear as the one item stored on the Windows Clipboard.) When working in any one of the Microsoft Office System applications, such as Word, you can display the Office Clipboard toolbar for use in copying, managing, and pasting information.

→ ## Method

To view and manage data stored on the Office Clipboard:

- CHOOSE: Edit, Office Clipboard

To move selected information to the Windows Clipboard:

- CLICK: Cut button (🖾), or press **CTRL** + **x**

To copy selected information to the Windows Clipboard:

- CLICK: Copy button (🖾), or press **CTRL** + **c**

To paste information from the Windows Clipboard into your document:

- CLICK: Paste button (🖾), or press **CTRL** + **v**

→ ## Practice

You will now open a document that discusses some flowcharting concepts. You will then practice using the Windows Clipboard. Ensure that you have completed the previous lesson and that no documents are open in the application window.

1. Open the WD0230 data file.

2. Save the file as "Flowchart" to your personal storage location.

3. To copy the second paragraph to the top, first you must select the text:
SELECT: the second paragraph
Hint: Triple-click in the paragraph
Your document should now appear similar to the one shown in Figure 2.16.

Figure 2.16

Text has been selected

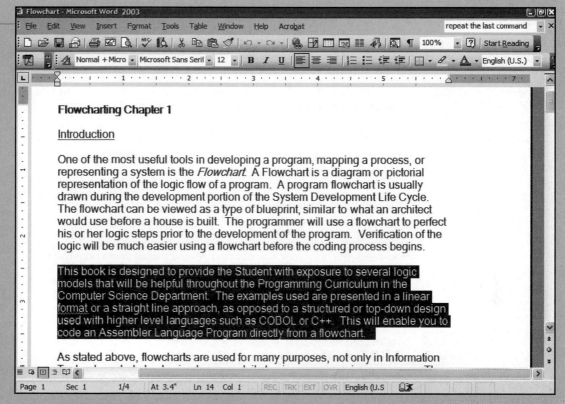

4. To copy the selection to the Clipboard:
   CLICK: Copy button ( ) on the Standard toolbar

5. MOVE: the insertion point to the beginning of the first paragraph (before the word "One").

6. CLICK: to place the insertion point.

7. To paste the contents of the Clipboard at the insertion point of the document:
   CLICK: Paste button ( )
   Your document should now appear similar to the one shown in Figure 2.17. Note the appearance of the Paste Options button ( ).

Figure 2.17

Text has been pasted into new location

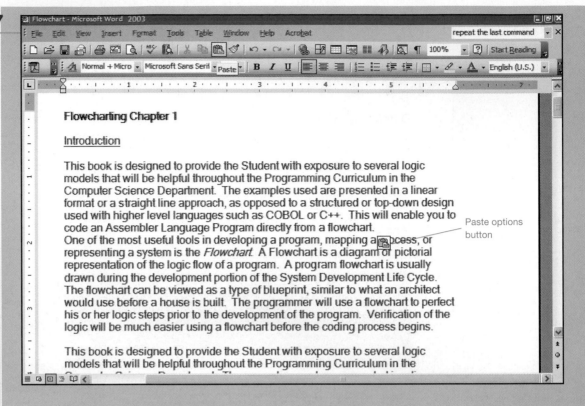

8. Let's see what happens when we click the Paste Options button.
CLICK: Paste Options button (📋▾)
Your screen should now appear similar to Figure 2.18. You will learn more about paste options in Chapter 6. For now, let's not change the current selection.

Figure 2.18

Paste Options

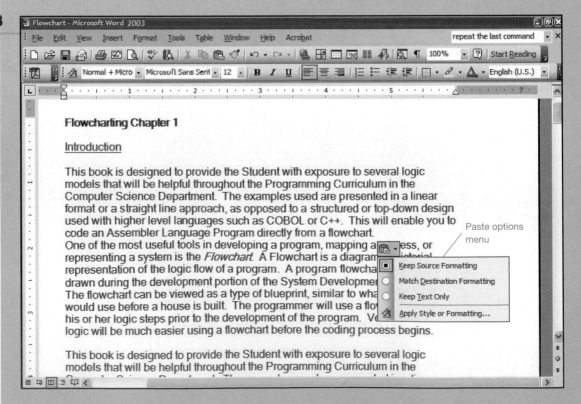

9. To remove the Paste Options menu:
CLICK: in the blank document area
Note that the Paste Options button (📋▾) remains visible.

10. To add a blank line after the paragraph:
CLICK: at the end of the paragraph you just pasted. The paragraph ends with the word "flowchart."
PRESS: `ENTER`

11. To change some of the copied text to uppercase:
SELECT: "Computer Science Department" appearing in the first paragraph
PRESS: `SHIFT` + `F3` once
The text should now read "COMPUTER SCIENCE DEPARTMENT."

12. Because we have already copied it to the top of the document, let's cut the entire third paragraph.
SELECT: the third paragraph

13. To cut the selected paragraph to the Clipboard:
CLICK: Cut button (✂) on the Standard toolbar
Note that the paragraph is removed from the document.

14. To move to the bottom of the document and add a blank line:
PRESS: `CTRL` + `END`
PRESS: `ENTER`

15. To paste the contents of the Clipboard at the insertion point of the document:
CLICK: Paste button (📋)
The paragraph is inserted at the bottom of the document. (*Note:* It may be necessary for you to delete an extra blank line.)

16. When information is placed in the Clipboard, it can be pasted multiple times. To illustrate:
PRESS: `ENTER`
CLICK: Paste button (📋)
Note that the same paragraph has been pasted twice (Figure 2.19).

Figure 2.19

Pasting a selection multiple times

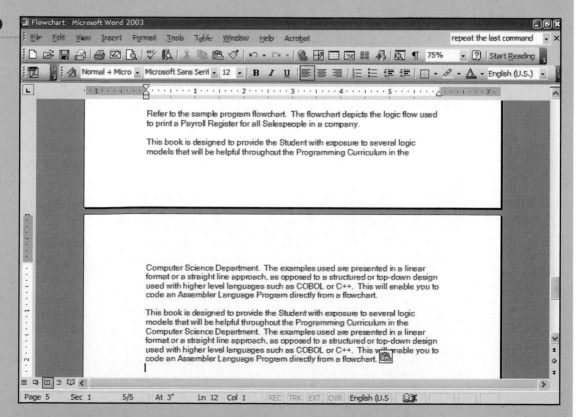

17. Let's view the contents of the Office Clipboard:
CHOOSE: Edit, Office Clipboard
The Clipboard task pane shows the contents of the Office Clipboard (Figure 2.20). The Office Clipboard contains the most recent item you copied to the Clipboard.

Figure 2.20

Office Clipboard

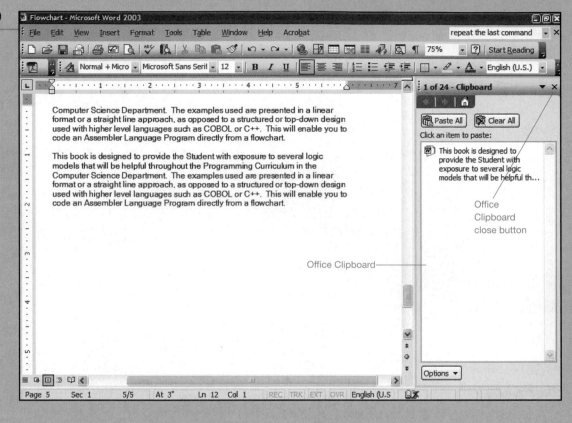

18. To close the Office Clipboard:
CLICK: the Clipboard's Close button, as indicated in Figure 2.20

19. Proceed to the next lesson

2.3.2 Using Drag and Drop

→ **Feature**

You can use the mouse, and bypass the Clipboards altogether, to drag and drop information from one location in your document to another. Although you cannot perform multiple pastes, the drag and drop method provides the easiest and fastest way to copy and move selected text and graphics short distances.

→ **Method**

To copy or move text using the drag and drop method:

• SELECT: the text that you want to copy or move

If you want to perform a copy operation, hold down the **CTRL** key. If you are moving text, do not hold down additional keys.

• DRAG: the selection to the target destination

Release the mouse button. (*Note:* If you are performing a copy operation, release the **CTRL** key after releasing the mouse button.)

→ Practice

You will now practice using drag and drop. Ensure that you have completed the previous lesson and that the "Flowchart" document is displaying.

1. Select the first sentence of the first paragraph.

2. Position the mouse pointer over the selected text. Note that the pointer shape is a left-pointing diagonal arrow and not an I-beam. To move this sentence using drag and drop:
CLICK: left mouse button and hold it down
The mouse pointer changes shape to include a phantom insertion point at the end of the diagonal arrow. This dotted insertion point indicates where the selected text will be inserted.

3. Drag the phantom insertion point to the beginning of the second paragraph. At this point, your document should appear similar to the one shown in Figure 2.21.

Figure 2.21

Positioning the phantom insertion point

Phantom insertion point

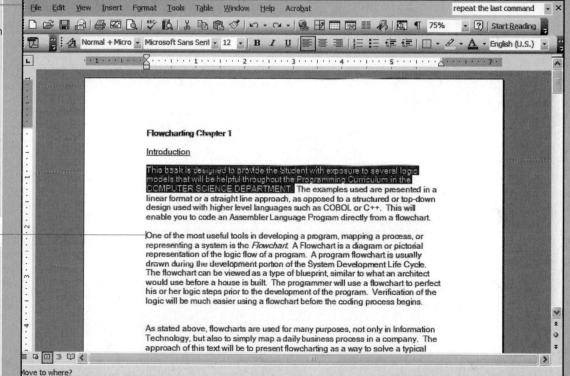

4. Release the left mouse button. Note that the sentence is inserted at the mouse pointer, causing the existing text to wrap to the next line. Your document should now appear similar to the one shown in Figure 2.22.

Figure 2.22

The selected
sentence was
moved using
drag and drop

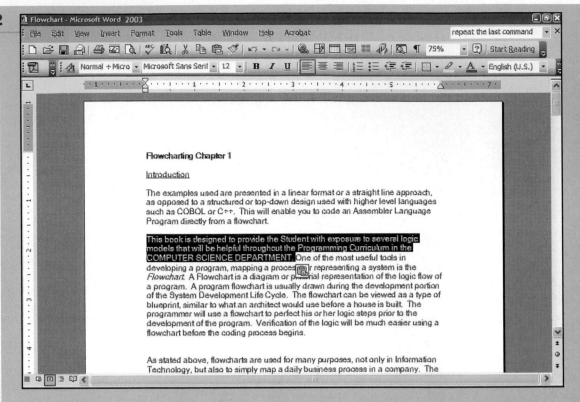

5. To deselect the text and move the insertion point to the top of the document:
PRESS: `CTRL` + `HOME`

6. The drag and drop method can also be used to copy text. To illustrate:
SELECT: the subtitle "<u>Introduction</u>" in the first paragraph

7. To copy this word:
PRESS: `CTRL` and hold it down

8. Position the mouse pointer over the selected text and then drag the selection to the blank line
below the first paragraph.

9. Release the left mouse button and then the `CTRL` key.

10. The copied text is currently selected. To change the copied text to uppercase:
PRESS: `SHIFT` + `F3`
PRESS: `SHIFT` + `F3` again
PRESS: `HOME`
PRESS: `ENTER`
Your document should now appear similar to Figure 2.23. (*Note:* You may have to insert a blank
line between the subtitle and following paragraph.)

Figure 2.23

Using drag and
drop to copy text

Copied text

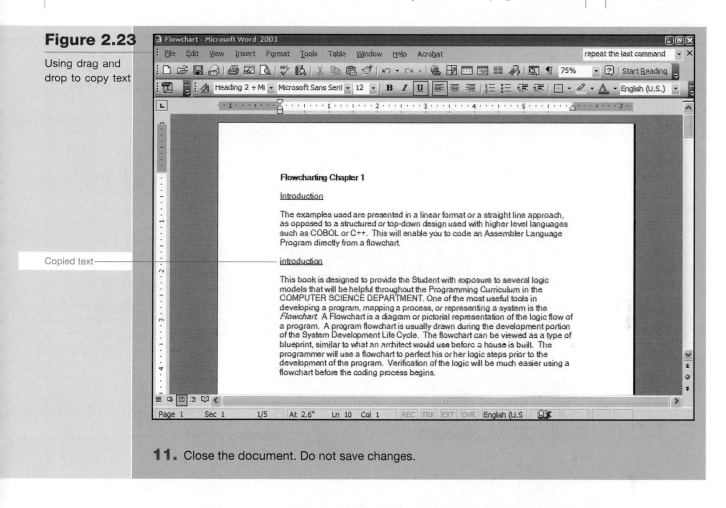

11. Close the document. Do not save changes.

2.4   What is the easiest method of moving text and graphics a short
distance?

2.4 Proofing Your Work

Although Word checks your documents for spelling and grammar errors as you type, you might want to
wait to proof your work until after you have finished typing what you want to say. The **Spelling and
Grammar command** analyzes your document all at once for spelling and grammar errors and reports the
results. Word's **Thesaurus** feature is useful for pinpointing the most effective words for getting your message across. The **Research tool** gives you access to several reference books such as a dictionary, stock quotes,
and an encyclopedia. We describe all three of these proofing tools in this module.

2.4.1 Using The Spelling and Grammar Checker and Research Tool

→ **Feature**

Although it is not a substitute for reading a document carefully, Word's spelling and grammar checker
can help you locate some of the more obvious errors quickly. When Word performs a spelling check,
it begins by comparing each word to entries in Word's main dictionary, which contains more than
100,000 words. If a word cannot be found, the spell checker attempts to find a match in a custom

dictionary that you may have created. Custom dictionaries usually contain proper names, abbreviations, and technical terms. Word's grammar checker contains grammatical rules and style considerations for different occasions. Word offers the following styles of grammar checking: Casual, Standard (the default setting), Formal, Technical, and Custom. You can also customize Word to check only for specific rules and wording styles. In addition, the Research feature allows you look up word meanings, look up similar words, and translate words into another language.

→ ## Method

- CLICK: Spell and Grammar button (🗹)

  or

- CHOOSE: Tools, Spelling and Grammar

- CLICK: Research button (📖)

  or

- CHOOSE: Tools, Research

- When a misspelled word is found, you can: accept Word's suggestion, change the entry, ignore the word and the suggested alternatives provided by Word, or add the term to the AutoCorrect feature or custom dictionary. When a grammar error is detected, you can accept Word's suggestion, change the entry, or ignore the sentence. When you select a word and click the Research button, you have a choice of several reference books that allow you to look up the definition of the word, use the Thesaurus to look for similar words, or translate the word into a different language.

→ ## Practice

After opening an existing document, you will perform a spelling and grammar check and display some statistics about your document. You will then look up a word definition and translate English words into French. Ensure that Word is loaded and that the application window is maximized.

1. Open the WD0240 data file.

2. Save the document as "Birthday" to your personal storage location.

3. To start the spelling check:
CLICK: Spelling and Grammar button (🗹)
When Word finds the first misspelled word, it displays a dialog box (Figure 2.24) and waits for further instructions. In the dialog box, Word applies red to spelling selections and green to grammar selections.

4. To correct the misspelled word "welcom," ensure that the correct spelling of the word appears in the *Suggestions* text box and then:
CLICK: Change command button
CONTINUE: spell checking until all errors are corrected

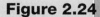

Figure 2.24

Spelling and
Grammar dialog
box

Misspelled word

Highlighted
suggestion

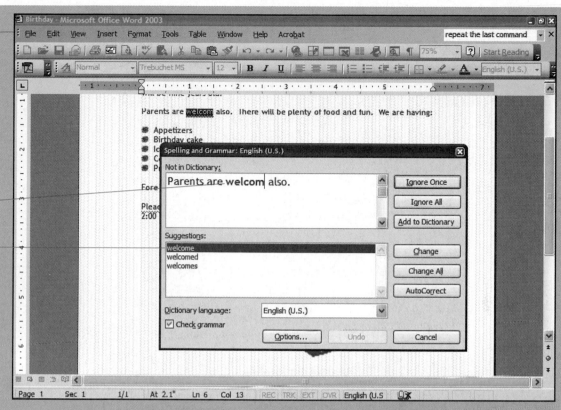

5. Word has now detected a grammar error (Figure 2.25). The dialog box shows the phrase and suggests why it was flagged. In this case, Word suggests that the sentence's subject and verb do not agree. Word also provides two suggestions for how the sentence might be reworded. To accept the selected suggestion:
CLICK: Change command button

Figure 2.25

Checking for
grammar

Click to accept
highlighted
suggestion

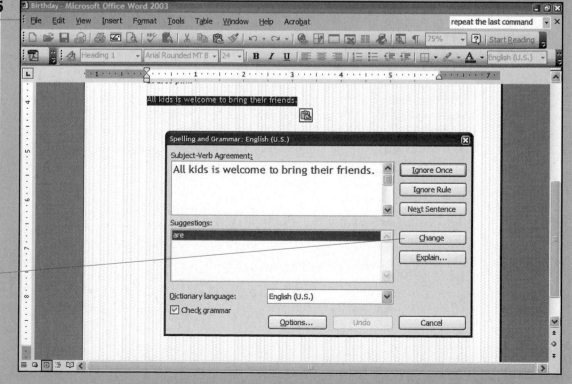

6. After Word has finished checking the spelling and grammar, a message dialog box will appear. To clear this dialog box:
CLICK: OK command button

7. The Word Count command is another useful tool that provides some basic document statistics. To display the Word Count dialog box:
CHOOSE: Tools, Word Count
The dialog box in Figure 2.26 should now appear.

Figure 2.26

Word Count
dialog box

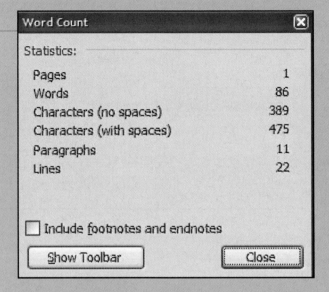

8. To close the Word Count dialog box:
CLICK: Close command button

9. Save and close the document.

2.4.2 Using the Thesaurus

→ **Feature**

A thesaurus provides quick access to synonyms, words with similar meanings, and antonyms, words with opposite meanings, for a given word or phrase. Word provides a built-in thesaurus for those times when you have found yourself with the perfect word at the tip of your tongue—only to have it stay there!

→ **Method**

To look up a word in the Thesaurus:
- SELECT: a word

- CHOOSE: Tools, Language, Thesaurus (or press **SHIFT** + **F7**)

  Select the desired word in the *Replace with Synonym* list box.

- CLICK: Replace command button

→ ## Practice

You will now practice using the Thesaurus.

1. Ensure that the "Flowchart" document you created earlier is open.

2. Using the mouse, select the word "useful" in the first sentence.

3. CHOOSE: Tools, Language, Thesaurus
The Thesaurus task pane should now appear, as shown in Figure 2.27.

Figure 2.27

Thesaurus task pane

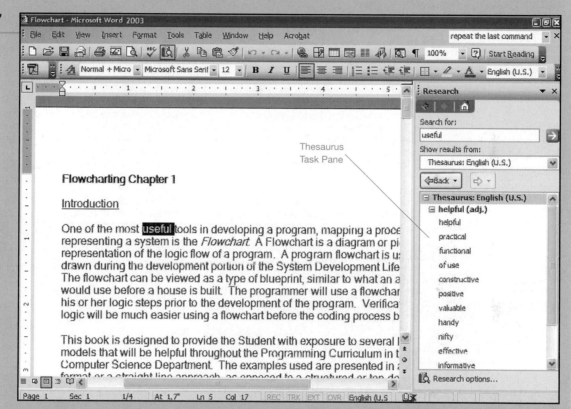

4. To replace the word "useful" with "valuable":
CLICK: the drop-down arrow next to "valuable" in the *Thesaurus* list box
CHOOSE: Insert

5. Let's find a synonym for the word "diagram," appearing in the second sentence in the first paragraph. To begin:
SELECT: "diagram"

6. To start the thesaurus using the keyboard method:
PRESS: SHIFT + F7

7. In the *Thesaurus* list box:
DOUBLE-CLICK: "drawing"
A list of synonyms for drawing appears
The Thesaurus task pane should now appear similar to the one shown in Figure 2.28.

Figure 2.28

Displaying synonyms for "drawing"

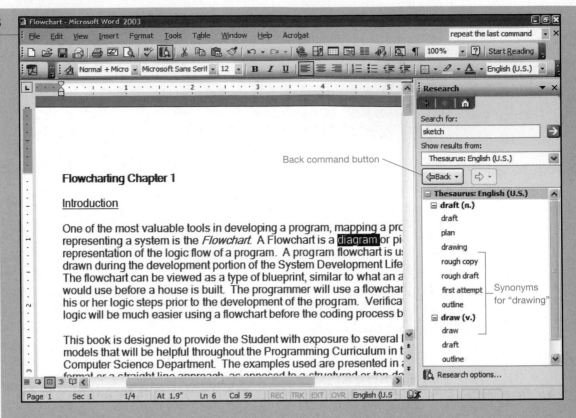

8. You decide not to change the word. To display the previous list of synonyms:

CLICK: ⟵Back ▾ command button

9. Save the "Flowchart" document and leave it open for the next exercise. Close the Research Pane.

2.4.3 Using the Research Tool

→ **Feature**

The Research tool allows you to look up word meanings, translate a word into a different language, use the Encarta Encyclopedia, and more. To gain the full benefit of the Research tool, you will need an Internet connection.

→ **Method**

To perform various actions on a word:

- SELECT: a word

- CHOOSE: Tools, Research

- CHOOSE: the Research tool you want to use by selecting it from the Show results from: drop-down list.

→ **Practice**

You will now practice using the Research tool. Ensure that you have completed the previous exercise and that the "Flowchart" document is open.

1. SELECT: the word "valuable" in the first sentence.

2. CLICK: the Research tool icon (🔲)
The Research task pane appears as shown in Figure 2.29.

Figure 2.29

The Research
task pane

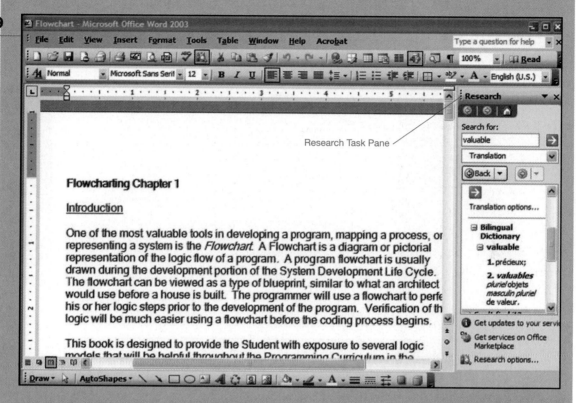

Research Task Pane

3. CLICK: the drop-down arrow next to the *Show results from:* drop-down list.

4. CHOOSE: "Translation." Ensure that from "English" to "French" are selected in the From and To text boxes.

5. You will note that the French word for valuable is "*précieux*." You will not change the word at this time. (*Note:* You may need to scroll down to see the translation.)

6. CLICK: the Research tool selection drop-down arrow and choose Encyclopedia: English (U.S.). Your screen should be similar to the one shown in Figure 2.30.

Figure 2.30

Research task pane showing English Encyclopedia options

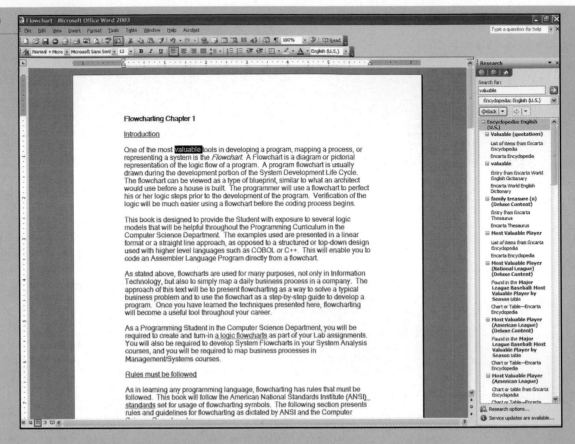

7. Scroll down to view the various options in the Encyclopedia Research Tool. You will not make a change now.

(Note that the options available in the Research task pane are hyperlinks. These links will take you to various resources on the Internet. If you do not have an Internet connection, you will be unable to enjoy the full benefit of the Research feature of Microsoft Office System.)

8. Close the Flowchart document without saving changes.

2.5 What is the purpose of the Thesaurus tool?

Chapter
summary

Before you can modify, cut, or copy text, you must know how to select it. Word is based on the "select and then do" approach to editing. Word includes a set of powerful features for modifying your work. The Find and Replace commands simplify the process of locating the information you need and making multiple changes at once throughout a document. You can easily reorganize a document using the Cut, Copy, and Paste commands. You can even drag and drop information short distances. Before sending your document out to others, you should always check it for spelling errors. You can perform this check either as you type or all at once after you have finished typing. You can also use the Thesaurus to find just the right word to convey your message. Finally, the Research tool allows you to access a variety of features, such as a language translator, on encyclopedia, stock quotes, and more.

Command Summary

Many of the commands and procedures appearing in this chapter are summarized in the following table.

Skill Set	To Perform this Task...	Do the Following...
Modifying Text	Undo your last action	CLICK: Undo button (🔙▼), or CHOOSE: Edit, Undo, or PRESS: CTRL + z
	Undo the last several actions	CLICK: down arrow next to the Undo button (🔙▼) CLICK: an action in the drop-down list to execute that action and all actions above
	Repeat the last action	CHOOSE: Edit, Repeat
	Find text	CHOOSE: Edit, Find
	Replace text	CHOOSE: Edit, Replace
	Copy text to the Clipboard	CLICK: Copy button (🗐)
	Move text to the Clipboard	CLICK: Cut button (✂)
	Paste text from the Clipboard	CLICK: Paste button (📋)
	Drag and drop text (copy)	PRESS: CTRL and then drag the selected text to a new location
	Drag and drop text (move)	DRAG: the selected text to a new location
Proofing a Document	Correct spelling and grammar errors as you type	RIGHT-CLICK: any word or phrase with a wavy red or green underline CHOOSE: an option from the right-click menu
	Check a document for spelling and grammar errors all at once	CLICK: Spelling and Grammar button (✔)
	Use the Thesaurus	CHOOSE: Tools, Language, Thesaurus
	Use the Research tool	CHOOSE: Tools, Research or click Research button (📖)

Key Terms

This section specifies page references for the key terms identified in this chapter. For a complete list of definitions, refer to the Glossary provided immediately after the Appendix in this learning guide.

drag and drop, *p. WD 68*

Office Clipboard, *p. WD 68*

Repeat command, *p. WD 56*

Research tool, *p. WD 75*

Selection bar, *p. WD 50*

Spelling and Grammar command, *p. WD 75*

Thesaurus, *p. WD 75*

Undo command, *p. WD 50*

Windows Clipboard, *p. WD 68*

Chapter
q u i z

Short Answer

1. What are the two methods of copying and moving information?

2. What can you do to remove a red wavy underline from a document?

3. What procedure would you use to move the insertion point efficiently to page 2, line 16?

4. Besides a word count, what other statistics appear in the Word Count dialog box?

5. What procedure selects a single sentence?

6. What procedure selects an entire document?

7. In Word, when might you want to use the Thesaurus?

8. Name two functions available by using the Research tool.

9. What menu command enables you to replace text in a document?

10. What happens when you type over a selection of text?

True/False

1. _____ When replacing text in Word, you can instruct Word to retrieve whole words.

2. _____ To move to the end of a document, press END .

3. _____ To move a selection of text using drag and drop, hold down CTRL before dragging.

4. _____ You can select a single word by double-clicking it.

5. _____ Scrolling moves the insertion point.

6. _____ Drag and drop is used for moving text between documents.

7. _____ In Word, you can search for words but not phrases.

8. _____ Word's grammar checker offers several styles of grammar checking.

9. _____ A thesaurus provides quick access to synonyms.

10. _____ Once information is placed in the Clipboard, it can be pasted multiple times.

Multiple Choice

1. In relation to a document, where is the Selection bar located?

   a. Top
   b. Bottom
   c. Left
   d. Right

2. You can select a word by:

   a. Single-clicking
   b. Double-clicking
   c. Both a. and b.
   d. None of the above

3. Which of the following allow you to copy information from one location to another in a document?

   a. The Clipboard
   b. Cut, copy, and paste
   c. Drag and drop
   d. All of the above

4. Which of the following operations moves text from the Clipboard?

   a. Cut   c. Paste
   b. Copy   d. Drag and drop

5. Which of the following provides a list of synonyms?

   a. Find command

   b. Replace command

   c. Thesaurus

   d. Spelling and Grammar command

6. Which of the following enables you to paste data multiple times?

   a. Windows Clipboard

   b. Office Clipboard

   c. Drag and drop

   d. Both a. and b.

7. To display statistics about a document:

   a. CHOOSE: Insert, Statistics

   b. CHOOSE: Tools, Spelling and Grammar

   c. CHOOSE: Tools, Statistics

   d. CHOOSE: Tools, Word Count

8. Which of the following cannot be selected?

   a. Letter

   b. Word

   c. Line

   d. Selection bar

9. Which of the following enables you to make multiple changes in a document at once?

   a. Find command

   b. Replace command

   c. Drag and drop

   d. Copy command

10. What should you always do before submitting a document to others?

   a. use the Undo command

   b. use the Replace command

   c. spell check the document

   d. launch the Thesaurus

Hands-On exercises

step by step

1. Proofing a Document

In this exercise, you will open a document and proofread it using the various tools available in Word.

1. Open the WD02HE01 data file.

2. Save the document as "Ceramics Flyer" to your personal storage location.

3. Move the cursor to the top of the document.

4. Click the Spelling and Grammar toolbar button (✓).

5. Replace misspelled words as necessary, then close the Spelling and Grammar dialog box.

6. To replace every instance of "ceramic" with "pottery," do the following:
CHOOSE: Edit, Replace
TYPE: **ceramic** in the *Find what:* text box
TYPE: **pottery** in the *Replace with:* text box

7. Perform this step if you see "Font: Bold" beneath the *Replace with:* text box.
PRESS: [CTRL] + **b** twice to remove the formatting command.

8. CLICK: Replace All command button. Word should have made four replacements.

9. Select the second paragraph by triple-clicking within the paragraph.

10. Using drag and drop, move the second paragraph in front of the first paragraph. Your screen should be similar to Figure 2.31.

11. Deselect the text and add a blank line after the first paragraph.

Figure 2.31

"Ceramics Flyer" document with new paragraph location

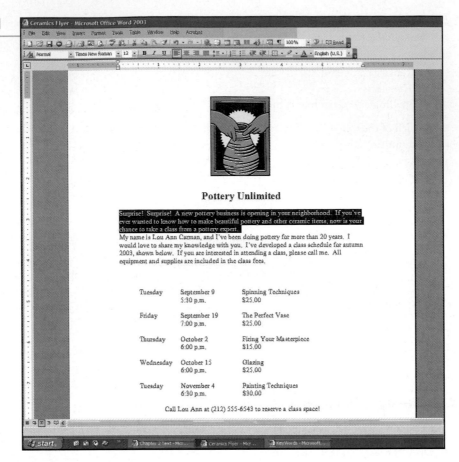

12. Save the file and leave it open for the next exercise.

step by step

2. Using Thesaurus

In this exercise, you will use Thesaurus.

1. Select the word "knowledge" in the second sentence of the second paragraph.

2. Open the Thesaurus:
CHOOSE: Tools, Language, Thesaurus

3. CLICK: the drop-down arrow next to the word "experience" from the list of synonyms in the Thesaurus task pane.
CHOOSE: Insert

4. In a similar manner, substitute the word "professional" for the word "expert" in the first paragraph.

5. In a similar manner, substitute the word "enterprise" for the word "business" in the second sentence of the first paragraph.

6. Display the word count for the file.
CHOOSE: Tools, Word Count

7. Save and close the file.

ep by step ▶

3. Using the Research Tool

When using the Research tool, you are entering a "live" Web site which can only be used with an Internet connection. Since its contents are ever changing, you may not get the same definitions for any one word. In this exercise, you use the Research tool to search the Encyclopedia for additional information.

1. Open the file WD02HE03 document.

2. Save the file as "Glazing" to your personal storage location.

3. Select the word "kiln" in the first sentence.

4. CHOOSE: Tools, Research

5. CLICK: drop-down arrow next to the Research tool selection text box.

6. CHOOSE: Encyclopedia: ENGLISH (U.S.). Your screen should be similar to the one shown in Figure 2.32.

7. Follow the "Use in Pottery" link until you find the articles about pottery and then select the Introduction paragraph.

8. CHOOSE: Edit, Copy

9. CLICK: the Back arrow twice until you are returned to your document.

10. Place the insertion point at the beginning of the first paragraph, before the word "Glazing."

11. CLICK: Paste button on the toolbar. Your screen should be similar to Figure 2.32.

Figure 2.32

Paragraph copied from Internet into document

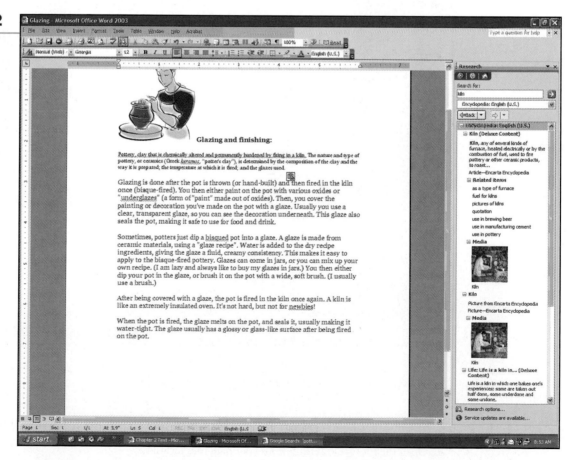

12. Save and close the file.

4. Using Find and Replace

In this exercise, you will open a document and, using Find and Replace, make corrections to the document.

1. Open the WD02HE04 document from your data file location.

2. Save the file as "Mailing List" to your personal storage location.

3. Ensure that your cursor is at the top of the document.

4. Using Find and Replace, make the following changes in the document:

Replace the zip code **43222** with **43228**

Replace the last name **Miller** with **Hemenway**

Replace the first name **Bob** with **Patty**

Replace the street name **Mirrow** with **Mirror**

Replace the zip code **43111** with **43219**

5. Save the document. Your completed document should be similar to that shown in Figure 2.33.

Figure 2.33

Completed
Mailing List
document

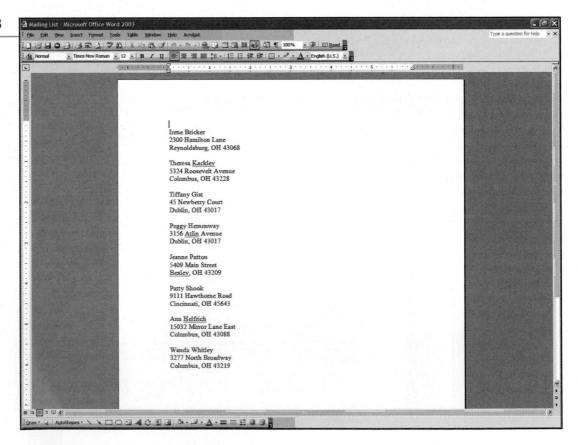

6. Save your changes and close the document.

5. Spell Check, Thesaurus, and Moving and Copying Information

1. Open the file WD02HE05 from your data files location.

2. Save the file as "History" to your personal storage location.

3. Spell check the document and correct any errors. Ignore all foreign words.

4. Move the third and fourth paragraphs up and place them just before the first paragraph. Remove or add blank lines as necessary to format the document properly.

5. Using Thesaurus, replace the word "advent" in the first sentence with a word of your choosing.

6. Select the word "Celadon" in the second heading.

7. Using Research, go to the Encarta World Dictionary. Read the definition of celadon and then close the Research tool. Your finished document should be similar to Figure 2.34.

Figure 2.34

Revised History document

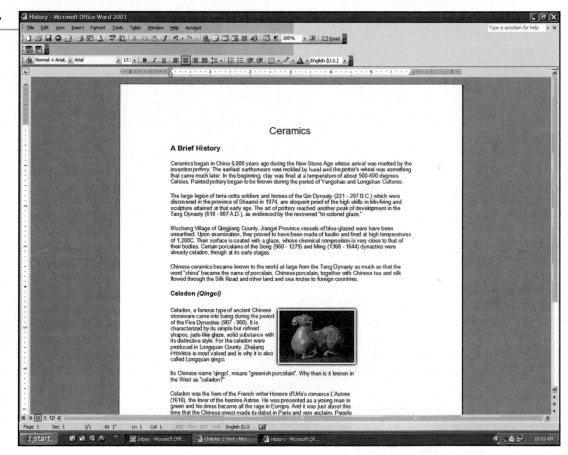

8. Print, save, and close the file.

6. Using Undo and Redo

1. Open the "Fitness" document created earlier in this module.

2. Cut the first paragraph from the document.

3. CLICK: the Undo button

4. CLICK: the Redo button

5. CLICK: the Undo button again

6. Practice making whatever changes you wish in the document. Use Undo and Redo until you are comfortable with them.

7. Close the document without saving changes.

Case Study   TRI-STATE COLLEGE

Renee Fronk has been hired as a teaching assistant in the Computer Science Department at a large community college in Ohio. Her job is to help faculty prepare new course materials, revise existing course materials, and research the Internet as required.

In the following case problems, assume the role of Renee as she helps the faculty in the department prepare course materials.

1. One of Renee's first duties is to revise the syllabus for a course on Microsoft Project. This project will involve spell checking the document, moving text, and using Find and Replace.

- Open the file WD02CS01 from your data files location.

- Save the file as "Syllabus MCT093" to your personal storage location.

- Spell check the document and correct mistakes as necessary.

- In the third line of the heading, change "2002" to "2004."

- In the textbook paragraph, replace *"Microsoft Project 2000 Step by Step"* with *"Microsoft Project 2002 Step by Step."*

- Move the textbook paragraph above the Course Description paragraph.

- Add a blank line if necessary to format the paragraph properly.

- Using Find and Replace, replace all occurrences of "Microsoft Project" with "Microsoft Project 2002."

- In the textbook paragraph, delete the second instance of "2002." The first page of your final document should be similar to the one shown in Figure 2.35.

Figure 2.35

Revised document

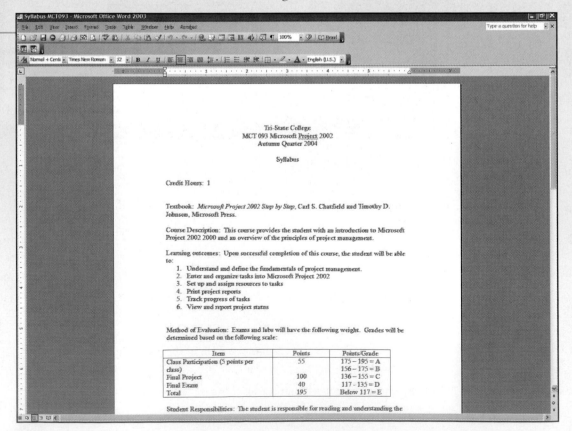

- Save, print, and close the file.

2. The department chairperson of the Computer Science Department has asked Renee to write a notice to the faculty in the department asking them to provide her with their posted office hours.

- Create a blank document and type the text shown below:

   (insert current date here)

   Dear Faculty:

   Libby has asked me to collect office hours from all of you. These hours are to be posted outside your offices so that students know when you are available.

   Please either send this information to me or to Libby directly. You may submit the information through e-mail if you wish.

   Thank you.
   Renee Fronk
   Teaching Assistant

- Save the document as "FacultyLetter" to your personal storage location.

- Using Thesaurus, substitute an appropriate word for "collect" in the first paragraph.

- Delete the word "either" in the second paragraph.

- Add a third paragraph that says "**Thank you for your cooperation.**"

- Spell check the document and correct any errors.

- Save, print, and close the document.

3. One of the faculty members has asked Renee to search the Internet for articles on using laptops in the classroom. Search the Internet and combine and summarize at least three articles. Run spell check and use Thesaurus to substitute at least six words in the document. Save the document as "Laptops" to your personal storage location. Print and then close document.

4. One of the faculty members in the department is serving on a college-wide assessment committee. She has drafted a document to be presented to the Board of Trustees and has asked Renee to make some changes.

- Open WD02CS02 from your data files location.

- Save the file as "Assessment" to your personal storage location.

- Move the second paragraph to the first paragraph position, and add a blank line if necessary to separate the paragraphs.

- In the fourth paragraph, change "seven-member . . ." to "nine-member . . ."

- Using Thesaurus, replace the word "jurisdiction" in the last paragraph with a suitable word of your choice.

- Search for and replace all instances of "Vice President for Academic Affairs" with "Provost."

- Run spell check and correct any errors.

- Save, print, and close the document

SelfCheck

2.1. You select a single sentence by holding the `CTRL` key and left-clicking once anywhere within the sentence.

2.2. Word defines a paragraph as any portion of text that is followed by a hard return.

2.3. The difference between Find and Replace is that Find allows you to find specific text or formatting characteristics in a document; Replace allows you to quickly and easily make several changes at once.

2.4. The easiest method of moving text and graphics a short distance is using Drag and Drop.

2.5. The purpose of the Thesaurus tool is to help you look up synonyms and antonyms for a word in your document.

Microsoft® Office Word® 2003

CHAPTER 3

Enhancing a Document's Appearance

PREREQUISITES

To successfully complete this chapter, you must be able to position the insertion point, select and change text, use Save and Save As, use the toolbar, and use the menu bar. You should understand the basics of file management, such as creating a folder on your disk.

LEARNING OBJECTIVES

After completing this chapter, you will be able to:

- Change page margins

- Change the look of text using character formatting

- Change the look of paragraphs using indenting, alignment, and spacing commands

- Create bulleted lists and numbered lists

- Set tabs

- Incorporate shading and borders in your documents

3.1 Setting Margins

By default, Word has margin settings of 1 inch on the top and bottom, and 1.25 inches on the left and right. For the times when these settings are unsuitable, Word provides an easy way to change its default margin settings. When you change the **margins** in a document, you can apply the changes to the entire document or from the point where you are currently situated. Margin changes are made from the File, Page Setup dialog box shown in Figure 3.1.

Figure 3.1

Page Setup
Dialog Box

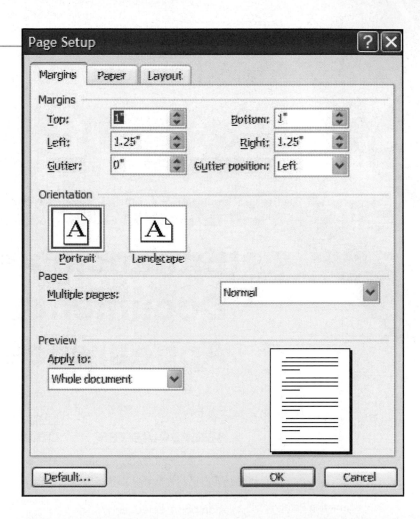

3.1.1 Setting Margins

→ **Feature**

There will be times when the default margins in Word do not meet your needs. Word provides a simple method for changing margins on all four sides of your document, as well as controlling when the new margins take effect. If you choose to apply the new margin settings to the whole document, the entire document will reflect the new margins. If you select *This point forward,* the new margins will take effect at the top of the next page. Margins are measured in inches and are calculated from the left edge of the page.

→ ## Method

To change margins in your document:

• CLICK: File, Page Setup

• CLICK: *Margins* tab, if necessary

• CLICK: in each of the *Margins* spin boxes and type a value, or click the up or down arrows to choose a setting

→ ## Practice

In this lesson, you will change the page margins for an existing document.

1. Ensure that you have started Word.

2. Open the file WD0301 from your data files location.

3. Save the document as "Travel Information" to your personal storage location. This document has 1″ margins on all four sides.

4. To change the margins:
Choose: File, Page Setup
Click: in each of the four margin boxes and change the setting to 2
Your Page Setup dialog box should look like the one shown in Figure 3.2.
Click: OK command button

Figure 3.2

Page Setup dialog box with margins changed to 2″

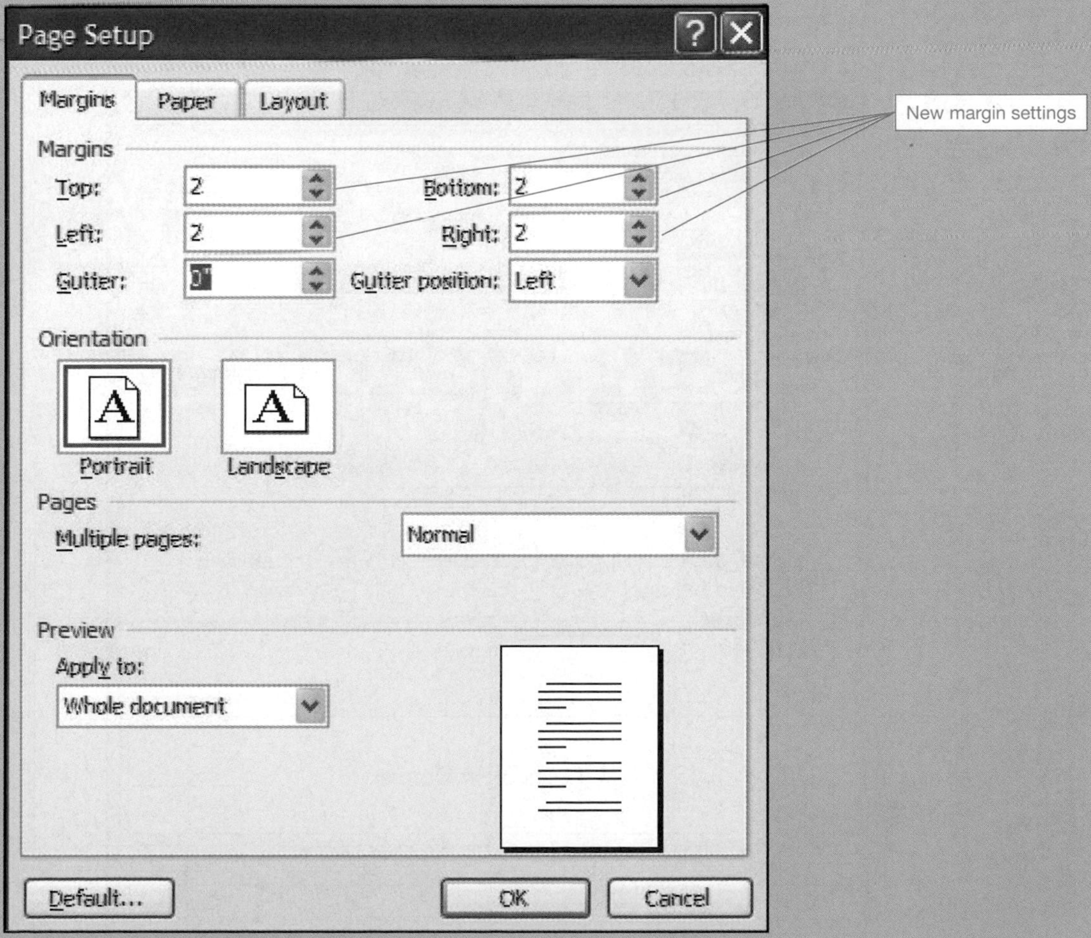

New margin settings

Page Setup

Margins   Paper   Layout

Margins

Top: 2   Bottom: 2

Left: 2   Right: 2

Gutter: 0   Gutter position: Left

Orientation

Portrait   Landscape

Pages

Multiple pages: Normal

Preview

Apply to:

Whole document

Default...   OK   Cancel

5. Scroll through the document and look at the new margin settings.

6. CLICK: Undo button (⤺▾) to return the margins to their previous settings.

7. Position the insertion point on page 2, to the left of the "Airlines" heading
CHOOSE: File, Page Setup
CLICK: in top margin box and change the value to 2
CLICK: in the *Apply to:* section and choose *This point forward*
CLICK: OK command button
Word will force a section break and start a new page at the insertion point location. You will learn more about section breaks in Chapter 4 of this learning module.

8. Close the document without saving changes.

 **SelfCheck**

3.1 What does *This point forward* mean in the margins dialog box?

3.2 Formatting Characters

Character formatting includes selecting typefaces, font sizes, and attributes such as bold, italic, underline, and others. Word's character formatting commands are accessed through the Font dialog box shown in Figure 3.3.

Figure 3.3

Font dialog box

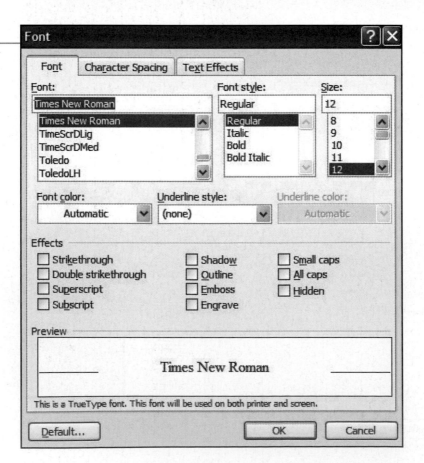

You can also access many of the font formatting commands using the Formatting toolbar and special shortcut keys. Table 3.1 summarizes some of the more common mouse and keyboard methods for choosing character formatting commands.

Table 3.1

Character Formatting Summary

Toolbar button	Keyboard shortcut	Description
B	CTRL + b	Makes the selected text bold
I	CTRL + i	Makes the selected text italic
U	CTRL + u	Makes the selected text underlined
A ▾		Changes the font color of the selected text
Times New Roman ▾	CTRL + SHIFT + f	Specifies a font or typeface
12 ▾	CTRL + SHIFT + p	Specifies a point size for the font (*Note:* 72 points = 1 inch)
	CTRL + [	Decreases point size by 1 point
	CTRL +]	Increases point size by 1 point
	CTRL + SHIFT + a	Changes the case of the selected text
	CTRL + F3	Deletes the selection
	CTRL + Space Bar	Removes all character formatting

3.2.1 Bolding, Italicizing, and Underlining Text

→ **Feature**

The bold, italic, and underline attributes help to emphasize important text.

→ **Method**

To make text bold:
• SELECT: the text
• CLICK: Bold button (**B**)
  or
• PRESS: CTRL + b

To make text italic:
• SELECT: the text
• CLICK: Italic button (*I*)
  or
• PRESS: CTRL + i

To underline text:
• SELECT: the text
• CLICK: Underline button (U)
  or
• PRESS: CTRL + u

When your cursor is positioned within text that has font formatting applied, the appropriate attribute button is highlighted on the formatting toolbar. To remove the font formatting, click the attribute button again, so it is not highlighted and the attribute is removed.

→ Practice

You will now open an existing document and apply bold, italic, and underline attributes. Make sure that no documents are open in the application window.

1. Open the WD0321 file from your data files location.

2. Save the file as "Teaching" to your personal storage location. Your document should appear similar to the one shown in Figure 3.4.

Figure 3.4

"Teaching" document before editing

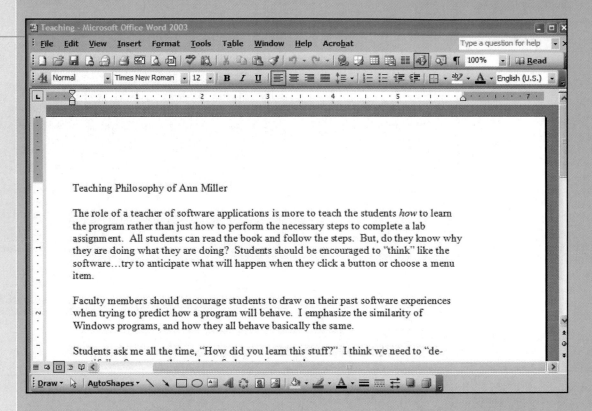

3. To bold the title
SELECT: the document title
CLICK: Bold button (**B**)

4. To add italic text:
PRESS: END to move to the end of the title line
PRESS: ENTER to create a blank line

CLICK: Italic button (*I*)
TYPE: the current date
CLICK: Italic button (*I*) again to stop italicizing

5. To italicize existing text:
Select: the text "perform the necessary steps" in the first sentence of the first paragraph.
CLICK: Italic button (*I*)
CLICK: anywhere in the document to deselect the text

6. In a similar manner, perform the formatting changes indicated below. Use the formatting toolbar buttons or the keyboard shortcuts.

Text to be formatted:	*Formatting to apply:*
similarity of Windows programs	Bold
"How did you learn this stuff?"	Italic
real-world examples	Underline
"think outside the box"	Bold and Italic

Your document should now appear similar to the one shown in Figure 3.5.

Figure 3.5

"Teaching"
document after
editing

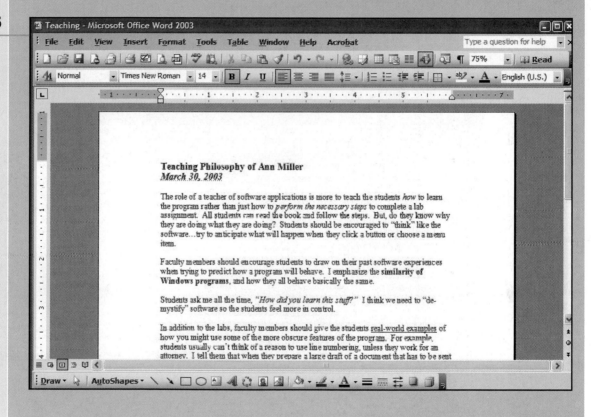

7. Save the "Teaching" document and leave it open for the next lesson.

3.2.2 Changing Fonts, Font Sizes, and Colors

→ **Feature**

A **font** is defined as all the symbols and characters of a particular style of print. Font size is measured in points (72 points = 1 inch). By selecting fonts and font sizes, you give your message impact and the right tone. By selecting colors other than black, you can visually enhance your document's appearance. Remember, it is best to select text first, and then apply font formatting to it.

→ ## Method

To select a typeface:

- CLICK: Font drop-down arrow (Times New Roman ▾)
- SELECT: the desired font

To change font size:

- CLICK: the Font Size drop-down arrow (12 ▾)
- SELECT: the desired point size

To change font color:

- CLICK: Font Color button (A▾) to select the most recently used color
- CLICK: Font Color drop-down arrow (A▾) to display a palette of colors from which you can choose

→ ## Practice

You will now change some of the fonts, point sizes, and font colors in the "Teaching" document. Make sure you have completed the previous lesson and the "Teaching" document is open.

1. SELECT: the main title line and the date line.

2. To display a list of available fonts:
CLICK: Font drop-down arrow (Times New Roman ▾)
Figure 3.6 shows an example of the Font drop-down list. Your list may be different; this is not a problem.

Figure 3.6

Font drop-down list

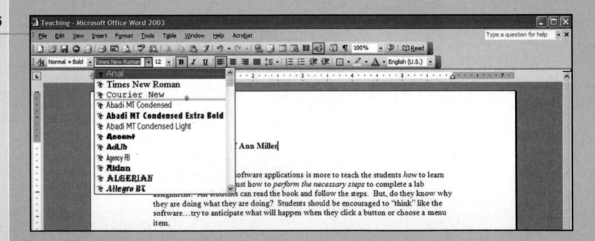

3. Scroll through the font choices by clicking the up and down arrows on the drop-down list's scroll bar, or by dragging the scroll box.

4. SELECT: Arial (or another font that is available on your computer). To select a font, click on the displayed name.

5. To display the range of available font sizes:
CLICK: Font Size drop-down arrow (12 ▾)
SELECT: 16-point font size

6. To apply a different font color to the title and subtitle:
CLICK: Font Color drop-down arrow (A▾)
CHOOSE: sea green (third row, fourth column)
CLICK: in the document to deselect the text. The title and subtitle should be similar to those shown in Figure 3.7. Note that the Font Color button now displays sea green because that is the most recently applied color.

Figure 3.7

New color applied

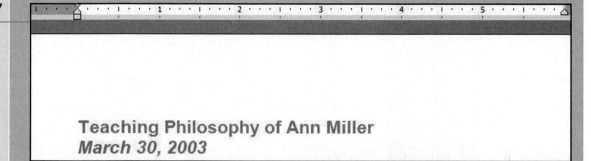

Teaching Philosophy of Ann Miller
March 30, 2003

7. Save and close the document.

3.2.3 Applying Styles

→ # Feature

Styles are collections of character and paragraph formatting commands that make it easy to format your document. Styles also help ensure that your documents are formatted consistently. Word comes with a number of built-in styles that you can use in your documents. For many people, Word's built-in styles are all they need. Each of these styles includes several formatting instructions that you can apply to document paragraphs with just a few mouse clicks.

→ # Method

To apply styles:

- CLICK: in a paragraph or select multiple paragraphs
- CLICK: down arrow on the Style button ([Normal ▾])
- CHOOSE: a style from the *Style* drop-down list

To clear formatting attributes:

- CHOOSE: Clear Formatting from the *Style* drop-down list

→ # Practice

This lesson practices applying styles and clearing formatting attributes. Ensure that no documents are open in the application window.

1. Open the WD0323 document from your data files location. This document describes the origins and future of GPS systems.

2. Save this document as "GPS" to your personal storage location. Your screen should now be similar to the one shown in Figure 3.8. All text in the document is formatted in the Normal style.

Figure 3.8

The "GPS"
document

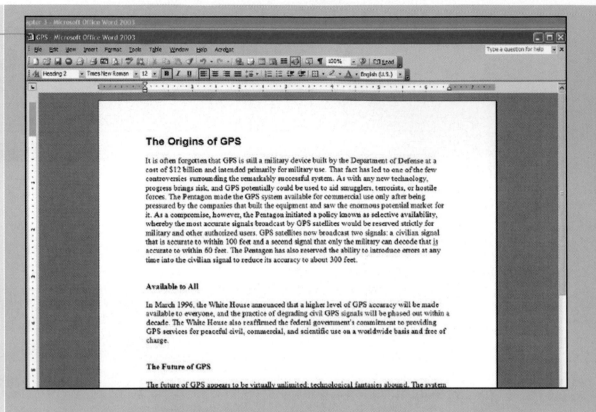

3. Let's begin by applying a heading style to the three headings in the document.
CLICK: anywhere in the heading "The Origins of GPS"
Because Heading 1 is a paragraph style, you do not need to select the entire heading before applying the style.

4. CLICK: down arrow on the Style button (Normal ▾)
Your screen should appear similar to the one shown in Figure 3.9.

Figure 3.9

Style menu

Style menu

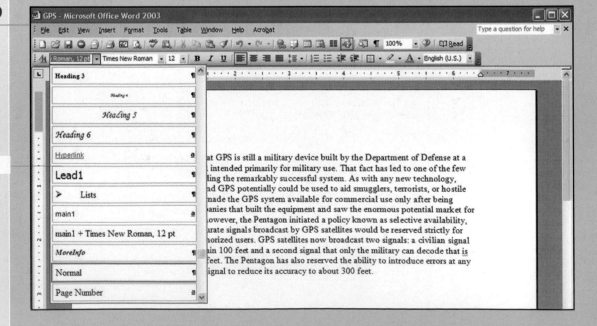

5. To apply the Heading 1 style:
CHOOSE: Heading 1

6. To clear formatting from a paragraph:
CLICK: down arrow on the Style button
CHOOSE: Clear Formatting from the *Style* drop-down list.
The formatting should have been removed from the heading.

7. Let's undo the previous command:
CLICK: Undo button ( )
The Heading 1 style is reapplied.

8. In a similar manner, apply the Heading 2 style to the other two headings in the document. Your document should appear similar to the one shown in Figure 3.10.

Figure 3.10

New styles applied

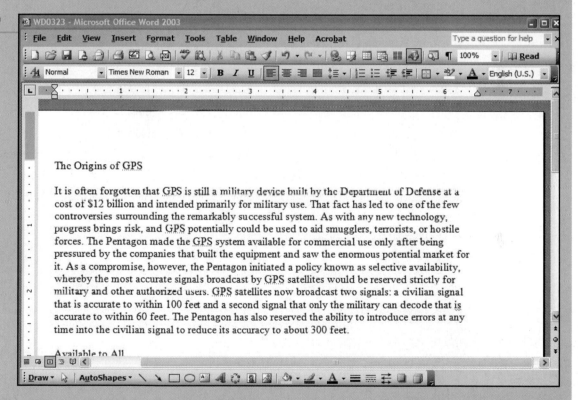

9. This time, let's display the entire style list available in the Normal template. To do so, hold down the **SHIFT** key while clicking the Style drop-down arrow.
PRESS: **SHIFT** and hold it down
CLICK: down arrow on the Style button (Normal)
A greater selection of styles appears.

10. To remove the style list without making a selection:
CLICK: in your document, away from the style menu

11. Save, print, and close the document.

3.2.4 Using the Format Painter

→ **Feature**

The **Format Painter** allows you to copy the formatting styles and attributes from one area in your document to another. This not only speeds up formatting operations, but also ensures consistency among the different areas of your document.

→ **Method**

To copy formatting to another area in your document:

- SELECT: the text with the desired formatting attributes
- CLICK: Format Painter ( ) on the Standard toolbar
- SELECT: the text that you want to format

To copy formatting to several areas in your document:

- SELECT: the text with the desired formatting attributes
- DOUBLE-CLICK: Format Painter ( ) on the Standard toolbar
- SELECT: the text that you want to format
- Repeat procedure until you have formatted the desired amount of text
- CLICK: Format Painter ( ) to deselect it

→ **Practice**

You will now practice using the Format Painter.

1. Open the WD0324 data file.

2. Save the file as "Grooming" to your personal storage location.

3. Begin by formatting the first heading, "Introduction."
   SELECT: the heading "Introduction"
   CLICK: Bold button (**B**) to add bold effects
   CLICK: down arrow on the Font button (Times New Roman ▼) and choose Comic Sans MS
   CLICK: down arrow on the Font Size button (12 ▼) and choose 16-point type
   CLICK: the down arrow on the Font Color button (A ▼) and choose red (third row, first column)
   CLICK: outside the text to deselect it
   Your document should appear similar to the one shown in Figure 3.11.

Figure 3.11

"Grooming" document with first heading formatted

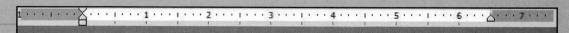

How to groom a dog

Introduction

Regularly grooming your dog can keep him free of parasites and improve his general appearance as well. During grooming you also have the opportunity to check the condition of the dog's skin, eyes, ears, coat and teeth. Deciding on how often to groom your dog is up to you, however it should be at least once a week.

Brushing can be a pleasant routine for the dog as well as the owner. You should have a specific place you wish to do the brushing. A table or chair will suffice. Lift the dog up onto the table or chair and talk to him. Reassure that all is well. It is important that you and your dog remain calm. Let the dog sniff the tools you will use. Doing this will allow the dog to associate the tools with a pleasant experience.

Required Tools

Tools you will need to brush and groom are comb, brush, nail clippers and scissors.

How to Start

Begin by brushing against the grain (so to speak). This helps to loosen dead hair and to stimulate the skin. It is important to have the proper brush. Short bristles are for short and medium haired dogs and long bristles are for long haired dogs. Use a flannel cloth to bring out the shine in your dog's coat after brushing.

4. To copy the formatting attributes to the remaining eight headings:
Ensure your cursor is positioned within the Introduction subtitle. You do not have to select the title.
DOUBLE-CLICK: Format Painter button (🖋)
By double-clicking the button, you are able to format multiple sections of text.
SELECT: the next heading, "Required Tools"
Notice that the selected text is formatted and the Format Painter is still active.

5. In a similar manner, select the text of the remaining headings and apply the new formatting. You should select these headings:

How to Start
Nail-Clipping
Bathing
Cleaning Ears
Eye Care
Dental
Summary

Your document, displayed in two-page view, should appear similar to Figure 3.12.
(*Note:* To display your document in two-page view, click the drop-down arrow on the Zoom button (125% ▾) and select Two Pages.)

Figure 3.12

"Grooming" document in two-page view

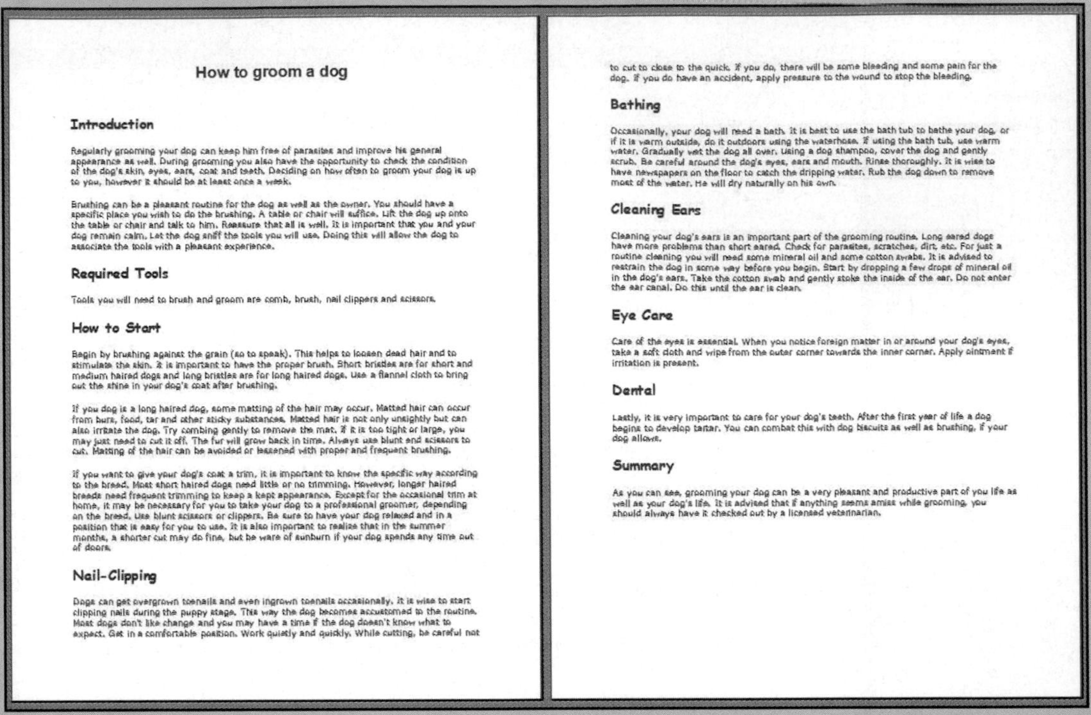

6. Click on the Format Painter button (🖌) to deactivate the feature.

7. To finish the document:
SELECT: the title "How to groom a dog"
CLICK: the Font Color button (A▾) to change the color to red.

8. Save, print, and keep the document open for the next lesson.

SelfCheck

3.2 Describe how to easily display a list of styles available in the Normal template.

3.2.5 Highlighting Text for Review

→ **Feature**

When others will be reviewing your document online, you will probably want to highlight certain areas of the text that need special attention. Word's Highlight tool (✐▾), located on the Formatting toolbar, allows you to select a highlight color and drag across the text to be highlighted. If you intend to print your document, you should use a lighter highlight color.

→ **Method**

To activate the highlighter:

• CLICK: Highlight button (✐▾)

To change the highlight color:

• CLICK: Highlight button drop-down arrow (✐▾)

• CHOOSE: an alternate color or choose none to remove existing highlighting

→ ## Practice

You will now practice highlighting text in the "Grooming" document

1. Ensure that you have completed the previous lesson and that the "Grooming" document is open.

2. Begin by selecting a color for the highlighter
CLICK: Highlight drop-down arrow ( )
SELECT: bright green
Word's Highlight tool is now activated and ready to use. Note that the mouse pointer has changed to a highlighter pointer.

3. SELECT: the first sentence in the second paragraph. The sentence now appears highlighted in bright green.

4. SELECT: the phrase "matting of the hair may occur" in the second paragraph under the "How to Start" heading
Your document should be similar to the one shown in Figure 3.13.

Figure 3.13

"Grooming" document with highlighting

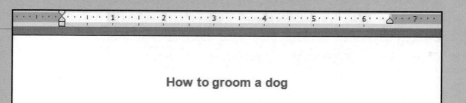

How to groom a dog

Introduction

Regularly grooming your dog can keep him free of parasites and improve his general appearance as well. During grooming you also have the opportunity to check the condition of the dog's skin, eyes, ears, coat and teeth. Deciding on how often to groom your dog is up to you, however it should be at least once a week.

Brushing can be a pleasant routine for the dog as well as the owner. You should have a specific place you wish to do the brushing. A table or chair will suffice. Lift the dog up onto the table or chair and talk to him. Reassure that all is well. It is important that you and your dog remain calm. Let the dog sniff the tools you will use. Doing this will allow the dog to associate the tools with a pleasant experience.

Required Tools

Tools you will need to brush and groom are comb, brush, nail clippers and scissors.

How to Start

Begin by brushing against the grain (so to speak). This helps to loosen dead hair and to stimulate the skin. It is important to have the proper brush. Short bristles are for short and medium haired dogs and long bristles are for long haired dogs. Use a flannel cloth to bring out the shine in your dog's coat after brushing.

If you dog is a long haired dog, some matting of the hair may occur. Matted hair can occur from burs, food, tar and other sticky substances. Matted hair is not only unsightly but can also irritate the dog. Try combing gently to remove the mat. If it is too tight or large, you may just need to cut it off. The fur will grow back in time. Always use blunt end scissors to cut. Matting of the hair can be avoided or lessened with proper and frequent brushing.

If you want to give your dog's coat a trim, it is important to know the specific way according to the breed. Most short haired dogs need little or no trimming. However, longer haired breeds need frequent trimming to keep a kept appearance. Except for the occasional trim at home, it may be necessary for you to take your dog to a professional groomer, depending on the breed. Use blunt scissors or clippers. Be sure to have your dog relaxed and in a position that is easy for you to use. It is also important to realize that in the summer months, a shorter cut may do fine, but be ware of sunburn if your dog spends any time out of doors.

5. Deactivate the Highlight tool:
CLICK: Highlight button ( )

6. To remove the second instance of highlighting:
SELECT: the text "matting of the hair may occur"
CLICK: Highlight drop-down arrow ( )
CHOOSE: None

7. In a similar manner, remove the highlighting from the first sentence of the second paragraph.

8. Save and close the document.

3.3 Formatting Paragraphs

Paragraph formatting involves changing alignment, line spacing, indentation, and tab settings for a paragraph. To apply paragraph formatting commands to a paragraph, position the insertion point anywhere in the paragraph—you do not need to select any text—and then issue the desired command.

Paragraph formatting commands are accessed through the Paragraph dialog box, from the Format menu, using the mouse, and using keyboard shortcut combinations. The Paragraph dialog box (Figure 3.14) is useful for entering specific measurements and accessing the full range of paragraph formatting options.

Figure 3.14

Paragraph dialog box

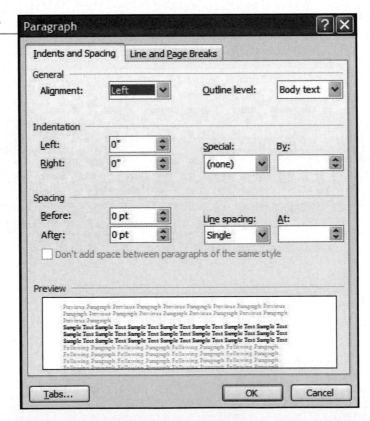

3.3.1 Revealing a Paragraph's Formatting

→ **Feature**

If you are working with someone else's document, you may want to inspect it first to see how it has been formatted. In Word you can do this with a simple command. Word stores paragraph formatting information in the **paragraph mark** (¶), which is inserted at the end of a paragraph when you press (ENTER). By default, paragraph marks and other nonprinting characters are hidden from view. By revealing these codes, you can more thoroughly check a document for errors.

→ Method

To display a paragraph's formatting:

- CHOOSE: Format, Reveal Formatting

  or

- PRESS: SHIFT + F1
- CLICK: in the paragraph whose formatting you want to reveal

To display paragraph marks and all other nonprinting characters:

- CLICK: Show/Hide button (¶) on the Formatting toolbar

→ Practice

You will now open a document that discusses how to start a home business. This is a public document provided by the Small Business Administration. Ensure that no documents are open in the application window.

1. Open the WD0325 data file.

2. Save the document as "HomeBusiness" to your personal storage location.

3. Show the document's nonprinting characters by doing the following:
CLICK: Show/Hide button (¶) on the Standard toolbar
Your screen should appear similar to the one shown in Figure 3.15.

Figure 3.15

Displaying paragraph marks and other nonprinting characters

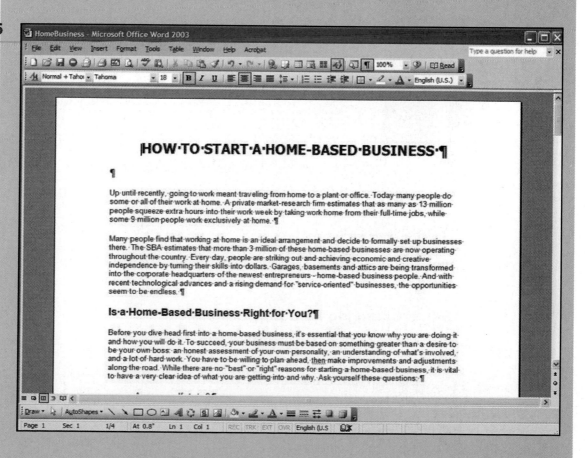

Word

4. To hide the symbols:
CLICK: Show/Hide button (**¶**)

5. To reveal a paragraph's formatting:
CHOOSE: Format, Reveal Formatting
or
PRESS SHIFT + F1

6. Position the insertion point anywhere in the document title.
Your screen should be similar to the one shown in Figure 3.16.

Figure 3.16

Revealing
formatting
characteristics of
the title

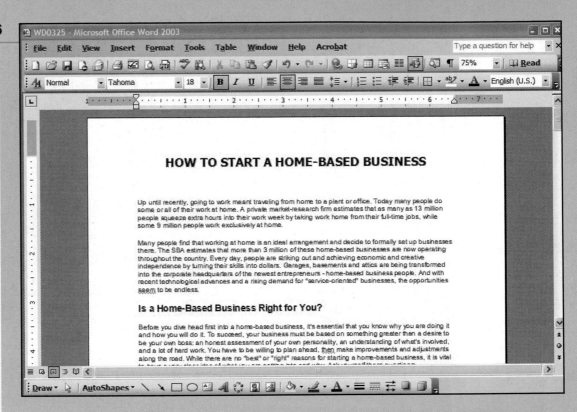

7. Click in other paragraphs of the document to reveal their formatting.

8. Close the task pane:
CHOOSE: View, Task Pane

3.3.2 Changing Paragraph Alignment

 ## Feature

Justification refers to how the text aligns within the left and right margins. *Left justification* aligns text against the left margin but leaves jagged right edges, similar to that of a typewriter. *Center justification* centers the text between the left and right margins. If your left and right margins are not even, the text may not appear centered on the page, but it will be centered between the margins. *Right justification* aligns the text against the right margin and leaves a jagged left edge. *Full justification* aligns text at both the left and right margins by adding spacing between words on the line.

→ # Method

To apply left justification:

- CLICK: Align Left button (▤)

  or

- PRESS: CTRL + l

To apply center justification:

- CLICK: Center button (▤)

  or

- PRESS: CTRL + e

To apply right justification:

- CLICK: Align Right button (▤)

  or

- PRESS CTRL + r

To full justify text:

- CLICK: Justify button (▤)

  or

- PRESS: CTRL + j

→ # Practice

You will now practice changing paragraph alignment in the "HomeBusiness" document. Ensure that you have completed the previous exercise and that the "HomeBusiness" document is open.

1. Position the insertion point in the first paragraph.

2. CLICK: Center button (▤)
The paragraph is immediately centered between the left and right margins.

3. In a similar manner, center the second paragraph.

4. Position the insertion point in the first subheading.
CLICK: Align Right button (▤)
The text is immediately aligned against the right margin.

5. In a similar manner, right-align the remaining subheadings.

6. To move to the top of the first page:
PRESS: CTRL + HOME
Your document, displayed in two-page view, should be similar to the one shown in Figure 3.17.

Figure 3.17

Aligning
paragraphs

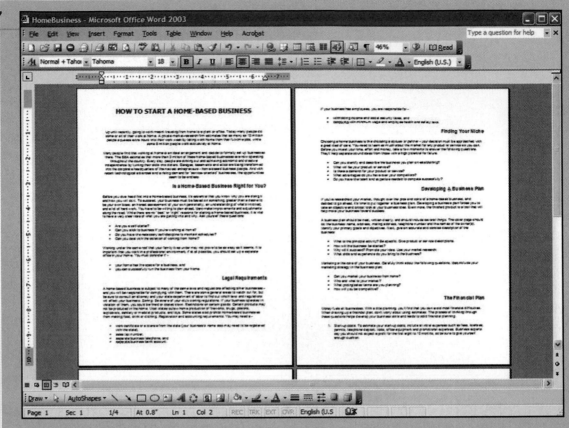

7. Save the document and leave it open for the next lesson.

3.3.3 Indenting Paragraphs

→ # Feature

Indenting a paragraph means to move a body of text in from the page margins. When you indent a paragraph, you temporarily change the text's positioning relative to the left and right margins. You can indent a paragraph on the left or right side, or on both sides.

→ # Method

To increase or decrease the left indent of an entire paragraph:

• CLICK: Increase Indent button ()

or

• CLICK: Decrease Indent button ()

To customize the left and right indents:

• DRAG: the indent markers on the Ruler

→ ## Practice

You will now practice indenting text in the "HomeBusiness" document. Ensure that you have completed the previous exercise and that the "HomeBusiness" document is open.

1. Position the cursor at the beginning of the paragraph under the subheading "Legal Requirements."

2. To increase the left indent:
CLICK: Increase Indent button (⬚) once.
Your document should appear similar to the one shown in Figure 3.18.

Figure 3.18

Indenting a
paragraph

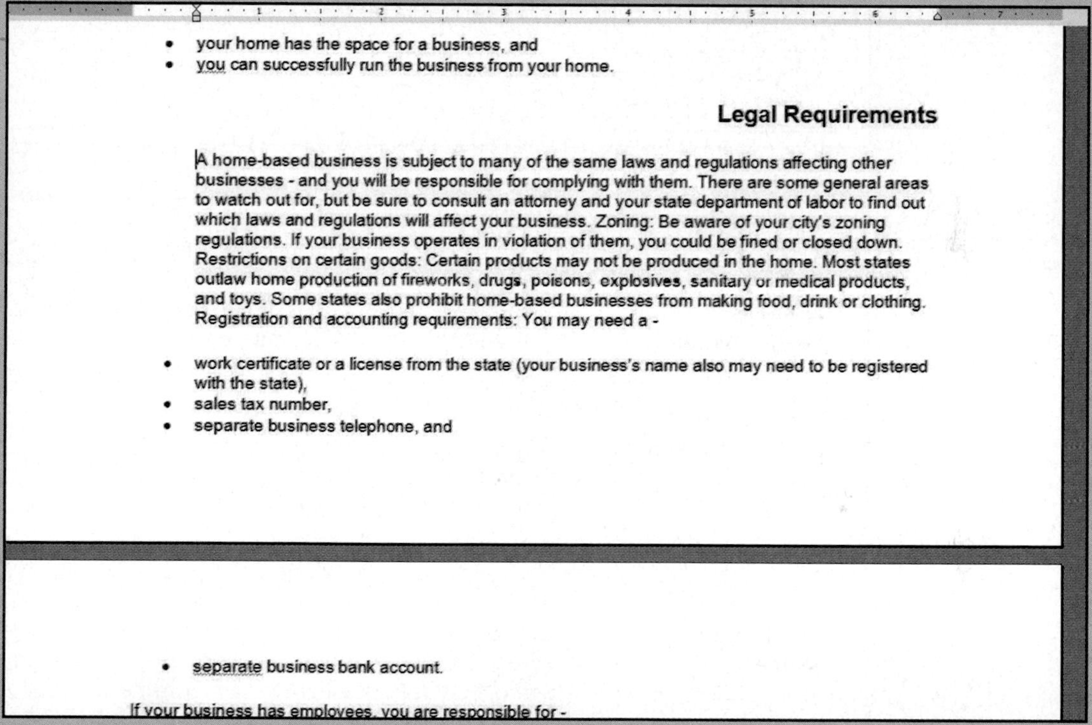

- your home has the space for a business, and
- you can successfully run the business from your home.

Legal Requirements

A home-based business is subject to many of the same laws and regulations affecting other businesses - and you will be responsible for complying with them. There are some general areas to watch out for, but be sure to consult an attorney and your state department of labor to find out which laws and regulations will affect your business. Zoning: Be aware of your city's zoning regulations. If your business operates in violation of them, you could be fined or closed down. Restrictions on certain goods: Certain products may not be produced in the home. Most states outlaw home production of fireworks, drugs, poisons, explosives, sanitary or medical products, and toys. Some states also prohibit home-based businesses from making food, drink or clothing. Registration and accounting requirements: You may need a -

- work certificate or a license from the state (your business's name also may need to be registered with the state),
- sales tax number,
- separate business telephone, and

- separate business bank account.

If your business has employees, you are responsible for -

3. To customize the indent position, you can drag the indent markers on the Ruler. These markers are labeled in Figure 3.19 and described in Table 3.2.

Figure 3.19

Indent markers
on Ruler

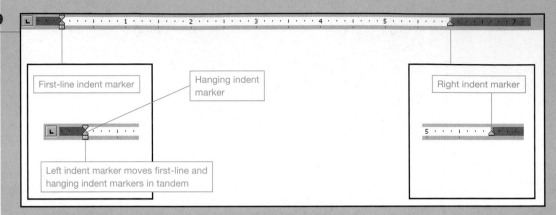

Table 3.2

Indent Markers

Type	Description
First-line indent marker	This indent marker moves only the first line of a paragraph in from the left margin. This paragraph format is often used in documents to avoid having to press the TAB key at the start of each new paragraph.
Hanging indent marker	This indent marker moves all but the first line of a paragraph in from the left margin, leaving the first-line indent marker in its current position.
Left indent marker	The left indent marker moves the first-line and hanging indent markers in tandem.
Right indent marker	The right indent marker moves the body of the entire paragraph in from the right margin. Left and right indents are often used together to set quotations apart from normal body text in a document.

To indent the paragraph 1″ from the right margin:
DRAG: the right indent marker to the left by 1″ (to 5 ¹/₂″ on the Ruler). Your screen should appear similar to the one shown in Figure 3.20.

Figure 3.20

Right-indenting
a paragraph

- your home has the space for a business, and
- you can successfully run the business from your home.

Legal Requirements

A home-based business is subject to many of the same laws and regulations affecting other businesses - and you will be responsible for complying with them. There are some general areas to watch out for, but be sure to consult an attorney and your state department of labor to find out which laws and regulations will affect your business. Zoning: Be aware of your city's zoning regulations. If your business operates in violation of them, you could be fined or closed down. Restrictions on certain goods: Certain products may not be produced in the home. Most states outlaw home production of fireworks, drugs, poisons, explosives, sanitary or medical products, and toys. Some states also prohibit home-based businesses from making food, drink or clothing. Registration and accounting requirements: You may need a -

- work certificate or a license from the state (your business's name also may need to be registered with the state),

4. To remove the left indent:
   CLICK: Decrease Indent button (⬅️) twice.

5. To remove the right indent:
   DRAG: the right indent marker back to the right margin (6 ¹/₂″ on the Ruler)

6. Position the insertion point at the end of the "HomeBusiness" document.

7. Insert a hanging indent for the new paragraph:
   DRAG: hanging indent marker to 1 ¹/₂″ on the Ruler
   (Make sure that the tip of your mouse points to the triangle and not to the bottom rectangle when dragging.) If performed correctly, the Ruler should appear as it does in Figure 3.21.

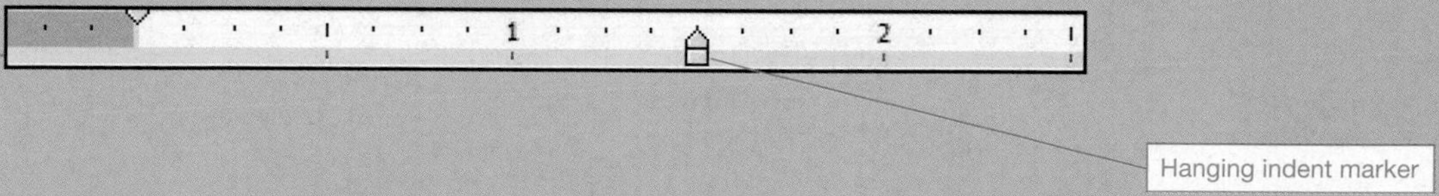

Figure 3.21

Hanging indent marker at the 1 1/2″ position

Hanging indent marker

8. TYPE: Conclusion:

9. PRESS: `TAB`

10. TYPE: **In order start a successful home business, you must be motivated, a self-starter, have sufficient funds to cover typical start-up costs, have a solid business plan, and be flexible.**
    Your document should appear similar to the one shown in Figure 3.22.

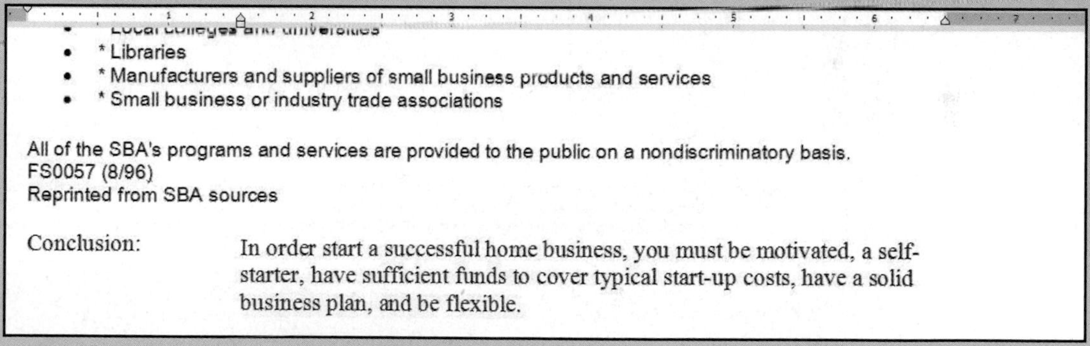

Figure 3.22

Creating a hanging indent

11. Save the "HomeBusiness" document and leave it open for the next lesson.

3.3.4 Changing Line Spacing

→ **Feature**

Changing a document's line spacing can make it easier to read. The standard choices for line spacing are 1.0, 1.5, 2.0, 2.5, and 3.0 spacing, but you are not limited to these.

→ **Method**

To change the line spacing using the toolbar:

• CLICK: Line Spacing drop-down arrow (📶▾)

• CHOOSE: an option from the drop-down menu

To select a specific line spacing option other than what is available on the toolbar:

- CHOOSE: Format, Paragraph
- CLICK: down arrow next to the *Line spacing* drop-down list box
- SELECT: *the desired spacing*
- CLICK: OK command button

→ ## Practice

We will now practice changing the line spacing in the "HomeBusiness" document. Ensure you have completed the previous lesson and the "HomeBusiness" document is open.

1. Move the insertion point to the first paragraph.

2. First, change the paragraph alignment back to left:
CLICK: Align left button (▤)

3. Change the line spacing to double:
CLICK: Line Spacing drop-down arrow (▤▾)
Your screen should be similar to the one shown in Figure 3.23.

Figure 3.23

Changing line spacing

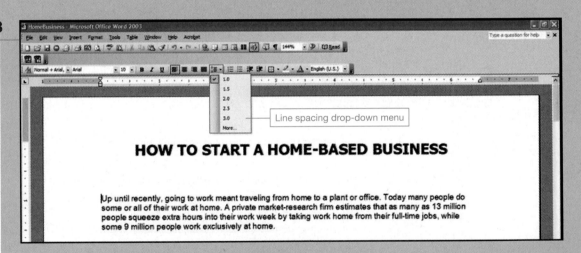

4. CHOOSE: 2.0 from the drop-down menu
Only the paragraph in which the insertion point was located is double-spaced (Figure 3.24).

Figure 3.24

First paragraph changed to double-spaced

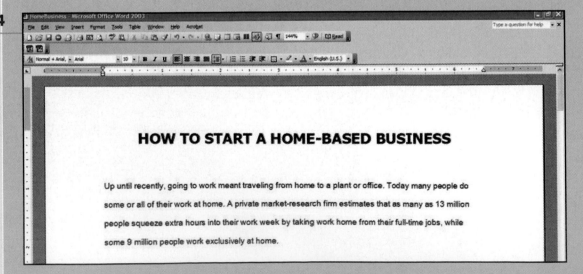

5. In a similar method, change the line spacing of the first paragraph to 1.5.

6. In a similar method, return the first paragraph to single spacing.

7. Double-space the entire document:
PRESS: `CTRL` + a (to select the entire document)
CLICK: Line Spacing drop-down arrow (≣▾)
CHOOSE: 2.0 from the drop-down menu

8. With the entire document still selected, let's return the spacing to single.
CHOOSE: Format, Paragraph
The Paragraph dialog box appears as shown in Figure 3.25.

Figure 3.25

Paragraph dialog box

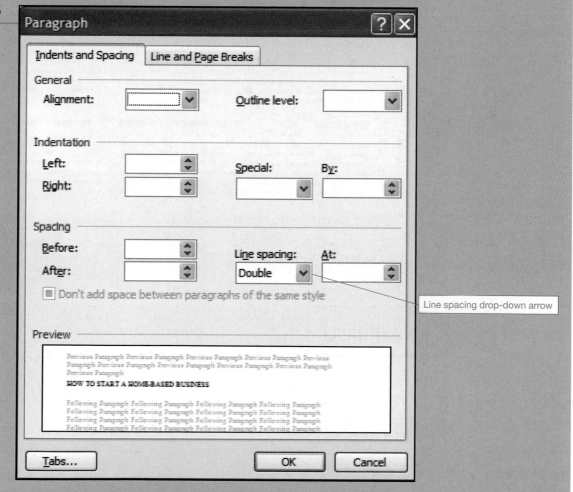

Line spacing drop-down arrow

9. CLICK: Line spacing drop-down arrow
CHOOSE: *Single* from the drop-down list
CLICK: OK command button

10. Position the insertion point in the second paragraph
CLICK: Align Left button (≣)
The first page of your document should appear similar to the one shown in Figure 3.26.

Figure 3.26

First page of document

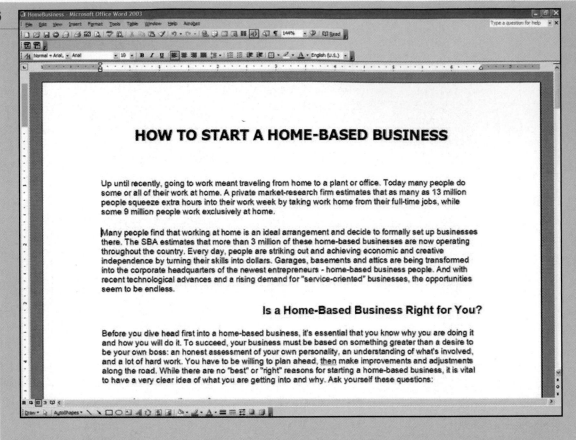

11. Save and close the "HomeBusiness" document.

 **3.3** Describe how to change line spacing in a document.

3.4 Creating Lists

Word provides several features for managing lists of items. In this module, we describe how to create bulleted and numbered lists and numbered outlines. We also discuss how to arrange lists of information by changing your document's tab settings.

3.4.1 Creating Bulleted and Numbered Lists

→ **Feature**

Word provides a utility for automatically creating lists with leading bullets or numbers. **Bullets** can be selected from a variety of shapes and symbols. Numbered lists can use numbers, Roman numerals, or letters.

→ ## Method

To create a bulleted list:

- CLICK: Bullets button (▤)

To create a numbered list:

- CLICK: Numbering button (▤)

To modify the bullet symbol or numbering scheme:

- CHOOSE: Format, Bullets and Numbering

The last bullet or numbering scheme you select from the Format, Bullets and Numbering dialog box becomes the default symbol until you change it to something else.

→ ## Practice

You will now begin a new document and create bulleted and numbered lists.

1. To begin a blank document:
CLICK: New button (▢)

2. TYPE: **Meeting Agenda**
PRESS: **ENTER** twice
(*Note:* Depending on your AutoCorrect settings, Word may apply a heading style to the title. This is not a problem.)

3. To create a bulleted list:
CLICK: Bullets button (▤)
A bullet appears, and the indent markers are moved on the Ruler.

4. Enter the following text, pressing **ENTER** after each entry
Attendance
Approval of Minutes
Introduction of Guests
Approval of Financial Statements
Curriculum Changes
New Personnel
Adjournment

5. Note that Word automatically starts each new line with a bullet when you press **ENTER**. To turn bullets off, ensure that your insertion point is below the last entry and press **ENTER**. Your document should be similar to the one shown in Figure 3.27.
Because the previous line was blank, Word turned off bullet formatting. You can also click the Bullets button to turn off bullet formatting.

Figure 3.27

Bulleted list

Bullets

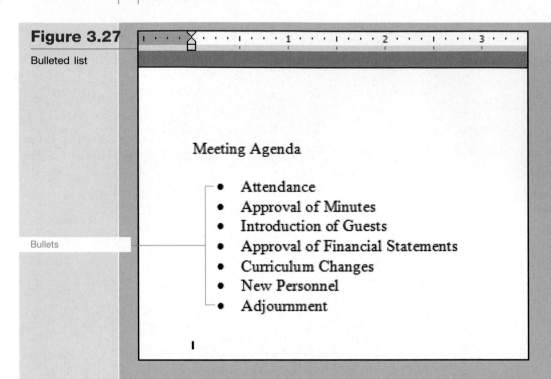

Meeting Agenda

- Attendance
- Approval of Minutes
- Introduction of Guests
- Approval of Financial Statements
- Curriculum Changes
- New Personnel
- Adjournment

6. In the next example, you will create a numbered list after you have already entered information into your document. To begin:
PRESS: **ENTER** three times

7. Enter the following lines of text, pressing **ENTER** after each entry:
Ensure quorum
Advise that minutes will be sent electronically
Limit guest introductions to 5 minutes total
Advise that budget is balanced and on target
New technology: Nuclear Medicine
New personnel list is for information only

8. Using the mouse pointer, select the text you entered in step 7.

9. CLICK: Numbering button (⊟)
The selected text is automatically numbered and indented.

10. To use letters in the list instead of numbers, with your cursor on the first numbered item
CHOOSE: Format, Bullets and Numbering
This opens the Bullets and Numbering dialog box as shown in Figure 3.28

Figure 3.28

Bullets and
numbering dialog
box, *Numbered*
tab

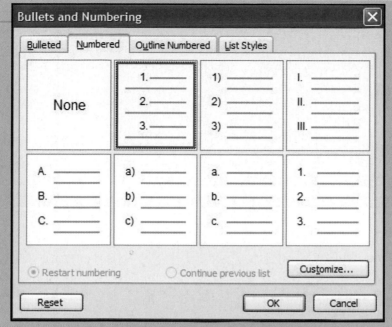

11. SELECT: the numbering scheme that begins with a)
    This scheme is in the second row, second column.

12. CLICK: OK command button
    CLICK: anywhere in the document to remove the highlighting, if necessary
    Your document should be similar to the one shown in Figure 3.29

Figure 3.29

Bulleted and
numbered lists

Bulleted List

Numbered List

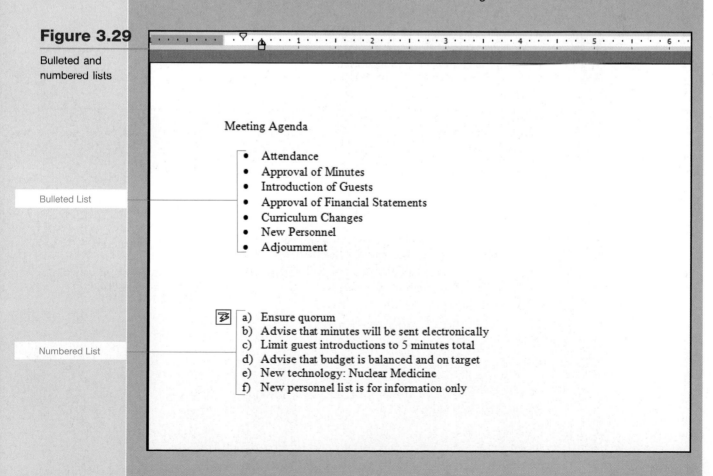

13. To add an item to the numbered list, position the cursor after item f).

14. PRESS: [ENTER]
TYPE: **Remind of next month's meeting date**
Note that Word automatically continues the numbering sequence.

15. Position the cursor after item b), then:
PRESS: [ENTER]
TYPE: **Confirm e-mail addresses of Board members**
Note that Word renumbers the list when you insert new entries.
Your document should be similar to the one shown in Figure 3.30.

Figure 3.30

Revised
document

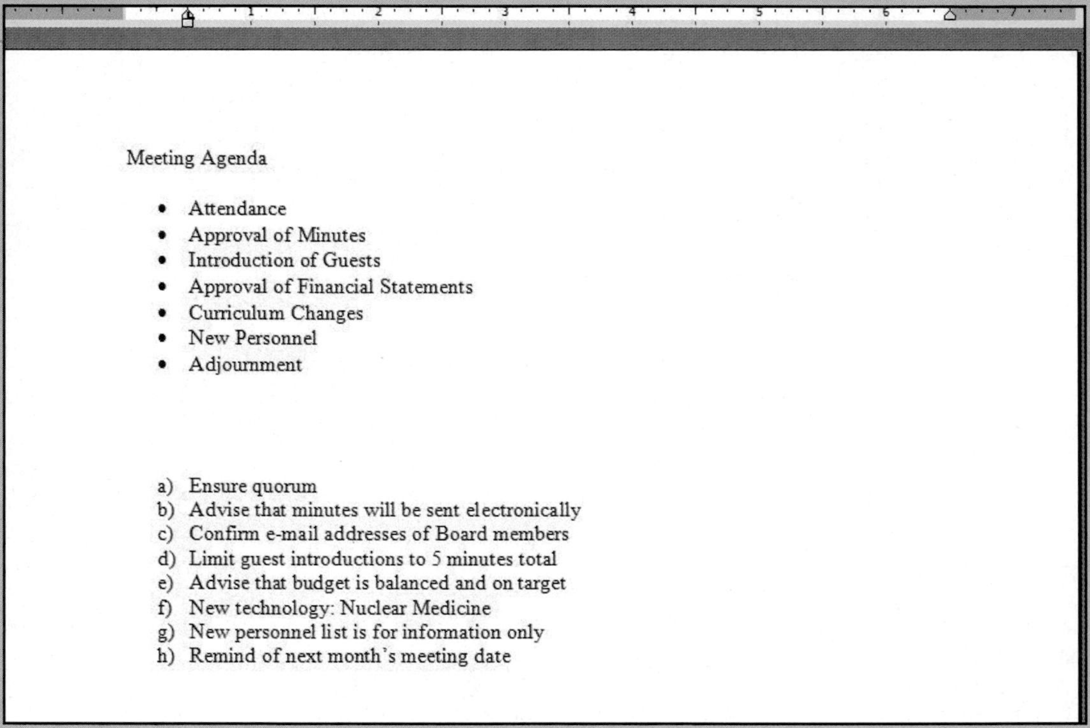

Meeting Agenda

- Attendance
- Approval of Minutes
- Introduction of Guests
- Approval of Financial Statements
- Curriculum Changes
- New Personnel
- Adjournment

a) Ensure quorum
b) Advise that minutes will be sent electronically
c) Confirm e-mail addresses of Board members
d) Limit guest introductions to 5 minutes total
e) Advise that budget is balanced and on target
f) New technology: Nuclear Medicine
g) New personnel list is for information only
h) Remind of next month's meeting date

16. Save the document as "Meeting Agenda" and close the document.

3.4.2 Creating a Numbered Outline

→ **Feature**

Have you ever created an outline for a document and then had to retype the outline numbers when your outline changed? If so, you will appreciate Word's ability to manage numbered outlines.

→ **Method**

- CHOOSE: Format, Bullets and Numbering
- CLICK: *Outline Numbered* tab
- SELECT: an outline style
- CLICK: OK command button

→ **Practice**

In this lesson, you will create an outline numbered list. Ensure that no documents are displaying in the application window.

1. Open the WD0326 document from your data files location.

2. Save the file as "Wedding" to your personal storage location.

3. Place the insertion point at the end of the document.
CHOOSE: Format, Bullets and Numbering
CLICK: *Outline Numbered* tab
The Bullets and Numbering dialog box appears as shown in Figure 3.31. There are seven outline styles from which you can choose.

Figure 3.31

Bullets and Numbering dialog box, *Outline Numbered tab*

You select this style in the next step

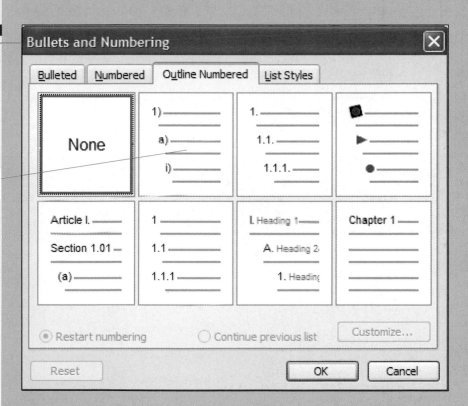

4. We will select the first style (located to the right of the None box. This style will use numbers for level one headings, letters for level two headings, and Roman numerals for level three headings.
SELECT: 1) a) i) style located in the first row, second column
CLICK: OK command button

5. The insertion point should be blinking to the right of 1).
TYPE: **Invitations**
PRESS: ENTER

6. To insert two demoted items:
PRESS: TAB
TYPE: **Select invitations**

7. PRESS: ENTER
TYPE: **Mail invitations on April 1**
Note that when you press ENTER, the next item is automatically indented at the same level as the previous item.

8. To promote the next item:
   PRESS: `ENTER`
   PRESS: `SHIFT` + `TAB`
   Your document should be similar to the one shown in Figure 3.32.

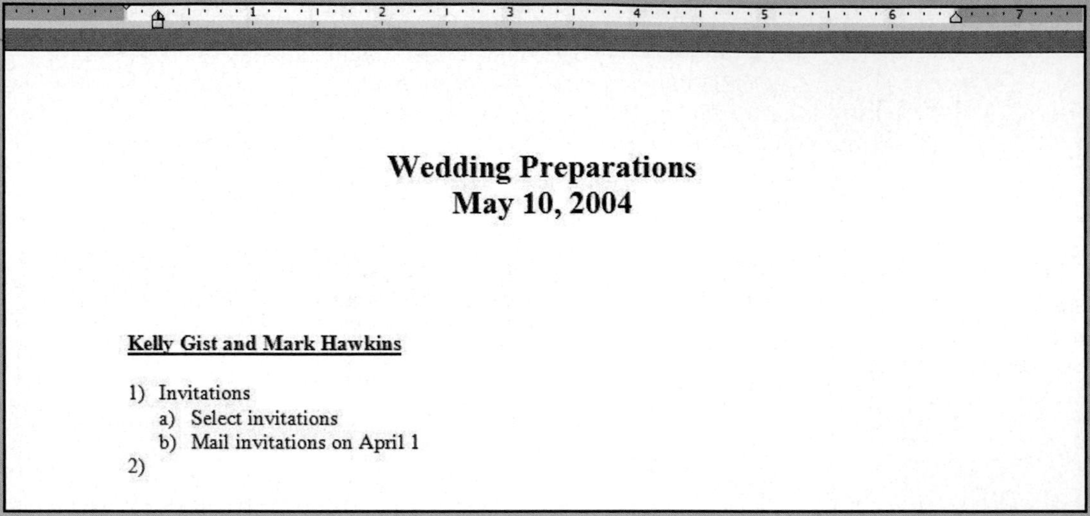

Figure 3.32

Typing a numbered outline

Wedding Preparations
May 10, 2004

Kelly Gist and Mark Hawkins

1) Invitations
   a) Select invitations
   b) Mail invitations on April 1
2)

9. Complete the outline by referring to Figure 3.33.

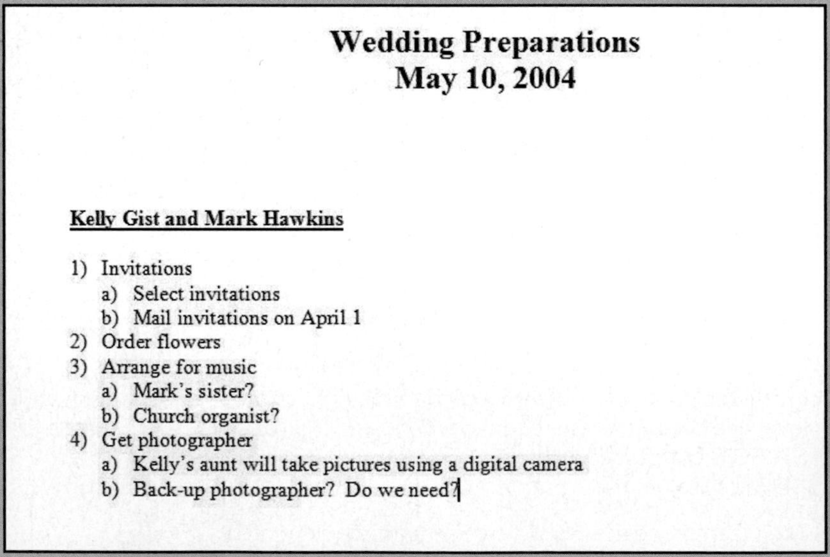

Figure 3.33

Completed outline

Wedding Preparations
May 10, 2004

Kelly Gist and Mark Hawkins

1) Invitations
   a) Select invitations
   b) Mail invitations on April 1
2) Order flowers
3) Arrange for music
   a) Mark's sister?
   b) Church organist?
4) Get photographer
   a) Kelly's aunt will take pictures using a digital camera
   b) Back-up photographer? Do we need?

10. Save and close the revised document.

3.4 What happens when you insert an item between two existing items in an outline numbered list?

Word

3.5 Setting and Modifying Tabs

Text that is aligned properly is easier to read and easier to understand. Using the Tabs feature, you can set several types of tabs and add dot leaders.

3.5.1 Setting Tabs in a New Document

→ ## Feature

Tabs allow you to neatly arrange and align text and numbers on a page. There are four basic tab types: left, center, right, and decimal. By default, Word has left-aligned tabs every one-half inch. Each of the four tab types can also have **leaders**, which are dotted, dashed, or solid lines that fill the space between text and tab stops. Leaders are commonly used in tables of contents to visually join the section headings with page numbers.

→ ## Method

To select a tab type:

- CLICK: the Tab alignment button (⬜) located on the left side of the Ruler until the tab symbol you want appears

- CLICK: the desired location on the Ruler to set the tab stop

To remove a tab:

- DRAG: the tab stop down and off the Ruler

To create a custom tab that includes a tab leader:

- CHOOSE: Format, Tabs to display the Tabs dialog box

→ ## Practice

In this module, you will exercise practice setting tabs. Ensure that no documents are open in the application window.

1. To begin a new document:
   CLICK: New button (⬜)

2. To enter the current date:
   CHOOSE: Insert, Date and Time
   SELECT: The month, date, and year format (the third down)

3. PRESS: **ENTER** four times
   TYPE: **Conference Attendees:**
   PRESS: **ENTER** two times

4. TYPE: **Thank you for registering for the Annual Mid-West Conference on Technical College Leadership. We have an exciting schedule this year, with several nationally known keynote speakers. You should have received an information packet with hotel information, rental car information, and tour events in the beautiful city of Columbus, Ohio. We have finalized room locations with the hotel for the various events. These are listed below:**
   PRESS: **ENTER** twice
   Save the document as "Conference" to your personal storage location and keep it open for the next steps.
   In the next few steps, you will set tabs and type text so that your document resembles Figure 3.34 when completed.

Figure 3.34

"Conference" document

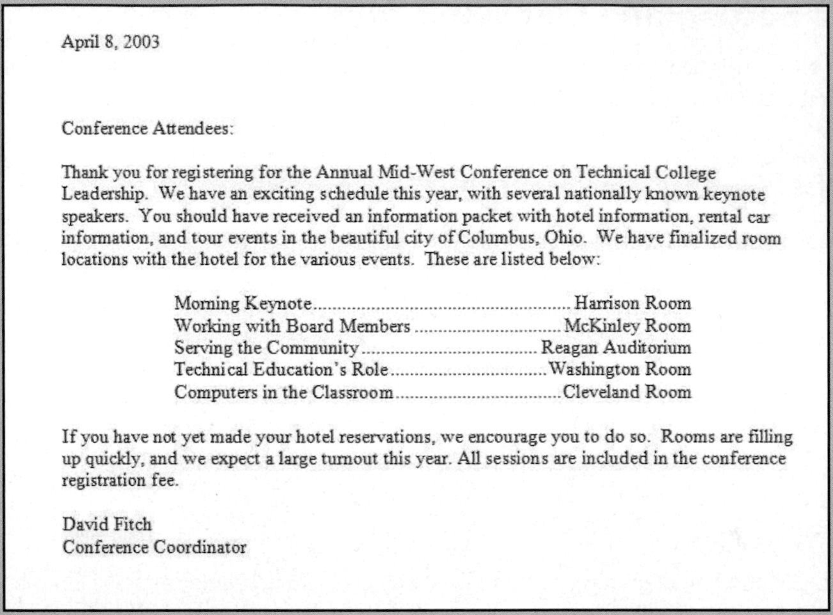

> April 8, 2003
>
> Conference Attendees:
>
> Thank you for registering for the Annual Mid-West Conference on Technical College Leadership. We have an exciting schedule this year, with several nationally known keynote speakers. You should have received an information packet with hotel information, rental car information, and tour events in the beautiful city of Columbus, Ohio. We have finalized room locations with the hotel for the various events. These are listed below:
>
> | Morning Keynote | Harrison Room |
> | Working with Board Members | McKinley Room |
> | Serving the Community | Reagan Auditorium |
> | Technical Education's Role | Washington Room |
> | Computers in the Classroom | Cleveland Room |
>
> If you have not yet made your hotel reservations, we encourage you to do so. Rooms are filling up quickly, and we expect a large turnout this year. All sessions are included in the conference registration fee.
>
> David Fitch
> Conference Coordinator

5. To specify a tab position for the event name:
CLICK: Tab Alignment button until the left-aligned tab symbol (⌞L⌟) appears (*Note:* This symbol may already be displaying.)

6. CLICK: at the 1″ marker on the Ruler
(*Hint:* If you position the tab incorrectly, you can drag it along the Ruler using the mouse, or you can drag it off the ruler and start again.)

7. To specify a location for the room name:
CLICK: Tab Alignment button until the right-aligned tab symbol (⌐⌐) appears
CLICK: at the 5 ¹/₂″ marker on the Ruler
The Ruler should appear as it does in Figure 3.35.

Figure 3.35

Changing tab settings

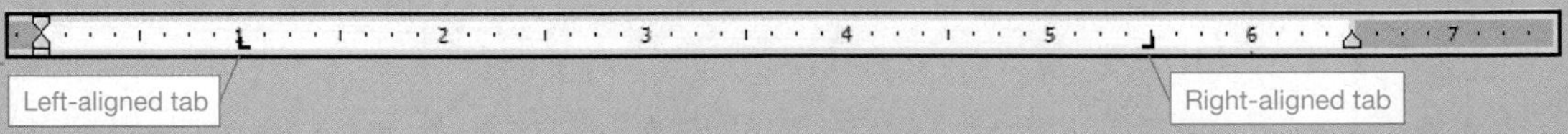

Left-aligned tab   Right-aligned tab

8. Now, edit the right-aligned tab to include a dot leader.
CHOOSE: Format, Tabs
SELECT: 5.5 in the *Tab stop position* list box
SELECT: 2 in the *Leader* area
The dialog box should appear similar to the one shown in Figure 3.36.

Figure 3.36

Tabs dialog box

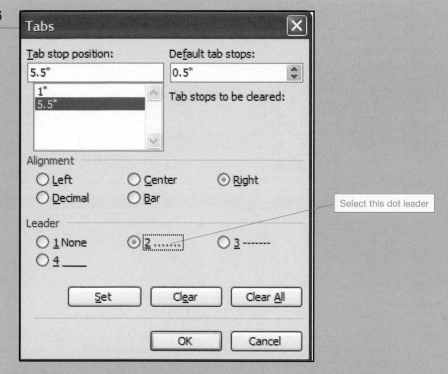

9. CLICK: OK command button

10. CLICK: Show/Hide button (¶)

11. Enter the first row of information:
PRESS: TAB to move the insertion point to the first tab stop
TYPE: **Morning Keynote**
PRESS: TAB
TYPE: **Harrison Room**
PRESS: ENTER
Note that each press of the TAB key results in the tab symbol (➜) as shown in Figure 3.37.

Figure 3.37

Tab symbols

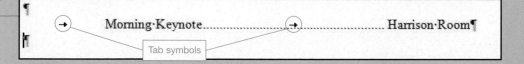

¶
➜   Morning·Keynote..................➜.....................Harrison·Room¶
¶

Tab symbols

12. Save the document as "Room Locations" to your personal storage location.

13. Continue entering the information shown in Figure 3.38.

Figure 3.38

Data entered

Working with Board Members .... McKinley Room
Serving the Community .... Reagan Auditorium
Technical Education's Role .... Washington Room
Computers in the Classroom .... Cleveland Room

14. CLICK: Show/Hide button (¶)

15. PRESS: (ENTER) twice

16. TYPE: If you have not yet made your hotel reservations, we encourage you to do so. Rooms are filling up quickly, and we expect a large turnout this year. All sessions are included in the conference registration fee.

17. PRESS: (ENTER) twice
TYPE: **David Fitch**
PRESS: (ENTER)
TYPE: **Conference Coordinator**
Your final document should be similar to the one shown in Figure 3.39.

Figure 3.39

Completed "Room Locations" document

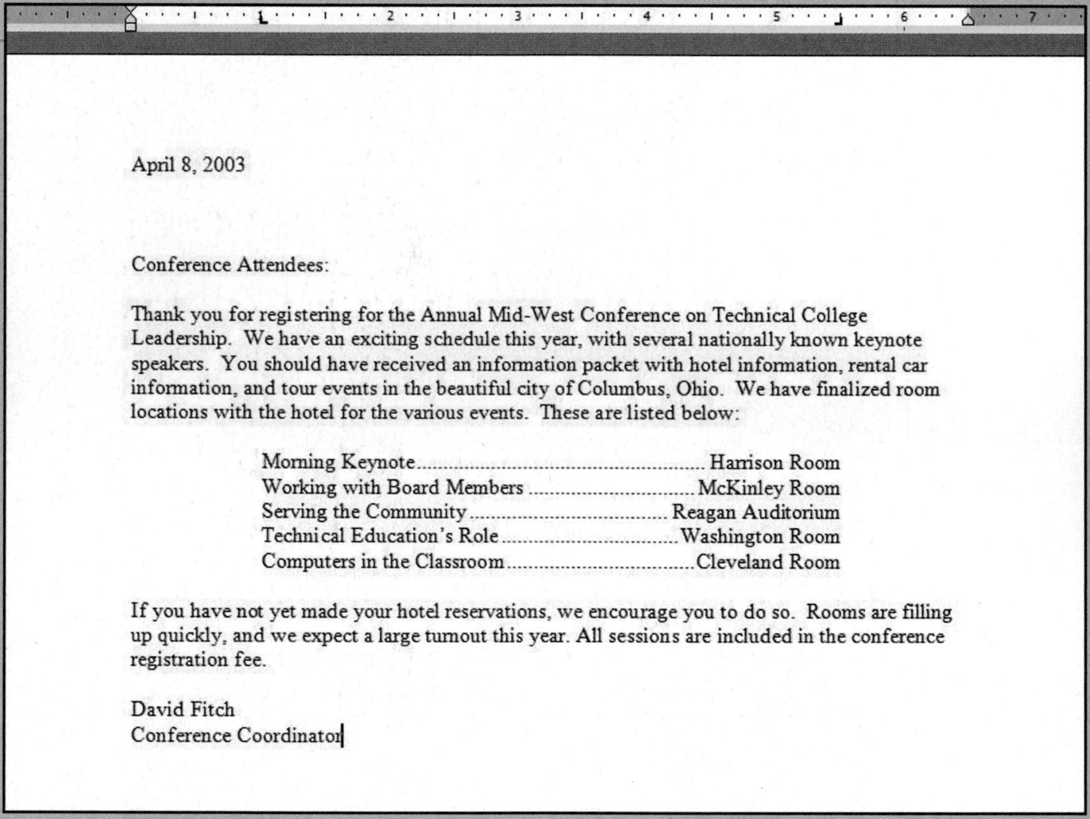

> April 8, 2003
>
>
> Conference Attendees:
>
> Thank you for registering for the Annual Mid-West Conference on Technical College Leadership. We have an exciting schedule this year, with several nationally known keynote speakers. You should have received an information packet with hotel information, rental car information, and tour events in the beautiful city of Columbus, Ohio. We have finalized room locations with the hotel for the various events. These are listed below:
>
> | | |
> |---|---|
> | Morning Keynote | Harrison Room |
> | Working with Board Members | McKinley Room |
> | Serving the Community | Reagan Auditorium |
> | Technical Education's Role | Washington Room |
> | Computers in the Classroom | Cleveland Room |
>
> If you have not yet made your hotel reservations, we encourage you to do so. Rooms are filling up quickly, and we expect a large turnout this year. All sessions are included in the conference registration fee.
>
> David Fitch
> Conference Coordinator

18. Save the document to your personal storage location.

19. Close the document.

3.5 Describe how to set dot leaders.

3.6 Applying Borders and Shading

Documents that incorporate interesting visual effects do a better job of engaging readers than those that use plain formatting. You have already learned how to use character and paragraph formatting commands to add visual emphasis to words and paragraphs. In this module, you will learn how to add shading and page borders to make your document even more appealing.

3.6.1 Adding Shading and Paragraph Borders

→ Feature

Word's Borders and Shading feature provides other methods of emphasizing text. However, unless your shading contrasts sufficiently from your text, it may be difficult to read.

→ Method

To add shading to text:

- CHOOSE: Format, Borders and Shading
- CLICK: *Shading* tab
- CLICK: a color in the *Fill* palette or choose an option from the *Style* drop-down list
- SELECT: Text or Paragraph in the *Apply to* drop-down list
- CLICK: OK command button

To add borders to text:

- CHOOSE: Format, Borders and Shading
- CLICK: *Borders* tab

To position the border:

- CLICK: an image in the *Setting* area

  or

- CLICK: on the diagram in the *Preview* area

To customize the border, perform one or more of the following procedures:

- SELECT: a style in the *Style* list box
- SELECT: a color from the *Color* drop-down list
- SELECT: a rule width from the *Width* drop-down list
- CLICK: OK command button

→ Practice

In this module, you will open an existing file and apply shading and borders to paragraphs. Ensure that no documents are open in the application window.

1. Open the WD0327 file.

2. Save the document as "Internet Security" to your personal storage location.
   Note that there are three headings in the document. You will add shading to each of these.

3. To shade the first heading:
   CLICK: the insertion point anywhere within the heading "Introduction"
   CHOOSE: Format, Borders and Shading
   SELECT: *Shading* tab
   Your screen should appear similar to the one shown in Figure 3.40.

Figure 3.40

Borders and
Shading dialog
box, *Shading* tab

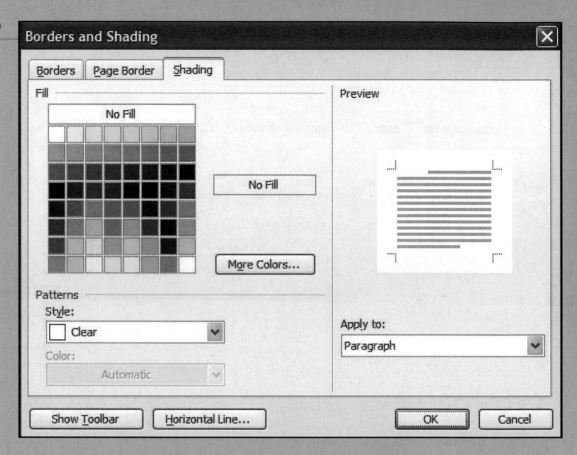

4. In the *Fill* palette:
   CLICK: light green (last row, fourth column)

5. Look at the *Apply to* drop-down list. Ensure that it shows *Paragraph*.
   (*Note:* By choosing *Paragraph*, the shading will extend from the left margin to the right margin. If
   Paragraph is not selected, click the drop-down arrow and select it.)

6. CLICK: OK command button

7. In a similar manner, add the same color shading to the remaining two headings, "Immediate Attention" and "Top Vulnerabilities to Windows Systems."
   Your document, displayed in two-page view, should be similar to Figure 3.41.

Figure 3.41

"Internet Security" document with shaded headings

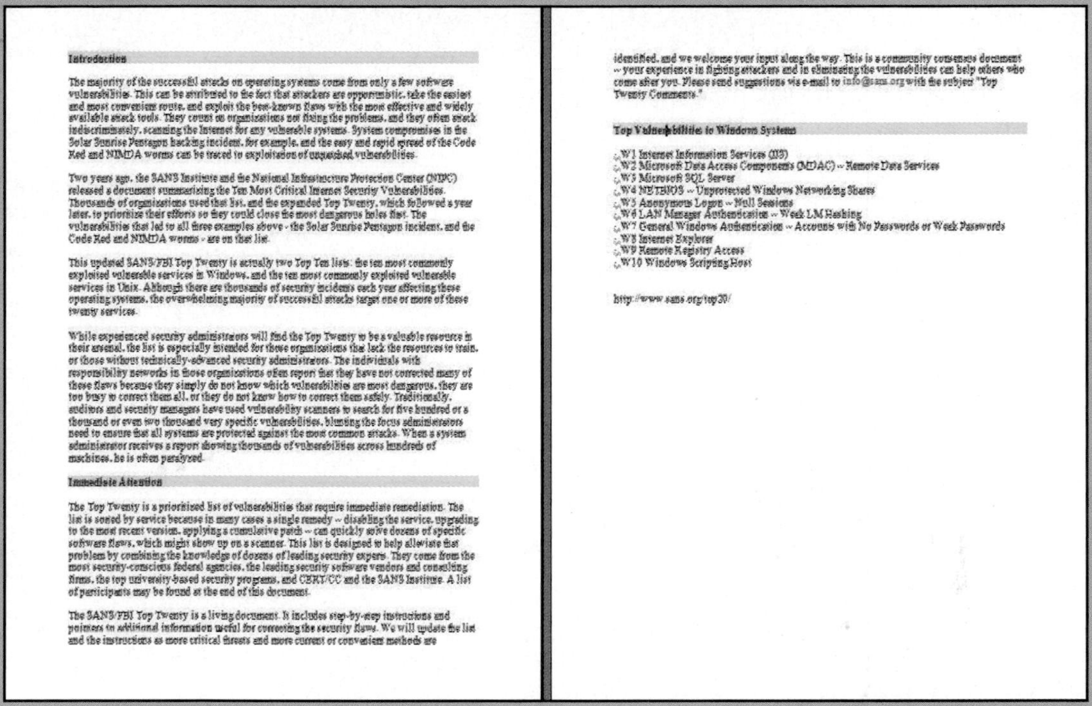

Introduction

The majority of the successful attacks on operating systems come from only a few software vulnerabilities. This can be attributed to the fact that attackers are opportunistic, take the easiest and most convenient route, and exploit the best-known flaws with the most effective and widely available attack tools. They count on organizations not fixing the problems, and they often attack indiscriminately, scanning the Internet for any vulnerable systems. System compromises in the Solar Sunrise Pentagon hacking incident, for example, and the easy and rapid spread of the Code Red and NIMDA worms can be traced to exploitation of unpatched vulnerabilities.

Two years ago, the SANS Institute and the National Infrastructure Protection Center (NIPC) released a document summarizing the Ten Most Critical Internet Security Vulnerabilities. Thousands of organizations used that list, and the expanded Top Twenty, which followed a year later, to prioritize their efforts so they could close the most dangerous holes first. The vulnerabilities that led to all three examples above - the Solar Sunrise Pentagon incident, and the Code Red and NIMDA worms - are on that list.

This updated SANS/FBI Top Twenty is actually two Top Ten lists: the ten most commonly exploited vulnerable services in Windows, and the ten most commonly exploited vulnerable services in Unix. Although there are thousands of security incidents each year affecting these operating systems, the overwhelming majority of successful attacks target one or more of these twenty services.

While experienced security administrators will find the Top Twenty to be a valuable resource in their arsenal, the list is especially intended for those organizations that lack the resources to train, or those without technically-advanced security administrators. The individuals with responsibility networks in those organizations often report that they have not corrected many of these flaws because they simply do not know which vulnerabilities are most dangerous, they are too busy to correct them all, or they do not know how to correct them safely. Traditionally, auditors and security managers have used vulnerability scanners to search for five hundred or a thousand or even two thousand very specific vulnerabilities, blunting the focus administrators need to ensure that all systems are protected against the most common attacks. When a system administrator receives a report showing thousands of vulnerabilities across hundreds of machines, he is often paralyzed.

Immediate Attention

The Top Twenty is a prioritized list of vulnerabilities that require immediate remediation. The list is sorted by service because in many cases a single remedy -- disabling the service, upgrading to the most recent version, applying a cumulative patch -- can quickly solve dozens of specific software flaws, which might show up on a scanner. This list is designed to help alleviate that problem by combining the knowledge of dozens of leading security experts. They come from the most security-conscious federal agencies, the leading security software vendors and consulting firms, the top university-based security programs, and CERT/CC and the SANS Institute. A list of participants may be found at the end of this document.

The SANS/FBI Top Twenty is a living document. It includes step-by-step instructions and pointers to additional information useful for correcting the security flaws. We will update the list and the instructions as more critical threats and more current or convenient methods are identified, and we welcome your input along the way. This is a community consensus document -- your experience in fighting attackers and in eliminating the vulnerabilities can help others who come after you. Please send suggestions via e-mail to info@sans.org with the subject "Top Twenty Comments."

Top Vulnerabilities to Windows Systems

W1 Internet Information Services (IIS)
W2 Microsoft Data Access Components (MDAC) -- Remote Data Services
W3 Microsoft SQL Server
W4 NETBIOS -- Unprotected Windows Networking Shares
W5 Anonymous Logon -- Null Sessions
W6 LAN Manager Authentication -- Weak LM Hashing
W7 General Windows Authentication -- Accounts with No Passwords or Weak Passwords
W8 Internet Explorer
W9 Remote Registry Access
W10 Windows Scripting Host

http://www.sans.org/top20/

8. Save your work.
9. Now add borders to each of these headings.
(*Note:* You could have added shading and borders at the same time while the Format, Borders and Shading dialog box was open. For learning purposes, however, we are performing the actions separately.)
10. To add borders to the first heading "Introduction":
CLICK: anywhere within the first heading "Introduction"
CHOOSE: Format, Borders and Shading
SELECT: *Borders* tab
The dialog box shown in Figure 3.42 should appear.

Figure 3.42

Borders and
Shading dialog
box, *Borders* tab

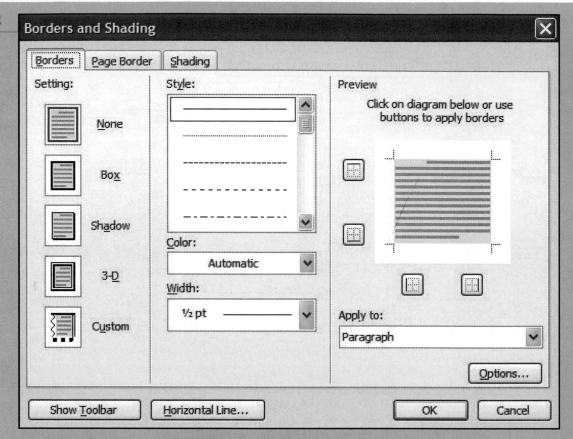

11. To add borders to the top and bottom of the paragraph:
CLICK: *Box* in the *Setting* area
CLICK: the left and right of the image in the *Preview* area
(*Note: This action turns off lines for the left and right side of the paragraph, which is what we want. Ensure that your dialog box looks like Figure 3.43.*)

Figure 3.43

Borders and Shading dialog box, *Borders* tab

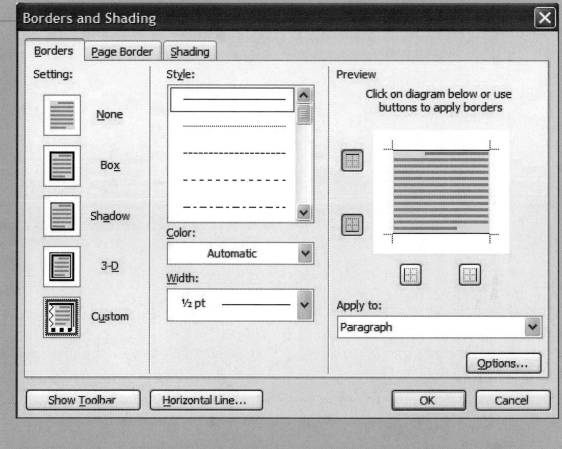

12. CLICK: OK command button

13. In a similar manner, apply the same borders to the other two headings.

14. Save the document and leave it open for the next lesson.

3.6.2 Applying Page Borders

→ **Feature**

Page borders are very effective in adding interest to pages, particularly for flyers and newsletters. Word provides several choices of page borders, including lines (also called *rules*) and graphics that are repeated around the page.

→ **Method**

To add a page border:

- CHOOSE: Format, Borders and Shading
- CLICK: *Page Border* tab
- CHOOSE: an option in the *Setting* area or
- CHOOSE: a graphic from the *Art* drop-down list
- SELECT: a color from the *Color* drop-down list (optional)
- SELECT: a rule width from the *Width* drop-down list
- CLICK: OK command button

→ **Practice**

In this module, you will add a page border to the "Internet Security" document. Ensure that you have completed the previous lesson and that the "Internet Security" document is open in the application window.

1. To insert a page border:
CHOOSE: Format, Borders and Shading
CLICK: *Page Border* tab

2. Let's choose the 3-D graphic in the *Setting* area:
CLICK: *3-D* graphic in the *Setting* area.
Your screen should appear similar to the one shown in Figure 3.44.

Figure 3.44

Borders and Shading dialog box, *Page Border* tab

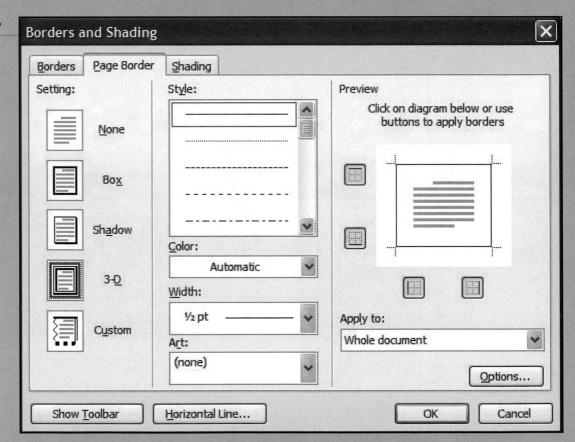

3. Change the width of the line:
CLICK: the *Width* drop-down list
SELECT: 3 pt

4. CLICK: OK command button
Your document, displayed in two-page view, should be similar to the one shown in Figure 3.45.

Figure 3.45

"Internet Security" document with page borders applied

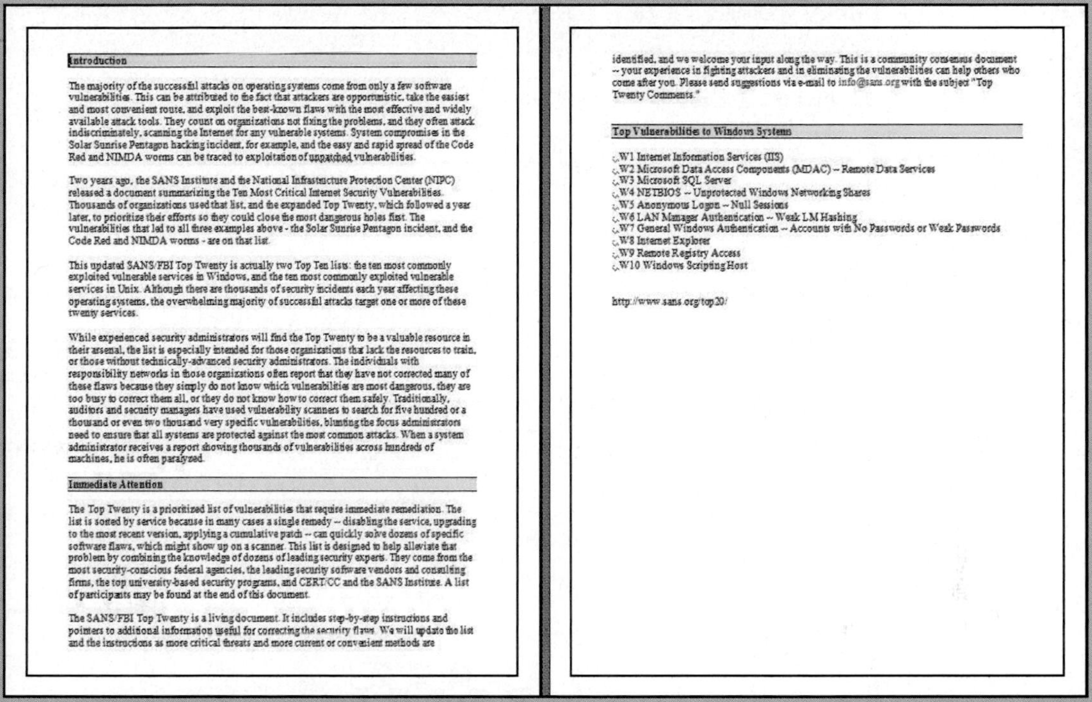

Introduction

The majority of the successful attacks on operating systems come from only a few software vulnerabilities. This can be attributed to the fact that attackers are opportunistic, take the easiest and most convenient route, and exploit the best-known flaws with the most effective and widely available attack tools. They count on organizations not fixing the problems, and they often attack indiscriminately, scanning the Internet for any vulnerable systems. System compromises in the Solar Sunrise Pentagon hacking incident, for example, and the easy and rapid spread of the Code Red and NIMDA worms can be traced to exploitation of unpatched vulnerabilities.

Two years ago, the SANS Institute and the National Infrastructure Protection Center (NIPC) released a document summarizing the Ten Most Critical Internet Security Vulnerabilities. Thousands of organizations used that list, and the expanded Top Twenty, which followed a year later, to prioritize their efforts so they could close the most dangerous holes first. The vulnerabilities that led to all three examples above - the Solar Sunrise Pentagon incident, and the Code Red and NIMDA worms - are on that list.

This updated SANS/FBI Top Twenty is actually two Top Ten lists: the ten most commonly exploited vulnerable services in Windows, and the ten most commonly exploited vulnerable services in Unix. Although there are thousands of security incidents each year affecting these operating systems, the overwhelming majority of successful attacks target one or more of these twenty services.

While experienced security administrators will find the Top Twenty to be a valuable resource in their arsenal, the list is especially intended for those organizations that lack the resources to train, or those without technically-advanced security administrators. The individuals with responsibility networks in those organizations often report that they have not corrected many of these flaws because they simply do not know which vulnerabilities are most dangerous, they are too busy to correct them all, or they do not know how to correct them safely. Traditionally, auditors and security managers have used vulnerability scanners to search for five hundred or a thousand or even two thousand very specific vulnerabilities, blunting the focus administrators need to ensure that all systems are protected against the most common attacks. When a system administrator receives a report showing thousands of vulnerabilities across hundreds of machines, he is often paralyzed.

Immediate Attention

The Top Twenty is a prioritized list of vulnerabilities that require immediate remediation. The list is sorted by service because in many cases a single remedy -- disabling the service, upgrading to the most recent version, applying a cumulative patch -- can quickly solve dozens of specific software flaws, which might show up on a scanner. This list is designed to help alleviate that problem by combining the knowledge of dozens of leading security experts. They come from the most security-conscious federal agencies, the leading security software vendors and consulting firms, the top university-based security programs, and CERT/CC and the SANS Institute. A list of participants may be found at the end of this document.

The SANS/FBI Top Twenty is a living document. It includes step-by-step instructions and pointers to additional information useful for correcting the security flaws. We will update the list and the instructions as more critical threats and more current or convenient methods are identified, and we welcome your input along the way. This is a community consensus document -- your experience in fighting attackers and in eliminating the vulnerabilities can help others who come after you. Please send suggestions via e-mail to info@sans.org with the subject "Top Twenty Comments."

Top Vulnerabilities to Windows Systems

- W1 Internet Information Services (IIS)
- W2 Microsoft Data Access Components (MDAC) -- Remote Data Services
- W3 Microsoft SQL Server
- W4 NETBIOS -- Unprotected Windows Networking Shares
- W5 Anonymous Logon -- Null Sessions
- W6 LAN Manager Authentication -- Weak LM Hashing
- W7 General Windows Authentication -- Accounts with No Passwords or Weak Passwords
- W8 Internet Explorer
- W9 Remote Registry Access
- W10 Windows Scripting Host

http://www.sans.org/top20/

5. Now, change the page border to a repeating graphic:
CHOOSE: Format, Borders and Shading
CLICK: *Page Border* tab, if necessary
CLICK: *Art* drop-down arrow
SELECT: any border style
An example is shown in Figure 3.46.

Figure 3.46

Borders and
Shading dialog
box with art
graphic selected

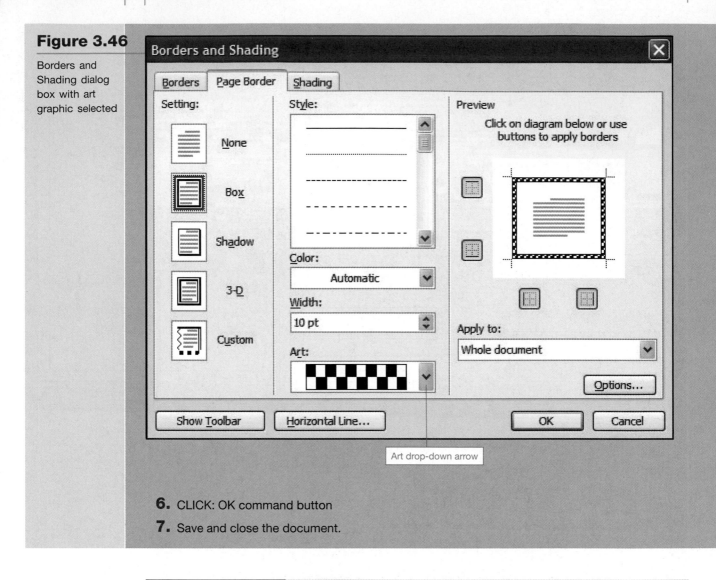

Art drop-down arrow

6. CLICK: OK command button

7. Save and close the document.

 **SelfCheck**

3.6 How do you apply a page border?

Chapter

summary

Word's formatting commands can be used to create compelling documents. Font formatting, such as bold-face, italic, and underlining, emphasizes important text, and your selection of fonts and font colors contributes to the overall message. You can further enhance your documents using paragraph formatting.

Command Summary

Many of the commands and procedures appearing in this chapter are summarized in the following table:

Skill Set	To Perform This Task . . .	Do the Following . . .
Changing Margins	Change margins of the current document	SELECT: File, Page Setup CLICK: *Margins* Tab
Modifying Text	Bold text	CLICK: Bold button (**B**)
	Italicize text	CLICK: Italic button (*I*)
	Underline text	CLICK: Underline button (U)
	Select a font	CLICK: Font drop-down arrow (Times New Roman ▾)
	Change font size	CLICK: Font Size drop-down arrow (12 ▾)
	Change font color	CLICK: Font Color button (A▾) to apply the most recently selected color, or CLICK: Font Color drop-down arrow (A▾) to choose from a palette of colors
	Highlight text	CLICK: Highlight button (✐▾)
	Clear formatting	CHOOSE: Clear Formatting from the *Style* drop-down list (Normal ▾)
	Copy formatting options to another area	CLICK: Format Painter button (✔)
	Copy formatting options to several areas	DOUBLE-CLICK: Format Painter button (✔)
Modifying Paragraphs	Show/Hide paragraph marks	CLICK: Show/Hide button (¶)
	Reveal a paragraph's formatting	CLICK: in the paragraph PRESS: SHIFT + F1
	Left-align a paragraph	CLICK: Align Left button (▤)
	Center-align a paragraph	CLICK: Center button (▤)
	Right-align a paragraph	CLICK: Align Right button (▤)
	Justify a paragraph	CLICK: Justify button (▤)
	Increase indentation	CLICK: Increase Indent button (▤)
	Decrease indentation	CLICK: Decrease Indent button (▤)
	Customize the left and right indents	DRAG: the indent markers on the Ruler
	Create a first-line or hanging indent	Drag the first-line indent marker for first-line indentation, and drag the hanging indent marker for hanging indentation
	Create a bulleted list	CLICK: Bullets button (▤)

Create a numbered list	CLICK: Numbering button (▤)
Specify bullet symbols or numbering schemes	CHOOSE: Format, Bullets and Numbering
Create a numbered outline	CHOOSE: Format, Bullets and Numbering CLICK: *Outline Numbered* tab
Change line spacing	CLICK: Line Spacing drop-down arrow (▤▾). CHOOSE: an option from the drop-down menu
Set tabs	SELECT: a tab type using the Tab Alignment button CLICK: the desired location on the Ruler to set the tab stop
Create a tab leader	CHOOSE: Format, Tabs
Remove tabs	DRAG: tab stop down and off the Ruler
Apply styles	CHOOSE: a style from the *Style* drop-down list (Normal ▾)
Shade selected words and paragraphs	CHOOSE: Format, Borders and Shading CLICK: *Shading* tab
Apply borders	CHOOSE: Format, Borders and Shading CLICK: *Borders* tab
Create a page border	CHOOSE: Format, Borders and Shading CHOOSE: *Page Border* tab

Key Terms

This section specifies page references for the key terms identified in this chapter. For a complete list of definitions, refer to the Glossary at the back of this learning guide.

Chapter
quiz

Short Answer

1. Describe how to change the color of a text selection to green.

2. What is a style, and how do styles help you?

3. What is *character formatting?*

4. What is the significance of the paragraph symbol?

5. Describe how to set line spacing to 1.5 lines.

6. Describe how to change page margins.

7. Describe the four types of tabs you can set in a document.

8. How do you shade and add a border to a paragraph?

9. How do you add a page border?

10. How do you right-align a paragraph?

True/False

1. _____ To set page margins, you click the Format, Page Margins menu.

2. _____ You cannot add a dot leader to a tab after the tab has been set.

3. _____ A style is a collection of paragraph and character formatting commands.

4. _____ To number text after it has been typed, you must select it and then click the Numbering button.

5. _____ One method to create a hanging indent involves dragging the hanging indent marker on the Ruler.

6. _____ You cannot control the width of a page border.

7. _____ To place a border around a paragraph, you must first select the paragraph.

8. _____ The Format Painter copies all formatting commands except font color.

9. _____ Bullets and numbering cannot be customized.

10. _____ You can preview your font selections in the Font dialog box.

Multiple Choice

1. To set page margins, choose:
   a. Format, Page Setup
   b. File, Page Setup
   c. Insert, Margins
   d. Edit, Page Margins

2. To remove a tab stop from the Ruler:
   a. Drag the tab stop down and off the Ruler
   b. Click Edit, Tab Stop
   c. Select the tab stop and press **DELETE**
   d. None of the above

3. Which of the following line spaces cannot be applied to a document?
   a. 3.0
   b. 1.0
   c. .5
   d. 2.0

4. To display a document's paragraph marks:
   a. Choose, View, Paragraph Marks
   b. Click Show/Hide button
   c. Choose Edit, View Marks
   d. None of the above

5. To create a tab leader, you must use the:
   a. Tabs dialog box
   b. Ruler
   c. Period (.) key
   d. Any of the above

6. Which of the following moves all but the first line of a paragraph in from the left margin, leaving the first-line indent marker in its current position?
   a. Hanging indent marker
   b. Left indent marker
   c. Right indent marker
   d. None of the above

7. Which of the following enables you to copy formatting styles and attributes?

   a. Styles
   b. Tabs
   c. Font dialog box
   d. Format Painter

8. Character formatting involves choosing:

   a. Typefaces
   b. Font sizes
   c. Text attributes
   d. All of the above

9. Which of the following is a collection of character and paragraph formatting commands?

   a. Format Painter
   b. Font characteristics
   c. Style
   d. Bulleted list

10. To use the Format Painter on multiple selections, you must first:

   a. Double-click the Format Painter
   b. Triple-click the Format Painter
   c. Single-click the Format Painter
   d. None of the above

Hands-On
exercises

step by step

1. Setting Tabs and Using Dot Leaders

In this exercise, you set tabs and use dot leaders to type a table of contents.

1. Launch Word and ensure that a blank document appears in the application window.

2. To set tabs:
SELECT: left tab alignment button (L) on the Ruler
CLICK: 1″ mark on the Ruler
SELECT: right tab alignment button (⌐) on the Ruler
CLICK: 6″ mark on the Ruler

3. To add a dot leader:
CHOOSE: Format, Tabs
CLICK: 6″ in the Tab Stop Position area
CHOOSE: 2 in the Leader section of the Tabs dialog box
CLICK: OK command button

4. To enter text:
Using Figure 3.47 as a guide, enter text as indicated. Center the title "Table of Contents."
Remember to press TAB before and after each topic entry.
Press ENTER twice after each entry.

Figure 3.47

Table of Contents document

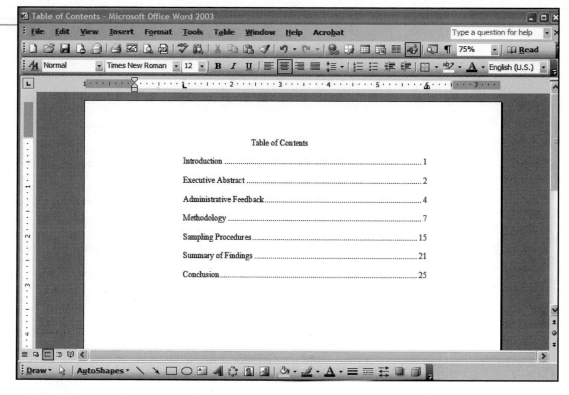

5. Save the document as "Table of Contents" to your personal storage location.

step by step

2. Formatting Characters

In this exercise, you will apply character formatting to a document.

1. Open WDHE02 from your data files location.

2. Save the document as "Project Timelines" to your personal storage location.

3. Format the title:
   SELECT: the title text "Project Timelines"
   CLICK: Font Size drop-down list (12 ▾)
   CHOOSE: 18
   CLICK: Bold button (**B**).

4. Format the three column headings:
   DOUBLE-CLICK: Project column heading
   CLICK: Bold button (**B**)
   CLICK: Underline button (<u>U</u>)

5. In a similar manner, format the other two column headings. Your document should be similar to the one shown in Figure 3.48.

Figure 3.48

"Project Timelines" document

Project Timelines

Project	Completion	Update
Engineering Building	September 2004	Architect hired Schematics developed
Administration Annex	October 2004	Framing underway Permit hearing scheduled
Remodel Data Center	January 2005	Interviewing architects
South Parking Lot	Not established	Waiting on approval of funds

6. Save and close the document.

step by step

3. Creating Bulleted and Numbered Lists

In this exercise, you will create a bulleted list and then change it to a numbered list.

1. Open WDHE03 from your data files location.

2. Save the document as "Staff Changes" to your personal storage location.

3. Create a bulleted list:
SELECT: all five paragraphs (excluding the title)
CLICK: Bullets button ()

4. Change the bullet symbol:
CHOOSE: Format, Bullets and Numbering
CLICK: the check mark bullet symbol. If the check mark bullet is not available, choose another symbol.
CLICK: OK command button
Your document should be similar to the one shown in Figure 3.49.

Figure 3.49

"Staff Changes" document with check mark bullets applied

Staff Changes Update

✓ Food Service Assistants: Two positions were added to the high school because of the cafeteria's success. They new assistants are **Jeanne Patton** and **Al Simmons**.

✓ Bus Drivers: Several new bus drivers were hired, including **Suzanne May, Vicki Christian, Cathy Caudill, Mike Snider,** and **Tom Erney.**

✓ Teachers: Three Computer Science Faculty were hired to handle the 20% increase in the department's enrollment. They are **Mary Insabella, Doug Yoder,** and **Candice Spangler.**

✓ Teaching Assistants: Two general-purpose teaching assistants have been hired to help all faculty. They include **Lisa Davis** and **Lori Rich.**

✓ Administrators: The following administrators have been hired to oversee the academic programs in the business area: **Tiffany Gist** and **Renee Stackhouse.**

5. Change bulleted list to numbered list.
   SELECT: the five paragraphs
   CLICK: Numbering button (⊟)
   Your document should be similar to the one shown in Figure 3.50.

Figure 3.50

Bulleted list
changed to
numbered list

Staff Changes Update

1. Food Service Assistants: Two positions were added to the high school because of the cafeteria's success. They new assistants are **Jeanne Patton** and **Al Simmons**.

2. Bus Drivers: Several new bus drivers were hired, including **Suzanne May, Vicki Christian, Cathy Caudill, Mike Snider,** and **Tom Erney**.

3. Teachers: Three Computer Science Faculty were hired to handle the 20% increase in the department's enrollment. They are **Mary Insabella, Doug Yoder,** and **Candice Spangler**.

4. Teaching Assistants: Two general-purpose teaching assistants have been hired to help all faculty. They include **Lisa Davis** and **Lori Rich**.

5. Administrators: The following administrators have been hired to oversee the academic programs in the business area: **Tiffany Gist** and **Renee Stackhouse**.

6. Save and close the document.

on your own　

4. Creating a Hanging Indent

In this exercise, you will open a bibliographic document and apply hanging indent formatting to each of the entries.

1. Ensure that a blank document appears in the application window.

2. Open WDHE04 from your data files location.

3. Save the document as "Bibliography" to your personal storage location.

4. Create a hanging indent at the .5″ mark for each of the four paragraphs. Your document should be similar to the one shown in Figure 3.51.

Figure 3.51

"Bibliography"
document with
hanging indents

Bibliography

Anspaugh, Janeen A. (2000). *Communications for the New Century* (pp.23-32). New York, NY: Liberty Press.

Davis, Jared M. (2001). *Preparing International Business Documents*. Vancouver, British Columbia, Canada: Maple Leaf Publishing.

Geiger, Ricardo J. (2000). *Communicating Internationally* (pp. 6-14). Sacramento, CA: Mainstay Publishing House

Nakagawa, Lisa M. (1999). *Managing Conflict*. New Orleans, LA: Sutherland & Gaines Publishing.

5. Save and close the file.

on your own ▶

5. Applying Borders and Shading

In this exercise, you will apply paragraph borders and shading to a document.

1. Open WDHE05 from your data files location.

2. Save the document as "Search Engines" to your personal storage location.

3. There are six subheadings in the document. To apply borders and shading to each topic:
   CLICK: in the first topic "WHAT ARE SEARCH ENGINES?"
   Apply a box border on all four sides and 10% gray shading to the paragraph.

4. In a similar manner, apply the same formatting to the other five subheadings.
   (*Hint:* Use the Format Painter to copy the formatting.)

5. Change the border width to 1 point for each subtitle.
   (*Hint:* Change it for one heading and use the Format Painter to copy it to the other headings.)
   Your document should be similar to the one shown in Figure 3.52.

Figure 3.52

"Search Engines"
document

WHAT ARE SEARCH ENGINES?

Search engines are huge databases of web page files that have been assembled automatically by machine.

There are two types of search engines:

1. **Individual.** Individual search engines compile their own searchable databases on the web.
2. **Meta.** Metasearchers do not compile databases. Instead, they search the databases of multiple sets of individual engines.

HOW DO SEARCH ENGINES WORK?

Search engines compile their databases by employing "spiders" or "robots" ("bots") to crawl through web space from link to link, identifying and perusing pages. Sites with no links to other pages may be missed by spiders altogether. Once the spiders get to a web site, they typically index most of the words on the publicly available pages at the site. Web page owners may submit their URLs to search engines for "crawling" and eventual inclusion in their databases.

Whenever you search the web using a search engine, you're asking the engine to scan its index of sites and match your keywords and phrases with those in the texts of documents within the engine's database.

It is important to remember that when you are using a search engine, you are NOT searching the entire web as it exists at this moment. You are actually searching a portion of the web, captured in a fixed index created at an earlier date.

How much earlier? It's hard to say. Spiders regularly return to the web pages they index to look for changes. When changes occur, the index is updated to reflect the new information. However, the process of updating can take a while, depending upon how often the spiders make their rounds and then, how promptly the information they gather is added to the index. Until a page has been both "spidered" AND "indexed," you won't be able to access the new information.

NOTE: While most search engine indexes are not "up to the minute" current, they have partnered with specialized news databases that are. For late breaking news, look for a "news" tab somewhere on the search engine or directory page. Examples include:

---

6. Save, print, and close the document.

6. Add borders, shading, and lines with color

In this exercise, you will open an existing document and format it with color, borders, and shading.

1. Open WDHE06 from your data files location.

2. Save the document as "Board Roles" to your personal storage location.

3. Place a border around the title using the following formats:

   - Center the Title

   - Create a border using the Shadow style with 10% gray shading

   - Change the border color to Red, 1 ½ pt.

4. In a similar manner, place a Red 1 ½ pt border on the top only of the following paragraphs. (*Hint:* Use Format Painter to accomplish this quickly!)

   Role of the Board
   Specifically, the Board:
   Meetings
   Remuneration

5. Save, print, and close the file.

CaseStudy   PLANNING A BOARD RETREAT FOR MID-WEST COLLEGE

Mid-West College is a two-year comprehensive community college located in central Ohio. With an enrollment of more than 30,000 students, the college has recently increased the membership of its Board of Directors from seven to ten members. Board members at this college have many important responsibilities, including approving the college budget, hiring personnel, approving new degree programs, and negotiating with various campus unions.

The president of the college has asked her executive assistant, Jeanne Patton, to plan a board retreat for April 2004. The purpose of the retreat is to orient the new board members to the college and to their responsibilities as board members. In addition, it will provide an opportunity for college administrators to socialize with the board members in an informal setting.

Jeanne begins preparing for the board retreat by preparing a checklist of the various tasks she must complete to plan the retreat.

In this case study, assume the role of Jeanne as she prepares various documents using Microsoft Word.

1. Jeanne starts by creating a blank document in Word. She decides that she will create a checklist using the bullets feature of Word. She uses the square box bullet and enters the following list (shown in Figure 3.53).

Figure 3.53

"Board Retreat" document

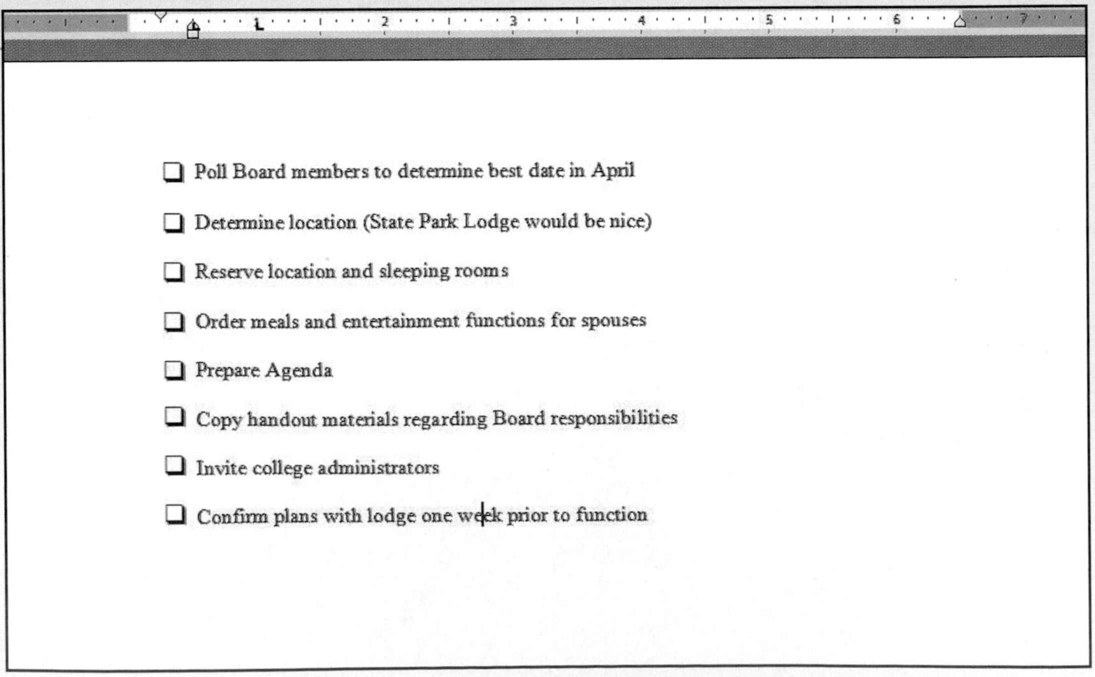

- ❑ Poll Board members to determine best date in April
- ❑ Determine location (State Park Lodge would be nice)
- ❑ Reserve location and sleeping rooms
- ❑ Order meals and entertainment functions for spouses
- ❑ Prepare Agenda
- ❑ Copy handout materials regarding Board responsibilities
- ❑ Invite college administrators
- ❑ Confirm plans with lodge one week prior to function

Jeanne decides the document would look better double spaced, so she changes the spacing to double. Jeanne saves the document as "Board Retreat" to her personal storage location.

2. Jeanne has discussed the board retreat agenda with the president. They have decided on a draft agenda, shown in Figure 3.54.

Figure 3.54

Draft Board
Agenda

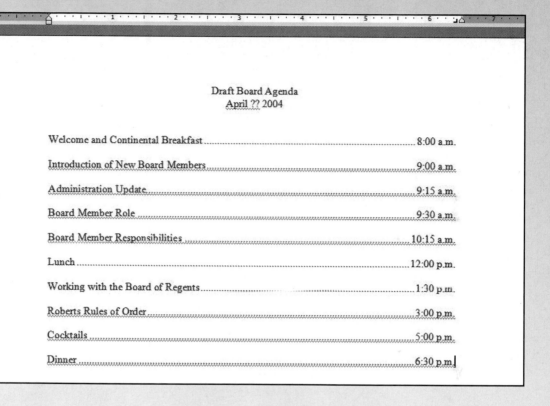

- As Jeanne creates the document, she applies the following formatting characteristics:
  Set the left and right margins to 1 inch.
  Title: Times New Roman, Bold, 18-point font
  Right-align tab at 6.5″ mark on Ruler, with dot leader 2
  Double spacing of agenda items

- Jeanne saves the document as "Draft Agenda" to her personal storage location.

3. Now, Jeanne wants to revise a document describing Board member roles and responsibilities that she prepared several months ago. She applies borders and shading to several areas of the document. Additionally, she uses Word's built-in styles. The finished document is shown in Figure 3.55.

Figure 3.55

"Board Roles"
document

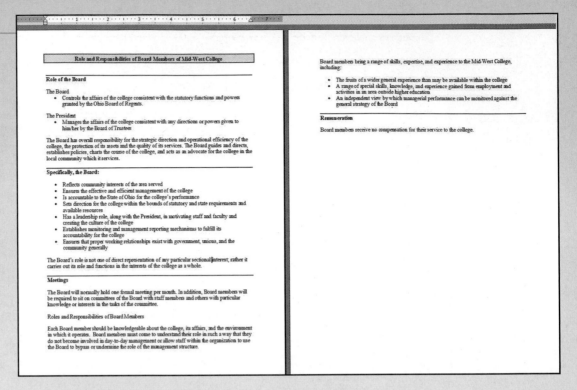

- Jeanne starts by opening the document WDHE06. This is the document she created several months ago. She saves the document as "Board Roles" to her personal storage location.

- She applies the following formatting:
  Title: Heading 2 style, centered
  First Subheading "Role of the Board": 3-point border on top, red

- Using Format Painter, she copies the formatting to the following subheadings:
  "Specifically, the Board"
  "Meetings"
  "Remuneration"

- Jeanne applies bold formatting to each of the subheadings.

- To make the document title stand out more, Jeanne applies a red 3-pt. border around it, as well as 10% gray shading.

- Satisfied with the document's appearance, Jeanne saves and closes the document.

4. The Agenda has been finalized, and Jeanne opens the document and makes several changes. The final document is shown in Figure 3.56.

Figure 3.56

"Final Agenda"
document

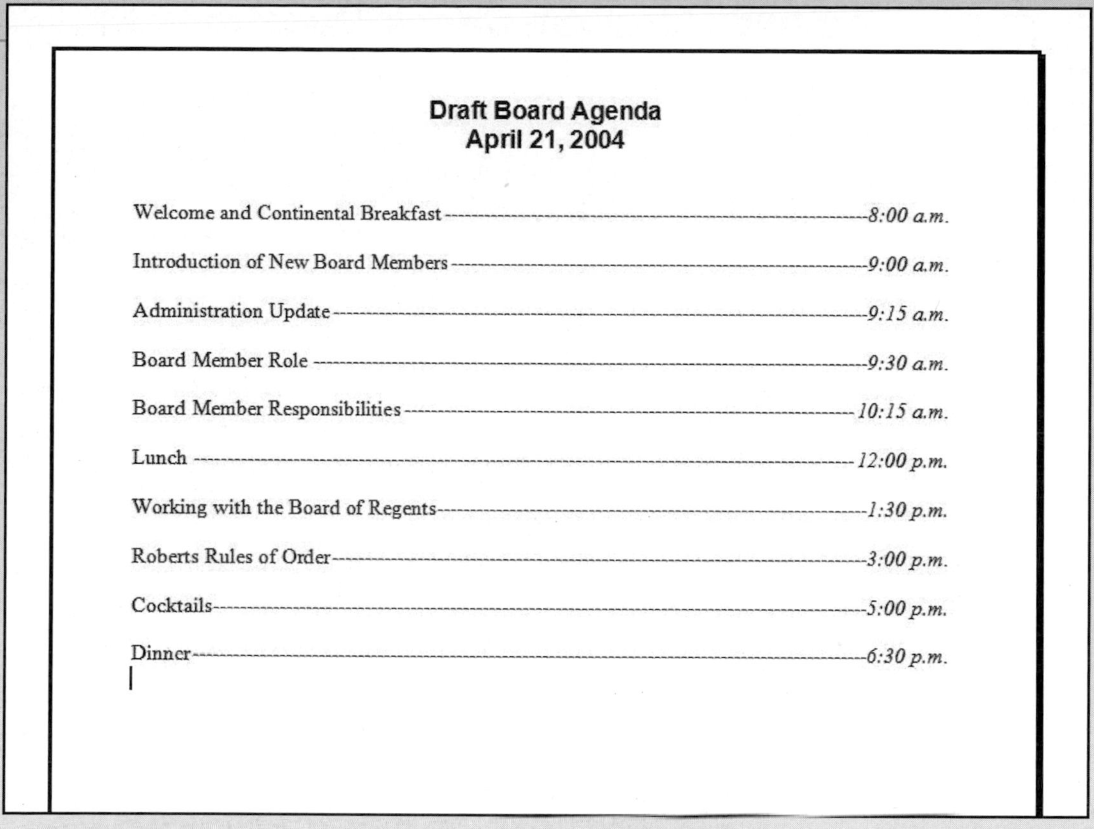

Draft Board Agenda
April 21, 2004

Welcome and Continental Breakfast --8:00 a.m.

Introduction of New Board Members --9:00 a.m.

Administration Update --9:15 a.m.

Board Member Role ---9:30 a.m.

Board Member Responsibilities --10:15 a.m.

Lunch --12:00 p.m.

Working with the Board of Regents---1:30 p.m.

Roberts Rules of Order--3:00 p.m.

Cocktails---5:00 p.m.

Dinner---6:30 p.m.

- She opens the "Draft Agenda" document created earlier and saves the document as "Final Agenda."

- Jeanne decides first to apply a page border around the document. She chooses the following border characteristics:
  2 1/4 points thick
  Black
  Shadow style

- She enters the date for the retreat as April 21, 2004.

- She formats the document title and date with the following font characteristics:
  Arial
  14 points
  Bold

- Jeanne changes the dot leader style to 3.

- She decides to run Spelling and Grammar check on the document to ensure that there are no typographical or grammatical errors. When she is finished, there are no grammar or spelling errors marked.

- As a final touch, Jeanne applies Italic formatting to each time.

- Jeanne saves and closes the document.

Answers to Self-Check Questions

3.1 What does *This point forward* mean in the margins dialog box? When changing margins in a document, selecting *This Point Forward* means that the margin change will not take effect until the next page.

3.2 Describe how to easily display a list of styles available in the Normal template. By holding down the Shift key (SHIFT) as you click the drop-down arrow on the Style button (Regular + Arial ▾), you can display a list of all styles available in the template.

3.3 Describe how to change line spacing in a document. Click the drop-down arrow on the Line Spacing button (▤▾) on the Formatting toolbar. Select the desired spacing.

3.4 What happens when you insert an item between two existing items in an outline numbered list? The remaining items are automatically renumbered.

3.5 Describe how to set dot leaders. Choose the Format, Tabs dialog box and select the desired leader.

3.6 How do you apply a page border? Choose Format, Borders and Shading. Select the Page tab and choose the desired border.

CHAPTER 4

Printing and Web Publishing

PREREQUISITES

To successfully complete this chapter, you must be able to format characters and paragraphs, create lists, and apply borders. You should also know how to save, open, close, and print your files.

LEARNING OBJECTIVES

After completing this chapter, you will be able to:

- Adjust page and margin settings and control pagination

- Insert page numbers and create headers and footers

- Insert section breaks

- Prepare a document for posting on a Web server

4.1 Previewing and Printing Documents

This module focuses on outputting your document creations. Most commonly, you will print a document for inclusion into a report or other such document.

4.1.1 Previewing a Document

→ **Feature**

Before sending a document to the printer, you can preview it using a full-page display that closely resembles the printed version. In this Preview display mode, you can move through the document pages and zoom in and out on desired areas.

→ **Method**

- CLICK: Print Preview button (⬛)

  or

- CHOOSE: File, Print Preview

→ **Practice**

You will now open a three-page document and preview it on the screen. Ensure that no documents are displayed in the application window.

1. Open WD0401 from your data files location.

2. Before continuing, save the file as "Ergonomics" to your personal storage location.

3. To preview how the document will appear when printed:
CLICK: Print Preview button (⬛)
Your screen should now appear similar to the one shown in Figure 4.1.

Figure 4.1

Previewing a
document

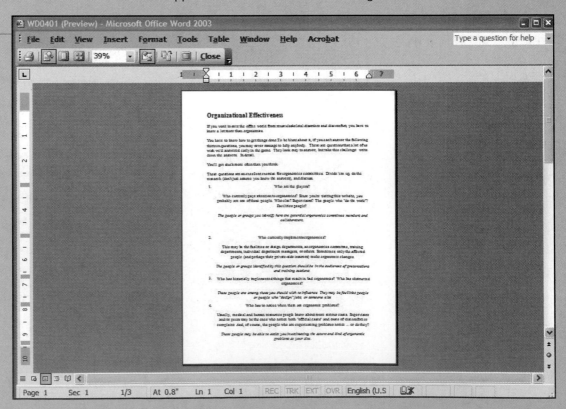

→ **Practice**

4. To display multiple pages at once:
   CLICK: Multiple Pages button () in the print preview toolbar

5. In the drop-down menu, point with the mouse to the icon located on the second row, in the middle position. If you click this icon, you will be able to preview four pages (2 x 2) of a document at once. Because this document has only three pages, you will see only three pages.
   CLICK: the icon located in the second row, in the middle position
   Small representations, called *thumbnails,* of the document's pages now appear in the Preview window. Your screen should now appear similar to the one shown in Figure 4.2.

Figure 4.2

Previewing three pages at once

One page button

Close button

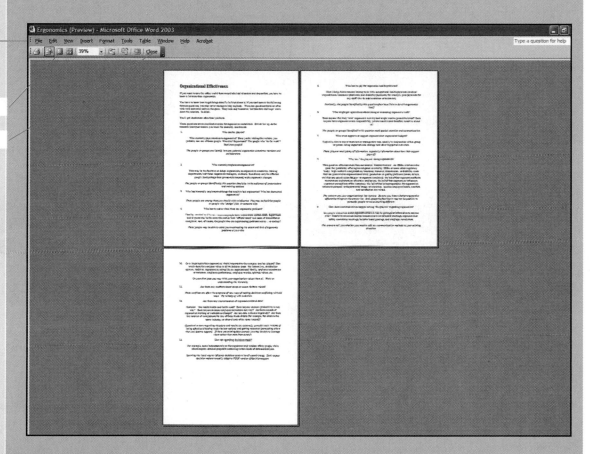

6. To redisplay a single page:
   CLICK: One Page button (🔲) in the toolbar

7. To zoom in on the document, move the magnifying glass mouse pointer over the document area and then click once.

8. To zoom out on the display, click the mouse pointer once again.

9. To exit preview mode:
   CLICK: Close button (Close) on the Print Preview toolbar

10. Continue to the next lesson.

4.1.2 Printing a Document

→ # Feature

When you are satisfied with a document's appearance, it is time to send it to the printer.

→ # Method

- CLICK: Print button (⊞)

  or

- CHOOSE: File, Print

→ # Practice

You will now send the "Ergonomics" document to the printer.

1. Assuming that you are satisfied with the layout of the document, let's send it to the printer. Do the following:
CHOOSE: File, Print
The dialog box displayed in Figure 4.3 appears. You can use this dialog box to specify what to print and how many copies to produce. (*Note:* As you know from previous lessons, the quickest way to send the current document to the printer is to click the Print button (⊞) on the Standard toolbar.)

Figure 4.3

Print dialog box

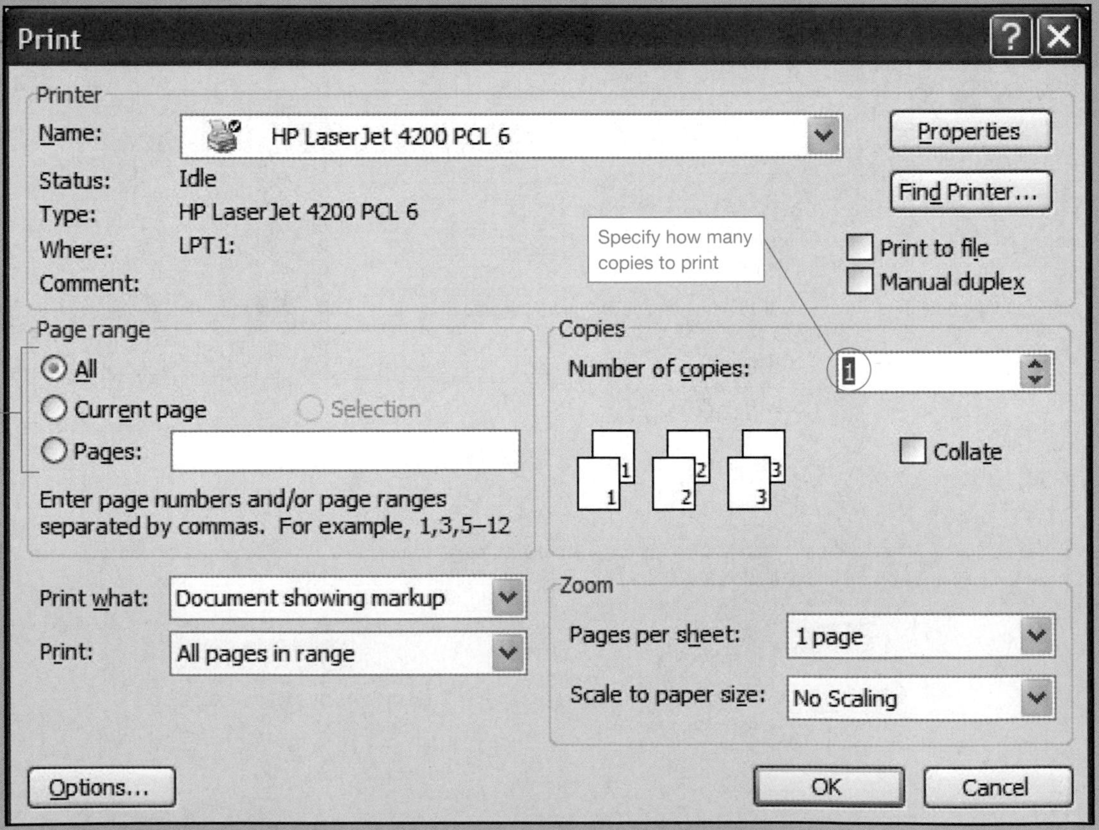

Specify how much of the document to print.

2. If you do not have access to a printer, click the Cancel button. If you have a printer connected to your computer and want to print out the document, do the following:
CLICK: OK command button
After a few moments, the document will appear at the printer.

3. Keep the document open for the next lesson.

 **4.1**   What is the procedure for printing your work?

4.2 Customizing Print Options

Now that you know how to create, edit, and apply character and paragraph formatting commands, it's time to think about finalizing your work for others to see. To present your work in the most flattering way, you may want to change the layout of your document before printing.

Your document's page layout is affected by many factors, including the margins or white space desired around the edges of the page, the size of paper you are using, and the page orientation. *White space* is that area of the page that is blank. Fortunately for us, Word provides a single dialog box, called the Page Setup dialog box, for controlling all of these factors. This module includes lessons on setting margins, changing page orientation, and controlling pagination.

4.2.1 Adjusting Margins

→ **Feature**

As discussed in Chapter 3, Word allows you to set the top, bottom, left, and right margins for a page. In addition, you can set a gutter margin to reserve space for binding a document. The **gutter** is where pages are joined in the center for binding or hole-punched for a ring binder. Word provides default settings of 1.25 inches for the left and right margins and 1 inch for the top and bottom margins. The gutter margin is initially set at 0 inches, as most documents are not bound.

→ **Method**

To change a document's margins:

• CHOOSE: File, Page Setup

• CLICK: *Margins* tab to display the settings page for margins

• Specify a gutter margin if binding the document and select the top, bottom, left, and right margins.

→ **Practice**

Ensure that you have completed the previous lesson and that the "Ergonomics" document is open in the application window.

1. Save a copy as "Printing Practice" to your personal storage location.

2. To change the margins from the default settings to an even 1 inch around the entire page:
CHOOSE: File, Page Setup
CLICK: *Margins* tab
The Page Setup dialog box should now appear, as shown in Figure 4.4.

Figure 4.4

Page Setup
dialog box,
Margins tab

Left margin spin
box

Gutter spin box

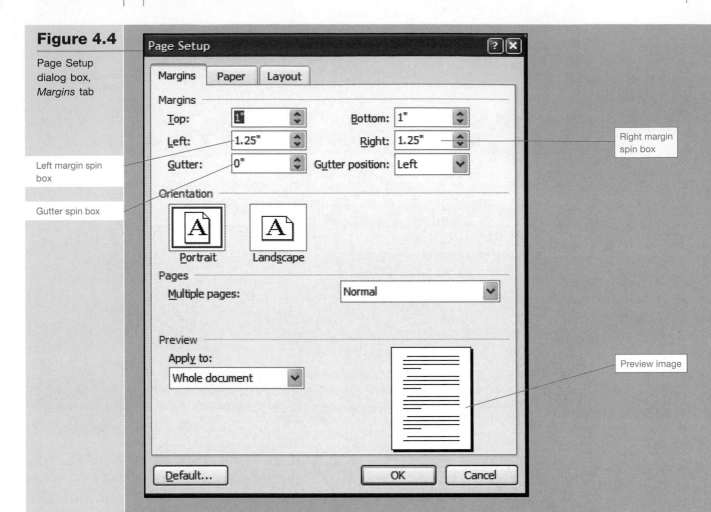

Right margin
spin box

Preview image

3. To change the left and right margins to 1 inch:
   CLICK: down arrow beside the *Left* margin spin box repeatedly, until the value decreases to 1 inch
   CLICK: down arrow beside the *Right* margin spin box repeatedly, until the value decreases to 1 inch
   (*Note:* As you click the symbols, the *Preview* area below shows the effect of the change on your document.)

4. To illustrate the use of a gutter, increase the counter in the *Gutter* text box to 0.5 inches:
   CLICK: up arrow beside the *Gutter* text box repeatedly, until the value increases to 0.5 inches
   Note that the gutter is represented in the *Preview* area.

5. Reset the Gutter margin to 0 inches.

6. To leave the Page Setup dialog box:
   CLICK: OK command button

7. Save the document, keeping it open for use in the next lesson.

4.2.2 Changing Page Orientation

→ Feature

If you consider your typical document printed on an 8.5-inch-by-11-inch piece of paper, text usually flows across the 8.5-inch width of the page. In this case, your document is said to have a **portrait orientation** (8.5 inches wide and 11 inches tall). When text flows across the 11-inch side of the page, the document is said to have a **landscape orientation** (11 inches wide and 8.5 inches tall). In Word, it is easy to switch between portrait and landscape orientation.

→ Method

To change a document's orientation:

- CHOOSE: File, Page Setup
- CLICK: *Margins* tab
- CLICK: *Portrait* or *Landscape* option button in the *Orientation* area

→ Practice

You will now practice displaying your document using a landscape orientation. The "Printing Practice" document should be open in the application window.

1. To specify a landscape orientation:
CHOOSE: File, Page Setup
CLICK: *Margins* tab, if it is not already displaying

2. SELECT: *Landscape* button in the *Orientation* area
Note that the *Preview* area changes with your selection.

3. To proceed:
CLICK: OK command button

4. At this point, the page may be too wide to fit in the current view. To remedy this problem:
CLICK: Zoom drop-down arrow (100% ▾) on the Standard toolbar
CHOOSE: Page Width
Your screen should now appear similar to the one shown in Figure 4.5.

Figure 4.5

Print Layout view with a landscape orientation

Landscape orientation

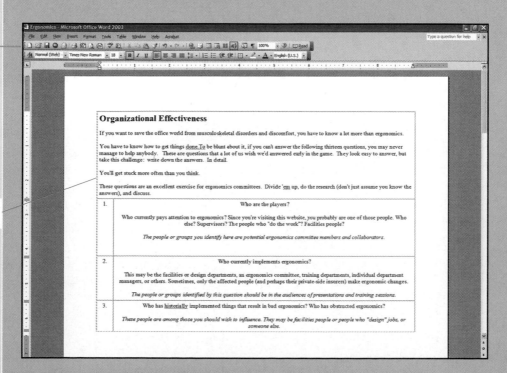

5. Let's return your document to a portrait orientation.
CHOOSE: File, Page Setup
SELECT: *Portrait* button
CLICK: OK command button

6. Close but do not save the document.

4.2.3 Controlling Pagination

→ ## Feature

Word automatically repaginates a document as you insert and delete text. In Word's Normal view, a dotted line appears wherever Word begins a new page, sometimes splitting an important paragraph or a list of items. Rather than leaving the text on separate pages, you can either insert a hard page break before the text or instruct Word to keep certain lines together. To prevent sentences from being separated from their paragraphs by page breaks, you will want to protect against widows and orphans. A **widow** is created when the last sentence in a paragraph flows to the top of the next page. An **orphan** is created when the first sentence of a paragraph begins on the last line of a page. Widows and orphans make the reader work harder to keep up with the flow of the text.

→ ## Method

To force a hard page break:

Position the insertion point at the beginning of the line that you want moved to the top of the next page.

- PRESS: CTRL + ENTER
  or
- CHOOSE: Insert, Break and select the *Page Break* option button

To control text flow:

- CHOOSE: Format, Paragraph
- CLICK: *Line and Page Breaks* tab

To prevent against widows and orphans, ensure that the *Widow/Orphan control* check box is selected.

To prevent a page break from occurring within the selected paragraph:

- SELECT: *Keep lines together* check box so that a check appears

To prevent a page break from occurring within the current selection, ensure that you performed step 3 and then:

- SELECT: *Keep with next* check box so that a check appears
- CLICK: OK command button

→ ## Practice

In this lesson, you will practice customizing pagination settings.

1. Open WD0404 from your data files location.

2. Save the file as "DTPbrochures" to your personal storage location.

3. Ensure that you are in Print Layout view.

4. Position the insertion point one line beneath the line "Author email: desktoppub.guide@miningco. com." In the next step, you will force a page break at the insertion point in order to create a title page for the document. The text above the page break will display alone on a single page.

5. To insert a page break at this location:
PRESS: `CTRL` + `ENTER`
Your document should now appear similar to the one shown in Figure 4.6. Notice that a dotted line, containing the words "Page Break," now appears above the insertion point. Note also that the insertion point is now positioned at the top of page 2.

Figure 4.6

Inserting a page break

Inserted page break

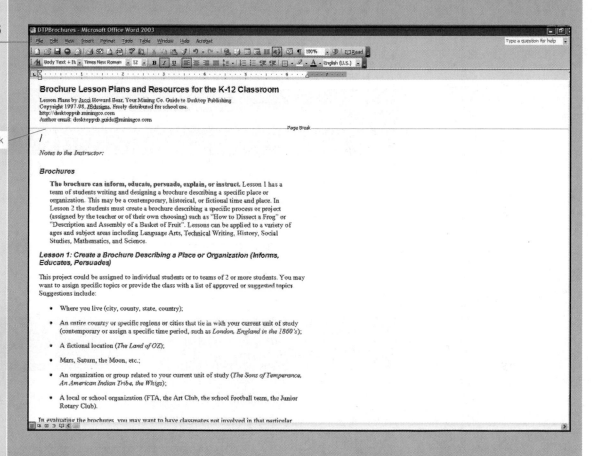

6. Let's practice deleting the page break. Position the insertion point on the line containing the words "Page Break" by clicking on the line once.

7. PRESS: `DELETE` to delete the page break

8. To restore the page break to the document:
CHOOSE: Edit, Undo Clear

9. Move the insertion point to about halfway down on page 3. Note the Lesson 1 heading. Let's in-sert a page break at this location:
Position the insertion point at the beginning of the Lesson 1 heading.
PRESS: `CTRL` + `ENTER`

10. Let's use the Paragraph dialog box to instruct Word to display the Lesson 2 heading with the en-tire following paragraph.
SELECT: the Lesson 2 heading and the entire paragraph immediately after it
Your document should now appear similar to the one shown in Figure 4.7.

Figure 4.7

Selecting paragraphs that you want to display together

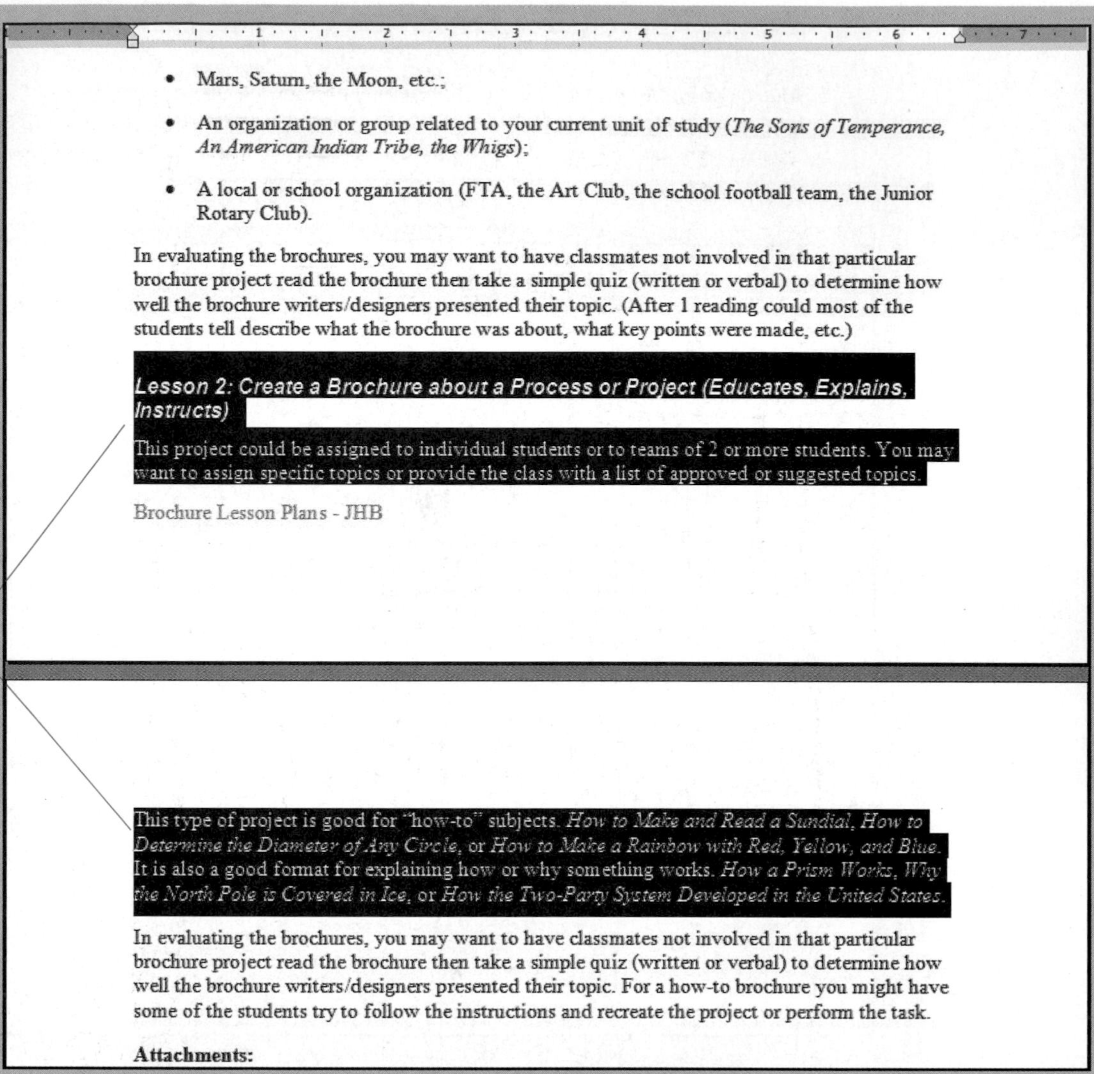

Selected text

- Mars, Saturn, the Moon, etc.;

- An organization or group related to your current unit of study (*The Sons of Temperance, An American Indian Tribe, the Whigs*);

- A local or school organization (FTA, the Art Club, the school football team, the Junior Rotary Club).

In evaluating the brochures, you may want to have classmates not involved in that particular brochure project read the brochure then take a simple quiz (written or verbal) to determine how well the brochure writers/designers presented their topic. (After 1 reading could most of the students tell describe what the brochure was about, what key points were made, etc.)

Lesson 2: Create a Brochure about a Process or Project (Educates, Explains, Instructs)

This project could be assigned to individual students or to teams of 2 or more students. You may want to assign specific topics or provide the class with a list of approved or suggested topics.

Brochure Lesson Plans - JHB

This type of project is good for "how-to" subjects. *How to Make and Read a Sundial, How to Determine the Diameter of Any Circle*, or *How to Make a Rainbow with Red, Yellow, and Blue*. It is also a good format for explaining how or why something works. *How a Prism Works, Why the North Pole is Covered in Ice*, or *How the Two-Party System Developed in the United States*.

In evaluating the brochures, you may want to have classmates not involved in that particular brochure project read the brochure then take a simple quiz (written or verbal) to determine how well the brochure writers/designers presented their topic. For a how-to brochure you might have some of the students try to follow the instructions and recreate the project or perform the task.

Attachments:

11. CHOOSE: Format, Paragraph
CLICK: *Line and Page Breaks* tab
The Paragraph dialog box should appear similar to the one shown in Figure 4.8.

Figure 4.8

Paragraph dialog box, *Line and Page Breaks* tab

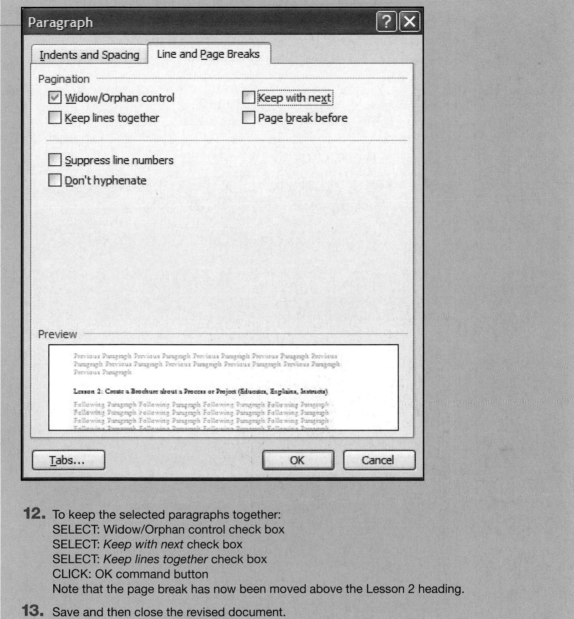

12. To keep the selected paragraphs together:
    SELECT: Widow/Orphan control check box
    SELECT: *Keep with next* check box
    SELECT: *Keep lines together* check box
    CLICK: OK command button
    Note that the page break has now been moved above the Lesson 2 heading.

13. Save and then close the revised document.

 **4.2** In inches, how wide are the left and right margins by default?

4.3 Inserting Headers and Footers

A document **header** and **footer** appear at the top and bottom of each page. The header often contains the title or section headings for a document, whereas the footer might show the page numbers or copyright information. Adding a header or footer produces a more professional-looking document and makes longer documents easier to read.

4.3.1 Inserting Page Numbers

→ **Feature**

In Word, you position page numbers in a document's header or footer. You can align the page number with the left, center, or right margin. To view inserted page numbers, you must preview or print the document or switch to Print Layout view.

→ **Method**

To insert page numbers:

- CHOOSE: Insert, Page Numbers
- SELECT: an option from the *Position* drop-down list box
- SELECT: an option from the *Alignment* drop-down list box
- PRESS: `ENTER`
  or
- CLICK: OK

→ **Practice**

You will now insert page numbers in an existing three-page document. No documents should be open in the application window.

1. Open the WD0405 student file. Ensure that you are in Print Layout view.

2. Save the file as "Glass Ceiling" to your personal storage location.

3. CHOOSE: Insert, Page Numbers
The dialog box shown in Figure 4.9 should appear on your screen.

Figure 4.9

Page Numbers dialog box

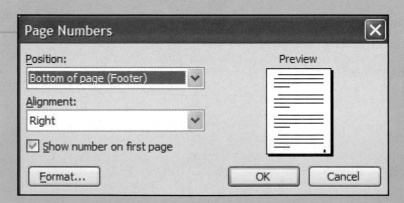

4. Note that "Bottom of page (Footer)" is selected in the *Position* box and "Right" is selected in the *Alignment* box. To insert the page number with these default settings:
CLICK: OK command button

5. You can only view inserted page numbers in Print Layout view, the current view mode. To view the page number on the bottom on Page 1, do the following:
DRAG: the horizontal scroll box to the bottom of Page 1
If you look closely, you will see the page number in the bottom-right corner of the page (Figure 4.10). The page number appears dimmed only on screen; it will not appear dimmed in the printed document.

Figure 4.10

Viewing the inserted page number

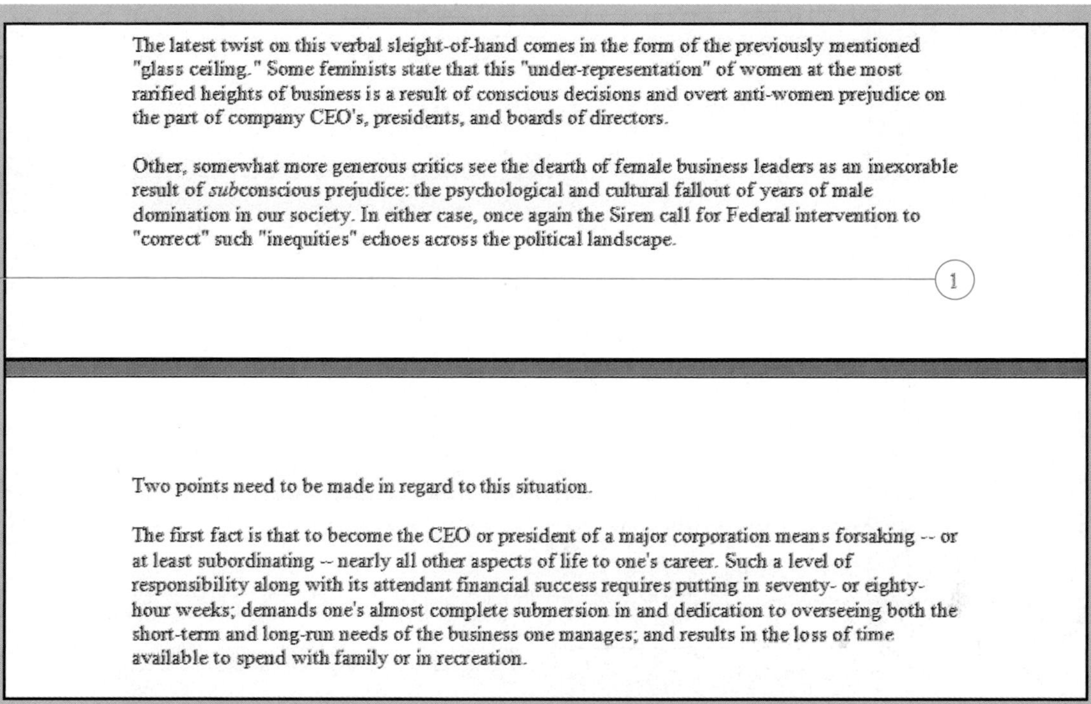

Inserted page number

The latest twist on this verbal sleight-of-hand comes in the form of the previously mentioned "glass ceiling." Some feminists state that this "under-representation" of women at the most rarified heights of business is a result of conscious decisions and overt anti-women prejudice on the part of company CEO's, presidents, and boards of directors.

Other, somewhat more generous critics see the dearth of female business leaders as an inexorable result of *subconscious* prejudice: the psychological and cultural fallout of years of male domination in our society. In either case, once again the Siren call for Federal intervention to "correct" such "inequities" echoes across the political landscape.

1

Two points need to be made in regard to this situation.

The first fact is that to become the CEO or president of a major corporation means forsaking -- or at least subordinating -- nearly all other aspects of life to one's career. Such a level of responsibility along with its attendant financial success requires putting in seventy- or eighty-hour weeks; demands one's almost complete submersion in and dedication to overseeing both the short-term and long-run needs of the business one manages; and results in the loss of time available to spend with family or in recreation.

6. Save the revised document and leave it open for the next lesson.

7. To prepare for the next lesson:

PRESS: CTRL + HOME to move the insertion point to the top of the document

4.3.2 Creating Headers and Footers

→ **Feature**

By default, the information that you include in a header or footer prints on every page in your document.

→ **Method**

To insert a header and footer:

• CHOOSE: View, Header and Footer

• Edit and format the header and footer using the regular formatting commands and the buttons on the Header and Footer toolbar.

• CLICK: Close button on the Header and Footer toolbar

→ **Practice**

You will now create a header in the "Glass Ceiling" document. You will also edit the existing footer to include additional information.

1. To edit the document's header:
CHOOSE: View, Header and Footer
When you choose this command, Word displays the Header and Footer toolbar, creates a framed editable text area for the header and footer, and dims the document's body text. Your screen should now appear similar to the one shown in Figure 4.11. Figure 4.12 identifies the buttons in the Header and Footer toolbar.

Word

Figure 4.11

Viewing a
document's
header and footer

> Header
>
> Russell Madden
>
> If glass ceilings existed, they would allow people to see through to the world above them. Because glass is clear, those existing under such a ceiling might not, at first, even notice that a barrier was in place which separated them from higher levels. Yet if they tried to pass through, they would quickly learn that the ceiling prevented any such rise.
>
> This analogy has been offered by some people to describe the alleged condition which is supposed to keep women and minorities from achieving any but token positions at the highest echelons of corporate America. Most individuals concerned with this problem cite it as evidence of discrimination; a situation which therefore should be corrected by an application of affirmative action laws.
>
> Yet even if what such advocates of "equality" claimed about glass ceilings were true, they would not be justified in using immoral means to achieve a purportedly positive end.

Figure 4.12

Header and
Footer toolbar

2. The insertion point is blinking in the document's header area.
   TYPE: **Shattering the Glass Ceiling**

3. To format the header, do the following:
   SELECT: header text
   CHOOSE: Arial from the *Font* drop-down list
   CHOOSE: 14 from the *Font Size* drop-down list
   CLICK: Bold button (**B**)
   CLICK: Center button (≣)

4. To view the footer:
   CLICK: Switch Between Header and Footer button (🗗) on the Header and Footer toolbar

5. The page number, inserted in the last lesson, appears at the far right-hand side of the first line in the footer area (Figure 4.13). Your insertion point should appear flashing at the left edge.

Figure 4.13

Viewing a
document's footer

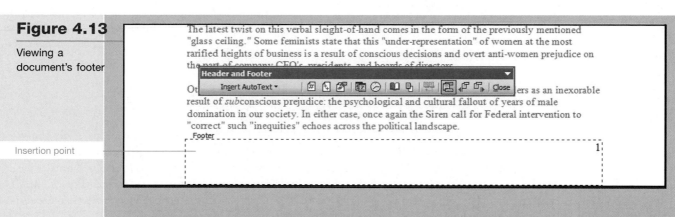

Insertion point

Let's now enter information about when the document was last printed:
TYPE: **Printed on**
PRESS: Space Bar

6. To place the date and time in the footer and have them automatically updated when you print the document:
CLICK: Insert Date button (📅) on the Header and Footer toolbar
PRESS: Space Bar
TYPE: **at**
PRESS: Space Bar
CLICK: Insert Time button (🕐) on the Header and Footer toolbar

7. To format the footer, you must first select the text in the footer. Because the footer includes inserted fields, the easiest way to do this is to use the Edit, Select All command.
CHOOSE: Edit, Select All to select the footer text

8. Issue the following character formatting commands:
SELECT: Arial from the *Font* drop-down list (Times New Roman ▾)
CLICK: Bold button (**B**)
Your screen should now appear similar to the one shown in Figure 4.14 (with a different date and time in the footer, of course). Congratulations, you have finished creating and formatting a header and footer!

Figure 4.14

Completing the
footer

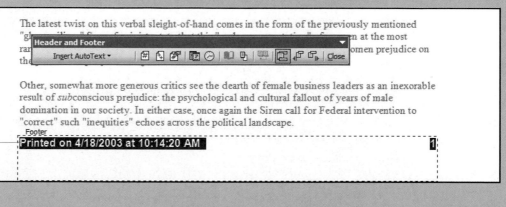

Formatted footer

9. To return to your document:
CLICK: Close button on the Header and Footer toolbar

10. Scroll through the document to view the headers and footers.

11. Save and then close the document.

In Addition

Once a header/footer is created you can open it/them by double-clicking in the header/footer area as opposed to choosing view, Header and Footer.

 **4.3** How do you insert page numbers into a document?

4.4 Using Sections to Apply Varied Formatting

Simple documents contain the same formatting—headers, footers, page numbers, margins, and so on—throughout the document. As your documents become more complex, you will need to use additional and varied formatting. Word enables you to divide a document into sections, which can then be formatted as individual documents within a larger document. This ability is especially useful in documents that include major topics or chapters, because you can format each topic with its own header and footer. Sections are also useful in desktop published documents to incorporate varied column formatting.

4.4.1 Inserting Section Breaks

→ **Feature**

By default, a document contains one section as referenced by the "Sec 1" indicator on the Status bar. A **section break** marks the beginning of a new section. To vary document formatting, such as headers and footers within a document, you must divide it into sections.

→ **Method**

Position the insertion point where you want the section break to occur.

- CHOOSE: Insert, Break
- SELECT: an option in the *Section breaks* area
- CLICK: OK command button

→ **Practice**

In this exercise, you will open a long document and divide it into six sections. Ensure that Word is loaded and that no documents are open in the application window.

1. Open the WD0406 data file. This file is a copy of a file you used earlier in this chapter.

2. Save the document as "Brochure Lesson Plans" to your personal storage location.

3. To prepare for inserting section break codes, switch to Normal view. In this view mode, it is easier to see inserted section break codes and to position the insertion point. (*Note:* Remember pressing the Show/Hide button will display section and page breaks in Print Layout view.)

4. Scroll through the document to become familiar with its contents. In the following steps, you will divide the document as follows, with each section beginning on a new page:

Section	Contents
1	Title page with author information
2	Brochures heading and lesson descriptions
3	Lesson 1
4	Lesson 2
5	Attachment A
6	Attachment B

5. Let's begin by inserting a section break just before the "Brochures" subheading. Position the insertion point at the beginning of the "Brochures" subheading, located on page 1.

6. To insert a section break at this location:
CHOOSE: Insert, Break

Figure 4.15

Section break
dialog box

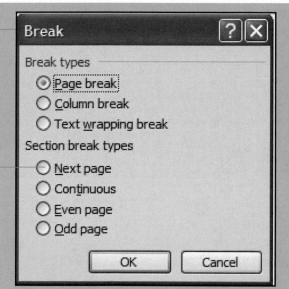

You will choose this
option in step 7

Your screen should now appear similar to the one shown in Figure 4.15.

7. Let's insert a section break that begins on a new page.
   SELECT: *Next page* option
   CLICK: OK command button
   Your document should now appear similar to the one shown in Figure 4.16. At this point, the entire document below the section break is part of Section 2.

Figure 4.16

Inserting a
section break

Section break

Brochure Lesson Plans and Resources for the K-12 Classroom

Lesson Plans by Jacci Howard Bear, Your Mining Co. Guide to Desktop Publishing
Copyright 1997-98, JBdesigns, Freely distributed for school use.
http://desktoppub.miningco.com
Author email: desktoppub.guide@miningco.com

···Section Break (Next Page)·············

Brochures

The brochure can inform, educate, persuade, explain, or instruct. Lesson 1 has a
team of students writing and designing a brochure describing a specific place or
organization. This may be a contemporary, historical, or fictional time and place. In
Lesson 2 the students must create a brochure describing a specific process or project
(assigned by the teacher or of their own choosing) such as "How to Dissect a Frog" or
"Description and Assembly of a Basket of Fruit". Lessons can be applied to a variety of
ages and subject areas including Language Arts, Technical Writing, History, Social
Studies, Mathematics, and Science.

---

8. Prepare to insert the next section break by positioning the insertion point one line above the Lesson 1 heading on page 3. Ensure that you are on page 3, and not on the Lesson 1 heading on page 2.

9. To insert a section break at this location:
   CHOOSE: Insert, Break
   SELECT: *Next page* option
   CLICK: OK command button

10. Prepare to insert the next section break by positioning the insertion point one line above the Lesson 2 heading on page 6.

11. To insert a section break at this location:
CHOOSE: Insert, Break
SELECT: *Next page* option
CLICK: OK command button

12. In a similar manner, insert next page section breaks at the Attachment A and Attachment B subheadings.

13. Save the revised document and keep it open for use in the next lesson.

14. In preparation for the next exercise, move the insertion point to the top of the document. The insertion point is now positioned in Section 1.

4.4.2 Varying Headers and Footers by Section

→ **Feature**

Once you have divided a document into sections, you can embellish the document with varied headers and footers. By default, the headers and footers in a multisection document are linked. This means that if you type your name into the header for Section 1, all remaining sections will also include your name. To create a unique header or footer, you must break the link to the previous section.

→ **Method**

To create a unique header or footer in the current section:

• Position the insertion point in the header or footer of the current section.

• CLICK: Same as Previous button (⌨) to deselect it

• Proceed by typing text into the header or footer.

→ **Practice**

The following exercise involves creating headers for the "Brochure Lesson Plans" document that include the current topic and page number. You will also create a footer with the following text: "Formatted by *your name*." The footer will remain the same for each of the six sections. The insertion point should be positioned at the top of the "Brochure Lesson Plans" document in Section 1.

1. Let's begin by creating the header for the first section.
CHOOSE: View, Header and Footer
The insertion point should be blinking inside the Section 1 header.

2. Let's type the topic heading "Brochure Lesson Plans" and the current page number in the right-aligned position.
CLICK: Align Right button (▤) on the Standard toolbar
TYPE: **Brochure Lesson Plans**,
PRESS: Space Bar
TYPE: **page**
PRESS: Space Bar
CLICK: Insert Page Number button (▣) on the Header and Footer toolbar

3. On your own, format the text in the header using Arial, 10 point, bold. With no text selected, the Section 1 header should appear similar to the header shown in Figure 4.17.

Figure 4.17

Viewing the inserted header and footer

Viewing the Section 1 header

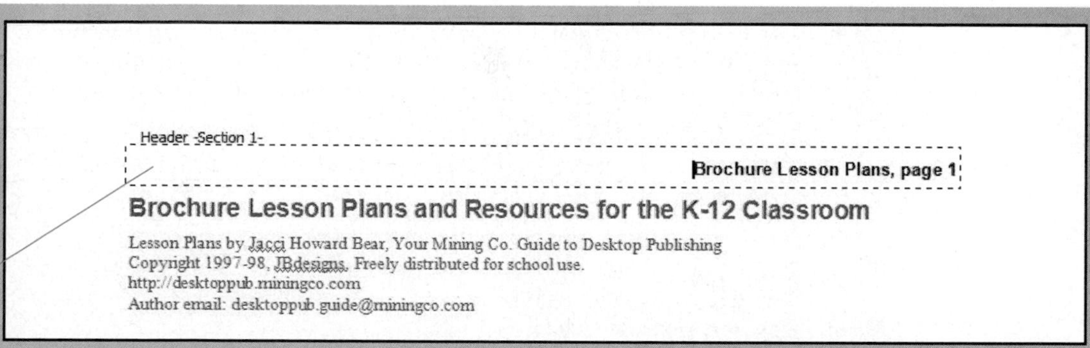
Header -Section 1-
Brochure Lesson Plans, page 1
Brochure Lesson Plans and Resources for the K-12 Classroom
Lesson Plans by Jacci Howard Bear, Your Mining Co. Guide to Desktop Publishing
Copyright 1997-98, JBdesigns. Freely distributed for school use.
http://desktoppub.miningco.com
Author email: desktoppub.guide@miningco.com

4. To define the header for Section 2:
   CLICK: Show Next button ( ) on the Header and Footer toolbar
   Note the "Same as Previous" setting in the header identifier area (Figure 4.18). Because this setting is in effect, the Section 2 header is currently identical to the Section 1 header.

Figure 4.18

Viewing the Section 2 header

Note the "Section 2" designation

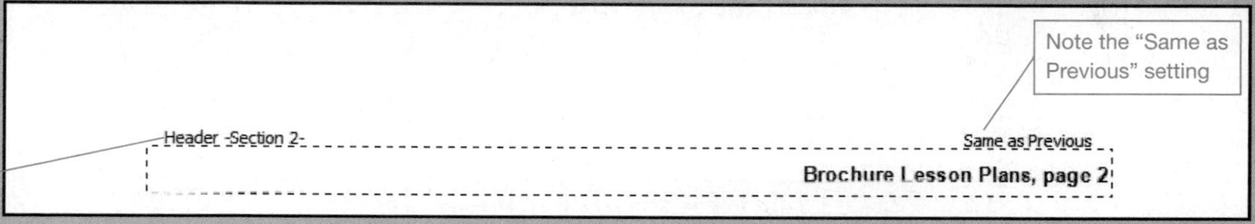
Note the "Same as Previous" setting
Header -Section 2-
Same as Previous
Brochure Lesson Plans, page 2

5. To create a unique header for Section 2, you must click the Same as Previous button ( ) on the Header and Footer toolbar to toggle off the Same as Previous setting.
   CLICK: Same as Previous button ( ) to deselect this setting
   Note that the "Same as Previous" designation no longer appears in the header identifier area.
6. SELECT: "Brochure Lesson Plans" in the header area
   TYPE: **Lesson Descriptions**
   The Section 2 header should appear similar to the one shown in Figure 4.19.

Figure 4.19

Viewing the Section 2 header

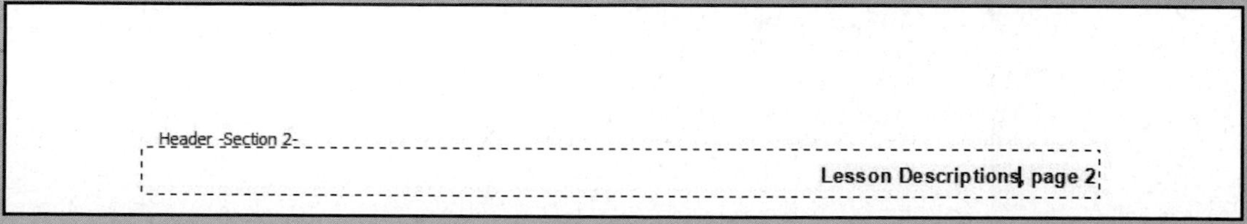
Header -Section 2-
Lesson Descriptions, page 2

7. Now, let's edit the Section 3 header.
   CLICK: Show Next button ( )
8. Remember, before you edit the header to reflect the current topic, you must detach it from the previous header.
   CLICK: Same as Previous button ( ) to deselect this setting
   SELECT: "Lesson Descriptions" in the header area
   TYPE: **Lesson 1**
9. To edit the Section 4 header:
   CLICK: Show Next button ( )
   CLICK: Same as Previous button ( ) to deselect this setting
   SELECT: "Lesson 1" in the header area
   TYPE: **Lesson 2**

10. In a similar manner, edit the Sections 5 and 6 headers to read Attachment A and Attachment B, respectively. The headers are complete! Now let's define the footer. Because the same footer will appear throughout the document, you need only create one footer, in Section 1.

11. To prepare to edit the footer:
DRAG: the vertical scroll box to the top of the vertical scroll bar
CLICK: in the Section 1 header area

12. To view the Section 1 footer:
CLICK: Switch Between Header and Footer button (⊡) on the Header and Footer toolbar
The insertion point should be blinking in the Section 1 footer area (Figure 4.20).

Figure 4.20

Viewing the
Section 1 footer

The insertion point
positioned in the
Section footer

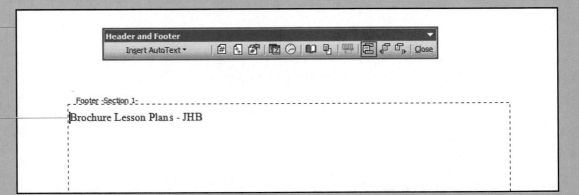

13. You will begin editing the footer by pressing (ENTER). This will force extra space to appear between the body text and the footer text.
PRESS: (ENTER)
TYPE: **Formatted by** *Your Name*
(*Note:* Delete the existing text "Brochure Lesson Plans – JHB")

14. On your own, format the footer using 10-point Arial. With no text selected, the footer should appear similar to the one shown in Figure 4.21.

Figure 4.21

Completed
Section 1 footer

15. Now that you are done defining the headers and footers for this document:
CLICK: Close button on the Header and Footer toolbar

16. Switch to Print Layout view so that you can view the document's headers and footers. Note that the Section 1 header and footer appear on the title page. Because title pages do not typically include a header or footer, in the next lesson we will show you how to change the format of the first page of the document.

17. Move the insertion point to the top of page 2. Your screen should appear similar to the one shown in Figure 4.22.

Figure 4.22

Viewing the
inserted header

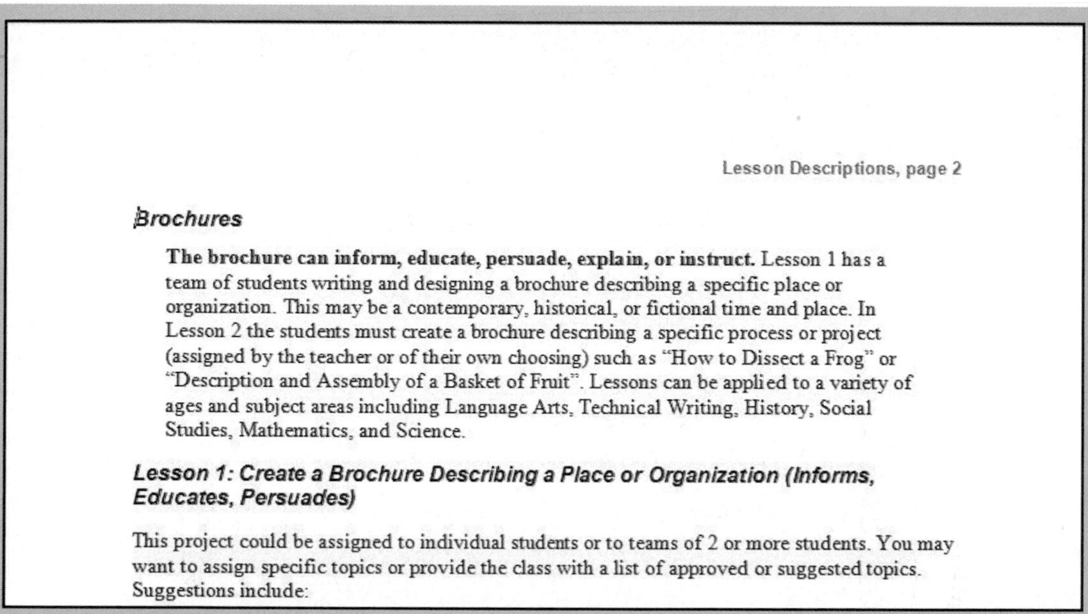

Lesson Descriptions, page 2

Brochures

The brochure can inform, educate, persuade, explain, or instruct. Lesson 1 has a
team of students writing and designing a brochure describing a specific place or
organization. This may be a contemporary, historical, or fictional time and place. In
Lesson 2 the students must create a brochure describing a specific process or project
(assigned by the teacher or of their own choosing) such as "How to Dissect a Frog" or
"Description and Assembly of a Basket of Fruit". Lessons can be applied to a variety of
ages and subject areas including Language Arts, Technical Writing, History, Social
Studies, Mathematics, and Science.

**Lesson 1: Create a Brochure Describing a Place or Organization (Informs,
Educates, Persuades)**

This project could be assigned to individual students or to teams of 2 or more students. You may
want to assign specific topics or provide the class with a list of approved or suggested topics.
Suggestions include:

18. Save the revised document.

19. To prepare for the next lesson, move the insertion point to the beginning of the "Brochure Lesson Plans" document.

4.4.3 Varying Page Setup Options by Section

→ Feature

In Word, you can format document sections uniquely using the Page Setup dialog box. For example, you may want to change an individual section's margins or orientation or further customize the section's header and footer.

→ Method

Position the insertion point in the section you want to change.

- CHOOSE: File, Page Setup
- CLICK: *desired tab* and then make your changes

Ensure that "This section" is selected in the *Apply to* drop-down list.

- CLICK: OK command button

→ Practice

In this lesson, you will use the Page Setup dialog box to remove the header and footer from the first page of Section 1. Ensure that you have completed the previous lesson and that the insertion point is positioned at the top of the "Brochure Lesson Plans" document.

1. To prevent the header and footer from printing on the first page of Section 1, the document's title page, you must begin by displaying the *Layout* tab of the Page Setup dialog box.
CHOOSE: File, Page Setup
CLICK: *Layout* tab
The Page Setup dialog box should now appear similar to the one shown in Figure 4.23.

Figure 4.23

Page Setup dialog box *Layout* tab

Different first page checkbox

Note that "This section" is selected. As a result your selections will only affect the current section.

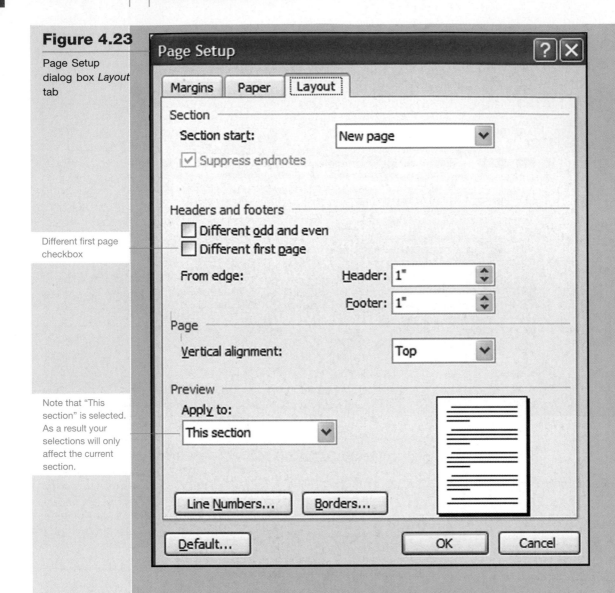

2. CLICK: *Different first page* check box

3. To proceed:
   CLICK: OK command button
   Note that the header and footer no longer appear on the first page.

4. Let's take a look at the header identifier for the first page of Section 1.
   CHOOSE: View, Header and Footer
   Notice that the header identifier now reads "First Page Header -Section 1-," as shown in Figure 4.24.

Figure 4.24

First page header

First Page Header -Section 1-

Brochure Lesson Plans and Resources for the K-12 Classroom

Lesson Plans by Jacci Howard Bear, Your Mining Co. Guide to Desktop Publishing
Copyright 1997-98, JBdesigns. Freely distributed for school use.
http://desktoppub.miningco.com
Author email: desktoppub.guide@miningco.com

5. Because it is our intention to keep the first page header and footer blank, let's close the Header and Footer toolbar.
CLICK: Close button on the Header and Footer toolbar

6. Save and then close the "Brochure Lesson Plans" document.

In Addition CHANGING PAGE ORIENTATION WITH SECTION BREAKS

To change the page orientation for a portion of a document, you can use section breaks. This procedure is useful when your document or report includes a table that is wider that the default page width. To change the orientation of a portion of a document from portrait to landscape, or vice versa, position the insertion point in the section you want to change and then choose File, Page Setup. Then, click the *Margins* tab and select a button in the *Orientation* area. To complete the procedure, select This section from the *Apply to* drop-down list and click the OK command button.

 **SelfCheck**   **4.4**   For what purposes are sections used?

4.5 Publishing to the Web

The **Internet** is a vast collection of computer networks that spans the entire planet, made up of many smaller networks connected by standard telephone lines, fiber optics, and satellites. The term **intranet** refers to a private and usually secure local- or wide-area network that uses Internet technologies to share information. To access the Internet, you need a network or modem connection that links your computer to your account with a university's or an Independent Service Provider's (ISP) network.

Once you are connected to the Internet, you can use Web browser software, such as Microsoft Internet Explorer or Netscape Navigator, to access the **World Wide Web.** The Web provides a visual interface for the Internet and lets you search for information by simply clicking on highlighted words and images, known as **hyperlinks.** When you click a link, you are telling your computer's Web browser to retrieve a page from a Web site and display it on your screen. Not only can you publish your documents on the Web, but you can also incorporate hyperlinks directly within a document to facilitate navigating among documents.

4.5.1 Apply a Web Theme

→ **Feature**

Microsoft Office System includes more than 30 themes for optimizing the look of your documents in Word and on the Web. A theme determines what colors and text fonts are used in a document, as well as the appearance of other graphical elements, such as bullets and horizontal lines.

→ **Method**

- CHOOSE: Format, Theme from Word's Menu bar
- SELECT: a theme in the *Choose a Theme* list box
- CLICK: OK command button

→ **Practice**

You will now apply a Web theme to an existing document. Ensure that Word is loaded and that no documents are displaying.

1. Open the WD0407 data file.

2. Save the document as "Front Page Themes" to your personal storage location. Your document should appear similar to the one shown in Figure 4.25.

Figure 4.25

"Front Page
Themes"
document

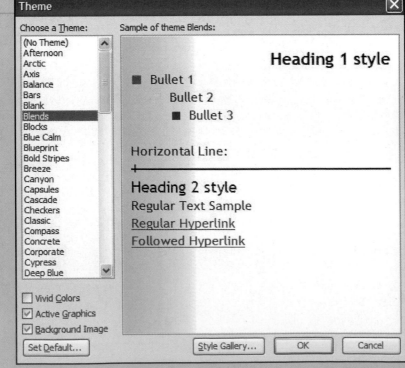

> |To Apply a FrontPage Theme
>
> On the FrontPage Explorer's **Views** bar, click the **Themes** button.
> Click on different themes in the scrolling list box.
>
> The **Theme Preview** pane lets you preview the different components of the theme, as they will appear on
> your Web pages. You can preview a theme before applying it by selecting it from the list of themes.
>
> Before applying a theme, you can select theme options that affect the appearance of the theme's
> components. Selecting **Vivid Colors** will apply brighter colors to text and graphics, selecting **Active
> Graphics** will animate certain theme components, and selecting **Background Image** will apply a
> background image to the pages in your current FrontPage web.
>
> For this lesson, select **Vivid Colors** and **Background Image**.
> From the list of themes, select a theme you like, then click the **Apply** button.
>
> The selected theme is applied to all of the pages in your current FrontPage web. In the next section of
> this lesson, you will see how the selected theme gives your pages a consistent appearance.
>
> **Opening Pages in the FrontPage Editor**
>
> Now that the overall layout of **My Own Web** is determined, you will add content to each of the pages.
> While pages are created and managed in FrontPage Explorer, designing and editing pages is all done in
> the FrontPage Editor.
>
> The **FrontPage Editor** is used to create, edit, and view pages. All text, styles, and page formatting is
> based on Hypertext Mark-up Language (HTML) standards.

3. Let's apply a Web theme to this document.
CHOOSE: Format, Theme

4. To view some of the different themes, click their names in the *Choose a Theme* list box.

5. Before continuing:
CLICK: Blends in the *Choose a Theme* list box

The Theme dialog box, similar to the one shown in Figure 4.26, should now appear.

Figure 4.26

Theme dialog box

6. To apply this theme to the document:
CLICK: OK command button
With the insertion point at the top of the document, your document should now appear similar to the one shown in Figure 4.27.

Figure 4.27

Applying the "Blends" theme

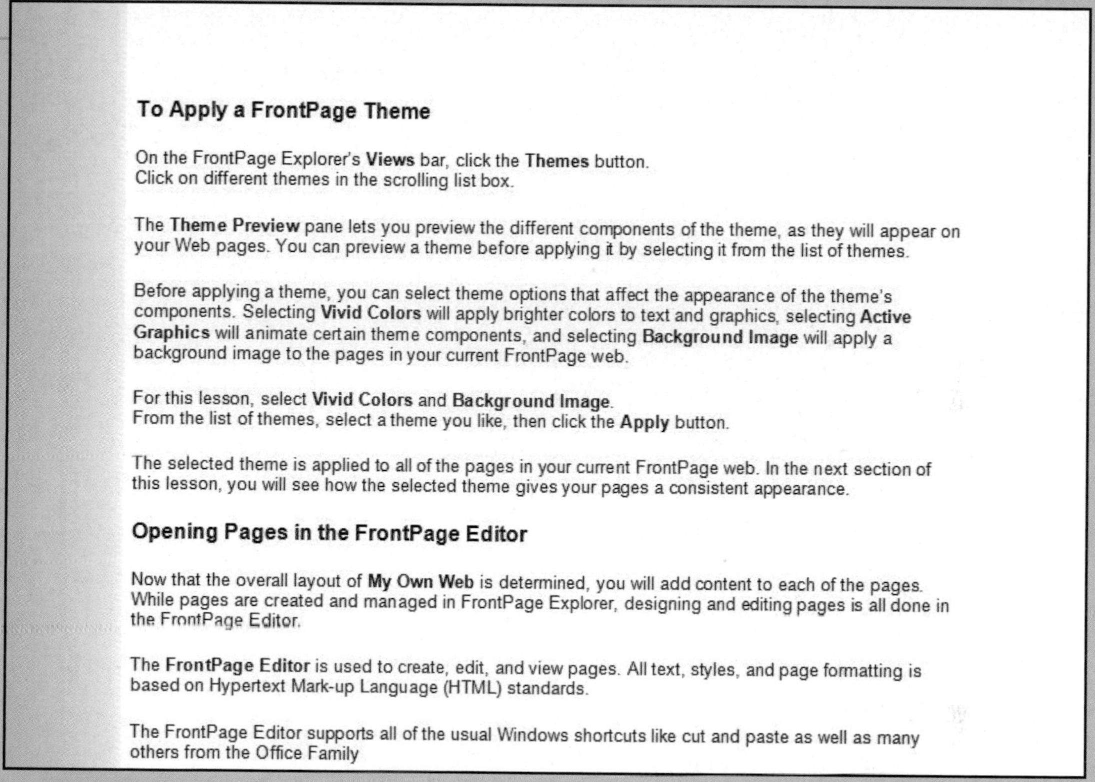

To Apply a FrontPage Theme

On the FrontPage Explorer's **Views** bar, click the **Themes** button.
Click on different themes in the scrolling list box.

The **Theme Preview** pane lets you preview the different components of the theme, as they will appear on your Web pages. You can preview a theme before applying it by selecting it from the list of themes.

Before applying a theme, you can select theme options that affect the appearance of the theme's components. Selecting **Vivid Colors** will apply brighter colors to text and graphics, selecting **Active Graphics** will animate certain theme components, and selecting **Background Image** will apply a background image to the pages in your current FrontPage web.

For this lesson, select **Vivid Colors** and **Background Image**.
From the list of themes, select a theme you like, then click the **Apply** button.

The selected theme is applied to all of the pages in your current FrontPage web. In the next section of this lesson, you will see how the selected theme gives your pages a consistent appearance.

Opening Pages in the FrontPage Editor

Now that the overall layout of **My Own Web** is determined, you will add content to each of the pages. While pages are created and managed in FrontPage Explorer, designing and editing pages is all done in the FrontPage Editor.

The **FrontPage Editor** is used to create, edit, and view pages. All text, styles, and page formatting is based on Hypertext Mark-up Language (HTML) standards.

The FrontPage Editor supports all of the usual Windows shortcuts like cut and paste as well as many others from the Office Family

7. Save the revised document and leave it open.

8. To prepare for the next lesson, ensure that the insertion point is positioned at the top of the document.

4.5.2 Saving and Opening Web Pages

→ ## Feature

Word makes it easy to convert a document for display on the World Wide Web. The process involves saving the document to Hypertext Markup Language **(HTML)** format for publishing to a Web server. Once the file has been saved using the proper format, you may upload it to your company's intranet or to a Web server.

→ ## Method

To save a document into HTML format for Web publishing:
• CHOOSE: File, Save as Web Page

To open a Web page in Word:
• CHOOSE: File, Open

→ **Practice**

You will now save the "Front Page Themes" document to HTML for publishing on the Web.

1. To preview the "Front Page Themes" document as a Web page in a Web browser:
CHOOSE: File, Web Page Preview
The document should be displaying in your browser and should look similar to the one shown in Figure 4.27, shown in the last lesson. You may need to maximize the browser window (□).

2. To close your browser:
CLICK: its Close button (✕)

3. To save the current document as a Web page:
CHOOSE: File, Save as Web Page
The Save As dialog box appears with some additional options (Figure 4.28). Note that "Single File Web Page" appears as the file type in the *Save as type* drop-down list box.

Figure 4.28

Save as Web
Page dialog box

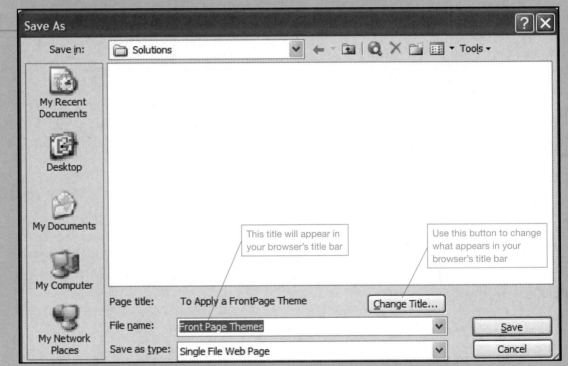

This title will appear in your browser's title bar

Use this button to change what appears in your browser's title bar

4. Using the *Save in* drop-down list box or the Places bar:
SELECT: *your storage location,* if not already selected

5. To proceed with the conversion to HTML:
CLICK: Save command button

6. Close the "Front Page Themes" document, saving any changes.

7. CHOOSE: File, Open

8. Using the *Look in* drop-down list box or the Places bar:
SELECT: *your storage location,* if not already selected

9. SELECT: All Web Pages from the *Files of type* drop-down list
The Open dialog box should now appear similar to Figure 4.29. As you can see from the file listing, Word automatically created a file named "Front Page Themes.htm" in your storage location.

Figure 4.29

Displaying Web pages in the file list

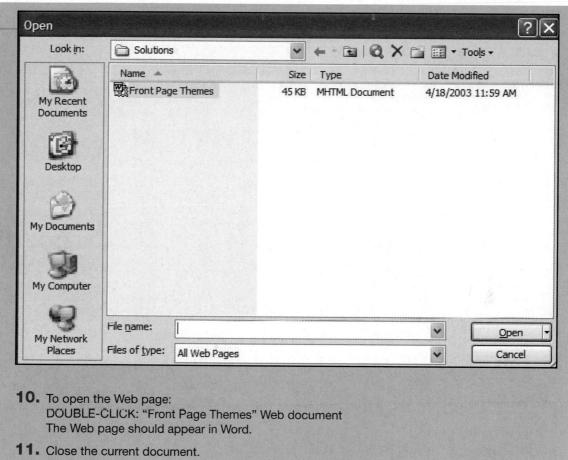

10. To open the Web page:
DOUBLE-CLICK: "Front Page Themes" Web document
The Web page should appear in Word.

11. Close the current document.

 **SelfCheck**   **4.5**   Why might you want to convert a Word document to HTML?

Chapter
summary

Depending on your output requirements, you may want to change one or more page layout settings before printing. Using the Page Setup dialog box, you can improve the layout of your document by changing margins and switching between portrait and landscape modes. You can further improve a document using headers, footers, and page numbers; these elements help provide a structure for your document in order to keep your audience focused. You may even choose to divide a document into sections in order to vary these settings within a document. After you have formatted your document so that it looks the way you want, you can print it or even publish it on your personal or company Web site. Before publishing a document to a Web site, you must save it in HTML.

Command Summary

Many of the commands and procedures appearing in this chapter are summarized in the following table.

Skill Set	To Perform this Task . . .	Do the Following . . .
Printing Documents	Preview a document	CLICK: Print Preview button (🔍), or CHOOSE: File, Print Preview
	Print a document	CLICK: Print button (🖨), or CHOOSE: File, Print
Formatting Documents	Change margins	CHOOSE: File, Page Setup CLICK: *Margins* tab and then adjust the settings in the *Margins* area
	Change page orientation	CHOOSE: File, Page Setup CLICK: *Margins* tab CLICK: *Portrait* or *Landscape* button
	Insert page numbers	CHOOSE: Insert, Page Numbers
	Create a header or footer	CHOOSE: View, Header and Footer
	Insert a section break	CHOOSE: Insert, Break SELECT: an option in the *Section breaks* area
	Format first-page headers and footers differently	CHOOSE: File, Page Setup CLICK: *Layout* tab CLICK: *Different first page* check box
	Vary page setup options by section	CHOOSE: File, Page Setup CLICK: *desired tab* CHOOSE: "This section" from the *Apply to* drop-down list
Customizing Paragraphs	Insert a page break	PRESS: CTRL + ENTER, or CHOOSE: Insert, Break
	Control pagination	CHOOSE: Format, Paragraph CLICK: *Line and Page Breaks* tab
Working with Web Pages	Save a document as a Web page	CHOOSE: File, Save as Web Page
	Open a Web Page in Word	CHOOSE: File, Open and then navigate to your storage location SELECT: Web Pages and Web Archives from the *Files of type* drop-down list DOUBLE-CLICK: the file you want to open
	Preview a Web page	CHOOSE: File, Web Page Preview
	Apply a theme	CHOOSE: Format, Theme

Key Terms

This section specifies page references for the key terms identified in this chapter. For a complete list of definitions, refer to the Glossary provided immediately after the Appendix in this learning guide.

footer, *p. WD 161*

gutter, *p. WD 155*

header, *p. WD 161*

HTML, *p. WD 175*

hyperlinks, *p. WD 173*

Internet, *p. WD 173*

intranet, *p. WD 173*

landscape orientation, *p. WD 157*

orphan, *p. WD 158*

portrait orientation, *p. WD 157*

section break, *p. WD 166*

widow, *p. WD 158*

World Wide Web, *p. WD 173*

Chapter
quiz

Short Answer

1. How do you create a Web document from a standard Word document?

2. What is the difference between a document that prints with a portrait orientation versus one that prints with a landscape orientation?

3. What is a Web theme?

4. What is a page break?

5. In Word, what is a widow?

6. How is the term "gutter" used in Word?

7. What is the difference between the Internet and an intranet?

8. What is the procedure for viewing headers and footers on the screen?

9. In Word, how do you insert a hard page break?

10. How wide are a document's top and bottom margins by default?

True/False

1. _____ Using the Insert, Page Numbers command, page numbers are inserted in the header or footer area.

2. _____ The Header and Footer toolbar automatically appears when you create a header or footer.

3. _____ Section breaks always mark the beginning of a new page.

4. _____ Once a page number has been inserted, it is no longer possible to apply character formatting to it.

5. _____ By default, a footer appears at the top of the page.

6. _____ It is not possible to vary margins within a document.

7. _____ Page breaks are always used when printing documents in a landscape orientation.

8. _____ You can delete a page break by positioning the insertion point on the break and pressing DELETE.

9. _____ You can align page numbers with the left, center, and right margins.

10. _____ In Word, you can format headers and footers using regular formatting commands.

Multiple Choice

1. Which of the following are commonly found on Web pages?

  a. Hyperlinks
  b. Internet
  c. Intranet
  d. All of the above

2. Which of the following do you use to change margins?

  a. Standard toolbar
  b. Formatting toolbar
  c. Page Setup dialog box
  d. Paragraph dialog box

3. To force a page break, press:

  a. `CTRL` + `BREAK`
  b. `CTRL` + `ALT`
  c. `CTRL` + `ENTER`
  d. None of the above

4. To create a footer, choose:

  a. View, Footer
  b. View, Header and Footer
  c. Insert, Header and Footer
  d. Both a and b

5. To enable varied formatting within a document, Word allows you to divide a document into:

  a. Master documents
  b. Outline views
  c. Multiple documents
  d. Sections

6. In which view is the header/footer displayed along with the body of the document?

  a. Normal view
  b. Print Layout view
  c. Print Preview mode
  d. Both b and c

7. Which of the following can you change using the Page Setup dialog box?

  a. Margins
  b. Page orientation
  c. First-page headers and footers
  d. All of the above

8. By default, your documents print with:

  a. 1 inch top and bottom margins
  b. 1.25 inches left and right margins
  c. A portrait orientation
  d. All of the above

9. Switching between portrait and landscape modes involves the:

  a. Print Layout view
  b. Page Setup dialog box
  c. Header and Footer toolbar
  d. None of the above

10. By default, the information you store in a header or footer prints:

  a. On just the first page
  b. On every other page
  c. On every page
  d. None of the above

Hands-On
exercises

step by step

1. Modifying Page Setup Options for Printing

In this exercise, you will open an existing document, add page breaks, add a header, preview, and then print the document.

1. Open the WD04HE01 data file. This document contains instructions on how to prepare a résumé for e-mailing.

2. Save the document as "Text Resume" to your personal storage location.

3. To insert a page break:
Place your cursor at the beginning of the "Step 5: . . ." line.
PRESS: `CTRL` + `ENTER`
Place your cursor at the beginning of the "Step 9: . . ." line.
PRESS: `CTRL` + `ENTER`

4. In this step, you insert a header that includes the name of the document.
   CHOOSE: View, Header and Footer
   TYPE: **Preparing a Plain Text Resume** in the Header area
   CLICK: Align Right button (⊟)
   PRESS: (ENTER) to add a line separating the header text from the document text
   CLICK: Close button on the Header and Footer toolbar

5. To preview the document:
   CLICK: Print Preview button (🔍)
   CLICK: Multiple Pages button (▦) to display all three pages.
   CLICK: Close button on the Print Preview toolbar

6. Save the revised document. A portion of the completed document appears in Figure 4.30.

Figure 4.30

"Text Resume" document

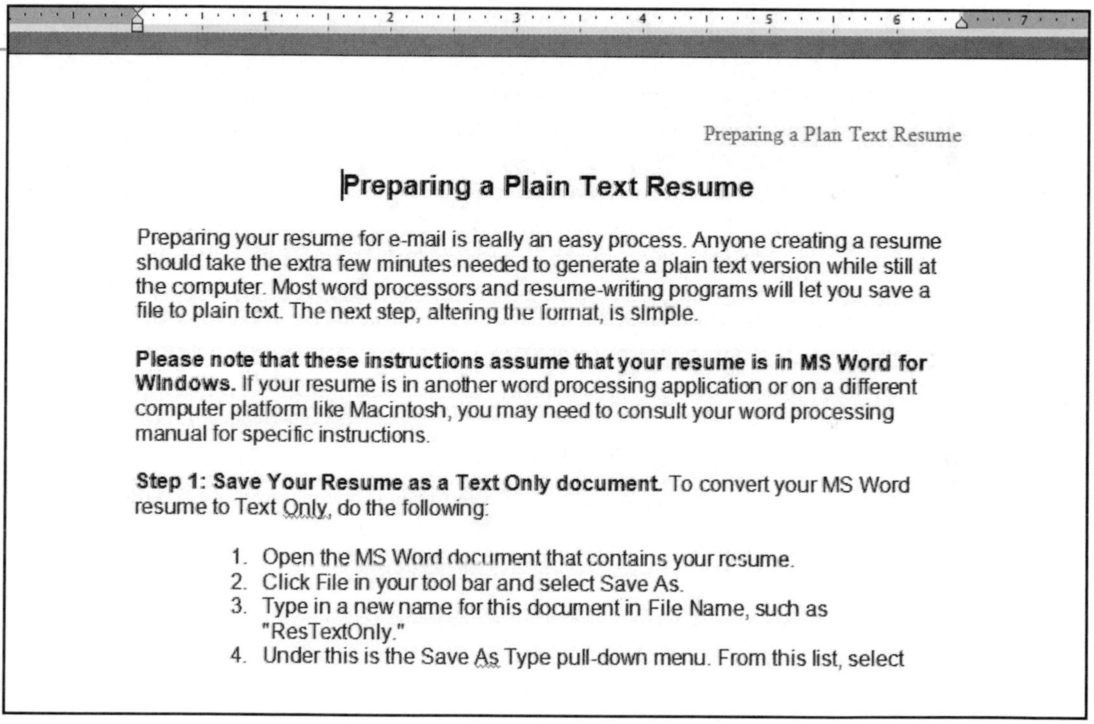

> Preparing a Plan Text Resume
>
> # Preparing a Plain Text Resume
>
> Preparing your resume for e-mail is really an easy process. Anyone creating a resume should take the extra few minutes needed to generate a plain text version while still at the computer. Most word processors and resume-writing programs will let you save a file to plain text. The next step, altering the format, is simple.
>
> **Please note that these instructions assume that your resume is in MS Word for Windows.** If your resume is in another word processing application or on a different computer platform like Macintosh, you may need to consult your word processing manual for specific instructions.
>
> **Step 1: Save Your Resume as a Text Only document.** To convert your MS Word resume to Text Only, do the following:
>
> > 1. Open the MS Word document that contains your resume.
> > 2. Click File in your tool bar and select Save As.
> > 3. Type in a new name for this document in File Name, such as "ResTextOnly."
> > 4. Under this is the Save As Type pull-down menu. From this list, select

7. Print and then close the document.

step by step

2. Inserting Section Breaks, Changing Margins, and Creating Headers

In this exercise, you will work with a long document and insert section breaks, change margins, and create headers.

1. Open WD04HE02 from your data files location.

2. Save the document as "Cell Phone Danger" to your personal storage location.

3. Switch to Print Layout view if necessary.

4. Do the following to divide the document into sections:
   Position the insertion point at the beginning of the subheading "Danger! Danger!"
   CHOOSE: Insert, Break
   SELECT: Next Page under Section Break Types
   CLICK: OK command button

5. In a similar manner, create the same type of section break at the following subheading locations:

"Government Steps In"
"Are You Dangerous?"
"Police Report Data Sought"
"Playing for Keeps"
"National Consensus"
"Jury Still out on Driver Distraction"

You should have a total of eight sections. Ensure that your sections are correct before continuing with this exercise.

6. To change the document's margins:
PRESS: [CTRL] + [HOME] to move to the top of the first page
CHOOSE: File, Page Setup
CREATE: 1.5″ margins on the top, bottom, left, and right
CLICK: OK command button

7. To insert the first section header:
CHOOSE: View, Header and Footer
CLICK: Align Right button (⊟)
TYPE: **Cell Phone Dangers, page**
CLICK: Insert Page Number button (⊞) on the Header and Footer toolbar

8. Format the header text as Arial, 14 point, bold.

9. To insert the second section header:
CLICK: Show Next button (⊡)
CLICK: Same as Previous button (⊞) to deselect it
Replace the text "Cell Phone Dangers" with "Danger! Danger!"
Be careful not to delete the page number.

10. Using steps similar to those outlined in item 9, create unique headers for each section. Use the subheading as the header text.
(*Note:* For the Section 8 header, type **Jury Still Out**.)

11. Close the Header and Footer toolbar.

12. Format the document subheadings:
Format each subheading with Arial, 18 point, bold. The first six pages of your document should be similar to those shown in Figure 4.31.

Figure 4.31

"Cell Phone Dangers" document

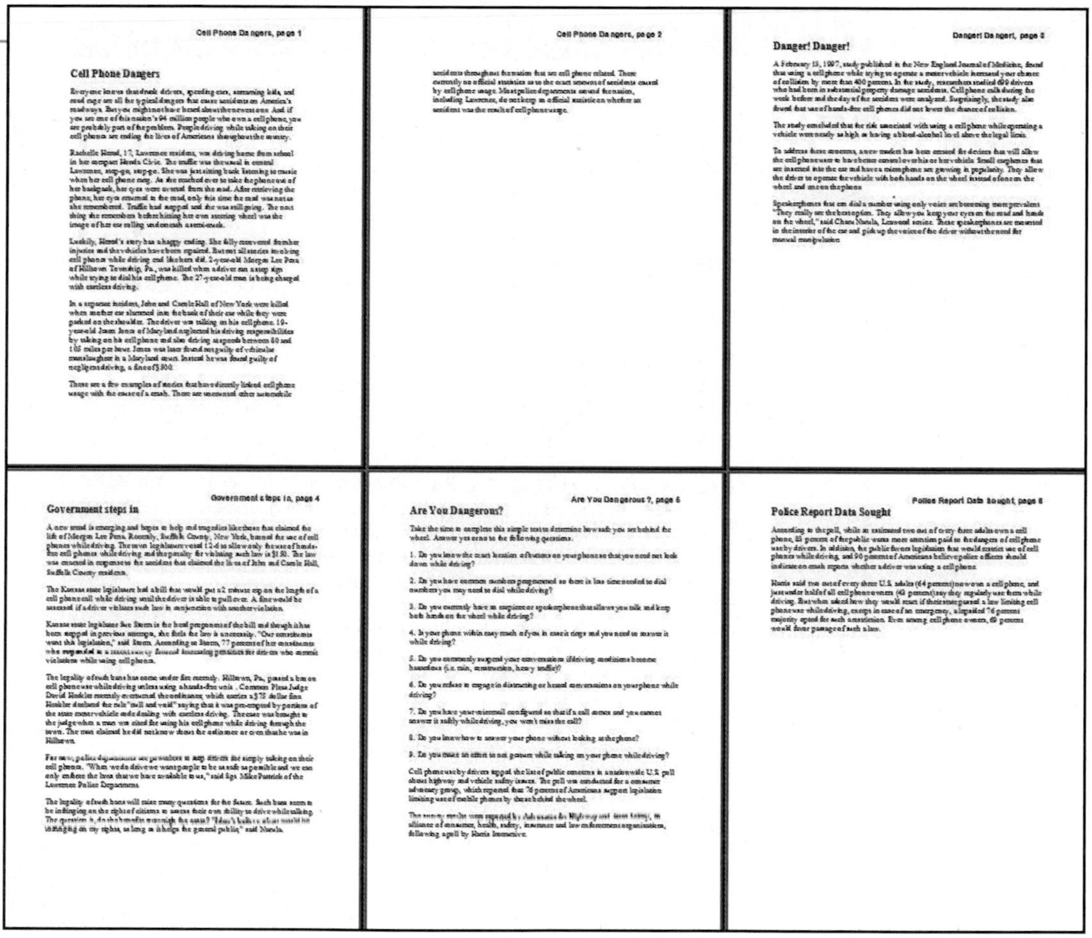

13. Save, print, and close the document.

3. Saving a Document as a Web Page and Using a Theme

In this exercise, you will open an existing document, save it as a Web page, and apply a Web theme.

1. Open the WD04HE03 data file.

2. Save the document as "Digital Photography" to your personal storage location.

3. Apply a Web theme to your document:
CHOOSE: Format, Theme
SELECT: Sunflower from the *Choose a Theme* list box, or choose another if Sunflower theme is not available
CLICK: OK command button

4. Add bullets to your document:
SELECT: the second through fourth paragraphs
CLICK: Bullets button (≡) on the Formatting toolbar

5. Add a blank line between the bulleted paragraphs:
Position your cursor at the end of each bulleted paragraph and press **SHIFT** + **ENTER**. This creates a blank line without adding another bullet. Your document should be similar to the one shown in Figure 4.32.

Figure 4.32

"Digital
Photography"
document

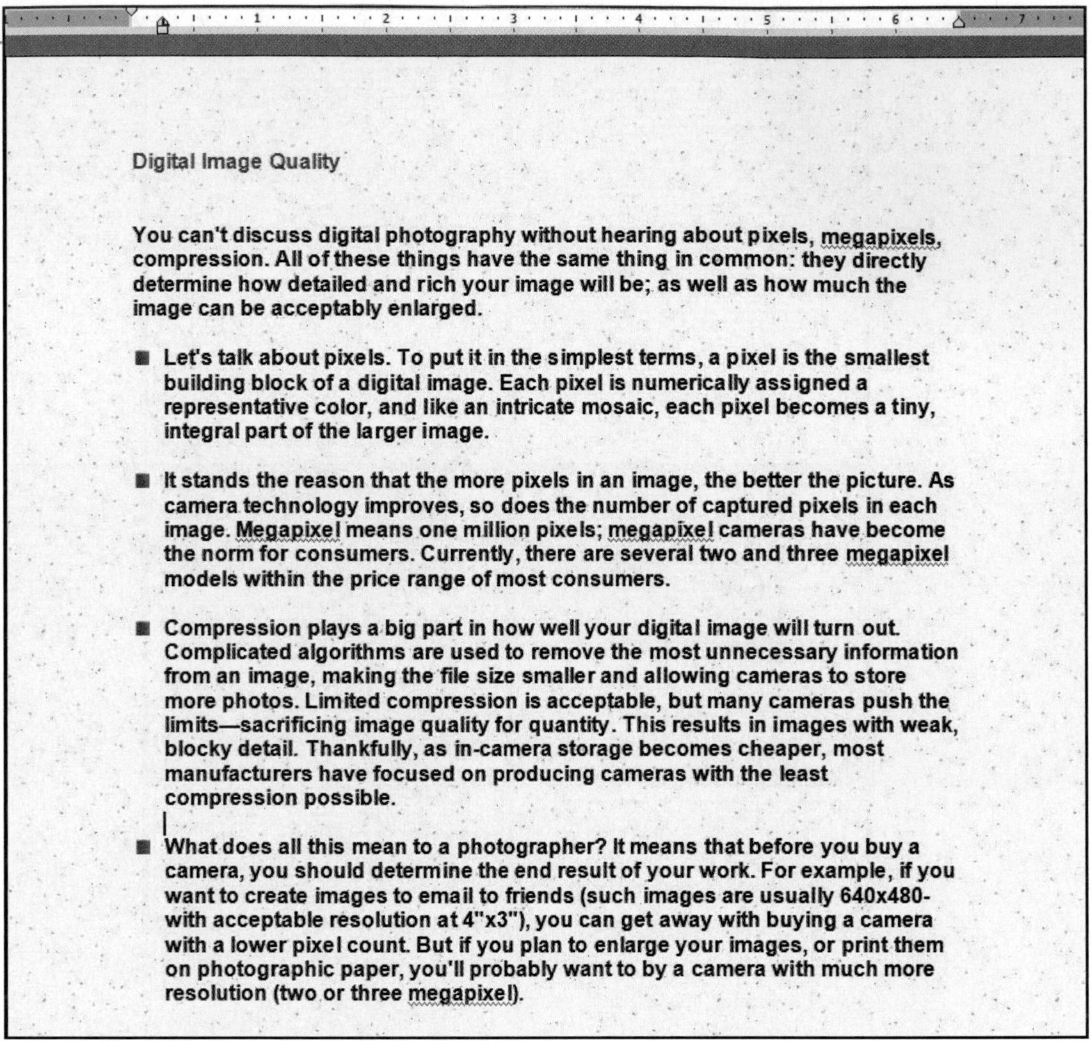

> **Digital Image Quality**
>
> You can't discuss digital photography without hearing about pixels, megapixels, compression. All of these things have the same thing in common: they directly determine how detailed and rich your image will be; as well as how much the image can be acceptably enlarged.
>
> - Let's talk about pixels. To put it in the simplest terms, a pixel is the smallest building block of a digital image. Each pixel is numerically assigned a representative color, and like an intricate mosaic, each pixel becomes a tiny, integral part of the larger image.
>
> - It stands the reason that the more pixels in an image, the better the picture. As camera technology improves, so does the number of captured pixels in each image. Megapixel means one million pixels; megapixel cameras have become the norm for consumers. Currently, there are several two and three megapixel models within the price range of most consumers.
>
> - Compression plays a big part in how well your digital image will turn out. Complicated algorithms are used to remove the most unnecessary information from an image, making the file size smaller and allowing cameras to store more photos. Limited compression is acceptable, but many cameras push the limits—sacrificing image quality for quantity. This results in images with weak, blocky detail. Thankfully, as in-camera storage becomes cheaper, most manufacturers have focused on producing cameras with the least compression possible.
>
> - What does all this mean to a photographer? It means that before you buy a camera, you should determine the end result of your work. For example, if you want to create images to email to friends (such images are usually 640x480- with acceptable resolution at 4"x3"), you can get away with buying a camera with a lower pixel count. But if you plan to enlarge your images, or print them on photographic paper, you'll probably want to by a camera with much more resolution (two or three megapixel).

6. Preview the document as a Web page:
   CHOOSE: File, Web Page Preview
   Close the Web browser.

7. Add a blank line after the first paragraph:
   Position the cursor at the end of the first paragraph.
   PRESS: (SHIFT) + (ENTER) to add a blank line

8. Save the document as a Web page:
   CHOOSE: File, Save as Web Page
   Ensure that the file is named "Digital Photography"
   CLICK: Save command button

on your own

4. Changing Margins and Page Orientation

In this exercise, you will open a document and change margins and page orientation.

1. Open the WD04HE04 data file.

2. Save the document as "Style Guide" to your personal storage location.

3. Set the top and bottom margins to .5″ and the left and right margins to 1″.

4. Locate the "Benefits of a Style Guide" heading. Insert a section break at this heading and change the page orientation to landscape.

5. At the "Support for a Style Guide" heading, create another section break and return the orientation to portrait.

6. Locate the heading "How to Improve Consistency Beyond Style Guides" heading. Select the heading and the following paragraph and apply Keep with Next and Keep Lines Together. Your document, displayed in print preview, should be similar to the one shown in Figure 4.33.

Figure 4.33

"Style Guide" document

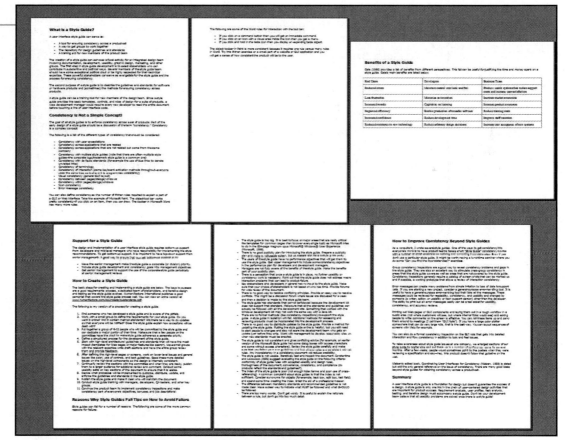

7. Close the print preview window.

8. Save and close the document.

n your own

5. Formatting a New Document

In this exercise, you will practice using some commands from previous chapters, as well as several page layout commands.

1. Start a new document and then switch to Print Layout view.

2. Set the following page dimensions:

Paper Orientation:	Portrait
Top Margin:	1 inch
Bottom Margin:	1 inch
Left Margin:	1 inch
Right Margin:	1 inch

3. Enter the information shown in Figure 4.34. (*Hint:* Use tabs.)

Figure 4.34

Company Budget document

ABC REALTY INC.

Revenue
2003

Commercial Properties	$125,500,000
Residential Properties	35,000,000
Leased Properties	875,000
Total Revenue	**$161,375,000**

Expenses

Insurance	$50,000
Salaries	750,000
Commissions	15,500,000
Office Supplies	25,000
Office Equipment	20,000
Utilities	15,000
Leased Automobiles	50,000
Travel	250,000
Advertising & Promotion	25,000,000
Total Expenses	**41,660,000**
Net Income	**$119,715,000**

4. Apply the shading and borders of your choice to the title "ABC REALTY INC."

5. Save the document as "Company Budget" to your personal storage location. Figure 4.35 shows a portion of the completed document.

Figure 4.35

"Company Budget" document formatted

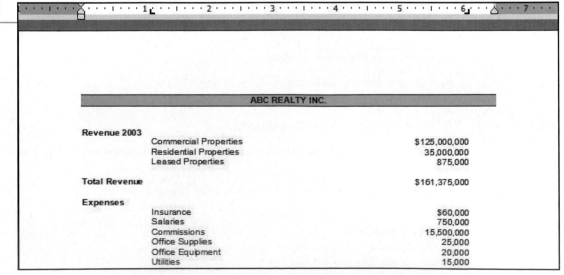

6. Preview and print the document.

your own

6. Formatting a Newsletter

In this exercise, you will open the WD04HE06 student file and format it to create a presentable newsletter. Change the orientation of the newsletter to landscape. The header should include the text "Sunshine Farm" and should appear in a large, boldfaced font with 15 percent light yellow shading. The footer should include the current date in the left-aligned position and the current page number in the right-aligned position. Issue a Keep with Next command so that the "Sunshine Farm Brewery" heading is not isolated at the bottom of page 1.

Finally, format all the headings in the newsletter with light yellow shading that spans from the left to the right margin. The first page of the newsletter should appear similar to the one shown in Figure 4.36. Save the document as "Sunshine Farm" and then preview and print your work. Close the document.

Figure 4.36

"Sunshine Farm" document

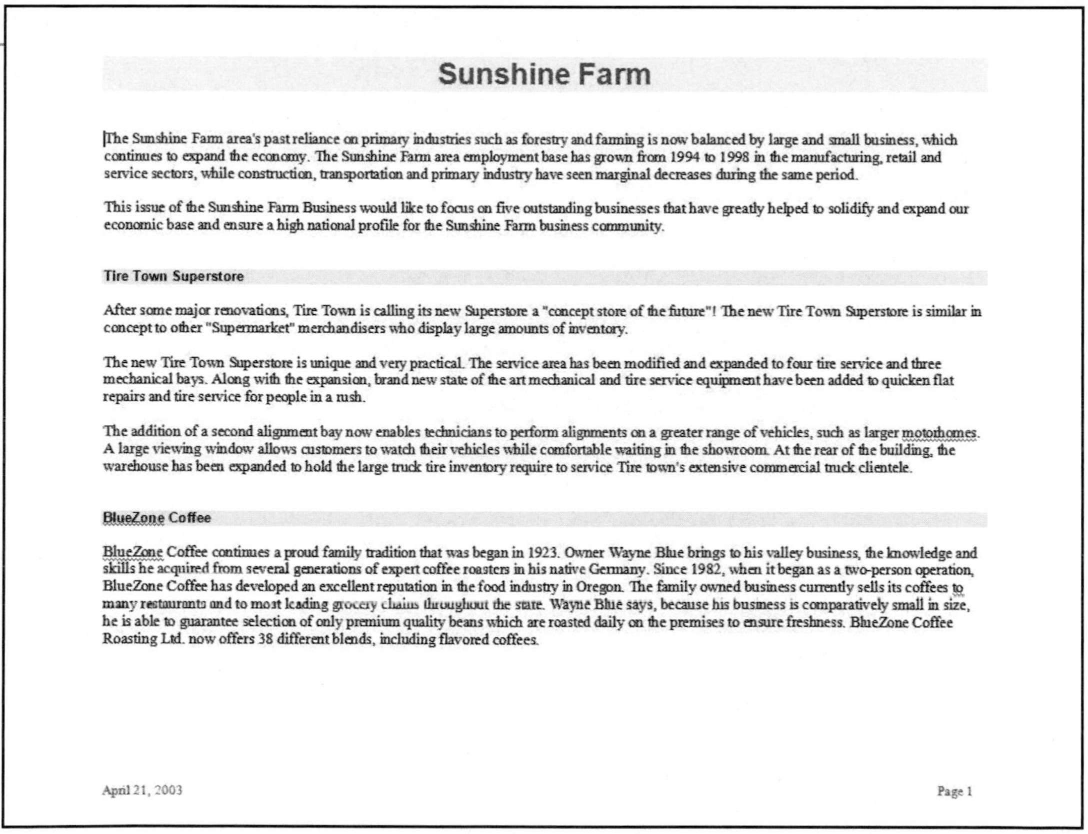

Sunshine Farm

The Sunshine Farm area's past reliance on primary industries such as forestry and farming is now balanced by large and small business, which continues to expand the economy. The Sunshine Farm area employment base has grown from 1994 to 1998 in the manufacturing, retail and service sectors, while construction, transportation and primary industry have seen marginal decreases during the same period.

This issue of the Sunshine Farm Business would like to focus on five outstanding businesses that have greatly helped to solidify and expand our economic base and ensure a high national profile for the Sunshine Farm business community.

Tire Town Superstore

After some major renovations, Tire Town is calling its new Superstore a "concept store of the future"! The new Tire Town Superstore is similar in concept to other "Supermarket" merchandisers who display large amounts of inventory.

The new Tire Town Superstore is unique and very practical. The service area has been modified and expanded to four tire service and three mechanical bays. Along with the expansion, brand new state of the art mechanical and tire service equipment have been added to quicken flat repairs and tire service for people in a rush.

The addition of a second alignment bay now enables technicians to perform alignments on a greater range of vehicles, such as larger motorhomes. A large viewing window allows customers to watch their vehicles while comfortable waiting in the showroom. At the rear of the building, the warehouse has been expanded to hold the large truck tire inventory require to service Tire town's extensive commercial truck clientele.

BlueZone Coffee

BlueZone Coffee continues a proud family tradition that was began in 1923. Owner Wayne Blue brings to his valley business, the knowledge and skills he acquired from several generations of expert coffee roasters in his native Germany. Since 1982, when it began as a two-person operation, BlueZone Coffee has developed an excellent reputation in the food industry in Oregon. The family owned business currently sells its coffees to many restaurants and to most leading grocery chains throughout the state. Wayne Blue says, because his business is comparatively small in size, he is able to guarantee selection of only premium quality beans which are roasted daily on the premises to ensure freshness. BlueZone Coffee Roasting Ltd. now offers 38 different blends, including flavored coffees.

April 21, 2003   Page 1

CaseStudy   THE CENTURION HELP DESK

Bonnie Armintrout has just been hired by the Centurion Publications Company. This company publishes custom textbooks for the K–12, or kindergarten through twelfth grade, educational market. During the past 10 years, the company has enjoyed much success and growth. Doug Yoder, company president, believes the size of the company warrants a full-featured Help Desk, complete with trained support staff who can answer employees' questions. Doug has hired Bonnie to lead the Help Desk. Because this is a new department for Centurion, Bonnie must build it from scratch.

In this case study, assume the role of Bonnie as she uses the various features of Word to develop materials for the newly created department.

1. Bonnie decides that the one of her first tasks should be to build a Web page for the company's intranet. The final document will be similar to the one shown in Figure 4.37.

Figure 4.37

"CPCWeb" document

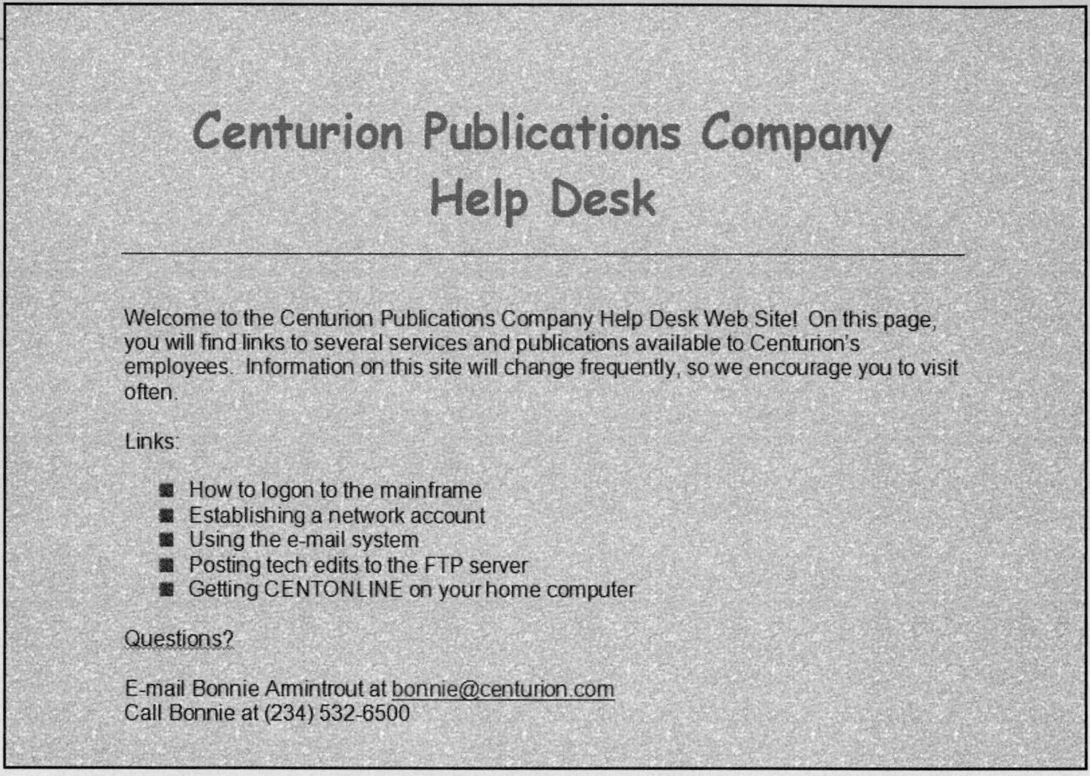

Centurion Publications Company
Help Desk

Welcome to the Centurion Publications Company Help Desk Web Site! On this page, you will find links to several services and publications available to Centurion's employees. Information on this site will change frequently, so we encourage you to visit often.

Links:

- How to logon to the mainframe
- Establishing a network account
- Using the e-mail system
- Posting tech edits to the FTP server
- Getting CENTONLINE on your home computer

Questions?

E-mail Bonnie Armintrout at bonnie@centurion.com
Call Bonnie at (234) 532-6500

Bonnie has drafted the content of the page in Microsoft Word and now needs to modify it for the Web. She opens the file WD04HE07 and saves it as "CPCWeb." She then applies the following formatting to the document:

Center the two title lines and apply the Comic Sans font, 26 points, bold. Apply the Sandstone Web theme. If this theme is not available, choose another. Change the font color of the two title lines to green. Preview the page in your Web browser, then close the browser window. Save as a Web Page and close the document.

2. Bonnie decides that the Help Desk should have its own letterhead, which should include a listing of some of the services that the Help Desk provides. She has designed the letterhead shown in Figure 4.38. (*Hint:* Bonnie inserts the letterhead information in a header and sets center tabs in positions 1.75″, 3″, and 4.5″. She also sets a right tab in position 6.5 inches.) She saves this file as "Help Desk Letterhead." Use your own judgment for font selections and sizes. (*Hint:* The border width is 1.5 points.)

Figure 4.38

"Help Desk Letterhead" document

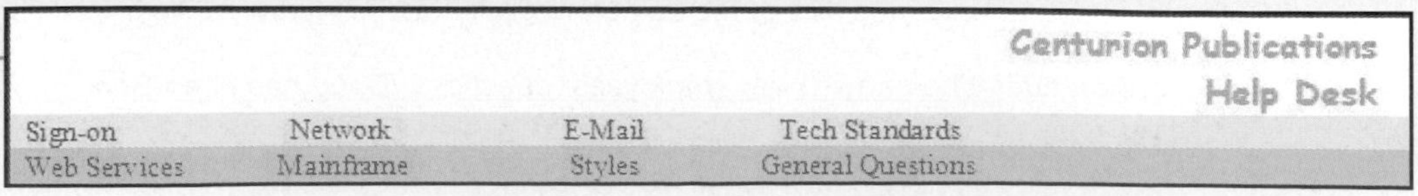

Centurion Publications
Help Desk

Sign-on	Network	E-Mail	Tech Standards
Web Services	Mainframe	Styles	General Questions

3. Bonnie has decided to develop a follow-up form to be used when the caller's problem cannot be immediately resolved. This form will contain information describing the problem, who took the call and when, who initiated the call, and the promised resolution date. Using what you have learned in this and previous chapters, design a form to contain that information. To begin creating the document, open the "Help Desk Letterhead" file you created. Be sure to use shading, paragraph borders, tabs, and font formatting. The form might look something like the one shown in Figure 4.39. Save the document as "Follow-up."

Figure 4.39

"Follow-up" document

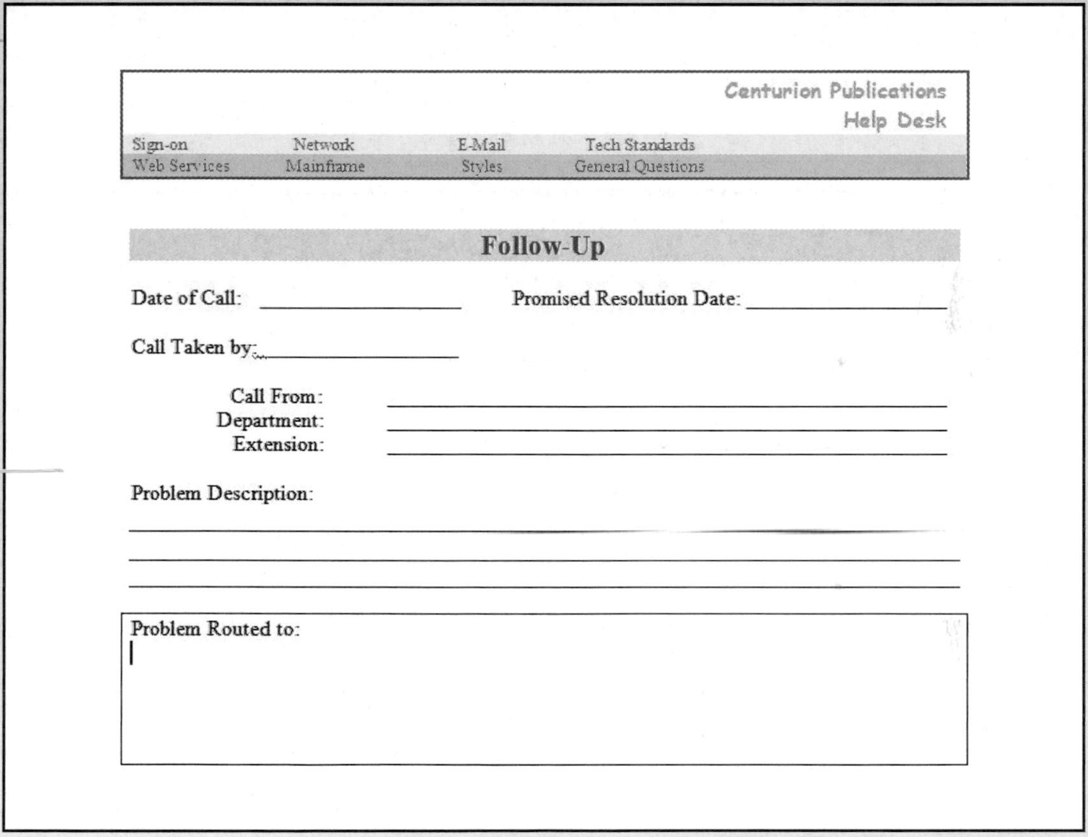

Centurion Publications
Help Desk

Sign-on	Network	E-Mail	Tech Standards
Web Services	Mainframe	Styles	General Questions

Follow-Up

Date of Call: ____________ Promised Resolution Date: ____________

Call Taken by: ____________

Call From: ____________
Department: ____________
Extension: ____________

Problem Description:

Problem Routed to:

4. Bonnie has begun working on a company newsletter that will be distributed monthly. She has several articles and wants to complete the newsletter by dividing it into sections and adding page numbering. Open the document WDC504 and make the following changes:

   At the beginning of each new article (except the first one), create a next page section break. Create a header with the article name on the left side and the page number aligned right for each section break. Your completed newsletter, in print preview, should be similar to the one shown in Figure 4.40. Save and close the document.

Figure 4.40

"Draft Newsletter" document

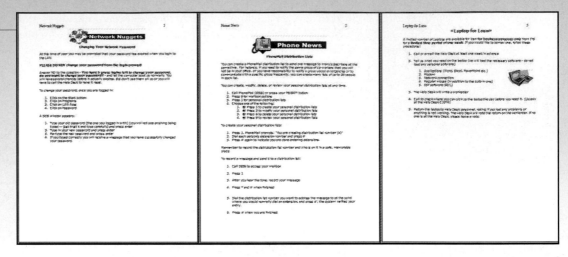

Answers to Self-Check Questions

4.1 What is the procedure for printing your work? Click the Print button ( ) to send your work directly to the printer or choose File, Print to display the Print dialog box. Using the Print dialog box, you can specify what to print and how many copies to produce.

4.2 In inches, how wide are the left and right margins by default? By default, the left and right margins are 1.25 inches. In contrast, the top and bottom margins are 1 inch each.

4.3 How do you insert page numbers in a document? Choose Insert, Page Numbers. If the Header and Footer toolbar is displayed, click the Insert Page Number button ( ).

4.4 For what purposes are sections used? Sections are useful for varying the formatting within a document.

4.5 Why might you want to convert a Word document to HTML? You must convert your documents to HTML before you can post them on a Web site or your company's intranet.

Notes

Notes

Microsoft® Office Excel®

2003

CHAPTER 1

Creating a Worksheet

PREREQUISITES

Although this chapter assumes no previous experience using Microsoft Office Excel 2003, you should be comfortable using a keyboard and mouse in the Microsoft Windows environment. You should be able to launch and exit programs and perform basic file management operations, such as opening and closing documents.

LEARNING OBJECTIVES

After completing this chapter, you will be able to:

- Describe the different components of the application and workbook windows

- Select commands using the Menu bar, toolbars, and right-click menus

- Enter text, dates, numbers, and formulas in a worksheet

- Edit and erase cell data

- Use the Undo and Redo commands

- Start a new blank workbook

- Save, open, and close a workbook

1.1 Getting Started with Excel 2003

Microsoft Office Excel 2003 is an electronic spreadsheet program that enables you to store, manipulate, and chart numeric data. Researchers, statisticians, and businesspeople use spreadsheets to analyze and summarize mathematical, statistical, and financial data. Closer to home, you can use Excel to create a budget for your monthly living expenses, analyze returns in the stock market, develop a business plan, or calculate your student loan payments.

Excel 2003 enables you to create and modify worksheets—the electronic version of an accountant's ledger pad—and chart sheets. A **worksheet** (Figure 1.1) is divided into vertical columns and horizontal rows. The rows are numbered and the columns are labeled from A to Z, then AA to AZ, and so on to column IV. The intersection of a column and a row is called a **cell.** Each cell is given a **cell address,** like a post office box number, consisting of its column letter followed by its row number (for example, B4 or FX400). Excel 2003 allows you to open multiple worksheets and chart sheets within its application window.

Figure 1.1

An electronic worksheet

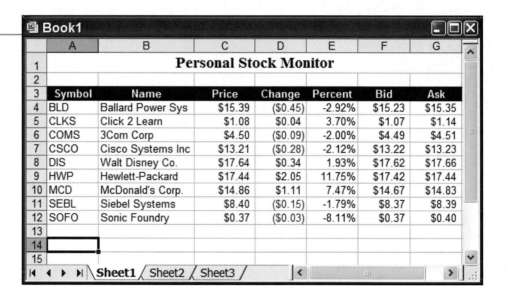

A **chart sheet** (Figure 1.2) displays a chart graphic that is typically linked to data stored in a worksheet. When the data is changed, the chart is updated automatically to reflect the new information. Charts may also appear alongside their data in a worksheet.

Figure 1.2

A chart sheet

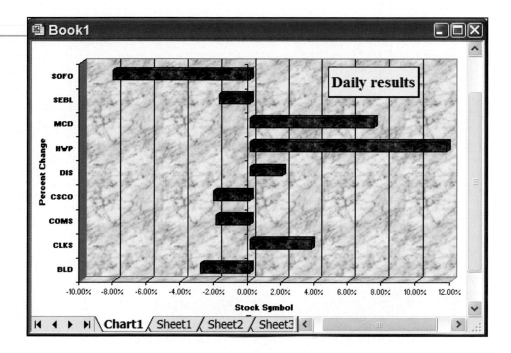

Related worksheets and chart sheets are stored together in a single disk file called a **workbook.** You can think of an Excel 2003 workbook file as a three-ring binder with tabs at the beginning of each new page or sheet. In this module, you will learn to load Microsoft Office Excel 2003 and will then proceed through a guided tour of its primary components.

1.1.1 Loading and Exiting Excel

→ Feature

Microsoft Office Excel 2003 is an application software program that runs under the Microsoft Windows operating system. To load Excel 2003 in Windows XP, click the Start button (*start*) on the taskbar to display the Windows Start menu. Then, choose the All Programs menu option. In the menu that appears, choose Microsoft Office by either clicking or highlighting the menu option, and then click Microsoft Office Excel 2003. After a few moments, the Excel 2003 application window appears.

When you are finished doing your work, close the Excel 2003 application window so that your system's memory is freed for use by other Windows applications. To do so, choose the File, Exit command or click on the Close button (X) appearing in the top right-hand corner. These methods are used to close most Microsoft Windows applications.

→ Method

To load Excel:

• CLICK: Start button (*start*)

• CHOOSE: All Programs → Microsoft Office

• CLICK: Microsoft Office Excel 2003

To exit Excel:

• CHOOSE: File → Exit from Excel's Menu bar

  or

• CLICK: its Close button (X)

→ ## Practice

You will load Microsoft Office Excel 2003 using the Windows Start menu and practice closing the application. Ensure that you have turned on your computer and that the Windows desktop appears.

1. Position the mouse pointer over the Start button (*start*) appearing in the bottom left-hand corner of the Windows taskbar and then click the left mouse button once. The Start menu appears.

2. Position the mouse pointer over the All Programs menu option. Notice that you do not need to click the left mouse button to display the list of programs in the fly-out or cascading menu. (*Note:* If you are using a version of Windows prior to XP, click the Programs menu option.)

3. Move the mouse pointer horizontally to the right until it highlights an option in the All Programs menu. You can now move the mouse pointer vertically within the menu to select an application.

4. Position the mouse pointer over the Microsoft Office program group and then move the highlight into the fly-out or cascading menu, similar to the graphic shown in Figure 1.3. (*Note:* Even if you are using Windows XP, the desktop theme, color scheme, and menu options may appear differently on your screen than in Figure 1.3.)

Figure 1.3

Highlighting an option in the Microsoft Office program group

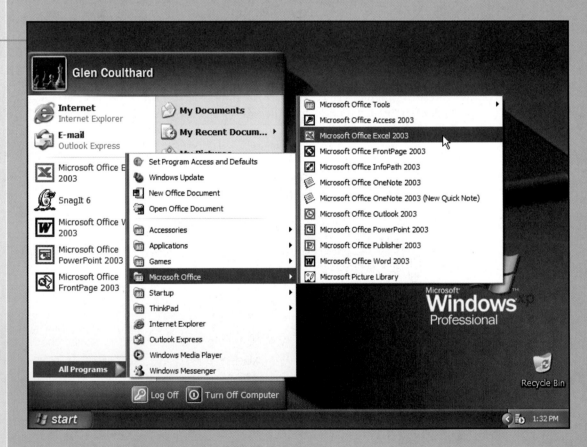

5. Position the mouse pointer over the Microsoft Office Excel 2003 menu option and then click the left mouse button once. After a few seconds, the Excel 2003 application window appears (Figure 1.4).

Figure 1.4

Microsoft Office
Excel 2003
application
window

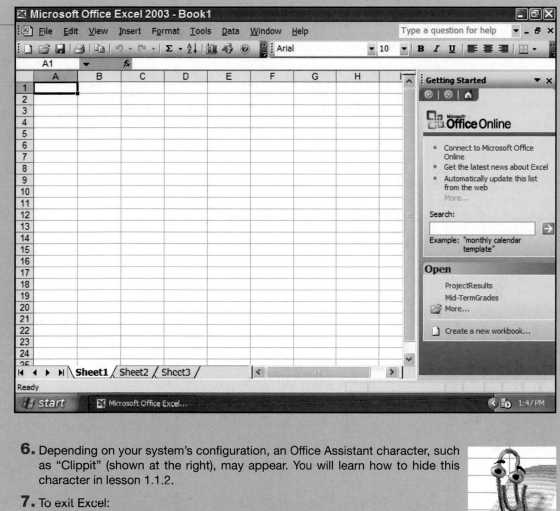

6. Depending on your system's configuration, an Office Assistant character, such as "Clippit" (shown at the right), may appear. You will learn how to hide this character in lesson 1.1.2.

7. To exit Excel:
CLICK: its Close button () in the top right-hand corner
Assuming that no other applications are running and displayed, you are returned to the Windows desktop.

In Addition SWITCHING AMONG APPLICATIONS

A button appears on the Windows taskbar for each running application or open document. Switching among your open Microsoft Office System applications involves clicking on a taskbar button and is as easy as switching channels on a television set.

1.1.2 Touring Excel

Feature

The Excel 2003 **application window** acts as a container for your worksheet and chart windows. It also contains the primary components for working in Excel, including the *Windows icons, Menu bar, toolbars, task pane, Name Box, Formula bar,* and *Status bar.* The components of a worksheet **document window** include *scroll bars, sheet tabs, Tab Split bar,* and *Tab Scrolling bar.* Figures 1.5 and 1.6 identify several of these components.

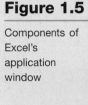

Practice

In a guided tour, you will explore the features of the Excel application window and a worksheet window. Ensure that the Windows desktop appears before you begin.

1. Load Excel 2003, referring to the previous lesson if necessary.

2. Excel's application window is best kept maximized to fill the entire screen, as shown in Figure 1.5. As with most Microsoft Windows applications, you use the Windows Title bar icons—Minimize (🗕), Maximize (🗖), Restore (🗗), and Close (❌)—to control the display of a window using the mouse. Figure 1.5 labels some of the components of Excel's application window.

Figure 1.5

Components of Excel's application window

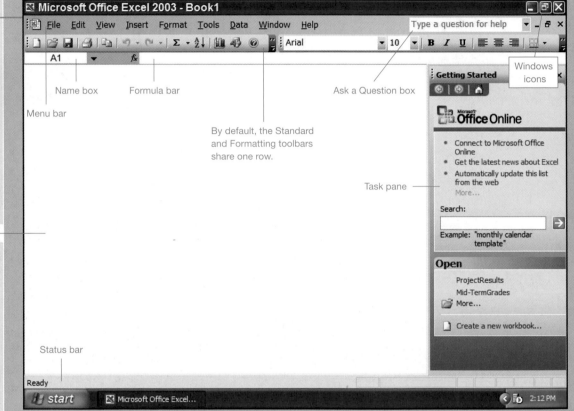

3. Below the Windows icons for the Excel application window, there are additional icons for minimizing, restoring, and closing the worksheet window. To display the worksheet as a window within the work area:
CLICK: its Restore button (🗗)
A worksheet window should now appear in the work area. Figure 1.6 labels the components found in a typical worksheet window.

Figure 1.6

Components of Excel's worksheet window

Cell pointer

Row frame area

Mouse pointer

Worksheet cell

Tab Scrolling arrows

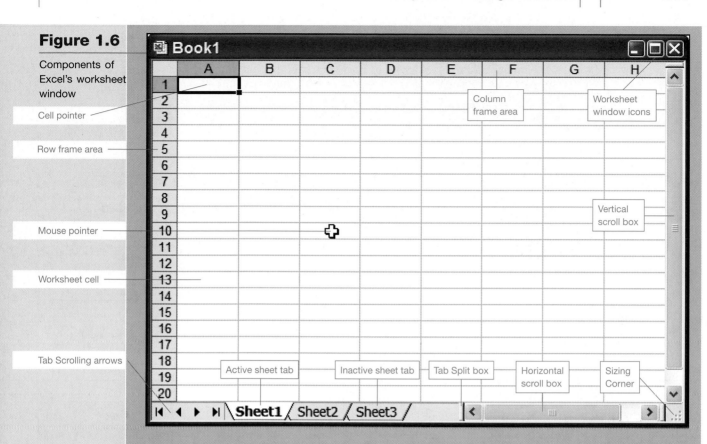

Column frame area

Worksheet window icons

Vertical scroll box

Active sheet tab   Inactive sheet tab   Tab Split box   Horizontal scroll box   Sizing Corner

Sheet1 / Sheet2 / Sheet3

4. Let's return the worksheet window to its maximized state:
CLICK: its Maximize button (□)

5. The Menu bar groups Excel menu commands for easy access. To execute a command, click once on the desired Menu bar option and then click again on the command. (*Note:* Commands that appear dimmed are not available for selection. Commands that are followed by an ellipsis (. . .) will display a dialog box. If a pull-down menu displays a chevron (☒) at the bottom, additional commands are displayed when it is selected.)

To practice using the Menu bar:
CHOOSE: Help
This instruction tells you to click the left mouse button once on the Help option appearing in the Menu bar. The Help menu appears, as shown here. (*Note:* All menu commands that you execute in this guide begin with the instruction "CHOOSE.")

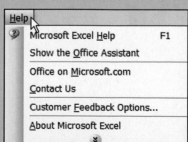

Help

② Microsoft Excel Help   F1
Show the Office Assistant
Office on Microsoft.com
Contact Us
Customer Feedback Options...
About Microsoft Excel
☒

6. To display other pull-down menus, move the mouse to the left over other Menu bar options. As each option is highlighted, a menu appears with its associated commands.

7. To leave the Menu bar without making a command selection:
CLICK: in a blank area of the Title bar
(*Hint:* You can also click in a worksheet cell to leave the Menu bar.)

8. Excel provides context-sensitive *right-click menus* for quick access to relevant menu commands. Rather than searching for the appropriate command in the Menu bar, you can position the mouse pointer on any object, such as a cell, graphic, or toolbar button, and right-click the mouse to display a list of commonly selected commands.

To display a cell's right-click menu:
RIGHT-CLICK: cell A1
The pop-up menu shown in Figure 1.7 should appear.

Figure 1.7

Displaying the right-click menu for a cell

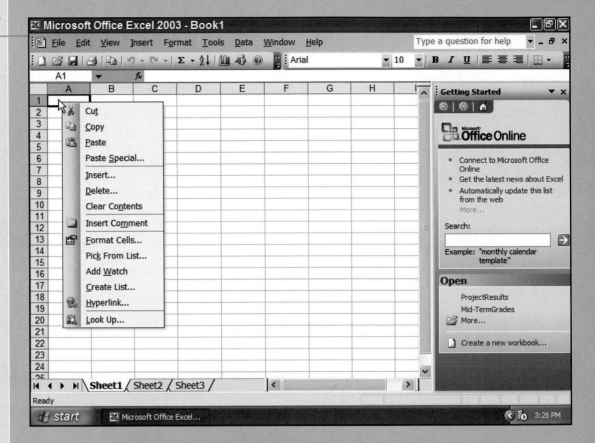

9. To remove the cell's right-click menu from the screen:
PRESS: ESC (or click on an empty portion of the Title bar)

10. If an Office Assistant character appears on your screen, do the following to hide it from view:
RIGHT-CLICK: *the character*
CHOOSE: Hide from the right-click menu
(*Note:* The character's name may appear in the command, such as "Hide Clippit.")

1.1.3 Displaying Menus, Toolbars, and the Task Pane

→ **Feature**

Software programs often become more difficult to learn with the addition of each new command or feature. In an attempt to reduce complexity, Microsoft incorporates **adaptive menus** that display only a subset of the most commonly used commands. Although the menus are shorter and less intimidating, this feature can sometimes frustrate novice users who cannot find desired commands by scanning the menus. Likewise, the Standard and Formatting toolbars share a single row under the Menu bar, displaying only a few of the many buttons available. However, you may find that learning to use Excel 2003 is greatly enhanced when the full menus and toolbars are displayed at all times. Finally, the **task pane** is positioned on the right side of your screen and provides convenient access to relevant commands and options. When you first start Excel 2003, the Getting Started task pane appears automatically, but you can choose to hide (and redisplay) the task pane using the View menu command.

→ **Method**

To disable the adaptive menus feature and display the Standard and Formatting toolbars on separate rows:

- CHOOSE: Tools → Customize
- CLICK: *Options* tab
- SELECT: *Show Standard and Formatting toolbars on two rows* check box
- SELECT: *Always show full menus* check box
- CLICK: Close command button

To display or hide a toolbar:

- CHOOSE: View → Toolbars
- CHOOSE: *a toolbar* from the menu

To display and hide the task pane:

- CHOOSE: View → Task Pane

  or

- CLICK: its Close button (✖)

→ **Practice**

In this lesson, you will disable the adaptive menus feature, display the Standard and Formatting toolbars on separate rows, and toggle the display of the task pane. Ensure that you have completed the previous lesson.

1. To begin, display the Tools menu:
CHOOSE: Tools
You should now see the Tools pull-down menu. (*Hint:* When a desired command does not appear on a menu, you can extend the menu to view all of the available commands by waiting a short period or by clicking on the chevron (☒) at the bottom of the pull-down menu.)

2. Let's turn off the adaptive menus feature and customize the Standard and Formatting toolbars. Do the following:
CHOOSE: Customize from the Tools pull-down menu
CLICK: *Options* tab
The Customize dialog box should now appear (Figure 1.8).

Excel

Figure 1.8

Customize dialog
box: *Options* tab

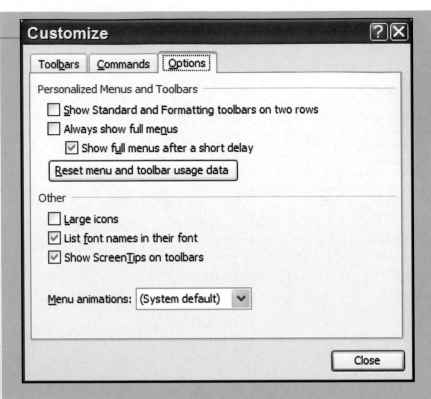

3. On the *Options* tab of the Customize dialog box:
SELECT: *Show Standard and Formatting toolbars on two rows* check box
SELECT: *Always show full menus* check box
(*Note:* An option is activated when its check box is selected, as shown by a check mark (✓)
displayed in the center of the box.)

4. To close the dialog box:
CLICK: Close command button
Figure 1.9 displays the Standard and Formatting toolbars as they should now appear on your
screen. The Standard toolbar provides access to file management and editing commands, as well
as special features such as wizards. The Formatting toolbar lets you access cell formatting commands.

Figure 1.9

Standard toolbar

Formatting
toolbar

5. To hide the task pane:
CHOOSE: View → Task Pane
(*Note:* When a toolbar or the task pane is displayed, a check mark appears beside the option in the pull-down menu, as shown here.)

6. To redisplay the task pane:
CHOOSE: View → Task Pane
Your screen should now appear similar to the one shown in Figure 1.10.

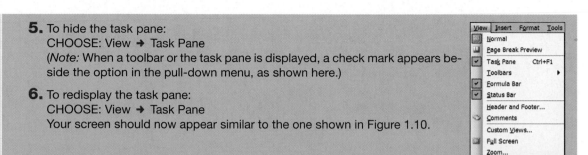

Figure 1.10

Customizing the application window

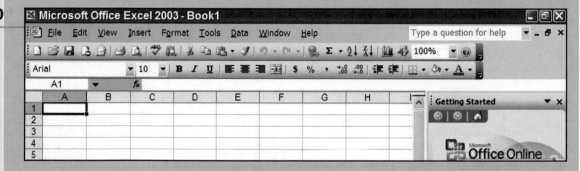

Important: For the remainder of this learning guide, we assume that the adaptive menus feature has been disabled and that the Standard and Formatting toolbars are displayed on separate rows.

In Addition MOVING TOOLBARS

You can move toolbars around the Excel application window using the mouse. A *docked* toolbar appears attached to one of the window's borders. An *undocked* or *floating* toolbar appears in its own window, complete with a Title bar and Close button (⊠). To float a docked toolbar, drag its Move bar (▌) at the left-hand side toward the center of the window. To redock the toolbar, drag its Title bar toward the window's border until it attaches itself automatically.

1.1 How do you turn the adaptive menus feature on or off?

1.2 Creating Your First Worksheet

You create a worksheet by entering text labels, numbers, dates, and formulas into the individual cells. To begin entering data, first move the cell pointer to the desired cell in the worksheet. Then type the information that you want to appear in the cell. Complete the entry by pressing **ENTER** or by moving the cell pointer to another cell. In this module, you will learn how to navigate a worksheet, enter several types of data, and construct a simple formula expression.

1.2.1 Moving the Cell Pointer

→ Feature

The **cell pointer** is the cursor used to select a cell in the worksheet using either the mouse or keyboard. When you first open a new workbook, the *Sheet1* worksheet tab is active and the cell pointer is positioned in cell A1. As you move the cell pointer around the worksheet, Excel displays the current cell address in the **Name Box,** as shown here.

The Name Box displays the currently selected cell address.

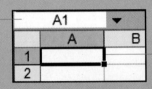

The cell pointer appears as a highlighted border around a cell.

→ Method

Some common keystrokes for navigating a worksheet include:

- **⬆**, **⬇**, **⬅**, and **➡**
- **HOME**, **END**, **PgUp**, and **PgDn**
- **CTRL** + **HOME** to move to cell A1
- **CTRL** + **END** to move to the last cell in the active worksheet area
- **F5** (GoTo) key for moving to a specific cell address

→ Practice

You will now practice moving around an empty worksheet. Ensure that Excel is loaded and a blank worksheet appears.

1. With the cell pointer in cell A1, move to cell D4 using the following keystrokes:
PRESS: **➡** three times
PRESS: **⬇** three times
Notice that the cell address, D4, is displayed in the Name Box and that the column (D) and row (4) headings in the frame area appear highlighted.

2. To move to cell E12 using the mouse:
CLICK: cell E12
(*Hint:* Position the cross mouse pointer (⬤) over cell E12 and click the left mouse button once.)

3. To move to cell E124 using the keyboard:
PRESS: [PgDn] until row 124 is in view

PRESS: [↑] or [↓] to select cell E124

(*Hint:* The [PgUp] and [PgDn] keys are used to move up and down a worksheet by as many rows as fit in the current document window.)

4. To move to cell E24 using the mouse, position the mouse pointer on the vertical scroll box and then drag the scroll box upward to row 24, as shown in Figure 1.11. Then click cell E24 to select the cell.

Figure 1.11

Dragging the
vertical scroll box

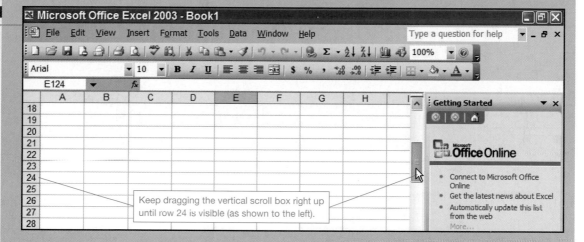

Keep dragging the vertical scroll box right up until row 24 is visible (as shown to the left).

5. To move quickly to a specific cell address, such as cell AE24:
CLICK: once in the Name Box
TYPE: **ae24**
PRESS: [ENTER]

The cell pointer moves to cell AE24. (*Hint:* Because cell addresses are not case sensitive, you need not use capital letters when typing a cell address.)

6. To move the cell pointer in any direction until the cell contents change from empty to filled, from filled to empty, or until a border is encountered, press [CTRL] with an arrow key. For example:
PRESS: [CTRL]+[→] to move to column IV
PRESS: [CTRL]+[↓] to move to row 65536

The cell pointer now appears in the bottom right-hand corner of the worksheet. Notice, also, that "IV65536" appears in the Name Box.

7. To move back to cell A1:
PRESS: [CTRL]+[HOME]

1.2.2 Entering Text

→ **Feature**

Text labels are the titles, headings, and other descriptive information that you place in a worksheet to give it meaning and enhance its readability. Although a typical worksheet column displays fewer than nine characters, a single cell can store thousands of words. With longer entries, the text simply spills over the column border into the next cell, if it is empty. If the adjacent cell is not empty, the text will be truncated at its right border. Fortunately, you can also increase the cell's display or column width to view more of its information.

→ ## Method

To enter text into the selected cell:

- TYPE: **your text**
- PRESS: **ENTER**

→ ## Practice

In this lesson, you will create a worksheet by specifying text labels for the row and column headings.

1. Ensure that the cell pointer is positioned in cell A1 of the *Sheet1* worksheet.

2. Let's begin the worksheet by entering a title. As you type the following entry, watch the Formula bar:
TYPE: **Income Statement**
Your screen should appear similar to the one shown in Figure 1.12.

Figure 1.12

Typing text into the Formula bar

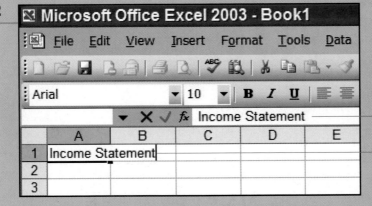

Your entry appears in the Formula bar as you type.

The cursor or insertion point shows where the next character typed will appear.

3. To enter the text into the cell, you press **ENTER** or click the Enter button (☑) in the Formula bar. To cancel an entry, you press **ESC** or click the Cancel (☒) button. Let's accept the entry:
PRESS: **ENTER**
Notice that the text entry is longer than the column's width and must spill over into column B. This is acceptable as long as you do not place anything in cell B1. You may also increase the width of column A.

After you press **ENTER**, the cell pointer moves down to the next row. If your pointer remains in cell A1, change this behavior using the Tools, Options command from the Menu bar. In the Options dialog box, click the *Edit* tab and ensure that the *Move selection after Enter* check box is selected with "Down" as the *Direction*, as shown in Figure 1.13.

Figure 1.13

Options dialog box: *Edit* tab

Select these options to change the behavior of the cell pointer after pressing the Enter key.

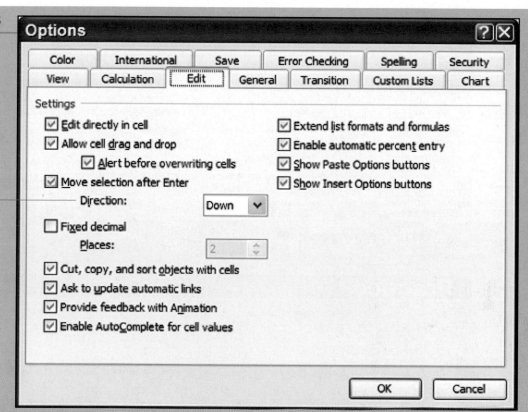

4. Move the cell pointer to cell B3.

5. Enter the following text label:
TYPE: **Revenue**
PRESS: ⬇
Notice that pressing ⬇ has the same result as pressing **ENTER**.

6. To finish entering the row labels:
TYPE: **Expenses**
PRESS: ⬇
TYPE: **Profit**
PRESS: **ENTER**
All of the textual information is now entered into the worksheet, as shown in Figure 1.14.

Figure 1.14

Entering text into a worksheet

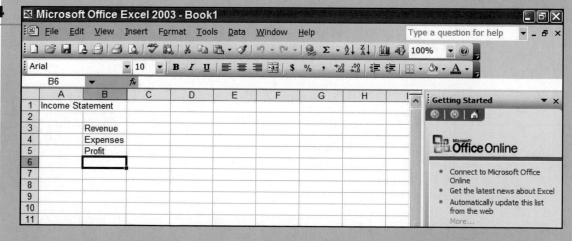

1.2.3 Entering Dates

→ # Feature

Date values are often used in worksheets as column headings, but they also appear in row entries such as invoice transactions and purchase orders. You enter date values into a cell using one of the common date formats recognized by Excel, such as mm/dd/yy (3/31/04) or dd-mmm-yy (31-Mar-04). Excel treats a date (or time) as a formatted number or value. Consequently, you can use date values to perform arithmetic calculations, such as finding out how many days have elapsed between two calendar dates.

→ # Method

To enter a date value into the selected cell:

- TYPE: *a date,* such as **3/31/04**
- PRESS: ENTER

→ # Practice

You will now add date values into your worksheet as column headings. Ensure that you have completed the previous lesson.

1. Move to cell C2.

2. To enter a month and year combination as a date value, you can use the format mmm-yyyy. For example:
TYPE: **Mar-2004**
PRESS: ➡
Excel reformats the value to appear as "Mar-04." Why wouldn't you type "Mar-04" in the first place? The answer is that Excel must make certain assumptions about your entries. If you type "Mar-04," Excel assumes that you want March 4 of the current year, which may or may not be 2004. By entering a year value using all four digits, you avoid having Excel misinterpret your entry.

3. Starting in cell D2, do the following:
TYPE: **Apr-2004**
PRESS: ➡
TYPE: **May-2004**
PRESS: ➡
TYPE: **Jun-2004**
PRESS: ENTER

4. Move the cell pointer to cell C2 and compare your work with the worksheet shown in Figure 1.15. Looking in the Formula bar, notice that the date entry reads "3/1/2004" and not "Mar-04." As illustrated by this example, a cell's appearance on the worksheet can differ from its actual contents.

Figure 1.15

Entering date values into a worksheet

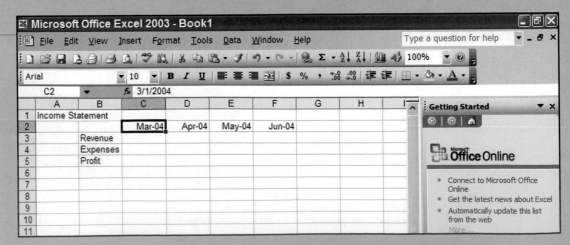

1.2.4 Entering Numbers

→ ## Feature

Numbers are entered into a worksheet for use in performing calculations, preparing reports, and creating charts. You can enter a raw or unformatted number, such as 3.141593, or a formatted number, such as 37.5% or $24,732.33. It is important to note that phone numbers, Social Security numbers, and zip codes are not treated as numeric values, because they are never used in performing mathematical calculations. Numbers and dates are right-aligned in a cell, as opposed to text, which aligns with the left border of a cell.

→ ## Method

To enter a number into the selected cell:

- TYPE: *a number,* such as **$9,987.65** or **12.345%**
- PRESS: **ENTER**

→ ## Practice

You will now add some numbers to the worksheet. Ensure that you have completed the previous lesson.

1. Move to cell C3.

2. To enter a value for March's revenue, do the following:
TYPE: **112,500**
PRESS: **→**
Notice that you placed a comma (,) in the entry to separate the thousands from the hundreds. Excel recognizes symbols such as commas, dollar signs, and percentage symbols as numeric formatting.

3. Starting in cell D3, do the following:
TYPE: **115,800**
PRESS: **→**
TYPE: **98,750**
PRESS: **→**
TYPE: **112,830**
PRESS: **ENTER**

4. Move the cell pointer to cell C3 and compare your work with the worksheet shown in Figure 1.16. Notice that the Formula bar reads "112500" without a comma separating the thousands. Similar to date values, numeric values may be formatted to display differently than the actual value stored.

Figure 1.16

Entering numbers into a worksheet

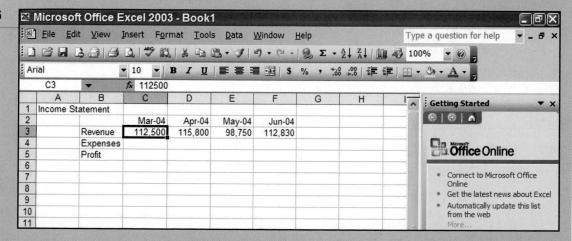

1.2.5 Entering Formulas

→ **Feature**

You use formulas to perform calculations, such as adding a column of numbers or calculating a mortgage payment. A **formula** is an expression, containing numbers, cell references, and/or mathematical operators, that is entered into a cell to display a calculated result. The basic mathematical operators ("+" for addition, "−" for subtraction, "/" for division, and "*" for multiplication) and rules of precedence from your high school algebra textbook also apply to an Excel formula. As a refresher, Excel calculates what appears in parentheses first, exponents second, multiplication and division operations (from left to right) third, and addition and subtraction (again from left to right) last.

→ **Method**

To enter a formula into the selected cell:

- TYPE: = (an equal sign)

- TYPE: *a formula*, such as **a4+b4**

- PRESS: [ENTER]

→ **Practice**

You will now enter formulas into the Income Statement worksheet. Ensure that you have completed the previous lesson.

1. Move to cell C4. Notice that the first step in entering a formula is to move to the cell where you want the result to display.

2. To tell Excel that what follows is a formula, first type an equal sign:
   TYPE: =

3. In order to calculate March's expenses, you will now multiply the cell containing the monthly revenue (cell C3) by 60%. Do the following:
   TYPE: **c3*60%**
   Your screen should appear similar to the worksheet shown in Figure 1.17. Notice that the formula's cell address is color-coded and that this coding corresponds to the cell borders highlighted in the worksheet. This feature, called **Range Finder,** is especially useful when you need to identify whether a calculation is drawing data from the correct cells.

Figure 1.17

Typing a formula expression into the Formula bar

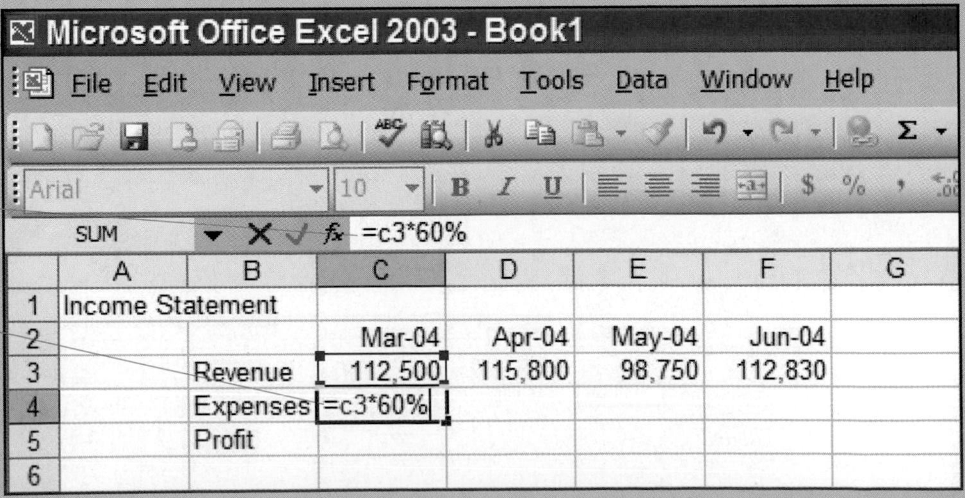

The expression is built in the Formula bar.

Notice that the blue-highlighted cell address "c3" in the formula expression corresponds with the cell outline immediately above.

	A	B	C	D	E	F	G
1	Income Statement						
2			Mar-04	Apr-04	May-04	Jun-04	
3		Revenue	112,500	115,800	98,750	112,830	
4		Expenses	=c3*60%				
5		Profit					
6							

4. To complete the entry and move to the next cell:
PRESS: ➡
The result, 67500, appears in the cell.

5. Let's use a method called *pointing* to enter the formula into cell D4. With pointing, you use the mouse or keyboard to point to the cell reference that you want to include in an expression. To illustrate:
TYPE: =
PRESS: ⬆
Notice that a dashed marquee appears around cell D3 and that the value "D3" appears in the Formula bar.

6. To finish entering the formula:
TYPE: *60%
PRESS: ➡
The result, 69480, appears in the cell.

7. For May's calculation, use the mouse to point to the desired cell reference. Do the following:
TYPE: =
CLICK: cell E3
Notice that a dashed marquee surrounds cell E3 to denote its selection.

8. To complete the formula:
TYPE: *60%
PRESS: ➡
The result, 59250, appears.

9. Last, enter the formula for December by typing:
TYPE: =f3*.6
PRESS: ENTER
The result, 67698, appears in cell F4. Notice that the value .6 may be used instead of 60% to yield the same result. Your worksheet should now appear similar to the one shown in Figure 1.18.

Figure 1.18

Entering formulas into a worksheet

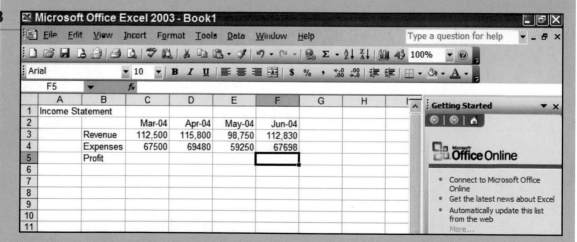

10. To finish the worksheet:
SELECT: cell C5

11. You will now enter a formula to calculate the profit by subtracting expenses from revenues for each month. Do the following:
TYPE: **=c3–c4**
Notice that "c3" appears in blue and "c4" appears in green, as shown below.

	A	B	C
1	Income Statement		
2			Mar-04
3		Revenue	112,500
4		Expenses	67500
5		Profit	=c3-c4
6			

> Excel's color-coding of cell references in a formula makes it easier to spot potential errors.

12. On your own, enter formulas into cells D5, E5, and F5 using both the typing and pointing methods. (*Hint:* In the next chapter, you will learn easier methods for entering multiple formulas into your worksheet.) When completed, your worksheet should appear similar to the one shown in Figure 1.19.

Figure 1.19

Completing the worksheet

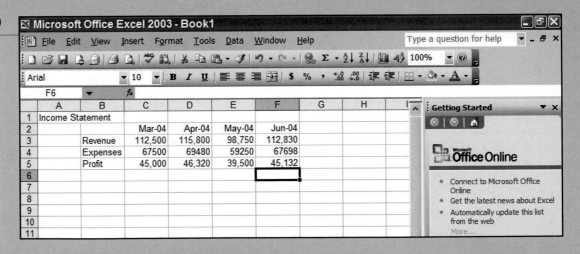

13. To illustrate the power of an electronic worksheet, let's change a cell's value and watch all the formulas that reference that cell recalculate their results automatically. Do the following:
SELECT: cell F3
TYPE: **100,000**
PRESS: **ENTER**
Notice that the Expense calculation for Jun-04 (cell F4) is immediately updated to 60000 and the Profit cell now displays 40,000.

14. To conclude the module, you will close the worksheet without saving the changes. (*Note:* You will learn how to save a worksheet later in this chapter.) From the Menu bar:
CHOOSE: File → Close
The following dialog box appears.

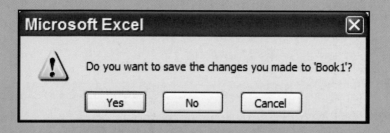

15. CLICK: No command button
There should be no workbooks open in the application window.

In Addition REFERENCING CELLS IN A FORMULA

Two types of cell addresses (also called *cell references*) can be entered into formulas: *relative* and *absolute.* A relative cell address, such as B4, is one that is relative in position to other cells on the worksheet. When copied within a formula to the next column, for example, the relative cell address "B4" adjusts automatically to become "C4." An absolute cell address, on the other hand, refers to a specific cell in the worksheet and does not adjust when copied. Absolute cell addresses contain dollar signs, such as $B$4. It is important to note that Excel defaults to using relative cell addresses in formulas. Relative and absolute cell referencing is covered in Chapter 4.

1.2 Explain why a phone number is not considered a numeric value in an Excel worksheet.

1.3 Editing the Worksheet

What if you type a label, a number, or a formula into a cell and then decide it needs to be changed? Novices and experts alike make data entry errors when creating a worksheet. Fortunately, Excel provides several features for editing information that has already been entered. In this module, you will learn how to modify existing cell entries, erase the contents of a cell, and undo a command or typing error.

1.3.1 Editing a Cell's Contents

→ **Feature**

You can edit information either as you type or after you have entered data into a cell. Your ability to edit a worksheet effectively is an extremely valuable skill. In many occupations and businesses, you will be asked to modify and maintain existing worksheets, rather than create new ones from scratch. Indeed, most worksheets are prepared by revising standard or template-generated worksheets with up-to-date information. To this end, the editing methods presented in this lesson will benefit you as a relatively new user of Excel.

→ **Method**

To edit cell contents:

- To edit data as you type, press **BACKSPACE** and then correct the typographical error or spelling mistake.

- To replace a cell's contents entirely, select the cell and then type over the original data. When you press **ENTER** or select another cell, the new information overwrites the existing data.

- To edit a cell in which the text is too long or complicated to retype, double-click the cell to perform **in-cell editing.** In this mode, the flashing insertion point appears ready for editing inside the cell. Alternatively, you can press the **F2** (Edit) key or click in the Formula bar to enter Edit Mode, in which you edit the cell's contents in the Formula bar. Regardless, once the insertion point appears, you perform your edits using the arrow keys, **DELETE**, and **BACKSPACE**.

→ **Practice**

In this lesson, you will create a simple inventory worksheet and then practice modifying the data stored in the worksheet cells. Ensure that no workbooks are open in the application window.

1. To display a new workbook and worksheet:
   CLICK: New button (⬜) on the Standard toolbar
   A new workbook, entitled "Book2," appears in the document area and the task pane is hidden. (*Note:* As an alternative to using the toolbar, you can start a new workbook by clicking the *Create a new workbook* option under the *Open* heading in the Getting Started task pane.)

2. SELECT: cell A1, if it is not already selected
   Your screen should appear similar to the one shown in Figure 1.20. (*Note:* For the remainder of this guide, you may use either the keyboard or mouse to move the cell pointer.)

Figure 1.20

Displaying a new workbook

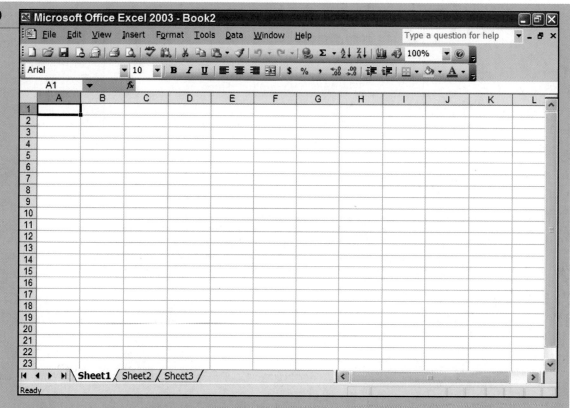

3. Let's enter a title for this worksheet:
TYPE: **Otaga's Food Warehouse**
PRESS: ⊙
TYPE: **Inventory List**
PRESS: (ENTER)

4. SELECT: cell A4

5. Now let's add some column headings:
TYPE: **Code**
PRESS: ➡
TYPE: **Product**
PRESS: ➡
TYPE: **Quantity**
PRESS: ➡
TYPE: **Price**
PRESS: (ENTER)

6. On your own, complete the worksheet as displayed in Figure 1.21. If you make a typing error, use (BACKSPACE) to correct your mistake prior to pressing (ENTER) or an arrow key.

Figure 1.21

Creating an inventory worksheet

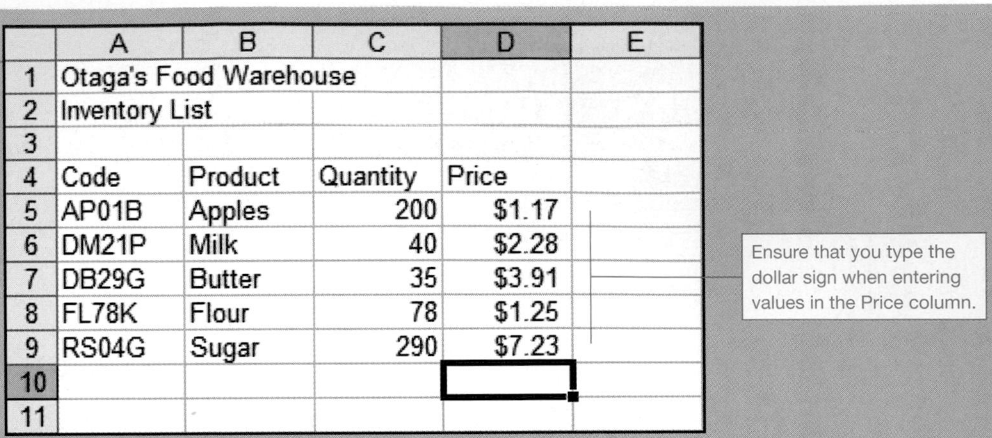

	A	B	C	D	E
1	Otaga's Food Warehouse				
2	Inventory List				
3					
4	Code	Product	Quantity	Price	
5	AP01B	Apples	200	$1.17	
6	DM21P	Milk	40	$2.28	
7	DB29G	Butter	35	$3.91	
8	FL78K	Flour	78	$1.25	
9	RS04G	Sugar	290	$7.23	
10					
11					

> Ensure that you type the dollar sign when entering values in the Price column.

7. To begin editing this worksheet, let's change the column heading in cell D4 to read "Cost" instead of "Price." To replace the existing entry:
SELECT: cell D4

8. TYPE: **Cost**
PRESS: **ENTER**
Notice that the new entry overwrites the existing cell contents. (*Hint:* If you start typing an entry in the wrong cell, you can press **ESC** to exit Edit mode and restore the previous value.)

9. You activate in-cell editing by double-clicking a cell. To practice, let's change the quantity of butter from 35 to 350 packages:
DOUBLE-CLICK: cell C7
Notice that the Status bar now reads "Edit" in the bottom left-hand corner, instead of the word "Ready." A flashing insertion point also appears inside the cell, as shown in Figure 1.22.

Figure 1.22

Performing in-cell editing

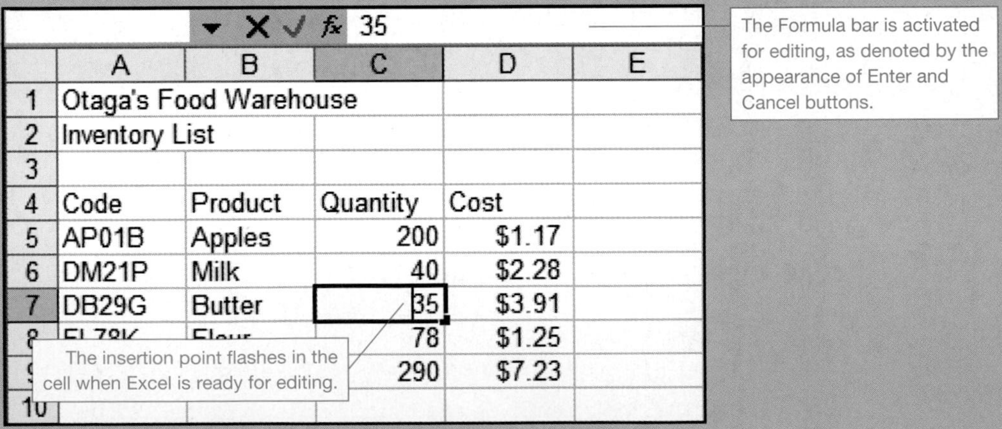

▼ ✕ ✓ *fx* 35

	A	B	C	D	E
1	Otaga's Food Warehouse				
2	Inventory List				
3					
4	Code	Product	Quantity	Cost	
5	AP01B	Apples	200	$1.17	
6	DM21P	Milk	40	$2.28	
7	DB29G	Butter	35	$3.91	
8	FL78K	Flour	78	$1.25	
9			290	$7.23	
10					

> The Formula bar is activated for editing, as denoted by the appearance of Enter and Cancel buttons.

> The insertion point flashes in the cell when Excel is ready for editing.

10. To add a "0" to the end of the cell's contents:
PRESS: [END] to move the insertion point to the far right
TYPE: **0**
PRESS: [ENTER]
Notice that the Status bar once again reads "Ready" in the bottom left-hand corner.

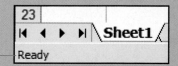

The current mode is displayed on the Status bar.

11. You can also activate Edit Mode by pressing the [F2] (Edit) key or by clicking the I-beam mouse pointer inside the Formula bar. In this step, you edit one of the product codes. Do the following:
SELECT: cell A6
Notice that the text "DM21P" appears in the Formula bar.

12. To modify "DM" to read "DN," position the I-beam mouse pointer over the Formula bar entry, immediately to the left of the letter "M." Click the left mouse button and drag the mouse pointer to the right until the "M" is highlighted, as shown in Figure 1.23.

Figure 1.23

Editing an entry in the Formula bar

	A6	▼ X ✓ fx	D**M**21P	
	A	B	Formula Bar D	E
1	Otaga's Food Warehouse			
2	Inventory List			
3				
4	Code	Product	Quantity	Cost
5	AP01B	Apples	200	$1.17
6	DM21P	Milk	40	$2.28
7	DB29G	Butter	350	$3.91
8	FL78K	Flour	78	$1.25
9	RS04G	Sugar	290	$7.23
10				
11				

Drag the I-beam mouse pointer form left to right over the letter "M."

13. Now that the desired letter is selected:
TYPE: **N**
PRESS: [ENTER]
The letter "N" replaces the selected letter in the Formula bar and cell.

1.3.2 Selecting and Erasing Cell Contents

→ **Feature**

You can quickly erase a single cell, a group of cells, or the entire worksheet with a few simple keystrokes. To erase the selected cell's contents, simply press the [DELETE] key. To erase the contents of more than one cell, use the mouse to drag over the desired area or cell range prior to pressing [DELETE]. Besides a cell's contents, you can delete specific characteristics of a cell, such as its formatting or attached comments. A **comment** is a special floating text box that you can attach to a worksheet cell. To display its text, you move the mouse pointer over the small red indicator that will appear in the upper right-hand corner of a cell containing a comment.

→ **Method**

To erase the contents of a cell or group of cells:

• SELECT: the cell or cell range

• PRESS: [DELETE]

To remove a cell's contents and/or its attributes:

• CHOOSE: Edit → Clear → *command*

• The *command* options include:

All	Removes the cell contents and other attributes
Formats	Removes the cell formatting only
Contents	Removes the cell contents only ([DELETE])
Comments	Removes the cell comments only

→ **Practice**

You will now practice erasing information that is stored in the inventory worksheet. Ensure that you have completed the previous lesson.

1. SELECT: cell A2

2. To delete the subtitle:
PRESS: [DELETE]
Notice that you need not press [ENTER] or any other confirmation key. Pressing [DELETE] removes the contents of the cell immediately.

3. SELECT: cell A9

4. In order to delete more than one cell at a time, you first select the desired range of cells. In this step, you will select the cells from A9 to D9. Do the following:
PRESS: [SHIFT] and hold it down
CLICK: cell D9
RELEASE: [SHIFT]
The four cells should now appear highlighted, as shown in Figure 1.24.

Figure 1.24

Selecting a group of cells to erase

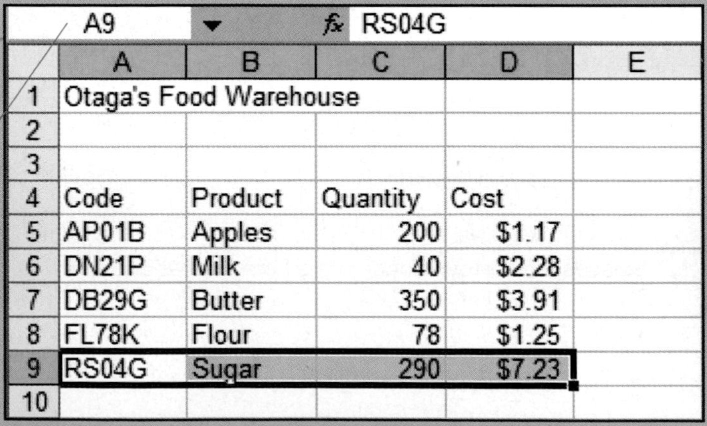

The Name box shows that the active cell is A9, displayed with a white background in the highlighted selection.

A9	▼	*fx* RS04G		
	A	**B**	**C**	**D**	**E**
1	Otaga's Food Warehouse				
2					
3					
4	Code	Product	Quantity	Cost	
5	AP01B	Apples	200	$1.17	
6	DN21P	Milk	40	$2.28	
7	DB29G	Butter	350	$3.91	
8	FL78K	Flour	78	$1.25	
9	RS04G	Sugar	290	$7.23	
10					

5. To erase all of the cell information, including contents and formatting:
CHOOSE: Edit → Clear → All
All of the entries in the selected cell range are deleted from the worksheet.

6. To erase the dollar values in the Cost column:
CLICK: cell D5 and keep the mouse button pressed down
DRAG: the mouse pointer downward to cell D8
Your screen should now appear similar to the one shown in Figure 1.25.

Figure 1.25

Selecting cells using the mouse

The Name box shows that four rows (4R) and one column (1C) are currently selected in the worksheet.

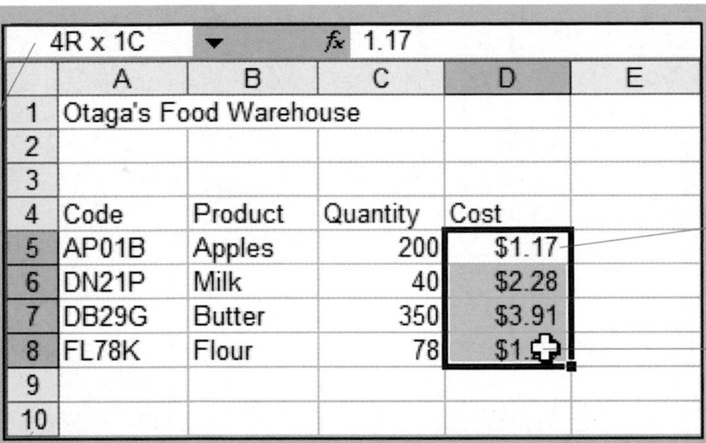

4R x 1C ▼			*fx* 1.17	
	A	B	C	D	E
1	Otaga's Food Warehouse				
2					
3					
4	Code	Product	Quantity	Cost	
5	AP01B	Apples	200	$1.17	
6	DN21P	Milk	40	$2.28	
7	DB29G	Butter	350	$3.91	
8	FL78K	Flour	78	$1.5	
9					
10					

The active cell in this selection is D5, the first selected cell.

After clicking cell D5, keep the mouse button depressed and drag the mouse pointer down to cell D8. Once the desired cells are highlighted, you may release the mouse button.

7. Release the mouse button when the cells are highlighted.

8. PRESS: `DELETE` to remove the contents of the cell range

9. PRESS: `CTRL` + `HOME` to move the cell pointer to cell A1

1.3.3 Using Undo and Redo

→ Feature

The **Undo command** allows you to cancel up to your last 16 actions. The command is most useful for immediately reversing a command or modification that was mistakenly performed. If an error occurred several steps before, you can continue "undoing" commands until you return the worksheet to its original state prior to the mistake. Although it sounds somewhat confusing, you can use the Redo command to undo an Undo command. The **Redo command** allows you to reverse an Undo command that you performed accidentally.

→ Method

To reverse an action or command:

- CLICK: Undo button (🔄▾)

    or

- CHOOSE: Edit → Undo

    or

- PRESS: `CTRL` + z

To reverse an Undo command:

- CLICK: Redo button (↻▾)

    or

- CHOOSE: Edit → Redo

Excel

→ **Practice**

Let's practice reversing some editing mistakes using the Undo command. Ensure that you have completed the previous lesson.

1. SELECT: cell A5
Your worksheet should appear similar to the one shown in Figure 1.26.

Figure 1.26

Selecting cell A5

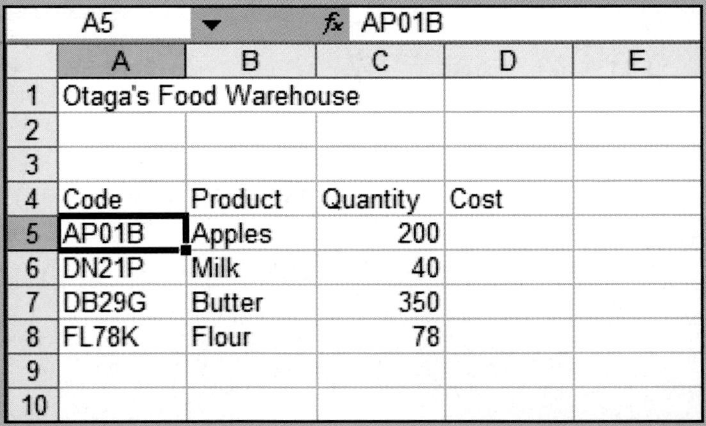

	A5	▼	f_x	AP01B	
	A	**B**	**C**	**D**	**E**
1	Otaga's Food Warehouse				
2					
3					
4	Code	Product	Quantity	Cost	
5	AP01B	Apples	200		
6	DN21P	Milk	40		
7	DB29G	Butter	350		
8	FL78K	Flour	78		
9					
10					

2. In order to practice using the Undo command, let's delete the contents of the cell:
PRESS: DELETE

3. To undo the last command or action performed:
CLICK: Undo button (⤺▾) on the Standard toolbar
(*Caution: The tip of the mouse pointer should be placed over the curved arrow and not on the attached down arrow.*)

4. SELECT: cell C5

5. To modify the quantity of apples:
TYPE: **175**
PRESS: ENTER

6. To undo the last entry using a keyboard shortcut:
PRESS: CTRL + z
The value 175 is replaced with 200 in cell C5. (*Hint: This shortcut keystroke is useful for quickly undoing a command or incorrect entry.*)

7. Now let's make two modifications to the worksheet:
SELECT: cell B5
TYPE: **Oranges**
PRESS: ⬇
TYPE: **Juice**
PRESS: ENTER

8. Let's view the history that Excel has been tracking for the Undo command. To begin, position the mouse pointer over the down arrow attached to the Undo button (⤺▾) on the Standard toolbar. Then click the down arrow once to display the drop-down list of "undoable" or reversible commands, as shown in Figure 1.27.

Figure 1.27

Displaying
reversible
commands

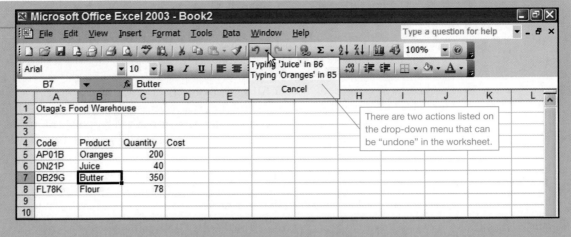

There are two actions listed on the drop-down menu that can be "undone" in the worksheet.

9. Move the mouse pointer slowly downward to select the two entries, as shown here.

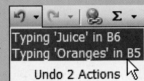

10. To perform the Undo operation, ensure that both items are highlighted and then do the following:
CLICK: "Typing 'Oranges' in B5" Undo option
(*Hint:* To remove the Undo drop-down menu, click the Title bar or the button's attached down arrow again.)

11. To conclude this module, close the worksheet without saving the changes. Do the following:
CHOOSE: File → Close

12. When the dialog box appears:
CLICK: No command button

 **SelfCheck**   **1.3** Why is worksheet editing such a valuable skill?

1.4 Managing Your Files

Managing the workbook files that you create is an important skill. The workbook you are using exists only in the computer's RAM (random access memory), which is highly volatile. If the power to your computer goes off, any changes that you have made to the workbook are lost. For this reason, you need to save your workbook permanently to the local hard disk, a network drive, or a removable disk. Creating, saving, opening, and closing workbooks are considered file management operations.

Saving your work to a named file on a disk is similar to placing it into a filing cabinet. For important workbooks (ones that you cannot risk losing), you should save your work every 15 minutes, or whenever you are interrupted, to protect against an unexpected power outage or other catastrophe. Saving a file without closing it is like placing a current copy in a filing cabinet. When naming workbook files, you can use up to 255 characters, including spaces, but it is wise to keep the length under 20 characters. You cannot, however, use the following characters or symbols:

$$\backslash \ / \ : \ ; \ * \ ? \ " < > |$$

In this module, you will practice creating a new workbook, saving and closing workbooks, creating workbook folders, and opening existing workbooks.

*Important: In this guide, we refer to the files that have been created for you as the **student data files**. Depending on your computer or lab setup, these files may be located on a removable diskette, in a folder on your hard disk, or on a network server. If necessary, ask your instructor or lab assistant where to find these data files. To download the Advantage Series' student data files from the Internet, visit our Web site at:*

http://www.advantageseries.com

You will also need to identify a storage location, such as a removable disk or hard-drive subdirectory, for the files that you create, modify, and save.

1.4.1 Beginning a New Workbook

→ Feature

There are three ways to create a new workbook. First, you can start with a blank workbook and enter all of the data from scratch. This is the method that you have used in the previous lessons. Next, you can select a workbook **template** that provides preexisting data and design elements. A template is a timesaving utility that promotes consistency in both design and function. Lastly, you can employ a **wizard** to help lead you step-by-step through the creation of a particular type of workbook.

→ Method

To display a new blank workbook:

• CLICK: New button (🗋)

To begin a workbook using a template or wizard:

• CHOOSE: File → New

→ **Practice**

In this example, you will use a workbook template to create a new workbook for an invoicing application. Ensure that no workbooks are displayed in the application window.

1. To create a workbook using a template, first display the New Workbook task pane:
CHOOSE: File → New
The New Workbook task pane appears, as shown here.

2. Using the hand mouse pointer (🖑):
CLICK: "On my computer. . ." under the *Templates* heading

3. The blank Workbook template icon appears on the *General* tab of the Templates dialog box. Excel uses this template when you click the New button (🗋) on the Standard toolbar. To view the custom templates that are shipped with Excel and stored locally on your computer, do the following:
CLICK: *Spreadsheet Solutions* tab
Your screen should now appear similar to the one shown in Figure 1.28. (*Note:* Depending on how Excel was installed and configured on your system, different template options may appear in your dialog box.)

Figure 1.28

Displaying solutions in the Templates dialog box

When you choose the "Complete Install" option during setup, Excel 2003 provides the *General* and *Spreadsheet Solutions* tabs for organizing your workbook templates.

4. To create a new workbook based on the Sales Invoice template:
DOUBLE-CLICK: Sales Invoice template icon ( )
(*Note:* If you or your lab administrator has not installed the workbook templates, you must skip to step 6.)

5. Excel loads the template and displays the workbook shown in Figure 1.29. Scan the contents of the worksheet using the horizontal and vertical scroll bars. If the selected template cannot be found, Excel attempts to locate and install it. (*Note:* A dialog box may appear warning that the template may contain a **macro virus.** A virus is a hostile program that is secretly stored and shipped inside another program or document. As this template is from Microsoft and not from an unknown source, you can safely enable the macros.)

Figure 1.29

New workbook based on the Sales Invoice template

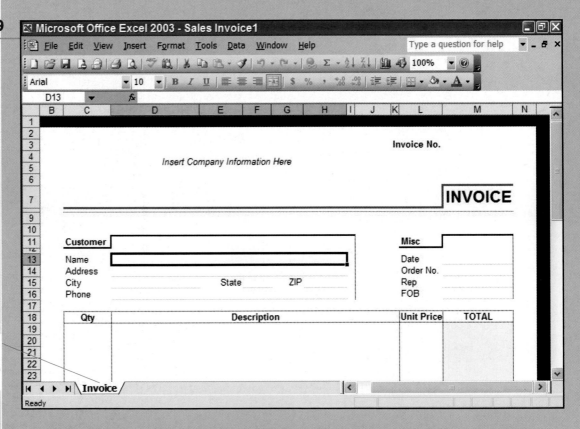

The Sales Invoice template contains a single worksheet tab named "Invoice."

6. The workbook templates provided by Excel contain many advanced features. Rather than introducing these features now, let's close the workbook and continue our discussion of file management:
CHOOSE: File → Close
CLICK: No command button, if asked whether to save the changes

In Addition ACCESSING OTHER WORKBOOK TEMPLATES

Besides the templates that ship with the Microsoft Office System, additional templates are available for free on the Internet. In the New Workbook task pane are two options that you may use to download such templates. First, the *On My Web sites* . . . option lets you retrieve workbook templates stored on Web servers around the world. This option is especially useful for retrieving shared templates from a company intranet. Second, the *Templates home page* option launches a Microsoft Web page dedicated to providing support and content for Microsoft Office users. Before creating a new workbook from scratch, you can peruse these templates to search for a possible starting point.

1.4.2 Saving and Closing

→ Feature

Many options are available for saving a workbook to a permanent storage location. The File, Save command and the Save button (🖫) on the toolbar allow you to overwrite an existing disk file with the latest version of a workbook. The File, Save As command enables you to save a workbook to a new filename or storage location. You can also specify a different file format for the workbook, such as an earlier version of Excel, using the Save As command. This is especially handy when you need to share a workbook with associates who haven't upgraded to the latest version. Once you have finished using a workbook, make sure you close the file to free up valuable system resources (RAM) in your computer.

→ Method

To save a workbook:

- CLICK: Save button (🖫)

  or

- CHOOSE: File → Save

  or

- CHOOSE: File → Save As

To close a workbook:

- CLICK: its Close button (✕)

  or

- CHOOSE: File → Close

→ Practice

You will now practice saving and closing a workbook. Identify a storage location for your personal workbook files. If you want to use a diskette or other removable storage medium, insert the media into the drive now.

1. To create a new workbook from scratch:
CLICK: New button (🗋)
TYPE: **My First Workbook** into cell A1
PRESS: ENTER

2. To save the new workbook:
CLICK: Save button (🖫)
(*Note:* If the current workbook has not yet been saved, Excel displays the Save As dialog box regardless of the method you chose to save the file. The filenames and folder directories that appear in your Save As dialog box will differ from those shown in Figure 1.30.)

Excel

Figure 1.30

Save As dialog box

Lists the files that you have most recently worked with

Lists common desktop shortcuts

Excel's default working folder for storing files

Provides access to the resources on your computer

Lists files and folders stored on your intranet or Internet Web server

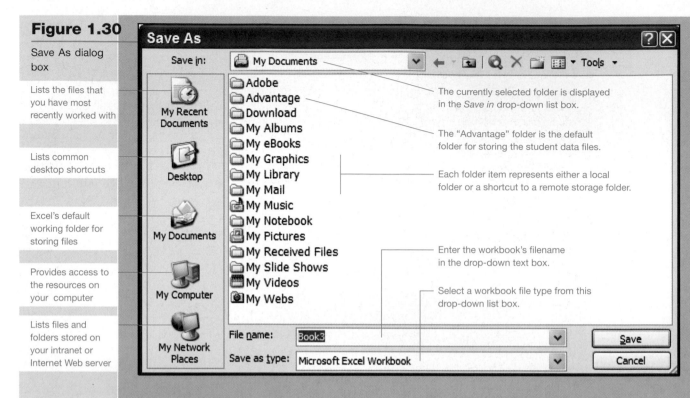

The currently selected folder is displayed in the *Save in* drop-down list box.

The "Advantage" folder is the default folder for storing the student data files.

Each folder item represents either a local folder or a shortcut to a remote storage folder.

Enter the workbook's filename in the drop-down text box.

Select a workbook file type from this drop-down list box.

3. The **Places bar,** located along the left border of the dialog box, provides convenient access to commonly used storage locations. To illustrate, let's view the resources available on your computer:
CLICK: My Computer button in the Places bar

4. Now let's display the available resources using the *Save in* drop-down list box. Do the following:
CLICK: down arrow attached to the *Save in* drop-down list box
Your screen will appear similar, but not identical, to the one shown in Figure 1.31.

Figure 1.31

Navigating the storage areas using the *Save in* drop-down list box

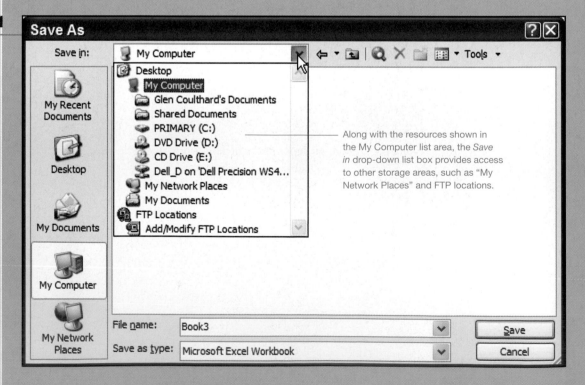

Along with the resources shown in the My Computer list area, the *Save in* drop-down list box provides access to other storage areas, such as "My Network Places" and FTP locations.

5. To browse the local hard drive:
SELECT: your local hard disk, usually labeled (C:)
The list area displays the folders and files stored in the root directory of your local hard disk.

6. To drill down and display the contents of a particular folder:
DOUBLE-CLICK: Program Files folder
This folder acts as a container for your application program folders and files. Figure 1.32 shows how full this folder can become.

Figure 1.32

The Program Files folder of the author's hard drive (C:)

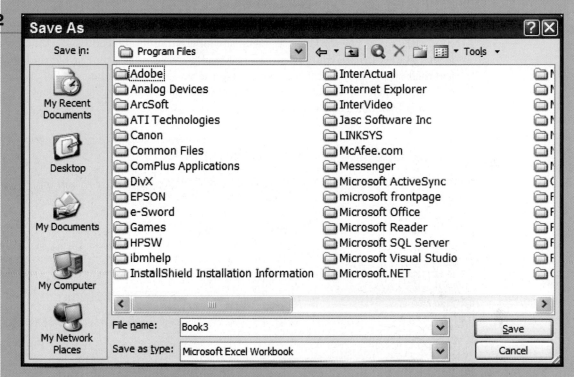

7. To return to the previous display:
CLICK: Back button (⬅ ▾) in the dialog box

8. Now, using either the Places bar or the *Save in* drop-down list box:
SELECT: *a storage location for your personal workbook files*
(*Note:* In this guide, we save files either to the My Documents folder or to a new folder you will create in lesson 1.4.4. However, your instructor or lab assistant may request that you save your workbook files to a removable disk or to a specified directory for your class work.)

9. Let's give the workbook file a unique name. Position the I-beam mouse pointer over the workbook name in the *File name* text box and then:
DOUBLE-CLICK: the *workbook name,* "Book3" in this example
The entire workbook name should appear highlighted.

10. To type over and replace the existing workbook name:
TYPE: **My First Workbook** as shown below

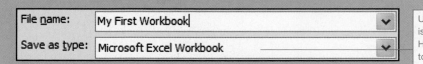

Using the default file type is recommended. However, you can choose to save a workbook in a different file format using this drop-down list box.

11. To complete the procedure:
CLICK: Save command button
When you are returned to the worksheet, notice that the workbook's name now appears in the Title bar.

12. Let's close the workbook:
CHOOSE: File → Close

There are times when you will need to save an existing workbook under a different filename. For example, you may want to create a backup copy or different version of the same workbook on your disk. You may instead want to use one workbook as a template for creating future workbooks that are similar in style and format. Rather than retyping an entirely new workbook, you can retrieve an old workbook, edit its content, and then save it under a different name using the Save As command on the File menu. Additionally, you can display the New Workbook task pane and select the "From existing workbook . . ." option to create a new workbook based on an existing file.

1.4.3 Opening an Existing Workbook

→ # Feature

You use the Open dialog box to search for and retrieve existing workbooks that are stored on your local hard disk, a removable storage device, a network server, or on the Web. If you want to load an existing workbook when you first start Excel, click the Start button (*start*) and then choose the Open Office Document command on the All Programs menu. Or, if you have recently used the workbook, display the Start menu and then try the My Recent Documents command, which lists the most recently used files.

→ # Method

To open an existing workbook:

• CLICK: Open button ( )

   or

• CHOOSE: File → Open

→ # Practice

You will now retrieve a student data file named EX0143 that displays the market penetration for snowboard sales by Canadian province. To complete this exercise, you will need to know the storage location for the Advantage student data files.

1. Ensure that there are no workbooks displayed in the application window. Then, display the Open dialog box:
CLICK: Open button ( )

2. Using the Places bar or the *Look in* drop-down list box, locate the folder containing the Advantage student data files. (*Note:* In this guide, we retrieve the student data files from a folder named "Advantage.") Your screen should appear similar to the one shown in Figure 1.33 before proceeding.

Figure 1.33

Viewing the
student data files
for the Microsoft
Office Excel 2003
tutorial

3. To view additional file information in the dialog box:
CLICK: down arrow beside the Views button (⊞▾)
The drop-down list shown at the right appears.

4. CHOOSE: Details
Each workbook is presented on a single line with additional file information, such as its size, type, and date.
(*Hint:* You can sort the filenames in this list area by
clicking on one of the column heading buttons.)

5. To return to a multicolumn list format:
CLICK: down arrow beside the Views button (⊞▾)
CHOOSE: List
Your screen should look like the one shown in Figure
1.33 once again.

6. Let's open one of the workbooks:
DOUBLE-CLICK: EX0143
The dialog box disappears and the workbook is loaded into the application window, as shown in
Figure 1.34. (*Note:* The "EX0143" filename reflects that this workbook is used in lesson 1.4.3 of
the Microsoft Office Excel 2003 learning guide.)

Figure 1.34

Opening the
EX0143
workbook

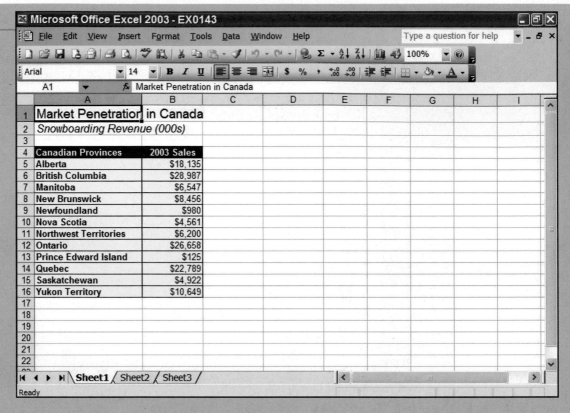

7. Let's prepare this worksheet for tracking sales in 2004:
   SELECT: cell B4
   TYPE: **2004 Sales**
   PRESS: `ENTER`

8. To remove the existing 2003 data:
   SELECT: cell B5
   PRESS: `SHIFT`
   CLICK: cell B16
   The cell range from B5 through B16 should now appear highlighted.

9. PRESS: `DELETE` to remove the cell contents (but retain the formatting)
   Your screen should now appear similar to the one shown in Figure 1.35. Notice that the selected range remains highlighted and that the only the data is removed. The cell's fill color and number formatting remain intact.

Figure 1.35

Modifying the
EX0143
workbook

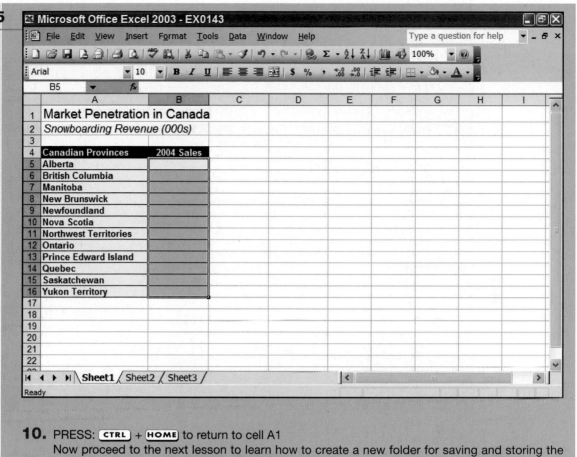

10. PRESS: `CTRL` + `HOME` to return to cell A1
    Now proceed to the next lesson to learn how to create a new folder for saving and storing the
    modified workbook.

In Addition OPENING AND SAVING FILES OF DIFFERENT FORMATS

In the Open and Save As dialog boxes, you will notice a drop-down list box named *Files of type* and
Save as type respectively. These list boxes allow you to select different file formats for opening and
saving your files. For instance, you can save a workbook so that users with an earlier version of Excel
are able to open and edit its contents. You can also open a file that was created using another spreadsheet software program, such as Lotus or Quattro Pro.

1.4.4 Creating a Workbook Folder

→ ## Feature

Storage folders help you organize your work. They also make it easier to find documents and back up your
data. For example, you can use a folder to collect all of the workbooks related to a single fiscal period. You
can also specify a folder to hold all of your personal documents, such as résumés and expense reports.
Although Windows Explorer should be used for most folder management tasks, Excel enables you to create a new folder from within the Save As dialog box. After you navigate to where you want the folder to
appear, click the Create New Folder button ( ) and then complete the steps presented below.

→ ## Method

To create a new workbook folder:

- CLICK: Create New Folder button (🗀) in the Save As dialog box
- TYPE: *a name* for the new folder
- CLICK: OK command button

→ ## Practice

You will now create a folder for storing the workbooks that you will create in the remaining pages of this tutorial. Ensure that you have completed the previous lesson.

1. You may create a new folder for your workbooks using the Save As command on the File menu. To begin:
CHOOSE: File → Save As

2. This exercise assumes that you are able to create folders on your computer's local hard disk. If this is not the case, you may substitute a removable media drive for the My Documents folder. To begin, use the Places bar to select the desired location for the new folder:
CLICK: My Documents folder button in the Places bar

3. To create a subfolder in the My Documents folder:
CLICK: Create New Folder button (🗀)
Your screen should now appear similar to the one shown in Figure 1.36.

Figure 1.36

Creating a new folder in the Save As dialog box

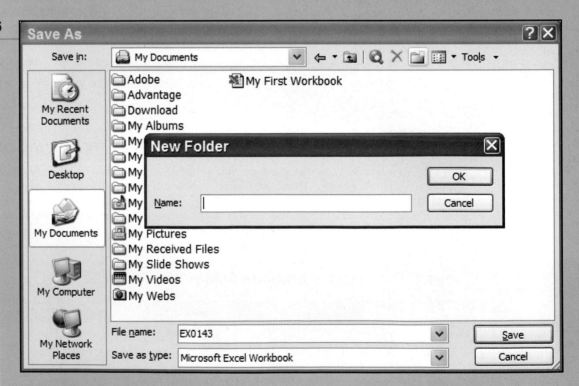

4. In the New Folder dialog box:
TYPE: **My Workbooks**
CLICK: OK command button
You are immediately transferred into the new folder, as shown in the *Save in* drop-down list box.

5. Now you can save the workbook in the new folder. Let's choose a different filename for the workbook. If it is not already selected:
DOUBLE-CLICK: "EX0143" in the *File name* text box
The filename should appear highlighted before you proceed.

6. To replace the existing workbook name:
TYPE: **Snowboarding 2004** as shown below

File name:	Snowboarding 2004	⌄
Save as type:	Microsoft Excel Workbook	⌄

7. To complete the procedure:
CLICK: Save command button

8. Let's close the workbook:
CHOOSE: File → Close

9. To exit Microsoft Office Excel 2003:
CHOOSE: File → Exit

Excel

In Addition   RENAMING AND DELETING A WORKBOOK FOLDER

Besides creating a workbook folder using the Open or Save As dialog boxes, you can rename and delete folders displayed in the list area. To rename a folder, right-click the folder and then choose Rename from the shortcut menu that appears. The folder's name will appear in Edit Mode within the list area. Type the new name and press (ENTER). (*Hint:* You can also click on a folder twice slowly in order to edit a folder's name.) To delete a folder, right-click the desired folder and choose the Delete command. You will be asked to confirm the folder deletion in a dialog box. Make sure that you do not accidentally delete a folder containing files that you want to keep! To avoid this, you should open a folder and view its contents before performing the Delete command.

 **1.4** In the Open and Save As dialog boxes, how do the List and Details views differ? Name two other views that are accessible from the Views button

Chapter
summary

Microsoft Office Excel 2003 is an electronic spreadsheet program. Spreadsheet software is used extensively in business for performing statistical analyses, summarizing numerical data, and publishing reports. Over the past two decades, spreadsheet software has proven to be the most robust and indispensable power tool for white-collar workers. You create a worksheet in Excel by typing text, numbers, dates, and formulas into cells. Editing the contents of a worksheet is also an important skill because of the frequency with which most worksheets are reused and modified. File management tasks—creating, saving, and opening workbook files, and creating a workbook folder for storing your work—are also key to your efficient and productive use of Excel 2003.

Command Summary

Many of the commands and procedures appearing in this chapter are summarized in the following table.

Skill Set	To Perform this Task...	Do the Following...
Using Excel	Launch Microsoft Office Excel 2003	CLICK: Start button (*start*) CHOOSE: All Programs → Microsoft Office CLICK: Microsoft Office Excel 2003
	Exit Microsoft Excel	CLICK: its Close button (☒) *or* CHOOSE: File → Exit
	Close a workbook	CLICK: its Close button (☒) *or* CHOOSE: File → Close
	Customize menus and toolbars	CHOOSE: Tools → Customize
Managing Workbooks	Create a new workbook	CLICK: New button (▢) *or* CHOOSE: File → New SELECT: an option from the New Workbook task pane
	Use a template to create a new workbook	CHOOSE: File → New CLICK: "On my computer . . ." under the *Templates* area of the New Workbook task pane CLICK: *Spreadsheet Solutions* tab in the Templates dialog box DOUBLE-CLICK: *a template*
	Locate and open an existing workbook	CLICK: Open button (▢) *or* CHOOSE: File → Open
	Open files of different formats	SELECT: a format from the *Files of type* drop-down list box in the Open dialog box
	Save a workbook	CLICK: Save button (▢) *or* CHOOSE: File → Save
	Save a workbook using a different filename, location, or format	CHOOSE: File → Save As
	Create a new folder while displaying the Save As dialog box	CLICK: Create New Folder button (▢)
Working with Cells and Cell Data	Navigate to a specific cell	CLICK: in the Name Box TYPE: *cell address*
	Enter text labels, numbers, and dates	TYPE: *an entry*
	Enter a formula	TYPE: *=expression*
	Replace the current cell's contents with new data	TYPE: *new entry*

Activate Edit Mode to revise a cell's contents	DOUBLE-CLICK: in the desired cell *or* CLICK: in the Formula bar *or* PRESS: **F2** (Edit) key
Delete the current cell's contents	PRESS: **DELETE**
Delete all information (contents, formatting, and other attributes) associated with a cell	CHOOSE: Edit → Clear → All
Reverse or undo a command or series of commands	CLICK: Undo button (⟲▾) *or* CHOOSE: Edit → Undo *or* PRESS: **CTRL** + **z**
Reverse or undo an Undo command	CLICK: Redo button (⟳▾) *or* CHOOSE: Edit → Redo

Excel

Key Terms

This section specifies page references for the key terms identified in this chapter. For a complete list of definitions, refer to the Glossary at the back of this learning guide.

adaptive menus, *p. EX 9*

application window, *p. EX 5*

cell, *p. EX 2*

cell address, *p. EX 2*

cell pointer, *p. EX 12*

chart sheet, *p. EX 2*

comment, *p. EX 25*

document window, *p. EX 5*

formula, *p. EX 18*

in-cell editing, *p. EX 22*

macro virus, *p. EX 32*

Name Box, *p. EX 12*

Places bar, *p. EX 34*

Range Finder, *p. EX 18*

Redo command, *p. EX 27*

task pane, *p. EX 9*

template, *p. EX 30*

Undo command, *p. EX 27*

wizard, *p. EX 30*

workbook, *p. EX 2*

worksheet, *p. EX 2*

Chapter
q u i z

Short Answer

1. Explain the difference between an application window and a document or workbook window.

2. Where do toolbars appear in the application window?

3. What is the fastest method for moving to cell BE1762?

4. What is significant about how dates are entered into a worksheet?

5. How do you enter a formula into a cell? Provide an example.

6. What does it mean to use *pointing* to enter cell addresses in a formula?

7. How would you reverse the past three commands executed?

8. How do you create a new workbook based on a template?

9. How would you save a copy of the currently displayed workbook onto a diskette?

10. How would you save a workbook using Excel 2003 so that a person with Excel 95 is able to open and edit the file?

True/False

1. _____ The cell reference "AX100" is an acceptable cell address.

2. _____ Pressing CTRL+SHIFT moves the cell pointer to cell A1.

3. _____ An Excel worksheet contains more than 68,000 rows.

4. _____ After a formula has been entered into a cell, you cannot edit the expression.

5. _____ A formula may contain both numbers and cell references, such as =A1*B7-500.

6. _____ Pressing DELETE erases the contents and formatting of the currently selected cell.

7. _____ Pressing CTRL + z will undo the last command executed.

8. _____ You can create a new folder from within the Save As dialog box.

9. _____ You access Excel's workbook templates using the Templates button (▣) on the Standard toolbar.

10. _____ You can open workbook files that have been created using earlier versions of Excel.

Multiple Choice

1. Which mouse shape is used to select cells in a worksheet?

  a. Arrow (↰)
  b. Cross (✛)
  c. Hand (☝)
  d. Hourglass (⌛)

2. Excel displays the current cell address in the:

  a. Name Box
  b. Standard toolbar
  c. Status bar
  d. Title bar

3. Using a mouse, you move around a worksheet quickly using the:

  a. Scroll bars
  b. Status bar
  c. Tab Scrolling arrows
  d. Tab Split bar

4. When you enter a text label, Excel justifies the entry automatically between the cell borders as:

  a. Centered
  b. Fully justified
  c. Left-aligned
  d. Right-aligned

5. When you enter a date, Excel justifies the entry automatically between the cell borders as:

  a. Centered
  b. Fully justified
  c. Left-aligned
  d. Right-aligned

6. Which keyboard shortcut lets you modify the contents of a cell?

  a. CTRL
  b. SHIFT
  c. F2
  d. F5

7. Which is the correct formula for adding cells B4 and F7?

  a. =B4+F7
  b. @B4+F7
  c. $B4:F7
  d. =B4*F7

8. To save the current workbook using a different filename:

  a. CHOOSE: File, Save
  b. CHOOSE: File, Save As
  c. CLICK: Save button (▣)
  d. CHOOSE: File, Rename

9. To open a new blank workbook:
   a. CLICK: New button (▣)
   b. CHOOSE: File, Open
   c. CHOOSE: File, Start
   d. CHOOSE: File, Template

10. To reverse an Undo command:
   a. CHOOSE: Edit, Go Back
   b. CHOOSE: File, Reverse Undo
   c. CLICK: Reverse button (↶▾)
   d. CLICK: Redo button (↷▾)

Hands-On
exercises

step by step

1. Creating a New Worksheet

This exercise lets you practice fundamental worksheet skills, including entering labels, numbers, dates, and formulas. You also practice saving your workbook.

1. Load Microsoft Office Excel 2003 and ensure that a blank worksheet is displayed.

2. To hide the task pane:
   CHOOSE: View ➔ Task Pane

3. Enter a title label for the worksheet in cell A1:
   TYPE: **Wally Burger's Fast Food**
   PRESS: ⬇

4. In cell A2, enter another label:
   TYPE: **Today is:**
   PRESS: ➡

5. In cell B2, enter today's date:
   TYPE: *your date* using the format dd-mmm-yy
   PRESS: **ENTER**
   (*Hint:* The date March 31, 2004 would be entered as 31-Mar-04.)

6. Complete the worksheet as it appears in Figure 1.37. (*Note:* Depending on how your computer is configured, the worksheet's date values may appear formatted differently on your screen.)

Figure 1.37

Wally Burger's Fast Food worksheet

These labels are entered into column A only, even though their text spills over into column B.

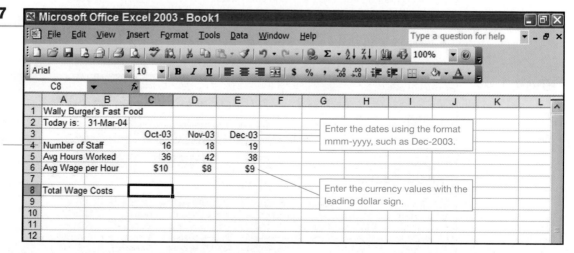

7. Now let's calculate the "Total Wage Costs" for October 2003.
   SELECT: cell C8, as shown in Figure 1.37
   TYPE: **=c4*c5*c6**
   PRESS: ➡
   The value $5,760 appears in cell C8.

8. Enter similar formulas into cells D8 and E8 using the pointing method. Which is the least costly month in terms of wages paid?

9. Modify the value in cell C4 to read "18" staff. Which month has the lowest wage cost now?

10. Let's save the workbook to your personal storage location:
CHOOSE: File ➔ Save As

11. On your own, navigate the Save As dialog box using the Places bar and *Save in* drop-down list box to locate your personal storage location for saving workbook files. When you are ready to proceed, name the workbook "**Wally Burger**" and compare the finished workbook to the one shown in Figure 1.38.

Figure 1.38

Completed "Wally Burger" workbook

![Screenshot of Microsoft Office Excel 2003 - Wally Burger workbook. Cell C5 is selected showing value 36. The worksheet contains the following data.]

The workbook's file name appears in the Title bar of the Excel 2003 application window.

	A	B	C	D	E
1	Wally Burger's Fast Food				
2	Today is:	31-Mar-04			
3			Oct-03	Nov-03	Dec-03
4	Number of Staff		18	18	19
5	Avg Hours Worked		36	42	38
6	Avg Wage per Hour		$10	$8	$9
7					
8	Total Wage Costs		$6,480	$6,048	$6,498

12. Close the workbook before proceeding.

step by step

2. Modifying a Worksheet

In this exercise, you enter and edit text labels in an existing worksheet, enter numbers and dates, select and delete a cell range, and use the Undo command.

1. Open the workbook named EX01HE02, located in the Advantage student data files location, to display the worksheet in Figure 1.39.

Figure 1.39

Opening the EX01HE02 workbook

![Screenshot of Microsoft Office Excel 2003 - EX01HE02 workbook. Cell A1 is selected showing "ABC Realty". The worksheet contains the following data.]

	A	B	C	D	E	F	G
1	**ABC Realty**						
2							
3	Listing	Date	Agent	Contact	Address	City	Price
4	21234	3/25/2004	Brown	270-535-1254	9800 Salmon Rd.	Nelson	$225,900
5	21455	4/1/2004	Griffiths	270-558-4695	468 Cherry Lane	Vernon	$324,800
6	21512	4/15/2004	Griffiths	270-558-4695	9002 Rockland St.	Vernon	$349,900
7	21513	4/21/2004	Brown	270-535-1254	#17-123 Main St.	Cranbrook	$185,500
8	21526	5/12/2004	Stevens	270-532-6545	21546 Anjou Dr.	Winfield	$272,000

2. To save the workbook to your personal storage location:
CHOOSE: File → Save As

3. On your own, navigate the Save As dialog box using the Places bar and *Save in* drop-down list box to locate your personal storage location for saving workbook files. When you are ready, name the workbook "**ABC Realty**" and proceed to the next step.

4. To change the "Contact" column heading to read "Phone":
SELECT: cell D3
TYPE: **Phone**
PRESS: (ENTER)

5. To correct a spelling mistake that occurs in the "City" column:
SELECT: cell F8
PRESS: (F2) to enter Edit mode

6. To change the name from "Winfield" to "Wimfield," do the following:
PRESS: (←) six times until the cursor appears to the left of the letter "n" in "Winfield"
PRESS: (DELETE)
TYPE: **m**
PRESS: (ENTER)

7. To modify the address in a listing:
SELECT: cell E7
Notice that the cell contents now appear in the Formula bar.

8. To change the street name from "Main" to "Elm," position the I-beam mouse pointer over "Main" in the Formula bar and then double-click. Your screen should appear similar to Figure 1.40 before proceeding.

Figure 1.40

Modifying cell contents in the worksheet

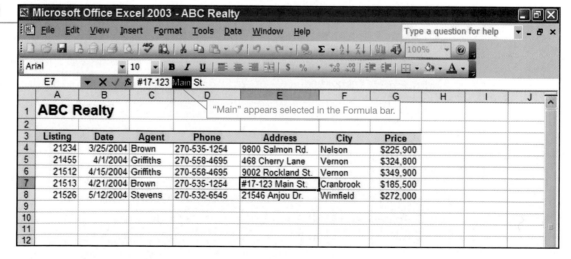

9. To replace the selected text:
TYPE: **Elm**
PRESS: (ENTER)
(*Note:* Rather than pressing (ENTER), you can also click the Enter button (☑) in the Formula bar.)

10. To erase both the contents and formatting in the "Price" column, do the following:
SELECT: cell G3
PRESS: (SHIFT)
PRESS: (↓) five times to select the desired cell range
RELEASE: (SHIFT)

11. To erase the cell range:

CHOOSE: Edit → Clear → All

Your screen should now appear similar to the one shown in Figure 1.41

Figure 1.41

Erasing a cell range in the worksheet

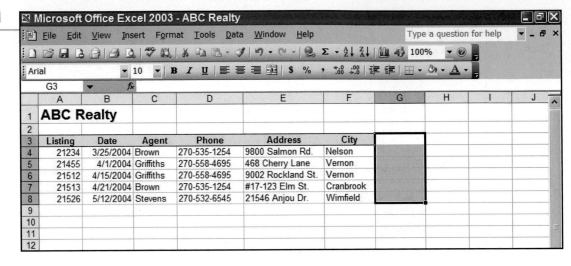

12. To undo this last command:

CLICK: Undo button ( ) on the Standard toolbar

The data and formatting reappear in the cell range.

13. Enter the following data for a new listing into row 9 of the worksheet, starting in cell A9:

Listing:	**21561**
Date:	**05/22/2004**
Agent:	**Kramer**
Phone:	**270-532-9764**
Address:	**1515 Michael Dr.**
City:	**Mission**
Price:	**$151,900**

14. Save and then close the workbook.

step by step

3. Entering Formulas

After creating a worksheet that includes text and values, you enter formulas to perform calculations and then save the workbook to your personal storage location.

1. To display a new workbook:

CLICK: New button ( )

2. Enter the company name in cell A1:

TYPE: **Johnson's Sport Mart**

PRESS: ⬇

TYPE: **Today is:**

PRESS: ➡

3. In cell B2, enter today's date:

TYPE: *your date* using the format dd-mmm-yy

PRESS: **ENTER**

(*Hint:* The date March 31, 2004 would be entered as 31-Mar-04.)

4. Complete the worksheet as it appears in Figure 1.42.

Figure 1.42

Johnson's Sport
Mart worksheet

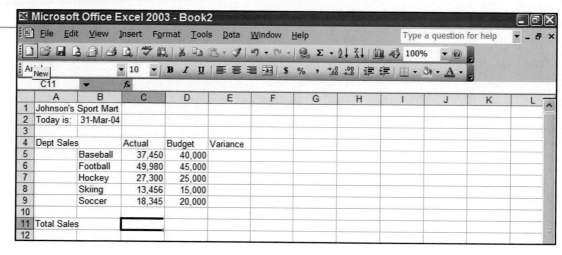

5. To begin, calculate the total sales for the "Actual" column:
SELECT: cell C11
TYPE: **=c5+c6+c7+c8+c9**
PRESS: (ENTER)
(*Hint:* There are easier methods for summing a column that you learn in the next chapter.)

6. Use a similar formula to display the sum of the "Budget" column in cell D11.

7. Now calculate the sales variance:
SELECT: cell E5
TYPE: **=c5−d5**
PRESS: (ENTER)
The value -2550 appears in the worksheet.

8. Using the same method, calculate the remaining variances for cells E6 through E9, and E11.

9. Let's save the workbook to your personal storage location:
CHOOSE: File → Save As

10. On your own, navigate the Save As dialog box using the Places bar and *Save in* drop-down list box to locate your personal storage location for saving workbook files. When you are ready to proceed, name the workbook "**Johnson**" and compare the finished workbook to Figure 1.43.

Figure 1.43

Completed
"Johnson"
workbook

Microsoft Office Excel 2003 - Johnson											
	A	B	C	D	E	F	G	H	I	J	K	L
1	Johnson's Sport Mart										
2	Today is:	31-Mar-04									
3											
4	Dept Sales		Actual	Budget	Variance						
5		Baseball	37,450	40,000	-2,550						
6		Football	49,980	45,000	4,980						
7		Hockey	27,300	25,000	2,300						
8		Skiing	13,456	15,000	-1,544						
9		Soccer	18,345	20,000	-1,655						
10											
11	Total Sales		146,531	145,000	1,531						
12											

E11 ▾ *fx* =C11-D11

11. On your own, change some values in the "Actual" and "Budget" columns and view the calculated results.

12. Close the workbook without saving your changes.

 on your own

4. Personal Monthly Budget

To practice working with text, values, and formulas, ensure that Excel is loaded and then display a blank workbook. You will now begin creating a personal budget. Enter a title that contains the words "My Monthly Budget." Under this title, include your name and the current month. Now enter the following expense categories and a reasonable amount for each:

- Rent/Mortgage
- Food
- Clothing
- Car expenses
- Utilities
- Education
- Entertainment

In the same column as the above labels, enter the words "Total Expenses." Then, beneath the column of numbers, enter a formula that sums the column. Now add a new column next to these budget figures that displays the percentage share for each budget category of the total expenses. For example, you would divide the value for Food by the Total Expenses value to calculate its share of the budget. (*Hint:* The division operator is specified using the forward slash symbol (/) on your keyboard.) Don't worry about formatting the results as percentages. Figure 1.44 provides an example of a completed worksheet.

Figure 1.44

Completing the "My Budget" workbook

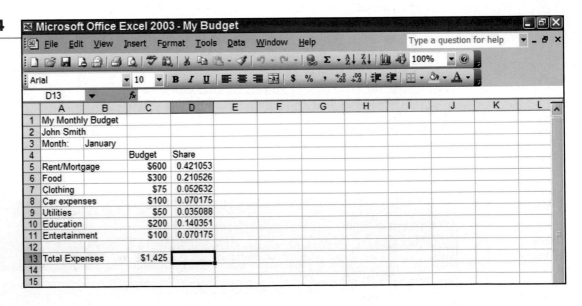

Experiment with increasing and decreasing the budget expense figures to see their effect on the percentage share calculations. When completed, save the workbook as "My Budget" to your personal storage location and then close the workbook.

 on your own

5. My Grade Book

To practice working with data and formulas, open the EX01HE05 workbook (Figure 1.45). Before continuing, save the workbook as "My Grade Book" to your personal storage location. Enter sample marks into column D of the worksheet.

Figure 1.45

Opening the EX01HE05 workbook

	A	B	C	D	E	F
1	My Grade Book					
2						
3	Business Computer Systems			MARK	OUT OF	%
4		assigment #1			30	
5		mid-term test			120	
6		assignment #2			45	
7		final exam			100	
8		TERM PERCENTAGE:				
9						
10	Pacific Rim Studies			MARK	OUT OF	%
11		assigment #1			50	
12		mid-term test			30	
13		assignment #2			50	
14		final exam			80	
15		TERM PERCENTAGE:				
16						
17	AVERAGE OF BOTH COURSES:					
18						

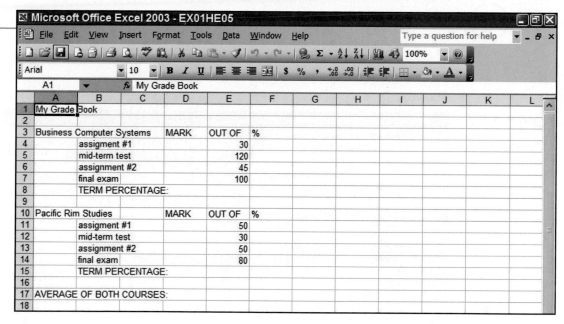

Enter formulas that calculate the percentage grade for each test or assignment by dividing the "MARK" column by the "OUT OF" column. Then, enter formulas that calculate the Term Percentages for each course. The results should display in cells F8 and F15. (*Hint:* You will need to use parentheses to group data in your formula equation. Specifically, you must divide the total course marks achieved by the total marks possible. This is a lengthy formula!) Finally, enter a formula that calculates the average percentage of both courses for display in cell F17. You will need to add together the two course percentages within parentheses and then divide the sum by 2. An example of the completed worksheet appears in Figure 1.46. Adjust some of the sample marks to check that the formulas are working correctly.

Figure 1.46

Completed "My Grade Book" workbook

	A	B	C	D	E	F
1	My Grade Book					
2						
3	Business Computer Systems			MARK	OUT OF	%
4		assigment #1		27	30	90.00%
5		mid-term test		100	120	83.33%
6		assignment #2		42	45	93.33%
7		final exam		88	100	88.00%
8		TERM PERCENTAGE:				87.12%
9						
10	Pacific Rim Studies			MARK	OUT OF	%
11		assigment #1		49	50	98.00%
12		mid-term test		24	30	80.00%
13		assignment #2		39	50	78.00%
14		final exam		68	80	85.00%
15		TERM PERCENTAGE:				85.71%
16						
17	AVERAGE OF BOTH COURSES:					86.42%
18						

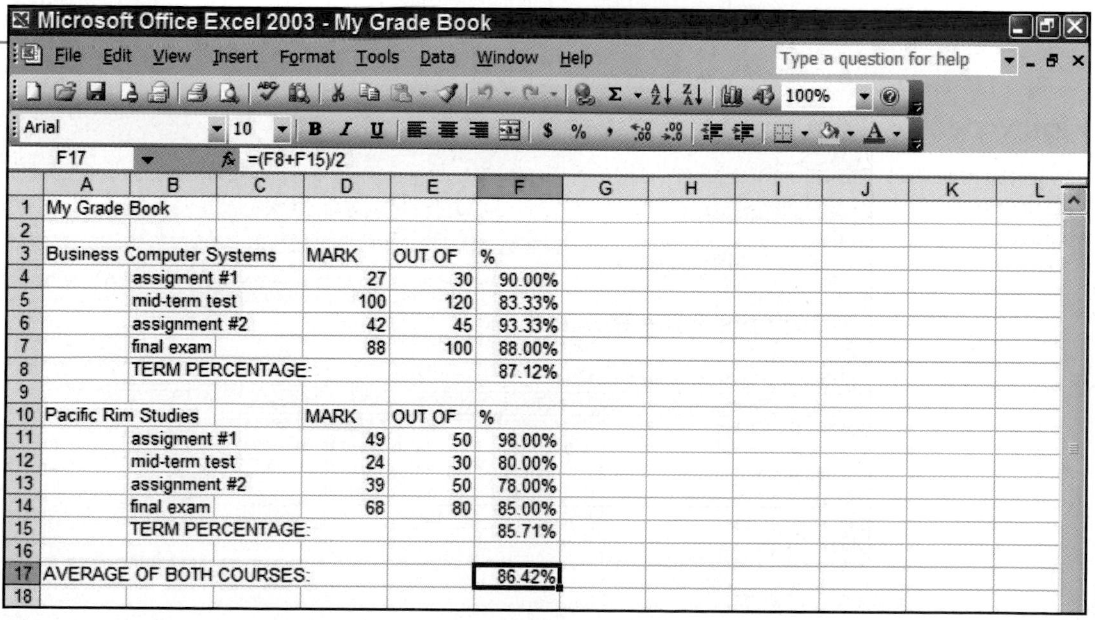

Save the completed workbook to your personal storage location and then close the workbook.

Excel

on your own

6. My Questionnaire

You now assume the role of market researcher and finalize the analysis of a questionnaire using Excel 2003. To begin, open the EX01HE06 workbook (Figure 1.47). Save the workbook as "My Questionnaire" to your personal storage location. Review the contents of the worksheet.

Figure 1.47

Opening the EX01HE06 workbook

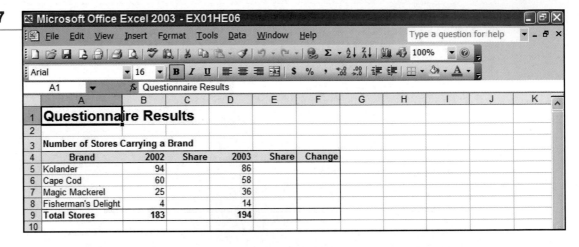

The "Kolander" brand of frozen fish has recently been renamed to "For the Halibut," and you immediately make this change in the worksheet. You also notice that the "Capetown Cod" brand is mistakenly entered as "Cape Cod," requiring you to edit another cell. You now calculate the market shares held by each brand in the years 2002 and 2003. For each brand in column C and E, enter a formula that divides a brand's results by the total number of stores in row 9. Don't worry about formatting the results as percentages. Lastly, calculate the percentage change that resulted for each brand between 2002 and 2003. The required formula may be described as: *(BrandResult2003 − BrandResult2002) / BrandResult2002*. (*Hint:* Do not enter this formula into the worksheet verbatim. You must replace these arguments with the appropriate cell addresses.) Check your work against the completed worksheet shown in Figure 1.48.

Figure 1.48

Completed "My Questionnaire" workbook

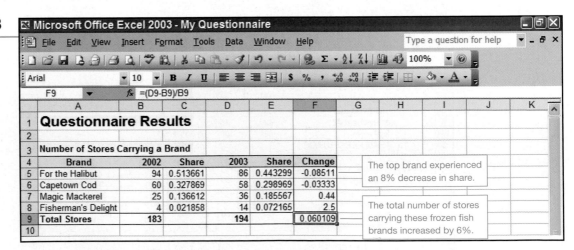

Save the workbook to your personal storage location. Close the workbook and exit Microsoft Office Excel 2003.

CaseStudy   PACWEST TOURS

PacWest Tours is a small, privately owned bus charter company operating in the Pacific Northwest. The company's business consists primarily of local sightseeing tours and meeting destination-based transportation needs, such as airport and hotel transfers. Earlier this year, PacWest added a third luxury coach to their fleet of buses and retained two full-time and three part-time drivers. Besides the drivers, PacWest employs a full-time dispatcher and a mechanic. Samuel Wong, the general manager, started the company and oversees all aspects of its operation.

Administratively, PacWest operates with minimal paperwork and performs manual record keeping. All bookings are handwritten into a scheduling chart, and the drivers fill out travel logs at the end of each trip. Invoices and receipts are simply turned over to a bookkeeping service, as Samuel cannot afford a staff accountant. Recently, however, Samuel has been finding it increasingly difficult to obtain the information he needs to make key decisions. To remedy this problem, he has hired Renee Duvall, the daughter of one of his drivers, as an office assistant and computer operator. Samuel wants Renee to use Microsoft Office Excel 2003 to create a worksheet that will enable him to compare the monthly efficiency of his fleet of buses. You see, Samuel has an opportunity to purchase an additional luxury coach for well below market value. As a cost-conscious businessman, Samuel wants to have a clear understanding of how his current equipment is performing before spending any more money.

In the following case problems, assume the role of Renee and perform the same steps that she identifies. You may want to reread the chapter opening before proceeding.

1. Renee decides to create a new worksheet that she can use as a template for each month's report. She begins by loading Microsoft Office Excel 2003 and displaying a blank workbook. Her first step will be to enter the title and the row and column headings. Then, the workbook needs to be saved to disk so that it can be retrieved later as a starting point for the monthly reports.

Renee creates the worksheet shown in Figure 1.49 and then saves it as "Fleet Stats" to her personal storage location.

Figure 1.49

Completing the
"Fleet Stats"
workbook

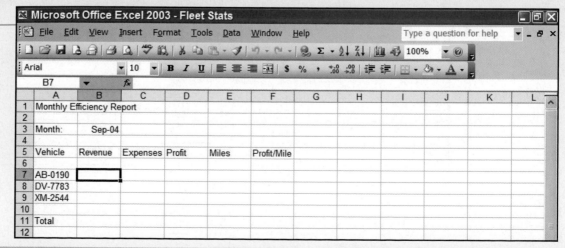

2. Satisfied that this format will provide Samuel with the information he needs, Renee begins to fill in the first month's figures. Most of the data she uses is taken directly from the monthly revenue and expense summaries prepared by the bookkeeping service. The driver's travel logs provide the rest of the data. After entering the information shown in Figure 1.50, Renee saves the workbook as "Sep-04 Stats" to her personal storage location.

Figure 1.50

Completing the "Sep-04 Stats" efficiency report

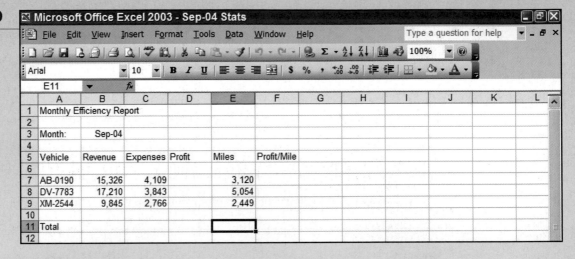

3. Now, Renee enters the formulas for the worksheet:

- She constructs formulas for display in row 11 that add the values appearing in the "Revenue," "Expenses," and "Miles" columns. The three formulas are entered into cells B11, C11, and E11.

- She enters formulas in cells D7, D8, and D9 that calculate the Profit by subtracting a bus's Expenses from the Revenue it generated. She then enters a sum formula for the column in cell D11.

- She calculates and displays the Profit per Mile in cells F7, F8, F9, and F11. The calculation she uses is simply the Profit from column D divided by the Miles in column E.

Unfortunately, Samuel has already left for the day. Renee decides to finish her work and go home; she saves the workbook as "Sep-04 Results" and then closes it. She is already looking forward to showing off her new creation (as shown in Figure 1.51) to Samuel in the morning.

Figure 1.51

Completing the "Sep-04 Results" workbook

Microsoft Office Excel 2003 - Sep-04 Results

	A	B	C	D	E	F	G	H	I	J	K	L
1	Monthly Efficiency Report											
2												
3	Month:	Sep-04										
4												
5	Vehicle	Revenue	Expenses	Profit	Miles	Profit/Mile						
6												
7	AB-0190	15,326	4,109	11,217	3,120	3.595192						
8	DV-7783	17,210	3,843	13,367	5,054	2.644836						
9	XM-2544	9,845	2,766	7,079	2,449	2.890568						
10												
11	Total	42,381	10,718	31,663	10,623	3						
12												

F11   =D11/E11

4. The next morning, Renee opens the "Sep-04 Results" workbook and asks Samuel to take a look at it. He is very pleased with the report and amazed at how quickly Excel can perform the calculations. Samuel asks Renee what it would take to produce this report for another month. She explains that all she needs to do is enter the month's revenues, expenses, and miles into the appropriate cells; Excel then recalculates the worksheet automatically. Samuel is impressed, realizing that he will finally have some decent information on which to base business decisions.

After mulling over the worksheet, Samuel decides it would be prudent to purchase the fourth luxury coach. With some minor modifications, he realizes that the workbook information would come in handy during his meeting with the bank's loan officer. Samuel asks Renee to make some revisions. First, the title of the report, explains Samuel, should read "PacWest Tours." The "Monthly Efficiency Report" title should be moved down to row 2. Furthermore, the buses should be identified by their names instead of their registration numbers. The bus names are Runner (AB-0190), Wanderer (DV-7783), and Zephyr (XM-2544). Samuel also asks Renee to change the column heading from "Vehicles" to "Fleet." The worksheet should now appear as shown in Figure 1.52.

Figure 1.52

Completing the "Sep-04 Summary" workbook

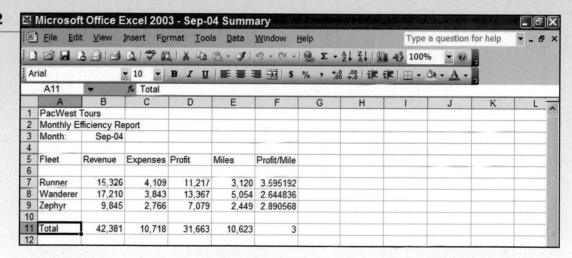

Renee makes the requested changes. She then saves the workbook as "Sep-04 Summary" and closes the workbook. As a last step, she exits Microsoft Office Excel 2003.

Answers to Self-Check Questions

SelfCheck

1.1 How do you turn the adaptive menus feature on or off? Choose the Tools, Customize command and then check the *Always show full menus* check box to turn the adaptive menus feature off. Remove the check to turn the feature back on.

1.2 Explain why a phone number is not considered a numeric value in an Excel worksheet. Although it contains numbers, a phone number is never used to perform mathematical calculations.

1.3 Why is worksheet editing such a valuable skill? Most worksheets in use today are revisions and updates of older worksheets. As a novice user, you often spend more time updating existing worksheets than constructing new ones.

1.4 In the Open and Save As dialog boxes, how do the List and Details views differ? Name two other views that are accessible from the Views button. The List view uses a multicolumn format. The Details view displays one file per row. Furthermore, the Details view displays other information, including the file size, type, and modification date. The other views that appear on the drop-down menu include: Thumbnails, Tiles, Icons, Properties, Preview, and WebView.

Microsoft® Office Excel®

2003

Modifying a Worksheet

CHAPTER OUTLINE

PREREQUISITES

To successfully complete this chapter, you must be able to perform basic data entry and file management operations in Excel. Besides entering text, numbers, dates, and formulas into a worksheet, you will be asked to open, save, and close workbooks. You must also know how to use the toolbar, Menu bar, and right-click shortcut menus in Excel.

LEARNING OBJECTIVES

After completing this chapter, you will be able to:

- Use several "Auto" features provided by Excel for entering and editing data and formulas

- Copy and move information using the Windows and Office Clipboards, and the drag and drop method

- Use the AutoFill feature and Fill commands to duplicate and extend data and formulas

- Insert and delete cells, rows, and columns

- Hide, unhide, and adjust rows and columns

2.1 Entering and Reviewing Data

Even new users can quickly learn to create workbooks and enter data using Microsoft Office Excel 2003. More experienced spreadsheet users know how to apply Excel's features efficiently and effectively in performing routine tasks. In this module, you are introduced to some popular Excel tools and methods that can help speed your learning and make you a more productive spreadsheet user. In addition to selecting and manipulating worksheet cells, you learn to use three of Excel's "Auto" features—*AutoComplete, AutoCalculate,* and *AutoSum.* These timesaving tools facilitate your entry of repetitive data in a worksheet and help you to construct and enter formulas for performing common calculations.

2.1.1 Selecting Cells and Ranges

→ Feature

A **cell range** is a single cell or rectangular block of cells. Each cell range has a beginning cell address in the top left-hand corner and an ending cell address in the bottom right-hand corner. To use a cell range in a formula, you separate the two cell addresses using a colon. For example, the cell range B4:C6 references the six shaded cells shown below. Notice that the current or active cell, B4, does not appear shaded in this graphic.

→ Method

To select a cell range using the mouse:

- CLICK: the cell in the top left-hand corner
- DRAG: the mouse pointer to the cell in the bottom right-hand corner

To select a cell range using the keyboard:

- SELECT: cell in the top left-hand corner
- PRESS: SHIFT and hold it down
- PRESS: *an arrow key* to extend the range highlighting
- RELEASE: SHIFT

→ Practice

In this exercise, you will open a workbook, save it to your personal storage location, and practice selecting single and multiple cell ranges. Ensure that Excel 2003 is loaded before proceeding.

1. Open the Advantage student data file named EX0210.

2. In the next two steps, you will save the workbook file as "My Gift List" to your personal storage location. Do the following:
CHOOSE: File → Save As
TYPE: **My Gift List** (but do not press [ENTER])

3. Using the *Save in* drop-down list box or the Places bar:
SELECT: *your personal storage location* (for example, the My Documents or My Workbooks folder, as shown in Figure 2.1)
CLICK: Save command button
(*Note:* Most lessons in this guide begin by opening an Advantage student data file and then saving it to your personal storage location using a new filename.)

Figure 2.1

Saving the
EX0210
workbook

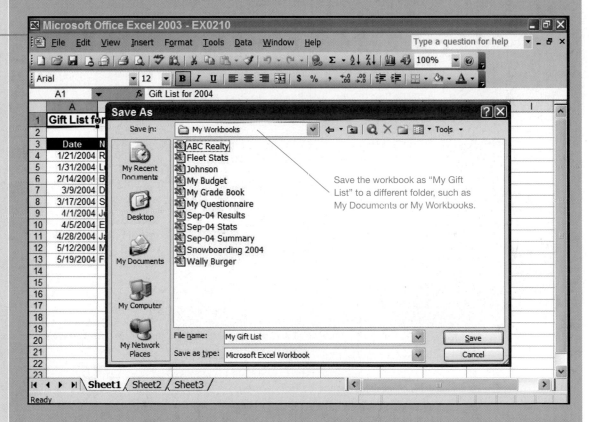

4. You will now practice selecting cell ranges. To begin:
SELECT: cell A3
(*Hint:* The word SELECT tells you to place the cell pointer at the identified cell address using either the keyboard or the mouse.)

5. To select the range from cell A3 to E3 using the keyboard:
PRESS: (SHIFT) and hold it down
PRESS: ➡ four times
Although it is not explicitly stated in the above instruction, you release the (SHIFT) key once the range is selected. Your screen should appear similar to the one shown in Figure 2.2.

Figure 2.2

Selecting the cell range A3:E3

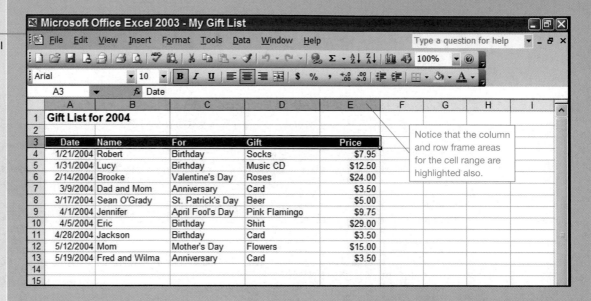

6. You learned in the previous chapter that the (CTRL) + (HOME) combination moves the cell pointer to cell A1. Pressing the (HOME) key by itself moves the cell pointer to column A within the same row. To illustrate, let's move the cell pointer back to cell A3:
PRESS: (HOME)

7. To select the same cell range, but more quickly and efficiently:
PRESS: (SHIFT) and hold it down
PRESS: (CTRL) + ➡ together
Notice that the entire cell range is selected. You may remember from the last chapter that the (CTRL) + arrow combination moves the cell pointer until the cell contents change from empty to filled or from filled to empty.

8. To select a cell range using the mouse:
CLICK: cell C6 and hold down the left mouse button
DRAG: the mouse pointer to E8 (and then release the mouse button)
Notice that the column letters and row numbers in the frame area appear highlighted for the selected cell range, as shown in Figure 2.3.

Figure 2.3

Selecting a cell range using the mouse

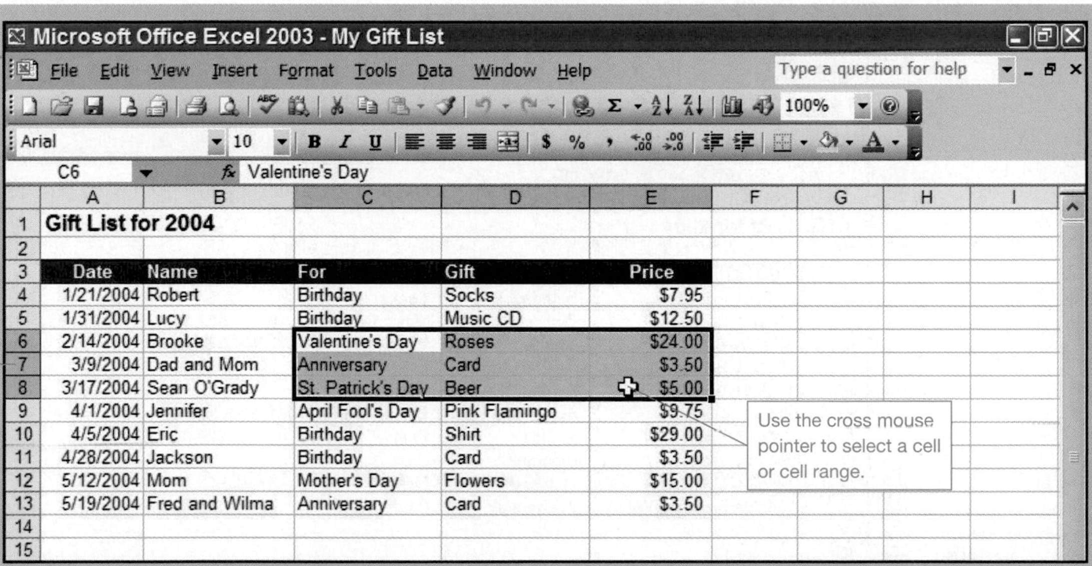

The row and column frame areas are highlighted, making it easy to identify the selected cell range.

Use the cross mouse pointer to select a cell or cell range.

9. For novice users, there is a mouse method easier than dragging a cell range for selection. To demonstrate, you will now select the cell range from B10 to D13:
CLICK: cell B10
PRESS: SHIFT and hold it down
CLICK: cell D13
The range between the two cells should now appear highlighted. (*Note:* Remember to release the SHIFT key after the last selection is made.)

10. You can also select multiple cell ranges on a worksheet. To begin:
DRAG: from cell A6 to cell E6
PRESS: CTRL and hold it down
DRAG: from cell A9 to cell E9
You should see two separate cell ranges highlighted on the worksheet. (*Note:* Release the CTRL key after making the cell range selection.)

11. To select a third cell range:
PRESS: CTRL and hold it down
DRAG: from cell A12 to cell E12
(*Note:* Release the CTRL key after making the selection.) Your screen should now look similar to the one shown in Figure 2.4.

12. To move the cell pointer to cell A1:
PRESS: CTRL + HOME

Figure 2.4

Selecting multiple cell ranges using the CTRL key

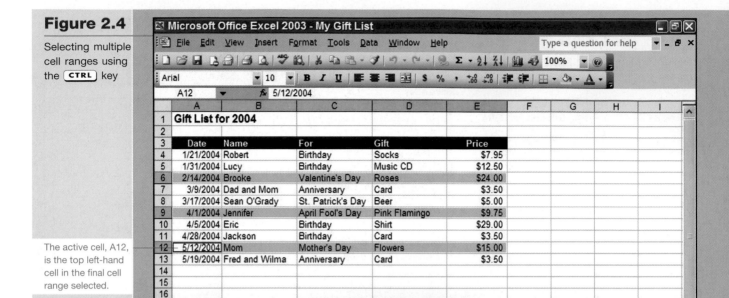

The active cell, A12, is the top left-hand cell in the final cell range selected.

2.1.2 Entering Data Using AutoComplete

→ **Feature**

The **AutoComplete** feature second-guesses what you are typing into a worksheet cell and suggests how to complete the entry. After analyzing your first few keystrokes and scanning the same column for similar entries, AutoComplete tacks on the remaining letters when it thinks it has found a match. You can accept the AutoComplete entry, or you can ignore its suggestion and continue typing. This feature can greatly reduce the number of repetitive entries you make in a worksheet.

→ **Method**

By default, the AutoComplete feature is turned on. If, however, you view its helpfulness as an intrusion, you can turn it off. To do so:

- CHOOSE: Tools → Options

- CLICK: *Edit* tab in the dialog box

- SELECT: *Enable AutoComplete for cell values* check box to toggle AutoComplete on (☑) or off (☐)

→ **Practice**

You now practice using Excel's AutoComplete feature to enter data. Ensure that the "My Gift List" workbook is displayed.

1. SELECT: cell A14

2. To add a new entry to the worksheet:
TYPE: **6/2/2004**
PRESS: ➡
TYPE: **Anda**
PRESS: ➡

3. You will now enter the word "Birthday" into cell C14. After typing the first letter, Excel notices that there is only one other entry in the column that begins with the letter "B" and makes the assumption that this is the word you want to enter. To demonstrate:
TYPE: **B**
Notice that Excel completes the word "Birthday" automatically, as shown in Figure 2.5.

Figure 2.5

The AutoComplete feature completes the C14 cell entry for "Birthday"

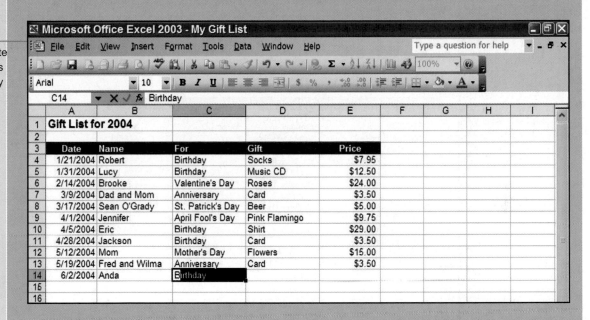

4. To accept the completed word:
PRESS: ➡

5. For the remaining cells in the row:
TYPE: **Shoes**
PRESS: ➡
TYPE: **$19.95**
PRESS: **ENTER** to move to the next row
PRESS: **HOME** to move to the first column (A)
Your cell pointer should now appear in cell A15.

6. Let's add another entry to the worksheet. Do the following:
TYPE: **6/5/2004**
PRESS: ➡
TYPE: **Trevor and Ann**
PRESS: ➡

7. You can also use Excel's AutoComplete feature to display a sorted list of all the unique entries in a column. To illustrate:
RIGHT-CLICK: cell C15 to display its shortcut menu
CHOOSE: Pick From List

AutoComplete generates the list and then displays its results in a pop-up list box, as shown in Figure 2.6.

Figure 2.6

Entering data using the AutoComplete pick list

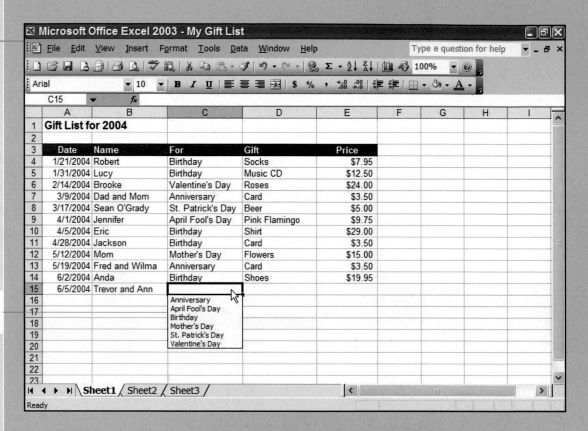

Displaying the AutoComplete "Pick From List" Feature

8. To make a selection:
   CLICK: Anniversary in the pick list

9. As an alternative to choosing the Pick From List command in the right-click menu, Excel provides a shortcut key combination. To demonstrate:
   CLICK: cell D15
   PRESS: ALT + ⬇ to display the column's pick list

10. To select an item:
    CLICK: Flowers in the pick list

11. To complete the row:
    PRESS: ➡
    TYPE: $15.00
    PRESS: ENTER

12. Save the workbook and keep it open for use in the next lesson. (*Hint:* The fastest methods for saving a workbook include clicking the Save button (🖫) or pressing CTRL + s.)

2.1.3 Using AutoCalculate and AutoSum

→ **Feature**

Using Excel's **AutoCalculate** feature, you can view the calculated result of a selected range of values in the Status bar. This feature is useful for checking the result of a calculation, such as summing a cell range, without actually having to store its value in the worksheet. If, on the other hand, you need to store the calculated result, click the **AutoSum** button ($\Sigma \cdot$) on the Standard toolbar. With the AutoSum feature, Excel reviews the surrounding cells, guesses at the range you want to sum, and then places a SUM function (described in a later chapter) into the active cell.

→ **Method**

To use the AutoCalculate feature:

- SELECT: the range of values that you want to calculate

To use the AutoSum feature:

- SELECT: the cell where you want the result to appear
- CLICK: AutoSum button ($\Sigma \cdot$)

→ **Practice**

Using the same worksheet, you will now practice viewing AutoCalculate results and entering an addition formula using AutoSum. Ensure that you have completed the previous lesson and that the "My Gift List" workbook is displayed.

1. Imagine that you want to know how much money to set aside for gifts in April. To find the answer quickly, do the following:
SELECT: cell range from E9 to E11
Notice that only the April values are selected in the Price column.

2. Review the Status bar. Notice that "Sum=$42.25" now appears near the right-hand side of the Status bar, as shown in Figure 2.7.

Figure 2.7

Using the AutoCalculate feature

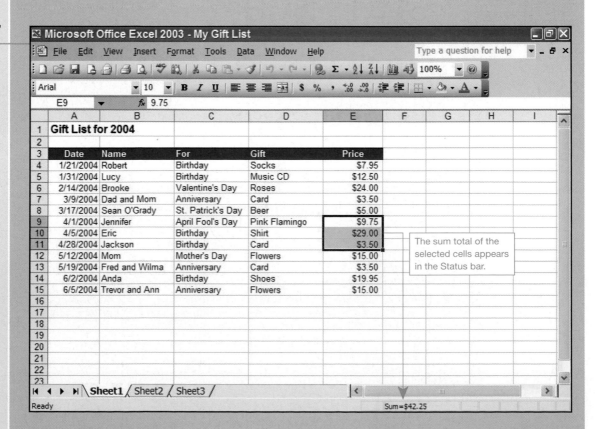

The sum total of the selected cells appears in the Status bar.

Excel

3. Let's perform another calculation:
SELECT: cell E4
PRESS: SHIFT and hold it down
PRESS: CTRL + ⬇
All of the cells under the Price column heading should now be selected. Assuming that you completed the previous lessons, the Status bar will now display "Sum=$148.65."

4. Using the AutoCalculate feature, you can also view the result of other calculations in the Status bar. To demonstrate, let's calculate the average value of gifts in the selected cell range:
RIGHT-CLICK: "Sum = $148.65" in the Status bar
Your screen should now appear similar to the one shown in Figure 2.8.

Figure 2.8

Displaying the right-click menu for the AutoCalculate feature

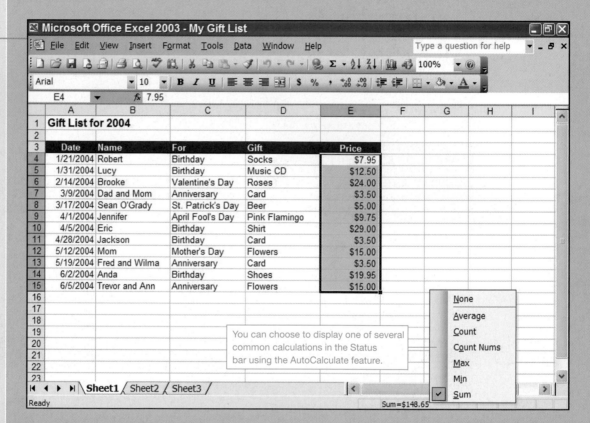

5. In the AutoCalculate right-click menu:
CHOOSE: Average
The Status bar now displays "Average=$12.39."

6. To make the Status bar display the sum of the selected cell range, do the following:
RIGHT-CLICK: "Average=$12.39" in the Status bar
CHOOSE: Sum

7. SELECT: cell D16

8. Let's enter a text label for the next calculation:
TYPE: **Total Cost**
PRESS: ➡

9. The quickest way to sum a row or column of values is using the AutoSum button (Σ⁃) on the Standard toolbar. Make sure that you click the sigma (Σ) portion of the button, rather than the down arrow (⁃). To demonstrate:

CLICK: AutoSum button (Σ ▾) once
A built-in function called SUM is entered into the cell, along with the range that Excel assumes you want to sum (Figure 2.9).

Figure 2.9

Using the AutoSum button (Σ ▾) to sum a cell range

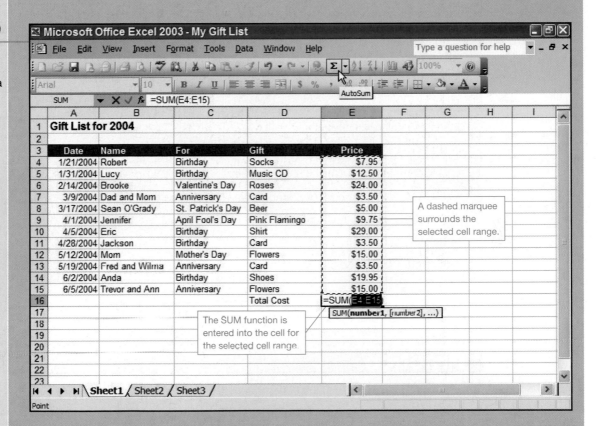

10. To accept the highlighted cells as the desired range:
CLICK: AutoSum button (Σ ▾) again
The result, $148.65, now appears in cell E16. (*Note:* You can also press **ENTER** or click the Enter button (☑) in the Formulas bar to accept the AutoSum entry.)

11. Let's change one of the column entries. Do the following:
SELECT: cell E14
TYPE: **$119.95**
PRESS: **ENTER**
Notice that the AutoSum result in cell E16 is recalculated automatically and now displays $248.65.

12. Save the workbook by clicking the Save button (🖫).

In Addition ACCESSING OTHER "AUTO" CALCULATIONS USING THE AUTOSUM BUTTON (Σ ▾)

Similar to AutoCalculate's right-click menu that allowed you to display an average value, AutoSum provides alternative calculations from the drop-down arrow attached to its button (Σ ▾). Click the down arrow to display a list of possible functions, such as Average and Count. When you select one of these function commands, Excel inserts the function into the cell with the appropriate range parameters, similar to SUM.

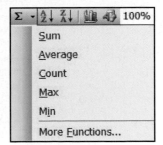

2.1.4 Inserting and Deleting Cells

→ ## Feature

You can insert a new, empty cell or cell range in the middle of existing data without destroying the data. Excel allows you to insert a cell range by pushing the existing range down or to the right. This feature is especially useful because it updates all the affected cell references used in formulas automatically. Similarly, Excel updates formulas when you delete a cell or cell range. Unlike clearing or erasing a cell's contents, deleting a cell or cell range does not leave a gap of empty cells behind.

→ ## Method

To insert a cell or cell range:

- SELECT: the desired cell or cell range
- CHOOSE: Insert → Cells
- SELECT: *Shift cells right* or *Shift cells down* option button
- CLICK: OK command button

To delete a cell or cell range:

- SELECT: the desired cell or cell range
- CHOOSE: Edit → Delete
- SELECT: *Shift cells left* or *Shift cells up* option button
- CLICK: OK command button

→ ## Practice

You will now practice inserting and deleting cells. Ensure that the "My Gift List" workbook is displayed.

1. Let's insert a new item into the worksheet in the proper ascending date order. To begin:
SELECT: cell range from A9 to E9

2. To insert a new range of cells:
CHOOSE: Insert → Cells
The Insert dialog box appears, as shown in Figure 2.10.

Figure 2.10

Inserting a range of cells using the Insert dialog box

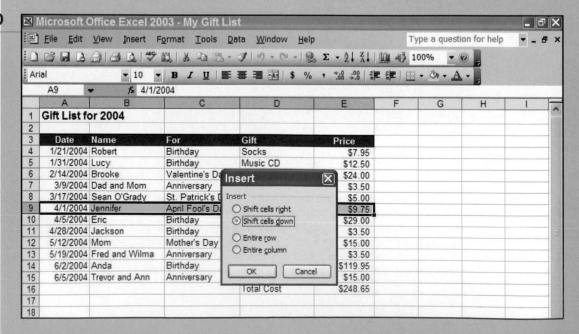

3. To complete the procedure:
SELECT: *Shift cells down* option button, if it is not already selected
CLICK: OK command button
The existing data is pushed down to make space for the new cells. Notice that the Insert Options icon (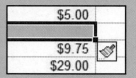) appears attached to the right side of the cell range, as shown here. You can use this icon to choose formatting options for the newly inserted cells. Because we want to keep the default formatting for the new row, you may ignore the Insert Options icon (⟨⟩) for now.

4. Make sure that the cell range from A9 to E9 remains selected. Now let's enter a new item:
TYPE: 3/31/2004
PRESS: ENTER
The cell pointer moves to the next available cell in the selected range, even though you pressed ENTER and not ➡. When you select a range for data entry, the cell pointer is confined to that range when you insert data using ENTER.

5. To complete the row item with an Anniversary entry:
TYPE: **Tim and Starr**
PRESS: ENTER
TYPE: **An**
PRESS: ENTER
TYPE: **Mirror**
PRESS: ENTER
TYPE: **$37.00**
PRESS: ENTER
Notice that the cell pointer wraps around to the beginning of the selected range and that the "Total Cost" value in cell E17 is updated.

6. Now let's remove Jackson's birthday from the list:
SELECT: cell range from A12 to E12

7. To delete the selected cells:
CHOOSE: Edit ➜ Delete
The Delete dialog box, similar to the Insert dialog box, is displayed, as shown in Figure 2.11.

Figure 2.11

Deleting a range of cells using the Delete dialog box

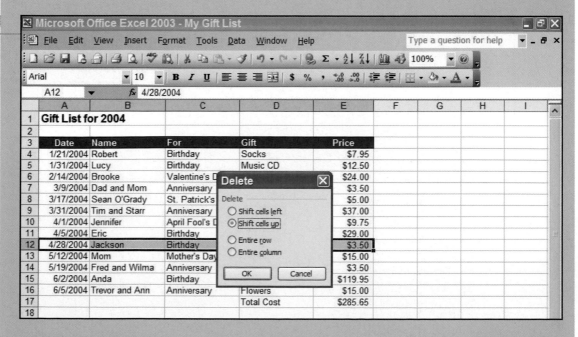

8. To complete the procedure
   SELECT: *Shift cells up* option button, if it is not already selected
   CLICK: OK command button
   The remaining cells slide up one row to close the gap and the "Total Cost" value in cell E16 is updated to $282.15.

9. PRESS: CTRL + HOME to move to cell A1

10. Save and then close the workbook.

 **SelfCheck**

2.1 Which of the "Auto" features enables you to sum a range of values and display the result in the Status bar?

2.2 Copying and Moving Data

Excel 2003 provides several tools for copying, moving, and pasting data. Like the "Auto" features, these tools can help you reduce the number of repetitive entries you are required to make. For example, once you enter a formula to sum one column of values, you can duplicate that formula to sum the adjacent columns. There are three primary methods for copying and moving data. First, you can cut or copy a single piece of data from any application and store it on the **Windows Clipboard.** Then, you can paste the data into any other worksheet, workbook, or application. Second, you can choose the **Office Clipboard** to collect up to 24 items and then paste the stored data singularly or as a group into any other Office 2003 application. Last, you can use **drag and drop** to copy and move cell information short distances using the mouse. In this module, you will practice duplicating cell contents and extending data and formulas in a worksheet.

2.2.1 Using the Windows Clipboard

 ### Feature

The Windows Clipboard is a software feature provided by the Windows operating system and is shared by the applications running on your computer. A limitation of this Clipboard is that it can hold only a single piece of data at any given time. Its advantage is that you can use it effectively to copy and move data among a variety of software programs. Once data exists on the Clipboard, it may be pasted multiple times and into multiple applications. The contents of the Clipboard are wiped clean, however, when the computer is turned off. When you perform a simple cut, copy, and paste operation in Excel, you are using the Windows Clipboard. Your alternatives are to use either the Office Clipboard (discussed in the next lesson) for copying multiple items at once or the mouse for quick drag and drop editing.

→ ## Method

Task description	Menu command	Toolbar button	Keyboard shortcut
Move data from the worksheet to the Clipboard	Edit, Cut	✂	CTRL + X
Place a copy of the selected data on the Clipboard	Edit, Copy	📋	CTRL + C
Insert data stored on the Clipboard into the worksheet	Edit, Paste	📋▾	CTRL + V

Excel

→ ## Practice

Using the Windows Clipboard, you will now practice copying and pasting data in a worksheet. The steps for moving data are identical to those for copying, except that you use the Cut command instead of Copy. Ensure that no workbooks are displayed in the application window.

1. Open the data file named EX0220 to display the workbook shown in Figure 2.12.

Figure 2.12

Opening the
EX0220 workbook

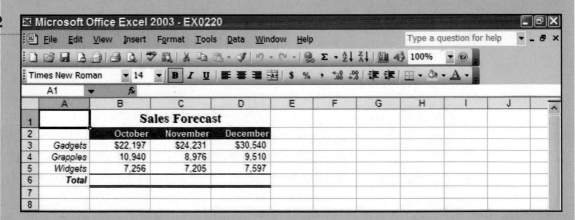

2. Save the file as "Sales Forecast" to your personal storage location.

3. To calculate totals for row 6 in the worksheet:
SELECT: cell range from B6 to D6
CLICK: AutoSum button ($\Sigma \cdot$)
The results appear immediately in the selected range (Figure 2.13). Notice that you can fill an entire cell range using the AutoSum feature.

Figure 2.13

Entering totals using the AutoSum button ($\Sigma \cdot$)

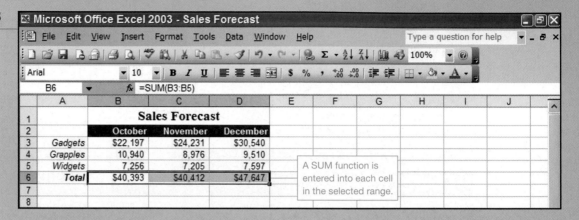

4. You will now use the Copy command to duplicate some cells in the worksheet. To begin:
SELECT: cell range from A2 to D6
Notice that all the data is selected, except for the title in row 1.

5. To copy the range selection to the Windows Clipboard:
CLICK: Copy button on the Standard toolbar
The range that you want to copy appears surrounded by a dashed marquee, or moving border, as shown in Figure 2.14.

Figure 2.14

Selecting and copying a range to the Clipboard

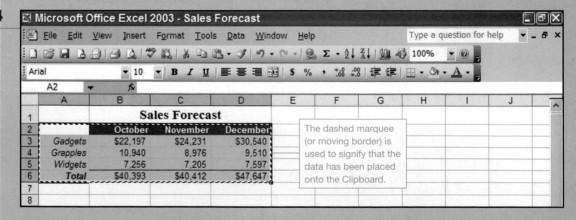

6. Now select the top left-hand corner of the worksheet location where you want to place the copied data. Do the following:
SELECT: cell A9

7. To paste the data from the Clipboard into the worksheet:
CLICK: Paste button ($\Box \cdot$)
Make sure that you click the clipboard portion of the Paste button ($\Box$) and not the down arrow ($\cdot$). Once the data is pasted, notice that the Paste Options icon ($\Box$) is displayed at the bottom right-hand corner of the new cell range. This icon allows you to select advanced formatting and paste options. For our purposes, you may ignore this icon and proceed to the next step.

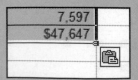

8. While the dashed marquee moves around the original cell range (A2:D6), the data on the Windows Clipboard remains available for pasting. Let's continue pasting the copied data into the worksheet using a shortcut keystroke:
SELECT: cell A16
PRESS: **CTRL** + **v** to paste the data
Your screen should now appear similar to the one shown in Figure 2.15.

Figure 2.15

Copying and pasting data in a worksheet

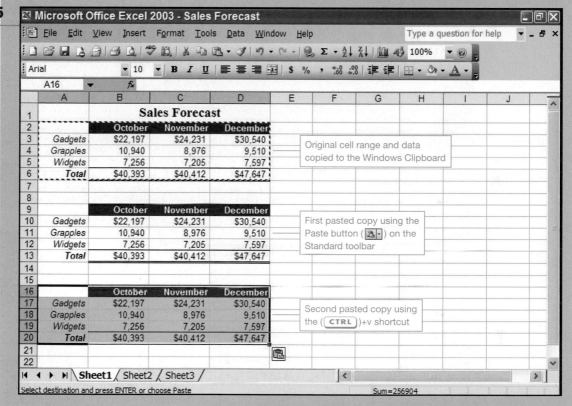

9. To remove the dashed marquee:
PRESS: **ESC**
Notice that the Paste button on the toolbar is now dimmed and unavailable for selection. In other words, the data is no longer available for pasting into the worksheet.

10. To return to cell A1:
PRESS: **CTRL** + **HOME**

2.2.2 Using the Office Clipboard

→ Feature

The Office Clipboard allows you to collect up to 24 data items and then paste them into Microsoft Office 2003 applications, such as Word, Excel, Access, and PowerPoint. For all intents and purposes, you work with the Office Clipboard in the same way you use the Windows Clipboard. In fact, the last item that you cut or copy to the Office Clipboard will be the one and only item stored on the Windows Clipboard. To copy an item to the Office Clipboard, first display the Clipboard task pane by choosing the Office Clipboard command on the Edit menu. Depending on your system's configuration, the Clipboard task pane may open automatically when you perform two copy operations in succession.

→ ## Method

To use the Office Clipboard:

- CHOOSE: Edit → Office Clipboard

→ ## Practice

You will now practice using the Office Clipboard and the Clipboard task pane. Ensure that you have completed the previous lesson and that the "Sales Forecast" workbook is displayed.

1. To demonstrate using the Office Clipboard:
CHOOSE: Edit → Office Clipboard
The Clipboard task pane appears docked at the right side of the application window, as shown in Figure 2.16. (*Hint:* Remember that, unlike the Windows Clipboard, the Office Clipboard can store up to 24 items and then paste them all at the same time.)

Figure 2.16

Displaying the Clipboard task pane

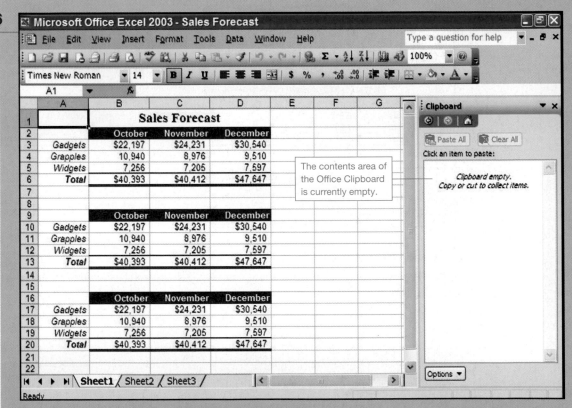

2. If the contents area of the Clipboard task pane is not empty:
CLICK: Clear All button (Clear All) in the task pane

3. Now let's add data items to the Office Clipboard:
SELECT: cell A3
CLICK: Copy button ( )
Notice that the contents area of the Clipboard task pane now shows "Gadgets" and its title bar reads "1 of 24 –Clipboard."

4. To continue adding items:
SELECT: cell B3
CLICK: Copy button (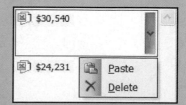)
SELECT: cell C3
CLICK: Copy button ()
SELECT: cell D3
CLICK: Copy button ()
The task pane's title bar now reads "4 of 24," as shown in Figure 2.17. (*Note:* If you were to continue adding items, the first item ("Gadgets," in our example) would be overwritten by the 25th item collected.)

Figure 2.17

Clipboard task pane after collecting four items

Pastes all of the items appearing in the list box vertically into the worksheet

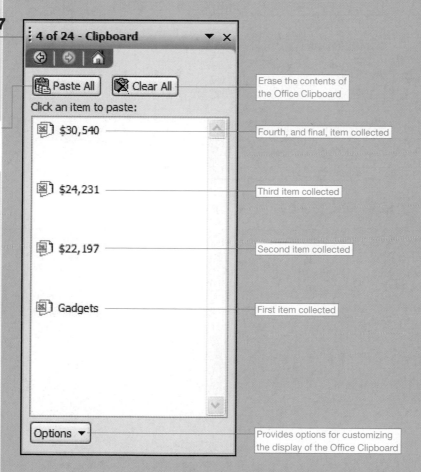

Erase the contents of the Office Clipboard

Fourth, and final, item collected

Third item collected

Second item collected

First item collected

Provides options for customizing the display of the Office Clipboard

5. Position the mouse pointer over one of the data items in the Clipboard task pane. The item will appear highlighted with a border and an attached down arrow at the right-hand side. On your own, click the down arrow to display the pop-up menu shown here. You use this menu to paste a single item from the list or to remove an item that you no longer need. To remove the pop-up menu, click the attached down arrow a second time.

6. Now let's use the Paste All button () to insert all of the collected data items into the worksheet. Do the following:
SELECT: cell F2
CLICK: Paste All button () in the Clipboard task pane
The contents of the Office Clipboard are pasted vertically into a single column in the worksheet; each data item is placed into its own row, as shown in Figure 2.18. Notice that the first item added to the Office Clipboard appears in the first row of the pasted cell range.

Figure 2.18

Pasting items from the Office Clipboard into the worksheet

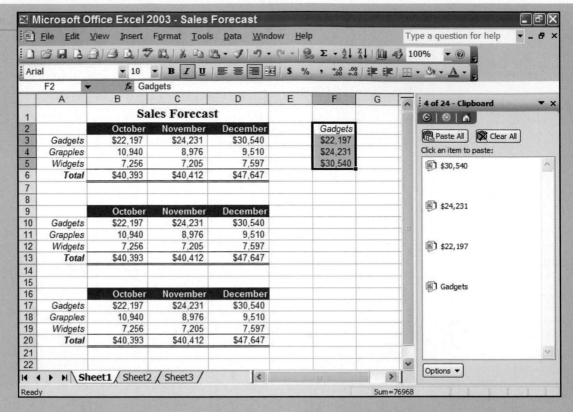

7. Let's prepare for another copy operation by clearing the Office Clipboard. Do the following:
CLICK: Clear All button (Clear All) in the Clipboard task pane

8. You will now collect, reorder, and then paste information from rows 3 through 5. The key to this step is to collect the data in the order that you want to paste it later. Therefore, to reorder the row data, do the following:
SELECT: cell range A5 through D5 ("Widgets")
PRESS: CTRL + c
SELECT: cell range A3 through D3 ("Gadgets")
PRESS: CTRL + c
SELECT: cell range A4 through D4 ("Grapples")
PRESS: CTRL + c
You should now see three items listed in the Clipboard task pane.

9. Now paste the results on top of an existing data area in the worksheet:
SELECT: A10
CLICK: Paste All button (Paste All)
Notice that you need only select the top left-hand corner of the desired target range. Your screen should now appear similar to the one shown in Figure 2.19.

Figure 2.19

Pasting the row items into the worksheet

Notice that the rows are ordered differently than the original cell range in rows 3 through 5.

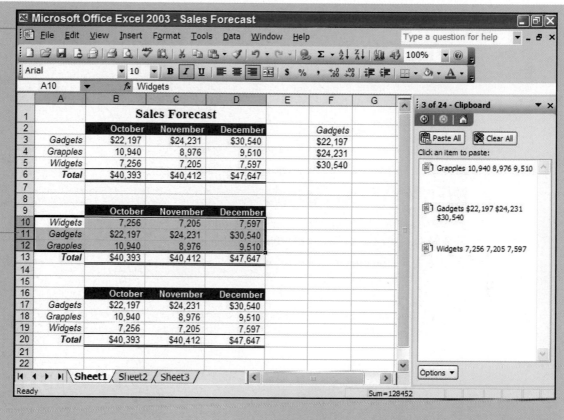

10. To clear the Office Clipboard and close the Clipboard task pane:
CLICK: Clear All button (Clear All)
CLICK: its Close button ([X])

11. Move the cell pointer to cell A1.

12. Save the workbook and keep it open for use in the next lesson.

In Addition USING THE OFFICE CLIPBOARD TO EXCHANGE
DATA IN OFFICE 2003

The Office Clipboard is an excellent tool for sharing data among the Office 2003 applications. You can copy worksheet data to the Office Clipboard and then paste the contents into a Word document or a PowerPoint presentation. You can also collect rows of data from an Access database and place them into your worksheet for analysis. When you need to transfer data, consider using the Office Clipboard instead of performing more complex linking and importing routines.

2.2.3 Using Drag and Drop

→ **Feature**

When you use the mouse to perform a drag and drop operation, you bypass the Windows and Office Clipboards altogether. The drag and drop method offers an efficient way to copy and move data from one location in your worksheet to another. Although you cannot perform multiple pastes or collect multiple items, the drag and drop method is the easiest and fastest way to copy and move a cell's contents short distances.

→ Method

To use drag and drop:

- SELECT: the cell range that you want to copy or move

- Position the mouse pointer over the border of the cell range until a white arrow over a four-pronged cross (⊹) appears.

- If you want to perform a copy operation, hold down the [CTRL] key.

- DRAG: the cell range by the border to the target destination

- Release the mouse button and, if necessary, the [CTRL] key.

→ Practice

Using the mouse, you will now practice dragging and dropping a cell range in the worksheet. Ensure that you have completed the previous lesson and that the "Sales Forecast" workbook is displayed.

1. Let's practice moving the data that was copied to column F in the previous lesson. Do the following:
SELECT: cell range from F2 to F5

2. Position the mouse pointer over a border of the selected cell range until a white diagonal arrow over a four-pronged cross (⊹) appears, as shown here.

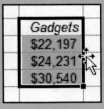

3. CLICK: left mouse button and hold it down
DRAG: mouse pointer downward until the ToolTip displays "F9:F12"
Before you release the mouse pointer to complete the drag and drop operation, your screen will appear similar to the one shown in Figure 2.20.

4. Release the mouse button to complete the drag and drop operation.

Figure 2.20

Using drag and drop to move cell data

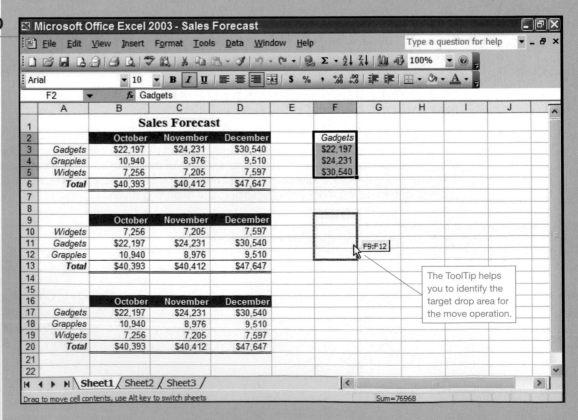

5. You will now copy the selected cell range back to its original location. To begin, ensure that the cell range from F9 to F12 is highlighted.

6. Position the mouse pointer (↖) over a border of the cell range. Then:
PRESS: CTRL and hold it down
You should notice a plus sign added to the diagonal arrow mouse pointer (↖).

7. CLICK: left mouse button and hold it down
DRAG: mouse pointer upward to F2:F5
The target cell range should appear as shown here.

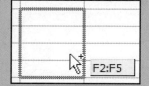

8. Release the mouse button and CTRL key to complete the copy operation. Your screen should appear similar to the one shown in Figure 2.21.

9. Save and then close the workbook.

Figure 2.21

Completing the "Sales Forecast" worksheet

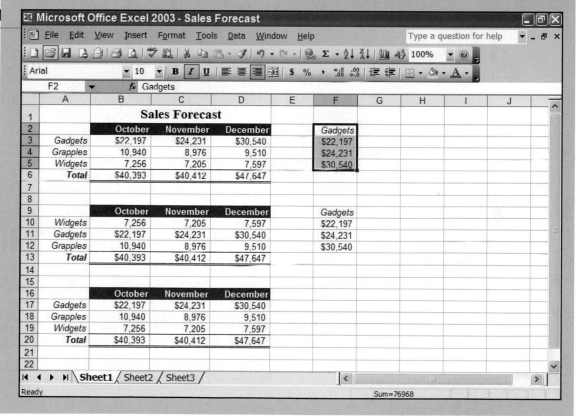

2.2.4 Creating a Series Using AutoFill

→ # Feature

Excel's **AutoFill** feature allows you to enter a data series into a worksheet. Whether a mathematical progression of values (1, 2, 3, . . .) or a row of date headings (Jan, Feb, Mar, . . .), a **series** is a sequence of data that follows a pattern. This feature is a real time-saver and reduces the potential for making data entry errors.

→ ## Method

To use AutoFill:

- SELECT: the cell range containing the data you want to extend

- DRAG: the **fill handle,** which is a black square that appears in the lower right-hand corner of the cell range, to extrapolate the series

- Release the mouse button to complete the operation.

→ ## Practice

In this exercise, you create a new workbook and then extend the contents of cells using the fill handle and the AutoFill feature. Ensure that no workbooks appear in the application window.

1. To display a new workbook:
CLICK: New button (⬜)

2. Let's enter some source data from which you will create a series:
SELECT: cell A3
TYPE: **Jan**
PRESS: ⬇
TYPE: **Period 1**
PRESS: ⬇
TYPE: **Quarter 1**
PRESS: **ENTER**
Each of these entries will become the starting point for creating three series that extend across their respective rows.

3. To extend the first entry in row 3:
SELECT: cell A3

4. Position the mouse pointer over the small black square (the fill handle) in the bottom right-hand corner of the cell pointer. The mouse pointer will change to a black cross when positioned correctly. (*Hint:* Figure 2.22 identifies the fill handle and mouse pointer.)

Figure 2.22

Using a cell's fill handle

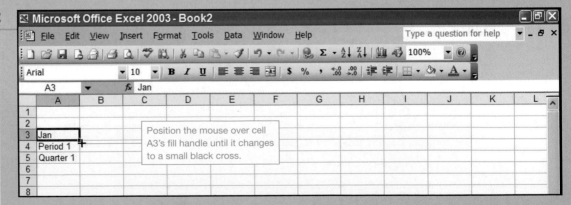

5. CLICK: left mouse button and hold it down
DRAG: the mouse pointer to column F, until the ToolTip displays "Jun"

6. Release the mouse button to complete the AutoFill operation. The AutoFill Options icon (⊞) appears in the bottom right-hand corner of the range (shown here) to provide additional fill options. For our purposes, you may ignore this icon and proceed to the next step.

7. Let's extend the next two rows:
SELECT: cell A4
DRAG: fill handle for cell A4 to column F
SELECT: cell A5
DRAG: fill handle for cell A5 to column F
(*Note:* Always release the mouse button after dragging to the desired location.) Notice that Excel recognizes the word "quarter"; it resumes at Quarter 1 after entering Quarter 4, as shown in Figure 2.23.

Figure 2.23

Using AutoFill to complete cell ranges

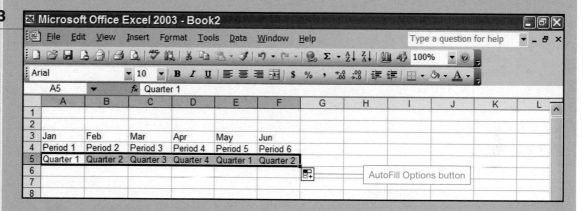

8. You can also extend a date series using the fill handle:
SELECT: cell A7
TYPE: **Sep-2003**
PRESS: ➡
TYPE: **Dec-2003**
PRESS: **ENTER**

9. To extend the range using the same increment (every three months), select both cells and then drag the range's fill handle:
SELECT: cell range from A7 to B7
DRAG: fill handle for the range to column F, as shown in Figure 2.24
When you release the mouse button, quarterly dates to Dec-2004 appear in the cell range.

Figure 2.24

Extending an incremental date series

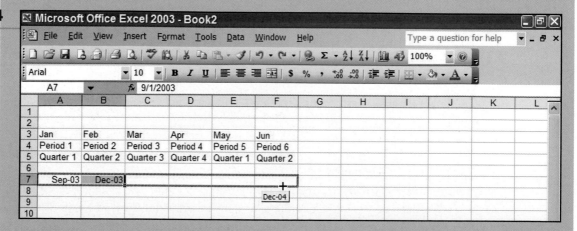

10. You can also extract a nonlinear series from a range of values:
   SELECT: cell A9
   TYPE: **12**
   PRESS: ➡
   TYPE: **15**
   PRESS: ➡
   TYPE: **17**
   PRESS: ⟨ENTER⟩
   Notice that there is not a static incrementing value in this example.

11. To continue this range of values:
   SELECT: cell range from A9 to C9
   DRAG: fill handle for the range to column F
   Excel calculates a "best guess" for the next few values. Your worksheet should now appear similar to the one shown in Figure 2.25.

12. Save the workbook as "My Series" to your personal storage location and then close the workbook.

Figure 2.25

Completing the "My Series" workbook

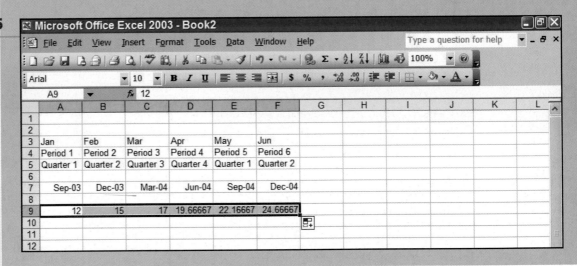

2.2.5 Extending a Cell's Contents

→ **Feature**

Another method for extending the contents of a cell is to use the Edit → Fill commands. These commands are especially useful for extending a formula across a row or down a column, saving you a tremendous amount of time compared to manual entry. If you prefer using the mouse, you can use a cell's fill handle to perform the same function, as covered in the previous lesson.

→ **Method**

To extend cell contents:

• SELECT: the desired cell range, ensuring that the data you want to copy is located in the top left-hand corner of the cell range (or in the bottom right-hand corner for filling up and to the left)

• CHOOSE: Edit → Fill → Right (or Left) to copy across a row

   or

• CHOOSE: Edit → Fill → Down (or Up) to copy down (or up) a column

→   **Practice**

In this exercise, you will open a cash flow worksheet and then copy and extend the formulas stored in it. Ensure that no workbooks appear in the application window.

1. Open the data file named EX0225 to display the workbook shown in Figure 2.26.

Figure 2.26

Opening the
EX0225 workbook

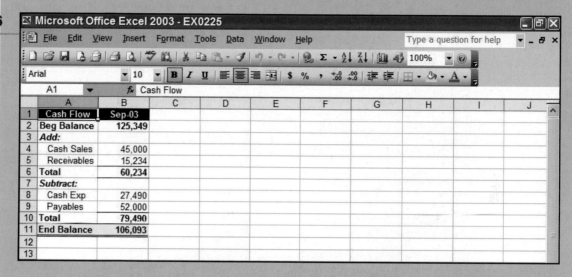

2. Save the file as "My Filled Cells" to your personal storage location.

3. To extend the date headings using the AutoFill feature:
SELECT: cell B1
DRAG: fill handle from cell B1 to column E
When you release the mouse button, the formatted date headings are entered into the columns up to Dec-03.

4. In this worksheet, the beginning balance for a new month is the ending balance from the previous month. To enter this formula into column C:
SELECT: cell C2
CLICK: Bold button (**B**) to apply boldface to the cell
TYPE: =b11
PRESS: ⌈ENTER⌋
The result "106,093" from cell B11 appears in the C2.

5. To copy and extend this formula to the right:
SELECT: cell range from C2 to E2
Notice that the top left-hand cell in the selected range contains the formula and formatting that you want to copy.

6. CHOOSE: Edit → Fill → Right

For the moment, only zeroes will appear in the remaining cells, as shown in Figure 2.27.

Figure 2.27

Extending cells using the Edit, Fill, Right command

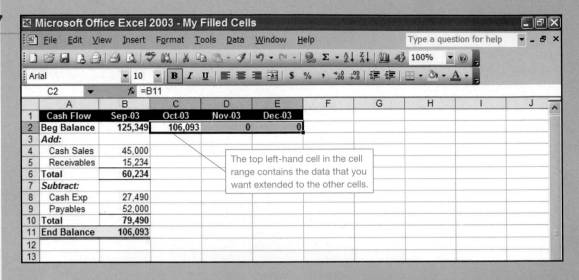

7. To extend the formulas for multiple ranges:

SELECT: cell range from B6 to E6

PRESS: CTRL and hold it down

SELECT: cell range from B10 to E10

SELECT: cell range from B11 to E11

When all the ranges are highlighted, release the CTRL key.

8. To fill each row with formulas from column B:

CHOOSE: Edit → Fill → Right

Your worksheet should now appear similar to the one shown in Figure 2.28.

Figure 2.28

Filling multiple ranges with formulas stored in the leftmost column

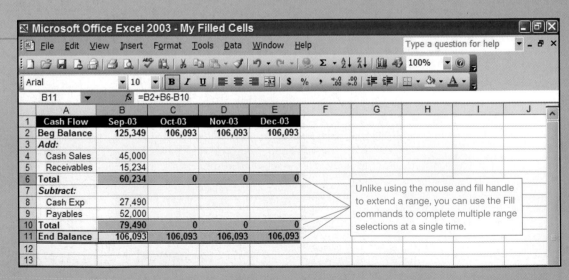

9. On your own, enter sample values into the worksheet (rows 4, 5, 8, and 9) and observe how the formulas recalculate the totals.

10. Save and then close the workbook.

 **SelfCheck**   **2.2** Which method would you use to copy several nonadjacent, or not beside one another, values for placement into a single worksheet column?

2.3 Modifying Rows and Columns

By adjusting the row heights and column widths in a worksheet, you can enhance the worksheet's appearance for both viewing and printing—in much the same way a textbook employs white space or a document uses double-spacing to make the text easier to read. You can also reorganize or modify the structure of a worksheet by inserting and deleting rows and columns. This module introduces you to the tools provided by Excel 2003 for revising and manipulating the appearance and structure of a worksheet.

2.3.1 Changing Column Widths

→ Feature

Previously, you were exposed to entering long text labels into a cell and watching as characters spilled over the cell borders into adjacent columns. For numeric entries, the data cannot extend beyond a column's borders. Instead, a series of number signs (#) fill the cell, informing you that the column is not wide enough to display the value. Fortunately, you can increase and decrease the width of your worksheet columns to allow for varying lengths of text labels, numbers, and dates. To speed the editing process, you can select and change more than one column width at a time. Excel can even calculate the best or **AutoFit** width for a column based on its existing entries. The maximum width for a column is 255 characters.

→ Method

To change a column's width using the mouse:

• DRAG: its right borderline in the frame area

To change a column's width using the menu:

• SELECT: a cell in the column that you want to format

• CHOOSE: Format → Column → Width

• TYPE: *value*, such as 12, for the desired width

To change a column's width to its best fit:

• DOUBLE-CLICK: its right borderline in the frame area

  or

• CHOOSE: Format → Column → AutoFit Selection

→ Practice

In this lesson, you open a workbook used to summarize the income earned by organizers of the Kettle Valley Craft Fair. You then change the worksheet's column widths to better view the data stored therein. Before proceeding, ensure that no workbooks are open in the application window.

Excel

1. Open the data file named EX0230 to display the workbook shown in Figure 2.29.

Figure 2.29

Opening the
EX0230 workbook

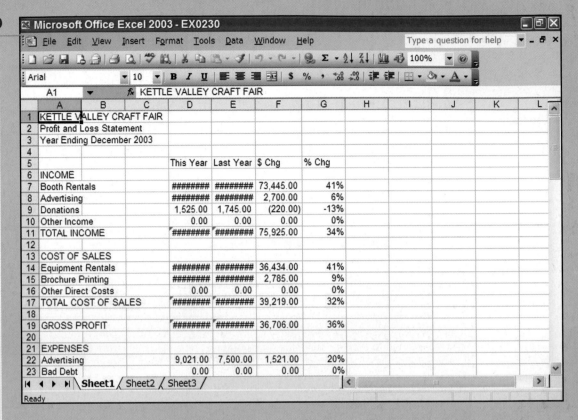

2. Save the file as "My Craft Fair" to your personal storage location.

3. In columns D and E of the worksheet, notice that some cells contain a series of "#" symbols. These symbols inform you that the columns are not wide enough to display the contents. To adjust the width of column D using a command from the Menu bar, first:
SELECT: cell D1
Notice that you need not select the entire column to change its width; in fact, you can choose any cell within the column.

4. CHOOSE: Format → Column → Width
The Column Width dialog box appears, as shown in Figure 2.30. Notice that 8.43 characters is the default column width.

Figure 2.30

Column Width
dialog box

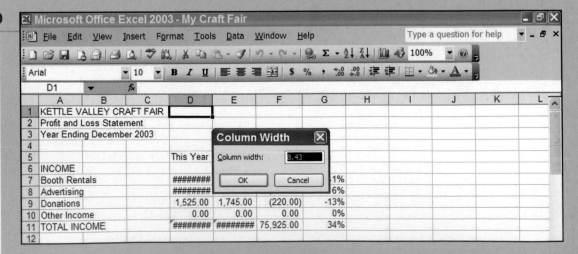

5. Enter the desired width as measured in characters:
TYPE: **12**
PRESS: (ENTER)
or
CLICK: OK
All of the values stored in column D should now be visible.

6. Now let's adjust the width for column E using the mouse. In the frame area, position the mouse pointer over the borderline between columns E and F. The mouse pointer changes shape (✛) when positioned correctly, as shown in Figure 2.31.

7. CLICK: the borderline and hold down the mouse button
DRAG: the mouse pointer to the right to increase the width to 12.00
Notice that the width (in characters and pixels) is displayed in a ToolTip. Your screen should now appear similar to Figure 2.31.

Figure 2.31

Changing a column's width using the mouse

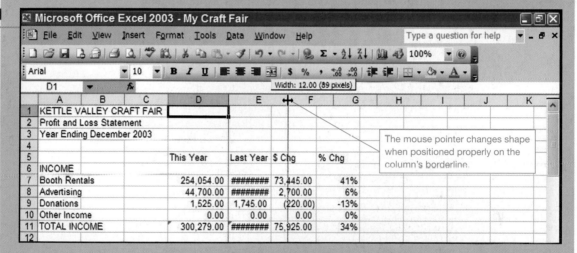

The mouse pointer changes shape when positioned properly on the column's borderline.

8. Release the mouse button to finalize the new column width setting.

9. The AutoFit feature enables you to find the best width for a column based on its existing cell entries. To demonstrate this feature, you must first select an entire column as the basis for the width calculation. Let's adjust column A to its best-fit width:
SELECT: column A
(*Hint:* This instruction tells you to move the mouse pointer over the "A" in the column frame area and click once. When done properly, the entire column appears highlighted, as shown in Figure 2.32.)

Figure 2.32

Selecting column A using the mouse

Use the black down arrow in the column frame area to select the entire column using the mouse.

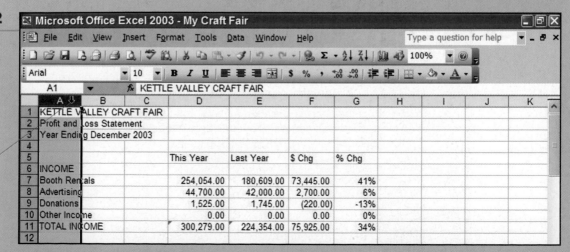

10. To calculate the best-fit width and make the change:
CHOOSE: Format → Column → AutoFit Selection
Notice that the column's width has been adjusted so that it can comfortably hold the longest cell entry.

11. PRESS: [HOME] to remove the column highlighting

12. Save the workbook and keep it open for use in the next lesson.

In Addition DOUBLE-CLICKING TO AUTOFIT A COLUMN'S WIDTH OR A ROW'S HEIGHT

After you become comfortable using the mouse to select the frame borderlines, try double-clicking the right frame borderline of a column or the bottom frame borderline of a row to AutoFit its width or height. You can select multiple columns or rows and change them all to their best-fit measurements by double-clicking any one of the selected cell's borderlines.

2.3.2 Changing Row Heights

→ ## Feature

You can change the height of any worksheet row to customize the borders and line spacing in a worksheet. What's more, a row's height is adjusted automatically when you increase or decrease the font size of information appearing in the row. A row's height is measured in points, where 72 points is equal to one inch. The larger the font size that you select for a given cell, the larger its row height.

→ ## Method

To change a row's height manually using the mouse:

• DRAG: its bottom borderline in the frame area

To change a row's height using the menu:

• SELECT: a cell in the row that you want to format

• CHOOSE: Format → Row → Height

• TYPE: *value*, such as 20, for the desired height in points

To change a row's height to its best fit:

• DOUBLE-CLICK: its bottom borderline in the frame area

  or

• CHOOSE: Format → Row → AutoFit

→ ## Practice

You now change some row heights in the worksheet to improve the spacing between data. Ensure that you have completed the previous lesson and that the "My Craft Fair" workbook is displayed.

1. Ensure that cell A1 is selected in the worksheet. In the next two steps, you will change the line spacing for the entire worksheet. As with most formatting commands, you must first select the cell range for which you want to apply formatting. To select the entire worksheet:
CLICK: Select All button (■) in the top left-hand corner of the frame area (see Figure 2.33)

2. With the entire worksheet highlighted:
CHOOSE: Format → Row → Height
Your screen should now appear similar to the one shown in Figure 2.33.

Figure 2.33

Row Height dialog box

Click the Select All button to select the entire worksheet.

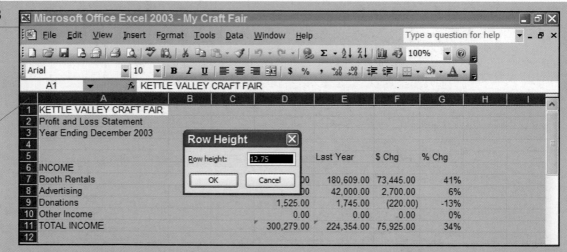

3. Enter the desired height as measured in points:
TYPE: **20**
PRESS: **ENTER**
or
CLICK: OK
Notice that the rows are enlarged, providing more white space.

4. To remove the selection highlighting:
CLICK: cell A1

5. Let's change the height of row 4 using the mouse. To begin, position the mouse pointer over the borderline between rows 4 and 5. Then:
CLICK: the borderline and hold down the mouse button
DRAG: the mouse pointer up to decrease the height to 9.00 points
As when you changed the column width, the mouse pointer changes shape and a yellow ToolTip appears with the current measurement, as shown in Figure 2.34.

Figure 2.34

Changing a column's width using the mouse

The mouse pointer changes shape when positioned properly on the row's borderline.

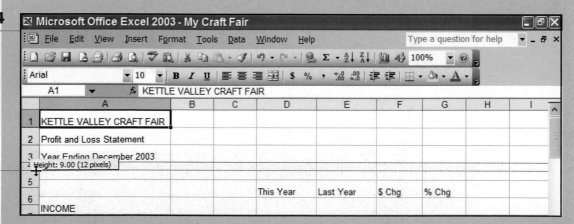

6. Release the mouse button to finalize the new row height setting.

7. Let's practice adjusting a row to its best-fit height:
SELECT: row 5
(*Hint*: This instruction tells you to move the mouse pointer over the "5" in the row frame area and click once. When this is done properly, the entire row will appear highlighted, as shown in Figure 2.35.)

8. CHOOSE: Format → Row → AutoFit
The row height is adjusted automatically, as shown in Figure 2.35.

Figure 2.35

Using AutoFit to change a row's height

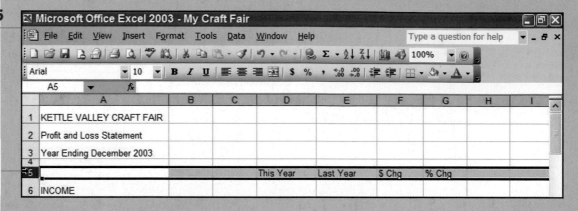

Use the black arrow in the row frame area to select the entire row.

9. PRESS: CTRL + HOME to move the cell pointer to cell A1

10. Save the workbook and keep it open for use in the next lesson.

2.3.3 Inserting and Deleting Rows and Columns

→ ## Feature

You insert and delete rows and columns to affect the structure of a worksheet. In doing so, however, you must be careful not to change areas in your worksheet unintentionally. Deleting column B, for example, removes all of the data in the entire column, not just the cells that are currently visible on your screen.

→ ## Method

To insert or delete a row:

- RIGHT-CLICK: *row number* in the row frame area

- CHOOSE: Insert or Delete

To insert or delete a column:

- RIGHT-CLICK: *column letter* in the column frame area

- CHOOSE: Insert or Delete

→ ## Practice

In this lesson, you will practice inserting and deleting rows and columns. Ensure that you have completed the previous lessons and that the "My Craft Fair" workbook is displayed.

1. After adjusting the width for column A earlier in the module, you may have noticed that columns B and C do not contain any data. Before deleting rows or columns, however, it is always wise to check your assumptions. To do so:
CLICK: cell B1
PRESS: CTRL + ↓
The cell pointer scoots down to row 65536. If there were data in the column, the cell pointer would have stopped at the cell containing the data.

2. To check whether there is any data in column C:
PRESS: ➡
PRESS: CTRL + ⬆
The cell pointer scoots back up to row 1, not stopped by any cells containing data. You can now be certain that neither column B nor column C contains data.

3. Let's delete these two columns from the worksheet. To begin:
CLICK: column B in the frame area and hold down the mouse button
DRAG: the mouse pointer right to highlight column C as well, as shown in Figure 2.36

Figure 2.36

Selecting two columns in the worksheet

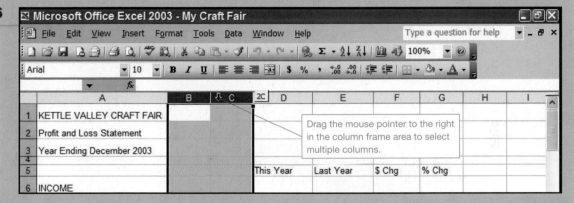

4. Release the mouse button after the two columns appear highlighted.

5. To delete these two columns:
RIGHT-CLICK: column C in the frame area
Notice that you need only right-click one of the selected column letters. Your screen should now appear similar to the one shown in Figure 2.37.

Figure 2.37

Displaying the right-click menu for the selected columns

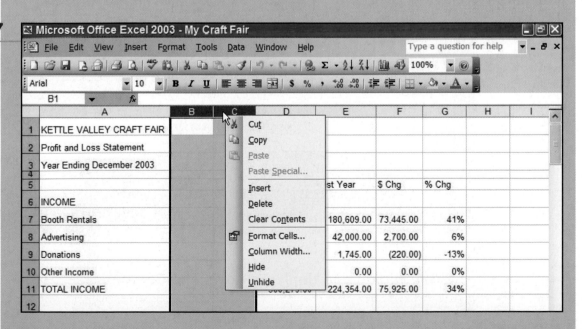

6. On the right-click menu:
CHOOSE: Delete
The blank columns are removed, but the column selection remains highlighted in case you want to apply additional formatting commands.

7. To insert a row:
RIGHT-CLICK: row 8 in the frame area
CHOOSE: Insert
A new row is inserted at row 8, pushing down the existing rows. The Insert Options icon (🗹) also appears below the newly inserted row.

8. To enter some new information:
SELECT: cell A8
TYPE: **Food Pavilion**
PRESS: ➡
TYPE: **55800**
PRESS: ➡
TYPE: **43750**
PRESS: **ENTER**

9. To copy the formulas for calculating the annual increase:
SELECT: cell range D7 to E8

10. CHOOSE: Edit → Fill → Down
The results, 12,050.00 and 28%, now appear in row 8, as shown in Figure 2.38.

Figure 2.38

Inserting and deleting rows in the "My Craft Fair" workbook

Entering data and extending formulas into the newly inserted row

11. PRESS: **CTRL** + **HOME** to move the cell pointer to cell A1

12. Save the workbook and keep it open for use in the next lesson.

2.3.4 Hiding and Unhiding Rows and Columns

→ **Feature**

Instead of deleting a row or column, you can modify a worksheet so that some of the data are not displayed. For example, you may want to hide rows and columns that contain sensitive data, such as salaries or commissions. You can also temporarily hide detailed information if you do not want it included in a particular report.

→ ## Method

To hide a row or column:

• RIGHT-CLICK: the frame area of the desired row or column

• CHOOSE: Hide

To unhide a row or column:

• SELECT: the rows or columns on both sides of the hidden row or column

• RIGHT-CLICK: the frame area of the selected rows or columns

• CHOOSE: Unhide

→ ## Practice

In this lesson, you will practice hiding and unhiding worksheet information. Ensure that you have completed the previous lessons and that the "My Craft Fair" workbook is displayed.

1. Let's hide columns D and E from displaying. Do the following:
CLICK: column D in the frame area
DRAG: the mouse pointer right to also highlight column E

2. To hide the selected columns:
RIGHT-CLICK: either column D or E in the frame area
CHOOSE: Hide
Notice that the column frame area in Figure 2.39 now shows A, B, C, and then F.

Figure 2.39

Hiding two
columns in the
worksheet

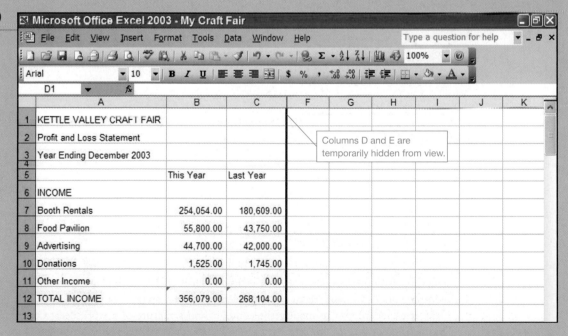

3. To hide several rows in the worksheet:
SELECT: rows 6 through 11 in the frame area
RIGHT-CLICK: any one of the selected rows (6 through 11) in the frame area
CHOOSE: Hide
The row frame area now displays a gap between row 5 and row 12.

4. To unhide columns D and E, you must select the columns on either side. For example:
CLICK: column C in the frame area
DRAG: the mouse pointer right to also highlight column F
Your screen should appear similar to the one shown in Figure 2.40.

Figure 2.40

Selecting columns in order to unhide the hidden columns

Notice the gap between rows 5 and 12 in the frame area. Rows 6 through 11 are temporarily hidden from view.

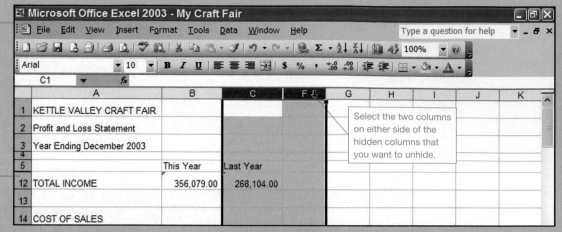

Select the two columns on either side of the hidden columns that you want to unhide.

5. Let's use the Menu bar to unhide the columns:
CHOOSE: Format → Column → Unhide
The columns reappear on the worksheet.

6. To unhide the rows:
SELECT: rows 5 through 12
CHOOSE: Format → Row → Unhide
The rows reappear on the worksheet. (*Hint:* Besides using the menu, you can right-click in the selected frame area and choose the Unhide command.)

7. PRESS: CTRL + HOME to move the cell pointer to cell A1

8. Save and then close the workbook.

9. Exit Microsoft Office Excel 2003.

 **SelfCheck**   **2.3**   Why must you be careful when deleting rows or columns?

Chapter
summary

Rarely will you begin and complete a worksheet without ever needing to correct an entry or modify its structure. Even professional spreadsheet users revisit their creations in order to adapt them to changing requirements or to make them more efficient. Fortunately, Excel provides several features and tools that make it easier for you to modify the contents and structure of a worksheet. One helpful set of "Auto" features includes AutoComplete for typing matching entries in a column and AutoSum and AutoCalculate for entering formulas. You also use the AutoFill feature to enter a series of data by dragging a cell range's fill handle. Like most Windows applications, Excel provides the standard Cut, Copy, and Paste commands for manipulating a worksheet's contents. The three approaches discussed in this chapter for copying and moving data include: the Windows Clipboard, the Office Clipboard, and the drag and drop method. You also learned to modify the structure of a worksheet by inserting and deleting cells, rows, and columns. Especially important for report presentation is your ability to adjust a worksheet's row heights and column widths and even hide (and unhide) rows and columns temporarily. You are well on your way to becoming a proficient spreadsheet user!

Command Summary

Many of the commands and procedures appearing in this chapter are summarized in the following table.

Skill Set	To Perform this Task...	Do the Following...
Creating and Revising Formulas	Enter the SUM function using the AutoSum button	SELECT: a cell to place the result CLICK: AutoSum button (Σ ▾)
	Display the sum result of a calculation using AutoCalculate	SELECT: a cell range and view the result in the Status bar
Working with Cells and Cell Data	Insert a cell or cell range	SELECT: the desired cell range CHOOSE: Insert → Cells
	Delete a cell or cell range	SELECT: the desired cell range CHOOSE: Edit → Delete
	Insert data using AutoComplete	RIGHT-CLICK: the desired cell CHOOSE: Pick From List SELECT: the desired data
	Copy or move data using the toolbar	SELECT: the desired cell or range CLICK: Copy (🗐) or Cut (✂) SELECT: the target cell or range CLICK: Paste button (📋 ▾)
	Move data using drag and drop	SELECT: the desired cell or range DRAG: the selection by its border
	Copy data using drag and drop	SELECT: the desired cell or range PRESS: CTRL and hold it down DRAG: the selection by its border
	Display the Clipboard task pane	CHOOSE: Edit → Office Clipboard
	Clear the Office Clipboard	CLICK: Clear All button (🗙 Clear All)
	Paste all of the contents from the Office Clipboard into the worksheet	CLICK: Paste All button (📋 Paste All)
	Create a data series using the fill handle	SELECT: the desired range DRAG: the fill handle
	Copy a formula across a row or down a column	SELECT: the range to fill, with the formula in the top left-hand corner CHOOSE: Edit → Fill → Right (or Down)
Formatting and Printing Worksheets	Change a cell's column width	CHOOSE: Format → Column → Width TYPE: *width* in characters
	Change a cell's row height	CHOOSE: Format → Row → Height TYPE: *height* in points
	Insert and delete columns	RIGHT-CLICK: a column's frame area CHOOSE: Insert or Delete
	Insert and delete rows	RIGHT-CLICK: a row's frame area CHOOSE: Insert or Delete
	Hide a row or column	RIGHT-CLICK: in the frame area CHOOSE: Hide
	Unhide a row or column	SELECT: rows or columns on either side of the hidden row or column RIGHT-CLICK: the frame selection CHOOSE: Unhide

Excel

Key Terms

This section specifies page references for the key terms identified in this chapter. For a complete list of definitions, refer to the Glossary at the back of this learning guide.

AutoCalculate, *p. EX 65*

AutoComplete, *p. EX 62*

AutoFill, *p. EX 79*

AutoFit, *p. EX 85*

AutoSum, *p. EX 65*

cell range, *p. EX 58*

drag and drop, *p. EX 70*

fill handle, *p. EX 80*

Office Clipboard, *p. EX 70*

series, *p. EX 79*

Windows Clipboard, *p. EX 70*

Chapter

q u i z

Short Answer

1. What visible feature differentiates the active cell in a selected cell range?

2. How do you select more than one cell range at a time?

3. Where does Excel's AutoComplete feature get the values to display in a pick list?

4. What are the two choices for shifting existing data when you insert a new cell or cell range?

5. Name the two types of Clipboards and explain how they differ.

6. What is the primary difference between using the Clipboards and using the drag and drop method to copy information?

7. What is the fastest way to place five years' worth of quarterly headings at the top of your worksheet (that is, Jan-04, Mar-04, Jun-04, . . .)?

8. What does "########" in a cell indicate?

9. What is meant by a "best fit" or "AutoFit" column width?

10. In what circumstances might you want to hide a row or column?

True/False

1. _____ You use `ALT` to select multiple cell ranges in a worksheet.

2. _____ Excel's AutoComplete feature allows you to sum a range of values and place the result into a worksheet cell.

3. _____ You use the Edit ➜ Clear command to delete the contents of a cell and the Edit ➜ Delete command to delete the actual cell.

4. _____ You can collect up to 32 items for pasting using the Office Clipboard.

5. _____ The Windows Clipboard can store only a single item for pasting.

6. _____ When you drag and drop a cell range using the `CTRL` key, a plus sign appears, indicating that you are using the copy feature.

7. _____ To copy and extend a formula to adjacent cells, you can use either the fill handle or the Edit ➜ Fill ➜ Right command.

8. _____ When you insert a column, the existing column is pushed to the left.

9. _____ When you insert a row, the existing row is pushed down.

10. _____ You unhide rows and columns using the Window ➜ Unhide All command.

Multiple Choice

1. You hold down this key to select multiple cell ranges using the mouse:
   a. `ALT`
   b. `CTRL`
   c. `SHIFT`
   d. `PRTSCR`

2. This feature allows you to view the sum of a range of values without entering a formula into a worksheet cell:
   a. AutoCalculate
   b. AutoComplete
   c. AutoTotal
   d. AutoValue

3. The AutoSum feature enters this function into a cell to sum a range of values:
   a. ADD
   b. SUM
   c. TOTAL
   d. VALUE

4. If you want to delete cells from the worksheet, you select the desired range and then choose this command:
   a. Edit ➜ Clear ➜ All
   b. Edit ➜ Clear ➜ Cells
   c. Edit ➜ Cells ➜ Delete
   d. Edit ➜ Delete

5. To perform a drag and drop operation, you position the mouse pointer over the selected cell or cell range until it changes to this shape:
   a. ⇖
   b. ✛
   c. ┿
   d. ✛

6. What menu command allows you to copy a formula in the active cell to a range of adjacent cells in a row?
   a. Edit ➜ Copy ➜ Right
   b. Edit ➜ Fill ➜ Down
   c. Edit ➜ Fill ➜ Right
   d. Edit ➜ Extend ➜ Fill

7. To select an entire column for editing, inserting, or deleting:
   a. PRESS: `ALT` + ⬇ with the cell pointer in the column
   b. DOUBLE-CLICK: a cell within the column
   c. CLICK: the column letter in the frame area
   d. CHOOSE: Edit ➜ Select Column

8. The height of a row is typically measured using these units:
   a. Characters
   b. Fonts
   c. Picas
   d. Points

9. To change a column's width using the mouse, you position the mouse pointer into the column frame area until it changes to this shape:
   a. ┿
   b. ✛
   c. ▷
   d. ┿

10. Row 5 is hidden on your worksheet. To unhide the row, you must make this selection before issuing the appropriate menu command:
    a. Rows 4 and 6
    b. Rows 1 through 4
    c. Row 4
    d. Row 6

Hands-On
exercises

step by step

1. Entering Data Using "Auto" Features

In this exercise, you practice using Excel's "Auto" features to enter information and calculate results. Specifically, you use AutoComplete to enter data into a column, AutoCalculate to display a calculated total, and then AutoSum to insert the calculated result into the worksheet.

1. Load Microsoft Office Excel 2003.

2. Open the data file named EX02HE01 to display the workbook shown in Figure 2.41.

Figure 2.41

Opening the
EX02HE01
workbook

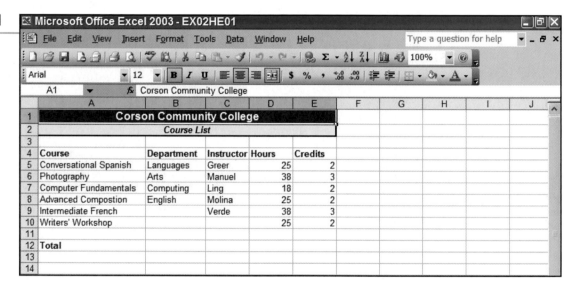

3. Save the workbook as "My Course List" to your personal storage location.

4. To complete this worksheet, you must enter some additional information for "Intermediate French." To begin:
SELECT: cell B9
TYPE: **L**
PRESS: (ENTER)
Notice that the word "Languages" is inserted automatically.

5. To enter some data for the "Writer's Workshop," do the following:
RIGHT-CLICK: cell B10
CHOOSE: Pick From List
A pick list appears with four options, as shown in Figure 2.42.

Figure 2.42

Displaying a cell's pick list

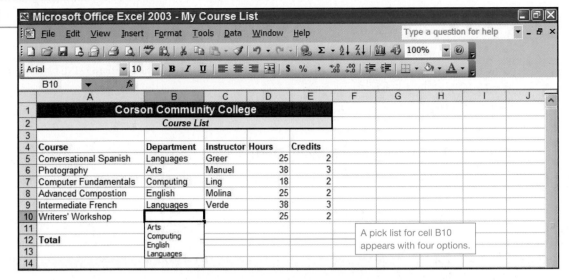

6. CLICK: English in the pick list

7. To access a column's AutoComplete pick list using the keyboard:
   SELECT: cell C10
   PRESS: ALT + ↓
   PRESS: ↓ four more times to highlight "Molina"
   PRESS: ENTER

8. Now let's use the AutoCalculate feature to sum the total number of hours in column D without placing an entry into the worksheet. Do the following:
   SELECT: cell range from D5 to D10
   What result is displayed in the Status bar?

9. To enter a formula into the worksheet that sums the Hours column:
   SELECT: cell D12
   CLICK: AutoSum button (Σ ▾)
   Excel reviews the worksheet and highlights its best guess of the range you want to sum, as shown in Figure 2.43.

Figure 2.43

Summing a column of values using the AutoSum button (Σ ▾)

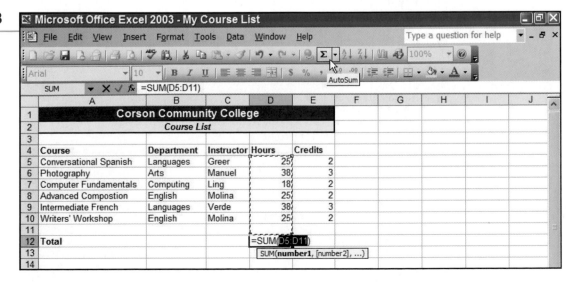

10. To accept the cell range:
CLICK: AutoSum button (Σ ▾) again
The answer, 169, now appears in the cell.

11. On your own, total the values in column E and place the result in cell E12 using the AutoSum button (Σ ▾).

12. Save and then close the workbook.

step by step

2. Copying and Moving Data

You will now practice copying and moving data using Excel's AutoFill feature, drag and drop, and Edit Fill commands.

1. Open the data file named EX02HE02 to display the workbook shown in Figure 2.44.

Figure 2.44

Opening the
EX02HE02
workbook

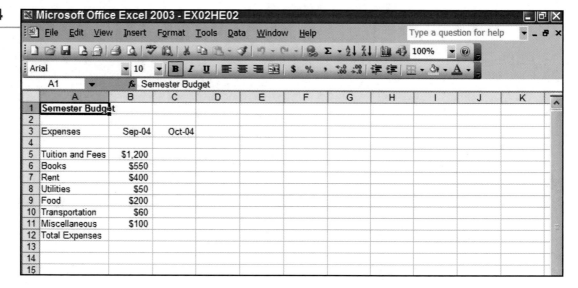

2. Save the workbook as "Semester Budget" to your personal storage location.

3. Using the AutoFill feature's fill handle, extend the dates in cells B3 and B4 out to December 2004 in the same row.

4. Using the drag and drop method, move the contents of cell A12 to cell A13. (*Hint:* Select cell A12 and then drag its cell border down one row.)

5. You will now extend several budget items to the new columns (Nov-04 and Dec-04). First, select the cell range from cell B7 to E11.

6. To copy the budget values to the rest of the highlighted range:
CHOOSE: Edit ➜ Fill ➜ Right
Your screen should now appear similar to the one shown in Figure 2.45.

Figure 2.45

Moving and extending data ranges

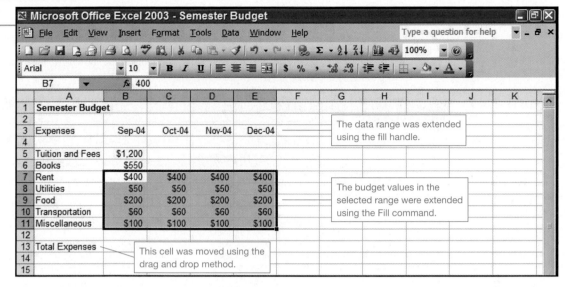

7. Using the AutoSum button (Σ▾), total the values in column B and display the result in cell B13. (*Hint:* Select cell B13 first and then click the AutoSum button (Σ▾) on the Standard toolbar.)

8. Copy the formula in cell B13 using the Copy button (🖹). The cell contents are placed onto the Windows Clipboard.

9. Select the cell range from C13 to E13.

10. Paste the contents of the Clipboard into the selected cells by clicking the Paste button (🖹▾).

11. PRESS: ESC to remove the dashed marquee
PRESS: CTRL + HOME to move to cell A1
Your screen should now appear similar to Figure 2.46.

Figure 2.46

Completed "Semester Budget" workbook

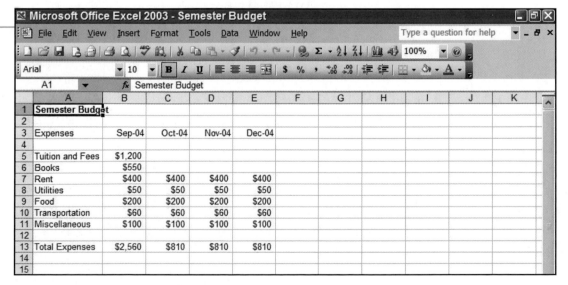

12. Save and then close the "Semester Budget" workbook.

3. Modifying a Worksheet's Structure

In this exercise, you will practice modifying the appearance and structure of an existing worksheet.

1. Open the data file named EX02HE03 to display the workbook shown in Figure 2.47.

Figure 2.47

Opening the
EX02HE03
workbook

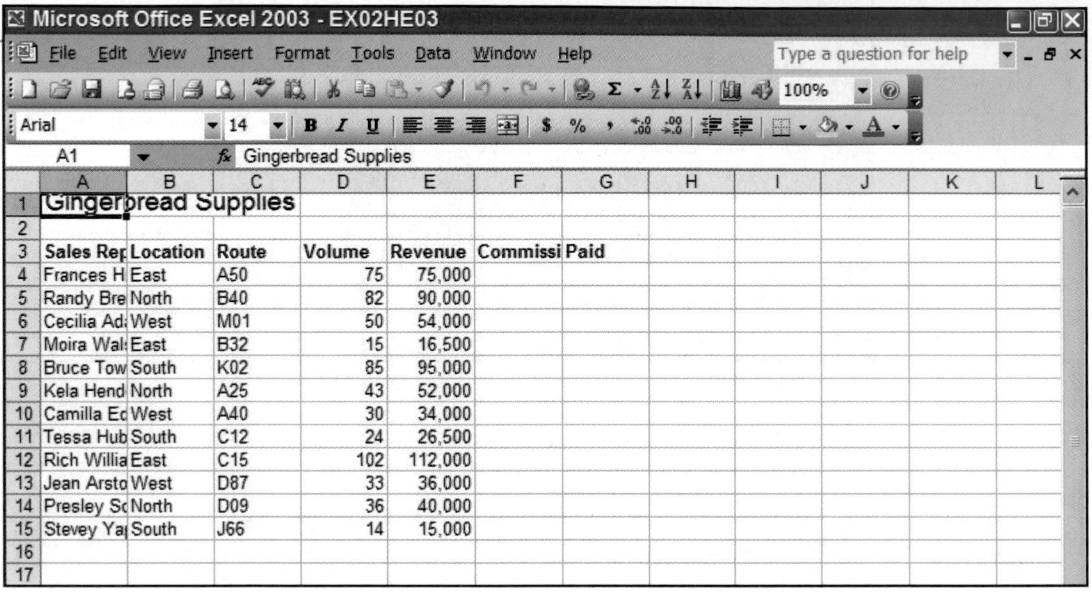

	A	B	C	D	E	F	G
1	Gingerbread Supplies						
2							
3	Sales Rep	Location	Route	Volume	Revenue	Commissi	Paid
4	Frances H	East	A50	75	75,000		
5	Randy Bre	North	B40	82	90,000		
6	Cecilia Ad	West	M01	50	54,000		
7	Moira Wal	East	B32	15	16,500		
8	Bruce Tow	South	K02	85	95,000		
9	Kela Hend	North	A25	43	52,000		
10	Camilla Ed	West	A40	30	34,000		
11	Tessa Hub	South	C12	24	26,500		
12	Rich Willia	East	C15	102	112,000		
13	Jean Arsto	West	D87	33	36,000		
14	Presley Sc	North	D09	36	40,000		
15	Stevey Ya	South	J66	14	15,000		

Microsoft Office Excel 2003 - EX02HE03. Cell A1: Gingerbread Supplies.

2. Save the workbook as "Sales Force" to your personal storage location.

3. You may have noticed that the title in cell A1 is difficult to read. Adjust the height for row 1 to its "best fit" or "AutoFit" height.

4. The sales representatives' names are truncated by the "Location" entries in column B. Therefore, adjust the width of column A to ensure that all the names are visible.

5. Change the column width for columns B through D to 8 characters.

6. Change the column width for columns E through G to 10 characters.

7. Change the height of rows 2 through 15 to 15.00.

8. In cell F4, enter a commission rate of 5%.

9. In cell G4, multiply the commission rate (F) by the Revenue (E). Your worksheet should now appear similar to the one shown in Figure 2.48.

Figure 2.48

Adjusting rows
and columns and
entering a formula

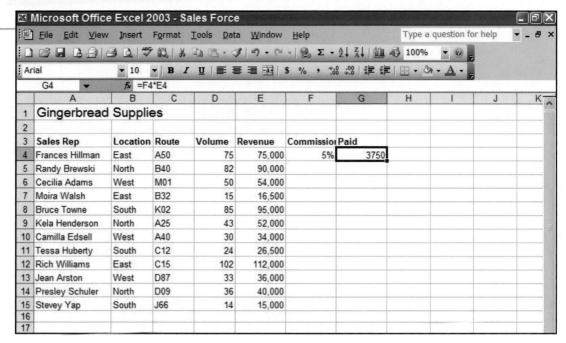

10. Using the Edit → Fill → Down command, copy the entries in cells F4 and G4 down their respective columns to row 15.

11. Remove the route information by deleting column C.

12. Remove the information for Bruce Towne by deleting the cell range A8 to F8 and then close up the gap.

13. Hide the Revenue column from displaying in the worksheet and then return the cell pointer to cell A1. Your worksheet should now appear similar to the one shown in Figure 2.49.

Figure 2.49

Completed "Sales
Force" workbook

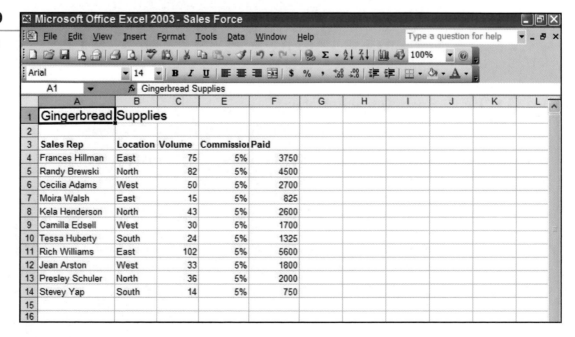

14. Without placing a formula on the worksheet, calculate the total volume of sales generated by these sales reps. What is this value?

15. Save and then close the workbook.

on your own

4. Sparkle Ski-Free Manufacturing

Sparkle Ski-Free Manufacturing recently computerized the production scheduling for their four plants in Brookview, Cedar Hill, Newton, and Westside. The supervising foreman has entered in three years of results for each of the plants and has asked you to project the future production totals. You open the EX02HE04 workbook that he created and save it as "Sparkle Projection" to your personal storage location.

After expanding column A to 12 characters, you decide to use the AutoFill feature's fill handle to extend a row of data. Select each cell range individually, starting with B3 to D3, and drag the range's fill handle to column G in order to extrapolate the series. Using the AutoSum button (Σ ▾), total the units produced for each year and place the results into row 8, as shown in Figure 2.50.

Figure 2.50

Filling data ranges and calculating totals

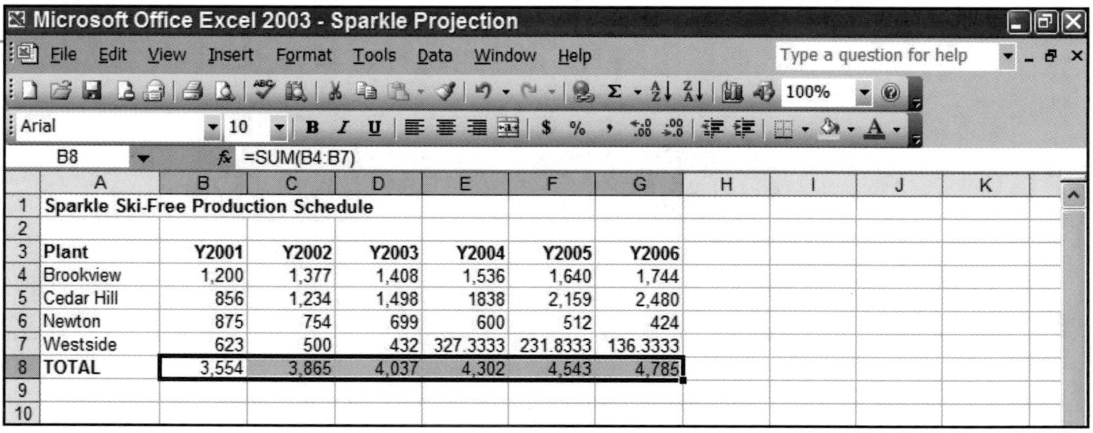

Microsoft Office Excel 2003 - Sparkle Projection										
	A	B	C	D	E	F	G	H	I	J	K
1	Sparkle Ski-Free Production Schedule										
2											
3	Plant	Y2001	Y2002	Y2003	Y2004	Y2005	Y2006				
4	Brookview	1,200	1,377	1,408	1,536	1,640	1,744				
5	Cedar Hill	856	1,234	1,498	1838	2,159	2,480				
6	Newton	875	754	699	600	512	424				
7	Westside	623	500	432	327.3333	231.8333	136.3333				
8	TOTAL	3,554	3,865	4,037	4,302	4,543	4,785				
9											
10											

B8 = =SUM(B4:B7)

To display only the total results for the projected years, hide rows 4 through 7 and columns B through D. Only three values should now appear on the worksheet under their column headings. Save and then close the workbook.

on your own

5. Ouchi Office Assistance

A friend of yours has just accepted a position at Ouchi Office Assistance. In addition to her general administrative duties, she must help the accountant prepare monthly income statements. Because she seemed quite nervous about the new position, you offered to help her develop an Excel worksheet. You open the EX02HE05 workbook that she has been using and save it as "Ouchi OA" to her personal storage location.

After adjusting the column widths, you review the structure of the worksheet. To begin, you insert a row above Expenses and label it "Total Revenue." Then, you use the AutoSum feature to sum the revenues for September and October. Continuing in this manner, you adjust and insert rows, data, and formulas so that the worksheet appears similar to Figure 2.51. Then, you save and close the workbook.

Figure 2.51

Modifying a
worksheet's
structure and
appearance

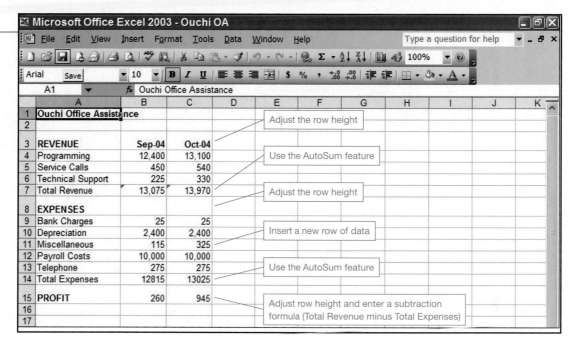

n your own

6. Running Diary

It is May and you are finally getting around to the New Year's resolution you made to get into shape. To motivate yourself, you decide to create a running diary using Microsoft Office Excel 2003. Open the data file named EX02HE06 (Figure 2.52) and then save it as "My Running Diary" to your personal storage location.

Figure 2.52

Opening the
EX02HE06
workbook

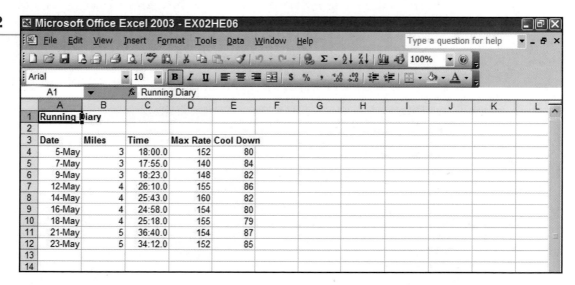

Given your current statistics, you would like to project how long it will take you to reach 10 miles. To do so, select the cell range from B4 through B12. Drag the fill handle for the range downward until the ToolTip displays a value over 10. Press (CTRL) + (HOME) to return to the top of the worksheet. To make it easier to count the number of runs, insert a new column A with the column heading "Run" and then move the title "Running Diary" back into cell A1 using drag and drop. Number each run in the column, using the fill handle to make the process faster. *How many runs will it take you to reach 10 miles?* Using Excel's AutoCalculate feature, find out how many miles you've run as of May 23. *How many miles have you run thus far?*

Impressed with your computer knowledge, your running partner asks you to track her running statistics also. Rather than create a new worksheet, you copy and paste the column headings beside your own, so that they begin in column H. Save and close the workbook and then exit Excel 2003.

CaseProblems   BEAVERTON FINANCIAL SERVICES

Beaverton Financial Services, Inc., is the largest private insurance company in Oregon state. The company has always maintained a high profile in the community by sponsoring youth programs and providing assistance to local charities. This sense of community was one of the main attractions for James Wyndham, who recently joined the company as its internal business manager.

James recently assumed responsibility for generating the monthly profitability reports for one of Beaverton Financial's longest-standing clients, a local car dealership for whom the company tracks financing, insurance, and after-market sales results. With this increase in workload, James knows that he must streamline operations and find a more efficient method for summarizing the data he receives. Fortunately, his new computer just arrived with Microsoft Office Excel 2003 installed. Upon reviewing some of the car dealership's past data James identifies an opportunity to use Microsoft Office Excel 2003 for generating its reports.

In the following case problems, assume the role of James and perform the same steps that he identifies. You may want to reread the chapter opening before proceeding.

1. James decides to focus his attention on one report that is generated for the car dealership at the end of each month. He calls a good friend, whom he knows has several months' experience using Excel, and describes what he needs. He then sends his friend a fax of the actual report to help clarify the discussion. The next day, James receives an e-mail attachment from his friend that contains a workbook called EX02CP01. He opens the workbook (Figure 2.53) using Excel 2003 and then saves it as "PROFIT" to his personal storage location.

Figure 2.53

Opening the
EX02CP01
workbook

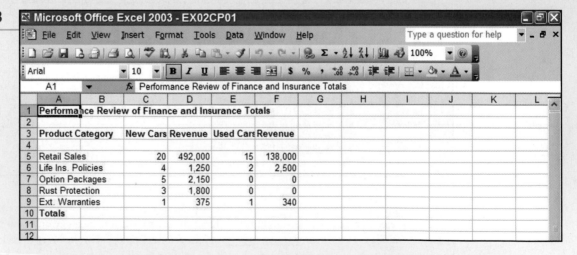

The PROFIT report, which is the car dealer's own abbreviation for a "Profitability Review of Finance and Insurance Totals," summarizes the number of new and used cars that are sold in a given month, including the number of financing, insurance, warranty, and rust protection packages. After reviewing the worksheet, James decides to make a few additions and modifications.

- In cell A1, edit the title to read "Profitability Review of Finance and Insurance Totals."

- In cells G3 and H3, enter the headings "Total Cars" and "Revenue," respectively.

- In cell G5, enter a formula that adds the number of new car sales to the number of used car sales.

- In cell H5, enter a formula that adds the revenue for new car sales to the revenue for used car sales.

- Using the fill handle, copy the formulas in cells G5 and H5 down their respective columns to row 9.

- Using the AutoSum feature, sum the values in columns C through H and place the results in row 10.

Save the workbook and keep it open for use in the next problem.

2. Wednesday morning does not start out well for James. The owner of the dealership calls to request that Beaverton Financial no longer track the sale of "Rust Protection" packages. He also asks James to hide the "Used Cars" columns in the report. Fortunately, James remembers how to remove and hide cells, rows, and columns. He also feels that this is a great opportunity to adjust some of the worksheet's column widths and row heights. Specifically, James performs the following steps:

- Select the "best fit" or "AutoFit" width for column A. Notice that the width is adjusted to handle the length of the title in cell A1.

- Specify a column width of 18 characters for column A.

- Specify a column width of 10 characters for columns C through H.

- Specify a row height of 7.50 points for row 4.

- Ensure that column B is empty, then delete the entire column.

- Select the cell range (A8:G8) for Rust Protection. Then choose the Edit → Delete command to remove the cells from the worksheet and shift the remaining cells upward.

- Select columns D and E for the Used Cars data, then hide the columns (i.e., keep them from displaying).

Move the cell pointer to cell A1. Your screen should appear similar to the one shown in Figure 2.54. Save the workbook and keep it open for use in the next problem.

Figure 2.54

Manipulating columns and rows in a worksheet

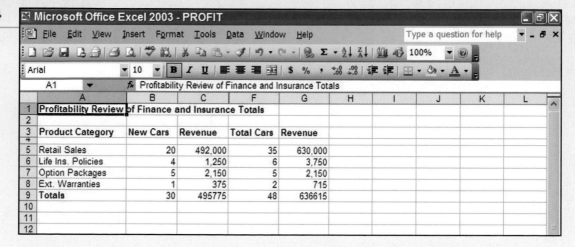

3. James decides that it would be helpful to develop a projection for next month's PROFIT report. Rather than create a new worksheet, he unhides columns D and E and then copies the data from cells A3 through G9 to the Windows Clipboard. He moves the cell pointer to cell A12, pastes the data, and then presses ESC to remove the dashed marquee. To complete the operation, James adjusts row 13 to match the height of row 4.

In order to start with a clean slate, James selects cells B14 through E17 and erases the cell contents in the range. Then he selects cell B14 and enters a formula that shows an increase of 20% over the value stored in cell B5. In other words, he multiplies the value in cell B5 by 1.2. Next, James copies the formula to the remaining cells in the range, as shown in Figure 2.55. To ensure that the projection area works properly, James changes some of the values in the original table area. Satisfied that the bottom projection table updates automatically, he saves and closes the workbook.

Figure 2.55

Creating a projection based on an existing range of cells

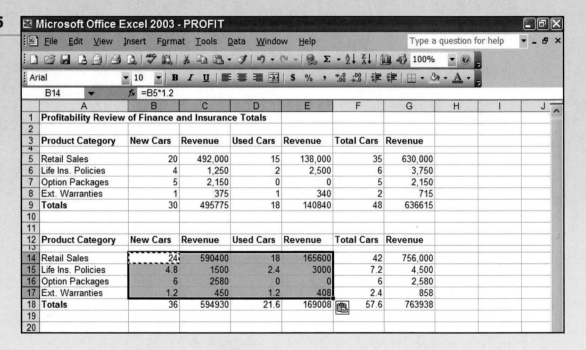

4. James opens a second workbook, EX02CP04, that he received from his friend. He then saves the workbook, shown in Figure 2.56, as "Car Buyers" to his personal storage location. This particular workbook stores customer information from each sale made in the month.

Figure 2.56

Opening the
EX02CP04
workbook

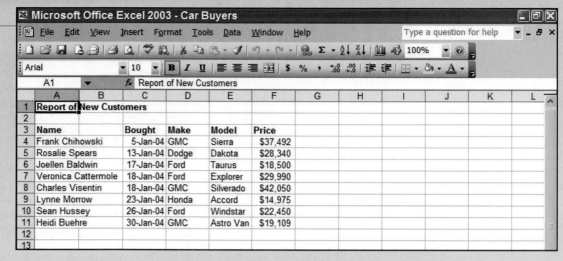

James reviews the worksheet and decides to make a few changes. First, he inserts a new column A and moves the title back into cell A1. He then enters 1 into cell A4 and 2 into cell A5. Using the mouse, James selects both cells and then drags the range's fill handle downward to continue numbering the customers. *What is the number of the last customer, Heidi Buehre?* He then moves to cell E12 and displays the AutoComplete pick list. *What vehicles are listed in the pick list and in what order do they appear?* To remove the pick list, James presses the ⌨ **ESC** key. Finally, James uses Excel's AutoCalculate feature to sum the purchase price of all vehicles sold in January without having to enter a formula into the worksheet. *What is the total value of vehicles purchased?*

Ready to go home for the day, James saves and closes the workbook and then exits Microsoft Office Excel 2003.

Excel

Answers to Self-Check Questions

2.1 Which of the "Auto" features enables you to sum a range of values and display the result in the Status bar? AutoCalculate

2.2 Which method would you use to copy several nonadjacent (not beside one another) values for placement into a single worksheet column? The Office Clipboard would provide the fastest method. After displaying the Clipboard task pane, clear the Clipboard and then collect up to 24 items in the desired sequence. You would then move to the target range and paste these items into a single column using the Paste All button ([Paste All]).

2.3 Why must you be careful when deleting rows or columns? You must be careful because if you delete the entire row or column, you may inadvertently delete data that exists farther down a column or farther across a row. Ensure that a row or column is indeed empty before deleting it.

Microsoft® Office Excel®

2003

CHAPTER 3

 # Formatting and Printing

CHAPTER OUTLINE

3.1 Enhancing a Worksheet's Appearance

3.2 Applying and Removing Formatting

3.3 Printing and Web Publishing

3.4 Customizing Print Options

Chapter Summary

Chapter Quiz

Hands-On Exercises

Case Study

PREREQUISITES

To successfully complete this chapter, you must be comfortable performing basic data entry and editing tasks. You will be asked to modify worksheet information using toolbar buttons, Menu commands, and right-click shortcut menus. Web publishing is also introduced in this chapter, so you should know how to launch your Web browser software for viewing Web pages.

LEARNING OBJECTIVES

After completing this chapter, you will be able to:

- Format cell entries to appear boldface or italic and with different typefaces and font sizes

- Format numeric and date values

- Format cells to appear with borders, shading, and color

- Preview and print a worksheet

- Publish a worksheet to the World Wide Web

- Define page layout options, such as margins, headers and footers, and paper orientation, for printing your worksheets

3.1 Enhancing a Worksheet's Appearance

Most people realize how important it is to create worksheets that are easy to read and pleasing to the eye. Clearly, a visually attractive worksheet will convey information better than an unformatted one. With Excel's formatting capabilities, you can enhance your worksheets for publishing online or for printing. In addition to choosing from a variety of fonts, styles, and cell alignments, you can specify decimal places and add currency and percentage symbols to values. The combination of these features enables you to produce professional-looking spreadsheet reports and presentations.

3.1.1 Applying Fonts, Font Styles, and Colors

→ ## Feature

Applying **fonts** to titles, headings, and other worksheet cells is often the most effective means for drawing a reader's attention to specific areas in your worksheet. You can also specify font styles, such as boldface and italic, adjust font sizes, and select colors. Do not feel obliged, however, to use every font that is available to you in a single worksheet. Above all, your worksheets must be easy to read—too many fonts, styles, and colors are distracting. As a rule, limit your font selection for a single worksheet to two or three common **typefaces,** such as Times New Roman and Arial.

→ ## Method

To apply character formatting to the contents of a cell, select the desired cell range and then use any of the following:

- CLICK: *Font* list box (Arial ▼)
- CLICK: *Font Size* list box (10 ▼)
- CLICK: Bold button (**B**)
- CLICK: Italic button (*I*)
- CLICK: Underline button (U̲)
- CLICK: Font Color button (A̲ ▼)

To display the *Font* formatting options:

- SELECT: cell range to format
- CHOOSE: Format → Cells
- CLICK: *Font* tab in the Format Cells dialog box
- SELECT: the desired font, font style, size, color, and effects

→ ## Practice

In this lesson, you will open and format a workbook that tracks a mutual fund portfolio. Before proceeding, ensure that Excel is loaded.

1. Open the data file named EX0310 to display the workbook shown in Figure 3.1.

Figure 3.1

Opening the
EX0310
workbook

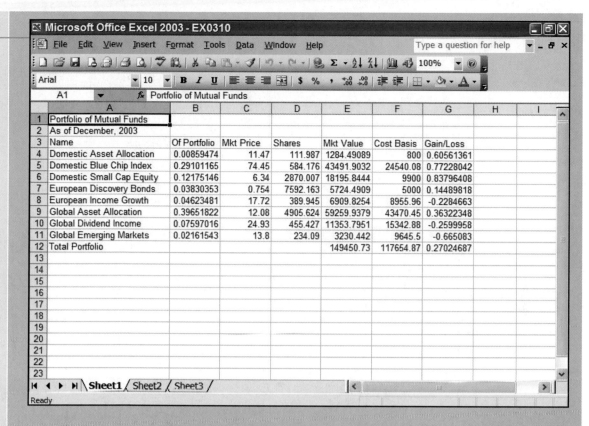

2. Save the file as "My Portfolio" to your personal storage location.

3. Your first step is to select the cell range to format. Do the following to begin formatting the column labels:
SELECT: cell range from A3 to G3

4. Let's make these labels bold and underlined:
CLICK: Bold button (**B**)
CLICK: Underline button (U)

5. Now format the title labels in cells A1 and A2:
SELECT: cell range from A1 to A2

6. To change the typeface used in the cells:
CLICK: down arrow attached to the *Font* list box (Arial ▾)
(*Note:* The fonts that appear in the list box are available for your use in Excel 2003. Some fonts are loaded with Windows and Microsoft Office, and a variety of other fonts may appear in the list from other application programs that you have installed.) Your screen will appear similar, but not identical, to the one shown in Figure 3.2.

Figure 3.2

Selecting a typeface from the Font list box

The typeface names appearing in your *Font* drop-down list box will differ from the ones displayed here.

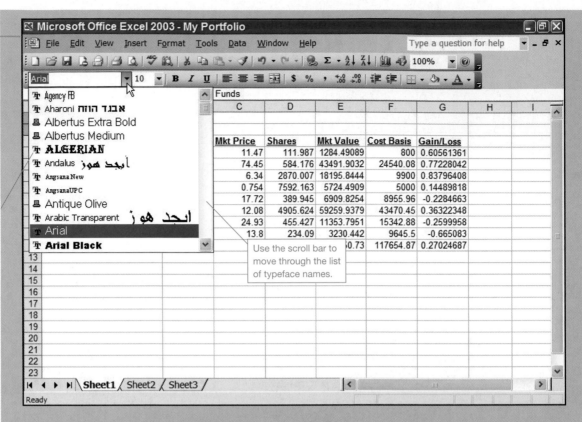

7. Using the scroll bars attached to the drop-down list box to move through the list of typeface names:
   SELECT: Times New Roman

8. To increase the font size:
   CLICK: down arrow attached to the *Font Size* list box (10 ▾)
   SELECT: 14
   The two cells now appear formatted using a 14-point, Times New Roman typeface; the row heights have also been adjusted automatically.

9. Besides the toolbar buttons, you can use the Format Cells dialog box to apply formatting to the selected cell range. To illustrate:
   SELECT: cell A1
   CHOOSE: Format → Cells
   CLICK: *Font* tab
   The Format Cells dialog box (Figure 3.3) displays the current formatting options for the active cell.

Figure 3.3

Format Cells
dialog box, *Font*
tab

The font or typeface
is Times New
Roman, as you
selected previously
using the *Font* drop-
down list box.

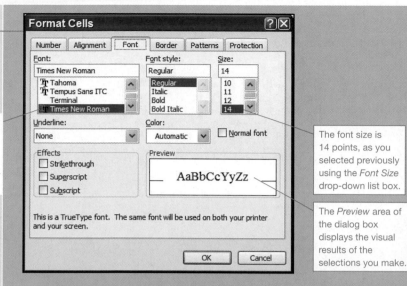

The font size is
14 points, as you
selected previously
using the *Font Size*
drop-down list box.

The *Preview* area of
the dialog box
displays the visual
results of the
selections you make.

10. To add some additional flare to the title:
SELECT: *any typeface* from the *Font* list box
SELECT: Bold in the *Font style* list box
SELECT: 16 in the *Size* list box
SELECT: Blue from the *Color* drop-down list box
CLICK: OK command button
The title in cell A1 should now stand out from the rest of the data.

11. You can also use shortcut keys to apply formatting. To demonstrate:
SELECT: cell range from A12 to G12
PRESS: **CTRL** + **b** to apply boldface

12. Save the workbook and keep it open for use in the next lesson.

In Addition COMMON SHORTCUT KEYS FOR FORMATTING YOUR
WORKSHEETS

To help speed up formatting operations, select the desired cell range and then use the following key
combinations:

- **CTRL** + **b** to apply boldface

- **CTRL** + **i** to apply italic

- **CTRL** + **u** to apply underlining

- **CTRL** + **SHIFT** + **f** to select a font typeface

- **CTRL** + **SHIFT** + **p** to select a font point size

3.1.2 Formatting Numbers and Dates

→ **Feature**

Numeric formats improve the appearance and readability of numbers in a worksheet by inserting dollar signs, commas, percentage symbols, and decimal places. Although a number or date may appear
formatted on the worksheet, the underlying value that is stored in the cell (and seen in the Formula bar)
does not change. Excel stores date and time entries as values and, therefore, allows you to customize
their display as you do numbers.

→ Method

To apply number formatting, select the desired cell range and then use one of the following:

- CLICK: Currency Style button ($)
- CLICK: Percent Style button (%)
- CLICK: Comma Style button (,)
- CLICK: Increase Decimal button
- CLICK: Decrease Decimal button

To display the number formatting options:

- SELECT: cell range to format
- CHOOSE: Format → Cells
- CLICK: *Number* tab
- SELECT: a number or date format from the *Category* list box
- SELECT: formatting options for the selected category

→ Practice

You will now apply number, currency, percentage, decimal place, and date formatting to the worksheet. Ensure that you have completed the previous lesson and that the "My Portfolio" workbook is displayed.

1. In reviewing the worksheet, notice that the Of Portfolio and Gain/Loss columns in the worksheet contain data that is best represented using a percent number format. The Of Portfolio column (B) displays the proportional share of an investment compared to the total portfolio. The Gain/Loss column (G) calculates the performance gain or loss. To display these calculated results as percentages, do the following:
SELECT: cell range from B4 to B11
PRESS: CTRL and hold it down
SELECT: cell range from G4 to G12

2. Release the CTRL key after the last range is selected. Notice that these two ranges are highlighted independently—ready for formatting. (*Note:* You will no longer be reminded to release the CTRL key when dragging the cell pointer over a range.)

3. To apply a percent style:
CLICK: Percent Style button (%)

4. To display the percentages with two decimal places:
CLICK: Increase Decimal button twice
Your worksheet should now appear similar to the one shown in Figure 3.4.

Figure 3.4

Applying percent formatting to multiple cell ranges

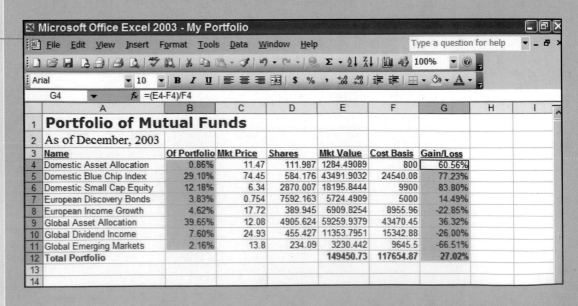

5. Let's apply some further number formatting:
SELECT: cell range from C4 to C11
CHOOSE: Format → Cells
CLICK: *Number* tab

6. In the Format Cells dialog box that appears:
SELECT: Currency in the *Category* list box
SELECT: 4 in the *Decimal places* spin box
SELECT: Black ($1,234.3210) in the *Negative numbers* list box
Your dialog box should now appear similar to the one shown in Figure 3.5.

Figure 3.5

Format Cells
dialog box,
Number tab

After selecting the
desired category for
numeric formatting,
customize the
display using the
other options in the
dialog box.

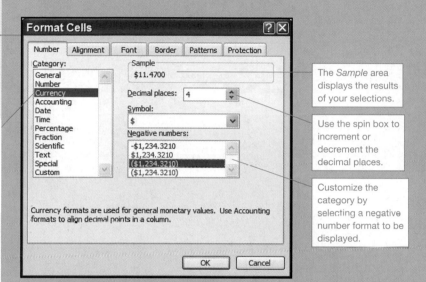

The *Sample* area
displays the results
of your selections.

Use the spin box to
increment or
decrement the
decimal places.

Customize the
category by
selecting a negative
number format to be
displayed.

7. To apply the formatting options:
CLICK: OK command button

8. To increase the decimal places in the Shares column:
SELECT: cell range from D4 to D11
CLICK: Increase Decimal button (⬆.0/.00)

9. To format the Currency style of remaining values:
SELECT: cell range from E4 to F12
CLICK: Currency Style button (⟨$⟩)

10. Depending on your system, the columns may not be wide enough to display the
formatted values. With the cell range still selected:
CHOOSE: Format → Column → AutoFit Selection
You should now see all the data contained in the column, as shown in Figure 3.6.

Figure 3.6

Formatting values in the worksheet

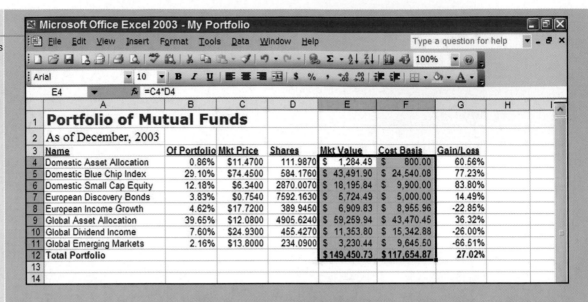

11. Now let's create a notes area:
SELECT: cell A14
TYPE: **Notes**
PRESS: ⬇

12. To enter the first note or comment:
TYPE: **31-Dec-2003**
PRESS: ➡
TYPE: **The market rebounded from a low of 7,200 in October.**
PRESS: ENTER

13. SELECT: cell A15
In the Formula bar, notice that the date reads 12/31/2003.

14. To format the date to appear differently on the worksheet:
CHOOSE: Format ➜ Cells
SELECT: Date in the *Category* list box, if it is not already selected

15. To apply a new format, select one of the listed versions:
SELECT: "March 14, 2001" in the *Type* list box
CLICK: OK command button
(*Note:* The *Type* list box displays the date formats for March 14, 2001. Keep in mind that you are selecting a display format and not a date value to insert into the worksheet.) Your screen should now appear similar to the one shown in Figure 3.7.

16. Save the workbook and keep it open for use in the next lesson.

Figure 3.7

Applying number
and date formats

The actual value
stored in the cell,
12/31/2003, appears
in the Formula bar.

The value currently
displayed in cell A15
is "December 31,
2003."

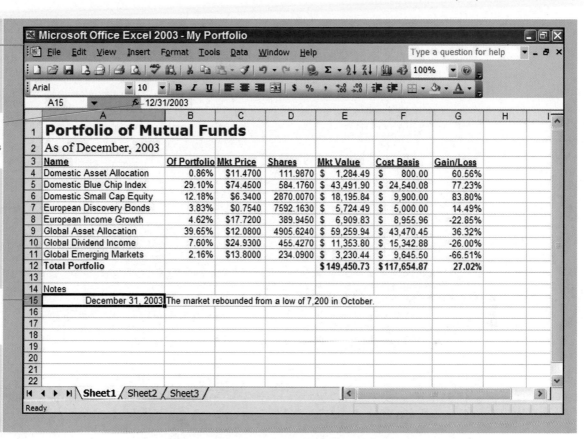

3.1.3 Aligning, Merging, and Rotating Cells

→ **Feature**

You can change the **cell alignment** for any type of data entered into a worksheet. By default, Excel aligns text against the left edge of a cell and values against the right edge. Not only can you change these default alignments, but you can also merge or combine data across cells. Rotating text within a cell allows you to fit longer text entries into a narrow column.

→ **Method**

To align and merge data, select the desired cell range and then use one of the following:

- CLICK: Align Left button (⊞)

- CLICK: Center button (⊞)

- CLICK: Align Right button (⊞)

- CLICK: Merge and Center button (⊞)

To display the alignment formatting options:

- SELECT: cell range to format

- CHOOSE: Format → Cells

- CLICK: *Alignment* tab

- SELECT: an option to align, merge, or rotate cells

→ Practice

You will now practice aligning, merging, and rotating text in cells. Ensure that you have completed the previous lessons in the module and that the "My Portfolio" workbook is displayed.

1. The easiest way to align a cell's contents is to use the buttons on the Formatting toolbar. To illustrate, let's manipulate the "Notes" title in cell A14:
SELECT: cell A14
CLICK: Bold button (**B**)
CLICK: Underline button (U)

2. To practice changing a cell's alignment:
CLICK: Align Right button (≣)
CLICK: Align Left button (≣)
CLICK: Center button (≣)
Notice the change in alignment that takes place with each mouse click.

3. You can change the cell alignment for number and date values also:
SELECT: cell A15
CLICK: Center button (≣)
The date appears centered under the column heading for "Notes."

4. Perhaps more interesting is your ability to merge cells together and then center their contents over a range. Do the following:
SELECT: cell range from A1 to G1
CLICK: Merge and Center button (≣)
Notice that the title is now centered over the table area, as shown in Figure 3.8. (*Note:* The merged cell is still considered to be cell A1. The next cell in the same row is cell H1.)

Figure 3.8

Aligning and merging cells

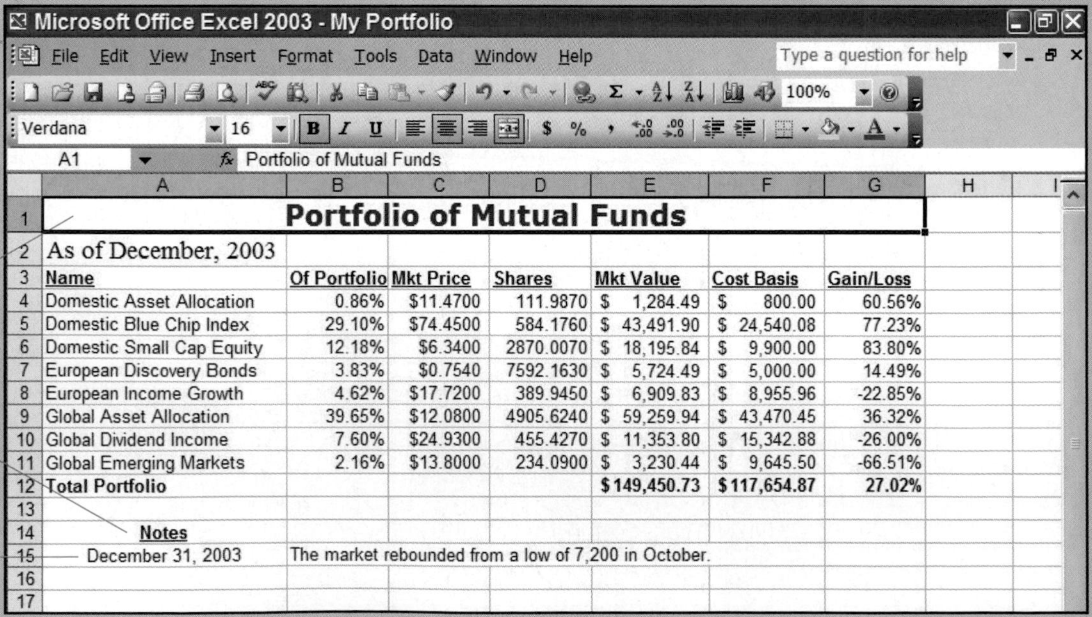

The title is centered in cell A1, which is a merged cell over the range A1:G1

The text is centered in cell A14.

The date value is centered in cell A15.

Microsoft Office Excel 2003 - My Portfolio

A1   *fx* Portfolio of Mutual Funds

	A	B	C	D	E	F	G	H
1	**Portfolio of Mutual Funds**							
2	As of December, 2003							
3	**Name**	**Of Portfolio**	**Mkt Price**	**Shares**	**Mkt Value**	**Cost Basis**	**Gain/Loss**	
4	Domestic Asset Allocation	0.86%	$11.4700	111.9870	$ 1,284.49	$ 800.00	60.56%	
5	Domestic Blue Chip Index	29.10%	$74.4500	584.1760	$ 43,491.90	$ 24,540.08	77.23%	
6	Domestic Small Cap Equity	12.18%	$6.3400	2870.0070	$ 18,195.84	$ 9,900.00	83.80%	
7	European Discovery Bonds	3.83%	$0.7540	7592.1630	$ 5,724.49	$ 5,000.00	14.49%	
8	European Income Growth	4.62%	$17.7200	389.9450	$ 6,909.83	$ 8,955.96	-22.85%	
9	Global Asset Allocation	39.65%	$12.0800	4905.6240	$ 59,259.94	$ 43,470.45	36.32%	
10	Global Dividend Income	7.60%	$24.9300	455.4270	$ 11,353.80	$ 15,342.88	-26.00%	
11	Global Emerging Markets	2.16%	$13.8000	234.0900	$ 3,230.44	$ 9,645.50	-66.51%	
12	Total Portfolio				$ 149,450.73	$ 117,654.87	27.02%	
13								
14	Notes							
15	December 31, 2003	The market rebounded from a low of 7,200 in October.						
16								
17								

5. Let's merge and center the subtitle in cell A2 using the dialog box:
SELECT: cell range from A2 to G2
CHOOSE: Format → Cells
CLICK: *Alignment* tab
The Format Cells dialog box appears, as shown in Figure 3.9.

Figure 3.9

Format Cells
dialog box,
Alignment tab

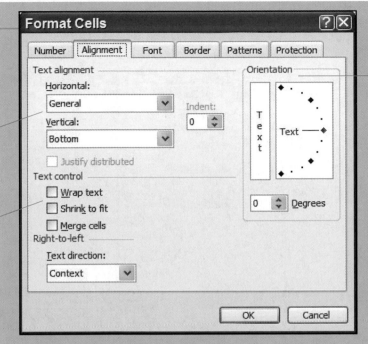

Use controls in the
Text alignment area
to align text
horizontally and
vertically within a cell.

Use controls in the
Text control area to
change the way long
text entries are
displayed in a cell.

Use the dialog box
controls in the
Orientation area to
adjust the angle of
text displayed in a
cell.

6. In the Format Cells dialog box:
   SELECT: Center from the *Horizontal* drop-down list box
   SELECT: *Merge cells* check box
   CLICK: OK command button

7. Let's practice splitting up a merged cell without using the Undo command. Ensure that cell A2 (which now covers the area to G2) is still selected and then do the following:
   CHOOSE: Format → Cells
   The last tab that was selected in the dialog box *(Alignment)* is displayed automatically.

8. To split the merged cell:
   SELECT: *Merge cells* check box so that no (✓) appears
   CLICK: OK command button
   The entry remains centered but only between column A's borders.

9. Now let's practice rotating text. Do the following:
   SELECT: cell range from B3 to G3
   CHOOSE: Format → Cells

10. You set the rotation for text by clicking and dragging in the *Orientation* area of the dialog box. You can also specify a positive value in the *Degrees* spin box to angle text from bottom left to upper right. In this step, use the mouse to select an angle of 30 degrees:
    DRAG: the "Text" line in the *Orientation* area to 30 degrees, as shown in Figure 3.10

Excel

Figure 3.10

Rotating text using the Format Cells dialog box

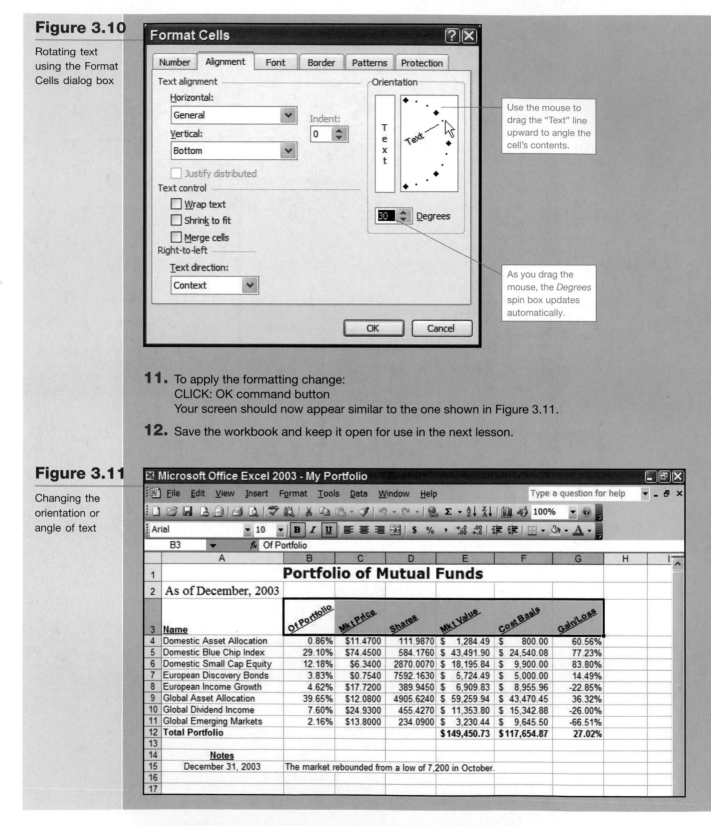

11. To apply the formatting change:
CLICK: OK command button
Your screen should now appear similar to the one shown in Figure 3.11.

12. Save the workbook and keep it open for use in the next lesson.

Figure 3.11

Changing the orientation or angle of text

In Addition DISPLAYING LONG TEXT ENTRIES IN A CELL

Excel provides several tools for working with long text entries. First, you can increase the row height of a cell and align its contents vertically between the top and bottom borders. You can then wrap the text to display in a single cell. Second, you can use the (ALT) + (ENTER) key combination to place a hard carriage return or line feed within a cell. Third, you can shrink an entry to fit between a column's borders.

3.1.4 Adding Borders and Shading

→ **Feature**

As with the other formatting options, you use borders, patterns, shading, and colors to enhance a worksheet's readability. The **gridlines** that appear in the worksheet window are nonprinting lines, provided only to help you line up information. Borders are used to place printed gridlines on a worksheet and to separate data into logical sections. These formatting options also enable you to create professional-looking invoice forms, memos, and tables.

→ **Method**

To apply borders or coloring, select the desired cell range and then:

- CLICK: Borders button (⊞▾)
- CLICK: Fill Color button (◌▾)

To display the border and patterns formatting options:

- SELECT: cell range to format
- CHOOSE: Format → Cells
- CLICK: border or patterns tab
- SELECT: borders or pattern, shading, and fill color options

→ **Practice**

In this exercise, you will format a worksheet by applying borders and fill coloring to selected cell ranges. Ensure that you have completed the previous lessons and that the "My Portfolio" workbook is displayed.

1. Move to cell A1.

2. In order to better see the borders that you will apply in this lesson, let's remove the gridlines from the worksheet display. To do so:
CHOOSE: Tools → Options
CLICK: *View* tab
Your dialog box should appear similar to the one shown in Figure 3.12.

Figure 3.12

Options dialog box, *View* tab

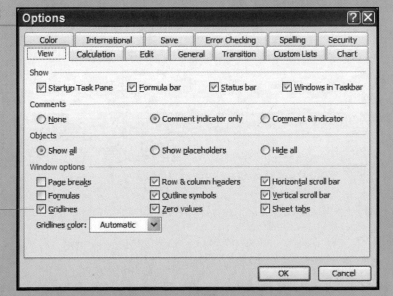

To remove the gridlines from displaying on the worksheet, deselect this check box option.

3. To proceed:
SELECT: *Gridlines* check box, so that no (☑) appears
CLICK: OK command button
Your worksheet should now appear similar to the one shown in Figure 3.13.

Figure 3.13

Removing the gridlines

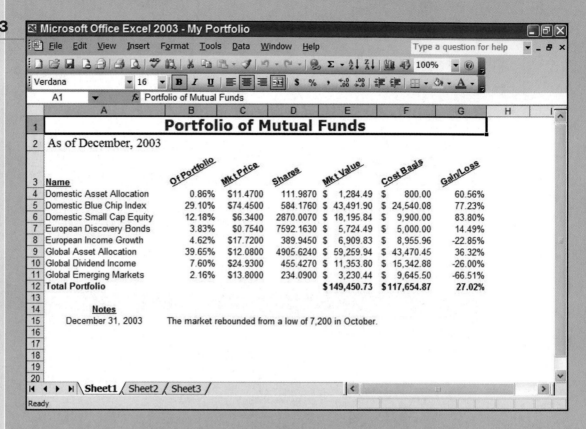

4. Now let's apply some borders:
SELECT: cell range from A12 to G12
(*Hint:* Use the column and row frame highlighting to help you line up the cell range.)

5. To display the border options available:
CLICK: down arrow attached to the Borders button (⊞▾)
A drop-down list of border options appears, as shown below.

6. You can choose from a variety of preset border options or choose to draw your own borders. For this step, let's use the preset borders:
SELECT: Top and Double Bottom Border (▤) in the drop-down list
CLICK: cell A1 to remove the selection highlighting
A border now separates the data from the summary information in row 12. (*Note:* Clicking the Underline button (U̲) underlines only the words in a cell, whereas applying borders underlines the entire cell.)

Excel

7. To outline the "Notes" area:
SELECT: cell range from A14 to G18
CLICK: down arrow attached to the Borders button (⊞⁻)
SELECT: Outside Borders button (▢)

8. Now let's apply a new fill color (sometimes called *shading*) to the "Notes" area. Ensure that the cell range from A14 to G18 is still selected and then do the following:
CLICK: down arrow attached to the Fill Color button (🎨⁻)
A drop-down list of colors appears, as shown below.

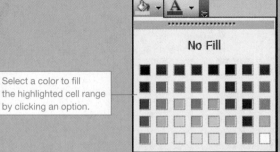

Select a color to fill the highlighted cell range by clicking an option.

9. SELECT: a light yellow color from the drop-down list
CLICK: cell A1 to remove the selection highlighting
The "Notes" area should now appear on a colored background.

10. To enhance the title in cell A1:
CLICK: down arrow attached to the Fill Color button (🎨⁻)
SELECT: a dark blue color from the drop-down list

11. To better see the title, you will need to adjust the text color:
CLICK: down arrow attached to the Font Color button (A⁻)
SELECT: white from the drop-down list
Your screen should now appear similar to the one shown in Figure 3.14.

Figure 3.14

Applying borders and colors to a worksheet

Formatted with a dark blue fill color and white font color

Formatted with a top and double bottom border

Formatted with an outline border and light yellow fill color

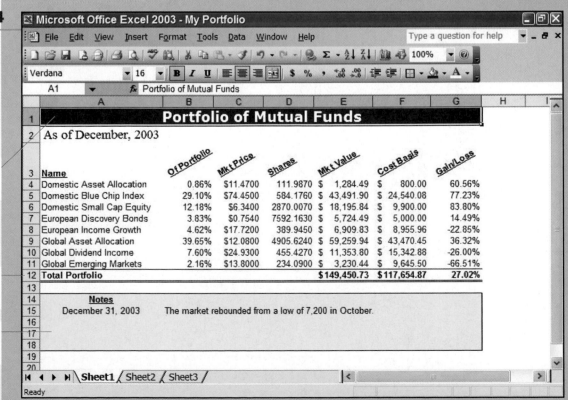

12. To turn the worksheet gridlines back on:
CHOOSE: Tools → Options
CLICK: *View* tab
SELECT: *Gridlines* check box, so that a check (☑) appears
CLICK: OK command button
Notice that the gridlines do not show through the cells that have been colored.

13. Let's practice drawing a border using the Borders toolbar:
CLICK: down arrow attached to the Borders button (⊞▾)
CHOOSE: Draw Borders
The Borders toolbar appears, as shown with labels below. (*Note:* The Borders button may appear differently than the graphic shown above, because it defaults to displaying the last border selection made.)

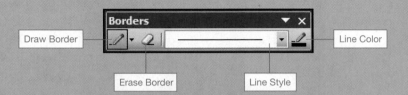

14. DRAG: the Borders toolbar by its Title bar so that cells E3 to E12 are visible (see Figure 3.15)

15. The Draw Borders button (✏▾) is set for "Draw Border," by default, which places an outline border around a cell range. Alternatively, you can choose the "Draw Border Grid" option (shown to the right) in order to place a border around each cell in a range.

Let's accept the default selection of "Draw Border" and use the pencil mouse pointer (✏) to draw an outline border:
CLICK: in the middle of cell E3
DRAG: downward to the middle of cell E11
The border extends as you move the mouse pointer down.

16. Release the mouse button to finish drawing the line. In addition to outlining the cell range, the border extends on an angle to follow the rotated text in cell E3. Your screen should now appear similar to the one shown in Figure 3.15.

Figure 3.15

Drawing a border
around a cell
range

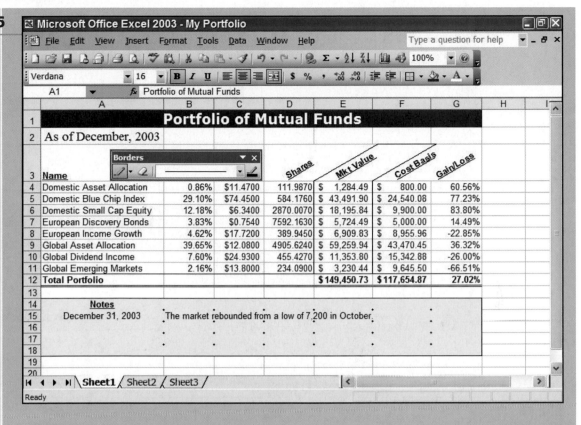

17. To close the Borders toolbar:
CLICK: its Close button (☒)

18. Save and then close the workbook.

 SelfCheck   **3.1** What is the basic difference between using the Underline button
(☐) and the Borders button (☐▾)?

3.2 Applying and Removing Formatting

Microsoft Excel provides a wealth of formatting commands for improving the appearance of a worksheet, its individual cells, and the contents within those cells. In addition to selecting formatting options individually, you can use the Format Painter button (⌗) and the Edit, Paste Special command to copy formatting characteristics. These tools, along with Excel's AutoFormat feature and Smart Tag button, can help you apply formatting commands to a worksheet consistently and more efficiently. In this module, you will work with these tools and also learn how to remove formatting characteristics from a worksheet.

3.2.1 Using Format Painter

→ **Feature**

Are you tired of selecting the same commands over and over? Excel 2003 understands these frustrations and provides an incredible time-saver for formatting your worksheets. With only a few clicks, the **Format Painter** feature allows you to copy the formatting styles and attributes from one area of your worksheet to another. Not only does Format Painter help speed up formatting procedures, but it also ensures formatting consistency within your workbooks. Now you can rest assured that all of your worksheet titles, headings, and data are formatted using the same fonts, sizes, colors, alignments, and numeric styles.

→ ## Method

To copy formatting from one cell range to another:

- SELECT: the cell range with formatting you want to copy

- CLICK: Format Painter button (🗗) on the Standard toolbar

- SELECT: the cell range that you want to format

→ ## Practice

You will now use Format Painter to copy formatting from one area of a worksheet to another. Ensure that no workbooks are open in the application window.

1. Open the data file named EX0320 to display the workbook shown in Figure 3.16.

Figure 3.16

Opening the
EX0320
workbook

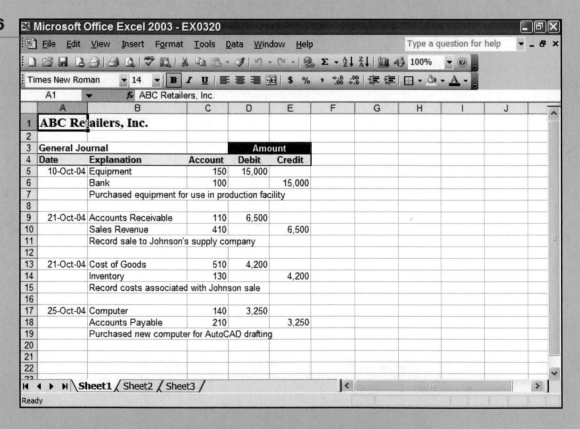

2. Save the file as "ABC Retailers" to your personal storage location.

3. You will now apply formatting commands to the first journal entry in the worksheet. After the formatting is completed, you will copy the set of formatting options to the other journal entries. To begin:
SELECT: cell A5

4. To change the date formatting:
CHOOSE: Format → Cells
CLICK: *Number* tab
SELECT: Date in the *Category* list box

SELECT: 3/14/2001 in the *Type* list box
CLICK: OK command button
(*Hint:* You may have to scroll down the *Type* list to find the date option. Do not select the first option in the list box, which appears as "*3/14/2001.") The cell entry now appears as 10/10/2004.

5. To emphasize the account numbers and explanation:
SELECT: cell range from C5 to C6
CLICK: Bold button (B)
SELECT: cell B7
CLICK: Italic button (I)

SELECT: Green from the Font Color button (A-)

6. To show the values in the Amount column as currency:
SELECT: cell range from D5 to E6
CLICK: Currency Style button ($)

7. To change the width of columns D and E, ensure that the cell range from D5 to E6 remains selected. Then, do the following:
CHOOSE: Format → Column → AutoFit Selection
The journal entry now appears formatted, as shown in Figure 3.17.

Figure 3.17

Formatting the
first journal entry

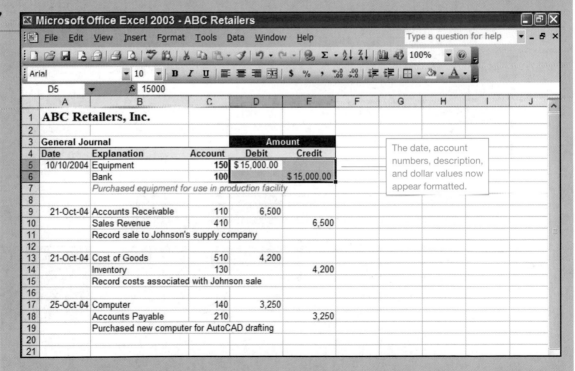

8. Using Format Painter, let's copy the formatting from this journal entry to another journal entry in the worksheet. Do the following:
SELECT: cell range from A5 to E7

9. To copy the formatting attributes:
CLICK: Format Painter button (🖌) on the Standard toolbar
Notice that a dashed marquee, sometimes referred to as a moving border, appears around the selected range.

10. To apply the formatting to the next journal entry:
CLICK: cell A9 using the Format Painter mouse pointer (⊹🖌)
(*Note:* You need only click the top left-hand cell in the target range.) Notice that the contents of the range remain the same, but the cells' formatting changes.

11. You can apply more than one coat to your worksheet using Format Painter. To demonstrate, ensure that the cell range A9 through E11 remains highlighted and then do the following:
DOUBLE-CLICK: Format Painter button (⚞)
Double-clicking the toolbar button locks it into active mode, even after you apply the first coat to a target cell range.

12. With the Format Painter button (⚞) toggled on, you can apply multiple formatting coats. Do the following:
CLICK: cell A13
CLICK: cell A17
The remaining journal entries have been formatted. Your screen should now appear similar to the one shown in Figure 3.18.

Figure 3.18

Applying a formatting coat using Format Painter

The dashed marquee surrounds the source cell range containing the formatting that was copied.

The Format Painter mouse pointer

Microsoft Office Excel 2003 - ABC Retailers

A17   10/25/2004

	A	B	C	D	E
1	**ABC Retailers, Inc.**				
2					
3	General Journal			**Amount**	
4	Date	Explanation	Account	Debit	Credit
5	10/10/2004	Equipment	150	$ 15,000.00	
6		Bank	100		$ 15,000.00
7		*Purchased equipment for use in production facility*			
8					
9	10/21/2004	Accounts Receivable	110	$ 6,500.00	
10		Sales Revenue	410		$ 6,500.00
11		*Record sale to Johnson's supply company*			
12					
13	10/21/2004	Cost of Goods	510	$ 4,200.00	
14		Inventory	130		$ 4,200.00
15		*Record costs associated with Johnson sale*			
16					
17	10/25/2004	Computer	140	$ 3,250.00	
18		Accounts Payable	210		$ 3,250.00
19		*Purchased new computer for AutoCAD drafting*			
20					
21					

13. To unlock or toggle this feature off:
CLICK: Format Painter button (⚞)

14. To better view your handiwork, do the following:
PRESS: CTRL + HOME

15. Save the workbook and keep it open for use in the next lesson.

In Addition PAINTING FORMATS USING THE INSERT OPTIONS ICON (⚞)

After inserting a new cell or cell range using the Insert ➔ Cells command, you may notice that the Insert Options icon (⚞) appears near the bottom right-hand corner of the range. By clicking the down arrow attached to this icon, you display the pop-up menu shown here. Notice that you may copy and apply the formatting styles from either above or below the newly inserted cell range, or you may clear the formatting entirely.

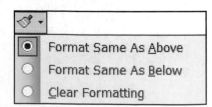

- ⦿ Format Same As <u>A</u>bove
- ○ Format Same As <u>B</u>elow
- ○ <u>C</u>lear Formatting

3.2.2 Removing Formatting Attributes

→ ## Feature

Feel confident in formatting your worksheet to your heart's content. If you realize later that your font and color selections are less than desirable, you can safely remove the formatting without affecting the contents of your cells. The fastest and easiest method for removing formatting is to click the Undo button (⟲▾) immediately after choosing a formatting command. When the Undo command is inappropriate or unavailable, you can remove any cell's formatting by choosing the Edit → Clear → Formats command.

→ ## Method

To remove the formatting characteristics from a cell range while leaving its contents intact:

- SELECT: the desired cell range

- CHOOSE: Edit → Clear → Formats

→ ## Practice

You will now practice removing formatting characteristics from a cell range. Ensure that you have completed the previous lessons and that the "ABC Retailers" workbook is displayed.

1. Let's demonstrate the effects of entering data into a formatted cell. In this example, you will attempt to enter a value into a cell that is formatted to display a date. Do the following:
SELECT: cell A17
TYPE: **1000**
PRESS: [ENTER]
The cell displays 9/26/1902. (*Note:* Excel 2003 stores dates as sequential numbers starting with "1" as January 1, 1900. The serial date value for January 1, 2004, for example, is 37,987.)

2. You will now remove the formatting from this cell:
SELECT: cell A17
CHOOSE: Edit → Clear → Formats
The cell now displays the correct value, 1000.

3. The Clear → Formats command on the Edit menu removes all formatting from a cell range. To remove a single formatting characteristic, you must modify that specific characteristic. To illustrate, let's remove the green color from the journal entry's explanatory note:
SELECT: cell B19
CLICK: down arrow attached to the Font Color button (A▾)
SELECT: Automatic from the drop-down list
The text retains the italic formatting but defaults to the black color.

4. To remove the italic formatting:
CLICK: Italic button (*I*) once
(*Note:* Several formatting commands are toggled on and off by clicking their respective toolbar buttons.)

5. To remove all of the formatting characteristics for the last two journal entries, do the following:
SELECT: cell range from A13 to E19
CHOOSE: Edit → Clear → Formats
Notice that the date in cell A13 is stored as a value, 38281, as shown in Figure 3.19. In the next lesson, you will use a new method to reapply formatting to the journal entries.

Figure 3.19

Removing formatting using the Clear → Formats command

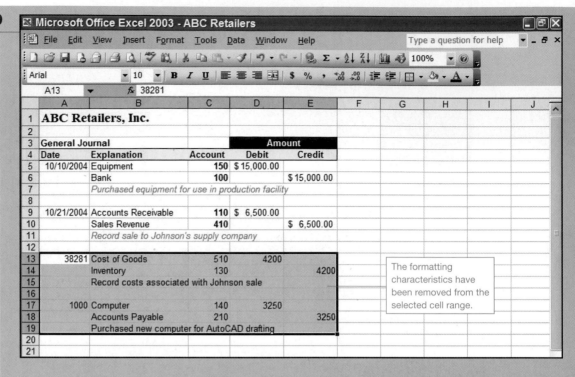

6. Save the workbook and keep it open for use in the next lesson.

3.2.3 Using the Paste Special Command

→ **Feature**

The Paste Special command on the Edit menu allows you to copy portions or characteristics of a cell or cell range to another area in your worksheet. Some of these characteristics include cell values, formulas, comments, and formats. Like the Format Painter feature, this command is useful for copying formatting options from one cell range to another. Additionally, you can use the Paste Special command to convert formulas into values, and transpose the orientation of values stored in a row or column.

→ **Method**

To copy and paste formatting characteristics:

- SELECT: the cell or range whose formatting you want to copy
- CLICK: Copy button (⬚)
- SELECT: the cells where you want to apply the formatting
- CHOOSE: Edit → Paste Special
- SELECT: *Formats* option button
- CLICK: OK command button

→ **Practice**

You will now practice copying and pasting formatting characteristics using the Paste Special command. Ensure that you have completed the previous lessons and that the "ABC Retailers" workbook is displayed.

1. In order to paste formatting characteristics, you must first copy them to the Clipboard. Do the following:
   SELECT: cell range from A9 to E11
   CLICK: Copy button (⬚)
   A dashed marquee or moving border appears around the selected range. (*Note:* All information in the range is copied to the Clipboard, including the individual cell values and formatting characteristics.)

2. To paste only the formatting information back to the worksheet, select the target range and then display the Paste Special dialog box:
   SELECT: cell A13
   CHOOSE: Edit → Paste Special
   The Paste Special dialog box, shown in Figure 3.20, provides several intermediate and advanced features. (*Hint:* You can also display this dialog box by clicking the down arrow attached to the Paste button (⬚▾) and choosing Paste Special from the drop-down menu.)

Figure 3.20

The Paste Special dialog box

Use the *Formats* option button to paste only the formatting characteristics from a cell range.

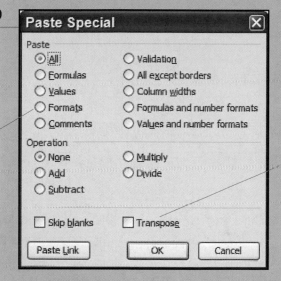

The *Transpose* check box allows you to change the column or row orientation of the selected cell range.

3. To paste the formatting from A9:E11 into cell A13:
   SELECT: *Formats* option button
   CLICK: OK command button
   The formatting is applied.

4. To format the last journal entry:
   SELECT: cell A17
   CLICK: down arrow (▾) attached to the Paste button (⬚▾)
   CHOOSE: Paste Special from the drop-down menu

5. In the Paste Special dialog box:
   SELECT: *Formats* option button
   CLICK: OK command button

6. To complete the copy and paste operation:
   PRESS: ESC

7. SELECT: cell A17
   TYPE: **10/25/2004**
   PRESS: ENTER
   Your worksheet should now appear similar to the one shown in Figure 3.21.

Excel

Figure 3.21

Completing the
"ABC Retailers"
workbook

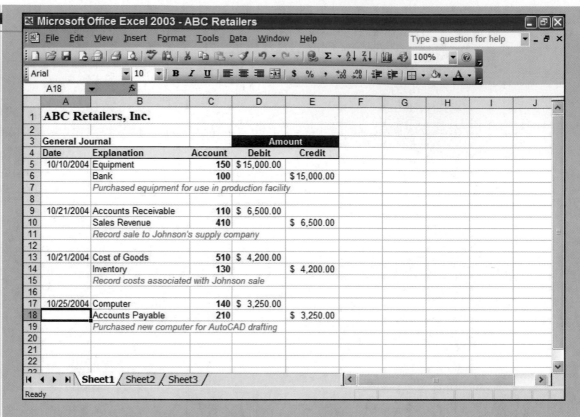

8. Save and then close the workbook.

In Addition PASTING FORMATS USING THE PASTE OPTIONS ICON (📋)

After completing a copy and paste operation using the Copy
(📋) and Paste (📋▾) buttons on the toolbar, you may notice
the Paste Options icon (📋) appear near the bottom right-
hand corner of the pasted range. By clicking the down arrow
attached to this icon, you display a pop-up menu with the options shown here. Notice that you may select the Formatting
Only option button to paste only the formatting of the copied
cell range, similar to making the selection from the Paste
Special dialog box.

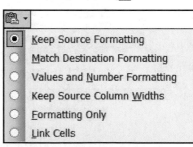

3.2.4 Using the AutoFormat Command

→ **Feature**

Rather than spend time selecting formatting options, you can use the **AutoFormat** feature to quickly
apply an entire group of formatting commands to a cell range. The AutoFormat command works best
when your worksheet data is organized using a table layout, with labels running down the left column
and across the top row. After you specify one of the predefined table formats, Excel proceeds to apply fonts, number formats, alignments, borders, shading, and colors to the selected range. It is an excellent way to ensure consistent formatting across worksheets.

→ **Method**

- SELECT: cell range to format

- CHOOSE: Format → AutoFormat

- SELECT: an option from the list of samples

→ **Practice**

You will now apply a predefined table format to an appliance sales worksheet. Ensure that no workbooks are open in the application window.

1. Open the data file named EX0324 to display the worksheet shown in Figure 3.22.

Figure 3.22

Opening the
EX0324
workbook

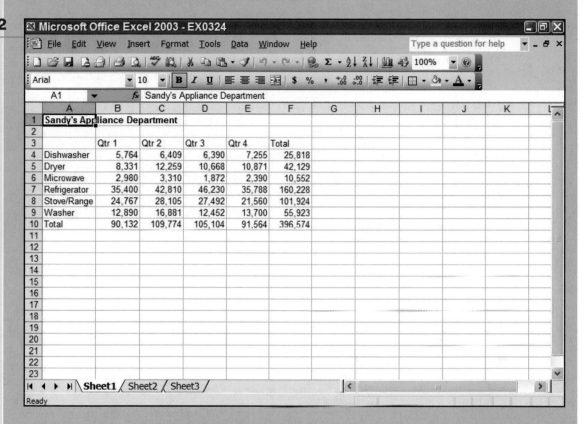

2. Save the workbook as "Sandy's Appliances" to your personal storage location.

3. To apply an AutoFormat style to specific cells in a worksheet, you first select the cell range that you want to format. Do the following:
SELECT: cell range from A3 to F10
(*Hint:* As long as the table layout does not contain blank rows or columns, you can place the cell pointer anywhere within the table. In this step, you select the entire range to make sure the formatting is applied to all cells.)

4. To display the AutoFormat options:
CHOOSE: Format → AutoFormat
The AutoFormat dialog box appears as shown in Figure 3.23.

Figure 3.23

AutoFormat dialog box

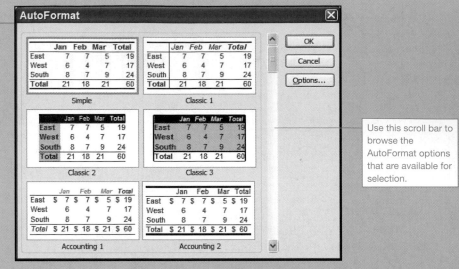

5. After scrolling the list in the AutoFormat dialog box, do the following:
SELECT: Colorful 2 option
CLICK: OK command button

6. To remove the selection highlighting from the range:
CLICK: cell A1
Your worksheet should now appear similar to the one shown in Figure 3.24.

Figure 3.24

Applying an AutoFormat

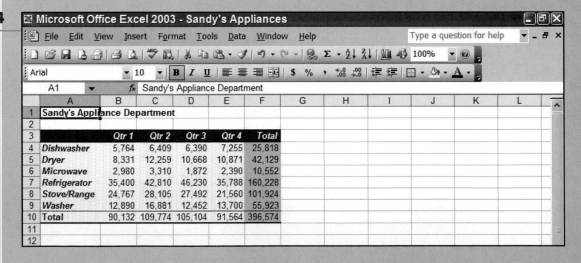

7. On your own, place the cell pointer within the table area and then apply some of the other Auto-Format options, such as Classic 2.

8. Save and then close the workbook.

In Addition SPECIFYING FORMATTING OPTIONS USING AUTOFORMAT

Using the AutoFormat dialog box, you can specify which formatting options to apply to a range. Click the Options command button to expand the dialog box. You can then select or deselect a variety of format check boxes, including *Number, Border, Font, Patterns, Alignment,* and *Width/Height.* Only those formatting options that are selected will be applied to the range.

 **3.2** How might you ensure that related worksheets and workbooks are formatted consistently?

3.3 Printing and Web Publishing

There are several methods available for outputting your worksheet creations. Most commonly, you will print a worksheet to be inclusion in a report or other such document. However, the Internet is a strong publishing medium unto itself. With the proper access, anyone can become an author and publisher for a global audience. This module introduces you to previewing and printing workbooks using traditional tools, as well as to publishing workbooks electronically on the World Wide Web.

For those of you new to the online world, the **Internet** is a vast collection of computer networks that spans the entire planet. This worldwide infrastructure is made up of many smaller networks connected by standard telephone lines, fiber optics, cable, and satellites. The term **intranet** refers to a private and usually secure local or wide area network that uses Internet technologies to share information. To access the Internet, you need a network or modem connection that links your computer to your account on the university's network or an independent service provider (ISP).

Once you are connected to the Internet, you can use Web browser software, such as Microsoft Internet Explorer or Netscape Navigator, to access the **World Wide Web.** The Web provides a visual interface for the Internet and lets you search for information by clicking on highlighted words and images, known as **hyperlinks.** When you click a link, you are telling your computer's Web browser to retrieve a page from a Web site and display it on your screen. Not only can you publish your workbooks on the Web, but you can also incorporate hyperlinks directly within a worksheet to facilitate navigating between documents.

3.3.1 Previewing and Printing a Worksheet

→ **Feature**

Besides the **Normal view** that you have used thus far to view your worksheets, Excel provides two additional views for adjusting the appearance of your printed worksheet. In **Print Preview** mode, the worksheet is displayed in a full-page WYSIWYG (What You See Is What You Get) window with margins, page breaks, and headers and footers. You can use this view to move through the workbook pages, zoom in and out on desired areas, and modify layout options, such as print margins and column widths. When satisfied with its appearance, you can send the workbook to the printer directly from this window. Similar to Print Preview, **Page Break Preview** lets you view and adjust the layout of information on particular pages. In Page Break Preview mode, you set the print area and page breaks for a workbook. In this lesson, you use Print Preview and the Print command.

→ **Method**

To preview a workbook:

- CLICK: Print Preview button (🔍)
  or
- CHOOSE: File → Print Preview

To print a workbook:

- CLICK: Print button (🖨)
  or
- CHOOSE: File → Print

→ **Practice**

You will now open a relatively large workbook, preview it on the screen, and then send it to the printer. Ensure that no workbooks are displayed in the application window.

1. Open the data file named EX0330.

2. Save the workbook as "Published Titles" to your personal storage location.

3. To preview how the workbook will appear when printed:
CLICK: Print Preview button ( )
Your screen should now appear similar to the one shown in Figure 3.25.

Figure 3.25

Previewing a
workbook

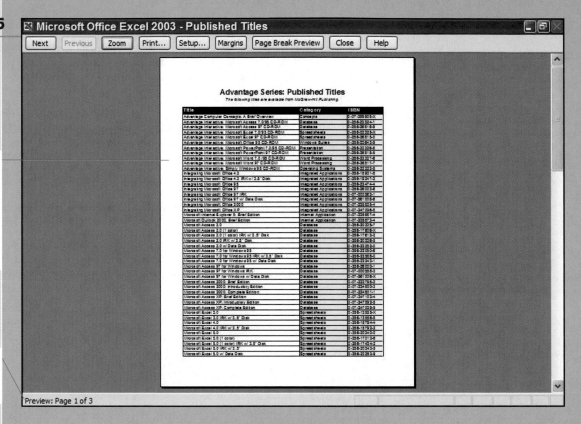

Print Preview mode
displays the page as
it will appear when
printed. If your
printer does not
support color, the
page appears with
shades of gray, as
shown here.

Identifies that you
are in Preview mode
and viewing "Page 1
of 3" total pages.

4. At the top of the Print Preview window, Excel provides a row of buttons for performing various functions. To display the next page in the Print Preview window:
CLICK: Next button in the toolbar

5. To return to the first page:
CLICK: Previous button in the toolbar

6. To zoom in on the worksheet, move the magnifying glass mouse pointer ( ) over the worksheet area and then click once. Your screen should appear similar to the one shown in Figure 3.26.

Figure 3.26

Zooming in on the worksheet

After zooming in on an area of the worksheet, use the horizontal and vertical scroll bars to adjust the window.

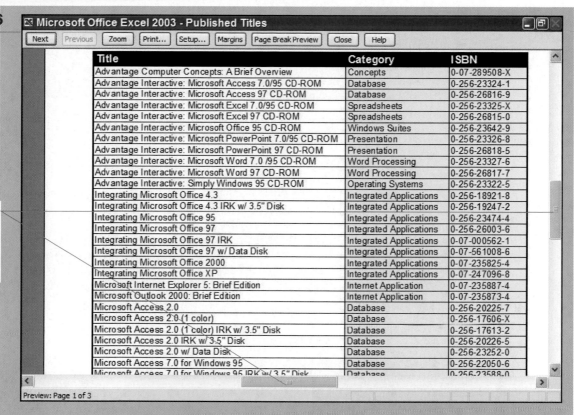

7. To zoom out on the display, click the mouse pointer once again.

8. On your own, practice zooming in and out on different areas of the page and using the scroll bars to position the window.

9. Assuming that you are satisfied with how the workbook appears, you can send it to the printer from Print Preview. To demonstrate:
   CLICK: Print button
   You are returned to Normal view and the Print dialog box appears, as shown in Figure 3.27. You can use this dialog box to select the desired printer, specify what pages to print, and input how many copies to produce. (*Note:* The quickest method for sending the current worksheet to the printer with the default options selected is to click the Print button (🖨) in Normal view.)

Figure 3.27

Print dialog box

Specify how much of the selection to print.

Specify what to print: range selection, worksheet(s), or the entire workbook.

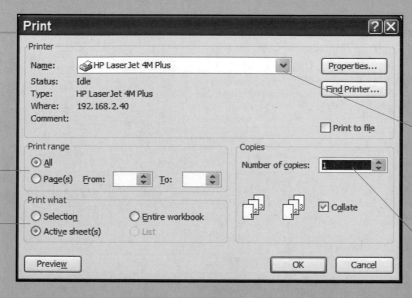

Select a printer name from this drop-down list box. This feature is especially useful if you are attached to a network and can choose from a variety of printers.

Specify how many copies to print.

10. If you do not have access to a printer, click the Cancel command button and proceed to the next lesson. If you have a printer connected to your computer and want to print the worksheet, do the following:
CLICK: OK command button
After a few moments, the worksheet will appear at the printer.

3.3.2 Previewing and Publishing to the Web

→ ## Feature

Excel 2003 makes it easy to convert and publish a workbook for display on the World Wide Web. The process involves saving the workbook in HTML (Hypertext Markup Language) format for publishing to a Web server. You can choose to publish a single worksheet or an entire workbook, complete with graphics and hyperlink objects. After files have been saved using the proper format, you may upload them to your company's intranet or to a Web server. Excel's **Web Page Preview** mode allows you to see how your work will appear when displayed in a Web browser, prior to your saving and uploading it to the Web.

→ ## Method

To save a worksheet as a Web page:

• CHOOSE: File → Save as Web Page

To view a worksheet as a Web page:

• CHOOSE: File → Web Page Preview

→ ## Practice

You will now practice saving and viewing a worksheet as an HTML Web document. Ensure that you have completed the previous lesson and that the "Published Titles" workbook is displayed.

1. To save the current worksheet as a Web page:
CHOOSE: File → Save as Web Page
The Save As dialog box appears with some additional options, as shown in Figure 3.28. Notice that "Single File Web Page" appears as the file type in the *Save as type* drop-down list box.

Figure 3.28

Save As dialog box for a Web page

"Single File Web Page" is the default setting in the *Save as type* drop-down list box.

Use this button to save and "FTP" the Web page directly to a Web server connected to the Internet.

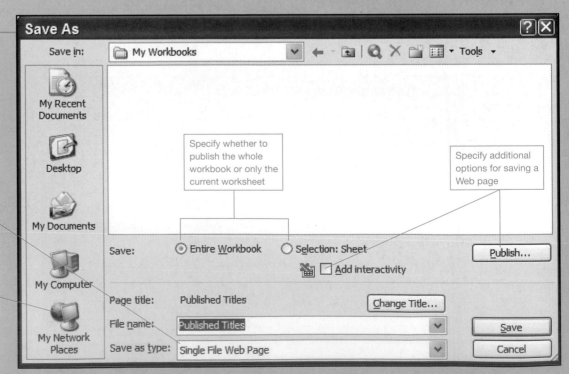

2. Using the *Save in* drop-down list box or the Places bar:
SELECT: *your personal storage location,* if not already selected (*Note:* To publish or post your workbook Web page directly to an intranet or to the Internet, you would click the My Network Places button shown in Figure 3.28 and then select your server location.)

3. In the *Save as type* drop-down list box:
SELECT: Web Page
(*Note:* If you choose "Single File Web Page," as shown in Figure 3.28, Excel 2003 creates an Internet Explorer archive file, which may not be accessible using other Web browsers. Therefore, we recommend that you create a standard HTML markup page for viewing in this lesson.)

4. To proceed with saving the workbook as a Web page:
CLICK: Save command button
The workbook document is saved as "Published Titles.htm" to your personal storage location.

5. To preview how the workbook will appear in a Web browser:
CHOOSE: File → Web Page Preview
After a few moments, the workbook appears displayed in your Web browser's window. Figure 3.29 shows how the worksheet Web page is displayed using Internet Explorer.

Figure 3.29

Viewing a worksheet as a Web page

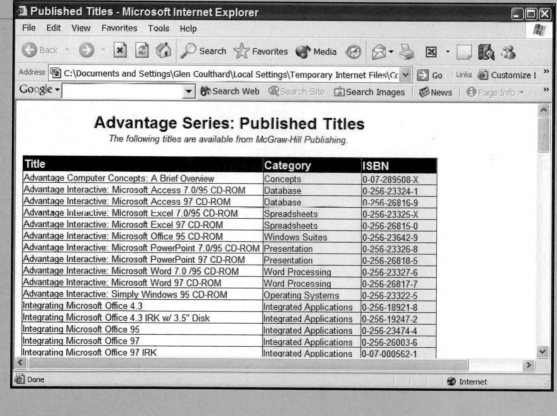

6. To close the Web browser window:
CLICK: its Close button (☒)

7. Close the "Published Titles" workbook. If asked, you need not save the changes.

In Addition PUBLISHING AN INTERACTIVE WEB PAGE

With Microsoft Internet Explorer and the Office Web Components, you can save a workbook as an interactive Web page, allowing users to enter, edit, and format data in your worksheet using their Web browsers. To create an interactive worksheet Web page, select the *Add interactivity* check box option in the Save As dialog box (see Figure 3.28) and then click the Publish command button to specify further options.

3.4 Customizing Print Options

For maximum control over the appearance of your printed worksheets, define the page layout settings using the File, Page Setup command. In the dialog box that appears, you can specify margins, headers, footers, and whether gridlines or row and column headings should appear on the final printed output. To make the process more manageable, Excel organizes the page layout settings into four tabs (*Page, Margins, Header/Footer,* and *Sheet*) in the Page Setup dialog box. The features and settings accessible from these tabs are discussed in the following lessons.

3.4.1 Adjusting Page and Margin Settings

→ ## Feature

You use the *Page* tab in the Page Setup dialog box to specify a worksheet's paper size, print scale, and print orientation, such as portrait or landscape. The *Margins* tab allows you to select the top, bottom, left, and right page **margins,** and to center the worksheet both horizontally and vertically on a page. You can also manipulate the page margins while viewing a worksheet in Print Preview mode.

→ ## Method

- CHOOSE: File ➔ Page Setup
- CLICK: *Page* and/or *Margins* tabs
- SELECT: the desired page layout options

→ ## Practice

In this lesson, you will open and print a workbook that summarizes a company's amortization expense. Ensure that no workbooks are open in the application window.

1. Open the data file named EX0340 to display the workbook shown in Figure 3.30.

Figure 3.30

Opening the
EX0340
workbook

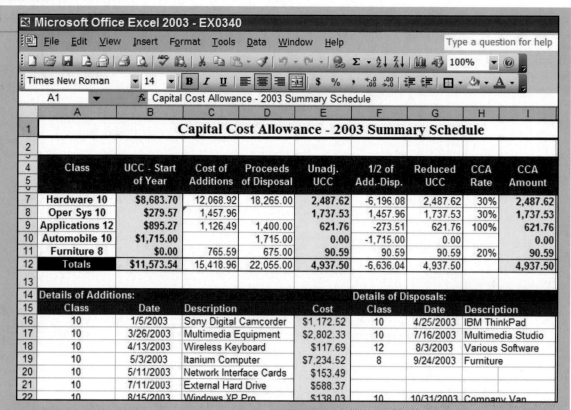

2. Save the file as "CCA Schedule" to your personal storage location.

3. To begin, let's display the worksheet using Print Preview mode:
CLICK: Print Preview button (🔍)

4. Practice zooming in and out on the worksheet using the Zoom command button and the magnifying glass mouse pointer (🔍).

5. To view the second page of the printout:
CLICK: Next command button
Notice that a portion of the worksheet's CCA table is truncated from printing on the first page and is displayed on the second page.

6. To exit from Print Preview mode:
CLICK: Close button

7. In order to fit the worksheet on a single page, let's adjust the page layout settings. To begin:
CHOOSE: File → Page Setup
CLICK: *Page* tab, if it is not already selected
Your screen should now appear similar to the one shown in Figure 3.31.

Figure 3.31

Page Setup
dialog box, *Page*
tab

Specify a portrait
(tall) or landscape
(wide) page
orientation.

Specify whether to
scale or shrink the
contents to fit the
page.

Specify printer
settings, such as
paper size and print
quality.

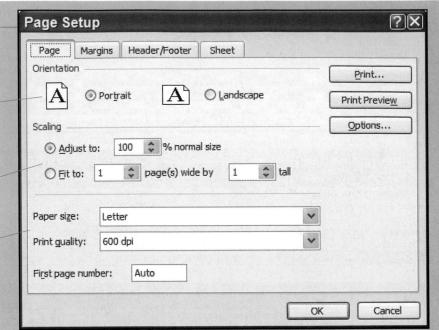

8. In the *Orientation* area:
   SELECT: *Landscape* option button

9. To ensure that a worksheet prints on a single page, you specify scaling options in the Page Setup dialog box. In the *Scaling* area:
   SELECT: *Fit to* option button

10. Now specify "1" for *page(s) wide by* and then clear the *tall* spin box using **DELETE**. (*Hint:* You clear the *tall* option in order to let Excel calculate the best height for the page.) The *Scaling* area now appears as shown here.

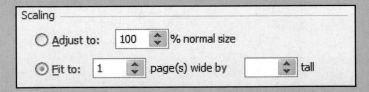

11. For narrower worksheets, you can center the printout between the left and right page margins. To do so, you make a check box selection on the *Margins* tab. Do the following:
    CLICK: *Margins* tab
    Your screen should now appear similar to the one shown in Figure 3.32.

Figure 3.32

Page Setup
dialog box,
Margins tab

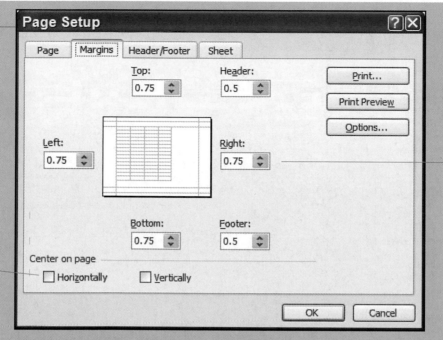

You can specify the
top, left, right, and
bottom margins
using the spin boxes
in this area. You can
also increase or
decrease the space
provided for the page
header and page
footer, discussed
further in the next
lesson.

Use these check
boxes to center the
worksheet vertically
and/or horizontally
on the printed page.

12. To proceed:
SELECT: *Horizontally* check box in the *Center on page* area

13. CLICK: Print Preview command button
As shown in Figure 3.33, the entire worksheet now appears centered between the margins on a
single printed page.

Figure 3.33

Previewing a
worksheet after
setting page
options

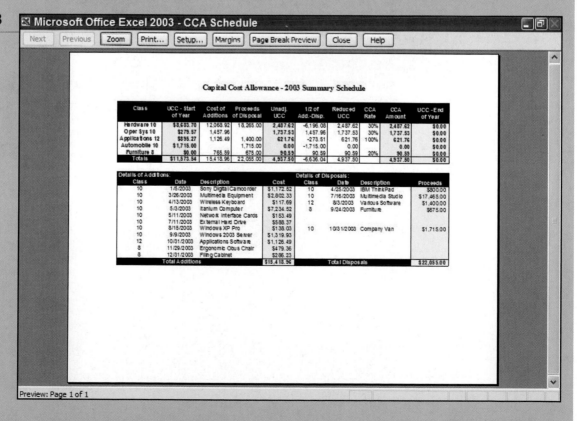

14. To exit from Print Preview mode and return to the worksheet:
CLICK: Close button

3.4.2 Inserting Headers and Footers

→ # Feature

Descriptive information, such as the current date at the top or bottom of a page, can add a lot to your worksheet's presentation. The contents of a **header** (at the top of a page) or **footer** (at the bottom of a page) repeat automatically for each page that is printed. Some suggested uses for these areas include displaying your name, copyright information, the words "confidential" or "first draft," or page numbering. You may simply want to place the workbook's filename in the header so that you can easily find it again on your hard disk.

→ # Method

- CHOOSE: File → Page Setup
- CLICK: *Header/Footer* tab
- SELECT: a predefined header or footer
  or
  CLICK: Custom Header button to design a new header
  or
  CLICK: Custom Footer button to design a new footer

→ # Practice

You now add a custom header and footer to the worksheet. Ensure that you have completed the previous lesson and that the "CCA Schedule" workbook is displayed in Print Preview mode.

1. To display the Page Setup dialog box:
CHOOSE: File → Page Setup
The dialog box appears, displaying the last tab that was selected.

2. To add headers and footers to the printed page:
CLICK: *Header/Footer* tab

3. To select a footer for printing at the bottom of each page:
CLICK: down arrow attached to the *Footer* drop-down list
Your screen should now appear similar to the one shown in Figure 3.34.

Figure 3.34

Page Setup dialog box, *Header/Footer* tab

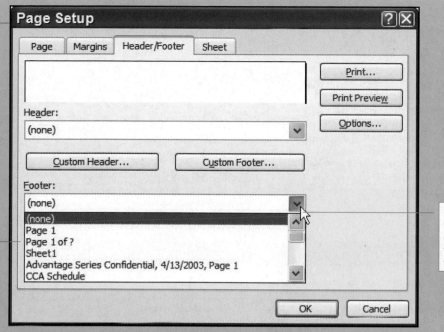

The Footer drop-down list box provides some predefined options.

Use the mouse to display the drop-down list box and then to scroll through the options provided.

4. In the *Footer* drop-down list box:
SELECT: "CCA Schedule, Page 1" option
After you make the selection, you should see the workbook's filename "CCA Schedule" appear centered in the footer preview area, and the words "Page 1" should appear right-aligned, as shown below.

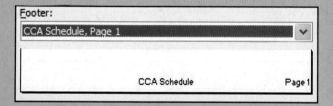

5. Now let's create a custom header:
CLICK: Custom Header command button
Figure 3.35 shows the Header dialog box and labels the buttons used for inserting information into the different sections.

Figure 3.35

Custom Header dialog box

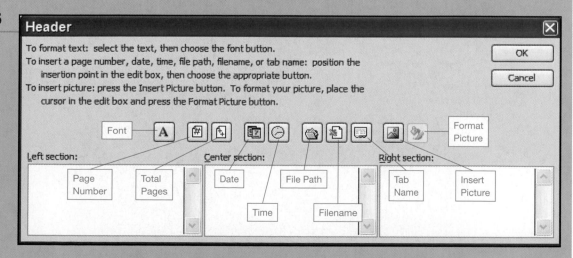

6. To create a header that prints your name at the left margin:
CLICK: the mouse pointer in the *Left section* area
TYPE: **Created by: *your name***
(*Hint:* Enter your name rather than the text "your name.")

7. Now place the date against the right margin:
CLICK: the mouse pointer in the *Right section* area
TYPE: **Printed on:**
PRESS: Space Bar once
CLICK: Date button (🖃) as labeled in Figure 3.35

8. To complete the dialog box:
CLICK: OK command button
You will see the custom header appear in the preview area, as shown in Figure 3.36. (*Note:* Your name and the current date will appear in the *Header* preview area.)

Figure 3.36

Page Setup dialog box, *Header/Footer* tab

The *Header* preview area displays the results of your custom selections.

The *Footer* preview area displays the results of your selection from the drop-down list box.

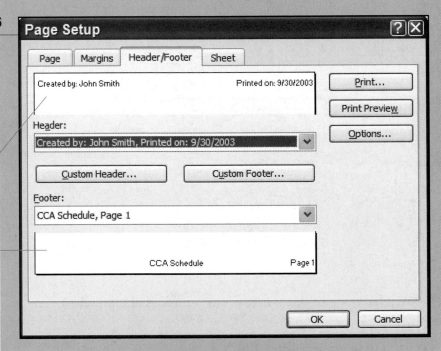

9. To display the worksheet in Print Preview mode:
CLICK: Print Preview command button
Notice the newly inserted header and footer in the Print Preview window shown in Figure 3.37.

Figure 3.37

Displaying the
header and footer
in Print Preview
mode

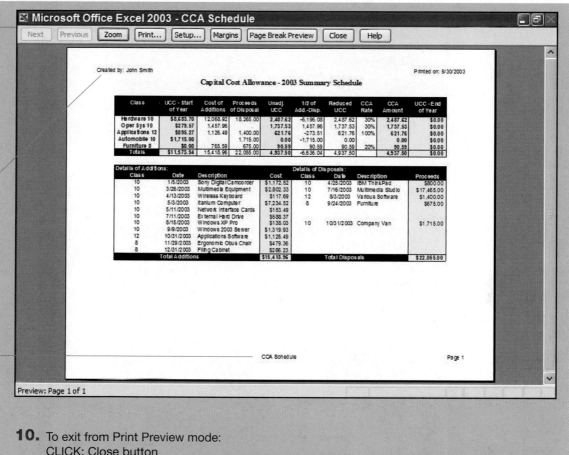

The header appears
at the top of the
apage.

The footer appears
at the bottom of the
page.

Excel

10. To exit from Print Preview mode:
CLICK: Close button

3.4.3 Selecting Worksheet Content to Print

→ **Feature**

From the Print dialog box, you can choose to print an entire workbook, a single worksheet, or a specified cell range. Alternatively, you can preselect a cell range to print by first specifying the print area. Other print options that are available from the Page Setup dialog box include printing the worksheet gridlines or row and column headings.

→ **Method**

To specify a print area:

• SELECT: *a cell range*

• CHOOSE: File → Print Area → Set Print Area

To clear a print area:

• CHOOSE: File → Print Area → Clear Print Area

To select from the general print options:

• CHOOSE: File → Print

• SELECT: one of the following *Print what* option buttons—*Selection, Active sheet(s)*, or *Entire workbook*

• SELECT: *Number of copies* to print

To specify whether to print gridlines or row and column headings:

- CHOOSE: File → Page Setup
- CLICK: *Sheet* tab
- SELECT: *Gridlines* check box to toggle the printing of gridlines
- SELECT: *Row and column headings* check box to print the frame area

→ Practice

In this lesson, you will practice selecting print options and setting print areas. You also have the opportunity to print the worksheet. Ensure that you have completed the previous lesson and that the "CCA Schedule" workbook is displayed.

1. You will often find the need to print specific ranges in a worksheet, rather than the entire workbook. This need is filled by first setting a print area. To practice selecting a cell range for printing:
SELECT: cell range from A1 (a merged cell) to J12
CHOOSE: File → Print Area → Set Print Area

2. Now that you have defined a specific cell range as the print area:
CLICK: Print Preview button ( )
Notice that only the selected range is previewed for printing, as shown in Figure 3.38.

Figure 3.38

Previewing a selected print area

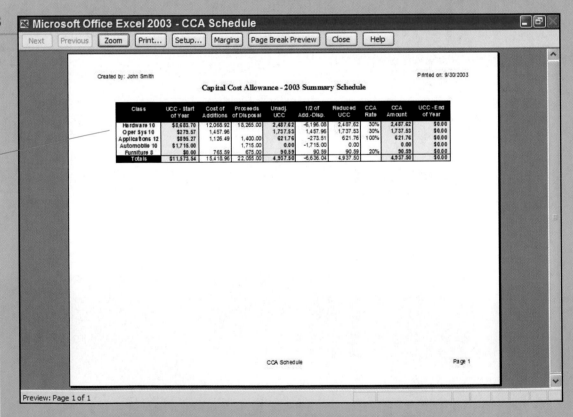

Only a portion of the worksheet now appears in the Print Preview window.

3. To return to the worksheet:
CLICK: Close button

4. To return to printing the entire worksheet:
CHOOSE: File → Print Area → Clear Print Area
This command removes the print area definition.

5. Let's view some other print options:
CHOOSE: File → Page Setup
CLICK: *Sheet* tab
Your screen should now appear similar to the one shown in Figure 3.39.

Figure 3.39

Page Setup
dialog box, *Sheet*
tab

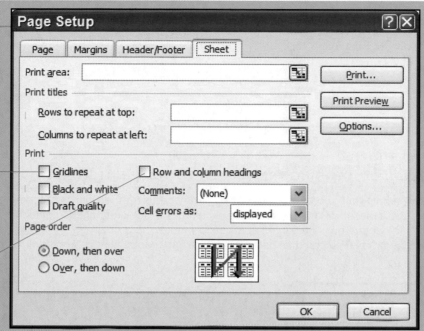

Select this check
box to print gridlines
for your worksheet.

Select this check
box to print row and
column frame
headings.

6. Sometimes printing the gridlines or row and column headings is useful for reviewing a worksheet
for errors. To demonstrate:
SELECT: *Gridlines* check box in the *Print* area
SELECT: *Row and column headings* check box
CLICK: Print Preview command button
Figure 3.40 shows that the printed worksheet now looks similar to the screen display, with the
exception of the header and footer. (*Note:* All page setup options are saved along with the work-
book file.)

Figure 3.40

Print previewing
with gridlines and
row and column
headings

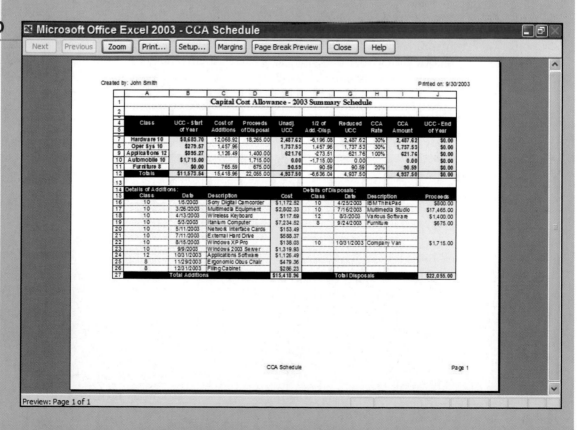

7. If you have a printer connected to your computer, perform the following actions. Otherwise, proceed to the next step.
CLICK: Print command button
CLICK: OK, when the Print dialog box appears

8. If necessary, close the Print Preview window.

9. Move to cell A1. Then save and close the "CCA Schedule" workbook.

10. Exit Microsoft Office Excel 2003.

In Addition SENDING THE SCREEN TO THE PRINTER

Did you know that you can capture a screen image using the Print Screen key on your keyboard? When you press the Print Screen key, the current full-screen image is copied to the Windows Clipboard. To capture only the current application window, hold down `CTRL` + `ALT` and then press the Print Screen key. You can then paste this image into a document or workbook for printing.

3.4 How would you create a custom footer that displayed your name against the left page border and your company's name against the right page border?

Chapter
summary

To enhance the appearance of worksheets, Excel 2003 offers many features and shortcuts that help you apply formatting to cells. You can select from various character formatting commands to change a cell's font typeface and size or to apply boldface, italic, and character underlining to its contents. The readability of numbers and dates is improved when you format values using currency and percent symbols, commas, and decimal places. Furthermore, you can change the appearance of a cell by aligning its contents, surrounding it with borders, or filling it with color. Lastly, you can apply professionally designed table formats to quickly change your worksheet's appearance. After the worksheet is formatted with your preferences, you can use various options to customize its output to the printer or for publishing to the World Wide Web.

Command Summary

Many of the commands and procedures appearing in this chapter are summarized in the following table.

Skill Set	To Perform this Task...	Do the Following...
Formatting and Printing Worksheets	Apply font typefaces, font sizes, and font styles	CHOOSE: Format → Cells CLICK: *Font* tab
	Apply number formats	CHOOSE: Format → Cells CLICK: *Number* tab
	Increase and decrease decimal places	CLICK: Increase Decimal button (⬚) CLICK: Decrease Decimal button (⬚)
	Modify a cell's alignment	CHOOSE: Format → Cells CLICK: *Alignment* tab
	Merge a range of cells	CHOOSE: Format → Cells CLICK: *Alignment* tab CLICK : *Merge cells* check box

Formatting and Printing Worksheets (con't)	Add borders, patterns, and shading using the menu	CHOOSE: Format → Cells CLICK: *Border* or *Patterns* tab
	Add borders and fill colors using the Formatting toolbar	CLICK: Borders button (⊞▾) CLICK: Fill Color button (🎨▾)
	Copy formatting from one range to another using the toolbar	SELECT: the desired range CLICK: Format Painter button (🖌) SELECT: the target range
	Copy formatting from one range to another using the Clipboard	SELECT: the desired range CLICK: Copy button (📋) SELECT: the target range CHOOSE: Edit → Paste Special SELECT: *Formats* option button
	Clear formatting that appears in a range	SELECT: the desired range CHOOSE: Edit → Clear → Formats
	Use AutoFormat	CHOOSE: Format → AutoFormat SELECT: *a predefined format*
	Preview a worksheet	CLICK: Print Preview button (🔍), or CHOOSE: File → Print Preview
	Print a worksheet	CLICK: Print button (🖨), or CHOOSE: File → Print
	Print the selected cell range, active worksheet, or the entire workbook	CHOOSE: File → Print SELECT: *the desired option button*
	Set the worksheet area to print	SELECT: the desired range CHOOSE: File → Print Area → Set Print Area
	Clear the selected print area	CHOOSE: File → Print Area → Clear Print Area
	Specify worksheet orientation and paper size	CHOOSE: File → Page Setup CLICK: *Page* tab
	Specify print margins and placement on a page	CHOOSE: File → Page Setup CLICK: *Margins* tab
	Define headers and footers for printing	CHOOSE: File → Page Setup CLICK: *Header/Footer* tab
	Take a snapshot of the screen and store it on the Clipboard	PRESS: Print Screen key
Workgroup Collaboration	Save worksheet as an HTML document	CHOOSE: File → Save as Web Page
	Preview worksheet as a Web page	CHOOSE: File → Web Page Preview

Key Terms

This section specifies page references for the key terms identified in this chapter. For a complete list of definitions, refer to the Glossary at the back of this learning guide.

AutoFormat, *p. EX 134*

cell alignment, *p. EX 119*

fonts, *p. EX 112*

footer *p. EX 146*

Format Painter, *p. EX 127*

gridlines, *p. EX 123*

header, *p. EX 146*

HTML, *p. EX 140*

hyperlinks, *p. EX 137*

Internet, *p. EX 137*

intranet, *p. EX 137*

margins, *p. EX 142*

Normal view, *p. EX 137*

Print Preview, *p. EX 137*

Page Break Preview, *p. EX 137*

typefaces, *p. EX 112*

Web Page Preview, *p. EX 140*

World Wide Web, *p. EX 137*

Chapter
quiz

Short Answer

1. Why should you limit the number of typefaces used in a worksheet?

2. Name two methods for specifying decimal places in a worksheet.

3. How do you split a merged cell?

4. How do you apply multiple coats using the Format Painter tool?

5. Name two color settings that you can change in a worksheet.

6. How do you keep gridlines from displaying in a worksheet?

7. How do you make gridlines print in a worksheet?

8. What should you do prior to sending a worksheet to the printer?

9. Name the tabs in the Page Setup dialog box.

10. How do you create a Web page from a standard Excel worksheet?

True/False

1. _____ The **B** button stands for bold. The **U** button stands for underline. The **I** button stands for incline.

2. _____ You use the *Number* tab in the Format Cells dialog box to select date and time formatting options.

3. _____ Whenever you merge cells, the contents must also be centered.

4. _____ You can remove formatting from a cell range by choosing the Edit ➔ Clear ➔ Formats command.

5. _____ The AutoFormat command works best when your data is organized using a table layout.

6. _____ You can only zoom in and out on a worksheet in Print Preview mode using the mouse.

7. _____ You can view a worksheet as it would appear in a Web browser, before or after saving it as a Web page.

8. ____ The two options for page orientation are *Picture* and *Landscape*.

9. ____ You can access the Page Setup dialog box directly from Print Preview mode.

10. ____ To convert a worksheet for display on the World Wide Web, you save the workbook as a "Web Page" in HTML format.

Multiple Choice

1. To change the text color of a cell entry:
   a. CLICK: Fill Color button (⬛▾)
   b. CLICK: Font Color button (A▾)
   c. CLICK: Text Color button (◀)
   d. You cannot change the text color of a cell entry.

2. Excel stores date and time entries as:
   a. Formats
   b. Formulas
   c. Labels
   d. Values

3. To merge a range of cells, select the *Merge cells* check box on this tab of the Format Cells dialog box:
   a. *Alignment* tab
   b. *Margins* tab
   c. *Merge* tab
   d. *Number* tab

4. To remove only a cell's formatting, you can:
   a. CHOOSE: Format ➜ Clear
   b. CHOOSE: Edit ➜ Clear ➜ Formats
   c. CHOOSE: Edit ➜ Formats ➜ Clear
   d. CHOOSE: Format ➜ Cells ➜ Clear

5. To copy a cell's formatting characteristics to another cell, you can:
   a. Use the AutoFormat feature
   b. Use the AutoPainter feature
   c. Use the Format Painter feature
   d. Use the Edit ➜ Paste Formats command

6. To select one of Excel's prebuilt table formats:
   a. CHOOSE: Format ➜ AutoFormat
   b. CHOOSE: Format ➜ AutoTable
   c. CHOOSE: Format ➜ TableFormat
   d. CHOOSE: Format ➜ Table

7. To produce gridlines on your printed worksheet:
   a. SELECT: *Gridlines* check box in the Page Setup dialog box
   b. CHOOSE: File ➜ Print ➜ Gridlines
   c. CLICK: Underline button (U) on the Formatting toolbar
   d. Both a and b above

8. To identify a specific cell range on the worksheet for printing:
   a. CHOOSE: File ➜ Print Range
   b. CHOOSE: File ➜ Print Area ➜ Set Print Area
   c. CHOOSE: File ➜ Set Print Area
   d. CHOOSE: File ➜ Set Print Range

9. To print data at the top of each page, you create the following:
   a. Footer
   b. Footnote
   c. Header
   d. Headline

10. To save the current worksheet as a Web page:
   a. CLICK: Save button 🖫
   b. CHOOSE: File ➜ Save as Web Page
   c. CHOOSE: File ➜ Save as HTML
   d. CHOOSE: File ➜ Publish to Web

Hands-On
exercises

step by step

1. Performing Character and Numeric Formatting

In this exercise, you will use Excel's character and numeric formatting commands to enhance the appearance of a monthly bookstore report.

1. Load Microsoft Office Excel 2003.

2. Open the data file named EX03HE01 to display the worksheet shown in Figure 3.41.

Figure 3.41

Opening the EX03HE01 workbook

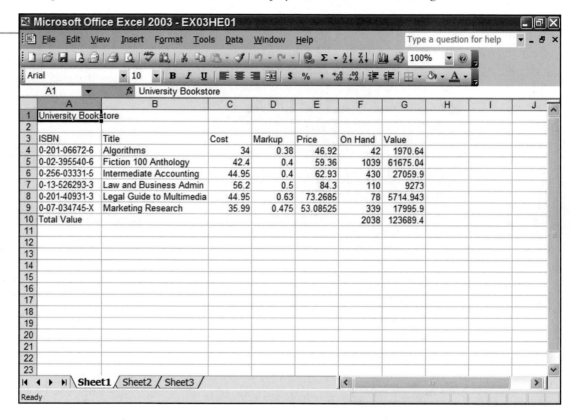

3. Save the workbook as "Bookstore" to your personal storage location.

4. Make sure that cell A1 is selected and then display the Format Cells dialog box.

5. On the *Font* tab in the dialog box, select a font with a point size of 16.

6. Then, apply a dark red font color and boldface to the selection. When you are ready to proceed, click the OK command button.

7. Use the Merge and Center button (⊞) to center the title across the width of the worksheet (A1:G1).

8. Apply percentage formatting to the cell range from D4 to D9.

9. With the cell range still highlighted, increase the decimals in the percentage formatting to include two additional decimal places. Your worksheet should now appear similar to the one shown in Figure 3.42.

Figure 3.42

Applying cell formatting

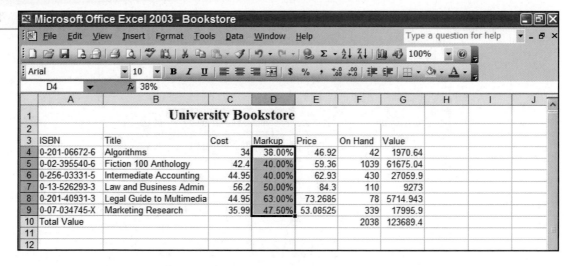

10. Apply currency formatting to the cell range from C4 to C10. (*Hint:* You include cell C10 in the range so that you can later copy this column's formatting to other ranges in the worksheet.)

11. Use the Format Painter button (⊿) to copy this range's formatting to columns E and G.

12. Use Format ➔ Column ➔ AutoFit Selection command to change the width of column G.

13. Use the Formatting toolbar to format the column headings in row 3, as shown in Figure 3.43.

Figure 3.43

Completing the "Bookstore" workbook

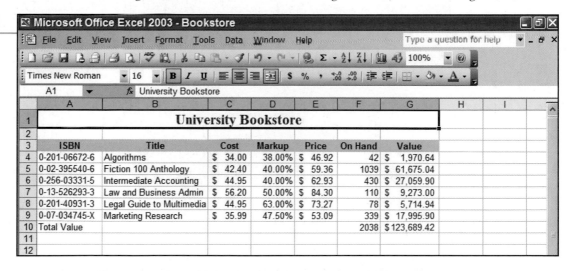

14. To better see the results of your formatting:
CLICK: cell A1
You now have a much nicer-looking report!

15. Save and then close the workbook.

2. Enhancing a Worksheet's Readability

Incorporating some skills learned in Chapter 2, you will now practice modifying a worksheet and applying formatting commands in order to make it easier to read and understand.

1. Open the workbook named EX03HE02. This workbook contains quarterly inventory information, as shown in Figure 3.44.

Figure 3.44

Opening the
EX03HE02
workbook

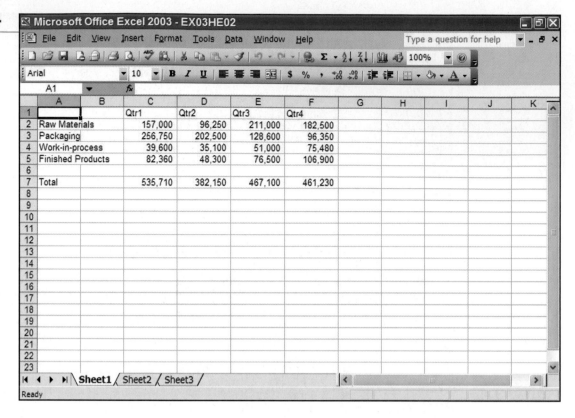

2. Save the workbook as "Cost Analysis" to your personal storage location.

3. Adjust the width of column A to 18 characters.

4. Delete column B.

5. Adjust columns B through E to their best-fit widths.

6. Format the headings in row 1 to appear boldface and centered in their respective columns.

7. Format the "Total" label in cell A7 to appear boldface and italic.

8. Insert two rows at the top of the worksheet for entering a title. (*Hint:* Rather than performing the Insert command twice to insert two rows, you can select rows 1 and 2 first and then perform the command once.) Your worksheet should now appear similar to Figure 3.45.

Figure 3.45

Inserting rows in
the worksheet

To insert two rows,
select rows 1 and 2
before choosing the
Insert → Rows
command from the
menu.

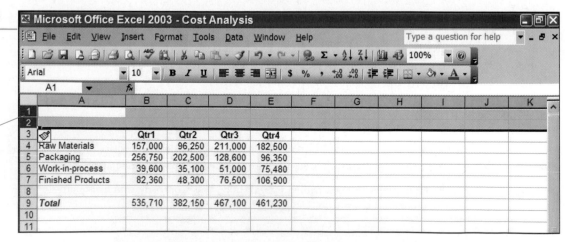

9. Enter a title for the worksheet:
SELECT: cell A1
TYPE: **Inventory Cost Analysis**
PRESS: (ENTER)

10. Merge and center the title in cell A1 between columns A and E.

11. Format the title to appear with a larger and more unique font. Apply boldface and a dark blue color to the font text on a light yellow background fill. Then, surround the merged cell with a Thick Box border.

12. To bring out the Total row, apply a Top and Double Bottom border to cells A9 through E9. With the cell range highlighted, assign a light gray background fill color.

13. To remove the selection highlighting and view the results, as shown in Figure 3.46:
CLICK: cell A3

14. Save and then close the workbook.

Figure 3.46

Completing the "Cost Analysis" workbook

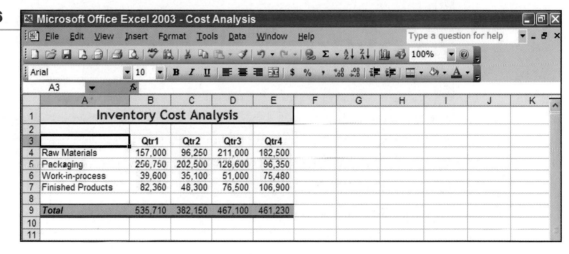

ep by step

3. Formatting and Printing a List

In this exercise, you will use the AutoFormat command, modify the formatting attributes selected, and then customize the page layout for printing.

1. Open the workbook named EX03HE03 to display the worksheet shown in Figure 3.47.

Figure 3.47

Opening the
EX03HE03
workbook

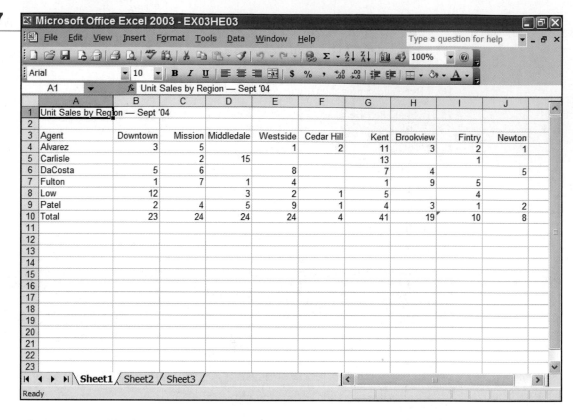

2. Save the workbook as "Unit Sales Summary" to your personal storage location.

3. Apply the "Classic 3" AutoFormat style to the cell range from A3 to K10.

4. Rotate the column headings from cell B3 to K3 so that they appear similar to those of the worksheet shown in Figure 3.48. Then, set the width of columns B through K to 8 characters.

5. Format the worksheet title in cell A1 to make it stand out from the table information. Your screen should appear similar to the one shown in Figure 3.48.

Figure 3.48

Applying the
"Classic 3"
AutoFormat

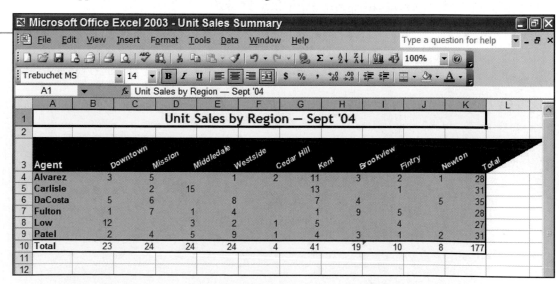

6. Display the Page Setup dialog box. Use the *Page* tab to change the page orientation to *Landscape* and to fit by "1" page wide.

7. Use the *Margins* tab in the Page Setup dialog box to center the worksheet horizontally on the page.

8. Use the *Header/Footer* tab to add a custom footer that prints the workbook's filename aligned left and the page number aligned right with the word "Page."

9. Add a custom header that shows the company name, "Detroit Distributions Inc.," aligned left and the current date aligned right.

10. Preview the worksheet. Your screen should now appear similar to the one shown in Figure 3.49.

Figure 3.49

Previewing the completed worksheet

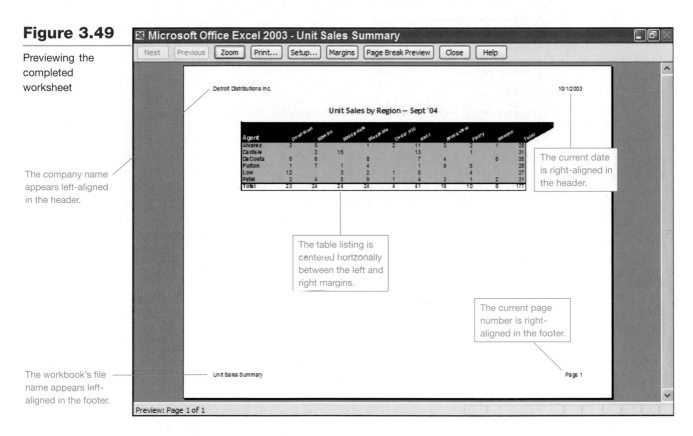

The company name appears left-aligned in the header.

The table listing is centered horizonally between the left and right margins.

The current date is right-aligned in the header.

The current page number is right-aligned in the footer.

The workbook's file name appears left-aligned in the footer.

11. Print a copy of the worksheet.

12. Save and then close the workbook.

 your own

4. Financial Data Table

To practice formatting and manipulating data, open the workbook named EX03HE04 and make a copy of the file by saving the workbook as "Financial Data" to your personal storage location. On your own, resize all of the columns to ensure that the data is visible. Insert a new row at the beginning of the worksheet and enter the worksheet title "Boston Consolidated Group." Using fonts, colors, alignment, borders, and background fills, format the titles in rows 1 and 2 to stand out from the rest of the data. Figure 3.50 shows one possible solution.

Figure 3.50

Formatting the title rows in a worksheet

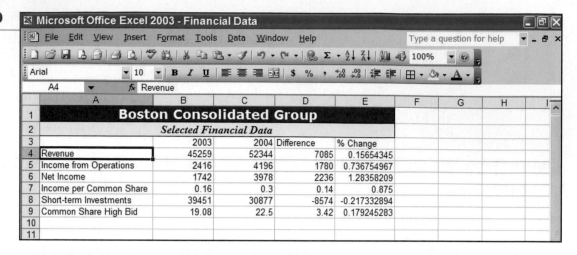

Format the data in columns B through D with currency formatting and two decimal places, except for the date headings. Format the data in column E with percent formatting and two decimal places. Center and apply boldface to the column headings in row 3. Apply boldface and italics to the cell range from A4 to A9. Before proceeding, adjust the column widths and row heights as required. Now use the Page Setup dialog box to center the worksheet between the page margins for printing. Preview and then print the worksheet. When you are ready to proceed, save and then close the workbook.

on your own

5. Personal Expense Comparison

To practice working with formatting and page layout options, use Excel 2003 to create a monthly expense comparison worksheet. After displaying a blank workbook, enter the following column headings in a single row: **Expense, January, February,** and **Change**. Then enter the following expense categories in a single column under the "Expense" heading.

- Rent/Mortgage
- Food
- Clothing
- Transportation
- Utilities
- Education
- Entertainment

For both the January and February columns, enter some reasonable data. Add the label "Total" below the last expense category and then use AutoSum to calculate totals for the monthly columns. Create formulas to calculate the difference for each expense category. Use the AutoFormat "Accounting 2" option to format the worksheet to appear similar to the one shown in Figure 3.51. Save the workbook as "My Expenses" to your personal storage location.

Figure 3.51

Creating an
expense
worksheet

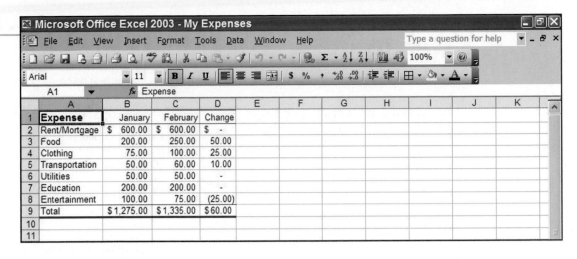

For printing purposes, add a custom footer that prints the current date, your name, and the page number at the bottom of each page. When you are finished, preview and print the worksheet with gridlines and row and column headings. Then, save and close the workbook.

your own

6. Reproducing a Formatted Worksheet

In this exercise, place yourself in the position of a new employee for an accounting firm. Your manager calls you into her office, hands you a color-printed page, and asks you to reproduce its contents in a worksheet. The page appears as it would in Print Preview mode in Figure 3.52. (*Note:* Do not worry if the screen graphic is not clear enough to copy its contents accurately. This exercise requires that you focus on formatting cells and selecting page layout options.)

Figure 3.52

Original
worksheet to
reproduce in
Excel 2003

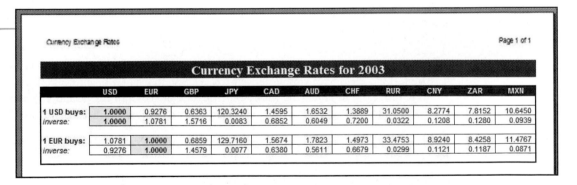

After entering data, adjusting column widths, applying borders and fill colors, and formatting cells, you prepare the worksheet for printing. Ensure that you add a header "Currency Exchange Rates," as shown in Figure 3.52, and center the worksheet between the left and right margins of a landscape page. Then, send the worksheet to your printer. When you are finished, save the workbook as "My Reproduction" to your personal storage location and then close it. Lastly, exit Microsoft Office Excel 2003.

Excel

CaseStudy SPINNERS!

Spinners! is an independently owned sidewalk store that is located in the downtown core of Randall, West Virginia. Established in 1974, Spinners! has successfully sold record albums, eight-track tapes, cassettes, and audio CDs. Recently, the store began stocking movie videos and DVDs. For the past 25 years, the company's most prominent business strategy has been a commitment to stocking a music selection with broad audience appeal. Spinners! has always taken pride in their large inventory and in providing personalized customer service.

With the recent announcement that a discount superstore chain is moving into the area, Spinners! is facing increased competitive pressures. Stacy Marvin, the store's owner and general manager, realizes that in order to stay competitive, she needs to be able to track and analyze her inventory costs, stock levels, and sales trends quickly and accurately. In a meeting with Justin Lee, her senior sales associate, she discusses some possible ideas for combating the new competitor. In addition to handling many of the purchasing and receiving duties, Justin is also the primary contact person for suppliers. As Stacy's most trusted employee, Justin has complete access to the company's accounting software and Microsoft Office Excel 2003, both of which are loaded on the office's personal computer.

In the following case problems, assume the role of Justin and perform the same steps that he identifies.

1. Stacy asks Justin to prepare a worksheet that will summarize the company's current stock levels. He begins by launching Microsoft Office Excel 2003 so that a new blank workbook is displayed. As shown in Figure 3.53, he enters the worksheet title, row and column labels, and inventory values for each category. (*Note:* Column A's width has been adjusted slightly so that you can see the text label entries.)

Figure 3.53

Creating an inventory worksheet

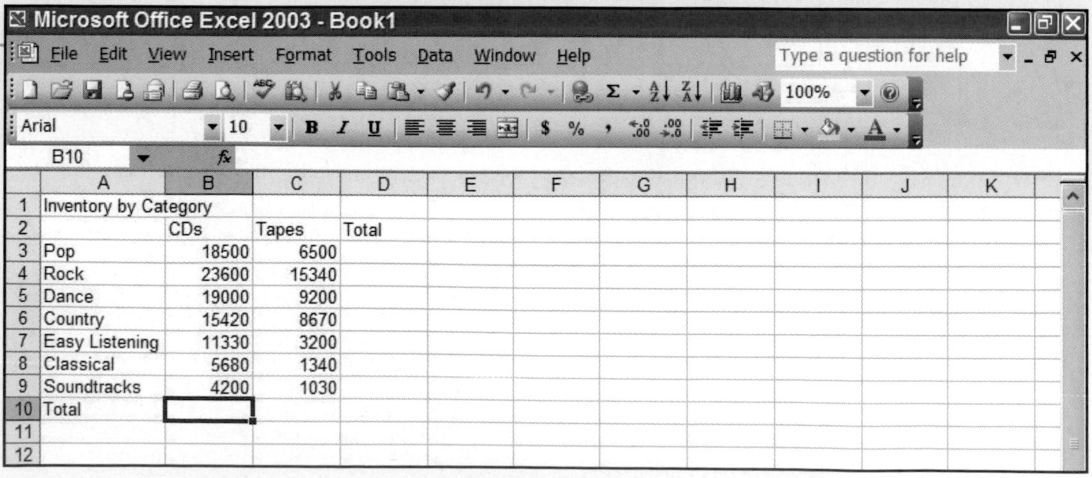

	A	B	C	D
1	Inventory by Category			
2		CDs	Tapes	Total
3	Pop	18500	6500	
4	Rock	23600	15340	
5	Dance	19000	9200	
6	Country	15420	8670	
7	Easy Listening	11330	3200	
8	Classical	5680	1340	
9	Soundtracks	4200	1030	
10	Total			
11				
12				

Using the AutoSum feature, Justin has Excel 2003 calculate totals for both the row and column values. He then selects the cell range from A2 to D10 and applies the "Classic 2" AutoFormat style. Not yet satisfied, he merges and centers the title in row 1 between columns A and D and then applies formatting to make it stand out from the rest of the worksheet. Justin saves the workbook as "Spinners Inventory1" to his personal storage location and prints a copy to show to Stacy.

2. After reviewing the worksheet, Stacy asks Justin to make the following adjustments:

- Insert a new row for "World Music" at row 9, enter 4100 for CDs and 3500 for Tapes, and ensure the totals are updated.

- Adjust the width of column A to 15 characters and then change the height of row 1 to 24 points. Increase the title's font size to fit snugly within the new row height.

- Make the values appear with dollar signs and commas, but with no decimal places.

- Adjust the width of columns B, C, and D to at least 10 characters wide.

After Justin finishes customizing the worksheet (Figure 3.54), he saves the workbook as "Spinners Inventory2" and then closes it.

Figure 3.54

Customizing the inventory worksheet

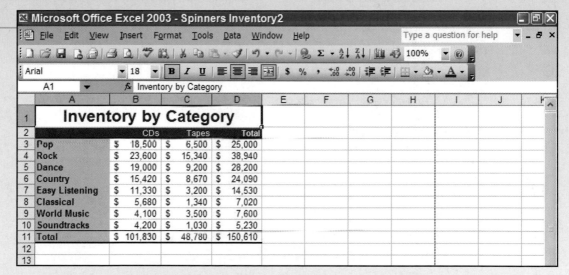

3. The next day, Stacy assigns Justin the task of completing the company's Advertising Schedule worksheet that she started a few days earlier. Justin opens the workbook named EX03CP03 and then saves it as "Spinners Advertising" to his personal storage location. According to the sticky notes attached to Stacy's printout of the worksheet, Justin needs to enter the following three new promotions:

- Back-to-School: 1 newspaper ad on August 27 for $500

- Rocktober Blitz: 6 radio spots on October 11 for $2,900

- Christmas: 3 TV ads starting December 1 for $9,000

After entering the new data, Justin formats the worksheet by applying the Currency style to the "Cost" column and increasing the width of the column. He then decreases the decimal places shown to 0. Using the Format Cells dialog box, Justin changes the date values in column C to appear in a "dd-mmm-yy" format and then adjusts the column's width to 10 characters.

Noticing that Stacy placed an extra column between the "Theme" and "Date" columns, Justin deletes column B and then resizes column A to display using its best-fit width. He also selects a new typeface, font size, and alignment for the column headings and title, as shown in Figure 3.55. Justin prints, saves, and then closes the workbook.

Figure 3.55

Formatting the "Spinners Advertising" workbook

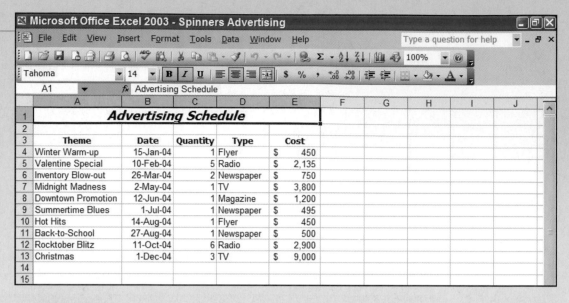

4. Having completed his work for Stacy, Justin opens one of his pet worksheet projects named EX03CP04. This workbook contains a sales transaction analysis that summarizes information from the store's point-of-sale equipment. He immediately saves the workbook as "Spinners Daily Sales" to his personal storage location.

To speed the formatting process, Justin uses the AutoFormat feature to apply a combination of table formatting attributes to the worksheet. Then, to distinguish the cells containing the times of day from the rest of the worksheet area, Justin applies a dark red fill color to the background of Row 1 and makes the font color white. Next he increases the width for all of the columns to give the worksheet a roomier look. He then adds some column borders to separate the data. At the top of the worksheet, Justin inserts a new row and then enters the title "Sales Transactions by Time Period." He merges and centers the title over the columns and then applies formatting to make the title stand out from the data, as in the worksheet shown in Figure 3.56.

Figure 3.56

Formatting the "Spinners Daily Sales" workbook

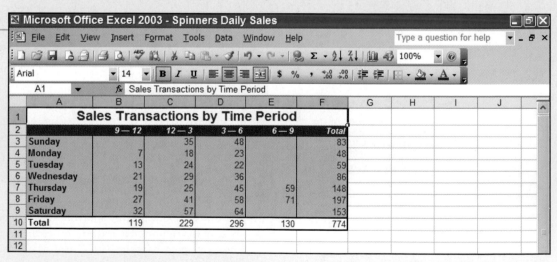

To prepare for printing, Justin adds a custom header that places the company name at the center of the page. He then adds a custom footer that contains the words "Prepared by *your name*" on the left, the date in the center, and the page number on the right-hand side. Next, he adjusts the page setup so the worksheet is centered horizontally on the page. After printing the worksheet, Justin saves it as a Web page (but not as a Single File Web Page archive) and views it using his Web browser. He closes the Web browser when he is ready to proceed. Satisfied that he has put in a full day, Justin saves and closes the workbook and exits Microsoft Office Excel 2003.

Answers to Self-Check Questions

SelfCheck

3.1   What is the basic difference between using the Underline button ($\underline{u}$) and the Borders button (▦)? When you apply an underline to a cell, only the words in the cell appear underlined. When you apply a border underline to a cell, the entire cell is underlined. Also, borders may be applied to each side of a cell, such as top, bottom, left, and right.

3.2   How might you ensure that related worksheets and workbooks are formatted consistently? Use the same predefined AutoFormat style to format data in all of the worksheets.

3.3   How does the Print Preview display mode differ from the Web Page Preview display mode? Print Preview appears in the Excel application window and displays the workbook as it will appear when printed. Web Page Preview uses the computer's default Web browser to display an HTML rendering of the current worksheet.

3.4   How would you create a custom footer that displayed your name against the left page border and your company's name against the right page border? In the Page Setup dialog box, click the Custom Footer command button on the *Header/Footer* tab. Then, enter your name into the left text box and your company's name into the right text box of the Footer dialog box.

Excel

Notes

Microsoft®Office**Excel**®

2003

CHAPTER **4**

 Analyzing Your Data

PREREQUISITES

To successfully complete this chapter, you must be able to enter values, dates, and simple formulas into a worksheet. You will be asked to select multiple cell ranges, modify worksheet information, and access Excel 2003 features using the toolbar and menus. The final module on creating embedded charts assumes no prior charting knowledge, but you do need to know how to preview and print a worksheet.

LEARNING OBJECTIVES

After completing this chapter, you will be able to:

• Create, modify, remove, and apply range names

• Understand absolute and relative cell addresses

• Use natural language formulas in a worksheet

• Use mathematical and statistical functions, such as SUM, AVERAGE, COUNT, MIN, and MAX

• Use date functions, such as NOW and TODAY

• Embed, move, and size a chart on a worksheet

• Preview and print a chart

4.1 Working with Named Ranges

In its simplest form, a cell range can be defined as a single cell, such as B4. Still, the term "cell range" is more commonly used to describe a "from here to there" area on a worksheet. A range can also cover a three-dimensional area, crossing more than one worksheet within a workbook. In a new workbook, Excel provides three worksheets named *Sheet1, Sheet2,* and *Sheet3.* It may help you to think of a worksheet as a tear-off page on a notepad, with the notepad representing the workbook. You access the worksheets in a workbook by clicking on the tabs appearing along the bottom of the document window.

A cell range can also be given a nickname, or **range name,** that can later be used in constructing formulas. For example, the formula expression **=Revenue-Expenses** is far easier to understand than **=C5-C6**. Working with cell references from more than one worksheet adds another level of complexity. For example, if the value for Revenue is stored on *Sheet1* and the value for Expenses is stored on *Sheet2,* the formula would read **=Sheet1!C5-Sheet2!C6**. Notice that the worksheet name is separated from the cell address using an exclamation point (!). By default, range names already contain this information, making them far easier to remember than these cryptic expressions. In this module, you will learn how to name ranges and how to work with different types of cell references.

4.1.1 Naming Cell Ranges

→ Feature

By naming individual cells and groups of cells in a worksheet, you make the worksheet, and the formulas contained therein, much easier to read and construct. There are two ways to name a cell range. One way is to click in the Name Box, located at the far left of the Formula bar, and then type a unique name with no spaces. The second way is to use a menu command to create names automatically from the row and column headings appearing in a worksheet. Once a range is named, you may select the cells that it represents in the worksheet by choosing its entry in the Name Box.

→ Method

To name a cell range using the Name Box:

- SELECT: the desired range
- CLICK: in the Name Box
- TYPE: range_name, such as "**Profit**," without spaces

To name a cell range using the Menu bar:

- SELECT: the desired range, including the row and column headings
- CHOOSE: Insert → Name → Create

→ Practice

You will now name several cell ranges appearing in an existing worksheet using the methods described above. Before proceeding, ensure that Microsoft Office Excel 2003 is loaded.

1. Open the data file named EX0410 to display the worksheet shown in Figure 4.1.

Figure 4.1

Opening the
EX0410 workbook

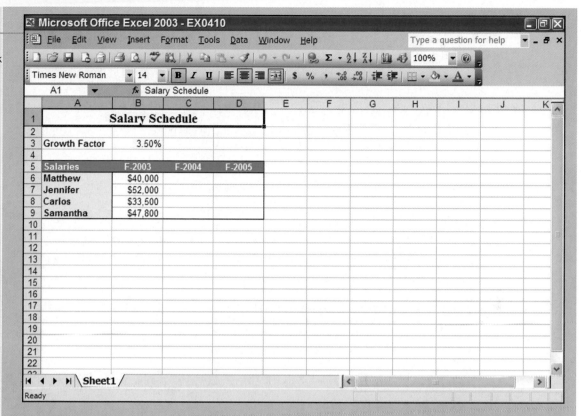

2. Save the workbook as "Salaries" to your personal storage location.

3. To increase Matthew's salary by the growth factor appearing in cell B3, perform the following steps:
SELECT: cell C6
TYPE: =b6*(1+b3)
PRESS: ENTER
The answer, 41400, appears in cell C6.

4. Now put yourself in the place of another user who needed to review this worksheet. To understand the calculation in cell C6, that person would first have to track down each cell address referenced by the formula. A better approach is to name the cells that are commonly referred to in formulas. Let's name the cell containing the growth factor before entering a formula to increase Jennifer's salary:
SELECT: cell B3
CLICK: in the Name Box with the I-beam mouse pointer
TYPE: **Growth** (as shown in Figure 4.2)

Figure 4.2

Naming a cell
range

Define a range name
using the Name Box.

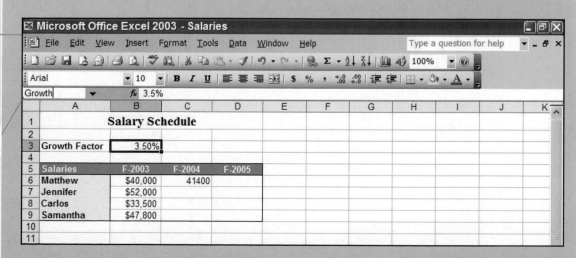

5. PRESS: [ENTER]
You have now created a named range called "Growth" that you can use in place of the cell address when entering formulas.

6. To use the range name:
SELECT: cell C7
TYPE: =b7*(1+Growth)
PRESS: [ENTER]
The answer, 53820, appears. A new user reading this formula would be better able to decipher its objective.

7. You can also use range names to navigate within your worksheet:
CLICK: down arrow attached to the Name Box
SELECT: Growth in the drop-down list that appears
The cell pointer moves immediately to cell B3.

8. Now update the growth factor:
TYPE: **5%**
PRESS: [ENTER]
The worksheet cells containing formulas are updated.

9. Another method for creating range names uses the existing heading labels in your worksheet. You can use this method effectively when the data is organized in a table layout. To demonstrate:
SELECT: cell range from A5 to D9
Notice that the selected range includes the fiscal years across the top row and the employee names down the leftmost column.

10. To specify that the heading labels be used in naming the ranges:
CHOOSE: Insert → Name → Create

11. In the Create Name dialog box, ensure that the *Top row* and *Left column* check boxes appear selected as shown in Figure 4.3.

Figure 4.3

Creating range names from worksheet values

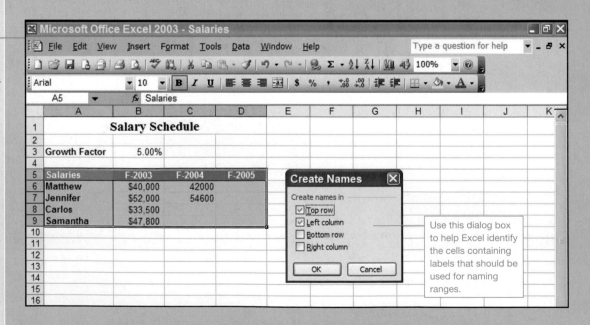

12. To complete the operation:
CLICK: OK command button

13. Now let's practice selecting named ranges:
CLICK: down arrow attached to the Name Box
Many range names now appear in the drop-down list, as shown in Figure 4.4.

Figure 4.4

Displaying range names in the Name Box

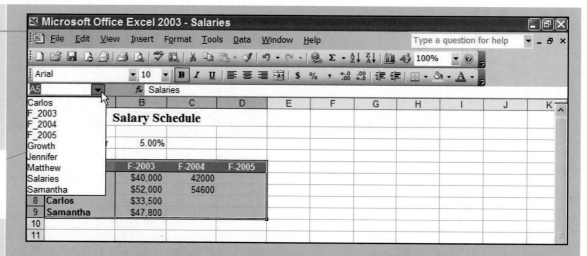

Excel 2003 creates these range names using the column and row heading labels.

14. To move the cell pointer to one of the row ranges:
CLICK: Jennifer in the drop-down list
The cell range from B7 to D7 appears selected.

15. To display one of the column ranges:
CLICK: down arrow attached to the Name Box
CLICK: F_2004 in the drop-down list
(*Note*: The label "F_2004" is used as the column heading instead of the value 2004, because Excel can create range names only from labels, not values. You must also beware of conflicts with cell addresses. For example, the range name "F2004" is unacceptable because it refers to an actual cell address on the worksheet.)

16. Finally, let's select the entire data area in the table:
CLICK: down arrow attached to the Name Box
CLICK: Salaries in the drop-down list
The range from cell B6 to D9 is highlighted.

17. PRESS: CTRL + HOME to remove the selection highlighting

18. Save the workbook and keep it open for use in the next lesson.

4.1.2 Managing Range Names

→ **Feature**

Once you have created range names, you can easily modify and delete them using the Define Name dialog box. Another useful Excel feature is the ability to paste a list of range names into your worksheet. You can then refer to this list, as you would a legend on a road map, when you are building formula expressions or when you need to jump to a particular spot in the worksheet.

→ **Method**

To display the Define Name dialog box:

• CHOOSE: Insert → Name → Define

To paste range names into the worksheet:

• CHOOSE: Insert → Name → Paste

→ Practice

You will now practice deleting and pasting range names. Ensure that you have completed the previous lesson and that the "Salaries" workbook is displayed.

1. You manipulate range names using the Define Name dialog box. To illustrate, let's delete the yearly range names that were created in the last lesson. Do the following:
CHOOSE: Insert → Name → Define
The dialog box shown in Figure 4.5 should now appear on the screen

Figure 4.5

The Define Name dialog box

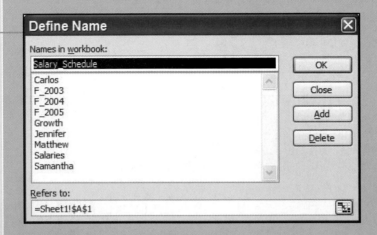

2. To remove the "F_2003" range name:
SELECT: F_2003 in the *Names in workbook* list box
Notice that the range address "=Sheet1!$B$6:$B$9" appears in the *Refers to* text box. (*Note:* If necessary, you can edit the cell references appearing in this text box. The significance of dollar signs in the range address is discussed in the next lesson.)

3. CLICK: Delete command button

4. To remove the remaining yearly range names:
SELECT: F_2004 in the list box
CLICK: Delete command button
SELECT: F_2005 in the list box
CLICK: Delete command button

5. To dismiss the dialog box:
CLICK: Close command button

6. To help you document and double-check the cell references in a worksheet, Excel 2003 enables you to paste a list of all named ranges into the worksheet. To demonstrate this technique:
SELECT: cell A12
CHOOSE: Insert → Name → Paste
CLICK: Paste List command button

7. To remove the selection highlighting:
PRESS: CTRL + HOME
Your screen should now appear similar to the one shown in Figure 4.6.

Figure 4.6

Pasting a list of range names into the worksheet

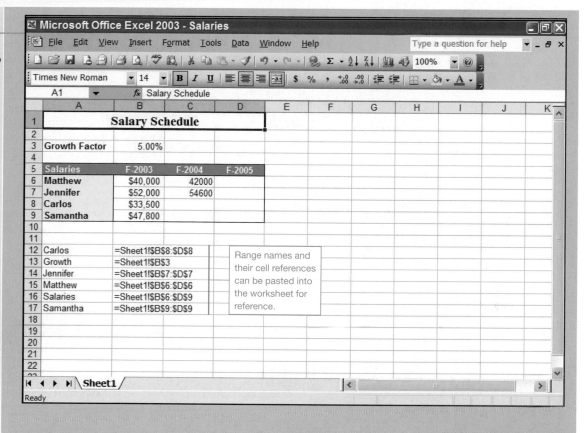

8. Save the workbook and keep it open for use in the next lesson.

In Addition MAKING EFFICIENT USE OF RANGE NAMES

Range names facilitate the entry of formulas and functions in a worksheet. By using range names in place of cell references, you are less likely to make data-entry errors when constructing complex formulas. For those cells on a worksheet to which you must refer frequently, consider naming the cell ranges immediately. You can always delete, rename, or redefine these range names at a later date.

4.1.3 Using References in Formulas

→ Feature

There are two types of cell references that you can enter into formulas: *relative* and *absolute*. The difference between the two types becomes especially important when you start copying and moving formulas in your worksheet. A **relative cell address** in a formula adjusts itself automatically when copied, because the cell reference is relative to where it sits in the worksheet. An **absolute cell address** always refers to an exact cell location in the worksheet.

→ Method

The formulas that you have entered so far have all used relative cell references—Excel's default. To specify an absolute reference, you precede each column letter and row number in a cell address with a dollar sign. For example, to make cell B5 an absolute cell reference, you type $B$5. A **mixed cell address,** on the other hand, locks only a portion of a cell address by placing the dollar sign ($) before either the address's column letter or row number, such as B$5. Sometimes it helps to vocalize the word "absolutely" as you read a cell address, so you would read $B$5 as "absolutely column B and absolutely row 5."

→ **Practice**

In this lesson, you will practice using relative and absolute cell addressing in performing simple copy and paste operations. Ensure that you have completed the previous lesson and that the "Salaries" workbook is displayed.

1. Let's begin by reviewing the formula in cell C6:
SELECT: cell C6
Review the expression "=B6*(1+B3)" in the Formula bar. You can vocalize the formula in cell C6 as "take the value appearing one cell to my left and then multiply it by 1 plus the value appearing three rows up and one column to the left." Notice that you need to use cell C6 as a point of reference for this formula to make any sense. This is an example of a relative cell reference.

2. Let's copy the formula in cell C6 to cell D6:
CLICK: Copy button (⊞) on the Standard toolbar
SELECT: cell D6
CLICK: Paste button (⊞)
PRESS: ESC to remove the dashed marquee, or moving border
The result, 42000, appears in cell D6, as shown in Figure 4.7. This, however, is not the desired result. The value has not been incremented by the growth factor of 5% in cell B3.

Figure 4.7

Copying a formula with relative cell addresses

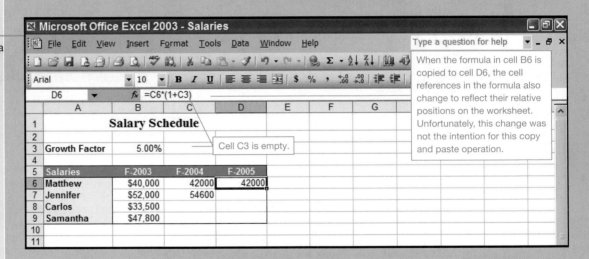

3. In the Formula bar, notice that the formula "=C6*(1+C3)" does not perform the correct calculation. Copying and pasting has modified the cell addresses by automatically adjusting the column letters. To ensure that Excel does not change a cell address during a copy operation, you need to make it absolute. Let's begin again:
PRESS: DELETE to remove the formula in cell D6

4. Move the cell pointer to cell C6. Now position the I-beam mouse pointer over the cell address B3 in the Formula bar and then click the left mouse button once.

5. To change the growth factor reference into an absolute address, you type dollar signs in front of the column letter and row number. You may also use the following shortcut method:
PRESS: F4 (ABS key; ABS stands for absolute)
Notice that B3 now appears as $B$3, as shown in Figure 4.8.

Figure 4.8

Changing a cell address from relative to absolute

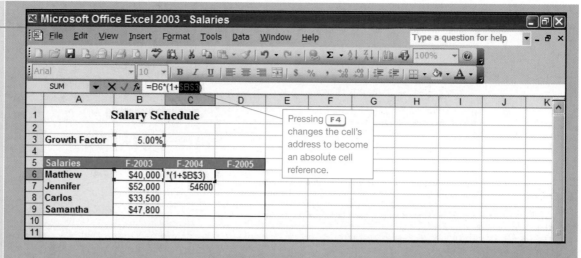

6. Continue pressing **F4** to see how Excel cycles through possible combinations of relative, absolute, and mixed cell addressing.

7. Before proceeding, ensure that $B$3 appears in the Formula bar and then press **ENTER** or click the Enter button (☑).

8. Copy and paste the formula stored in cell C6 back into cell D6. Remember to press **ESC** to remove the dashed marquee. The correct result, 44100, now appears in the cell.

9. Range names are defined using absolute cell addresses. To illustrate, remember that you used a range name, Growth, in constructing the formula for cell C7. On your own, copy the formula in cell C7 to cell D7, as shown in Figure 4.9. The formula calculates correctly.

Figure 4.9

Copying and pasting a formula with a range name

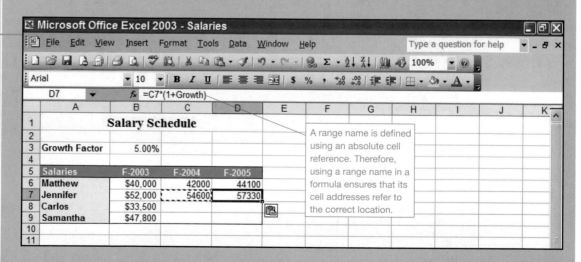

10. To continue:
    PRESS: **ESC** to remove the dashed marquee

11. PRESS: **CTRL**+**HOME** to move to cell A1

12. Save and then close the worksheet.

Excel

4.1.4 Entering Natural Language Formulas

→ **Feature**

Another alternative to cell references is a special type of expression called a **natural language formula**. Like a range name, a natural language formula allows you to build a formula using the row and column labels from the active worksheet. In effect, a natural language formula uses implicit range names. In order for natural language formulas to work effectively, however, the worksheet must be organized in a table format with distinctly labeled rows and columns.

→ **Method**

- SELECT: the cell where you want the result to appear

- TYPE: = (an equal sign)

- TYPE: an expression, such as **Revenue-Expenses**, using the actual row and column labels

- PRESS: ENTER

→ **Practice**

You will now use natural language formulas to calculate an expression in a worksheet. Ensure that no workbooks are open in the application window.

1. Open the data file named EX0414.

2. Save the workbook as "Natural" to your personal storage location.

3. Before you begin, you will need to review some configuration settings:
CHOOSE: Tools → Options
CLICK: *Calculation* tab
This tab, as shown in Figure 4.10, enables you to specify calculation options and dictate whether Excel recognizes labels in formulas.

Figure 4.10

Options dialog box, *Calculation* tab

Select this option to have Excel recalculate the formulas in your worksheet whenever you change a value.

Ensure that this check box is selected before attempting to enter a natural language formula.

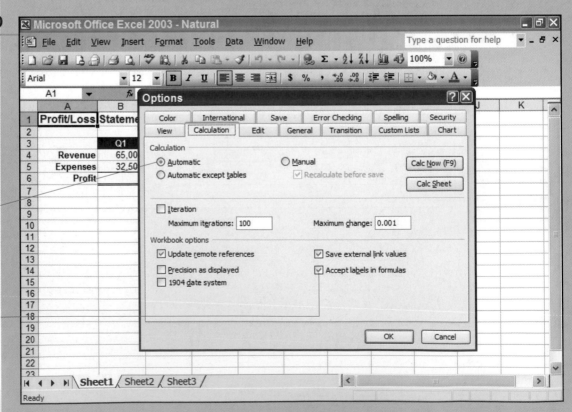

4. On the *Calculation* tab of the Options dialog box:
CLICK: *Automatic* option button, if it is not already selected
CLICK: *Accept labels in formulas* check box so that a ✔ appears
CLICK: OK command button

5. This worksheet does not contain any named ranges. You will, however, calculate the profit for Q1 using a natural language formula. To proceed:
SELECT: cell B6
TYPE: **=Revenue-Expenses**
PRESS: ➡
The result, 32500, appears in the cell.

6. To proceed, enter the same natural language formula into cell C6. Excel again calculates the result correctly.

7. Now try copying the formula in cell C6 to cells D6 and E6. As illustrated, you can copy and paste natural language formulas as well. Your worksheet should now appear similar to the one shown in Figure 4.11.

Figure 4.11

Entering and copying natural language formulas

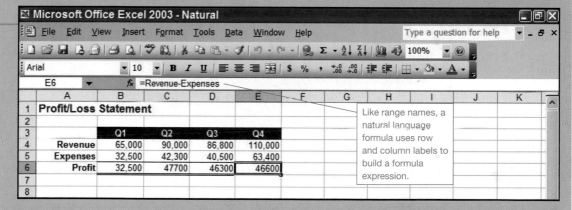

8. To confirm that "Revenue" and "Expenses" are not range names:
CHOOSE: Insert ➔ Name ➔ Define
Notice that there are no range names defined in the dialog box.

9. CLICK: Close command button

10. Save and then close the workbook.

4.1 Why is "AD2002" an unacceptable name for a cell range?

4.2 Using Built-In Functions

This module introduces you to Excel's built-in **functions.** Do not let the word "function" conjure up visions of your last calculus class; functions are merely shortcuts that you use in place of entering lengthy and complicated formulas. Functions are incredible time-savers that can increase your productivity in creating worksheets.

There are several methods for entering a function into a worksheet cell. To begin with, you can type a function name, preceded by an equal sign (**=**), and then enter its **arguments** (labels, values, or cell references). Many functions are quite complex, however, and all require that you remember the precise order, called **syntax,** in which to enter arguments. An easier method is to search for and select a function from the Insert Function dialog box shown in Figure 4.12. You access this dialog box by choosing the Insert ➜ Function command or by clicking the Insert Function button (f_x). In addition to organizing Excel's functions into tidy categories (further described in Table 4.1), the Insert Function dialog box lets you view a function's syntax, along with a brief description.

Figure 4.12

Insert Function
dialog box

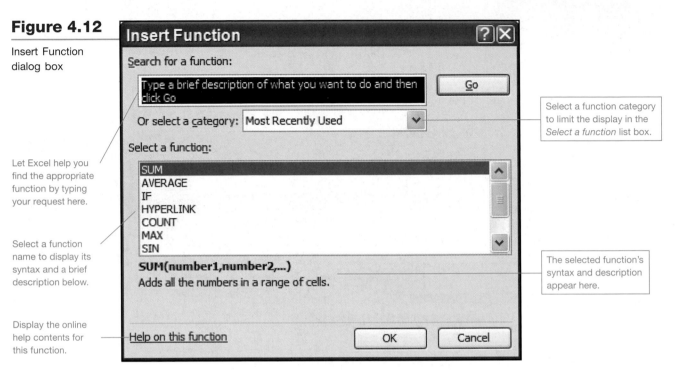

Let Excel help you find the appropriate function by typing your request here.

Select a function name to display its syntax and a brief description below.

Display the online help contents for this function.

Select a function category to limit the display in the *Select a function* list box.

The selected function's syntax and description appear here.

Table 4.1

Function
Categories

Category	Description
Financial	Determine loan payments, present and future values, depreciation schedules, and rates of return
Date & Time	Perform date and time calculations; input the current date and/or time into a cell
Math & Trig	Sum a range of values; perform trigonometric calculations; determine absolute and rounded values
Statistical	Determine the average, median, minimum, and maximum values for a range; calculate statistical measures, such as variance and standard deviation
Lookup & Reference	Look up and select values from a range; return the active cell's column letter and row number
Database	Perform mathematical and statistical calculations on worksheet values in a table or list format
Text	Manipulate, compare, format, and extract textual information; convert values to text (and vice versa)
Logical	Perform conditional calculations using IF statements; compare and evaluate values
Information	Return information about the current environment; perform error-checking and troubleshooting

4.2.1 Adding Values (SUM)

→ ## Feature

You use the SUM function to add the values appearing in a range of cells. SUM is the most frequently used function in Excel 2003, saving you from having to enter long addition formulas such as "=A1+A2+A3…+A99." As you have already seen, the AutoSum button (Σ ▾) inserts the SUM function into a worksheet cell automatically, guessing at the range argument to use. If entering the function manually, you can use a block of cells, such as A3:A8, as the range argument, or enter individual cell addresses separated by commas, as in A3,A5,A7.

→ ## Method

=SUM(*range*)

→ ## Practice

You now practice entering the SUM function. Ensure that no workbooks appear in the application window.

1. Open the data file named EX0420 to display the worksheet shown in Figure 4.13.

Figure 4.13

Opening the
EX0420
workbook

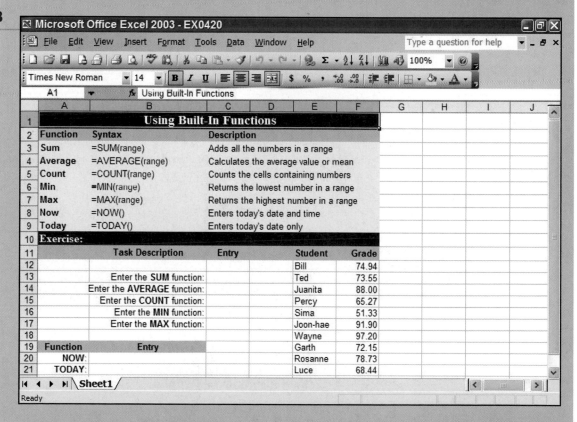

2. Save the workbook as "Functions" to your personal storage location.

3. Let's total the grade values in column F. Do the following:
SELECT: cell C13

4. To enter the SUM function:
TYPE: **=sum(f12:f21**
Notice that the cell range is highlighted with Excel's Range Finder feature (shown in Figure 4.14) as you enter the function arguments.

Figure 4.14

Entering the SUM function

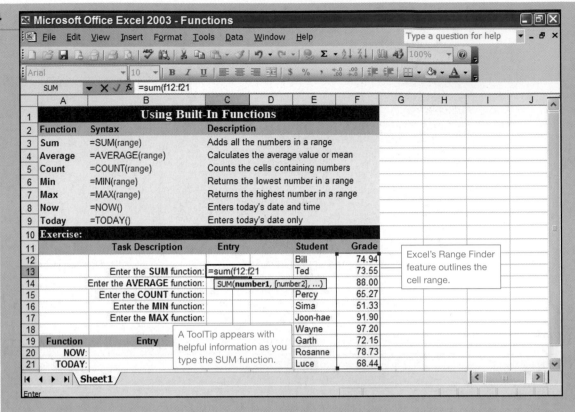

5. To complete the function:
   PRESS: ENTER
   If you forget to add the right-hand parenthesis for a function (as we did here on purpose), Excel 2003 will automatically add the parenthesis and complete your entry. The result, 761.51, should now appear in the cell. (*Note:* You can enter a function's name and arguments using either lowercase or uppercase letters.)

6. Let's change Percy's grade from 65.27:
   SELECT: cell F15

7. To enter the revised grade:
   TYPE: **75.27**
   PRESS: ENTER
   The new SUM result displays 771.51 in cell C13.

8. Save the workbook and keep it open for use in the next lesson.

4.2.2 Calculating Averages (AVERAGE)

→ **Feature**

You use the AVERAGE function to compute the average value, sometimes called the arithmetic mean, for a range of cells. This function adds together all of the numeric values in a range and then divides the sum by the number of cells used in the calculation. You can use a block of cells, such as A3:A8, as the range argument or enter individual cell addresses separated by commas, as in A3,A5,A7.

→ **Method**

=AVERAGE(*range*)

→ Practice

In this exercise, you will calculate the average value for a named range in a worksheet. Ensure that you have completed the previous lesson and that the "Functions" workbook is displayed.

1. To make it easier to enter functions, let's name the cell ranges on your worksheet. First, name the range that contains the grade values:
SELECT: cell range from E11 to F21
Noticed that you include the column headings, Student and Grade, in the selection.

2. CHOOSE: Insert → Name → Create
Your screen should now appear similar to the one shown in Figure 4.15.

Figure 4.15

Naming a cell range on the worksheet

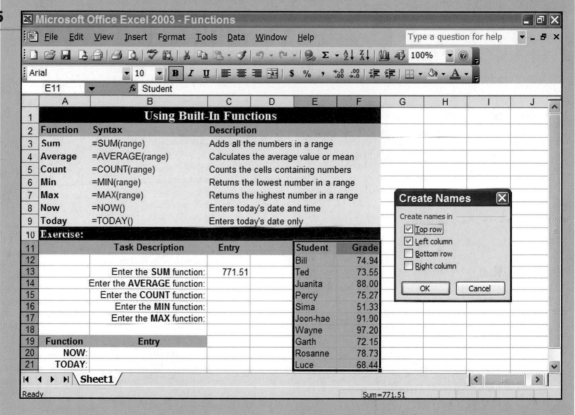

3. In the Create Names dialog box:
CLICK: *Top row* check box, if it is not already selected
CLICK: *Left column* check box, if it is not already selected
CLICK: OK command button

4. To view the range names that have been created:
CLICK: down arrow attached to the Name Box
The Name Box appears with each of the students' names, along with Grade and Student, as shown here.

5. In the *Name* drop-down list box:
SELECT: Garth
Your cell pointer should now be positioned in cell F19. Notice also that the Name Box displays the name "Garth"

6. To select the entire "Grade" range:
CLICK: down arrow attached to the Name Box
SELECT: Grade in the drop-down list
The cell range from F12 to F21 is selected.

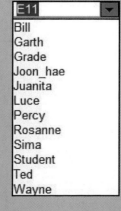

7. Let's use the range name to calculate the average grade:
SELECT: cell C14
TYPE: **=average(grade)**
Notice again how the Range Finder feature highlights the cell range.

8. PRESS: `ENTER`
The result, 77.151, appears in the cell.

9. To determine the average of a list of nonadjacent values, separate the items in the list using commas. To illustrate:
SELECT: cell D14
TYPE: **=average(Bill,Ted,Sima,Rosanne)**
Your worksheet should appear similar to the one shown in Figure 4.16.

Figure 4.16

Averaging a list of nonadjacent cells

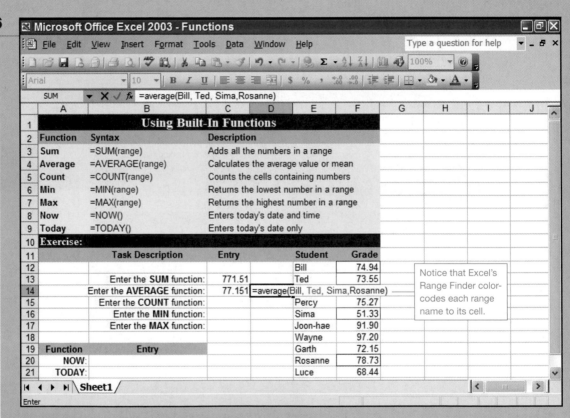

10. PRESS: `ENTER` to enter the function into cell D14
The average of these students' grades is 69.6375.

4.2.3 Counting Values (COUNT)

→ **Feature**

The COUNT function counts the number of cells in a range that contain numeric or date values. This function ignores cells containing text labels. You can use this function to determine how many entries are present in a worksheet column. As with SUM and AVERAGE, you can use a block of cells, such as A3:A8, as the range argument or enter individual cell addresses separated by commas, as in A3,A5,A7.

→ # Method

=COUNT(*range*)

→ # Practice

You will now enter the COUNT function in the "Functions" workbook. Ensure that you have completed the previous lessons and that the "Functions" workbook is displayed.

1. Now move the cell pointer to where you want the COUNT function's result to appear. Do the following:
SELECT: cell C15

2. Let's use the mouse to help count the number of entries in a range:
TYPE: =count(

3. Using the mouse, position the cell pointer over cell F12. Then:
CLICK: cell F12 and hold down the left mouse button
DRAG: mouse pointer to cell F21
Notice that as you drag the mouse pointer, the range is entered into the function as an argument. When you reach cell F21, the argument displays the range name "Grade," as shown in Figure 4.17.

Figure 4.17

Using the mouse to select a cell range

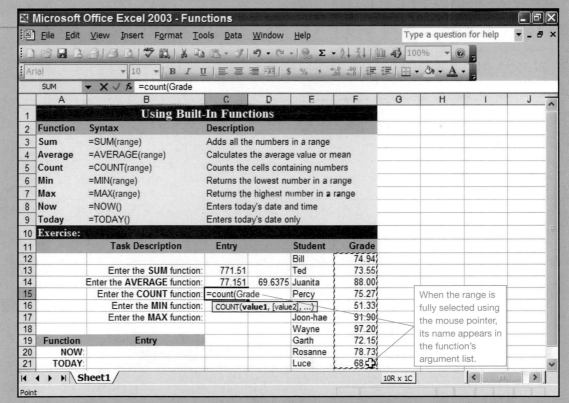

4. Release the mouse button.

5. To complete the function entry:
TYPE:)
PRESS: (ENTER)
The result, 10, appears in cell C15.

6. Save the workbook and keep it open for use in the next lesson.

In Addition THE DIFFERENCE BETWEEN COUNT AND COUNTA

The COUNT function has a second cousin named the COUNTA function. Whereas COUNT tallies the cells containing numbers and dates, COUNTA counts all nonblank cells. The primary difference, therefore, is that the COUNTA function includes text labels in its calculations.

4.2.4 Analyzing Values (MIN and MAX)

→ ## Feature

You use the MIN and MAX functions to determine the minimum (lowest) and maximum (highest) values in a range of cells. These functions are useful in pulling information from your worksheet, such as the highest mark appearing in a teacher's grade book. You can use a block of cells as the range argument, such as A3:A8, or enter individual cell addresses separated by commas, as in A3,A5,A7.

→ ## Method

=MIN(*range*)
=MAX(*range*)

→ ## Practice

In this lesson, you will use the Function Arguments dialog box to calculate the minimum and maximum grades in a range. Ensure that you have completed the previous lessons in this module and that the "Functions" workbook is displayed.

1. To calculate the lowest grade achieved:
   SELECT: cell C16
   TYPE: **=min(grade)**
   PRESS: ➡
   The result, 51.33, appears.

2. To find the lowest grade achieved among three students:
   TYPE: **=min(Wayne,Garth,Luce)**
   PRESS: **ENTER**
   The result, 68.44, appears.

3. Now let's use Excel's Function Arguments dialog box to calculate the maximum value in a range. Do the following:
   SELECT: cell C17
   TYPE: **=max(**
   Ensure that you include the open parenthesis "(" at the end of the function name.

4. To display the Function Arguments dialog box:
   CLICK: Insert Function button ([*fx*]) in the Formula bar
   The Function Arguments dialog box appears, as shown in Figure 4.18.

Figure 4.18

Function
Arguments dialog
box

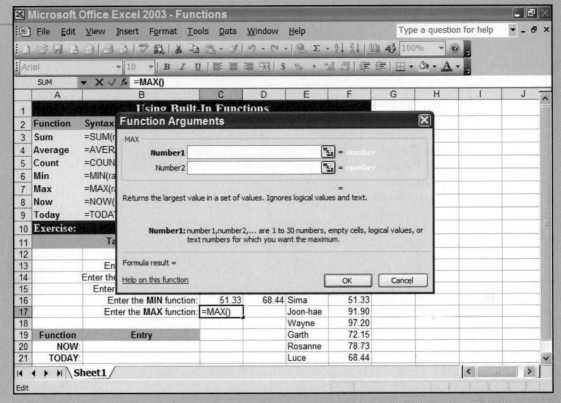

5. In the *Number1* argument text box:
TYPE: **grade**
Notice that the actual cell contents appear at the right of the text box and that the result is calculated immediately, as shown in Figure 4.19.

Figure 4.19

Entering
arguments for the
MAX function

The calculated
formula result
appears here.

Actual values from the cell
range appear here.

Calculated result

Function Arguments dialog box showing:

MAX

Number1 grade   = {74.94;73.55;88;75

Number2   = number

= 97.2

Returns the largest value in a set of values. Ignores logical values and text.

Number1: number1,number2,... are 1 to 30 numbers, empty cells, logical values, or text numbers for which you want the maximum.

Formula result =   97.2

Help on this function   OK   Cancel

6. To complete the entry:
CLICK: OK command button
The result, 97.2, is placed into the cell.

7. To find the maximum grade achieved among three students:
SELECT: cell D17
TYPE: **=max(**
CLICK: Insert Function button ([*fx*])

8. In the Function Arguments dialog box:
TYPE: **Juanita**
PRESS: TAB
TYPE: **Ted**
PRESS: TAB
TYPE: **Luce**
Notice that the Formula bar displays the function as you build it in the Function Arguments dialog box (shown in Figure 4.20).

Figure 4.20

Entering arguments into the Function Arguments dialog box

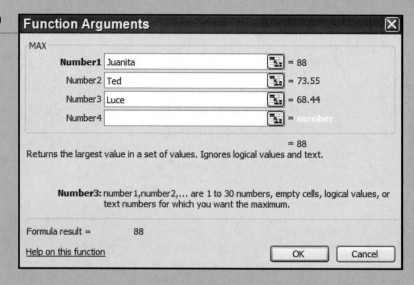

```
Function Arguments                                    ⊠
┌─ MAX ──────────────────────────────────────────────
│   Number1  Juanita                      [▦] = 88
│   Number2  Ted                          [▦] = 73.55
│   Number3  Luce                         [▦] = 68.44
│   Number4                               [▦] = number
│                                              = 88
│ Returns the largest value in a set of values. Ignores logical values and text.
│
│       Number3: number1,number2,... are 1 to 30 numbers, empty cells, logical values, or
│                text numbers for which you want the maximum.
│
│ Formula result =        88
│ Help on this function              [   OK   ]  [ Cancel ]
```

9. To complete the entry:
CLICK: OK command button
The result, 88, appears in the cell.

4.2.5 Calculating Dates (NOW and TODAY)

→ **Feature**

You use the NOW and TODAY functions to display the date and time in your worksheets. The NOW function returns the current date and time as provided by your computer's internal clock. The way the function's result appears in a worksheet cell is determined by the date and time formatting selected. Unlike the NOW function, the TODAY function provides only the current date. Neither of these functions requires an argument.

→ **Method**

=NOW( )
=TODAY( )

→ **Practice**

In this exercise, you will insert the NOW and TODAY functions into the worksheet. Ensure that you have completed the previous lessons in this module and that the "Functions" workbook is displayed.

1. To start this lesson, let's practice using the Insert Function dialog box to search for a function. First, position the cell pointer where you want the result to appear:
SELECT: cell B20

2. Now display the Insert Function dialog box:
CLICK: Insert Function button (f_x)
(*Hint:* You can also choose the Insert → Function command on the menu.)

3. In the *Search for a function* text box:
TYPE: **to display the current time**
CLICK: Go command button

4. In the *Select a function* list box:
CLICK: NOW function
The dialog box should now appear similar to Figure 4.21.

Figure 4.21

Searching for a function "to display the current time"

Type your request for a function here and then click the Go command button to perform the search.

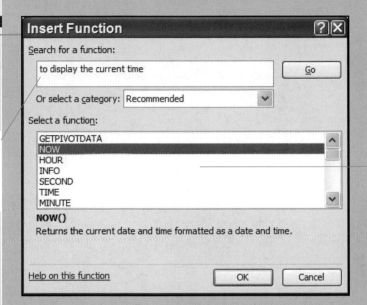

The results of the function search appear in this list box. Click on a function to display its description below the list box.

5. With the NOW function selected in the *Select a function* list box, read the description that starts with "Returns the current date and time."

6. To insert the NOW function into cell B20:
CLICK: OK command button

7. The Function Arguments dialog box appears, as shown in Figure 4.22, asking for confirmation:
CLICK: OK command button
The date is displayed in cell B20 using the "mm/dd/yyyy" format, depending on your default settings. The time is typically displayed using the "hh:mm" 24-hour clock format.

Figure 4.22

Function
Arguments dialog
box for the NOW
function

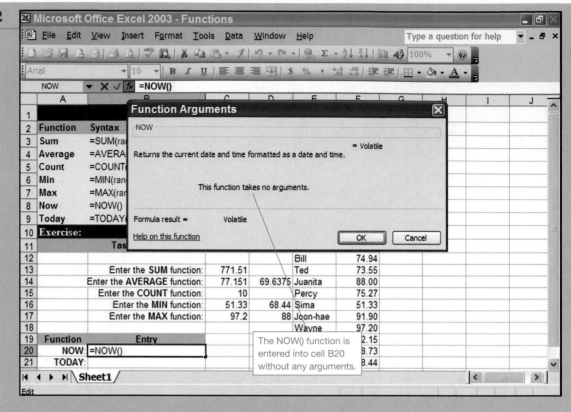

8. To display only the time in the cell, you must reformat the entry:
SELECT: cell B20, if it is not already selected
CHOOSE: Format → Cells
CLICK: *Number* tab

9. Now select a time format:
SELECT: Time in the *Category* list box
SELECT: 1:30:55 PM in the *Type* list box
Figure 4.23 shows the selections in the Format Cells dialog box.

Figure 4.23

Formatting the
display of the
current time

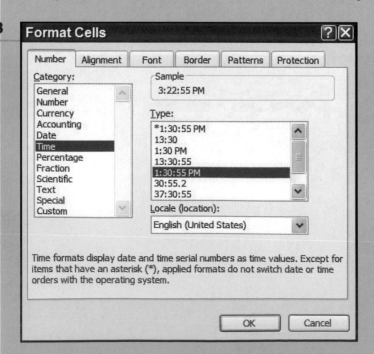

10. CLICK: OK command button

11. To recalculate the NOW function:
PRESS: **F9** (CALC key)
You should see the cell value change to the current time. (*Hint:* You can use **F9** to recalculate all formulas and functions in a worksheet.)

12. To select a function for entering the current date:
SELECT: B21
CLICK: Insert Function button (**fx**)

13. To display a list of the available function categories, as shown in Figure 4.24, do the following:
CLICK: down arrow attached to the *Or select a category* drop-down list box

Figure 4.24

Displaying the
function
categories

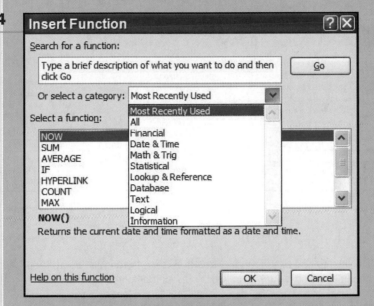

14. In the category drop-down list box:
SELECT: Date & Time

15. Scroll through the *Select a function* list box and then:
SELECT: TODAY
CLICK: OK command button

16. The Function Arguments dialog box asks for confirmation:
CLICK: OK command button
The current date now appears in cell B21.

17. As you did in formatting the time, use the Format Cells dialog box to select a "dd-mmm-yy" date format. Your worksheet should now appear similar to the one shown in Figure 4.25.

18. Save and then close the workbook.

Figure 4.25

Completing the "Functions" workbook

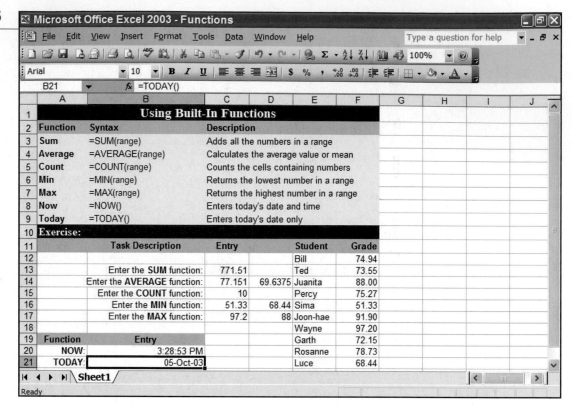

In Addition   THE IF FUNCTION

The IF function is arguably one of the most useful of Excel's functions. Using the IF function allows you to employ conditional logic in your worksheets. Specifically, you can test for a condition and then, depending on the result, perform one of two calculations. Because the IF function is used to solve more complex problems, it is covered in Chapter 6 of the Advantage Series' Introductory and Complete editions.

4.2   When might you use the Function Arguments dialog box or Insert Function dialog box to enter a function into the worksheet?

4.3 Creating an Embedded Chart

Since the earliest versions of spreadsheet software became available, users have been able to display their numerical data using graphs and charts. Although these graphics were acceptable for in-house business reports and school projects, they often lacked the depth and quality required by professional users. Until now! You can confidently use Excel 2003 to produce visually stunning worksheets and charts that are suitable for electronic business presentations, color print masters, published reports, and Web pages.

Many types of charts are available for presenting your worksheet data to engineers, statisticians, business professionals, and other audiences. Some popular business charts—line charts, column charts, pie charts, and XY scatter plot diagrams—are described below.

- *Line Charts* When you need to plot trends or show changes over a period of time, the **line chart** is the perfect tool. The angles of the line reflect the degree of variation, and the distance of the line from the horizontal axis represents the amount of the variation. An example of a line chart appears in Figure 4.26, along with some basic terminology.

Figure 4.26

A line chart

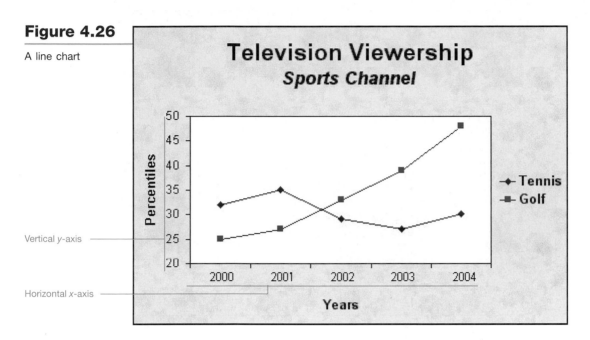

Vertical *y*-axis

Horizontal *x*-axis

- *Bar or Column Charts* When the purpose of the chart is to compare one data element with another data element, a **column chart** is the appropriate form to use. Like a line chart, a column chart (Figure 4.27) shows variations over a period of time. A **bar chart** also uses rectangular images, but the images run horizontally rather than vertically.

Figure 4.27

A column chart

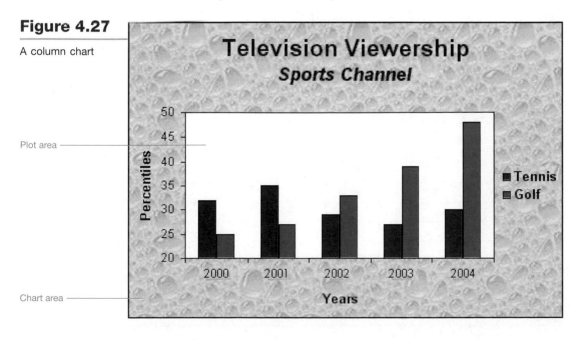

Plot area

Chart area

- *Pie Charts*   A **pie chart** shows the proportions of individual components compared to the total. Like a real pie (the baked variety), a pie chart is divided into slices or wedges. (In Excel 2003, you can even pull out the slices from the rest of the pie.) An example of a pie chart appears in Figure 4.28.

Figure 4.28

A pie chart

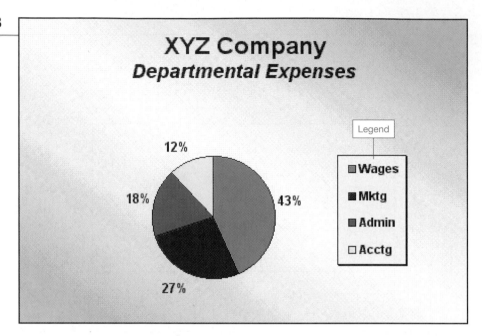

- *Scatter Plot Diagrams*   **XY charts,** which are commonly referred to as **scatter plot diagrams,** show how one or more data elements relate to another data element. Although they look much like line charts, XY charts show the correlation between elements and include a numeric scale along both the x- and y-axes. The XY chart in Figure 4.29 shows that worker productivity diminishes as stress levels increase.

Figure 4.29

An XY chart

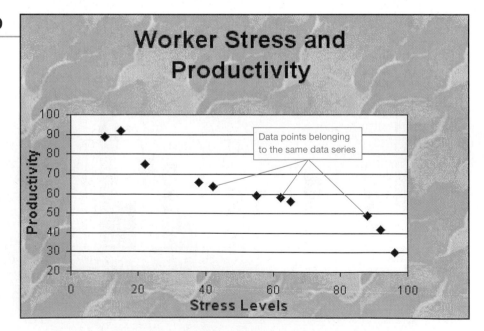

There are two methods for creating a chart in Excel 2003, differing primarily in the way the chart is stored and printed. First, you can create a new chart as a separate sheet in a workbook. This method works well for printing full-page charts and for creating computer-based presentations or electronic slide shows. Second, you can create an **embedded chart** that is stored on the worksheet. Embed a chart when you want to view or print the chart alongside the worksheet data. Whichever approach you choose, you can use the step-by-step features in Excel's **Chart Wizard** to construct the chart from existing worksheet data.

In this module, you will learn how to create and print an embedded chart.

4.3.1 Creating a Chart Using the Chart Wizard

→ ## Feature

Creating an impressive chart in Excel 2003 is surprisingly easy. To begin, select a range of cells that you want to plot and then launch the Chart Wizard. The wizard examines the selected range and then displays its dialog box. You make selections, such as choosing a chart type, and proceed through the steps to embed the chart on the worksheet. An embedded chart is actually placed over—not entered into—a cell range. Once it is embedded, you can move, size, and delete the chart at any time.

→ ## Method

- SELECT: the cell range to plot in a chart
- CLICK: Chart Wizard button (⊞)
- Complete the steps in the Chart Wizard.

→ ## Practice

You will now create and embed a new chart onto a worksheet.

1. Open the data file named EX0430 to display the worksheet in Figure 4.30.

Figure 4.30

Opening the
EX0430
workbook

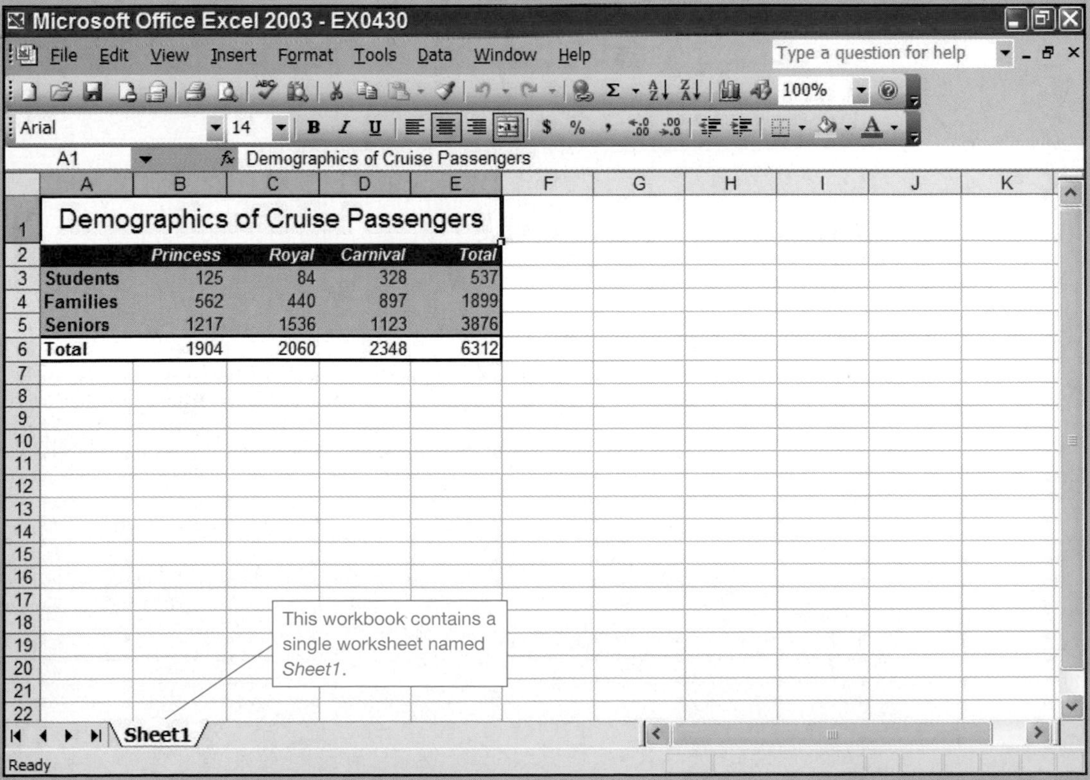

This workbook contains a single worksheet named *Sheet1*.

2. Save the workbook as "Cruising" to your personal storage location.

3. Let's plot the worksheet's demographic data. To begin, select both the column headings and the data area:
   SELECT: cell range from A2 to D5
   (**Caution:** Do not include the title in cell A1 or the "Total" cells in row 6 or column E in the range selection.)

4. To start the Chart Wizard:
   CLICK: Chart Wizard button (🔳) on the Standard toolbar
   The Chart Wizard dialog box appears, as shown in Figure 4.31.

Figure 4.31

Chart Wizard:
Step 1 of 4

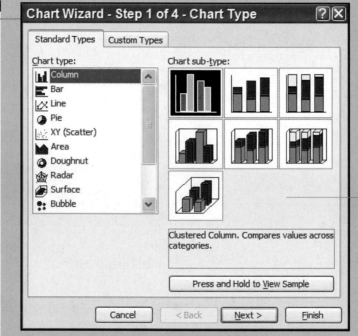

5. To see a sample of how Excel will plot this data:
   CLICK: "Press and Hold to View Sample" command button
   (*Note:* You must hold down the left mouse button to see the chart inside the *Sample* preview window. When you are finished viewing, release the mouse button.)

6. Let's select a different chart sub-type that amalgamates (adds together) the data series in a column. Do the following:
   SELECT: Stacked Column in the *Chart sub-type area,* as shown here
   (*Hint:* When you click on a chart sub-type, the chart's name and description appear above the "Press and Hold to View Sample" command button.)

7. Once again, preview a sample of the chart:
   CLICK: "Press and Hold to View Sample" command button

8. To continue creating the chart:
   CLICK: [Next>] to proceed to Step 2 of 4
   Your screen should now appear similar to the one shown in Figure 4.32.

Figure 4.32

Chart Wizard:
Step 2 of 4

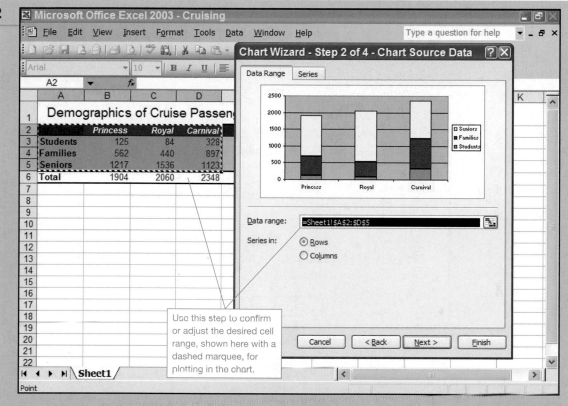

9. Because you selected the data range prior to launching the Chart Wizard, you can accept the default entry in Step 2 and proceed:
CLICK: Next> to proceed to Step 3 of 4

10. In Step 3 of 4 of the Chart Wizard:
TYPE: **Cruise Lines** into the *Category (X) axis* text box
TYPE: **Passengers** into the *Value (Y) axis* text box
(*Hint:* Click the I-beam mouse pointer into a text box and then type the appropriate text. You can also press **TAB** to move forward through the text boxes.) Notice that the preview area is immediately updated to display the new titles, as shown in Figure 4.33.

Figure 4.33

Chart Wizard:
Step 3 of 4

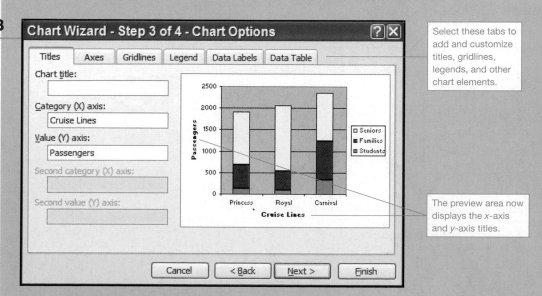

11. To proceed to the final step:
CLICK: Next>

12. In Step 4 of 4, you specify where you want to store the chart. To create an embedded chart:
CLICK: *As object in* option button, as shown in Figure 4.34
Notice that the current worksheet's name, *Sheet1,* already appears in the drop-down list box next to the option button.

Figure 4.34

Chart Wizard:
Step 4 of 4

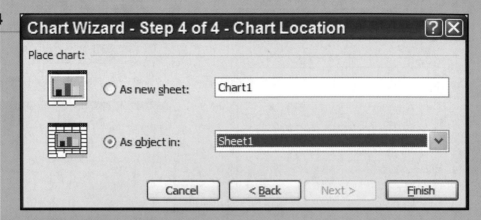

13. To complete the Chart Wizard:
CLICK: Finish
The embedded chart appears in the application window, as shown in Figure 4.35. (*Note:* You may also see Excel's Chart toolbar appear.)

Figure 4.35

Adding a chart as an embedded object to the worksheet

Excel's Range Finder feature displays the range plotted in the selected chart.

The Chart toolbar will appear when the chart object is selected.

The embedded chart object floats above the cells in the worksheet.

Size a chart by dragging one of the selection boxes that appear around the selected chart object.

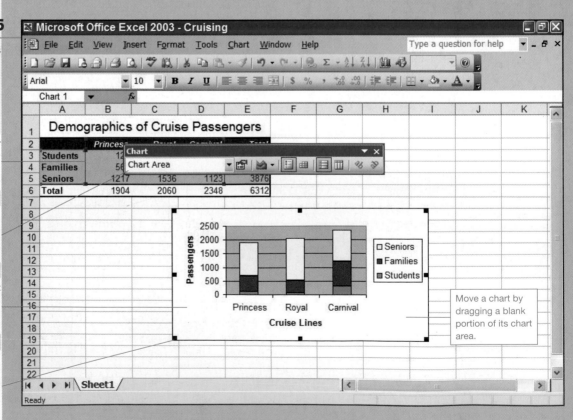

14. The black selection boxes (sometimes called "sizing handles") that surround the chart indicate that the chart is currently selected. Using the mouse, you can size the embedded chart by dragging these boxes. On your own, practice sizing the chart.

15. You can move the chart by dragging the object with the mouse. Position the white mouse arrow over a blank portion of the chart's background area. Then, drag the chart into position. Practice moving and sizing the chart to cover the range from cell A8 to E20, immediately beneath the data area.

16. To return focus to the worksheet:
CLICK: any cell visible in the worksheet area, such as cell A1
Notice that the selection boxes around the chart disappear, as shown in Figure 4.36.

Figure 4.36

Returning focus to the worksheet

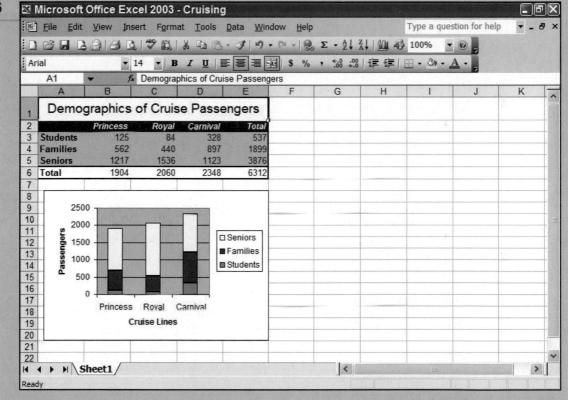

17. One of the most significant features of an Excel chart is that it remains dynamically linked to the data stored in the worksheet. To illustrate, let's update the "Carnival" column in the embedded chart:
SELECT: cell D5
TYPE: **400**
PRESS: (ENTER)
The chart is updated immediately to reflect the new data.

18. Save the workbook and keep it open for use in the next lesson.

4.3.2 Previewing and Printing an Embedded Chart

→ ## Feature

One of the primary reasons for embedding a chart on a worksheet is to view and print it alongside its worksheet data. You must ensure, however, that the print area (or worksheet range) includes the entire chart object. As you learned in the previous chapter, you can manipulate various page setup options, including margins, headers, and footers. Remember also to preview your worksheet and chart before sending it to the printer.

→ ## Method

- SELECT: a cell range that includes the chart
- CHOOSE: File → Print Area → Set Print Area
- CHOOSE: File → Print Preview

    or

- CHOOSE: File → Print

→ ## Practice

You will now preview and print an embedded chart along with its worksheet data. Ensure that you have completed the previous lesson and that the "Cruising" workbook is displayed.

1. To print the worksheet and embedded chart on the same page:
SELECT: cell range from A1 to F21
(*Note:* Depending on the size and placement of your chart object, you may need to increase or decrease this print range. Make sure that the entire object is covered in the highlighted range.)

2. CHOOSE: File → Print Area → Set Print Area
Your screen should appear similar to the one shown in Figure 4.37.

Figure 4.37

Specifying the worksheet range to be printed

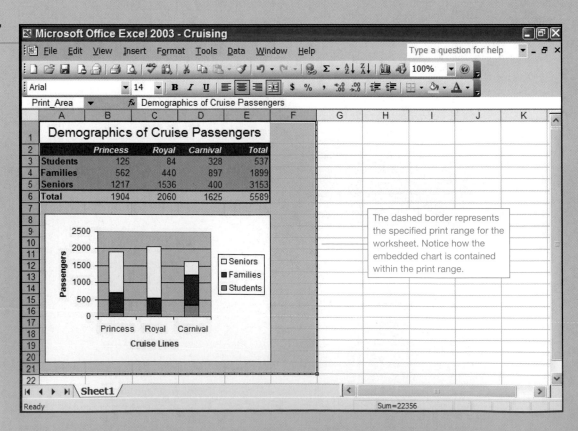

The dashed border represents the specified print range for the worksheet. Notice how the embedded chart is contained within the print range.

3. To preview the worksheet and chart:
CLICK: Print Preview button ()

4. To zoom in on the preview window:
CLICK: Zoom command button

5. On your own, scroll the preview window so that it appears similar to the one shown in Figure 4.38. Notice that the chart is printed immediately and seamlessly below the worksheet data. (*Note:* If you do not have a color printer specified as your default, the worksheet and chart will not appear in color as shown here.)

Figure 4.38

Previewing an embedded chart

Worksheet data area

Embedded chart object

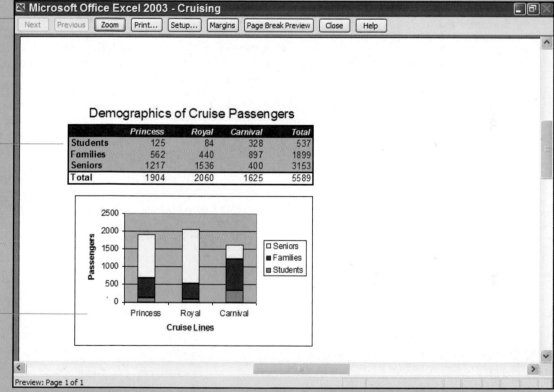

6. To print the chart from the Preview window:
CLICK: Print command button

7. If you do not have access to a printer, click the Cancel command button and proceed to the next step. If you have a printer attached to your computer and want to print this chart, do the following:
CLICK: OK command button

8. To remove the selection highlighting from the worksheet area:
CLICK: cell A1
(*Hint:* You may have noticed that we often select cell A1 prior to saving the workbook. The reason is that Excel saves and restores the cell pointer's position for the next time you open the workbook.)

9. Save and then close the workbook.

10. Exit Microsoft Office Excel 2003.

SelfCheck   **4.3** What must you ensure when selecting the print range for a worksheet that contains an embedded chart?

Chapter
summary

Excel 2003 provides powerful tools for analyzing and summarizing data. The ability to name cells and ranges for use in constructing expressions and navigating the worksheet increases accuracy and efficiency. You can also create formula expressions using either relative or absolute cell references. Specifying an absolute cell address by adding dollar signs ($) serves to anchor a cell reference to an exact location on the worksheet. The default, however, is to use relative cell addresses, which Excel can adjust automatically when you copy formulas to new locations in the worksheet.

Built-in functions, such as SUM and AVERAGE, are used as shortcuts to perform complex or lengthy calculations. Excel 2003 provides hundreds of functions, sorted alphabetically into categories for your convenience. You enter a function by typing directly into a worksheet cell or by displaying the Insert Function dialog box and then selecting the desired function. Another helpful productivity feature provided by Excel is the Function Arguments dialog box, which prompts you in entering the required arguments for a particular function.

Charts and graphics help to organize and present data and to convey meaning for the users of your worksheets. Most people agree that it is easier to infer trends and patterns from a line graph or bar chart than from a table of numerical data. Fortunately, Excel 2003's Chart Wizard makes it easy to produce and format a variety of chart types. You can even embed and print your charts alongside the data stored in a worksheet.

Command Summary

Many of the commands and procedures appearing in this chapter are summarized in the following table:.

Skill Set	To Perform this Task...	Do the Following...
Working with Cells and Cell Data	Name a cell range	SELECT: the desired range CLICK: in the Name Box TYPE: *range name*
	Create range names from labels appearing on the worksheet	SELECT: the desired range CHOOSE: Insert ➜ Name ➜ Create
	Modify and delete range names	CHOOSE: Insert ➜ Name ➜ Define
	Paste a list of range names onto the worksheet	CHOOSE: Insert ➜ Name ➜ Paste
Creating and Revising Formulas	Modify and use cell references (absolute, relative, and mixed)	SELECT: the desired cell CLICK: in the cell address in the Formula bar PRESS: F4 (ABS key) to apply reference type
	Recalculate formulas in a worksheet	PRESS: F9 (CALC key)
	Use the Insert Function dialog box to enter a function and its arguments	CLICK: Insert Function button (fx) SELECT: a category and function

	Use basic functions: • Sum a range of values • Average a range of values • Count the numeric and date values in a range • Find the lowest value in a range • Find the highest value in a range	**=SUM**(*range*) **=AVERAGE**(*range*) **=COUNT**(*range*) **=MIN**(*range*) **=MAX**(*range*)
	Use date functions: • Enter the current date and time • Enter today's date	**=NOW( )** **=TODAY( )**
Creating and Modifying Graphics	Use the Chart Wizard to create a chart	SELECT: the cell range to plot CLICK: Chart Wizard button (▥)
	Preview and print an embedded chart	SELECT: the desired range CHOOSE: File ➜ Print Area ➜ Set Print Area CLICK: Print Preview (▨) or Print (▨)

Key Terms

This section specifies page references for the key terms identified in this chapter. For a complete list of definitions, refer to the Glossary at the back of this learning guide.

absolute cell address, *p. EX 175*

arguments, *p. EX 179*

bar chart, *p. EX 193*

Chart Wizard, *p. EX 195*

column chart, *p. EX 193*

embedded chart, *p. EX 195*

functions, *p. EX 180*

line chart, *p. EX 193*

mixed cell address, *p. EX 175*

pie chart, *p. EX 194*

natural language formula, *p. EX 178*

range name, *p. EX 170*

relative cell address, *p. EX 175*

scatter plot diagrams, *p. EX 194*

syntax, *p. EX 180*

XY charts, *p. EX 194*

Chapter quiz

Short Answer

1. Why would you want to name a range of cells?

2. How do you place a list of range names into the worksheet?

3. Name the two primary types of cell references and explain how they differ.

4. In order for natural language formulas to work effectively, how should the worksheet be organized?

5. Which function would you use to extract the highest value from a range named "salary"? How would you enter the function?

6. Which function would you use to place only the current time in your worksheet? What else might you want to do after entering the function?

7. What is the name of the dialog box that you can use to select functions from categories? How do you access this dialog box?

8. What is the name of the dialog box that can help you to enter a function's arguments correctly? How do you access this dialog box?

9. Describe the four steps in creating a chart using the Chart Wizard dialog boxes.

10. What are the black boxes called that surround an embedded chart? For what are they used?

True/False

1. _____ Range names that you create use relative cell references.

2. _____ Cell addresses that you enter into formulas use, by default, absolute cell references.

3. _____ The "$s" in the cell reference $D$5 indicate an absolute cell reference.

4. _____ To ensure that a cell address appears in formulas as an absolute cell reference, move the cell pointer to the cell location and press [F4].

5. _____ You enter a function using parentheses instead of the equal sign.

6. _____ The SUM function appears in the Math & Trig function category of the Insert Function dialog box.

7. _____ The TODAY function updates the computer's internal clock to the current date and time.

8. _____ A pie chart shows the proportions of individual components compared to the total.

9. _____ The Chart Wizard allows you to place a chart on a separate sheet in the workbook or as an embedded object on a worksheet.

10. _____ You can move and size a chart object once it is embedded on the worksheet.

Multiple Choice

1. What menu command allows you to create range names using the labels that already appear in the worksheet?
   a. Edit → Name → Create
   b. Insert → Name → Create
   c. Insert → Name → Define
   d. Range → Name → Create

2. Which of the following symbols precedes an absolute cell reference?
   a. &
   b. @
   c. $
   d. #

3. In Edit mode, which key do you press to change a cell address to being absolute, relative, or mixed?
   a. [F2]
   b. [F3]
   c. [F4]
   d. [F9]

4. Which key do you press to recalculate or update a worksheet?
   a. [F2]
   b. [F3]
   c. [F4]
   d. [F9]

5. Which is the correct expression for adding the values stored in the cell range from A1 to A20?
   a. =ADD(A1+A20)
   b. =AutoSUM(A1,A20)
   c. =SUM(A1+A20)
   d. =SUM(A1:A20)

6. Which is the correct expression for determining the average of a range named "Units"?
   a. =AVERAGE(Units)
   b. =AVG(Units)
   c. =SUM(Units/Average)
   d. =UNITS(Average)

7. What does the COUNT function actually count?

   a. All of the cells in a range
   b. All of the cells containing data in a range
   c. Only those cells containing text and numbers
   d. Only those cells containing numeric or date values

8. Which button do you click to display the Insert Function dialog box?

   a. f_x
   b. 📊
   c. ↺▾
   d. Σ▾

9. What is the name of the step-by-step charting tool provided by Excel?

   a. Chart Master
   b. Chart Wizard
   c. Plot Master
   d. Plot Wizard

10. A chart may be created as a separate chart sheet or as an embedded object. In which step of the Chart Wizard do you specify how a chart is created and stored?

   a. Step 1
   b. Step 2
   c. Step 3
   d. Step 4

Hands-On
exercises

step by step

1. Creating and Using Range Names

In this exercise, you will practice working with named cell ranges in constructing formulas. To begin, you will use existing labels in the worksheet to define the range names automatically and then paste those names into the worksheet.

1. Open the data file named EX04HE01.

2. Save the workbook as "Departments" to your personal storage location.

3. To begin, name cell B8 "Total" using the Name Box in the Formula bar.

4. Use the existing worksheet labels in A2 through A7 to define range names for the data stored in cells B2 through B7. After choosing the Insert ➡ Name ➡ Create command, your screen should appear similar to the one shown in Figure 4.39.

Figure 4.39

Creating range names

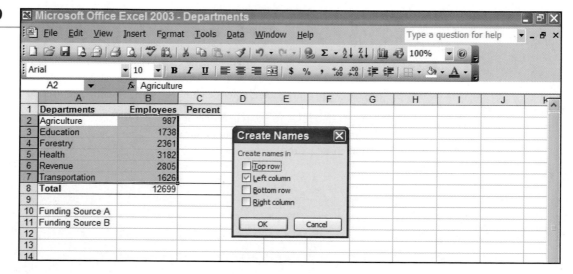

5. Starting in cell E2, paste a complete list of the range names that you just created into the worksheet.

6. Move to cell B10 in order to prepare for entering the first formula.

7. To enter a formula using the named cell ranges:
TYPE: **=**
CLICK: cell B3
Notice that "Education" appears in the Formula bar in place of the cell B3 reference.

8. To continue the formula:
TYPE: **+**
CLICK: cell B5
CLICK: Enter button (☑)
The expression now reads "=Education+Health" in the Formula bar.

9. Move to cell B11 to enter the next formula.

10. Using the typing or pointing method, enter an expression that totals the remaining departments not included in the previous formula. Before pressing (**ENTER**), your screen should appear similar to the one shown in Figure 4.40.

Figure 4.40

Entering a
formula using
named ranges

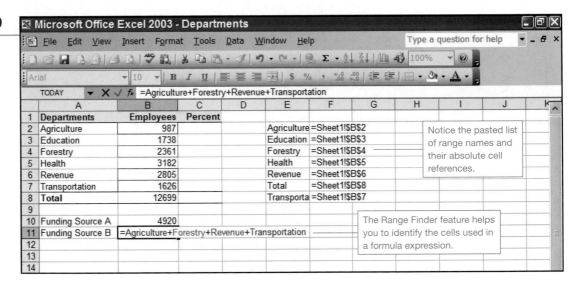

11. Ensure that you complete the formula entry by pressing (**ENTER**).

12. Now calculate the employment percentage for each department. Starting in cell C2, enter a formula that can be later used for copying. To do so, specify an absolute cell reference for the Total value and a relative cell reference for the Department value. (*Hint:* A range name provides an absolute cell reference. Therefore, you cannot use the range name "Agriculture" in the formula expression.)

13. Copy the formula in cell C2 to the remaining departments in column C using the fill handle, as shown in Figure 4.41. (*Hint:* The fill handle for a cell or cell range is the small black box in the bottom right-hand corner of the range selection.)

Figure 4.41

Using the fill
handle to copy a
formula

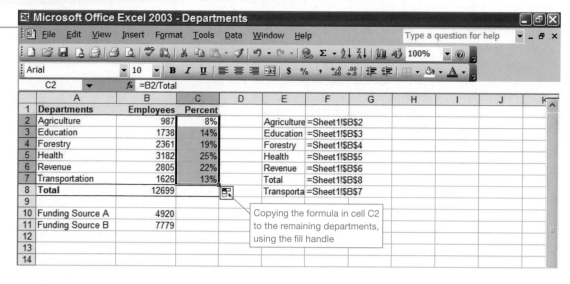

14. On your own, select the cells in the range C2:C8 and view the contents in the Formula bar. Notice that the relative cell references (B2, B3, . . . B8) adjust automatically. The range name "Total" remains absolute.

15. Save and then close the "Departments" workbook.

step by step

2. Entering Functions

You will now practice using some of Excel 2003's built-in functions to complete an existing worksheet. You also use the AutoFill feature to create a series and then the Fill command to copy formulas.

1. Open the data file named EX04HE02 to display the worksheet shown in Figure 4.42.

Figure 4.42

Opening the
EX04HE02
workbook

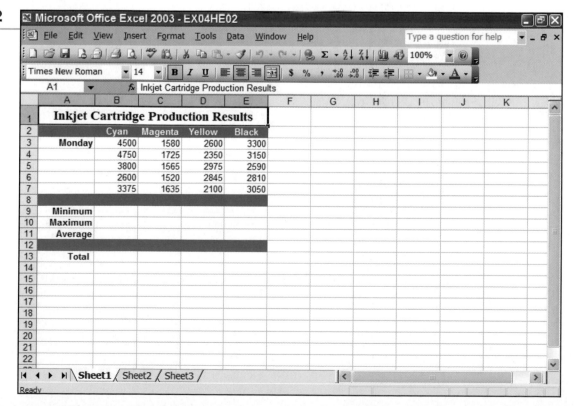

2. Save the workbook as "Inkjet Results" in your personal storage location.

3. Use the fill handle to complete a series listing the days of the week (Monday through Friday) in cells A3 to A7.

4. In cell B9, enter the following function to calculate the minimum production amount for cyan cartridges:
   TYPE: **=min(b3:b7)**
   PRESS: **ENTER**

5. Using the same approach, enter formulas in cells B10 and B11 to calculate the maximum and average production for cyan.

6. Select the cell range from B9 to E11 and then use the Edit → Fill → Right command to copy the formulas to columns C, D, and E.

7. Select the cell range from A2 to E7 and then use the Insert → Name → Create command to assign range names using the existing row and column labels, as shown in Figure 4.43.

Figure 4.43

Creating range names

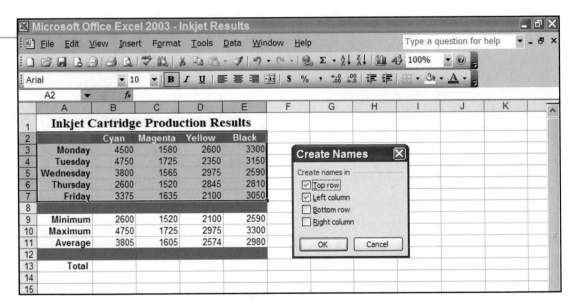

8. Paste a list of the range names starting in cell G2.

9. Adjust the widths for columns G and H to their best fit.

10. To calculate the total production for cyan cartridges:
    SELECT: cell B13
    TYPE: **=sum(cyan)**
    PRESS: **ENTER**

11. Using the same technique, calculate the totals for the Magenta, Yellow, and Black columns. (*Note:* You cannot use the Edit, Fill, Right command, because the named range "Cyan" uses an absolute cell reference.)

12. Figure 4.44 shows the completed worksheet. Save and then close the workbook.

Figure 4.44

Completing the "Inkjet Results" workbook

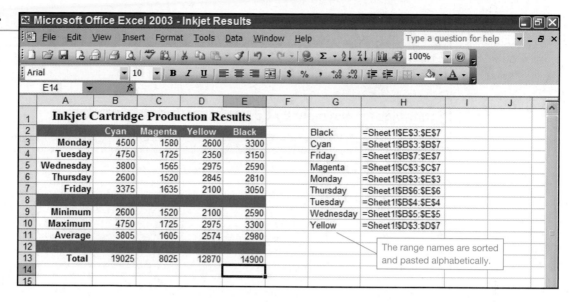

step by step

3. Creating an Embedded Chart

You will now practice creating an embedded column chart using Excel 2003's Chart Wizard. You will then print out this chart alongside its worksheet data.

1. Open the data file named EX04HE03.

2. Save the workbook as "Citywide Employment" to your personal storage location.

3. As shown in Figure 4.45, select the cell range from A3 to G5 for plotting the data in a chart. (*Note:* You do not include the "Total" row or "Total" column in the range selection.)

Figure 4.45

Selecting the data to plot in a chart

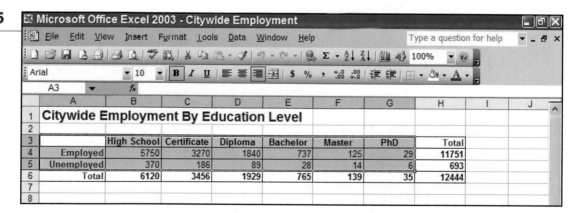

4. Launch the Chart Wizard by clicking its button (📊) on the Standard toolbar.

5. To display the two categories, Employed and Unemployed, side by side in a chart, select a "Column" chart type with a "Stacked Column" sub-type; then proceed to Step 2 of 4.

6. Accept the default range selection and then proceed to Step 3 of 4.

7. On the *Titles* tab of Step 3 in the Chart Wizard:
TYPE: **Education Level** into the *Category (X) axis* text box
TYPE: **Population** into the *Value (Y) axis* text box
Your screen should now appear similar to the one shown in Figure 4.46.

Figure 4.46

Completing Step
3 of the Chart
Wizard dialog
box

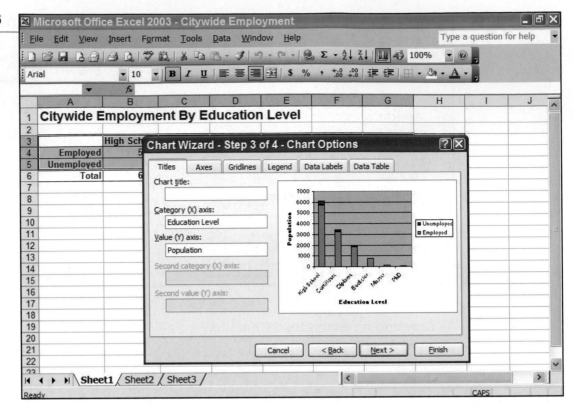

8. Proceed to the last step in the Chart Wizard dialog box.

9. In the last step of the dialog box, click the *As object in* option button and then click [Finish]. The chart object appears in the middle of the application window.

10. Move the embedded chart below the data area using the mouse pointer.

11. Enlarge the size of the embedded chart by dragging its selection boxes, so that it appears similar to the one shown in Figure 4.47. (*Note:* Because of their small values, categories such as "Master" and "PhD" do not show up well in this chart. Fortunately, Excel 2003 allows you to modify a chart's type and formatting at any time in order to improve its appearance.)

Figure 4.47

Sizing and
moving an
embedded chart

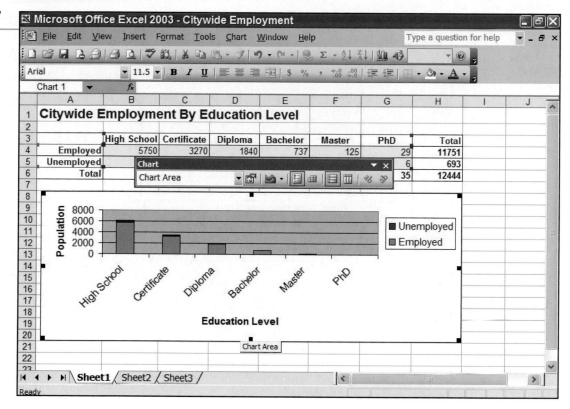

12. Save and then print the worksheet data and chart. When you are finished, close the "Citywide Employment" workbook.

on your own

4. Creating a Mortgage Rate Chart

In this exercise, your business associate has created a worksheet for you compiling mortgage rates from the previous six quarters. Your objective is to enhance the worksheet's presentation by embedding a line chart alongside or below the data. To begin, open the EX04HE04 workbook (Figure 4.48) and then save it as "Mortgage Rates" to your personal storage location.

Figure 4.48

Opening the
EX04HE04
workbook

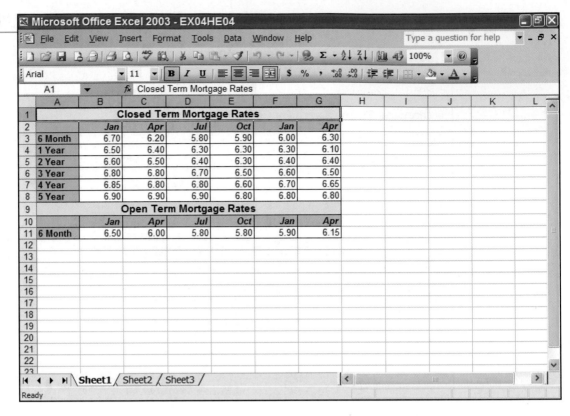

Using the data for closed term mortgage rates only, select the cell range from A2 to G8 and then launch the Chart Wizard. In the Chart Wizard dialog boxes, select a line chart with markers displayed at each data value and then add the title "Average Mortgage Rates" to the top of the chart. Embed the chart as an object and then move and size it to appear similar to the chart shown in Figure 4.49.

Figure 4.49

Embedding a line
chart into the
worksheet

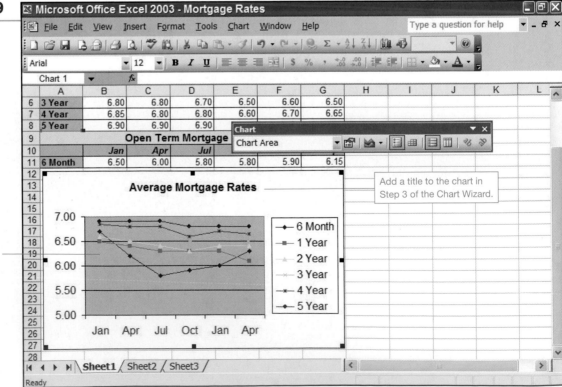

When you are satisfied with the results, set the print area to include both the data and the embedded chart object. Preview and then print the worksheet. Finally, save and then close the "Mortgage Rates" workbook.

on your own

5. Calculating Auto Fuel Statistics

In this exercise, you will practice naming ranges and entering functions. To begin, open the EX04HE05 workbook and then save it as "Auto Fuel" to your personal storage location.

Let's create some range names. Assign the name "Capacity" to the cell range B2:B7. Assign the name "City" to the cell range C2:C7. Assign the name "Hwy" to the cell range D2:D7. Paste a list of the range names in column F. In row 8, calculate the average for each column using their respective range names and the AVERAGE function. Format the new values to appear with two decimal places only. For more practice, enter a function in cell B10 that returns a count of the number of numerical entries in the "Capacity" range. In cell C10, display the minimum miles per gallon city rating. In cell D10, display the maximum miles per gallon highway rating. Then, place formatted descriptive labels above each calculation in row 9. Your worksheet should appear similar to the one shown in Figure 4.50.

Figure 4.50

Completing the "Auto Fuel" workbook

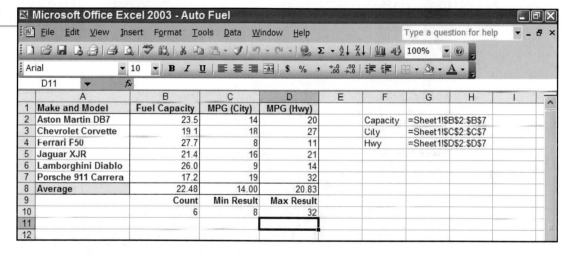

Preview and then print the worksheet using a landscape page orientation. When you are finished, save and then close the "Auto Fuel" workbook.

on your own

6. Displaying Expenses in a Pie Chart

For additional practice creating charts, open the EX04HE06 data file. Before continuing, save the workbook as "Expense Chart" to your personal storage location. Then, complete the worksheet by inputting your monthly expenses into the appropriate cells.

Using the Chart Wizard, create a pie chart of these expenses. Do not add a title to the chart. Save it as an embedded object in the worksheet. Once it appears on the worksheet, size the chart so that the information is easily read. Position the chart to the right of the worksheet data. Print the worksheet data and the chart on the same page, as shown in Figure 4.51. Remember to use the Set Print Area command and Print Preview to ensure that your settings are correct.

Figure 4.51

Plotting expenses using a pie chart

If you have not selected a color printer, the colored portions of your worksheet and chart will appear as shades of gray.

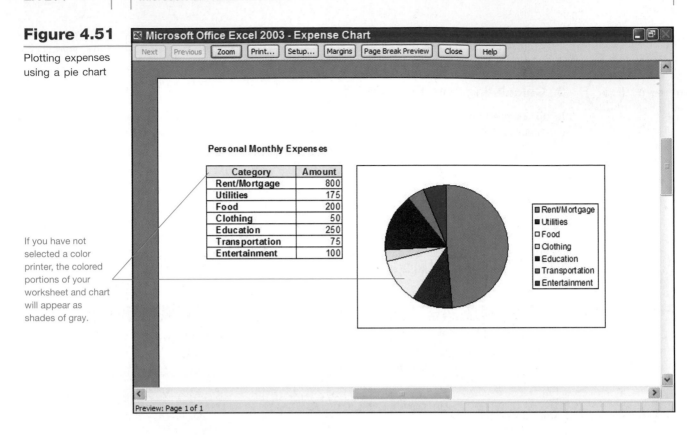

When you are satisfied with the results, send the worksheet and embedded chart to the printer. Save and then close the "Expense Chart" workbook. Then exit Microsoft Office Excel 2003.

CaseStudy   INTERIOR FOOTBALL LEAGUE (IFL)

The Interior Football League consists of eight elite football teams in as many communities. The IFL is run by a small group of dedicated volunteers who handle everything from coaching to administration. An ex-player himself, Doug Allen has volunteered for the organization for the past four years. In addition to fundraising, Doug is responsible for keeping records and tracking results for all of the teams in the league.

Shortly after the end of each season, the IFL publishes a newsletter that provides various statistics and other pertinent information about the season. In the past, this newsletter required weeks of effort, followed by days of typing results into a word processor. After enrolling in an Excel 2003 course, Doug now realizes that worksheets and charts can help him to complete his upcoming tasks. Specifically, he has recently learned how to use ranges and functions in Excel and now wants to use them to produce worksheets that can be incorporated into the newsletter.

In the following case problems, assume the role of Doug and perform the same steps that he identifies.

1. It is 8:00 on a Sunday evening when Doug decides to sit down at his home computer and spend some time working on the IFL newsletter. After loading Excel, he opens the EX04CP01 workbook that he has been using to project next year's attendance levels. Doug wants to communicate the fine growth in attendance that the IFL has been experiencing. Before continuing, he saves the workbook as "IFL Attendance" to his personal storage location.

   Having learned about range names, Doug's first step is to use the Name Box and apply a range name of "Factor" to cell C12. Then, he selects the cell range A2:B10 and uses the Insert ➔ Name ➔ Create command to create range names from the selection's row and column labels. To verify that the range names are correct, Doug selects cell E3 in the worksheet and then pastes a list of all existing named ranges. After returning to cell A1, Doug's worksheet appears similar to Figure 4.52.

Figure 4.52

Pasting range names into the worksheet

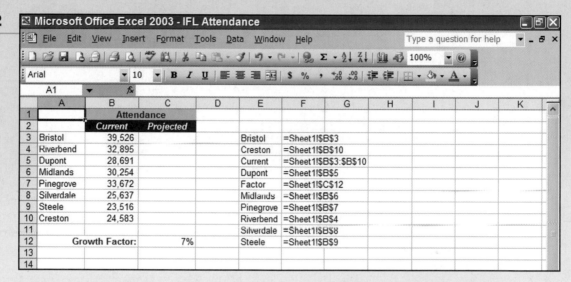

Doug remembers that to calculate next year's attendance using a growth factor formula, he will have to use both relative and absolute cell addresses. Otherwise, when he performs a copy operation, the formula's cell addresses will not be adjusted automatically. Doug wants to ensure that the formulas always use the value in cell C12 as the growth factor. Fortunately, he also remembers that a named range is, by default, an absolute reference. Therefore, using a relative cell address and the "Factor" range name, Doug can complete his task. To begin, he enters the formula **=b3*(1+Factor)** into cell C3. Notice that Doug typed "b3" and not "Bristol" into the cell. (*Hint:* The range name "Bristol" refers to the absolute cell address $B$3 and not to the relative cell address that is required for this calculation.) This formula calculates next year's projected attendance for Bristol.

Doug uses Excel's AutoFill feature to extend the formula in cell C3 for the rest of the teams. As shown in Figure 4.53, he uses the Format Painter to copy the numbering formats from column B to the new results in column C. Doug saves and then closes the workbook.

Figure 4.53

Formatting the
worksheet results

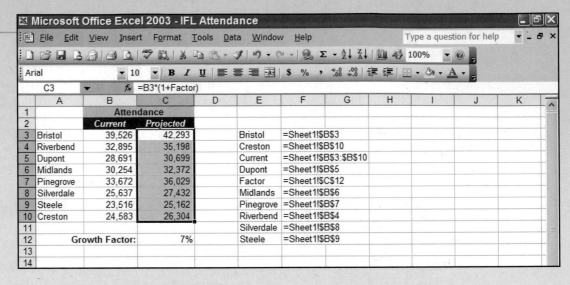

2. Last week, Doug began constructing a worksheet that shows the team standings at the end of the
   IFL's regular season play. To review the worksheet, he opens the EX04CP02 file and then saves it as
   "IFL Standings" to his personal storage location.

   With the teams already in the proper order, Doug wants to chart their results. He selects the cell
   range B2:C10 and then launches the Chart Wizard. In the first step, Doug selects a "Clustered bar
   with a 3-D visual effect" chart. In Step 3, Doug removes the chart title that appears in the dialog box.
   He then clicks the Finish command button. When the embedded chart appears in the application
   window, Doug sizes it so that all the team names are visible on the vertical axis. He then moves the
   chart so that it appears as shown in Figure 4.54.

Figure 4.54

Analyzing data
using an
embedded chart

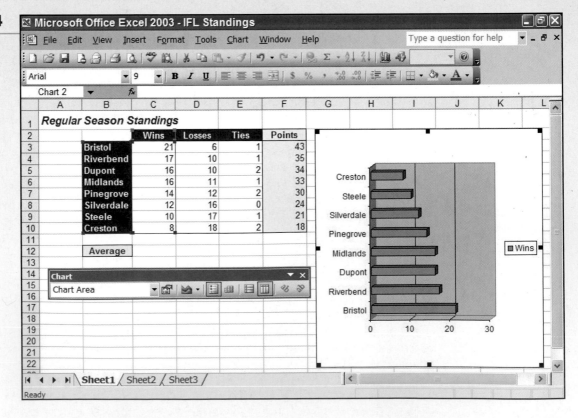

Continuing his work, Doug enters a formula into cell C12 that averages the values in that column. He uses the Edit → Fill → Right command to extend the formula across to column F. Finally, Doug prints the worksheet and chart using the landscape page orientation. He then saves and closes the workbook.

3. With the deadline for the season-end newsletter fast approaching, Doug is determined to finish the Team Statistics worksheet. He opens the EX04CP03 data file and then saves it as "IFL Team Stats" to his personal storage location.

After double-checking to make sure that the formulas in column D are correct, Doug copies the formula from cell D3 to the cell range D14:D21. He then uses the AutoSum button (Σ ▾) to enter SUM functions into cells C11 and C22 that sum the points for Offense and Defense, respectively. He applies boldface to the new results. In column G, Doug uses Excel's built-in functions to find the highest, lowest, and average number of points for both Offense and Defense. He names the two data ranges in column C (C3:C10 and C14:C21) and then enters the functions into the appropriate cells, as shown in Figure 4.55. When he is finished, Doug saves and then closes the workbook.

Figure 4.55

Completing the "IFL Team Stats" worksheet

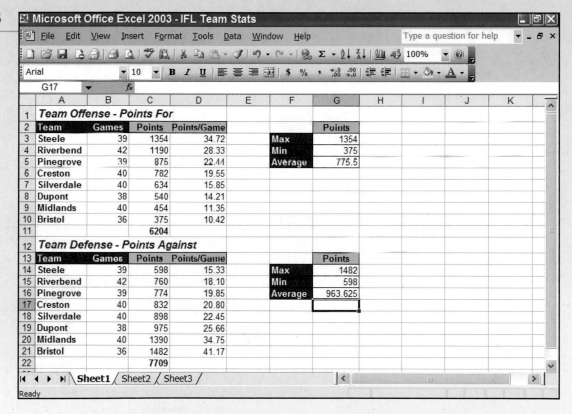

4. The final worksheet that Doug needs to compile is for the "Points Per Quarter" statistics. Doug opens the EX04CP04 data file and saves it as "IFL Scoring" in his personal storage location.

Using one of Excel's built-in functions, Doug calculates and displays the total points scored by the first team in column F. After entering the function, he uses the cell's fill handle to extend the formula to the rest of the teams. Next, he uses the appropriate function in row 11 to calculate the average for the first quarter. He formats the result to display with no decimal places and then extends the formula to cover columns C through F. Doug completes the worksheet using the MIN and MAX functions to calculate the high and low scores for each period. As before, he extends these functions to cover the remaining columns.

Satisfied with the results thus far, Doug decides to place an embedded stacked column chart under the data table. He sizes and positions the chart to appear similar to Figure 4.56. Doug then previews and prints the worksheet and chart on the same page. He saves and closes the workbook and then exits Microsoft Office Excel 2003.

Figure 4.56

Completing the "IFL Scoring" worksheet

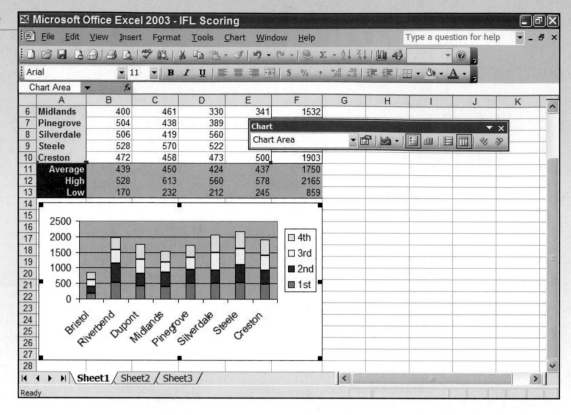

Answers to Self-Check Questions

4.1 Why is "AD2002" an unacceptable name for a cell range? You cannot name a cell range using an actual cell reference on the worksheet.

4.2 When might you use the Function Arguments dialog box or Insert Function dialog box to enter a function into the worksheet? If you need help entering the arguments in the correct order or if you cannot remember a function's name or proper syntax, you can use these tools to refresh your memory or to assist you in completing the task.

4.3 What must you do when selecting the print range for a worksheet that contains an embedded chart? Because charts do not appear in cells on a worksheet, you must be sure to select the print range to include these graphic objects. For example, select the cells that appear underneath the embedded chart that you want to print.

Notes

Notes

Notes

Notes

Notes

Notes

Microsoft®OfficePowerPoint®

2003

CHAPTER 1

Creating a Presentation

PREREQUISITES

Although this chapter assumes no previous experience using Microsoft Office PowerPoint 2003, you should be comfortable using a keyboard and mouse in the Microsoft Windows environment. You should be able to launch and exit programs and perform basic Windows file management operations, such as opening and closing documents.

LEARNING
OBJECTIVES

After completing this chapter, you will be able to:

• Describe the different components of the application window

• Select commands and options using the Menu bar and right-click menus

• Begin new presentations and add slides

• Insert slide text

• Save, open, and print a presentation

1.1 Getting Started with PowerPoint 2003

The most important part of any presentation is the presenter and his or her message. A presenter who is energetic, enthusiastic, and sensitive to the needs of his or her audience will likely connect with that audience and be well received. In addition, a presenter who is well prepared with carefully crafted visuals to support his or her message will be able to convey a high level of confidence about the topic.

For this reason, people in business, academia, and many other professions turn to Microsoft Office PowerPoint 2003 to improve their communication effectiveness. PowerPoint can help you to develop, manage, and deliver your presentation message. It is a presentation graphics program that enables you to create a variety of presentation media—onscreen slideshows to support "live" presentations with computer projection equipment, overhead transparencies or 35mm slides for situations where projection equipment is not available, audience handouts, and even online presentations for Web delivery.

PowerPoint 2003 enables you to add the visual aspect to your presentation delivery that will help your audience to better understand your message. Research has proven that people comprehend and remember more information when they hear and see that information. Therefore, your ability to express yourself in an interesting, visual way is becoming increasingly important. Presentation visuals guide the presenter as well as the audience; when designed and used effectively, they also add interest to a presentation.

For example, text is an important component of a presentation, and its effective use demands concise writing. The chosen fonts, sizes, colors, and alignment treatments all help to make words easier to read and their meaning easier to grasp. However, text is not enough. You need to select appropriate images to bring a sense of reality to what your audience sees and draw diagrams to help them understand processes you need to explain. When numbers are important, you need to know which charts or graphs to use for the points you need to make. Knowing what to do, and when to do it, requires visual communication skill. PowerPoint can help you develop that skill.

PowerPoint 2003 is also a media management tool because it allows you to display sounds and video clips as part of your presentation. Animation and other special effects can make your presentation more dynamic and compelling, but it is important to use these effects to support your message and not merely because they are available.

In this module, you will start Microsoft Office PowerPoint 2003 and proceed through a guided tour of its primary components.

1.1.1 Loading and Exiting PowerPoint

→ Feature

To load PowerPoint, begin at the Windows Start menu and click on the Start button (*start*) on the taskbar. Then choose the All Programs menu option, Microsoft Office, and click PowerPoint.

When you finish using PowerPoint, you should exit the program so your system's memory is freed for use by other Windows applications. To do so, choose the File, Exit command or click on the Close button (X) appearing in the top right-hand corner. These methods are used to close most Microsoft Windows applications.

→ Method

To load PowerPoint:

- CLICK: Start button (*start*)
- CHOOSE: All Programs → Microsoft Office
- CLICK: Microsoft Office PowerPoint 2003

To exit PowerPoint:

- CHOOSE: File → Exit from PowerPoint's Menu bar

  or

- CLICK: Close button (X) appearing in the top right-hand corner

→ ## Practice

You will now load Microsoft PowerPoint using the Windows Start menu.

1. Position the mouse pointer over the Start button (⊞ *start*) appearing in the bottom left-hand corner of the Windows taskbar and then click the left mouse button once. The Start menu appears.

2. Point to the All Programs command using the mouse and the list of programs will appear in a fly-out or cascading Programs menu. (*Note:* If you are using a version of Windows prior to XP, click the Programs menu option.)

3. Move the mouse pointer within the programs group until it highlights Microsoft Office. Then move the highlight into the fly-out or cascading menu to select Microsoft Office PowerPoint 2003 as shown in Figure 1.1.

Figure 1.1

Start Menu

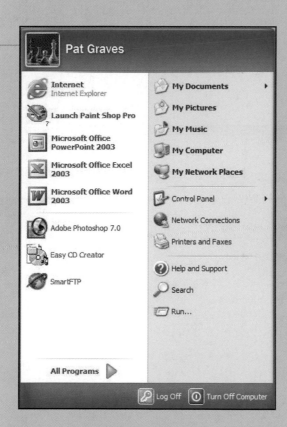

4. With Microsoft Office PowerPoint 2003 highlighted,
CLICK: the left mouse button once.
After a few seconds, the PowerPoint 2003 application window appears (Figure 1.2).

PowerPoint

Figure 1.2

Microsoft
PowerPoint
application
window

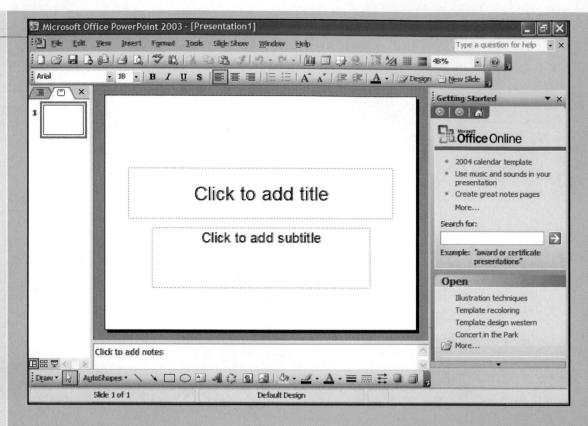

5. Depending on your system's configuration, an Office Assistant character, such as "Clippit," the animated paper clip, may be displaying. To hide this character from view, do the following:
RIGHT-CLICK: *the character*
CHOOSE: Hide from the right-click menu

1.1.2 Touring PowerPoint

→ **Feature**

The PowerPoint **application window** acts as a container for your presentation. It also contains the primary interface components for working in PowerPoint, including the *Windows icons, Menu bar, toolbars, task pane, View buttons,* and *Status bar.* Figure 1.3 identifies several of these components.

→ **Practice**

In a guided tour, you now explore the features of PowerPoint's application window. Ensure that you have already loaded PowerPoint.

1. PowerPoint's application window is best kept maximized to fill the entire screen, as shown in Figure 1.3. As with most Windows applications, you use the Windows Title bar icons—Minimize ( ), Maximize ( ), Restore ( ), and Close ( )—to control the display of a window using the mouse. Figure 1.3 labels some of the components of PowerPoint's application window.

Figure 1.3

Components of PowerPoint's application window

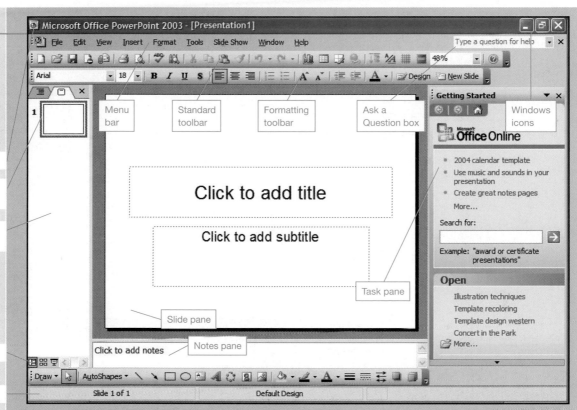

Title bar

Thumbnail of the current slide

Outline and slide tabs pane

View buttons

Status bar

→ **Practice**

2. The Menu bar contains the PowerPoint menu commands. To execute a command, click once on the desired Menu bar option and then click again on the command. Commands that appear dimmed are not available for selection at the moment. Commands that are followed by an ellipsis (. . .) will display a dialog box.
To practice working with the PowerPoint Menu bar:
CHOOSE: Help
This instruction tells you to click the left mouse button once on the Help option appearing in the Menu bar.

3. To display other pull-down menus, move the mouse to the left over other options in the Menu bar. As each option is highlighted, a pull-down menu appears with its associated commands. If a chevron (≥) appears at the bottom of a list, then additional menu items are available when you mouse over the chevron.

4. To leave the Menu bar without making a command selection:
CLICK: in a blank area of the Title bar at the top of the screen

5. PowerPoint provides context-sensitive *right-click menus* for quick access to menu commands. Rather than searching for the appropriate command in the Menu bar, you can position the mouse pointer on any object, such as a graphic or toolbar button, and right-click the mouse to display a list of commonly selected commands.
To display a slide's right-click menu:
RIGHT-CLICK: near the top of the large slide that appears centered on your screen (refer to Figure 1.4).

Figure 1.4

Right-click menu

Thumbnail of the current slide

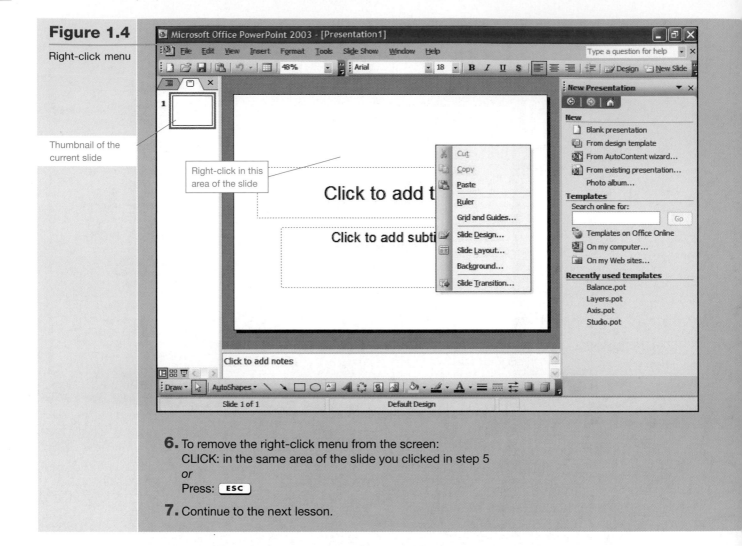

6. To remove the right-click menu from the screen:
   CLICK: in the same area of the slide you clicked in step 5
   or
   Press: ESC

7. Continue to the next lesson.

1.1.3 Customizing Menus and Toolbars

→ **Feature**

Some people argue that software becomes more difficult to learn with the addition of each new command or feature. In response to this sentiment, Microsoft developed adaptive menus that display only the most commonly used features. By default, Microsoft Office 2003 ships with the **adaptive menus** feature enabled. However, you may find this dynamic feature confusing and choose to turn off the adaptive menus. Likewise, the Standard and Formatting toolbars are positioned side-by-side in a single row. You may find it easier to locate buttons when these toolbars are positioned on separate rows. Also, the **task pane** is positioned on the right side of your screen, providing convenient access to relevant commands and options. Some new users find that the task pane is distracting and consumes too much of their workspace. Fortunately, you can hide (and redisplay) the task pane using the View menu command.

→ **Method**

To disable the adaptive menus feature and display the Standard and Formatting toolbars on separate rows:

- CHOOSE: Tools → Customize

- CLICK: *Options* tab

- SELECT: *Show Standard and Formatting toolbars on two rows* check box

- SELECT: *Always show full menus* check box

- CLICK: Close command button

To display or hide a toolbar:

- CHOOSE: View → Toolbars

- CHOOSE: a toolbar from the menu

To display or hide the task pane:

- CHOOSE: View → Task Pane
  or
- CLICK: its Close button (☒)

→ # Practice

In this lesson, you will disable the adaptive menus feature, display the Standard and Formatting tool-bars on separate rows, and toggle the display of the task pane. Ensure that you have completed the previous lesson.

1. To begin,
CHOOSE: Tools
You should now see the Tools pull-down menu.
(*Hint:* When a desired command does not appear on a menu, you can extend the menu to view all of the available commands by waiting for a short period or by clicking on the chevron (⊻) at the bottom of the pull-down menu.)

2. Let's turn off the adaptive menus feature and customize the Standard and Formatting toolbars so they display on separate rows.
CHOOSE: Tools → Customize from the pull-down menu
CLICK: *Options* tab
The Customize dialog box should now appear (Figure 1.5).

Figure 1.5

Customize dialog box: *Options* tab

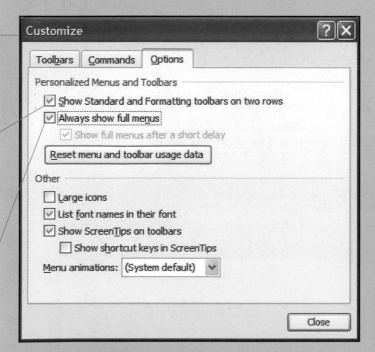

If you select this option, the Standard and Formatting toolbars will display on separate rows.

With this option selected, PowerPoint disables its adaptive menus feature and always displays completed menus.

3. On the *Options* tab of the Customize dialog box:
SELECT: *Show Standard and Formatting toolbars on two rows* check box
SELECT: *Always show full menus* check box
(*Note:* An option is selected when a check mark (☑) appears in the selection box.)

PowerPoint

4. To proceed:
CLICK: Close command button
Figure 1.6 displays the Standard and Formatting toolbars as they should now appear on your screen. The Standard toolbar provides access to file management and editing commands, in addition to special features. The Formatting toolbar lets you access formatting commands.

Figure 1.6

Standard toolbar

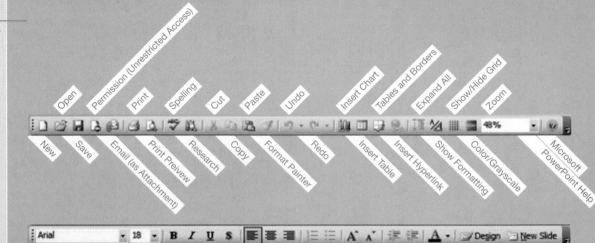

Formatting toolbar

5. The task pane is already displayed; to hide the task pane:
CHOOSE: View → Task Pane
(*Note:* When a toolbar or the task pane is displayed, a check mark (☑) appears beside the option in the pull-down menu. This step removes the check mark.)

6. To display the task pane:
CHOOSE: View → Task Pane
Your screen should now appear similar to Figure 1.7.

Figure 1.7

Customizing the application window

Standard toolbar

Formatting toolbar

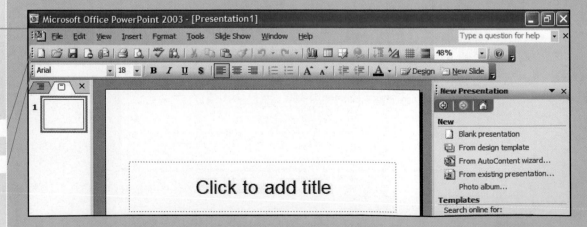

Important: *For the remainder of this learning guide, we assume that the adaptive feature has been disabled and that the Standard and Formatting toolbars are displayed on separate rows.*

In Addition MOVING TOOLBARS

You can move toolbars around the PowerPoint application window using the mouse. A *docked* toolbar appears attached to one of the window's borders. An *undocked* or *floating* toolbar appears in its own window, complete with a Title bar and Close button (☒). To float a docked toolbar, drag the Move bar (|) at the left-hand side toward the center of the window. To redock the toolbar, drag its Title bar toward a border until it attaches itself automatically.

1.1 How do you remove a right-click menu from view?

1.2 Starting a New Presentation

There are several ways to start a new PowerPoint presentation. If you are looking for content suggestions, start with the **AutoContent Wizard**. This wizard provides a quick and easy method for starting a new presentation. AutoContent presentations, consisting of 5 to 10 slides each, are available on a variety of topics. Once created, you simply customize the presentation content to meet your needs.

For design (not content) suggestions, consider starting a new presentation from a design template. A **design template** determines the look of your presentation by defining its color scheme, background, and use of fonts. If neither the AutoContent Wizard nor a design template sounds tempting, you can start a presentation from scratch by clicking the New button (▣). This procedure is described in module 1.3.

1.2.1 Using the AutoContent Wizard

→ **Feature**

If you are finding it difficult to express your thoughts or to decide how to organize your presentation, consider using the AutoContent Wizard to help you get started. After progressing through the Wizard's dialog boxes, you will have the basic framework for building a complete presentation.

→ **Method**

If the task pane is not displaying:

• CHOOSE: File → New

• CLICK: "From AutoContent wizard" link in the New Presentation task pane

→ **Practice**

You will now practice launching the AutoContent Wizard. Ensure that PowerPoint is loaded.

1. The New Presentation task pane should already be displaying on your screen. If not, choose File, New to display the New Presentation task pane as shown in Figure 1.8. Task panes contain textual links, called **hyperlinks,** for performing PowerPoint procedures.
Note: Your task pane may appear differently from Figure 1.8 if templates have not been used on the computer you are using.

Figure 1.8

New Presentation
task pane

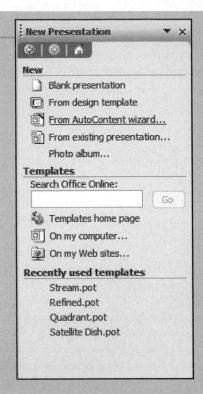

2. Move the mouse pointer over the hyperlinks in the task pane and note that a hand () appears. You will know you are pointing to a hyperlink when a hand appears. You select a link by clicking on it.

3. To select a link:
   From AutoContent wizard . . . link
   The initial AutoContent Wizard dialog box should now appear (Figure 1.9).

Figure 1.9

Initial
AutoContent
Wizard screen

4. The left side of the dialog box shows the steps through which the wizard will go to develop the presentation. To proceed to the next step, do the following:
CLICK: Next command button

5. In this step, you select the type of presentation you are going to give (Figure 1.10). When you click a category option button, a list of related presentations appears in the list box to the right. *Note:* Your screen may look slightly different.
Note: Your screen may look slightly different.

Figure 1.10

Selecting a
presentation type

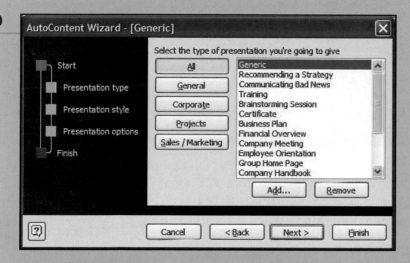

Do the following:
CLICK: Corporate button
SELECT: *Company Meeting* in the list box
CLICK: Next command button
You must now select an output option for the presentation (Figure 1.11).

Figure 1.11

Selecting an
output type

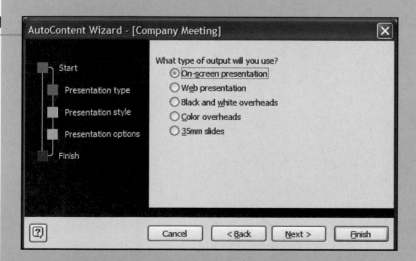

PowerPoint

6. SELECT: *On-screen presentation* option
CLICK: Next command button
Your screen should now appear similar to the one shown in Figure 1.12.

Figure 1.12

Defining the
opening slide

7. In this step, you enter the information you want to appear on the opening slide of your presentation.
CLICK: in the *Presentation title* text box
TYPE: **Marketing Results**
(*Note:* Leave the footer information blank for now and leave the checks displayed in the *Date last updated* and *Slide number* options.)

8. Do the following to proceed:
CLICK: Next command button
CLICK: Finish command button
At this point, as shown in Figure 1.13, the presentation is compiled with some content suggestions that you can edit to meet your needs. This view of your presentation is called **Normal view,** and it provides one place in which to build the different parts of your presentation. In Figure 1.13, we label and describe the different areas you see in Normal view.

Figure 1.13

Displaying a presentation in Normal view

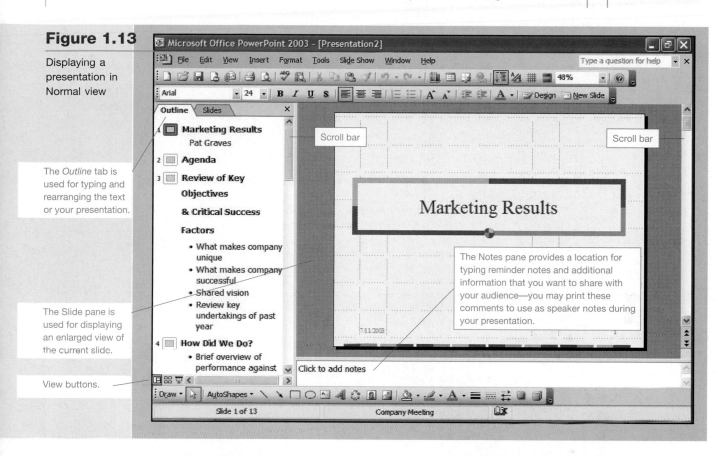

The *Outline* tab is used for typing and rearranging the text or your presentation.

The Slide pane is used for displaying an enlarged view of the current slide.

View buttons.

1.2.2 Viewing Your Presentation

→ **Feature**

Individual slides can be viewed one by one in the **Slide pane** by advancing through them using the Next Slide and Previous Slide buttons. Another way to move between slides is to use the **Outline and Slides pane,** where you can click on the slide icons or miniature images, called **thumbnails** to go to different slides. Another way to view all of the slides at one time is to use the **Slide Sorter** feature. Moving through your slides is called **navigating.**

→ **Method**

From the Slide pane:

- CLICK: Next Slide button (⬇) and Previous Slide button (⬆)

From the Outline and Slides pane:

- CLICK: *Outline* tab
- SELECT: Slide icon

From the Outline and Slides pane:

- CLICK: *Slides* tab
- SELECT: Slide thumbnail

From Slide Sorter view:

- CLICK: Slide Sorter button (⊞)
- SELECT: Slide thumbnail
- DOUBLE-CLICK: Slide to return to Normal view

→ **Practice**

You will now practice moving between slides using the above-listed methods.

1. On the lower right of the Slide pane, the Next Slide (⬇) and Previous Slide (⬆) buttons on the vertical scroll bar enable you to navigate through your presentation. To illustrate:
CLICK: Next Slide button (⬇) to view the second slide
CLICK: Previous Slide button (⬆) to view the first slide

2. Advance through the entire presentation by pressing the Next Slide button (⬇) twelve (12) times.

3. When slide 13 is displaying in the slide pane, do the following:
CLICK: *Slides* tab
Your screen should now appear similar to the one shown in Figure 1.14, with small thumbnail images of your presentation slides in the Outline and Slides pane at the left of your screen.
Note: You can navigate to different slides in your presentation by clicking on the thumbnail image or by dragging the slide scroll bar in the Outline and Slides pane.

Figure 1.14

Displaying the contents of the Outline and Slides pane

The Slides tab is used for displaying the slides in your presentation using thumbnails

Slide sorter

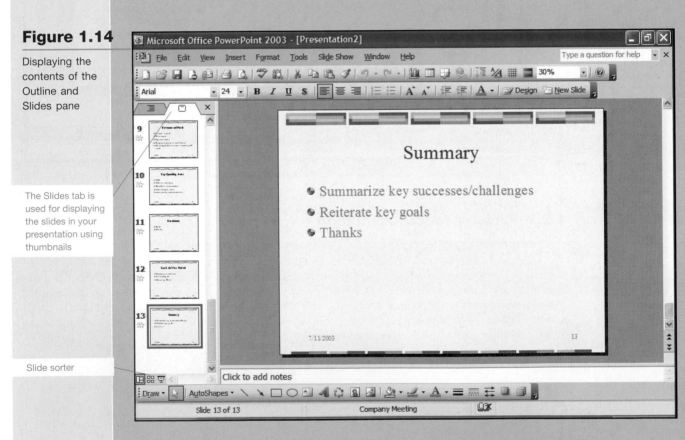

4. To see your presentation slides in the Slide Sorter view:
CLICK: Slide Sorter button (⊞)
Your screen should now appear similar to the one shown in Figure 1.15 with thumbnail images of your presentation slides filling the screen.

Figure 1.15

Displaying the
contents in Slide
Sorter View

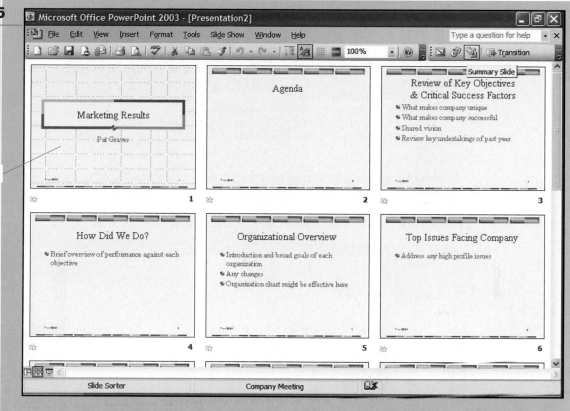

5. To return to Slide view:
   DOUBLE-CLICK: on any slide to return to that slide
   Note: You can adjust the size of these images by choosing a different magnification percentage in
   the Zoom box on the Standard toolbar.

6. To conclude this lesson, you will close the presentation without saving changes. From the Menu bar:
   CHOOSE: File → Close

7. In the dialog box that appears asking "Do you want to save the changes . . .":
   CLICK: No command button
   There should be no presentations open in the application window.

1.2.3 Using Design Templates

→ **Feature**

If you already have your content in mind but want to use an attractive background, PowerPoint provides a selection of **design templates** that you can use to start new presentations. These templates
help to establish a presentation theme with background graphics and color-coordinated fonts.

→ **Method**

To display the New Presentation task pane:

• CHOOSE: File → New

From the task pane under New Presentation:

• CLICK: From design template hyperlink

• CLICK: a design thumbnail in the Slide Design task pane

PowerPoint

→ **Practice**

You will now practice applying design templates. Ensure that no presentations are open.

1. Your first step is to display the New Presentation task pane.
CHOOSE: File → New

2. To select a design template:
CLICK: From design template hyperlink
The Slide Design task pane should appear with a selection of thumbnail designs (Figure 1.16) arranged by three categories: *Used in This Presentation, Recently Used, and Available for Use.*

Figure 1.16

Slide Design task pane

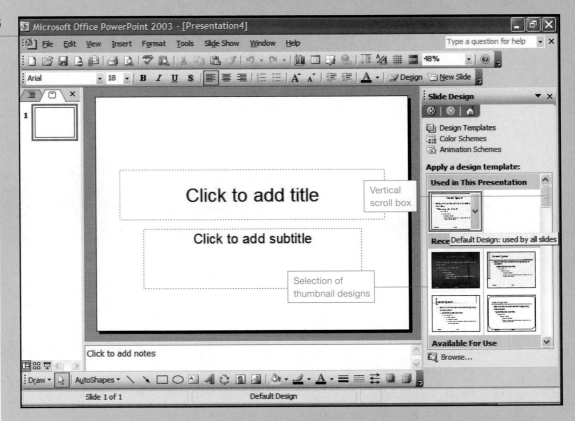

3. When you move the mouse pointer over a thumbnail in the Slide Design pane, its name appears. The thumbnails are arranged by their names in alphabetical order. Move your mouse pointer over the displayed thumbnails to view their names.

4. To view additional thumbnail designs:
DRAG: the vertical scroll box in the task pane down to the bottom of the list

5. Before continuing, drag the vertical scroll box back to the top of the vertical scroll bar.

6. When you point to a thumbnail, a drop-down arrow appears on the right slide of the thumbnail. You can click the drop-down arrow to display a selection of commands. To illustrate, point to a design template in the task pane.

7. CLICK: the thumbnail's drop-down arrow
The Slide Design task pane should now appear similar to the one shown in Figure 1.17.

Figure 1.17

Thumbnail with
associated menu

8. To view large thumbnails, do the following:
   CHOOSE: Show Large Previews from the drop-down menu

9. To redisplay small thumbnails:
   CLICK: a thumbnail's drop-down list
   CHOOSE: Show Large Previews to deselect the option

10. Locate the "Balance" design template. This template is mostly brown in color and should appear near the top of the thumbnails list.
    CLICK: its drop-down arrow
    CHOOSE: Apply to All Slides from the drop-down list
    (*Note:* You can also click on a slide layout thumbnail to apply its design to all slides.) Your screen should now appear similar to the one shown in Figure 1.18.

Figure 1.18

Applying the
"Balance" design
template

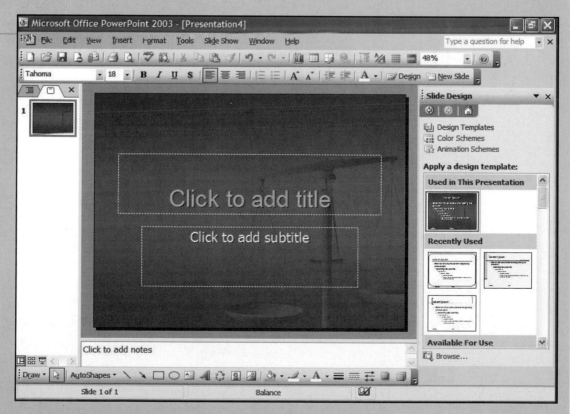

11. At this point, you could proceed with creating the presentation. However, to conclude this lesson, you will close the document without saving changes. From the Menu bar:
    CHOOSE: File → Close

PowerPoint

12. In the dialog box:
CLICK: No command button
There should be no presentations open in the application window.

1.2 How does starting a presentation with the AutoContent Wizard differ from starting a presentation using a design template?

1.3 Creating a Textual Presentation

When building a presentation, you will naturally need to add new slides. Part of the process of adding a new slide to a presentation involves selecting a layout for the slide. PowerPoint categorizes its selection of layouts according to whether they include text only, graphics only, or both text and graphics. PowerPoint uses **placeholders** to mark the location of text and graphics objects. This module concentrates on editing text-only slides. PowerPoint provides four text-only slide layouts, each of which appears labeled in Figure 1.19.

Figure 1.19

Text Layouts

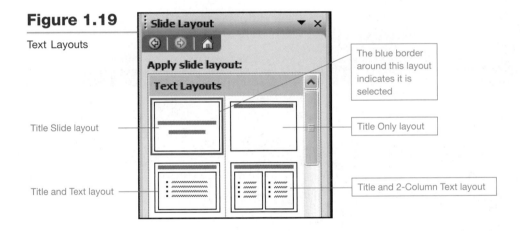

When working with text, you will need to write concisely. If you type more text than can fit in the place-holder, PowerPoint's **AutoFit feature** will automatically resize the placeholder to accommodate the text. In Chapter 2 you will learn how to adjust this feature and why it is important that your presentation has a consistent text size.

1.3.1 Beginning with a Blank Presentation

→ **Feature**

Rather than use the AutoContent wizard or a design template to start a new presentation, you may prefer to start from scratch. Blank presentations are just that—blank. They contain no content or design suggestions. By default, the first slide of a blank presentation uses the Title Slide layout. To develop your presentation, you create new slides by selecting the appropriate slide layout and filling in the text content.

→ **Method**

• CLICK: New button (⬜)

→ **Practice**

You will now start a blank presentation and practice selecting alternate layouts.

1. CLICK: New button (□)

A new, blank, presentation slide appears in the Slide pane. Note that the Title Slide layout is se-lected in the task pane (Figure 1.20), as indicated by the blue border. (*Hint:* Move the mouse pointer over a particular layout to see its name.)

Figure 1.20

Blank
presentation:
Title Slide layout

2. You can see the large, Slide pane view of other text layouts by clicking their thumbnails in the Slide Layout task pane.

CLICK: Title Only layout (located beside the Title Slide layout)

The Title Only layout now appears in the Slide pane (Figure 1.21).

Note: You will learn later to use the Notes pane below the Slide pane to make speaker notes. So disregard the "Click to add notes" instruction for now.

PowerPoint

Figure 1.21

Blank
presentation: Title
Only layout

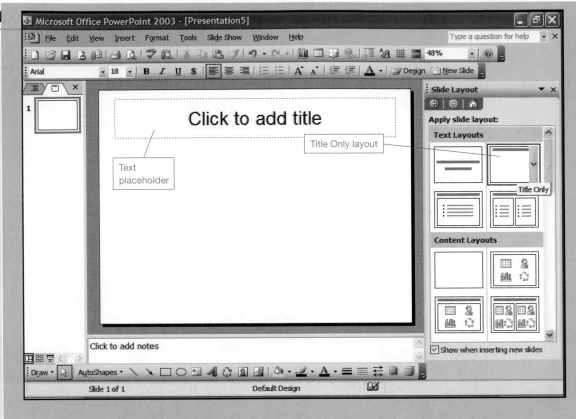

3. In the task pane, click the Title and Text layout, and then the Title and 2-Column Text layout to examine these layouts.

4. Before proceeding:
   CLICK: Title Slide layout in the task pane

5. Proceed to the next lesson.

1.3.2 Creating a Title Slide

→ **Feature**

PowerPoint provides two easy ways to enter slide text: typing directly into the placeholders on each slide or typing in the *Outline* tab. Once you understand the different methods, you can decide which technique you prefer to use.

→ **Method**

To add text to the Slide pane:
• CLICK: in a text placeholder and then begin typing

To add text using the Outline and Slides pane:
• CLICK: the *Outline* tab and then select the slide icon and begin typing the slide title

→ **Practice**

You will now add text using the Slide pane and the Outline and Slides pane.

1. The title placeholder is indicated by a single dotted line and the text "Click to add title." To type text into the title placeholder:
   CLICK: in the title placeholder

The insertion point should be blinking in the center of the title placeholder and the border line of the placeholder change to diagonal marks indicating the placeholder is ready to accept text.

2. Ensure that the outline is displaying in the Outline and Slides pane. If it is not, do the following:
CLICK: *Outline* tab by referring to Figure 1.22

Figure 1.22

Filling in the Title placeholder

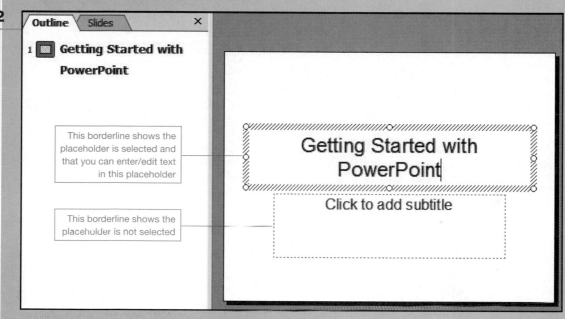

3. TYPE: **Getting Started with PowerPoint**
Note that the title text also appears on the Outline pane (Figure 1.22).

4. To type text into the subtitle placeholder:
CLICK: in the subtitle placeholder, marked by "Click to add subtitle"

5. TYPE: **By** *Your Name*
(*Note:* Be sure to substitute your actual name in place of words "your name.") Your screen should now appear similar to Figure 1.23. Although the message "Click to add notes" also appears on the bottom of the PowerPoint window, we are not going to enter them now.

Figure 1.23

Filling in the Subtitle placeholder

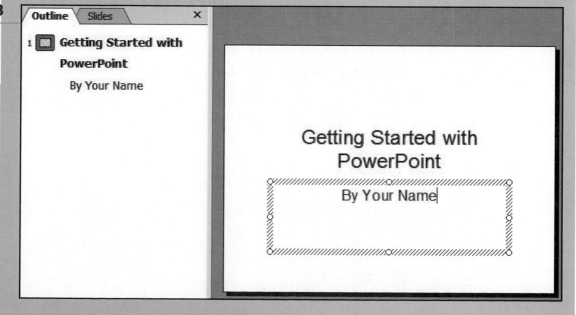

PowerPoint

6. Edit the text in the Title placeholder. This time, use the Outline pane.
SELECT: the text "Getting Started with" by dragging with the mouse over the text
The selected text should be highlighted in reverse color.

7. TYPE: **Introducing**
The title should now read "Introducing PowerPoint" in both the *Outline* tab and Slide pane.

8. CLICK: after your name in the *Outline* tab

9. PRESS: ENTER
The insertion point was moved down to the next line.

10. TYPE: **the name of your School/Business**
(*Note:* Be sure to substitute your actual school or business name in the subtitle, or just make one up.) The subtitle now contains two lines of text. Your screen should now appear similar to Figure 1.24.

Figure 1.24

Revised text

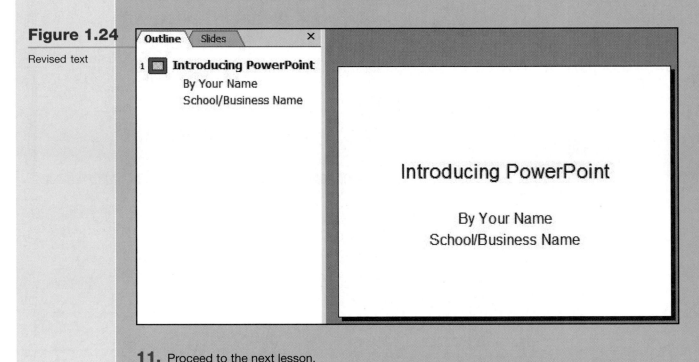

11. Proceed to the next lesson.

1.3.3 Inserting New Slides and Using the *Outline* Tab

→ **Feature**

New slides are inserted after the current, or displayed, slide. Select a layout for the slide and then edit text placeholders using the Slide pane or Outline and Slides pane. If you decide to remove a slide, you can easily delete it from the Outline and Slides pane or with the Edit menu.

→ **Method**

• CLICK: New Slide button (New Slide) to add a new slide

• CHOOSE: Edit → Delete Slide to delete a slide

   or

• SELECT: the slide icon in the Outline and Slides pane and press DELETE

To create a bulleted list in the Outline pane:

• CLICK: to begin typing at the current level

• PRESS: TAB to begin typing at a demoted (lower) outline level

• PRESS: SHIFT + TAB to begin typing at a promoted (higher) outline level

→ **Practice**

You will now practice inserting and deleting slides and typing text in the Outline pane. Ensure that you have completed the previous lessons in this module and that the "Introducing PowerPoint" slide is displaying in the Slide pane.

1. To insert a new slide after the current slide:
CLICK: New Slide button (New Slide) on the Formatting toolbar near the top right of your screen
Your screen should now appear similar to the one shown in Figure 1.25. PowerPoint automatically applied the Title and Text layout to the new slide.

Figure 1.25

Adding a
new slide

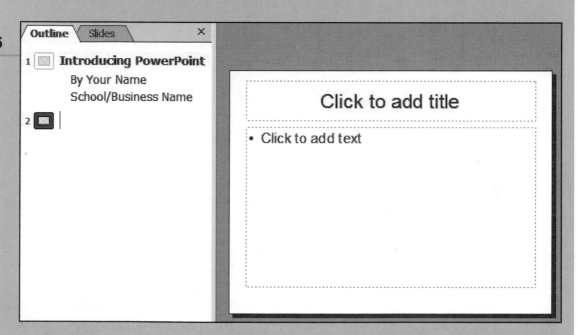

2. In the *Outline* tab, notice that the insertion point is blinking to the right of the slide 1 icon.
TYPE: **PowerPoint lets you create:**
PRESS: ENTER
Note that when you pressed ENTER, PowerPoint automatically inserted another slide (slide 3).

3. To demote the current outline level so that you can type a bulleted list on slide 2 (not slide 3), do the following:
PRESS: TAB to demote the current outline level
Your screen should now appear similar to the one shown in Figure 1.26.

PowerPoint

Figure 1.26

The bulleted list placeholder

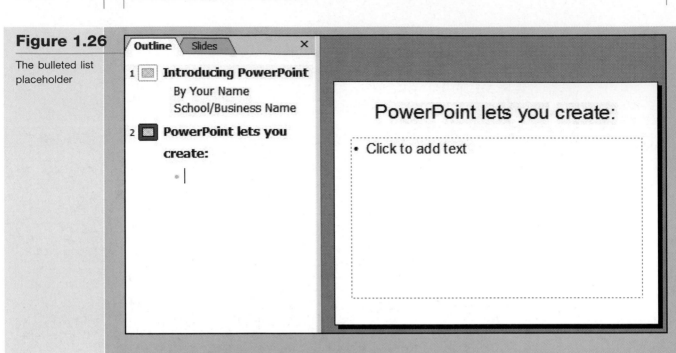

4. To create the bulleted list:
TYPE: **On-screen presentations**
PRESS: ENTER
TYPE: **Web presentations**
PRESS: ENTER
TYPE: **Overhead transparencies**
PRESS: ENTER
TYPE: **35mm slides**
PRESS: ENTER
TYPE: **Audience handouts**

5. Your screen should now appear similar to the one shown in Figure 1.27.

Figure 1.27

Typing a bulleted list in the Outline pane

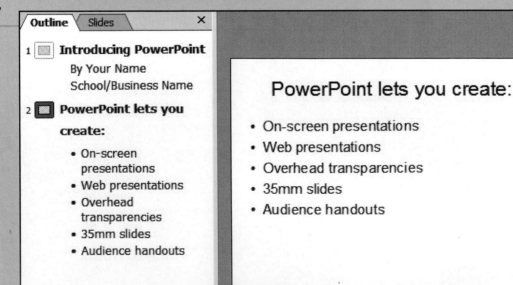

6. As a final step, let's use the Slide pane to add two more detailed items that relate to the first item in the bulleted list. They will be indented to the second outline level.
CLICK: to the right of the first bulleted item in the Slide pane to move your insertion point after the words on-screen presentations
PRESS: [ENTER]
PRESS: Tab to indent (demote) to a second outline level
TYPE: **Requires a projection device**
PRESS: [ENTER]
TYPE: **May include animation**
(*Note:* When you have demoted text to a second outline level and need to return to the first outline level, press [SHIFT] + [TAB] to promote the text.)

7. To insert a new slide after the current slide:
CLICK: New Slide button ([🗅 New Slide]) on the Formatting toolbar
CLICK: Title and 2-Column Text layout (its thumbnail appears in the Slide Layout task pane)
The presentation now includes three slides. Note that the Outline pane also includes three slide icons (Figure 1.28).

Figure 1.28

Inserting a third slide

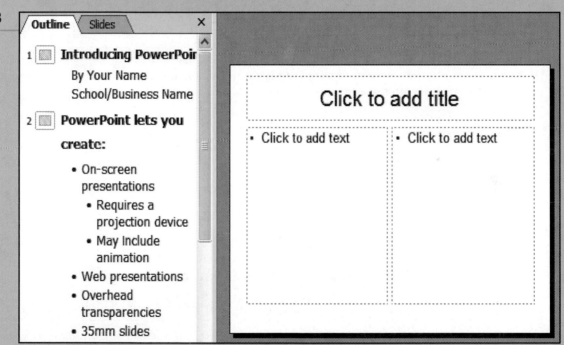

8. To delete the newly inserted third slide using the Outline pane:
CLICK: slide 3 icon located on the lower left of your screen
PRESS: [DELETE]
The slide 3 icon should no longer appear.

Note: The Outline pane and the Slide pane can be used interchangeably for entering and editing text. If you want to delete a slide while you are on the Slide pane, use the Edit Menu to access the Delete Slide option.

9. At this point, you could proceed with creating the presentation. However, to conclude this lesson, you will close the presentation without saving changes. From the Menu bar:
CHOOSE: File → Close

10. In the dialog box that appears:
CLICK: No command button

11. There should be no presentations open in the application window. Continue to the next lesson.

PowerPoint

 **1.3** What does it mean to demote or to promote text in a bulleted list?

1.4 Managing Files

Managing the presentation files that you create is an important skill. The presentation you create exists only in the computer's RAM (random access memory), which is highly volatile. In other words, if the power to your computer goes off, your presentation is lost. For safety and security, you need to save your presentation permanently to the local hard disk, a network drive, a removable disk, CDR, or CDRW.

Saving your work to a named file on a disk is like placing a paper document into a filing cabinet. When you name your files, you need to use logical file names so you can easily identify the presentation content. Just as you would with a paper filing system, you should develop organizational techniques to keep related files together so you can find them easily.

When you are developing your presentations, you should save your work at least every 15 minutes, or whenever you are interrupted, to protect against an unexpected power outage or other catastrophe. When naming your presentation files, you can use up to 255 characters, including spaces, but it is wise to keep the length under 20 characters. Furthermore, because they are special reserved characters, you cannot use any of the following characters in naming your presentations:

\ / : ; * ? " < > |

In the following lessons, you practice several file management procedures, including saving, closing, opening, and printing presentations.

*Important: In this guide, we refer to the files that have been created for you as the **student data files.** Depending on your computer or lab setup, these files may be located on a floppy disk, in a folder on your hard drive, or on a network server. If necessary, ask your instructor or lab assistant exactly where to find these data files. To download the Advantage Series' student data files from the Internet, visit the Advantage Series' Web site at:*

http://www.advantageseries.com

You will also need to identify a personal storage location, such as a removable disk or hard-drive subdirectory, for the files that you create, modify, and save.

1.4.1 Saving and Closing a Presentation

→ **Feature**

The File → Save command and the Save button (⊟) on the Standard toolbar allow you to save a file for the first time or to overwrite an existing file with the latest version of a presentation. The File, Save As command enables you to save a presentation to a new filename or storage location. Plus you can save your presentation in a different file format such as an earlier version of PowerPoint in case people you are working with have not yet updated to the latest version of PowerPoint. When you are finished working with a presentation, ensure that you close the file to free up the valuable RAM on your computer.

→ **Method**

To save an opened presentation:

- CLICK: Save button (⊟)
  or
- CHOOSE: File → Save
  or
- CHOOSE: File → Save As

To close an opened presentation:

- CLICK: its Close button (✕)
  or
- CHOOSE: File → Close

→ Practice

You will now practice saving and closing an opened presentation. Ensure that PowerPoint is loaded and that you have identified a storage location for your personal document files. If you want to use a disk, place it into the disk drive now.

1. So that we have a presentation to save, create a quick AutoContent presentation.
CHOOSE: File → New (🗋)
CLICK: From AutoContent wizard link in the task pane
CLICK: Finish command button
A presentation should now appear in the application window.

2. To save the new presentation:
CLICK: Save button (🖫)
(*Note:* If the current presentation has not been saved, PowerPoint displays the Save As dialog box, regardless of the method you choose to save the file.) The filenames and folder directories that appear in your Save As dialog box may differ from those shown in Figure 1.29.

Figure 1.29

Save As dialog box

The Places bar

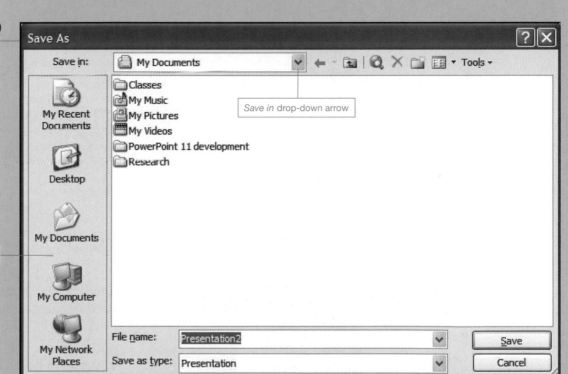

3. Let's navigate through the storage areas:
CLICK: down arrow attached to the *Save in* drop-down list box
Your screen may now appear similar, but not identical, to Figure 1.30.

PowerPoint

Figure 1.30

Navigating the
storage areas

My Documents
folder button

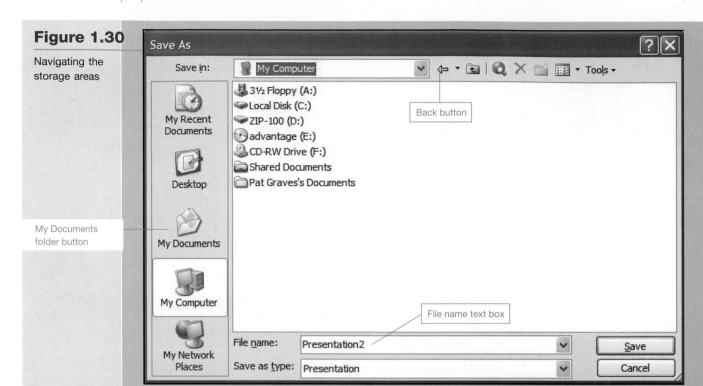

4. To browse the local hard disk:
   DOUBLE-CLICK: your local hard disk (▭) usually labeled C:
   The list area displays the folders and files stored in the root directory of your local hard drive.
   (*Note:* Your instructor may provide an alternate storage location if drive C: is not accessible.)

5. To open one of the folders:
   DOUBLE-CLICK: Program Files folder
   This folder contains the program files for several applications. Figure 1.31 shows how full of applications this folder can become.

Figure 1.31

The Program
Files folder of the
author's local
hard disk

6. To return to the previous display:
CLICK: Back button (‹Back) in the dialog box

7. The **Places bar**, located along the left border of the dialog box, provides convenient access to commonly used storage locations. To illustrate, let's view the files in your My Documents folder:
CLICK: My Documents folder button, as shown here

8. Now, using either the Places bar or the *Save in* drop-down list box:
SELECT: *a storage location for your personal files*
(*Note*: In this guide, we save files to the My Documents folder.)

9. Let's give the presentation a unique name that is more descriptive. Position the I-beam mouse pointer over the presentation name in the *File name* text box and then:
DOUBLE-CLICK: the *presentation name* to select it
The entire presentation name should appear highlighted.
TYPE: **Practice Presentation** as shown below

10. To complete the procedure:
CLICK: Save command button
Note that the presentation's name now appears in the program's Title bar (Figure 1.32).

Figure 1.32

The file name now appears in the program's Title bar

11. In this step, insert a title on the first slide.
CLICK: the title placeholder
TYPE: **Marketing Strategy**

12. To save the revised presentation:
CLICK: Save button (🖫)
There are times when you may want to save an existing presentation under a different filename. For example, you may want to keep different versions of the same presentation on your disk, or you may want to use one presentation as a template for future presentations that are similar in style and format. To do this, you can retrieve the original presentation file, edit the information, and then save it again under a different name using the File, Save As command.

13. Let's close the presentation:
CHOOSE: File → Close (✕)

In Addition MAKING A BACKUP

An important reason to use the Save As feature is to make a backup copy of your presentation. This is a second copy of your presentation saved in a different location. When you name it, you may want to add the word backup to your filename to distinguish this version from the original. Disks can become damaged, so this is an important safety procedure to ensure that your work is not lost.

PowerPoint

1.4.2 Opening an Existing Presentation

→ **Feature**

You use PowerPoint's Open dialog box to search for and retrieve existing presentations that are stored on your local hard drive, removable disks, CDs, a network server, or on the Web. If you want to load PowerPoint and an existing presentation at the same time, you can click on the Start menu and then go directly to the My Documents folder.

→ **Method**

To open an existing presentation:

- CLICK: Open button (⬚),
  or
- CHOOSE: File → Open

→ **Practice**

You will now open an existing file. Ensure that you have completed the previous lesson and that no presentations are displayed. You also should know the storage location for the student data files.

1. To display the Open dialog box:
CLICK: Open button (⬚)
The Open dialog box should now appear similar, but not identical, to Figure 1.33. The contents of your data files folder should be displayed.

Figure 1.33

Open dialog box

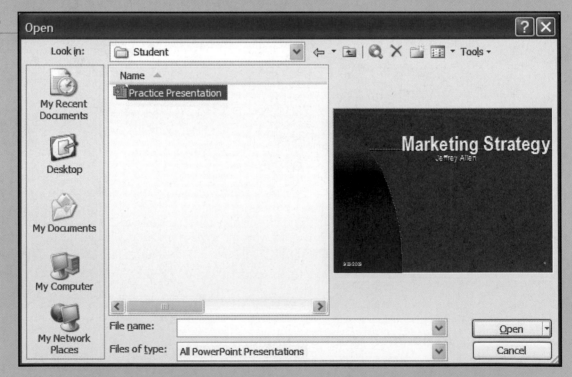

2. To open the PowerPoint file, "Practice Presentation," do the following:
DOUBLE-CLICK: "Practice Presentation"
The dialog box disappears and the presentation is loaded into the application window.

3. Proceed to the next lesson.

1.4.3 Creating a New File Folder

→ **Feature**

As files accumulate on your computer, you may want to create folders to help you better organize your work. For example, you may have one folder for your presentations and another for your reports and memos. Although Windows Explorer should be used for most folder management tasks, Power-Point allows you to create a new folder from the Save As dialog box. After you navigate to where you want the folder to appear, click the Create New Folder button (🗀) and then complete the steps below. Microsoft PowerPoint uses the Folder icon (🗀) to identify folders.

→ **Method**

To create a new folder, in the Save As dialog box:

- CLICK: Create New Folder button (🗀) in the Save As dialog box
- TYPE: *a folder name*
- CLICK: OK command button

To delete a folder, in the Save As dialog box:

- RIGHT-CLICK: a folder
- CHOOSE: Delete from the right-click menu

→ **Practice**

In this lesson, you create a folder named My Presentations in the My Documents folder. You then save the open file into the new folder.

1. To display the Save As dialog box:
   CHOOSE: File → Save As

2. This exercise assumes that you are able to create folders on your computer's local hard drive. If this is not the case, you may substitute a removable disk drive for the My Documents folder. To begin, use the Places bar to select the desired location for the new folder.
   CLICK: My Documents folder button

3. To create a new folder called My Presentations in the My Documents folder:
   CLICK: Create New Folder button (🗀)
   In the New Folder dialog box (Figure 1.34):
   TYPE: **My Presentations**

Figure 1.34

Creating a new folder

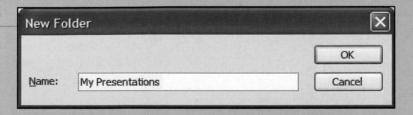

4. To finish creating the folder:
   CLICK: OK command button
   You are immediately transferred into the new folder, as shown in the *Save in* drop-down list box. Your screen should now appear similar to Figure 1.35.

PowerPoint

Figure 1.35

My Presentations folder

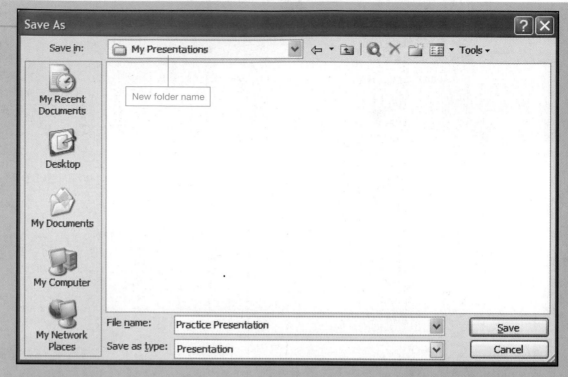

5. To save the open file to the new folder, using the same filename:
   CLICK: Save command button
   It is that easy to keep your files organized!

6. Proceed to the next lesson.

1.4.4 Previewing and Printing a Presentation

→ **Feature**

Clicking the Print button (🖨) sends your presentation directly to the printer with each slide printed on a separate piece of paper. You have many other print options, however, when you choose File, Print to display the Print dialog box options. You can select your print media—slides, audience handouts, notes pages, or your presentation's outline—and the number of copies to print. You can select whether to print your presentation using grayscale (shades of gray) or black. Each of these options can be inspected before printing by using **Print Preview**. In this lesson, we will cover how to preview and print slides.

→ **Method**

To preview presentation slides before printing:

- CHOOSE: File → Print Preview
- CHOOSE: File → Print → Preview button (🔍)

To preview other slide printing options before printing:

- CHOOSE: File → Print → Preview button (🔍)

To send a presentation directly to the printer with one slide on a page:

- CLICK: Print button (🖨)

To customize one or more print options:

- CHOOSE: File → Print

→ **Practice**

You will now send a presentation to the printer. Ensure that the PowerPoint file, "Practice Presentation," is displaying. (*Note:* If you do not have a printer installed, review the following steps without performing them.)

1. Let's open the "Practice Presentation" file and then preview and print the presentation:
CLICK: Open button (🖼), select the appropriate folder, such as My Documents or My Presentations, from your personal storage location
SELECT: "Practice Presentation" and click the Open button.
CHOOSE: File → Print

Figure 1.36

Print dialog box

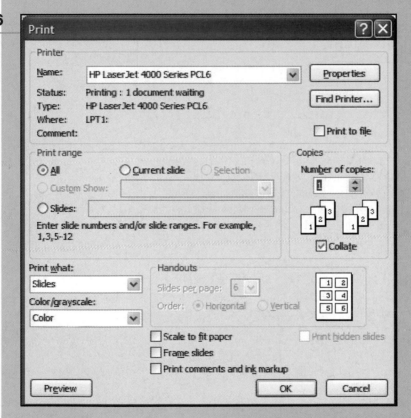

The Print dialog box displayed in Figure 1.36 appears.

2. Note that "Slides" is the current selection in the *Print what* drop-down list. To see other printing options,
CLICK: *Print what* drop-down arrow
The additional options of Handouts, Notes Pages, and Outline View are displayed.

3. To remove the drop-down list:
PRESS: ESC

4. If you do not have access to a printer, click the Cancel button. This presentation has nine slides, so it will print on nine pages if you print using the Slides option. If you have a printer connected to your computer and want to print the nine slides on separate pages, do the following:

PowerPoint

CLICK: OK command button
The Print dialog box will disappear and, after a few moments, the presentation will print.

5. Close the presentation without saving.

In Addition PRINTING AUDIENCE HANDOUTS

When you want to print multiple slides on one page, choose the handout option. Then you can choose 2, 3, 4, 6, or 9 slides to be printed on a page in a horizontal or vertical format. Slides printed in this miniature form are useful for audience handouts or for your own use when proofreading your presentation content, because they use fewer pages than when printing full-size slides on separate pages.

 **1.4** Why would you want to save a file under a different filename?

Chapter
summary

You have several options when starting a new presentation. For content suggestions, you might start a presentation using the AutoContent Wizard. For design suggestions, consider starting a presentation from a design template. You may also choose to start with a blank presentation in which you disregard PowerPoint's content and design suggestions altogether.

After inserting a new slide, you can add text to it by clicking a text placeholder or by typing in the Outline pane. In addition to creating presentations, it is important to know how to execute common file management procedures, including saving, opening, closing, and printing presentations.

Command Summary

Many of the commands and procedures appearing in this chapter are summarized in the following table.

Objective	To Perform this Task	Do the Following
Creating Presentations	Begin with the AutoContent wizard	CHOOSE: File → New CLICK: From AutoContent wizard link in the task pane
	Begin with a design template	CHOOSE: File → New CLICK: From design template link in the task pane
	Begin with a blank presentation	CLICK: New button (⬜)
	Insert slides	CLICK: New Slide button (⬜ New Slide)
	Delete a selected slide	CHOOSE: Edit → Delete Slide
Inserting and Modifying Text	Add text to the Slide pane	CLICK: in a text placeholder and then type
	Add text to the Outline pane	PRESS: (ENTER) to insert a new slide or continue typing at the same level PRESS: (TAB) to begin typing at a demoted (lower) level PRESS: (SHIFT) + (TAB) to begin typing at a promoted (higher) level

Managing files	Save a presentation	CLICK: Save button ([ ])
	Save as a new presentation	CHOOSE: File → Save As
	Close a presentation	CLICK: Close button ([X]), or CHOOSE: File → Close
	Open an existing presentation	CLICK: Open button ([ ]), or CHOOSE: File → Open
	Create a new file folder	RIGHT-CLICK: an empty part of the Open or Save dialog box CHOOSE: File → New TYPE: a folder name
Previewing and Printing Presentations	Preview a presentation	CHOOSE: File → Print Preview CHOOSE: File → Print → Preview button
	Print a presentation	CLICK: Print button ([ ]), or CHOOSE: File → Print
	Print slides in a variety of formats	CHOOSE: File → Print SELECT: an option from the *Print what* drop-down list

Key Terms

This section specifies page references for the key terms identified in this chapter. For a complete list of definitions, refer to the Glossary provided immediately after the Appendix in this learning guide.

adaptive menus, *p. PP 6*

application window, *p. PP 4*

AutoContent Wizard, *p. PP 9*

AutoFit feature, *p. PP 18*

design template, *p. PP 9*

hyperlinks, *p. PP 9*

navigating, *p. PP 13*

Normal view, *p. PP 12*

Outline and Slides pane, *p. PP 13*

placeholders, *p. PP 18*

Places bar, *p. PP 29*

Print Preview, *p. PP 32*

Slide pane, *p. PP 13*

Slide Sorter, *p. PP 13*

task pane, *p. PP 6*

thumbnails, *p. PP 13*

Chapter
quiz

Short Answer

1. Describe an advantage of displaying both the Standard and Formatting toolbars.

2. Explain the purpose of the AutoContent Wizard.

3. What is the difference between the Slide pane and the Task pane?

4. What happens when you click the New button ([ ])?

5. What are the characteristics of Normal view?

6. How do you delete a slide from a presentation?

7. Describe the type of placeholders provided for text slides.

8. What is a slide layout?

9. What does PowerPoint's AutoFit feature do if you type too much text in a placeholder?

10. What is the difference between choosing File, Print and clicking the Print button (⊡)?

True/False

1. _____ To create a blank presentation, choose File, New.

2. _____ Placeholders are inserted on slides when you choose a slide layout.

3. _____ Clicking the New button (⊡) starts a presentation from a design template.

4. _____ In Normal view, the Outline pane is larger than the Slide pane.

5. _____ You can tell that text is a hyperlink in the task pane because your mouse pointer will change to a hand (⌐) when you point to it.

6. _____ Design template thumbnails are miniature images displayed in the task pane.

7. _____ You can delete the current slide using the Menu bar Edit, Delete Slide option.

8. _____ PowerPoint's AutoFit feature automatically resizes placeholders to accommodate typed text.

9. _____ You can add text in both the Outline pane and Slide pane.

10. _____ Inserted slides are placed before the current slide.

Multiple Choice

1. Which of the following provides content suggestions?

   a. AutoContent Wizard
   b. Blank presentation
   c. Design template
   d. Slide Show view

2. To apply an attractive background to a presentation, you should apply an alternate:

   a. AutoLayout
   b. Placeholder
   c. Design template
   d. All of the above

3. To save a presentation using a different name, choose:

   a. File ➜ Save
   b. File ➜ Save As
   c. File ➜ Print
   d. All of the above

4. Filenames should be no longer than this many characters:

   a. 8
   b. 15
   c. 20
   d. 50

5. Organizing your files by subject requires the use of [the]:

   a. Outline pane
   b. Slide pane
   c. Folders
   d. All of the above

6. Which of the following mark the location of slide objects?

   a. Folders
   b. Placeholders
   c. Hyperlinks
   d. Fonts

7. When you demote a text item on a bulleted list,

   a. That item is indented one outline level to the right
   b. That item is indented one outline level to the left
   c. Pressing the (ENTER) key will enable you to add another bullet list item at the previous outline level
   d. None of the above

8. You can move between the slides of your presentation by:

    a. Clicking on the previous/next buttons at the bottom of the slide pane scrollbar

    b. Clicking on the slide icon in the outline tab

    c. Clicking on the slide thumbnail in the slide tab

    d. All of the above

9. The Places bar is useful when:

    a. Saving and opening

    b. Formatting text

    c. Inserting slides

    d. All of the above

10. The Print dialog box is displayed when you:

    a. Click the Print button (⊞)

    b. Choose File, Print

    c. Click the New button (▯)

    d. All of the above

Hands-On
exercises

 step by step

1. Editing an AutoContent Presentation

Tech Solutions is company that develops creative yet easy-to-use Web sites for small businesses featuring products available for purchase. Whenever a new client contracts with Tech Solutions, a planning session is held with client representatives and two developers from Tech Solutions.

    Eric Svensson has been asked to lead this brainstorming session for a new client, Decorative Arts, a company selling jewelry and objects such as pottery, sculptures, and paintings. In this exercise, you are to assume Eric's role and perform the steps listed below.

1. Start a new presentation and launch the AutoContent Wizard. Make the following choices when prompted:

    • In the General category, select the "Brainstorming Session" presentation.

    • For the output option, select "On-screen presentation."

    • Type: **Web Site Planning** in the *Presentation title* text box.

    • Type: **Decorative Arts** in the *Footer* text box and then click the Finish command button to compile the presentation.

2. Delete the existing text from the subtitle placeholder on the first slide and then type **your name**.

3. Using the Outline tab, delete slide 3. Then, delete the newly positioned slide 7 (and slide 8 if a blank slide shows up in this position.)
(*Note:* Click the OK command button if prompted.)

4. On slide 2 (Agenda), delete the first and last bulleted items, Overview and Next Steps.

5. On slide 3 (Brainstorming Objectives), edit the text as follows:

    • **Identify content for site**

        • **Products—jewelry and home interior?**

        • **Display ideas?**

        • **Feature/product naming?**

        • **Promotion ideas?**

        • **New process for ordering?**

    • **Define top requirements and restrictions**

6. The slide should appear similar to the one shown in Figure 1.37.

PowerPoint

Figure 1.37

Brainstorming
Objectives
revised bulleted
list

7. Save the presentation as "Decorative Arts" to your personal storage location.

8. Print and then close the presentation.

step by step

2. Adding and Editing Slides

Amie Jefferson works for Creative Communication Services, a company that sells presentation equipment to educational institutions and businesses. Amie frequently goes on location to demonstrate presentation products and their benefits to potential clients.

Today Amie is working on an idea she has to help people understand why it is so important for them, as presenters, to communicate their message to audiences with visual images in the form of presentation slides. She has titled this presentation Visual Communication and has already finished several slides. In this exercise, assume the role of Amie in adding and editing four more slides.

1. Open the PP01HE02 presentation.

2. Save the presentation as "Visual Communication" to your personal storage location.

3. Display slide 4 and you will see that the bulleted list placeholder is positioned on the slide but the text has not been entered. So type the following four items as shown in Figure 1.38:

- **Cognitive psychology**

- **Human-computer studies**

- **Reading and language**

- **Educational research**

Figure 1.38

Visual
Communication
bulleted list

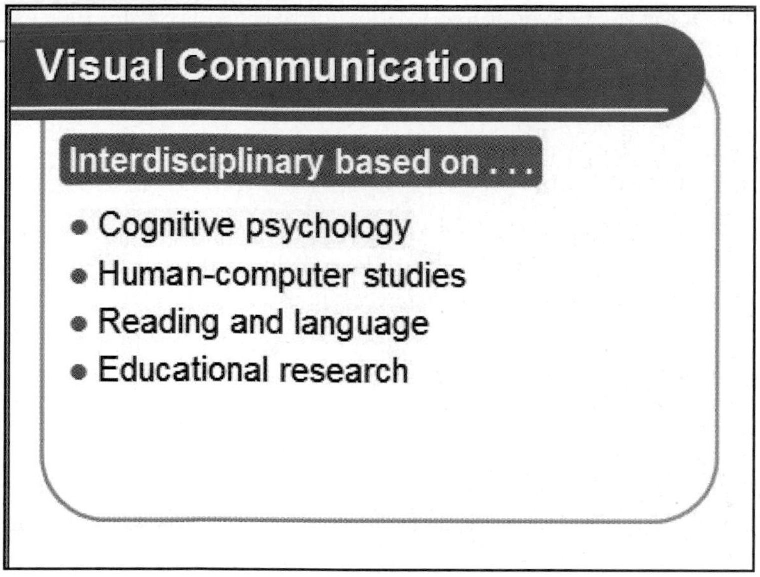

4. Display slide 5 and repeat the process to type these two items:

  - **Thinking is below level of consciousness**

  - **We are conscious of thoughts, but they may be difficult to describe**

5. Display slide 7 and then insert a new slide with the title **Perception**. Type these items (press the
[**TAB**] key to indent to the second bullet level).

  - **An active process necessary to assign meaning**

  - **Visual properties—figure (perceived object) and ground (surrounding background)**

    - **patterns and groupings**

    - **shading**

    - **continued visual lines**

6. Now insert a new slide with the title **Spatial Cues**. Repeat the same process:

  - **Alignment, blank space, columns/rows**

  - **Influence the way readers see text**

    - **what they attend to**

    - **the order they scan**

    - **the importance they assign to information**

    - **the relationships between elements**

7. Notice that for the last slide Amie used a Title slide layout and that this slide will be shown as she makes her concluding comments.

8. Save, print handouts with six slides on a page, and then close the revised presentation.

step by step ▶

3. Writing Bulleted Lists

In her job at Creative Communication Services, Amie Jefferson often educates people about the equipment necessary to project presentations prepared with PowerPoint. She has prepared six slides for this presentation but needs to add three more. In this exercise, assume Amie's role to add these slides and write the bulleted lists.

1. Open the PP01HE03 presentation.

2. Save the presentation as "Hardware" to your personal storage location.

3. Display slide 2 and insert a new slide.

4. The title for slide 3 is **Projection Equipment**. Amie wants people to think about where presentations will be given because that is such an important consideration for the type of equipment purchased. People might travel to remote locations to give presentations, or they might need the flexibility of using the same equipment in different rooms at the same location. They may have a room that will be dedicated to training or group events where equipment could be permanently installed. Based on this information, think about how you would create a bulleted list from this information. Figure 1.39 shows an example to use as your guide in completing slide 3.

Figure 1.39

Projection
Equipment
bulleted list

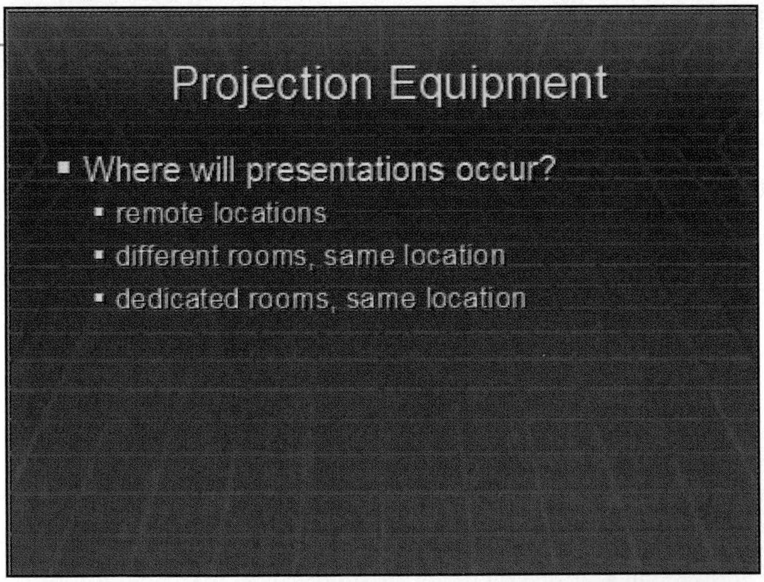

Projection Equipment

- Where will presentations occur?
    - remote locations
    - different rooms, same location
    - dedicated rooms, same location

5. Now Amie wants to create two more slides. Here is the information she needs to include in each slide. Read the following paragraphs and decide how you would word the text for each slide and then create the slides. Write concisely and word each item as a phrase rather than a sentence.

The title for slide 4 is **Projector Selection**. Amie wants clients to understand that the first step is to determine their presentation needs for permanent, mobile, or portable units. It is best to look at the clarity of projected images in the location where the equipment will be used. Clients should consider both the cost and warranty as they decide which products to buy. They will also need to make replacement plans, especially if multiple units are purchased. Multiple units should be purchased over a period of time, so that all units do not wear out at the same time.

The title for slide 5 is **LCD (Liquid Crystal Display)**, which is the most common projector type. These units come in different sizes and can be ceiling mounted or portable. They range in weight from 9 to 24 pounds, but they can be even smaller. Most units have built-in speakers for presentations that display sound. Older models had one negative characteristic in that the lighting level, called room illumination, had to be reduced so colors would display effectively.

6. Notice that Amie again used a Title slide layout for her last slide to display while she makes her concluding comments.

7. Save, print handouts with six slides on a page, and then close the revised presentation.

4. Editing an AutoContent Presentation

Prepare a certificate using a layout that is already developed in PowerPoint.

1. Start a new presentation from the From AutoContent wizard link in the task pane. Select the General category and then Certificate as the type of presentation and then click on Finish. A three-slide presentation will appear. Delete slide 1.

2. Revise the text for either the Certificate of Excellence or the Certificate of Completion to make the certificate appropriate for your business or student organization.

3. Save the presentation as "Certificate" and print a copy. When you access the Print menu, be sure you put a check in front of *Scale to fit paper* so a small amount of blank space will appear around the edge of the paper. Your finished certificate should look something like that shown in Figure 1.40.

4. Close the presentation.

PowerPoint

Figure 1.40

Certificate

on your own

5. Revising an AutoContent Presentation

Prepare a presentation to be used for an orientation session at your place of employment or at the college you are attending. Use a PowerPoint AutoContent Wizard presentation for ideas, but reduce the number of slides from 10 to 6.

1. Start a new presentation from the From AutoContent wizard link in the task pane. Select the Corporate category and then Employee Orientation as the type of presentation. Click on Finish and a 10-slide presentation will appear.

2. Review the slides to determine which ones will not fit your situation and delete them. However, be sure to keep both the title slide and the summary slide.

3. Edit each slide to insert your own text.

4. Save the presentation as "Orientation" and print a handout copy with six slides on a page. Close the presentation.

on your own

6. Creating the Presentation

Using one of PowerPoint's design templates, create a presentation to promote a new fitness program being started where you work. Assume that you have been leading the group planning the activities that are scheduled after the end of the workday. You will be using a YMCA facility two blocks from your office.

Prepare a title slide and three slides with bulleted lists to help explain the benefits of the program to other employees. Make your points persuasive. You might mention that the program is a good way to avoid rush-hour traffic, because it would be better to exercise than to sit in a slow-moving car.

Write an ending slide that tells people when the program will start and whom to contact for more information. Be sure to include a phone number.

Save the presentation as "Fitness Program" to your personal storage location and print a handout copy with six slides on a page. Close the presentation.

CaseStudy   CAREER COUNSELOR PRESENTATION

Joe Santos is a career counselor at Prairie Community College. In addition to advising students in his office, he frequently talks to students in classes, organization meetings, or other special events. Joe has decided to develop a series of presentation slide shows, because many of the meeting rooms on his campus now have presentation equipment available for use.

Lately a lot of students have been asking Joe about how to handle themselves in interview situations, so he knows this is a timely topic that he can present to several different groups. Although Joe has limited experience with PowerPoint, he decides to use its Outline feature to organize his thoughts and prepare a few simple lists for his first presentation on business etiquette for job interviews. As he learns more about the software, he plans to add more graphic elements. In the following case, assume the role of Joe and perform the same steps that he identifies. You will select an appropriate design template and create six slides. Finally, you will save your presentation and print handouts.

1. Joe begins his presentation by selecting the design template "Beam." He enters the title and subtitle text as shown in Figure 1.41.

Slide 1: Title Slide layout
Title: **Business Etiquette for Your Job Interview**
Subtitle: **First Impressions are Important and Lasting**

PowerPoint

Figure 1.41

Business
Etiquette Title
slide

2. Using the Outline pane, Joe starts to develop slides describing what a job applicant should do before, during, and after a job interview. As some of the slides become too full, he divides the content into five different slides. Here is the text he enters for slides 2-6.

Slide 2: Title and Text layout
Title: **As You Arrive**

- **Treat all people you meet with courtesy**

- **Arrive at least 10 minutes before your appointment**

- **Arrive prepared**

- **Be sure your appearance and good grooming reflect respect for yourself and the situation**

Slide 3: Title and Text layout
Title: **Beginning the Interview**

- **Thank the interviewer for talking with you**

- **Remember to shake hands firmly**

- **Wait to sit down until the interviewer invites you to do so**

- **Sit up straight and keep your hands still**

- **Look the interviewer in the eye as you speak**

Slide 4: Title and Text layout
Title: **During the Interview**

- **Speak to be heard and enunciate clearly**

- **Listen carefully and remain attentive**

- **Respond to questions succinctly**

- Be prepared to take notes if necessary
- Be careful about gestures and body language—remain respectful

Slide 5: Title and Text layout
Title: **Ending the Interview**

- Watch for signals that the interview is over
- Make a positive statement about your interest in working for this company
- Shake hands again, firmly
- Exit with composure and maintain good posture as you walk away

Slide 6: Title and Text layout
Title: **After the Interview**

- Write a thank-you letter—VERY important!
- Express your interest in the job
- Indicate your appreciation for the interview
- Tell in your own words how much being employed by this company means to you
- Call back within a month if you have not been contacted

3. Save the presentation as "Business Etiquette" to your personal storage location.

4. So students can make notes as he is talking, Joe decides to print handouts with six slides on a page. He will prepare one black-and-white original and then photocopy the number he needs each time he gives this presentation.

5. Close the presentation.

Answers to Self-Check Questions

1.1 How do you remove a right-click menu from view? Click outside the right-click menu or press ⎋ ESC .

1.2 How does starting a presentation with the AutoContent Wizard differ from starting a presentation using a design template? Whereas the AutoContent Wizard provides content suggestions, a design template provides design, not content, suggestions. The AutoContent Wizard asks you a series of questions and then builds your slides based on the responses you give.

1.3 What does it mean to demote or to promote text in a bulleted list? To demote text, you show decreased importance or emphasis. Move the text to the right one outline level to show a subpoint under the existing bullet. To promote text, you show increased importance or emphasis. Move a second-level bulleted item to the first level, or make a first-level bulleted item become a slide title.

1.4 Why would you want to save a file under a different filename? You may want to keep different versions of the same presentation on your disk. You may want to use one presentation as a template for future presentations that are similar in style and format. You may want to make a backup copy of your presentation.

PowerPoint

Notes

Microsoft®Office**PowerPoint**®

2003

CHAPTER 2

Modifying and Running Presentations

PREREQUISITES

To successfully complete this chapter, you must be able to start presentations, insert slides, and insert slide text in placeholders. You will be asked to use basic file management operations to open, save, and close presentations. You should know how to select options from the toolbars, menus, and right-click menus.

LEARNING
OBJECTIVES

After completing this chapter, you will be able to:

- Format text and use different fonts

- Apply slide layouts and change slide order

- Add footer text

- Apply design templates and customize slide color schemes

- Start and run slide shows

2.1 Editing and Enhancing Your Presentation

Text is a very important part of your presentation and the particular font you use will impact the tone of your presentation. Fonts have personalities—some have a conservative appearance and are good for serious messages. Others are crisp and clear and convey a modern, contemporary tone. Still others are "fun" fonts, with a relaxed or even flamboyant style, that should be used for lighthearted messages.

Some fonts are much easier to read than others when projecting computer slides in color. Text always needs a strong color contrast against the background on which it appears. A shadow may be needed for even greater distinction between the text and the background color.

Understanding Typography Terms

To better understand the differences in typefaces, here is a discussion of some basic typography terms. Typography refers to the design of text characters.

Font/typeface

A font is a complete alphabet of uppercase and lowercase letters and all their related symbols, special characters, and punctuation marks. A typeface is the name given to a particular font such as Arial or Times New Roman. Be careful about mixing too many fonts in a presentation. One or two usually work well.

> Arial
> Times New Roman

Serif and sans serif

Most typefaces are divided into these two categories. Serifs are the cross strokes at the ends of letters that increase their readability in long passages of text; therefore, serif typefaces are commonly used for paragraph copy. Sans serif typefaces have no cross strokes at the ends of letters and have a crisp, no-frills appearance. The projector you are using, as well as the particular colors on your slides, will influence the readability of typefaces. Generally, sans serif typefaces are easier to read when projected.

Some Serif Typefaces	**Some Sans Serif Typefaces**
Times New Roman	Arial
Bookman Old Style	Tahoma
Georgia	Verdana

Script and display typefaces

These typefaces look like handwriting, calligraphy, or other unusual letterform designs and should be used only for special purposes. Rarely would one of these typefaces be used for the body of a presentation, because they are not very readable when projected. If you feel that a typeface like this is appropriate for your message, use it sparingly, as in slide titles; choose a body font that works well with the decorative title font and blends with its tone.

> Bradley Hand ITC
> **Forte**
> Jokerman
> Lucida Calligraphy

Part of a character (or letterform)

What makes each font distinctive is how the parts of the characters have been designed. These differences influence the appearance and readability of the text. All text aligns at the bottom on an imaginary "baseline." The main body of a letter is measured as the "x-height." The parts of a letter that stick up above the x-height are called ascenders; parts of letters that hang down below the baseline are called descenders. In some typefaces these letter parts have little variation in size; in others, the size differences can be dramatic. When letters are thick and chunky, they have more "weight" than regular text.

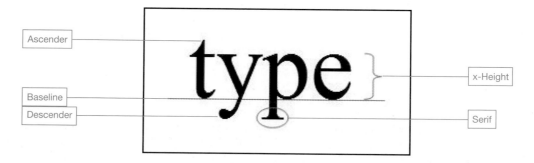

Attributes

Fonts can be varied for emphasis by applying boldface or italic attributes. Boldface conveys the strongest emphasis. A shadow attribute can sometimes provide a better definition to the letterforms and make text easier to read in the colors you are using. However, if the colors you have chosen lack contrast, a shadow treatment can make text appear blurry. Use of underlining should be limited to hyperlinks, because that use is now common for references to Web pages. The underline attribute also cuts through font descenders and, therefore, inhibits readability.

Arranging Text

Select fonts for your presentation that fit your topic and are easy to read in the colors you plan to use. Often the best approach is a simple one, using only one or two fonts.

Case

Limit the use of words spelled in all capital letters. Such words are more difficult to read than words with initial caps, in which only the first letter of each word is capitalized. Use initial caps for slide titles. For bulleted lists, use sentence case, in which only the first letter of each line of text is capitalized.

> THIS IS AN EXAMPLE OF TEXT PRINTED IN UPPERCASE (ALL CAPITAL) LETTERS. IT IS MUCH MORE DIFFICULT TO READ THAN TEXT PRINTED IN INITIAL CAPS. WE READ BY THE SHAPES OF WORDS—AND THAT SHAPE IS LOST WHEN LETTERS APPEAR TO BE THE SAME SIZE. PROOFREADING IS MORE DIFFICULT, TOO.

Distinctive slide titles

A slide's title text should have the dominant text treatment, because the viewer's eye should begin reading with the title. Make that text larger than the body text, perhaps bold or a different color than the body text. The title needs to have some distinguishing feature to separate it from the body text. Such a feature could also be a graphic treatment on the background (such as a different color for that part of the slide) or a drawn line that works as a divider to separate the title text from the body.

Descriptive slide titles

Keep title text short and concise. On occasion, titles may be long enough to word wrap on two lines, but they should generally be short enough—from three to five words—to fit on one text line. The consistent sizing of slide titles is also an important element of your slide show and contributes to the unity of your presentation.

PowerPoint

Concise writing

Bulleted lists must be concise. The "**Rule of 49**" will help you remember that you should have no more than 7 words of text on each bulleted item, no more than 7 lines of bulleted text on a slide, and therefore, no more than 49 words on a text slide. Consistent sizing of the body text contributes to unity in your presentation design.

Text sizes

Like desktop publishing software, presentation software such as PowerPoint uses point size as its standard unit of text measurement. One inch contains 72 points. Varying point sizes is an important way to signify levels of importance for your text. For example, the slide title should be the largest text on a slide (usually 36–44 points). The body text, as in a bulleted list, is smaller than the title (usually 24–28 points). The font you choose will influence the sizes that seem pleasing. Always remember, however, that you are preparing slides that will be seen from a distance.

Text alignment

For bulleted lists, left alignment is always a good treatment. You might vary where the text aligns, however, by indenting the position of the list to better fit your background or to complement other objects on the slides. Left, center, and right alignment are effective for slide titles. Both left and right alignment have the advantage of providing the viewer with a standard beginning or ending position for each of the lines of text that serves to anchor that text element. Centered titles are commonly used, but because each title varies in length, a standard beginning position cannot be achieved. Justified alignment is never appropriate for presentation slides.

Punctuation

Use publishing punctuation marks for a more professional appearance. Be sure to use "smart quotes," quotation marks that curve when placed on either side of the text you are quoting. Use an em dash (—) in place of two hyphens. These two punctuation treatments can be enabled with PowerPoint's AutoCorrect feature, so that they will automatically appear as you enter text.

In the next sections you will learn to apply various fonts and font attributes as you create and edit the presentations in Chapter 2.

2.1.1 Formatting Text on Slides

→ Feature

PowerPoint's Formatting toolbar provides many commands for changing text appearance. For example, you can select different typefaces, font sizes, and text attributes. You can also change **alignment** within a text placeholder.

→ Method

- To change a text attribute, use the appropriate button for Bold (B), Italic (I), Underline (U), or Shadow (S), on the Formatting toolbar
- To select an alternate typeface, use the *Font* drop-down list (Arial ▾) on the Formatting toolbar
- To change the current font size, use the *Font Size* drop-down list (32 ▾) on the Formatting toolbar
- To change paragraph alignment:

  CLICK: the Align Left (▤), Center (▤), or Align Right (▤) button on the Formatting toolbar

→ Practice

You will now open a presentation and practice changing text appearance using the Formatting toolbar. Ensure that no presentations are open in the application window.

1. Open the PP0210 data file to display a presentation based on the "Quadrant" design template.

2. Save the presentation as "Writing Effective Slides" to your personal storage location.

3. On the first slide, revise the text in the subtitle placeholder:
CLICK: the subtitle placeholder

Notice how the slide placeholder changes its appearance when you click inside to edit the text. You see diagonal slash marks in the placeholder border line when you are in position to insert or edit text.

TYPE: **Your Name**

TYPE: **Your University or College**

Your screen should now appear similar to the one shown in Figure 2.1, with your name and school displayed instead of the words "Your Name" and "Your University or College".

Figure 2.1

Title slide layout

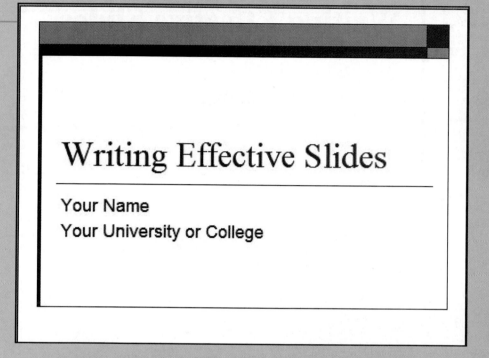

4. Apply the bold and shadow attributes to the title:

SELECT: the title words by dragging over the text with the mouse to highlight

CLICK: Bold button (B)

CLICK: Shadow button (S)

5. Apply an italic attribute to the subtitle:

SELECT: the subtitle words by dragging over the text with the mouse to highlight

CLICK: Italic button (I)

CLICK: outside the selected text to better view your modifications

Your Slide pane should appear similar to the one shown in Figure 2.2.

Figure 2.2

Applying character attributes to the title and subtitle

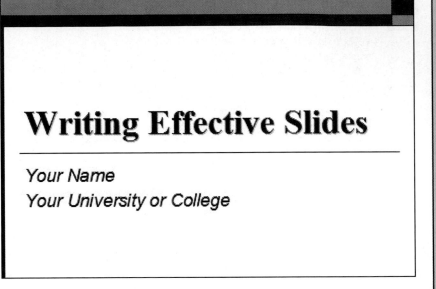

6. To change the font in the title placeholder:
   SELECT: the text in the title placeholder
   CLICK: down arrow beside the *Font* drop-down list (Arial ▼)
   SELECT: Impact (or another font that is available on your computer if you cannot find Impact)

7. With the text still selected, change the title's font size:
   CLICK: down arrow beside the *Font Size* drop-down list (32 ▼)
   SELECT: 66-point font size
   CLICK: Bold button (B) to turn off bold, because this font is already very bold

   Note that the enlarged text is too big to fit on one line in the placeholder and has word wrapped to two lines. A button, called the AutoFit Options button, is displaying on the slide (Figure 2.3).

Figure 2.3

Changing font
and font size

AutoFit
Options

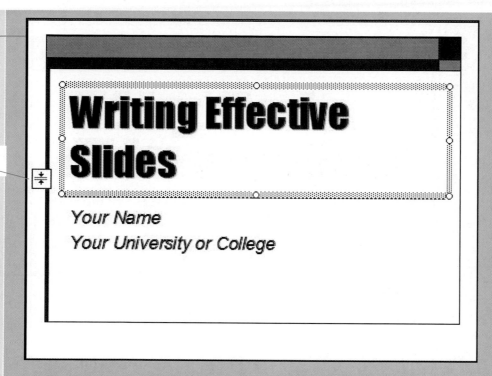

8. CLICK: AutoFit Options button (⬍▾)
   SELECT: *AutoFit Text to Placeholder* option
   Note that the title text now returns to one text line within the placeholder.

9. To practice changing alignment:
   CLICK: in the subtitle placeholder
   You may need to click again on the placeholder borderline so it has a dotted appearance. This indicates that the whole placeholder is selected and your change will affect everything in the placeholder. This item is currently left aligned in the placeholder.

10. To change from the current left alignment to right alignment:
    CLICK: Align Right button (▤) on the Formatting toolbar
    The item is positioned on the right side of the placeholder, as shown in Figure 2.4. This alignment position would fit nicely with the background graphics in this design template.

Figure 2.4

Changing
placeholder
alignment

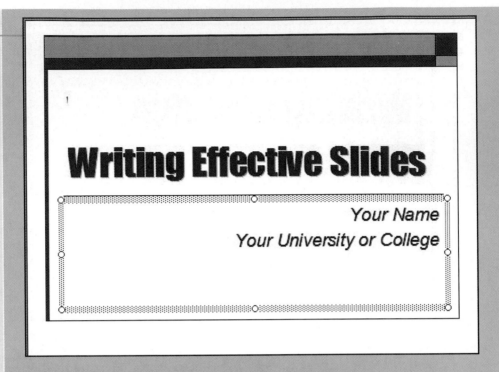

11. To move the subtitle placeholder back to its original position:
CLICK: Align Left button (▤) on the Formatting toolbar

12. To change the font on each of the other slide titles to match the Title slide font.
CLICK: slide 2 icon
SELECT: the title text
SELECT: the font Impact
Repeat this process for slides 3 and 4.

13. Save your presentation and continue to the next lesson.

2.1.2 Adding Footer Text

→ **Feature**

The Header and Footer command provides an easy way to display the date and time, slide number, or other, optional footer text on every slide in a presentation.

→ **Method**

- CHOOSE: View → Header and Footer
- CLICK: *Slide* tab to add information to slides
- SELECT: desired options
- CLICK: Apply to add information to only the current slide
  or
- CLICK: Apply to All to add information to all slides

→ ## Practice

In this lesson, you will use the Header and Footer command. Ensure that the "Writing Effective Slides" presentation is displaying.

1. View the first slide of the "Writing Effective Slides" presentation, if it is not displaying already.

2. CHOOSE: View → Header and Footer
CLICK: *Slide* tab in the Header and Footer window
Your screen should now appear similar to the one shown in Figure 2.5.

Figure 2.5

Header and
Footer dialog
box, *Slide* tab

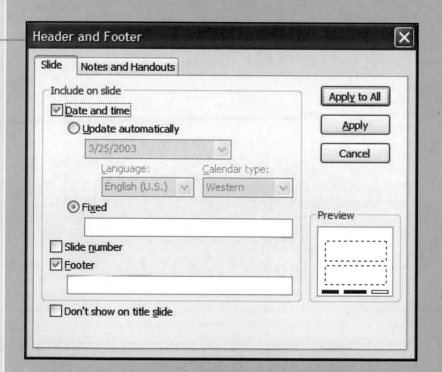

3. To insert the same date on every slide, ensure that the Fixed option button is selected and then do the following:
CLICK: in the text box located below the Fixed option button
TYPE: **the current date**

4. To insert the current slide number on the slide:
CLICK: *Slide number* check box

5. To insert footer text:
CLICK: *Footer* check box
CLICK: in the text box located below the *Footer* check box
TYPE: **Prepared by *Your Name***
Your Header and Footer dialog box should now appear similar to the one shown in Figure 2.6.

Figure 2.6

Making selections
in the Header
and Footer dialog
box

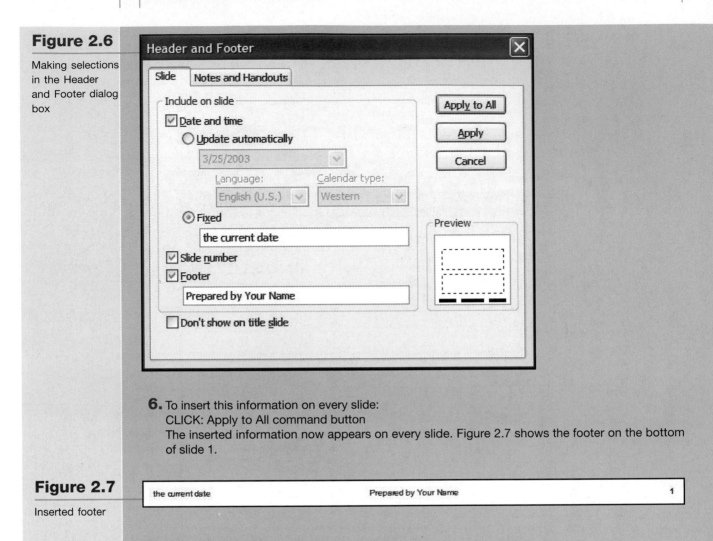

6. To insert this information on every slide:
   CLICK: Apply to All command button
   The inserted information now appears on every slide. Figure 2.7 shows the footer on the bottom
   of slide 1.

Figure 2.7

Inserted footer

| the current date | Prepared by Your Name | 1 |

7. Save your presentation and continue to the next lesson.

2.1.3 Checking Spelling and Using AutoCorrect

→ **Feature**

You may notice red, wavy lines appearing below your text while you work. PowerPoint does not
recognize your spelling of the underlined words. Proper names that are not found in Microsoft's dictionary will also be underlined with red, wavy lines.

Spell Checker, a shared utility that appears in all Microsoft Office applications, lets you perform a
spelling check on your presentation. The spelling checker scans slides, and when it finds a word that
does not appear in one of its dictionaries, it displays a list of similarly spelled words with the most likely
match. You may then select the proper spelling from these suggested words or retype the word. If the
word is already spelled correctly, you can choose to ignore the suggestions, add the word to a custom
dictionary, or insert the word into the AutoCorrect list.

The **AutoCorrect feature** can correct hundreds of common typographical and capitalization errors
as you type. You will find this feature extremely helpful if you habitually misspell particular words.
AutoCorrect also helps you use modern punctuation marks such as smart quotes (" "), an em dash (—)
and special symbols, such as © or ™. If you wish, you can turn on only selected options.

→ ## Method

To check spelling:

- CLICK: Spelling button (⌨)

  or

- CHOOSE: Tools → Spelling

To turn off an AutoCorrect option or add an AutoCorrect word:

- CHOOSE: Tools → AutoCorrect Options

→ ## Practice

Ensure that the "Writing Effective Slides" presentation is displayed. Use the spell checker to correct errors in the text and practice using the AutoCorrect feature.

1. To begin spell checking the entire presentation:
CLICK: Spelling button (⌨)

2. When PowerPoint finds a misspelled word, it displays the dialog box shown in Figure 2.8 and awaits further instructions.

Figure 2.8

Checking spelling

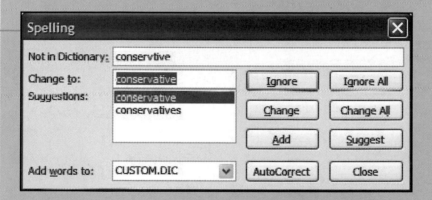

3. To change the misspelled word to the correctly spelled word "conservative," do the following:
CLICK: Change command button
(*Note:* If this is a word that you frequently misspell, consider adding it to your AutoCorrect list by clicking the AutoCorrect command button. The next time you misspell the word, PowerPoint will correct your mistake automatically.)

4. Continue correcting errors until spell check is completed.
CLICK: OK to close the message dialog box

5. To demonstrate how the AutoCorrect feature will correct errors as you type, let's intentionally enter a misspelled word. Go to slide 2 and position your insertion point at the end of the text in the second bulleted text line after "messages."
PRESS: ENTER
TYPE: **dispaly**
Notice how the first letter was automatically capitalized.
PRESS: Space bar
Notice that the spelling is automatically corrected to read "Display."

6. To review some of the other entries available in AutoCorrect:
CHOOSE: Tools → AutoCorrect Options
CLICK: AutoCorrect tab if it is not already selected

PowerPoint

In the dialog box that appears (Figure 2.9), the top part of the box displays the options that are already selected for automatic correction. The lower part of the box displays two columns: *Replace* and *With*. AutoCorrect replaces the entry (words or symbols) appearing in the *Replace* column with the entry in the *With* column. To customize this list for your own needs, you could add words you frequently misspell.

7. At the top part of the AutoCorrect dialog box, notice the capitalization option. Whenever you press the ⟨ENTER⟩ key, PowerPoint capitalizes the first word that you type. To disable this option:
CLICK: the (☑) to deselect *Capitalize first letter of sentences*
CLICK: OK command button

Figure 2.9

AutoCorrect
dialog box

Remove this check if
you do not want text
to be automatically
capitalized every
time you press the
⟨ENTER⟩ key.

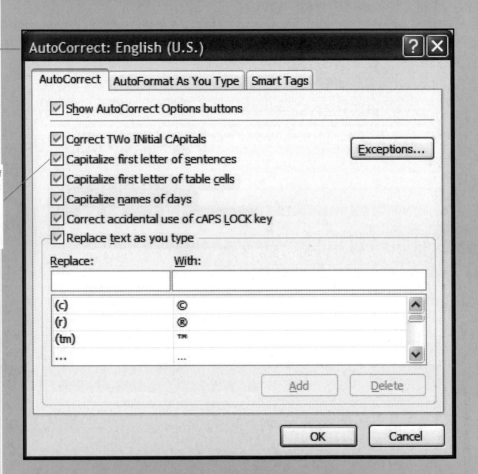

8. To review some of the other entries available in the *AutoFormat As You Type* tab:
CHOOSE: Tools → AutoCorrect Options
CLICK: *AutoFormat As You Type* tab
In the dialog box (Figure 2.10) that appears, you will see the punctuation marks, symbols, and AutoFit options that can be controlled.

Figure 2.10

AutoFormat As You Type options

AutoCorrect

AutoCorrect | AutoFormat As You Type | Smart Tags

Replace as you type
- ☑ "Straight quotes" with "smart quotes"
- ☑ Fractions (1/2) with fraction character (½)
- ☑ Ordinals (1st) with superscript
- ☑ Hyphens (--) with dash (—)
- ☑ Smiley faces :-) and arrows (==>) with special symbols
- ☑ Internet and network paths with hyperlinks

Apply as you type
- ☑ Automatic bulleted and numbered lists
- ☑ AutoFit title text to placeholder
- ☑ AutoFit body text to placeholder

Apply as you work
- ☑ Automatic layout for inserted objects

[OK]   [Cancel]

9. Delete the word "Display" and go back to the end of the previous bulleted item.
PRESS: **ENTER**
TYPE: **others are "friendly" for lighthearted messages**
Notice that the first letter of this line remained lowercase and the straight quotes you typed have been changed to smart quotes. Your slide should now appear similar to the one shown in Figure 2.11.

Figure 2.11

Slide with AutoCorrect changes

"Smart quotes"

The Personality of Fonts

- ☐ Each font has a personality
  - ■ some are conservative for serious messages
  - ■ others are "friendly" for lighthearted messages
- ☐ Be careful about mixing fonts
- ☐ Limit the number of different fonts used
- ☐ Use fonts consistently

the current date   Prepared by Your Name   2

10. Save the revised presentation and continue to the next lesson.

2.1.4 Using the Thesaurus

→ ## Feature

When you want to change a word to another word with a similar meaning, PowerPoint's **Thesaurus** can help to suggest a list of synonyms. The Thesaurus will open in the task pane and provide possible replacement words. It will also enable you to "dig deeper" into the meaning of the words by using the *Look up* option to access online reference materials.

→ ## Method

To use the Thesaurus

- CLICK: on the word you want to replace so your insertion point is on that word
- CHOOSE: Tools → Thesaurus

→ ## Practice

Ensure that the "Writing Effective Slides" presentation is displaying. Use the Thesaurus to select a different word.

1. On the third slide of the "Writing Effective Slides" presentation, place your insertion point on the word you want to look up.
CLICK: on the word "Emphasize"

2. To look up a synonym for this word:
CHOOSE: Tools → Thesaurus
Results will appear in the Research task pane (Figure 2.12).

Figure 2.12

Using Thesaurus

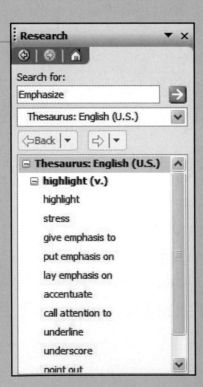

3. To use one of the words, move the mouse over the desired word and:
CLICK: the down arrow beside it
CLICK: Insert

4. To look up additional words:
CLICK: one of the words in the list of results
Note: You can look up words in other languages by using the Research pane and selecting Research options, which will bring up a number of Thesaurus options.

2.1.5 Changing Slide Order

→ **Feature**

It is easy to reorder slides in the *Outline* and *Slides* tabs, as well as the Slide Sorter window. The operation is a simple drag and drop to rearrange icons or thumbnails (small miniature images) representing your slides.

→ **Method**

- DRAG: slide icon (in *Outline* tab) or slide thumbnail (in *Slides* tab) up or down in the slide list

- DRAG: slide thumbnail (in Slide Sorter) in any direction in the slide list

→ **Practice**

You will now practice reordering slides in the *Outline* and *Slides* tabs and the Slide Sorter window. Ensure that you have completed the previous lesson and that the "Writing Effective Slides" presentation is displaying in Normal view. You can check whether your presentation is displaying in Normal view by choosing View, Normal from the menu.

1. To display the contents of the *Outline* tab, located on the left side of your screen:
CLICK: *Outline* tab

2. To move slide 3 so that it is positioned before slide 2, do the following:
CLICK: slide 3 icon
Notice that the slide's title and bulleted items are highlighted in reverse color (Figure 2.13).

Figure 2.13

Selecting a slide in the *Outline* tab

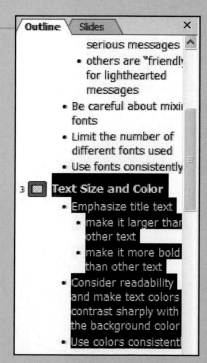

PowerPoint

3. Now drag the slide 3 icon upward in the *Outline* tab so that it is positioned above slide 2. As you drag the icon, the slide's title and bulleted items will move with it. A narrow horizontal bar will mark where the slide will be inserted when you release the mouse button.
DRAG: the slide 3 icon upward until the horizontal bar is one line above the slide 2 icon then release the mouse button.
The *Outline* tab, located on the left side of your screen, should now appear similar to the one shown in Figure 2.14.

Figure 2.14

Reordering slides
in the *Outline* tab

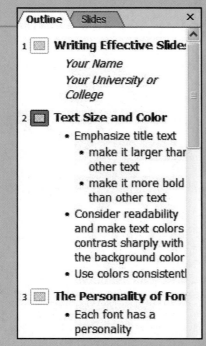

4. Now reorder slides using the *Slides* tab by moving slide 2 after slide 3.
CLICK: *Slides* tab

5. DRAG: the slide 2 thumbnail below slide 3
The presentation has now been returned to its original order.

6. Now reorder slides using the *Slide Sorter* window
CLICK: Slide Sorter button (⊞) in the View Buttons area at the lower left of your screen
Your screen should now appear similar to Figure 2.15 with thumbnail images of your presentation slides filling the screen. Practice moving the thumbnails and then return them to their original positions.
Note: You can adjust the size of these images by choosing a different magnification percentage in the Zoom box.

Figure 2.15

Reordering slides in the Slide Sorter

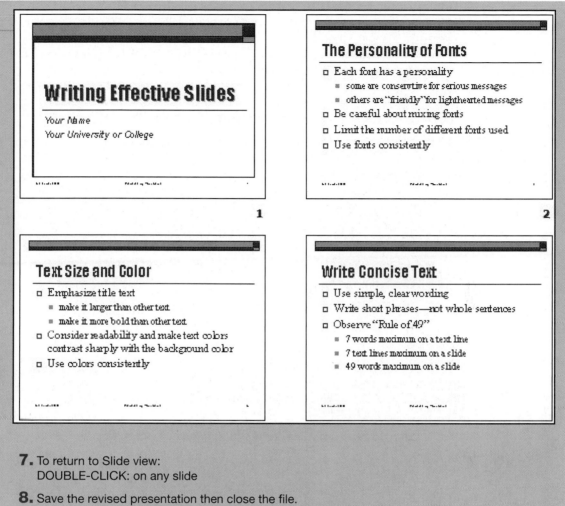

7. To return to Slide view:
   DOUBLE-CLICK: on any slide

8. Save the revised presentation then close the file.

 **SelfCheck**   **2.1** How do you rearrange slide order?

2.2 Changing a Presentation's Design

How your presentation looks can directly affect your audience's response to your message. If your message is buried in inconsistent design elements and varied colors that seem randomly applied, you risk losing the attention of your audience.

An easy way to give your presentation a consistent look is to apply one of PowerPoint's pre-existing design templates, as you learned in Chapter 1. Design templates control the overall design—the background graphics and text colors and fonts used as well as the positioning of text placeholders and other objects. For example, the title text will have a consistent treatment across all slides of the presentation because the font and its attributes are controlled by the design template title placeholder. The title text will be larger or bolder than other text because a viewer's eye should be drawn to that text before moving on to the information contained in the body of the slide, such as in a bulleted list.

Because the graphics and color schemes of PowerPoint's design templates have been designed by professionals, you can be confident that they work well together. However, you may find it important to adjust the current design scheme to meet your particular requirements for the theme and tone of your presentation. For example, you may want to match your company colors, establish an environmental theme, or use colors to match a seasonal promotion.

In this module, we focus on changing and customizing slide layouts, applying different design templates, and changing the current color scheme.

2.2.1 Applying Alternate Slide Layouts

→ ## Feature

You may find that an existing slide layout does not meet your needs. For example, you may decide that in addition to your bulleted list placeholder, you need a graph placeholder. In this case, you will want to change the existing slide layout to meet your new requirements.

→ ## Method

- CHOOSE: Format → Slide Layout

In the *Slides* tab:

- CLICK: the slides to which you want to apply the layout (press and hold down `CTRL` when selecting multiple slides)

In the Slide Layout task pane:

- CLICK: the layout you want

→ ## Practice

You will now begin a new presentation and practice changing slide layouts. Ensure that no presentations are open in the application window.

1. To create a new presentation based on the "Eclipse" design template:
   CHOOSE: File → New
   CLICK: "From Design Template" link in the New Presentation task pane

2. Find the "Eclipse" template thumbnail in the Slide Design task pane and then:
   CLICK: "Eclipse" template thumbnail

3. To insert text in the title placeholder:
   CLICK: the title placeholder (in the Slide pane)
   TYPE: **Telecommuting Issues**

4. To insert text in the subtitle placeholder:
   CLICK: the subtitle placeholder
   TYPE: *Your Name*
   Your screen should now appear similar to the one shown in Figure 2.16, with your name displaying instead of the words "Your Name."

Figure 2.16

This slide uses
the Title slide
layout

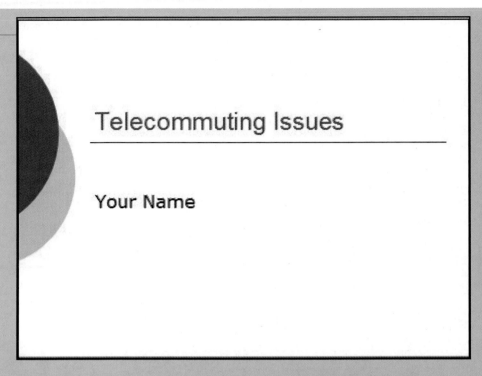

Telecommuting Issues

Your Name

5. Add a second slide to the presentation.
   CLICK: New Slide button (New Slide) on the Formatting toolbar
   The new slide is currently conforming to the Title and Text layout for a bulleted list.

6. Change the layout of this slide to the Title, Text, and Content layout. In the Slide Layout task pane, drag the vertical scroll bar downward to the Text and Content Layouts section, then CLICK: Title, Text, and Content layout
   The slide now includes placeholders for a title, bulleted list, and graph or other content.

7. To add a title to the slide:
   CLICK: title placeholder
   TYPE: **Home Office Needs**

8. To add content to the slide:
   CLICK: bulleted list placeholder (located on the left side of the slide)
   TYPE: **Good computer**
   PRESS: (ENTER)
   TYPE: **Online access with fast connection speed**
   PRESS: (ENTER)
   TYPE: **Printer and fax**
   PRESS: (ENTER)
   TYPE: **Phone with separate business line**
   PRESS: (ENTER)
   TYPE: **Comfortable chair**

   Your screen should now appear similar to the one shown in Figure 2.17. (*Note:* The graphic used for the bulleted items may appear differently on your computer.)

PowerPoint

Figure 2.17

This slide uses the Title, Text, and Content layout

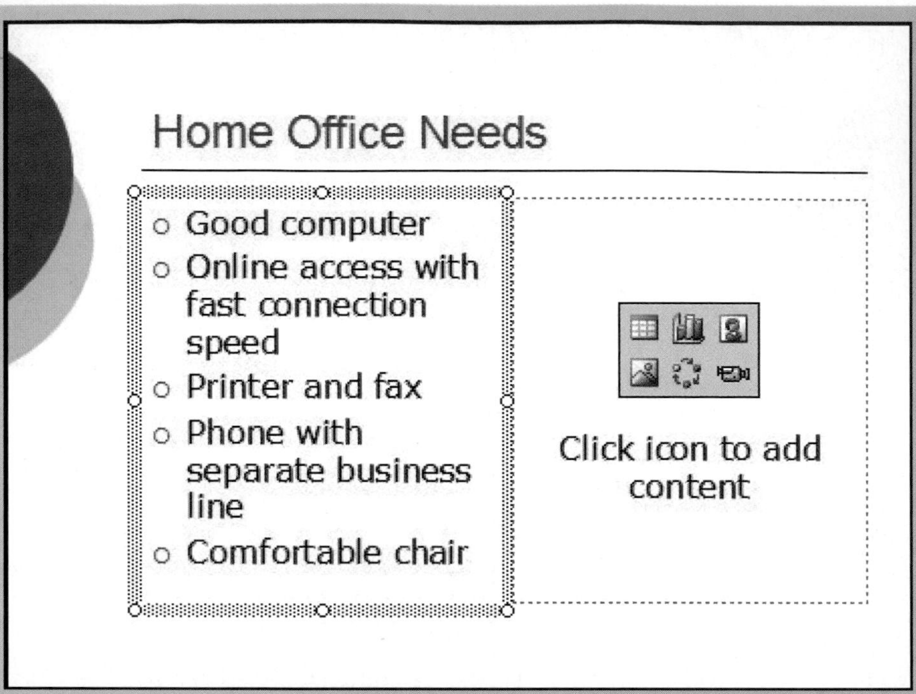

Home Office Needs

- Good computer
- Online access with fast connection speed
- Printer and fax
- Phone with separate business line
- Comfortable chair

Click icon to add content

9. Change the layout of the second slide to the Title and Text layout.
CLICK: Title and Text thumbnail at the top of the Slide Layout pane
The slide was changed to conform to the Title and Text layout. The text in the bulleted list has been enlarged, and the graph placeholder no longer appears (Figure 2.18).

Figure 2.18

Reapplying the Title and Text layout

Home Office Needs

- Good computer
- Online access with fast connection speed
- Printer and fax
- Phone with separate business line
- Comfortable chair

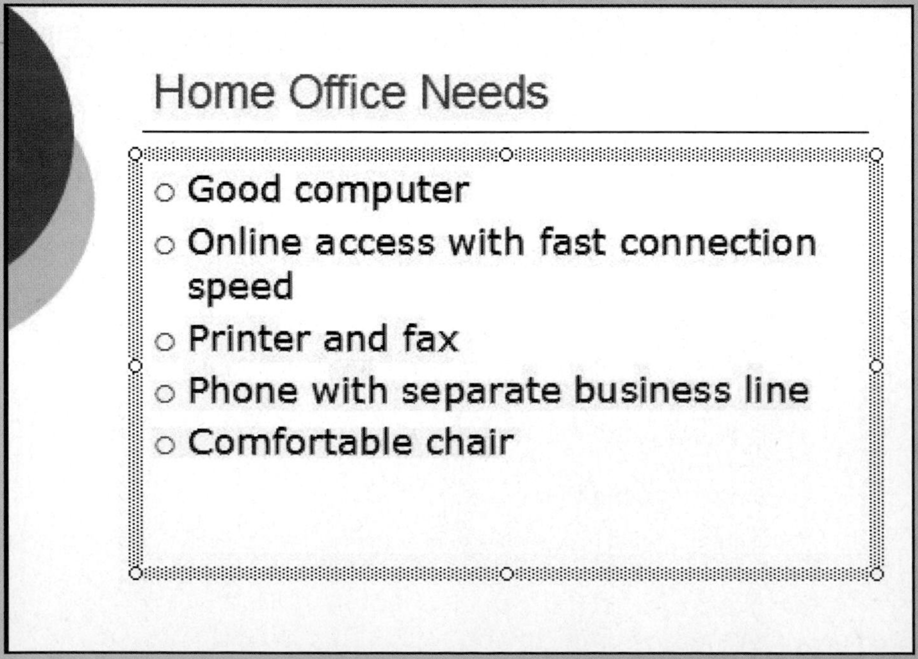

10. Using the Title and Text layout, add two more new slides to your presentation with this content:

On the Positive Side . . .
- **Your commute is short**
- **You can create an ideal work atmosphere**
- **You will eat out less and save money**
- **You may become closer to your family**

On the Negative Side . . .
- **Strong self-discipline is needed**
- **Setup may be expensive**
- **You will find no clear division between work time and nonwork time**
- **You may feel too isolated**
- **Family members may interfere**

11. Save the presentation as "Telecommuting Issues" to your personal storage location but do not close the presentation.

12. Continue to the next lesson.

2.2.2 Customizing Placeholders

→ # Feature

As you know, when you choose a layout for a new or existing slide, PowerPoint inserts an arranged group of placeholders on the slide. You can move, resize, and delete object placeholders to suit your needs. The appearance of the borderline of the placeholder will help you to judge whether you can edit the text inside the placeholder or resize or move the placeholder.

→ # Method

- Select a placeholder by clicking it.

- Move a selected placeholder by dragging it.

- Resize a selected placeholder by dragging its sizing handles.

- Delete a selected placeholder by pressing DELETE.

→ # Practice

You will now practice customizing the current slide layout. Ensure that you have completed the previous lesson in this module and that you are viewing slide 4 in the "Telecommuting Issues" presentation.

1. On the bulleted list slides of the "Telecommuting Issues" presentation, the bulleted items are aligned under the first letter of the title. Let's indent each bulleted list placeholder to the right by selecting it and resizing it to move the text to the right. To select the placeholder:
CLICK: in the bulleted list placeholder
As shown in Figure 2.19, the placeholder is surrounded by **sizing handles** (tiny circles on the borderline surrounding the object) and a borderline with diagonal slash marks, indicating that the text is ready for editing.

Figure 2.19

Selecting a sizing handle

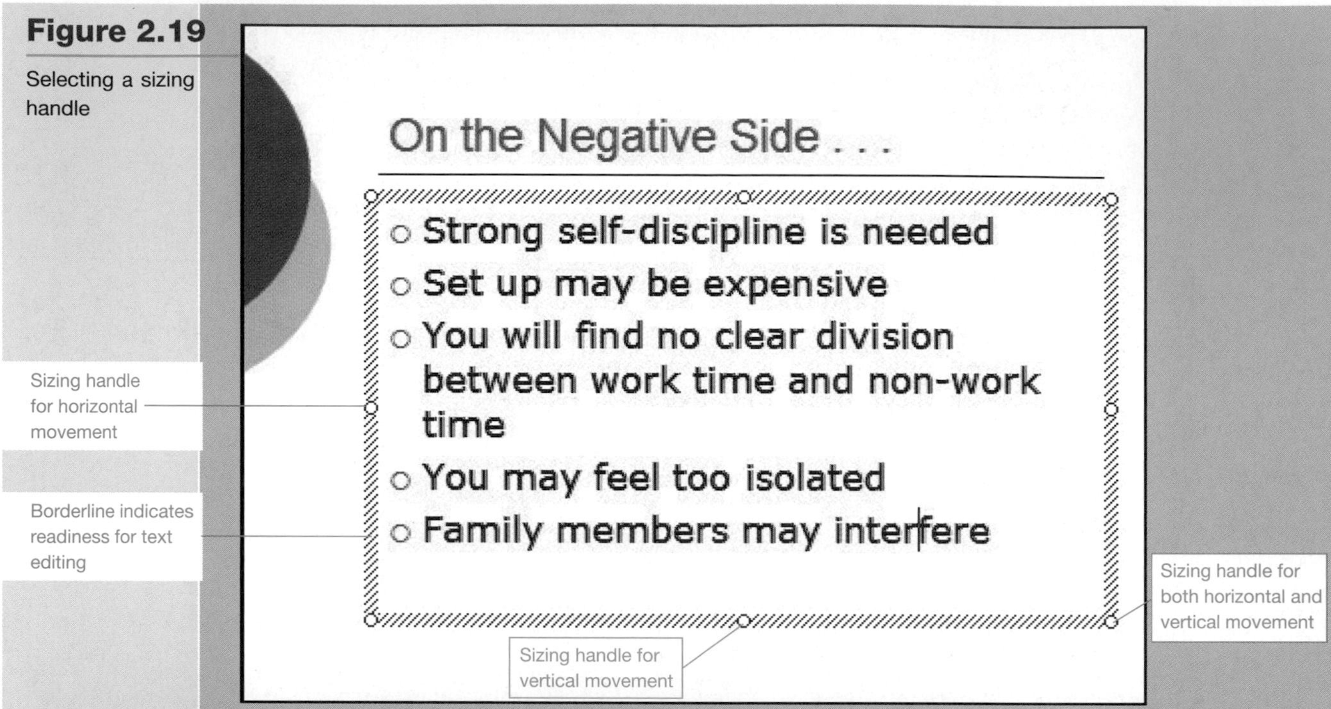

Sizing handle for horizontal movement

Borderline indicates readiness for text editing

Sizing handle for both horizontal and vertical movement

Sizing handle for vertical movement

On the Negative Side . . .

- ○ Strong self-discipline is needed
- ○ Set up may be expensive
- ○ You will find no clear division between work time and non-work time
- ○ You may feel too isolated
- ○ Family members may interfere

2. When you position the mouse pointer over a sizing handle, the pointer will change to a double-headed arrow (↔) showing the direction that you will resize if you move your mouse in that direction. In addition, the borderline around the selection becomes dotted. To practice resizing the placeholder:
DRAG: the sizing handle in the bottom-right corner (see Figure 2.19) inward until the placeholder looks like the one shown in Figure 2.20.

Figure 2.20

Resizing a slide object

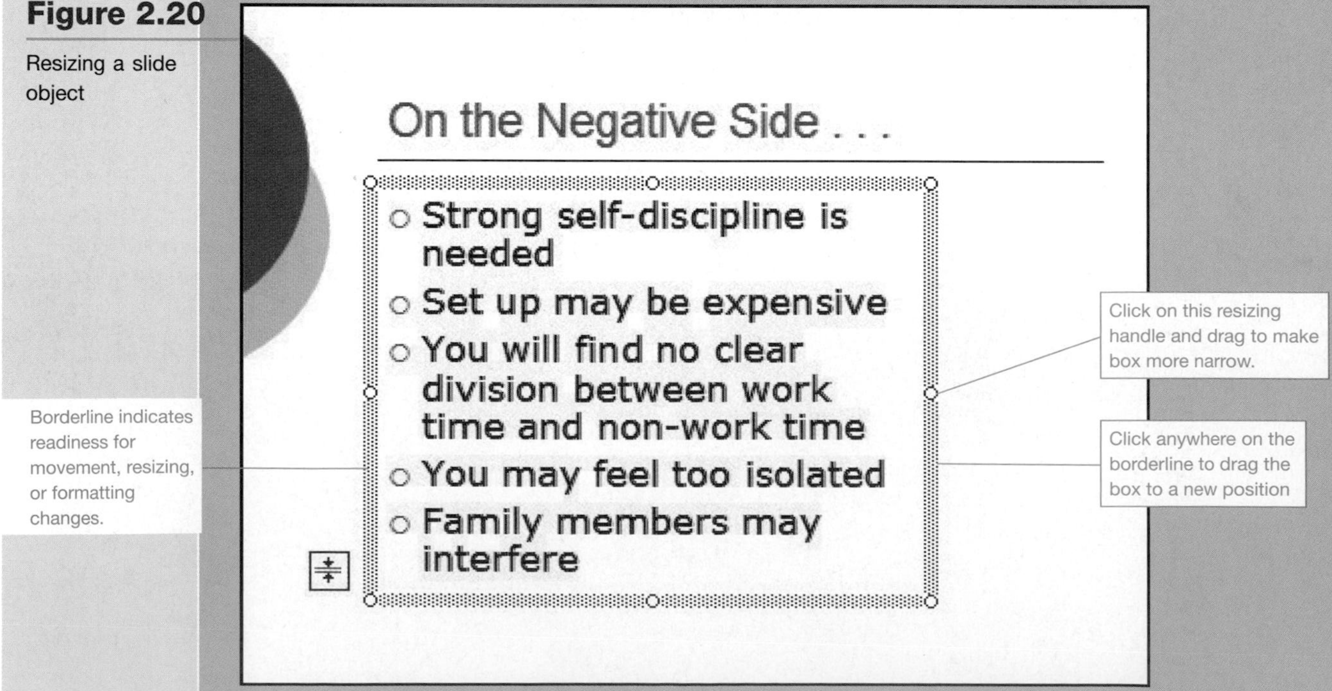

Borderline indicates readiness for movement, resizing, or formatting changes.

Click on this resizing handle and drag to make box more narrow.

Click anywhere on the borderline to drag the box to a new position

On the Negative Side . . .

- ○ Strong self-discipline is needed
- ○ Set up may be expensive
- ○ You will find no clear division between work time and non-work time
- ○ You may feel too isolated
- ○ Family members may interfere

3. To move the placeholder to the right without resizing it, position the mouse pointer anywhere on the placeholder borderline until a four-headed arrow (⊕) appears.
DRAG: the placeholder to the right

4. To restore the placeholder to its original shape and position:
CLICK: the curved part of the undo button (↶▾) twice

5. For precise positioning of the placeholder, using the ruler will allow you to better judge space and provides a way to position elements consistently across several slides. To display the ruler, CHOOSE: View → Ruler
Now position the left side of the bulleted placeholder on the 2.5-inch scale marker on the ruler. Select the middle sizing handle and you will see a vertical line that moves on the ruler as you move the handle.
Your screen should now appear similar to Figure 2.21.

Figure 2.21

Moving the bulleted list placeholder to the right

On the Negative Side . . .

○ Strong self-discipline is needed
○ Set up may be expensive
○ You will find no clear division between work time and non-work time
○ You may feel too isolated
○ Family members may interfere

PowerPoint

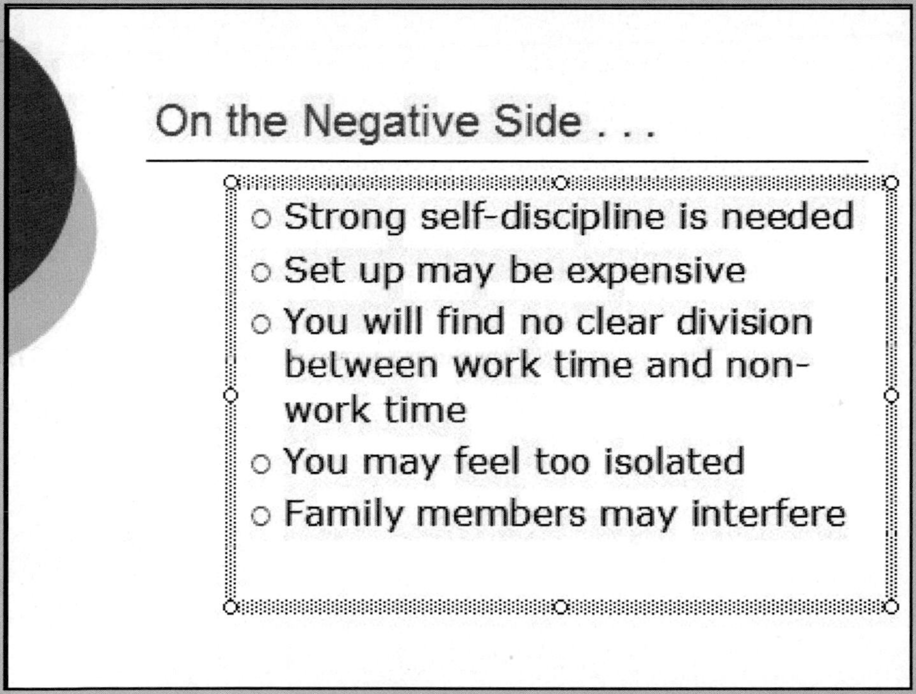

6. Repeat this adjustment for slide 3 of this presentation.

7. You can delete the text inside a placeholder or the entire selected placeholder. To practice deleting the placeholder text, ensure that you are on slide 4 and that your bulleted list placeholder is selected and displaying the dotted borderline:
PRESS: DELETE
The contents of the placeholder are now deleted. To delete the placeholder itself:
PRESS: DELETE again

8. To undo the two previous deletions:
PRESS: the curved part of the Undo button (↶▾) twice
Note: The appearance of the borderline is your visual cue for whether you are inside the placeholder ready to add or delete text or if you are ready to resize or move the placeholder.

9. Save the revised presentation and keep it open for the next lesson.

10. Continue with the next lesson.

In Addition CUSTOMIZING PLACEHOLDER POSITIONING

Placeholder position can be more efficiently controlled by using the Slide Master, because changes made on the Slide Master affect all slides created with that layout.

2.2.3 Applying Design Templates

→ **Feature**

Applying an alternate design template to a presentation involves selecting the design's thumbnail in the Slide Design task pane. Placeholder alignment, positioning, colors, and fonts vary. When you change to a different "look," you may want to make adjustments in these initial settings.

→ **Method**

- CHOOSE: Format → Slide Design

- CLICK: a design thumbnail in the Slide Design task pane

→ **Practice**

You will now practice applying design templates. Ensure that the "Telecommuting Issues" presentation is open.

1. Apply a different design template to the presentation.
CHOOSE: Format → Slide Design

2. Find the "Glass Layers" thumbnail in your Slide Design task pane template list on the right side of your screen. (*Note:* If this template is unavailable, select an alternate template.)

3. CLICK: "Glass Layers" thumbnail in the template list
The presentation's title slide should now appear similar to the one shown in Figure 2.22.
It is that easy to change the look of a presentation!

Figure 2.22

Applying an alternate design template

4. Save the revised presentation and close the file.

2.2.4 Customizing the Color Scheme

→ **Feature**

The colors you use in a presentation can influence how an audience responds to your message. Fortunately for us, Microsoft hired professional artists to compile PowerPoint's numerous color schemes. A **color scheme** is a set of eight colors that you can apply to your presentation. By using color schemes, you ensure that all the colors in your presentation are balanced and work well together. Color schemes also make it easy to apply a new set of colors to your presentation, just as templates make it easy to change its overall design. You can easily customize a color scheme to your particular needs, but always remember to exercise restraint so that your creativity does not overpower your message.

→ **Method**

To display a collection of color schemes in the Slide Design task pane:

• CHOOSE: Format → Slide Design

• CLICK: Color Schemes link near the top of the task pane

Perform this step if you want to apply the color scheme to a selection of slides:

• SELECT: the slides in the *Slides* tab (press and hold down the `CTRL` key while clicking multiple slides)

• CLICK: drop-down arrow on the color scheme

• CHOOSE: Apply to Selected Slides

Perform this step if you want to apply the color scheme to the entire presentation:

• CLICK: the color scheme

→ **Practice**

In this lesson, you apply a new color scheme and then customize it to meet your needs.

1. Open the PP0224 data file.

Figure 2.23

The first slide of the "E-Learning" presentation

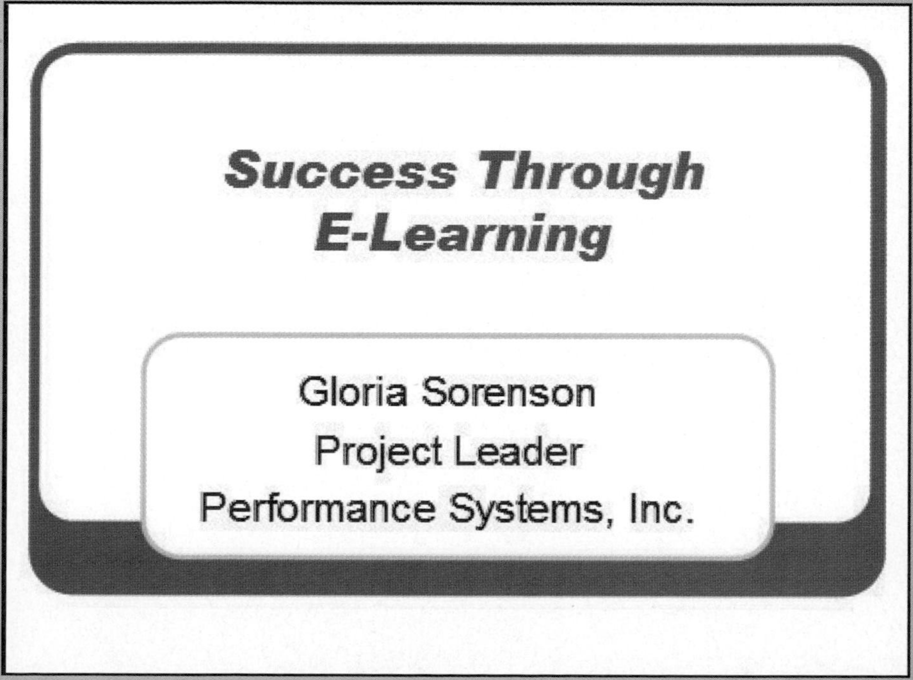

Success Through
E-Learning

Gloria Sorenson
Project Leader
Performance Systems, Inc.

PowerPoint

2. Save the presentation as "E-Learning" to your personal storage location. Your screen should now appear similar to Figure 2.23. The "Studio" design template is applied to this presentation.

3. Advance through the slides in this presentation in order to become familiar with their contents.

4. Let's apply an alternate color scheme to the presentation:
CHOOSE: Format → Slide Design
CLICK: Color Schemes link (located near the top of the Slide Design task pane)

Figure 2.24

Slide Design task
pane showing
color schemes

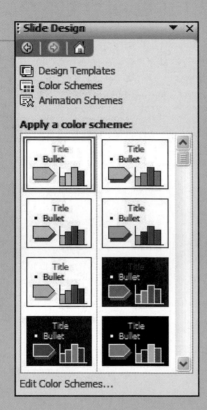

The Slide Design task pane should now appear similar to Figure 2.24. Note that the color scheme thumbnails you see in the task pane are all part of the "Studio" design template. You can use the scroll bar to see even more color combinations.

Figure 2.25

Applying an
alternate color
scheme

5. To experiment with different color schemes, do the following:
   CLICK: different color scheme thumbnails and those colors will be displayed on the Slide pane
   CLICK: the purple background (located in the second column of the fourth row)
   Your screen should now appear similar to the one shown in Figure 2.25.

Figure 2.26

Displaying a color
scheme's drop-
down menu

6. To display the drop-down menu:
   CLICK: arrow on the color scheme layout
   The color scheme and associated menu should now appear similar to Figure 2.26. To apply a color scheme only to certain slides, you must choose the *Apply to Selected Slides* option on this drop-down menu.

7. Let's apply another color scheme to the presentation.
   CLICK: color scheme with dark blue background (scroll down to the last row of available color scheme thumbnails)
   The new color scheme has now been applied to every slide in the presentation. Figure 2.27 shows the first slide of the presentation.

PowerPoint

Figure 2.27

Applying an alternate color scheme

8. On your own, view the revised presentation.

9. Save and close the revised presentation.

 **2.2** What is the procedure for moving and resizing object placeholders?

2.3 Running a Slide Show

When you are ready to make your presentation, PowerPoint provides several ways to help you do it. Whereas handouts, overhead transparencies, and 35-millimeter slides are static presentation media, on-screen presentations are dynamic, often incorporating special multimedia effects that help maintain an audience's attention. In this module, we discuss starting and running on-screen presentations.

Remember that the visual display of your presentation should support—and not dominate—its content. Any time you are using equipment to support your presentation, you should be very familiar with its use and control, as much as possible, where it is positioned so that your discussion and interaction with the audience can be as natural as possible. Because equipment often creates a barrier between the presenter and the audience, you should do all that you can to eliminate this possibility. Here are some "speaker tips" for using presentation equipment effectively:

• Plan for the electrical cords and cables coming to your equipment so you do not trip on or disconnect them.

• Position your equipment so the monitor is visible and the keyboard and mouse are accessible to you while facing the audience. Remote controls are convenient to use and allow you more freedom to move away from the equipment.

- Refer to, but do not read from, the monitor while speaking. A thorough rehearsal prior to your presentation will allow you to explain, rather than read, to your audience. Maintain eye contact with your audience.

- Do not turn to face the projection screen while you are talking. You may occasionally need to glance in that direction, but avoid speaking to the projected image.

- Rehearse with your equipment until you are able to quickly load your file and move smoothly from slide to slide within the presentation.

- Know how to navigate to selected slides in case someone has a question about a previously viewed slide.

- Have your title slide displayed at the beginning of your presentation so the audience does not have to watch your start up.

2.3.1 Starting Slide Shows

→ **Feature**

PowerPoint provides several ways to start slide shows. In this lesson, we describe how to start a **slide show** from within PowerPoint and from the Windows desktop.

→ **Method**

To start a slide show from within PowerPoint:

- CLICK: the slide on which you want to start in the *Outline* or *Slides* tab (or in the Slide Sorter window)
- CLICK: Slide Show button (🖳)

To start a slide show from the Windows desktop:

- RIGHT-CLICK: the presentation filename in My Computer or Windows Explorer
- CHOOSE: Show from the right-click menu

→ **Practice**

You will now open an existing presentation from within PowerPoint.

1. Open the PP0231 data file. (*Note:* You may need to use the Open dialog box to navigate to the location in which your student files are stored, such as your floppy diskette.)

2. Save this four-slide presentation as "Getting to Know" to your personal storage location.

3. At this point, slide 1 is the current slide.
CHOOSE: View → Slide Show (Figure 2.28)

Figure 2.28

The View menu

4. To illustrate that you can start a presentation on any slide, let's exit Slide Show view, display slide 2, and then switch back to Slide Show view.
PRESS: ESC to exit Slide Show view
CLICK: Next Slide button (⬇) on the vertical scroll bar to display slide 2

5. You can also start shows using the Slide Show button (🖵) located in the View Button area beneath the Outline and Slides pane.
CLICK: Slide Show button (🖵)
The second slide is now displaying in Slide Show view.

6. Before continuing:
PRESS: ESC to exit Slide Show view
The presentation is displaying in Normal view.

7. Display the first slide of the presentation in the Slide pane.

2.3.2 Navigating Slide Shows

→ **Feature**

Moving through your slide show is called navigating. Usually you will advance the slides in sequence (a linear order) by simply clicking with the mouse or using various keyboard commands. In Slide Show view, you can navigate a presentation using the keyboard or mouse. To navigate a presentation using the mouse, you must display a right-click menu in Slide Show view. Among the available commands on the right-click menu are options for navigating the slide show and ending the slide show.

→ **Method**

To navigate a slide show using the keyboard or mouse:

• PRESS: Space Bar, PgDn or ⬇ to display the next slide

• PRESS: PgUp or ⬆ to display the previous slide

• CLICK: to display the next slide

or

• RIGHT-CLICK: to display a navigational right-click menu

→ **Practice**

You will now practice navigating a running slide show. Ensure that the first slide of the "Getting to Know" presentation is displaying in Normal view.

1. To practice navigating the presentation using the keyboard, do the following:
CHOOSE: View → Slide Show
PRESS: Space Bar to display the next slide
PRESS: PgDn to display the next slide
PRESS: PgUp twice to display the previous slides

or

PRESS: ⬆ twice to display the previous slides

2. Explore some additional options that become available when you right-click a slide.
RIGHT-CLICK: anywhere on the current slide
The right-click menu shown in Figure 2.29 should now appear.

Figure 2.29

Right-click menu

3. To move to the next slide using the right-click menu:
   CHOOSE: Next
   Slide 2 should now appear.

4. To see a listing of the slides in your presentation and then move to a specific slide:
   RIGHT-CLICK: anywhere on the current slide
   CHOOSE: Go to Slide
   A pop-up list of your slides will now appear (Figure 2.30).

Figure 2.30

Go to Slide list

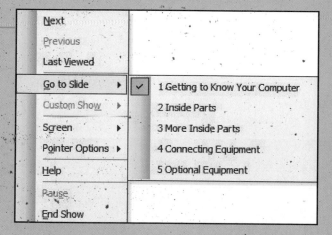

5. To display the third slide:
   CLICK: "More Inside Parts" title in the list box
   Slide 3 should now appear in Slide Show view.

6. To return to the previously viewed slide:
   RIGHT-CLICK: anywhere on the current slide
   CHOOSE: Go → Previous
   Slide 2 should reappear in the window.

7. In some presentations, a faint Slide Navigator box (Figure 2.31) will appear in the bottom-left corner of the screen showing arrow buttons for directional movement through your slides, an arrow button for the Arrow Options menu, and a menu button for the slide show right-click menu box. If you click the menu button, the right-click menu will appear.
   CLICK: menu button in the bottom-left corner of the window
   CLICK: anywhere on the screen to remove the menu

PowerPoint

Figure 2.31

Slide Navigator box

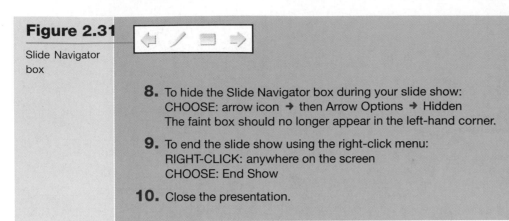

8. To hide the Slide Navigator box during your slide show:
CHOOSE: arrow icon → then Arrow Options → Hidden
The faint box should no longer appear in the left-hand corner.

9. To end the slide show using the right-click menu:
RIGHT-CLICK: anywhere on the screen
CHOOSE: End Show

10. Close the presentation.

SelfCheck

2.3   How can you go to a specific slide in Slide Show view?

Chapter
summary

Once created, your presentation can be changed with ease. You can apply alternate layouts to slides and modify existing layouts by manipulating the slide's placeholders. You can also modify the look of your slides by applying an alternate design template or changing the slide color scheme. When you are developing your slides, you can rearrange them using several methods, including the Slide Sorter. After your presentation is complete, you can view the presentation in Slide Show view and navigate the show using the keyboard or mouse.

Command Summary

Many of the commands and procedures appearing in this chapter are summarized in the following table.

Skill Set	To Perform this Task	Do the Following
Editing Presentations	Apply bold, italic, underline, or shadow text attributes	CLICK: Bold (**B**), Italic (*I*), Underline (U), or Shadow (S) buttons
	Change the current font	CLICK: down arrow beside the *Font* drop-down list (Arial)
	Change font size	CLICK: down arrow beside the *Font Size* drop-down list (32)
	Change text placeholder alignment	CLICK: Align Left button
CLICK: Align Center button
CLICK: Align Right button
	Add footer text	CHOOSE: View → Header and Footer
CLICK: *Slides* tab
	Use automatic correction features	CLICK: Spelling button
CHOOSE: Tools → AutoCorrect Options
	Change slide order	DRAG: the selected slide up or down in the Outline or Slides pane or Slide Sorter

Changing Presentation Designs	Apply a different layout	CHOOSE: Format → Slide Layout SELECT: the slides you want to format CLICK: a layout in the task pane
	Select a placeholder	CLICK: the placeholder
	Move a selected placeholder	POINT: to the placeholder until a double-headed arrow appears DRAG: the placeholder to a new location
	Resize a selected placeholder	DRAG: the placeholder's sizing handles
	Delete a selected placeholder	PRESS: [DELETE]
	Apply an alternate design template	CHOOSE: Format → Slide Design, or CLICK: Design button CLICK: thumbnail in the task pane
	Customize a color scheme	In Design task pane: CHOOSE: Color Schemes CLICK: thumbnail of color choice
Running a Slide Show	Start a slide show	CHOOSE: View → Slide Show, or CLICK: Slide Show button
	Use the keyboard to navigate a slide show	In Slide Show view: • PRESS: Space Bar, [PgDn] or [↓] to display the next slide • PRESS: [PgUp] or [↑] twice to display the previous slide
	Use on-screen navigation tools	In Slide Show view: CLICK: to advance to the next slide RIGHT-CLICK: to display slide navigation options

Key Terms

This section specifies page references for the key terms identified in this chapter. For a complete list of definitions, refer to the Glossary provided immediately after the Appendix in this learning guide.

alignment, *p. PP 50*

AutoCorrect feature, *p. PP 56*

color scheme, *p. PP 71*

Rule of 49, *p. PP 50*

sizing handles, *p. PP 67*

Slide Show, *p. PP 75*

Spell Checker, *p. PP 56*

Thesaurus, *p. PP 60*

Chapter
quiz

Short Answer

1. Describe the procedure for changing the size of a text selection from 24 points to 28 points and for making it boldface.

2. How do you create a footer?

3. If you do not want PowerPoint to capitalize the first letter after you press the (ENTER) key, how can you stop this action?

4. Describe two different ways to reorder slides.

5. How do you apply a different layout to the current slide?

6. Describe how to resize a placeholder and check for precise positioning using the ruler.

7. Explain how to select a different color scheme for the design template you are using.

8. How do you start a slide show?

9. In Slide Show view, how do you advance to the next slide using the keyboard?

10. Describe how to use the right-click menu in Slide Show view to go to a different slide.

True/False

1. _____ Formatting text involves selecting font typefaces, sizes, and attributes.

2. _____ Fonts should be carefully selected to match the tone of the presentation.

3. _____ To add footer text to a presentation, choose View, Header and Footer.

4. _____ AutoCorrect settings make it easier to keep your text sizes consistent.

5. _____ Smart quotes are special punctuation marks that you must insert with the Insert menu.

6. _____ The borderline around a text placeholder looks different depending on whether you are editing its content or moving the placeholder.

7. _____ You resize placeholders by dragging their sizing handles.

8. _____ To apply a different design template, choose Format, Slide Design from the Menu bar.

9. _____ It is possible to change a slide's layout in Slide Show view.

10. _____ Changing an existing slide layout may involve moving and resizing object placeholders.

11. _____ In Slide Show view, you can navigate a presentation only by using the mouse.

Multiple Choice

1. Which of the following lets you select a different typeface?

   a. **B**

   b. 📊

   c. 32 ▾

   d. Arial ▾

2. Which text alignment option provides a consistent beginning point to anchor title text in the same position throughout a slide show?

   a. Left

   b. Center

   c. Right

   d. Justified

3. Text size is measured in points, and one inch contains this many points:

   a. 36
   b. 60
   c. 72
   d. 96

4. As you type, the AutoCorrect feature enables you to control whether to:

   a. Capitalize the first letter of sentences
   b. Change straight quotes to smart quotes
   c. Change double hyphens to an em dash
   d. All of the above

5. To delete an existing placeholder:

   a. Double-click the placeholder
   b. Select the placeholder and press (DELETE)
   c. Drag the placeholder to outside the Slide pane
   d. All of the above

6. Text slide layouts provide placeholders for:

   a. A Title slide showing placeholders for title and subtitle text
   b. Different layout choices for slide titles and one- or two-column bulleted lists
   c. Both a and b
   d. None of the above

7. Which of the following can you include in a footer on every slide?

   a. Date and time
   b. Current slide number
   c. Text
   d. All of the above

8. You can reorder slides in:

   a. Outline and Slides pane
   b. Slide sorter view
   c. Task pane view
   d. Both a and b

9. In Slide Show view, which of the following displays the previous slide?

   a. (PgUp)
   b. (⬆)
   c. Both a and b
   d. None of the above

10. Which of the following enables you to exit Slide Show view?

   a. View, Exit
   b. File, Close
   c. File, Exit
   d. (ESC)

Hands-On
exercises

step by step

1. Modifying a Presentation

Dr. Wayne Cavanaugh, Associate Chair for the College of Business, has drafted several text slides to help him explain career opportunities to transfer students considering a major in business. He also wants to encourage students to apply for admission and available scholarships.

In this exercise, assume that you are a graduate student whom Dr. Cavanaugh has asked to revise the presentation's design and color scheme. He wants you to talk next week to students who are visiting your campus and considering transferring for the next semester.

1. Open the PP02HE01 data file and then save it as "Business Careers" to your personal storage location. Your screen should appear similar to the one shown in Figure 2.32.

Figure 2.32

"Careers in Business" presentation

Careers in Business

Dr. Wayne Cavanaugh
Associate Chair
College of Business

2. Using Slide Show view, reorder the slides 4–8 in this order:

- Accounting

- Finance

- Information Systems

- Management

- Marketing

3. To display footer information on every slide except the title slide, do the following:
CHOOSE: View ➔ Header and Footer
TYPE: ***current date*** in the *Fixed* text box
CLICK: *Slide number* check box
TYPE: **Langley College** in the *Footer* text box
CLICK: *Don't show on title slide* check box
CLICK: Apply to All command button
On slide 2, the footer should appear similar to the one shown in Figure 2.33.

Figure 2.33

Inserted footer slide 2

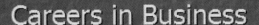

current date   Langley College   2

4. Save the revised presentation and continue with the next exercise.

2. Changing a Presentation's Design and Color Scheme

You decide to apply a different design template and color scheme to the presentation.

1. Assure that the "Business Careers" presentation is open and on slide 2. Apply the "Shimmer" design template to the presentation. (*Note:* If this template is not available on your computer, select an alternate one.) Your screen should now appear similar to the one shown in Figure 2.34.

Figure 2.34

Applying an alternate design template

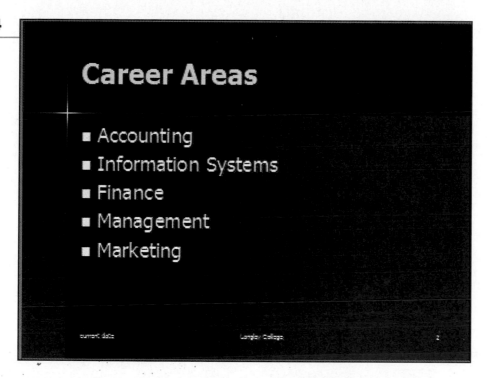

2. Modify the slide color scheme by selecting a light green background from the available choices so that your colors appear similar to those shown in Figure 2.35.

Figure 2.35

Modifying the
color scheme

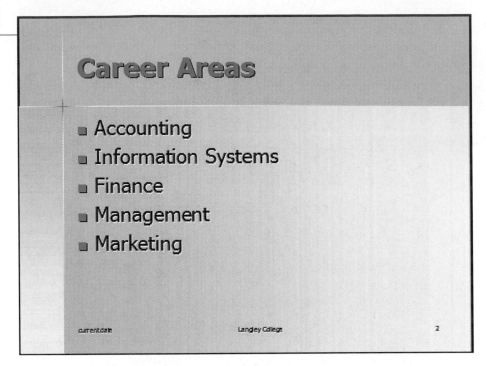

3. Use the CTRL key to select slides 1, 3, and 9, which use the Title Slide layout, in the Slide pane. Modify the slide color scheme for only these slides by choosing a dark green background from the available choices so your colors look like those shown in Figure 2.36.

Figure 2.36

Modifying the
colors of selected
slides

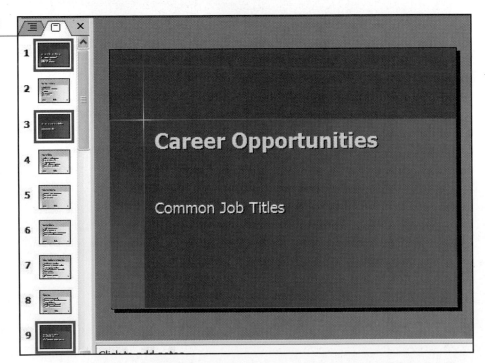

4. On slide 1, enlarge the title text to 54 points.

5. Resize the subtitle placeholder and add your name as shown in Figure 2.37.

Figure 2.37

Revised title slide text

6. Save the revised presentation and continue to the next exercise.

3. Starting and Navigating a Slide Show

Now examine the presentation in Slide Show view to be sure the slides are arranged in a logical sequence.

1. With slide 1 selected, start the presentation:
   CHOOSE: View → Slide Show

2. Use the keyboard or mouse to navigate through the presentation.

3. In case prospective students have questions about some of your slides, practice navigating to different slides in the series by using the right-click menu.

4. Print a handout with six slides on a page. On the Print dialog box, be sure to check *Scale to fit paper* and *Frame slides*. These settings will make the slides slightly larger and print a line around each slide on the page.

5. Close the presentation.

4. Modifying an AutoContent Presentation

n your own ▶

Alan Jacobson, City Manager, has decided to customize one of PowerPoint's AutoContent presentations. He will edit the content to insert his own text and make a few other changes. In this exercise, assume the role of Alan and perform the same steps he identifies.

1. Start a new presentation from the "From AutoContent Wizard" link in the task pane. Make the following selections as you advance through the wizard's steps:

   - In the Projects category, select the "Project Overview"

   - Ensure that the *On-screen presentation* option button is selected

   CLICK: the Finish command button
   Your screen should now appear similar to the one shown in Figure 2.38.

Figure 2.38

Generating an
AutoContent
presentation

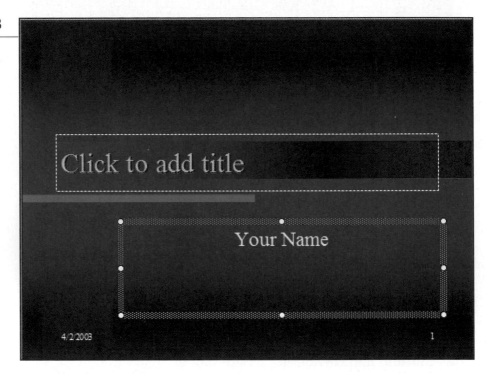

2. Type **A Concrete Solution** in the title placeholder. In the subtitle placeholder, type **The Walking Problem Resolved.**

3. Change the title placeholder to the font Arial Black and change the point size to 60. Change the subtitle text to Arial and make it bold.

4. Save the presentation as **Concrete Solutions** and resave after you complete each of the slides.

5. Click on the Slide Sorter button and then delete all slides except for these four slides: title slide "Concrete Solutions," "Description," "Team/Resources," and "Current Status."
   Note: Remember to hold down the CTRL key to select multiple slides.

6. Double-click on slide 2 to return to Normal view, then edit the content of slide 2 as shown in Figure 2.39.

Figure 2.39

Edited bulleted list

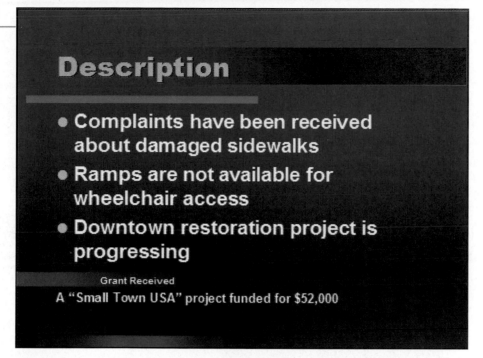

7. Edit the footer area so that the current date no longer appears.

8. Change slides 3 and 4 by replacing the slide content with this text.

Team/Resources

- J and J Construction, lowest bid
  - proposed drawings require approval by City Council
- Time frame, 5 weeks
  - removal of existing sidewalks and surface preparations, 3 weeks
  - installation of new sidewalks and landscaping improvements

Current Status

- J and J can begin once drawings are approved
  - 50% fee required before startup
  - 50% upon completion
- Time is "of the essence" to complete construction before summer tourist season.

9. Change all slide titles to the font Arial Black.

10. Check spelling and correct any errors. Examine the slides in Slide Sorter for any inconsistencies (Figure 2.40).

PowerPoint

Figure 2.40

Completed slides
in Slide Sorter

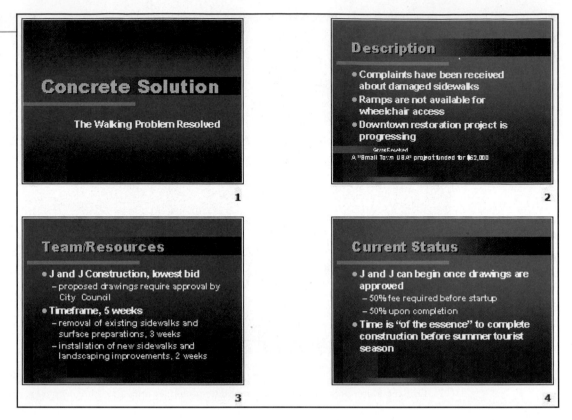

11. Save the presentation to your personal storage location.

12. Print a handout with six slides on a page. On the Print dialog box, be sure to check *Scale to fit paper* and *Frame slides*.

13. Close any presentations that remain open.

5. Creating the Presentation "Hometown Proud"

Create a presentation that describes your hometown community. Your presentation should include at least five slides. Use bulleted lists to describe characteristics that someone who is considering moving to your town would find important. For example, you could describe the schools, restaurants, athletic facilities, social activities, civic groups, and so on. Apply a design template that is appropriate for your message. (*Note:* Remember to keep your message professional.) Save your presentation as "Hometown" to your personal storage location. Print handouts and then close the presentation.

6. Creating the Presentation "Our New Business"

Create a presentation that could be used to promote a fictitious business that you and your family are opening. The presentation should include five slides. Guidelines for the five slides follow, but you must come up with the details. Be creative!

- Company Name
  Presented by: *Your Name*

- Contact information (address, phone number)

- What do we do? (services, features, or benefits)

- Where to purchase or obtain more information?

- Summary slide

Apply an appropriate design template and color scheme to the presentation. Adjust fonts as needed. Save your presentation as "New Business" to your personal storage location and then run the slide show. Print handouts and then close the presentation.

CaseStudy   MANAGING YOUR TIME

Matthew Norton, student organization president, was recently asked to speak about time management skills during Freshman Orientation Day. He has decided to prepare a slide show to help him explain important points to help these new students adapt to college life. In the following case, assume the role of Matthew and perform the steps that he identifies. You will select an appropriate design template, create slides, and add some of your own ideas. Finally, you will save your presentation and print handouts.

1. Matthew begins to develop his presentation by looking for a design template appropriate for this topic. He finds that the "Proposal" template effectively communicates the importance of budgeting time for work and other student activities.

2. Using the "Proposal" design template, Matthew enters the title and subtitle text as shown in Figure 2.41, with both the title and subtitle in boldface. Then Matthew saves the presentation as "Managing Time" to his personal storage location.

Figure 2.41

Title slide information

3. Matthew wants to begin the presentation with some thought-provoking questions that will get the students' attention. He thinks of three widely used sayings that reflect misconceptions about time. He decides to show these thoughts on a separate question and answer slide. He enters the following text for slides 2 and 3. He resaves the presentation once these slides are complete.

Questions
- **How does time "fly"?**
- **Can you "save" time?**
- **Can you "manage" your time?**

Answers
- **Time does not fly**
  - **It progresses consistently**
- **Time cannot be saved**
  - **All people have equal time**
- **You cannot manage time**
  - **You can manage what you do in the time you have**

4. The next concept that Matthew wants to cover concerns activity planning. He has observed many students who procrastinate and do not allow enough time to complete their class assignments. They then wonder why they feel so behind all the time or get poor grades because they rushed to complete their assignments. The students attending this Freshman Orientation Day received their first semester and work-study schedules right before Matthew's session, so he prepared a handout to help students master this concept. Matthew will have the students fill in their daily activities after he talks about weekly planning and creating to-do lists. Matthew uses the following text for slides 4–6 and resaves the presentation after he finishes each slide.

Planning
- **Prepare a weekly schedule**
  - **Classes and work hours**
- **Decide time needed for class preparation (2–4 hours each)**
  - **Schedule throughout the week**
- **Plan fun activities for after the work is done! Reward yourself!**

Daily To-Do
- **When the work day ends . . .**
  - **Plan for the next day**
  - **Make a list of activities**
  - **Prioritize so essential activities are finished first**

Be Flexible but Firm
- **Allow for unexpected things**
- **Learn to say no**

5. When he reviews the presentation, Matthew decides the slide titles should be emphasized more, so he applies the bold attribute to all slide titles.

6. Matthew decides to use the Title Slide layout for slide 7 so he can emphasize his ending comments. In the title placeholder, he types the words **Best Wishes as You Begin Your College Career** and allows the placeholder to AutoFit the text on two lines. He then deletes the subtitle placeholder, because it is not needed on this slide.

7. Matthew practices his presentation using Slide view and enters a few thoughts about personal stories and certain situations he wants to remember to mention in the Notes pane below the Slide pane. He may print these pages as reminders to use while he is presenting. For now, he is using this helpful area to record the ideas he is thinking about.

8. Matthew likes the looks of the presentation, so he saves it for the final time. In case of equipment or disk failure, he makes a backup copy on another disk. He prints a handout page showing slides 1–6 to use for speaker notes during his presentation. Then he closes the completed "Managing Time" presentation.

Answers to Self-Check Questions

SelfCheck

2.1 How do you rearrange slide order? Use the Outline and Slides pane or Slide Sorter view to drag and drop slide icons or thumbnails.

2.2 What is the procedure for moving and resizing object placeholders? To move a placeholder, position the mouse pointer over the placeholder until a four-headed arrow appears. Then drag the placeholder to a new location. You resize placeholders by dragging the object's sizing handles.

2.3 How can you go to a specific slide in Slide Show view? Right-click anywhere on the slide and then choose Go, Slide Navigator from the right-click menu. Then, click the slide you want to display and click the Go To command button.

Notes

Microsoft® Office PowerPoint®

2003

CHAPTER 3

◎ Adding and Editing Graphic Images

PREREQUISITES

To successfully complete this chapter, you must be able to start new presentations, select a template, apply alternate slide layouts, and move and resize object placeholders. You should also know how to use toolbars, the Menu bar, right-click menus, navigate a slideshow and to manage your files.

LEARNING OBJECTIVES

After completing this chapter, you will be able to:

- Insert clip art and pictures

- Create and modify objects using drawing tools

- Layer and recolor AutoShapes and other drawing objects

- Insert text boxes and add text to AutoShapes

- Use alignment, rotating, ordering, and grouping features

- Insert and format WordArt

3.1 Inserting Clip Art and Photographs

A picture is worth a thousand words! Although that phrase may be overused, its truth is undeniable. Graphics can help you communicate in ways that words alone cannot. When a viewer first sees a slide, his or her eye will scan the perceived image, seeing first shapes, then more complex patterns, and then text. Because you want to help your audience understand and remember your message, you can use this natural tendency to help people focus on the particular elements you want to emphasize. You can help people see relationships between concepts or apply meaning and relevance to your data.

Graphics can grab attention and also entertain. Although we are accustomed to constantly changing images displayed daily on television and the Internet and in other forms of entertainment, it is good to remember that a presentation's main purpose is not to entertain. Your goal is to convey a message—one that informs, educates, or persuades—and your visual images need to support that message. You hope your presentation will be enjoyable for your audience, but more important, it should be carefully crafted to help you make your points.

Repeated graphics on all slides of a presentation should be rather subdued, because they are the background for all of your message content. Use graphics for a valid reason, blend their colors appropriately for your color scheme, and carefully select shapes and images that fit the tone of your presentation.

At least one-half of the slides in your presentation should have some type of graphic. In this chapter we will focus on using lines, shapes, and ready-made art called clip art, as well as photographs, to communicate in a more visual way. In Chapter 4, we will take a look at tables, charts and graphs, and diagrams.

Sources for Graphic Images

PowerPoint provides for your use a large collection of images arranged in a Clip Art or Photograph category. Some of this professionally prepared artwork is installed with the program and other images are available from searching Microsoft's collection online. PowerPoint's Clip Art task pane is used to search for these images.

Each image has a different effect and will influence the tone of your presentation—some are humorous drawings, some are sophisticated drawings, and others are photographs of real objects or people. Consider the needs of your presentation as you make your selections. As a licensed user of Microsoft Office, you are authorized to use these images in your presentations.

You may also insert drawings and photographs from your own files. You may freely use photographs that you have taken; however, copyright laws govern the use of pictures that have been published, including those published on the Internet.

Think about what you do in writing a research paper when you quote an author's words. You arrange those words in quotation marks or indent them to distinguish them from your own. You also give credit to the author by making a reference citation. Apply this same idea to the use of images for in-class assignments. For example, if in an academic setting you create a slide show based on your class research project and you find an image on the Internet that you place on a slide, you may cite the resource as you would a quote in a written research paper. However, this same image could not be used in a slide show that was to be used commercially to advertise a product for a company. You would need permission to use the image and perhaps be required to pay a fee for the rights to use the image.

Many Web sites provide collections of free or inexpensive images; CD collections are also available for purchase. You should be sure that your licensing agreement authorizes you to use the images in the way you need to use them.

Graphic File Formats

Graphic images are classified into two main categories: *bitmap* images, also called paint-type or raster images, and *vector* images, also called outline images. These formats affect how a computer displays the images' colors and how the images can be edited. A computer uses pixels (picture elements or dots) arranged in a grid of rows and columns to create everything we see on a computer screen.

Bitmap Graphics

The bitmap graphics format is well suited to photographs because realistic images consist of many different colors and gradual color changes. The image will have a fixed size expressed in a pixel width and height, such as 240×200 pixels. A "map" is made of each individual colored pixel; this map resembles colored squares on graph paper. Bitmap graphics are thus "resolution dependent." When they are displayed on a PowerPoint slide and resized at a larger size, the image will look "grainy" or jagged, because the size of the pixels themselves has increased. Bitmap images can be reduced in size and still usually display correctly.

PowerPoint's Picture toolbar can be used with bitmap images to adjust the brightness and contrast, to convert a color image to black and white or grayscale, or to create transparent areas. However, to change specific colors in a bitmap, you need a program that can edit photos, such as Microsoft Paint or Adobe Photoshop. Common bitmap formats include:

- .bmp   Microsoft Windows Bitmap

- .jpg   Joint Photographic Experts Group

- .gif   Graphics Interchange Format

Vector Graphics

Line and shape drawings are usually saved in a vector graphics format. Vector graphics are made up of mathematical formulas describing the points and paths of lines used in the image and their respective fill colors. Therefore, these images are not resolution dependent—they can be scaled up or down in size without quality being reduced. Because these graphics require less storage space, their file sizes are usually smaller. Common vector formats include:

- .wmf   Windows Metafile Format

- .png   Portable Network Graphics

3.1.1 Inserting Clip Art

→ **Feature**

PowerPoint allows you to insert drawings, pictures, photographs, charts, sounds, movies, and other types of media files into your presentation. PowerPoint refers to these files as media *clips.* In this lesson, we will focus on inserting clip art, one type of media clip, in your presentations. A **clip art** image is a computer graphic or picture that you can insert in your presentation usually without having to pay royalties or licensing fees to the artist or designer. PowerPoint provides several methods for inserting clip art in your presentations. You can go directly to a selection of images, search for the right image using a typed keyword, or display a categorical listing of the clips that accompany all Microsoft Office applications.

→ **Method**

To go directly to a selection of clip art images:
- CLICK: a content placeholder
- CLICK: Insert Clip Art button (⊞) on the Drawing toolbar

To search for a clip using the Clip Art task pane:
- CHOOSE: Insert → Picture → Clip Art

    or

- CLICK: Insert Clip Art button (⊞) on the Drawing toolbar
- TYPE: a search keyword in the *Search for* box
- CLICK: Search command button in the task pane

To display a categorical listing of Microsoft Office clip art:
- CHOOSE: Insert → Picture → Clip Art

    or

- CLICK: Insert Clip Art button (⊞) on the Drawing toolbar
- CLICK: "Organize clips" link in the task pane
- DOUBLE-CLICK: Office Collections in the Collection List pane

To go to Microsoft's Online collection:
- CHOOSE: Insert → Picture → Clip Art

or

- CLICK: Insert Clip Art button (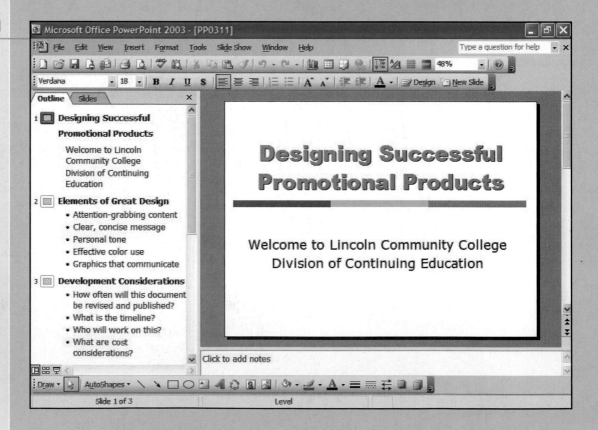) on the Drawing toolbar
- CLICK: "Clip art on Office Online" link in the task pane
- CLICK: a category

or

- TYPE: a search keyword

→ **Practice**

You will now open a short presentation that currently contains three slides. Your objective will be to locate clip art for slides 1 and 3 of the presentation. Ensure that no presentations are open in the application window.

1. Open the PP0311 data file.

2. Save the presentation as "Designing Products" to your personal storage location. Your screen should now appear similar to the one shown in Figure 3.1. If the task pane is displaying on the right side of your screen, close it now by clicking its Close button (⌐x⌐).

Figure 3.1

"Designing
Products"
presentation

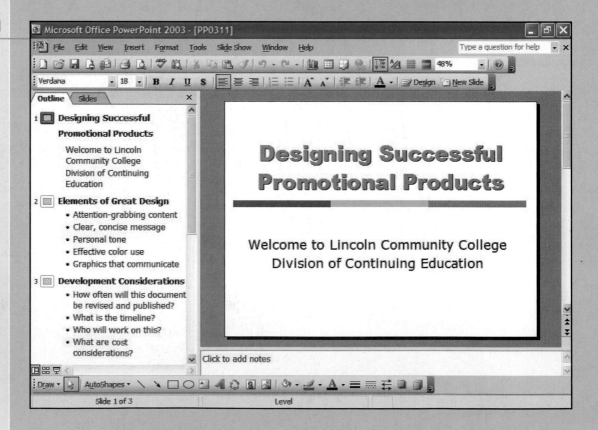

3. Go to the second slide and search for an appropriate image:
CLICK: on the *Slides* tab in the Outline and Slides pane
(*Note:* More space is now available in the Slide pane.)
CLICK: on slide 2 thumbnail
CHOOSE: Insert → Picture → Clip Art
The Insert Clip Art task pane should now appear on the right side of the screen.

4. Promotional products need to communicate well, so search for a communication-related image:
TYPE: **communication** in the *Search for* box
Your screen should now appear similar to the one shown in Figure 3.2.

Figure 3.2

Searching for images using the Clip Art task pane

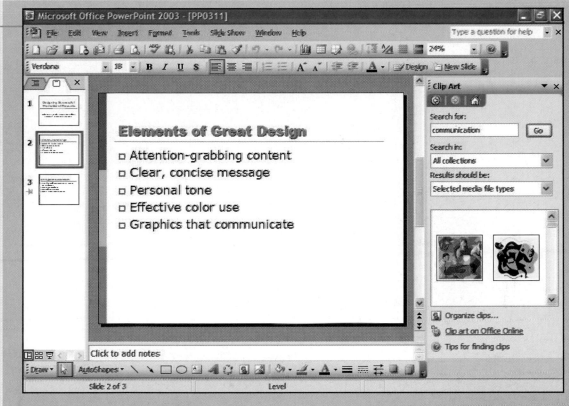

5. To proceed with the search:
CLICK: Go button
The Insert Clip Art task pane should now appear similar to the one shown in Figure 3.3.

Figure 3.3

Search results for communication-related clips

Click to expand area of search results

Catalogs all of the clips on your computer by category

Click to select only one of the available collections if you want to restrict your search:
My Collections
Office Collections
Web Collections

Click to limit the media type in your search:
Clip Art
Photographs
Movies
Sounds

Connects you to Microsoft's Office Online Clip Art and Media Collection

6. Practice pointing with the mouse at the different clips in the task pane. Note that for each clip a yellow pop-up description appears detailing the image's associated keywords, dimensions in pixel width and height, and file size and type.

7. When you click an image, it will be inserted on the current slide. In the task pane, locate the first image shown in Figure 3.3 and then do the following:
CLICK: the image shown in Figure 3.3
The image was inserted in the middle of the current slide, and the Picture toolbar also appeared. The image is surrounded with sizing handles. The green dot above the image is used to rotate it and will not be used in this exercise.

After you insert clip art and other graphics objects, you will often need to move, resize, or otherwise format them to fit the specific needs of your presentation. The methods for moving and resizing graphics objects are the same as for manipulating placeholders, a topic we discussed in Chapter 2 (lesson 2.2.2). The current slide appears in Figure 3.4.

Figure 3.4

Communication image as it first appears

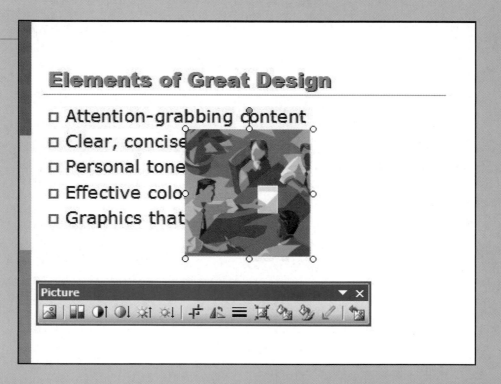

8. The floating Picture toolbar should also be displayed. Because we are not going to use the Picture toolbar in this lesson, you may close it.
CLICK: the Picture toolbar's Close button (⊠)

9. Resize and move the image to the right. Resize the bulleted list placeholder so that your slide appears similar to the one shown in Figure 3.5.

Figure 3.5

Moving and resizing a clip art image

10. Insert another image on slide 3 of this presentation, but this time use a content placeholder. To display slide 3:
PRESS: Next Slide button (⬇)
The Content placeholder icons on slide 3 appear in Figure 3.6.

Figure 3.6

Content placeholder icons

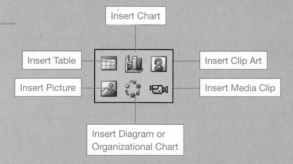

11. To insert a clip art image:
CLICK: Insert Clip Art button (🖳) in the content placeholder
The Select Picture dialog box will appear.

12. To search for the clip:
TYPE: **computer** in the *Search for* box
CLICK: Go button

13. Locate the clip shown in Figure 3.7 and then do the following:
CLICK: the clip
CLICK: OK command button
(*Note:* If the clip pictured in Figure 3.7 is not available, select an alternate clip.)

14. While referring to Figure 3.7, move and resize the image as necessary. Change the font size to 28 points to match slide 2 then resize the bulleted list placeholder so that the text word wraps as shown.

PowerPoint

Figure 3.7

Using the clip art placeholder

15. Before concluding this lesson, let's create a new slide and then look at how to display a categorical listing of clips.
    CLICK: New Slide button (New Slide)
    CLICK: Title Only layout from Slide Layout pane
    CLICK: Back button on the task pane to return to Clip Art task pane
    CLICK: Organize clips link at the bottom of the task pane
    The Clip Organizer appears in Figure 3.8.

Figure 3.8

Microsoft Clip Organizer

Contents of the Collection List will vary on different computers.

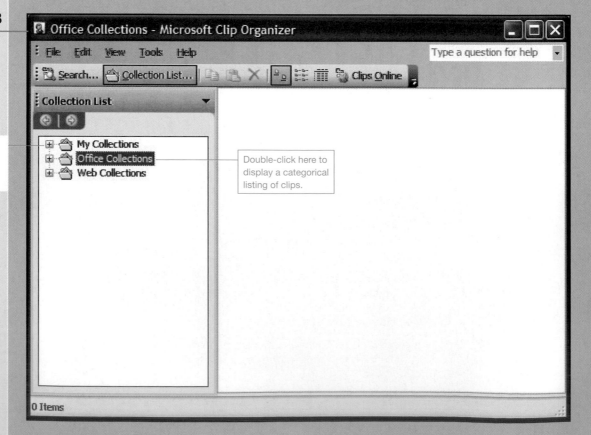

16. To display a categorical listing of Microsoft Office clips:
DOUBLE-CLICK: Office Collections folder in the left pane
A list of categories should appear in the left pane.
The dialog box should now appear similar to the one shown in Figure 3.9.

Figure 3.9

Categorical clip
art listing

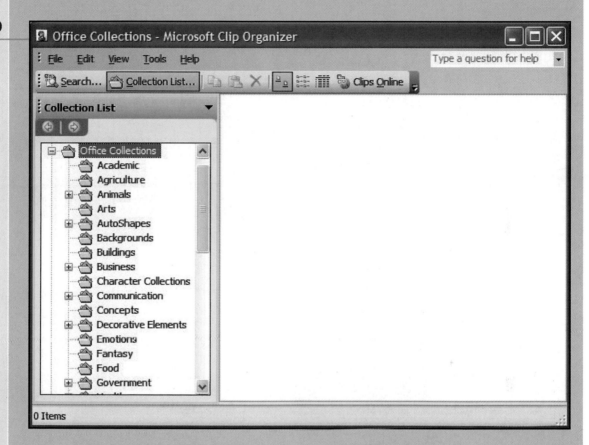

17. To display the contents of a category in the right pane, simply click a category. To illustrate:
CLICK: Buildings category in the left pane
The dialog box should now appear similar to the one shown in Figure 3.10.

Figure 3.10

Images from
the Buildings
category

18. To insert a clip from the Clip Organizer on a slide, you must copy it to the clipboard and then paste it on your slide. To illustrate, point to the lighthouse, pictured in Figure 3.10. Note that a drop-down arrow appears.
CLICK: drop-down arrow associated with the lighthouse clip
CHOOSE: Copy from the menu

19. Minimize the Clip Organizer dialog box by clicking its Minimize button (■).

20. CLICK: Paste button (▣)
The lighthouse clip should now appear on the current slide.

21. To undo the paste procedure:
CHOOSE: Edit → Undo Paste

22. To close the Clip Organizer:
RIGHT-CLICK: its button on the taskbar (located on the bottom of your screen)
CHOOSE: Close from the right-click menu

In Addition SEARCHING TIPS

If you know that you only want to see clip art images, and no photographs, movies, or sounds, then you can speed up the search process by selecting that media type only when you start your search. If you are connected to the Internet, PowerPoint will automatically include search results from Microsoft's Office Online. Clips that came from this source will display a small world icon in the thumbnail corner that does not reproduce when you use the image. You can visit the site yourself by clicking the link at the bottom of the Clip Art task pane.

Indicates online clip

23. To search for photographic images only, change your search results to Photographs only and search for "computer." On your own, practice inserting a photograph and resizing it.

24. Delete slide 4 from your presentation.

25. Save and then close the revised presentation.

3.1.2 Inserting Pictures from Files

→ **Feature**

Digital images, captured with a camera or scanned from photo prints, can easily be inserted into a PowerPoint presentation. Once inserted, the image can be moved, resized, or edited to meet your particular needs.

→ **Method**

- CHOOSE: Insert → Picture → From File
- SELECT: the desired disk drive and filename
- CLICK: Insert command button

→ **Practice**

You will now practice inserting a picture object from a file. Ensure that no presentations are open in the application window.

1. To begin a blank presentation and then select the Title Only layout in the task pane:
CLICK: New button ()
CLICK: Title Only layout in the task pane

2. Let's edit the title placeholder:
CLICK: in the title placeholder
TYPE: **Picture Adjustments**

3. To insert a photograph that we have provided for you:
CHOOSE: Insert → Picture → From File
The Insert Picture dialog box should appear similar, but not identical, to the one shown in Figure 3.11. You'll always need to select the location where the images are stored.

PowerPoint

Figure 3.11

Insert Picture
dialog box with
images displayed
as thumbnails

4. To insert a file named PP0312 from the student files location:
SELECT: *the location of your student files*
SELECT: PP0312 from the Insert Picture dialog box
CLICK: Insert command button
The picture is inserted on the slide and appears selected. The Picture toolbar also appears (Figure 3.12).
CLICK: the corner handles and drag them to resize and make the picture slightly larger, as shown in Figure 3.13.

Figure 3.12

Picture toolbar

Figure 3.13

"Picture
Adjustments" first
slide

5. Save the presentation as "Picture Adjustments" to your personal storage location.

6. Keep the presentation open and continue to the next lesson.

3.1.3 Cropping and Editing Pictures

→ **Feature**

If photographs are too dark, they can be improved in appearance with adjustments in brightness and contrast using the Picture toolbar. They can be edited to remove extra portions of the image through **cropping** and adding border lines to frame the image. They can even be converted from color to **grayscale** or **washout**.

→ **Method**

When you have inserted a picture, choose the following methods to edit it:

- CLICK: Color (⊞) to change from Automatic coloring to Grayscale, Black and White, or Washout

- CLICK: More Contrast (▣) or Less Contrast (▣) to sharpen or soften colors

- CLICK: More Brightness (▣) or Less Brightness (▣) to add or remove light in the picture

- CLICK: Crop (⌗) to trim the picture edges

- CLICK: Rotate (▣) to angle the picture 90 degrees to the left

- CLICK: Line Style (☰) to place a border around the picture

- CLICK: Compress Pictures (▣) to reduce the image file size

- CLICK: Format Picture (▣) to control many settings, including size and position, from one dialog box

PowerPoint

- CLICK: Set Transparent Color ( ) to make one color in an image transparent (effective for simple images on a white background)

- CLICK: Reset Picture ( ) to restore the image to its original state before editing

- CLICK: Insert Picture ( ) to add another picture
  (*Note:* Recolor Picture ( ) is not available when the image is in a bitmap graphic format.)
  CLICK: Insert command button

→ **Practice**

You will now practice editing pictures. Ensure that the "Picture Adjustments" presentation is open in the application window. So you can observe the results of the changes you are about to make, let's use two copies of an image and position them as shown in Figure 3.14.

1. Create a new slide with a Title Only layout:
CLICK: New slide button (New Slide)
CLICK: Title Only layout in the task pane

2. Let's edit the title placeholder:
CLICK: in the title placeholder
TYPE: **Contrast/Brightness**

3. To insert a file named PP0313 from the student files location:
SELECT: *the location of your student files*
SELECT: PP0313 from the Insert Picture dialog box
CLICK: Insert command button
The picture is inserted on the slide and appears selected. When the picture is selected, the Picture toolbar appears (see Figure 3.12).

4. Now reposition the first picture and make a duplicate copy:
DRAG: this picture without resizing (be sure you see the four-tipped arrow before trying to move the picture) to the left
PRESS: CTRL + **d** to duplicate the picture and move the second picture to the right of the screen

Figure 3.14

Two pictures for comparison of editing changes

Contrast/Brightness

5. Now make changes to the picture on the right:
CLICK: to select the picture
CLICK: the More Brightness button (🔆) 3–4 times to make the room furnishings more visible (notice that this reduces the distant hills showing through the windows)
CLICK: the More Contrast button (🔆) 3–4 times to sharpen the color in the image
CLICK: the Less Brightness button (🔆) or the Less Contrast button (🔆) if you change the image too much
CLICK: the Reset Picture button (🔆) if you need to go back to the original version of the image

6. After you are satisfied with the changes in the second image, add borders to both of the pictures:
CLICK: the picture on the left
CLICK: the Line Style button (≡) and select a 3-point line
CLICK: the picture on the right
CLICK: the Line Style button (≡) and select a 6-point line
In the next module, you will gain even more experience in changing these lines. For now, you need only to notice that the line provides a more distinctive edge to the picture and, depending on your use, may improve the appearance of the picture in your presentation. You will need to determine the appropriate line thickness based on the colors you are using and the size of the image.

7. Now let's make a copy of this slide so you can practice two more picture adjustments. A quick way to do this is to duplicate the slide using either the Slide Sorter window or the *Slides* tab.
CLICK: the slide thumbnail in the *Slides* tab
PRESS: CTRL + **d** to duplicate and create slide 3
DOUBLE-CLICK: to bring slide 3 to the slide pane

8. Change the slide 3 title to **Washout and Crop.**

9. Now modify the picture on the left:
CLICK: the picture on the left
CLICK: the Color button (🎨) and try both the Grayscale and Black & White treatments; then return to Automatic
(*Note:* The Grayscale treatment will change a color picture into a picture with only shades of gray; Black & White will change the picture into a line art image, because only solid black areas will show.)
CLICK: the Color button (🎨) and select Washout
The image colors have a very faint appearance. You might use an effect like this as a subtle background effect when you are placing text over the image.

10. Now modify the picture on the right:
CLICK: the picture on the right
CLICK: the Crop button (🔲)
You will notice that the markings on the edges of the picture look different. Now when you resize the edges of the picture, you are cropping, or trimming, the picture.
DRAG: the sides of the picture until you have focused on the two chairs and ottoman between them
CLICK: somewhere else on the slide to turn off the crop tool
DRAG: the picture up slightly as shown in Figure 3.15
Use this technique to focus your audience's attention on important elements of the picture and to remove any unnecessary details.

Figure 3.15

Washout example
and cropped
picture

11. Create a new slide with a Title Only layout:
CLICK: New slide button ( New Slide)
CLICK: Title Only layout in the task pane

12. Let's edit the title placeholder:
CLICK: in the title placeholder
TYPE: **Transparent Color**

13. Using the Clip Art task pane, search for "candle." You may not find the same image as shown on
the left in Figure 3.16, but find an image that has a solid-colored background.
CLICK: the search thumbnail to insert the picture

14. As you did before, arrange two copies of this picture:
DRAG: the picture to the left without resizing (*Note:* be sure you see the four-tipped arrow before
trying to move the picture.)
PRESS: (CTRL) + **d** to duplicate the picture and move the second picture to the right of the screen

Figure 3.16

Making a solid-color background transparent

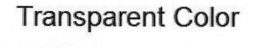

15. Now remove the background of the picture on the right in Figure 3.16:
CLICK: the picture on the right
The Picture toolbar should be available. If it does not pop up, then
CHOOSE: View → Toolbars → Picture
CLICK: the Set Transparent Color button (), and your mouse pointer changes to an eraser
CLICK: the solid-colored background on the image, and it becomes transparent
This tool can erase only one color; if you click somewhere else on the image, the background color will return, and the new color will be transparent. However, it is an effective tool in situations in which you want to remove solid-colored areas.

In Addition REMOVING MULTIPLE COLORS

Because PowerPoint's Set Transparent Color button ( ) can remove only one color, you might prefer to use a photo editing program such as Microsoft Photo Editor or Microsoft Paint to edit the picture even further by painting color or by removing pixels with an eraser tool. When using a program like this, be sure to magnify the image so you can work in detail.

16. Save your presentation and continue to the next lesson.

3.1.4 Making and Inserting Screen Captures

→ **Feature**

A screen capture is a copied image of the contents displayed on a computer screen, regardless of the program used to create that image. You can capture an entire screen or only the active window. Commonly used for computer documentation, screen captures (such as the figures in this book) can also be used for presentations. For example, you might want to show the home page of a particular Web site when you cannot be connected to the Internet to actually load the site.

PowerPoint

→ # Method

Screen captures are made by placing a copy of the current screen display in your clipboard:

- PRESS: the PRTSCR key on your keyboard to capture the entire computer display
- PRESS: the ALT + PRTSCR to capture the active window only

To use this image, go to the location where you want to place the captured image:

- PRESS: Copy button (⊡)
- Resize or crop the image as needed

→ # Practice

You will now practice making a screen capture. Ensure that the "Picture Adjustments" presentation is open in the application window.

1. Create a new slide with a Title Only layout:
CLICK: New slide button (⊡ New Slide)
CLICK: Title Only layout in the task pane

2. Let's edit the title placeholder:
CLICK: in the title placeholder
TYPE: **Screen Capture**

3. To make a capture of your computer's current open window:
PRESS: ALT + PRTSCR

4. To add this image to your current slide:
CLICK: Paste button (⊡)

5. Move the image below your title placeholder. You may need to make it slightly smaller. To keep your resizing in accurate proportions, hold down the SHIFT key as you drag the handles to resize. Match the positioning in Figure 3.17.

6. Save and then close the revised presentation.

Figure 3.17

Screen capture example

3.2 Using Drawing Tools to Illustrate Concepts

While PowerPoint's drawing tools allow you to add decorative enhancements to your slides, their most important function is to help you make your points more effectively. Well-designed graphics can help you communicate the message of your presentation in a more visual way. For example, you might want to use text to label parts of an image with arrows pointing to particular places, or you might want to arrange text on a rectangle with a contrasting color to draw attention to that information. Emphasis could be added to slide titles by adding a line below the text in a color that blends with your slide color scheme.

When drawing, you create objects such as lines, arrows, and text boxes. These objects are automatically stacked in individual layers as you add them to your slides. You see the stacking order when objects overlap. This stacking order can be changed by moving an object forward or backward one layer at a time or to the top or bottom of the objects in the stack. Objects you draw can also be grouped so they function as one object.

In this module, you will learn how to insert and manipulate a variety of graphic objects.

3.2.1 Creating, Coloring, Ordering, and Aligning

→ Feature

Lines, arrows, rectangles, ovals, and other shapes are easy to create using tools on the Drawing toolbar. When you select a tool, you draw with that tool by moving your mouse. Adjustments for line style, **fill colors,** and sizing can be made using other tools or menu selections. You can move and copy objects using standard drag and drop techniques. These objects can draw the viewer's attention to specific areas or simply enhance a presentation's visual appearance.

→ Method

- CLICK: a drawing tool button on the Drawing toolbar
- CLICK: to start drawing with the tool
- DRAG: to complete drawing the object in the size you want
- CLICK: the Fill Color button (⬛▾) to select different colors
- CLICK: the Line Color button (✏▾) to select different line colors
- DRAG: the object to move it
- PRESS: `CTRL` + **d** to duplicate an object

→ Practice

You will now create a line and a rectangle, adjust size and colors, reorder layer positioning, and duplicate an object. Ensure that no documents are open in the application window.

1. Open the PP0321 data file.

2. Save the document as "Desert Valley Realty" to your personal storage location. The presentation should now appear similar to the one shown in Figure 3.18. In the next few steps, you will emphasize the title and make the pictures look more distinctive.

PowerPoint

Figure 3.18

"Desert Valley Realty" title slide

3. To add graphics, you must use the Drawing toolbar. By default, this toolbar is positioned along the bottom of the application window.
Note: If this toolbar is not displaying,
CHOOSE: View → Toolbars → Drawing

4. Create a horizontal line and position it below the presentation title to emphasize that text. Be sure to drag the mouse horizontally left to right. Dragging slightly upward or downward will create a slanted line. Holding the **SHIFT** key down while dragging will constrain the angle of the line, making it easier to draw a straight line. Do the following:
CLICK: Line button (◻) on the Drawing toolbar
Position the mouse pointer below the first letter, in the title, "D."

5. DRAG: the cross-hair pointer to the right so that the line extends to the right edge of the slide. To complete the operation, release the mouse button.

6. Change the line's formatting characteristics. With the line still selected:
CLICK: Line Color button (◻▾) to access the pop-up menu (Figure 3.19)
CLICK: the third color from the right, a teal color, from the row of small color samples that make up the palette of this design template

Figure 3.19

Line Color pop-up menu

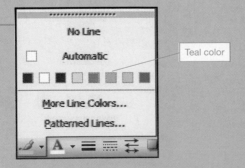

Teal color

7. To change the weight (thickness) of the line to 6 points:
CLICK: the Line Style button (▤)
SELECT: 6 pt from the *Line Style* pop-up menu (Figure 3.20)

Figure 3.20

Line Style pop-up menu

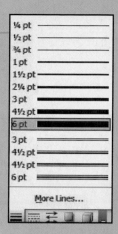

8. Now create a rectangle that will soon be placed behind the picture to frame it:
CLICK: Rectangle button (▢)
DRAG: to create a rectangle over the picture and make it slightly larger than the picture

9. Now let's recolor this rectangle and change it to a **gradient,** or range of blended colors, fill that will complement the slide background.
CLICK: Fill Color button (▨▾)
SELECT: Fill Effects
CLICK: *Gradient* tab

10. Now match the colors to the ones used on the background, as shown in Figure 3.21. Leave the Transparency setting at 0%.
CLICK: *Shading styles* Diagonal up
CLICK: Variant top row, left (Notice the border line that shows selection.)

Figure 3.21

Fill Effects dialog box

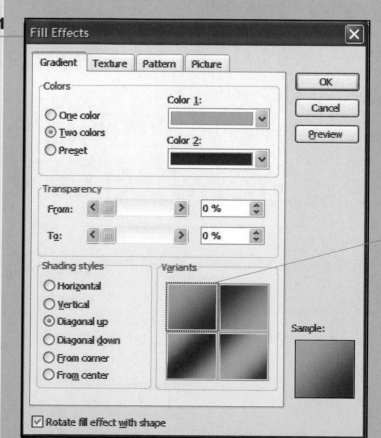

This gradient is in the opposite direction from the slide background colors, so this treatment will create an interesting effect behind the picture.

11. Change the thickness (weight) of the line to 6 points and the color to brown:
CLICK: the Line Style button (▤)
SELECT: 6 pt from the *Line Style* drop-down list
CLICK: the Line Color button (▨▾)
SELECT: brown, the third color from the left

12. The rectangle object appears surrounded by eight white circles (Figure 3.22). These circles, called **sizing handles,** work the same way as those of the placeholders you adjusted in a previous lesson to modify the height and width of the object. These handles appear only when an object is selected. The green circle is a **rotation handle** that lets you change the angle of the object. You will use it in the next lesson.

Figure 3.22

Gradient fill applied with line color and thickness changed

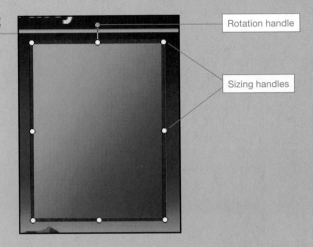

Rotation handle

Sizing handles

13. Let's move the selected rectangle behind the woman's picture:
CLICK: Draw button (Draw▾) on the Drawing toolbar
CHOOSE: Order → Send to Back

14. Adjust the size and position of the rectangle to evenly frame the picture. If you need to make only slight movements, you can use the arrow keys to gently "nudge" an object into position.
CLICK: away from the object
Your screen should now appear similar to the one shown in Figure 3.23.

Figure 3.23

"Desert Valley Realty" adjusted title slide

15. Now copy the rectangle and position it behind the picture on slide 2 (Figure 3.24).
    CLICK: to select the rectangle
    PRESS: CTRL + **c** to copy
    CLICK: ➡ to go to slide 2
    PRESS: CTRL + **v** to paste
    (*Note:* Resize the bulleted list placeholder as necessary to fit beside the image.)

16. Repeat steps 13 and 14 to adjust order so the rectangle is behind the picture; then adjust the rectangle size.

17. Repeat steps 15, 13, and 14 for slide 3.

Figure 3.24

Slides 2 and 3

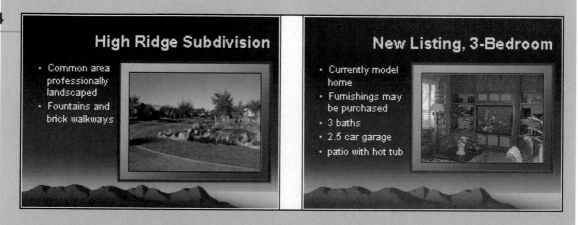

18. Save the presentation and continue to the next lesson.

3.2.2 Aligning with Rulers, Grids, and Guides

→ ## Feature

You can achieve precise positioning of objects on your slides by using rulers, **grids,** or guides. These features can help you achieve consistency in the positioning of objects from slide to slide.

→ ## Method

To use the ruler:

- CHOOSE: View → Ruler

   To use a grid or guide:

- CHOOSE: View → Grid and Guides

   or

- CLICK: Draw (Drawing toolbar), Grid and Guides

- SELECT: Grid and Guides

→ ## Practice

You will now use these methods to check the alignment of the objects you added to the "Desert Valley Realty" presentation.

1. On slide 1, add the Ruler as shown in Figure 3.25. The Ruler displays on the top and left and is measured from 0 at the midpoint of the slide.

Figure 3.25

Ruler

2. As you move your mouse pointer over the slide, you will see its position marked with a straight line on the Ruler at the top and left. These measurements can help you position objects.

3. Turn off the Ruler:
CHOOSE: View → Ruler

4. Now add guides to your slide pane. Guides are fine marks that cross the entire slide to help with placing objects. They display only on the slide while you are working and not on the slide when you view it in a slide show.
CLICK: Draw (in the Drawing toolbar)
SELECT: Grid and Guides from the Grid and Guides dialog box (Figure 3.26):
CLICK: *Display grid on screen* (☑)
CLICK: drop-down list and choose ½₄
CLICK: OK command button

Figure 3.26

Grid and Guides dialog box

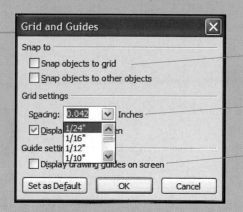

Snap to can help you align your objects by sliding them to the nearest grid point.

Grid settings control how far apart the alignment points appear.

The *Guide* appears as one vertical and one horizontal line that you can position to help with judging alignment.

5. Your slide should now look like the one shown in Figure 3.27. Examine the positioning of slide objects on the three slides to see if you need to make any adjustments for consistent placement.

Figure 3.27

Grid displayed on slide 2

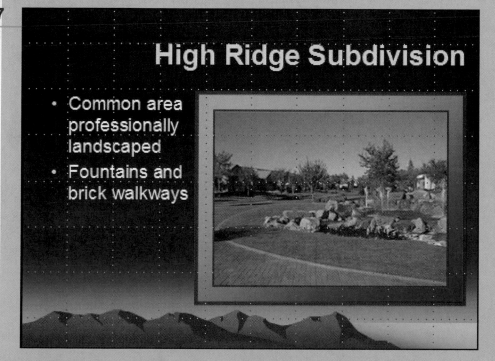

6. Save your presentation.

7. Now let's make the Snap feature available:
CLICK: Draw button → Grid and Guides
From the *Grid and Guides* dialog box:
CLICK: *Snap objects to grid* (if not selected)
SELECT: *Display grid on screen*
CLICK: drop-down list and choose ⅕″
CLICK: OK command button

8. Now move one of the objects on your slide to see how the Snap feature has changed your placement. As you move it, the object will align only on the grid, as it "snaps" to the closest vertical and horizontal grid points.
(*Note:* To temporarily disable the Snap feature, press [ALT] as you drag the object.)

9. Turn off the Grid and Snap features and add a Guide:
CLICK: Draw → Grid and Guides
From the *Grid and Guides* dialog box:
CLICK: to disable the Snap feature
CLICK: to turn off the Grid feature
CLICK: *Display drawing guides on screen*
CLICK: OK command button

10. Guides are fine horizontal and vertical lines (Figure 3.28) that you can reposition by dragging them to a particular location. For example, you could use these lines to check the position of slide titles or bullet lists for consistency across several slides.

Figure 3.28

Guide displayed on slide 2

11. Close your presentation without saving these last changes.

3.2.3 Using Drawing Tools and AutoShapes

→ ## Feature

PowerPoint's Drawing toolbar has convenient buttons for line, arrow, rectangle, and oval tools, and many other shapes are available through the **AutoShapes** menu. Objects that you draw can help to focus the viewer's attention to specific areas, illustrate with diagrams, or simply enhance a presentation's visual appearance.

→ ## Method

- CLICK: a tool button on the Drawing toolbar or in the AutoShapes menu
- CLICK: on a slide to begin drawing the object
- DRAG: the object's sizing handles to size the object
- DRAG: the center of the object to move it

→ ## Practice

You will now insert and manipulate drawing objects. Ensure that no documents are open in the application window.

1. Open the PP0323 data file.

2. Save the document as "Trace Enterprise" to your personal storage location. The title slide should now appear similar to the one shown in Figure 3.29. In the next few steps, you are going to add the shapes to slides 2–4. In the next lesson you will add more text.

Figure 3.29

"Trace Enterprise" title slide

3. To add graphics, you must use the Drawing toolbar. By default, this toolbar is positioned along the bottom of the application window.
(*Note:* If this toolbar is not displayed, right-click an existing toolbar and then select Drawing from the pop-up menu.)

4. Go to slide 2 and create an AutoShapes rectangle with rounded corners (Figure 3.30). To begin:
CLICK: AutoShapes button ([AutoShapes▾]) on the Drawing toolbar
SELECT: Basic Shapes
SELECT: Rounded Rectangle

Figure 3.30

AutoShapes menu with Basic Shapes selected

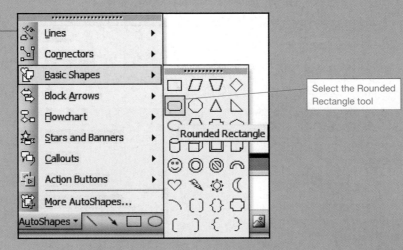

Select the Rounded Rectangle tool

5. The pop-up menu disappears and your mouse pointer changes to a small crosshair as you move it over the slide area. Hold down your left mouse button as you click and drag to create the box shown in Figure 3.31.

Figure 3.31

Rounded rectangle with handles

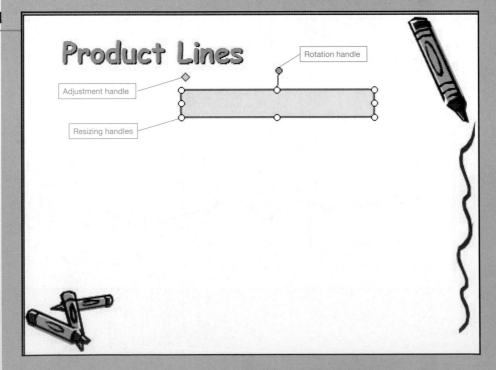

6. The rounded rectangle appears surrounded by the eight white circles called sizing handles that only appear when the object is selected. As you learned in the previous lesson, you use these handles to modify the height and width of the object using the mouse. The yellow diamond is an **adjustment handle** that lets you change the appearance, not the size, of most AutoShapes. The green circle is a rotation handle that lets you angle objects on the screen.

7. In the previous lesson you learned to use the Fill and Line tools, so let's use the Format AutoShape dialog box to adjust these settings for this shape, as shown in Figure 3.32.
   CHOOSE: Format → AutoShape
   CLICk: *Colors and Lines* tab
   (*Note:* You can also double-click an object to display this dialog box.)
   CLICK: the Color box and select a gold color to match the crayon images on the slide background

Figure 3.32

Format AutoShape dialog box, *Colors and Lines* tab

8. Before closing this dialog box, adjust the size of the rounded rectangle.
   CLICK: *Size* tab
   SELECT: .6″ for height and 4.25″ for width, as shown in Figure 3.33.
   CLICK: OK command button

Figure 3.33

Format
AutoShape dialog
box, *Size* tab

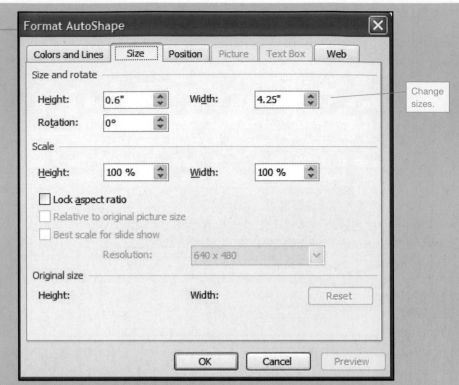

9. Now duplicate the rounded rectangle and position the duplicate copy below the first rectangle:
   PRESS: **CTRL** + **d** to duplicate and then reposition the second rounded rectangle
   PRESS: **CTRL** + **d** three more times to create a total of five rounded rectangles

10. Now use a "lasso" technique to select all five rounded rectangles so they can be aligned with each other.
    CLICK: Select objects tool ( )
    CLICK: above and to the left of the first rectangle and hold down the left mouse button
    DRAG: down and to the right to draw a broken line around all five rectangles, as shown in Figure 3.34
    RELEASE: the mouse button to select them all as shown in Figure 3.35

Figure 3.34

Lasso selection
technique

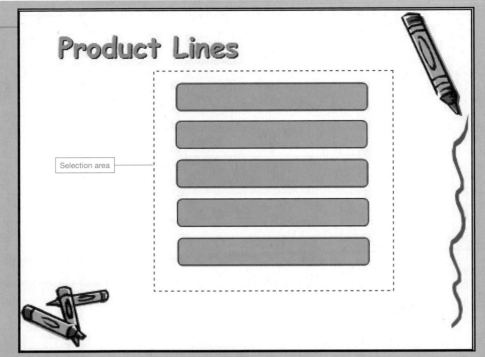

11. With all five objects selected:
    CLICK: Draw button → Align or Distribute → Distribute Vertically
    CLICK: Draw button → Align or Distribute → Align Left
    Now the five boxes are aligned evenly with each other.
    CLICK: in any blank space on the slide to turn off the selection handles

Figure 3.35

Multiple select objects and alignment options

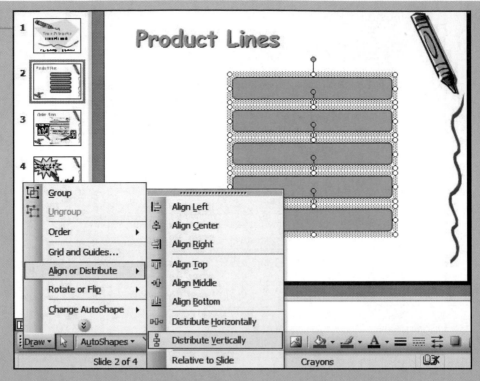

12. At the bottom of this slide, draw a wavy line to match the purple line on the right. To begin:
CLICK: AutoShapes button (AutoShapes▾) on the Drawing toolbar
SELECT: Lines
SELECT: Scribble (Figure 3.36)
Draw a wavy line to connect the crayon on the lower left to the wavy line on the right

Figure 3.36

Line options

Use the Sribble line tool to draw a line with a pen as you move the mouse.

13. Adjust the line style to make it thicker and change the line color.
CLICK: Line Color button and change to purple
CLICK: Line Style button and, from the pop-up menu, change the thickness to 6 points

14. On slide 3, the form displayed contains text that is too small to read. Therefore, you need to position callout boxes to describe key portions of the form. In this step, you will create the callout shapes. To begin:
CLICK: AutoShapes button (AutoShapes▼) on the Drawing toolbar
SELECT: Callouts
SELECT: Rectangular Callout (Figure 3.37)
Drag a box on the left side of the form image. Adjust where the callout points by dragging the adjustment handle at the tip of the callout.

Figure 3.37

Callout shapes

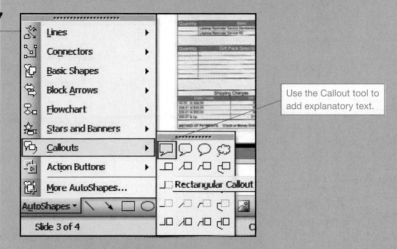

15. Duplicate the callout box and position the second callout on the right side of the form. Adjust the point by dragging the adjustment handle at the tip of the callout as shown on Figure 3.38.
PRESS: CTRL + **d** to duplicate then adjust

Figure 3.38

Image with rectangular callouts

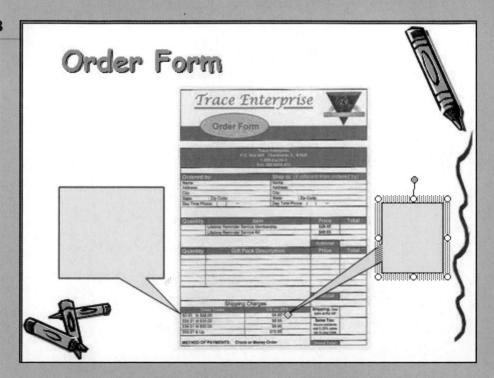

16. On slide 4, create a star shape in the upper left of the slide. To begin:
CLICK: AutoShapes button ([AutoShapes▾]) on the Drawing toolbar
SELECT: Stars and Banners
SELECT: Explosion 1 (Figure 3.39)
Draw a star shape at the upper left of the slide about halfway across the slide. Move the star to let some of the points extend off the edge of the slide.

Figure 3.39

Stars and
Banners

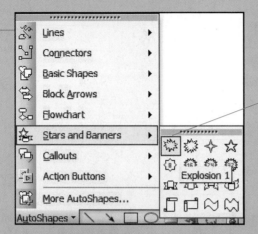

This star shape has random points.

17. Add a black shadow to make the shape more distinctive. In the Drawing toolbar:
CLICK: on Shadow Style (▣) button
SELECT: Shadow Style 5 (Figure 3.40)

Figure 3.40

Shadow Style

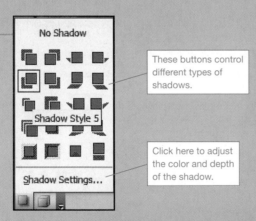

These buttons control different types of shadows.

Click here to adjust the color and depth of the shadow.

18. A shadow appears, but it is not black. To change the color,
CLICK: Shadow Style (▣) button
SELECT: Shadow Settings, and a separate toolbar appears (Figure 3.41)
CLICK: Shadow Color and select black
CLICK: Semitransparent Shadow option so the color is solid black
CLOSE: Shadow Settings box

Figure 3.41

Shadow Settings

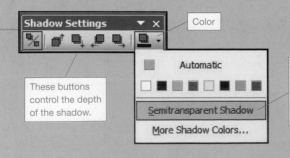

These buttons control the depth of the shadow.

Because this menu item is highlighted, the current shadow is semitransparent; click to remove this treatment and make the shadow a solid color.

19. Now draw an AutoShapes arrow and angle it on the screen.
    CLICK: AutoShapes button (AutoShapes ▾) on the Drawing toolbar
    SELECT: Block Arrows
    SELECT: Right Arrow (Figure 3.42)

Figure 3.42

Block Arrows

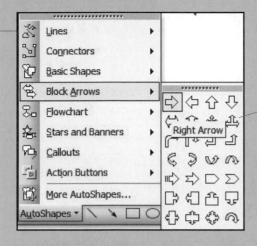

All of these arrows can be rotated

20. Draw a Block arrow at the bottom of the star shape and change its color to red as shown in Figure 3.43.
    CLICK: Fill color button (◻▾) then select red

Figure 3.43

Star and red arrow

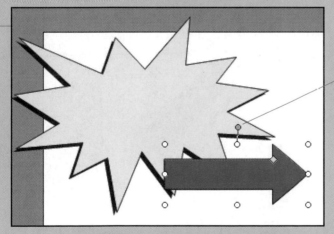

Use the rotation handle to make the arrow point down.

21. Save the revised presentation and keep it open for use in the next lesson.

3.2.4 Rotating and Grouping Objects

→ **Feature**

In PowerPoint, you can control how objects are layered on a slide. That is, you can control whether an object is positioned in front of or behind another object or in front of or behind text. When an image is composed of multiple objects, you might want to group the objects together before moving, copying, or resizing the image.

PowerPoint

→ ## Method

To change where an object appears in relation to other objects and text:

- SELECT: an object
- CLICK: Draw button (Draw▼) on the Drawing toolbar
- SELECT: Order
- SELECT: an option from the Order menu

To create a single object out of a group of objects:

- DRAG: with the mouse pointer, the lasso technique, to select the objects to be grouped
- CLICK: Draw button (Draw▼) on the Drawing toolbar
- SELECT: Group

→ ## Practice

You will rotate an object and adjust the order of the two objects on slide 4 of the "Trace Enterprise" presentation. Then, you will group the rounded rectangles on slide 2 to form a single object.

1. Ensure that the "Trace Enterprise" presentation is open and that you are currently on slide 4.

2. With the arrow selected, rotate it downward:
CLICK: Rotation handle (green dot handle) and drag to make the arrow point downward

3. Because you created the arrow after you created the star, the arrow is stacked on top of the star. To change this layering and reorder the arrow behind the star
CLICK: Draw button
SELECT: Order

Figure 3.44

Changing order
of objects

As you draw, all objects are stacked—use these options to adjust layering order.

SELECT: Send to Back (Figure 3.44):

4. Now go to slide 2 and select the five rounded rectangles.
DRAG: over all five rectangles to lasso and select them
(*Note:* Another way to select multiple items is to press the **SHIFT** key as you click on each different item you want to select.)

5. All five of the rectangles show sizing and rotation handles. To create a single object out of these five objects:
CLICK: Draw button () on the Drawing toolbar
CHOOSE: Group
The rectangles are now joined into one object and now the group of rectangles has one set of sizing handles, as shown in Figure 3.45.

Figure 3.45

Grouped objects with one set of sizing handles

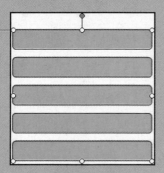

6. Save the revised presentation and keep it open for use in the next lesson.

SelfCheck   **3.2** When is it helpful to use to grids or guides?

PowerPoint

3.3 Inserting Text and WordArt

When building presentations in PowerPoint, you will usually insert text in a slide's existing title, subtitle, and bulleted list placeholders. However, when you want to label a drawing object, picture, or chart, you will need greater control over where text is positioned. In this module, you will learn how to add text to AutoShape objects, position text using text boxes, and create decorative text treatments with WordArt.

3.3.1 Adding Text on AutoShapes

→ **Feature**

When used appropriately, AutoShapes help to grab your audience's attention. As such, they serve as the perfect backdrop for the words and phrases that need special emphasis.

→ **Method**

To add text to an AutoShape:

- CLICK: the AutoShape
- TYPE: *the text you want to insert*

To invoke text wrapping inside the AutoShape:

- CLICK: the AutoShape
- CHOOSE: Format → AutoShape
- CLICK: *Text Box* tab
- CLICK: *Word wrap text in AutoShape* check box
- CLICK: OK command button

→ **Practice**

In this lesson, you insert text inside the AutoShape objects on slides 2, 3, and 4.

1. Ensure that the "Trace Enterprise" presentation is open and you are currently on slide 2.

2. CLICK: once to select the grouped rectangles
CLICK: the top rectangle to select it
(*Note:* Different handles indicate a subselection.)
TYPE: **Scrapbook Layouts**

3. Repeat this process for each of the remaining boxes and enter the following text:
TYPE: **Scissors and Punches**
TYPE: **Albums and Paper**
TYPE: **Ribbons and Tapes**
TYPE: **And Lots More!**

4. Even though the rectangles are grouped, you need to lasso the whole group to change the text attributes:
DRAG: around all five rectangles
CLICK: Bold button (B)

CLICK: Left alignment button (≡)
Your rectangles should appear as Figure 3.46.

Figure 3.46

AutoShape
rectangles with
text

5. While referring to Figure 3.47, enter text in the Callout boxes on slide 3 and change font sizes and alignment.

Figure 3.47

Callout boxes with text

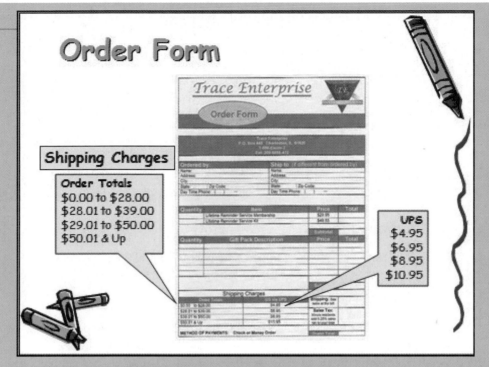

6. In the left callout box, change to left alignment and change the font size:
CLICK: the callout box
CLICK: Left Align button (≣)
CHOOSE: 18 point size
TYPE: the following text and make "Order Totals" bold:

Order Totals
$0.00 to $28.00
$28.01 to $39.00
$29.01 to $50.00
$50.01 & Up

7. In the right callout box, change to right alignment and change the font size:
CLICK: the callout box
CLICK Right Align button (≣)
CHOOSE: 18 point size
TYPE: the following text and make "UPS" bold:

UPS
$4.95
$6.95
$8.95
$10.95

8. Adjust the sizes and positions of the callout boxes if necessary.
(*Note:* You will add the text for Shipping Charges in the next lesson.)

9. Now go to slide 4 and add text to the star object:
CLICK: the star object
CLICK: Center button (▤)
CHOOSE: 28 point size, bold
TYPE: the following text:

8–5 Monday–Saturday
454 Madison Street
355-4802

10. Adjust the size of the star, if necessary, so the text does not word wrap.

In Addition AUTOSHAPE WORDWRAP ADJUSTMENTS

If text that you enter in an AutoShape extends outside the AutoShape, turn on the text-wrapping feature.
RIGHT-CLICK: AutoShape object
SELECT: Format Placeholder from the right-click menu
CLICK: *Text Box* tab
Here you can adjust the text anchor point, the internal margins, word wrapping, resizing of the shape, and rotation of text.

11. Save the revised presentation and keep it open for the next lesson.

3.3.2 Adding Text Using Text Boxes

→ ## Feature

Text boxes are used to position text anywhere on a slide. They act as containers for text and can hold more than one paragraph. They can also be formatted with their own text attributes and alignment.

→ ## Method

- CLICK: Text Box button (▤) on the Drawing toolbar

- CLICK: in your document to create a text box that enlarges as you type, *or*
  DRAG: with the mouse to establish the size of the text box

→ ## Practice

You will now practice inserting a text box. Ensure that you have completed the previous lesson and that slide 1 of the "Trace Enterprise" presentation is displaying.

1. Use the Text Box tool to insert some additional text on the bottom of slide 1:
CLICK: Text Box button (▤) on the Drawing toolbar

2. To insert a text box in the bottom left-hand of the slide that will enlarge as you type:
CLICK: near the bottom left-hand corner of the slide
(*Note:* You will have an opportunity to move the text box later.) The insertion point should be blinking inside a text box, as shown below:

3. TYPE: **Phone 702-616-5544**

4. Repeat this process to add the fax number:
CLICK: Text Box button (⊞) on the Drawing toolbar
CLICK: near the bottom right-hand corner of the slide
TYPE: **Fax 702-616-6576**

5. Refer to Figure 3.48 while dragging the text boxes into position and aligning them.
CLICK: both text boxes while holding down the **SHIFT** key to select them both
CLICK: Draw button (Draw▾) on the Drawing toolbar
SELECT: Align or Distribute
SELECT: Align Bottom

Figure 3.48

Title slide with
text boxes

6. Go to slide 3 to add a text box above the callout box on the left. Follow these steps:
CLICK: Text Box button (⊞) on the Drawing toolbar
CLICK: above the callout box on the left
TYPE: **Shipping Charges** then highlight this text

7. Now format the text and change the text box fill color:
Make the text 24 points and bold.
CLICK: the Fill Color button (▣▾) on the Drawing toolbar and select the same yellow color to match the callout box seen in Figure 3.49.

PowerPoint

Figure 3.49

Text box with
color fill

8. Save your presentation and keep it open for the next lesson.

3.3.3 Using WordArt for Special Effects

→ ## Feature

WordArt provides many possibilities for dramatic, eye-catching text arrangements. The WordArt Gallery provides many color and shape choices to get you started, and all of these designs can be customized even further, with different fill effects, coloring techniques, and shapes. Although these unusual treatments are fun, use WordArt sparingly in your presentation.

→ ## Method

- CLICK: Insert WordArt button (◢) on the Drawing toolbar

- SELECT: the WordArt style that has the best shape for your purpose (although you may change it later)

- TYPE: your text and adjust the font and attributes as needed

- CLICK: Format WordArt button (▣) to change the object's fill and line colors

- CLICK: WordArt Shape button (▣) to change the object's shape

→ ## Practice

You will now practice inserting WordArt on slide 4 of the "Trace Enterprise" presentation. You will make adjustments to the text, fonts, colors, and rotation of this object.

1. Ensure that the "Trace Enterprise" presentation is open and you are currently on slide 4.

2. To insert WordArt:
CLICK: WordArt button (◢) on the Drawing toolbar, and the WordArt Gallery will appear, as displayed in Figure 3.50.

Figure 3.50

WordArt Gallery

Select a style.

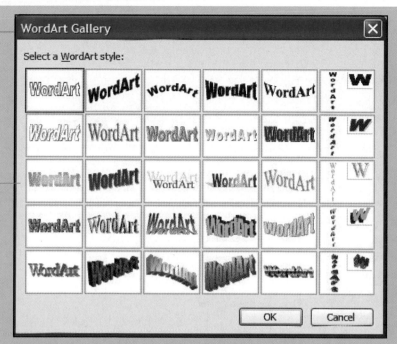

3. Select a style that seems most suitable for your purpose
CLICK: OK command button
(*Note:* All of these designs can be changed in their treatment of shape and color to better match your overall presentation design.)
The Edit WordArt Text dialog box will appear as displayed in Figure 3.51.

Figure 3.51

Edit WordArt Text dialog box

Type your text and change text attributes as needed.

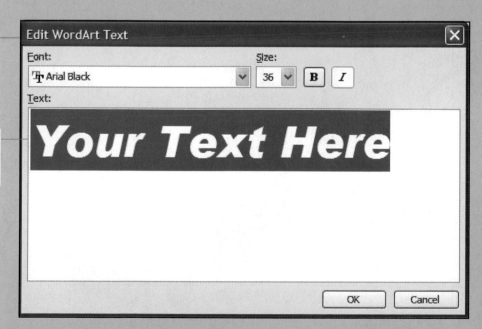

4. Enter text, change the font, and adjust attributes
TYPE: Sale Now!
SELECT: Comic Sans MS
SELECT: 36 points, bold, remove italic
CLICK: OK command button

5. Now adjust the appearance of the WordArt to better match your slide color scheme. Be sure the WordArt is selected; then, from the WordArt toolbar:
CLICK: Format WordArt button ([]) then select the *Colors and Lines* tab
SELECT: a gold color to match the other gold used in the presentation
CLICK: OK command button

6. Now with the WordArt selected, change the shadow color to black:
CLICK: Shadow Style button ([]) and select Shadow Settings
SELECT: a black color and remove the semitransparent setting
CLICK: Shadow button ([]) again and select Shadow Style 5, as displayed in Figure 3.52, to match the direction of the shadow used on the star shape
(*Note:* You may need to adjust the depth of the shadow for a pleasing appearance.)

Figure 3.52

Adjust WordArt shadow

7. Use a different WordArt shape to make the text angle:
CLICK: WordArt Shape button ([]) and select the Slant Up shape

8. Now resize the WordArt to make it larger and position all objects as shown in Figure 3.53.

Figure 3.53

Slide 4 completed

9. Examine all of your slides and make any necessary final adjustments. Save your presentation for the last time and close it.

In Addition CHANGING WORDART

To modify WordArt, simply double click the WordArt object and the toolbar will appear for easy editing.

 **SelfCheck** | **3.3** When would it be better to use a text box instead of a bulleted list placeholder?

Chapter
summary

Most people recognize the benefit of using graphics to improve the effectiveness of their presentations. PowerPoint makes it possible to insert many types of graphic objects, including clip art, photographs, shapes, and WordArt on your slide. It also allows you to label the graphic objects you draw. Objects are often more effective at conveying information than text alone, and when used effectively, help hold your audience's attention.

Command Summary

Many of the commands and procedures appearing in this chapter are summarized in the following table.

Skill Set	To Perform this Task	Do the Following
Inserting Clip Art and Photographs	Go directly to a selection of clip art images	CLICK: a content placeholder CLICK: Insert Clip Art button (▣)
	Search for a clip using the Clip Art task pane	CHOOSE: Insert → Picture → Clip Art, or click the Insert Clip Art button (▣) on the Drawing toolbar TYPE: a search keyword in the *Search for* text box CLICK: Search command button in the task pane CHOOSE: all media types or select only the type of media you need
	Display a categorical listing of Microsoft Office clip art	CHOOSE: Insert → Picture → Clip Art, or CLICK: the Insert Clip Art button (▣) on the Drawing toolbar CLICK: "Organize Clips" link in the task pane DOUBLE-CLICK: Office Collections in the Collection List pane
	Insert a picture	CHOOSE: Insert → Picture → From File

PowerPoint

Inserting and Modifying Draw Objects	Insert a draw object	CLICK: an object button on the Drawing toolbar CLICK: on the slide to insert the object
	Size and move objects	SELECT: object DRAG: object's handles to size, and DRAG: object to move
	Delete an object	PRESS: `DELETE`
	Format an AutoShape object	RIGHT-CLICK: an AutoShape object CHOOSE: Format AutoShape command
	Fill an AutoShape	CLICK: Fill Color button (⬛▾)
	Scale and rotate an AutoShape	RIGHT-CLICK: an AutoShape object CHOOSE: Format AutoShape command CLICK: *Size* tab, or DRAG: resize and rotation handles
	Change the order of objects	CLICK: Draw button (Draw▾) on Drawing toolbar SELECT: Order SELECT: multiple objects
	Group objects	CLICK: Draw button (Draw▾) on Drawing toolbar SELECT: Group
Inserting Text Boxes and WordArt	Create a text box	CLICK: Text Box button (📄) CLICK: on the slide to create a text box object
	Add text to an AutoShape	CLICK: the AutoShape Type: *Your text*
	Wrap text within AutoShapes	RIGHT-CLICK: the AutoShape SELECT: Format AutoShape CLICK: *Text Box* tab SELECT: *Word wrap text in AutoShape* check box
	Insert WordArt	CLICK: Insert WordArt button (📄) TYPE: *Your text*
	Edit WordArt	DOUBLE-CLICK: WordArt object SELECT: Format, Shape, or Alignment from the WordArt toolbar SELECT: Shadow and 3D options from the Drawing toolbar

Key Terms

This section specifies page references for the key terms identified in this chapter. For a complete list of definitions, refer to the Glossary provided immediately after the Appendix in this learning guide.

Chapter
q u i z

Short Answer

1. Describe the procedure to search for a photograph image.

2. What information displays if you mouse over an image in the Clip Art task pane?

3. How do you insert a picture from a file into your presentation?

4. Explain how to draw a rectangle on a slide.

5. Describe how to make a round circle.

6. For what is an AutoShape adjustment handle used?

7. How can you duplicate an AutoShape object?

8. For what purpose are text boxes used?

9. How do you add text to AutoShapes?

10. What is WordArt and how can you use it effectively?

True/False

1. _____ An image search procedure can be streamlined if you search only for the desired media type.

2. _____ To change the layering of objects, click the Draw button (Draw▾) and then select the Order option.

3. _____ Gradient coloring blends colors to show a gradual change.

4. _____ Adjustment handles are used for sizing AutoShapes.

5. _____ Text can be added to AutoShapes.

6. _____ To move an object, drag the object's sizing handles.

7. _____ To scale and rotate an object, use the *Size* tab in the Format AutoShape dialog box.

8. _____ To draw AutoShape objects, click the Draw button (Draw▾) on the Drawing toolbar.

9. _____ Text boxes can be formatted with text attributes and alignment options.

10. _____ Once a WordArt design is selected from the WordArt Gallery, its shape cannot be changed.

PowerPoint

Multiple Choice

1. To insert a picture file in your presentation:

a. CHOOSE: Insert → Picture → From File

b. CLICK: Insert Picture button

c. CHOOSE: File → Insert

d. All of the above

2. In the Picture toolbar, the Color button (🖼️) options include:

a. Automatic, grayscale, black and white, washout

b. Automatic, black and gray, transparent

c. Full color, gray shading, transparent

d. None of the above

3. To control whether an object is layered in front of or behind another, use this command:

a. Group

b. Ungroup

c. Order

d. Rotate

4. To check alignment of objects on a slide, use the:

a. Ruler

b. Grid

c. Guides

d. All of the above

5. Fill colors for shapes include:

a. Solid and gradient colors

b. Patterns

c. Textures

d. All of the above

6. Which of the following can change the shape, not the size, of an object?

a. Slide Master

b. Adjustment handle

c. Sizing handle

d. All of the above

7. To delete an existing clip art image:

a. Right-click the image and choose Cut

b. Select the image and press ⟨DELETE⟩

c. Drag the image to outside the Slide pane

d. Both a and b

8. If you do not want to use a bulleted list, which of the following should you use to enter text on a slide?

a. Text Box tool

b. Design template

c. Text placeholder

d. Slide Master

9. To display the Format AutoShape dialog box, do this to the AutoShape:

a. Click

b. Double-click

c. Right-click

d. Both b and c

10. Bitmap formats, commonly used for photographs, include:

a. .png

b. .wmf

c. .jpg

d. All of the above

Hands-On

exercises

step by step

1. Creating Graphics: Lines and Shapes

This exercise will guide you through the use of many more drawing tools in addition to the ones you learned to use in this chapter. An essential part of learning to communicate in a more visual way is understanding the shapes you can use, how to color them in interesting ways to blend with your slide show color scheme, and how to layer objects effectively. After you are comfortable drawing, then you can begin to add meaning to your slide show with the graphics you create.

In this exercise, you will work with a PowerPoint presentation organized by the particular type of drawing tool being used on each of six slides. Samples of shapes created with different drawing techniques are arranged on the left. You should use the blank space on the right of each slide to practice making those same shapes. One sample slide is shown in Figure 3.54.

Experiment to learn how each of the samples is created by trying different tools. Change line colors and thicknesses as well as fill colors and effects.

Figure 3.54

Line examples
and practice area

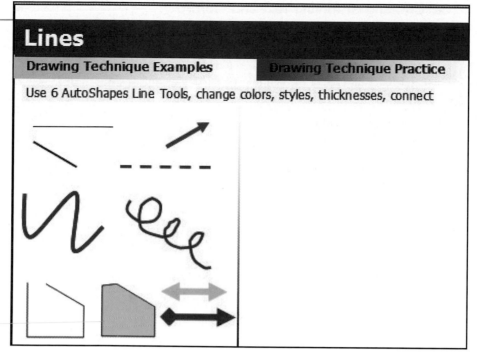

The (**SHIFT**) key is an important drawing tool. Here is what happens when you hold down the (**SHIFT**) key as you use these tools:

- Line: keeps lines straight

- Rectangle: makes square boxes

- Ellipse: makes round circles

- Other shapes and pictures: maintains correct up/down, left/right size relationships

1. Open the PP03HE01 presentation.

2. Save it as "Drawing 1" to your personal storage location.

3. For this exercise, close your task pane, because you will be using only drawing tools, related menus, and dialog boxes.

4. Here is a list of the slides and the skills you will practice on each one:

- Lines: Use six AutoShapes Line Tools, change colors, styles, thicknesses, connect

- Rectangles: Use Rectangle tool, different fills and lines, layer, align, change order, group

- Ovals and Circles: Use Ellipse tool, different fills and lines, duplicate, align, layer, group, ungroup

- AutoShapes, Basic Shapes: Use different fill and line colors, use Shadow and 3D

- AutoShapes, Block Arrows: Use different fill and line colors, rotate, adjust thickness and point

- AutoShapes, Stars and Banners: Use different fill and line colors, use 3D, combine shapes

5. Save your changes and close the presentation.

PowerPoint

2. Creating Graphics: Text and WordArt

In this exercise, you will work with a PowerPoint presentation organized by the particular type of text or WordArt treatment being used on each of five slides. Samples of the different techniques are arranged on the left. You should use the blank space on the right to practice making those same shapes.

Figure out how each of the samples is created. Experiment with the fonts and try changing colors and fill effects.

1. Open the PP03HE02 presentation.

2. Save it as "Drawing 2" to your personal storage location.

3. For this exercise, close your task pane, because you will be using only drawing tools, related menus, and dialog boxes.

4. Here is a list of the slides and the skills you will practice on each one:

Text Boxes, Decorative Fonts: Create text samples (24 points), handwriting, calligraphy, or unusual fonts

Text Boxes, Angled Text: Use Rotate and Flip to angle text in different directions

Text Boxes, Reverse Text: Use dark backgrounds with white or yellow text and bold, chunky fonts

WordArt: Use different shapes, textures, and pattern fills

WordArt: Use different shapes, gradients, and picture fills

Use picture file PP03HE02 to fill the word "POOL," as shown in Figure 3.55.

5. Save your changes and then close the presentation.

Figure 3.55

WordArt with gradient and picture fills

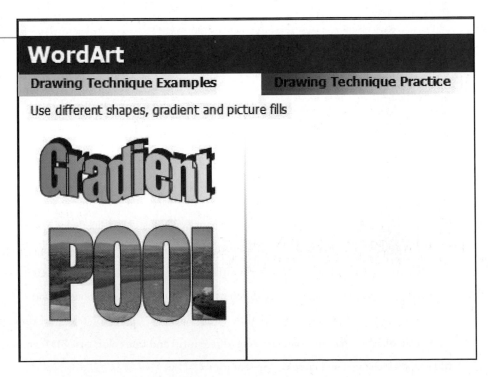

3. Creating a Presentation: "Concert in the Park"

Stephanie Nimmons is preparing for an upcoming concert to be given by her high school music group. She wants to create a slide show that she can use to announce this upcoming event at a school assembly next week. In this exercise, assume the role of Stephanie and perform the same steps that she identifies.

1. Start a new presentation using the "Refined" template. Save it as "Concert" to your personal storage location.

2. Rather than use the Title slide placeholders to enter text, Stephanie decides to make this slide look more dramatic, with large photos and WordArt. She uses the white lines on the slide background as a guide for positioning the photographs.

3. For the Title slide, find the two photographs (or similar ones) shown in Figure 3.56. Search for photographs only and first use the keywords "sheet music" to find the music pages. Use the sizing handles to stretch the photograph to match the size of the white lines.

4. Search for "violin" to find the musical instrument; resize it as necessary and position it on the left.

5. Use WordArt to enter the text **Concert in the Park** on two lines. Change the font to Forte (or a similar font), the color to red, and the alignment left. Change the shadow to a solid black. Position this text over the sheet music on the right and resize as shown.

Figure 3.56

"Concert in the Park" Title slide

6. Insert a new slide and use the Title and Text layout.

7. In the title placeholder type the slide title **Music to Celebrate the Season**. Change the font to Forte in 44 points.

8. In the bulleted list, type the following musical arrangement names. Use Arial at 24 points, bold, and resize the placeholder to move it to the right and lower on the slide.

- Vivaldi—Spring Allegro from Four Seasons
- Bach—Air for Strings in G
- Beethoven—Symphony No. 5 in C Minor
- Mozart—Symphony No. 25 in G Minor

9. Draw a rectangle on the left of the slide and make it red. Align it with the white lines on the slide background, then adjust the order to send it behind the title text.

10. Search for musical notes (clip art only, not photographs).

11. Adjust object positions to match those shown in Figure 3.57.

Figure 3.57

Bullet list with graphics

12. Insert a new slide and use the Title Only layout.

13. In the title placeholder type the slide title **When and Where?** Change the font to Forte in 44 points.

14. Draw an AutoShapes Bevel rectangle, found in Basic Shapes, and change the color to white. Type the text using Arial, 24 points, boldface, and left alignment.
Anderson Park
Sunday, June 16
3:00–4:30 p.m.
Bring your lawn chairs!

15. Duplicate this rectangle and change the font to 18 points. Edit the text and then resize the rectangle and align it with the bottom white line of the slide background.
Donations accepted to support our school music programs

16. Now use an AutoShapes tool to add an 8-point star. Change the fill color to red with no line color and use the adjustment handle to make sharp points.

17. Adjust object positions to match those shown in Figure 3.58.

Figure 3.58

AutoShapes with text

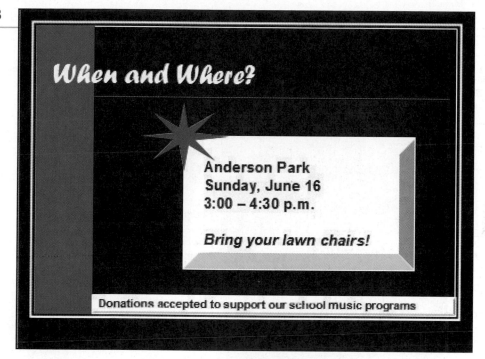

18. Save your presentation and print a notes page with three slides on a page. Close the "Concert" presentation.

on your own

4. Creating Business Logos

Start a blank presentation and save it as "Business logos." Insert two slides on which you can develop four business logos using PowerPoint's drawing tools. Use a variety of techniques to layer shapes, lines, WordArt, and text boxes to develop original designs.

Some ideas for business names follow, but you may also select your own names. As you design each logo, consider what you would expect to be an appropriate theme, based on the name of the business.

- Giorgio's Pizza

- Miller & Miller Consulting

- Tranquil Interiors

- Pure Water Systems

Save your presentation and print a handout with two slides on a page. Close your presentation.

5. Creating Advertising Flyers for Gardenside Nurseries

Create four slides, similar to the ones displayed in Figures 3.59–3.62, that could be printed as color flyers to advertise seasonal specials for a local store called Gardenside Nurseries. Design the first slide and then duplicate it, make revisions, and edit the text to easily create the other four slides.

1. Start with a blank presentation and add a photo for the first slide. Find a seasonal picture with a vertical orientation that can be stretched to fit on the left of the slide.

Figure 3.59

Spring ad

2. Insert WordArt for the name of the season. Use a bright yellow and make the color 30% semitransparent. Remove a shadow if one is present and change the font to Comic Sans MS. Rotate the WordArt and position it as shown. Resize if necessary.

3. Use a text box to add the company name using Comic Sans MS in 54-point type. Stretch the box to fill the right side of the slide and change its color to bright yellow.

4. Add the remaining text using three different text boxes with no fill color. In the first two, use Arial at 18 points; in the third, use Arial at 14 points.

5. Create a guarantee logo by using two AutoShapes in colors to match your picture. Add two small single-flower images. Once completed, group these objects together so they form a single object.

6. Save your presentation as "Gardenside Nurseries" to your personal storage location. Continue to save after each slide is complete.

7. Go to Slide Sorter and press (CTRL) + d to duplicate the slide. Double-click slide 2 to return to Normal view.

8. Now revise the text and WordArt as shown on Figure 3.60. Replace the picture with one appropriate for summer. Change the color fill on the company name box.

Figure 3.60

Summer ad

9. Repeat this duplication process using Slide Sorter to create and then edit the fall and winter slides, as shown in Figures 3.61 and 3.62.

Figure 3.61

Fall ad

Figure 3.62

Winter ad

10. Save and close the presentation.

6. Creating a Presentation about Procrastination

Create a new presentation with an appropriate design template and name it "Procrastination." Decide how you could first "tell the story" to define procrastination and then explain how to avoid it. Take a humorous approach and use amusing clip art images to help make your points. Instead of using bulleted lists, add needed text using text boxes or AutoShapes.

Save your presentation. Print handouts with six slides on a page and then close the presentation.

CaseStudy   HOMES FOR HUMANITY

Homes for Humanity is a not-for-profit agency in your hometown that works to provide affordable homes for those who cannot obtain housing funding through conventional methods. Many people throughout the community donate their time, money, and supplies to build these homes. Each prospective homeowner must be approved and must be involved with the building process.

Kristen Goodman is a volunteer worker who not only helps during construction time but also works diligently to help raise funds for each project. In this case, assume the role of Kristen as she develops a presentation she can use when she talks to various civic groups to get the necessary funds and volunteer workers for the next house.

1. Kristen begins the presentation by selecting the Pixel design template and typing the title and sub-title text shown in Figure 3.63. She saves the presentation as "Homes" to her personal storage location.

   (*Note:* The house will be added after she completes slide 2.)

Figure 3.63

"Homes for Humanity" Title slide

2. To make the point about an organization dedicated to building homes, Kristen adds title text to slide 2 and draws a simple house using colors to match the design template color scheme. She groups the elements of the house so that it can be easily copied as one object. She then adds text boxes to label the three goals of the organization and the date the organization was founded (Figure 3.64).

Figure 3.64

Slide 2: The goals

3. Kristen copies the house and pastes it on the Title slide. She resizes it so that it fits at the left of the title.

4. Save the presentation, and resave after each slide is complete.

5. On the third slide, Kristen wants to dramatically show how severe the shortage of housing is for people in low-income households. The finished slide is shown in Figure 3.65. Following are the steps she used to create it:

   • She finds a clip art image of a single house and reduces it in size.

   • She then duplicates that house until she has 10 houses stacked vertically.

   • She selects those 10 houses and groups them.

   • She duplicates the grouped houses until 100 houses are displayed.

   • She checks for horizontal and vertical alignment.

6. Kristen uses three text boxes on the left in Arial at 18 points and colors them as shown.

7. She decides to use either the rectangle tool to make several rectangles or the freeform tool to color the area that will be behind the rectangles. After the areas are covered for the 36 and 64 home numbers, she sends those colored rectangles behind the houses by using the order command.

Figure 3.65

Slide 3: The need

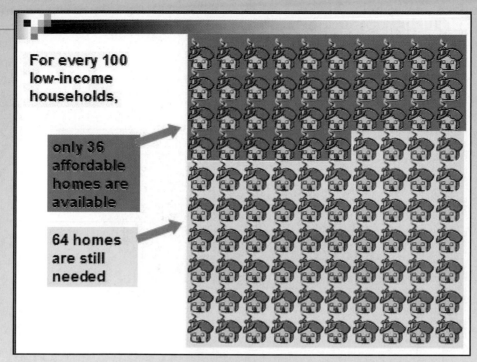

8. Kristen next considers how to show that the process of building these homes has several tasks that must be accomplished and each one builds on the previous task. So she thought a stair-step diagram would help to communicate this point.

9. Kristen makes the first rectangle using an AutoShapes Cube, adjusting its height to .85″ and its width to 5.25″. She then positions this shape at the bottom of the slide. She duplicates the shape four times and positions the duplicated shapes evenly.

10. Before entering the text, Kristen selects all of the shapes and changes the font size to 24, the type style to bold, and the alignment to left. She then types the text shown in Figure 3.66.

Figure 3.66

Slide 4: The process

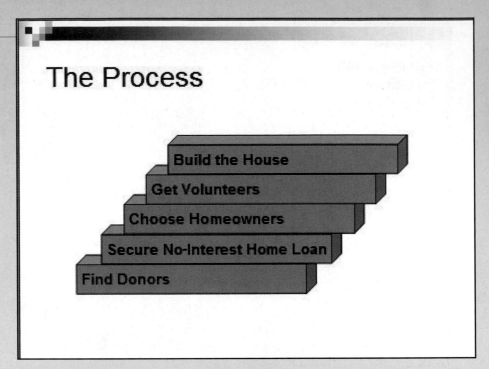

11. From her own experiences as a volunteer, Kristen can describe the challenges of building and what it is like to work on a construction site. She has four pictures to arrange evenly on this slide. The pictures are larger than displayed on Figure 3.67, so she must resize them to fit as shown in the figure. On this slide, insert picture files PP03C01, PP03C02, PP03C03, and PP03C04.

Figure 3.67

Slide 5: The activities

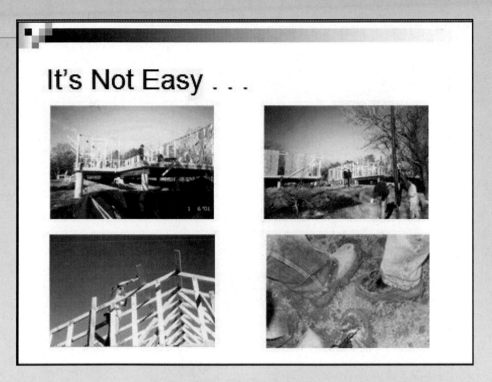

12. The concluding slide is a simple one (Figure 3.68), but it will help Kristen appeal to the audience to become involved by donating their time or resources. Kristen inserts picture file PP03C05 then uses the Clip Art task pane to search for an appropriate photo showing a family moving into a house. She then adds a rectangle with the summary comment in Arial, bold, at 44 points and a blue fill color.

Figure 3.68

Slide 6: The results

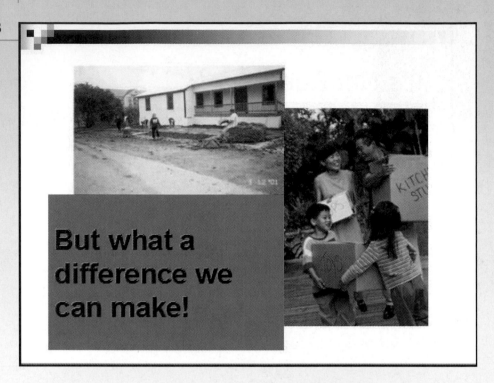

But what a difference we can make!

13. Kristen examines the presentation one more time to check the positioning of all objects on the slides. She then saves the presentation for the final time and closes it.

Answers to Self-Check Questions

3.1 How can you search for photographs but not clip art images, movies, or sounds? At the time you activate the search, specify the media file type that you want to use instead of searching for all media types.

3.2 When is it helpful to use grids and guides? Grids and guides allow you to examine alignment of objects on the screen. They are especially useful in checking positioning between slides that have similar elements that should be positioned consistently.

3.3 When would it be better to use a text box instead of a bulleted list placeholder? Text boxes are commonly used for labeling AutoShapes and adding text in various locations on a slide. When compared to text placeholders, text boxes provide greater flexibility.

Microsoft®OfficePowerPoint®

CHAPTER 4

Creating Tables, Charts, and Diagrams

CHAPTER OUTLINE

PREREQUISITES

To successfully complete this chapter, you must be able to start new presentations, insert slides, insert and format slide text, and apply alternate layouts. You must also know how to use toolbars, the Menu bar, right-click menus, and drawing tools and how to manage your files.

LEARNING OBJECTIVES

After completing this chapter, you will be able to:

- Create and format tables to organize information in columns and rows

- Select appropriate chart types for different situations

- Develop charts using different layout techniques

- Create organizational charts

- Draw customized diagrams to show processes and relationships

4.1 Creating Tables

Tables are useful for organizing words and numbers in a grid for easy interpretation and comparison. Tables are composed of columns and rows, and the intersection of a column and row is called a **cell**.

For presentation visuals you should keep your tables as simple and as easy to read as possible. Limit the number of rows and columns, because placing too much information in the table will necessitate text that is too small to read easily. However, row and column background colors can be changed to highlight the information in different ways, such as to differentiate column headings from the body of a table. Always be careful to emphasize column headings more than the body text of a table. And blend the colors you use with the overall color scheme of your presentation.

Various alignment techniques will make your slides easier to read and interpret accurately. Text is usually left-aligned (titles and column headings are sometimes centered) and numbers are usually right-aligned or decimal aligned. Right alignment of numbers is essential when the numbers have an arithmetic value; left alignment is useful when the numbers are used for identification, as in a catalog item number.

If the table looks cluttered on your slide, you can resize or reposition the table or remove grid lines between table rows and columns. Columns and rows can be inserted, too, but editing the table for correct placement can be time consuming. In this module, you will create the table pictured in Figure 4.1.

Figure 4.1

A PowerPoint table

Course Registration Fees

Title	Location	Cost
Desktop Publishing	Main campus	$159
Web Design	Main campus	159
Beginning HTML	East campus	139
Advanced HTML	East campus	139

4.1.1 Creating the Table Structure

→ **Feature**

If you already know how to create and insert tables in Microsoft Word, you will see that inserting them in PowerPoint is very similar. Before inserting a table on a slide, first consider how many columns your table will require. If you insert and delete columns after you have added data, you disrupt the established format of the table, and getting it to fit within the slide table boundaries can be a little tedious. You need not worry about the length of your table, because you can easily add rows as you go without changing the structure of the table.

→ ## Method

To insert a table using the Insert Table button (⊞):

- Be sure the slide in which you want to insert the table is displayed.
- CLICK: Insert Table button (⊞) on the Standard toolbar and hold it down
- DRAG: the grid pattern to the desired number of rows and columns
- RELEASE: the mouse button

To insert a table using a preset slide layout:

- CHOOSE: Format → Slide Layout
- CLICK: a slide Content Layout in the task pane that includes the Insert Table button (⊞)
- CLICK: Insert Table button (⊞)
- Define the number of columns and rows in the Insert Table dialog box.
- CLICK: OK command button

→ ## Practice

You will now insert a table on a slide by editing a table placeholder. Ensure that no presentations are open in the application window.

1. To begin a blank presentation and apply the Title and Content layout:
CLICK: New button (⬜)
CLICK: Title and Content layout in the Slide Layout task pane
Your screen should now appear similar to the one shown in Figure 4.2.

PowerPoint

Figure 4.2

Title and Content layout

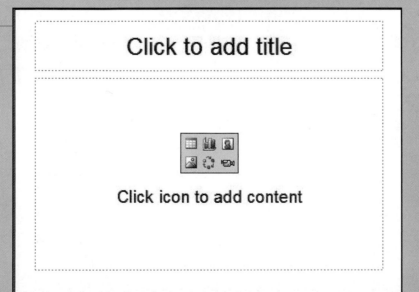

2. To add the slide title:
CLICK: the title placeholder
TYPE: **Course Registration Fees**
Highlight the text and then:
CLICK: the Bold button ([B])

3. To begin creating the table:
CLICK: Insert Table button (▦) in the content placeholder
The Insert Table dialog box should now appear, as shown in Figure 4.3.

Figure 4.3

Insert Table
dialog box

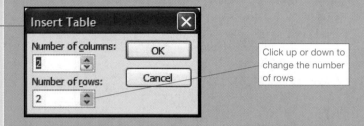

4. Let's create a table that contains two columns and four rows. To increase the number of rows:
PRESS: [TAB] to select the number in the *Number of rows* box
TYPE: **5** (or click the up arrow three times)
CLICK: OK command button
PowerPoint places a table with five rows and two columns in the table placeholder. The Tables and Borders toolbar should also appear. This toolbar provides a number of convenient shortcuts for formatting tables. In addition, the Draw Table tool, which looks like a pencil, is now activated. You would use this tool if you were going to draw the table one cell at a time.

5. DRAG: the Tables and Borders toolbar below the Formatting toolbar. Your screen should now appear similar to the one shown in Figure 4.4. (*Note:* The Tables and Borders toolbar will appear only when your insertion point is inside the table.)

Figure 4.4

Inserted table

Insertion point

It is important that you know how to select table cells, rows, and columns before you perform most procedures involving tables. The procedures for selecting items in a table are summarized in Table 4.1.

Table 4.1

Table selection methods

To select this...	Do this...
The contents of the cell in the next column	PRESS: `TAB`
The contents of the cell in the previous column	PRESS: `SHIFT`+`TAB`
A row	CLICK: in the desired row CLICK: Table on the Tables and Borders toolbar CHOOSE: Select Row
A column	CLICK: in the desired column CLICK: Table on the Tables and Borders toolbar CHOOSE: Select Column
A range of cells, rows, or columns	DRAG: the mouse over the cells, rows, or columns
An entire table	CLICK: in the table CLICK: Table on the Tables and Borders toolbar CHOOSE: Select Table

6. Save the presentation as "Course Registration Fees" to your personal storage location and keep it open for use in the next lesson.

4.1.2 Navigating a Table and Entering Data

→ **Feature**

Each cell in a table can contain more than one paragraph and can be formatted with its own unique text attributes and paragraph formatting commands. In fact, you can think of a table cell as a miniature document page.

→ **Method**

- PRESS: `TAB` to move to the next cell on the right (if the insertion point is in the last table cell, pressing `TAB` inserts a new row)

  or

- PRESS: `CTRL`+`TAB` to move the insertion point to the next tab stop within a cell
- PRESS: ⬆, ⬇, ⬅, or ➡ to move around a table

→ **Practice**

You will now enter some information into the table. Ensure that you have completed the previous lesson and that the "Course Registration Fees" presentation is displaying.

1. Position the insertion point in the first cell of the first column, if it is not already there.

PowerPoint

2. Let's enter some information into the table:

TYPE: **Title**

PRESS: `TAB` to move to the adjacent cell

TYPE: **Cost**

PRESS: `TAB`

Note that the last `TAB` takes you to the first column of the next row.

3. In the same manner, enter the following items.

Desktop Publishing	$159
Web Design	159
Beginning HTML	139
Advanced HTML	139

4. Your table should now appear similar to the one shown in Figure 4.5. (*Note:* If you accidentally pressed `TAB` after typing in the last cell and inserted a new row, choose Edit, Undo from the menu.)

Figure 4.5

Table with text

Course Registration Fees

Title	Cost
Desktop Publishing	$159
Web Design	159
Beginning HTML	139
Advanced HTML	139

5. Save the revised presentation and keep it open for use in the next lesson.

In Addition MERGING AND SPLITTING CELLS

The ability to merge and split cells is extremely useful when customizing a table to your exact specifications. Merge is used to combine two or more cells into one cell; split is used to create additional cells from one cell. To merge or split cells, select the cells you want to merge or split before clicking the Table menu button (▣) on the Tables and Borders toolbar. Then choose Merge Cells or Split Cells from the drop-down menu. You can also merge cells by using the eraser tool to remove the line separating cells.

4.1.3 Formatting Table Cells

→ **Feature**

Text attributes and paragraph formatting commands help make your tables more attractive and easier to read. When formatting tables, you can choose to format an entire table, a selection of rows or columns, or a selection of cells.

→ **Method**

- Apply text attributes and paragraph formatting commands to tables the same way you apply them to other text.

- Use the Tables and Borders toolbar to apply special table attributes affecting cells.

- Drag the column and row borders to adjust their widths or heights.

→ **Practice**

You will now practice several table formatting procedures. Ensure that you have completed the previous lessons in this module and that the "Course Registration Fees" presentation is displaying. The insertion point should be positioned in the table.

1. Perform the following steps to format the table column heading text:
   CLICK: in the first cell and drag across to select both cells in the first row
   CHOOSE: 32 from the *Font Size* drop-down list (32 ▼)
   CLICK: Bold button (B)

2. Now right-align the Cost column, because it contains numbers:
   CLICK: in the first cell of the second column and drag down to select all cells in that column
   CLICK: Align Right button (☰)

3. Use Figure 4.6 as your guide for column heading and row shading adjustments:
   CLICK: in the first cell of the first row and drag across to highlight that row
   CLICK: the Fill Color button (🎨▼) on the Tables and Borders toolbar and select a teal color (second from right)

Figure 4.6

Column headings emphasized with shading and font attributes

Course Registration Fees

Title	Cost
Desktop Publishing	$159
Web Design	159
Beginning HTML	139
Advanced HTML	139

PowerPoint

CLICK: the Font Color button (▲·) to change the text to white

CLICK: the Shadow button (s) to make the heading text more distinct on the colored background

4. Now highlight the third row and change the fill color to a lighter blue (fourth color from right). Repeat for the fifth row. Your table should now display color on alternating rows, as shown in Figure 4.6.

5. If you look closely, you will notice that the text in each of the cells is aligned with the top border rather than the middle of each cell. To vertically center all the data in the table:
CLICK: Table menu button (▤) on the Tables and Borders toolbar
SELECT: Select Table
CLICK: Center Vertically button (▤) on the Tables and Borders toolbar
Your text should now be centered vertically in all the rows.

6. Now insert a column. With your insertion point on any row in the first column:
CLICK: Table menu button (▤) on the Tables and Borders toolbar
SELECT: Insert Columns to the Right (Figure 4.7)

Figure 4.7

Table menu

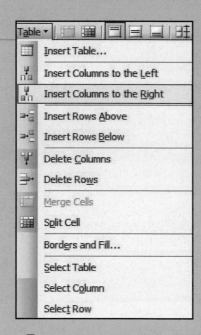

7. Your table will expand off the right side of your slide, as shown in Figure 4.8.
CLICK: on the column edges so horizontal resizing arrows appear
DRAG: the column edges until the whole table once again fits on your slide.

Figure 4.8

Inserting a column

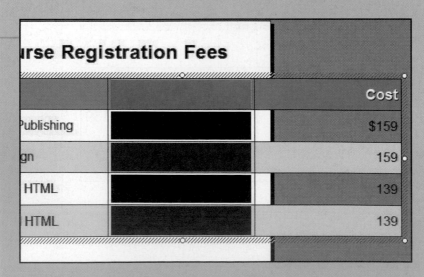

8. Now add the text for this column and resize the columns as needed so that the text does not word wrap in any cell and the columns are evenly spaced.
TYPE: the following text:
Location
Main campus
Main campus
East campus
East campus

9. Because you have applied row shading, the border lines within the whole table are no longer essential. To remove the table lines:
CLICK: Table menu button (▣) on the Tables and Borders toolbar
SELECT: Select Table
CLICK: All Borders (▦▾) button
CLICK: No Border button (▢) from the border options shown in Figure 4.9

Figure 4.9

Border option buttons

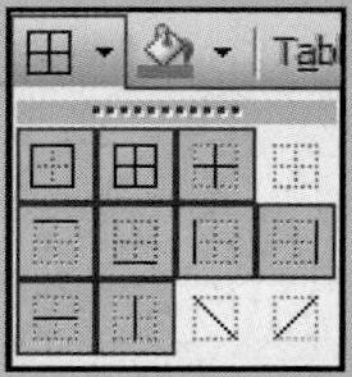

10. Now apply lines at the top and bottom of the column heading row:
CLICK: to select the column heading row
CLICK: Top Border (▭) button
CLICK: Bottom Border (▭) button

11. Your finished table should now appear similar to the one shown in Figure 4.10.

Figure 4.10

Completed table

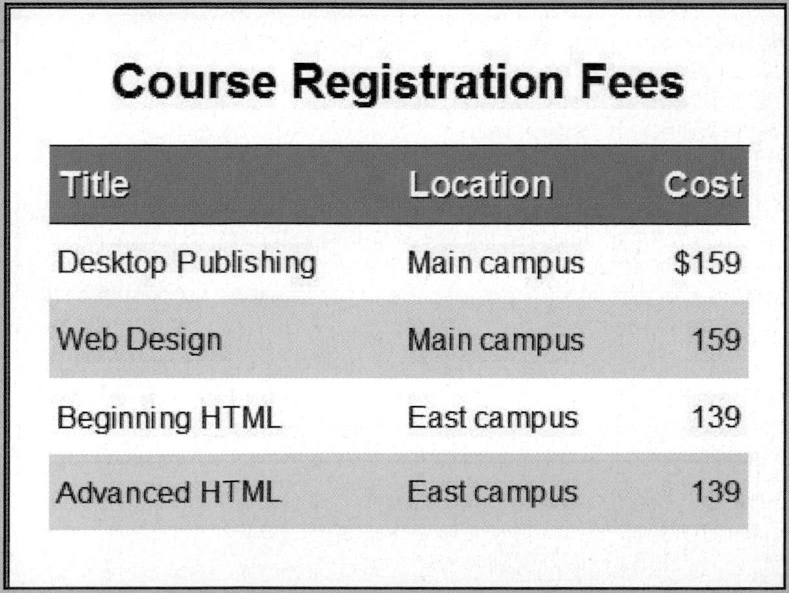

Course Registration Fees

Title	Location	Cost
Desktop Publishing	Main campus	$159
Web Design	Main campus	159
Beginning HTML	East campus	139
Advanced HTML	East campus	139

12. Save and then close the revised "Course Registration Fees" presentation.

In Addition INSERTING AND DELETING COLUMNS AND ROWS

When you insert columns and rows, the inserted column or row takes on the formatting of the previous column or row. For example, if the current row has a height of 18 points, the inserted row will be set at a height of 18 points. Inserted columns can appear to the left or right of the selected column, and inserted rows appear above or below the selected row. To insert and delete columns, use the options on the Table menu, accessed from the Tables and Borders toolbar.

4.1.4 Sizing and Moving a Table

→ **Feature**

Once a table is created, it can be resized or repositioned on the slide. The row size can be no smaller than the current font size being used. When the whole table is made smaller, the column size relationships will be maintained, but the information in the columns may word wrap as the columns become more narrow.

→ **Method**

- DRAG: sizing handles vertically to make rows more narrow
- DRAG: sizing handles horizontally to make the table more narrow
- DRAG: the table border line to move it

→ **Practice**

You will now practice reducing the size of a table by removing a table column, resizing the table to fit the remaining content, and moving the table to a new position on the slide. Ensure that you have completed the previous lessons in this module and that the "Course Registration Fees" presentation is displaying. The insertion point should be positioned in the table.

1. To reduce the table size, remove the Location column:
CLICK: on any word in the Location column
CHOOSE: Delete Column from the Table menu
The table will now have two columns.

2. Now reduce the size of the table:
CLICK: the bottom center sizing handle and drag up to make the rows more narrow
CLICK: the right middle sizing handle and drag to the left to make the table smaller
Resize the table if necessary to avoid word wrapping.
(*Note:* You can also reduce extra space in the columns by double-clicking the vertical line between columns when the insertion point changes to double arrows for resizing.)

3. Assume that you need to insert a picture on the left of the slide and move the table to the right of the screen:
CLICK: the table border line then drag the table to the right
Your table should now appear similar to the one shown in Figure 4.11.

Figure 4.11

Table in a
reduced size

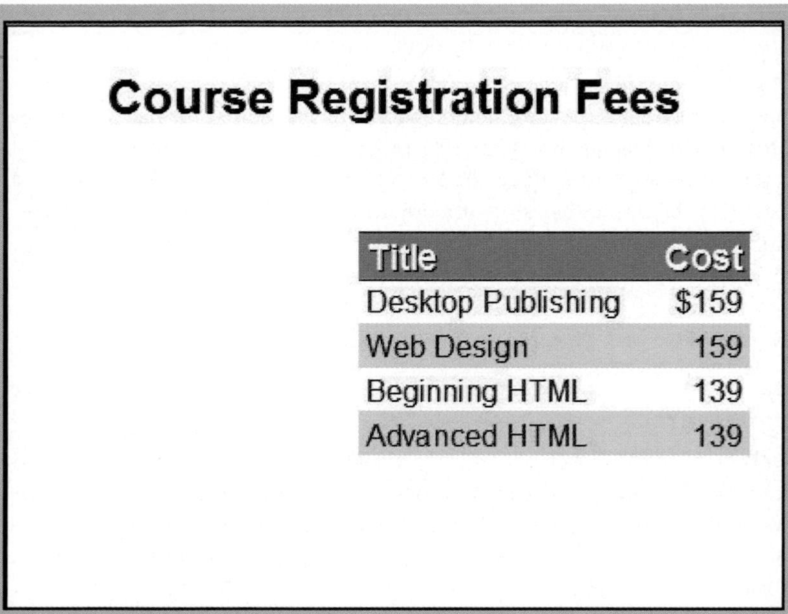

Course Registration Fees

Title	Cost
Desktop Publishing	$159
Web Design	159
Beginning HTML	139
Advanced HTML	139

4. Save and then close the revised "Course Registration Fees" presentation.

SelfCheck

4.1 How can the width of a table column be changed?

4.2 Creating Charts for Numeric Information

Numeric information can be made easier to interpret when it is shown as charts that visually represent the data. When viewers can compare the sizes of bars or pie slices, they can more readily understand the relationships between the numbers. When viewers can follow the up and down movement of a line chart, they can more easily visualize a trend over time.

The words "chart" and "graph" are often used interchangeably as forms of displaying numeric information. However, in this module we will make a clear distinction between these terms. **Microsoft Graph** is the program within Office Systems 2003 that is used to create charts; **charts** are objects such as bar, pie, line, or bubble charts used to show data and data relationships that are embedded, or saved, in your presentation. As you are working in PowerPoint, the switch to this program is so seamless that you will barely notice a difference other than the new menu and toolbar items that become available.

Selecting a Chart Type

Which chart type is most appropriate? It depends on the situation. The ideal chart is the one that presents your data most clearly. Microsoft Graph can produce more than 12 different types of charts in a variety of layouts.

In this module you will create four of the most common charts. The next paragraphs explain the reasons for choosing each chart and provide some design tips for each one.

Column chart:

Column charts are among the most common and are well suited for making comparisons of data in categories or for showing changes over time. The categories are usually shown along the bottom of the chart (*x*-axis) and the values are shown along the left side (*y*-axis). Therefore columns (or bars) appear in different heights based on the size of the value. If more than one data series is used, then the columns are clustered. Some design tips for column charts include:

- Use five or fewer bars (or bar clusters) whenever possible.

- Show values above bars when precise numbers are needed.

- If data are not time dependent, arrange from low to high or from high to low for easy interpretation and greater emphasis.

Bar chart:

Bar charts serve the same purpose as column charts, but their categories are shown in horizontal bars instead of vertical columns. The categories are listed along the left (*y*-axis) and the values are shown along the bottom (*x*-axis). The column chart design tips also apply to bar charts except that bar chart values are shown at the end of the bars.

Line chart:

When you need to show changes in quantities over time, use a line chart. More data points can be shown on a line than on a column chart, and multiple lines can be compared. Some design tips for line charts include:

- Make lines thicker and data points larger than default sizes.

- If using more than one line, be sure the line colors contrast.

- Add callout boxes to label the most important numbers.

Pie chart:

To show the percentage of each data value in a whole quantity, use a pie chart. The data can be shown as actual values or percentages. Some design tips for pie charts include:

- Use seven or fewer slices (seven numbers).

- Arrange data from small to large or from large to small.

- Begin ordering slices from either the twelve o'clock or the three o'clock position.

- Emphasize a single slice by exploding it, pulling it out, and using the brightest color for that slice.

Understanding Chart Elements

Charts are made up of many elements and these can usually be formatted individually using Graph menus and buttons:

Data: counted or measured information

Data labels: words that identify data

Legend: shows color to identify each data series

x-Axis: horizontal scale

y-Axis: vertical scale

Tick marks: small marks that indicate points on a scale

Gridlines: background lines to aid interpretation of quantities

Chart area: the entire chart, including the plot area, the legend, and chart title if used

Plot area: the area created by the *x*- and *y*-axes

3-D effect: the illusion of depth

Maintaining Visual Integrity

As a presenter, you have a responsibility to be accurate and truthful in the display of your data's proportions. Be careful when resizing charts that you do not distort their size relationships. Coordinate chart colors with the colors of your presentation, and beware of special effects that could distort meaning or make the chart difficult to interpret. Simple designs are often the best.

Add text as necessary for titles, labels, and scale indicators. Include sources when needed for credibility and authenticity.

4.2.1 Creating Column Charts

→ **Feature**

The Microsoft Graph program enables you to produce great-looking charts from within PowerPoint. Graph does not replace a full-featured spreadsheet application such as Microsoft Excel, but it does provide a convenient tool for embedding simple charts into presentations. All types of charts are inserted in the same way.

→ **Method**

Each of the following methods can be used to launch Microsoft Graph:

- CLICK: Insert Chart button (▦) on the Standard toolbar

  or

- CLICK: Insert Chart button (▦) in a content placeholder

  or

- CHOOSE: Insert → Chart from the menu

  or

- CHOOSE: Insert → Object and then select Microsoft Graph Chart

To edit an inserted chart:

- DOUBLE-CLICK: the chart object

→ **Practice**

You will now start a new presentation and create a column chart by editing a chart placeholder. Ensure that no presentations are open in the application window.

1. To begin a new presentation and apply a design template:
CLICK: New button (▯)
CLICK: Design button (▱ Design)
CLICK: the Blends design template thumbnail in the task pane

2. Change the presentation color scheme:
CLICK: the Color Schemes hyperlink in the task pane
CLICK: the color scheme thumbnail on the lower left

3. On slide 1 which automatically uses the Title Slide layout, add title and subtitle text and change the alignment and position of the subtitle text:
CLICK: in the title placeholder
TYPE: **Chart Sampler**
CLICK: in the subtitle placeholder
TYPE: these four words and press **ENTER** after each word
Column
Bar
Line
Pie
DRAG: the subtitle placeholder sizing handles to increase the size of the box, then move it to the right
CLICK: Left Align button (▤)
Your screen should now appear similar to the one shown in Figure 4.12.

PowerPoint

Figure 4.12

Chart Sampler
Title slide

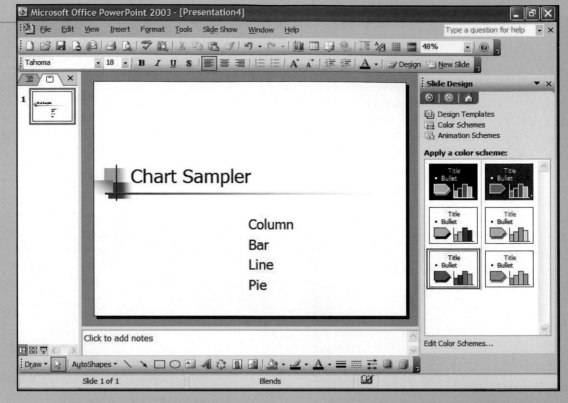

4. CLICK: the New Slide button (⬛ New Slide), then
CLICK: on the Title and Content layout
In the title placeholder:
TYPE: **Outdoor Activity Participation**

5. To insert a chart:
CLICK: Insert Chart button (📊) in the content placeholder as shown in Figure 4.13.

Figure 4.13

Title and Content
layout

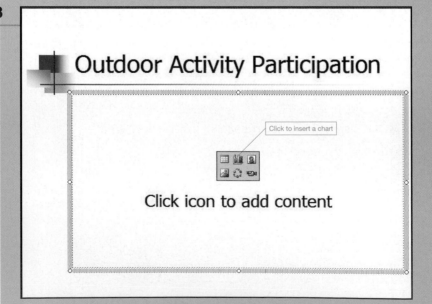

6. Now the Graph program is loaded, and your screen should appear similar to the one shown in Figure 4.14 with Graph buttons added to your Standard toolbar. A **datasheet** also appears in a separate window with sample data displayed in the chart. As you do in an electronic spreadsheet, you add and edit data in the datasheet; because the chart is embedded, the visual representation of the data on the slide changes automatically. Figure 4.15 shows the datasheet both as it first appears and as it will look after you edit it.

Figure 4.14

Inserting a chart

Data sheet

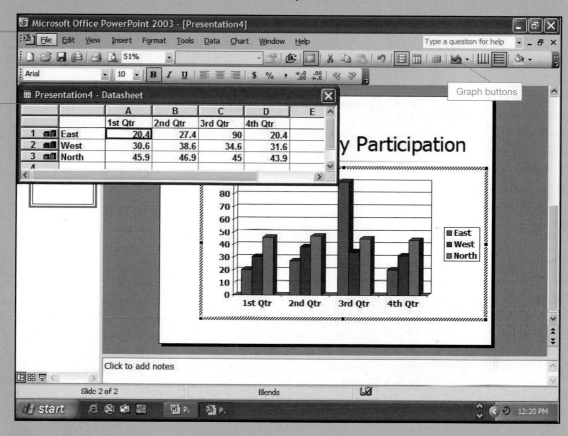

Figure 4.15   *Before*

Editing the datasheet

Click here to select the entire datasheet.

			A	B	C	D	E
			1st Qtr	2nd Qtr	3rd Qtr	4th Qtr	
1		East	20.4	27.4	90	20.4	
2		West	30.6	38.6	34.6	31.6	
3		North	45.9	46.9	45	43.9	

Presentation4 - Datasheet

After

Click between the column buttons then drag to widen the columns.

Double click the column buttons to clear the columns.

Presentation4 - Datasheet

			A	B	C	D	E
			Camping	Bicycling	Swimming	Walking	
1		Male	18	23	25	26	
2		Female	22	18	15	22	
3							

PowerPoint

7. Now delete all the data that currently appears in the datasheet. Notice that when you move your mouse pointer over the datasheet, it changes to a plus.
CLICK: the upper-left corner of the datasheet (refer to the "Before" image in Figure 4.15)
PRESS: DELETE
The datasheet should be empty and the columns are removed from the chart. The columns will appear again as you add numbers to the datasheet.

8. To enter data into the datasheet, you click on the appropriate cell in the datasheet. In this step, you enter the names of the data series and the category names.
CLICK: in the cell to the right of the number 1
TYPE: **Male**
PRESS: ENTER
The insertion point automatically moved to the cell below.
TYPE: **Female**
PRESS: ENTER
CLICK: in the cell in the first row below the A button
TYPE: these words in columns A–D, **Camping, Bicycling, Swimming, Walking,** and press TAB to move between columns.

9. Now prepare to enter the data. (*Note:* Be sure that the (Num Lock) key has been pressed.)
PRESS: CTRL + HOME
The insertion point automatically moved to where you will type in the first data value (18).

10. To enter the data, refer to Figure 4.15 and use the TAB or arrow keys to move between columns.
TYPE: these numbers:
18   23   25   26
22   18   15   22

11. To hide the datasheet and view the inserted chart:
CLICK: anywhere in the background of your slide
DRAG: the chart slightly to the left
Your screen should now appear similar to the one shown in Figure 4.16.

Figure 4.16

Inserted chart

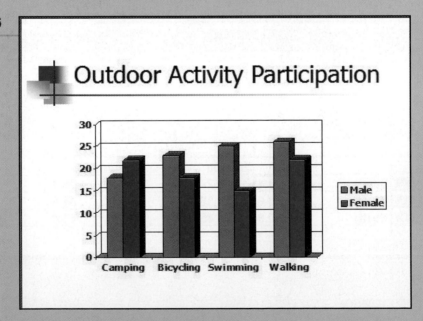

12. Save the presentation as "Chart Sampler" to your personal storage location and continue with the next lesson.

4.2.2 Applying Chart Types

→ # Feature

After you have created a chart, you may decide that you want to use a different chart type to better display your information. Microsoft Graph provides more than 12 different chart types and each of these have a selection of subtypes from which to choose.

→ # Method

The following methods can each be used to modify chart type:

- CLICK: Chart Type button ( ) on the Standard toolbar

  or

- CHOOSE: Chart → Chart Type and then select Microsoft Graph Chart

The second method enables you to access all the subchart designs.

→ # Practice

You will now duplicate a chart and modify the chart type to change its appearance. Ensure that the "Chart Sampler" presentation is open in the application window.

1. To look at this same information in a different way, let's make a duplicate of this slide and then change the chart type. In the Outline and Slides pane:
CLICK: slide 2
PRESS: CTRL + d to duplicate the slide

2. Now on slide 3.
DOUBLE-CLICK: on the chart so you can make changes to it
CHOOSE: Chart → Chart Type from the Menu bar
The Chart Type dialog box should appear (Figure 4.17).

Figure 4.17

Chart Type dialog box

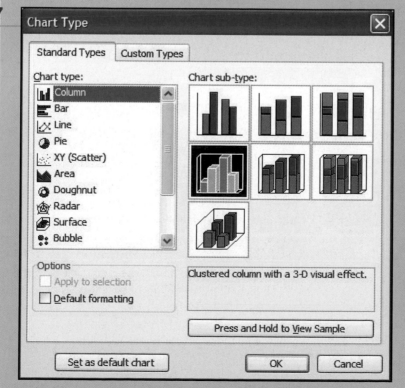

PowerPoint

3. The Column chart has seven different subtypes. The one you are currently using has a 3-D appearance, showing depth, and the ones on the top row have a 2-D, or flat, appearance.
(*Note:* As you try out different subtypes, you can click the Press and Hold button to see how your chart would look in this arrangement.)
SELECT: the first Bar on the first row
CLICK: OK command button

4. Because your chart is now selected, Graph buttons appear on the Standard toolbar. Currently the By Row button (⊞) is selected so the chart is now displaying a bar for each data point in the series clustered by category. This arrangement allows easy comparison of male and female data in each of the categories.
CLICK: the By Column button (⊞) and notice how the chart is changed to display bars for each category, clustered by series. This arrangement allows comparison of data for all categories for the male then female series as shown in Figure 4.18.

Figure 4.18

Displaying an alternate chart type

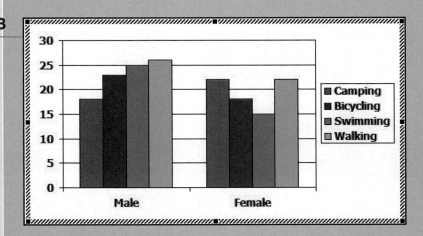

(*Note:* As you are developing your charts, you may want to try out different treatments such as this one to determine which one best reflects the data you want to emphasize.)

5. Save the presentation as "Chart Sampler" to your personal storage location and continue to the next lesson.

4.2.3 Creating Bar and Line Charts

→ **Feature**

The Microsoft Graph program creates bar and line charts in the same way it creates column charts.

→ **Method**

The methods used to launch Microsoft Graph are the same as were described in the previous lesson.

→ **Practice**

You will now create a new slide with a bar chart and modify the chart type to create a line chart. Ensure that the "Chart Sampler" presentation is open in the application window.

1. With slide 3 selected:
CLICK: the New Slide button (New Slide), then
CLICK: on the Title and Content layout
In the title placeholder:
TYPE: **Weber Sales by Region**

2. To insert a chart:
CLICK: Insert Chart button (⊞) in the content placeholder.
CHOOSE: Chart → Chart Type from the Menu bar
CLICK: Bar chart type
SELECT: the first chart subtype
CLICK: OK command button

3. Now clear your datasheet and enter the information shown in Figure 4.19. Adjust the width of column C by dragging the edge of the column button.
(*Note:* You can tell that columns and rows are empty when the datasheet buttons look flat. If the buttons have a raised appearance, then the Graph program will display empty space on the chart that is created to show this data.)

Figure 4.19

Slide 4 datasheet

Flat buttons mean empty cells.

Chart Sampler - Datasheet		A	B	C	D	E	F
		Eastern	Southern	Midwestern	Plaines	Western	
1 ▬	Consumer	4.25	6.5	4.5	5.25	7.25	
2 ▬	Industrial	9.5	5	6	6.25	5.75	
3							
4							

4. When the data is entered, click on any blank area of the slide. Figure 4.20 shows the bar chart (horizontal bars) for this information.

Figure 4.20

Bar chart

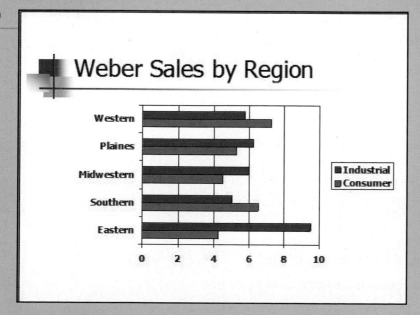

PowerPoint

5. To create a line chart from this same data, let's make a duplicate of this slide and then change the chart type. In the Outline and Slides pane:
CLICK: slide 4
PRESS: CTRL + **d** to duplicate the slide

6. Now on slide 5:
DOUBLE-CLICK: on the chart so you can make changes to it
CHOOSE: Chart → Chart Type from the Menu bar
CLICK: Line chart type
SELECT: the first Chart subtype on the second row (line with markers displayed at each data value).
CLICK: OK command button
The line chart box should appear (Figure 4.21).

Figure 4.21

Line chart

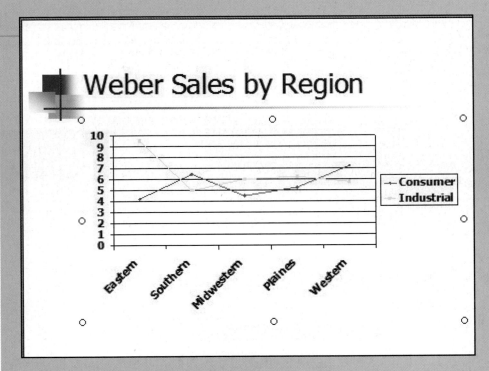

7. Save the presentation as "Chart Sampler" to your personal storage location and continue to the next lesson.

4.2.4 Creating Pie Charts

→ **Feature**

The Microsoft Graph program creates pie charts in the same way it creates column charts.

→ **Method**

The methods used to launch Microsoft Graph are the same as described in the previous lessons.

→ Practice

You will now create a new slide with a pie chart. Ensure that the "Chart Sampler" presentation is open in the application window.

1. With slide 5 selected:
CLICK: the New Slide button (New Slide), then
CLICK: on the Title and Content layout
In the title placeholder:
TYPE: **Our Market Share**

2. To insert a chart:
CLICK: Insert Chart button ( ) in the content placeholder
CHOOSE: Chart → Chart Type from the Menu bar
CLICK: Pie chart type
SELECT: the second chart subtype on the first row (Pic with 3-D visual effect)
CLICK: OK command button

3. If you compare your datasheet with the pie image, you can see that the pie is displaying the data by row (East). Although data exists in the datasheet for the West and North data series, it is ignored because a pie chart can display only the numbers for one data series (Figure 4.22).

Figure 4.22

Pie chart default datasheet

Data from rows 2 and 3 are not displayed

		A	B	C	D	E
		1st Qtr	2nd Qtr	3rd Qtr	4th Qtr	
1	East	20.4	27.4	90	20.4	
2	West	30.6	38.6	34.6	31.6	
3	North	45.9	46.9	45	43.9	
4						

Chart Sampler - Datasheet

4. Instead of clearing your datasheet, this time let's use a different method of replacing the existing words and numbers with your new information. Enter the information shown in Figure 4.23 and delete the row content that is not used. Resize the columns so you can see all of the words at the top.

Figure 4.23

Pie chart datasheet

		A	B	C	D	E
		Us	Competitor 1	Competitor 2	Competitor 3	
1	3-D Pie 1	25	23	20	15	
2						
3						

Chart Sampler - Datasheet

5. Your pie chart slide should appear similar to the one shown in Figure 4.24.

Figure 4.24

Pie chart

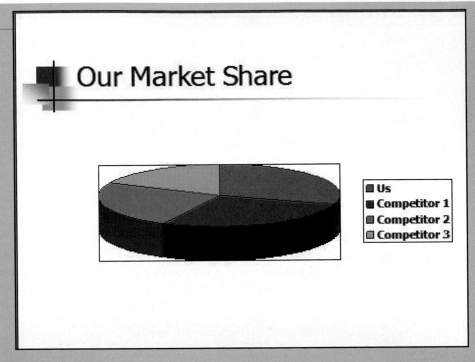

6. Save the presentation as "Chart Sampler" to your personal storage location and continue to the next lesson.

4.2.5 Formatting Chart Elements

→ **Feature**

You can format charts to improve their appearance by changing colors, legend and label positioning, and line thicknesses. Often the colors used in your presentation will influence the types of changes you need to increase both attractiveness and the visibility of chart elements.

→ **Method**

The techniques used will vary for each of the five charts you completed in the previous lessons of this module.

→ **Practice**

Ensure that the "Chart Sampler" presentation is open in the application window. You will modify each of the charts in this series.

1. With slide 2 selected:
DOUBLE-CLICK: the chart so you can make modifications
CLICK: to select the chart walls area, as shown in Figure 4.25

Figure 4.25

Chart walls

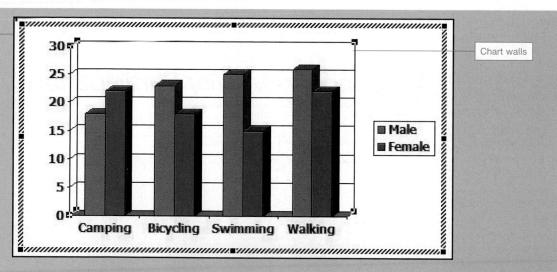

2. With the walls selected:
   CHOOSE: Format → Selected Walls
   CLICK: Fill Effects button
   CLICK: *Two colors*
   For Color 1, choose light turquoise
   For Color 2, choose sky blue
   For Shading style, choose Horizontal
   For Variant, choose the lighter blue at the top
   CLICK: OK command button to accept these colors and then click OK again to apply the gradient color to the chart walls

3. Move the legend and change its fill color to white:
   DRAG: the legend to the left above the bars as shown in Figure 4.26 chart so you can make modifications
   CHOOSE: Format → Selected Legend
   CLICK: the white color
   CLICK: OK command button to accept this color
   CLICK: any blank area outside the chart to return to the slide

4. Now add an AutoShapes arrow to highlight one of the bars:
   CLICK: the AutoShapes menu
   SELECT: Block Arrow, and Left Arrow
   Make a short arrow above the chart and then rotate it and move it into position above the walking bars, as shown in Figure 4.26.

PowerPoint

Figure 4.26

Slide 2: Column
chart with
colored walls

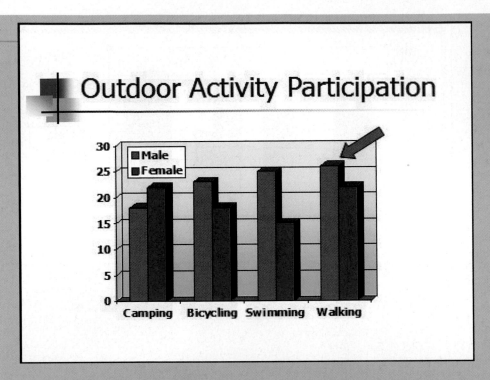

5. On slide 3, add numbers for precise interpretation above all the bars. When using this technique,
you do not need to include gridlines. With slide 3 selected:
DOUBLE-CLICK: the chart so you can make modifications
CHOOSE: Chart Options
CHOOSE: Gridlines tab and remove the check for *Major gridlines* (Figure 4.27)

Figure 4.27

Chart options
dialog box

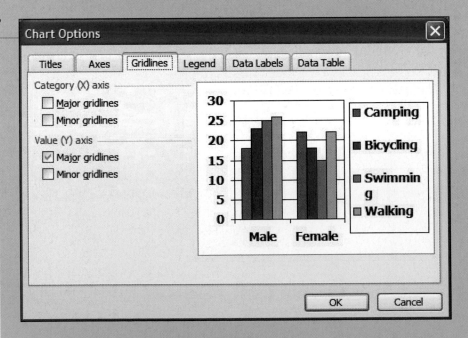

CLICK: *Data Labels* tab and click *Value*
CLICK: OK command button
Now the numbers are displayed above each column with no grid lines, as shown in Figure 4.28.

Figure 4.28

Slide 3: Column
chart with
numbers and no
grid lines

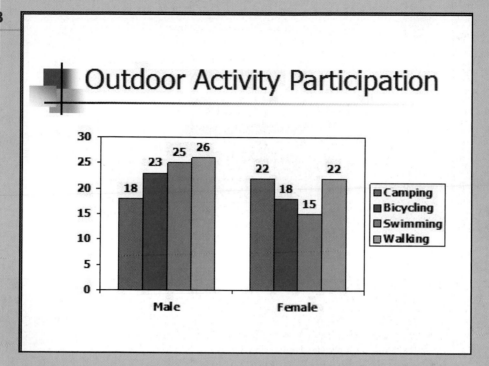

6. With slide 4 selected, change the chart type to add a 3-D appearance to the bars.
   DOUBLE-CLICK: the chart so you can make modifications
   CHOOSE: Chart → Chart Type
   CLICK: the first Bar subtype on the second row (Clustered bar with a 3-D visual effect)
   CLICK: OK command button

7. Now change the bar colors to add gradient colors:
   CLICK: any bar in the Consumer series
   CHOOSE: Format → Selected Data Series
   CLICK: Fill Effects → Gradient → Two-colors
   For Color 1, choose sea green
   For Color 2, choose light green
   For Shading style, choose Vertical
   For Variants, choose the light to dark color so the bars will end in the darkest color
   CLICK: OK command button to accept these colors and OK again to apply them
   Repeat these steps for the Industrial series but use two shades of blue (light blue and pale blue).

8. Your slide 4 should now look like the one shown in Figure 4.29.

Figure 4.29

Slide 4: Bar chart with 3-D appearance and gradient colors

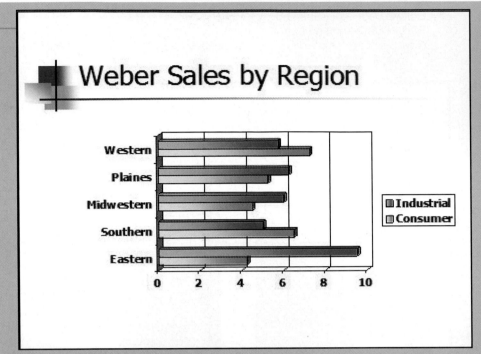

9. On slide 5, the lines can barely be seen, so the line colors and thickness should be changed.
   DOUBLE-CLICK: the chart so you can make modifications
   CLICK: anywhere on the Consumer series line in the chart area
   CHOOSE: Format → Selected Data Series
   For *Line*, choose color teal and thickest weight
   For *Marker,* choose Foreground and Background color of blue and increase the size to 14 points
   These settings are shown in Figure 4.30.

Figure 4.30

Format Data Series dialog box

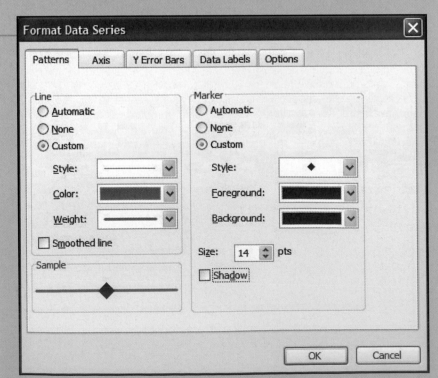

10. Now repeat this process to improve the appearance of the Industrial line. Select the line color of light orange, the Foreground and Background color of plum, and the marker size of 10 points.

11. Now select the legend so it can be repositioned.
CHOOSE: Format → Selected Legend → *Placement* tab
CLICK: *Top*
CLICK: OK command button
Now the legend is positioned above the chart, and the chart has expanded in size.
CLICK: to select the legend and resize it so the two labels are not so close together
CLICK: on a blank area of your slide
CLICK: to select the line chart and move it slightly to the left and down

12. Add callout boxes to emphasize the beginning and ending numbers on the Consumer series.
CHOOSE: the AutoShapes menu → Callouts → Rectangular Callout
CLICK: on your slide and drag to estimate the size you need near the first data marker
TYPE: **4,250,000** and make this text bold
Adjust the position of this callout and the point.
Duplicate this callout, position the second callout near the last data marker, and edit the text **7,250,000**.

13. Your slide should now look similar to the one shown in Figure 4.31.

Figure 4.31

Slide 5: Line chart with thicker lines, legend moved, and callouts added

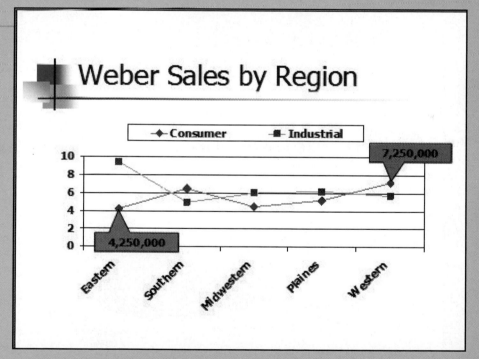

14. Pie slice sizes are usually easier to interpret when the labels are positioned directly beside each slice. In addition, the plot area line around the pie serves no purpose and should be removed. With slide 4 selected:
DOUBLE-CLICK: the chart so you can make modifications
CLICK: the plot area line around the pie
CHOOSE: Format → Selected Plot Area
CHOOSE: Border → None
CLICK: OK command button

15. Now show data category labels and percentages:
CHOOSE: Chart → Chart Options → Legend tab
CLICK: to remove Show legend
CLICK: *Data Labels* tab
CLICK: Category name and Percentage
CLICK: to Show leader lines
CLICK: OK

16. The labels are now word wrapping in an awkward way, so make the text smaller.
CLICK: on any of the pie slice labels
CHOOSE: Format → Selected Data Labels
SELECT: a 16-point size

17. The legend is no longer needed, so delete it. Drag each of the slice labels slightly away from the pie, so the leader lines will appear.

18. To emphasize that Competitor 1 has recently increased, explode that slice and add a callout box.
CLICK: to select the Competitor 1 slice (you may need to click more than once to select only this slice) and drag it slightly away from the other slices
CLICK: on a blank area of the slide outside the chart
CLICK: the AutoShapes menu
SELECT: Callout, Line Callout 3
TYPE: **Increase of 2%**

19. Adjust the positioning of the callout as necessary, so that your slide looks like Figure 4.32.

Figure 4.32

Slide 6: Pie chart with data labels, percentages, exploded slice, and callout box

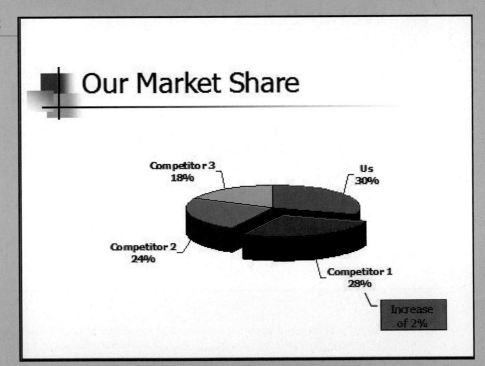

20. Your chart improvements are now complete. Save "Chart Sampler" for the final time and close the presentation.

4.2 Which chart type is best suited for comparing two data series with four categories?

4.3 Creating Diagrams for Processes and Relationships

Diagrams can help to communicate your message using very few words. They are made up of shapes connected in some way to help people understand a process or see a particular relationship. Often connecting lines or arrows show the path or sequence needed.

Following are the six different diagrams that PowerPoint provides in its Diagram Gallery and their main functions:

- *Organization Chart:* shows superior/subordinate or line-of-authority relationships

- *Cycle Diagram:* displays a process that occurs in a continuous cycle

- *Radial Diagram:* shows a central, or core, concept with related concepts like spokes of a wheel

- *Pyramid Diagram:* shows a foundational element and then each subsequent element builds on the previous one

- *Venn Diagram:* indicates overlapping relationships

- *Target Diagram:* displays steps to reach a goal

Each of these diagrams can be formatted using preset styles or customized. If these designs do not meet your needs, you can always create your own diagram using drawing tools.

4.3.1 Accessing the Diagram Gallery

→ Feature

PowerPoint's **Diagram Gallery** provides six different diagram types for the purposes outlined above. This lesson will focus on the **organization chart** for the purpose of showing a hierarchy of superior/subordinate relationships of an organization's employees.

→ Method

- CLICK: Insert Diagram or Organization Chart button (⬡) in a content placeholder

  or

- CLICK: Insert Diagram or Organization Chart button (⬡) on the Drawing toolbar

  or

- CHOOSE: Insert → Picture → Organization Chart from the menu

→ Practice

You will now insert an organization chart on a slide by editing an organization chart placeholder. Ensure that no presentations are open in the application window.

1. To begin a blank presentation and apply the Title and Content layout:
   CLICK: New button (🗋)
   CLICK: Title and Content layout

2. CLICK: in the title placeholder
   TYPE: **XYZ Corporation**

3. CLICK: Insert Diagram or Organization Chart button (⬡) in the content placeholder
   The Diagram Gallery dialog box, as shown in Figure 4.33, should now appear.

PowerPoint

Figure 4.33

Diagram Gallery
dialog box

Organization
Chart

Pyramid
Diagram

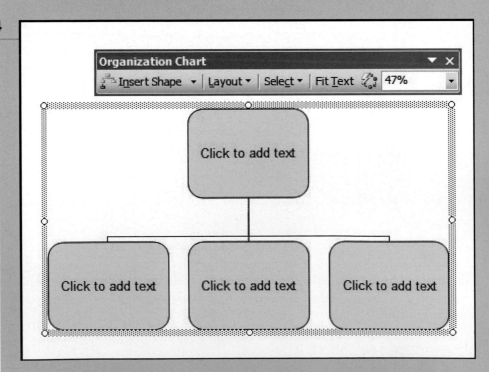

Cycle Diagram

Radial Diagram

Target Diagram

Venn Diagram

Diagram Gallery

Select a diagram type:

Organization Chart
Used to show hierarchical relationships

OK   Cancel

4. To create an organization chart, the currently selected option:
CLICK: OK command button
Your screen should now appear similar to the one shown in Figure 4.34. Note that the Organization
Chart toolbar is currently floating in the window. (*Note:* You can move a toolbar by dragging it by its
Title bar.) You should see four boxes in the chart area. The topmost box should already be selected,
and the handles should look a little different than other handles you have learned to use.

Figure 4.34

Organization
Chart beginning
structure

Organization Chart

Insert Shape ▾ | Layout ▾ | Select ▾ | Fit Text 🔧 47% ▾

Click to add text

Click to add text   Click to add text   Click to add text

5. In the next few steps, you will edit the content of the organization chart boxes.
CLICK: in the topmost chart box, which is the superior position for this chart
TYPE: **William Sanders**
PRESS: ENTER
TYPE: **President**

6. CLICK: the far left box, located in the second row of the chart
(*Note:* Because the three chart shapes on this row are below the superior box, they are considered subordinate positions.)
TYPE: **Alonzo Rodrigues**
PRESS: ENTER
TYPE: **VP Marketing**

7. CLICK: the box in the center of the second row
TYPE: **Jared Emerson**
PRESS: ENTER
TYPE: **VP Operations**

8. CLICK: the box on the right of the second row
TYPE: **Marianne Jefferson**
PRESS: ENTER
TYPE: **VP Accounting**

9. Edit the organization chart to include a new box below the President's box.
CLICK: the President's chart box
CLICK: Insert Shape drop-down arrow on the Organization Chart toolbar
The toolbar and associated drop-down menu appear in Figure 4.35. Be sure when you are adding positions that you have selected the correct box before you insert another shape. Your choices affect how the new boxes are connected (subordinate, coworker, or assistant).

Figure 4.35

Organization
Chart toolbar

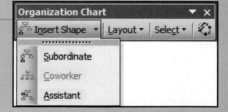

10. To add a new box to the chart:
CHOOSE: Assistant from the drop-down menu

11. CLICK: in the newly inserted box
TYPE: **Amie Reese**
PRESS: ENTER
TYPE: **Assistant**
The new box is added below the superior level and above the subordinate level to indicate that Amie Reese is an assistant to William Sanders.

12. On the Organization Chart toolbar,
CLICK: the AutoFormat button (⬚)
From the Organization Chart Style Gallery:
CLICK: Bookend Fills
CLICK: Outside the organization chart, near the upper-left corner of the slide
Adjust sizing of the organization chart if necessary. It should now appear similar to the one shown in Figure 4.36.

Figure 4.36

Completed organization chart

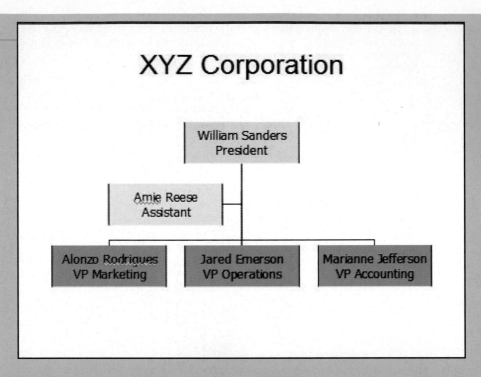

13. Save the presentation as "Organization chart" to your personal storage location.

14. Close the presentation.

4.3.2 Creating Custom Diagrams with Drawing Tools

→ Feature

If PowerPoint's Diagram Gallery does not provide the diagram structure that you need, then you can use drawing tools to create your own design. The AutoShapes collection provides a variety of rectangle, oval, and even flowchart shapes designed for this purpose. You can connect the shapes using lines or arrows.

→ Method

- CLICK: the AutoShapes tool that you want to use and draw an appropriate size on your slide
- TYPE: text to label each shape
- CLICK: an AutoShapes line or arrow to add connecting lines

→ Practice

You will now create three diagrams using drawing tools. Ensure that no presentations are open in the application window.

1. To begin a blank presentation and apply the Title Only layout:
CLICK: New button (🗋)

CLICK: Title Only layout
TYPE: **Sequential Diagram** in the slide title placeholder and make it bold

2. CHOOSE: AutoShapes → Basic Shapes → Rounded Rectangle
   CLICK: and drag to create a rectangle on the left of the slide
   With the rectangle selected:
   TYPE: **Part 1**
   CHOOSE: bold and change the font size to 32

3. PRESS CTRL + d twice to create two more rectangles and position them as shown in Figure 4.37
   Edit the text for **Part 2** and **Part 3**.

4. Add arrows to connect the rectangles:
   CHOOSE: AutoShapes → Block Arrows → Bent Arrow
   CLICK: and drag to create an arrow pointing right
   CHOOSE: Draw menu → Rotate or Flip → Flip Vertical to make the arrow point correctly
   CLICK: the Fill Color button and choose a contrasting color for the arrow
   PRESS: CTRL + d to duplicate this block arrow and position the second arrow between parts 2 and 3

Figure 4.37

Sequential
diagram

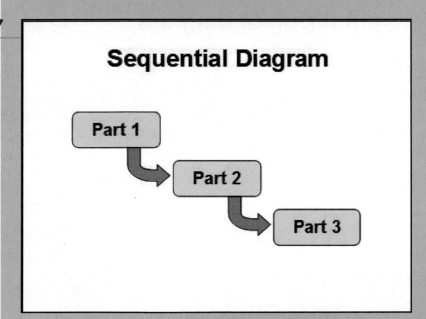

5. To begin a new slide and apply the Title Only layout:
   CLICK: New button ([D])
   CLICK: Title Only layout
   TYPE: **Input/Output Diagram** in the slide title placeholder and make it bold

6. CHOOSE: AutoShapes → Basic Shapes → Rectangle
   CLICK: and drag to create a rectangle on the left of the slide
   With the rectangle selected:
   TYPE: **Item 1**
   Make the text bold and change the font size to 24.

PowerPoint

7. With the rectangle selected:
PRESS: CTRL + **d** to create a second rectangle and position it below the first rectangle
PRESS: CTRL + **d** twice more to create two more rectangles and position them as shown in Figure 4.38
Edit the text for **Item 2**, **Item 3**, and **Item 4**.

8. With one of the rectangles selected:
PRESS: CTRL + **d** twice to create two more rectangles
Position one rectangle in the center of the slide and resize as shown in Figure 4.38.
Edit the text for **Process**.
Position one rectangle on the right of the slide.
Edit the text for **Results**.

9. Add lines to connect the rectangles:
CLICK: Line tool and drag to connect the Item 1 rectangle to the Process rectangle
Repeat for all other lines shown in Figure 4.38.

Figure 4.38

Input/Output
diagram

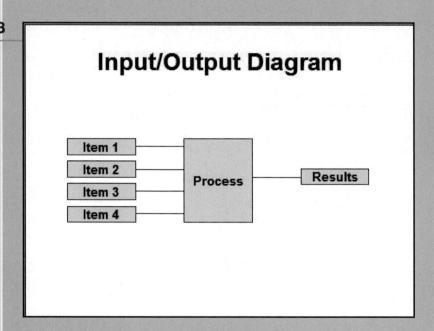

10. To begin a new slide and apply the Title Only layout:
CLICK: New button ( )
CLICK: Title Only layout
TYPE: **Stair Step Diagram** in the slide title placeholder and make it bold

11. CHOOSE: AutoShapes → Basic Shapes → Cube
CLICK: and drag to create a cube, a rectangle shape that looks like a stair step on the lower left of the slide
With the rectangle selected:
TYPE: **Foundation concept** and make it bold and change the font size to 24
CLICK: Align Left button

12. With the rectangle shape selected:
PRESS: `CTRL` + **d** to create a second rectangle shape and position it above the first rectangle shape and indented slightly
Edit the text for **Second concept**.

13. With the second rectangle shape selected:
PRESS: `CTRL` + **d** twice to create two more rectangles
Position them above the previous rectangles and indent them slightly.
Edit the text for **Third concept** and **Fourth concept**.

14. Make any necessary adjustments in the positioning of the rectangle shapes so your design is similar to the one shown in Figure 4.39.

Figure 4.39

Stair step
diagram

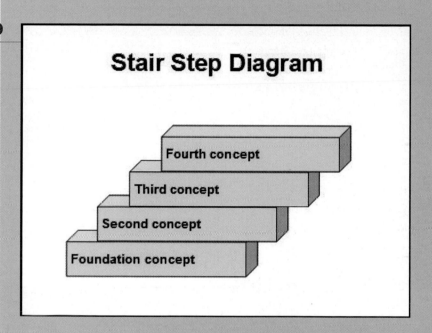

15. Save your presentation as "Diagrams" to your personal storage location.

16. Close your presentation

 **4.3**   What is the purpose of an organization chart?

Chapter
summary

PowerPoint provides several methods for making your presentations more understandable and interesting. Tables give order to your data by arranging your information in rows and columns. Charts show data in a visual way so viewers can better judge values and make comparisons between data series. Diagrams and organization charts show processes and hierarchy relationships. All of these elements must be carefully designed and formatted for easy interpretation and the greatest impact within your overall message.

Command Summary

Many of the commands and procedures appearing in this chapter are summarized in the following table.

Skill Set	To Perform this Task	Do the Following
Inserting a Table and Modifying Formats	Insert a table from the Standard toolbar	CLICK: Insert Table button (▢)
	Insert a table using a content placeholder	CHOOSE: Format, Slide Layout CLICK: a slide layout that includes the Insert Table button (▢) CLICK: Insert Table button (▢)
	Format text	SELECT: text Apply text attributes CLICK: Alignment button (▤) and Center Vertically button (▤) in Tables and Borders toolbar
	Add or remove border lines and row/column shading	CLICK: Border button (⊞▾) in Standard toolbar or Tables and Borders toolbar CLICK: Fill color button (🔳▾) in Drawing toolbar or Tables and Borders toolbar
	Resize a table	CLICK: sizing handles and adjust table size
Insert a Chart	Insert a chart	CLICK: Insert Chart button (📊) on the Standard toolbar or CLICK: Insert Chart button (📊) in a content placeholder or CHOOSE: Insert ➔ Chart from the menu or CHOOSE: Insert ➔ Object and then select Microsoft Graph Chart
	Edit chart content	DOUBLE-CLICK: chart object and revise information in the datasheet
	Apply a chart type	DOUBLE-CLICK: chart object CHOOSE: Chart ➔ Chart Type ➔ Chart subtype or CLICK: Chart Type button (📊▾)
	Format chart element colors	DOUBLE-CLICK: chart object SELECT: data series, or SELECT: walls or area behind chart CLICK: Fill color button to select a different color CHOOSE: Format ➔ Selected Data Series
	Format chart element legend and labels	DOUBLE-CLICK: chart object CHOOSE: Format ➔ Selected Chart area CHOOSE: Chart ➔ Chart Options

| Diagrams | Insert a diagram or organization chart | CLICK: Insert Diagram or Organization Chart button (⬚) in a content placeholder, or CHOOSE: Insert → Picture → Organization Chart |
| | Draw a diagram | SELECT: AutoShapes tools to draw a custom diagram |

Key Terms

This section specifies page references for the key terms identified in this chapter. For a complete list of definitions, refer to the Glossary provided at the back of this learning guide.

3D effect, *p. PP 166*

charts, *p. PP 166*

datasheet, *p. PP 169*

diagram, *p. PP 183*

Diagram Gallery, *PP 183*

grid lines, *p. PP 166*

labels, *p. •PP 166*

legend, *p. PP 166*

Microsoft Graph, *p. PP 165*

organization chart, *p. PP 183*

x-axis, *p. PP 166*

y-axis, *p. PP 166*

Chapter
q u i z

Short Answer

1. What is the procedure for changing the width of a table column?

2. Describe how to insert a column after a table has been created.

3. What techniques can you use to increase the readability of table content?

4. What is the purpose of the Microsoft Graph program?

5. Describe what it means to maintain visual integrity.

6. For pie charts, explain whether data labels or legends are easier to interpret.

7. Explain the most appropriate use of a line chart.

8. In what order should columns and bars be arranged?

9. Describe how to insert an organization chart on a slide.

10. Sketch a diagram showing a sequential process consisting of four parts.

True/False

1. _____ It is possible to apply character and paragraph formatting commands to your PowerPoint tables.

2. _____ Table text can be centered vertically or horizontally in a cell.

3. _____ Descriptive text should be left-aligned in table cells.

4. _____ Datasheet numbers can be changed only when a chart is created.

PowerPoint

5. _____ To insert a chart, double click on the datasheet.

6. _____ You edit a chart by double-clicking on the chart placeholder.

7. _____ A legend is necessary even when one data series is used.

8. _____ The colors used in charts should blend with the colors of your overall presentation.

9. _____ Organization charts are often used to represent spreadsheet data.

10. _____ When drawing diagrams, it is important to keep the diagram simple, so that it is easy to interpret.

Multiple Choice

1. Which of the following row alignments are possible with tables?

  a. Top
  b. Middle
  c. Bottom
  d. All of the above

2. If your insertion point is in the first column of a three-column table, press this key to move to the next cell to the right:

  a. TAB
  b. SHIFT + TAB
  c. PgUp
  d. PgDn

3. How do you activate the Microsoft Graph program in order to make changes to a chart?

  a. Choose Chart ➔ Chart Options from the menu
  b. Click the Graph button on the Drawing toolbar
  c. Double-click the placeholder that contains the chart
  d. Choose Data ➔ Graph from the menu

4. A chart is made up of two associated components:

  a. A data series and data markers
  b. A datasheet and a chart
  c. A datasheet and a data series
  d. None of the above

5. Which of the following changes can be made to a chart after it has been created?

  a. Choosing a different chart type
  b. Changing the color of a data series
  c. Removing grid lines
  d. All of the above

6. To compare values across categories, you should use a:

  a. Column chart
  b. Line chart
  c. Organization chart
  d. Pie chart

7. The chart type most suitable for showing a given quantity divided into parts is the:

  a. Column chart
  b. Line chart
  c. Organization chart
  d. Pie chart

8. Which of the following statements about charts is false?

  a. Chart types include both two-dimensional and three-dimensional options.
  b. The size of lines and data markers on line charts can be modified.
  c. The data you have will not influence the type of chart you choose.
  d. Almost every part of the chart can be formatted.

9. Which of the following is used to identify the colors that distinguish one data series from another?

  a. The labels on the x-axis
  b. The legend
  c. The key
  d. The labels on the y-axis

10. To edit an organization chart and add a new position:

  a. Choose Subordinate from the Insert Shape menu to add a position below a superior shape
  b. Choose Assistant from the Insert Shape menu to add a position below a superior shape but above a subordinate shape
  c. Choose Left Hanging and click where you want the shape to appear
  d. Either a. or b.

Hands-On
exercises

ep by step

1. Creating a Table

Randal Jackson works for Hadden Marketing Consultants, a company providing retail customer service solutions. He has been asked to add a table to an existing presentation to promote one of the company's training conferences. In this exercise, assume the role of Randal and perform the steps listed below.

1. Open the PP04HE01 presentation.

2. Save the presentation as "Customer Service Conference" to your personal storage location. Your screen should now appear similar to the one shown in Figure 4.40.

Figure 4.40

"Customer Service Conference" title slide

3. Display slide 4 and then click the Insert Table button (▦) in the content placeholder.

4. Create a table that contains two columns by eight rows.

5. Select the entire table and do the following:

   • Check to see that the font is Arial with a point size of 24 in bold (reduce size slightly if text word wraps on your computer).

   • Center the text vertically within each cell.

   • Expand the table on both sides to make room for the content (the edges should match the horizontal line endings at the bottom of the slide).

   • Make the first column more narrow by dragging the line between the two columns to the left (refer to Figure 4.41).

6. Type the text pictured in Figure 4.41.

Figure 4.41

Table before color adjustments

7. Change the background and font color in selected cells (refer to Figure 4.42):

   • Highlight all cells in the first column and change the fill color to a medium blue.

   • Repeat this process for the Registration and Lunch cells.

   • Highlight the morning session titles and change the fill color to white and the text color to dark blue.

   • Repeat this process for the afternoon session titles.

   • Now select the entire table and click on the No Border button (▦) to remove all the lines in the table.

   The slide should now appear similar to the one shown in Figure 4.42.

Figure 4.42

Table with color
adjustments

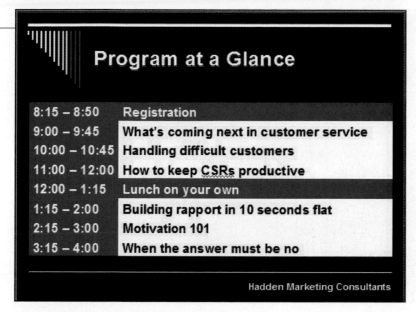

8. Save and then close the revised presentation.

2. Creating Charts

Northern Financial Networks provides mortgage options for residential properties. Justin Kirby is making changes to an existing presentation that he uses in talking to prospective clients about their refinancing or home equity loan options. In this exercise, assume the role of Justin and perform the same steps that he identifies.

1. Open the PP04HE02 data file.

2. Save the presentation as "Refinancing" to your personal storage location. The first slide of the presentation appears similar to the one shown in Figure 4.43.

Figure 4.43

"Refinancing" Title
slide

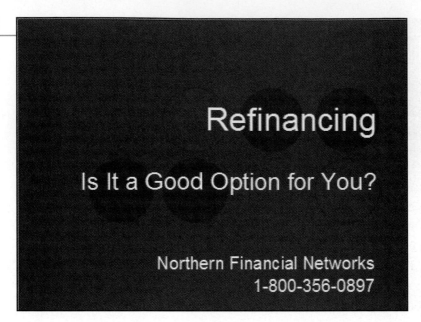

3. Display slide 3 and then click the Insert Chart button (⊞) in the content placeholder.

4. Create a graph that contains the mortgage rates from 1994–2003. Refer to the datasheet in Figure 4.44.

Figure 4.44

Refinancing
mortgage rate
datasheet

		A	B	C	D	E	F	G	H	I	J
		1994	1995	1996	1997	1998	1999	2000	2001	2002	2003
1	3-D Colum	7.25	9.5	7.25	8.25	7	6.75	8.5	7	6.5	5.5
2											
3											
4											

30-Year Fixed Mortgage Rates

1994	1995	1996	1997	1998	1999	2000	2001	2002	2003
7.25	9.5	7.25	8.25	7.0	6.75	8.5	7.0	6.5	5.5

Source: Interest.com

5. View the data as a column chart, as shown in Figure 4.45.

Figure 4.45

30-Year Fixed
Mortgage Rates
slide

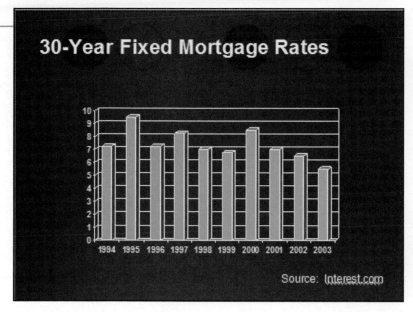

6. Duplicate this slide and then change the chart to a line chart. Adjust the thickness of the line and consider whether the line chart better reflects the information.

7. Save and then close the "Refinancing" presentation.

3. Creating a Diagram

As the founder of Crisman Associates, a small advertising firm, Ashley Powers frequently explains to clients her company's commitment to each project in which it becomes involved. She uses her notebook computer when talking to one or two people and has a small projector she uses when she meets with three or more people. For this exercise, assume the role of Ashley and perform the following steps.

1. Open the PP04HE03 presentation.

2. Save the presentation as "Advertising" to your personal storage location. Your screen should now appear similar to the one shown in Figure 4.46.

Figure 4.46

"Advertising" Title slide

3. Display slide 3 and click on the Insert Diagram or Organizational Chart button (⬚) in the Drawing toolbar, then select the Target diagram.

4. TYPE: the three labels:
Top circle: **Effective Timing**
Center circle: **Carefully Crafted Message**
Back circle: **Appropriate Outlets**

5. The default appearance of this diagram is shown in Figure 4.47. As you can see, it needs to be adjusted to make the text more readable and to give the colors on the target more variety.

Figure 4.47

Unformatted
diagram

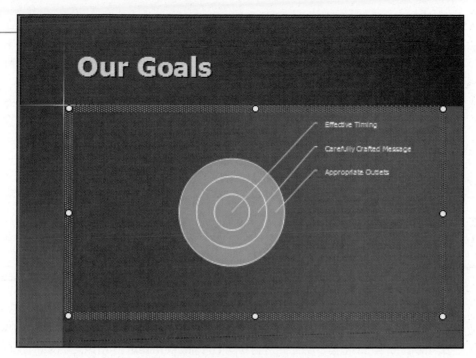

6. Highlight each text item and change the font to bold at 24 points.

7. From the Diagram toolbar, select Layout, Fit Diagram to Contents. Now the border line around the target is smaller. Move the target to the left to balance both the target and the text on the slide.

8. From the Diagram toolbar, select the AutoFormat button and choose 3-D Color. Your slide should now appear similar to the one shown in Figure 4.48.

Figure 4.48

Formatted
diagram

4. Creating a Diagram

A friend of yours, Danny Diego, operates a small but very successful sandwich shop called Danny's Deli, near your campus. The business is so successful that customers frequently wait for seating or to pick up carry-out sandwiches.

Danny has asked you to prepare two signs that can be posted in the waiting area to be seen by all customers. In this exercise, you will prepare the first sign, which explains Danny's philosophy for success.

As Danny was talking about the content for this sign, you realized that what he described could be best portrayed using an input/output diagram. You also decided to use a red, white, and blue color scheme to match the colors of the Danny's Deli sandwich shop, which features red and white checkered table cloths.

You decide to use PowerPoint to create the sign as a slide that you will print in color. Start with a blank slide and design the slide elements as follows:

1. Draw a blue rectangle at the top of the slide then add a narrow rectangle with a red and white checkered pattern fill that is positioned at the top of the blue rectangle.

2. Duplicate this patterned rectangle and position the second one below the blue rectangle.

3. Insert a clip art image that reflects this type of sandwich business.

4. Insert text for **Danny's Deli** and **Only the best . . .** using the Forte font and appropriate sizes.

5. Insert an AutoShapes rectangle and type **The finest meats** in Arial, 20 point, bold. Duplicate this rectangle and edit the text for **The freshest breads**. Repeat this process for each of the other boxes shown in Figure 4.49. Resize and reposition each box as shown. Check alignment.

Figure 4.49

Danny's Deli diagram

6. Add blue arrows by creating one and then duplicating others. Position them appropriately.

7. Insert a clip art image to reflect good customer service.

8. Save the presentation as "Weekly Deli Specials" and continue to the next exercise.

5. Creating a Table

In this exercise you will add another slide to your Weekly Deli Specials presentation to make the second sign for Danny's Deli.

1. Be sure that your first slide is selected in the Outline and Slide pane and then duplicate the slide. On slide 2, delete the diagram and other objects on the lower part of the slide to make room for a table.

2. Edit the text at the top of the slide to change it to **Weekly Specials.**

3. Insert a four-column, five-row table. The sandwich names are set in 28-point type, but the sandwich ingredients are set in 20-point type. Type the text as shown in Figure 4.50.

Figure 4.50

"Weekly Specials" table

4. Align the table rows on the bottom. Add alternate row shading of yellow and light brown. Use a 6-point table border in red.

5. Adjust the table size if necessary. Add the comment at the bottom below the table.

6. Save the presentation to your personal storage location and print both slides. Close the presentation.

6. Creating a Chart

You were recently asked to speak to your local community college about employment concepts. The person asking you to talk wants you to give an overview of emerging jobs and then focus on management opportunities, including a discussion of salaries.

1. Open the PP04HE06 data file and save it as "Employment" to your personal storage location.

2. On slide 3, create a chart using the datasheet information displayed in Figure 4.51.

Figure 4.51

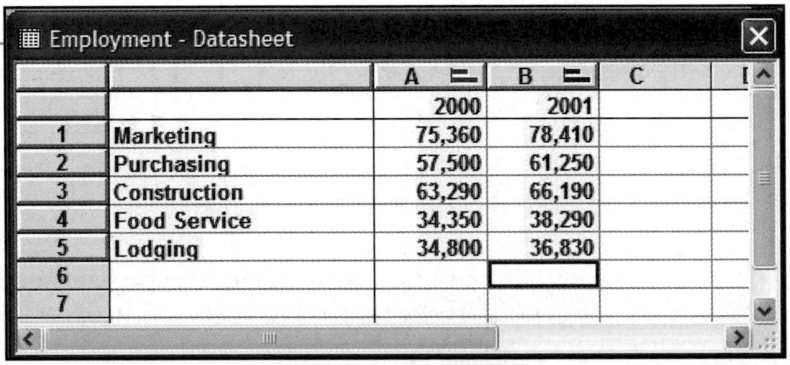

"Employment" datasheet

		A ▭ 2000	B ▭ 2001	C	I
1	Marketing	75,360	78,410		
2	Purchasing	57,500	61,250		
3	Construction	63,290	66,190		
4	Food Service	34,350	38,290		
5	Lodging	34,800	36,830		
6					
7					

3. Make these adjustments to the chart so that it looks like the example shown in Figure 4.52:

- The datasheet information is currently displayed by row. Change this by clicking on the By Column button (▦).

- Change the chart type to a horizontal bar.

- Remove the grid lines.

- With the Value axis selected, format the axis so that the numbers have no decimal place.

- Select one of the data series by clicking on one of the bars, then choose Format, Data Series, *Options* tab. Change the gap width to 50 to make the bars thicker.

- Insert the picture in the plot area. Select the plot area and then choose Fill, Fill Effects, *Picture* tab. Click Picture then select PP04EX06B from the data files.

- Select the 2001 data series and change the color to a plum color.

4. From Chart Options, select the *Data Labels* tab and then choose Value so that the numbers are displayed at the end of each bar.

5. Move the legend closer to the plot area.

6. Save your slide show and print a handout copy on one page.

Figure 4.52

Completed
"Employment"
slide

CaseStudy   BEAVER RUN RESORT AND CONFERENCE CENTER

Joyce Kennedy is a marketing manager for Beaver Run Resort and Conference Center in Breckenridge, Colorado. The condominium units at this resort facility are individually owned, and the owners belong to a Homeowners' Association that helps to manage the property. At the Annual Homeowners' Meeting, Joyce is one of several speakers who will present information. Joyce will showcase recent renovations at the resort and inform homeowners about ongoing issues, such as expenditures and guest satisfaction. She will also discuss some of the trends in the resort industry. Joyce has started to develop her presentation, and the opening slide is shown in Figure 4.53.

Joyce opens the PP04CS04 presentation and saves it as "Beaver Run" to her personal storage location. She reviews the remaining slides in the presentation and now has the necessary information to complete slides 5–8. Assume the role of Joyce and perform the steps she identifies to complete these slides.

PowerPoint

Figure 4.53

Beaver Run
Resort and
Conference
Center Title slide

1. The Homeowners' Association's total expenditures are divided into six categories. Therefore, Joyce decides to display this data in a 3-D pie chart on slide 6. The datasheet numbers are displayed in Figure 4.54.

Figure 4.54

Financial
Performance
datasheet

		A	B	C	D
		3-D Pie 1			
1	Utilities	732,000			
2	Maintenance	663,000			
3	Administration	344,000			
4	Fixed	205,000			
5	Janitorial	193,000			
6	Security	136,000			
7					

Beaver Run Case - Datasheet

2. Joyce adjusts the pie chart to remove the legend and add labels and percentages. The label text must be a smaller size so that the text will not word wrap. Joyce then adjusts the 3-D view of the pie so that the slices are less flat and easier to see. Joyce's final step for this slide is to add the subtitle text, as shown in Figure 4.55.

Figure 4.55

Financial Performance pie chart

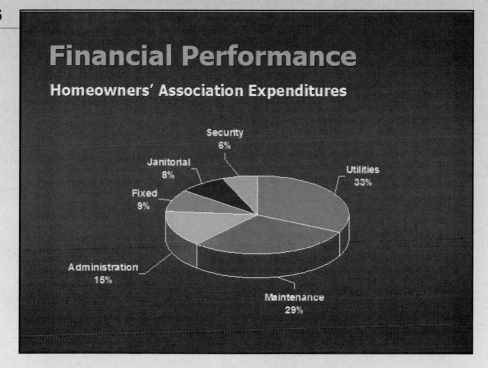

3. To improve the quality of guest services, the staff at Beaver Run during the past few weeks have been surveying guests about their satisfaction with the many services offered. These surveys have been compiled, and Joyce wants to feature those services with the highest average scores. She will then explain the staff's plans to improve the five areas that received lowest scores.

4. Refer to Figures 4.56 and 4.57 to prepare tables on slides 6 and 7.

Figure 4.56

Services Report—
Highest Ratings

**Services Report—
Highest Ratings**

Hotel shuttle service	4.49	
Quality of meeting rooms	4.26	5 points possible
Beaver Run staff	4.25	
Concierge/guest services	4.22	
Banquet services	4.22	
Reservations	4.22	
Front desk	4.21	

Figure 4.57

Services Report—
Lowest Ratings

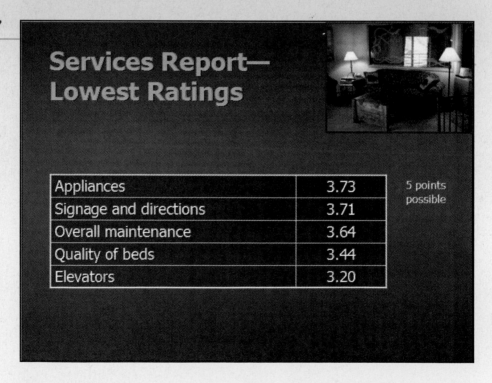

**Services Report—
Lowest Ratings**

Appliances	3.73	5 points possible
Signage and directions	3.71	
Overall maintenance	3.64	
Quality of beds	3.44	
Elevators	3.20	

5. Ten years ago people made reservations at the resort by calling the resort directly or by booking reservations through a travel agent. However, the Internet has had a tremendous impact on the tourist industry, and many more people are booking reservations online with a variety of Web sites that have been developed for this purpose. Because people tend to shop around for the best value, prices must be competitive.

6. Joyce wants to show visually that learning how to deal with this trend has been somewhat uncertain and that its future impact cannot be predicted. However, it is clear that the Beaver Run Web site must be easy to use and that Beaver Run's values offered must be in line with those of other comparable properties for Beaver Run to remain competitive.

7. Refer to Figure 4.58 to prepare the diagram Joyce designed for slide 8. Use AutoShapes and choose a shadow treatment for all the elements that make up the diagram. Then add the subtitle text.

Figure 4.58

Sales and
Marketing

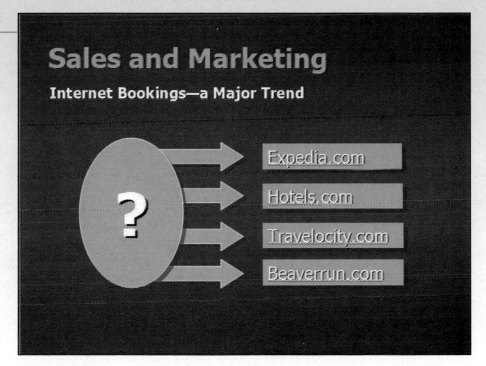

Answers to Self-Check Questions

4.1   How can the width of a table column be changed? Drag the column edges to the left or right.

4.2   Which chart type is best suited for comparing two data series with four categories? The column (or bar) chart is well suited to make this type of comparison using a clustered arrangement.

4.3   What is the purpose of an organization chart? An organization chart is a drawing showing a hierarchy of relationships, such as the superior-subordinate or line-of-authority relationships among a company's employees.

Notes

Microsoft®Office Access®

2003

CHAPTER 1

⊕ # Working with Access

CHAPTER OUTLINE

PREREQUISITES

Although you need no previous experience using Microsoft Office Access 2003 to this chapter, you should be comfortable working with the mouse and keyboard in the Microsoft Windows environment. You should be able to launch and exit programs and perform basic file management operations, such as opening and closing documents.

LEARNING OBJECTIVES

After completing this chapter, you will be able to:

- Understand basic database terminology

- Describe the different components of the Access 2003 application window and the Database window

- Select commands and perform actions using the keyboard and mouse

- Open various database objects, including tables, queries, forms, and reports, for display

- View, edit, and print data in a datasheet

- Insert and delete records in a datasheet

- Open and close a database

1.1 Getting Started with Access 2003

Microsoft Office Access 2003 is a database program that enables you to enter, store, analyze, and present data. For end users, power users, and software developers alike, Access provides easy-to-use yet powerful tools most often associated with higher-end **database management systems (DBMS)**. In fact, Access offers scalability never before seen in desktop database software to meet needs ranging from simple to complex. At the desktop level, Access can help you manage your personal information or collect data for a research study. At the corporate and enterprise level, Access can retrieve and summarize data stored on servers located throughout the world. Access also enables you to create and publish dynamic Web-based forms and reports for delivery over the Internet.

Although this is not a database theory course, a familiarity with some basic terms will help you become more productive using Access 2003. The word **database,** for example, refers to a collection of related information, such as a company's accounting data. The primary object in a database for collecting and storing data is called a **table.** As shown in Figure 1.1, tables are organized into rows and columns similar to an electronic spreadsheet. An individual entry in a table (for example, a person's name and address) is called a **record** and is stored as a horizontal row. Each record in a table is composed of one or more fields. A **field** holds a single piece of data. For example, the Students table shown in Figure 1.1 divides each person's record into vertical columns or fields for StudentID, LastName, FirstName, Major, Address, and City.

Figure 1.1

An Access table
in Datasheet view

Each column
represents a field.

Each row represents
a record.

	StudentID	LastName	FirstName	Major	Address	City
+	1	Stedman	Alan	Business	3710 Bush St.	Seattle
+	2	Hernandez	Pete	Business	1485 Sonama Way	Redmond
+	3	Mohr	Judy	Arts	100 Bosley Lane	Redmond
+	4	Buggey	Diana	Science	20 Cactus Lane	Redmond
+	5	Seinfeld	Casey	Arts	17 Windy Way	Bellevue
+	6	Alomar	Sandra	Business	PO Box 1465	Kirkland
+	7	Fernandez	Rosa	Science	151 Greer Rd.	Seattle
+	8	Peters	Bob	Arts	200 Union St.	Seattle

Record: |◄ ◄   1   ► ►| ►✳ of 65

1.1.1 Loading and Exiting Access

→ **Feature**

Microsoft Office Access 2003 is an application software program that runs under the Microsoft Windows operating system. To load Access 2003 in Windows XP, click the Start button (*start*) on the taskbar to display the Windows Start menu. Then, choose the All Programs menu option. In the menu that appears, choose Microsoft Office by either clicking or highlighting the menu option and, then, click Microsoft Office Access 2003. After a few moments, the Access 2003 application window appears.

When you are finished doing your work, close the Access 2003 application window so that your system's memory is freed for use by other Windows applications. To do so, choose the File, Exit command or click on the Close button (✕) appearing in the top right-hand corner. These methods are used to close most Microsoft Windows applications.

→ **Method**

To load Access:

- CLICK: Start button (*start*)

- CHOOSE: All Programs → Microsoft Office

- CLICK: Microsoft Office Access 2003

To exit Access:

- CHOOSE: File → Exit from the Access Menu bar

  or

- CLICK: its Close button (X)

→ Practice

You will now load Microsoft Office Access 2003 using the Windows Start menu. Ensure that you have turned on your computer and that the Windows desktop now appears.

1. Position the mouse pointer over the Start button (start) appearing in the bottom left-hand corner of the Windows taskbar and then click the left mouse button once. The Start menu appears.

2. Position the mouse pointer over the All Programs menu option. Notice that you do not need to click the left mouse button to display the list of programs in the fly-out or cascading menu. (*Note:* If you are using a version of Windows prior to XP, click the Programs menu option.)

3. Move the mouse pointer horizontally to the right until it highlights an option in the All Programs menu. You can now move the mouse pointer vertically within the menu to select an application.

4. Position the mouse pointer over the Microsoft Office program group and then move the highlight into the fly-out or cascading menu, similar to the graphic shown in Figure 1.2. (*Note:* Even if you are using Windows XP, the desktop theme, color scheme, and menu options may appear differently on your screen than in Figure 1.2.)

Figure 1.2

Highlighting an option in the Microsoft Office program group

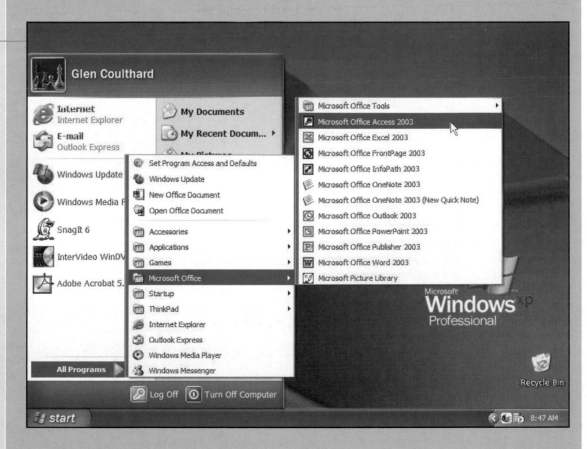

5. Position the mouse pointer over the Microsoft Office Access 2003 menu option and then click the left mouse button once. After a few seconds, the Access 2003 application window appears (Figure 1.3).

Figure 1.3

Microsoft Office Access 2003 application window

The *work area* is like the top of your desk. You open data tables, forms, and reports for editing and viewing in this area.

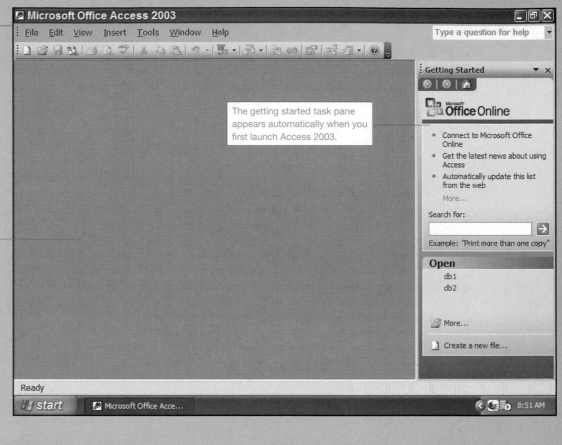

The getting started task pane appears automatically when you first launch Access 2003.

6. To exit Access:
CLICK: its Close button () in the top right-hand corner
Assuming that no other applications are running and displayed, you are returned to the Windows desktop.

In Addition SWITCHING AMONG APPLICATIONS

A button appears on the Windows taskbar for each "running" application or open document. Switching among your open Microsoft Office System applications is as easy as clicking on a taskbar button, like switching channels on a television set.

1.1.2 Opening a Database File at Startup

→ ## Feature

There are several methods for opening an existing database file in Access 2003. First, you can load Access and then click the Open button ( ) on the toolbar to display the Open dialog box. You can achieve the same result by clicking the "More . . ." option under the *Open* heading in the *Getting Started task pane*. A **task pane** (see Figure 1.3) is the window area that appears docked at the right side of your screen. The Getting Started task pane is displayed automatically when you first start Microsoft Office Access 2003. Once displayed, use the Open dialog box to search for and retrieve a database file that is stored on your computer's local hard disk, a removable disk, a network server, or on the Web.

If you want to load Access 2003 and open an existing database at the same time, click the Start button (*start*) and then choose the Open Office Document command on the All Programs menu. You can also double-click an Access filename that is displayed in Windows Explorer.

→ Method

To display the Open dialog box:

- CLICK: Open button (⬜) on the toolbar,

    or

- CHOOSE: File → Open from the Menu bar,

    or

- CLICK: "More . . ." option under the *Open* heading in the Getting Started task pane

    To retrieve a database file using the Open dialog box:

- SELECT: *the desired folder* from the Places bar, located along the left border of the dialog box, or from the *Look in* drop-down list box

- DOUBLE-CLICK: *the desired file* from the list area

→ Practice

You will now practice navigating your computer's storage areas using the Open dialog box. Ensure that the Windows desktop appears.

1. Load Microsoft Office Access 2003, referring to the previous lesson if necessary.

2. To open an existing database:
CLICK: Open button (⬜) on the toolbar
The Open dialog box appears, as shown in Figure 1.4.

Figure 1.4

Open dialog box

Lists the files with which you have most recently worked.

Lists common desktop shortcuts.

The default folder for storing your work

Provides access to the resources on your computer

Lists files and folders stored on your intranet or Internet Web server

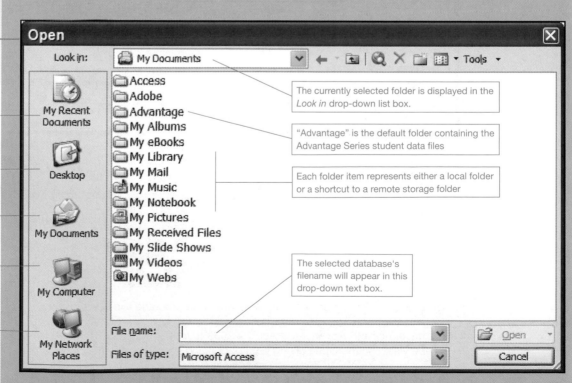

The currently selected folder is displayed in the *Look in* drop-down list box.

"Advantage" is the default folder containing the Advantage Series student data files

Each folder item represents either a local folder or a shortcut to a remote storage folder

The selected database's filename will appear in this drop-down text box.

- CLICK: Minimize button (▪) to minimize a window
- CLICK: Restore button (🗗) to restore a maximized window

→ **Practice**

In a guided tour, you will now explore several interface features of the Access application window. Ensure that you have completed the previous lesson and that the Open dialog box is displayed in the application window.

1. To begin, let's open a database file using the Open dialog box:
DOUBLE-CLICK: AC0100
Depending on your computer's configuration, the warning dialog box in Figure 1.7 may appear.

Figure 1.7

A warning dialog box may display when you open a database file

2. If the dialog box shown in Figure 1.7 appears:
CLICK: Enable Macros command button to proceed
After the database is loaded into the application window, your screen should appear similar to the one shown in Figure 1.8. (*Note:* The AC0100 filename reflects that this file is used in Chapter 1 of the Microsoft Office Access 2003 learning guide.)

Figure 1.8

Access application and Database windows

Menu bar

Database toolbar

Database window

Work area

Status bar

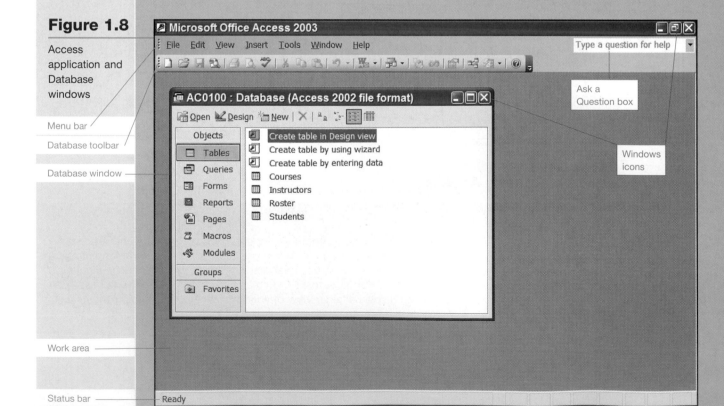

3. The Database window is best displayed as a floating window in the work area, although it may be maximized to fill the entire application window. You control the display of the application and Database windows by clicking their respective Title bar or Windows icons: Minimize (), Maximize (□), Restore (🗗), and Close (☒).

4. The Menu bar groups commands for easy access. To execute a command, click once on the desired Menu bar option and then click again on the command. (*Note:* Commands that appear dimmed are not available for selection. Commands that are followed by an ellipsis (. . .) display a dialog box. If a pull-down menu displays a chevron (⅀) at the bottom, additional commands are displayed when the chevron is selected.)
To practice using the Menu bar:
CHOOSE: Help
This instruction tells you to click the left mouse button once on the Help option appearing in the Menu bar. The Help menu appears, as shown here. (*Note:* All menu commands that you execute in this guide begin with the instruction "CHOOSE.")

Help	
Microsoft Access Help	F1
Show the Office Assistant	
Office on Microsoft.com	
Microsoft Access Developer Resources	
Contact Us	
Sample Databases...	▶
Check for Updates	
Detect and Repair...	
Activate Product...	
Customer Feedback Options...	
About Microsoft Access	

5. To display the other pull-down menus, move the mouse to the left, over top of the other Menu bar options. As each option is highlighted, a menu appears with its associated commands.

6. To leave the Menu bar without making a command selection:
CLICK: in a blank portion of the Access work area
(*Hint:* You can also click in a blank area of the Title bar.)

7. Access provides context-sensitive *right-click menus* for quick access to relevant menu commands. Rather than searching for the appropriate command in the Menu bar, you can position the mouse pointer on a database object and right-click to display a list of commonly selected commands for that object.
To display the right-click menu for a table object:
RIGHT-CLICK: Students in the list area of the Database window
Your screen should now appear similar to the one shown in Figure 1.9.

Figure 1.9

Right-click menu for a table object

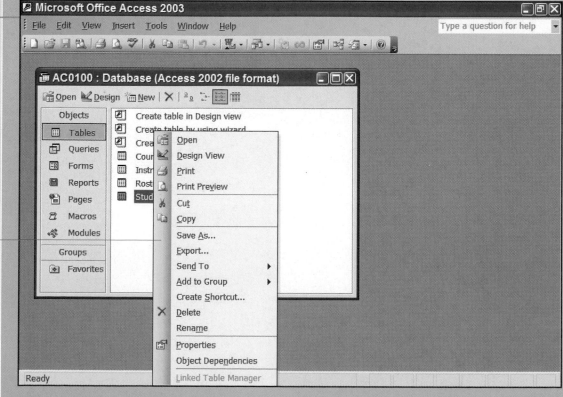

This pop-up menu appears when you right-click the Students table object.

8. To remove the right-click menu without making a selection:
PRESS: ‹ ESC › (or click on a blank portion of the work area.)

9. If an Office Assistant character (as shown here) appears on your screen as you proceed through any part of this tutorial, do the following to hide it from view:
RIGHT-CLICK: *the character*
CHOOSE: Hide from the right-click menu
(*Note:* The character's name may appear in the command, as in "Hide Clippit.")

1.1.4 Working in the Database Window

→ # Feature

The Access 2003 **Database window** is your command control center; it provides the interface to your database. The **Objects bar,** located along the left border, organizes the available database objects into seven categories named *Tables, Queries, Forms, Reports, Pages, Macros,* and *Modules.* Most of your time is spent working with objects in the Database window. When you are more familiar with Access 2003, you can customize the Database window by defining your own groups to appear alongside the Favorites folder in the **Groups bar.**

→ # Method

To peruse the objects in a database:

• CLICK: *the category buttons* in the Objects bar

→ # Practice

In this lesson, you will practice selecting objects for display in the Database window. Ensure that the AC0100 Database window is displayed.

1. To begin, let's practice manipulating the Database window in the work area. Using the mouse, drag the Title bar of the Database window to move the window. Do the following:
DRAG: the Database window to the center of the work area

2. Now, place the mouse pointer over the bottom right-hand corner of the Database window. The mouse pointer changes shape to a diagonal double-headed sizing arrow. To decrease the size of the window:
DRAG: the sizing corner inward, as shown in Figure 1.10

Figure 1.10

Sizing the
Database window

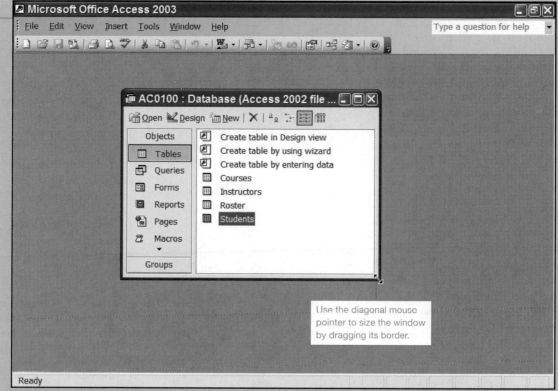

Use the diagonal mouse
pointer to size the window
by dragging its border.

3. When you are satisfied with the size of the window, release the mouse button to complete the operation. (*Hint:* Because your system's resolution and font selections may differ from the author's, these mouse techniques may be necessary to adjust the windows in your work area so that they look similar to the screen figures in this tutorial.)

4. On your own, return the Database window to its original size and location, so that it appears similar to Figure 1.11. Familiarize yourself with the features and components labeled in the figure.

Figure 1.11

Access 2003
Database window

Objects bar

Active category
button

Inactive category
button

Groups bar

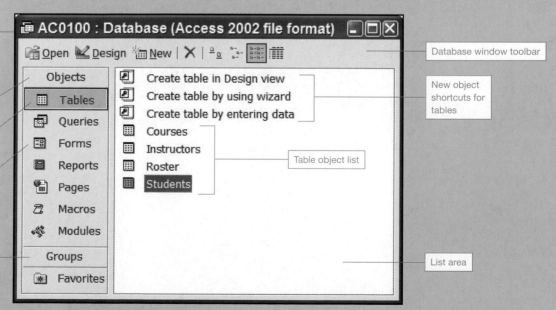

Database window toolbar

New object
shortcuts for
tables

Table object list

List area

Access

5. Table objects are the primary element of a database and are used to store and manipulate data. A single database file may contain several tables. To display the contents of a table object, ensure that the Tables button in the Objects bar is selected and then do the following:

DOUBLE-CLICK: Students in the list area

The Students table appears in a row-and-column layout called a *datasheet,* as shown in Figure 1.12. You will learn how to navigate and manipulate the contents of a datasheet in the next module.

Figure 1.12

Datasheet
window for the
Students table
object

		StudentID	LastName	FirstName	Major	Address	City	Zip
	+	1	Stedman	Alan	Business	3710 Bush St.	Seattle	99900
	+	2	Hernandez	Pete	Business	1485 Sonama V	Redmond	99780
	+	3	Mohr	Judy	Arts	100 Bosley Lan	Redmond	99780
	+	4	Buggey	Diana	Science	20 Cactus Lane	Redmond	99804
	+	5	Seinfeld	Casey	Arts	17 Windy Way	Bellevue	98180
	+	6	Alomar	Sandra	Business	PO Box 1465	Kirkland	97080
	+	7	Fernandez	Rosa	Science	151 Greer Rd.	Seattle	99890
	+	8	Peters	Bob	Arts	200 Union St.	Seattle	99850
	+	9	Rinaldo	Sandy	Arts	1871 Orrinton R	Redmond	99704
	+	10	Finklestein	Sue	Business	888 Burrard St.	Seattle	99904
	+	11	Mortimer	Bruce	Science	235 Johnston S	Redmond	99704
	+	12	Jung	Chris	Science	1005 West 9th ,	Redmond	99780
	+	13	Abu-Alba	Benji	Arts	122 Cordova Av	Bellevue	98200
	+	14	Stockton	Gretta	Arts	4210 Bush St.	Seattle	99900
	+	15	Sakic	Eric	Arts	875 Cordova Av	Bellevue	98180
	+	16	Modano	Joey	Science	36 Primore St.	Kirkland	97780
	+	17	Francis	Mike	Business	875 Broadway	Maryland	92250
	+	18	Hillman	Frances	Business	29 Redmond Rc	Redmond	99850
	+	19	Brewski	Randy	Science	190 Greer Rd.	Seattle	99890
	+	20	Walsh	Moira	Arts	909 West 18th ,	Seattle	99900

Record: ◄◄ ◄ 1 ► ►► ►* of 65

6. To close the Students datasheet:

CLICK: its Close button (☒) in the top right-hand corner of the datasheet window

7. A **query** is a question you ask of your database. The answer, which may draw data from more than one table in the database, typically displays a datasheet of records. To see a list of the stored queries:

CLICK: Queries button in the Objects bar

8. The stored query in this database links and extracts data from the Courses and Instructors tables. To display the results of the query:

DOUBLE-CLICK: Courses Query in the list area

Your screen should now appear similar to the one shown in Figure 1.13. The first two columns in this query display information from the Courses table, and the remaining two columns extract information from the Instructors table.

Figure 1.13

Datasheet
window for the
Courses Query
object

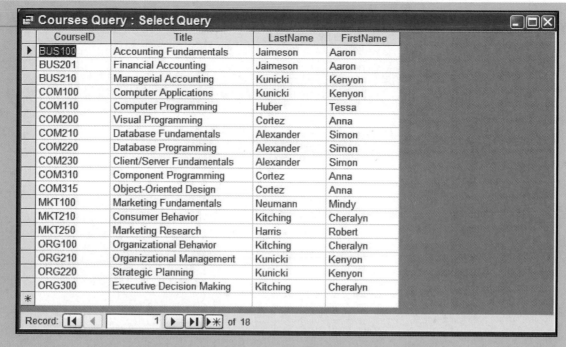

9. After reviewing the query, close the displayed datasheet:
   CLICK: its Close button ( )

10. Unlike a table's column and row layout, a **form** generally displays one record at a time. To see a list of the stored form objects:
   CLICK: Forms button in the Objects bar

11. To display a form:
   DOUBLE-CLICK: Student Input Form in the list area
   Your screen should now appear similar to the one shown in Figure 1.14.

Figure 1.14

Form window for
the Student Input
Form object

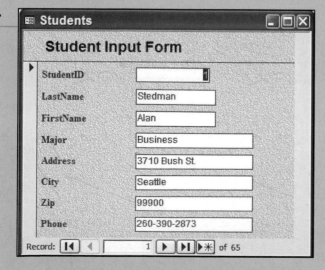

12. To close the Student Input Form:
   CLICK: its Close button ( )

13. Whereas you use datasheets and forms to input and modify data, you create **reports** to present, summarize, and print data. To see a list of the stored report objects in the database:
CLICK: Reports button in the Objects bar

14. To view a report as it will appear when printed:
DOUBLE-CLICK: Students by Major in the list area
The report appears in the Print Preview window, as shown in Figure 1.15.

Figure 1.15

Print Preview window for the Students by Major report object

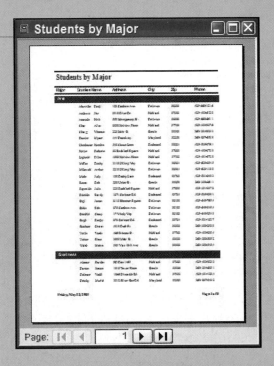

15. To close the Print Preview window:
CLICK: its Close button (✖)

16. To return to displaying the table objects:
CLICK: Tables button in the Objects bar
(*Note:* If you are proceeding to the next module, keep the database open for use in the next lesson.)

In Addition ADDITIONAL DATABASE OBJECTS

The Objects bar lets you access a variety of database objects. In addition to *Tables, Queries, Forms,* and *Reports,* it offers the *Pages* category to link to external Internet-ready database objects called *data access pages.* The *Macro* category stores objects that you use to automate frequently performed procedures. For even greater control, you can write code *modules* using Visual Basic for Applications (VBA), a subset of the Microsoft Visual Basic programming language.

1.1   How do you close a window that appears in the Access work area?

1.2 Viewing and Printing Your Data

Much like an electronic worksheet, a table object stores data in a series of rows and columns called a **datasheet.** Each row represents an individual record, and each column represents a field. The intersection of a row and column is called a **cell.** This **Datasheet view** mode lets you display and work with many records at once. Learning how to navigate, customize, and print datasheets is fundamental to working effectively with Access 2003.

1.2.1 Moving Around a Datasheet

→ Feature

To properly manage the data stored in a table object, you must know how to efficiently move the selection cursor to view all parts of a table. As with most Access 2003 features, both mouse and keyboard methods are available for moving the cursor in a datasheet window. Try both methods and then select the one that appeals to you most in a given situation.

→ Method

Keystroke	Task Description
⬆, ⬇	Moves to the previous or next record
⬅, ➡	Moves cursor to the left or to the right
CTRL + ⬇	Moves to the bottom of a field column
CTRL + ⬆	Moves to the top of a field column
PgUp, PgDn	Moves up or down one screen
HOME	Moves to the first (leftmost) field in a record
END	Moves to the last (rightmost) field in a record
CTRL + HOME	Moves to the top (first record and first field)
CTRL + END	Moves to the bottom (last record and last field)

→ Practice

Using the Students table, you will now practice moving the cursor around a datasheet. Ensure that the AC0100 Database window is displayed. If it is not, open the AC0100 database from your student data files location.

1. Ensure that the Tables button in the Objects bar is selected. To display the Students datasheet, do the following:
   DOUBLE-CLICK: Students in the list area
   The Students data table is loaded into the computer's memory and displayed in Datasheet view. Depending on your screen size, you may see more or fewer records than those shown in Figure 1.16.

Figure 1.16

Datasheet
window

The table name is
displayed in the
Datasheet
window's Title bar.

This triangle symbol
marks the current
or active record.

The navigation area
displays the current
record number (4)
and the local
number of records
(65).

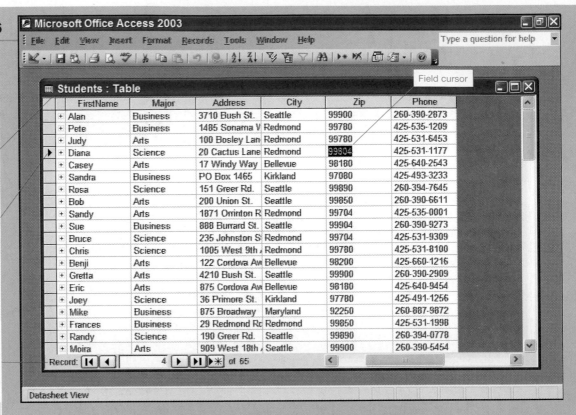

2. Notice the flashing cursor that appears in the leftmost field of the first record. To move this cursor to the last field column in the current record, do the following:
PRESS: `END`
The cursor is now positioned in the Phone column.

3. To move one field to the left and down to the fourth record:
PRESS: `←` once
PRESS: `→` three times
Your screen should now appear similar to the one shown in Figure 1.16. (**Caution:** If pressing a cursor movement key does not yield the expected result, you may have activated Access's Edit mode accidentally. To return to navigating between records and fields, press `F2` or `ENTER` to exit the Edit mode.)

4. To move the cursor down by one screen at a time:
PRESS: `PgDn` twice

5. To move to the top left-hand corner of the datasheet window:
PRESS: `CTRL` + `HOME`

6. Position the mouse pointer over the scroll box on the vertical scroll bar and then drag the scroll box downward. Notice that a yellow Scroll Tip appears, identifying the current record number. Release the mouse button when you see "Record: 25 of 65" in the Scroll Tip, as shown here. (*Note:* Although the window pans downward, this method does not move the cursor. Looking in the navigation area, you will see that the first record, 1, remains the active or current record.)

Kirkland	97900
Bellevue	98100
Seattle	99890
Kirkland	97800
Seattle	99904
Seattle	99900	Record: 25 of 65
Bellevue	98000

7. As illustrated in Figure 1.16, Access provides a navigation area in the bottom left-hand corner of the Datasheet window. To use this area to navigate the records in a datasheet:

CLICK: Last Record button (▶|) to move to the bottom of the datasheet (record 65)
CLICK: First Record button (|◀) to move to the top of the datasheet (record 1)

8. Access allows you to open a number of datasheet windows at the same time. To display another table, make the Database window active by clicking on it or by using the following menu command:
CHOOSE: Window → AC0100 : Database (Access 2002 file format)

9. To display the Roster table:
DOUBLE-CLICK: Roster in the list area
The Roster Datasheet window appears, overlapping the other two windows, as shown in Figure 1.17. Like the Students table, the Roster table contains a field named StudentID. This common field enables a link to be established between the two tables.

Figure 1.17

Opening the Roster Datasheet window

Students Datasheet window

AC0100 Database window

Roster Database window

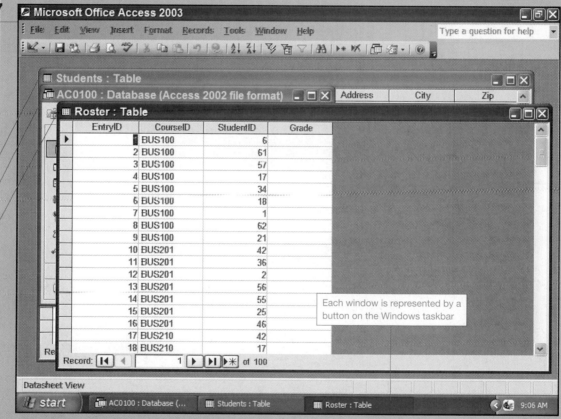

10. To display the Students datasheet once again:
CHOOSE: Window → Students : Table
(*Hint:* You can also click the "Students : Table" button that appears on the Windows taskbar at the bottom of the screen.)

11. Within the Students Datasheet window, you can display course and grade information from the Roster table using *subdatasheets*. A **subdatasheet** lets you browse related data that is stored in another table without having to open another Datasheet window. In a sense, a subdatasheet provides a "picture-in-picture" view of your data. To demonstrate, let's drill down and display the courses and grades for Ms. Rosa Fernandez. Do the following:
CLICK: Expand button (⊞) in the left-hand column of StudentID 7
Your screen should now appear similar to the one shown in Figure 1.18.

Figure 1.18

Displaying a subdatasheet

Displaying related records from the Roster table in a subdatasheet

		StudentID	LastName	FirstName	Major	Address	City	Zip
►	+	1	Stedman	Alan	Business	3710 Bush St.	Seattle	99900
	+	2	Hernandez	Pete	Business	1485 Sonama V	Redmond	99780
	+	3	Mohr	Judy	Arts	100 Bosley Lan	Redmond	99780
	+	4	Buggey	Diana	Science	20 Cactus Lane	Redmond	99804
	+	5	Seinfeld	Casey	Arts	17 Windy Way	Bellevue	98180
	+	6	Alomar	Sandra	Business	PO Box 1465	Kirkland	97080
	−	7	Fernandez	Rosa	Science	151 Greer Rd.	Seattle	99890

Students : Table

	EntryID	CourseID	Grade
	55	COM200	86.00
	66	COM210	74.00
*	(AutoNumber)		0.00

		StudentID	LastName	FirstName	Major	Address	City	Zip
	+	8	Peters	Bob	Arts	200 Union St.	Seattle	99850
	+	9	Rinaldo	Sandy	Arts	1871 Orrinton R	Redmond	99704
	+	10	Finklestein	Sue	Business	888 Burrard St.	Seattle	99904
	+	11	Mortimer	Bruce	Science	235 Johnston S	Redmond	99704
	+	12	Jung	Chris	Science	1005 West 9th ,	Redmond	99780
	+	13	Abu-Alba	Benji	Arts	122 Cordova Aw	Bellevue	98200
	+	14	Stockton	Gretta	Arts	4210 Bush St.	Seattle	99900
	+	15	Sakic	Eric	Arts	875 Cordova Aw	Bellevue	98180
	+	16	Modano	Joey	Science	36 Primore St.	Kirkland	97780

Record: |◄ ◄ 1 ► ►| ►* of 65

12. Using the mouse, do the following:
CLICK: in a cell in the first row of the subdatasheet
Notice that the record navigation area in the Datasheet window shows Record 1 of 2. Clicking the First Record (|◄) or Last Record (►|) buttons will move the cursor in this subdatasheet only.

13. To collapse the subdatasheet:
CLICK: Collapse button (−) for StudentID 7
The record navigation area shows Record 1 of 65 once again.

14. On your own, expand the subdatasheets for three records in the Students Datasheet window. When finished, collapse all of the subdatasheets and then return to the top of the Students datasheet by pressing CTRL + HOME.

15. To clean up the work area, let's close the Roster Datasheet window:
CHOOSE: Window → Roster : Table
CLICK: its Close button (✕)
(*Note:* The display of a subdatasheet does not depend on both datasheets being open in the work area, as they were in this exercise.)

16. Keep the Students Datasheet window open for use in the next lesson.

In Addition MOVING TO A SPECIFIC RECORD NUMBER

Access displays the current record number alongside the navigation buttons in the bottom left-hand corner of a Datasheet window. To move to a specific record in the datasheet or subdatasheet, double-click the mouse pointer in this text box, type a record number, and then press ENTER. The cursor immediately moves to the desired record.

1.2.2 Adjusting Column Widths and Row Heights

→ **Feature**

By adjusting the column widths and row heights in a datasheet, you can enhance its appearance for both viewing and printing in much the same way that you use double-spacing in a document to make text easier to read. To change the width of a column in Datasheet view, use the sizing mouse pointer (⬌) to drag its borderline in the **field header area.** You can also have Access scan the contents of the column and recommend the best width. Rows behave somewhat differently. When you adjust a single row's height in the *record selection area*, Access updates all of the rows in the datasheet. Figure 1.19 labels the field header and record selection areas for a datasheet.

→ **Method**

To change a column's width using the mouse:

- DRAG: its right borderline in the field header area

To change a column's width using the menu:

- SELECT: a cell in the column that you want to format
- CHOOSE: Format → Column Width
- TYPE: **the desired width (in characters)**

To change the default row height using the mouse:

- DRAG: Its bottom borderline in the record selection area

To change the default row height using the menu:

- CHOOSE: Format → Row Height
- TYPE: **the desired height (in points)**

→ **Practice**

In this lesson, you will adjust column widths and row heights in a datasheet. Ensure that the Students datasheet is displayed.

1. In order to change the width of the Zip column, you must first select a cell in the Zip column. To do so:
PRESS: `END`
PRESS: `←`

2. To reduce the width of the Zip column using the menu:
CHOOSE: Format → Column Width
The Column Width dialog box appears, as shown here. Notice that the default width is 15.6667 characters at the *Normal* font size.

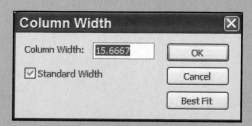

Access

3. Although you can type the desired width, let's ask Access to calculate the best width for the column:
CLICK: Best Fit command button
The column's width is decreased in the Datasheet window.

4. You will now adjust the width of the Address column using the mouse. In the field header area, position the mouse pointer over the borderline between the Address and City fields. The mouse pointer changes shape (↔) when positioned correctly, as shown below.

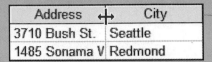

Field header area; the mouse pointer is positioned on the borderline between the two columns.

5. CLICK: the borderline and hold down the mouse button
DRAG: the mouse pointer to the right to increase the width (to approximately the beginning of the word "City")

6. You can also set the best-fit width for a column using the mouse. To adjust the width of the Major column:
DOUBLE-CLICK: the borderline between Major and Address
The Major column is sized automatically to its best-fit width.

7. To reposition the cursor:
PRESS: CTRL + HOME

8. On your own, size the StudentID, LastName, and FirstName columns to their best-fit widths.

9. Now change the row height setting in the Datasheet window:
CHOOSE: Format → Row Height
The Row Height dialog box appears, as shown here. Notice that the default row height is 12.75 points.

10. To spread out the row contents in the Datasheet window:
TYPE: **18**
PRESS: ENTER or CLICK: OK
All of the rows in the datasheet are updated to reflect the formatting change. Your worksheet should now appear similar to the one shown in Figure 1.19.

Figure 1.19

Formatting the
Datasheet
window

The column *field header area*
contains the field names.

The *record selection
area* contains row
selector buttons.

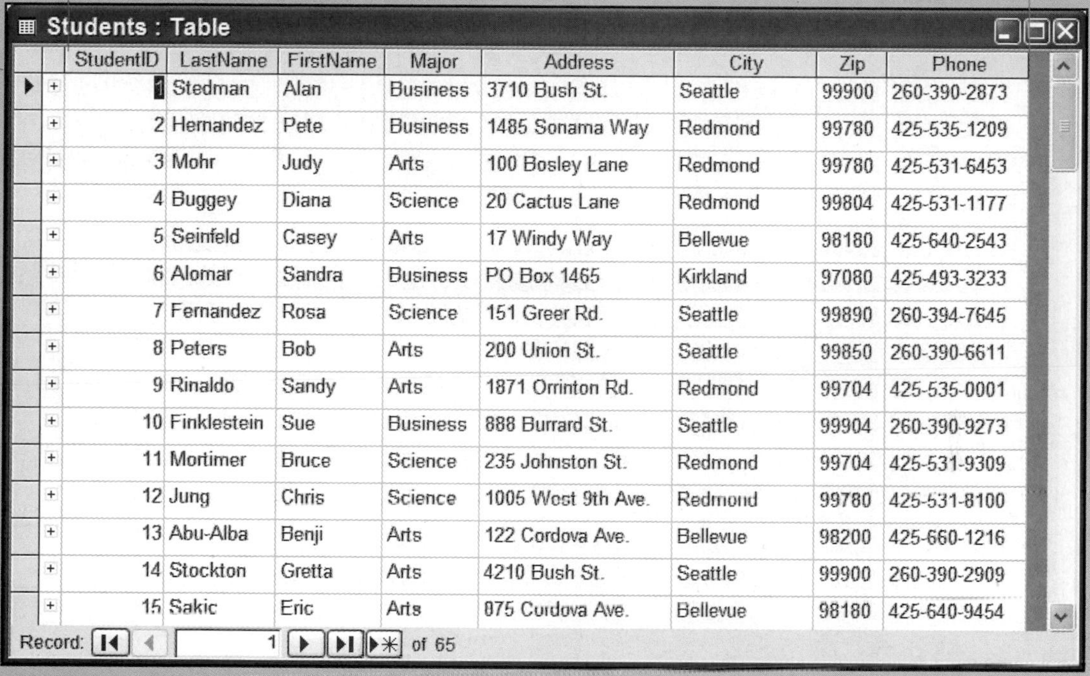

		StudentID	LastName	FirstName	Major	Address	City	Zip	Phone
▶	+	1	Stedman	Alan	Business	3710 Bush St.	Seattle	99900	260-390-2873
	+	2	Hernandez	Pete	Business	1485 Sonama Way	Redmond	99780	425-535-1209
	+	3	Mohr	Judy	Arts	100 Bosley Lane	Redmond	99780	425-531-6453
	+	4	Buggey	Diana	Science	20 Cactus Lane	Redmond	99804	425-531-1177
	+	5	Seinfeld	Casey	Arts	17 Windy Way	Bellevue	98180	425-640-2543
	+	6	Alomar	Sandra	Business	PO Box 1465	Kirkland	97080	425-493-3233
	+	7	Fernandez	Rosa	Science	151 Greer Rd.	Seattle	99890	260-394-7645
	+	8	Peters	Bob	Arts	200 Union St.	Seattle	99850	260-390-6611
	+	9	Rinaldo	Sandy	Arts	1871 Orrinton Rd.	Redmond	99704	425-535-0001
	+	10	Finklestein	Sue	Business	888 Burrard St.	Seattle	99904	260-390-9273
	+	11	Mortimer	Bruce	Science	235 Johnston St.	Redmond	99704	425-531-9309
	+	12	Jung	Chris	Science	1005 West 9th Ave.	Redmond	99780	425-531-8100
	+	13	Abu-Alba	Benji	Arts	122 Cordova Ave.	Bellevue	98200	425-660-1216
	+	14	Stockton	Gretta	Arts	4210 Bush St.	Seattle	99900	260-390-2909
	+	15	Sakic	Eric	Arts	875 Curdova Ave.	Bellevue	98180	425-640-9454

Record: ◀◀ ◀ 1 ▶ ▶▶ ▶* of 65

1.2.3 Previewing and Printing

→ **Feature**

Before sending a datasheet to the printer, you can preview it using a full-page display that resembles
the printed output. In Print Preview mode, you can move back and forth through the pages, zoom in
and out on desired areas, and modify page layout options such as print margins and page orientation.
Once you are satisfied with your datasheet's appearance, you may then send it to the printer with a
single mouse click.

→ **Method**

To preview the current Datasheet window:

• CLICK: Print Preview button (🔍)

  or

• CHOOSE: File → Print Preview

To print the current Datasheet window:

• CLICK: Print button (🖨)

  or

• CHOOSE: File → Print

Access

→ ## Practice

You will now use the Print Preview mode to display the Students datasheet. Ensure that you have completed the previous lesson and that the Students datasheet is displayed.

1. To preview how the datasheet will appear when printed:
CLICK: Print Preview button ([🔍]) on the toolbar
The Datasheet window becomes the Print Preview window, as shown in Figure 1.20.

Figure 1.20

Displaying the Students datasheet in the Print Preview window

The Print Preview toolbar replaces the Database toolbar.

Navigation buttons allow you to move among the preview pages.

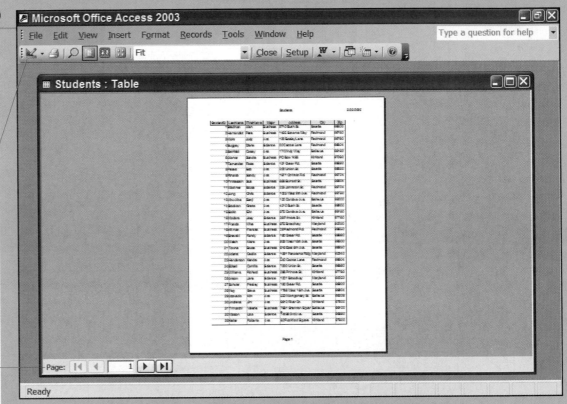

2. To move through the pages to print, click the navigation buttons at the bottom of the window. Let's practice:
CLICK: Next Page button ([▶])
CLICK: Last Page button ([▶|])
CLICK: First Page button ([|◀])

3. To zoom in on, or magnify, the Print Preview window, move the magnifying glass mouse pointer over the column headings, centered between the margins, and then click once. The Print Preview window should now appear similar to the one shown in Figure 1.21.

Figure 1.21

Zooming in on the Students datasheet

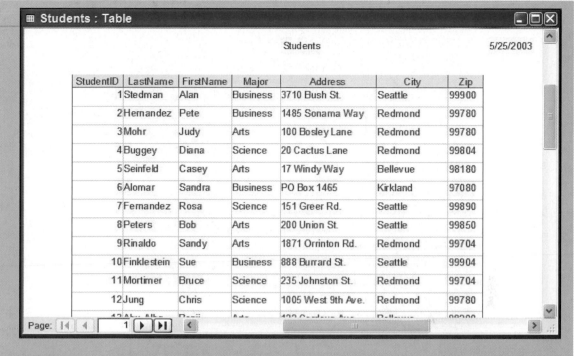

4. To zoom back out on the page:
   CLICK: anywhere on the page in the Print Preview window

5. You can change the page setup to landscape orientation in order to print more columns of data on each page. Do the following:
   CHOOSE: File → Page Setup
   CLICK: *Page* tab
   The Page Setup dialog box appears as shown in Figure 1.22. (*Note:* You can also display this dialog box by clicking the Setup command button on the Print Preview toolbar.)

Figure 1.22

Page Setup dialog box: *Page* tab

Use the *Margins* tab to adjust the top, botton, left, and right margins for the printed page.

Use the *Page* tab to change the page orientation, paper size, and source tray for the printer.

6. In the *Orientation* area of the Page Setup dialog box:
SELECT: *Landscape* option button
CLICK: OK command button
Notice that the Print Preview window is dynamically updated.

7. On your own, zoom in and out on the Print Preview window using the magnifying glass mouse pointer. All the field columns should appear on a single page.

8. There are two ways to close the Print Preview window. First, you can click the Close button (☒), which closes both the Print Preview window and the Students Datasheet window. Second, you can click the Close button (Close) in the Print Preview toolbar, which returns you to the Datasheet window. To return to the Students datasheet:
CLICK: Close button (Close) in the toolbar

9. Now let's close the Students Datasheet window:
CLICK: its Close button (☒)
The following dialog box appears.

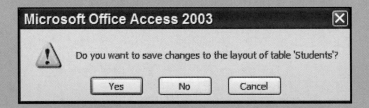

10. Because you have made changes to the layout of the Datasheet window, Access asks you to either save or discard the formatting changes. Let's discard the changes for now:
CLICK: No command button
The AC0100 Database window should now appear as the only open window in the work area.

11. Rather than opening a datasheet for previewing or printing, you can use a shortcut from the Database window. To illustrate:
RIGHT-CLICK: Courses in the list area
CHOOSE: Print Preview
The Courses table object is now displayed in a Print Preview window. (*Note:* To send the datasheet to the printer, choose the Print command from the right-click menu. It is a good idea, however, to preview a page first to ensure that it will print as expected.)

12. To close the Print Preview window:
CLICK: its Close button (☒)

　　1.2　Describe two methods for moving the cursor to the last record in a large datasheet

1.3 **Manipulating Table Data**

Maintaining a database is difficult work. Updating the contents of a table, adding and deleting records, and fixing mistakes can take a tremendous amount of time. Fortunately, Access provides some tools and features that can help you manipulate data productively. In this module, you learn to enter, edit, and delete data in Datasheet view.

1.3.1 Selecting and Editing Data

→ **Feature**

You can edit information either as you type an entry or after you have placed data into a table. In Datasheet view, changes are made by selecting the data or cell and then issuing a command or typing over the existing data. Unlike other applications in Office System 2003, you do not choose the File → Save command in Access 2003 to save your work. Your editing changes are saved automatically when you move the cursor to another record.

→ **Method**

Some points to keep in mind when editing in Datasheet view:

- Press **F2** to enter and exit Edit mode for the selected cell.

- If you start typing while data is selected, you will replace the entire selection with the text you type.

- If the flashing cursor or insertion point is positioned in a field's cell but no data is selected, the text you type will be inserted in the cell.

- With the cursor or insertion point positioned in a cell, you may press **BACKSPACE** to remove characters to the left of the insertion point or press **DELETE** to remove characters to the right.

→ **Practice**

In this lesson, you will practice editing data in a table's datasheet. Ensure that the AC0100 Database window is displayed. If not, open the AC0100 database from your student data files location.

1. In the Database window, ensure that the Tables button in the Objects bar is selected. Then do the following:
DOUBLE-CLICK: Instructors in the list area
The Instructors Datasheet window is displayed, as shown in Figure 1.23.

Figure 1.23

Displaying the Instructors datasheet

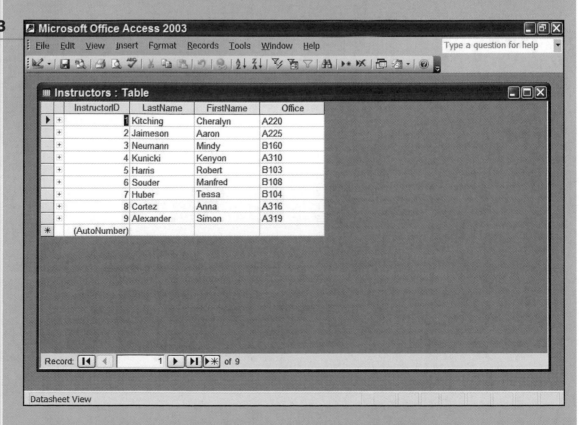

2. To position the cursor in the Office column of the first record:
PRESS: ➡ three times
Notice that the cell's contents "A220" are highlighted.

3. To update the Office number:
TYPE: **B**
Notice that a pencil icon (🖉) appears in the row's selector button, as shown below. This icon indicates that you are now editing the data and have not yet saved the changes.

The pencil icon tells you that the record's contents have been changed.

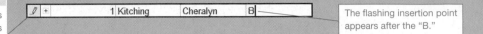

The flashing insertion point appears after the "B."

4. To complete the entry:
TYPE: **113**
PRESS: **ENTER**
The new office number replaces the selection. When you press **ENTER**, the cursor moves to the next available field (which, in this case, is the first field of the next record. Notice also that the pencil icon is no longer visible in the row's selector button.

5. Rather than retyping an entire cell's contents, you can modify the individual characters in a cell. To illustrate, let's edit the record data for InstructorID 4. First, position the I-beam mouse pointer to the right of the last name "Kunicki" and then click once. A flashing insertion point (shown below) appears to the right of the trailing letter "i," which means that you are ready to edit the cell's contents. (*Hint:* You can also position the insertion point by first selecting the cell using the cursor keys and then pressing **F2** to enter Edit mode. Pressing **F2** a second time will toggle the in-cell Edit mode off.)

The triangle tells you that this is the active record in the datasheet.

Flashing insertion point   I-beam mouse pointer

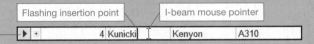

6. To replace the final "i" in Kunicki with a "y," do the following:
PRESS: **BACKSPACE**

Notice that the pencil icon (🖉) appears in the row selector button, warning you that the record has been changed.

7. To continue:
TYPE: **y**

8. To complete the in-cell editing for the LastName field:
PRESS: **ENTER**
The cursor moves to the next field, but the pencil icon remains displayed in the row selector button, as shown below.

The pencil icon tells you that the record's changes have not yet been saved.

🖉 | + | 4 | Kunicky | Kenyon | A310

9. To save the changes you have made to a record, move the cursor to another record in the datasheet. To illustrate:
PRESS: ⬇
The pencil icon disappears. (*Note:* When working in Edit mode, pressing **HOME**, **END**, ⬅, and ➡ moves the insertion point within the cell. Press **F2** to toggle out of Edit mode in order to use these keys for cursor navigation around the entire datasheet.)

10. When you move the mouse pointer over a cell, it changes shape to an I-beam, so that you may easily position the insertion point between characters. In order to select an entire cell for editing, you position the mouse pointer over the top or left grid line of a cell and click once. You will know that the mouse pointer is properly positioned when it changes shape to a cross (⊹). To select the contents of the LastName field for InstructorID 7, position the mouse pointer as shown below.

Position the mouse pointer over the cell's left grid line.

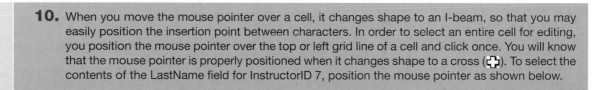

11. To select the cell:
CLICK: left mouse button once
The cell's contents ("Huber") are highlighted in reverse video (typically, white text on a black background), as shown in Figure 1.24.

Figure 1.24

Selecting an entire cell in a datasheet

Active record

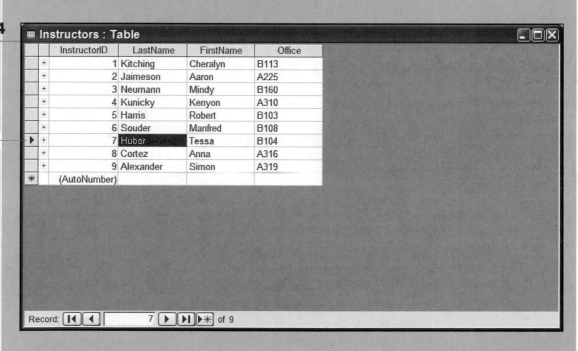

12. Let's assume that Tessa got married recently and has decided to change her name. Do the following:
TYPE: **Moss**
The pencil icon appears in the row's selector button, as shown here.

| 𝒫 | + | 7 | Moss| | Tessa | B104 |

13. To save the changes:
PRESS: ⬇ to move to the next record

In Addition SAVING YOUR CHANGES

Rather than moving to another row, you can save the changes you make to the current record by pressing (SHIFT) + (ENTER). This keyboard shortcut allows you to write the changes permanently to the disk without having to move to another record.

1.3.2 Using the Undo Command

→ ## Feature

The **Undo command** allows you to reverse mistakes during editing. Unlike other Microsoft Office Suite products, Access does not offer a multiple undo capability when editing in Datasheet view. Therefore, you must remember to choose the Undo command immediately after making a mistake. In this lesson, you will practice editing and undoing changes in a Datasheet window.

→ ## Method

To reverse the last action performed, do any one of the following:

* CHOOSE: Edit → Undo

  or

* CLICK: Undo button (🔄)

  or

* PRESS: CTRL + z

(*Note:* The menu command's name changes to reflect the action that may be reversed. For example, on the Edit pull-down menu, the command may read Undo Current Field/Record, Undo Delete, or Undo Saved Record.)

→ ## Practice

Using the Undo command, you will now practice reversing common editing procedures. Ensure that you have completed the previous lesson and that the Instructors datasheet is displayed.

1. You've just been informed that "Robert Harris" prefers to go by the name "Bobby." Let's edit the table:
SELECT: the FirstName cell for InstructorID 5
(*Hint:* This instruction asks you to click the top or left grid line of the FirstName cell. When this task is done correctly, the cell containing "Robert" is highlighted, as shown below.)

2. TYPE: **Bobby**
PRESS: ENTER
The cursor moves to the next field in the current record.

3. To undo the last edit using the Menu bar:
CHOOSE: Edit → Undo Current Field/Record
The contents revert back to "Robert," yet the cursor remains in the Office field column.

4. Now let's delete a cell entry for Anna Cortez:
SELECT: the Office cell for InstructorID 8, as shown below

5. To remove the entry:
PRESS: DELETE

6. To save the changes and move to the next record:
PRESS: ⬇
Your screen should appear similar to the one shown in Figure 1.25.

Figure 1.25

Deleting an entire cell's contents

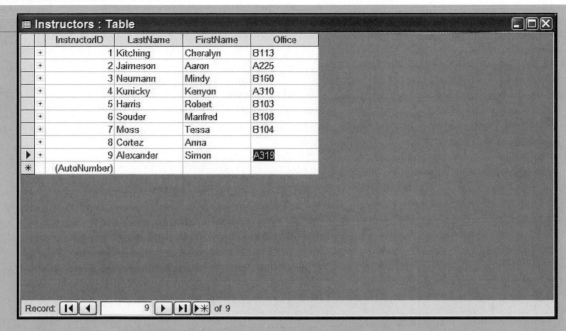

7. Even though this change has been saved and recorded to disk, Access lets you reverse the deletion. Do the following:
CLICK: Undo button ( )
The Office assignment is restored for Anna Cortez. (*Note:* In this step, clicking the toolbar button executes the Edit, Undo Saved Record command.)

8. PRESS: **CTRL** + **HOME** to return to the first record in the datasheet

In Addition USING **ESC** TO UNDO CHANGES

Instead of choosing the Undo command from the menu, you can undo changes in the current field by pressing **ESC** once. Pressing **ESC** a second time will undo all of the unsaved changes made to the current record.

1.3.3 Adding Records

→ **Feature**

In Datasheet view, you add new records to the blank row appearing at the bottom of a datasheet. If the text "(AutoNumber)" appears in a cell, ignore its contents and press **ENTER**, **TAB**, or ➔ to bypass the cell and move to the next field. Any cell containing an *AutoNumber* field is incremented automatically by Access when a new record is added to the table.

→ **Method**

To position the cursor in a blank row at the bottom of the datasheet, ready for the insertion of a new record, use any one of the following methods:

- CLICK: New Record button ( ) on the toolbar

  or

- CLICK: New Record button ( ) in the record navigation bar

  or

- CHOOSE: Insert ➔ New Record from the Menu bar

→ **Practice**

In this lesson, you will insert two records into the Instructors datasheet. Ensure that the Instructors datasheet is displayed.

1. To position the cursor at the bottom of the datasheet:
CLICK: New Record button (⯈⁑) on the toolbar
The AutoNumber entry in the first field of the new record is selected, as shown below.

> | ▶ | | (AutoNumber) | | | |

2. Ignore this field and let Access handle the entry for the InstructorID column. To move to the next field:
PRESS: TAB
(*Note:* You can also press ENTER to move to the next field. The convention in this guide, however, is to use TAB to move the cursor forward and SHIFT + TAB to move the cursor backward. The ENTER key is sometimes used to complete in-cell editing.)

3. Let's enter the new record information:
TYPE: **Melville**
PRESS: TAB
Notice that the AutoNumber entry for the InstructorID column is calculated and entered automatically.

4. To complete the entry:
TYPE: **Herman**
PRESS: TAB
TYPE: **C230**
Your screen should now appear similar to the one shown in Figure 1.26. Notice that the pencil icon appears in the current row's selector button and that a new row was added to the datasheet, as denoted with an asterisk in its selector button.

Figure 1.26

Adding a new record

The pencil icon appears because the new record has not yet been saved.

The asterisk indicates that this row provides a new blank record.

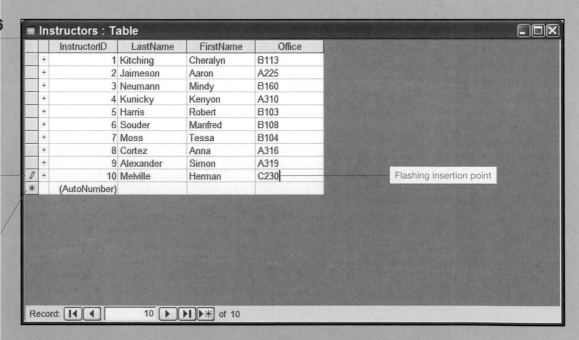

		InstructorID	LastName	FirstName	Office
	+	1	Kitching	Cheralyn	B113
	+	2	Jaimeson	Aaron	A225
	+	3	Neumann	Mindy	B160
	+	4	Kunicky	Kenyon	A310
	+	5	Harris	Robert	B103
	+	6	Souder	Manfred	B108
	+	7	Moss	Tessa	B104
	+	8	Cortez	Anna	A316
	+	9	Alexander	Simon	A319
⌀	+	10	Melville	Herman	C230|
*		(AutoNumber)			

Instructors : Table

Flashing insertion point

Record: ⏮ ◀ 10 ▶ ⏭ ▶⁎ of 10

5. To save the record and move to the next row:
PRESS: TAB
(*Note:* Again, you can also press ENTER to move the cursor.)

6. Remembering to allow Access to complete the AutoNumber cell, add the following two records to the datasheet:

InstructorID: **11**
LastName: **Shaw**
FirstName: **Bernard**
Office: **C240**

InstructorID: **12**
LastName: **Conrad**
FirstName: **Joseph**
Office: **C320**

7. Move the cursor to the next blank row to ensure that the last record is saved.

8. To return to the top of the datasheet:
PRESS: CTRL + HOME
Your datasheet should now appear similar to the one shown in Figure 1.27.

Figure 1.27

Adding records to
the Instructors
datasheet

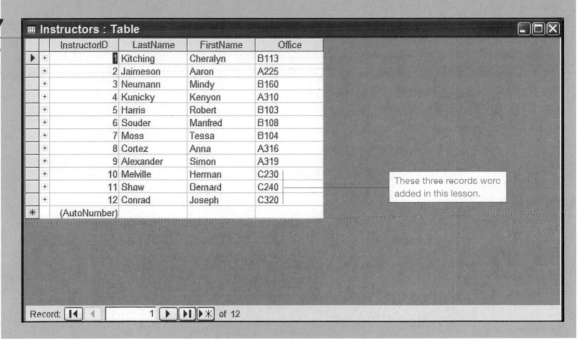

1.3.4 Deleting Records

→ **Feature**

In Datasheet view, Access provides several methods for removing records from a table. To do so efficiently, however, you must learn how to select multiple records in a datasheet. In this lesson, you highlight records using the mouse to drag the pointer in the **record selection area,** sometimes called the *row selector buttons.* Refer to the diagram below for clarification on the parts of a Datasheet window.

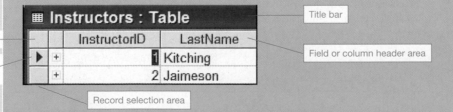

→ # Method

To delete a record or records in a datasheet:

- SELECT: a record or group of records
- CLICK: Delete Record button ([⬛])

   or

   PRESS: [DELETE]

   or

   CHOOSE: Edit → Delete Record

→ # Practice

You will now practice selecting and removing records from a datasheet. Ensure that you have completed the previous lesson and that the Instructors datasheet is displayed.

1. To practice selecting records in the datasheet, do the following:
CLICK: Select All button ([ ]) in the upper left-hand corner of the datasheet
All of the datasheet's records should now appear in reverse video (white on black), as shown in Figure 1.28.

Figure 1.28

Selecting all of the records in a datasheet

The Select All button for the datasheet

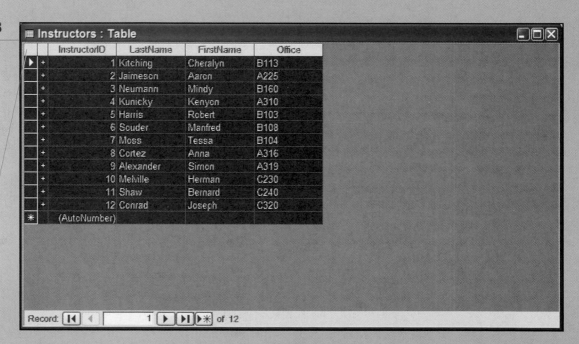

2. To remove the highlighting:
PRESS: [HOME]

3. To select the record for InstructorID 3, position the mouse pointer to the left of the desired record in the record selection area. The mouse pointer changes shape to a black horizontal right-pointing arrow (→). When the pointer is positioned over the row selector button properly, click the left mouse button once to select the entire row. It should now appear highlighted, as shown below.

4. Let's remove the selected record from the table:
CLICK: Delete Record button (⊠) on the toolbar
A confirmation dialog box appears, as shown in Figure 1.29. (*Caution:* Access displays this dialog box whenever you delete records. Clicking the Yes command button permanently removes the record. Clicking the No button returns the datasheet to its previous state.)

Figure 1.29

Removing a record from the datasheet

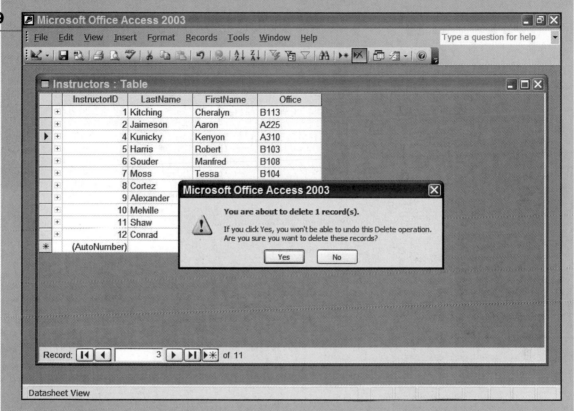

5. To confirm the deletion:
CLICK: Yes command button
Notice that the InstructorID field in the first column does not contain a dynamic record count. In other words, the remaining records are not renumbered to fill the gap left by deleting InstructorID 3.

6. You can also delete numerous records with a single command. To illustrate, click once in the record selection area for Manfred Souder's entry (InstructorID 6) and hold down the left mouse button. Then drag the mouse pointer downward to Anna Cortez's record (InstructorID 8). Release the mouse button to display the selected records, as seen here.

Mouse pointer ———

+		5 Harris	Robert	B103
▶ +		6 Souder	Manfred	B108
+		7 Moss	Tessa	B104
⇨ +		8 Cortez	Anna	A316
+		9 Alexander	Simon	A319

7. To delete the selected records:
PRESS: `DELETE`
CLICK: Yes to confirm the deletion of three records
Your screen should now appear similar to the one shown in Figure 1.30.

Figure 1.30

Deleting multiple records from the datasheet

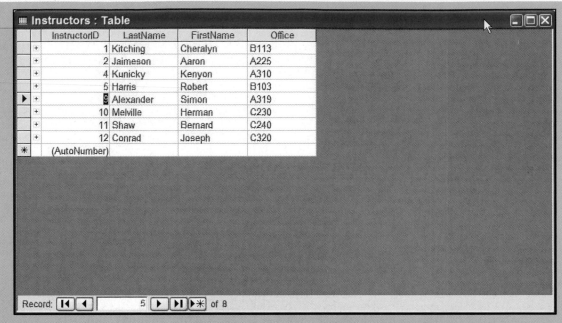

8. To close the Instructors datasheet:
   CLICK: the Close button (X) on the Datasheet window
   You should now see the Database window for the AC0100 database.

9. To close the AC0100 database:
   CLICK: the Close button (X) on the Database window

10. To exit Microsoft Office Access 2003:
    CHOOSE: File → Exit

 **1.3** When does Access save the editing changes that you have made to a record?

Chapter
summary

Microsoft Office Access 2003 is a full-featured database management application for desktop computers. Database software enables you to store and manipulate large amounts of data, such as inventory items and customer mailing lists. When you first open a database using Access, you are presented with the main control center, called the Database window. From this one window, you can create and display a variety of database objects, including tables, forms, queries, and reports. The main type of object used for storing and manipulating data is the table, or datasheet. In a Datasheet window, you can enter, edit, and delete field and record data. With the Undo command, you can immediately reverse your last action. Access 2003 also lets you preview and print a table's contents as they are displayed in the Datasheet window.

Command Summary

Many of the commands and procedures appearing in this chapter are summarized in the following table.

Skill Set	To Perform this Task...	Do the Following...
Using Access	Launch Microsoft Office Access 2003	CLICK: Start button (🔲 start) CHOOSE: All Programs → Microsoft Office CLICK: Microsoft Office Access 2003
	Exit Microsoft Office Access 2003	CLICK: its Close button (✖) or CHOOSE: File → Exit
	Open a database	CLICK: Open button (🗁) SELECT: the desired folder DOUBLE-CLICK: a database file
	Close a database	CLICK: its Close button (✖), or CHOOSE: File → Close
Creating and Using Databases	Select and open database objects using the Objects bar	CLICK: the desired object category DOUBLE-CLICK: the desired object
	Navigate to a specific record	DOUBLE-CLICK: in the navigation text box TYPE: desired record number PRESS: ENTER
	Adjust a column's width in a datasheet	DRAG: a column's right borderline in the field header area, or CHOOSE: Format → Column Width
	Adjust the height of all rows in a datasheet	DRAG: a row's bottom borderline in the record selection area, or CHOOSE: Format → Row Height
	Expand/collapse subdatasheets in a Datasheet window	CLICK: Expand button (⊞) CLICK: Collapse button (⊟)
	Preview a datasheet for printing	CLICK: Print Preview button (🔍), or CHOOSE: File → Print Preview
	Print a datasheet	CLICK: Print button (🖨), or CHOOSE: File → Print
	Change the page orientation for a printed document	CHOOSE: File → Page Setup CLICK: *Page* tab SELECT: Portrait or Landscape
Viewing and Organizing Information	Toggle Edit mode on and off for editing a datasheet cell	PRESS: F2 (Edit key)
	Reverse or undo the most recent change or mistake	CLICK: Undo button (↩), or CHOOSE: Edit → Undo
	Save the editing changes to the current record	PRESS: SHIFT + ENTER, or Move the cursor to the next record.
	Add a new record to a datasheet	CLICK: New Record buttons (▶✱ or ▶✱), or CHOOSE: Insert → New Record
	Delete selected record(s) from a datasheet	CLICK: Delete Record button (✖), or PRESS: DELETE, or CHOOSE: Edit → Delete Record

Access

Key Terms

This section specifies page references for the key terms identified in this chapter. For a complete list of definitions, refer to the Glossary at the end of this learning guide.

application window, *p. AC 7*

cell, *p. AC 15*

database, *p. AC 2*

database management system (DBMS), *p. AC 2*

Database window, *p. AC 10*

datasheet, *p. AC 15*

Datasheet view, *p. AC 15*

field, *p. AC 2*

field header area, *p. AC 19*

form, *p. AC 13*

Groups bar, *p. AC 10*

Objects bar, *p. AC 10*

Places bar, *p. AC 6*

query, *p. AC 12*

record, *p. AC 2*

record selection area, *p. AC 31*

report, *p. AC 14*

subdatasheet, *p. AC 17*

table, *p. AC 2*

task pane, *p. AC 4*

Undo command, *p. AC 28*

Chapter
q u i z

Short Answer

1. Describe situations in which you might use a database.

2. Define the following terms: *table, record,* and *field*.

3. What is an *object* in Microsoft Office Access 2003? Provide examples.

4. Which database object is used to collect and store data?

5. Which database object displays in Print Preview mode when opened?

6. Why is the Database window referred to as a *control center?*

7. How do you select the entire contents of a cell in a datasheet?

8. How do you select all of the records displayed in a datasheet?

9. What is the procedure for adding a record in Datasheet view?

10. What is the procedure for deleting a record in Datasheet view?

True/False

1. _____ DBMS stands for database backup and management system.

2. _____ When you first launch Access 2003, the Getting Started task pane appears.

3. _____ A *form* is a database object that displays multiple records in a column-and-row layout.

4. _____ A *query* allows you to ask questions of your data and to combine information from more than one table.

5. _____ The column widths of a datasheet cannot be adjusted after information has been entered into the cells.

6. _____ Changing the height of one row in a datasheet affects the height of every row.

7. ____ If you want to fit more field columns on a single printed page, you can select landscape orientation for printing.

8. ____ If you make a mistake while editing a field, you can press `ESC` to undo the error.

9. ____ In a datasheet, the *record selection area* is the gray area at the top of each column.

10. ____ Access 2003 allows you to delete several records at once.

Multiple Choice

1. Which of the following buttons does not appear in the Objects bar?
  a. Forms
  b. Modules
  c. Programs
  d. Reports

2. Which database object do you use to display information for one record at a time?
  a. Table
  b. Form
  c. Query
  d. Report

3. In a datasheet, the intersection of a row and a column is called a:
  a. Cell
  b. Cursor
  c. Form
  d. Record

4. In a datasheet, what does each column represent?
  a. Database
  b. Table
  c. Record
  d. Field

5. In a datasheet, which mouse pointer do you use to select a cell by clicking on its gridline?
  a. ⇧
  b. ↖
  c. ⌛
  d. I

6. In a datasheet, which icon appears at the left side of a record while it is being edited?
  a. Asterisk (✳)
  b. Pencil (✐)
  c. Pointer (▶)
  d. Selector (☐)

7. When editing a record, which keystroke allows you to save the changes without leaving the current record?
  a. `CTRL` + `ENTER`
  b. `CTRL` + `ALT`
  c. `ALT` + `ENTER`
  d. `SHIFT` + `ENTER`

8. Which of the following will not reverse the last action performed?
  a. CHOOSE: Edit → Undo
  b. CLICK: Undo button (↺▾)
  c. PRESS: `CTRL` + x
  d. PRESS: `ESC`

9. Any cell containing this type of field is incremented automatically by Access when a new record is added.
  a. AutoElevate
  b. AutoIncrement
  c. AutoNumber
  d. AutoValue

10. The row selector buttons in a datasheet are located in the:
  a. Row selection area
  b. Record selection area
  c. Field selection area
  d. Table selection area

Hands-On
exercises

step by step   ### 1. Navigating a Datasheet

In this exercise, you will practice fundamental database skills, such as opening a database, displaying a table, and navigating through a datasheet using the mouse and keyboard.

1. Ensure that you have turned on your computer and that the Windows desktop appears. Load Microsoft Office Access 2003 using the Windows Start menu.

2. Use the Open button (🗐) on the Database toolbar to display the Open dialog box.

3. Using either the Places bar or the *Look in* drop-down list box:
   SELECT: *the folder location* of your Advantage student data files
   DOUBLE-CLICK: AC01HE in the list area
   The Database window appears, as shown in Figure 1.31. (*Note:* The "HE" in the database filename stands for Hands-On Exercises.)

Figure 1.31

Opening the AC01HE database

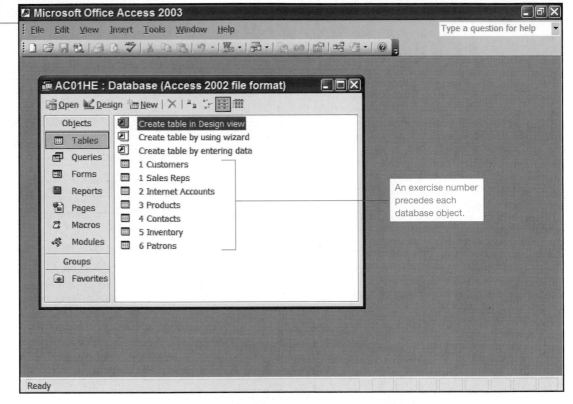

4. Ensure that the *Tables* button in the Objects bar is selected. Then, open the "1 Sales Reps" table in Datasheet view to display 12 records and 5 field columns in a Datasheet window.

5. To move to the second field of the third record:
   PRESS: ⬇ two times
   PRESS: ➡ once
   The cursor should now highlight the name "Louis."

6. Now move to the last record using the mouse:
   CLICK: Last Record button (▶|)
   Notice that the cursor moves to the last record in the same column to highlight the name "Masterson."

7. To quickly move to the top of the datasheet using the keyboard:
   PRESS: CTRL + HOME

8. Each sales rep in this table is responsible for servicing specific customer accounts. You can display the customer accounts for each sales rep in a subdatasheet. To do so, drill down and display the customers assigned to Peter Fink (SalesRep A14). Once completed, your screen should appear similar to the one shown in Figure 1.32.

Figure 1.32

Expanding a datasheet to display a sales rep's customers

This subdatasheet displays data from the "1 Customers" table.

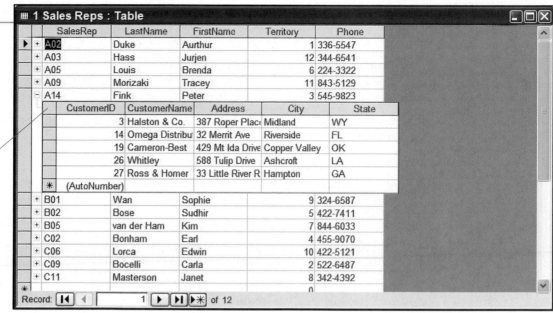

9. On your own, practice opening a few more subdatasheets. When you are finished, hide each subdatasheet by clicking the Collapse button (⊟) in the left-hand column.

10. Close the "1 Sales Reps" Datasheet window by clicking its Close button (☒).

2. Formatting a Datasheet

In this exercise, you will practice adjusting a datasheet's column widths and row heights before previewing it for printing. Ensure that the AC01HE Database window is displayed.

1. Open the "2 Internet Accounts" table for display in Datasheet view. Ensure that your screen appears similar to the one shown in Figure 1.33 before you proceed.

Figure 1.33

Displaying the "2 Internet Accounts" datasheet

2 Internet Accounts : Table

Customer	Username	Address	City	Zip	Phone	Amount	Billing
Ann Harris	ahariss	123 W. Rose	Lodi	95240	339-1997	$19.95	CK
Bo Bailey	bbailey	1 Merriwether	Victor	95244	367-3665	$24.95	DD
Bonnie Mar	bmar	7855 "E" St.	Victor	95244	367-5443	$24.95	DD
G. T. Morris	gmorris	P.O. Box 9844	Ripon	95336	264-5221	$19.95	DD
Jose Cuervo	jcuervo	56 Mar Vista Dr	Ripon	95336	264-1489	$19.95	CC
Kaley Lewis	klewis	St. John's Clinic	Lodi	95240	339-6552	$24.95	CK
Liz Schuler	lschuler	599 W. Walnut	Lodi	95240	367-6548	$24.95	CC
Sam Yee	syee	944 E. Fifth St.	Victor	95244	267-3125	$19.95	CK
Tom Sawyer	tsawyer	5065 Villa Arroy	Ripon	95336	264-9552	$19.95	CC
Vu Nguyen	vnguyen1	P.O. Box 3992	Lodi	95242	339-9254	$24.95	CK
Van Nguyen	vnguyen2	11 N. Weber	Victor	95244	367-2114	$19.95	DD

Record: ◄ ◄ 1 ► ►► ►* of 11

2. Select any cell in the Address field column. Then, display the Column Width dialog box using the menu. Lastly, adjust the width of the Address field column by having Access 2003 calculate its best width.

3. Now use the mouse to adjust the width of the Phone column. In the field header area, position the mouse pointer (↔) over the borderline between the Phone and Amount fields and then drag the borderline to decrease its width (to approximately the end of the word "Phone").

4. Use the mouse to set the best-fit width for the Zip column by double-clicking the borderline between Zip and Phone in the field header area.

5. Adjust the width of the City column so that it is more narrow.

6. Change the row height setting for all the rows in the datasheet. Display the Row Height dialog box using the menu and then enter **15** as the desired height. When finished, your screen should appear similar to the one shown in Figure 1.34.

Figure 1.34

Sizing rows and columns in a datasheet

2 Internet Accounts : Table

Customer	Username	Address	City	Zip	Phone	Amount	Billing Type
Ann Harris	ahariss	123 W. Rose	Lodi	95240	339-1997	$19.95	CK
Bo Bailey	bbailey	1 Merriwether	Victor	95244	367-3665	$24.95	DD
Bonnie Mar	bmar	7855 "E" St.	Victor	95244	367-5443	$24.95	DD
G. T. Morris	gmorris	P.O. Box 9844	Ripon	95336	264-5221	$19.95	DD
Jose Cuervo	jcuervo	56 Mar Vista Dr	Ripon	95336	264-1489	$19.95	CC
Kaley Lewis	klewis	St. John's Clinic	Lodi	95240	339-6552	$24.95	CK
Liz Schuler	lschuler	599 W. Walnut	Lodi	95240	367-6548	$24.95	CC
Sam Yee	syee	944 E. Fifth St.	Victor	95244	267-3125	$19.95	CK
Tom Sawyer	tsawyer	5065 Villa Arroyo	Ripon	95336	264-9552	$19.95	CC
Vu Nguyen	vnguyen1	P.O. Box 3992	Lodi	95242	339-9254	$24.95	CK
Van Nguyen	vnguyen2	11 N. Weber	Victor	95244	367-2114	$19.95	DD

Record: ◀◀ ◀ 1 ▶ ▶◀ ▶※ of 11

7. Use the Print Preview button (🔍) on the toolbar to see what the datasheet will look like when printed.

8. Zoom in and out on the Print Preview window using the magnifying glass mouse pointer.

9. If you have a printer connected to your computer, print the datasheet using the following instruction. Otherwise, proceed to step 10.
   CLICK: Print button (🖨) on the toolbar

10. Close the Print Preview window by clicking the Close button (Close) in the toolbar. The "2 Internet Accounts" datasheet remains displayed.

11. Now close the Datasheet window by clicking its Close button (✕). The following dialog box appears.

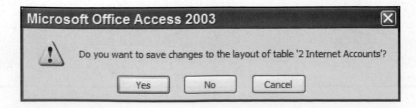

Microsoft Office Access 2003

⚠ Do you want to save changes to the layout of table '2 Internet Accounts'?

Yes   No   Cancel

12. Save the layout changes by clicking the Yes command button, so that the datasheet displays using the new column and row settings the next time it is opened.

3. Editing Data in a Datasheet

In this exercise, you will edit data in an existing datasheet and practice using the Undo command. Ensure that the AC01HE Database window is displayed before proceeding.

1. Open the "3 Products" table for display in Datasheet view. Ensure that your screen appears similar to the one shown in Figure 1.35 before you proceed.

Figure 1.35

Displaying the "3 Products" datasheet

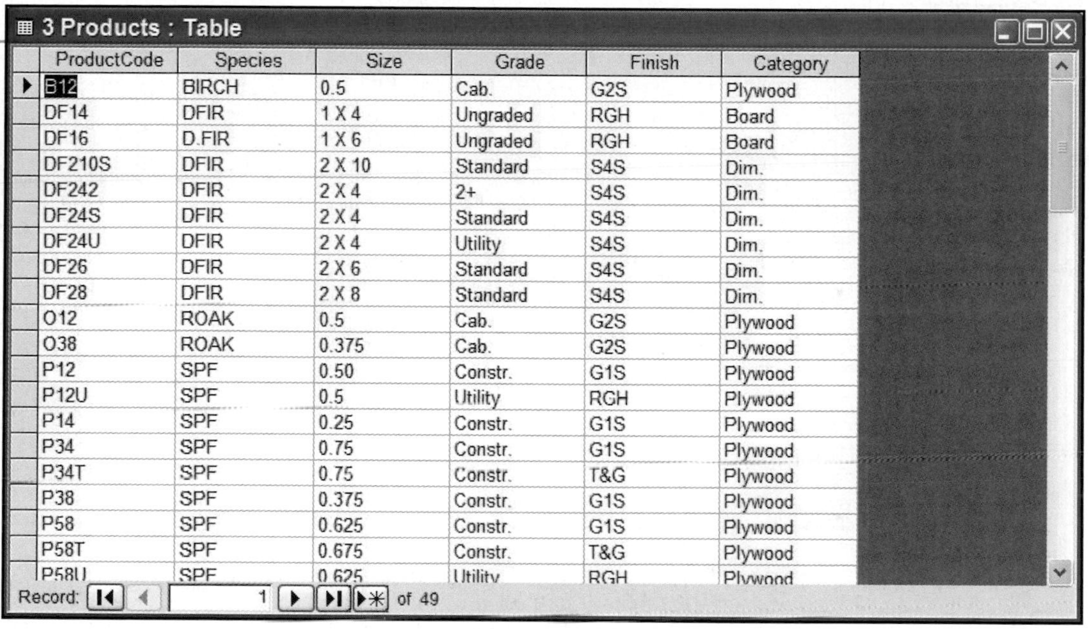

ProductCode	Species	Size	Grade	Finish	Category
B12	BIRCH	0.5	Cab.	G2S	Plywood
DF14	DFIR	1 X 4	Ungraded	RGH	Board
DF16	D.FIR	1 X 6	Ungraded	RGH	Board
DF210S	DFIR	2 X 10	Standard	S4S	Dim.
DF242	DFIR	2 X 4	2+	S4S	Dim.
DF24S	DFIR	2 X 4	Standard	S4S	Dim.
DF24U	DFIR	2 X 4	Utility	S4S	Dim.
DF26	DFIR	2 X 6	Standard	S4S	Dim.
DF28	DFIR	2 X 8	Standard	S4S	Dim.
O12	ROAK	0.5	Cab.	G2S	Plywood
O38	ROAK	0.375	Cab.	G2S	Plywood
P12	SPF	0.50	Constr.	G1S	Plywood
P12U	SPF	0.5	Utility	RGH	Plywood
P14	SPF	0.25	Constr.	G1S	Plywood
P34	SPF	0.75	Constr.	G1S	Plywood
P34T	SPF	0.75	Constr.	T&G	Plywood
P38	SPF	0.375	Constr.	G1S	Plywood
P58	SPF	0.625	Constr.	G1S	Plywood
P58T	SPF	0.675	Constr.	T&G	Plywood
P58U	SPF	0.625	Utility	RGH	Plywood

3 Products : Table

Record: 1 of 49

2. Using the keyboard, position the cursor in the Species column of the third record. What data is stored in this cell?

3. Let's change this cell value to match the standard abbreviation. With the entry selected, enter the new data:
TYPE: **DFIR**

4. Save the changes by moving the cursor to the next record. Notice that the pencil icon in the record selection area disappears.

5. Now let's edit the product code of record number 4. (*Hint:* Glance at the navigation bar in the Datasheet window to see the current record number.) Position the I-beam mouse pointer to the right of the product code "DF210S," as shown here. Then, click once to position the flashing insertion point to the right of the letter "S."

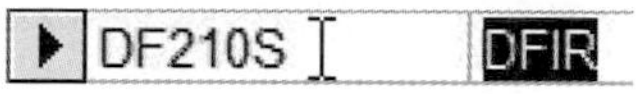

DF210S   DFIR

6. To delete the final "S" in DF210S and save the change:
PRESS: (BACKSPACE)
PRESS: (↓)

7. SELECT: Grade cell for record 1 using the mouse
(*Hint:* Position the mouse pointer over the cell's left gridline so that the pointer changes to a cross shape (✛). Then, click the left mouse button once to select the entire cell.)

8. Replace the cell's contents with the new Grade code "Utility" and then save the changes using the (SHIFT) + (ENTER) key combination.

9. To end the in-cell Edit mode:
PRESS: (F2)

10. Now delete the entry in the last field column of the first row. Move to the next record to save your changes. Your screen should now appear similar to the one shown in Figure 1.36.

Figure 1.36

Editing cells in the "3 Products" datasheet

	ProductCode	Species	Size	Grade	Finish	Category
	B12	BIRCH	0.5	Utility	G2S	
▶	DF14	DFIR	1 X 4	Ungraded	RGH	Board
	DF16	DFIR	1 X 6	Ungraded	RGH	Board
	DF210	DFIR	2 X 10	Standard	S4S	Dim.
	DF242	DFIR	2 X 4	2+	S4S	Dim.
	DF24S	DFIR	2 X 4	Standard	S4S	Dim.
	DF24U	DFIR	2 X 4	Utility	S4S	Dim.
	DF26	DFIR	2 X 6	Standard	S4S	Dim.
	DF28	DFIR	2 X 8	Standard	S4S	Dim.
	O12	ROAK	0.5	Cab.	G2S	Plywood
	O38	ROAK	0.375	Cab.	G2S	Plywood
	P12	SPF	0.50	Constr.	G1S	Plywood
	P12U	SPF	0.5	Utility	RGH	Plywood
	P14	SPF	0.25	Constr.	G1S	Plywood
	P34	SPF	0.75	Constr.	G1S	Plywood
	P34T	SPF	0.75	Constr.	T&G	Plywood
	P38	SPF	0.375	Constr.	G1S	Plywood
	P58	SPF	0.625	Constr.	G1S	Plywood
	P58T	SPF	0.675	Constr.	T&G	Plywood
	P58U	SPF	0.625	Utility	RGH	Plywood

3 Products : Table

Record: 2 of 49

11. Reverse the previous cell deletion using the Undo command.

12. Close the Datasheet window.

on your own

4. Adding and Deleting Records

As the most junior board member in the local chamber of commerce, you have been granted responsibility for maintaining a list of volunteer groups in the community. Fortunately, your predecessor used Microsoft Office Access 2003 to store information for each of the contact groups. You must now add and delete some data in the "4 Contacts" table, shown in Figure 1.37. Before proceeding, ensure that the AC01HE Database window is displayed.

Figure 1.37

Displaying the "4 Contacts" datasheet

ID	Volunteer Group	Contact	Address	City	Phone 1	P
1	Downtown Rotary	John Reusche	6717 Cherokee Rd.	Silverdale	478-4802	
2	Silverdale Arts Commission	Jan Neely & Laurie Berg	425 N. El Dorado St.	Silverdale	937-7488	
3	Sierra Middle Sch. Ptsa	Michelle Turnbeaugh	777 Elaine Dr.	Silverdale	477-0205	473-8
4	Lady Bugs	Rachael Pappas	1660 W.Sonora St.	Silverdale	943-5288	
5	American Diabetes Assn.	Penny Knapp	9883 Weeping Willow	Silverdale	474-4581	478-5
6	Delta Rotary	Gary Giovanetti	318 E. Vine Street	Silverdale	957-6650	465-1
7	Silverdale Chamber Of Comm.	Patti Glico	445 W. Weber Ave. #220	Silverdale	547-2960	931-3
8	Assistance League	Teresa Perry	137 Mc Kelley	Silverdale	477-5915	
9	National Council	Janice Colombini	18543 E. Front St.	Centerville	887-3338	
10	Convey, Bill	Bill Convey	3014 Country Club Blvd.	Silverdale	948-3300	463-0
11	Annunciation 5th Grade	Julie Mulligan	9119 Casterbridge Dr	Silverdale	952-2460	946-5
12	Silverdale Police Youth Activ.	Connie Wyman	22 E. Market St.	Silverdale	937-8472	478-9
13	Commodore Sktn Skills	Shirley Lopez	112 E. Sonoma St.	Silverdale	943-6270	
14	Matsuya, Susie & Mike	Susie Matsuya	2828 Appling Circle	Silverdale	953-4238	952-6
15	St. Lukes Parent Club	Maria J. Castellanos	437 Cordoba Lane	Silverdale	468-3598	473-3
16	El Dorado Kiwis Club	John Monte	5334 Rivera Court	Silverdale	474-4680	466-2
17	Pinawa B.P.W.	Jackie Soupe	P.O. Box 2324	Pinawa	368-6765	
18	Silverdale Chorale	Maxine Garrison	7707 N. Pershing Ave.	Silverdale	951-3551	477-2
19	Alder Market	Kitty Rustler	151 W. Alder St.	Silverdale	943-2093	943-1
20	SJ Co 4-H Club Council	Sharon Ross	420 S. Wilson Way	Silverdale	468-2094	477-7

Record: 1 of 66

After opening the "4 Contacts" table for display in Datasheet view, enter two new records to the bottom of the datasheet. Noticing that the first column contains an AutoNumber entry, you ignore the field and proceed to enter the information for two volunteer groups, as shown below.

Group: **Silverdale Search and Rescue**
Contact: **Amy McTell**
Address: **P.O. Box 1359**
City: **Silverdale**
Phone 1: **474-9636**

Group: **Historical Society**
Contact: **Craig Burns**
Address: **3528 Pacific Ave.**
City: **Silverdale**
Phone 1: **945-6621**

When reviewing your work, you notice that a record was inadvertently entered twice—IDs 60 and 61. You select ID 61 (also record 61) and remove the record from the table using the Delete Record button (⊠). The datasheet now appears similar to Figure 1.38. Satisfied with your work, close the Datasheet window and return to the Database window.

Figure 1.38

Adding and deleting records in a datasheet

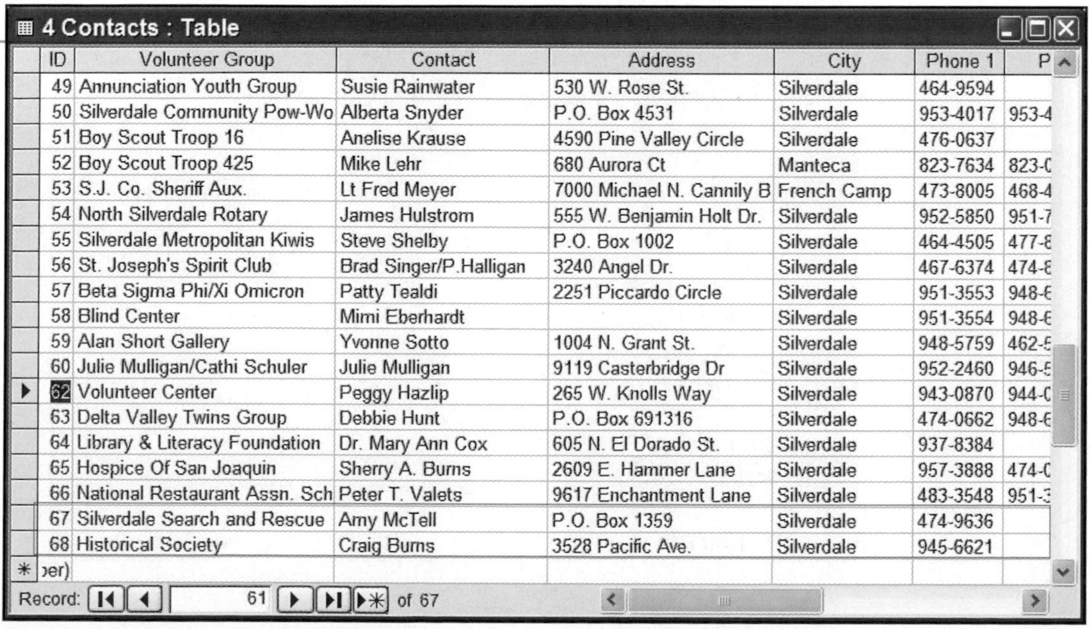

ID	Volunteer Group	Contact	Address	City	Phone 1	P
49	Annunciation Youth Group	Susie Rainwater	530 W. Rose St.	Silverdale	464-9594	
50	Silverdale Community Pow-Wo	Alberta Snyder	P.O. Box 4531	Silverdale	953-4017	953-4
51	Boy Scout Troop 16	Anelise Krause	4590 Pine Valley Circle	Silverdale	476-0637	
52	Boy Scout Troop 425	Mike Lehr	680 Aurora Ct	Manteca	823-7634	823-0
53	S.J. Co. Sheriff Aux.	Lt Fred Meyer	7000 Michael N. Cannily B	French Camp	473-8005	468-4
54	North Silverdale Rotary	James Hulstrom	555 W. Benjamin Holt Dr.	Silverdale	952-5850	951-7
55	Silverdale Metropolitan Kiwis	Steve Shelby	P.O. Box 1002	Silverdale	464-4505	477-8
56	St. Joseph's Spirit Club	Brad Singer/P.Halligan	3240 Angel Dr.	Silverdale	467-6374	474-8
57	Beta Sigma Phi/Xi Omicron	Patty Tealdi	2251 Piccardo Circle	Silverdale	951-3553	948-6
58	Blind Center	Mimi Eberhardt		Silverdale	951-3554	948-6
59	Alan Short Gallery	Yvonne Sotto	1004 N. Grant St.	Silverdale	948-5759	462-5
60	Julie Mulligan/Cathi Schuler	Julie Mulligan	9119 Casterbridge Dr	Silverdale	952-2460	946-5
62	Volunteer Center	Peggy Hazlip	265 W. Knolls Way	Silverdale	943-0870	944-0
63	Delta Valley Twins Group	Debbie Hunt	P.O. Box 691316	Silverdale	474-0662	948-6
64	Library & Literacy Foundation	Dr. Mary Ann Cox	605 N. El Dorado St.	Silverdale	937-8384	
65	Hospice Of San Joaquin	Sherry A. Burns	2609 E. Hammer Lane	Silverdale	957-3888	474-0
66	National Restaurant Assn. Sch	Peter T. Valets	9617 Enchantment Lane	Silverdale	483-3548	951-3
67	Silverdale Search and Rescue	Amy McTell	P.O. Box 1359	Silverdale	474-9636	
68	Historical Society	Craig Burns	3528 Pacific Ave.	Silverdale	945-6621	

Record: 61 of 67

5. Previewing a Datasheet

To practice navigating and formatting a table's datasheet, open the table object named "5 Inventory" in the AC01HE database. Experiment with the various mouse and keyboard methods for moving the cursor in the datasheet. After you have familiarized yourself with the table, use the keyboard to reposition the cursor to the first field of the first record.

Resize the ProductID, Description, and Suggested Retail columns to their best fit. Adjust the OnHand and Cost columns to 12 characters. Change the height of all the rows to 14 points. Now, use Print Preview to see how the datasheet will look when it is printed. Change the page setup to landscape orientation so that all the columns fit on a single page, as shown in Figure 1.39. If they do not, adjust the widths of the remaining columns until they do. When you are satisfied with the appearance of the page, print a copy. Then, close the Datasheet window and save the layout changes.

Figure 1.39

Previewing a datasheet with a landscape print orientation

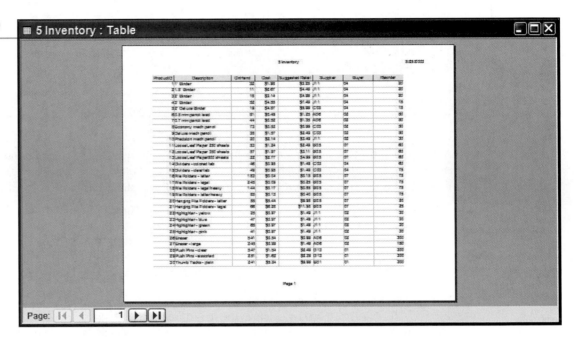

6. Manipulating Data in a Datasheet

To practice manipulating table data, open the table object named "6 Patrons" in the AC01HE database. Now make the following editing changes to the datasheet:

• Change the spelling of guest ID 2 from "Neely" to "Neally"

• Change the Interest of guest ID 6 from "Tennis" to "Golf"

• Change the Hometown of guest ID 8 from "Clonkurry" to "Mount Isa"

• Change the Best Time of guest ID 22 to "11:30 AM"

Make the following addition:
Guest: **Ric Fernando**
Hometown: **Manila**
State: (*leave blank*)
Co: **PHI**
Interest: **Golf**
Room#: **B311**
#Stay: **1**
Best Time: **1:00 PM**

Finally, delete the record for guest ID 15 and then move the cursor to the top of the datasheet. Your screen should appear similar to the one shown in Figure 1.40. Once finished, close the Datasheet window and the AC01HE Database window.

Figure 1.40

Editing the "6 Patrons" datasheet

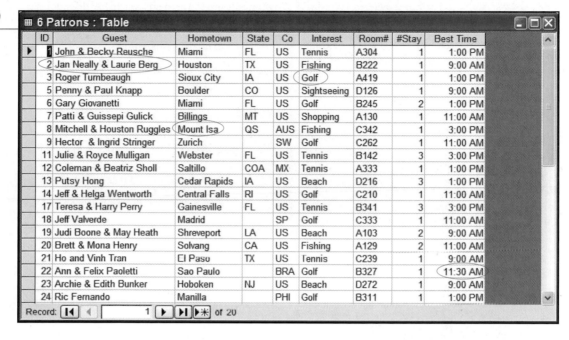

ID	Guest	Hometown	State	Co	Interest	Room#	#Stay	Best Time
1	John & Becky Reusche	Miami	FL	US	Tennis	A304	1	1:00 PM
2	Jan Neally & Laurie Berg	Houston	TX	US	Fishing	B222	1	9:00 AM
3	Roger Turnbeaugh	Sioux City	IA	US	Golf	A419	1	1:00 PM
5	Penny & Paul Knapp	Boulder	CO	US	Sightseeing	D126	1	9:00 AM
6	Gary Giovanetti	Miami	FL	US	Golf	B245	2	1:00 PM
7	Patti & Guissepi Gulick	Billings	MT	US	Shopping	A130	1	11:00 AM
8	Mitchell & Houston Ruggles	Mount Isa	QS	AUS	Fishing	C342	1	3:00 PM
9	Hector & Ingrid Stringer	Zurich		SW	Golf	C262	1	11:00 AM
11	Julie & Royce Mulligan	Webster	FL	US	Tennis	B142	3	3:00 PM
12	Coleman & Beatriz Sholl	Saltillo	COA	MX	Tennis	A333	1	1:00 PM
13	Putsy Hong	Cedar Rapids	IA	US	Beach	D216	3	1:00 PM
14	Jeff & Helga Wentworth	Central Falls	RI	US	Golf	C210	1	11:00 AM
17	Teresa & Harry Perry	Gainesville	FL	US	Tennis	B341	3	3:00 PM
18	Jeff Valverde	Madrid		SP	Golf	C333	1	11:00 AM
19	Judi Boone & May Heath	Shreveport	LA	US	Beach	A103	2	9:00 AM
20	Brett & Mona Henry	Solvang	CA	US	Fishing	A129	2	11:00 AM
21	Ho and Vinh Tran	El Paso	TX	US	Tennis	C239	1	9:00 AM
22	Ann & Felix Paoletti	Sao Paulo		BRA	Golf	B327	1	11:30 AM
23	Archie & Edith Bunker	Hoboken	NJ	US	Beach	D272	1	9:00 AM
24	Ric Fernando	Manilla		PHI	Golf	B311	1	1:00 PM

Record: |◄ ◄ 1 ► ►| ►* of 20

CaseStudy   PROGRESSIVE SOLUTIONS LEARNING CENTER

Joanna Walsh just started a new job with the Progressive Solutions Learning Center, a company that specializes in career and life skills training. As an administrative assistant, Joanna knew that she would be expected to answer phones, write and edit letters, and organize meetings. However, on her first day, Karen Chase, the office director, informed her of some additional expectations: "You will be using Access 2003 to manage our basic seminar information. Our instructors will call you if they have a problem or need to modify the database for any reason. For instance, you may be asked to look up student phone numbers and inform students when a seminar is canceled." Because she has never used database software before, Joanna immediately enrolled in an evening course on Microsoft Office Access 2003 at the local community college. Having attended the first lesson, she now feels ready to open and view the contents of her company's database.

In the following case problems, assume the role of Joanna and perform the same steps that she identifies.

1. Midway through the morning, Joanna receives a phone call from an agitated instructor: "Hello, Joanna? My name is Mary Sterba and I teach the Safety in the Workplace seminars. Due to a family emergency, I cannot make my TR145 seminar this Tuesday. Please call the students and ask if they can transfer into TR146 the following week."

Access

Knowing that all the information she needs is stored in Access, Joanna loads the AC01CP database located in her Advantage student data files folder. From the Database window, she opens the Trainers table and locates Mary Sterba's record. She expands the subdatasheet for Mary's record and verifies that she is indeed scheduled to teach both the TR145 and TR146 seminars. Next, she expands the subdatasheet for TR146, as shown in Figure 1.41, to ensure that it does not have more than 10 students registered. Joanna then collapses the subdatasheet for TR146 and expands the TR145 subdatasheet in order to write down the names and phone numbers of all students registered in the canceled class. She will use the list to call the students later and reschedule them into the next seminar. After completing her first task using Access 2003, Joanna closes the Trainers table.

Figure 1.41

Drilling down into a table's data using subdatasheets

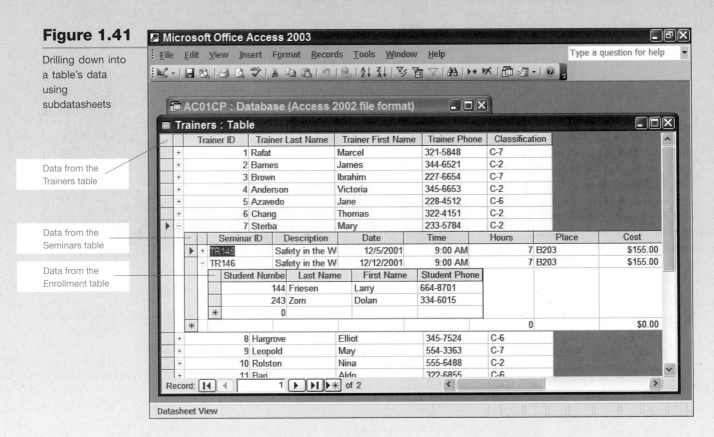

2. Later that day, Karen Chase, the office director, asks Joanna to produce a printout of the currently scheduled seminars. Joanna opens the Seminars table in the AC01CP database and adjusts the column width of the Description field so that the entire title is visible. To provide some additional white space in the printout, she adjusts the height of all the rows to 16 points. Using Print Preview to view the datasheet, Joanna notices that not all columns fit on a single page. To compensate, she changes the page setup to use landscape orientation and adjusts the datasheet's column widths as necessary. When she is satisfied with the appearance of the datasheet (Figure 1.42), Joanna prints a copy for Karen. Then she closes the Seminars table, saving the formatting changes she has made.

Figure 1.42

Previewing the
Seminars
datasheet

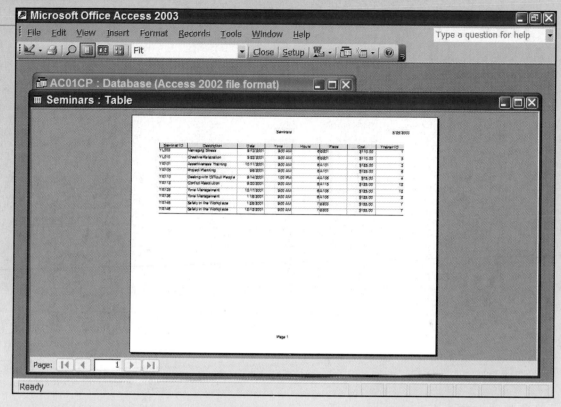

3. Joanna phones the five students whose phone numbers she wrote down earlier that day and
determines that the students are all indeed able to switch to the later "Safety in the Workplace" seminar. To update the database, Joanna begins by opening the Enrollment table. She locates the five students' records and changes the Seminar ID for each record from TR145 to TR146. She then switches
to the Database window, without closing the datasheet, and opens the Seminars table. To finish the
task, Joanna ensures that no students are registered in seminar TR145 and then deletes the record. Finally, she closes both Datasheet windows.

4. Toward the end of the day, Joanna receives two phone calls from people wishing to register for seminars. After writing down the information, Joanna is ready to update the database. She opens the Enrollment table and adds two new records, as shown in Figure 1.43.

Student Number: **501**
Last Name: **Haldane**
First Name: **Chris**
Student Phone: **577-9685**
Seminar ID: **TR135**

Student Number: **502**
Last Name: **Zhou**
First Name: **Shih-Chang**
Student Phone: **345-6087**
Seminar ID: **TR146**

Joanna saves the records and closes the datasheet. Then she closes the Database window and exits
Microsoft Office Access 2003.

Figure 1.43

Adding students
to the Enrollment
table

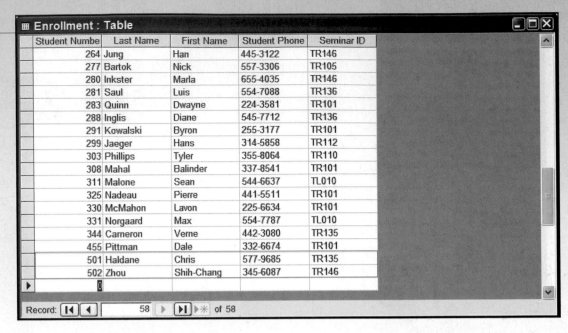

Answers

to self-check questions

1.1 How do you close a window that appears in the Access work area? Click on its Close button (☒).

1.2 Describe two methods for moving the cursor to the last record in a large datasheet. Here are three methods. First, you can use the cursor movement keys **CTRL** + **↓** or **CTRL** + **END** to move the cursor to the last record. Second, you can use the mouse to click the Last Record button (▶|). Third, you can scroll the window by dragging the vertical scroll box and then click in a field of the last record. (*Note:* You must click in the record's row in order to move the cursor. Otherwise, you simply scroll the window.)

1.3 When does Access save the editing changes that you have made to a record? Editing changes to a record are saved permanently to disk when the cursor is moved to another record or when the user presses the **SHIFT** + **ENTER** combination.

Microsoft® Office Access® 2003

CHAPTER 2

⊕ # Creating a Database

PREREQUISITES

To successfully complete this chapter, you must know how to open database objects appearing in the Database window. Most importantly, you must be able to display and navigate a table's datasheet using the mouse and keyboard. You should also be able to perform basic editing in a datasheet, including adding and deleting records.

LEARNING OBJECTIVES

After completing this chapter, you will be able to:

- Create a new database from scratch

- Create a new database using a wizard

- Define table objects for storing data

- Specify a primary key and indexes

- Rename, delete, and move fields

- Print a table's structure

2.1 Designing Your First Database

Desktop database software has existed since the first personal computer was introduced by IBM in the early 1980s. Since that time, many database programs and applications have been developed for both personal and business use. Whatever your particular data management needs, rarely will you require a truly unique application. Refining or customizing an existing database application is a more common practice. Microsoft Office Access 2003 allows you to take advantage of what others before you have learned and accomplished. Using the Access 2003 wizards, you can develop an entire database application in less time than it takes to read this module.

2.1.1 Planning a Database

→ Feature

Many people who have worked with computer databases can attest to the 90/10 rule of database design: place 90 percent of your effort into properly designing a database in order to spend only 10 percent of your time maintaining or changing it. As you probably can infer from this rule, many problems arising in database management are traceable to a faulty design. In this lesson, you will learn some strategies for planning a well-designed database.

→ Method

Here are five steps to designing a better database:

Determine your output requirements. State your expectations in terms of the queries and reports desired from the application. It is often helpful to write out questions, such as "How many customers live in Kansas City?" and to sketch out reports on a blank piece of paper.

Determine your input requirements. From the output requirements, identify the data that must be collected, stored, and calculated. You should also review any existing paper-based forms used for data collection in order to get a better idea of what data are available.

Determine your table structures. Divide and group data into separate tables and fields for flexibility in searching, sorting, and manipulating data. Review the following example to see what fields can be separated out of a simple address:

Ensure that each record can be identified using a unique code or field, such as Order Number or Customer ID. This code need not contain information related to the subject—a numeric field that is automatically incremented works fine.

Determine your table relationships. Rather than entering or storing the same information repeatedly, strive to separate data into multiple tables and then relate the tables using a common field. For example, in a table containing book information (Books), an AuthorID field would contain a unique code that could be used to look up the author's personal data in a separate table (Authors). Without such a design, you would need to type an author's name and address each time you added one of his or her works to the Books table.

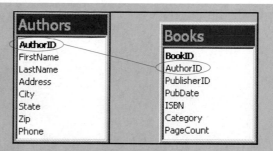

By incorporating common fields into your table structures, you can establish relationships among the tables for sharing data. This process, called *normalizing* your data, enhances your efficiency and reduces potential data redundancy and entry errors.

Test your database application. Add sample records to the table using both datasheets and forms and then run queries and produce reports to test whether the application is robust and accurate. In addition to ensuring the validity and integrity of data, you want the information to be readily accessible.

2.1.2 Starting a New Database

→ Feature

Access provides two main options for creating a new database. First, you can choose to create a blank structure and then add the database objects appropriate for your specific application. The creation of an empty database structure is the focus of this lesson. The second option, discussed in the next lesson, is to select a starting point from a group of professionally designed database templates. Unlike other Office 2003 applications, which allow you to open multiple documents simultaneously, Access allows you to work with only one database at a time. Therefore, before starting a new database, you must ensure that there is no active database displayed in the application window's work area.

→ Method

To create an empty database structure:

- CLICK: New button (□)

    or

- CHOOSE: File → New

- CLICK: "Blank database" option under the *New* area in the New File task pane

→ Practice

In this lesson, you will create a new database file for storing table objects.

1. Ensure that you have turned on your computer and that the Windows desktop appears. Load Microsoft Office Access 2003 using the Windows Start menu.

2. To create a new database application, start by ensuring that the New File task pane (shown in Figure 2.1) is displayed:
CLICK: New button (□) on the toolbar

Figure 2.1

New File task
pane

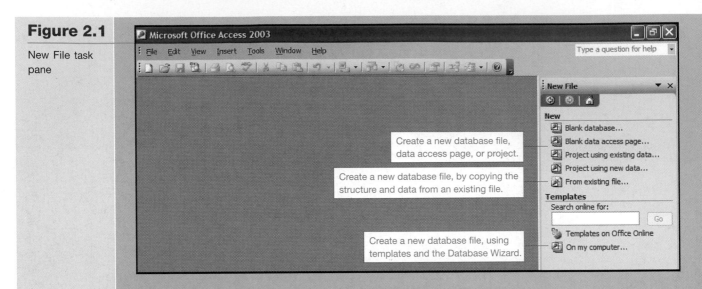

3. Using the hand mouse pointer (👆):
CLICK: Blank database, located under the *New* heading

4. You use the File New Database dialog box (Figure 2.2) to select a storage location and filename
for permanently saving the database structure. Using the Places bar or the *Save in* drop-down
dialog box, select your personal storage location.

Figure 2.2

File New
Database dialog
box

Places bar ———

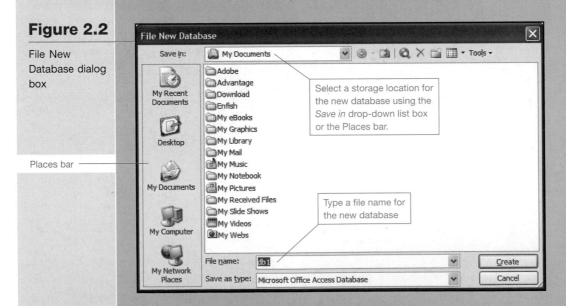

5. On your own, select the existing filename (by default, "db1") that appears in the *File name* text box
using the mouse. (*Hint:* Double-click or drag over the filename using the I-beam mouse pointer.)

6. To create the new database file:
TYPE: **My Phone Book** to replace the existing filename
CLICK: Create command button
A new Database window appears in the work area, as shown in Figure 2.3. Notice that the Title
bar reads "My Phone Book : Database (Access 2002 – 2003 file format)." Nothing more than an
empty shell at this point, the Database window contains no objects except the default New Object
shortcuts. (*Note:* To facilitate information sharing among users of legacy applications, Access
2003 also allows you to create database files using the Access 2000 file format.)

Figure 2.3

Creating a blank
database named
"My Phone Book"

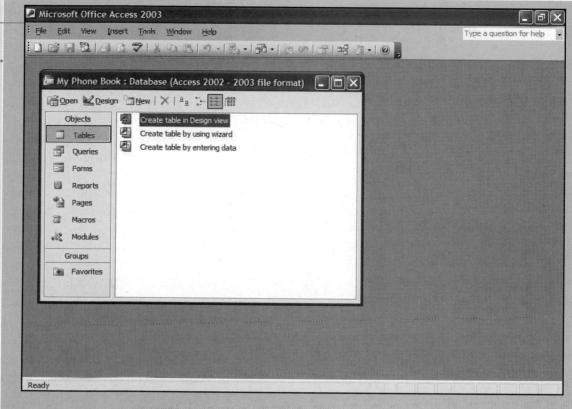

7. You learn how to add table objects to an empty database in the next module. For now, close the
Database window and proceed to the next lesson:
CLICK: its Close button (✕)

2.1.3 Employing the Database Wizard

→ **Feature**

Besides creating an empty database structure and then populating it with objects, Access 2003 can
lead you in the step-by-step generation of a new database using the **Database Wizard.** This wizard
provides access to professionally designed templates for creating complete database applications.
Each template contains tables, queries, forms, and reports, as well as a main menu called a *switchboard* that makes the application's features easier to access.

→ **Method**

- CLICK: New button (▣)

  or

- CHOOSE: File → New

- CLICK: "On my computer" option under the *Templates* area in the New File task pane

- CLICK: *Databases* tab in the Templates dialog box

- DOUBLE-CLICK: a database wizard (▨)

Using the Access 2003 Database Wizard, you will now create an inventory control application from scratch. Ensure that Access is loaded and that no Database window is displayed.

1. Let's begin by ensuring that the New File task pane is displayed:
CLICK: New button (▣) on the toolbar

2. Using the hand pointer (🖑) of the mouse:
CLICK: On my computer, located under the *Templates* heading

3. The Blank Database template icon appears selected on the *General* tab of the Templates dialog box. This is the template used by Access when you click the "Blank database" option under the *New* heading. To list the Database Wizard templates that are available on your computer, do the following:
CLICK: *Databases* tab
Your screen should now appear similar to the one shown in Figure 2.4. (*Note:* Depending on how Access 2003 was installed and configured on your system, different template options may appear in your dialog box. If you have not installed any database templates, you cannot perform the steps in this lesson.)

Figure 2.4

Templates dialog box: *Databases* tab

By default, Access 2003 provides the *General* and *Databases* tabs for organizing database templates.

You may also search for database templates on the Microsoft Office Online Web site.

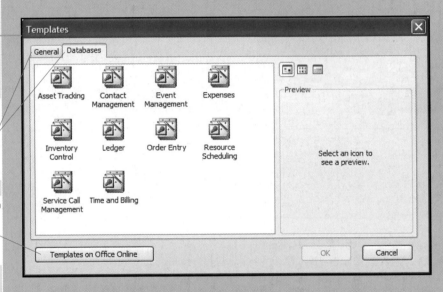

4. Using the appropriate Database Wizard template, let's create an inventory database application:
DOUBLE-CLICK: Inventory Control wizard (📷)

5. In the File New Database dialog box that appears, use the Places bar or the *Save in* drop-down list box to select your personal storage location. Then, select the name that appears in the *File name* text box using the mouse.

6. Now select the name (usually "Inventory Control" with the number "1" appended) that appears in the *File name* text box and do the following:
TYPE: **My Inventory** to replace the existing filename
CLICK: Create command button
Wait patiently as Access 2003 displays your new Database window and prepares the Database Wizard dialog box, shown in Figure 2.5.

Figure 2.5

Database Wizard
dialog box for
creating an
Inventory Control
database

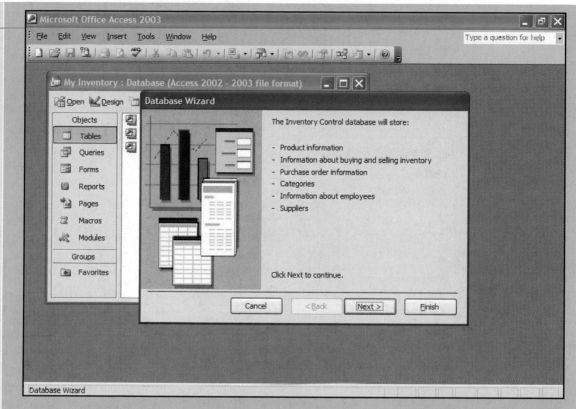

7. The opening screen of the Database Wizard dialog box provides information about the Inventory Control wizard. After reading its contents, proceed to the next step:
CLICK: Next>

8. Your first task in the Database Wizard, as shown in Figure 2.6, is to select fields for collecting and storing information in the database. Optional fields appear in italic type. On your own, click on the names listed in the *Tables in the database* list box. The field names for the selected table appear in the *Fields in the table* list box. To proceed:
CLICK: Next>

Figure 2.6

Inventory Control
Database Wizard:
select fields

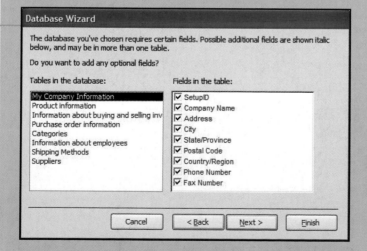

9. To select a screen appearance for your forms, click on each option in the dialog box to see a preview and then:
SELECT: Sumi Painting, as shown in Figure 2.7
CLICK: [Next>]

Figure 2.7

Inventory Control
Database Wizard:
select screen
appearance

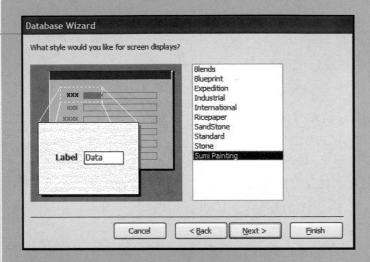

10. To select a page layout for your printed reports, click on each option in the dialog box to see a preview and then:
SELECT: Soft Gray, as shown in Figure 2.8
CLICK: [Next>]

Figure 2.8

Inventory Control
Database Wizard:
select report
appearance

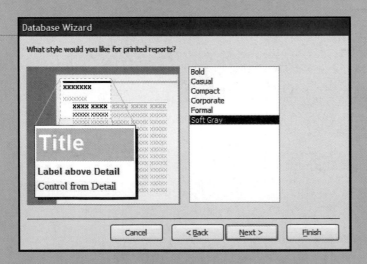

11. You can also specify the title of the database and whether to include a logo or picture. To accept the defaults ("Inventory Control"):
CLICK: [Next>]

12. At the finish line, you tell Access 2003 to create and display the database. Ensure that the *Yes, start the database* check box is selected and then do the following:
CLICK: [Finish]
The Database Wizard creates the database based on your selections. Depending on the power of your system, this process can take a few minutes.

13. In this particular wizard, Access 2003 displays a dialog box asking you to furnish some company data. Do the following:
CLICK: OK command button to continue

14. Using the [TAB] key to move forward through the text boxes in the My Company Information window, type the information shown in Figure 2.9. When you are ready to proceed:
CLICK: its Close button ([X])

Figure 2.9

Furnishing the
wizard with
company
information

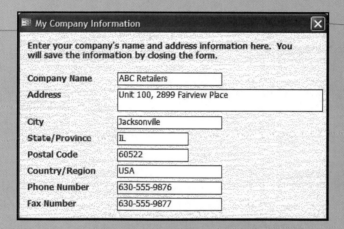

Click here when you are finished
entering data into the form window.

15. The Main Switchboard (Figure 2.10) for the Inventory Control application is displayed. On your own, click on the menu buttons to access and display the forms and reports created by the Database Wizard. (*Note:* If you move into a submenu, click the Return to Main Switchboard menu button to move back to the main window.)

Access

Figure 2.10

Main Switchboard for the Inventory Control application

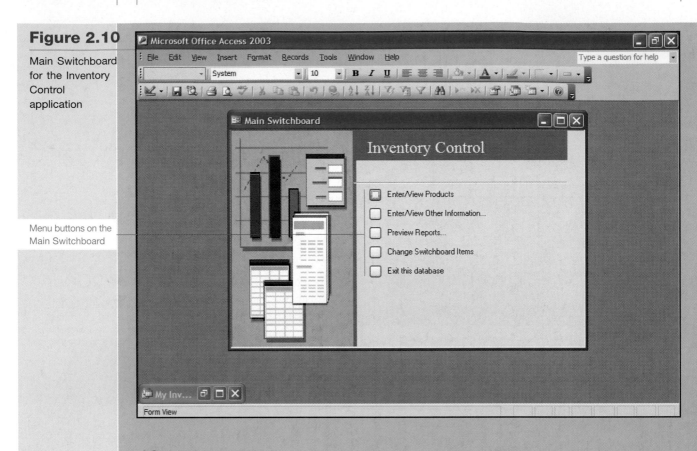

Menu buttons on the Main Switchboard

16. Before proceeding, close any display or preview windows that appear for a form or a report by clicking their Close buttons (⊠).

17. Let's examine the database objects that were created by the Database Wizard for this application. From the Menu bar:
CHOOSE: Window → My Inventory : Database (Access 2002 – 2003 file format)

18. In the Database window, click on the various buttons in the Objects bar to view the table, query, form, and report objects. You may need to scroll the list area or adjust the size of the Database window to see all of the object names. When you are finished, close the application:
CLICK: the Close button (⊠) for the Database window
Notice that the Main Switchboard, which appears as a form object, also disappears when you close the Database window.

In Addition ACCESSING OTHER DATABASE TEMPLATES

Besides the templates that ship with Microsoft Office System 2003, additional templates are available free on the Internet. For example, in the New File task pane, clicking the *Templates on Office Online* option launches a Microsoft Web page in your default browser. Before creating a new database from scratch, you can peruse these templates to search for a possible starting point and save yourself some time.

2.1 What two objects are most closely associated with the output of a database application?

2.2 Creating a Simple Table

An Access 2003 database file is simply a container for storing database objects. After creating an empty database structure, the next step is to define the table objects for storing data. Each table in your database should contain information about a single topic or subject. In an automobile industry database, for example, one table may contain a list of car dealerships while another table contains a list of manufacturers. Although these tables deal with different subjects, they are both related to the automobile industry. In this module, you will learn two methods for quickly populating a database structure with table objects. What these methods may lack in power and flexibility, they make up for in speed and ease of use.

2.2.1 Creating a Table Using the Table Wizard

→ Feature

Access 2003 provides the **Table Wizard** to help you create a table structure, in much the same way that you created a complete application using the Database Wizard. Rather than defining a new table from scratch, you build it by picking and choosing fields from existing personal and business tables. This method lets you quickly populate an empty database structure with reliable and usable table objects.

→ Method

In the Database window, select the Tables button and then:

* DOUBLE-CLICK: Create table by using wizard

  or

* CLICK: New button (⬜) on the Database window toolbar
* DOUBLE-CLICK: Table Wizard in the New Table dialog box

→ Practice

After opening a new database, you will create a table object using the Table Wizard. Before continuing, ensure that no Database window is displayed.

1. To create a new database using the New File task pane:
   CLICK: New button (⬜) on the toolbar
   CLICK: Blank database, under the *New* heading in the task pane

2. In the File New Database dialog box that appears, use the Places bar or the *Save in* drop-down list box to select your personal storage location. Then, select the name that appears in the *File name* text box using the mouse.

3. TYPE: **My Business** into the *File name* text box to replace the existing filename
   CLICK: Create command button
   The My Business Database window will appear.

4. Your next step is to add table objects to the empty database structure. To use the Table Wizard, ensure that the Tables button is selected in the Objects bar and then do the following:
   DOUBLE-CLICK: Create table by using wizard
   The Table Wizard dialog box appears, as shown in Figure 2.11.

Access

Figure 2.11

Table Wizard
dialog box

The "My Business"
Database window

Select a category in
order to display
tables appropriate
for your application.

Select one of the
prebuilt tables to
display the fields
that are available.

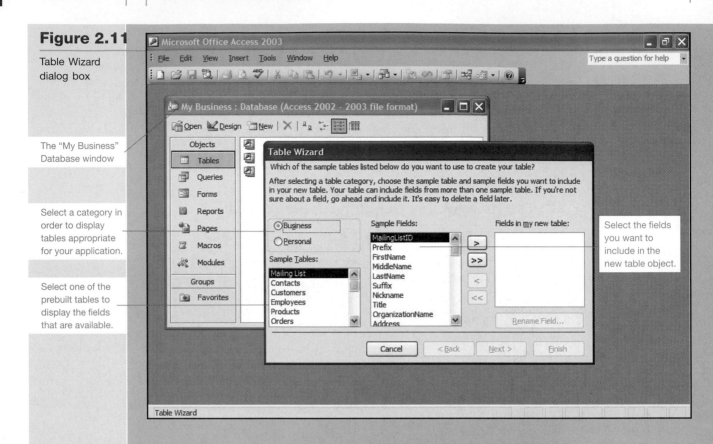

Select the fields
you want to
include in the
new table object.

---

5. By default, the *Business* option button is chosen in the Table Wizard dialog box. As a result, only business-related table structures appear in the *Sample Tables* list box. To view the Personal tables:
CLICK: *Personal* option button

6. On your own, scroll the *Sample Tables* list box to view the available table structures.

7. Let's create a new table in which to store the company's product information:
CLICK: *Business* option button
SELECT: Products in the *Sample Tables* list box
Notice that the fields for this table structure now appear in the *Sample Fields* list box, as shown here.

8. To specify fields for your new table, select individual field names in the *Sample Fields* list box and then click ⟩ to move them to the *Fields in my new table* list box. You can also select all fields by clicking ⟩⟩. For this step, let's include all of the suggested fields:
CLICK: Include All button (⟩⟩)

9. To proceed to the next step:
CLICK: Next>
Your screen should now appear similar to the one shown in Figure 2.12.

Figure 2.12

Specifying a table name in the Table Wizard dialog box

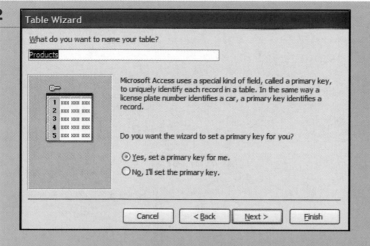

10. Let's accept the default selections in this dialog box and proceed to the next step:
CLICK: Next>

11. Ensure that the *Enter data directly into the table* option button is selected in the final dialog box and then do the following:
CLICK: Finish
The new table, called "Products," appears in a Datasheet window ready to accept data, as shown in Figure 2.13.

Figure 2.13

Products
Datasheet
window

The new Products table is displayed in Datasheet view so that you can begin entering data.

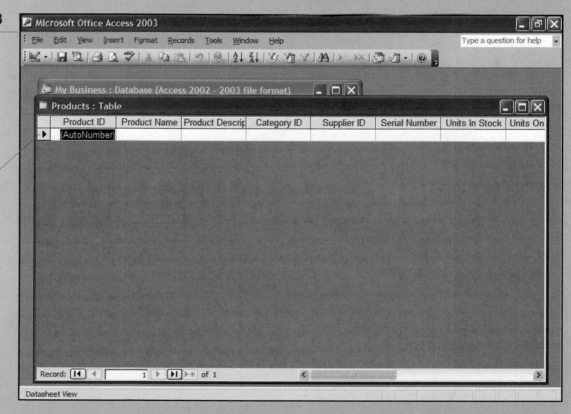

12. Close the Products Datasheet window. You should now see the Products table object in the Database window.

2.2.2 Creating a Table in Datasheet View

→ **Feature**

Using Datasheet view, you create a table by typing information into a blank datasheet, just as you would when entering data into an Excel worksheet. When you save the table, Access 2003 creates the table structure and assigns the proper data types to each field based on the information you have entered. This method lets novice users create tables without an in-depth understanding of table structures and data types.

→ **Method**

In the Database window, select the *Tables* button and then:

- DOUBLE-CLICK: Create table by entering data

  or

- CLICK: New button (New) on the Database window toolbar
- DOUBLE-CLICK: Datasheet View in the New Table dialog box

→ **Practice**

In this lesson, you will create a new table in Datasheet view for storing supplier information. Ensure that you have completed the previous lesson and that the My Business Database window is displayed.

1. To create a table using Datasheet view, ensure that the Tables button is selected in the Objects bar and then do the following:
DOUBLE-CLICK: Create table by entering data
A blank Datasheet window appears with several field columns and blank records.

2. Let's begin by renaming the column headings in the field header area.
Using the column select pointer (>) of the mouse:
DOUBLE-CLICK: Field1
The field or column name appears selected in the field header row, as shown here.

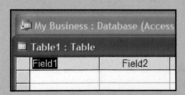

3. Now type the new field name:
TYPE: **SupplierID**
PRESS: (ENTER)
The new field name, SupplierID, appears in the field header area.

4. To continue renaming fields in the Datasheet window:
DOUBLE-CLICK: Field2
TYPE: **Company**
DOUBLE-CLICK: Field3
TYPE: **Contact**
DOUBLE-CLICK: Field4
TYPE: **Phone**
PRESS: (ENTER)
The cursor should now appear in the first field of the first record.

5. On your own, enter the two records appearing in Figure 2.14.

Figure 2.14

Entering records in Datasheet view

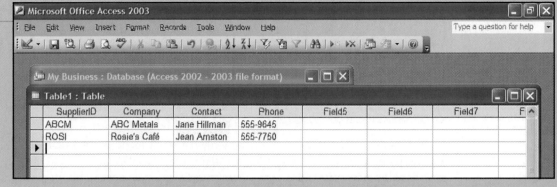

6. To save and name the new table structure:
CLICK: Save button (🖫) on the toolbar
TYPE: **Suppliers** into the Save As dialog box
PRESS: **ENTER** or CLICK: OK
An Alert dialog box appears, as shown in Figure 2.15.

Figure 2.15

Defining a new table based on the contents of a datasheet

Access 2003 offers to define a primary key for the table. A primary key holds a unique value for identifying, locating, and sorting records in a table.

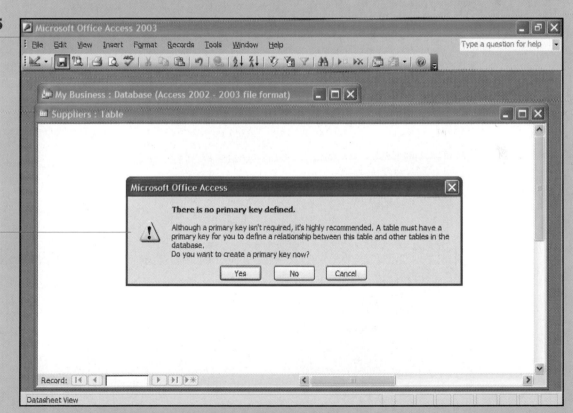

7. To allow Access to define a primary key for the table:
CLICK: Yes command button
After a few moments, Access displays the datasheet for the Suppliers table, complete with a new AutoNumber primary key field named "ID" in the left-hand column.

8. Close the Suppliers Datasheet window. You should now see the Suppliers table object in the Database window.

9. Close the Database window.

 **2.2** How do you specify the name of a field when creating a table in Datasheet view?

2.3 Using the Table Design View

If all of your database needs are satisfied by the templates found in the Database and Table Wizards, you are already on your way to developing desktop database applications that are robust. To unlock the real power behind Access 2003, however, you must delve into the inner workings of an Access table structure. Using Design view, you create a table by specifying its properties, characteristics, and behaviors down to the field level. Although this method requires the greatest understanding of database design, it is well worth the effort in terms of creating efficient custom table structures.

2.3.1 Creating a Table in Design View

→ Feature

Table Design view allows you to get down to the nuts and bolts of designing and constructing a table. In Design view, you create the table structure manually, specifying the field names, data types, and indexes. After some practice, you will find that this method affords the greatest power and flexibility in designing and modifying table objects.

→ Method

In the Database window, select the Tables button and then:

• DOUBLE-CLICK: Create table in Design view

    or

• CLICK: New button (New) on the Database window toolbar

• DOUBLE-CLICK: Design View in the New Table dialog box

→ Practice

You will now create a new table structure in Design view. Ensure that no Database window is displayed in the work area.

1. To create a new database using the New File task pane:
CLICK: New button (☐) on the toolbar
CLICK: Blank database, under the *New* heading in the task pane

2. In the File New Database dialog box that appears, use the Places bar or the *Save in* drop-down list box to select your personal storage location. Then, select the name that appears in the *File name* text box using the mouse.

3. TYPE: **My Library** into the *File name* text box to replace the existing filename
CLICK: Create command button
The My Library Database window will appear.

4. Because tables are the foundation for all your queries, forms, and reports, you need to create at least one table before creating any other database object. To add a new table to the database:
CLICK: New button (New) on the Database window toolbar
The New Table dialog box (Figure 2.16) offers an alternative to selecting a New Object shortcut in the list area of the Database window.

Figure 2.16

New Table dialog box

Click the New button on the Database window toolbar to display the New Table dialog box.

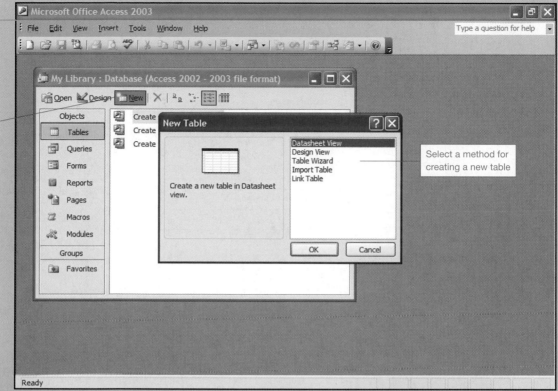

Select a method for creating a new table

5. CLICK: Design View in the list area to select it
CLICK: OK command button
The table Design window (Figure 2.17), which is divided into a **Field Grid pane** and a **Field Properties pane,** appears in **Design view.** This window is used to add, delete, and rename fields for the table structure; set a field's data type; specify a field's properties or characteristics; and choose a primary key for organizing and sorting a table.

6. To define the first field in the table, ensure that the insertion point appears in the Field Name column and then do the following:
TYPE: **BookID**
PRESS: TAB to move to the Data Type column
Your screen should now appear similar to the one shown in Figure 2.17. (*Note:* Access provides specific rules for naming fields in a table. First, names cannot exceed 64 characters in length. Second, names should not contain special symbols or punctuation, such as a period or exclamation point. Third, names cannot begin with a space and, in our opinion, should not contain spaces. Descriptive single-word names are best.)

Access

Figure 2.17

Table Design window

Use the Field Grid pane to define the fields that you want in the table.

When a field is selected in the Field Grid pane, the Field Properties pane is used to display and set its characteristics, such as size and display format.

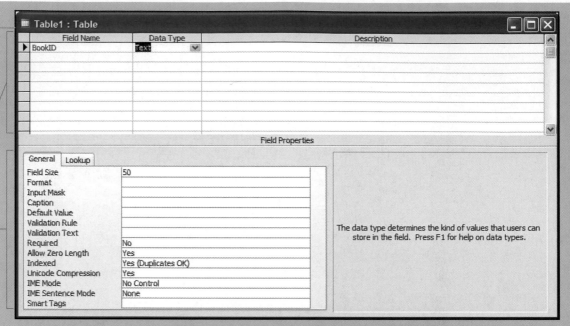

7. By default, Access inserts "Text" as the data type for the BookID field. The data type you select determines the kind of values that you will be able to enter into the field. To view the other data type options, described further in Table 2.1, do the following:
CLICK: down arrow attached to the field
The drop-down list shown here is displayed.

Table 2.1

Data Types

Type	Description
Text	Alphanumeric data, up to 255 characters; used for entering text and numbers that are not required for calculation, such as zip codes and phone numbers
Memo	Alphanumeric data, up to 65,535 characters; used to store notes, comments, or lengthy descriptions
Number	Numeric data that are used to perform mathematical calculations
Date/Time	Dates and times
Currency	Numeric data with a leading dollar sign; used to store and calculate monetary values up to four decimal places
AutoNumber	Numeric value that increments automatically; used for assigning a unique value to a record, which makes it a perfect *primary key* field
Yes/No	Logical or Boolean values for toggling (turning on and off) yes/no or true/false results

Type	Description
OLE Object	Object linking and embedding (OLE) field for storing objects (Excel worksheets and Word documents), graphics, or other binary data up to one gigabyte (GB) in size
Hyperlink	Text or numbers stored as a hyperlink address; used to store Web site addresses, also called URLs, such as http://www.advantageseries.com/
Lookup Wizard	A link to another table or to a static list of values for inserting data into the current table; selecting this option launches the Lookup Wizard.

8. For the BookID field's data type:
SELECT: AutoNumber
PRESS: TAB

9. The *Description* column allows you to store a helpful comment describing the contents of the field. This comment will also appear in the Status bar when you select the field in Datasheet view. To proceed:
TYPE: **Unique code generated by Access**
PRESS: ENTER to move to the next row

10. On your own, complete the Field Grid pane as displayed in Figure 2.18. Notice that the longer field names, such as AuthorSurname, contain mixed case letters to enhance their readability. When finished, keep the table Design window displayed and proceed to the next lesson.

Figure 2.18

Completing the Field Grid pane

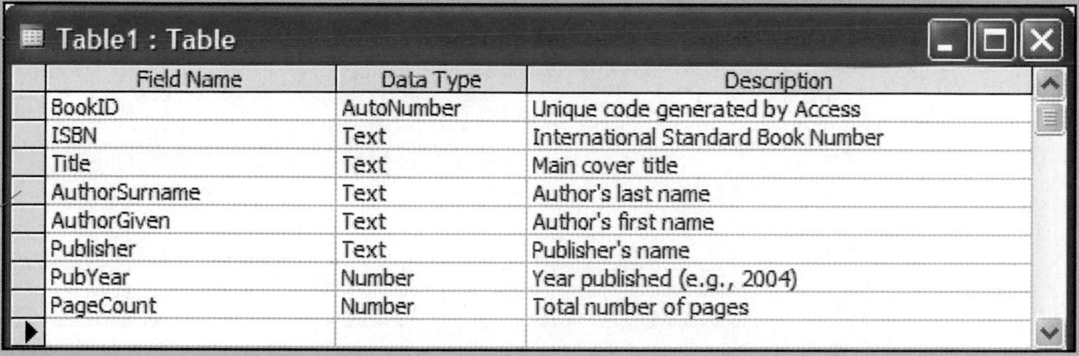

Row selection area of the Field Grid pane

Field Name	Data Type	Description
BookID	AutoNumber	Unique code generated by Access
ISBN	Text	International Standard Book Number
Title	Text	Main cover title
AuthorSurname	Text	Author's last name
AuthorGiven	Text	Author's first name
Publisher	Text	Publisher's name
PubYear	Number	Year published (e.g., 2004)
PageCount	Number	Total number of pages

In Addition FIELD NAMING CONVENTIONS

Besides the Access rules for naming fields, some naming conventions are used by programmers to convey specific information about fields and database objects. For example, the prefix "str" is often used to denote a text or string data type (such as strName) and the prefix "bln" is used to name a Boolean Yes/No field (such as blnMailingList). Furthermore, a group of database objects may be named tblBooks (table), qryBooks (query), frmBooks (form), and rptBooks (report) to describe the different types of objects related to a single subject. The important concept here is to remain consistent in whatever naming scheme you select.

2.3.2 Assigning a Primary Key

→ # Feature

In creating a table structure, you need to specify a field (or fields) that will uniquely identify each and every record in the table. This field, called the **primary key,** is used by Access in searching for data and in establishing relationships between tables. Once a field is defined as the primary key, its datasheet is automatically indexed, or sorted, into order by that field. Access also prevents you from entering a duplicate value or a **null value** (nothing) into a primary key field. An **AutoNumber** data type automatically increments sequentially as each new record is added to a table, making this data type one of the best choices for a primary key.

→ # Method

In table Design view:

- SELECT: the desired field using the row selection area
- CLICK: Primary Key button (⬚) on the toolbar

   or

- CHOOSE: Edit → Primary Key

→ # Practice

You will now assign a primary key field for the table created in the last lesson. Ensure that you have completed the previous lesson and that the table Design window is displayed.

1. To select a field for the primary key:
CLICK: row selector button for BookID
(*Hint:* Position the mouse pointer in the row selection area of the Field Grid pane and click the row selector button next to the BookID field.)

2. To assign a primary key:
CLICK: Primary Key button (⬚)
Your screen should now appear similar to the one shown in Figure 2.19.

Figure 2.19

Setting the primary key

Selecting a field in the Field Grid pane and then making it the primary key field for the table.

Notice that the field is indexed (sorted) and does not allow duplicate entries.

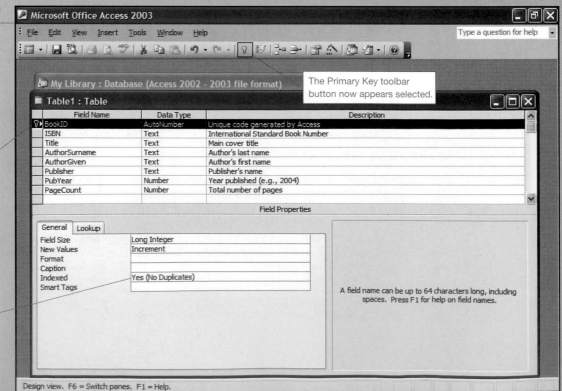

3. Now that you have assigned the primary key, you can save the table structure. Do the following:
CLICK: Save button (⊞)

4. In the Save As dialog box that appears:
TYPE: **Books**
PRESS: ENTER or CLICK: OK
Notice that the Title bar for the table Design window displays the table's name. Keep the window displayed for use in the next lesson.

2.3.3 Defining and Removing Indexes

→ ## Feature

An **index**, like the primary key, is a special mechanism for dynamically organizing and ordering the data stored in a table. By defining indexes, you can speed up the search and sort operations for running queries and reports. However, you do not want to create indexes for all fields, as this would slow down the common activities of adding and editing records. As a rule, index only the fields that you use frequently in searching for and sorting data, such as a Surname or Company Name field.

→ ## Method

To define an index in table Design view:

- SELECT: the desired field using the row selection area
- SELECT: *Indexed* text box in the Field Properties pane
- CLICK: down arrow attached to the *Indexed* text box
- SELECT: an indexing option

To remove an index in table Design view:

- CLICK: Indexes button (☞) on the toolbar
- RIGHT-CLICK: the desired field's row selector button
- CHOOSE: Delete Rows

→ ## Practice

In this lesson, you will create two indexes to complement the primary key and remove an existing index that was created by Access. Ensure that you have completed the previous lessons and that the Design window for the Books table is displayed.

1. Most people search for a book based on its title or author. Therefore, let's create indexes for these fields in the Books table. To begin:
SELECT: Title row selector button in the Field Grid pane

2. Using the I-beam mouse pointer:
CLICK: in the *Indexed* text box in the Field Properties pane
You should now see a drop-down arrow attached to the text box.

3. With the flashing insertion point in the *Indexed* text box, you may select an indexing option from the drop-down list box. To proceed:
CLICK: down arrow attached to the *Indexed* text box
Your screen should now appear similar to the one shown in Figure 2.20.

Figure 2.20

Setting an index

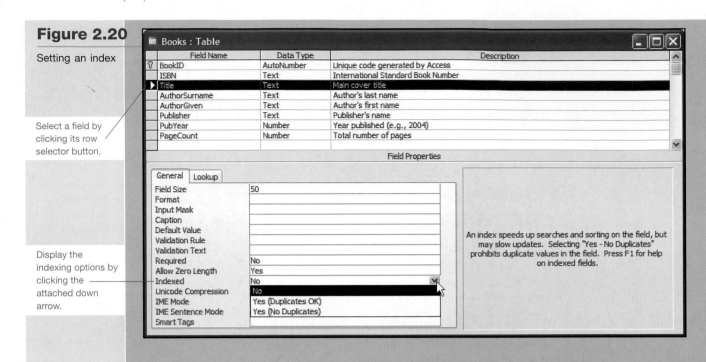

Select a field by
clicking its row
selector button.

Display the
indexing options by
clicking the
attached down
arrow.

4. Because you do not want to limit the possibility of duplicate entries (different authors may have written books with the same title):
   SELECT: Yes (Duplicates OK)

5. Let's define another index for the table:
   SELECT: AuthorSurname in the Field Grid pane
   CLICK: in the *Indexed* text box in the Field Properties pane

6. From the drop-down list attached to the *Indexed* text box:
   SELECT: Yes (Duplicates OK)

7. Save the table structure:
   CLICK: Save button (🖫)
   (*Note:* It is a good habit to save the table after each major change.)

8. To display the associated indexes for the Books table:
   CLICK: Indexes button (📝)
   The Indexes window appears as shown in Figure 2.21.

Figure 2.21

Indexes window
for the Books
table

List of available
indexes

Index properties for
selected index

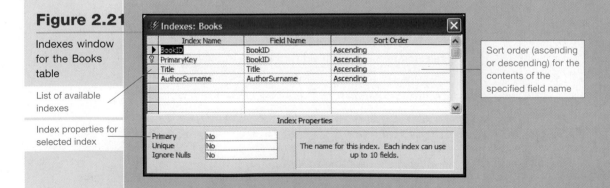

Sort order (ascending
or descending) for the
contents of the
specified field name

9. As illustrated in Figure 2.21, Access automatically creates indexes for fields that contain the letters "ID" in their names. The BookID field, for example, is the primary key but also the name of an index. To remove the BookID index using the row select mouse pointer (➡):
   RIGHT-CLICK: BookID row selector button

10. In the right-click menu that appears:
CHOOSE: Delete Rows
The BookID index is removed but the BookID primary key remains.

11. Close the Indexes window.

12. To clean up the Access 2003 work area, save and then close the table Design window. Finally, close the My Library Database window.

In Addition SETTING FIELD PROPERTIES

Every field in a table has a set of properties. A field property is a specific characteristic of a field or data type that enables you to provide greater control over how your data is entered, stored, displayed, and printed. Some common properties include *Field Size, Format, Decimal Places, Input Mask, Default Value, Required,* and *Indexed*. You set a field's properties using the Field Properties pane in the table Design window.

2.3 What is an AutoNumber field? Why is it useful as a primary key?

2.4 Modifying a Table

A database is a dynamic entity. It is not uncommon for the initial design requirements to change once a database is set in front of users. Fortunately Access enables you to modify a table's structure quickly and efficiently. Adding, deleting, and changing field specifications in table Design view are similar to editing records in a datasheet. Nonetheless, you should not perform structural changes hastily. When you modify a table's structure, you also affect the forms and reports that are based on the table.

2.4.1 Inserting and Deleting Fields

→ **Feature**

After displaying a table structure in Design view, you can easily add and remove fields. Adding a field is as simple as entering a field name and data type on a blank row in the Field Grid pane. Removing a field deletes the field from the Field Grid pane but also deletes all the data stored in the field. Be extra careful when deleting existing fields!

→ **Method**

To insert a field in table Design view:

• SELECT: an empty row in the Field Grid pane

• Type a field name, select a data type, and enter a description.

To delete a field in table Design view:

• RIGHT-CLICK: row selector of the field you want to remove

• CHOOSE: Delete Rows

→ **Practice**

In this lesson, you will insert and remove fields in an existing table structure. Ensure that no Database window is displayed.

1. Open the database named AC0240, located in your Advantage student data files location.

2. This database contains a single table object, named Books, that is based on the table structure you created in the last module. To display the table in Datasheet view:
DOUBLE-CLICK: Books
Your screen should now appear similar to the one shown in Figure 2.22.

Figure 2.22

Displaying the
Books datasheet

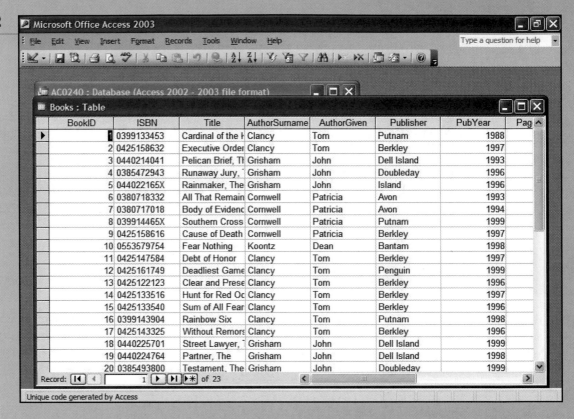

3. With the Datasheet window displayed:
CLICK: View – Design button ( ) on the toolbar
(*Note:* Although the toolbar button is named View, we include the mode name "– Design" for clarity.)

4. Let's add a new field to the table structure that will store a reviewer's synopsis for each book. In the Field Grid pane:
CLICK: in the *Field Name* column of the next empty row, so that the insertion point appears as shown here

PageCount
▶

5. Now enter the new field name:
TYPE: **Synopsis**
PRESS: TAB

6. Because the contents of the field will be entered mostly in paragraph form, select Memo as the field's data type:
CLICK: down arrow attached to the Data Type cell
SELECT: Memo
PRESS: TAB

7. In the Description column:
TYPE: **Reviewer's synopsis or abstract**
PRESS: ENTER
The field information should appear as shown below.

▶ Synopsis	Memo	Reviewer's synopsis or abstract

8. You can insert a new field between two existing fields by right-clicking the desired row selector button and choosing the Insert Rows command. Similarly, you can delete an existing field using the right-click menu. To demonstrate, let's remove the PageCount field:
RIGHT-CLICK: row selector button for PageCount
Your screen should now appear similar to the one shown in Figure 2.23.

Figure 2.23

Displaying a field's right-click menu

Right-click menu for the PageCount field

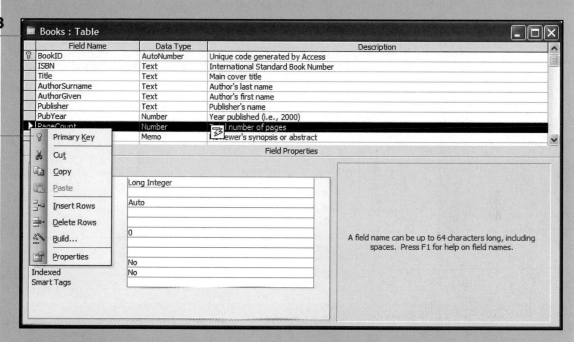

9. From the right-click menu:
CHOOSE: Delete Rows
An Alert confirmation dialog box appears, as shown below.

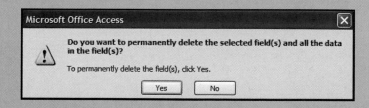

10. To confirm that the deletion will also remove all the data in the field:
CLICK: Yes command button

11. Let's save the table before proceeding:
CLICK: Save button (⊞)

12. Now switch back to the Datasheet window:
CLICK: View – Datasheet button (⊞▾)

13. To enter a brief synopsis for the first record:
PRESS: END to move to the last field column
PRESS: SHIFT + F2 to zoom the window
Your screen should now appear similar to the one shown in Figure 2.24.

Figure 2.24

Using the Zoom window to enter data into a memo field

Entering a memo using the Zoom window, accessed by pressing `SHIFT`+`F2`

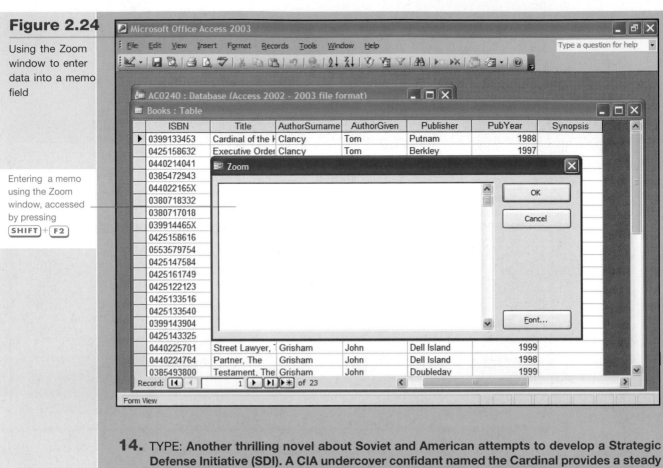

14. TYPE: **Another thrilling novel about Soviet and American attempts to develop a Strategic Defense Initiative (SDI). A CIA undercover confidant named the Cardinal provides a steady stream of Soviet secrets. Once compromised, however, the Cardinal must be pulled to safety, a task assigned to Jack Ryan and John Clark, an ex-Navy SEAL.**

15. To complete the entry and save the record:
CLICK: OK command button
PRESS: ⬇ to move to the next record

16. Close the Datasheet window.

2.4.2 Renaming and Moving Fields

→ **Feature**

In addition to modifying a table's structure, renaming and moving fields in Design view affect the display of a datasheet. You may have noticed that the columns in Datasheet view follow the field names and display order appearing in Design view. More importantly, however, you can speed up most database operations by moving frequently used fields (those used as primary keys or in indexes) to the top of a table structure.

→ **Method**

To rename a field, edit the contents of the Field Name column as you would modify a cell entry in a datasheet.

To move a field, click the field's row selector button and then drag it to the target location.

→ **Practice**

You will now practice renaming and moving fields in table Design view. Ensure that the AC0240 Database window is displayed.

1. To display the Books table object in Design view:
SELECT: Books in the list area, if it is not already selected
CLICK: Design button (🖳▾) on the Database window toolbar

2. Let's rename the Author fields. Using the I-beam mouse pointer:
CLICK: to the right of "AuthorSurname" in the Field Name column
The flashing insertion point should appear to the right of the name.

3. To remove the "Surname" portion of the cell entry:
PRESS: [BACKSPACE] seven times

4. TYPE: **Last**
The cell entry should now read "AuthorLast," as shown here with the insertion point.
▶ AuthorLast

5. To complete the entry:
PRESS: ⬇

6. To remove the "Given" portion of the "AuthorGiven" field name:
PRESS: [F2] (Edit mode)
PRESS: [BACKSPACE] five times
TYPE: **First**
The cell entry now reads "AuthorFirst."
▶ AuthorFirst

7. To complete the entry:
PRESS: ⬇
Your screen should now appear similar to the one shown in Figure 2.25.

Figure 2.25

Renaming fields in the Field Grid pane

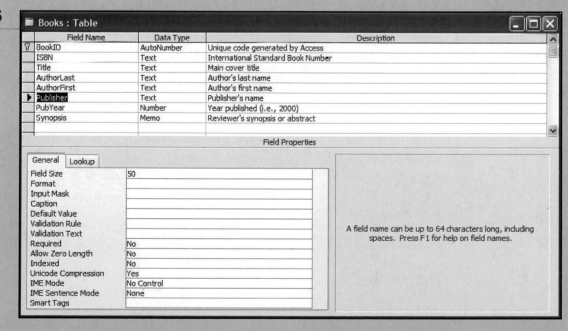

8. Let's move the ISBN field below the AuthorFirst field. To begin:
CLICK: row selector button for ISBN

Access

9. Using the arrow mouse pointer:
DRAG: row selector button for ISBN downward until a bold grid line appears below the Author-First field

10. Release the mouse button. Your screen should now appear similar to the one shown in Figure 2.26.

Figure 2.26

Moving the ISBN
field in the Field
Grid pane

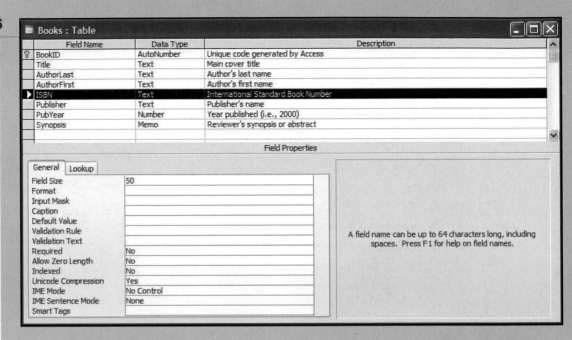

11. To save and then view the changes in Datasheet view:
CLICK: Save button (⊞)
CLICK: View – Datasheet button (⊞▾)
Notice that the field header area displays the new field names in the modified field order.

12. Close the Datasheet window.

2.4.3 Printing a Table's Design Structure

→ **Feature**

Access provides a special tool called the **Documenter** that allows you to preview and print various design characteristics of your database objects, including a table's structure and field properties. This tool is especially useful when you are planning or revising a table's field specification.

→ **Method**

- CHOOSE: Tools → Analyze → Documenter
- CLICK: *Tables* tab
- SELECT: the desired object or objects
- CLICK: Options command button
- SELECT: the desired options
- CLICK: OK command button to preview the report
- CLICK: Print button (⬛) to print the report

→ ## Practice

In this lesson, you will prepare a documentation printout of the Books table. Ensure that the AC0240 Database window is displayed. (*Note:* If you have not already done so, this lesson requires that you install the Documenter feature from the Office System 2003 installation media.)

1. Before launching the Access Documenter, ensure that the Books table appears selected in the Database window. Then, do the following:
   CHOOSE: Tools → Analyze → Documenter
   The Documenter window appears as shown in Figure 2.27. (**Caution:** If you have not yet installed the Documenter feature, a warning dialog box is displayed.)

Figure 2.27

Documenter window

Click the check box to include an object in the Documenter's report.

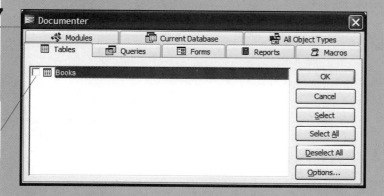

2. To print the design structure for the Books table object, ensure that the *Tables* tab is selected and then:
   SELECT: *Books* check box so that a ✓ appears

3. To specify the report options for the Documenter:
   CLICK: Options command button
   The Print Table Definition dialog box appears, as shown in Figure 2.28.

Figure 2.28

Print Table Definition dialog box

These items will be selected in the next few steps.

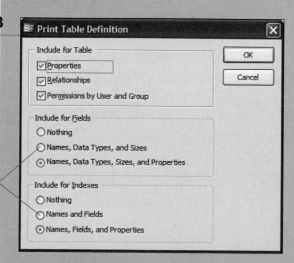

4. For this example, let's specify that only the table structure is printed. In the *Include for Table* area, remove all the selections so that no ✓ appears in any of the check boxes.

5. In the *Include for Fields* area:
   SELECT: *Names, Data Types, and Sizes* option button

Access

6. In the *Include for Indexes* area:
SELECT: *Names and Fields* option button
CLICK: OK command button

7. To preview the report printout:
CLICK: OK command button

8. To maximize the report's Object Definition window:
CLICK: its Maximize button (☐)

9. On your own, zoom in on the report by clicking the mouse pointer over the page. Then, move, size, and scroll the Object Definition window to make it appear similar to the one shown in Figure 2.29.

Figure 2.29

The maximized Object Definition window

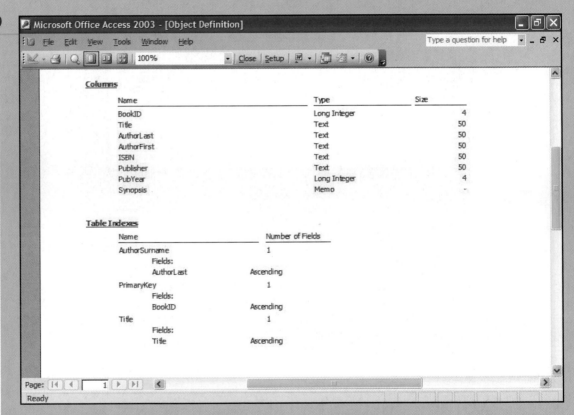

10. To print the documentation report:
CLICK: Print button (🖨) on the toolbar

11. To restore the Object Definition window to the smaller size:
CLICK: its Restore button (🗗)

12. Close the Object Definition window. Then, close the AC0240 Database window. Exit Microsoft Office Access 2003.

2.4 What happens to your table's data if you delete a field in table Design view?

Chapter
s u m m a r y

Microsoft Office Access 2003 provides several tools to help novice users create new database applications. The Database Wizard offers a variety of professionally designed template solutions for common database problems. After guiding you through a few simple steps in the wizard, Access creates a comprehensive set of database objects, including tables, forms, and reports, that you can put to use immediately. If you prefer having more control, you can opt to create an empty database and then populate it with standard tables using the Table Wizard. Another straightforward method involves designing a table simply by entering data into a Datasheet window. You can also use Design view in order to develop a custom table object. In the table Design window, you add, delete, rename, move, and manipulate fields and indexes individually, in addition to specifying each field's properties and characteristics. The Documenter helps you quickly document the design of database objects.

Command Summary

Many of the commands and procedures appearing in this chapter are summarized in the following table.

Skill Set	To Perform this Task . . .	Do the Following . . .
Creating and Using Databases	Create a new empty database	CLICK: New button (◻) CLICK: Blank database option, under the *New* heading in the New File task pane
	Create a comprehensive application using the Database Wizard	CLICK: New button (◻) CLICK: On my computer option, under the *Templates* heading in the New File task pane CLICK: *Databases* tab in the Templates dialog box DOUBLE-CLICK: a database wizard (◻)
	Switch from Datasheet view to Design view	CLICK: View – Design button (◻▾)
	Switch from Design view to Datasheet view	CLICK: View – Datasheet button (◻▾)
	Launch the Documenter utility	CHOOSE: Tools → Analyze → Documenter
Creating and Modifying Tables	Create a table using the Table Wizard	SELECT: Tables object button DOUBLE-CLICK: Create table by using wizard
	Create a table in Datasheet view	SELECT: Tables object button DOUBLE-CLICK: Create table by entering data
	Create a table in Design view	SELECT: Tables object button DOUBLE-CLICK: Create table in Design view
	Save the table structure in Design view	CLICK: Save button (◻)
	Assign a primary key in Design view	SELECT: the desired field CLICK: Primary Key button (◻)
	Add a new field in Design view	SELECT: an empty row in the Field Grid pane TYPE: **field name**

Access

Remove a field in Design view	RIGHT-CLICK: row selector for the desired field CHOOSE: Delete Rows
Move a field in Design view	DRAG: a field's row selector button to its new location
Define an index in Design view	SELECT: the desired field SELECT: an indexing option in the *Indexed* property text box
Display the Indexes window	CLICK: Indexes button (⊞)
Remove an index displayed in the Indexes window	RIGHT-CLICK: row selector for the desired Index field CHOOSE: Delete Rows

Key Terms

This section specifies page references for the key terms identified in this chapter. For a complete list of definitions, refer to the Glossary at the end of this learning guide.

AutoNumber, *p. AC 68*

Database Wizard, *p. AC 53*

Design view, *p. AC 65*

Documenter, *p. AC 76*

Field Grid pane, *p. AC 65*

Field Properties pane, *p. AC 65*

index, *p. AC 69*

null value, *p. AC 68*

primary key, *p. AC 68*

Table Wizard, *p. AC 59*

Chapter

quiz

Short Answer

1. Name four Database Wizard templates that are available on your computer.

2. What is a switchboard?

3. Name the five steps to designing a better database.

4. Name three methods for creating a table in an Access database.

5. What are the two categories of Table Wizards?

6. What data storage types can be defined in a table structure?

7. What is the difference between the Text and Memo data types?

8. How does a primary key differ from an index?

9. When would you want to insert a row in a table structure?

10. Why must you be careful when changing a field's data type?

True/False

1. _____ In creating a new database using a template, you select either the *General* or *Wizards* tab in the Templates dialog box.

2. _____ In the Database Wizard, the optional fields that you may select for inclusion appear in italic.

3. _____ The process of dividing related data into separate tables in order to reduce data redundancy is called _normalizing_ your data.

4. _____ Like Word and Excel, you can open multiple Database windows in the Access 2003 work area.

5. _____ After selecting a sample table in the Table Wizard, you can specify only the fields that you want included in your new table.

6. _____ In table Design view, you define the names of fields in the Field Grid pane and select data types in the Field Properties pane.

7. _____ Field names cannot exceed 64 characters in length.

8. _____ What you type into the _Description_ column of the Field Grid pane appears in the Title bar of a table's Datasheet window.

9. _____ Access prevents you from entering duplicate values into a primary key field.

10. _____ You can print a table's structure using the Documenter tool.

Multiple Choice

1. In an application created using the Database Wizard, the main menu is presented as which of the following?

    a. A form, called a _switchboard_
    b. A report, called a _menu_
    c. A table, called a _switchboard_
    d. A query, called a _menu_

2. Which of the following is not a step presented in this chapter for designing a better database?

    a. Determine your input requirements
    b. Test your database application
    c. Create your tables using wizards
    d. Determine your table structures

3. You have the choice of either creating a table structure from scratch or using the following to lead you through the process.

    a. Assistant
    b. Coach
    c. Relation
    d. Wizard

4. Which data type would you use to store the price of an item within an inventory table?

    a. AutoNumber
    b. Currency
    c. Number
    d. Text

5. Which data type would you use to store a phone number?

    a. Currency
    b. Memo
    c. Number
    d. Text

6. What determines a table's default sort order in a datasheet?

    a. AutoNumber field
    b. Field order
    c. Index field
    d. Primary key

7. To display a window showing the table's primary key and indexes:

    a. CLICK: Indexes button ( )
    b. CLICK: Primary Key button ( )
    c. CLICK: View – Datasheet button ( )
    d. CLICK: View – Design button ( )

8. To delete a field in Design view, right-click the field's selector button and choose the following command:

    a. Delete Field
    b. Delete Rows
    c. Remove Field
    d. Remove Rows

9. You use this tool to generate a printout of a table's structure.

    a. Analyzer
    b. Designator
    c. Documenter
    d. Generator

10. When printing a table's structure, you use this dialog box to specify the desired options.

    a. Print Object Definition
    b. Print Table Definition
    c. Print Table Setup
    d. Print Setup Definition

Hands-On
exercises

step by step ▶

1. Creating a New Database

In this exercise you will practice creating a new database file and adding a table object using the Table Wizard.

1. Load Microsoft Office Access 2003 using the Windows Start menu.

2. Display the New File task pane and then click the "Blank database" option under the *New* heading to begin creating a new database.

3. In the File New Database dialog box:
   TYPE: **Acme Payroll** into the *File name* text box

4. Using the Places bar or the *Save in* drop-down dialog box, select your personal storage location. Then, do the following:
   CLICK: Create command button

5. To use the Table Wizard, ensure that the Tables button is selected in the Objects bar and then do the following:
   DOUBLE-CLICK: Create table by using wizard

6. You will now create a new table to store Acme's employee records. In the Table Wizard dialog box, select the *Business* option and then select "Employees" as the sample table on which to base your new table.

7. Include all of the suggested fields from the "Employees" table in your new table. Your screen should appear similar to the one shown in Figure 2.30.

Figure 2.30

Creating a new table using the Table Wizard

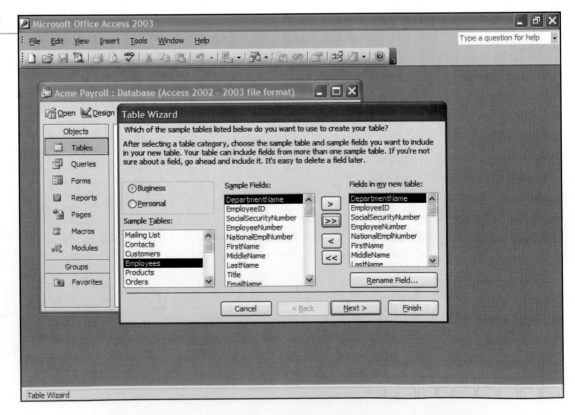

8. Now let's remove an unnecessary field. First scroll to the end of the *Fields in my new table* list. Then, do the following:
   SELECT: Photograph
   CLICK: Remove button ()

9. On your own, remove the Notes and OfficeLocation fields.

10. Complete the wizard so that the "Employees" table opens in Datasheet view, ready to accept data.

11. Close the Datasheet window.

12. Close the Database window.

2. Creating Table Objects

In this exercise, you will practice creating two new table objects in an existing database.

1. Open the database file named AC02HE. Ensure that the Tables button in the Objects bar is selected. Your screen should appear similar to the one shown in Figure 2.31.

Figure 2.31

Opening the
AC02HE
database

2. To create a new table in Datasheet view:
   DOUBLE-CLICK: Create table by entering data

3. To start, rename the column headings in the field header area:
   DOUBLE-CLICK: Field1
   TYPE: **City**
   DOUBLE-CLICK: Field2
   TYPE: **AreaCode**
   DOUBLE-CLICK: Field3
   TYPE: **DialUp**
   PRESS: (ENTER)

4. Now let's enter one record before saving the table:
   TYPE: **Arjuna**
   PRESS: (TAB)
   TYPE: **555**
   PRESS: (TAB)
   TYPE: **533-1525**

5. PRESS: (SHIFT) + (ENTER) to save the record
   Your screen should now appear similar to the one shown in Figure 2.32.

Figure 2.32

Creating a table
by entering data

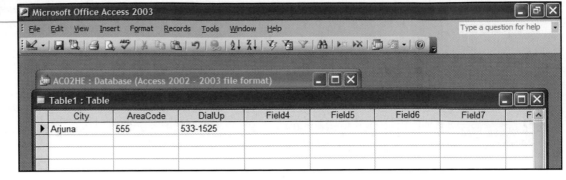

6. Save the new table structure as "Cities."

7. When prompted, let Access define a primary key for the new table.

8. Close the Datasheet window.

9. Create a second table in Design view for storing information about a company's personnel.

10. Define the table fields in the Design window's Field Grid area:
    TYPE: **SupportID**
    PRESS: ⟨ TAB ⟩ to move to the Data Type column
    SELECT: AutoNumber
    PRESS: ⟨ TAB ⟩
    TYPE: **Code to identify Tech Support personnel**
    PRESS: ⟨ ENTER ⟩ to move to the next row

11. Add two more fields to the table, as shown in Figure 2.33. First, add a Name field with a Text data type and the description "First and last name." Then, add a Local field with a Number data type and the description "4-digit phone local."

Figure 2.33

Creating a table
in table Design
view

Field Name	Data Type	Description
SupportID	AutoNumber	Code to identify Tech Support personnel
Name	Text	First and last name
Local	Number	4-digit phone local

12. Save the table structure as "TechSupport."

13. When prompted, let Access define a primary key for the new table.

14. Close the Datasheet window.

3. Creating Primary Keys and Indexes

In this exercise, you will add a primary key to an existing table object and then modify its indexes.

1. Ensure that the AC02HE Database window is displayed and that the Tables button in the Objects bar is selected.

2. Open the "3 Orders" table for display in Datasheet view. Your screen should appear similar to the one shown in Figure 2.34.

Figure 2.34

Displaying the
3 Orders
datasheet

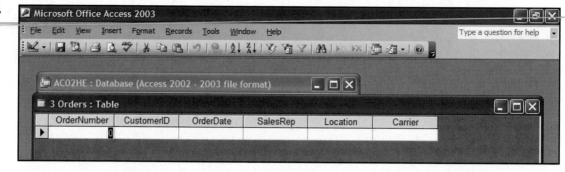

3. Change the display mode to Design view for the table object.

4. In Design view, assign the OrderNumber field as the primary key for the table. When completed, a key icon appears in the field's row selector button.

5. To speed up operations for finding a particular salesperson, create an index for the SalesRep field that allows for duplicate values. Your screen should now appear similar to the one shown in Figure 2.35.

Figure 2.35

Setting a primary
key and creating
an index

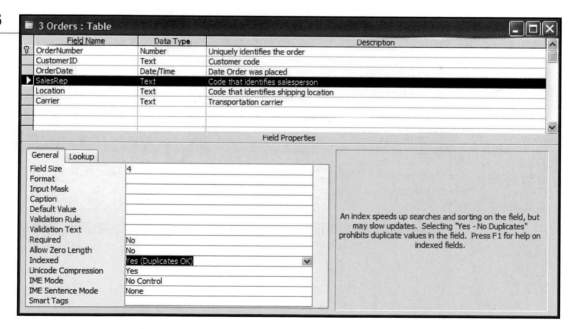

6. To display all the indexes for the table:
CLICK: Indexes button (📝)

7. In the Indexes window, remove the OrderDate index so that three entries are displayed only, as shown in Figure 2.36.

Figure 2.36

Viewing the indexes for a table

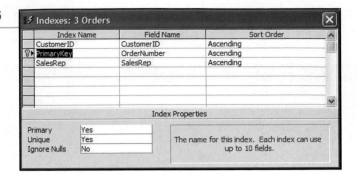

8. Close the Indexes window.

9. Save the table structure and then close the table Design window.

on your own

4. Modifying a Table's Structure

The majority of database design work involves editing the structure of existing databases. In this exercise, you practice modifying the table structure of the 4 Contacts table in the AC02HE database. To begin, open the 4 Contacts table in Design view so that all of the fields and their data types are displayed. Perform the following changes to the table structure:

• Change the field name for "Contact" to "ContactPerson"

• Add a new field named "Email" for storing e-mail addresses

• Delete the field named "Phone 2," including the data stored therein

• Move the "Phone 1" field to appear below the "Email" field

Your table Design window should now appear similar to the one shown in Figure 2.37.

Figure 2.37

Editing, deleting, and adding fields to the Field Grid pane

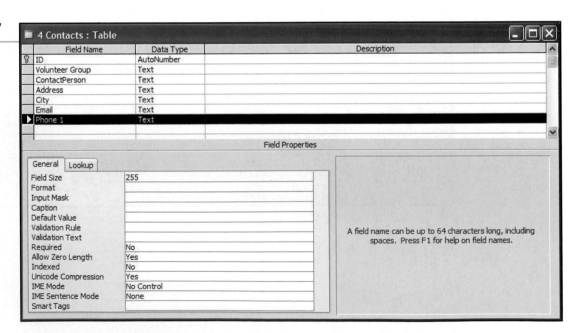

When you are satisfied with your work, save the changes and view the datasheet. Your screen should appear similar to the one shown in Figure 2.38. Before proceeding, close the 4 Contacts Datasheet window.

Figure 2.38

Viewing the changes made to a table in Datasheet view

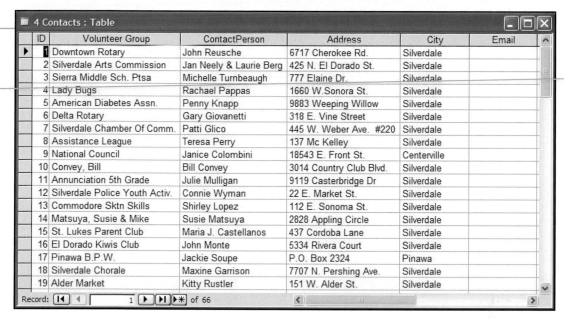

5. Modifying a Table's Indexes

To practice making changes to a table's indexes, open the 5 Inventory table in the AC02HE database. After changing to Design view, add a new field named Category between the existing Description and OnHand fields. Assign a data type of Number to the new field. Next, move the Reorder field so that it appears immediately after the OnHand field and then remove the SuggestedRetail field. To speed up your table search and sort operations, create an index for the Buyer field that allows duplicate entries. Finally, in the Indexes window, remove the extraneous index on ProductID. Make sure that you do not remove the primary key for this field. Your screen should now appear similar to the one shown in Figure 2.39. When you are finished, close the Indexes window. Then, save the table changes and close the table Design window.

Figure 2.39

Adding, moving, deleting, and indexing fields

Compare your work to the field names and order shown here.

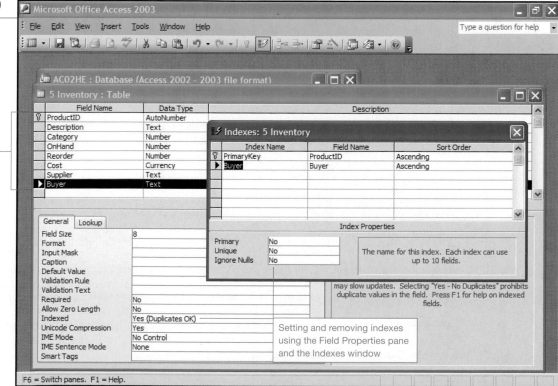

6. Creating a Table in Design View

In this exercise, use the table Design view to create a new table in the AC02HE database. If the Database window does not appear in the work area, open it now. Your new table should contain the following fields, complete with data types and descriptions.

- *PackageID:* This field, which automatically increments by one each time a new record is added, contains a unique code that identifies each promotional package.

- *Description:* This text field stores the name of each package.

- *Price:* This field stores the suggested price in dollars for each package.

- *Nights:* This field stores the number of nights for accommodations.

Save the table as "Valley Packages" to the database and let Access create a primary key. Now use the Documenter tool to preview (Figure 2.40) and print out the table's design structure. Then, close all of the open windows, including the Database window.

Figure 2.40

Previewing the Documenter's design report

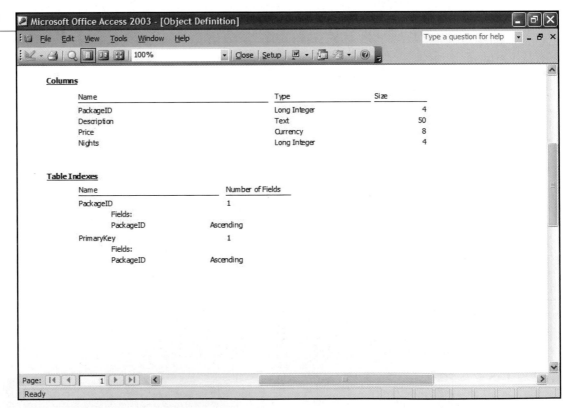

CaseStudy   McGAVIN TRUCKING, LTD.

McGavin Trucking, Ltd., operates a fleet of trucks in the Pacific Northwest. Last week, McGavin's management team asked the company's controller, Mike Lambert, to locate and summarize a variety of information about the business. After spending three days reviewing reports and searching through filing cabinets, Mike came to the realization that he needs a better information management system and decides to use Microsoft Access.

Mike starts the process by laying out his design ideas on paper. He wants to ensure that all of McGavin's relevant business information is collected, stored, and readied for processing. In order to reduce data redundancies, Mike splits the company information into three tables. The first table stores operational data for each truck in the fleet. The second table stores personnel data for each driver. The third and final table stores a detailed log of each delivery. Now Mike must launch Access, create a database structure, and initialize these tables.

In the following case problems, assume the role of Mike and perform the same steps that he identifies.

1. To begin, Mike creates a new blank database named "McGavin Trucking" and saves it to his *personal storage location*. Once the Database window appears, he proceeds to create the first table using the Table Wizard. After launching the wizard, Mike ensures that the *Business* option button is selected. He then scrolls the list of sample tables to find a suitable structure. From the list, Mike selects a table named "Assets" and then includes all of the fields for his new table. After proceeding to the next screen in the wizard's dialog box, he names the new table "Trucks" and lets Access set the primary key. In the final step, Mike opens the table in Design view in order to rename three of the fields. As shown in Figure 2.41, he changes "AssetID" to "TruckID," "AssetDescription" to "TruckDescription," and "AssetCategoryID" to "TruckCategoryID." He saves the changes to the table structure and closes the Trucks table.

Figure 2.41

Creating and then modifying the Trucks table

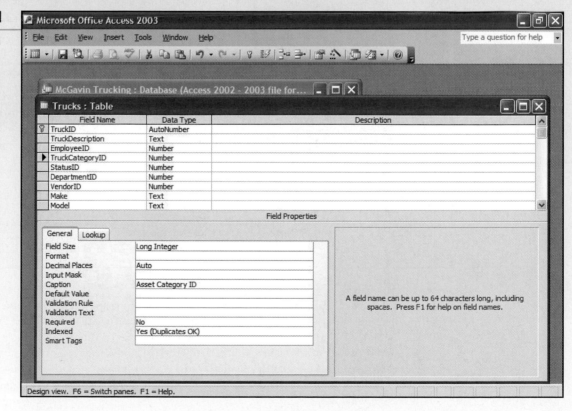

2. Mike decides to create the second table in Datasheet view. After double-clicking the appropriate New Object shortcut, he renames the column headings in the empty datasheet to create the following fields:

- Name

- Address

- Phone

- Classification

Mike saves the new table object as "Drivers" and lets Access define a primary key. Looking at the results shown in Figure 2.42, Mike decides to switch to Design view and rename the ID field "DriverID." He then saves the table structure and closes the table Design window.

Figure 2.42

Creating the Drivers table structure in Datasheet view

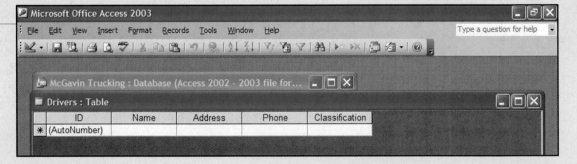

3. For the third table, Mike uses Design view to create the structure displayed in Figure 2.43. As shown in the screen graphic, Mike makes the TripID field the primary key. He then saves the table as "Trips" and closes the table Design window. Using the Access Documenter tool, he prints out the Trips table structure for later review.

Figure 2.43

Creating the Trips table structure in Design view

Field Name	Data Type	Description
TripID	AutoNumber	Identifies the delivery
TruckID	Number	Identifies the truck
Date	Date/Time	Date of the trip
Destination	Text	Delivery destination
Miles	Number	Round trip mileage
DriverID	Number	Identifies the driver
LoadWeight	Number	Weight in pounds

4. Later the same day, Mike realizes he needs to make a few structural changes to some of the tables. He begins by opening the Trips table in Design view and creating an index for the Destination field. Using the Indexes window, he removes the extra index on the TripID field that Access automatically created and then closes the window. In the Field Grid pane, Mike adds a new text field named "Pickup" between the Date and Destination fields. He then moves the DriverID field to appear immediately below the TruckID field, as shown in Figure 2.44. He saves the changes and closes the table Design window.

Figure 2.44

Modifying the
Trips table
structure

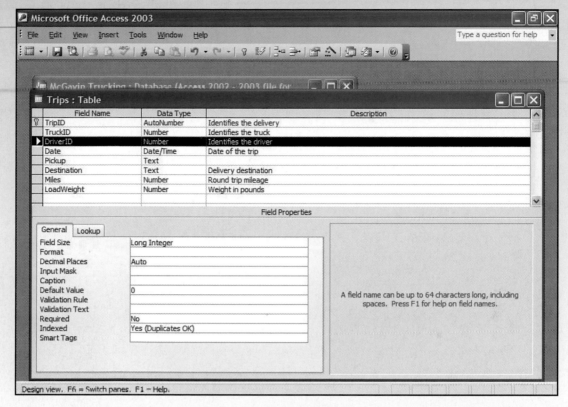

For the Trucks table, Mike opens the table in Design view and deletes the DepartmentID and BarcodeNumber fields. He then moves the Make and Model fields to be the third and fourth fields respectively. Satisfied with the progress he has made in setting up McGavin's new database, Mike saves his changes and exits Microsoft Office Access 2003.

Answers
to self-check questions

2.1 What two objects are most closely associated with the output of a database application? Query objects (the questions you ask of a database) and Report objects (the structured printed output from a database).

2.2 How do you specify the name of a field when creating a table in Datasheet view? You double-click the column name in the field header area and then type the desired field name.

2.3 What is an AutoNumber field? Why is it useful as a primary key? An AutoNumber field is a data type that automatically increments a numeric value each time a new record is added to a table. It is useful as a primary key because it already supplies a unique field value for identifying each record in a table.

2.4 What happens to your table's data if you delete a field in table Design view? The table data that is stored in the field is removed along with the field definition in Design view.

Notes

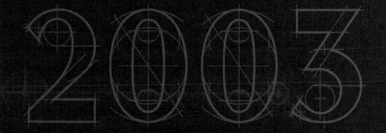

CHAPTER 3

⊕ **Organizing and Retrieving Data**

PREREQUISITES

To successfully complete this chapter, you must be comfortable performing basic data entry and editing tasks in the Datasheet window. You will be asked to modify the appearance of a datasheet using toolbar buttons, Menu commands, and right-click shortcut menus. You should also know how to view and print objects from the Database window.

LEARNING OBJECTIVES

After completing this chapter, you will be able to:

- Enhance the display and printing of a datasheet using fonts and special effects

- Sort the contents of a datasheet into ascending and descending order

- Find a record by entering search criteria and using wildcard characters

- Filter the records displayed in a datasheet using Filter For Input, Filter By Selection, and Filter By Form

- Create a query using the Simple Query Wizard

3.1 Customizing Datasheet View

Microsoft Office Access 2003 provides numerous options for customizing the appearance, or layout, of a datasheet. Because a datasheet is only a tool for viewing the data stored in an underlying table, you can manipulate the datasheet's column widths, row heights, and field order without affecting the table structure itself. Exceptions to this rule are when you rename or delete a column. These changes flow through to the structure of the table. Once the table is customized to your satisfaction, remember to save the layout changes by clicking the Save button (⊞) on the toolbar. Otherwise, the modifications are discarded when you close the Datasheet window.

3.1.1 Formatting a Datasheet

→ **Feature**

To enhance the readability of a datasheet, you may select fonts and apply special effects for onscreen display and printing. Any changes that you make affect the entire datasheet but do not affect other database objects such as forms and reports. After formatting the datasheet to suit your needs, save the layout changes for subsequent use.

→ **Method**

To format a datasheet, choose from the following options:

- CHOOSE: Format → Font to select font characteristics
- CHOOSE: Format → Datasheet to apply special visual effects

To save the format changes:

- CLICK: Save button (⊞) on the toolbar

  or

- CHOOSE: File → Save from the menu

→ **Practice**

In this lesson, you format and then save a datasheet's layout to appear with a custom font, color, and background.

1. Load Microsoft Access, if it is not already running.

2. Open the database named AC0300, found in your Advantage student data files location. Ensure that the *Tables* button is selected in the objects bar.

3. To display the Courses table in Datasheet view:
   DOUBLE-CLICK: *Courses* in the list area
   The Courses Datasheet window appears in the work area, as shown in Figure 3.1.

Figure 3.1

Displaying the
Courses
datasheet

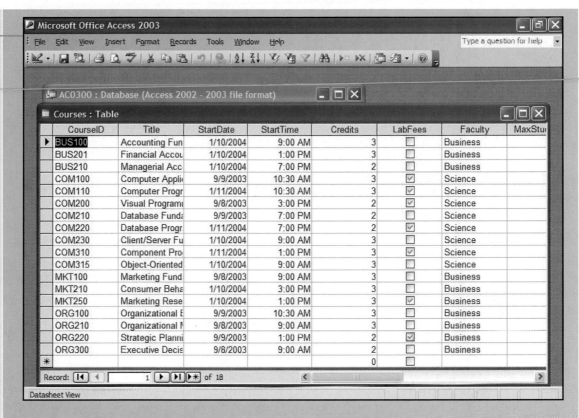

4. You can change the font characteristics of text displayed in a datasheet without affecting any other Datasheet window. To customize the Courses datasheet, do the following:
   CHOOSE: Format → Font
   The Font dialog box appears, similar but not identical to the one shown in Figure 3.2. In this one dialog box, you can change the font **typeface,** style, size, and text color.

5. Make the following selections in the Font dialog box:
   SELECT: Times New Roman in the *Font* list box
   SELECT: Regular in the *Font style* list box
   SELECT: 12 in the *Size* list box
   SELECT: Navy in the *Color* drop-down list box
   Notice that the *Sample* area, as shown in Figure 3.2, displays an example of the current selections.

Figure 3.2

Font dialog box

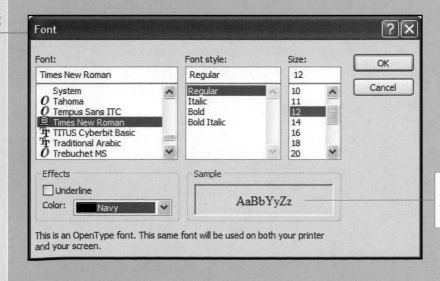

The *Sample* area provides a preview of the selections made in the Font dialog box.

Access

6. To accept the changes:
   CLICK: OK command button
   The Datasheet window is updated to display the font selections.

7. You can also enhance a datasheet by formatting the window characteristics such as gridlines and background matting. To begin:
   CHOOSE: Format → Datasheet
   The Datasheet Formatting dialog box shown in Figure 3.3 is displayed. Notice that the options selected in the screen graphic are the default settings for a Datasheet window.

Figure 3.3

Datasheet
Formatting dialog
box

The *Sample* area provides a preview of the selections made in the Datasheet Formatting dialog box.

8. After selecting a few options, you can better appreciate the resulting changes by viewing the *Sample* area of the dialog box. To begin:
   SELECT: *Raised* option button in the *Cell Effect* area
   Notice that this selection nullifies the other options in the dialog box—they are no longer available for selection.

9. Let's select a different formatting enhancement. Do the following:
   SELECT: *Flat* option button in the *Cell Effect* area
   SELECT: *Vertical* check box so that no ✓ appears
   SELECT: Teal in the *Gridline Color* drop-down list box

10. In the *Border and Line Styles* area of the dialog box:
   SELECT: *Horizontal Gridline* in the left-hand drop-down list box
   SELECT: *Dots* in the right-hand drop-down list box

11. To apply the changes:
   CLICK: OK command button
   The Datasheet window now appears with teal dots separating records in the datasheet as horizontal gridlines, as shown in Figure 3.4.

Figure 3.4

Formatting the
Courses
datasheet

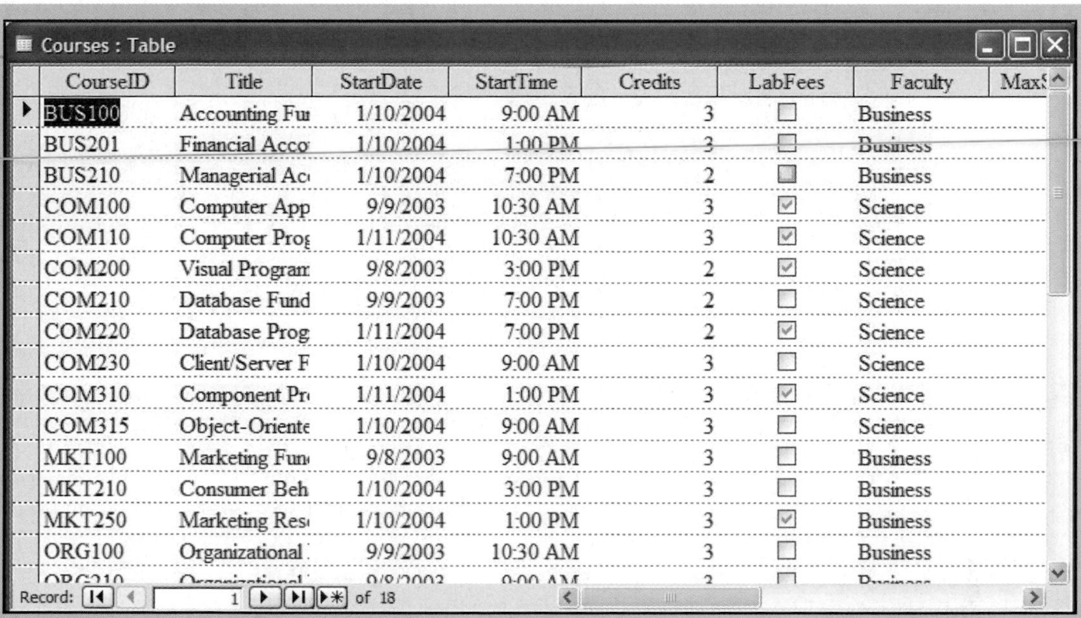

CourseID	Title	StartDate	StartTime	Credits	LabFees	Faculty	Max ^
BUS100	Accounting Fur	1/10/2004	9:00 AM	3	☐	Business	
BUS201	Financial Acco	1/10/2004	1:00 PM	3	☐	Business	
BUS210	Managerial Ac	1/10/2004	7:00 PM	2	☐	Business	
COM100	Computer App	9/9/2003	10:30 AM	3	☑	Science	
COM110	Computer Prog	1/11/2004	10:30 AM	3	☑	Science	
COM200	Visual Program	9/8/2003	3:00 PM	2	☑	Science	
COM210	Database Fund	9/9/2003	7:00 PM	2	☐	Science	
COM220	Database Prog	1/11/2004	7:00 PM	2	☑	Science	
COM230	Client/Server F	1/10/2004	9:00 AM	3	☐	Science	
COM310	Component Pr	1/11/2004	1:00 PM	3	☑	Science	
COM315	Object-Oriente	1/10/2004	9:00 AM	3	☐	Science	
MKT100	Marketing Fun	9/8/2003	9:00 AM	3	☐	Business	
MKT210	Consumer Beh	1/10/2004	3:00 PM	3	☐	Business	
MKT250	Marketing Res	1/10/2004	1:00 PM	3	☑	Business	
ORG100	Organizational	9/9/2003	10:30 AM	3	☐	Business	
ORG210	Organizational	9/8/2003	9:00 AM	2	☐	Business	

Record: 1 of 18

12. To save the formatting changes to the datasheet:
CLICK: Save button (🖫) on the toolbar

3.1.2 Changing the Field Column Order

→ **Feature**

Access 2003 determines the column order displayed in a Datasheet window from the field order in the underlying table structure. You may want to modify the column order in order to display fields side by side or to perform a multiple-field sort operation. One way to change the column order is to modify the field order in table Design view. An easier and less drastic method is to move fields by dragging their column headings in Datasheet view. This method does not affect the underlying table structure. Once the columns are positioned, you can save the field column order in the datasheet along with other customizing options.

→ **Method**

To change the field column order in Datasheet view:

• SELECT: the desired column in the field header area

• DRAG: the column heading to its new location

→ **Practice**

You will now practice selecting and moving columns in a datasheet. Ensure that you have completed the previous lesson and that the Courses Datasheet window is displayed.

1. Before moving fields in the datasheet, let's practice selecting columns and changing column widths. Do the following:
CLICK: CourseID in the field header area
Notice that the mouse pointer becomes a downward pointing arrow (⬇) when positioned properly on the column heading. The entire column should now appear highlighted.

2. Using the horizontal scroll bar, scroll the window by clicking the right scroll button (▷) so that the last field column, InstructorID, is visible.

3. To select all of the columns in the datasheet at once:
PRESS: (SHIFT) and hold it down
CLICK: InstructorID in the field header area
All of the columns should now appear highlighted. (*Note:* Although it is not explicitly stated, you should release the (SHIFT) key after clicking on the InstructorID column heading.)

4. You can now update the columns to their best-fit widths. To do so:
CHOOSE: Format → Column Width
CLICK: Best Fit command button
PRESS: (HOME) to remove the highlighting
The datasheet should now appear similar to the one shown in Figure 3.5.

Figure 3.5

Adjusting all columns to their best-fit width

CourseID	Title	StartDate	StartTime	Credits	LabFees	Faculty	MaxStudents	Min
BUS100	Accounting Fundamentals	1/10/2004	9:00 AM	3	☐	Business	120	
BUS201	Financial Accounting	1/10/2004	1:00 PM	3	☐	Business	60	
BUS210	Managerial Accounting	1/10/2004	7:00 PM	2	☐	Business	30	
COM100	Computer Applications	9/9/2003	10:30 AM	3	☑	Science	150	
COM110	Computer Programming	1/11/2004	10:30 AM	3	☑	Science	60	
COM200	Visual Programming	9/8/2003	3:00 PM	2	☑	Science	30	
COM210	Database Fundamentals	9/9/2003	7:00 PM	2	☐	Science	60	
COM220	Database Programming	1/11/2004	7:00 PM	2	☑	Science	30	
COM230	Client/Server Fundamentals	1/10/2004	9:00 AM	3	☐	Science	30	
COM310	Component Programming	1/11/2004	1:00 PM	3	☑	Science	25	
COM315	Object-Oriented Design	1/10/2004	9:00 AM	3	☐	Science	25	
MKT100	Marketing Fundamentals	9/8/2003	9:00 AM	3	☐	Business	120	
MKT210	Consumer Behavior	1/10/2004	3:00 PM	3	☐	Business	60	
MKT250	Marketing Research	1/10/2004	1:00 PM	3	☑	Business	30	
ORG100	Organizational Behavior	9/9/2003	10:30 AM	3	☐	Business	120	
ORG210	Organizational Management	9/8/2003	9:00 AM	3	☐	Business	60	

Record: ◄◄ ◄ 1 ► ►► ►* of 18

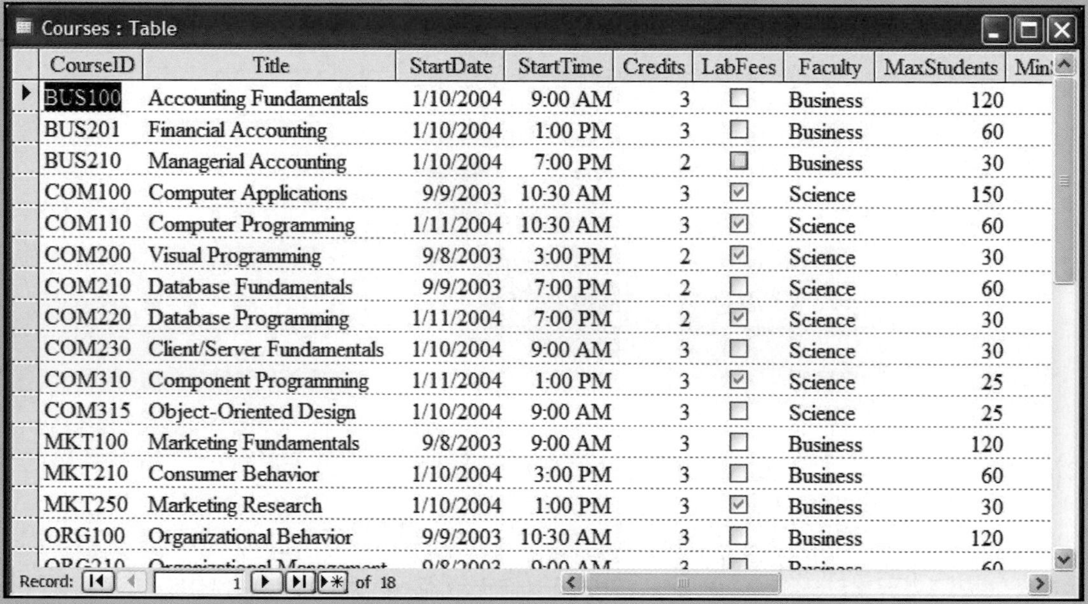

5. Let's practice moving columns in the datasheet. Using the horizontal scroll bar, scroll the window so that both the Faculty and DeptHead field columns are visible.

6. CLICK: DeptHead in the field header area

7. Position the white arrow mouse pointer (⇨) over the DeptHead field name. Then:
DRAG: DeptHead to the left so that the bold vertical gridline appears between the Faculty and MaxStudents field columns, as shown in Figure 3.6

Figure 3.6

Moving a field column

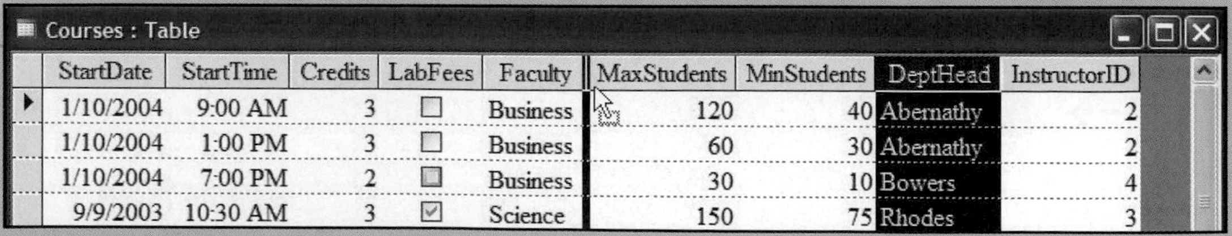

StartDate	StartTime	Credits	LabFees	Faculty	MaxStudents	MinStudents	DeptHead	InstructorID
1/10/2004	9:00 AM	3	☐	Business	120	40	Abernathy	2
1/10/2004	1:00 PM	3	☐	Business	60	30	Abernathy	2
1/10/2004	7:00 PM	2	☐	Business	30	10	Bowers	4
9/9/2003	10:30 AM	3	☑	Science	150	75	Rhodes	3

8. Release the mouse button to complete the move operation.

9. Now let's try moving two fields at the same time:
CLICK: Faculty in the field header area
PRESS: (SHIFT) and hold it down
CLICK: DeptHead in the field header area
Both columns should now appear highlighted.

10. You will now reposition the two field columns. Position the mouse pointer on one of the selected column headings. Then:
DRAG: Faculty (or DeptHead) to the left so that the bold vertical gridline appears between Title and StartDate

11. After releasing the mouse button:
PRESS: HOME to remove the highlighting
Your Datasheet window should now appear similar to the one shown in Figure 3.7.

Figure 3.7

Changing the field column order

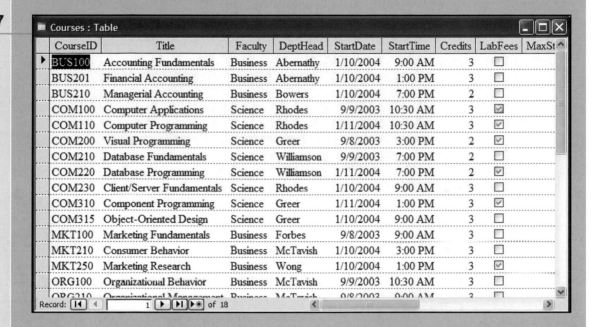

12. Save the layout changes by clicking the Save button (⊞).

3.1.3 Hiding and Unhiding Columns

→ **Feature**

Hiding columns in a datasheet is useful for temporarily restricting the display of sensitive data, such as salaries or commissions. You can also hide columns that you do not want displayed in a printout or that you are thinking about deleting permanently. Whatever your reasons, Access 2003 makes it easy to hide and unhide field columns in the Datasheet window.

→ **Method**

To hide a field column using the menu:

• SELECT: the desired column in the field header area

• CHOOSE: Format → Hide Columns

To hide a field column using the right-click menu:

• RIGHT-CLICK: the desired column in the field header area

• CHOOSE: Hide Columns

Access

To unhide a field column:

- CHOOSE: Format → Unhide Columns
- SELECT: the desired columns in the Unhide Columns dialog box
- CLICK: Close command button

→ **Practice**

In this lesson, you will hide and unhide columns in the active datasheet. Ensure that you have completed the previous lessons and that the Courses Datasheet window is displayed.

1. Let's assume that you have been asked to print out the Courses datasheet. However, the last three columns in this datasheet are for administrative eyes only and should not be included. Therefore, you must hide the last three field columns before printing. To begin:
PRESS: (END) to move the cursor to the last field column

2. Fortunately, the three columns, MaxStudents, MinStudents, and InstructorID, appear next to one another in the datasheet. To select the three columns:
CLICK: MaxStudents in the field header area
PRESS: (SHIFT) and hold it down
CLICK: InstructorID in the field header area
Remember to release the (SHIFT) key after you click InstructorID.

3. To hide the selected columns:
CHOOSE: Format → Hide Columns
The columns disappear from the Datasheet window display (Figure 3.8), although the data remain safely in the table object. (*Note:* You can also right-click a column in the field header area and choose the Hide Columns command.)

Figure 3.8

Hiding columns in
Datasheet view

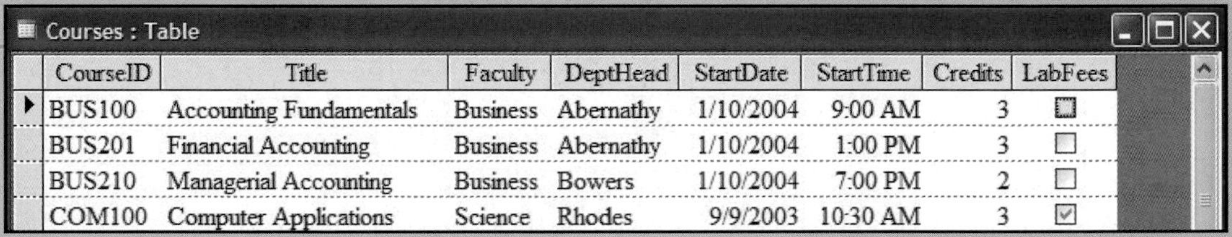

CourseID	Title	Faculty	DeptHead	StartDate	StartTime	Credits	LabFees
▶ BUS100	Accounting Fundamentals	Business	Abernathy	1/10/2004	9:00 AM	3	☐
BUS201	Financial Accounting	Business	Abernathy	1/10/2004	1:00 PM	3	☐
BUS210	Managerial Accounting	Business	Bowers	1/10/2004	7:00 PM	2	☐
COM100	Computer Applications	Science	Rhodes	9/9/2003	10:30 AM	3	☑

Courses : Table

4. To specify how the datasheet will now print:
CHOOSE: File → Page Setup
CLICK: *Page* tab
SELECT: *Landscape* option button
CLICK: OK command button

5. To preview the datasheet:
CLICK: Print Preview button ( ) on the toolbar

6. Using the magnifying glass mouse pointer, zoom in and out on the page. Notice that the hidden columns are not displayed in the Print Preview window, as shown in Figure 3.9.

Figure 3.9

Zooming in the
Print Preview
window

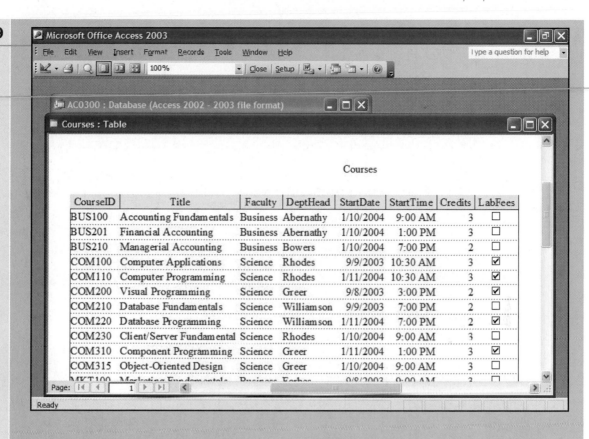

7. To return to the Datasheet window:
   CLICK: Close button (Close) on the toolbar

8. To unhide the columns:
   CHOOSE: Format → Unhide Columns
   The dialog box shown in Figure 3.10 appears.

Figure 3.10

Unhide Columns
dialog box

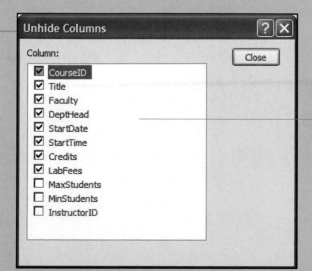

Field columns that are currently
displayed in the datasheet
appear in this list area with a
selected check box.

9. In the Unhide Columns dialog box:
SELECT: *MaxStudents* check box
SELECT: *MinStudents* check box
SELECT: *InstructorID* check box
CLICK: Close command button
Notice that the field columns are displayed once again.

10. Save the layout changes before proceeding.

3.1.4 Freezing and Unfreezing Columns

→ **Feature**

When you navigate a large table with many columns, the Datasheet window scrolls automatically to accommodate your cursor movements. The farther right you move the cursor, the more the columns scroll away from view at the left. To more easily identify the current record, Access 2003 lets you freeze or lock in place one or more columns, such as a company name or product number, along the left edge of the Datasheet window.

→ **Method**

To freeze a field column using the menu:

• SELECT: the desired column(s) in the field header area

• CHOOSE: Format → Freeze Columns

To freeze a field column using the right-click menu:

• RIGHT-CLICK: the desired column in the field header area

• CHOOSE: Freeze Columns

To unfreeze columns in a datasheet:

• CHOOSE: Format → Unfreeze All Columns

→ **Practice**

In this lesson, you will freeze and unfreeze columns in the active datasheet. Ensure that you have completed the previous lessons and that the Courses Datasheet window is displayed.

1. Let's use the right-click menu to freeze the CourseID field column from scrolling off the screen. Do the following:
RIGHT-CLICK: CourseID in the field header
A shortcut menu appears, as displayed in Figure 3.11.

Figure 3.11

Displaying the right-click shortcut menu for a column

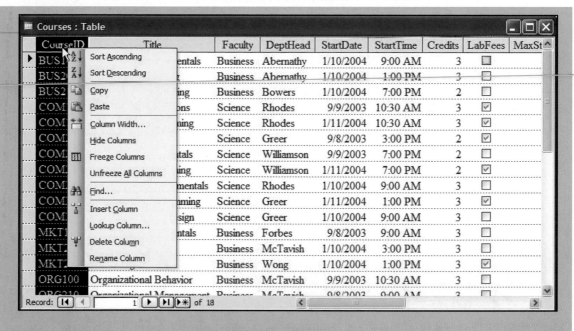

2. To freeze the column in the Datasheet window:
CHOOSE: Freeze Columns
Nothing appears to have happened to the column, but the effects are illustrated in the next few steps.

3. Remove the column highlighting:
PRESS: HOME
Notice that a vertical gridline appears between the CourseID and Title field columns.

4. To demonstrate the frozen column feature:
PRESS: END to move to the last field column
The CourseID column remains displayed at the left side of the window, as shown in Figure 3.12. This command is especially useful for displaying datasheets that contain many fields.

Figure 3.12

Freezing a column in a datasheet

CourseID	DeptHead	StartDate	StartTime	Credits	LabFees	MaxStudents	MinStudents	InstructorID
BUS100	Abernathy	1/10/2004	9:00 AM	3	☐	120	40	2
BUS201	Abernathy	1/10/2004	1:00 PM	3	☐	60	30	2
BUS210	Bowers	1/10/2004	7:00 PM	2	☐	30	10	4
COM100	Rhodes	9/9/2003	10:30 AM	3	☑	150	75	3

5. To unfreeze the CourseID column:
CHOOSE: Format → Unfreeze All Columns

6. PRESS: HOME

7. Save the layout changes and then close the Datasheet window.

8. To prove that the formatting changes were indeed saved:
DOUBLE-CLICK: *Courses* in the list area
The Datasheet window appears with the same text and window formatting and field column order.

9. Close the Datasheet window once again.

Access

 **3.1** Name two reasons for changing the field column order in a datasheet.

3.2 Sorting, Finding, and Maintaining Data

Information is *processed data*. This processing can take several forms, from analyzing, organizing, and summarizing data to presenting data in charts and reports. In this module, you will learn how to sort and arrange records into a precise and logical order. You will also find and replace data stored in a table. Finally, you will learn how to spell-check the contents of a table as you would a document in Microsoft Word or a worksheet in Microsoft Excel.

3.2.1 Sorting Records in a Datasheet

→ Feature

Records are displayed in the order in which they are originally entered into a table, unless a primary key has been assigned. With a primary key, records are arranged and displayed according to the contents of the primary key field. Even so, Access allows you to rearrange the records appearing in a datasheet into ascending (0 to 9; A to Z) or descending (Z to A; 9 to 0) order by the contents of any field. A field chosen to sort by is referred to as a **sort key.** Sorting is often your first step in extracting information from raw data. It allows you to better organize records and makes it easier to scan a datasheet for specific information.

→ Method

To sort data using the toolbar:

- SELECT: the desired column(s) in Datasheet view
- CLICK: Sort Ascending button (⊞) to sort in ascending order

  or

  CLICK: Sort Descending button (⊞) to sort in descending order

To sort data using the right-click menu:

- RIGHT-CLICK: the desired column in the field header area
- CHOOSE: Sort Ascending to sort in ascending order

  or

  CHOOSE: Sort Descending to sort in descending order

→ Practice

You will now practice sorting a table into ascending and descending order. Ensure that the AC0300 Database window is displayed.

1. To open the Students table in Datasheet view:
DOUBLE-CLICK: *Students* in the list area
Figure 3.13 shows the datasheet displayed in order by StudentID, the primary key field.

Figure 3.13

Displaying the
Students
datasheet

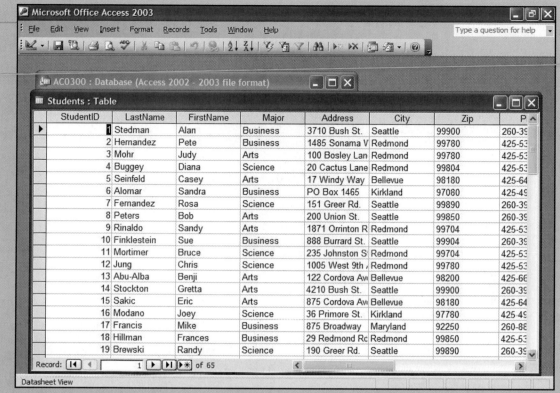

2. To sort the records into order by surname:
CLICK: LastName in the field header area
CLICK: Sort Ascending button ($\frac{A}{Z}\downarrow$) on the toolbar
The contents of the datasheet are sorted immediately.

3. Instead of selecting the entire field column, you can position the cursor in any cell within the desired column for sorting. To illustrate:
CLICK: in any cell within the Zip field column
CLICK: Sort Descending button ($\frac{Z}{A}\downarrow$)
The datasheet is sorted into descending order by ZIP code.

4. You can also sort a table by the contents of more than one column, if the columns are adjacent to one another. Access sorts a table starting with the values in the leftmost selected column and then, for identical values, the records are sorted further by the values appearing in the next column. For example, to sort the datasheet into order by major and then surname, you must move the first or primary sort key, Major, to the left of the secondary sort key, LastName. To begin:
CLICK: Major in the field header area
DRAG: Major to the left of LastName
When you release the mouse button, the Major column appears between the StudentID and LastName columns.

5. Now you must select both columns. Since the Major column is already highlighted, do the following:
PRESS: **SHIFT** and hold it down
CLICK: LastName in the field header area
The datasheet should appear similar to the one shown in Figure 3.14.

Access

Figure 3.14

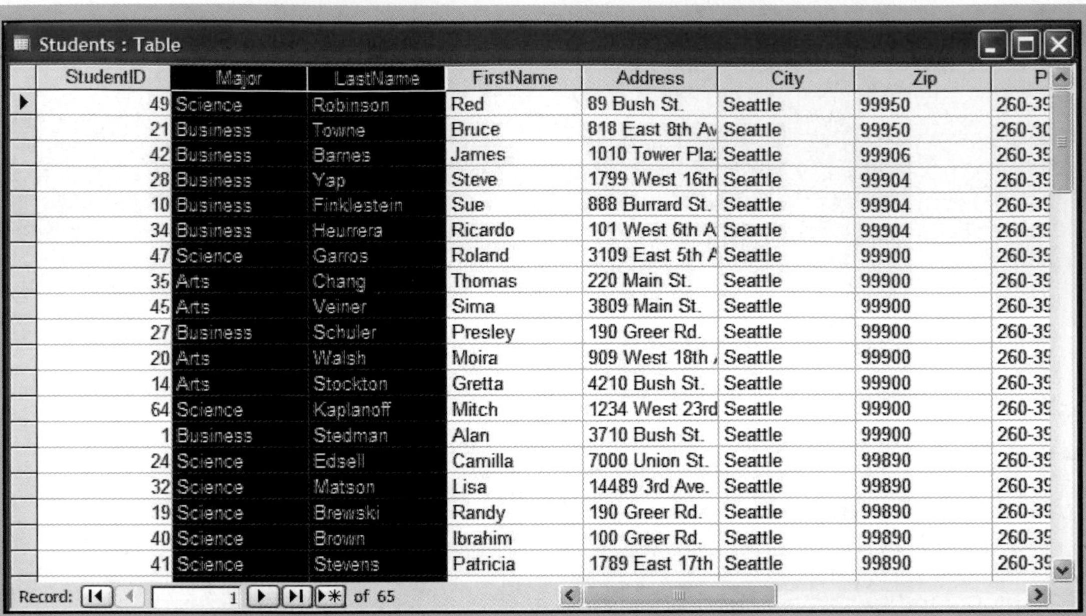

Moving and selecting columns for sorting

StudentID	Major	LastName	FirstName	Address	City	Zip	P
49	Science	Robinson	Red	89 Bush St.	Seattle	99950	260-39
21	Business	Towne	Bruce	818 East 8th Av	Seattle	99950	260-30
42	Business	Barnes	James	1010 Tower Pla:	Seattle	99906	260-39
28	Business	Yap	Steve	1799 West 16th	Seattle	99904	260-39
10	Business	Finklestein	Sue	888 Burrard St.	Seattle	99904	260-39
34	Business	Heurrera	Ricardo	101 West 6th A	Seattle	99904	260-39
47	Science	Garros	Roland	3109 East 5th A	Seattle	99900	260-39
35	Arts	Chang	Thomas	220 Main St.	Seattle	99900	260-39
45	Arts	Veiner	Sima	3809 Main St.	Seattle	99900	260-39
27	Business	Schuler	Presley	190 Greer Rd.	Seattle	99900	260-39
20	Arts	Walsh	Moira	909 West 18th A	Seattle	99900	260-39
14	Arts	Stockton	Gretta	4210 Bush St.	Seattle	99900	260-39
64	Science	Kaplanoff	Mitch	1234 West 23rd	Seattle	99900	260-39
1	Business	Stedman	Alan	3710 Bush St.	Seattle	99900	260-39
24	Science	Edsell	Camilla	7000 Union St.	Seattle	99890	260-39
32	Science	Matson	Lisa	14489 3rd Ave.	Seattle	99890	260-39
19	Science	Brewski	Randy	190 Greer Rd.	Seattle	99890	260-39
40	Science	Brown	Ibrahim	100 Greer Rd.	Seattle	99890	260-39
41	Science	Stevens	Patricia	1789 East 17th	Seattle	99890	260-39

Record: 1 of 65

6. To sort the datasheet by the contents of these columns:
CLICK: Sort Ascending button (☲↓)

7. Using the vertical scroll bar, scroll the window down to where the values in the Major column change from Arts to Business. Notice that the student records appear sorted by surname within each major.

8. Close the Datasheet window without saving the changes.

3.2.2 Performing a Simple Search

→ **Feature**

The Find command in Access 2003 lets you search an entire table for the existence of a few characters, a word, or a phrase. With large tables, this command is especially useful for moving the cursor to a particular record for editing. Most commonly, the Find command is used to locate a single record. Filters and query objects, discussed later in this chapter, are best used to locate groups of records matching specific criteria.

→ **Method**

- SELECT: a cell in the field column you want to search
- CLICK: Find button (🔍) on the toolbar

  or

  CHOOSE: Edit → Find
- SELECT: desired search options

→ **Practice**

In this lesson, you will attempt to find specific data stored in a table. Ensure that the AC0300 Database window is displayed.

1. Open the Students table in Datasheet view.

2. Finding data is much easier when the datasheet is sorted by the field in which you want to perform a search. To begin:
RIGHT-CLICK: LastName in the field header area
CHOOSE: Sort Ascending from the menu

3. Let's find the record for Jimmy Kazo:
CLICK: Find button (🏛) on the toolbar

4. In the Find and Replace dialog box that appears:
TYPE: **Kazo** in the *Find What* combo box
Notice that the LastName field already appears selected in the *Look In* drop-down list box, as shown in Figure 3.15.

Figure 3.15

Find and Replace dialog box: *Find* tab

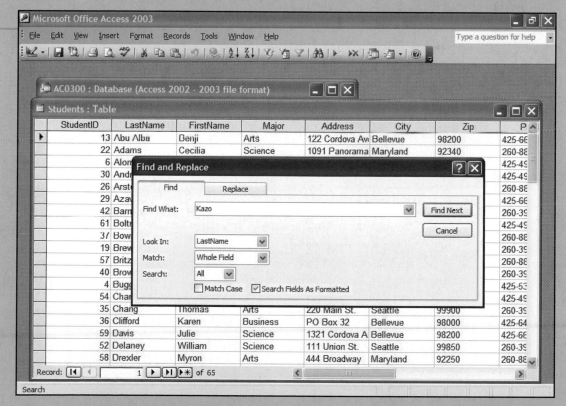

5. To proceed with the search:
CLICK: Find Next
The cursor moves down the column and stops on the first occurrence of "Kazo" in record 31. (*Note:* The Find and Replace dialog box does not disappear. Therefore, it may be necessary to drag it out of the way by its Title bar in order to view the selected record.)

6. You can continue the search for more entries for Kazo:
CLICK: Find Next
The following dialog box appears, stating that no more matches were found.

7. To dismiss the message box:
   CLICK: OK command button
   You are returned to the Find and Replace dialog box.

8. To end the search:
   CLICK: Cancel command button
   Notice that the cursor remains on record 31 (StudentID 56) for "Kazo."

9. Close the Datasheet window without saving the changes.

3.2.3 Specifying Search Patterns

→ ## Feature

Using the Find command, you can specify several options to control how a search is performed. You can also use **wildcard characters** to help locate words for which you are unsure of the spelling. These wildcards are also useful in defining search criteria for filters and queries.

→ ## Method

- Use the question mark (?) in place of a single character. For example, the search pattern "??S?" matches ROSI and DISC.

- Use the number symbol (#) in place of a single number. For example, the search pattern "##9" matches 349 and 109.

- Use the asterisk (*) to represent zero or more characters. For example, the search pattern "Sm*" yields entries beginning with the letters "Sm," such as Smith, Smythe, and Smallwood. You can also use the asterisk in the middle of a search pattern.

→ ## Practice

You will now practice using wildcards in building search criteria. Ensure that the AC0300 Database window is displayed.

1. Open the Students table in Datasheet view.

2. Your objective now is to find all the students who live on Shannon Square. To begin, select the Address column:
   CLICK: Address in the field header area

3. Let's change the width of the Address field column:
   CHOOSE: Format → Column Width
   TYPE: 25
   PRESS: [ENTER] or CLICK: OK command button

4. CLICK: Find button ([🔍])

5. In the Find and Replace dialog box:
   TYPE: *Shannon*
   Notice that the existing value, Kazo, in the combo box is replaced by the new entry (Figure 3.16).
   Using asterisks in this search criteria tells Access to find all occurrences of the word "Shannon" anywhere within a cell entry.

Figure 3.16

Searching for data using wildcards

6. To begin the search:
   CLICK: Find Next
   The cursor moves to Valerie Trimarchi's record, number 31.

7. To continue the search:
   CLICK: Find Next to move to Janos Sagi's record, number 43
   CLICK: Find Next to move to Mary Timerson's record, number 62
   CLICK: Find Next
   A dialog box appears stating that the search item was not found.

8. To accept the dialog box and proceed:
   CLICK: OK command button

9. To cancel the search:
   CLICK: Cancel

10. To return to the top of the datasheet:
    PRESS: CTRL + HOME

3.2.4 Performing a Find and Replace

→ **Feature**

The Replace command in Access lets you perform a global find and replace operation to update the contents of an entire table. Using the same process as Find, you enter an additional value to replace all occurrences of the successful match. Replace is an excellent tool for correcting spelling mistakes and updating standard fields, such as telephone area codes.

→ **Method**

To perform a find and replace operation:

• SELECT: a cell in the field column you want to search

• CHOOSE: Edit → Replace

• SELECT: desired search and replace options

Access

→ Practice

You will now practice using the Find and Replace feature. Ensure that you have completed the previous lesson and that the Students datasheet is displayed.

1. In the next few steps, you will replace the word "Science" in the Major field column with the word "CompSci." To begin:
CLICK: Major in the field header area

2. To proceed with the find and replace operation:
CHOOSE: Edit → Replace

3. On the *Replace* tab of the Find and Replace dialog box:
TYPE: **Science** in the *Find What* combo box
PRESS: **TAB**
TYPE: **CompSci** in the *Replace With* combo box
Your dialog box should now appear similar to the one shown in Figure 3.17.

Figure 3.17

Find and Replace
dialog box:
Replace tab

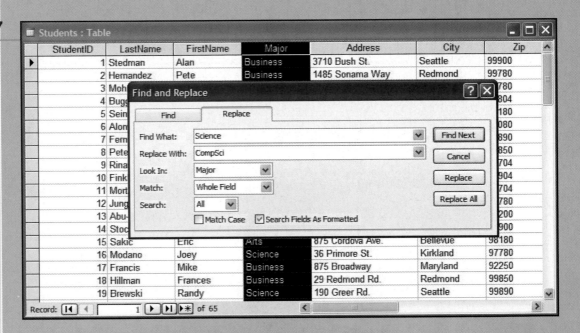

4. If you want to check the values you are about to replace, you can click the Replace command button to proceed one change at a time. For this step, however, let's change all of the values in a single step:
CLICK: Replace All command button
The following confirmation dialog box appears.

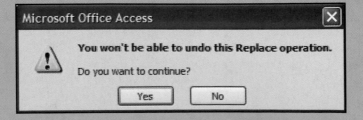

5. CLICK: Yes to accept and to remove the dialog box

6. To remove the Find and Replace dialog box:
CLICK: Cancel command button
Your datasheet should now contain "CompSci" in the Major field column, as shown in Figure 3.18.

Figure 3.18

Replacing a matching value in a datasheet

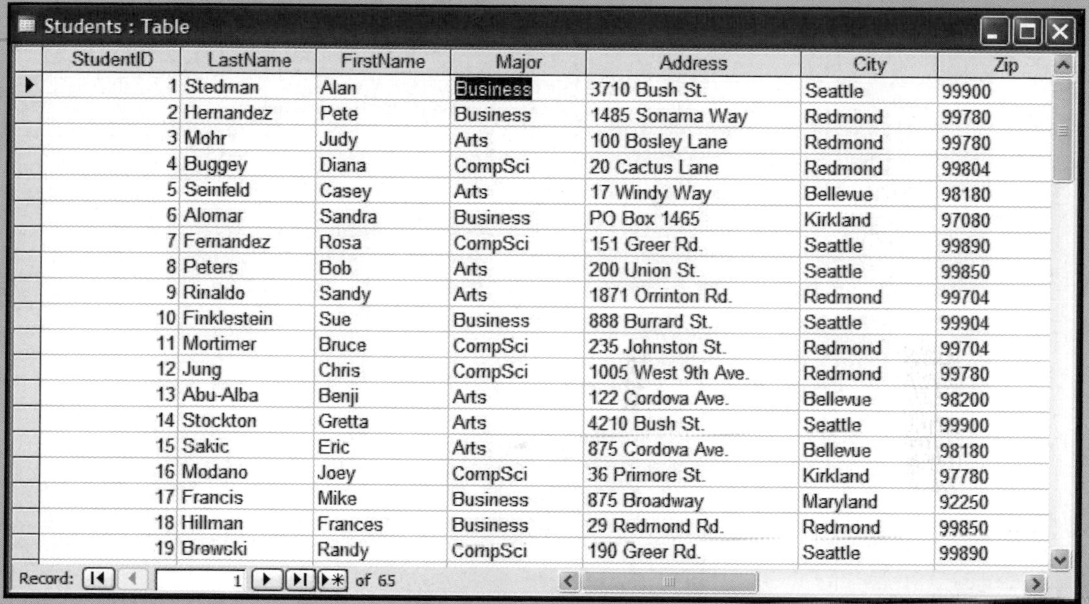

7. Keep the datasheet open for use in the next lesson.

3.2.5 Spell-Checking a Datasheet

→ **Feature**

You can check the spelling of entries in a datasheet in the same way that you spell-check a word processing document. With the Datasheet window displayed, click the Spelling button (icon) on the toolbar. A dialog box appears for each word that the Spelling Checker does not recognize or believes to be misspelled. You can correct the spelling, ignore the entry, or add the word to a custom dictionary.

→ **Method**

To perform a spelling check:

• CLICK: Spelling button (icon) on the toolbar

  or

• CHOOSE: Tools → Spelling from the menu

→ **Practice**

You will now practice spell-checking a datasheet. Ensure that you have completed the previous lesson and that the Students datasheet is displayed.

1. PRESS: CTRL + HOME to move to the top corner of the datasheet

2. To begin spell-checking the table contents:
CLICK: Spelling button (icon)
The Spelling Checker reads through the contents of the field and stops at the first word that it does not recognize, as shown in Figure 3.19.

Figure 3.19

Spell-checking a datasheet

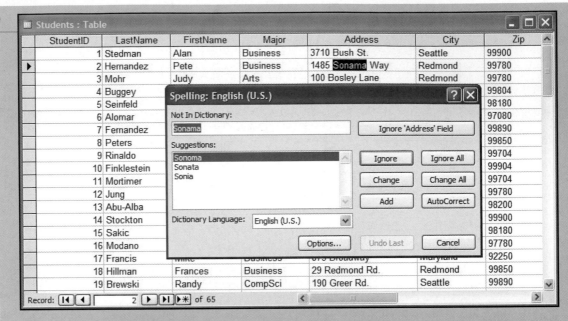

3. Because the Address field contains many names that will not likely appear in the spelling dictionary, let's tell the Spelling Checker to refrain from checking the contents of this field. Do the following:
CLICK: Ignore 'Address' Field command button

4. Similarly, the LastName field contains proper names not typically found in a dictionary. To ignore the word "Buggey" and other names in the field column:
CLICK: Ignore 'LastName' Field command button

5. The Spelling Checker now stops on the word "CompSci." Rather than ignore the entire field, let's ignore all the occurrences of this word only, because it is spelled correctly. Do the following:
CLICK: Ignore All command button

6. Now ignore checking the contents of the FirstName field:
CLICK: Ignore 'FirstName' Field command button
After proceeding through the remaining cells, the Spelling Checker displays the following dialog box.

7. To dismiss the dialog box:
CLICK: OK command button

8. Close the Datasheet window and save the layout changes.

 **SelfCheck**   **3.2** How do you perform a sort operation using more than one field column?

3.3 Using Filters

A **filter** is a tool that limits the display of records in a table using a simple matching criterion. Similar to a pasta strainer that lets water through but not the pasta, a filter allows only some records to pass through for display. Filtering is an excellent way to find a subset of records that match a particular value or range of values. Several methods are available for filtering records in a table: Filter For Input, Filter By Selection, Filter Excluding Selection, and Filter By Form, accessed using the Records, Filter command. In this module, you will learn how to define, apply, and remove filters.

3.3.1 Filtering for Input

→ ## Feature

Filtering displays a subset of records from a table. The **Filter For Input** method allows you to specify which records are let through. To apply this filter, you display a field's right-click menu and then type a value into the "Filter For:" text box. Finding matches to this value in the current field filters the datasheet. You may return to viewing all of the records by clicking the Apply/Remove Filter button (▽) at any time.

→ ## Method

To apply a filter using Filter For Input:

• RIGHT-CLICK: any cell in the desired field column

• CHOOSE: Filter For:

• TYPE: **filter criterion**

→ ## Practice

In this lesson, you will use the Filter For Input method to apply a filter. Ensure that the AC0300 Database window is displayed.

1. Open the Students table in Datasheet view.

2. Let's apply a filter to the datasheet that displays only those students with a last name beginning with the letter "S." Do the following:
RIGHT-CLICK: Stedman in the LastName field column
Your screen should now appear similar to the one shown in Figure 3.20.

Figure 3.20

Choosing the Filter For Input command

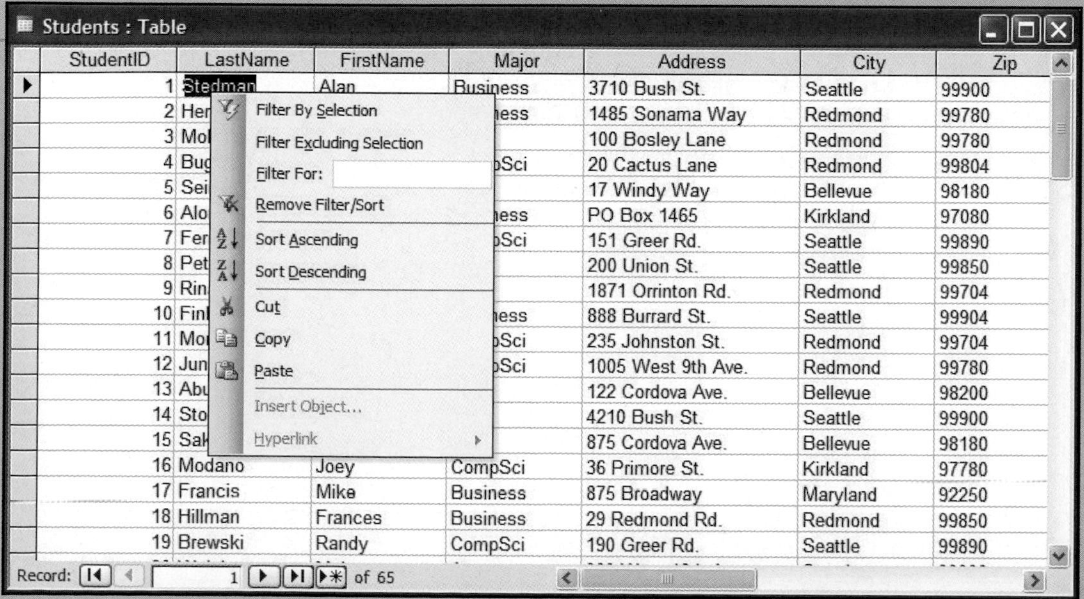

3. CHOOSE: Filter For:
A flashing insertion point should appear in the adjacent text box, as shown below.

Filter For:	

4. In the Filter For: text box:
TYPE: **s***
PRESS: **ENTER**
The datasheet (Figure 3.21) displays 8 of the original 65 records.

Figure 3.21

A filtered
datasheet

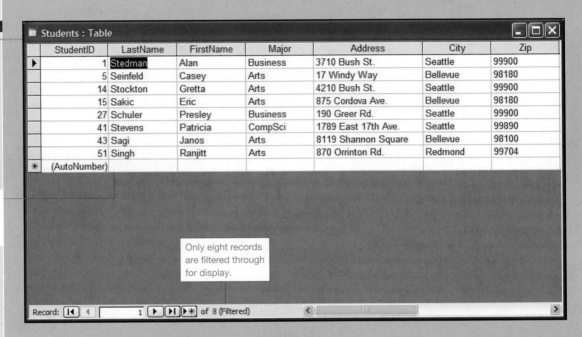

Displays only those
students with a last
name beginning
with "s."

StudentID	LastName	FirstName	Major	Address	City	Zip
1	Stedman	Alan	Business	3710 Bush St.	Seattle	99900
5	Seinfeld	Casey	Arts	17 Windy Way	Bellevue	98180
14	Stockton	Gretta	Arts	4210 Bush St.	Seattle	99900
15	Sakic	Eric	Arts	875 Cordova Ave.	Bellevue	98180
27	Schuler	Presley	Business	190 Greer Rd.	Seattle	99900
41	Stevens	Patricia	CompSci	1789 East 17th Ave.	Seattle	99890
43	Sagi	Janos	Arts	8119 Shannon Square	Bellevue	98100
51	Singh	Ranjitt	Arts	870 Orrinton Rd.	Redmond	99704
(AutoNumber)						

Only eight records
are filtered through
for display.

Record: 1 of 8 (Filtered)

5. Once the datasheet is filtered, you can sort the resulting subset of records using the appropriate toolbar buttons. To sort the filtered records:
CLICK: Sort Ascending button ($\frac{A}{Z}\downarrow$)
The datasheet now appears sorted by surname.

6. The Apply/Remove Filter button ($\triangledown$) on the toolbar acts as a toggle to turn on and off the current or active filter. To illustrate:
CLICK: Remove Filter button ($\triangledown$)
Notice that the datasheet remains sorted in ascending order by surname.

7. To reapply the last filter:
CLICK: Apply Filter button ($\triangledown$)
Notice that the toolbar button changes names depending on its toggle status.

8. Close the Datasheet window without saving the changes.

3.3.2 Filtering by Selection

→ ## Feature

Using the **Filter By Selection** method, you apply a filter based on a selected value from the datasheet. The selection may be an entire cell's contents or only a portion of the entry. Likewise, you use the **Filter Excluding Selection** method to display only those records that do not match the selected value.

→ ## Method

To apply a Filter By Selection:

- SELECT: all or part of an existing field entry
- CLICK: Filter By Selection button (🥢)

  or

  CHOOSE: Records → Filter → Filter By Selection

To apply a Filter Excluding Selection:

- SELECT: all or part of an existing field entry
- CHOOSE: Records → Filter → Filter Excluding Selection

→ ## Practice

In this lesson, you will use the Filter By Selection method to apply a filter. Ensure that the AC0300 Database window is displayed.

1. Open the Students table in Datasheet view.

2. To display only those students living in the city of Redmond:
DOUBLE-CLICK: "Redmond" in the City field column of the second record

3. To create a filter based on the selected text:
CLICK: Filter By Selection button (🥢)
A subset of 10 records is displayed in the Datasheet window, as shown in Figure 3.22.

Figure 3.22

Filtering a datasheet by selection

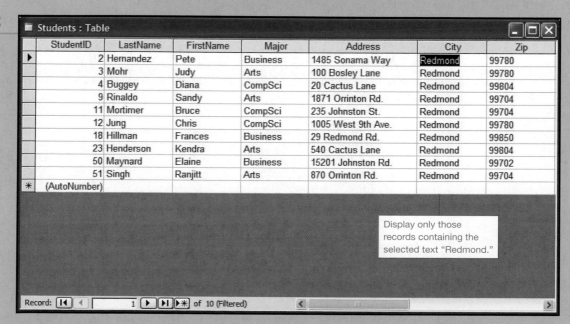

	StudentID	LastName	FirstName	Major	Address	City	Zip
▶	2	Hernandez	Pete	Business	1485 Sonama Way	Redmond	99780
	3	Mohr	Judy	Arts	100 Bosley Lane	Redmond	99780
	4	Buggey	Diana	CompSci	20 Cactus Lane	Redmond	99804
	9	Rinaldo	Sandy	Arts	1871 Orrinton Rd.	Redmond	99704
	11	Mortimer	Bruce	CompSci	235 Johnston St.	Redmond	99704
	12	Jung	Chris	CompSci	1005 West 9th Ave.	Redmond	99780
	18	Hillman	Frances	Business	29 Redmond Rd.	Redmond	99850
	23	Henderson	Kendra	Arts	540 Cactus Lane	Redmond	99804
	50	Maynard	Elaine	Business	15201 Johnston Rd.	Redmond	99702
	51	Singh	Ranjitt	Arts	870 Orrinton Rd.	Redmond	99704
*	(AutoNumber)						

Display only those records containing the selected text "Redmond."

Record: ◀◀ ◀ 1 ▶ ▶◀ ▶* of 10 (Filtered)

Access

4. To remove the filter:
CLICK: Remove Filter button (▽)

5. To display only those students who are *not* taking Arts as their major:
DOUBLE-CLICK: "Arts" in any cell of the Major field column
CHOOSE: Records → Filter
The following menu appears. You can access all Filter commands, except for the Filter For Input option, using this menu.

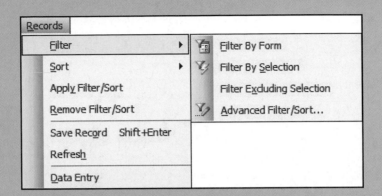

6. CHOOSE: Filter Excluding Selection
A subset of 42 records is displayed in the Datasheet window.

7. To remove the filter:
CLICK: Remove Filter button (▽)

8. To display only those students living in Seattle and taking CompSci as their major, you need to apply two filters to the datasheet. To begin:
DOUBLE-CLICK: "CompSci" in any cell of the Major field column
CLICK: Filter By Selection button (▽)
A subset of 20 records is displayed.

9. Without removing the filter:
DOUBLE-CLICK: "Seattle" in any cell of the City field column
CLICK: Filter By Selection button (▽)
Now a subset of 11 records is displayed, as shown in Figure 3.23. These records match the criteria specified in the previous two filter selections.

Figure 3.23

Filtering a datasheet using two filter specifications

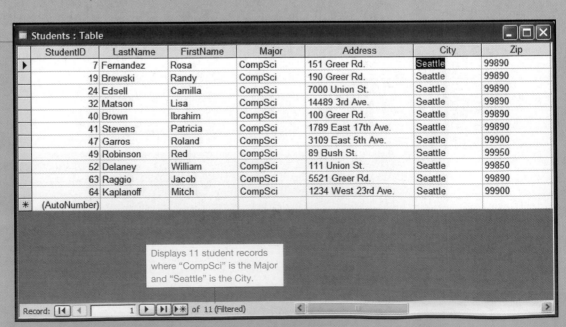

10. To continue, let's filter to find those students who live on Greer Road:
DOUBLE-CLICK: "Greer" in any cell of the Address field column
CLICK: Filter By Selection button ([icon])
Four students who live on Greer Road in Seattle are taking CompSci as their major.

11. To display all of the records once again:
CLICK: Remove Filter button ([icon])

12. Close the Datasheet window without saving the changes.

3.3.3 Filtering by Form

→ # Feature

For more detailed filtering operations, use the **Filter By Form** method to set multiple criteria. Unlike Filter For Input or Filter By Selection, a blank datasheet row appears in which you can enter or select the desired criteria. Once you have defined a filter, Access 2003 enables you to save it as a query object in the Database window.

→ # Method

To apply a Filter By Form:

• CLICK: Filter By Form button ([icon])

 or

 CHOOSE: Records → Filter → Filter By Form

• Enter the desired filtering criteria.

• CLICK: Apply/Remove Filter button ([icon])

To save a Filter By Form as a Query:

• Display the Filter By Form window.

• CLICK: Save As Query button ([icon])

→ # Practice

In this lesson, you will use the Filter By Form method to apply a filter. Ensure that the AC0300 Database window is displayed.

1. Open the Students table in Datasheet view.

2. To use the Filter By Form method for filtering a datasheet:
CLICK: Filter By Form button ([icon]) on the toolbar
Your screen should now appear similar to the one shown in Figure 3.24.

Figure 3.24

Creating a filter using Filter By Form

Filter/Sort toolbar

Use these tabs to specify criteria and filtering logic.

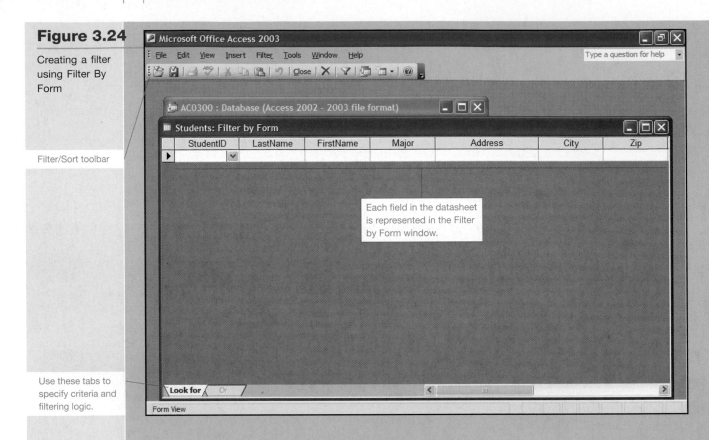

Each field in the datasheet is represented in the Filter by Form window.

3. Let's display only those students living in Kirkland who are taking Arts as their major. To begin:
CLICK: Major cell once, immediately below the field header area
Notice that a down arrow appears next to the cell. You use this arrow to access a drop-down list of unique values taken from the datasheet.

4. CLICK: down arrow attached to the Major field
The following list appears.

5. SELECT: Arts from the list of three values
The search criterion "Arts" is entered into the cell.

6. To specify the city criteria:
CLICK: City cell once
CLICK: down arrow attached to the City field
The following list appears.

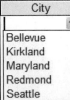

7. SELECT: Kirkland from the list of five values
The search criterion "Kirkland" is entered into the cell.

8. To apply the filter and display the results:
CLICK: Apply Filter button (▽)
A subset of six records is displayed, as shown in Figure 3.25.

Figure 3.25

Filtering a
datasheet using
Filter By Form

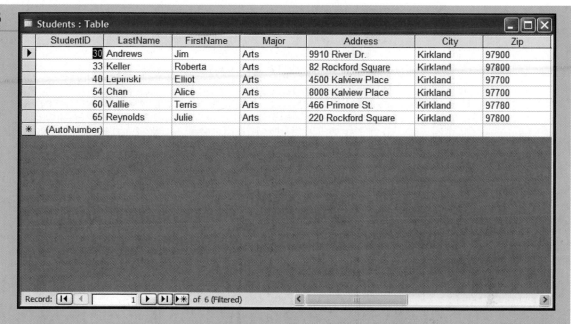

9. Let's return to the Filter By Form window:
   CLICK: Filter By Form button (▣)
   Notice that the same criteria appear in the window.

10. To save this filter as a query object:

    CLICK: Save As Query button (▣)
    TYPE: **Kirkland Arts Students**
    The dialog box should appear as shown here.

11. PRESS: ENTER

    or

    CLICK: OK command button

12. To specify a new filter:
    CLICK: Clear Grid button (✕)
    The existing filter criteria are removed from the window.

13. In addition to selecting values from the drop-down list, you can type values into the Filter By Form window. To illustrate, let's display only those students with a last name starting with the letter "m":
    CLICK: LastName cell once
    TYPE: **m***

14. CLICK: Apply Filter button (▽)
    A subset of seven records is displayed, as shown in Figure 3.26.

Figure 3.26

Filtering the datasheet by the LastName field

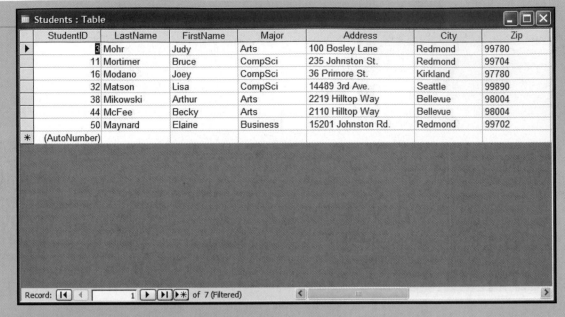

15. Close the Datasheet window without saving the changes.

16. Let's use the Filter By Form query you saved in step 10 to run this query from the Database window, first:
    CLICK: *Queries* button in the Objects bar
    You should see the "Kirkland Arts Students" query in the Database window.

17. DOUBLE-CLICK: Kirkland Arts Students in the list area
    A datasheet displaying the filtered results appears, similar to the datasheet shown in Figure 3.25.

18. Close the Datasheet window.

 **3.3** In a personnel table, how would you display a subset of those employees working in the accounting department?

3.4 Creating a Simple Query

A query is a question that you ask of your database, such as "How many customers live in Chicago?" or "What is the average age of employees in XYZ Corporation?" Using queries, you can prepare, view, analyze, and summarize your data. The results of a query may also be used when presenting data in forms and reports. You can also use special queries to perform advanced updating routines in your database.

   Although similar to filters, queries differ in several significant areas. Both filters and queries allow you to retrieve and display a subset of records, but queries also allow you to display data from multiple tables, to control which fields display and in what order they appear, and to perform calculations on selected field values. In addition, whereas filters provide a temporary view of a subset of records, queries are saved as independent database objects. Use the following statement as your guideline: *find* a record, *filter* a table, and *query* a database.

3.4.1 Creating a Query Using the Query Wizard

→ **Feature**

The **Simple Query Wizard** is a step-by-step tool that helps you retrieve data from one or more tables in a database. Unfortunately, the wizard does not allow you to specify search criteria or sort parameters. The type of query object created by the wizard is known as a **select query,** since you use it to select data for display. The results of the query are listed in a Datasheet window, sometimes referred to as a **dynaset.** Other types of queries include action queries for updating, adding, and deleting records in a database and parameter queries for accepting input from users.

→ **Method**

In the Database window, select the *Queries* button and then:

- DOUBLE-CLICK: Create query by using wizard

  or

- CLICK: New button (⊞ New) on the Database window toolbar
- DOUBLE-CLICK: Simple Query Wizard in the New Query dialog box

→ **Practice**

You will now use the Simple Query Wizard to extract data from two tables for display in a single Datasheet window. Ensure that the AC0300 Database window is displayed.

1. The options for creating a new query object are similar to the options for creating a new table object. You can start from scratch in query Design view or get helpful guidance from wizards. In the next few steps, you will use the Simple Query Wizard to create a query. To begin:
CLICK: *Queries* button in the Objects bar, if it is not already selected

2. To launch the Simple Query Wizard:
DOUBLE-CLICK: Create query by using wizard
The dialog box shown in Figure 3.27 appears.

Figure 3.27

Simple Query Wizard dialog box

Selecting a table or query updates the fields displayed in the list box below.

Select fields for display in the resulting query.

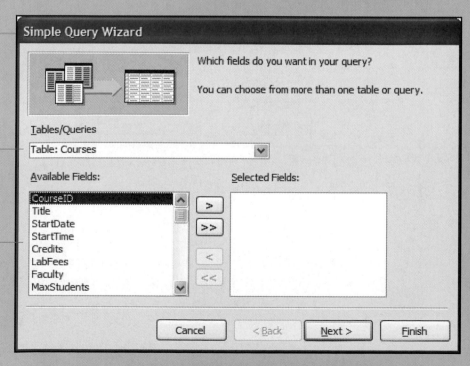

3. In order to display a listing of courses along with the instructor's name, you must select fields from two tables. To begin, ensure that "Table: Courses" is selected in the *Tables/Queries* drop-down list box.

4. In the *Available Fields* list box:
SELECT: CourseID
CLICK: Include button (>)
SELECT: Title
CLICK: Include button (>)

5. Now select a new table:
SELECT: Table: Instructors in the *Tables/Queries* drop-down list box
Notice that new fields are displayed in the associated list box.

6. In the *Available Fields* list box:
SELECT: LastName
CLICK: Include button (>)
SELECT: FirstName
CLICK: Include button (>)
Your screen should now appear similar to the one shown in Figure 3.28.

Figure 3.28

Selecting fields for display in the Simple Query Wizard

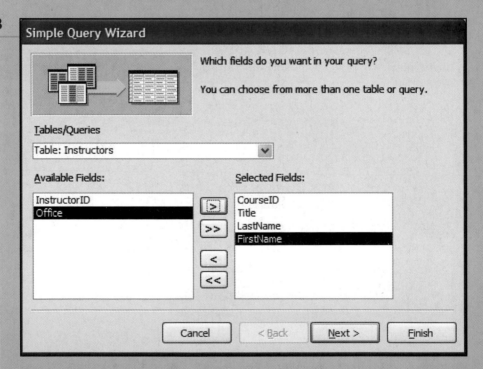

7. To proceed to the next step in the wizard:
CLICK: Next >

8. Now let's name the query:
TYPE: **Course Listing Query**

9. Ensure that the *Open the query to view information* option button is selected in the dialog box and then do the following:
CLICK: Finish
Your screen should appear similar to the one shown in Figure 3.29. Data in the first two columns is taken from the Courses table, and data in the last two columns is taken from the Instructors table.

Figure 3.29

Displaying
dynaset results
for a query

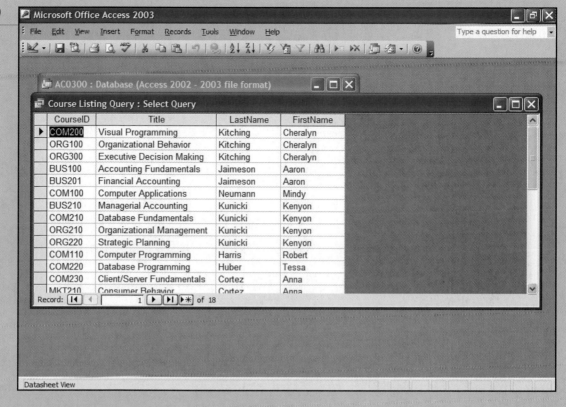

10. Keep the Datasheet window open and proceed to the next lesson.

3.4.2 Displaying the Query Design Window

→ **Feature**

The Simple Query Wizard makes it easy to get started creating queries. Modifying an existing query, however, requires that you use the query Design window. Discussed in Chapter 6 of our Introductory and Complete editions, the Design view is also used to create complex queries from scratch. In this lesson, you will learn some basic techniques for displaying and editing an existing query.

→ **Method**

If the query's Datasheet window is displayed:

• CLICK: View – Design button ( ) on the toolbar

In the Database window, select the *Queries* button and then:

• SELECT: the query object that you want to modify

• CLICK: Design button (Design) on the Database window toolbar

  or

• RIGHT-CLICK: the query object that you want to modify

• CHOOSE: Design View

Access

→ **Practice**

Using the query Design window, you will modify the query created in the last lesson. Ensure that you have completed the previous lesson and that the Course Listing Query Datasheet window is displayed.

1. Let's change the view mode for the Course Listing Query to Design view. Do the following:
CLICK: View – Design button (⬚▾)
Your screen should appear similar to the one shown in Figure 3.30 before proceeding.

Figure 3.30

Query Design window for the Course Listing Query object

The query Design grid, in the lower portion of the Design window, displays the fields, criteria, and sort specifications for the query.

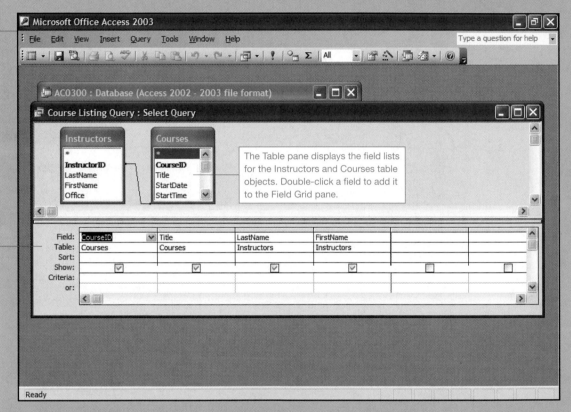

2. To add a field to the query:
DOUBLE-CLICK: Office in the Instructors table object
The field "Office" is added immediately to the next empty column in the query Design grid.

3. To display the resulting dynaset:
CLICK: View – Datasheet button (▦▾) on the toolbar
Notice that the Office column is now displayed in the datasheet.

4. To return to Design view:
CLICK: View – Design button (⬚▾)

5. Let's limit the display of courses to only those taught by instructors with offices in the "B" wing. To do so:
CLICK: in the *Criteria* text box of the Office column
TYPE: **B***
PRESS: ⬇ to complete the entry
Notice that the criteria specification is automatically changed by Access to **Like "B*"**. Your screen should now appear similar to the one shown in Figure 3.31.

Figure 3.31

Entering a criteria specification in the query Design window

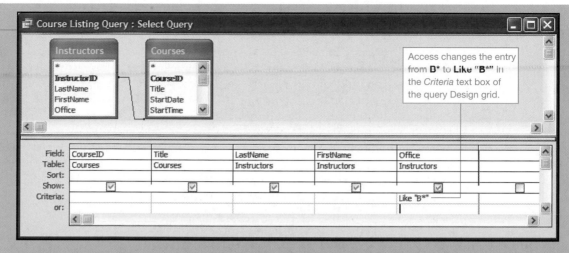

6. Let's save the query object:
   CLICK: Save button (⊟)

7. To view the resulting dynaset:
   CLICK: View – Datasheet button (▦▾)
   Only three records are displayed in the datasheet, as shown in Figure 3.32.

Figure 3.32

Displaying the results of a modified query object

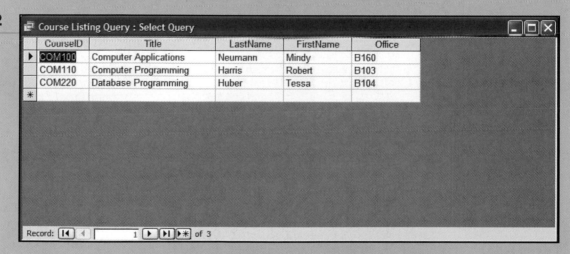

8. Close the Datasheet window for the Course Listing Query.

9. Close the AC0300 Database window.

In Addition SPECIFYING SEARCH CRITERIA IN QUERIES

Querying a database involves more than limiting its display to specific fields. Using query Design view, you can create and modify queries to extract records from tables that meet given criteria. You can also adjust the sorting order and perform calculations.

3.4 Name one way that a query's dynaset may differ from a table's datasheet.

Chapter
summary

One of the primary advantages of using a computerized database is the ability to manipulate, retrieve, and display information quickly and easily. Making your information pleasing to read requires the further ability to format and customize the results. Fortunately, you can spice up your datasheets by applying fonts, styles, and special effects. You can also improve your efficiency in working with a datasheet by moving, hiding, and freezing field columns in Datasheet view.

To help you turn raw data into information, the Sort, Find, and Filter commands enable you to organize, locate, and highlight records in a table. You can also use filters to limit the display of records in a table and queries to ask questions of your database. In addition to being able to draw data from multiple tables, queries enable you to specify complex search criteria and sort parameters. Queries are powerful database objects and the sole subject of more advanced chapters.

Command Summary

Many of the commands and procedures appearing in this chapter are summarized in the following table.

Skill Set	To Perform This Task . . .	Do the Following . . .
Creating and Using Databases	Enhance the text displayed in a datasheet using fonts and colors	CHOOSE: Format → Font
	Enhance the background and appearance of a Datasheet window	CHOOSE: Format → Datasheet
	Select a field column	CLICK: in the column's field header area
	Change the field column order in a datasheet	SELECT: the desired column DRAG: its column heading into position
	Hide a field column in a datasheet	SELECT: the desired column CHOOSE: Format → Hide Columns
	Unhide field columns in a datasheet	CHOOSE: Format → Unhide Columns SELECT: the columns to unhide
	Freeze or lock a field column into place in a datasheet	SELECT: the desired column CHOOSE: Format → Freeze Columns
	Unfreeze all of the locked columns in a datasheet	CHOOSE: Format → Unfreeze All Columns
	Save modifications and layout changes made to a datasheet	CLICK: Save button (🖫), or CHOOSE: File → Save
Viewing and Organizing Information	Sort a field column in a datasheet into ascending order	SELECT: the desired column CLICK: Sort Ascending button (🔼)
	Sort a field column in a datasheet into descending order	SELECT: the desired column CLICK: Sort Descending button (🔽)
	Find or locate a value or record in a datasheet	CLICK: Find button (🔍), or CHOOSE: Edit → Find
	Replace an existing value in a datasheet with a new value	CHOOSE: Edit → Replace

Filter a datasheet using the Filter For Input method	RIGHT-CLICK: a cell in the desired column CHOOSE: Filter For: TYPE: *a filter criterion*
Filter a datasheet using the Filter By Selection method	SELECT: a datasheet entry CLICK: Filter By Selection button (⧩)
Filter a datasheet using the Filter Excluding Selection method	SELECT: a datasheet entry CHOOSE: Records → Filter → Filter Excluding Selection
Filter a datasheet using the Filter By Form method	CLICK: Filter By Form button (▦) SELECT: the desired criteria
Toggle a filter on or off	CLICK: Apply/Remove Filter button (▽)
Save the criteria entered using Filter By Form as a query object	CLICK: Save As Query button (▤)
Create a query using the Simple Query Wizard	SELECT: *Queries* object button DOUBLE-CLICK: Create query by using wizard
Toggle between query Design view and Datasheet view	CLICK: View – Design button (▨▾) CLICK: View – Datasheet button (▦▾)

Key Terms

This section specifies page references for the key terms identified in this chapter. For a complete list of definitions, refer to the Glossary at the end of this learning guide.

dynaset, *p. AC 121*

filter, *p. AC 113*

Filter By Form, *p. AC 117*

Filter By Selection, *p. AC 115*

Filter Excluding Selection, *p. AC 115*

Filter For Input, *p. AC 113*

select query, *p. AC 121*

Simple Query Wizard, *p. AC 121*

sort key, *p. AC 104*

typeface, *p. AC 95*

wildcard characters, *p. AC 108*

Chapter
quiz

Short Answer

1. Name the three *Cell Effect* options for formatting a datasheet.

2. What command allows you to lock one or more columns of a datasheet in place? Name two ways to execute this command.

3. What are the two primary options for sorting a list?

4. What are wildcards? Provide an example of how they are used.

5. Name four methods for filtering records in a table.

6. When would you use the Find command rather than applying a filter?

7. How do the Filter For Input and Filter By Selection methods differ?

8. When would you apply a filter rather than creating a query?

9. What are two limitations of the Simple Query Wizard?

10. What type of query does the Simple Query Wizard create? What are two additional types of queries?

True/False

1. _____ You can change the color of a datasheet's background.

2. _____ In Datasheet view, click Save (□) to save your editing changes and click Save Layout (□) to save your formatting changes.

3. _____ To sort a datasheet by more than one column, you must first ensure that the columns are positioned next to one another.

4. _____ Once you have filtered a datasheet, you can then sort the results using the appropriate toolbar buttons.

5. _____ The search criteria ***osf*** would match "Microsoft."

6. _____ The search criteria **?crosof?** would match "Microsoft."

7. _____ You invoke the Filter Excluding Selection method by selecting text in a datasheet and then clicking a toolbar button.

8. _____ When viewing a table's data in Datasheet view, you can use a filter to limit the display of records in the active datasheet.

9. _____ When viewing a table's data in Datasheet view, you can use a query to limit the display of records in the active datasheet.

10. _____ You find a record, filter a table, and query a database.

Multiple Choice

1. In the Datasheet Formatting dialog box, which of the following is not an option in the *Border and Line Styles* drop-down list box?
   a. Datasheet Border
   b. Datasheet Underline
   c. Horizontal Gridline
   d. Vertical Gridline

2. Which of the following is not an option for customizing a Datasheet window?
   a. Freeze one column
   b. Hide one column
   c. Change one row's height
   d. Change one column's width

3. Which of the following is not a command that is selectable from a field column's right-click menu?
   a. Hide Columns
   b. Unhide Columns
   c. Freeze Columns
   d. Sort Descending

4. The process of restricting the display of records in a table to those matching a particular criterion is called:
   a. Filtering
   b. Restricting
   c. Sifting
   d. Sorting

5. Which of the following is not a type of filter method described in this chapter?

a. Filter By Example
b. Filter By Form
c. Filter By Selection
d. Filter For Input

6. What is the name of the Access 2003 tool that simplifies the process of creating a query object?

a. Database Wizard
b. Simple Filter Wizard
c. Simple Query Wizard
d. Table Wizard

7. A collection of records matching the parameters of a query is sometimes called a:

a. Dynaset
b. Field
c. Table
d. Grid

8. Which of the following criteria returns only those cities beginning with the letter "B"?

a. =B
b. B*
c. B?
d. B#

9. Which of the following criteria returns the name "Jones" as a match?

a. *ne*
b. J??nes
c. J#s
d. ?ne*

10. Which of the following statements is false?

a. A filter operation limits records displayed in a datasheet.
b. A query operation returns a Datasheet window of results.
c. A sort operation modifies the natural order of data in a table.
d. A find operation that is successful moves the cursor to the record.

Hands-On
exercises

ep by step

1. Formatting a Datasheet

In this exercise, you will enhance the appearance of a datasheet by applying fonts and specifying background special effects.

1. Load Microsoft Office Access 2003, if it is not already running.

2. Open the database file named AC03HE. Ensure that the *Tables* button in the Objects bar is selected, as shown in Figure 3.33.

Figure 3.33

Opening the
AC03HE
database

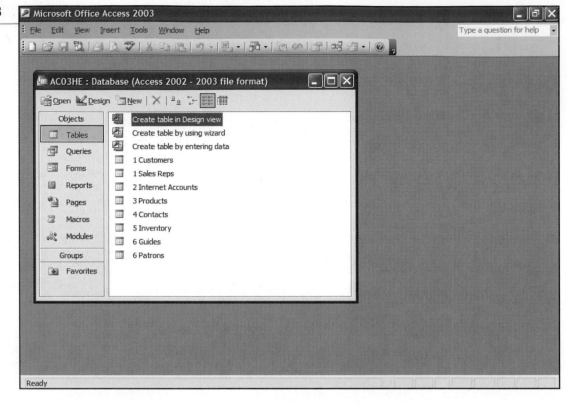

3. Open the "1 Customers" table in Datasheet view.

4. Using the Font dialog box, change the display font in the datasheet to Courier New with an 11-point font size. Apply a boldface font style and a maroon text color.

5. Using the Datasheet Formatting dialog box, change the appearance of the datasheet's background to display using the "raised" cell effect.

6. Modify the field columns in the datasheet to appear using their "best-fit" width.

7. Return to the top of the datasheet using (CTRL) + (HOME). Your screen should now appear similar to the one shown in Figure 3.34.

Figure 3.34

Formatting the "1 Customers" datasheet

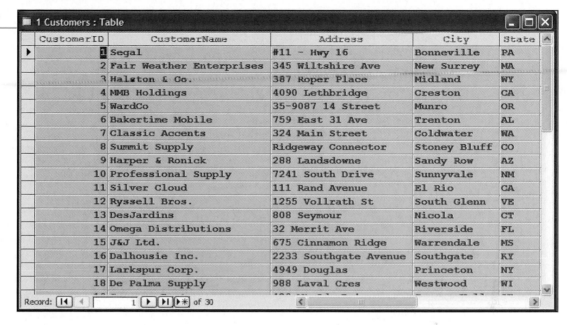

8. Move the SalesRep column so that it appears to the right of the CustomerID field.

9. PRESS: HOME to remove the highlighting

10. Using the Page Setup dialog box, specify a landscape print orientation.

11. Preview the datasheet in a Print Preview window.

12. Zoom in on the Print Preview window, as shown in Figure 3.35.

Figure 3.35

Previewing a formatted datasheet

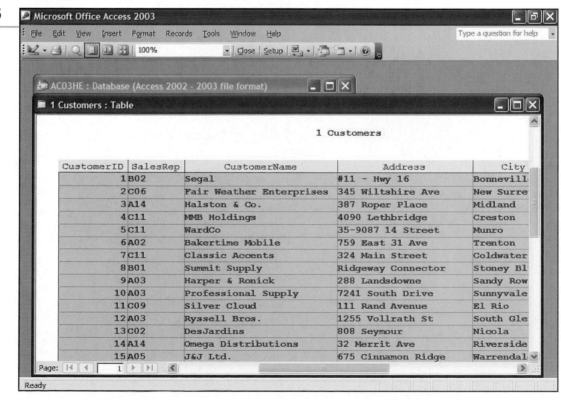

13. If you have a printer, print the datasheet by clicking the Print button (⊞). Last, click the Close button (⌧) in the toolbar.

14. Save the layout changes by clicking the Save button (⊞).

15. Close the Datasheet window.

2. Customizing a Datasheet

You will now practice customizing a datasheet using the Freeze, Hide, and Sort commands.

1. Ensure that the AC03HE Database window is displayed.

2. Open the "2 Internet Accounts" table object for display.

3. First, let's freeze the Username field column in the datasheet, so that it is always visible when you scroll the window. Notice that the column is moved to the far left of the Datasheet window.

4. To demonstrate the effect of freezing the Username column:
PRESS: (**END**) to move to the last field column
Notice that the Username column remains visible, as shown in Figure 3.36.

Figure 3.36

Freezing the Username column

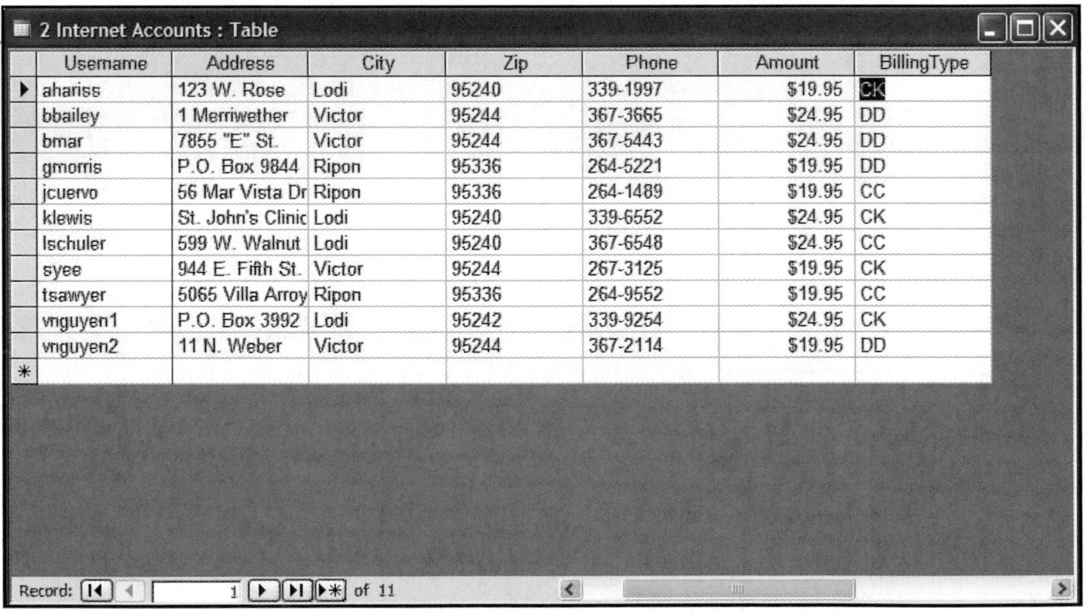

Username	Address	City	Zip	Phone	Amount	BillingType
▶ ahariss	123 W. Rose	Lodi	95240	339-1997	$19.95	CK
bbailey	1 Merriwether	Victor	95244	367-3665	$24.95	DD
bmar	7855 "E" St.	Victor	95244	367-5443	$24.95	DD
gmorris	P.O. Box 9844	Ripon	95336	264-5221	$19.95	DD
jcuervo	56 Mar Vista Dr	Ripon	95336	264-1489	$19.95	CC
klewis	St. John's Clinic	Lodi	95240	339-6552	$24.95	CK
lschuler	599 W. Walnut	Lodi	95240	367-6548	$24.95	CC
syee	944 E. Fifth St.	Victor	95244	267-3125	$19.95	CK
tsawyer	5065 Villa Arroy	Ripon	95336	264-9552	$19.95	CC
vnguyen1	P.O. Box 3992	Lodi	95242	339-9254	$24.95	CK
vnguyen2	11 N. Weber	Victor	95244	367-2114	$19.95	DD

2 Internet Accounts : Table

Record: 1 of 11

5. Unfreeze the Username field column before proceeding.

6. PRESS: (**END**) to move the cursor to the last field column
Notice that the column is no longer locked into position.

7. Hide the last two columns, Amount and BillingType, from displaying in the Datasheet window. (*Note:* Hidden columns are temporarily hidden in the Datasheet window, but they are not removed from the table object.)

8. Now sort the records into ascending order by the contents of the City field column.

9. Adjust the width of the Address column to its best-fit width by double-clicking the borderline between the Address and City columns.

10. To preview what the datasheet looks like when sent to the printer:
CLICK: Print Preview button (⊞) on the toolbar

11. On your own, use the magnifying glass mouse pointer to zoom in on the Print Preview window, as shown in Figure 3.37.

Figure 3.37

Previewing the "2 Internet Accounts" datasheet

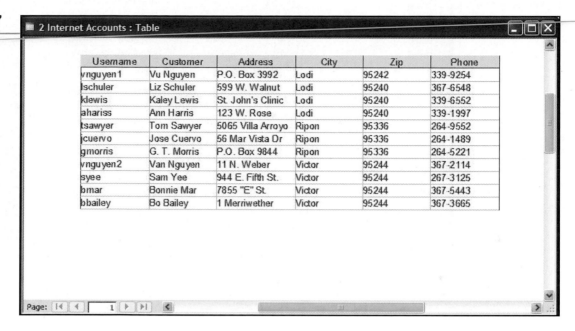

2 Internet Accounts : Table

Username	Customer	Address	City	Zip	Phone
vnguyen1	Vu Nguyen	P.O. Box 3992	Lodi	95242	339-9254
lschuler	Liz Schuler	599 W. Walnut	Lodi	95240	367-6548
klewis	Kaley Lewis	St. John's Clinic	Lodi	95240	339-6552
ahariss	Ann Harris	123 W. Rose	Lodi	95240	339-1997
tsawyer	Tom Sawyer	5065 Villa Arroyo	Ripon	95336	264-9552
jcuervo	Jose Cuervo	56 Mar Vista Dr	Ripon	95336	264-1489
gmorris	G. T. Morris	P.O. Box 9844	Ripon	95336	264-5221
vnguyen2	Van Nguyen	11 N. Weber	Victor	95244	367-2114
syee	Sam Yee	944 E. Fifth St.	Victor	95244	267-3125
bmar	Bonnie Mar	7855 "E" St.	Victor	95244	367-5443
bbailey	Bo Bailey	1 Merriwether	Victor	95244	367-3665

Page: 1

12. If you have a printer, print the datasheet by clicking the Print button (🖨). Last, click the Close button (Close) in the toolbar.

13. Unhide the Amount and BillingType field columns in the Datasheet window.

14. Save the layout changes by clicking the Save button (💾).

15. Close the Datasheet window.

3. Sorting, Finding, and Replacing Data

In this exercise, you will sort data using more than one column and practice using the Find and Replace commands.

1. Ensure that the AC03HE Database window is displayed.

2. Open the "3 Products" table for display in Datasheet view.

3. Perform a sort operation that displays the table in ascending order by Category and then by the ProductCode stored within each category. Your screen should now appear similar to the one shown in Figure 3.38.

Figure 3.38

Sorting a
datasheet by two
field columns

Category	ProductCode	Species	Size	Grade	Finish
Board	DF14	DFIR	1 X 4	Ungraded	RGH
Board	DF16	D.FIR	1 X 6	Ungraded	RGH
Board	SP14	SPF	1 X 4	Ungraded	S4S
Board	SP14R	SPF	1 X 4	Ungraded	RGH
Board	SP16	SPF	1 X 6	Ungraded	S4S
Board	SP18	SPF	1 X 8	Ungraded	S4S
Board	WP110	WPINR	1 X 10	Utility	RGH
Board	WP13	WPINE	1 X 3	Utility	RGH
Board	WP14	WPINE	1 X 4	Utility	RGH
Board	WP16	WPINE	1 X 6	Utility	RGH
Board	WP18	WPINE	1 X 8	Utility	RGH
Dimension	DF210S	DFIR	2 X 10	Standard	S4S
Dimension	DF242	DFIR	2 X 4	2+	S4S
Dimension	DF24S	DFIR	2 X 4	Standard	S4S
Dimension	DF24U	DFIR	2 X 4	Utility	S4S
Dimension	DF26	DFIR	2 X 6	Standard	S4S
Dimension	DF28	DFIR	2 X 8	Standard	S4S
Dimension	SP210	SPF	2 X 10	Standard	S4S
Dimension	SP212	SPF	2 X 12	Standard	S4S

3 Products : Table — Record: 1 of 49

4. Now let's find all of the products made from birch wood. Use the Find button and the Find and Replace dialog box to find "birch." (*Note:* By default, the Find command is not case sensitive.) What product category does the cursor stop on first?

5. Use the Find Next command button to determine if any of the other products are made from birch. When you are finished, close the Find and Replace dialog box.

6. You will now use the Replace command to replace all occurrences of the code "Dim." in the Category column with the word "Dimension." Move to the first field in the table and then open the Find and Replace dialog box.

7. On the *Replace* tab of the Find and Replace dialog box:
TYPE: **Dim.** in the *Find What* combo box
PRESS: (**TAB**)
TYPE: **Dimension** in the *Replace With* combo box
The Find and Replace dialog box appears in Figure 3.39.

Figure 3.39

Find and Replace
dialog box

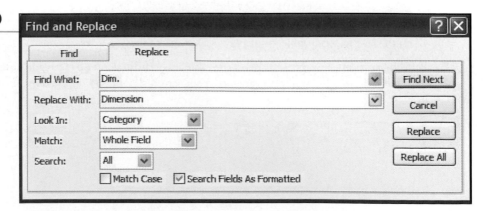

8. Proceed with the Find and Replace operation. When Access asks you to confirm the replacement:
CLICK: Yes command button

9. CLICK: Cancel to remove the Find and Replace dialog box

10. Close the Datasheet window without saving your layout changes. (*Note:* The Find and Replace changes are saved, but the repositioning of the Category column and the sort order are not saved.)

n your own

4. Working with Filters

Filtering provides an excellent method for displaying only those records that match a specific criterion. In this lesson, you will practice using the Filter For Input and Filter By Selection methods. To begin, open the "4 Contacts" table for display in Datasheet view. Then, perform the following steps:

- Apply a filter so that only the records containing the word "Club" in the VolunteerGroup field column are displayed. How many groups have "Club" as part of their name?

- Remove the current filter from displaying and then use Filter By Selection to extract those groups based in the city of Pinawa. How many groups contain "Pinawa" in the City field column?

- Remove the current filter and use the Filter By Selection method to display only those groups from the city of Centerville. How many groups contain "Centerville" in the City field column? Then, remove the filter so that all records are displayed.

- Remove the current filter and then use Filter Excluding Selection to view all groups from outside the city of Silverdale. Your screen should now appear similar to the one shown in Figure 3.40.

Figure 3.40

Using the Filter Excluding Selection method

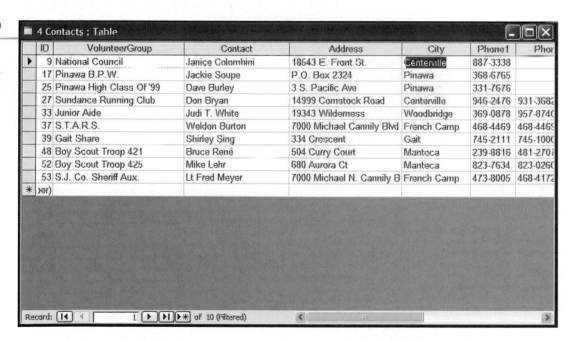

Before proceeding to the next lesson, remove the active filters and then close the Datasheet window without saving your changes.

5. Retrieving and Presenting Data

You will now practice organizing, retrieving, and manipulating data in the Datasheet window. Open the "5 Inventory" table in the AC03HE database. Perform the following database tasks:

- Using the Find and Replace command, change all records with a Supplier code of "G06" to a "J11" code.

- Use the Filter By Form method to display only those records with a Supplier "J11" code and a Buyer "02" code.

- Format the Datasheet window to display using a new and larger font.

- Hide the Reorder column.

- Adjust the widths of the remaining columns, so that no data is truncated.

- Move the Supplier column so that it appears as the first field.

- Sort the datasheet by the OnHand amount so that the record with the largest amount is at the top of the datasheet.

When you are finished (Figure 3.41), preview and then print a copy of the Datasheet window.

Figure 3.41

Filtering and formatting the "5 Inventory" datasheet

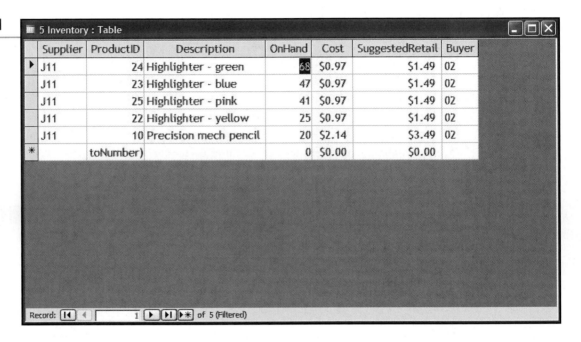

Lastly, close the Datasheet window and save your changes.

6. Using the Simple Query Wizard

You will now create a query object using the Simple Query Wizard. The objective of using a query in this exercise is to display data from two tables in the database. To begin, select the *Queries* button in the Objects bar and then launch the Simple Query Wizard. From the "6 Guides" table, include the GuideNumber and Guide fields. From the "6 Patrons" table, include the Guest, Hometown, and State fields. In the next step of the wizard, save the query as "Guides and Guests Query" and then open the query to view the results (Figure 3.42).

Figure 3.42

Displaying the
results of a
simple query

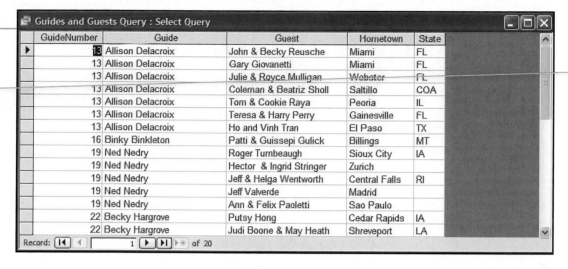

	GuideNumber	Guide	Guest	Hometown	State	
▶	13	Allison Delacroix	John & Becky Reusche	Miami	FL	
	13	Allison Delacroix	Gary Giovanetti	Miami	FL	
	13	Allison Delacroix	Julie & Royce Mulligan	Webster	FL	
	13	Allison Delacroix	Coleman & Beatriz Sholl	Saltillo	COA	
	13	Allison Delacroix	Tom & Cookie Raya	Peoria	IL	
	13	Allison Delacroix	Teresa & Harry Perry	Gainesville	FL	
	13	Allison Delacroix	Ho and Vinh Tran	El Paso	TX	
	16	Binky Binkleton	Patti & Guissepi Gulick	Billings	MT	
	19	Ned Nedry	Roger Turnbeaugh	Sioux City	IA	
	19	Ned Nedry	Hector & Ingrid Stringer	Zurich		
	19	Ned Nedry	Jeff & Helga Wentworth	Central Falls	RI	
	19	Ned Nedry	Jeff Valverde	Madrid		
	19	Ned Nedry	Ann & Felix Paoletti	Sao Paulo		
	22	Becky Hargrove	Putsy Hong	Cedar Rapids	IA	
	22	Becky Hargrove	Judi Boone & May Heath	Shreveport	LA	

Record: |◄ ◄ 1 ► ►| ►* of 20

Before printing the dynaset, enhance the datasheet by applying formatting commands and preview the contents of the Datasheet window. Then, save the layout changes and close the datasheet. Finally, close the Database window and exit Microsoft Office Access 2003.

CaseStudy   ARMSTRONG RENTALS

Ellie Floyd is the office supervisor for Armstrong Rentals, a rental and lease company that specializes in landscaping and gardening equipment. In addition to managing the administrative and inside sales staff, Ellie's recently expanded responsibilities include the company's record-keeping. The owner and manager of Armstrong Rentals, Sal Witherspoon, knows that Ellie just completed a course in Microsoft Office Access 2003. Because much of the record-keeping data is already stored in a database, Sal wants Ellie to become well versed in its operation, so that she can eventually take over the office's day-to-day management. To this end, Ellie has spent the past week familiarizing herself with the table objects in the company's Access 2003 database. Feeling confident that she now understands the nature of the table structures, she informs Sal that she is ready to begin.

In the following case problems, assume the role of Ellie and perform the same steps that she identifies.

1. To begin, Sal informs Ellie that he needs a formatted printout of Armstrong's equipment inventory. The data is stored in a table object named "Equipment" in the AC03CP database. While Sal thinks up other tasks for Ellie, she jots down a note to herself that Sal prefers all of his business correspondence and reports to appear with a 12-point Times New Roman font. She plans on opening the table in Datasheet view, applying the new font choice, and then removing the vertical gridlines from the Datasheet window. Sal now describes some more preferences. In addition to hiding the DatePurchased field column, Sal wants the Cost column to be positioned as the last column in the datasheet. Ellie makes an additional note to preview the datasheet, as shown in Figure 3.43, to ensure that the proper fields are hidden and positioned correctly. After printing the datasheet for Sal's review, Ellie saves the layout changes and closes the Datasheet window.

Access

Figure 3.43

Formatting the
"Equipment"
datasheet

2. Sal next asks Ellie to make some corrections to data stored in the "Rentals" table. She opens the datasheet and then sorts it into CustomerID sequence. Using the Find command, she locates the record for CustomerID 41. She changes the rental start date to 5/23/03 and the number of rental days to three. After returning to the top of the datasheet, Ellie moves to the Days column and then uses the Find and Replace command to change any records that have a value of zero in the Days field to the minimum rental of one day. Then Ellie uses the Filter By Selection method to display and print only the records that have a status of "Active," as shown in Figure 3.44. She closes the Datasheet window and saves the changes.

Figure 3.44

Editing and
filtering the
"Rentals"
datasheet

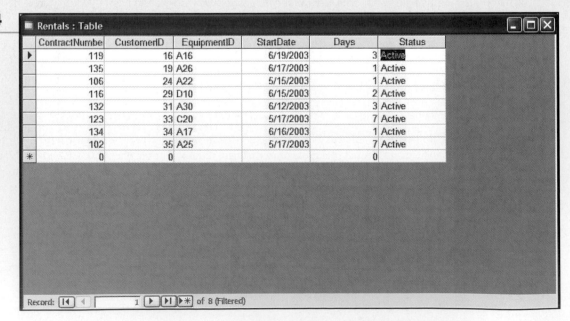

3. Before he leaves for the afternoon, Sal provides a list of questions for Ellie about Armstrong's customer base. To answer the questions, she must find, filter, and/or query the database. Using these methods, Ellie answers the following questions:

- Which customers are not eligible for a discount, as determined by a zero value in the Discount field?

- How many customers living in Pike Mountain have an account, as denoted by a check mark in the Account field column's check box?

- Which customer accounts are eligible for a discount of 10 percent on their rentals?

- How many customers are from outside the city of Kelly?

4. Finally, Ellie uses the Simple Query Wizard to create a "details" query that displays data from all three tables. She includes the following fields in the query and then saves it as "Customer Rentals Query."

Table	Field
Customers	Name
Rentals	StartDate
Rentals	Days
Rentals	Status
Equipment	Description

After the results are displayed (Figure 3.45), Ellie applies some formatting options, adjusts the column widths, saves the layout, and then prints the Datasheet window.

Figure 3.45

Resulting dynaset from a multitable query

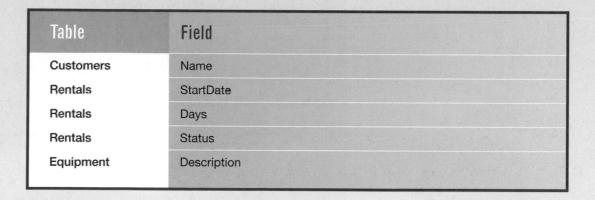

Name	StartDate	Days	Status	Description
Summit	6/16/2003	2	Reserved	High Vol Sprinkler
Finnigan	5/17/2003	7	Active	Water Level
Magnum	6/14/2003	6	Reserved	Brush Saw
Wagner	6/23/2003	5	Reserved	Trimmer
Sloan	6/1/2003	8	Complete	Tiller
Ladbroke	5/15/2003	1	Active	100' Hose
Chow	5/23/2003	3	Complete	Edger
Cordell	4/28/2003	2	Complete	Brush Saw
Boyd	4/28/2003	6	Complete	50' Hose
Phillips	6/12/2003	2	Complete	Cement Mixer
Cordell	6/30/2003	5	Reserved	50' Hose
Finnigan	6/23/2003	3	Reserved	Power Washer
Rafferty	5/2/2003	2	Reserved	Aerator
Sloan	3/1/2003	1	Complete	Water Level

Record: 1 of 36

Reflecting on the work she has already completed, Ellie closes all of the open windows, including the AC03CP Database window, and exits Microsoft Office Access 2003.

Access

Answers
to self-check questions

SelfCheck

3.1 Name two reasons for changing the field column order in a datasheet. Some reasons for changing the field order include customizing a datasheet's appearance for printing, displaying fields side by side in a datasheet, and arranging columns for performing multiple-field sort operations.

3.2 How do you perform a sort operation using more than one field column? You must first ensure that the columns are adjacent to one another. The leftmost column should contain the primary or first sort key. The next column(s) provides the secondary sort level(s). You must then select all of the columns involved in the sort operation and click the appropriate Sort button on the toolbar.

3.3 In a personnel table, how would you display a subset of those employees working in the Accounting department? Using Filter For Input, you enter "Accounting" as the criterion. Using Filter By Selection, you select "Accounting" from the datasheet. Using Filter By Form, you select "Accounting" from the drop-down list attached to the department field. You then apply and remove the filter by clicking on the Apply/Remove Filter button (▽) on the toolbar.

3.4 Name one way that a query's dynaset may differ from a table's datasheet. A query's dynaset may display results from two or more tables in the same Datasheet window.

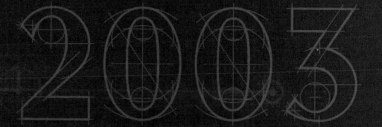

Microsoft® Office Access® 2003

CHAPTER 4

⊕ # Presenting and Managing Data

CHAPTER OUTLINE

4.1 Creating a Simple Form

4.2 Creating a Simple Report

4.3 Generating a Mailing Labels Report

4.4 Managing Database Objects

Chapter Summary

Chapter Quiz

Hands-On Exercises

Case Study

PREREQUISITES

This chapter assumes that you are familiar with creating, displaying, and editing table objects in Datasheet view. You should also know how Microsoft Office Access 2003 organizes and presents a database file's objects, including tables, queries, forms, and reports, in the Database window. Ensure also that you are familiar with printing and previewing a Datasheet window.

LEARNING OBJECTIVES

After completing this chapter, you will be able to:

- Create new forms and reports using the AutoForm and AutoReport Wizards

- Create new forms and reports using the Form and Report Wizards

- Navigate and edit data using a form

- Preview and print reports from the Database window

- Create a mailing labels report using the Label Wizard

- Rename, copy, and delete database objects

- Compact, repair, and convert a database file

4.1 Creating a Simple Form

An alternative to working with a screen full of records in a datasheet is to focus your attention on a single record at a time, using a form. Forms can be customized to display multiple records and to link with data stored in other tables. Some forms that you may find useful in your database applications include data entry forms that resemble their paper counterparts, switchboard forms that provide menus of choices, and custom dialog boxes that gather input from users. Forms serve many purposes in Microsoft Office Access 2003 and can enhance the productivity of both novice and expert users. In this module, you will learn to create forms using the Access 2003 **form wizards.**

4.1.1 Creating a Form Using the AutoForm Wizards

→ ## Feature

An **AutoForm Wizard** provides the fastest and easiest way to create a new form. Requiring minimal information from the user, the wizard analyzes a table's field structure, designs and builds the form, and then displays it in a **Form window.** There are actually five wizards from which to choose. First, the *Columnar AutoForm Wizard* displays data from one record in a single column, with each field appearing on a row. The *Tabular AutoForm Wizard* arranges data in a table format, with field labels as column headings and each row representing a record. Similarly, the *Datasheet AutoForm Wizard* creates a form of rows and columns resembling a datasheet. You can also choose from the *PivotTable* and *PivotChart AutoForm Wizards* for further options. If you choose to create an AutoForm by clicking the New Object button (⊞▾), Access creates a columnar form based on the open or selected table or query.

→ ## Method

To create a columnar form quickly:

• SELECT: a table or query object in the Database window

• CLICK: New Object: AutoForm button (⊞▾)

To create a form using an AutoForm Wizard:

• SELECT: *Forms* button in the Objects bar

• CLICK: New button (▤ New) on the Database window toolbar

• SELECT: a table or query from the drop-down list box

• DOUBLE-CLICK: an AutoForm Wizard

→ ## Practice

In this lesson, you will create forms using the New Object button and the Tabular AutoForm Wizard.

1. Load Microsoft Office Access 2003, if it is not already running.

2. Open the database file named AC0400, located in the Advantage student data files folder. The Database window in Figure 4.1 is displayed.

Figure 4.1

AC0400 Database window

3. To have Access create a form automatically, ensure that the *Tables* button is selected in the Objects bar and then:
   SELECT: Books in the table list area
   (*Hint:* You do not need to open the Books table. Click once on the table object so that it appears highlighted.)

4. Once a table (or query) is selected:
   CLICK: New Object: AutoForm button (📋▾)
   (*Hint:* The New Object button contains a list of wizards used in creating database objects. If the AutoForm image is not currently displayed on the face of the New Object button, click the attached down arrow to show the drop-down list appearing here. Then, select the AutoForm command.)

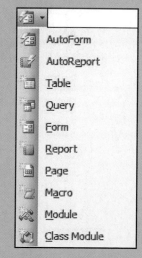

5. After a few seconds, Access displays the columnar form shown in Figure 4.2. Notice that each field appears on a separate row in the Form window. You will learn how to navigate and manipulate data in a form later in this module.

Access

Figure 4.2

A columnar form displays data for a single record

Formatting toolbar for forms and reports

Form View toolbar

Form window

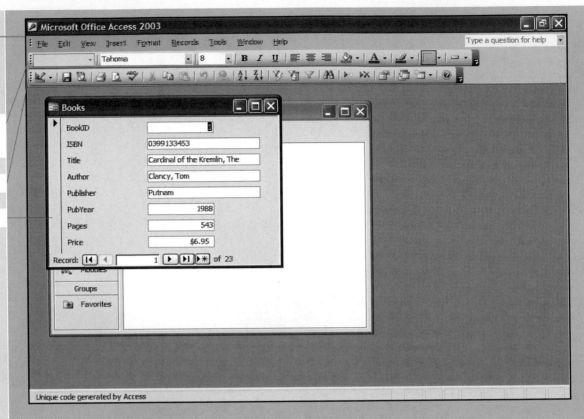

6. To close the form:
   CLICK: its Close button (X)
   The following Alert dialog box appears to inform you that the form object has not yet been saved.

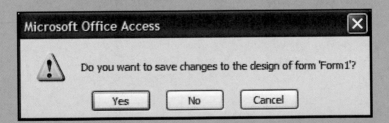

7. To proceed with saving and naming the form:
   CLICK: Yes command button

8. In the dialog box that appears:
   TYPE: **Books – Columnar** into the *Form Name* text box
   PRESS: ENTER
   or
   CLICK: OK

9. The new form object is stored in the *Forms* category of the Database window. To view the object:
   CLICK: *Forms* button in the Objects bar
   DOUBLE-CLICK: Books – Columnar in the list area
   The Form window appears as displayed previously.

10. Close the Form window.

11. Let's create a new form using a tabular layout. To begin:
    CLICK: *Tables* button in the Objects bar
    SELECT: Books in the list area, if not already selected

12. To access the other AutoForm Wizards:
CLICK: down arrow attached to the New Object button (▦▾)
CHOOSE: Form
The New Form dialog box appears, as shown in Figure 4.3.

Figure 4.3

New Form dialog box

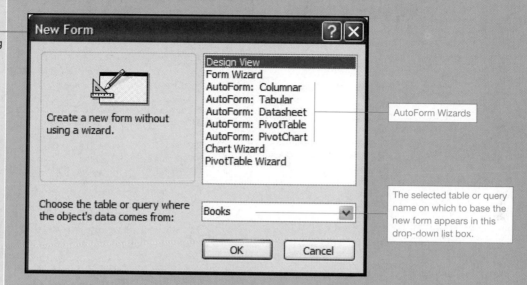

13. To create a new form using the Tabular AutoForm Wizard:
SELECT: AutoForm: Tabular
CLICK: OK command button
After a few moments, a tabular form similar to the one shown in Figure 4.4 is displayed.

Figure 4.4

A tabular form displays numerous records at the same time

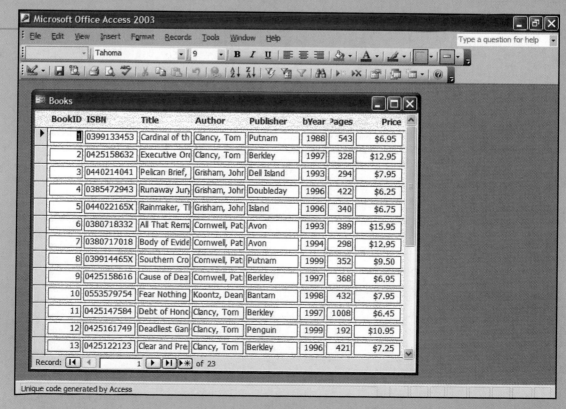

14. Close the Form window without saving the changes.

4.1.2 Creating a Form Using the Form Wizard

→ # Feature

The Form Wizard provides a step-by-step approach to creating a form from scratch. Even experienced users find the Form Wizard a handy way to get started in building a new form. Whereas an AutoForm Wizard generates a complete form using a set of default values, the Form Wizard allows you to pick and choose options from a series of dialog boxes. Using the Form Wizard, you specify what fields to display on the form and how you want it to look. The layout options include Columnar, Tabular, Datasheet, Justified, PivotTable, and PivotChart. The columnar and justified layouts are suited for viewing a single record at a time and work especially well for tables with few fields. The tabular and datasheet layouts are best used to display numerous records at a time.

→ # Method

In the Database window, select the *Forms* button and then:

- DOUBLE-CLICK: Create form by using wizard

  or

- CLICK: New button (New) on the Database window toolbar

- SELECT: a table or query from the drop-down list box

- DOUBLE-CLICK: Form Wizard

→ # Practice

You will now use the Form Wizard to create a standard form object. Ensure that the AC0400 Database window is displayed.

1. As with other database objects, you may create a form from scratch in Design view or get helpful guidance from the Access 2003 wizards. You access the Form Wizard using the New Form dialog box or by double-clicking a shortcut in the Database window. To begin:
CLICK: *Forms* button in the Objects bar

2. To launch the Form Wizard:
DOUBLE-CLICK: Create form by using wizard
The dialog box shown in Figure 4.5 appears.

Figure 4.5

Form Wizard
dialog box

Select a table or
query in order to
specify fields for
display.

Select the fields that
you want to display
on the new form.

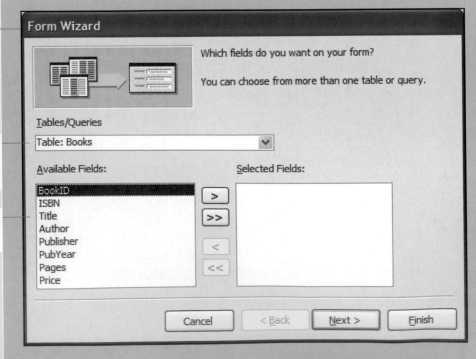

3. Let's create a form that displays the data from the Courses table:
SELECT: Table: Courses from the *Tables/Queries* drop-down list box
Notice that the table's fields are displayed in the associated list box.

4. In the *Available Fields* list box:
SELECT: Title
CLICK: Include button ( )
Notice that the Title field is no longer displayed in the *Available Fields* list box. (*Hint:* You can also double-click a field name to move it between the list boxes.)

5. Using the same process, add the Faculty, DeptHead, StartDate, and StartTime fields to the *Selected Fields* list box, in the order specified.

6. To proceed to the next step (Figure 4.6) in the wizard:
CLICK: Next >

Figure 4.6

Selecting a form layout

Preview area

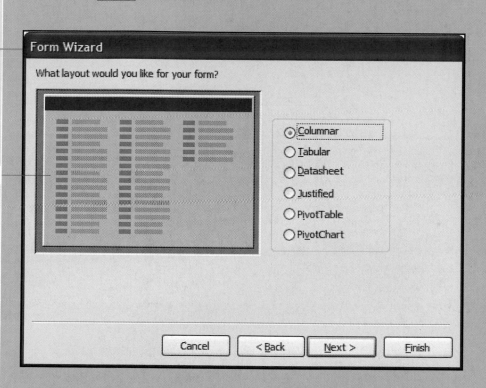

7. In this step, you will specify how to arrange the selected fields in the Form window. Notice that five of the six options (Columnar, Tabular, Datasheet, PivotTable, and PivotChart) mirror the AutoForm wizards. On your own, click the layout options one at a time to view their formats in the Preview area. When you are ready to proceed:
SELECT: *Justified* option button
CLICK: Next >

8. This step (Figure 4.7) allows you to specify a formatting style for the form. On your own, click the style names appearing in the list box in order to preview their formats. When you are ready to proceed:
SELECT: Sumi Painting
CLICK: Next >
(*Note:* The next time you use the Form Wizard, the options selected here will have become the default selections.)

Figure 4.7

Selecting a form style

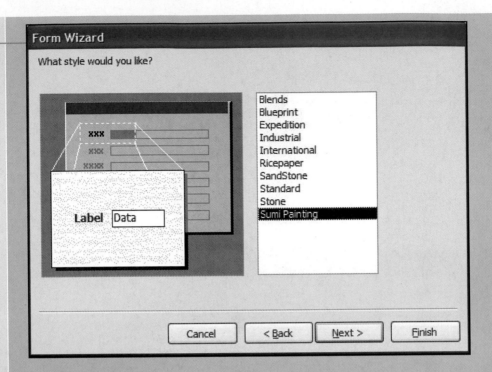

9. In the final step, you will name and then choose whether to display or modify the form. Do the following:

TYPE: **Courses – Form Wizard** in the text box

SELECT: *Open the form to view or enter information* option button, if it is not already selected

CLICK: Finish

The Form window displays only the fields selected in the Form Wizard using a justified (wrapping) layout, as shown in Figure 4.8.

Figure 4.8

A justified form created using the Form Wizard

The Courses — Form Wizard form is displayed in a Form window.

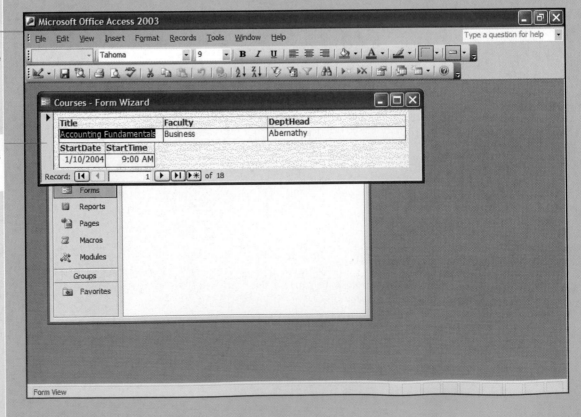

10. Close the Form window. Notice that the form name now appears in the Forms list area of the Database window.

4.1.3 Navigating Data Using a Form

→ **Feature**

An Access 2003 form provides the same navigational buttons that you find at the bottom of a Datasheet window. Use these buttons, along with the arrow keys (described further below), to move through the records in a table. To move among the fields on a form, press the arrow keys (⬆ and ⬇) or use TAB to move forward and SHIFT + TAB to move backward. You can also move quickly to the top of a form using HOME and to the last field on a form using END.

→ **Method**

Button	Keystroke	Description
⏮	CTRL + HOME	Moves to the first field of the first record
◀	PgUp	Moves to the previous record
▶	PgDn	Moves to the next record
⏭	CTRL + END	Moves to the last field of the last record

→ **Practice**

In this lesson, you will use the AutoForm Wizard to create a form and practice navigating records in the Form window. Ensure that the AC0400 Database window is displayed.

1. Let's begin by creating a new columnar form for the Courses table:
CLICK: *Tables* button in the Objects bar
SELECT: Courses in the list area

2. To launch the AutoForm Wizard:
CLICK: down arrow attached to the New Object button (⊞▾)
Notice that the New Object: Form icon appears on the face of the AutoForm button, because it was the last selection made.

3. From the drop-down menu:
CHOOSE: AutoForm
The Courses Form window appears, as shown in Figure 4.9.

Figure 4.9

Creating a
columnar
AutoForm for the
Courses table

Record selection
area

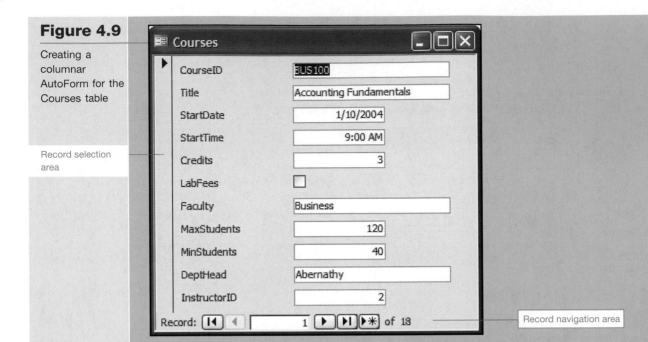

Record navigation area

4. To save the new form:
CLICK: Save button (◻)
TYPE: **Courses – AutoForm**
PRESS: ENTER

or

CLICK: OK

5. Using the form, let's display the last record in the table:
CLICK: Last Record button (▶|) at the bottom of the Form window
Notice that the record navigation area displays Record 18 of 18.

6. To move to record 15:
PRESS: PgUp three times

7. To move to the first field in the first record:
PRESS: CTRL + HOME

8. To move the cursor into the Title field:
PRESS: TAB

9. Like Datasheet view, Form view allows you to use the Find, Replace, and Sort commands. Let's use the Find command to locate all courses containing the word "database." Do the following:
CLICK: Find button (🔍)

10. In the Find and Replace dialog box:
TYPE: **database** in the *Find What* combo box
SELECT: Any Part of Field in the *Match* drop-down list box
Your screen should now appear similar to the one shown in Figure 4.10.

Figure 4.10

Using the Find command in Form view

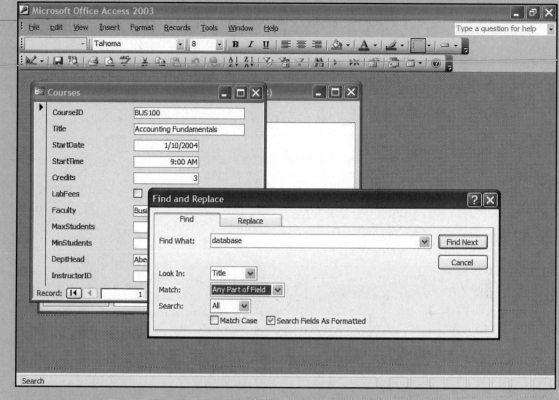

11. To proceed with the search procedure:
CLICK: Find Next command button

12. Access moves the cursor to the first matching record, "Database Fundamentals" in Record 7. If the Find and Replace dialog box is covering the form, move the window by dragging its Title bar.

13. In the Find and Replace dialog box, continue the search:
CLICK: Find Next command button
The next record, "Database Programming" in Record 8, is displayed.

14. CLICK: Cancel button to close the Find and Replace dialog box

15. Close the Form window.

4.1.4 Working with a Form

→ **Feature**

The methods for editing data in Form view are nearly identical to those for editing in Datasheet view. Nevertheless, many people find it easier to edit field data using a form, preferring the less cluttered interface and the ability to focus attention on a single record. After reading this lesson, you may also find it easier to add, delete, sort, and filter a table's records using a form.

→ **Method**

Toolbar buttons available for working with forms include the following:

• CLICK: New Record button (▶*) to add a new record

• CLICK: Delete Record button (▶◀) to remove a record

• CLICK: Sort Ascending button (A↓) to sort into ascending order

- CLICK: Sort Descending button (⤓) to sort into descending order

- CLICK: Print Preview button (🔍) to preview a form

- CLICK: Print button (🖨) to print a form

→ Practice

You will now practice sorting, adding, and deleting records, and previewing how a form will appear when printed. Ensure that you have completed the previous lesson and that the AC0400 Database window is displayed.

1. Let's start by displaying the form that you created in the last lesson:
CLICK: *Forms* button in the Objects bar
DOUBLE-CLICK: Courses – AutoForm in the list area

2. Using `PgDn` and `PgUp`, navigate through the records and take notice of the ascending CourseID sort order. To return to the first field in the first record, do the following:
PRESS: `CTRL` + `HOME`

3. Now let's sort the table's records into ascending order by course title. To begin:
PRESS: `TAB` to position the cursor in the Title field
CLICK: Sort Ascending button (⤒)

4. While the first record, "Accounting Fundamentals," remains displayed, press the `PgDn` and `PgUp` keys to see that the table is now sorted alphabetically by course title.

5. Let's add a new record to the table:
CLICK: New Record button (▶*) on the toolbar
An empty form appears, as shown in Figure 4.11, with "Record 19" in the record navigation area.

Figure 4.11

Adding a new
record using a
blank form

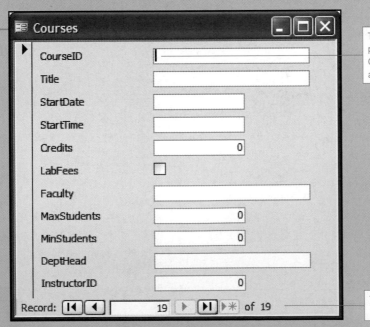

The flashing insertion point shows that the CourseID field is active and awaiting your entry.

The new record is number 19 of 19 total records.

6. Enter the information appearing in Figure 4.12. Use the `TAB` key to move forward and `SHIFT` + `TAB` to move backward, if necessary. As you type, notice the pencil icon (🖉) that appears in the record selection area of the form. When you reach the LabFees field, press the Space Bar to toggle the check box to "Yes." For the last field, InstructorID, enter the value but do not press `TAB` or `ENTER`. In other words, leave the insertion point in the InstructorID field.

Figure 4.12

Entering data into a new record

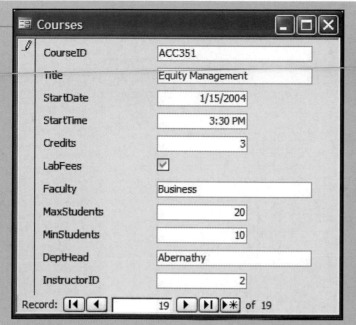

7. To save the record:
   PRESS: SHIFT + ENTER
   Notice that the pencil icon (✐) disappears from the record selection area.

8. Now let's remove a record from the table:
   PRESS: PgUp until you reach "Object-Oriented Design" in Record 14
   CLICK: Delete Record button (✕)
   The following dialog box appears.

9. To confirm the deletion:
   CLICK: Yes command button
   Notice that the record navigation area now shows 18 as the total number of records.

10. To preview how a form will print:
    CLICK: Print Preview button (🔍)

11. On your own, enlarge the Print Preview window and then use the magnifying glass mouse pointer to zoom in on the image. Your screen should appear similar to the one shown in Figure 4.13.

Figure 4.13

Previewing
a form

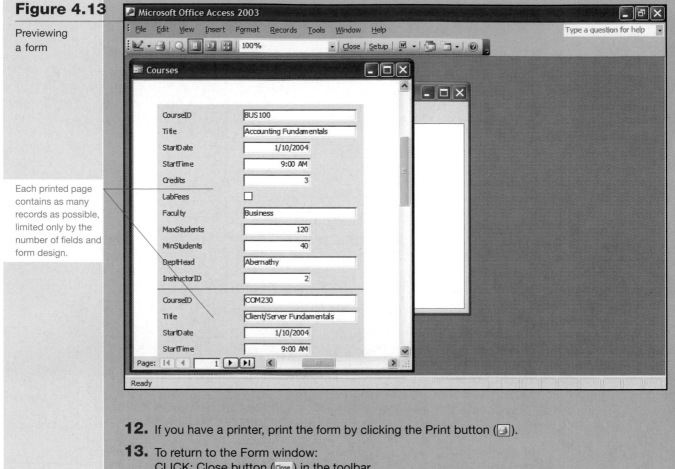

Each printed page
contains as many
records as possible,
limited only by the
number of fields and
form design.

12. If you have a printer, print the form by clicking the Print button (⊟).

13. To return to the Form window:
CLICK: Close button (⌐Close⌐) in the toolbar

14. You may have noticed that the Form window maintains the same size as the Print Preview window. On your own, practice resizing the Courses Form window to appear similar to the window's size and shape shown in Figure 4.12.

15. Close the Form window.

 **4.1** Name the layout options for designing a form using the Form Wizard.

4.2 Creating a Simple Report

A report provides a structured display format for presenting a table's data or a query's results. Although most reports are designed for printing, you can also save reports as graphic snapshots or as Web pages. To capture and retain the attention of readers, each report may contain a variety of design elements, such as fonts, lines, borders, colors, graphics, and white space. In addition to jazzing up reports, these elements combine with powerful features for summarizing data to present information clearly and concisely. Each day, people make important decisions using reports obtained from database management systems. Potential uses for reports in a typical business database application include invoices, mailing labels, address books, product catalogs, and inventory listings. In this module, you will learn to create reports using the Access 2003 **report wizards**.

4.2.1 Creating a Report Using the AutoReport Wizards

→ ## Feature

What AutoForm Wizards do for forms, AutoReport Wizards do for reports. Using an **AutoReport Wizard,** you can create a professionally designed report with the click of a button. Access 2003 provides two types of AutoReport wizards, Columnar and Tabular. Clicking the New Object button for a report (🖳▾) generates a relatively unattractive columnar report that presents data down a single column. The Tabular option, selected from the New Report dialog box, prepares a much nicer-looking report.

→ ## Method

To create a columnar report quickly:

• SELECT: a table or query object in the Database window

• CLICK: New Object: AutoReport button (🖳▾)

To create a report using an AutoReport Wizard:

• SELECT: *Reports* button in the Objects bar

• CLICK: New button (🖳 New) on the Database window toolbar

• SELECT: a table or query from the drop-down list box

• DOUBLE-CLICK: an AutoReport Wizard

→ ## Practice

In this lesson, you will create a columnar report using the AutoReport Wizard. Ensure that the AC0400 Database window is displayed.

1. The first step is to select a table or query for which you want to produce a report. To begin:
CLICK: *Tables* button in the Objects bar
SELECT: Instructors in the list area
(*Hint:* You do not need to open the Instructors table. Click once on the table object so that it appears highlighted.)

2. To generate a report using the AutoReport Wizard:
CLICK: New Object: AutoReport button (🖳▾) from the toolbar
(*Hint:* The New Object button contains a list of wizards used in creating database objects. To access the AutoReport button (🖳▾), click the attached down arrow and then select the command from the drop-down menu.)

3. Access 2003 opens a columnar report in the Print Preview window. Each field from the Instructors table appears on a separate row in the report. On your own, use the magnifying glass mouse pointer to zoom in and out on the report (Figure 4.14).

Figure 4.14

A columnar
report created
using the
AutoReport
Wizard

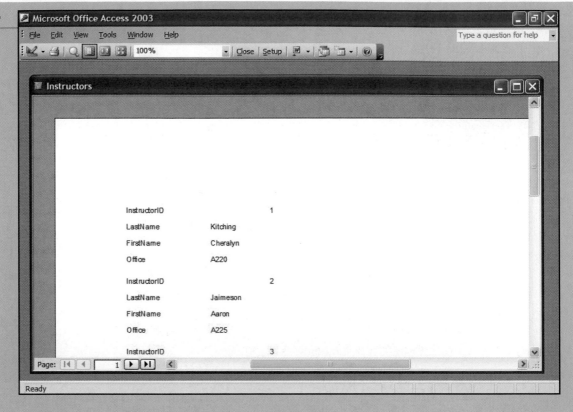

4. To close the report:
CLICK: its Close button (X)
The following dialog box appears, asking whether you want to save the new report.

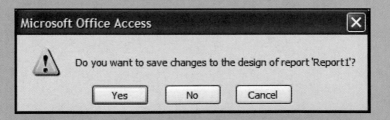

5. To save the report:
CLICK: Yes command button
TYPE: **Instructors – Columnar**
PRESS: ENTER

or

CLICK: OK

6. To view the new object in the Database window:
CLICK: *Reports* button in the Objects bar
DOUBLE-CLICK: Instructors – Columnar in the list area
The report opens up into the Print Preview window.

7. When you are finished viewing the report, close the Print Preview window by clicking its Close
button (X).

4.2.2 Creating a Report Using the Report Wizard

→ **Feature**

The Report Wizard lets you select options from a series of dialog boxes when constructing a new report. After selecting the fields to display, you determine the grouping and subtotal levels, sorting options, and presentation styles. Once a report has been created and saved, you can preview and print the report at any time.

→ **Method**

In the Database window, select the *Reports* button and then:

- DOUBLE-CLICK: Create report by using wizard

  or

- CLICK: New button (New) on the Database window toolbar

- SELECT: a table or query from the drop-down list box

- DOUBLE-CLICK: Report Wizard

→ **Practice**

You will now use the Report Wizard to create a tabular report. Ensure that the AC0400 Database window is displayed.

1. To launch the Report Wizard, ensure that the *Reports* button is selected in the Database window and then:
DOUBLE-CLICK: Create report by using wizard
The first dialog box of the Report Wizard appears. Notice the similarity between this dialog box and the Form Wizard shown in Figure 4.5.

2. To create a report that displays data from the Students table:
SELECT: Table: Students from the *Tables/Queries* drop-down list box

3. In the *Available Fields* list box, select the following fields to include in the report:
DOUBLE-CLICK: LastName
DOUBLE-CLICK: FirstName
DOUBLE-CLICK: Major
DOUBLE-CLICK: GradYear
DOUBLE-CLICK: GPA

4. To proceed to the next step in the wizard:
CLICK: Next >

5. In the second step of the wizard, Access 2003 lets you specify grouping levels so that you may better organize your data and perform subtotal calculations. To group the student records by the student's selected major:
DOUBLE-CLICK: Major in the list box
As shown in Figure 4.15, the layout preview area is updated to help you visualize the grouping options selected.

Access

Figure 4.15

Report Wizard
dialog box:
grouping levels

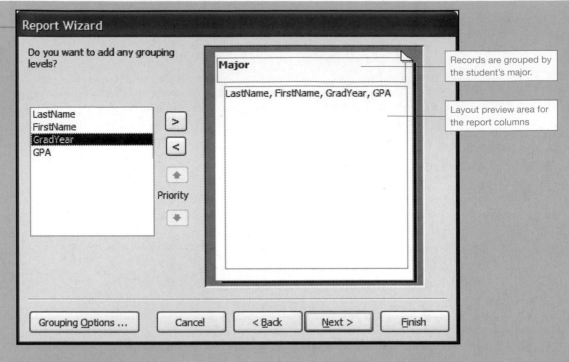

Records are grouped by
the student's major.

Layout preview area for
the report columns

6. To proceed to the next step:
CLICK: Next >

7. In this step, you will specify sorting options for the report. Since the report is already grouped
(and thus sorted) by major, let's further sort the report alphabetically by name. Do the following:
CLICK: down arrow attached to the first drop-down list box
SELECT: LastName
CLICK: down arrow attached to the second drop-down list box
SELECT: FirstName
The wizard's dialog box should now look like the one shown in Figure 4.16. (*Hint:* If necessary,
you can click the Sort Ascending button that appears to the right of each drop-down list box in
order to toggle between ascending and descending order.)

Figure 4.16

Report Wizard
dialog box:
sorting

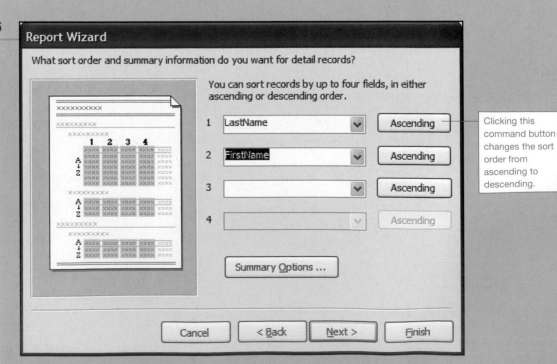

Clicking this
command button
changes the sort
order from
ascending to
descending.

8. If the selected table or query contains numeric or currency fields, you can also use this step in the Report Wizard dialog box to include summary calculations in the report. To illustrate:
CLICK: Summary Options command button
The Summary Options dialog box (Figure 4.17) is displayed showing the fields that are eligible for performing calculations.

9. There are four summary calculations from which to choose. The Sum option totals record values stored in a field, and the Avg option calculates the arithmetic mean or average. The Min and Max options find the minimum and maximum values in a field, respectively. For those fields you sum, you can also calculate each record's percent share of the total value.

   In the Students table, these calculations provide no real benefit toward better understanding the GradYear field. However, summarizing the student grade point averages might provide useful information. To proceed, complete the Summary Options dialog box to match the selections shown in Figure 4.17.

Figure 4.17

Report Wizard
dialog box:
Summary Options

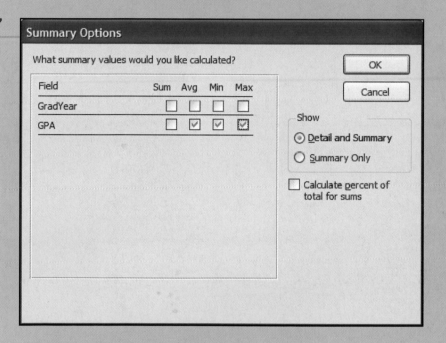

10. To accept the choices made in the Summary Options dialog box and proceed to the next step:
CLICK: OK command button
CLICK: Next >

11. You will now specify the desired layout and page orientation settings for the report. For grouping data, the Report Wizard provides nice formats for separating and organizing the information. Do the following:
SELECT: *Outline 1* option button in the *Layout* area
SELECT: *Portrait* option button in the *Orientation* area
Your screen should appear similar to the one shown in Figure 4.18.

Figure 4.18

Report Wizard
dialog box:
layout and
orientation
options

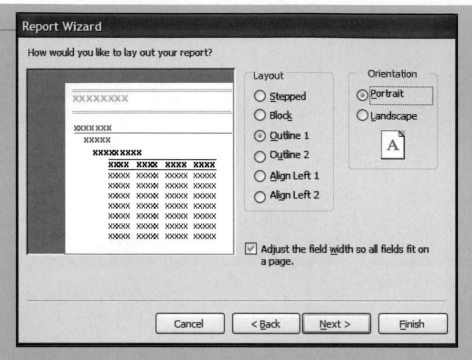

12. CLICK: Next > to proceed to the next step

13. As in the Form Wizard dialog box shown in Figure 4.7, you are now asked to select a style for your report. A style is a formatting template that Access 2003 applies to change the look and feel of a report. On your own, click on the style options in the list box to preview their formats. When you are ready to proceed:
SELECT: Corporate
CLICK: Next >

14. In the final step, name the report and determine whether to preview it or perform additional modifications. Do the following:
TYPE: **Students – By Major**
SELECT: *Preview the report* option button
CLICK: Finish
The report is displayed in the Print Preview window, as shown in Figure 4.19.

Figure 4.19

Previewing the report Students – By Major

Student records are grouped according to major.

Within each grouping by major, student records are sorted alphabetically, first by last name and then by first name.

Page navigation area

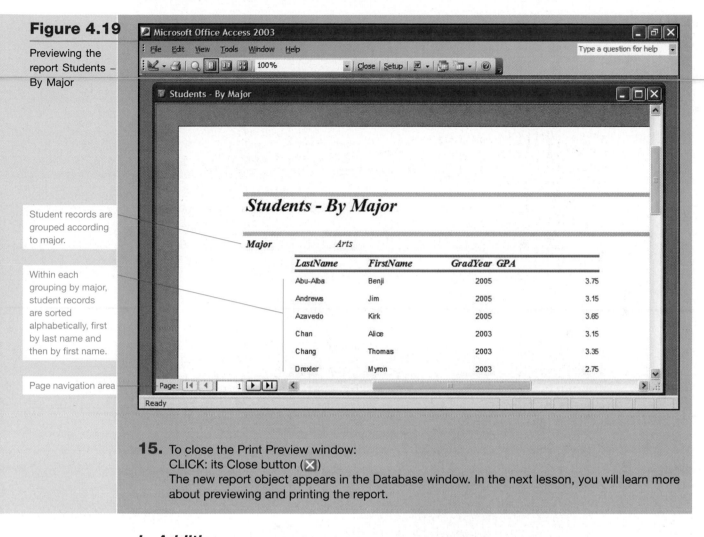

15. To close the Print Preview window:
CLICK: its Close button (✕)
The new report object appears in the Database window. In the next lesson, you will learn more about previewing and printing the report.

In Addition USING FORM AND REPORT DESIGN VIEWS

Although the form and report wizards let you immediately create usable objects, you may want to create a form or report from scratch or modify an existing object. Although the specifics are not covered in this chapter, you can further customize forms and reports in Design view.

4.2.3 Previewing and Printing a Report

→ Feature

Whereas you open tables, queries, and forms, you **preview** and print reports. Double-clicking a report object in the Database window opens the report for display in a Print Preview window. In this mode, you can navigate pages, zoom in and out, and modify page setup options. You can also send a report to the printer from the Print Preview window.

→ Method

To preview a report after selecting it in the Database window:

• CLICK: Print Preview button (🔍) to preview the report

   or

• CHOOSE: File → Print Preview

Access

To print a report after selecting it in the Database window:

- CLICK: Print button (🖨) to print the report

  or

- CHOOSE: File → Print

To specify print options:

- CHOOSE: File → Page Setup

→ # Practice

You will now display and print a report using the Print Preview window. Ensure that you have completed the previous lesson and that the *Reports* button is selected in the AC0400 Database window.

1. To display a report in Print Preview mode:
DOUBLE-CLICK: Students – By Major in the list area

2. Let's maximize the Print Preview window for a better view:
CLICK: its Maximize button (□)
Your screen should now appear similar to the one shown in Figure 4.20. (*Hint:* If your Print Preview window does not appear as shown, ensure that the "Fit" option is selected in the Zoom button (Fit ▾) on the toolbar. You can also click the One Page button (□) to yield the same effect.)

Figure 4.20

Maximized Print Preview window

The Zoom button displays "Fit" in order to shrink the report page to fit in a single screen.

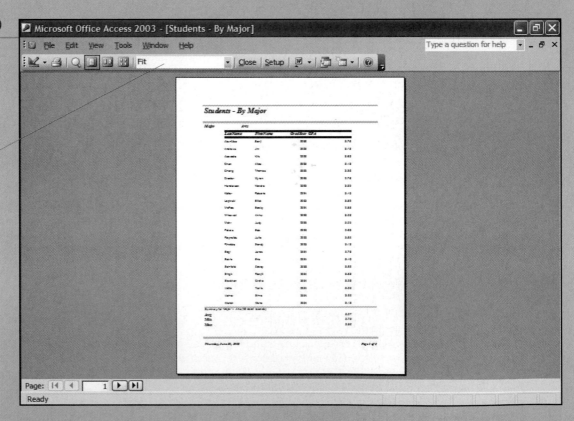

3. On your own, move among the pages using the navigation buttons appearing at the bottom of the Print Preview window. When you are ready to proceed, return to Page 1 of the report.

4. To view two pages of the report side by side:
CLICK: Two Pages button (□)
(*Hint:* For more options, choose the View, Pages command.)

5. On your own, zoom in and out on different areas of the preview. Take special note of the summary calculations appearing at the end of a category grouping, as shown in Figure 4.21.

Figure 4.21

Zooming in on the summary calculations

Mikowski	Arthur	2005	3.25
Mohr	Judy	2003	3.00
Peters	Bob	2003	2.95
Reynolds	Julie	2003	3.50
Rinaldo	Sandy	2003	3.15
Sagi	Janos	2004	2.75
Sakic	Eric	2004	3.15
Seinfeld	Casey	2005	3.50
Singh	Ranjitt	2004	3.65
Stockton	Gretta	2004	3.25
Vallie	Terris	2004	3.25
Veiner	Sima	2004	3.50
Walsh	Moira	2004	3.15

Summary for 'Major' = Arts (23 detail records)

Avg 3.27
Min 2.75
Max 3.80

Summary calculations appear at the end of each category grouping.

6. To view multiple pages:
CLICK: Multiple Pages button ()
SELECT: 1×3 Pages in the drop-down menu that appears, as shown here

1x3 Pages

7. To return to viewing a single page:
CLICK: One Page button ()

8. Now let's practice using the Zoom feature:
CLICK: down arrow attached to the Zoom button (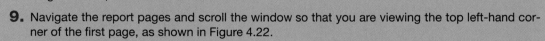)
SELECT: 150%
(*Hint:* You can also choose the View, Zoom command to change the magnification.)

9. Navigate the report pages and scroll the window so that you are viewing the top left-hand corner of the first page, as shown in Figure 4.22.

Figure 4.22

Manipulating the
Print Preview
window

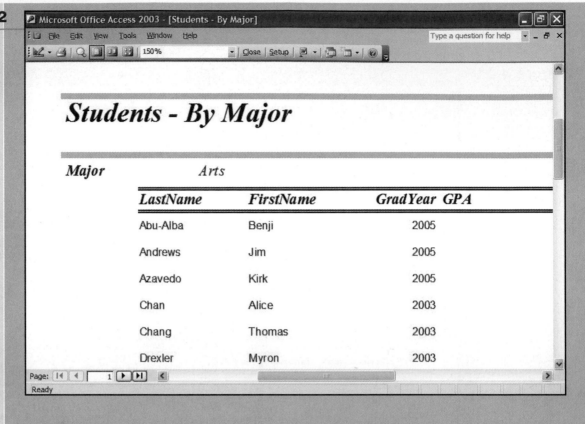

10. To restore the Print Preview window to a window:
CLICK: its Restore button (⟐)

11. If you have a printer, print the report by clicking the Print button (🖨).

12. Close the Print Preview window by clicking its Close button (✕). You are returned to the Database window.

In Addition PRINTING A REPORT FROM THE DATABASE WINDOW

You can preview or print a datasheet, query, form, or report by right-clicking the desired object in the Database window and then choosing a command. From the right-click or shortcut menu that appears, choose Print Preview to open the object in a Print Preview window or choose the Print command to send it directly to the printer.

4.2.4 Publishing HTML and XML Documents

→ **Feature**

The **World Wide Web** is an exciting medium for exchanging data. Using **Internet** technologies, the Web provides an easy-to-use multimedia interface for finding information stored on a Web server anywhere on the planet. Access 2003 makes it simple for you to tap the power of the Web. Once you have created a database object such as a table or report, you can export the object using **HTML** (Hypertext Markup Language) and **XML** (Extensible Markup Language) formats. Because HTML documents provide only a static representation or snapshot of a database, Access 2003 provides several additional tools, such as Data Access Pages, for creating dynamic real-time Web applications.

→ ## Method

After selecting an object in the Database window:

- CHOOSE: File → Export
- TYPE: **filename** for the Web document
- SELECT: HTML Documents or XML in the *Save as type* drop-down list box
- CLICK: Export command button

→ ## Practice

In this lesson, you will export database objects as HTML and XML documents. Ensure that you have completed the previous lessons and that the *Reports* button is selected in the AC0400 Database window.

1. To export a report for HTML publishing to the Web:
SELECT: Students – By Major
The object name must appear highlighted in the list area.

2. CHOOSE: File → Export
The Export Report dialog box appears, similar to the one shown in Figure 4.23.

Figure 4.23

Export dialog box

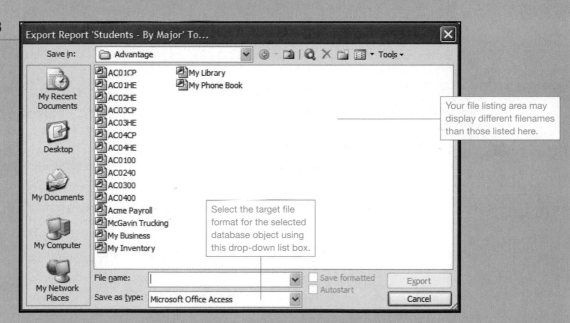

Export Report 'Students - By Major' To...

Save in: Advantage

My Recent Documents
Desktop
My Documents
My Computer
My Network Places

AC01CP
AC01HE
AC02HE
AC03CP
AC03HE
AC04CP
AC04HE
AC0100
AC0240
AC0300
AC0400
Acme Payroll
McGavin Trucking
My Business
My Inventory
My Library
My Phone Book

Your file listing area may display different filenames than those listed here.

Select the target file format for the selected database object using this drop-down list box.

File name:

Save as type: Microsoft Office Access

Save formatted
Autostart

Export
Cancel

3. Using the Places bar or the *Save in* drop-down list box, select your personal storage location. Then, in the *File name* text box:
TYPE: **Students – Web Page**

4. In the *Save as type* drop-down list box
SELECT: HTML Documents
(*Note:* The listing area will clear to display only the existing HTML documents in the target folder.)

5. To proceed with the export:
CLICK: Export command button
The HTML Output Options dialog box appears, as shown in Figure 4.24. This dialog box allows you to specify a template for enhancing the report's appearance, navigation, and formatting.

Access

Figure 4.24

HTML Output
Options dialog
box

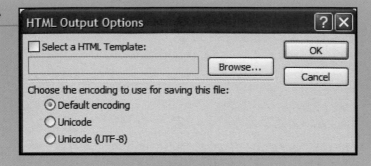

6. To continue without specifying an HTML template:
CLICK: OK command button

7. The export process creates one HTML document for each page of the report. You are then returned to the Database window. If you have access to Web browser software, open one of the pages for viewing. Click the hyperlinks appearing at the bottom of the page to navigate the report pages. Figure 4.25 provides an example of how the first page of the report is displayed using Internet Explorer. (*Note:* You can import the HTML pages into a Web application, such as Microsoft Office FrontPage 2003, in order to enhance their formatting.)

Figure 4.25

Viewing a report
page using
Internet Explorer

Access truncates
the Title during
export.

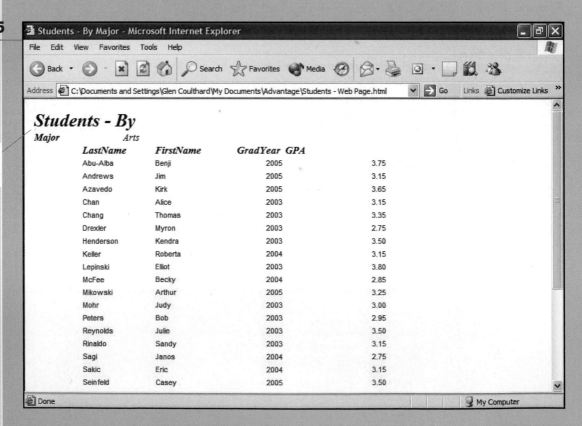

8. Now let's export a table object as an XML document. Do the following:
CLICK: *Tables* button in the Objects bar
SELECT: Courses in the table list area

9. To display the Export Table dialog box:
CHOOSE: File ➔ Export

10. Using the Places bar or the *Save in* drop-down list box, select your personal storage location. Then, in the *File name* text box:
TYPE: **Courses – XML** in the *File name* text box
SELECT: XML in the *Save as type* drop-down list box

11. To proceed with the export:
CLICK: Export command button
The Export XML dialog box appears, as shown in Figure 4.26. This dialog box allows you to specify the information and how it is to be exported.

Figure 4.26

Export XML dialog box

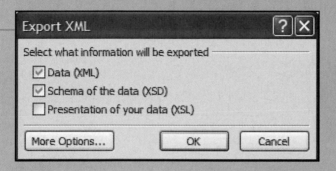

12. To proceed with the default selections:
CLICK: OK command button

13. The default selections shown in Figure 4.26 create two files—an XML document containing the table data and an XSD document containing the schema specifications. You are then returned to the Database window. If you have access to Web browser software or a text editor, open the Courses – XML page for viewing. Figure 4.27 shows an example of how Internet Explorer parses the information stored in an XML document for display.

Figure 4.27

Displaying an XML document using Internet Explorer

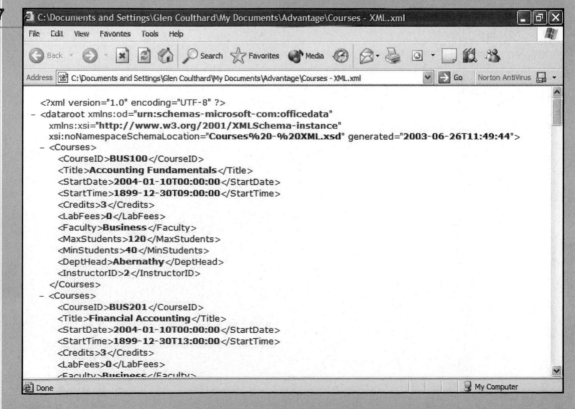

14. When you are ready to proceed, close the Internet Explorer application window (or text editor) and return to the AC0400 Database window.

In Addition SAVING A REPORT AS A SNAPSHOT

If you regularly need to print, photocopy, and distribute Access 2003 reports, consider sending a **report snapshot** instead. A snapshot, which is stored as a graphic metafile on a disk, contains a static image of each page in a report. To create a snapshot, select the desired report in the Database window and then choose the File, Export command. After specifying a name and storage location, select "Snapshot Format" as the file type. Once the snapshot file is saved, you can distribute it via electronic mail or post it to your Web site.

SelfCheck   **4.2**   What does the term "grouping data" refer to in a report?

4.3 Generating a Mailing Labels Report

Using your database to print mailing labels can save you a lot of time in preparing envelopes for greeting cards, birth announcements, or other special mailings. You can even keep track of your computer disks and files in a database and then prepare diskette labels (Avery Product Number 5296) using a report object. In this module, you will learn to create, format, and print mailing labels using the Label Wizard.

4.3.1 Creating a Report Using the Label Wizard

→ **Feature**

The Access 2003 **Label Wizard** provides an easy way for you to create a mailing labels report and print standard labels that fit on envelopes, packages, and diskettes. There are a variety of different uses for this wizard, and you may customize its output to meet your needs.

→ **Method**

In the Database window, select the *Reports* button and then:

- CLICK: New button () on the Database window toolbar
- SELECT: a table or query from the drop-down list box
- DOUBLE-CLICK: Label Wizard

→ **Practice**

You will now create a mailing labels report for the Students table. Ensure that the AC0400 Database window is displayed.

1. Let's generate mailing labels for the Students table. Begin by displaying the New Report dialog box (Figure 4.28):
SELECT: *Reports* button in the Objects bar
CLICK: New button (New) on the Database window toolbar

Figure 4.28

New Report dialog box

2. Now launch the Label Wizard for the Students table:
SELECT: Label Wizard in the list area
SELECT: Students in the *Choose the table . . .* drop-down list box
CLICK: OK command button
The first dialog box for the Label Wizard appears, as shown in Figure 4.29. You use this dialog box to specify the label size and format.

Figure 4.29

Label Wizard dialog box: type of label

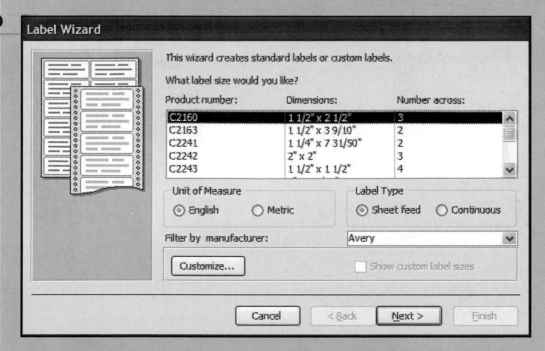

3. For a standard mailing labels report, let's confirm a few settings:
SELECT: English option button in the *Unit of Measure* area
SELECT: Sheet feed option button in the *Label Type* area
SELECT: Avery in the *Filter by manufacturer* drop-down list box
SELECT: 5160 in the *Product number* column
CLICK: Next >

4. In this step, you will select the font used for the labels. Do the following:
SELECT: Times New Roman from the *Font name* drop-down list box
SELECT: 10 from the *Font size* drop-down list box
Your screen should now appear similar to the one shown in Figure 4.30.

Figure 4.30

Label Wizard
dialog box: font
selection

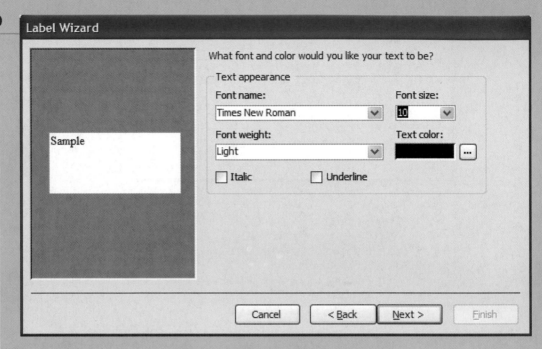

5. To proceed:
CLICK: Next >

6. You will now build the appearance of the label by entering text or selecting fields. In the *Available fields* list box:
DOUBLE-CLICK: FirstName
PRESS: Space Bar
DOUBLE-CLICK: LastName
PRESS: **ENTER**
Notice how you must enter spaces between fields and break the label into lines.

7. To finish creating the label:
DOUBLE-CLICK: Address
PRESS: **ENTER**
DOUBLE-CLICK: City
TYPE: , (a single comma)
PRESS: Space Bar
DOUBLE-CLICK: State
PRESS: Space Bar
DOUBLE-CLICK: Zip
Your label should now appear similar to the one shown in Figure 4.31.

Figure 4.31

Label Wizard
dialog box:
adding fields

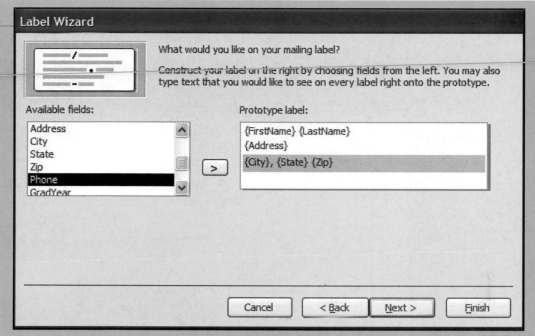

8. To proceed to the next step:
   CLICK: Next >

9. You are now asked to specify a sort order for the mailing labels. Common sort orders for mailing labels include by zip code and by alphabetical last name. To sort the labels by student name:
   DOUBLE-CLICK: LastName in the *Available fields* list box
   DOUBLE-CLICK: FirstName in the *Available fields* list box
   CLICK: Next >

10. In the final step, you name the mailing label report and specify whether to display or modify the label design. To accept the default selections:
    CLICK: Finish

11. If the following dialog box appears, you can ignore the warning and continue by clicking the OK command button.

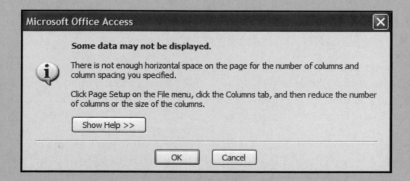

12. After a few moments, the mailing label report appears in the Print Preview window (Figure 4.32). On your own, zoom in and out on pages in the Print Preview window.

Figure 4.32

Label report generated by the Label Wizard

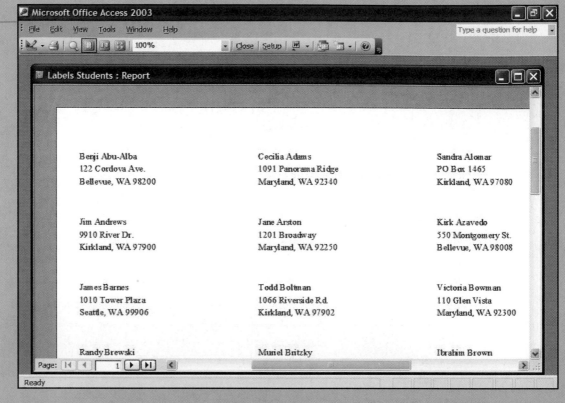

13. If you have a printer, print the report by clicking the Print button (🖨).

14. Close the Print Preview window by clicking its Close button (✖). You are returned to the Database window.

 **SelfCheck**   **4.3**   How could you use table and report objects to print diskette labels?

4.4 Managing Database Objects

As you continue to use Access 2003, you will create many databases and many database objects, and it is important that you know how to manage them properly. Effective file and disk management techniques also help you to secure and protect your data. In this module, you will learn to rename, copy, and delete objects in the Database window and to compress and repair a database file.

4.4.1 Renaming, Copying, and Deleting Objects

→ **Feature**

Like performing routine file management procedures using Windows Explorer, renaming, copying, and deleting the individual objects stored in a database is simple. In a sense, the Access 2003 wizards make it too easy to create database objects. Novice users commonly have Database windows overflowing with trial editions of objects. Users quickly create a form or report using a wizard only to find that they need to make a few improvements. Because creating a new wizard-generated object is often easier than editing the existing one, the Database window can become overpopulated quickly. To avoid capacity and performance issues, these trial objects should be removed from the Database window.

→ Method

After right-clicking the desired database object, choose from the following options:

- CHOOSE: Rename to rename an object,

  or

  PRESS: **F2**

- CHOOSE: Cut to move an object,

  or

  CLICK: Cut button (⊠)

- CHOOSE: Copy to copy an object,

  or

  CLICK: Copy button (⊠)

- CHOOSE: Paste to paste an object,

  or

  CLICK: Paste button (⊠)

- CHOOSE: Delete to remove an object,

  or

  CLICK: Delete button (⊠)

→ Practice

You will now practice managing objects in the AC0400 database. Ensure that the AC0400 Database window is displayed.

1. To begin, let's display the table objects:
CLICK: *Tables* button in the Objects bar

2. Let's practice adjusting the view options in the list area:
CLICK: Large Icons button (⊠) on the Database window toolbar
Your Database window should resemble the one shown in Figure 4.33.

Figure 4.33

Adjusting view options in the Database window

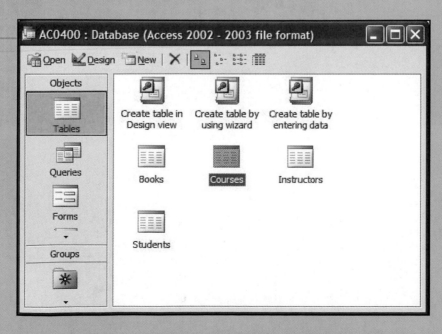

3. CLICK: Small icons button ( ) to view smaller icons
CLICK: Details button ( ) to view additional information
CLICK: List button ( ) to return to the standard view
(*Hint:* You can change the appearance and order in which the objects are displayed by choosing the View and the View, Arrange Icons commands.)

4. To rename the Books table object to Fiction:
CLICK: the name "Books" once so that it appears highlighted
CLICK: the name "Books" again to enter Edit mode, as shown here
(*Hint:* You can also select an object and press **F2** to enter Edit mode. Notice that you click the name and not the icon to rename an object.)

5. To rename the table object:
TYPE: **Fiction**
PRESS: **ENTER**

6. Let's create a copy of the Fiction object and name it Non-Fiction:
SELECT: Fiction, if it is not already selected
CLICK: Copy button ( ) on the toolbar
CLICK: Paste button ( ) on the toolbar
The Paste Table As dialog box appears, as shown in Figure 4.34.

Figure 4.34

Paste Table As
dialog box

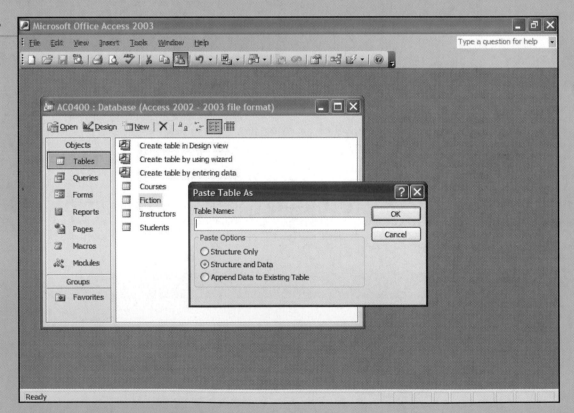

7. To complete the paste operation:
TYPE: **Non-Fiction** in the *Table Name* text box
SELECT: *Structure Only* option button
CLICK: OK command button
(*Note:* In this step, you will copy only the structure, because the data stored in the Fiction table is not required for the Non-Fiction table.)

8. To delete an object using the right-click menu:
RIGHT-CLICK: Non-Fiction
CHOOSE: Delete
The following dialog box appears.

Microsoft Office Access [X]

Do you want to delete the table 'Non-Fiction'?

For more information on how to prevent this message from displaying every time you delete an object, click Help.

[Yes] [No] [Help]

9. To confirm the deletion of the table object:
CLICK: Yes command button
The table object is removed from the Database window.

4.4.2 Compacting, Repairing, and Converting a Database

→ **Feature**

An Access 2003 database file is stored on the disk with the file extension .mdb. When you make several changes to a database, such as copying and deleting objects, the file may become fragmented. Compacting a database reorganizes and packs the file more closely together, and repairing a database verifies the reliability of objects. An added benefit for those tables that contain AutoNumber fields, and where records have been deleted from the end of the table, is that compacting resets the field to the next sequential value. As a result, the next record added to the table will have an AutoNumber value that is one more than the last record in the table. In addition to saving disk space and resetting AutoNumber fields, compacting a database improves a database's performance.

Before sharing a database with another user or using a database in another application, you may need to first convert the file to another version of Access. For example, an associate using Microsoft Access 97 will not be able to work with your database files unless you first convert them to the Access 97 file format. Both the Access 2000 and Access 2002–2003 file formats, however, are native to Microsoft Access 2002. Perhaps surprisingly, Microsoft Office Access 2003 defaults to creating databases in the Access 2000 file format to maintain compatibility with older software, although this can be changed using the Tools → Options command. Before compacting or converting a database, remember to use the Windows Explorer or another utility to back up your database file.

→ **Method**

To compact and repair a database:

• CHOOSE: Tools → Database Utilities → Compact and Repair Database

To convert a database to another version:

• CHOOSE: Tools → Database Utilities → Convert Database

Access

→ **Practice**

In this lesson, you will compact and then convert the AC0400 database file. Ensure that the AC0400 Database window is displayed.

1. To compact and repair the AC0400 database:
CHOOSE: Tools → Database Utilities
The menu commands for converting, compressing, repairing, and maintaining a database appear.

2. CHOOSE: Compact and Repair Database
The automated process begins and then ends rather quietly. You can witness its processing status by looking in the Status bar.

3. Let's convert the AC0400 database to the Access 2000 file format, in order to share it with users who do not yet own Microsoft Office Access 2003. Do the following:
CHOOSE: Tools → Database Utilities

4. CHOOSE: Convert Database → To Access 2000 File Format
The Convert Database Into dialog box appears, as shown in Figure 4.35, with a default name of "db1" for the new database.

Figure 4.35

Converting an Access database file

Notice that the Database window's Title bar displays the current file format version.

5. Using the Places bar and the *Save in* drop-down list box, select your personal storage location. Then, in the *File name* text box:
TYPE: **AC2K-0400**

6. To proceed with the conversion:
CLICK: Save command button
After a few moments, you will see the following dialog box.

7. To accept the warning dialog box:
   CLICK: OK command button

8. Before you can open the new Access 2000 database file, you must first close the AC0400 Database window. Close the AC0400 Database window now.

9. On your own, open the AC2K-0400 database from your personal storage location. The Database window should appear similar to the one shown in Figure 4.36.

Figure 4.36

Opening an
Access 2000
database file

10. Open a datasheet or report object for viewing. Notice that the conversion to the Access 2000 file format is relatively seamless to the end user. In fact, without the notification in the Title bar, you would be hard pressed to determine which version you were using.

11. Close all of the open windows, including the AC2K-0400 Database window, and then exit Microsoft Access.

In Addition BACKING UP THE DATABASE

One of the most important tasks you can perform after creating and adding data to a database is to make a backup copy of it to another storage location. Most people back up a database, along with their other important data files, using "My Computer," Windows Explorer, or a specialized backup program. An Access database is stored in a file ending with the extension .mdb or .mde. You can search for this file type using the Find, Files or Folders command on the Start (_start_) menu.

 **4.4** Name two operating system tools that you can use to back up a database.

Chapter
summary

The users of your database applications will be most familiar with its form and report objects. Forms are used for entering and editing data, whereas reports are used for presenting and displaying information. Besides offering a more attractive interface than datasheets, forms can help focus the user's attention on a single record at a time. Reports, which also offer a variety of attractive layouts, are primarily meant for printing. Because it is uncommon to limit a report to previewing on-screen, you must learn to match your printer's capabilities (color versus black-and-white, inkjet versus laser) with the report design and formatting options that are available. Access 2003 provides several wizards that make it easier to create forms, reports, and mailing labels. To enable easier database management, Access 2003 also provides commands for renaming, copying, and deleting objects, and compacting, repairing, and converting a database.

Command Summary

Many of the commands and procedures appearing in this chapter are summarized in the following table.

Skill Set	To Perform this Task . . .	Do the Following . . .
Creating and Modifying Forms	Create a new form using the AutoForm Wizard	SELECT: the desired table or query CLICK: New Object: AutoForm button
	Create a new form using the Form Wizard	CLICK: *Forms* button in the Objects bar DOUBLE-CLICK: Create form by using wizard
Producing Reports	Create a new report using the AutoReport Wizard	SELECT: the desired table or query CLICK: New Object: AutoReport button
	Create a new report using the Report Wizard	CLICK: *Reports* button in the Object bar DOUBLE-CLICK: Create report by using wizard
	Create a new mailing labels report using the Label Wizard	CLICK: *Reports* button in the Object bar CLICK: New button (New) SELECT: a table or query object from the drop-down list box DOUBLE-CLICK: Label Wizard
	Preview a report for printing	DOUBLE-CLICK: the report object, or CLICK: Print Preview button ( ), or CHOOSE: File → Print Preview
	Print a report	CLICK: Print button ( ), or CHOOSE: File → Print

Integrating with Other Applications	Export a report to HTML format for Web publishing	SELECT: the desired object CHOOSE: File → Export TYPE: **filename** for this version SELECT: HTML Documents in the *Save as type* drop-down list box CLICK: Save command button
	Export a report as a snapshot file for e-mail and Web distribution	SELECT: the desired object CHOOSE: File → Export TYPE: **filename** for this version SELECT: Snapshot Format in the *Save as type* drop-down list box CLICK: Save command button
Creating and Using Databases	Rename a database object	RIGHT-CLICK: the desired object CHOOSE: Rename
	Copy a selected database object	CLICK: Copy button ( ) CLICK: Paste button ( ) SELECT: a paste option
	Delete a database object	RIGHT-CLICK: the desired object CHOOSE: Delete
Using Access Tools	Compact and repair a database	CHOOSE: Tools → Database Utilities CHOOSE: Compact and Repair Database
	Back up and restore a database	Use Windows Explorer or "My Computer" to perform copy, backup, and restore operations for an Access database file (extension .mdb)
	Convert a database file to another file format version	CHOOSE: Tools → Database Utilities CHOOSE: Convert Database → *an option*

Key Terms

This section specifies page references for the key terms identified in this chapter. For a complete list of definitions, refer to the Glossary at the end of this learning guide.

AutoForm Wizard, *p. AC 142*

AutoReport Wizard, *p. AC 155*

Form window, *p. AC 142*

form wizards, *p. AC 142*

HTML, *p. AC 164*

Internet, *p. AC 164*

Label Wizard, *p. AC 168*

preview, *p. AC 161*

report snapshot, *p. AC 168*

report wizards, *p. AC 154*

World Wide Web, *p. AC 164*

XML, *p. AC 164*

Chapter
q u i z

Short Answer

1. Why create forms for use in a database application?

2. Name five types of AutoForm Wizards.

3. List the form options available in the New Form dialog box.

4. When would you choose a columnar or justified form layout?

5. When would you choose a tabular or datasheet form layout?

6. Why create reports for use in a database application?

7. Describe two types of AutoReport Wizards.

8. List the report options available in the New Report dialog box.

9. How do you create an Access 2003 report for publishing to the Web?

10. Describe two ways to remove objects in the Database window.

True/False

1. _____ The default AutoForm Wizard is the AutoForm: Columnar Wizard.

2. _____ The Form Wizard allows you to specify a sorting order.

3. _____ You can display data from more than one table in a form.

4. _____ In the Form window, pressing `CTRL` + `END` moves the cursor to the last field in the current record.

5. _____ The default AutoReport Wizard is the AutoReport: Tabular Wizard.

6. _____ The Report Wizard allows you to specify a sorting order.

7. _____ The information that you want summarized in a report can be extracted from either a table or a query.

8. _____ A tabular report prints several columns of information, with the field labels appearing down the left margin of the page.

9. _____ In the Database window, you can copy a table object's structure without duplicating the data stored in the table.

10. _____ You should regularly compact a database using Windows Explorer.

Multiple Choice

1. A form is used to display data from which of the following objects?

   a. Tables and/or queries
   b. Tables and/or reports
   c. Queries and/or reports
   d. Tables only

2. Which form layout is produced by default when selecting the AutoForm option from the New Object button?

   a. Circular
   b. Columnar
   c. Singular
   d. Tabular

3. Which of the following best describes a tabular form layout?

a. Data from a single record presented in a single column

b. Data from numerous records presented in a single column

c. Data from a single record presented in rows and columns

d. Data from numerous records presented in rows and columns

4. Which of the following best describes a justified form layout?

a. Data from a single record presented with stacked fields

b. Data from numerous records presented with stacked fields

c. Data from a single record presented in a single column

d. Data from numerous records presented in rows and columns

5. Which of the following performs the same action as pressing   in the Form window?

a. CLICK: ⏮

b. CLICK: ◀

c. CLICK: ▶

d. CLICK: ⏭

6. The Report Wizard provides the following options that are not available in the Form Wizard:

a. Grouping and Filtering

b. Outlining and Sorting

c. Grouping and Sorting

d. Outlining and Filtering

7. Which of the following is not a summary calculation available in the Summary Options dialog box of the Report Wizard?

a. Avg

b. Count

c. Max

d. Sum

8. This chapter presents which three options for exporting a table or report object for publishing to the Web?

a. ASP, CFML, and HTML

b. ASP, HTML, and Java

c. MDB, MDE, and XML

d. HTML, Snapshot, and XML

9. The Label Wizard enables you to create a report format using standard label sizes from this vendor.

a. Avery

b. Linux

c. Microsoft

d. Macromedia

10. Which of the following is *not* a paste option when copying a table object?

a. Structure Only

b. Structure and Data

c. Structure, Forms, and Reports

d. Append Data to Existing Table

Hands-On
exercises

1. Using AutoForm and AutoReport

In this exercise, you will create two new database objects using Access 2003's "Auto" wizards. First, using the AutoForm Wizard, you will create a columnar data entry form for a customers table. Then, you will create a tabular report using an AutoReport Wizard.

1. Load Microsoft Office Access 2003 using the Windows Start menu.

2. Open the database file named AC04HE. Ensure that the *Tables* button in the Objects bar is selected. Your screen should appear similar to the one shown in Figure 4.37.

Access

Figure 4.37

Opening the
AC04HE
database

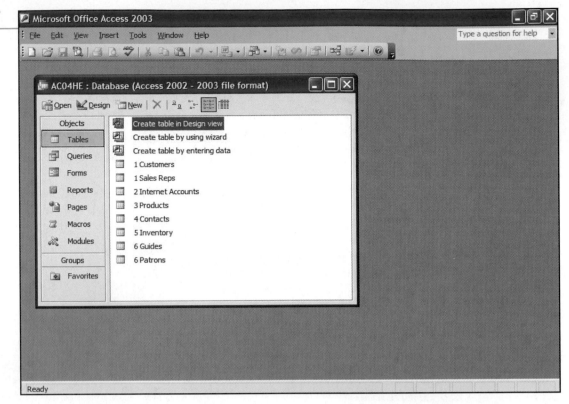

3. To create a data entry form for the Customers table, start by selecting the 1 Customers table object in the list area. (*Hint:* Click once on the name of the table. Do not double-click.)

4. Use the New Object: AutoForm button (⊞▾) to create a new columnar form. (*Hint:* If the AutoForm image is not displayed on the button face, click the attached down arrow and choose the AutoForm command.)

5. Let's save the new form shown in Figure 4.38:
   CLICK: Save button (🖫)
   TYPE: **Customer Data Entry Form**
   PRESS: (ENTER)
   or
   CLICK: OK

Figure 4.38

Customer Data
Entry Form
window

1 Customers	
CustomerID	1
CustomerName	Segal
Address	#11 - Hwy 16
City	Bonneville
State	PA
SalesRep	B02

Record: |◀ ◀ 1 ▶ ▶| ▶* of 30

6. Close the new Form window.

7. Now let's create a tabular report for the Customers table. After displaying the *Reports* list area, click the New button (⊞ New) on the Database window toolbar.

8. In the New Report dialog box, select the 1 Customers table object on which to base the new report. Then, select the AutoReport: Tabular option in order to create the report displayed in the Print Preview window shown in Figure 4.39.

Figure 4.39

Tabular
AutoReport
displayed in Print
Preview

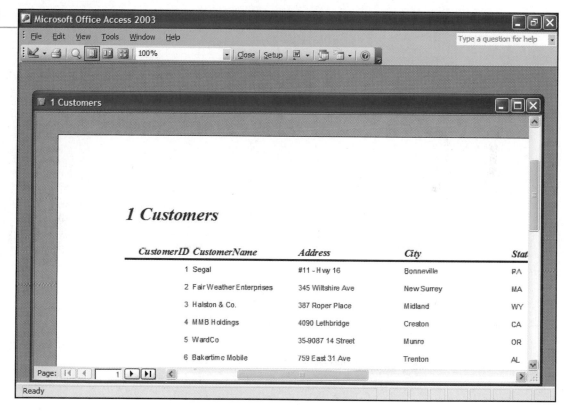

9. On your own, use the magnifying glass mouse pointer to zoom in and out on the report page.

10. Close the report's Print Preview window and save the report object as "Customer AutoReport," when prompted. The new report object should appear in the Database window.

2. Using the Report Wizard

The 2 Internet Accounts table contains a listing of current user accounts for an Internet service provider (ISP). In this exercise, you will create a report that groups and summarizes users according to where they live.

1. Ensure that the AC04HE Database window is displayed.

2. In the *Reports* list area of the Database window, launch the Access 2003 Report Wizard by double-clicking the "Create report by using wizard" option.

3. In the first step of the Report Wizard dialog box, select the 2 Internet Accounts table from the *Tables/Queries* drop-down list box.

4. Specify the following fields to include in the report: Customer, Username, City, Phone, and Amount. Then, proceed to the next step in the wizard.

5. Specify a grouping level by city, as shown in Figure 4.40, and then proceed to the next step in the wizard.

Figure 4.40

Specifying a grouping level

6. Specify an alphabetical sort order by the account's username. Then, specify a summary calculation that sums the contents of the Amount field. When ready, proceed to the next step.

7. Specify a report layout using the Align Left 1 style option with a landscape orientation. Then, proceed to the next step.

8. Select Soft Gray for your report style and then proceed to the next step in the wizard.

9. In the last step of the wizard, ensure that the *Preview the report* option button is selected and name the report object "Internet Accounts By City." When ready, complete the wizard by clicking [Finish].

10. Maximize the report's Print Preview window and then zoom out to 75%. Your screen should appear similar to the one shown in Figure 4.41.

Figure 4.41

Previewing the
report Internet
Accounts By City

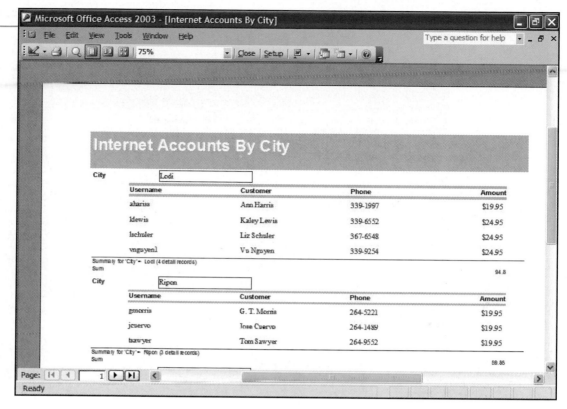

11. If you have a printer, print the report by clicking the Print button (▣).

12. Restore the Print Preview window and then close it to return to the Database window.

3. Using the Form Wizard

In this exercise, you will practice creating a tabular form using the Form Wizard and then working and navigating within the Form window.

1. Ensure that the AC04HE Database window is displayed.

2. In the *Forms* list area of the Database window, launch the Access 2003 Form Wizard by double-clicking the "Create form by using wizard" option.

3. In the Form Wizard dialog box, select the 3 Products table object and then include all of the fields on the new form. Proceed to the next step.

4. In the next two steps of the Form Wizard, select a Tabular layout and an Expedition style for the form.

5. In the last step of the wizard, enter the name "Products Tabular Form" and then open the form in Form view, as shown in Figure 4.42.

Figure 4.42

Displaying the
Products Tabular
Form

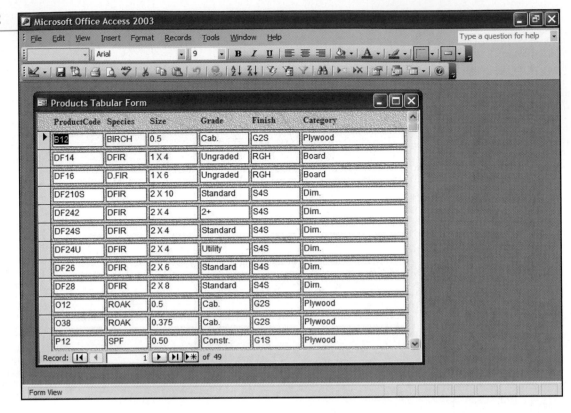

6. Enter the following data after clicking the New Record button ($\blacktriangleright\ast$):
   ProductCode: **DF99**
   Species: **DFIR**
   Size: **2 × 8**
   Grade: **Ungraded**
   Finish: **RGH**
   Category: **Dim.**

7. PRESS: (SHIFT) + (ENTER) to save the new record

8. Move to the first field in the first record. Then:
   PRESS: (TAB) to move to the Species field column

9. Using the Sort Descending button ($\frac{Z}{A}\downarrow$) on the toolbar, sort the table into descending order by the Species column.

10. To filter the information displayed in the form:
    DOUBLE-CLICK: SYP in the Species field column
    CLICK: Filter By Selection button ($\overline{\vee}$)
    Only records of the SYP species now appear in the new form.

11. If you have a printer, print the form by clicking the Print button ($\boxed{\triangleq}$).

12. Close the form by clicking its Close button ($\boxed{\times}$).

on your own

4. Generating a Mailing List Report

In this exercise, you will create a mailing labels report for all the records stored in the 4 Contacts table object. Start by displaying the *Reports* list area in the AC04HE Database window. Using the Access 2003 Label Wizard, create a mailing label report that prints the entire contents of the 4 Contacts table using Avery 5160 labels. Also, specify a 10-point, Tahoma font with normal weighting and a dark blue color. The prototype label should appear similar to the one shown in Figure 4.43. (*Note:* The state and zip code text, "MN 56300," is used to demonstrate your ability to enter static text into a mailing label report. In a real-world application, this data would be stored in a table object and then extracted from fields for inclusion in the report.)

Figure 4.43

Designing the
mailing label

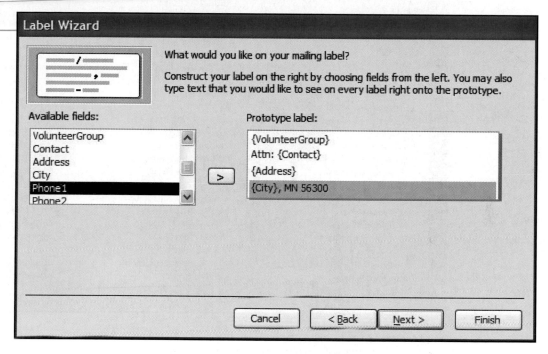

When finished, sort the report alphabetically by volunteer group. Then, name the mailing label report "Volunteer Mailing Labels" and display it in the Print Preview window as shown in Figure 4.44. (*Note:* If displayed, ignore the warning dialog box by clicking the OK command button.) If you have a printer, print the report and then close the Print Preview window to return to the Database window.

Figure 4.44

Previewing the mailing label report

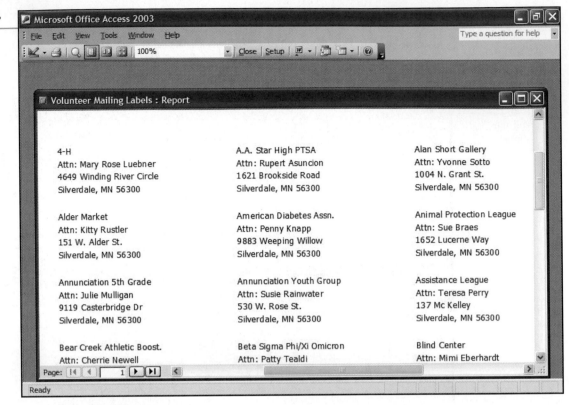

5. Creating an Inventory Form and Report

The 5 Inventory table object contains product information, including current stock levels, reorder quantities, costs, and suggested retail prices. Using the Form Wizard, create a justified form using the Blends style, as shown in Figure 4.45. Name the form "Inventory Input" for use in entering and editing data.

Figure 4.45

Displaying the Inventory Input form

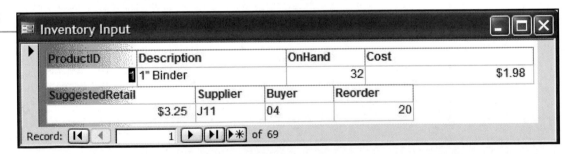

To practice working with the form, enter the following two records. (*Hint:* Access 2003 automatically adds the dollar signs to the Cost and SuggestedRetail values.) When you are finished, remember to save the last record by pressing (**SHIFT**) + (**ENTER**) and then close the Form window.

ProductID: (*Autonumber*)
Description: **Push Pins**
OnHand: **45**
Cost: **$2.00**
SuggestedRetail: **$4.00**
Supplier: **E01**
Buyer: **01**
Reorder: **20**

ProductID: (*Autonumber*)
Description: **Project Folders**
OnHand: **112**
Cost: **$9.00**
SuggestedRetail: **$13.00**
Supplier: **B05**
Buyer: **07**
Reorder: **40**

Using the Report Wizard, create a report for the 5 Inventory table object that is grouped by supplier and sorted by product description. Then, display the minimum and maximum values for the Cost and SuggestedRetail fields. For presentation, select a Block layout with a Casual style. Name the report "Supplier Summary" and then view the report in a maximized Print Preview window with a 100% zoom factor, as shown in Figure 4.46. If you have a printer, send a copy of the report to the printer. Then, restore and close the Print Preview window.

Figure 4.46

Previewing the
Supplier
Summary report

Grouped by Supplier
and sorted by
Description

Block layout with
Casual style
formatting

Minimum and
maximum summary
calculations for the
Cost and
SuggestedRetail
field columns

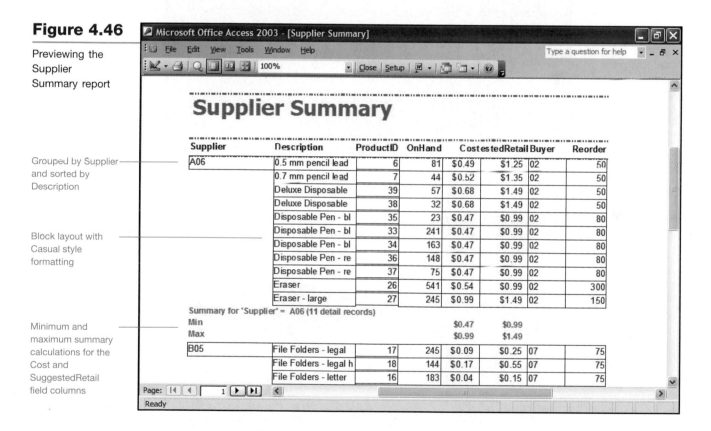

6. Creating a Data Entry Form

To make life easier for a company's front-counter clerks, you have been asked to create two data entry forms. The 6 Guides table object contains only a few fields, so create a tabular form using the International style and name it "Guides Data Entry," as shown in Figure 4.47. Then, for the 6 Patrons table, create a columnar form using the International style and name it "Patrons Data Entry." To test the usability of the forms, practice selecting records and editing data.

Figure 4.47

Displaying the
Guides Data
Entry form

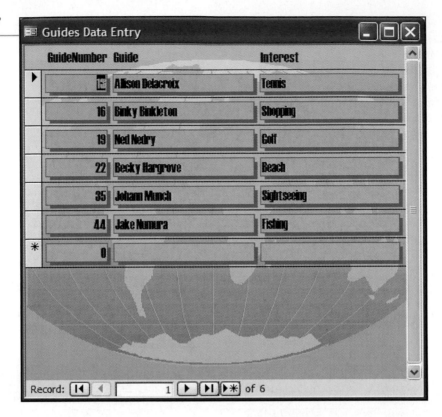

You have also been asked to create a report that includes all of the fields from the Patrons table and that groups the patrons according to interest. The report is to be sorted in order by the BestTime field. After specifying a layout and style, save the report as "Patrons By Interest." Then preview the report in the Print Preview window before sending it to the printer. When finished, close the AC04HE Database window and then exit Microsoft Office Access 2003.

CaseStudy   YOU'VE GOT BAGGAGE, INC.

Janice Marchant is the western regional sales representative for You've Got Baggage, Inc., a San Diego manufacturer of stylish travel gear. Although she has worked for the company only a short time, she enjoys the job and the challenges it presents. Janice works from her home in Boston with a notebook computer and fax machine but meets once a month with the national sales manager, John Lucci. Like all of the sales representatives at You've Got Baggage, Janice is responsible for tracking sales to the company's preferred clientele using Microsoft Office Access 2003. Now that she is getting the hang of entering data in Datasheet view, Janice wants to add a few form objects to facilitate data entry and enable her to focus on one customer at a time. She must also create and submit monthly reports listing the items that were sold and who purchased them. This information helps the management team of You've Got Baggage forecast demand levels and predict next season's sales figures.

In the following case problems, assume the role of Janice and perform the same steps that she identifies.

1. After launching Access 2003, Janice opens the AC04CP database that is stored in her data files folder. Wanting to get a better feel for the forms Access can create, she uses the AutoForm Wizard to generate a columnar form for the Customers table. She saves the form as "Customers − AutoForm" and then practices moving through the records using the navigation buttons in the Form window. Feeling comfortable with her creation, she closes the Form window.

Because the AutoForm Wizard did such a nice job with the form, Janice decides to create a new report. She selects the Customers table and launches the AutoReport Wizard using the toolbar. After perusing the report, she closes the window by clicking its Close button (❌) and then saves the report as "Customers − AutoReport." After letting the report sink in for a few moments, Janice concedes that it is not quite what she had hoped for. She displays the *Reports* list area in the Database window and then uses the right-click menu (Figure 4.48) to delete the AutoReport object from the Database window.

Figure 4.48

Deleting a report object

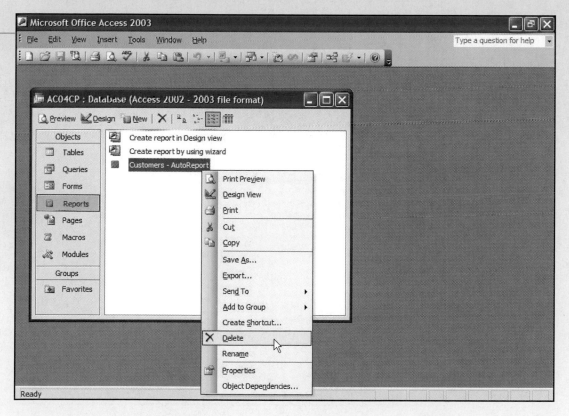

2. Being the adventurous type, Janice wants to create a new form layout for the Products table. To begin, she displays the *Forms* list area in the Database window and then double-clicks the "Create form by using wizard" shortcut. In the first step of the wizard, she selects the Products table and includes all of the fields. Then she specifies a columnar layout and the Stone style for the form. Janice names the new form "Products − Input Form" and opens it for display (Figure 4.49). After viewing the new form, she closes it by clicking its Close button (❌).

Figure 4.49

Displaying the
form Products –
Input Form

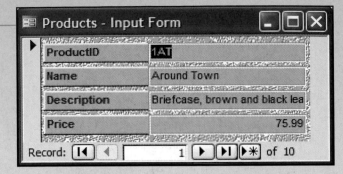

3. Janice wants to send out a mailing to all her preferred customers. Using the Customers table, she prepares a standard Avery 5160 mailing label. The font selected is Verdana with a 10-point font size. After specifying that the labels be sorted into ascending order by last name, she saves the report as "Customer Mailing." Figure 4.50 displays the results of the mailing labels report. Janice displays two pages in the Print Preview window and then sends the report to the printer. Then, she closes the Print Preview window to return to the Database window.

Figure 4.50

Previewing a
mailing labels
report

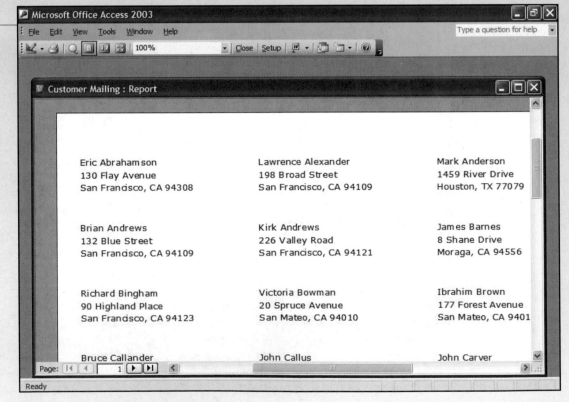

4. Janice's boss, John, commends her for the new reports but would like to see her customers grouped by the product that they purchased. Janice knows that the Report Wizard can help her produce this report. After launching the wizard, she selects the Customers table and includes all its fields for display in the report. Janice selects the ProductID field for grouping the contents of the report and the Last-Name field for sorting the report. She then selects a layout, page orientation, and style. In the last step of the Report Wizard, Janice names the report "Customers – By ProductID" and then opens it for display in the Print Preview window, similar to the report shown in Figure 4.51). Satisfied with the results, Janice prints and then closes the report.

Figure 4.51

A possible solution for the Customers – By Product ID report

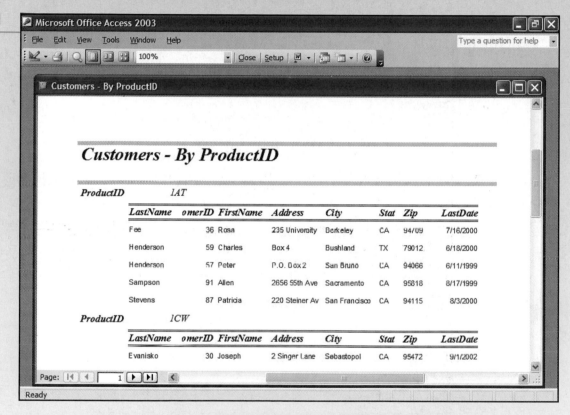

5. Janice, your report looks great!" John exclaims on the answering machine. "I'd like you to show Jose and Wendy how you produced it so quickly. They spend three days each month compiling their data." Janice is pleased that the report has gone over so well. She decides that, instead of faxing the pages to Jose and Wendy, she will export the report as an HTML document. In the Database window, Janice selects the "Customers – By ProductID" report object and chooses the File, Export command. After locating her personal storage folder and selecting the "HTML Documents" format, she clicks the Export command button and bypasses the dialog box asking for an HTML template. She opens the first page of the report in her Web browser (Figure 4.52) to view the results. Janice will inform her associates that they can preview the report after she finishes uploading it to her personal Web site. Then, she closes the AC04CP Database window and exits Microsoft Office Access 2003.

Figure 4.52

Displaying a static report using Internet Explorer

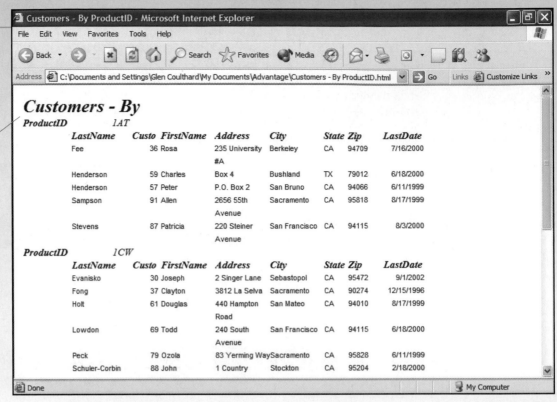

Unfortunately the Title is truncated during export.

Janice is pleased by her incredible progress with Microsoft Office Access 2003. She now understands how rewarding her job, and working from home, can be. Janice looks forward to learning more computer skills in the future.

Answers

to self-check questions

4.1 Name the layout options for designing a form using the Form Wizard. Columnar, Tabular, Datasheet, Justified, PivotTable, and PivotChart.

4.2 What does the term "grouping data" refer to in a report? You can arrange data so that it appears combined into categories in a report. The categories are based on field values and appear sorted into ascending order, by default. Grouping data also enables you to prepare subtotal calculations.

4.3 How could you use table and report objects to print diskette labels? You store the diskette names, titles, and other information in a table and then use a mailing labels report to print the information using the Avery 5296 diskette label.

4.4 Name two operating system tools that you can use to back up a database. Windows Explorer and "My Computer"

Notes

Notes

Notes

Notes

Notes

Notes

Microsoft® Office System 2003®

2003

CHAPTER 1

⊕ **Integrating Office Word and Office Excel**

PREREQUISITES

To successfully complete this chapter, you must know how to create, open, save, and print Office Word documents and Office Excel workbooks. You should also be comfortable performing basic editing tasks, such as selecting and deleting text, in both document paragraphs and worksheet cells.

LEARNING OBJECTIVES

After completing this chapter, you will be able to:

- Use the Office Clipboard to assemble a report from a variety of documents

- Link data in Office Excel to an Office Word document

- Embed data from Office Excel in an Office Word document

- Move, resize, delete, and edit shared objects

- Enhance an Office Word document with worksheets and charts created using Office Excel

1.1 Using the Office Clipboard

In Microsoft Office System 2003 applications, the Windows and Office Clipboards enable you to copy items from one location to another. While the **Windows Clipboard** can store only a single item at a time, the enhanced **Office Clipboard** can store up to 24 items simultaneously. The Office Clipboard is ideal for assembling reports that require excerpts from multiple documents. For example, you can copy an Excel 2003 chart, an Access 2003 table, and a PowerPoint 2003 slide to the Office Clipboard and then paste the entire collection of items into a Word 2003 document.

1.1.1 Activating the Office Clipboard

→ Feature

The Clipboard task pane is used for displaying and managing the contents of the Office Clipboard. This task pane automatically appears when you copy two items to the Clipboard without an intervening paste. The Clipboard task pane displays icons to represent each of the copied items. Be aware that the Windows Clipboard continues to trap the last cut or copied item even after the Office Clipboard is activated. In other words, the last item that was cut or copied to the Office Clipboard will also be stored as the single item on the Windows Clipboard.

→ Method

To display the Clipboard task pane:

Cut or copy two items in sequence without an intervening paste operation

or

- CHOOSE: Edit, Office Clipboard

→ Practice

You will now copy a range of worksheet cells and a chart to the Office Clipboard from an existing workbook created using Excel 2003. Ensure that you have installed Microsoft Office System 2003 and that the Windows desktop appears before you begin.

1. Load Microsoft Office Word 2003 using the Start menu (*start*).

2. From the Word 2003 Menu bar:
CHOOSE: File → Open

3. In the Open dialog box that appears, use the Places bar and the *Look in* drop-down list box to select the Advantage student data files folder. Your screen should appear similar, but not identical, to the one shown in Figure 1.1.

Figure 1.1

Open dialog box in Office Word

Places bar

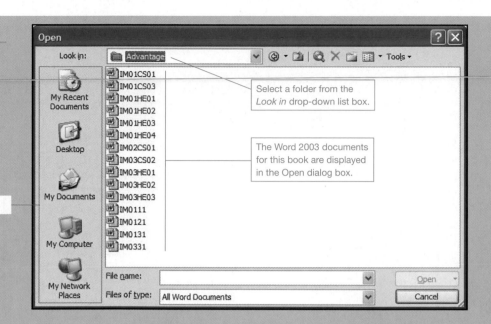

Select a folder from the *Look in* drop-down list box.

The Word 2003 documents for this book are displayed in the Open dialog box.

4. To open the IM0111 document file:
DOUBLE-CLICK: IM0111 in the list area
The document is opened in Microsoft Office Word 2003, as shown in Figure 1.2. (*Note:* The current date from your computer is displayed in the memo's "Date:" area.)

Figure 1.2

Opening the IM0111 document for display in Office Word

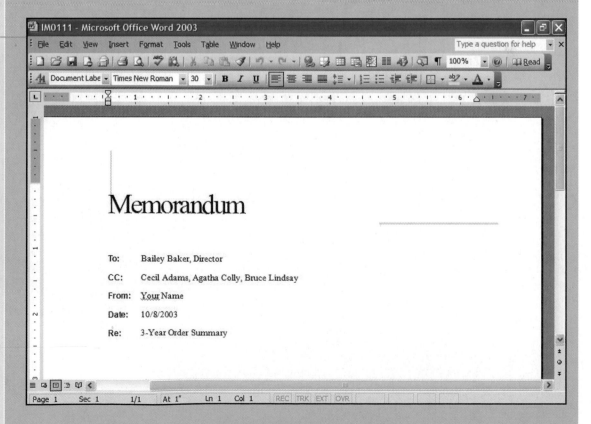

5. Save the document as "Summary Memo" to your personal storage location.

6. Load Microsoft Office Excel 2003 using the Start menu (start).

7. From the Excel 2003 Menu bar:
CHOOSE: File → Open

8. In the Open dialog box that appears, use the Places bar and the *Look in* drop-down list box to select the Advantage student data files folder. Your dialog box should appear similar, but not identical, to the one shown in Figure 1.3.

Figure 1.3

Open dialog box in Office Excel

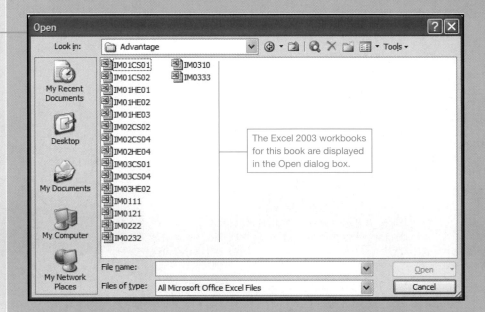

The Excel 2003 workbooks for this book are displayed in the Open dialog box.

9. To open the IM0111 workbook file:
DOUBLE-CLICK: IM0111 in the list area
The workbook is opened in Microsoft Office Excel 2003.

10. Save the workbook as "Orders Summary" to your personal storage location.

11. The Office Clipboard appears automatically when you copy two items simultaneously. You can also force its display, as illustrated in this step, using a menu command. Do the following:
CHOOSE: Edit → Office Clipboard
Your screen should now appear with the Clipboard task pane displayed, as shown in Figure 1.4.

Figure 1.4

Displaying the
Office Clipboard
in Office Excel

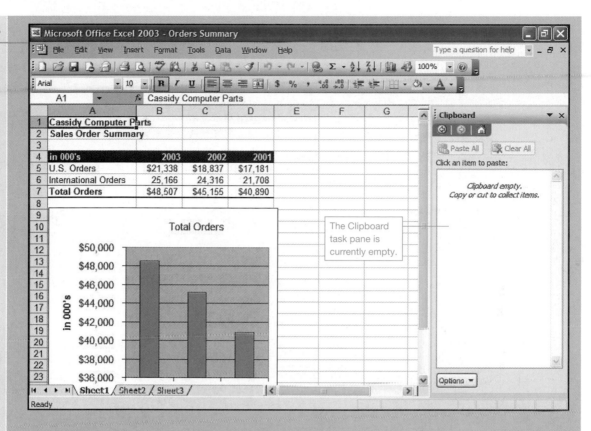

12. When the Office Clipboard is empty, the Paste All and Clear All buttons near the top of the task pane are not available for selection. However, if your Clipboard does contain items, do the following to clear its contents in preparation for the next few steps:
CLICK: Clear All button (🗑 Clear All) in the task pane

13. Let's copy some worksheet data to the Office Clipboard:
SELECT: cell range from A4 to D7
CLICK: Copy button (🗐) in the toolbar

14. An icon representing the Office Excel data now appears in the Clipboard task pane, along with a preview of the copied data. You should also see a moving border, called a dashed marquee, surrounding the cell range in the worksheet area.

15. You will now copy the chart to the Office Clipboard. To begin, select the chart as instructed below:
CLICK: a blank area on the background of the chart
(*Note:* You can actually click anywhere in the chart as long as the ScreenTip indicates "Chart Area.") When this task has been successfully completed, the chart object appears with **sizing handles,** tiny boxes that surround the object. Later, you will learn how to use these handles to resize an object.

16. To copy the chart to the Office Clipboard:
CLICK: Copy button (🗐) in the toolbar
Your screen should now appear similar to the one shown in Figure 1.5.

Figure 1.5

Copying items to the Office Clipboard

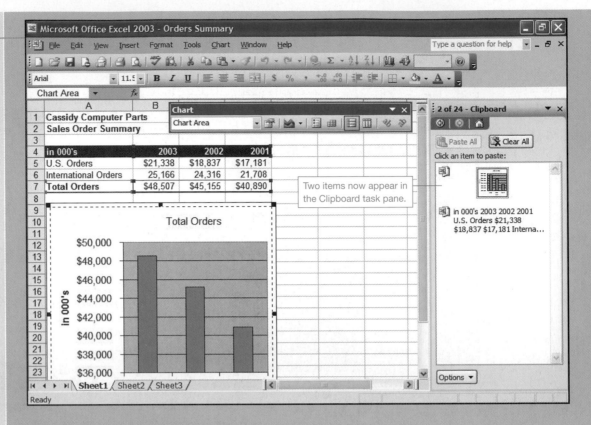

17. CLICK: cell A1 to remove the dashed marquee

18. Save the workbook, and continue to the next lesson.

1.1.2 Pasting and Clearing Clipboard Items

→ **Feature**

Whereas the contents of the Windows Clipboard are pasted by clicking the Paste button (📋▾) on the Standard toolbar, the contents of the Office Clipboard are pasted using the Clipboard task pane. You can insert or paste the items stored on the Office Clipboard into any one of the Microsoft Office System 2003 applications. Unlike the Windows Clipboard, the Office Clipboard enables you to paste items individually or as a group. You can also clear items from the Office Clipboard selectively or all at once.

→ **Method**

Use the Clipboard task pane to perform the following tasks:

- CLICK: on a single item in the Clipboard task pane to paste the item at the cursor position in the current document

- CLICK: Paste All command button (📋 Paste All) in the Clipboard task pane to paste all of the items as a group

- CLICK: Clear All command button () in the Clipboard task pane to clear all of the items from the Office Clipboard

- CLICK: an item's drop-down arrow and choose the Delete command in order to clear an individual item from the Office Clipboard

→ Practice

You will now paste the contents of the Office Clipboard into a Word 2003 document and then clear the contents of the Office Clipboard. Ensure that you have completed the previous lesson and that the "Summary Memo" document and "Orders Summary" workbook are both open.

1. You are most likely familiar with moving among applications using the Windows taskbar, as shown in Figure 1.6. To bring a running application to the foreground and make it active, click on the application's button displayed on the taskbar. Do the following to make the "Summary Memo" document in Word 2003 active:
CLICK: Summary Memo – Microsoft Office Word 2003
(*Note:* The complete descriptive text appears in a ScreenTip, as shown in Figure 1.6.)

Figure 1.6

Windows taskbar

| start | Summary Memo - Micr... | Microsoft Office Excel... | | 11:52 AM |

Start button   Microsoft Office Word 2003 application button   Microsoft Office Excel 2003 application button   Office Clipboard icon displays "active" status.

2. To position the insertion point at the end of the memo:
PRESS: CTRL + END

3. Let's paste the entire contents of the Office Clipboard into the Word document. To begin, display the Clipboard task pane:
CHOOSE: Edit, Office Clipboard

4. In the Clipboard task pane:
CLICK: Paste All command button, located near the top

5. To better view the results of the paste operation, move the insertion point to the top of the memo:
PRESS: CTRL + HOME

6. Now change the zoom factor to 50%:
CLICK: down arrow attached to the Zoom button (100% ▾)
CLICK: 50%
Your screen should now appear similar to the one shown in Figure 1.7. After pasting items between applications, you must typically move and resize the objects to better fit with the existing data. For example, the document in Figure 1.7 would look more uniform if the table were moved to the right and the size of the chart reduced. You will learn how to manipulate shared objects in module 1.3 of this chapter.

Integrating

Figure 1.7

Pasting Excel
2003 items into a
Word 2003
document

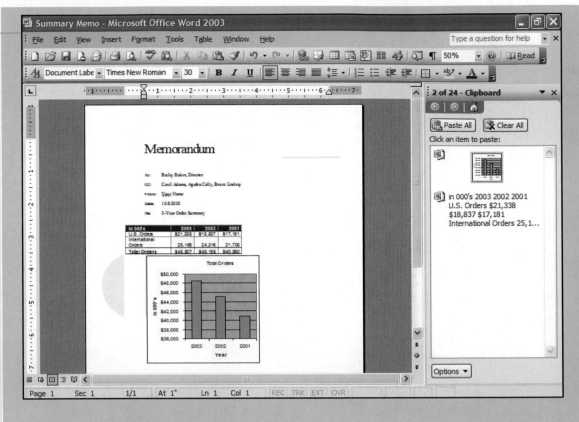

7. Let's restore the zoom factor to 100% for normal viewing:
   CLICK: down arrow attached to the Zoom button (100%)
   CLICK: 100%

8. Save and then close the "Summary Memo" document, without exiting Word 2003. (*Hint:* After clicking the Save button ( ), choose the File, Close command or click on the document's Close button ( ).) Notice that the Clipboard task pane remains displayed in the Word 2003 application window.

9. To clear the chart object from the Office Clipboard, position the mouse pointer over the item until it appears with an outline. Then click the arrow attached to its right border. As shown in Figure 1.8, a menu appears that allows you to paste or delete the item independently of the remaining objects stored on the Office Clipboard.

Figure 1.8

Displaying an object's menu in the Clipboard task pane

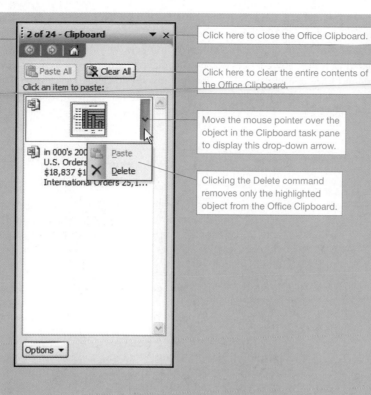

10. To remove the chart object from the Office Clipboard:
    CLICK: Delete command

11. On your own, remove the worksheet range object from the Office Clipboard using the same method. Then close the Clipboard task pane by clicking its Close button (☒).

12. Close Word 2003 and Excel 2003, and return to the Windows desktop.

 **1.1** Name two methods for activating the Office Clipboard and displaying the Clipboard task pane.

1.2 Pasting, Linking, and Embedding

Microsoft Office System 2003 lets you select from a variety of formats when pasting data into an application using the Windows or Office Clipboards. The easiest method is to allow each Office application to apply a default data format according to the application used to create the source data. For example, a paragraph written in Word 2003 is pasted into a workbook in Excel 2003 as a fully editable Word object, unless you specify otherwise. A cell range in Excel 2003, on the other hand, is pasted into a Word document using the **HTML** (HyperText Markup Language) format. Additionally, a PowerPoint 2003 slide is pasted into Word 2003 as a graphic image by default, using the portable network graphics (PNG) file format. The various data formats determine what you may do with the data once it has been pasted. There may be times when you do not want to use the default data formats, such as when you want data pasted as simple text. In this case, you can use the Office application's Paste Special command in order to select an alternative data format.

Not only must you consider data formats when copying and pasting data between applications, but you must also decide whether the pasted data will be updated by its original source application or in its new application. For example, when copying a cell range from Excel 2003 to Word 2003, you may specify that the data be updated to reflect any changes made in its original worksheet. Table 1.1 describes three ways to share data among Office applications. Each method involves copying the desired data from the **source document** (the document in which the data was first created) into the **destination document** (the document that receives the data).

Table 1.1

Three methods for sharing data among Office applications

Method	Description
Pasting	The easiest method for sharing information is to copy the desired data from the source document and then paste it into the destination document. In its purest form, **pasting** data involves inserting a static representation of the source data into the destination document.
Linking	In **linking,** you not only paste the data, but also establish a dynamic link between the source and destination documents. Thereafter, any changes made in the source document are automatically updated in the destination document.
Embedding	**Embedding** data involves inserting a source document into a destination document as an object. An embedded object is fully editable within the destination document using tools and features from its source application. For example, you can edit the pasted contents of an Excel 2003 cell formula from within the Word 2003 application window. Unlike linked data, an embedded object does not retain a connection to its source document; everything is contained in the destination document.

In the following lessons, we will explore the methods of pasting, linking, and embedding data between Office applications.

1.2.1 Pasting Data from Office Word to Office Excel

→ **Feature**

Pasting is the term used to describe the transfer of data from one application to another. When you paste data, your goal is to move data "from here to there." You do not link the source and destination documents, nor do you embed the data as an intelligent object. The data is simply copied from a source document to the Clipboard and then inserted into the destination document using a default format.

→ **Method**

To perform a copy and paste operation:

Copy data from the source document to the Clipboard.

Make the target application window active.

Move to the desired location in the destination document.

• CHOOSE: Edit → Paste from the Menu bar

or

• CLICK: Paste button ([icon])

→ # **Practice**

You will now practice copying and pasting data between Word 2003 and Excel 2003.

1. Load Microsoft Office Word 2003 using the Start menu (**start**).

2. Open the IM0121 document from the Advantage student data files folder, and then save it as "Student Memo" to your personal storage location. Ensure that your screen appears similar to the one shown in Figure 1.9 before proceeding.

Figure 1.9

"Student Memo" document

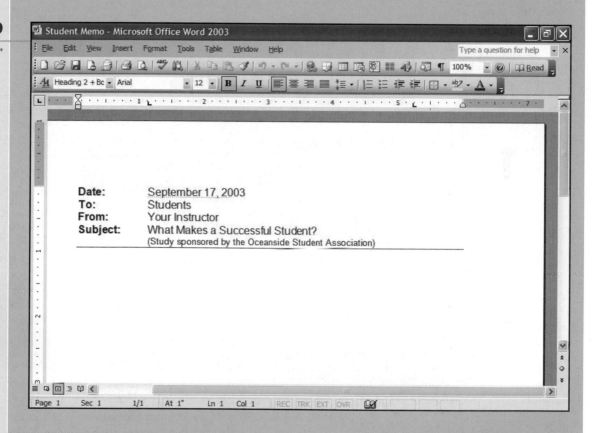

3. Load Microsoft Office Excel 2003 using the Start menu (**start**).

4. Open the IM0121 workbook from the Advantage student data files folder, and then save it as "Survey Results" to your personal storage location.

5. You will now copy the data stored in the Word document to the Clipboard. To begin, switch to the Word 2003 application window:
CLICK: "Student Memo – Microsoft Office Word 2003" button on the Windows taskbar
(*Hint:* The button's text will not be completely visible. However, you can position the mouse pointer over a taskbar button in order to display its name in a ScreepTip.)

6. Notice that the insertion point is currently blinking near the top of the document. To copy all of the textual data to the Clipboard:
PRESS: **SHIFT** and hold it down

7. Position the mouse pointer to the right of the parenthesis in ". . . Association)" and then click the left mouse button once. All of the text between the insertion point and where you clicked the mouse should now appear highlighted, as shown in Figure 1.10. Release the **SHIFT** key before proceeding.

Integrating

Figure 1.10

Selecting the data to copy

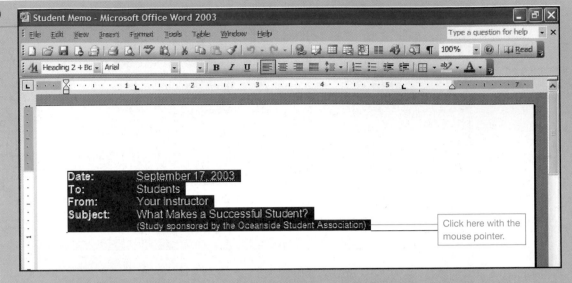

8. To copy the selected text to the Clipboard:
   CLICK: Copy button (🗎)

9. Now switch to the Excel 2003 application window:
   CLICK: Microsoft Office Excel 2003 button on the Windows taskbar

10. Ensure that the cell pointer appears in cell A1. Then, paste the data:
    CLICK: Paste button (🗎▾)
    (*Hint:* Make sure that you click the clipboard portion of the Paste button (🗎) and not the down arrow (▾).) As shown in Figure 1.11, the data is automatically divided into rows and columns in the worksheet.

Figure 1.11

Pasting the copied data into a worksheet

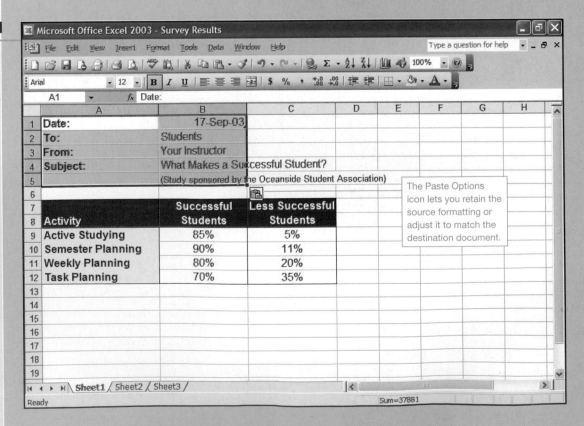

11. Once the data is pasted, you will notice that the Paste Options icon (🔳) is displayed at the bottom right-hand corner of the selected range. This icon allows you to select advanced formatting and paste options. To display the Paste Options menu (Figure 1.12):
CLICK: Paste Options icon (🔳)

Figure 1.12

Paste Options menu

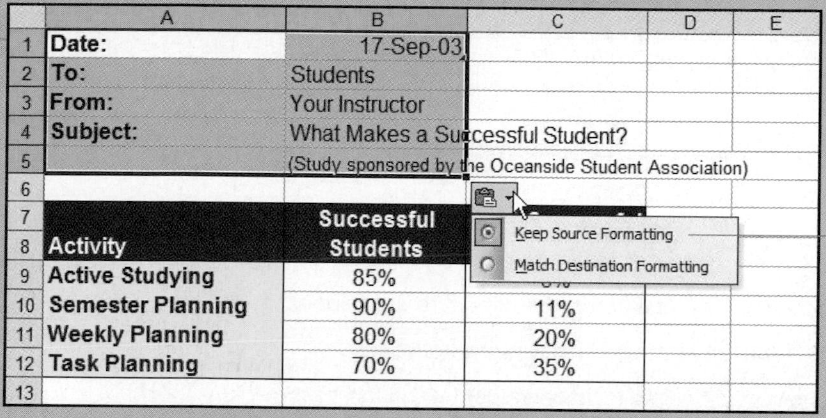

	A	B	C	D	E
1	Date:	17-Sep-03			
2	To:	Students			
3	From:	Your Instructor			
4	Subject:	What Makes a Successful Student?			
5		(Study sponsored by the Oceanside Student Association)			
6					
7		**Successful**	Keep Source Formatting		
8	**Activity**	**Students**	Match Destination Formatting		
9	**Active Studying**	85%			
10	**Semester Planning**	90%	11%		
11	**Weekly Planning**	80%	20%		
12	**Task Planning**	70%	35%		
13					

The Paste Options menu appears when you click the button.

12. The Paste Options menu displays "Keep Source Formatting" as the default selection. Unless you wish to change the pasted data's formatting to match the destination document, you can ignore this icon for now. To close the Paste Options menu:
CLICK: Paste Options icon (🔳) once again

13. Move to cell A1 to remove the selection highlighting.

14. Save the revised worksheet, and then continue to the next lesson.

In Addition CASCADING AND TILING WINDOWS

When copying and pasting data between application windows, it is often helpful to display those windows on the desktop simultaneously. There are two primary methods for arranging open application windows. First, the Cascade Windows command fans out the open windows like a deck of cards, so that only the Title bar is showing for most windows. Second, the Tile Windows Horizontally and Tile Windows Vertically commands arrange the open windows in rectangular tiles, in a pattern similar to that of floor tiles, to cover the entire desktop.

To cascade or tile open application windows on the desktop:

- RIGHT-CLICK: an empty portion of the taskbar

- CHOOSE: Cascade Windows

  or

  CHOOSE: Tile Windows Horizontally

  or

  CHOOSE: Tile Windows Vertically

Integrating

1.2.2 Linking Office Excel Data to an Office Word Document

→ Feature

Linking allows you to insert "live" data into a destination document that updates dynamically when data in the source document is modified. You link files when the data you need to include from a source document is either maintained by other users or needs to be inserted into multiple destination documents. Because Excel 2003 is largely an analysis tool for calculating and summarizing data, worksheets typically provide the source data for use in Word documents and PowerPoint presentations. The only caveat for linking is that the source document be accessible by the destination document, whether stored on the same computer or via a network connection.

→ Method

To link data between Office applications:

Copy data from the source document to the Clipboard.

Make the target application window active.

Move to the desired location in the destination document.

- CHOOSE: Edit → Paste Special from the Menu bar
- SELECT: *Paste link* option button
- SELECT: a data format in the *As* list box
- CLICK: OK command button

To update or refresh a linked object manually:

- RIGHT-CLICK: the linked object
- CHOOSE: Update Link from the menu

→ Practice

In this lesson, you will paste and link data stored in an Excel 2003 workbook into a Word 2003 document. Ensure that you have completed the previous lesson in this module.

1. Ensure that the "Student Memo" document is open in Word 2003 and that the "Survey Results" workbook is open in Excel 2003. To begin, make sure that the Excel 2003 application window is active.

2. Let's copy the "Activity" table to the Clipboard:
SELECT: cell range from A7 to C12
CLICK: Copy button (📋)

3. To make Word 2003 the active application window:
CLICK: "Student Memo – Microsoft Office Word 2003" button on the taskbar

4. To position the insertion point at the bottom of the document:
PRESS: CTRL + END

5. You will now paste the data into the Word 2003 document and, at the same time, establish a link between the data and its original Excel 2003 workbook file. To begin:
CHOOSE: Edit → Paste Special from the Word 2003 Menu bar
The Paste Special dialog box appears, as shown in Figure 1.13, showing a selection of possible data formats for inserting the data.

Figure 1.13

Paste Special
dialog box

Select the *Paste*
option button if you
do not want a link
established.

Select the *Paste link*
option button to
specify a dynamic
link with the data's
source file.

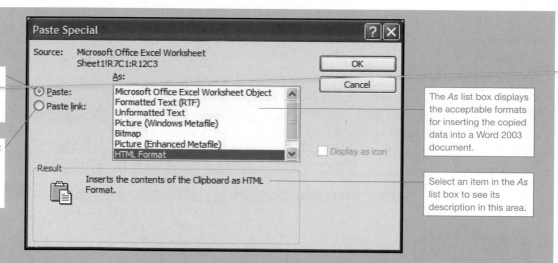

The *As* list box displays
the acceptable formats
for inserting the copied
data into a Word 2003
document.

Select an item in the *As*
list box to see its
description in this area.

6. To review the various data formats, click on each item in the *As* list box and then read the description appearing in the *Result* area. Table 1.2 further describes the formats listed in the *As* list box. Note that "HTML Format" is the currently selected option.

Table 1.2

Data Format
Options

Data Format	Description
Microsoft Office Excel Worksheet Object	The data is inserted as an embedded and self-aware Excel 2003 object that you can edit by double-clicking.
Formatted Text (RTF)	The data is inserted as an editable and formatted Word table.
Unformatted Text	The data is inserted as editable text, without any formatting applied.
Picture (Windows Metafile)	The data is inserted as a picture object using the older Windows Metafile format.
Bitmap	The data is inserted as a picture object for online viewing. This option takes up a lot of memory and disk space.
Picture (Enhanced Metafile)	The data is inserted as a picture object using the more recent Enhanced Metafile format.
HTML Format	The data is inserted as formatted text using the HTML format specification.
Unformatted Unicode Text	The data is inserted as editable text, without any formatting applied.

7. To insert the Excel 2003 data into Word using the HTML format:
SELECT: HTML Format in the *As* list box

8. To specify that the data be linked to its original source workbook:
CLICK: *Paste link* option button
Notice that the description in the *Result* area is updated.

9. To proceed:
CLICK: OK command button
The information is inserted in the memo, and the link is established. Your document should now appear similar to the one shown in Figure 1.14.

Figure 1.14

Pasting and linking data in Word 2003

The Excel 2003 data is pasted into the memo. Changes made in the "Survey Results" workbook will be reflected in this document as well.

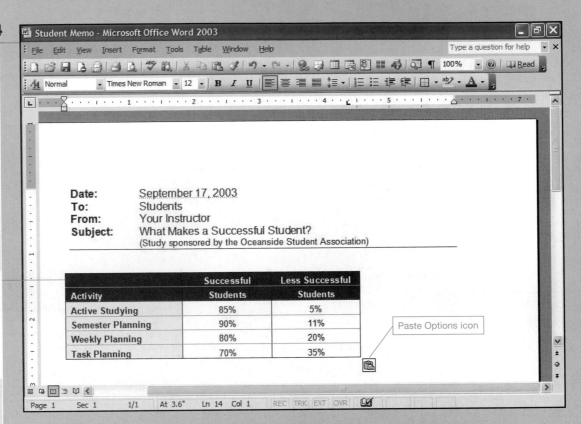

10. Because of the established link, any changes you make to the table data in the "Survey Results" workbook will be reflected in the "Student Memo" document. To illustrate, let's switch to Excel 2003 and make a few changes to the worksheet. To begin:
CLICK: Survey Results button on the taskbar

11. PRESS: ESC to remove the selection highlighting

12. Let's change two cell results in the table area:
SELECT: cell B12
TYPE: **90%**
PRESS: ➡
TYPE: **25%**
PRESS: ENTER
Your worksheet should now appear similar to the one shown in Figure 1.15.

Figure 1.15

Updating data in the "Survey Results" workbook

	A	B	C	D	E
1	Date:	17-Sep-03			
2	To:	Students			
3	From:	Your Instructor			
4	Subject:	What Makes a Successful Student?			
5		(Study sponsored by the Oceanside Student Association)			
6					
7		Successful	Less Successful		
8	Activity	Students	Students		
9	Active Studying	85%	5%		
10	Semester Planning	90%	11%		
11	Weekly Planning	80%	20%		
12	Task Planning	90%	25%		
13					
14					

Updating values in cells B12 and C12

13. Now let's view the "Student Memo" in Word 2003:
CLICK: "Student Memo – Microsoft Office Word 2003" button on the taskbar
Notice that 90% and 25% appear in the linked table object. (*Note:* If the changes do not appear, right-click the linked table object and then choose the Update Link command from the pop-up menu.)

Dynamic linking does not work in the opposite direction; it is a one-way relationship only. If you change a value in the linked table object in Word 2003, the "Survey Results" workbook is not updated. Furthermore, the next time you update the workbook in Excel 2003, any changes that you have made to values in the linked table object will be overwritten.

14. Save the document as "Linked Memo" to your personal storage location.

15. Close the "Linked Memo" document before proceeding.

1.2.3 Embedding Office Excel Data in an Office Word Document

→ **Feature**

Embedding enables you to place a fully editable version of the source data into the destination document. Moreover, when editing an embedded object, you use the actual commands and tools of the original **server application** (the application that was used to create the data) from within the current application's window. Understandably, a document containing embedded objects requires more disk space than one containing links.

→ **Method**

To embed data into an Office application:

Copy data from the source document to the Clipboard.

Make the target application window active.

Move to the desired location in the destination document.

• CHOOSE: Edit → Paste Special from the Menu bar

• SELECT: an "Object" list item, such as Microsoft Office Excel Worksheet Object, in the *As* list box

• CLICK: OK command button

Integrating

→ **Practice**

You will now embed an Excel 2003 worksheet range into a Word 2003 document. Ensure that you have completed the previous lessons in this module. No documents should be open in Word, and the "Survey Results" worksheet should be open in Excel. The Word window should be the active window.

1. Ensure that there are no documents open in the Word 2003 application window and that the "Survey Results" workbook is open in Excel 2003. To begin, make sure that Word 2003 is the active window.

2. In Word 2003, open the "Student Memo" document from your personal storage location.

3. PRESS: CTRL + END to move to the end of the document
Your screen should appear similar to the one shown in Figure 1.16.

Figure 1.16

Opening the "Student Memo" document

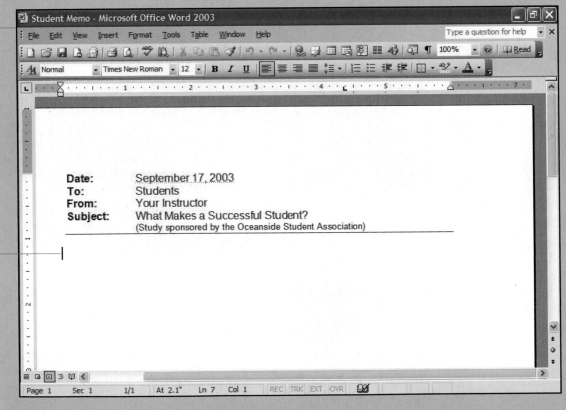

The insertion point should appear at the end of the document.

4. Let's switch to Excel 2003 in order to copy some data to the Clipboard. Do the following:
CLICK: Survey Results button in the taskbar

5. To copy the desired information to the Clipboard:
SELECT: cell range from A7 to C12
CLICK: Copy button ()

6. To switch back to Word 2003:
CLICK: "Student Memo – Microsoft Office Word 2003" button in the taskbar

7. To embed the worksheet range as an editable object:
CHOOSE: Edit → Paste Special
SELECT: Microsoft Office Excel Worksheet Object in the *As* list box, as shown in Figure 1.17

Figure 1.17

Selecting a data
format in the
Paste Special
dialog box

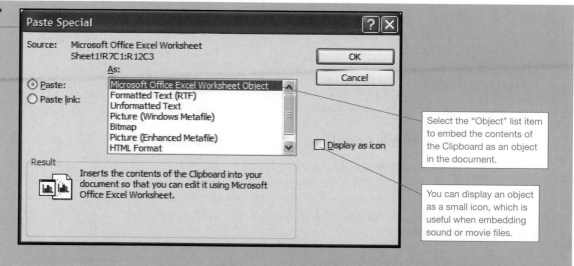

Select the "Object" list item
to embed the contents of
the Clipboard as an object
in the document.

You can display an object
as a small icon, which is
useful when embedding
sound or movie files.

8. To proceed:
CLICK: OK command button
The object appears in the document, as shown in Figure 1.18. Unlike in a linked table object, any changes that you make in the source workbook ("Survey Results") will have no effect on this embedded table.

Figure 1.18

Embedding a
table object into
Word 2003

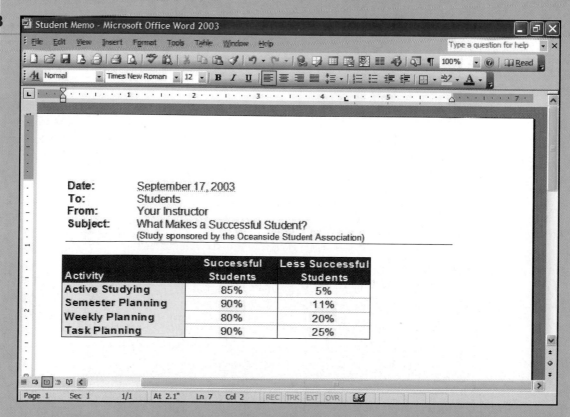

9. In the next module, you will learn more about editing linked and embedded objects. For now, save the document as "Embedded Memo" to your personal storage location.

10. Close the Word 2003 and Excel 2003 application windows.

Integrating

1.2. When you copy worksheet data from Excel 2003, what is the default data format for pasting that data into Word 2003?

1.3 Manipulating Shared Objects

Pasting, linking, and embedding data is the first step toward sharing data among your Microsoft Office System 2003 applications. Once you have inserted data, however, you must typically manipulate shared objects so that the data appears seamlessly alongside the document's existing content. This module describes methods for moving, resizing, deleting, and editing shared objects, regardless of whether the data is linked or embedded.

1.3.1 Moving, Resizing, and Deleting Shared Objects

→ Feature

After data is inserted into an Office document as a linked or embedded object, the object will appear with a border outline and *sizing handles*—small boxes (or circles) that you use to size an object, as shown here. If the border outline or sizing handles are not visible, you must first select the object by clicking on it once. After you have selected the object, you use the mouse to move and resize it to fit alongside the existing data or within the dimensions of the current document.

	2003	2004
Grommets	100	123
Grapples	56	52

→ Method

To select a shared object:

Position the mouse pointer over the object (or its placeholder icon) until a four-headed arrow (⊕) appears and then click once to select it.

After you select the object, use the following techniques to manipulate its appearance:

Move the selected object by dragging it with the mouse.

Resize the selected object by dragging its sizing handles.

Delete the selected object by pressing **DELETE**.

→ Practice

You will now practice selecting, moving, resizing, and deleting an embedded object in Word 2003.

1. Load Microsoft Office Word 2003 using the Start menu (**start**).

2. Open the IM0131 document from the Advantage student data files folder, and then save it as "Cruises" to your personal storage location.

3. To practice manipulating the embedded worksheet object, you must first select the object in the Word 2003 document. Do the following:
CLICK: once on the Microsoft Office Excel Worksheet Object, as identified in Figure 1.19

Figure 1.19

The "Cruises" document

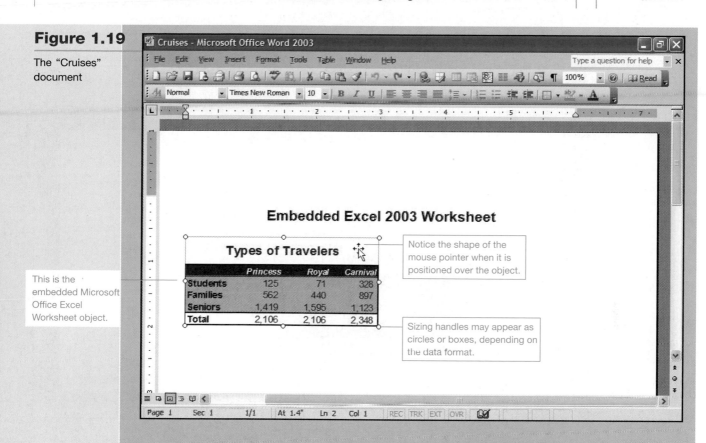

This is the embedded Microsoft Office Excel Worksheet object.

Embedded Excel 2003 Worksheet

Types of Travelers

	Princess	Royal	Carnival
Students	125	71	328
Families	562	440	897
Seniors	1,419	1,595	1,123
Total	2,106	2,106	2,348

Notice the shape of the mouse pointer when it is positioned over the object.

Sizing handles may appear as circles or boxes, depending on the data format.

4. To resize the selected object, position the mouse pointer over the sizing handle in the bottom right-hand corner. The mouse pointer changes to a double-headed arrow when positioned correctly. (*Hint:* When you select one of the corner sizing handles, the object is sized proportionally as you drag the mouse.)

5. DRAG: the sizing handle to the right about one inch
(*Hint:* Use the Ruler to guide your distance.)

6. To move the selected object, position the mouse pointer over the object until the mouse pointer changes to a four-headed arrow (✥).

7. DRAG: the object to the right so that it appears centered beneath the title, as shown in Figure 1.20

Figure 1.20

Resizing and moving an object

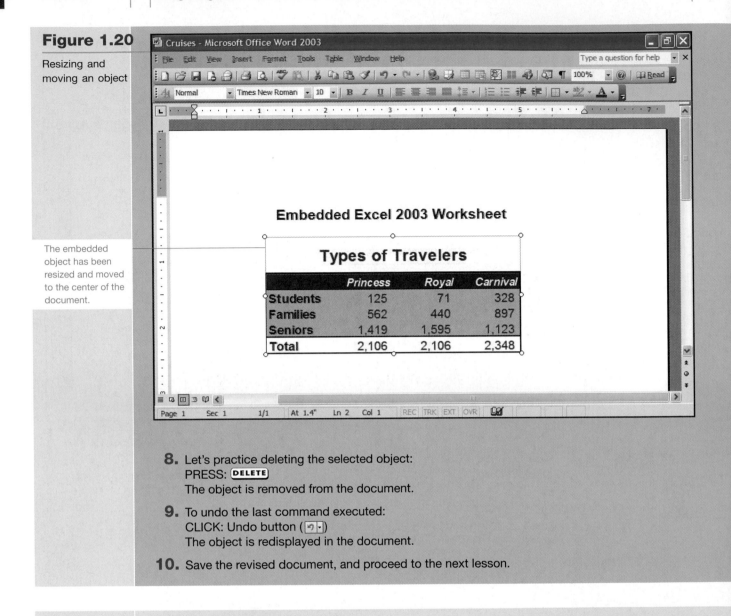

The embedded object has been resized and moved to the center of the document.

8. Let's practice deleting the selected object:
   PRESS: DELETE
   The object is removed from the document.

9. To undo the last command executed:
   CLICK: Undo button ( )
   The object is redisplayed in the document.

10. Save the revised document, and proceed to the next lesson.

1.3.2 Editing Shared Objects

→ # Feature

A special feature in Microsoft Office System 2003 called *visual editing* makes it easy to update embedded objects. With visual editing, double-clicking an embedded object causes the object's source application to temporarily replace the existing application's menus and toolbars with its own, so that you have full access to its editing features and capabilities. Visual editing allows you to edit, for example, an Excel 2003 object from within a Word 2003 document; as opposed to launching the object inside the Excel 2003 application window. Conversely, to edit a linked object, you must first switch to the source or server application in order to edit the original document. The linked object (in the destination document) is updated automatically when changes are made to the source document.

Method

To edit an embedded object:

- DOUBLE-CLICK: the object to enable visual editing

  Make the desired changes.

- CLICK: outside of the object to return to editing the document

To edit a linked object:

Open the original document inside of the server application.

Make the desired changes.

Save and then close the document and server application.

Practice

You will now practice editing an embedded object, since you have already edited a linked object in lesson 1.2.2. Ensure that you have completed the previous lesson and that the "Cruises" document is open in Word 2003.

1. To begin editing the embedded worksheet object:
DOUBLE-CLICK: the Microsoft Office Excel Worksheet Object
Your screen should now appear similar to Figure 1.21. Notice that the Word 2003 Menu bar and toolbars are replaced by those found in an Excel 2003 application window. The worksheet area is also bound by row and column headers to facilitate editing the data.

Figure 1.21

Editing an embedded object

The Menu bar and toolbars are replaced with Excel's, although this remains the Word 2003 application window.

The hashed border indicates that you are editing the embedded object using the "visual editing" feature.

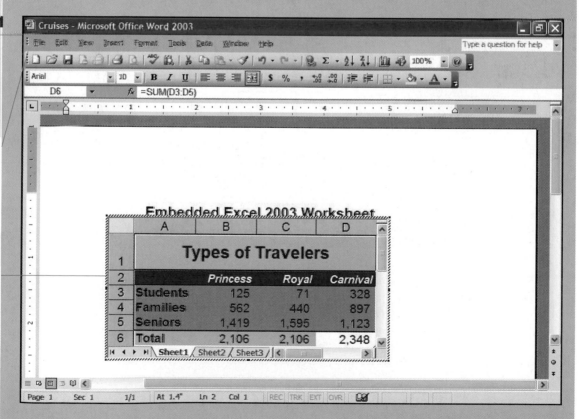

2. Now let's make some changes to the object's data:
SELECT: cell B3
TYPE: **150**
PRESS: **ENTER**
Note that the worksheet's "Total" row recalculates the value in cell B6, as expected.

3. You can perform many additional editing operations. For our purposes, however, let's finish editing the embedded object:
CLICK: the mouse pointer outside of the object
The object's hashed border outline disappears.

4. On your own, edit the embedded worksheet object to display the table's values with currency formatting and no decimal places. (*Hint:* Use the Format → Cells command or the toolbar buttons and .) When completed, return to the document so that your screen appears similar to the one shown in Figure 1.22.

Figure 1.22

Editing cell displays in an embedded worksheet object

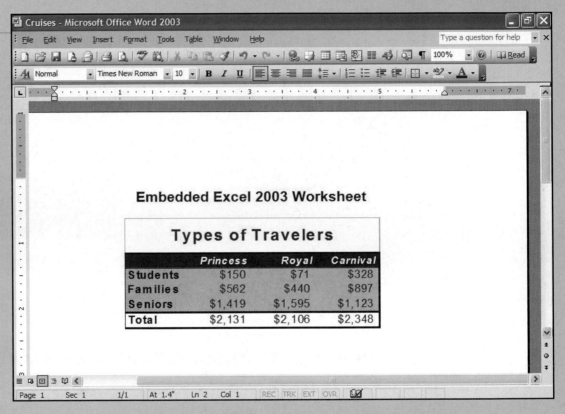

5. Save and then close the revised "Cruises" document.

6. Exit Microsoft Office Word 2003.

 **1.3** How do you proportionally resize a shared object?

1.4 Inserting Worksheets and Charts in Office Word

Inserting existing objects into a document, workbook, or presentation is relatively straightforward using either the Windows or Office Clipboards. You can also create new objects for insertion using the Insert → Object command from within a Microsoft Office System 2003 application window. There are several types of shared objects, including worksheets, charts, presentations, sound files, text files, and bitmap images from which you may choose. Once created, new objects are inserted automatically as embedded objects (as opposed to linked objects). In this module, you will learn how to insert new Excel 2003 worksheets and charts into a Word 2003 document.

1.4.1 Inserting a New Worksheet in Office Word

→ ## Feature

Word 2003 provides the table feature for separating data into rows and columns for display in a document. Although quite powerful for word processing software, Word's table feature pales in comparison to the strength of Excel 2003 for tabulating and analyzing numerical data. If you require the advanced calculation features found in Excel 2003, consider inserting a worksheet object into your Word 2003 document rather than using a table. Instead of loading Excel 2003, you may find it easier to insert a Microsoft Office Excel Worksheet object from within Word 2003, especially for smaller worksheets.

→ ## Method

To insert an Excel 2003 worksheet object into a Word 2003 document:

Position the insertion point or cursor at the location where you want the object inserted.

- CHOOSE: Insert → Object
- SELECT: Microsoft Office Excel Worksheet in the *Object type* list box
- CLICK: OK command button

In the Word 2003 application window, edit the worksheet using Excel 2003's menus and toolbar buttons.

- CLICK: outside of the embedded object to return to the Word 2003 menus and toolbar buttons

→ ## Practice

You will now embed a new worksheet object in a Word 2003 document.

1. Load Microsoft Office Word 2003 using the Start menu (*start*). A new document should appear in the application window.

2. Close the Getting Started task pane, if displayed, by clicking its Close button ([×]).

3. To insert a title for the new document:
   TYPE: **My Personal Budget**
   PRESS: **ENTER** twice

4. To insert a new worksheet object:
   CHOOSE: Insert → Object

5. In the Object dialog box, scroll the list box downward and then:
   SELECT: Microsoft Office Excel Worksheet in the *Object type* list box, as shown in Figure 1.23

Figure 1.23

Object dialog box: Excel Worksheet selected

Select the Microsoft Office Excel Worksheet object in the *Object type* list box.

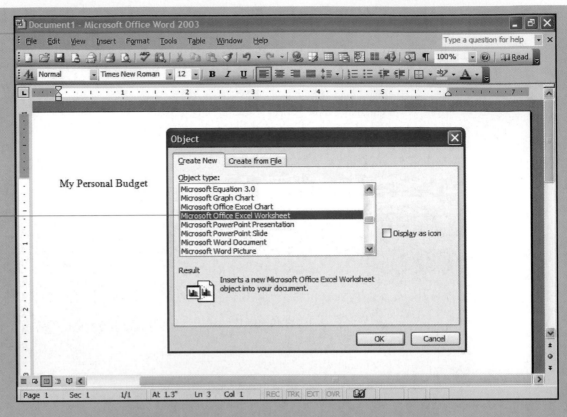

6. To embed the selected object in the new Word 2003 document:
CLICK: OK command button
A worksheet object appears in the document outlined by hashed borders as seen in Figure 1.24.

7. Complete the worksheet as shown in Figure 1.24. (*Hint:* Click in the appropriate cell and then type the required information. Apply formatting using the toolbar buttons.)

Figure 1.24

Completing the embedded worksheet object

Excel 2003's Menu bar

Microsoft Office Excel Worksheet object embedded into Word 2003 document

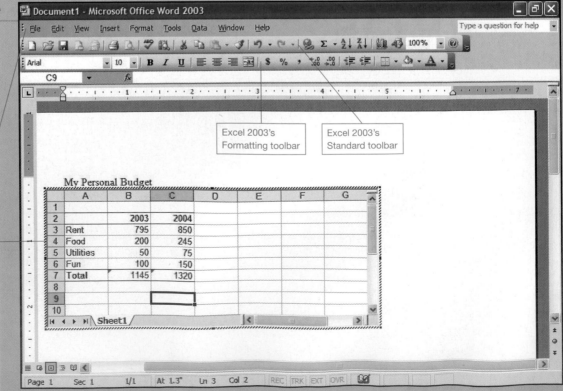

8. To return control to the Word 2003 application window:
CLICK: outside of the embedded object in the document area
Notice that the Menu bar and toolbars revert to those of Word 2003.

9. To resize the embedded object:
DOUBLE-CLICK: on the embedded object
The hashed border returns to the object, as do the Excel 2003 Menu bar and toolbars.

10. Using the sizing handles, resize the embedded object so that only columns A, B, and C are displayed, along with rows 1 through 7.

11. When you are ready to proceed:
CLICK: outside of the embedded object in the document area
Your screen should now appear similar to the one shown in Figure 1.25.

Figure 1.25

Resizing an
embedded object

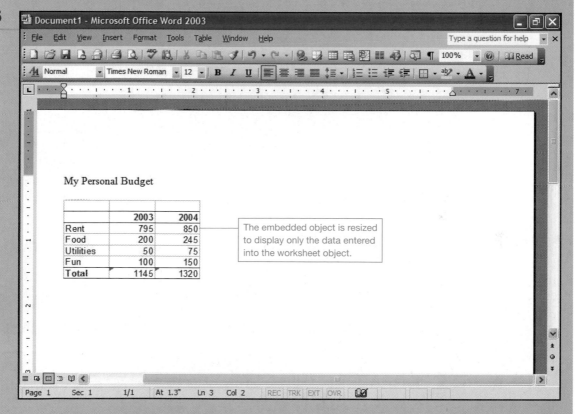

12. Save the document as "Embedded Budget" to your personal storage location, and then close the document.

1.4.2 Inserting a New Chart in Office Word

→ **Feature**

One of the key strengths of Excel 2003 is its ability to display numerical data using professionally designed charts and graphs. Excel 2003's charting capabilities are comprehensive, offering many styles, designs, and formats not available in other software products. As you might imagine, there are many opportunities for using these high-quality graphics in your other applications, such as Office Word documents and Office PowerPoint presentations. This lesson demonstrates how easy it is to incorporate an Excel 2003 chart into a Word 2003 document file.

→ ## Method

To insert an Excel 2003 chart object into a Word 2003 document:

Position the insertion point or cursor at the location where you want the object inserted.

- CHOOSE: Insert → Object
- SELECT: Microsoft Office Excel Chart in the *Object type* list box
- CLICK: OK command button

In the Word 2003 application window, edit the chart using Excel 2003's menus and toolbar buttons.

- CLICK: outside of the embedded object to return to the Word 2003 menus and toolbar buttons

→ ## Practice

You will now embed a new chart object in a Word 2003 document. Ensure that the Word 2003 application is open and that no documents appear in the work area.

1. To begin, display a new document in Word 2003:
CLICK: New Blank Document button ( )

2. To insert a title for the new document:
TYPE: **Charting My Budget**
PRESS: ENTER twice

3. To insert a new worksheet object:
CHOOSE: Insert → Object

4. In the Object dialog box, scroll the list box downward and then:
SELECT: Microsoft Office Excel Chart in the *Object type* list box, as shown in Figure 1.26

Figure 1.26

Object dialog box: Excel Chart selected

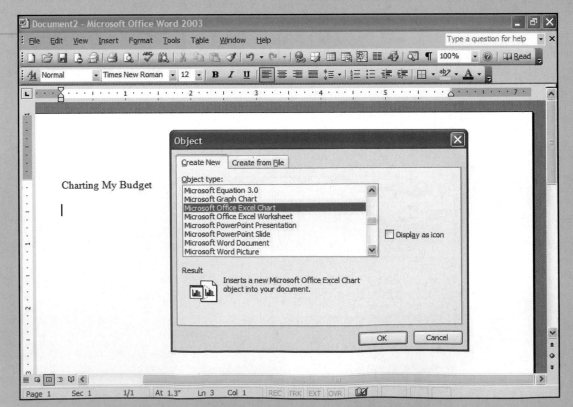

5. To embed the selected object in the new Word 2003 document:
CLICK: OK command button
A chart object appears in the document outlined by hashed borders as seen in Figure 1.27. (*Note:* Because this is not a lesson in building Excel 2003 chart objects, you will accept the default chart object and proceed to the next step.)

Figure 1.27

Embedding a chart object

Use the Chart toolbar and menus to edit the chart's source data and formatting.

The embedded chart object is outlined with a hashed border.

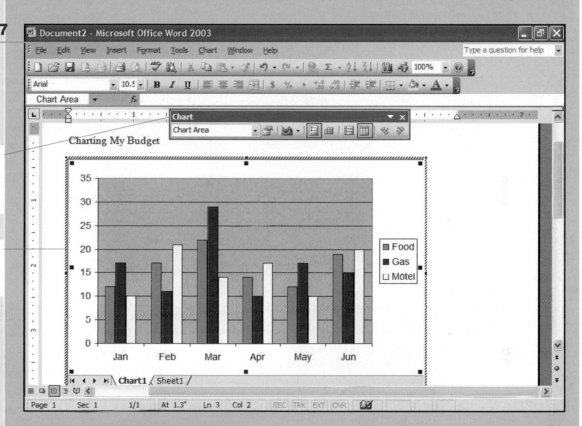

6. To return control to the Word 2003 application window:
CLICK: outside of the embedded object in the document area
Notice that the Menu bar and toolbars revert to those of Word 2003.

7. Save the document as "Embedded Chart" to your personal storage location, and then close the document.

8. Exit Microsoft Office Word 2003.

1.4 How do you activate the visual editing feature for embedded objects?

Chapter
summary

Microsoft Office System 2003 provides feature-rich individual applications for performing a variety of personal- and business-oriented tasks. However, the extensive power of Office is only truly realized when you exchange and share data between these exceptional applications. The easiest method for sharing data is to cut or copy and then paste the data using the Windows Clipboard, which is familiar to all users and accessible to all Windows applications. The Microsoft Office System 2003 provides an enhanced version of the Windows Clipboard called the Office Clipboard that can store up to 24 items at once. You can paste the stored items individually or as a group into any one of the Office applications.

In Microsoft Office System 2003, data is exchanged or shared using three primary methods: pasting, linking, and embedding. These three methods differ in how they relate source data and pasted data. With the pasting method, you insert the data stored on the Clipboard into the destination document using the default data format, which varies depending on the type of source data and the destination document. With the linking method, you insert data into the destination document and, at the same time, retain a dynamic link to the data in its original or source document. Any changes to the data in the source document flow through to update the contents of the destination document. With embedding, you insert the data along with information about what application should be used to maintain the document. Double-clicking an embedded object enables you to edit the source data using the appropriate application's menus and toolbars, without leaving the destination document. Besides editing its contents, you can also move, resize, and delete a shared object.

Command Summary

Many of the commands and procedures appearing in this chapter are summarized in the following table.

Skill Set	To Perform This Task . . .	Do the Following . . .
Using the Office Clipboard	Display the Office Clipboard	CHOOSE: Edit → Office Clipboard
	Paste the contents of the Office Clipboard as a group	CLICK: Paste All command button (Paste All) in the Clipboard task pane
	Clear the contents of the Office Clipboard	CLICK: Clear All command button (Clear All) in the Clipboard task pane
Pasting Data	Paste data from Word 2003 into Excel 2003, once the data appears on the Clipboard	CHOOSE: Edit, Paste, or CLICK: Paste button ( )
Linking Data	Insert a link to existing Microsoft Office System 2003 data once it appears on the Clipboard	CHOOSE: Edit → Paste Special SELECT: *Paste link* option button SELECT: a data format in the *As* list box CLICK: OK command button
	Edit linked data that appears in the destination document	Switch to the server application and update the source document.
	Update or refresh a linked object	RIGHT-CLICK: the linked object CHOOSE: Update Link
Embedding Data	Embed Excel 2003 data in Word 2003, once the data appears on the Clipboard	CHOOSE: Edit → Paste Special SELECT: Microsoft Office Excel Worksheet object in the *As* list box CLICK: OK command button

	Embed a new Microsoft Office System 2003 object, without using the Clipboard	CHOOSE: Insert → Object CLICK: *Create New* tab SELECT: the desired object in the *Object type* list box CLICK: OK command button
	Edit embedded data that appears in a destination document	DOUBLE-CLICK: the object and make your changes CLICK: outside of the object to conclude editing
Modifying Shared Objects	Resize an object	SELECT: the object DRAG: the object's sizing handles
	Move an object	DRAG: the object to a new location
	Delete an object	SELECT: the object PRESS: DELETE

Key Terms

This section specifies page references for the key terms identified in this chapter. For a complete list of definitions, refer to the Glossary at the end of this learning guide.

destination document, *p. IMO 10*

embedding, *p. IMO 10*

HTML, *p. IMO 9*

linking, *p. IMO 10*

Office Clipboard, *p. IMO 2*

pasting, *p. IMO 10*

server application, *p. IMO 17*

sizing handles, *p. IMO 5*

source document, *p. IMO 10*

Windows Clipboard, *p. IMO 2*

Chapter
quiz

Short Answer

1. What is meant by the term "linking"?

2. What is meant by the term "embedding"?

3. How do embedded objects differ from linked objects? Under what circumstances would you choose linking over embedding?

4. Describe the general procedure for embedding a new Excel 2003 chart object in a Word 2003 document.

5. What is the primary difference between the Windows Clipboard and the Office Clipboard?

6. How do you delete an embedded object?

7. How do you paste the contents of the Office Clipboard as a group?

8. How do you clear the contents of the Office Clipboard?

9. What is the procedure for editing a linked object?

10. What is the procedure for editing an embedded object?

True/False

1. _____ The destination document is the document that receives the data from another application.

2. _____ An embedded object is automatically updated when information in its source document changes.

3. _____ You should embed an object when the information needs to be updated by different people on a network.

4. _____ You can embed a new object or an existing object in a document.

5. _____ The Office Clipboard can store up to a maximum of 12 items.

6. _____ Linked objects are updated automatically each time the destination document is opened.

7. _____ Microsoft Office Word 2003 provides charting capabilities that are superior to those of Microsoft Office Excel 2003.

8. _____ The last item you copy to the Office Clipboard is always the only item stored on the Windows Clipboard.

9. _____ Objects that you insert by choosing the Insert → Object command are embedded automatically in the destination document.

10. _____ After double-clicking an embedded object to perform visual editing, the object's source application menus and toolbars replace the existing application's menus and toolbars.

Multiple Choice

1. When exchanging data between Microsoft Office System 2003 applications, the following document is the document in which the data was first entered:

   a. Source
   b. Destination
   c. Original
   d. Primary

2. To establish a link between a source document and a destination document, use which of the following commands?

   a. Tools → Link → Documents
   b. Tools → Link
   c. Edit → Link
   d. Edit → Paste Special

3. Which of the following is a Microsoft Office System 2003 feature that makes it easy to update embedded objects?

   a. Copy and Pasting
   b. Edit → Links
   c. Visual editing
   d. Tools → Maintain Links

4. Which of the following features would be the most helpful in assembling various data items into a single document?

   a. Windows Clipboard
   b. Office Clipboard
   c. Visual editing
   d. Paste Special

5. To enable automatic updates between source and destination documents, you must perform which of the following actions between the documents?

   a. Apply permissions
   b. Define a relationship
   c. Embed objects
   d. Establish a link

6. When you insert an Excel 2003 chart into a Word 2003 document:

   a. Word 2003 is the destination document (application)
   b. Excel 2003 is the destination document (application)
   c. The chart object is the destination document (application)
   d. The Word document is the source document (application)

7. When you want to update the data in a linked worksheet range:

    a. DOUBLE-CLICK: the worksheet range object

    b. RIGHT-CLICK: the worksheet range and choose Edit Object

    c. Edit the worksheet data in the destination document

    d. Edit the worksheet data in the source document

8. When you want to update the data in an embedded worksheet range:

    a. DOUBLE-CLICK: the worksheet range object

    b. RIGHT-CLICK: the worksheet range and choose Edit Object

    c. Edit the worksheet data in the destination document

    d. Edit the worksheet data in the source document

9. It is possible for you to do which of the following to an embedded object?

    a. Move

    b. Resize

    c. Delete

    d. All of the above

10. To specify the target format for pasting data into a destination document, use the following command:

    a. Insert Link

    b. Insert Object

    c. Paste Special

    d. Paste Unique

Hands-On
exercises

ep by step

1. Pasting and Clearing Clipboard Items

In this exercise, you will prepare a short document in Microsoft Office Word 2003 that incorporates two Excel 2003 data items. To accomplish this task, you must copy items to the Office Clipboard, paste the data into Word 2003, and then clear the contents of the Office Clipboard.

1. Load Microsoft Office Word 2003 using the Start menu (start).

2. Open the IM01HE01 document from the Advantage student data files folder, and then save it as "Toy Sales Letter" to your personal storage location. Your screen should appear similar to the one shown in Figure 1.28 before proceeding.

Integrating

Figure 1.28

"Toy Sales Letter" document

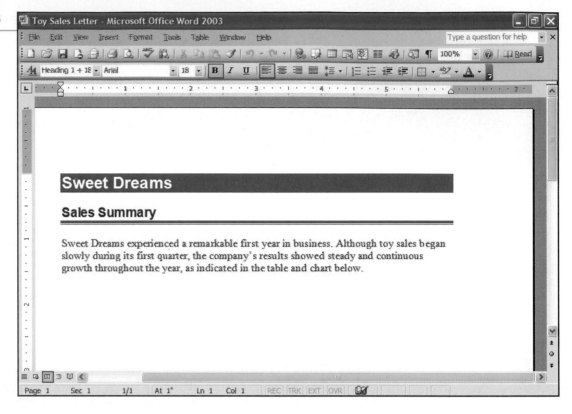

3. Load Microsoft Office Excel 2003 using the Start menu (start).

4. Open the IM01HE01 workbook from the Advantage student data files folder, and then save it as "Toy Sales Data" to your personal storage location. Your screen should appear similar to the one shown in Figure 1.29 before proceeding.

Figure 1.29

"Toy Sales Data" workbook

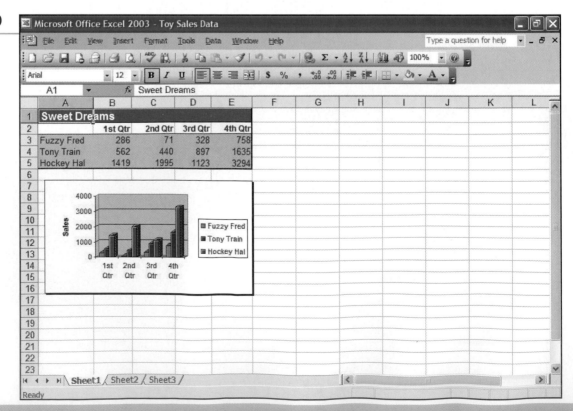

5. Use the Menu bar to display the Clipboard task pane in the Excel 2003 application window.

6. If the Clipboard task pane does not appear to be empty, clear all of the displayed items using the Clear All button (Clear All).

7. Copy the worksheet cell range from A1 to E5 to the Office Clipboard. If done properly, a partial view of the copied data will appear in the Clipboard task pane.

8. Select the chart object displayed on the worksheet by clicking on it once.

9. Copy the chart object to the Office Clipboard. Two items should now appear in the Clipboard task pane.

10. Switch to the "Toy Sales Letter" document in the Word 2003 application window.

11. Move the insertion point or cursor to the end of the document using the (CTRL) + (END) key combination.

12. Ensure that the Clipboard task pane is displayed and then use the Paste All button (Paste All) to insert the contents of the Office Clipboard into the Word 2003 document, as shown in Figure 1.30.

Figure 1.30

Pasting Excel 2003 data into a Word 2003 document

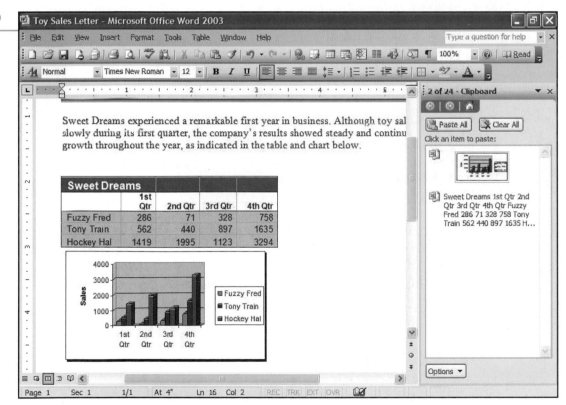

13. Clear the contents of the Office Clipboard using the Clear All button (Clear All).

14. Save, print, and then close the "Toy Sales Letter" document. Close the "Toy Sales Data" workbook, without saving any changes.

15. Exit Microsoft Office Word 2003 and Microsoft Office Excel 2003.

2. Inserting a Linked Chart in Word 2003

You are now tasked with preparing a document that incorporates a linked chart object. The chart is stored and will continue to be maintained within an Excel 2003 workbook.

1. Load Microsoft Office Word 2003 using the Start menu (start).

2. Open the IM01HE02 document from the Advantage student data files folder, and then save it as "Chairman Letter" to your personal storage location. Your screen should appear similar to the one shown in Figure 1.31 before proceeding.

Figure 1.31

"Chairman Letter" document

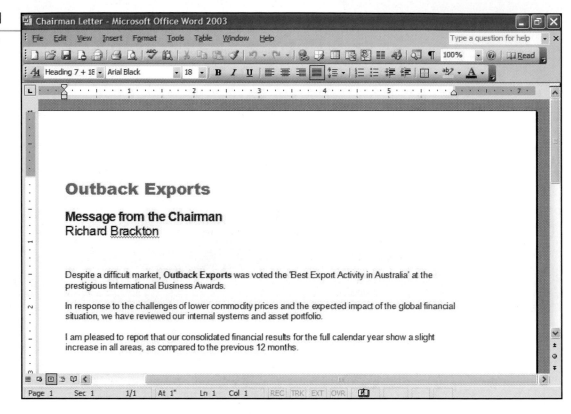

3. Load Microsoft Office Excel 2003 using the Start menu (start).

4. Open the IM01HE02 workbook from the Advantage student data files folder, and then save it as "Export Data" to your personal storage location. Your screen should appear similar to the one shown in Figure 1.32 before proceeding.

Figure 1.32

"Export Data"
workbook

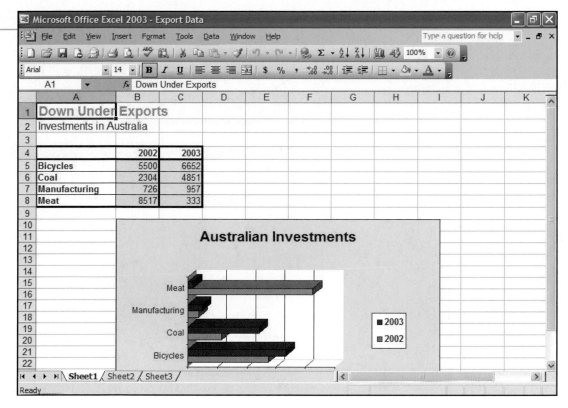

5. Copy the "Australian Investments" chart object to the Windows Clipboard.

6. Switch to the "Chairman Letter" document in the Word 2003 application window.

7. Move the insertion point or cursor to the end of the document using the CTRL + END key combination.

8. Using the Paste Special dialog box (Figure 1.33), paste the Excel 2003 chart object into the document and establish a link between the source data in the "Export Data" workbook and the destination document, "Chairman Letter."

Figure 1.33

Inserting a linked
object using the
Paste Special
dialog box

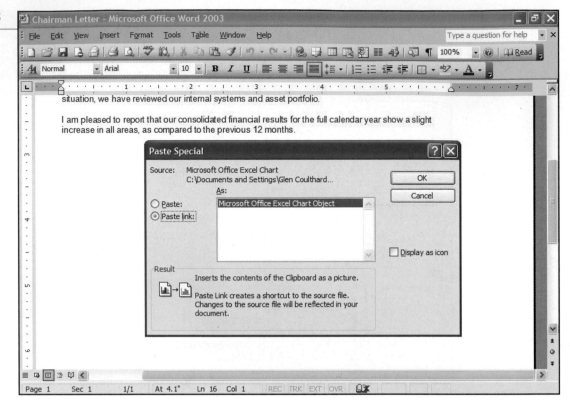

9. With the chart object now displayed in the Word 2003 document, switch back to the "Export Data" workbook in the Excel 2003 application window.

10. Change the "Meat" value for 2003 appearing in cell C8 from "333" to "9000." Notice that the chart is updated in the Excel 2003 application window.

11. Save the "Export Data" workbook.

12. Switch to the "Chairman Letter" document in the Word 2003 application window.

13. If necessary, right-click the linked chart object and choose the Update Link command to refresh the object's display, as shown in Figure 1.34. The chart object should be displayed with the new worksheet values.

Figure 1.34

Updating a linked
chart object

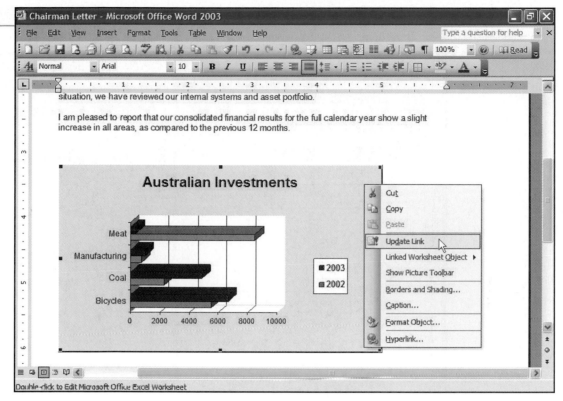

14. Save, print, and then close the "Chairman Letter" document.

15. Exit Microsoft Office Word 2003 and Microsoft Office Excel 2003.

3. Inserting and Manipulating Shared Objects

This exercise lets you practice embedding and linking Excel 2003 objects in a document and maintaining those objects from within Word 2003.

1. Load Microsoft Office Word 2003 using the Start menu (start).

2. Open the IM01HE03 document from the Advantage student data files folder, and then save it as "Flavors" to your personal storage location.

3. Load Microsoft Office Excel 2003 using the Start menu (start).

4. Open the IM01HE03 workbook from the Advantage student data files folder, and then save it as "Flavor Results" to your personal storage location.

5. To view both application windows on the desktop at the same time:
RIGHT-CLICK: a blank portion of the Windows taskbar
CHOOSE: Tile Windows Vertically
Your screen should now appear similar to the one shown in Figure 1.35. Notice that both the Office Word and Office Excel windows are displayed.

Integrating

Figure 1.35

Tiling windows vertically on the desktop

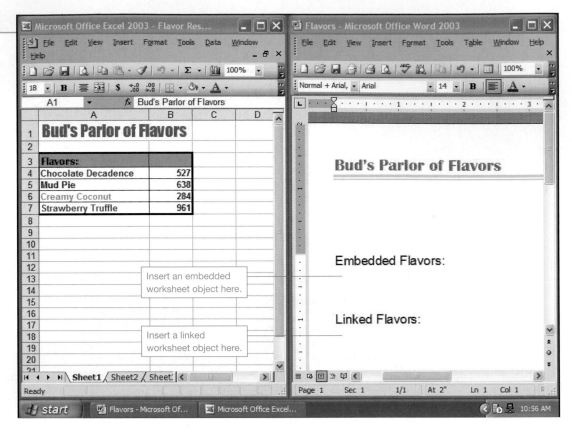

6. In the Excel 2003 worksheet, select and then copy the cell range from A3 to B7 to the Windows Clipboard.

7. Click within the Word 2003 application window and move the insertion point two rows beneath the "Embedded Flavors" heading.

8. Using the Paste Special command, paste the data as an embedded Microsoft Office Excel Worksheet Object.

9. Because the original source data remains on the Windows Clipboard, you can continue pasting the data. This time, position the insertion point two rows beneath the "Linked Flavors" heading.

10. Using the Paste Special command, paste the data as a linked object using the default data format. Your screen should now appear similar to the one shown in Figure 1.36.

Figure 1.36

Inserting objects

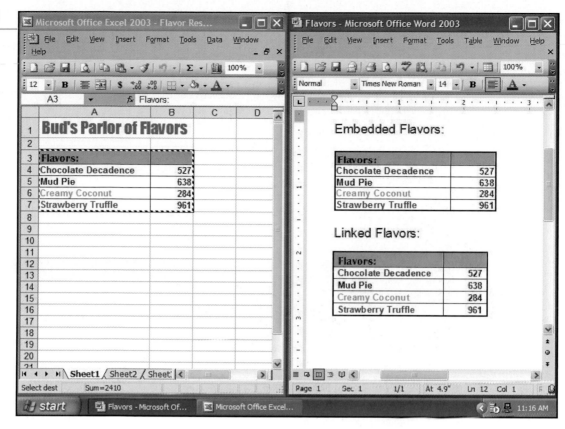

11. Edit the embedded object by changing the Chocolate Decadence value from "527" to "1000."

12. Edit the worksheet so that the Mud Pie value in cell B5 displays "750" rather than "638." Then, right-click the linked object in the "Flavors" document and choose Update Link to display the new amount.

13. Save, print, and then close the "Flavors" document.

14. Maximize and then exit the Microsoft Office Word 2003 application window.

15. Save and then close the "Flavor Results" workbook.

16. Maximize and then exit the Microsoft Office Excel 2003 application window.

n your own

4. Embedding New Excel 2003 Objects

Mary is an employee for The Software Edge, an online software retailer. She has been asked to prepare a Word 2003 document that outlines the number of software conventions the "Edge" employees must attend in the coming quarter. After assembling the required information, Mary performs the following steps.

- She loads Microsoft Office Word 2003 and labels a new document with the heading "Number of Software Edge Conventions."

- A few lines down in the document, she inserts a new Microsoft Office Excel Worksheet object and enters the following information, beginning in cell A1.

New York	15
Chicago	10
Dallas	12
Phoenix	10

- She then resizes the object, as shown here.

- After returning to the document, Mary moves the insertion point down a few lines below the embedded worksheet object.

- She inserts a second heading entitled "Software Edge Convention Expenses" at the insertion point, followed by two blank lines.

- At the insertion point, Mary inserts a new Microsoft Office Excel Chart object and then clicks outside of the chart to accept the default data. She will update the information another time.

- After Mary reduces the zoom factor to 75%, her document appears similar to the one shown in Figure 1.37.

Figure 1.37

Inserting objects into a Word 2003 document

Embedded Microsoft Office Excel Worksheet object

Embedded Microsoft Office Excel Chart object

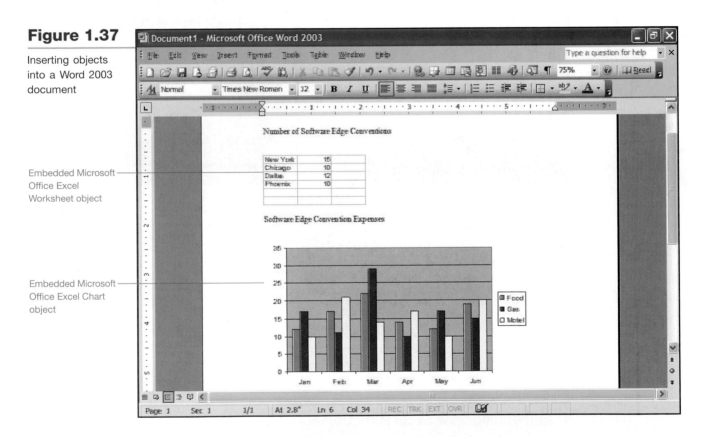

Mary saves the document as "Software Edge" and then prints it for review. Satisfied with her work to this point, Mary closes the document and then exits Microsoft Office Word 2003.

5. Pasting Between Word 2003 and Excel 2003

Your objective for this exercise is to create and copy two Word 2003 data items to the Office Clipboard. You will then insert these two items into a new Excel 2003 worksheet. To begin, load Microsoft Office Excel 2003 and then Microsoft Office Word 2003. Ensure that the Word 2003 application window is active and that the zoom factor is 100%.

Using Figure 1.38 as your guide, create a new Word 2003 document with the headings "My Favorite Animals" and "My Favorite Colors." Under the respective headings, type a bulleted list containing entries for your three favorite animals and three favorite colors. Display the Office Clipboard, and then copy the first heading ("My Favorite Animals"), along with its list, to the Office Clipboard. Then copy the next heading ("My Favorite Colors") and its list to the Office Clipboard. After pressing (CTRL) + (HOME) to return to the top of the document, your screen should appear similar to the one shown in Figure 1.38.

Figure 1.38

Copying items to the Office Clipboard

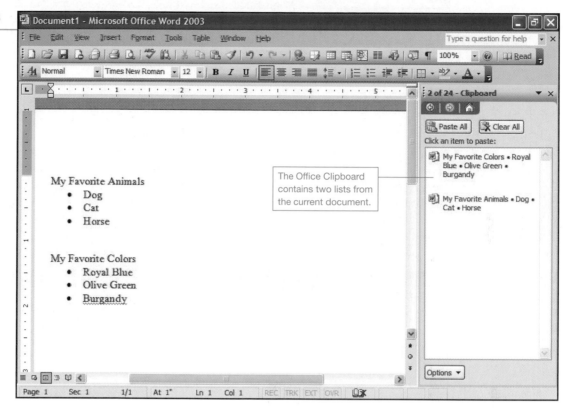

Switch to the Excel 2003 application window. Select cell B2 and then paste the "My Favorite Animals" data item into the worksheet. Next select cell E2 and paste the "My Favorite Colors" data item. Notice that each item in the list is entered on a separate row in the worksheet. To demonstrate pasting the entire group of items, select cell B7 and then click the Paste All button (Paste All). Save the workbook as "Favorites" to your personal storage location. Print and then close the workbook, and exit Microsoft Office Excel 2003. Finally, exit Microsoft Office Word 2003, without saving the document changes.

6. Pasting, Linking, and Embedding

This exercise provides additional practice in pasting, linking, and embedding objects in Microsoft Office Word 2003. As a junior research assistant, you are tasked with explaining to management how to prepare a Word 2003 document that incorporates data from Excel 2003. To this end, you have decided to copy a range of worksheet cells to a single Word 2003 document three times, in order to demonstrate each of the three insertion methods. To begin, create the Excel 2003 worksheet displayed in Figure 1.39, and save it as "Cities" to your personal storage location.

Figure 1.39

The "Cities"
workbook

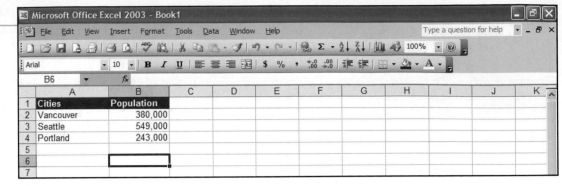

Load Microsoft Office Word 2003, and display a new document with the heading "City Statistics." Copy the cell range from A1 to B4 in the "Cities" workbook to the Windows Clipboard. A few lines below the heading, paste the Excel 2003 data into the Word 2003 document using the Paste button (⬛) on the Standard toolbar. Add a few additional lines and then paste the Excel 2003 data as a dynamic link. Finally, after adding some more lines, paste the Excel 2003 data as an embedded object. Your screen should appear similar to the one shown in Figure 1.40.

Figure 1.40

Pasting Excel
2003 data into a
new document

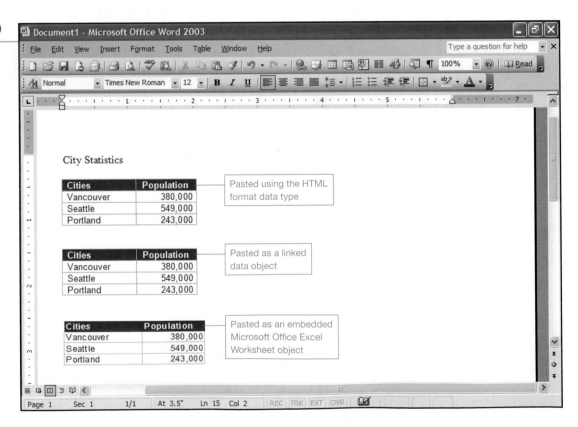

Using the appropriate methods, update the population of Seattle to display 575,000 people in each of the three objects. Save the document as "City Statistics," and then exit Microsoft Office Word 2003. Save the "Cities" workbook, and then exit Microsoft Office Excel 2003.

CaseStudy   ARBOR FORESTRY

Sam Houghton is a senior manager with Arbor Forestry, a major harvesting and value-added lumber company operating in the Pacific Northwest. Having worked with Microsoft Office over the past few years, Sam is quite comfortable creating documents in Word 2003 and basic worksheets in Excel 2003. Until recently, however, Sam had not realized how easy it was to exchange data between the Office applications. While discussing an unrelated issue, Sam noticed that his junior assistant was copying a range of worksheet cells and then pasting the data into a Word 2003 document. Completely impressed by this demonstration, Sam returned to his Advantage Series guides and learned how best to integrate Microsoft Office System 2003. He is now ready to practice his newly acquired skills using real documents and workbooks!

In the following case problems, assume the role of Sam and perform the same steps that he identifies.

1. Sam starts his day by opening a Word 2003 memo named IM01CS01. This memo is addressed to the production manager and describes the company's productivity levels over the past three months. Before proceeding, Sam saves the memo as "ProdQtr1" to his personal storage location. Rather than retype the productivity figures into a table, Sam decides to copy and paste the data from one of his existing Excel 2003 worksheets. He opens the IM01CS01 workbook and then displays the Office Clipboard's task pane. Starting with January's results, Sam copies each month's table to the Office Clipboard separately. Switching back to the "ProdQtr1" document, Sam moves the insertion point below the paragraph and pastes January's table, adds a blank line, pastes February's table, adds another blank line, and then inserts March's table. After changing the zoom factor to 50%, Sam saves the document, which now appears similar to the one shown in Figure 1.41. He clears the Office Clipboard and then closes the Clipboard task pane. Before proceeding to his next task, Sam closes the document and workbook but keeps the Word 2003 and Excel 2003 application windows open.

Figure 1.41

Pasting items
from the Office
Clipboard

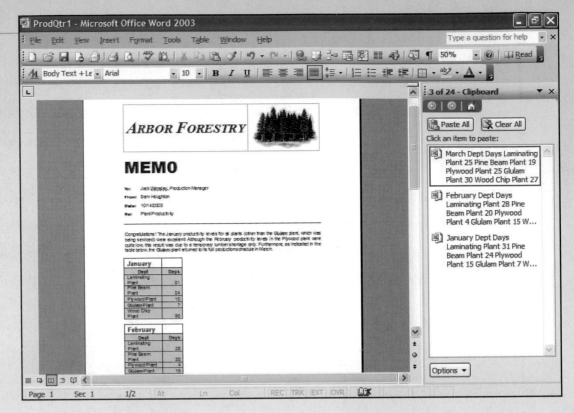

2. Each month, Sam must forward a memo to the personnel manager, Harold Brock, detailing the number of full-capacity production days at each of Arbor's plants. To begin this task, Sam creates a new Word 2003 document, shown in Figure 1.42, called "Personnel Memo." Be sure to set the zoom factor for the document window to 100%.

Figure 1.42

"Personnel
Memo" document

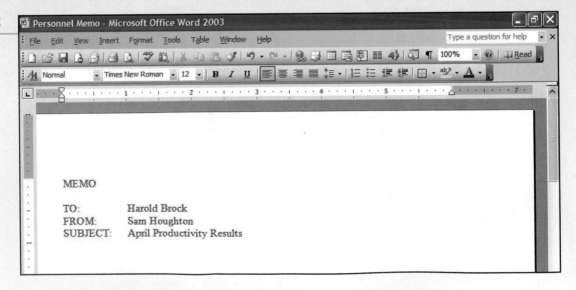

Sam opens the IM01CS02 Excel 2003 workbook and then saves it as "April-Prod" to his personal storage location. He copies the April results in cells A5 through B11 to the Windows Clipboard. Because this information may change, Sam decides to paste the data into the "Personnel Memo" as a linked object using the HTML format. To ensure that the link is active, Sam switches to the Excel 2003 application window and changes the value for cell B7 to "30." He then returns to Word 2003 to witness the dynamic flow-through updating, as shown in Figure 1.43. (*Note:* You may have to right-click on the object and choose Update Link to refresh the object.) After printing the memo, Sam saves and closes both the document and workbook. He keeps the Word 2003 and Excel 2003 application windows open for use in his next task.

Figure 1.43

Inserting a linked cell range from Excel 2003

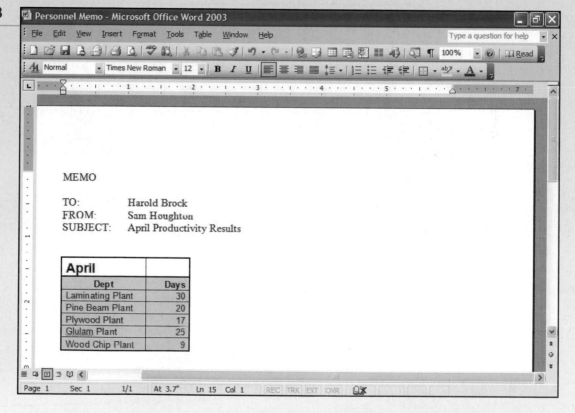

3. Sam wants to practice editing, resizing, and moving a shared object in a Word 2003 document. He retrieves the IM01CS03 document and saves it as "Conversions" to his personal storage location. Sam ensures that the zoom factor is 100% and then uses visual editing to modify the embedded table to read "800/900" in the first row of the "PLF Load" column. After clicking outside of the worksheet object, he increases the size of the table and moves it so that it is closer to the heading and centered between the margins. The document's contents should now appear similar to the one shown in Figure 1.44. He saves, prints, and then closes the "Conversions" document. Sam closes Microsoft Office Excel 2003 but leaves the Word 2003 application window open.

Integrating

Figure 1.44

"Conversions"
document

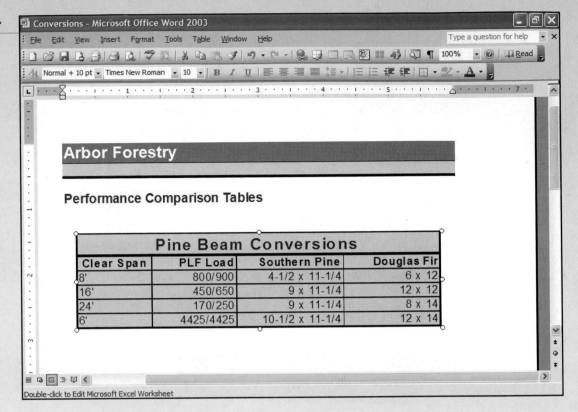

4. Sam must now complete a memo to the Purchasing Department regarding some electrical wire
needed for an upcoming sawmill installation. Sam opens the IM01CS04 document that has already
been started and then saves it as "Purchasing" to his personal storage location. He changes the zoom
factor to 75%. Rather than launching Excel 2003 to create the worksheet, Sam uses the Insert → Object
command to insert a worksheet range at the bottom of the memo. He adds the following data to the
object:

Number	Size	Stranding
SD18	18	16/30
SD19	19	16/30
SD20	20	30/40

At this point, Sam clicks outside the worksheet object in order to continue editing the memo. Upon
further review, Sam notices an important omission in the table. He edits the worksheet object to
include the fourth column shown here:

Amount
40 yds
20 yds
100 yds

After sizing the worksheet object (refer to Figure 1.45), Sam saves and prints the memo. He then closes Microsoft Office Word 2003. Sam is very pleased with the time he saves using the integration capabilities found in Microsoft Office System 2003.

Figure 1.45

"Purchasing" document

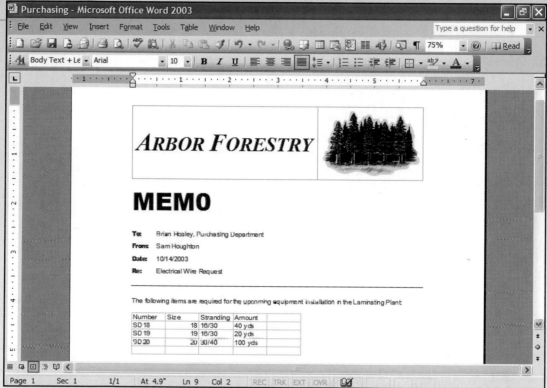

Self-Check Answers

1.1 Name two methods for activating the Office Clipboard and displaying the Clipboard task pane. Copy two items successively to the Clipboard or choose the Edit → Office Clipboard command.

1.2 When you copy worksheet data from Excel 2003, what is the default data format for pasting that data into Word 2003? HTML format.

1.3 How do you proportionally resize a shared object? To resize an object proportionally, drag one of its corner sizing handles inward or outward.

1.4 How do you activate the visual editing feature for embedded objects? Double-click the embedded object to activate visual editing.

Integrating

Notes

Microsoft® Office System 2003®

CHAPTER 2

Performing More Integration Tasks

PREREQUISITES

This chapter assumes that you already know how to create, save, edit, and print Word 2003 documents, Excel 2003 workbooks, and Power-Point 2003 presentations. You should also know how to view and print table data using Access 2003.

LEARNING OBJECTIVES

After completing this chapter, you will be able to:

- Develop an outline in Word 2003 and then convert the document into a Power-Point 2003 presentation

- Copy PowerPoint 2003 slides into Word 2003

- Copy an Excel 2003 chart into PowerPoint 2003

- Export Access 2003 reports to Word 2003

- Transfer an Excel 2003 list to Access 2003

2.1 Creating a Presentation from an Office Word Document

When you need to create longer documents, such as reports, term papers, or books like this one, Word 2003's Outline view helps you to organize your thoughts and plan your approach. You access Outline view in the same way that you access other views provided in Word 2003, by clicking on its button (▣) at the left-hand side of the horizontal scroll bar or by choosing the Outline command on the View menu. In this module, you learn how to use a Word 2003 outline as an efficient starting point for a PowerPoint 2003 presentation.

2.1.1 Creating an Outline Document in Word 2003

→ ## Feature

Most professional writers will concur that outlining is one of the key components of the writing process. Without a proper outline, the writer chances straying off topic, failing to organize facts and data logically, and missing key information. Fortunately, Word 2003 provides the Outline view to help professional and novice writers alike organize their thoughts and ideas. Furthermore, when you create a document in Outline view, Word 2003 automatically applies default heading styles to the various outline levels to ensure consistency in format and appearance.

→ ## Method

To view a document in Word 2003's Outline view:

- CHOOSE: View → Outline

  or

- CLICK: Outline View button (▣) located to the left of the horizontal scroll bar

To enter data into an outline in Word 2003:

- TYPE: **a desired topic**
- PRESS: `ENTER` to move the insertion point to a new heading at the same level in the outline
- CLICK: Demote button (→) to reduce the topic to a lower level

  or

- PRESS: `TAB`
- CLICK: Promote button (←) to increase the topic to a higher level

  or

- PRESS: `SHIFT` + `TAB`

→ ## Practice

You will now create an outline in Word 2003. Ensure that the Windows desktop appears before you begin.

1. Load Microsoft Office Word 2003 using the Start menu (*start*). A new document should appear in the application window.

2. Close the Getting Started task pane, if displayed, by clicking its Close button (☒).

3. To switch to Outline view:
CHOOSE: View → Outline
The insertion point should appear blinking on the first line of the outline (Figure 2.1). Notice that the Outlining toolbar is displayed and that "Heading 1" appears in the Style box on the Formatting toolbar.

Figure 2.1

Creating a document in Outline view

Outlining toolbar

End of Document marker

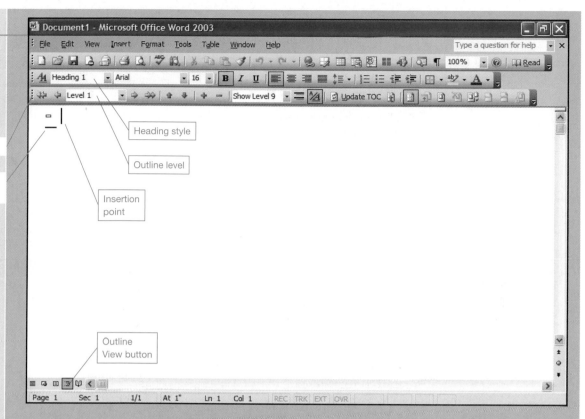

4. To begin typing the outline:
   TYPE: **Exploring the Internet**
   PRESS: **ENTER** to insert another heading

5. TYPE: **Popular Internet Search Tools**
   PRESS: **ENTER** to insert another heading

6. To begin a subtopic in the outline:
   CLICK: Demote button (→) on the Outlining toolbar
   Notice that "Heading 2" now appears in the Style box, along with "Level 2" in the Outline Level box.

7. To enter the subtopics:
   TYPE: **AltaVista**
   PRESS: **ENTER** to insert another heading
   TYPE: **Google**
   PRESS: **ENTER** to insert another heading
   TYPE: **MSN**
   PRESS: **ENTER** to insert another heading
   TYPE: **Yahoo!**
   PRESS: **ENTER** to move to the next line
   Your screen should now appear similar to the one shown in Figure 2.2.

Integrating

Figure 2.2

Entering subtopics in the outline

Main topic at Heading Level 1 in the outline

Subtopic at Heading Level 2 in the outline

8. To return to entering main topic headings:
CLICK: Promote button (⟸) on the Outlining toolbar

9. To continue the outlining process:
TYPE: **Downloading and Sharing Files**
PRESS: (ENTER)
TYPE: **Security, Privacy, and Copyright**

10. To view the main headings only:
CLICK: *Show Level* (Show All Levels ⏷) drop-down list box
SELECT: Show Level 1
Your outline should now appear similar to the one shown in Figure 2.3.

Figure 2.3

Collapsing the outline

The plus sign icon in an outline denotes a topic that contains subtopics and may be expanded.

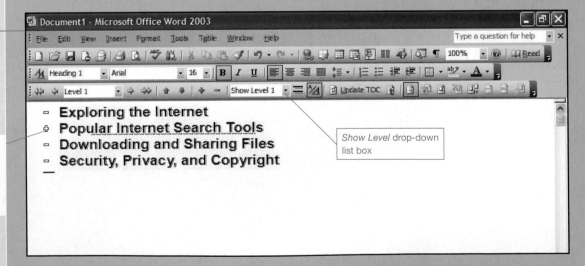

11. To redisplay the entire outline:
CLICK: *Show Level* (Show All Levels ⏷) drop-down list box
SELECT: Show All Levels

12. Save the document as "Internet Outline" to your personal storage location.

2.1.2 Converting an Outline Document into a Slide Presentation

→ **Feature**

Once you have created an outline document using Word 2003, you can easily convert the document into a presentation file using a single menu command. You may then edit, display, print, and save the slide contents in PowerPoint 2003. Because the two documents are not linked dynamically, any subsequent changes that you make to the original Word 2003 outline document will not be reflected in the PowerPoint 2003 presentation file.

→ **Method**

To send an outline document to PowerPoint 2003:

Open the outline document in Word 2003.

• CHOOSE: File → Send To → Microsoft Office PowerPoint

Edit and save the document in PowerPoint 2003.

→ **Practice**

In this exercise, you will convert a Word 2003 outline into a PowerPoint 2003 presentation. Ensure that you have completed the previous lesson and that the "Internet Outline" document is currently displayed in the Word 2003 application window.

1. To convert the displayed outline into a PowerPoint 2003 presentation:
CHOOSE: File → Send To
The menu shown in Figure 2.4 appears on your screen.

Figure 2.4

Send To menu options

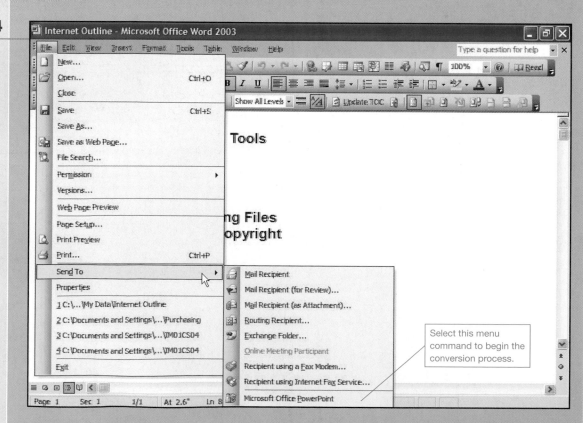

Select this menu command to begin the conversion process.

2. To proceed with the conversion:
CHOOSE: Microsoft Office PowerPoint
PowerPoint 2003 is loaded into memory, and after a few moments, the outline appears as a presentation in the application window (Figure 2.5).

Figure 2.5

"Summary Memo" document

Slide pane

During the conversion process, PowerPoint 2003 creates a new slide for each of the topics formatted using the "Heading 1" style.

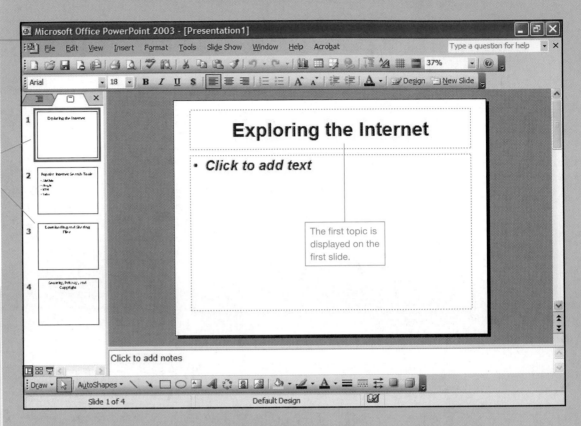

3. To improve the appearance of the presentation, let's apply one of PowerPoint 2003's professionally designed templates:
CHOOSE: Format → Slide Design
The Slide Design task pane appears on the right-hand side of the window.

4. On your own, scroll through the selection of design templates in the task pane, and then click on one (for example, "Radial") that you feel is appropriate for this presentation.

5. Move to the second slide in the presentation by clicking the Next Slide button (⬇) on the vertical scroll bar. If you selected the "Radial" design template, your screen will appear similar to the one shown in Figure 2.6. Otherwise, only the textual content will appear to be similar.

Figure 2.6

Applying a design template

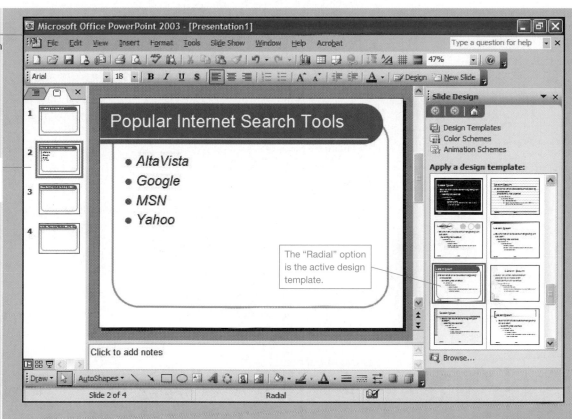

Slide 2 is the currently displayed slide.

The "Radial" option is the active design template.

6. Return to the first slide by clicking it in the Slide pane. Then, run the slide show by clicking the Slide Show button ().

7. Click the mouse on each slide to advance through the presentation. A black screen will appear when you are finished. Click the mouse one more time to exit the slide presentation and return to the PowerPoint 2003 application window.

8. Save the presentation as "Internet Slides" to your personal storage location.

9. Close the PowerPoint 2003 and Word 2003 application windows.

SelfCheck

2.1 How does PowerPoint 2003 determine the number of slides to add to a presentation when converting a Word 2003 outline document?

2.2 Integrating Office Powerpoint with Other Office Applications

Microsoft Office PowerPoint 2003 is a powerful application for creating presentations. When combined with other Office System applications, PowerPoint 2003 is easily extended beyond displaying simple slide shows. In this module, you will discover how to incorporate slide graphics from PowerPoint 2003 into reports, memos, and other documents created using Word 2003. You will also learn how to display business data stored in an Excel 2003 worksheet as a chart object on a slide.

Integrating

2.2.1 Copying Powerpoint 2003 Slides to Word 2003

→ **Feature**

A PowerPoint 2003 slide is a collection of text, pictures, clip art images, and other media. Using the Windows Clipboard, you may copy this collection as a single slide object and then paste it into your documents. In this lesson, you will learn how to insert a slide as a dynamically linked object that will update itself automatically when modified in PowerPoint 2003.

→ **Method**

To paste a PowerPoint 2003 slide into a Word 2003 document:

In PowerPoint 2003, select a slide in the Outline pane or Slide pane so that it appears in the work area.

- CHOOSE: Edit → Copy from the PowerPoint 2003 menu

Make Word 2003 the active application.

In Word 2003, position the insertion point where you want the object to be inserted.

- CHOOSE: Edit → Paste Special from the Word 2003 menu
- SELECT: a data type in the *As* list box
- CLICK: OK command button

→ **Practice**

In this lesson, you will open a four-slide presentation and then practice copying and pasting slides into a Word 2003 document. Ensure that the Windows desktop is displayed.

1. Load Microsoft Office Word 2003 using the Start menu (start). A new document should appear in the application window.

2. Close the Getting Started task pane, if displayed, by clicking its Close button ([×]).

3. Load Microsoft Office PowerPoint 2003 using the Start menu (start).

4. In PowerPoint 2003, open the IM0220 presentation file from the Advantage student data files folder, and then save it as "Operating Systems" to your personal storage location. Ensure that your screen appears similar to the one shown in Figure 2.7 before you proceed.

5. To copy the second slide into Word, you must first select the slide in either the Outline or Slide pane. For this step:
CLICK: slide 2 in the Slide pane, as shown in Figure 2.7

Figure 2.7

"Operating Systems" presentation

Select a slide by clicking on its thumbnail image in the Slide pane.

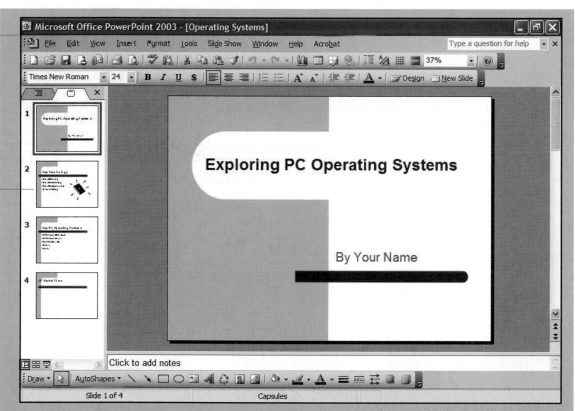

6. To copy this slide to the Clipboard:
CLICK: Copy button (⬛) on the Standard toolbar
(*Hint:* If you want to copy a group of slides to the Windows Clipboard, hold down the **CTRL** key and click on the slides you want to include.)

7. Make Word 2003 the active application.

8. To embed the slide as a dynamically linked object in Word 2003:
CHOOSE: Edit → Paste Special

9. In the Paste Special dialog box:
SELECT: *Paste link* option button
SELECT: "Microsoft PowerPoint Slide Object" in the *As* list box
Your screen should now appear similar to the one shown in Figure 2.8.

Integrating

Figure 2.8

Paste Special
dialog box

Select the *Paste link*
option to create a
dynamic link
between the source
data and the pasted
result.

Select an option to
determine the
format for pasting
the object into
Word 2003.

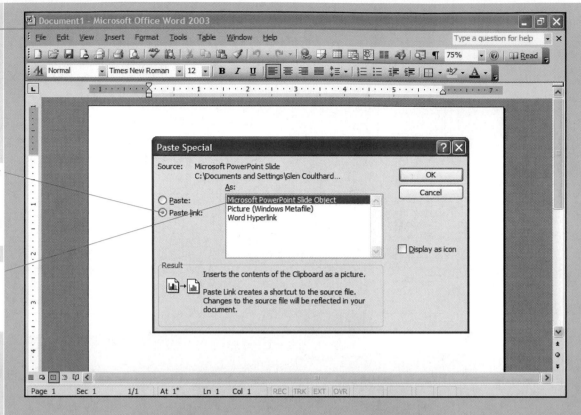

10. To proceed with pasting the object into the document:
CLICK: OK command button
The slide should now appear in the Word 2003 document.

11. Let's demonstrate the dynamic link by changing some text on the slide. Make PowerPoint 2003 the active application.

12. To change the text for the fourth bullet point on slide 2:
DOUBLE-CLICK: any part of the term "Time-sharing" to select it
TYPE: **Time-slicing**

13. Make Word 2003 the active application.

14. To update the linked content:
RIGHT-CLICK: the slide object in the Word 2003 document
CHOOSE: Update Link
Your screen should now appear similar to the one shown in Figure 2.9.

Figure 2.9

Updating linked information

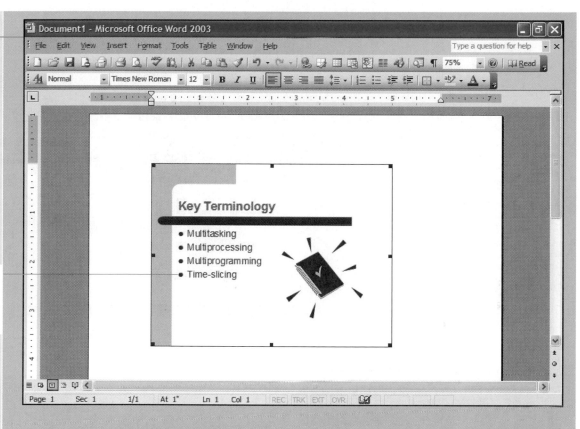

The text for this bullet point has been changed from "Time-sharing" to "Time-slicing."

15. Save the presentation as "Pasting Slides" to your personal storage location.

16. Close Microsoft Office Word 2003 but leave the PowerPoint 2003 application window displayed.

2.2.2 Copying an Excel 2003 Chart to Powerpoint 2003

→ # Feature

The Windows Clipboard is an amazing tool for transferring content among applications. However, it is the Paste Special command on each application's Edit menu that really enhances the Clipboard's inherent power. You have witnessed some of the Clipboard's capabilities in exchanging data among the Microsoft Office System 2003 applications. In this lesson, you will continue to use the Paste Special command in moving data created using Excel 2003 into a PowerPoint 2003 presentation.

→ # Method

To paste an Excel 2003 chart into a PowerPoint 2003 presentation:

In Excel 2003, select the desired chart object.

• CHOOSE: Edit → Copy from the Excel 2003 menu

Make PowerPoint 2003 the active application.

In PowerPoint 2003, position the insertion point on the slide where you want the object to be inserted.

• CHOOSE: Edit → Paste Special from the PowerPoint 2003 menu

• SELECT: a data type in the *As* list box

• CLICK: OK command button

Integrating

→ ## Practice

You will now embed an existing Excel 2003 chart object onto the last slide of the "Operating Systems" presentation. Ensure that the PowerPoint 2003 application window is displayed.

1. In PowerPoint 2003, select the fourth slide by clicking on it in the Slide pane. Your screen should appear similar to the one shown in Figure 2.10. Notice that the slide's content area under the title appears empty. You will embed a chart onto this slide in the next few steps.

Figure 2.10

Displaying the fourth slide in the presentation

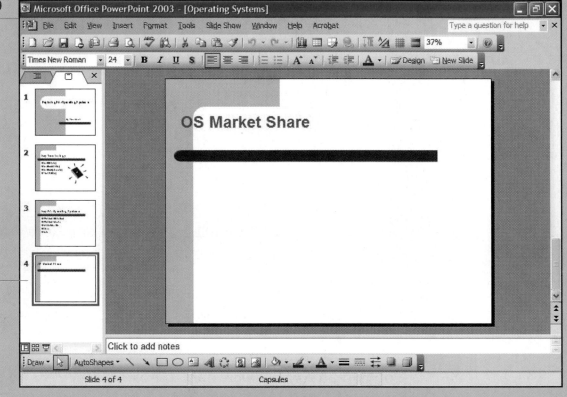

Click on the thumbnail image of the fourth slide to display it in the work area

2. Load Microsoft Office Excel 2003 using the Start menu (*start*). If necessary, maximize the worksheet window to fill the work area.

3. In Excel 2003, open the IM0222 workbook from the Advantage student data files folder, and then save it as "Market Share" to your personal storage location. Ensure that your screen appears similar to the one shown in Figure 2.11 before you proceed.

Figure 2.11

"Market Share" worksheet

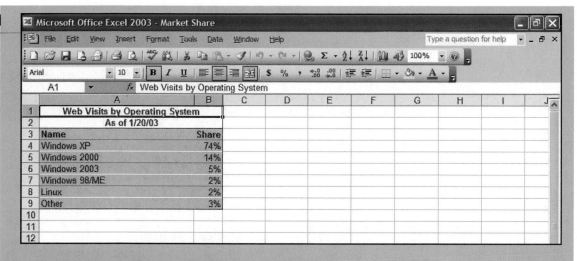

4. To view the chart object for this worksheet:
CLICK: *Sheet2* tab at the bottom of the worksheet window
The embedded chart object should appear selected on the *Sheet2* worksheet, as shown in Figure 2.12. (*Hint:* You can tell that an object is selected when black boxes, called selection handles, appear around its edges.)

Figure 2.12

"Market Share" embedded chart

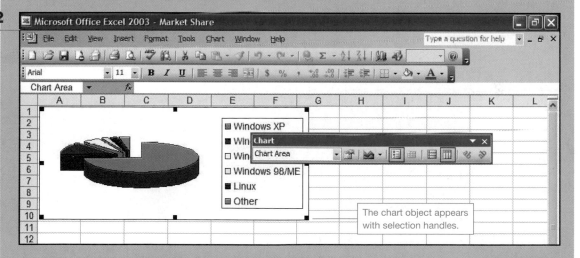

The chart object appears with selection handles.

5. To copy the selected chart to the Clipboard:
CLICK: Copy button (⬚) on the Standard toolbar

6. Make PowerPoint 2003 the active application.

7. To paste the chart object onto the destination slide:
CHOOSE: Edit ➔ Paste Special

8. In the Paste Special dialog box, ensure that the "Microsoft Office Excel Chart Object" option is selected in the *As* list box and then:
CLICK: OK command button

9. On your own, resize and move the chart object so that your slide appears similar to the one shown in Figure 2.13. (*Hint:* To remove the selection handles from view, click on the slide's background. To edit the Excel 2003 chart object using the "Visual Editing" feature, double-click the object on the slide.)

Figure 2.13

Pasting an Excel 2003 chart object onto a slide

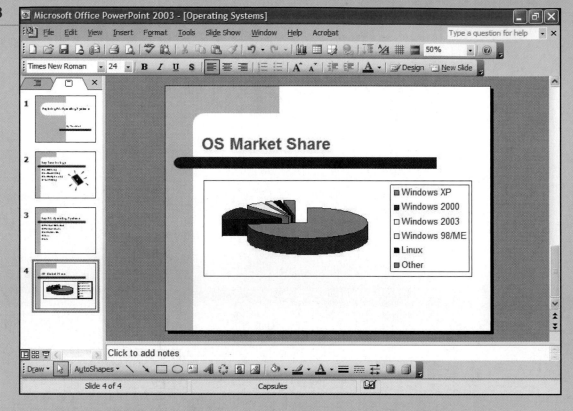

10. Save the presentation and then close Microsoft Office PowerPoint 2003.

11. Close the "Market Share" workbook without saving the changes.

12. Close Microsoft Office Excel 2003.

 **SelfCheck**

2.2 How would you edit a Microsoft Office Excel chart object that you had pasted onto a slide in PowerPoint 2003?

2.3 Integrating Office Access with Other Office Applications

Microsoft Office Access 2003 is the desktop database management system included in the Microsoft Office System suite of applications. You use Access 2003 to store and manage large amounts of data, such as invoice transactions, inventory items, and personal contacts. Although not as efficient or full-featured as Access 2003, Microsoft Office Excel 2003 also provides the ability to store, analyze, filter, query, and summarize data. Because it is the more familiar application to many users, Excel 2003 is often selected for creating and storing lists. However, users sometimes outgrow Excel 2003's database management features and must transfer their data into Access 2003. In this module, you will learn how to move and share data between Excel 2003 and Access 2003.

2.3.1 Exporting Access 2003 Reports to Word 2003

→ ## Feature

Although Access 2003 provides an effective reporting module for creating and printing standard summary reports, it does not provide the ability to analyze and manipulate data like Excel 2003. Furthermore, Access 2003 cannot match the formatting capabilities of Word 2003. One way around these shortcomings is to export your Access 2003 reports to either Excel 2003 or Word 2003 for further enhancement and fine-tuning.

→ ## Method

To export an Access 2003 report object to a Word 2003 document:

In Access 2003, preview the report that you want to export.

- CLICK: down arrow attached to the OfficeLinks button (📰▾) on the Print Preview toolbar
- CLICK: Publish It with Microsoft Office Word

→ ## Practice

You will now practice sending an Access 2003 report to Word 2003 for additional formatting. Ensure that the Windows desktop is displayed.

1. Load Microsoft Office Access 2003 using the Start menu (🏁 start).

2. Open the IM0230 database from the Advantage student data files folder. Ensure that your screen appears similar to the one shown in Figure 2.14 before you proceed.

Figure 2.14

IM0230 Database window

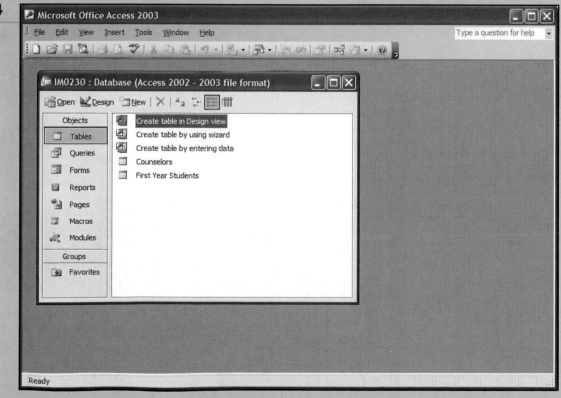

3. To begin, open the "First Year Students" report for display in the Print Preview window. Do the following:
CLICK: Reports button in the Objects bar
DOUBLE-CLICK: "First Year Students" report object in the list area

4. Maximize the report window and then:
SELECT: 75% from the *Zoom* (Fit ▾) drop-down list box

5. To send this report to Word 2003:
CLICK: down arrow attached to the OfficeLinks button (W ▾)
Your screen should now appear similar to the one shown in Figure 2.15.

Figure 2.15

Zooming and the OfficeLinks menu in the Print Preview window

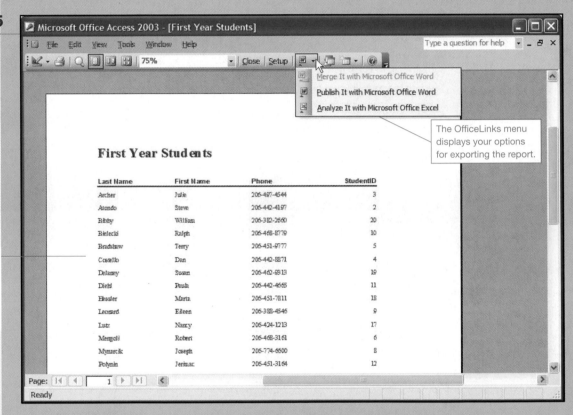

The OfficeLinks menu displays your options for exporting the report.

This report is displayed in a maximized Print Preview window with a zoom factor of 75%.

6. From the OfficeLinks menu:
CHOOSE: Publish It with Microsoft Office Word
After a few moments, Word 2003 is loaded, and the report is displayed in a document window. Notice in Word 2003's Title bar that the document is named "First Year Students," after the name of the report object in Access 2003.

7. If a portion of the title has been truncated in the conversion process to Word 2003, edit the title to read "First Year Students" rather than "First Year."

8. Let's apply some formatting to the columnar data:
SELECT: all of the data beneath the headings in the Last Name, First Name, Phone, and StudentID columns

9. To enlarge the font's point size for the selected information:
SELECT: 12 from the *Font Size* (12 ▾) drop-down list box

10. Move to the top of the document and then:
SELECT: 100% from the *Zoom* (100% ▾) drop-down list box
Your screen should now appear similar to the one shown in Figure 2.16.

Figure 2.16

Formatting an Access 2003 report in Word 2003

Insertion point

The row data is now formatted using a 12-point font size.

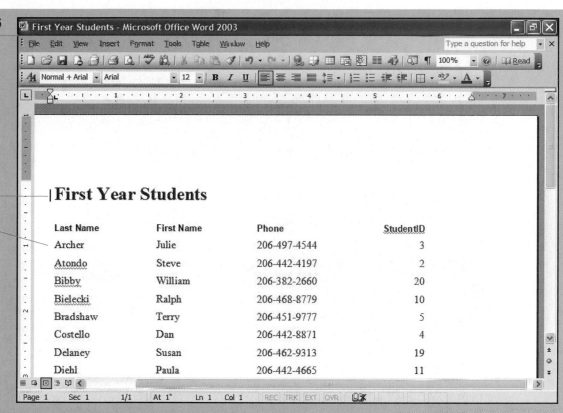

First Year Students

Last Name	First Name	Phone	StudentID
Archer	Julie	206-497-4544	3
Atondo	Steve	206-442-4197	2
Bibby	William	206-382-2660	20
Bielecki	Ralph	206-468-8779	10
Bradshaw	Terry	206-451-9777	5
Costello	Dan	206-442-8871	4
Delaney	Susan	206-462-9313	19
Diehl	Paula	206-442-4665	11

11. Save the document and then close Microsoft Office Word 2003.

12. When you return to the Access 2003 application window:
CLICK: Close button (⌐Close⌐) on the Print Preview toolbar
CLICK: Restore button (⌐⌐) to restore the Database window

13. Keep Microsoft Office Access 2003 open for use in the next lesson.

In Addition MAIL MERGING IN WORD 2003 WITH AN ACCESS 2003
DATA SOURCE

One of the most powerful features of word processing software is the ability to combine (merge) names and addresses with a standard document for printing. This process, called *mail merge,* can be a tremendous time-saver, because it allows you to use a single document to print personalized letters to multiple recipients. The merge process requires two files: the main document and the data source. The *main document* contains the standard text, graphics, and other objects that will stay the same from document to document. The *data source* contains the variable data, such as names and addresses, that will be merged into the main document. A data source is composed of a *header row, records,* and *fields.* Examples of popular data sources include Word 2003 tables, Excel 2003 worksheet lists, and Access 2003 table or query objects. For more information on merging, refer to the Microsoft Office Word 2003 Advantage Series learning guide.

2.3.2 Importing a Worksheet List into Access 2003

→ ## Feature

Microsoft Office Excel 2003 is an extraordinary spreadsheet application that allows you to perform mathematical computations, analyze and summarize vast quantities of numeric data, and plot data using professionally designed charts and graphs. As one of the most popular business applications in use today, Office Excel is the Swiss army knife of applications software. For instance, you can use Excel 2003 like a basic calculator to add together values. You can also use it as a comprehensive database management system to compile long lists of data, data that is usually better served stored in an Access 2003 database. Not until worksheet lists become too large for Excel 2003 is Access 2003 considered as a solution. Fortunately, Access 2003 provides the tools you need to quickly convert worksheet lists into manageable database tables.

→ Method

To import a worksheet list from Excel 2003 into Access 2003:

In Access 2003, click the *Tables* button in the Objects bar.

- CHOOSE: File → Get External Data → Import
- SELECT: the workbook file containing the worksheet list to import

Complete the steps in the Access 2003 Import Spreadsheet Wizard.

→ Practice

You will now practice converting an Excel 2003 worksheet list into an Access 2003 table object. Ensure that you have completed the previous lesson and that the IM0230 Database window is displayed in Access 2003.

1. Load Microsoft Office Excel 2003 using the Start menu (start).

2. In Excel 2003, open the IM0232 workbook file from the Advantage student data files folder, and then save it as "Counselors" to your personal storage location. Ensure that your screen appears similar to the one shown in Figure 2.17 before you proceed.

Figure 2.17

"Counselors" workbook

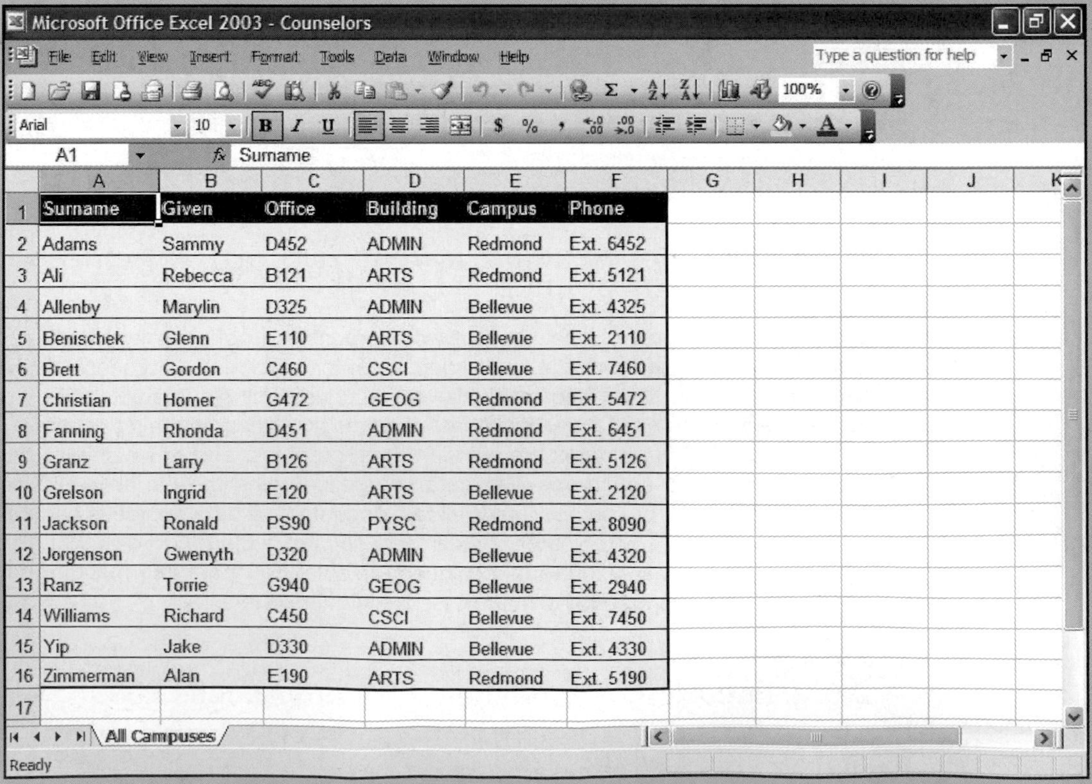

3. Let's convert the worksheet list shown in Figure 2.17 into an Access 2003 table object. In order to import data stored in the worksheet list, however, you must first close the workbook. To begin, close Microsoft Office Excel 2003, and do not save any changes to the workbook.

4. In the Access 2003 application window:
CHOOSE: File → Get External Data → Import
The Import dialog box appears, displaying Access database files in its list area.

5. In the Import dialog box, use the Places bar and the *Look in* drop-down list box to navigate to your personal storage location. Then do the following:
SELECT: Microsoft Excel from the *Files of type* drop-down list box

6. Peruse the list of file names and then:
DOUBLE-CLICK: "Counselors" in the list area
Your screen should now appear similar to the one shown in Figure 2.18.

Figure 2.18

Import Spreadsheet Wizard dialog box: Step 1

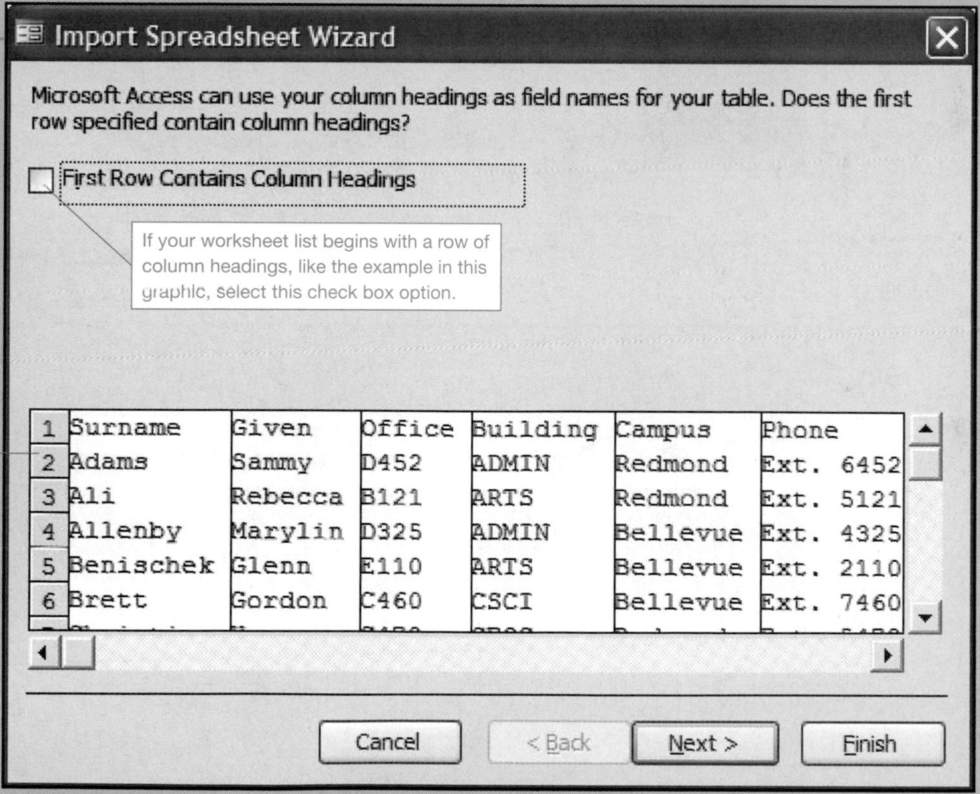

Actual data from the Excel 2003 workbook named "Counselors"

Import Spreadsheet Wizard

Microsoft Access can use your column headings as field names for your table. Does the first row specified contain column headings?

☐ First Row Contains Column Headings

If your worksheet list begins with a row of column headings, like the example in this graphic, select this check box option.

1	Surname	Given	Office	Building	Campus	Phone
2	Adams	Sammy	D452	ADMIN	Redmond	Ext. 6452
3	Ali	Rebecca	B121	ARTS	Redmond	Ext. 5121
4	Allenby	Marylin	D325	ADMIN	Bellevue	Ext. 4325
5	Benischek	Glenn	E110	ARTS	Bellevue	Ext. 2110
6	Brett	Gordon	C460	CSCI	Bellevue	Ext. 7460

[Cancel]   [< Back]   [Next >]   [Finish]

7. In the Import Spreadsheet Wizard dialog box:
SELECT: *First Row Contains Column Headings* check box so that a ✓ appears
CLICK: [Next >]

8. You must now specify whether to store the imported data in a new table or append the data to an existing table. Do the following:
SELECT: *In a New Table* option button
CLICK: [Next >]
The dialog box should now appear similar to the one shown in Figure 2.19.

Figure 2.19

Import
Spreadsheet
Wizard dialog
box: Step 3

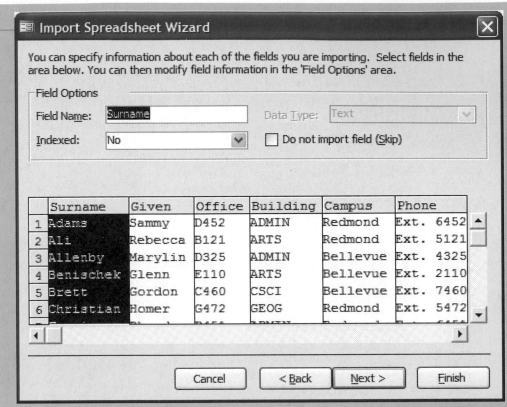

9. In this step of the Import Spreadsheet Wizard, you specify the field columns and confirm their data types for processing the worksheet list. By default, all columns are selected. To remove a column, you must select the column in the preview area and then click the *Do not import field (Skip)* check box. For this exercise, however, you will import all of the fields. Do the following:
CLICK: Next >

10. To allow Access 2003 to add an ID column in order to define a primary key for sorting and retrieving data:
SELECT: *Let Access add primary key* option button
CLICK: Next >

11. In the last step of the dialog box, you must name the new table object:
TYPE: **Counselors**
CLICK: Finish

12. A confirmation dialog box appears:
CLICK: OK command button to proceed

13. When you are returned to the Database window in Access 2003, a new table object named "Counselors" appears in the list area. To display the new table object:
DOUBLE-CLICK: Counselors
Your screen should now appear similar to the one shown in Figure 2.20.

Figure 2.20

"Counselors" datasheet

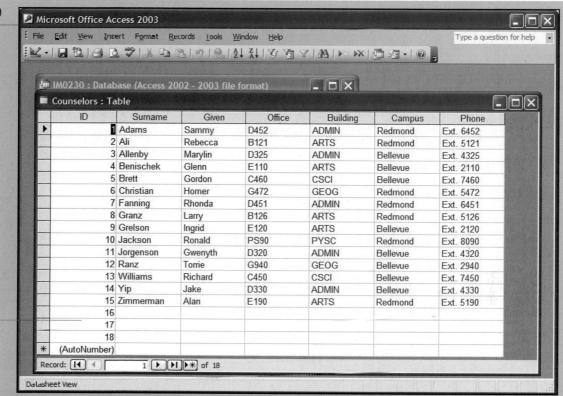

The conversion process adds a few blank rows in this example, which you would normally delete.

14. Close the "Counselors" Datasheet window by clicking its Close button (☒) and then close Microsoft Office Access 2003.

 **2.3** In what circumstances might you export a report created in Access 2003 to Word 2003?

Chapter
summary

Microsoft Office System 2003 provides an integrated suite of applications—each designed with different strengths to achieve specific results. Microsoft Office PowerPoint 2003, for example, is the most popular presentation software application in use today. PowerPoint 2003 allows you to create professional slide shows that combine text, graphics, and other media elements for local or online delivery. After spending time creating such intricate slide graphics, you may decide to incorporate them in your worksheets or report documents. Fortunately, Microsoft Office System 2003 provides several tools and features that allow you to integrate PowerPoint 2003 with other applications. You will also find tools and wizards, such as the OfficeLinks menu and the Import Spreadsheet Wizard in Access 2003, that help you perform specialized integration tasks.

Integrating

Command Summary

Many of the commands and procedures appearing in this chapter are summarized in the following table.

Skill Set	To Perform This Task . . .	Do the Following . . .
Converting a Word 2003 Outline to a PowerPoint 2003 Presentation	Switch to Outline view in Word 2003	CHOOSE: View → Outline, or CLICK: Outline View button (⊞)
	Create an outline in Word 2003's Outline view	PRESS: ENTER to insert a new heading at the same level, or CLICK: Demote button (→) to begin typing at a demoted (lower) level, or CLICK: Promote button (←) to begin typing at a promoted (higher) level
	Send a Word 2003 outline to PowerPoint 2003	CHOOSE: File → Send To → Microsoft Office PowerPoint
Integrating PowerPoint 2003 with Word 2003 and Excel 2003	Copy a PowerPoint 2003 slide to Word 2003	SELECT: a slide in the PowerPoint 2003 Outline or Slide pane CLICK: Copy button (📋) and then switch to the destination location in Word 2003 CHOOSE: Edit → Paste Special from Word 2003's Menu bar SELECT: a data type in the *As* list box SELECT: *Paste* or *Paste Link* option button CLICK: OK command button
	Copy an Excel 2003 chart to PowerPoint 2003	SELECT: a chart in Excel 2003 CLICK: Copy button (📋) and then switch to the destination slide in PowerPoint 2003 CHOOSE: Edit → Paste Special from PowerPoint 2003's Menu bar SELECT: a data type in the *As* list box SELECT: *Paste* or *Paste Link* option button CLICK: OK command button
Integrating Access 2003 with Word 2003 and Excel 2003	Export an Access 2003 report to Word 2003	DOUBLE-CLICK: a report object in the Access 2003 Database window to preview the report CLICK: down arrow attached to the OfficeLinks button (W▾) on the Print Preview toolbar SELECT: Publish It with Microsoft Office Word
	Importing an Excel 2003 worksheet into Access 2003	CHOOSE: File → Get External Data → Import from the Access 2003 Menu bar SELECT: an Excel 2003 workbook file to launch the Import Spreadsheet Wizard

Chapter

quiz

Short Answer

1. How must content in a Word 2003 document be formatted for successful conversion to slides in PowerPoint 2003?

2. What are some advantages to using Word 2003's Outline view for creating a new PowerPoint 2003 presentation?

3. How do you select multiple slides in PowerPoint 2003's Outline or Slide pane?

4. What is the procedure for exporting an Access 2003 report to Word 2003 for additional formatting?

5. Suggest some instances when you might want to import an Excel 2003 worksheet list into an Access 2003 database.

6. Suggest some instances when you might want to copy a PowerPoint 2003 slide into a Word 2003 document.

7. What is the procedure for editing a chart object after you have embedded it on a PowerPoint 2003 slide?

8. What are the three menu options displayed on the OfficeLinks button (⊞▾) in Access 2003?

9. What command enables you to paste and link an Excel 2003 worksheet into a Word 2003 document?

10. How do you copy an Excel 2003 chart object to the Windows Clipboard?

True/False

1. _____ You may only embed entire PowerPoint 2003 presentations, not individual slides, in Word 2003.

2. _____ To copy a worksheet range to the Windows Clipboard, use the Edit → Paste Special command.

3. _____ When importing an Excel 2003 worksheet list into Access 2003, you must specify an existing field column as the primary key.

4. _____ In Word 2003's Outline view, you can promote or demote a heading with the click of a toolbar button.

5. _____ After converting a Word 2003 outline to PowerPoint 2003, you may apply formatting and design templates as you would normally.

6. _____ You may move and resize an Excel 2003 chart object after pasting it onto a PowerPoint 2003 slide.

7. _____ In Word 2003, it is possible to "collapse" a document's outline so that only the main headings appear.

8. _____ In Outline view, Word 2003 automatically applies its own heading styles to the different levels in the outline.

9. _____ To link a PowerPoint 2003 slide to a Word 2003 document, you must choose the Edit → Paste Special command.

10. _____ Whether you are pasting an Excel 2003 chart into PowerPoint 2003 or into Word 2003, the procedure is basically the same.

Multiple Choice

1. To convert a Word 2003 outline into a Power-Point 2003 presentation, do the following:

   a. CHOOSE: File → Send To → PowerPoint

   b. CHOOSE: Insert → Object → Power-Point

   c. CHOOSE: Edit → Paste Special → Microsoft Office PowerPoint Object

   d. None of the above

2. In order for PowerPoint 2003 to easily convert a Word 2003 outline into slides, the Word 2003 document must be formatted using:

   a. Macros

   b. Objects

   c. Fonts

   d. Styles

3. To select a slide in PowerPoint 2003 for copying to the Clipboard, you must perform which of the following actions in PowerPoint 2003?

   a. Click the slide's icon in the Outline or Slide pane

   b. Double-click the slide's icon in the Outline or Slide pane

   c. Display the slide in Slide Show view

   d. None of the above

4. When you paste an Excel 2003 worksheet onto a PowerPoint slide:

   a. The workbook is the destination document

   b. The presentation is the destination document

   c. The presentation is the source document

   d. None of the above

5. When importing an Excel 2003 worksheet into Access 2003, you must first perform which of the following actions?

   a. Close the worksheet in Excel 2003

   b. Open the worksheet in Excel 2003

   c. Display a blank worksheet in Excel 2003

   d. None of the above

6. To import an Excel 2003 worksheet into Access 2003, do which of the following?

   a. CHOOSE: File → Search

   b. CHOOSE: File → Get External Data

   c. CHOOSE: View → External Data

   d. None of the above

7. To display the Outline view in Word 2003, do which of the following?

   a. CHOOSE: File → Send To → Outline

   b. CHOOSE: File → New → Outline

   c. CHOOSE: View → Outline

   d. Either b or c

8. To embed an existing Excel 2003 chart into a PowerPoint 2003 presentation, do which of the following?

   a. CHOOSE: Edit → Paste Special

   b. CHOOSE: View → Slide Sorter

   c. CHOOSE: View → Outline

   d. CHOOSE: Insert → Object

9. To export an Access 2003 report to Word 2003, do which of the following?

   a. CHOOSE: File → Send To → Microsoft Office Word

   b. CHOOSE: Data → Publish It with Microsoft Office Word

   c. CLICK: arrow attached to the OfficeLinks button (🆆▾)
CHOOSE: Publish It with Microsoft Office Word

   d. All of the above

10. When importing an Excel 2003 worksheet list into Access 2003 using the Import Spreadsheet Wizard, you are able to:

   a. Select which columns to import

   b. Name the imported table

   c. Specify a primary key for the imported table

   d. All of the above

Hands-On
exercises

tep by step

1. Sending a Word 2003 Outline to PowerPoint 2003

In this exercise, you are tasked with creating an outline in Word 2003 and then converting the outline into a PowerPoint 2003 presentation.

1. Load Microsoft Office Word 2003 using the Start menu (✪ start). A new document should appear in the application window.

2. Close the Getting Started task pane, if displayed, by clicking its Close button (☒).

3. Switch the display to Outline view.

4. Create the outline document shown in Figure 2.21, and then save it as "Sweet Dreams Outline" to your personal storage location.

Figure 2.21

"Sweet Dreams Outline" document

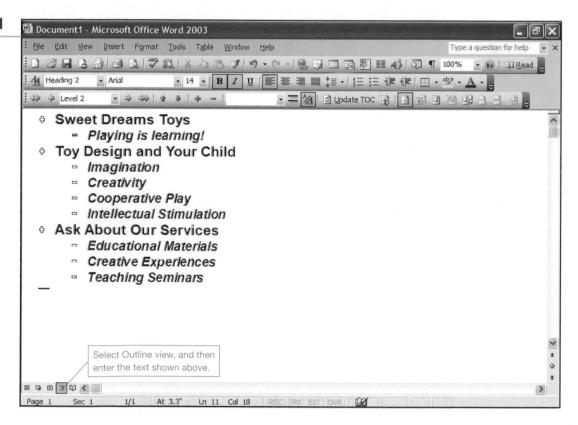

5. To convert the outline document to a presentation file:
CHOOSE: File → Send To → Microsoft Office PowerPoint
After a few moments, the Word 2003 outline appears as a PowerPoint 2003 presentation containing three slides.

6. To change the layout of the first slide from the Title and Text layout to a Title Slide layout, do the following:
CHOOSE: Format → Slide Layout
CLICK: Title Slide option in the *Text Layouts* area of the Slide Layout task pane

7. To apply a design template to the presentation:
CHOOSE: Format → Slide Design
CLICK: Crayons option in the Slide Design task pane
The presentation's title slide should now appear similar to the one shown in Figure 2.22.

Figure 2.22

Customizing a
presentation

8. Save the PowerPoint 2003 presentation as "Sweet Dreams Presentation" to your personal storage location.

9. Display the presentation as a full-screen slide show. Then print and close the presentation.

10. Exit Microsoft Office PowerPoint 2003 and Microsoft Office Word 2003.

2. Embedding a PowerPoint 2003 Slide in Word 2003

In this exercise, you will copy the contents of a slide in a PowerPoint 2003 presentation to the Windows Clipboard. Once placed on the Clipboard, you are tasked with pasting the slide image into a Word 2003 document.

1. Load Microsoft Office Word 2003 using the Start menu (*start*). A new document should appear in the application window.

2. Close the Getting Started task pane, if displayed, by clicking its Close button (✕).

3. Load Microsoft Office PowerPoint 2003 using the Start menu (*start*).

4. Open the IM02HE02 presentation from the Advantage student data files folder, and then save it as "Coal Exportation" to your personal storage location. Your screen should appear similar to Figure 2.23 before proceeding.

Figure 2.23

"Coal Exportation" presentation

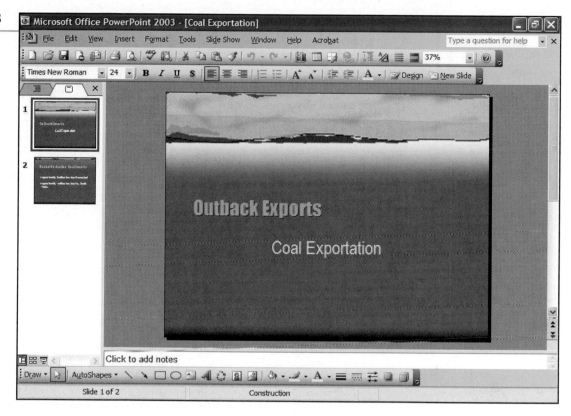

5. Select the second slide in the presentation and then copy it to the Windows Clipboard.

6. Make Word 2003 the active application.

7. Enter the title "Outback Exports" on the first line of the document and format it to display using the Heading 1 style format. Press (ENTER) three times before proceeding.

8. Paste the copied slide into the Word 2003 document as a "Microsoft Office PowerPoint Slide Object."

9. Using one of the proportional sizing corners, size the object to have a width of 3.5 inches. Scroll the window upward so that your screen appears similar to Figure 2.24.

Integrating

Figure 2.24

Embedding and sizing a slide object

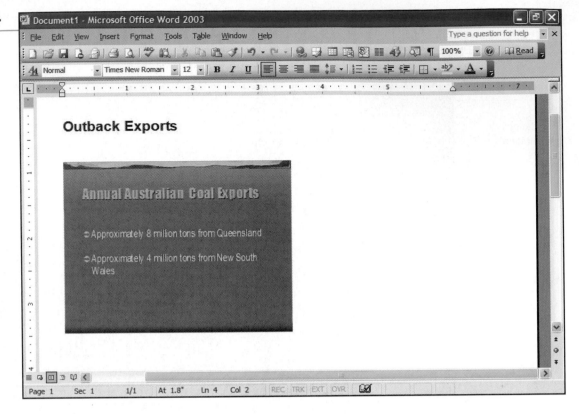

10. Edit the embedded slide object (without returning to Microsoft Office PowerPoint 2003) so that the first bullet point reads "10 million tons" and not "8 million tons."

11. Save the document as "Exports Slide" to your personal storage location, and then print the document.

12. Exit Microsoft Office Word 2003 and Microsoft Office PowerPoint 2003.

3. Exporting an Access 2003 Report to Word 2003

You will now practice exporting an Access 2003 report object to a Word 2003 document. The primary feature used in this exercise is the OfficeLinks button, which is found on the Access 2003 toolbars.

1. Load Microsoft Office Access 2003 using the Start menu (*start*).

2. Open the IM02HE03 database from the Advantage student data files folder.

3. Display the report objects in the Database window, and then preview the "Restaurant Report" report.

4. Maximize the report's Print Preview window and adjust the zoom factor so that your screen appears similar to the one shown in Figure 2.25.

Figure 2.25

Previewing the "Restaurant Report" report

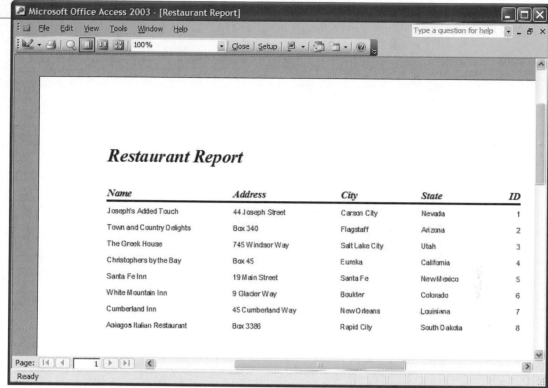

5. Using the OfficeLinks button (), send the report to Word 2003.

6. In Word 2003, center the report's title and then increase the font size of the column headings to 16 points.

7. Select the row data beneath the column headings and specify a 10-point font size. Your report should now appear similar to the one shown in Figure 2.26.

Integrating

Figure 2.26

Formatting the "Restaurant Report" document

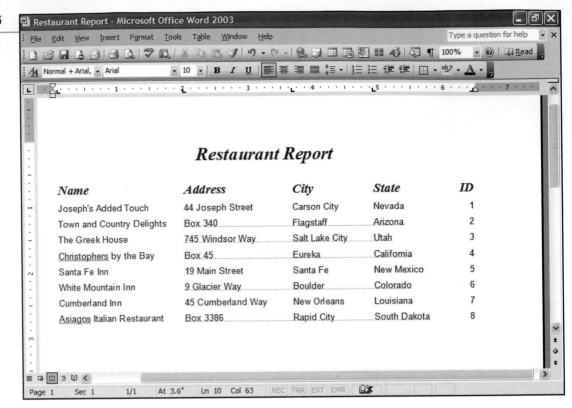

8. Save and then print the document.

9. Exit Microsoft Office Word 2003.

10. Before exiting Microsoft Office Access 2003, close the Print Preview and then restore the size of the Database window.

on your own

4. Using the Import Spreadsheet Wizard

Having recently completed a course in Microsoft Office System 2003, you have been asked by your supervisor to upsize the company's Excel 2003 worksheet list into an Access 2003 database. To begin, you load Microsoft Office Excel 2003. You then open the IM02HE04 workbook, shown in Figure 2.27, and save it as "Development Teams" to your personal storage location. Exiting Excel 2003, you are now ready to import the data into Access 2003.

Figure 2.27

"Development Teams" workbook

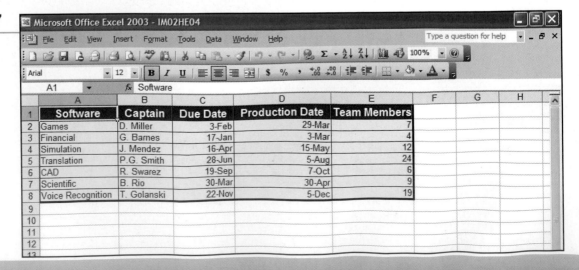

You now load Microsoft Office Access 2003 and then create a new blank database named "Development." To launch the Import Spreadsheet Wizard, use the File → Get External Data → Import command and then select the "Development Teams" workbook. Specify that the data appears only on the "Sheet1" worksheet and proceed to the next step of the wizard. You may then inform the wizard that the first column contains column headings, as shown in Figure 2.28.

Figure 2.28

Stepping through the Import Spreadsheet Wizard

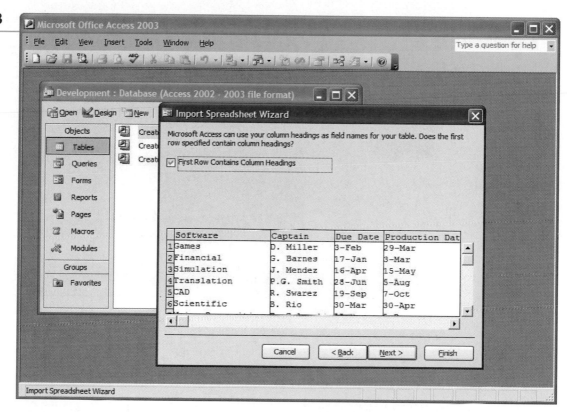

Continue accepting the default selections until you reach the last step of the Import Spreadsheet Wizard. Name the table "Teams," and then finish the wizard. After confirming the dialog box message, display the new Team table in Datasheet view and then print its contents. When finished, close the Datasheet window and exit Microsoft Office Access 2003.

5. Embedding Slides from a PowerPoint 2003 Presentation into Word 2003

You will now embed an entire PowerPoint 2003 presentation into a Word 2003 document. To begin, load Microsoft Office PowerPoint 2003. Open the IM02HE05 presentation file, and then save it as "Web Training" to your personal storage location. Display the presentation as a full-screen slide show and then return to the workspace. In the Outline or Slide pane, select all three slides in the presentation using the (CTRL) or (SHIFT) shortcut keys. Your screen should appear similar to the one shown in Figure 2.29 before proceeding.

Figure 2.29

Selecting slides
in the "Web
Training"
presentation

All three slides in the —
presentation are
selected, as
illustrated by the
blue box
surrounding each
slide's thumbnail
image.

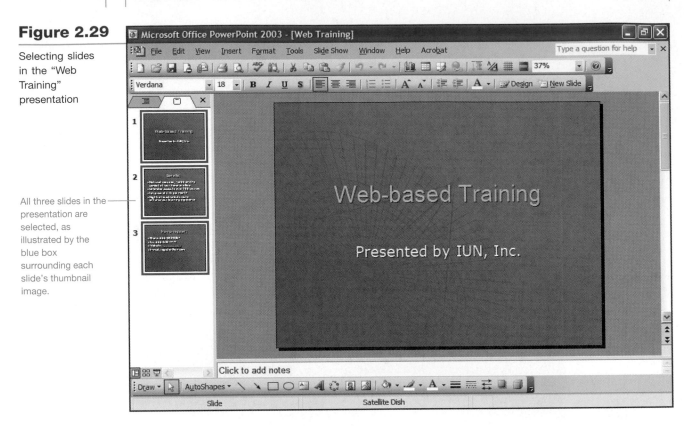

Copy the selected slides to the Windows Clipboard and then load Microsoft Office Word 2003, so that a new blank document is displayed. Using the Paste Special command (Figure 2.30), embed the slides as an icon representing a "Microsoft PowerPoint Presentation Object."

Figure 2.30

Embedding an
object to display
as an icon

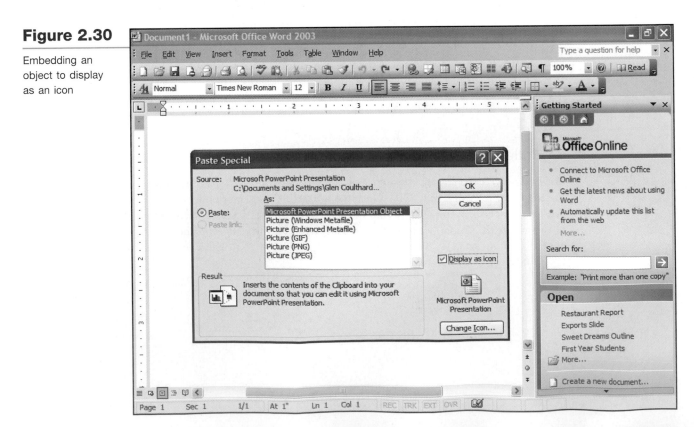

Once the slide icon is embedded in the document, double-click it to view the entire slide show from Word 2003. After proceeding through the slides, you are returned ro the document. Save the document as "Launch Presentation" to your personal storage location. Exit Microsoft Office Word 2003 and Microsoft Office PowerPoint 2003.

6. Embellishing an Access 2003 Report Using Word 2003

You have been asked by an associate to help format an existing Access 2003 report. Rather than work within Access 2003's report Design view, you have decided that it would be easier to export and format the report using Word 2003. To begin, you load Microsoft Office Access 2003. You then open the IM02HE06 database and display the "Animal Report" report object in the Print Preview window. After maximizing, zooming, and adjusting the view, your screen should appear similar to the one shown in Figure 2.31.

Figure 2.31

Previewing the "Animal Report" report

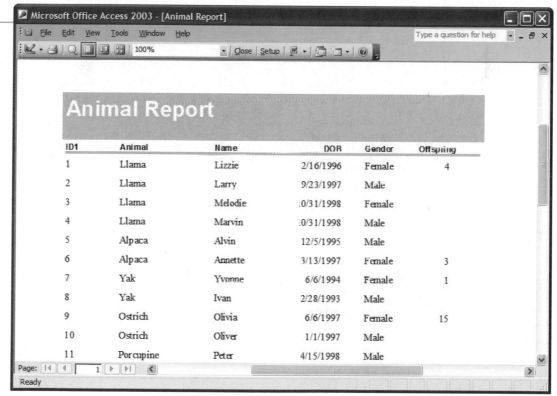

You are now ready to send the report object to Word 2003 using the OfficeLinks button (). Once the object has been converted, you realize that the title appears as white text on a white background. You immediately fix this problem by selecting the "invisible" title and then applying a dark red font color. You then perform various formatting enhancements to the report, so that it appears similar to the one shown in Figure 2.32.

Figure 2.32

Formatting the "Animal Report" document

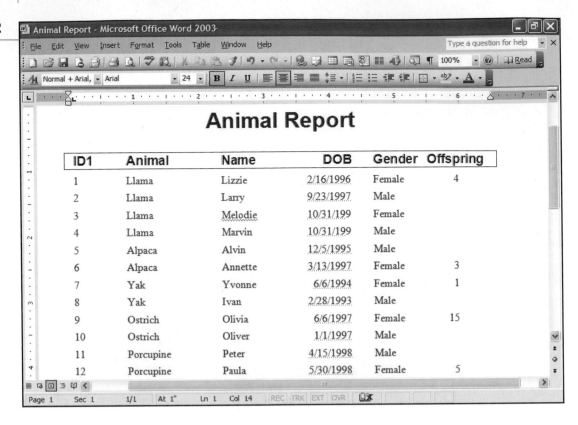

When finished, you save and then print the report. You then exit Microsoft Office Word 2003. Returning to Microsoft Office Access 2003, you close the Print Preview window and restore the Database window, so that it no longer appears maximized. You then exit Microsoft Office Access 2003.

CaseStudy   DEL'S DELICIOUS COOKIES

Del Paul is the owner of a successful cookie company. One of his marketing techniques involves delivering presentations at culinary trade shows. Del currently creates his presentations from scratch using PowerPoint 2003, even though much of the content already exists in Word 2003 documents. At a recent trade show, Del and his associates began discussing the integration features available in Microsoft Office System 2003. He was surprised learn that he already had the tools available to convert his Word 2003 outlines into PowerPoint 2003 presentation files. He also learned about the importing and exporting features available in Excel 2003 and Access 2003. Although impatient to return to his office and try these new features, Del is confident that he soon will be creating better presentations in less time, producing formatted database reports, and efficiently managing his inventory lists.

In the following case problems, assume the role of Del and perform the same steps that he identifies.

1. One of Del's immediate tasks is to prepare a presentation for an upcoming trade show. Rather than retyping the information he already has stored in a Word 2003 document, Del decides to convert the

Word 2003 outline into a PowerPoint 2003 presentation. To begin, Del opens the IM02CS01 document file and then saves it as "Cookies" to his personal storage location. The document appears in Figure 2.33.

Figure 2.33

"Cookies" document

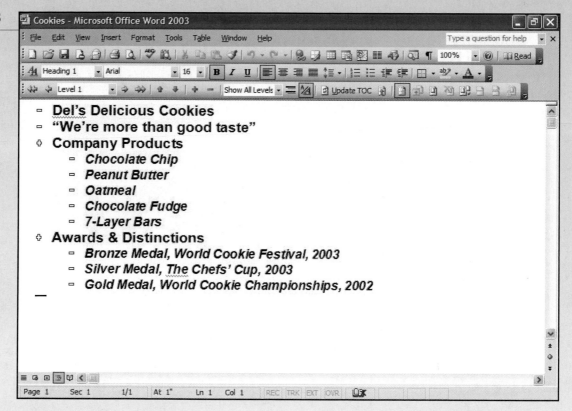

Before sending the outline to PowerPoint 2003, Del demotes the second heading entitled "We're more than good taste." He then converts the outline to a slide presentation. In PowerPoint 2003, Del applies the "Title Slide" layout to the first slide and selects the "Curtain Call" design template. After viewing the presentation as a full-screen slide show, he saves it as "Delicious Cookies" to his personal storage location. After making Word 2003 the active application, Del saves the outline document and then closes Microsoft Office Word 2003. He leaves the "Delicious Cookies" presentation file displayed in PowerPoint 2003.

2. Del would like to display one of his Excel 2003 charts as the final slide in the presentation. To this end, he inserts a new slide entitled "Del's Ingredients" at the end of the presentation. He selects the "Title Only" layout for the new slide. After loading Microsoft Office Excel 2003, Del opens the IM02CS02 workbook and then copies the embedded chart to the Windows Clipboard. He returns to the PowerPoint 2003 application window and embeds the chart on the slide. He then sizes and moves the chart object so that it appears similar to the one shown in Figure 2.34.

Figure 2.34

Embedding and sizing a chart object in PowerPoint 2003

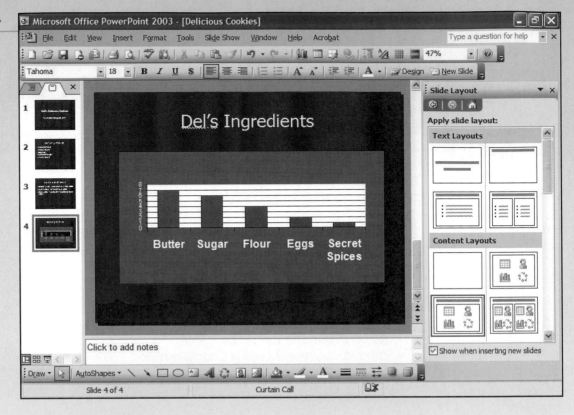

Del saves the revised presentation as "Delicious Cookies-Revised" to his personal storage location. He then closes both Microsoft Office PowerPoint 2003 and Microsoft Office Excel 2003. (*Note:* If prompted, do not save changes to the workbook file.)

3. Del created a simple report in Access 2003. However, he is not pleased with its appearance. He converts the report to Word 2003—an application he knows much better than Access 2003—in order to make the desired changes. To begin, Del loads Microsoft Office Access 2003 and then opens the IM02CS03 database. He previews the "Machine Ingredients" report and then publishes it to Word 2003.

Once the Access 2003 report has been converted to Word 2003, Del enhances the report's title, "Machine Ingredients," to display in the center of the page using a 22-point, Times New Roman font. He then adds italic formatting to the column headings and changes the row data beneath the headings to display using a 12-point, Times New Roman font. He saves and then prints the completed report, shown in Figure 2.35. When finished, Del exits Microsoft Office Word 2003 and Microsoft Office Access 2003.

Figure 2.35

"Machine
Ingredients"
report document

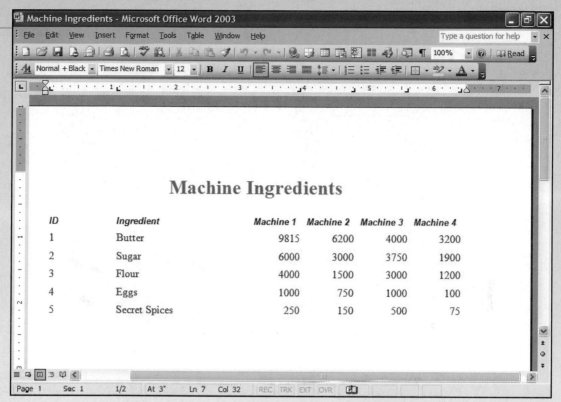

4. Last week, Del started entering a list of items into an Excel 2003 worksheet. He now realizes that it would be far more efficient to use Access 2003 to manage the data. To start the conversion, Del opens the IM02CS04 workbook and saves it as "Bowl Inventory" to his personal storage location. To prepare the worksheet for conversion, Del deletes the top four rows and the bottom three rows of the active range, so that the worksheet appears similar to the one shown in Figure 2.36. Having made such a drastic change to the workbook, he saves it again before proceeding.

Integrating

Figure 2.36

Editing the
worksheet prior
to importing into
Access 2003

The Import
Spreadsheet Wizard
works better with
worksheets that do
not have headings
and blank rows.

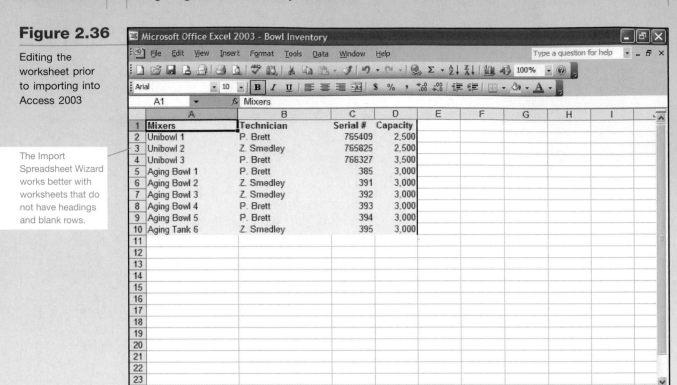

Next, Del loads Microsoft Office Access 2003 and creates a blank database named "Delicious
Cookies." He imports the "Bowl Inventory" worksheet into Access 2003 using the default settings
and then names the table "Bowl Inventory." When finished, Del displays the table in Datasheet view
(Figure 2.37).

Figure 2.37

The "Bowl
Inventory" table
in Datasheet view

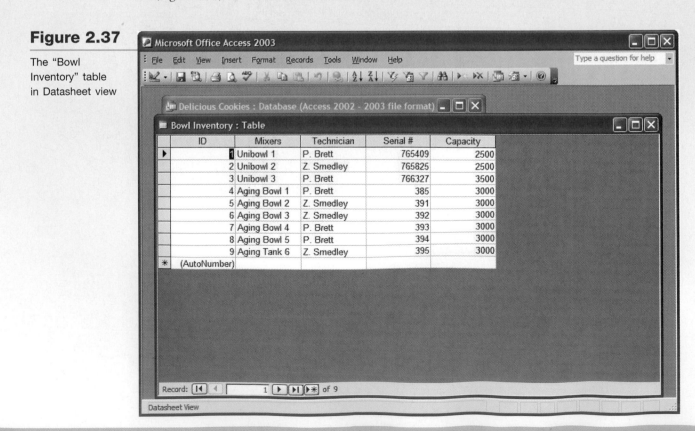

Satisfied with his efforts for the day, Del prints the table and then closes Microsoft Office Access 2003. Finally, he exits Microsoft Office Excel 2003 to display the Windows desktop.

Self–Check Answers

2.1   How does PowerPoint 2003 determine the number of slides to add to a presentation when converting a Word 2003 outline document? PowerPoint 2003 creates a new slide for each topic heading that is formatted using the "Heading 1" style.

2.2   How would you edit a Microsoft Office Excel chart object that you had pasted onto a slide in PowerPoint 2003? To edit an embedded object using Microsoft Office System's Visual Editing feature, you simply double-click the object.

2.3   In what circumstances might you export a report created in Access 2003 to Word 2003? You may choose to export an Access 2003 report to Word 2003 in order to apply additional formatting or to more easily include it in a report document.

Notes

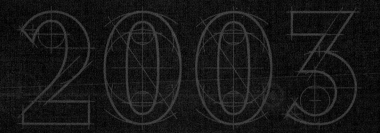

CHAPTER 3

Extending Office 2003 to the Web

PREREQUISITES

This chapter assumes that you know how to create, save, edit, and print Word 2003 documents, Excel 2003 worksheets, and PowerPoint 2003 presentations. You should also know how to view and print data using Access 2003. Finally, you should be familiar with using Web browser software to view HTML documents locally and on the Web.

LEARNING OBJECTIVES

After completing this chapter, you will be able to:

- Insert hyperlinks in Microsoft Office System 2003 documents, worksheets, and presentations

- Browse the Web from within an application using the Web toolbar

- Create HTML files from existing documents, worksheets, presentations, and databases

- Apply a Web theme and create a frames page in Word 2003

- Create an interactive worksheet page in Excel 2003 and customize a presentation in PowerPoint 2003

3.1 Using Hyperlinks

For readers new to the online world, the Internet is a collection of computer networks spanning the entire planet. The World Wide Web (or just "Web") is one of the most popular applications available on the Internet. The Web provides a graphical interface to the Internet, offering an interactive multimedia experience complete with text, graphics, sound, music, movies, and even virtual reality. Besides its entertainment value, the Web provides a medium for anyone to retrieve, share, transfer, and publish information. As the world's largest library, the Web boasts a collection of billions of interconnected documents stored on computers around the world. Once on line, you browse through Web content by clicking on tagged words and images, known as *hyperlinks*. Many features of the Web—including the ability to insert hyperlinks into documents, create HTML Web pages, and transfer data using XML—have now been incorporated into Microsoft Office System 2003. The focus of this module is to illustrate how you can insert and use hyperlinks within your documents, worksheets, and presentations.

3.1.1 Inserting Hyperlinks into Documents

→ Feature

There are many reasons for inserting a hyperlink into an Office 2003 document. For example, you can create a bibliography at the end of a report that allows the reader to click on a reference item and retrieve the full article's text from the Web. You may also want to provide an active e-mail link in the closing of a letter that allows readers to launch their default e-mail software with your e-mail address automatically inserted into the "To" field of a new message. You can even use hyperlinks to retrieve and open documents that are stored on your computer, on a computer's network, or on the Web. In this lesson, you will learn how to enter hyperlinks into a Word 2003 document.

→ Method

To insert a hyperlink by typing in an Office 2003 document:

- TYPE: a URL address (a *uniform resource locator*, or URL, is a valid address for a Web resource)

- PRESS: ENTER (or the Space Bar) to have the Office 2003 application automatically format the entry as a hyperlink

To insert a hyperlink using the toolbar:

- CLICK: Insert Hyperlink button (⬇)

Select an object, such as a Web page or another document, as the target value.

- CLICK: OK command button

To edit a hyperlink:

- RIGHT-CLICK: the displayed hyperlink

- CHOOSE: Hyperlink → Edit Hyperlink

→ Practice

You will now practice inserting and editing hyperlinks in a Word 2003 document. Ensure that the Windows desktop appears before you begin.

1. Load Microsoft Office Word 2003 using the Start menu (🏁 start). A new document should appear in the application window.

2. Close the Getting Started task pane, if displayed, by clicking its Close button (☒).

3. To enter a hyperlink by typing:
TYPE: **The Advantage Series**
PRESS: (ENTER)
TYPE: **www.advantageseries.com**
PRESS: (ENTER) twice
By default, Word 2003 formats hyperlinks to display using a blue, underlined, Times New Roman font. Your screen should now appear similar to the one shown in Figure 3.1.

Figure 3.1

Inserting a hyperlink by typing

Insertion point

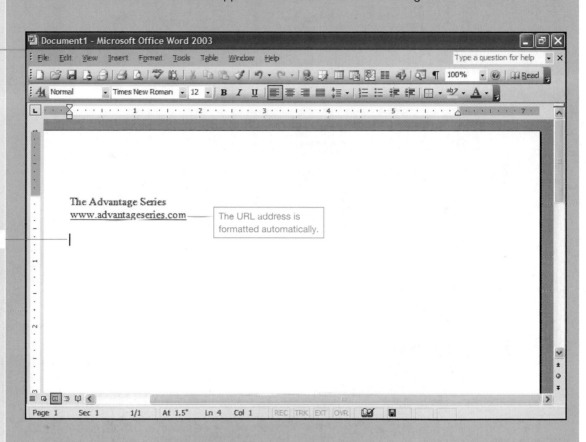

4. Position the I-beam mouse pointer over top of the "www.advantageseries.com" hyperlink. Note that a description of the hyperlink, called a *ScreenTip*, appears attached to the pointer, as shown below. (*Hint:* As the ScreenTip indicates, you must press and hold down the (CTRL) key and then click the link in order to display the web site.)

AutoCorrect Options button

The Advantage Series
www.advantageseries.com

http://www.advantageseries.com/
CTRL + click to follow link

ScreenTip

5. Although the automatic formatting is helpful, there may be times when you would rather Word 2003 keep its hands to itself. To undo the automatic formatting, press (CTRL) + **z** or click the Undo button ( ) on the toolbar. In this step, you will learn how to undo the hyperlink formatting using the AutoCorrect Options button. To begin, point to the AutoCorrect Options button using the mouse and then:
CLICK: down arrow attached to the AutoCorrect Options button
Your screen should now appear similar to the one shown in Figure 3.2.

Integrating

Figure 3.2

AutoCorrect
Options menu

AutoCorrect
Options button

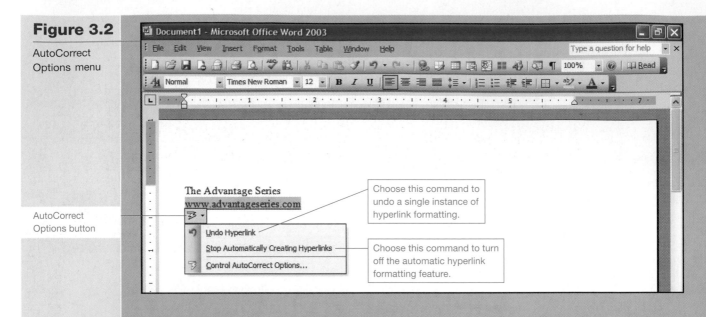

The Advantage Series
www.advantageseries.com

Undo Hyperlink

Stop Automatically Creating Hyperlinks

Control AutoCorrect Options...

Choose this command to undo a single instance of hyperlink formatting.

Choose this command to turn off the automatic hyperlink formatting feature.

6. To undo the hyperlink formatting for *www.advantageseries.com:*
CHOOSE: Undo Hyperlink
Notice that the font's blue color and underline have been removed.

7. Position the mouse pointer over the URL address once again. Notice that a ScreenTip no longer appears. To reapply the hyperlink formatting, point to the AutoCorrect Options button using the mouse and then:
CLICK: down arrow attached to the AutoCorrect Options button
CHOOSE: Redo Hyperlink

8. Your next step is to insert a hyperlink that opens an Excel 2003 workbook when clicked. To begin, ensure that the insertion point appears two lines below the existing text and then:
CLICK: Insert Hyperlink button (🔘) on the toolbar
The Insert Hyperlink dialog box appears.

9. Using the Places bar and the *Look in* drop-down list box, display the files stored in the Advantage student data files folder. When successful, your dialog box should appear similar to the one shown in Figure 3.3.

Figure 3.3

Insert Hyperlink
dialog box

Link to an existing
file or to a Web
page.

Link to a location
within the current
document.

Link to a new
document.

Create an e-mail
link.

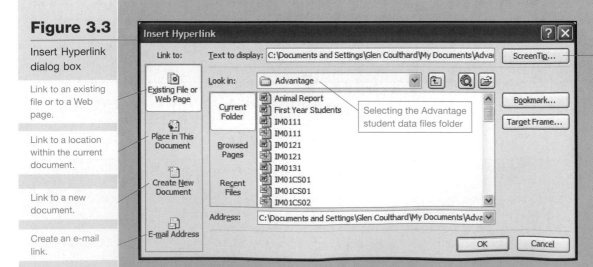

Change the text
in the ScreenTip
that displays.

Selecting the Advantage
student data files folder

10. In the Insert Hyperlink dialog box:
SELECT: "IM0310" workbook icon
CLICK: OK command button
A hyperlink to the workbook, complete with its path and filename, appears in the document, as shown in Figure 3.4.

Figure 3.4

Inserting a hyperlink to an Excel 2003 workbook

Your hyperlink's path will differ from the one shown here.

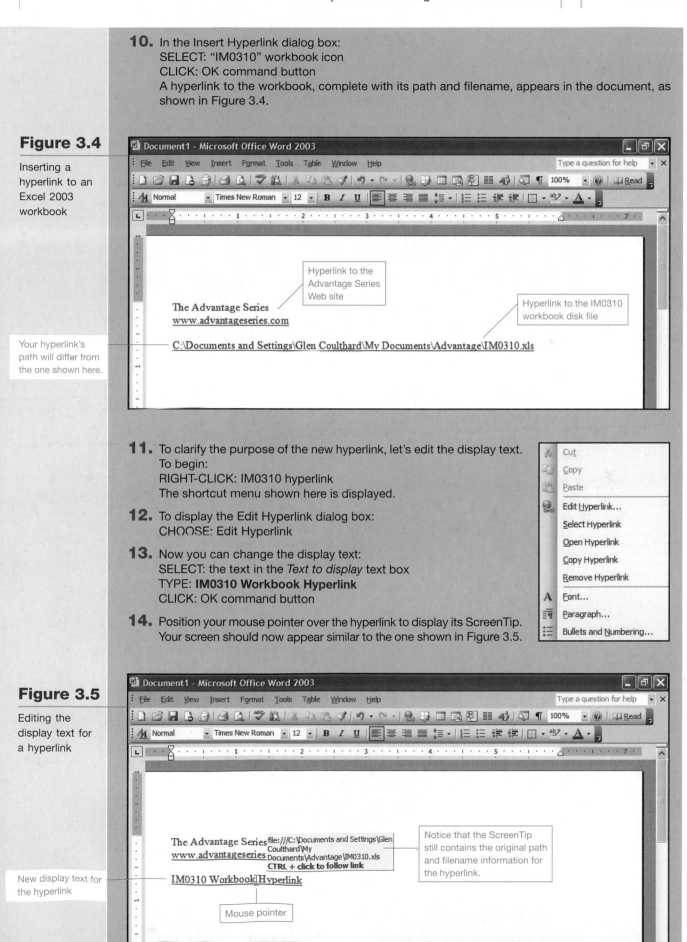

11. To clarify the purpose of the new hyperlink, let's edit the display text.
To begin:
RIGHT-CLICK: IM0310 hyperlink
The shortcut menu shown here is displayed.

12. To display the Edit Hyperlink dialog box:
CHOOSE: Edit Hyperlink

13. Now you can change the display text:
SELECT: the text in the *Text to display* text box
TYPE: **IM0310 Workbook Hyperlink**
CLICK: OK command button

14. Position your mouse pointer over the hyperlink to display its ScreenTip.
Your screen should now appear similar to the one shown in Figure 3.5.

Figure 3.5

Editing the display text for a hyperlink

New display text for the hyperlink

15. Save the document as "My Hyperlinks" to your personal storage location.

16. Keep the document open for use in the next lesson, in which you test the hyperlinks you have entered into the "My Hyperlinks" document.

3.1.2 Browsing Hyperlinks Using the Web Toolbar

→ # Feature

When you follow a hyperlink that references a local disk file (e.g., a workbook), the file is opened in its associated application (e.g., Microsoft Office Excel 2003). To return to the document containing the hyperlinks, click the Back button (⬦) on the Microsoft Office System 2003's **Web toolbar.** This tool-bar appears automatically when you browse to another Office application via a hyperlink. If you follow a Web-based URL hyperlink, your default Web browser (e.g., Internet Explorer) is launched and the Web page or resource is downloaded for display. To return to your document, click the Back button (⬦Back▾) on your Web browser's toolbar.

→ # Method

To display the Web toolbar:

• RIGHT-CLICK: any button on a toolbar

• CHOOSE: Web

To follow a hyperlink inserted into a document:

• PRESS: CTRL and hold it down

• CLICK: the desired hyperlink

To navigate using the Web toolbar:

• CLICK: Back button (⬦) to return to the previously displayed document

• CLICK: Forward button (⬦) to return to the document you were viewing prior to clicking the Back button

• CLICK: Start Page button (⌂) to display your Web browser's default or home page

To display a Web page from within an Office application:

• CLICK: in the Address box (C:\Documents and Settings\Glen Coulthard\My Documents\Advanta ▾)

• TYPE: **the desired URL address**

• PRESS: ENTER

→ # Practice

You will now practice following hyperlinks in an Office 2003 document. Ensure that you have completed the previous lesson before proceeding. (*Note:* Some of the steps in this lesson require that you have an active Internet connection.)

1. Let's display the hyperlinks you created in the last lesson:
PRESS: CTRL and hold it down
CLICK: "IM0310 Workbook Hyperlink" hyperlink
After a few moments, Microsoft Office Excel 2003 is loaded, and the IM0310 workbook is opened in the application window, as shown in Figure 3.6. Notice also that the Web toolbar is displayed.

Figure 3.6

Hyperlinking to an Excel 2003 workbook

Web toolbar

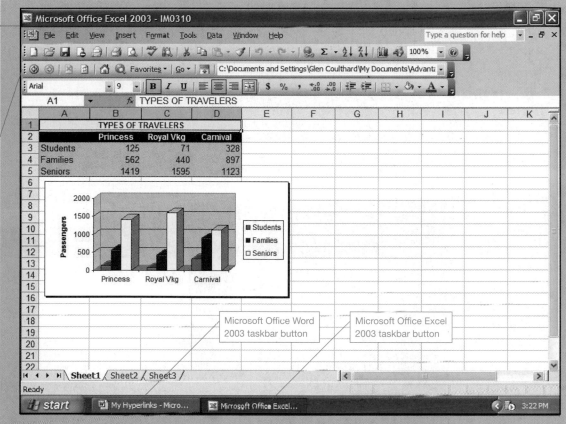

2. You can use the Web toolbar (Figure 3.7) to return to the Word 2003 document:
CLICK: Back button (⊙) on the Web toolbar

Figure 3.7

Web toolbar

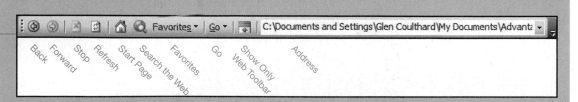

3. In the "My Hyperlinks" document, the "IM0310 Workbook Hyperlink" hyperlink appears purple (or an alternate color), as shown below. This is Office 2003's way of reminding you that you have already visited the hyperlink.

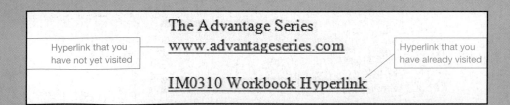

Integrating

4. Now let's follow the *www.advantageseries.com* hyperlink:
PRESS: **CTRL** and hold it down
CLICK: *www.advantageseries.com* hyperlink
(*Note:* To successfully perform this step, your computer must be connected to the Internet.) Your default Web browser software is loaded and the Advantage Series Web site is displayed, as shown in Figure 3.8.

Figure 3.8

Displaying the Advantage Series Web site

The URL address appears in the Address bar of Internet Explorer.

The taskbar shows that Word 2003, Excel 2003, and Internet Explorer are now open on the Windows desktop.

5. To return to the Word 2003 document:
CLICK: Back button (◯ Back ▾) on the Internet Explorer toolbar

6. To display the Web toolbar in the Word 2003 application window:
RIGHT-CLICK: any button on the Standard or Formatting toolbars
CHOOSE: Web from the right-click menu

7. You can use the Web toolbar to display other URL addresses. To illustrate:
CLICK: once in the Address box (C:\Documents and Settings\Glen Coulthard\My Documents\Advanta ▾) of the Web toolbar
The contents of the Address box should now appear selected.

8. To replace the selected text:
TYPE: **www.mhhe.com**
PRESS: **ENTER**
(*Note:* To successfully perform this step, your computer must be connected to the Internet.) You should now see the McGraw-Hill Higher Education Web site in your default Web browser software.

9. To return to the Word 2003 document:
CLICK: Back button (◯ Back ▾) on the Internet Explorer toolbar

10. To hide the Web toolbar in Word 2003:
RIGHT-CLICK: any button on the Standard or Formatting toolbars
CHOOSE: Web from the right-click menu

11. Save the document and then exit Microsoft Office Word 2003.

12. Exit Microsoft Office Excel 2003.

In Addition SEARCHING THE WEB

To display a search page where you can enter keywords for locating information on the Web, click the Search the Web button (🔍) on the Web toolbar. You can also type **www.google.com** into the Address box () and then press (**ENTER**). Google is one of the most popular Web-based search engines available on the Internet.

> **SelfCheck**
>
> **3.1** Provide an example of when you might use a hyperlink in an Office document to access information on the Web.

3.2 Saving Documents to HTML and XML

Browsing through hyperlinks and using search engines are critical skills required to use the World Wide Web effectively. The majority of people, however, have little interest in learning the "nuts and bolts" of TCP/IP and FTP, or how to code Web pages in HTML or XML. With Microsoft Office System 2003, you can put these acronyms aside and focus on publishing your content to the Web. Office 2003 takes care of the intricacies involved in converting documents, workbooks, and presentations to the HTML and XML Web-based formats. In this module, you will learn how to save your work to HTML and XML, as opposed to using native Office 2003 file types—.DOC, .XLS, and .PPT.

3.2.1 Saving Documents, Workbooks, and Presentations to HTML

→ **Feature**

Microsoft Office System 2003 makes it easy to convert your documents, workbooks, and presentations for display on the Web. The process involves saving your work in HTML (Hypertext Markup Language) for publishing to a local intranet or to a Web server. You can typically customize the publishing process by changing the page title and specifying the data to include, such as a particular worksheet in a workbook. Once the file (or files) is saved in the HTML Web format, you may then upload it to your company's server.

→ **Method**

To preview how your work will appear as a Web page:

• CHOOSE: File → Web Page Preview

To convert and save your work to the HTML Web format:

• CHOOSE: File → Save as Web Page

Integrating

→ **Practice**

You will now save a PowerPoint 2003 presentation to the HTML format. It is important to remember that the same steps outlined in this lesson can be used to convert Word 2003 documents and Excel 2003 workbooks. Before proceeding, ensure that the Windows desktop is displayed.

1. Load Microsoft Office PowerPoint 2003 using the Start menu (start).

2. In PowerPoint 2003, open the IM0321 presentation file from the Advantage student data files folder, and then save it as "Travel" to your personal storage location. Ensure that your screen appears similar to the one shown in Figure 3.9 before proceeding.

Figure 3.9

"Travel"
presentation

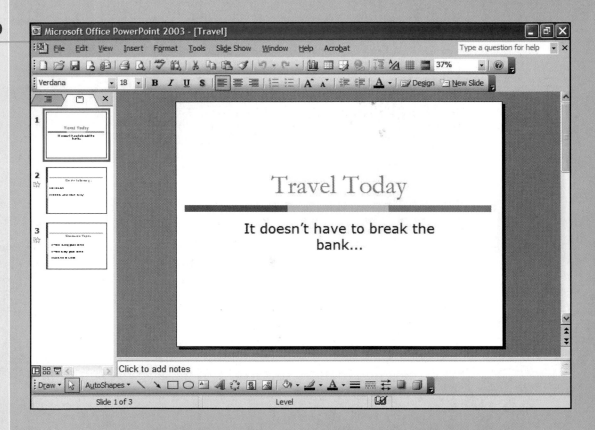

3. Before converting the file, let's preview how the presentation will appear using Web browser software. Do the following:
CHOOSE: File → Web Page Preview
After a few moments, the presentation is displayed in your default Web browser software. Notice that the presentation's name "Travel" appears in the Web browser's Title bar. Figure 3.10 shows the presentation as it will appear in Microsoft Internet Explorer.

Figure 3.10

Displaying a Web Page Preview

Click the items in this pane to navigate to the desired slide graphics.

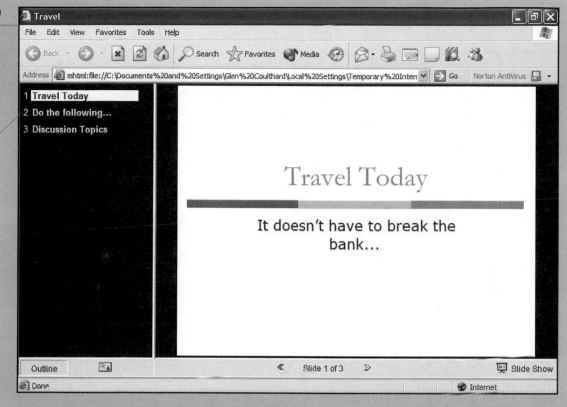

4. On your own, click the menu items in the left-hand navigation pane to display the slides in the presentation. When you are finished, close your Web browser's application window in order to return to PowerPoint 2003.

5. Now that you have previewed the presentation, let's save it to the HTML Web format. To begin:
CHOOSE: File → Save as Web Page
A dialog box appears with two command buttons, Publish and Change Title, that are not normally found in the Save As dialog box.

6. In the Save As dialog box, use the Places bar and the *Save in* drop-down list box to select your personal storage location.

7. Let's change the title that appears in the Web browser's Title bar:
CLICK: Change Title command button
TYPE: **Travel Tips by Rosalyn Peters**
Your screen should now appear similar to the one shown in Figure 3.11.

Figure 3.11

Save As and Set Page Title dialog boxes

You can save the presentation as a single Web page (more easily transported) or as multiple Web pages (better compatibility with Web servers).

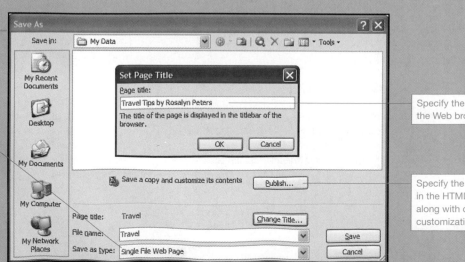

Specify the text to appear in the Web browser's Title bar.

Specify the slides to include in the HTML presentation, along with other customization options.

Integrating

8. CLICK: OK command button to proceed

9. There are actually two types of HTML file formats that you may choose from in the Save As dialog box. The "Single File Web Page" option creates an MHT file—a Microsoft-proprietary format that combines the HTML code into a single file to facilitate transporting. The "Web Page" option creates HTM files that offer better compatibility with the various types of Web servers. Therefore, do the following to select the HTML file format:
SELECT: "Web Page" in the *Save as type* drop-down list box

10. Now display the custom publishing options:
CLICK: Publish command button
The Publish as Web Page dialog box appears, as shown in Figure 3.12.

Figure 3.12

Publish as Web Page dialog box

Specify the data (slides) you want to publish for the Web.

Change this option if you need to support older Web browsers or alternate technologies.

Select this check box to display the result in your Web browser.

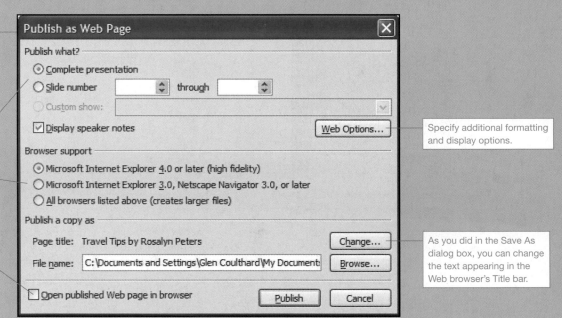

Specify additional formatting and display options.

As you did in the Save As dialog box, you can change the text appearing in the Web browser's Title bar.

11. For this lesson, you will accept the default selections for publishing the complete presentation, along with speaker notes. To open the published presentation in your Web browser:
SELECT: *Open published Web page in browser* check box, so that a ✓ appears
CLICK: Publish command button
After the conversion is finished processing, the presentation is displayed in your Web browser software, similar to the Web Page Preview display shown previously in Figure 3.10.

12. On your own, navigate the pages in the Web-based slide presentation. Then exit your Web browser software.

13. When you return to PowerPoint 2003, save the presentation.

14. Exit Microsoft Office PowerPoint 2003.

In Addition WEB EDITING

With more recent versions of Internet Explorer, you can edit the HTML files that you have created using Office 2003 applications. To do so, choose the "Edit with Microsoft Office *application*" command from the File menu. The HTML file opens in its source application (Word 2003, Excel 2003, or PowerPoint 2003). After editing the HTML file and saving your changes, exit the source application. Then, click the Refresh button (🖼) in Internet Explorer to view the revised page.

3.2.2 Saving Documents and Workbooks to XML

→ ## Feature

Aside from saving the odd HTML Web document, most users will continue to use the native .DOC and .XLS binary file formats of Word 2003 and Excel 2003 for their day-to-day work. However, Microsoft is banking on the popularity of XML (Extensible Markup Language) to solve specific data format issues and to enhance the interoperability of Office 2003 with other software. XML is arguably the best option for transmitting structured data across the Internet. With the XML features in Microsoft Office System 2003, you are able to expose your data to other software applications and Web services. You can also import XML documents for manipulation within Word 2003 or Excel 2003.

→ ## Method

To convert and save your work to the XML Web format:

- CHOOSE: File → Save As

- SELECT: an XML format (such as "XML Document," "XML Spreadsheet," or "XML Data") in the *Save as type* drop-down list box

- CLICK: Save command button

→ ## Practice

You will now save a Word 2003 table document as an XML file. Ensure that the Windows desktop appears before you begin.

1. Load Microsoft Office Word 2003 using the Start menu (start).

2. In Word 2003, open the IM0322 document file from the Advantage student data files folder, and then save it as "My Hardware" to your personal storage location. Your screen should appear similar to the one shown in Figure 3.13 before proceeding.

Figure 3.13

"My Hardware" document

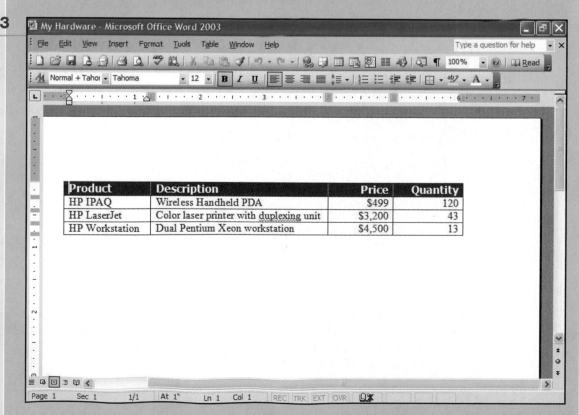

Product	Description	Price	Quantity
HP IPAQ	Wireless Handheld PDA	$499	120
HP LaserJet	Color laser printer with duplexing unit	$3,200	43
HP Workstation	Dual Pentium Xeon workstation	$4,500	13

Integrating

3. To save this Word 2003 document as an XML document:
CHOOSE: File → Save As

4. In the Save As dialog box, use the Places bar and the *Save in* drop-down list box to select your personal storage location.

5. Accept the default file name and then:
SELECT: XML Document from the *Save as type* drop-down list box
CLICK: Save command button
A file named "My Hardware.xml" is saved to the file folder you specified in Step 4.

6. Exit Microsoft Office Word 2003.

3.2.3 Displaying an Access 2003 Table on the Web

→ **Feature**

Microsoft Office Access 2003 makes it simple for you to tap the power of the Web. Once you have created a database object such as a table or report, you can export the object using HTML (Hypertext Markup Language) and XML (Extensible Markup Language) formats. Because HTML documents provide only a static representation, or snapshot, of a database, Access 2003 provides several additional tools, such as *data access pages*, for creating dynamic real-time Web applications. A **data access page** is an interactive Web page that enables you to use Web browser software to view and edit data stored in an Access 2003 database. Because these pages are stored in HTML files, separate from the database file, you can use them locally or upload them to a network or Web server. The only stipulation is that you require a recent version of Internet Explorer to edit the data displayed on a data access page. Otherwise, you are able only to view, not to change, the Access 2003 data.

→ **Method**

To export an Access 2003 object from the Database window:

• SELECT: the desired object

• CHOOSE: File → Export

• TYPE: **filename** for the Web document

• SELECT: "HTML Documents" or "XML" in the *Save as type* drop-down list box

• CLICK: Export command button

To create a data access page using an Access 2003 wizard:

• CLICK: Pages button in the Objects bar

• DOUBLE-CLICK: *Create data access page by using wizard* item in the list area

Complete the prompts in the Data Access Page Wizard.

To preview a data access page in your Web browser software:

• CLICK: Pages button in the Objects bar

• DOUBLE-CLICK: the desired page object in the list area

• CHOOSE: File → Web Page Preview

→ **Practice**

You will now use a wizard to create a data access page and then preview the page in your Web browser. Ensure that the Windows desktop appears before you begin.

1. Load Microsoft Office Access 2003 using the Start menu (*start*).

2. In Access 2003, open the IM0323 database file from the Advantage student data files folder.

3. In the Database window:
CLICK: Pages button in the Objects bar
Ensure that your screen appears similar to the one shown in Figure 3.14 before proceeding.

Figure 3.14

Displaying the
Pages list area

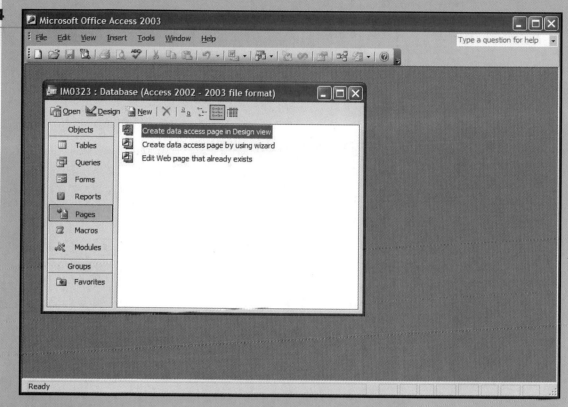

4. To launch the Data Access Page Wizard:
DOUBLE-CLICK: *Create data access page by using wizard* item in the list area

5. In the Page Wizard dialog box:
CLICK: Include All button (>>) to select all of the fields for display
Your screen should now appear similar to the one shown in Figure 3.15.

Figure 3.15

Page Wizard
dialog box:
Step 1

Because this
database contains
only one table
object, you
accepted the
default selection in
this drop-down
list box.

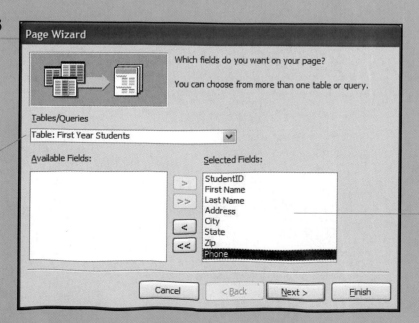

All of the fields in the "First
Year Students" table object
are selected for display on
the data access page.

Integrating

6. CLICK: [Next >] to proceed

7. In this step of the wizard, you specify the grouping levels. To accept the default selection and leave the settings unchanged:
CLICK: [Next >]

8. You may now specify the sort order for the table data. Do the following:
CLICK: down arrow attached to the first sort drop-down list box
SELECT: Last Name
CLICK: down arrow attached to the second sort drop-down list box
SELECT: First Name
Your screen should now appear similar to the one shown in Figure 3.16.

Figure 3.16

Page Wizard
dialog box:
Step 3

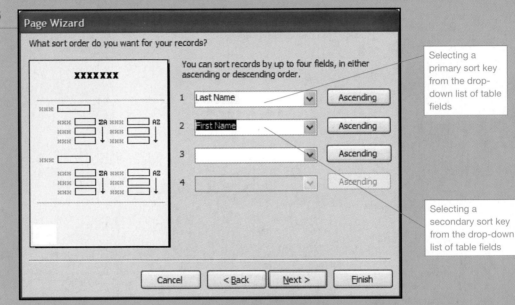

9. CLICK: [Next >] to proceed

10. In the last step of the wizard, you specify the title that will appear on the data access page. Do the following:
TYPE: **Student Listing**

11. In order to open, rather than modify, the new data access page:
CLICK: *Open the page* option button
CLICK: [Finish]
The data access page should now appear in its own window, as shown in Figure 3.17. This window provides a preview of how the data access page will appear in your Web browser software.

Figure 3.17

Displaying the
data access page

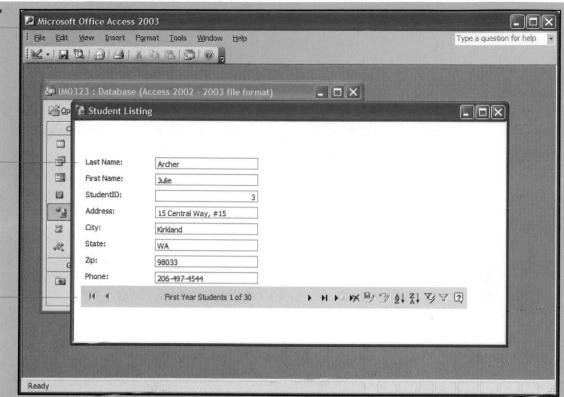

The fields selected
for sorting appear
at the top of the
data access page.

Use the navigation
bar to move
through the records
in the table, to add
and delete records,
to change the sort
order, and to apply
filters.

12. To save the data access page:
CLICK: Save button ( ) on the toolbar

13. In the Save As Data Access Page dialog box, use the Places bar and the *Save in* drop-down list
box to select your personal storage location.

14. To complete the save operation:
CLICK: Save command button

15. A dialog box may appear asking if you would like to set this folder as the default location for data
access pages. If so, do the following:
CLICK: No command button

16. Another dialog box may appear informing you that the path name to the data access page is
absolute. If so, do the following:
CLICK: OK command button

17. To preview the data access page using your Web browser software:
CHOOSE: File → Web Page Preview
Figure 3.18 shows the data access page in Microsoft Internet Explorer. Any changes that you
make to the data will be reflected automatically in the underlying "First Year Students" table
object in the database.

Figure 3.18

Displaying the data access page using Internet Explorer

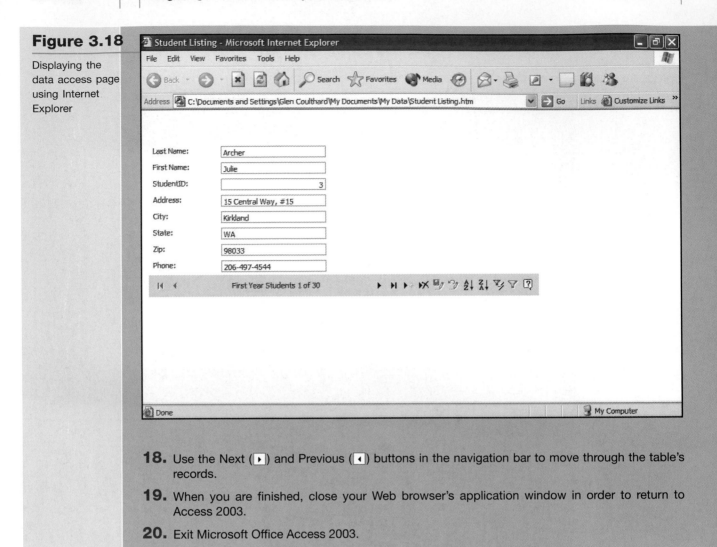

18. Use the Next (▶) and Previous (◀) buttons in the navigation bar to move through the table's records.

19. When you are finished, close your Web browser's application window in order to return to Access 2003.

20. Exit Microsoft Office Access 2003.

 **SelfCheck** 3.2 How do you convert a document, worksheet, or presentation to the HTML Web format?

3.3 Preparing Web Pages Using Office 2003

Microsoft Office System 2003 applications provide several features for customizing Web pages. In Word 2003, for example, you can apply Web themes to spruce up the visual appearance of your documents online. You can also divide a document into an HTML frameset for easier navigation. In Excel 2003, you can add interactivity to a worksheet, so that other users can edit it online. In PowerPoint 2003, you can customize a presentation's appearance and the location of its navigation buttons. In this module, you will prepare and customize documents, worksheets, and presentations for publishing to the Web and for display using Web browser software.

3.3.1 Applying Web Themes to Word 2003 Documents

→ **Feature**

Office 2003 includes approximately 30 themes for optimizing the look of your documents in Word 2003 and for display on the Web. A theme, sometimes called a *Web theme*, provides a coordinated set of colors, fonts, and other formatting characteristics that you can apply to a document. Themes bring together the visual facets of creativity and design into a nice, manageable package. It also does not hurt that Microsoft hired professional designers to create these themes. If you cannot find the theme you need for a particular presentation locally, consider browsing to the Office 2003 Web site and evaluating the publicly available templates and themes.

→ **Method**

To apply a theme to a document:

- CHOOSE: Format → Theme from Word 2003's Menu bar
- SELECT: a theme in the *Choose a Theme* list box
- CLICK: OK command button

→ **Practice**

You will now apply a Web theme to an existing Word 2003 document. Ensure that the Windows desktop appears before you begin.

1. Load Microsoft Office Word 2003 using the Start menu (start).

2. In Word 2003, open the IM0331 document file from the Advantage student data files folder, and then save it as "Web Theme" to your personal storage location.

3. To change the display to view the entire width of the document:
CLICK: down arrow attached to the Zoom button (100% ▾) on the Standard toolbar
SELECT: Page Width
Ensure that your screen appears similar to the one shown in Figure 3.19 before proceeding.

Figure 3.19

"Web Theme" document

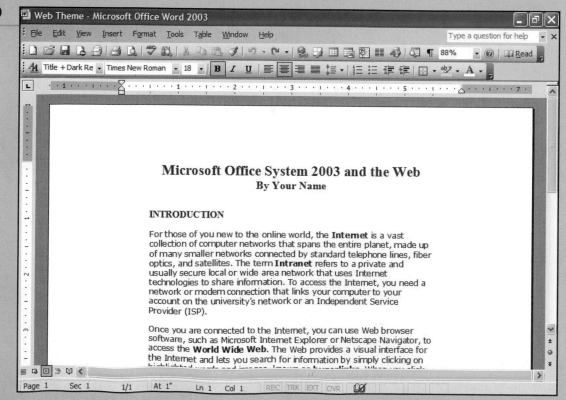

4. Scroll through the document to become familiar with its contents.

5. Before saving this document as an HTML Web page, let's apply a theme designed specifically for displaying Web pages. To begin:
CHOOSE: Format → Theme
The Theme dialog box appears with a list of professionally designed Web themes.

6. To view a visual representation of a theme, click on its name in the *Choose a Theme* list box. (*Note:* Depending on your installation of Office 2003, some themes may need to be installed before you can view them in the Preview area.) Before proceeding:
SELECT: Corporate in the *Choose a Theme* list box
Your dialog box should now appear similar to the one shown in Figure 3.20.

Figure 3.20

Theme dialog box

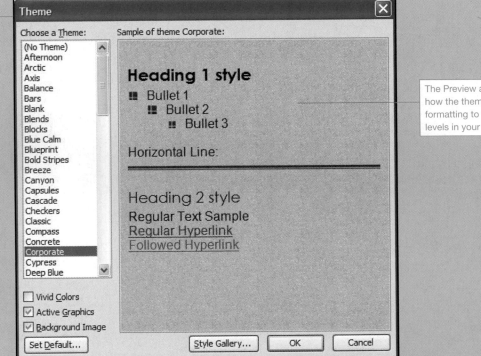

The Preview area shows how the theme applies formatting to the various levels in your document.

7. To apply this theme to the entire document:
CLICK: OK command button
Your screen should now appear similar to the one shown in Figure 3.21.

Figure 3.21

Applying the
Corporate theme

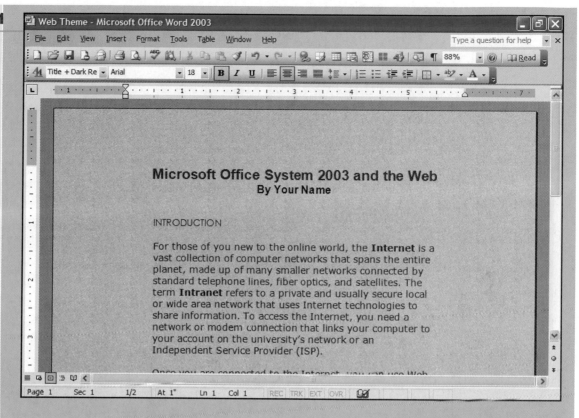

8. Save the revised "Web Theme" document, and keep it open for use in the next lesson. Next, you will learn how to create a table of contents for the Web page.

3.3.2 Creating a Framed Table of Contents in Word 2003

→ # Feature

Word 2003 lets you create a separate area on a Web page for displaying a table of contents. The items appearing in this framed area are simply hyperlinks that, when clicked, take you to bookmarked pages on the Web. The table of contents area is displayed in a **frame;** a frame refers to the split window that displays more than one HTML Web page at the same time. If the headings in your document are formatted using Word 2003's heading styles, you can easily create a framed table of contents for your document. Most often, a frames page, or frameset, includes a narrow frame on the left for navigation controls and hyperlinked bookmarks. The larger frame to its right displays the content that you are interested in viewing.

→ # Method

To create a table of contents in a frame:

● CHOOSE: Format → Frames → Table of Contents in Frame

Edit the hyperlinks in the table of contents frame, as necessary.

Save the frames page or frameset.

→ # Practice

You will now create a new frames page that includes a table of contents frame on the left side of the screen and a document on the right. Ensure that Word 2003 is the active application and that the insertion point is positioned at the top of the document.

Integrating

1. To create a table of contents frame for the "Web Theme" document:
CHOOSE: Format → Frames → Table of Contents in Frame
Word 2003's document window (shown in Figure 3.22) should now appear split into two. On the left side of the window, a framed area displays hyperlinks to the three headings in the document. In the right side of the window, the original document remains unchanged.

Figure 3.22

Creating a table of contents frame

This frame contains hyperlinks to the document's headings.

The insertion point is currently in the table of contents frame area.

The Frames toolbar contains buttons that allow you to create, delete, and customize a frame.

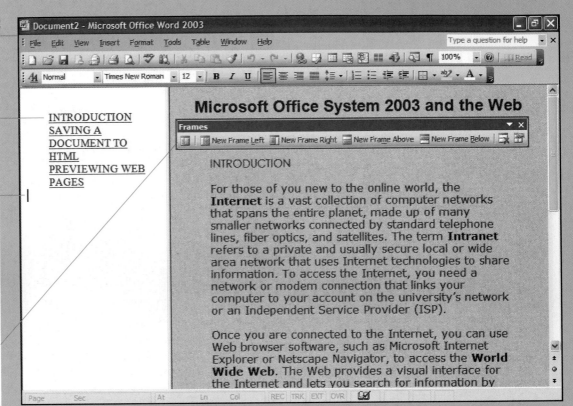

2. To hide the Frames toolbar:
CLICK: its Close button (☒)

3. On your own, position the insertion point at the end of each hyperlink and press **ENTER** to insert a blank line for spacing and visual clarity. When completed, your document should appear similar to the one shown in Figure 3.23.

Figure 3.23

Editing the table of contents frame area

Blank lines have now been inserted between the hyperlinks.

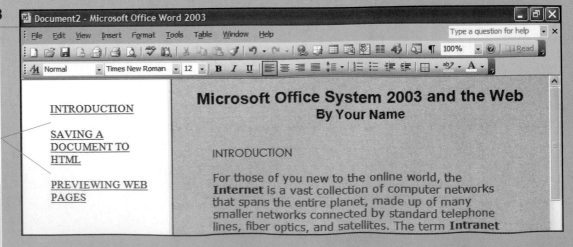

4. Save the document as "Web Frames" to your personal storage location.

5. Practice following the hyperlinks by pressing CTRL and then clicking on an item in the table of contents frame area. When you click a hyperlink, the insertion point is moved into the content frame area. Therefore, to return to the table of contents frame, you must first click in the frame to make it active. You may then press CTRL and hold it down as you click another hyperlink.

6. When you are ready to proceed:
CHOOSE: File → Save as Web Page

7. In the Save As dialog box, leave the name as "Web Frames" and then:
SELECT: "Web Page" in the *Save as type* drop-down list box
CLICK: Save command button

8. On your own, load your Web browser software and open the "Web Frames" HTML Web page stored in your personal folder. Practice clicking the hyperlinks in the table of contents frame area. Your screen should appear similar to the one shown in Figure 3.24.

Figure 3.24

Viewing the "Web Frames" HTML Web page using Internet Explorer

These hyperlinks have already been visited, as indicated by their purple color.

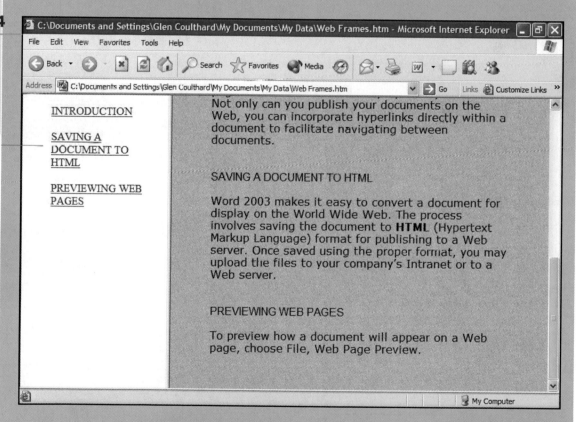

9. Exit Microsoft Internet Explorer.

10. Exit Microsoft Office Word 2003.

Integrating

3.3.3 Creating an Interactive Web Page Using Excel 2003

→ # Feature

Using Microsoft Office Excel 2003, the worksheets, charts, and PivotTables that you publish to the Web can be much more than static snapshots. Excel 2003 employs three special components, called *Web components*, for publishing these interactive objects. This lesson focuses on the **Spreadsheet Office Web component,** which makes it possible for anyone to update a worksheet using their Web browser software. This capability is extremely valuable, especially when corporate-wide data must be shared among a large number of people.

→ # Method

To create an interactive Web page:

- CHOOSE: File → Save as Web Page
- SELECT: *Selection: Sheet* option button
- SELECT: *Add interactivity* check box
- CLICK: Publish command button

To export a modified worksheet back to Excel 2003:

- CLICK: Export to Microsoft Office Excel button (🎇) on the worksheet object's toolbar

→ # Practice

You will now add interactivity to an Excel worksheet. Ensure that the Windows desktop appears before you begin.

1. Load Microsoft Office Excel 2003 using the Start menu (🏁 start).

2. In Excel 2003, open the IM0333 workbook file from the Advantage student data files folder, and then save it as "Highlights" to your personal storage location. Your screen should now appear similar to the one shown in Figure 3.25.

Figure 3.25

"Highlights" workbook

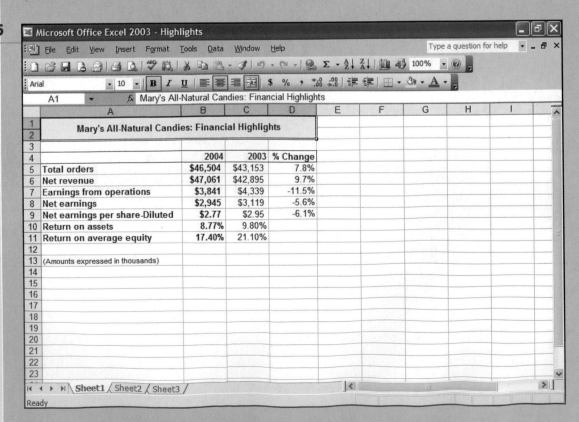

3. Let's save this worksheet as a Web page with interactivity. Do the following:
CHOOSE: File → Save as Web Page

4. In the Save As dialog box, use the Places bar and the *Save in* drop-down list box to select your personal storage location.

5. Ensure that "Web Page" appears in the *Save as type* text box. Then:
SELECT: *Selection: Sheet* option button
SELECT: *Add interactivity* check box so that a ✓ appears
Notice that Excel 2003 replaces the file name with "Page.htm." Your Save As dialog box should now appear similar to the one shown in Figure 3.26.

Figure 3.26

Saving an Excel 2003 worksheet as a Web page

The default file name for the worksheet is "Page.htm."

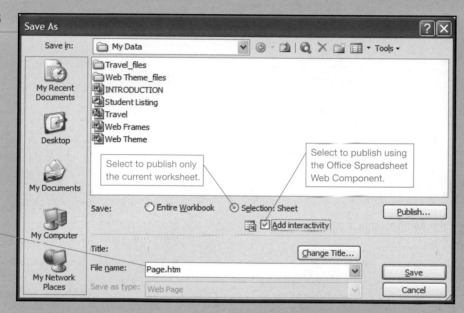

6. To customize how Excel 2003 saves the worksheet as a Web page:
CLICK: Publish command button
The entire *Sheet1* worksheet is selected and the Publish as Web Page dialog box appears, as shown in Figure 3.27.

Figure 3.27

Publish as Web
Page dialog box

Select to specify
that the Web page
includes the
Spreadsheet Office
Web component.

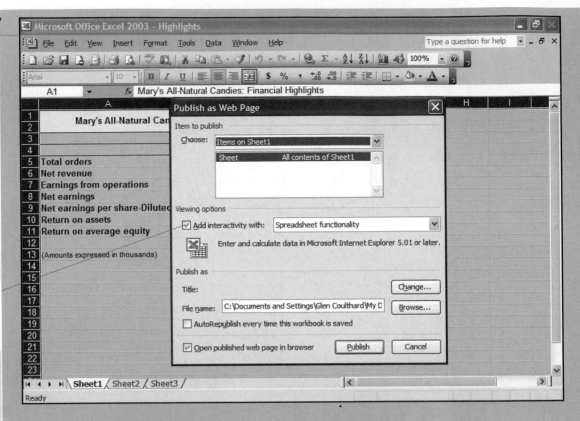

7. Ensure that both the *Add interactivity with* check box and the *Open published web page in browser* check box are selected in the Publish as Web Page dialog box. Then:
CLICK: Publish command button
Figure 3.28 displays the "Highlights" workbook as an interactive Web page in Internet Explorer.

Figure 3.28

Displaying an
Excel 2003
worksheet as an
interactive Web
page

Spreadsheet Office
Web Component
toolbar

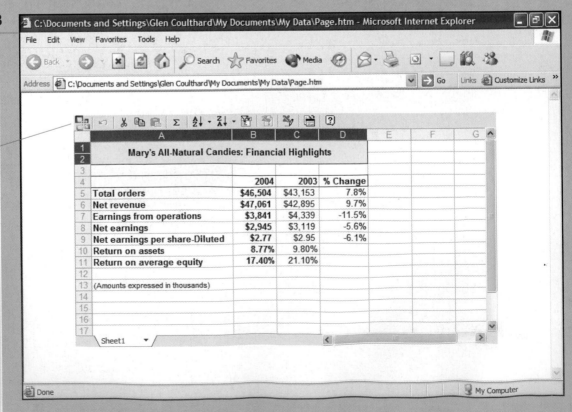

8. Let's change a few numbers in this worksheet:
   CLICK: cell B5 (Total Orders for 2004)
   TYPE: 50678
   PRESS: (ENTER)
   Notice that the "% Change" value in cell D5 changed when you updated the worksheet.

9. To export your change back into Excel 2003:
   CLICK: Export to Microsoft Office Excel button ( )
   A new copy of Excel 2003 is loaded into memory, along with the worksheet. Because the worksheet is opened in read-only mode, you must save it to a different file name if you need to make changes.

10. Exit the Microsoft Office Excel 2003 application window displaying the read-only worksheet.

11. Exit Microsoft Internet Explorer.

12. Exit Microsoft Office Excel 2003, without saving the workbook's changes.

3.3.4 Customizing a Web Presentation Using PowerPoint 2003

→ **Feature**

When you save a presentation to HTML, PowerPoint 2003 automatically creates a navigation frame for the presentation and a frame for viewing any associated notes pages. From within PowerPoint 2003, you have control over several features of your published presentation, including whether to display the notes frame. You can also change the colors that are used in the navigation pane and determine whether animated effects should be visible in the Web browser software.

→ **Method**

To customize a Web presentation:

• CHOOSE: File → Save as Web Page

• CLICK: Publish command button

• CLICK: Web Options command button

→ **Practice**

You will now practice customizing an existing presentation for publishing on the Web. Ensure that the Windows desktop appears before you begin.

1. Load Microsoft Office PowerPoint 2003 using the Start menu (start).

2. In PowerPoint 2003, open the IM0334 presentation file from the Advantage student data files folder, and then save it as "RCMelon" to your personal storage location.

3. To preview the presentation in your Web browser:
   CHOOSE: File → Web Page Preview
   Figure 3.29 shows how the presentation appears in Microsoft Internet Explorer.

Integrating

Figure 3.29

"RCMelon" presentation in Internet Explorer

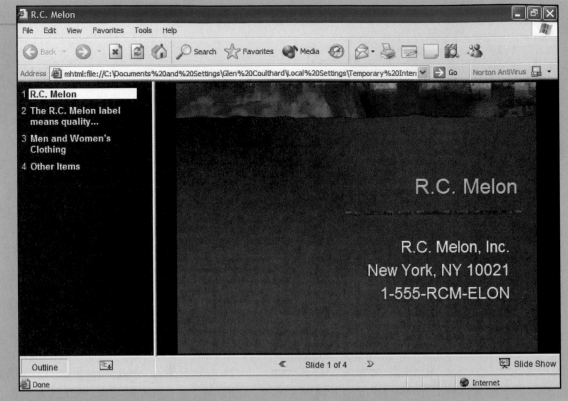

4. Let's customize the presentation by changing the background color appearing in the left frame. To begin, exit Microsoft Internet Explorer and return to the PowerPoint 2003 application window.

5. To save the presentation as a Web page:
CHOOSE: File → Save as Web Page
The Save As dialog box appears.

6. To customize the way in which PowerPoint 2003 saves the presentation as a Web page:
CLICK: Publish command button
The Publish as Web Page dialog box appears, as shown in Figure 3.30.

Figure 3.30

Customizing a presentation using the Publish as Web Page dialog box

Publish as Web Page

Publish what?
- ⦿ Complete presentation
- ◯ Slide number [ ] through [ ]
- ◯ Custom show: [   ]

☑ Display speaker notes   [Web Options...]

Browser support
- ⦿ Microsoft Internet Explorer 4.0 or later (high fidelity)
- ◯ Microsoft Internet Explorer 3.0, Netscape Navigator 3.0, or later
- ◯ All browsers listed above (creates larger files)

Publish a copy as
Page title: R.C. Melon   [Change...]

File name: C:\Documents and Settings\Glen Coulthard\My Document [Browse...]

☑ Open published Web page in browser   [Publish] [Cancel]

7. To change the appearance of the navigation bar:
CLICK: Web Options command button
The Web Options dialog box should appear.

8. Let's display the navigation text using the same color scheme as the presentation. Do the following:
CLICK: down arrow attached to the *Colors* drop-down list box
SELECT: "Presentation colors (text color)"
Notice that the sample area displays the new color selection, as shown in Figure 3.31.

Figure 3.31

Web Options dialog box

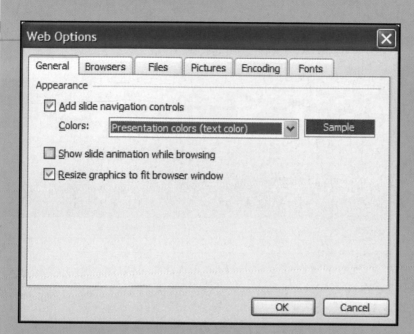

9. CLICK: OK command button to proceed

10. To view the modified presentation in your Web browser, ensure that the *Open published Web page in browser* check box is selected and then:
CLICK: Publish command button
After a few moments, the presentation is opened for display in your Web browser. Figure 3.32 shows the presentation as it would appear in Microsoft Internet Explorer.

Figure 3.32

Viewing the modified presentation in Internet Explorer

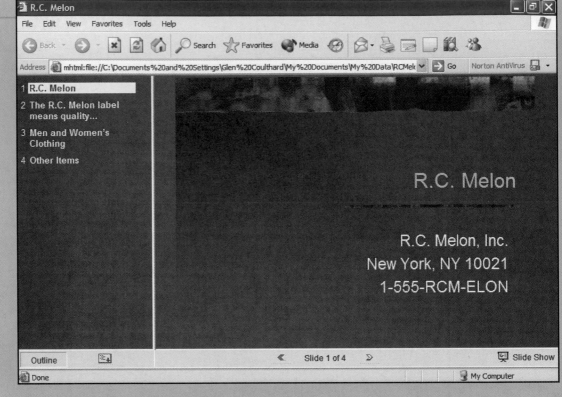

11. On your own, peruse the presentation by clicking on the hyperlinks in the left frame area. When you are ready to proceed, exit Microsoft Internet Explorer.

12. Exit Microsoft Office PowerPoint 2003, and save the changes to the presentation file.

In Addition POSTING FILES TO WEB SERVERS

To make your Web pages available for others to see using their Web browser software, you can use the Save As dialog box to post (or copy) them to a special computer, called a **Web server.** To use the Save As dialog box for this purpose, the server must support *Web Folders*, a Windows system extension that enables users to browse Web servers using the Open and Save As dialog boxes. For more information, talk to your company's system administrator or your *Internet Service Provider (ISP)* to determine the options that best suit your needs.

 **3.3** Explain why you might want to use frames for a Web page.

Chapter
summary

Microsoft Office System 2003 is truly a Web-enabled productivity suite of "best-in-class" applications. However, the developers of Microsoft Office System 2003 also understand that their users are not always proficient with all of the applications or with the Internet and Web page development. For this reason, they have instituted several key features in Office 2003 that enable you to accomplish high-level tasks with a minimum of effort. Inserting a fully functioning hyperlink into a Word 2003 document, for example, requires only that you type a URL or e-mail address. Exporting a document or workbook to an XML data file is as easy as saving a file normally. Creating an HTML Web page in Word 2003, Excel 2003, or PowerPoint 2003 involves the same menu command (File ➔ Save as Web Page) in all applications. As you can see, amazing functionality is accessible even with rudimentary knowledge of the many features! Now imagine how much more you may accomplish if you continue your studies beyond this text!

Command Summary

Many of the commands and procedures appearing in this chapter are summarized in the following table.

Skill Set	To Perform This Task . . .	Do the Following . . .
Working with Hyperlinks	Insert a hyperlink to a Web or an e-mail address	TYPE: **URL** or **e-mail address** PRESS: (ENTER) (or the Space Bar)
	Insert a hyperlink to an existing file	CLICK: Insert Hyperlink button (🔖) CLICK: File command button DOUBLE-CLICK: a file in the list area CLICK: OK command button
	Edit a hyperlink	RIGHT-CLICK: a hyperlink CHOOSE: Edit Hyperlink
	Browse using the Web toolbar	CLICK: Back button (🔘) to display the previously viewed document CLICK: Forward button (🔘) to display the next document CLICK: Start Page button (🏠) to display the Web browser's Home page
Working with Word 2003	Save a Word 2003 document as an HTML Web page	CHOOSE: File ➔ Save as Web Page
	Apply a theme	CHOOSE: Format ➔ Theme
	Create a table-of-contents frames page	CHOOSE: Format ➔ Frames ➔ Table of Contents in Frame
	Export a Word 2003 document to an XML file	CHOOSE: File ➔ Save As SELECT: "XML Document" in the *Save as type* drop-down list box CLICK: Save command button
Working with Excel 2003	Save an Excel 2003 worksheet as an HTML Web page	CHOOSE: File ➔ Save as Web Page
	Create an interactive Web-based worksheet	CHOOSE: File ➔ Save as Web Page SELECT: *Selection: Sheet* option button SELECT: *Add interactivity* check box CLICK: Publish command button CLICK: Publish command button
	Export an Excel 2003 document to an XML file	CHOOSE: File ➔ Save As SELECT: "XML Spreadsheet" or "XML Data" in the *Save as type* drop-down list box CLICK: Save command button

Working with PowerPoint 2003	Save a PowerPoint 2003 presentation as an HTML Web page(s)	CHOOSE: File → Save as Web Page
	Customize a Web-based PowerPoint 2003 presentation	CHOOSE: File → Save as Web Page CLICK: Publish command button CLICK: Web Options command button
Working with Access 2003	Create a data access page using Access 2003	CLICK: Pages button in the Objects bar DOUBLE-CLICK: "Create data access page by using wizard" object in the list area and then follow the wizard prompts
	Preview a data access page in your Web browser	CLICK: Pages button in the Objects bar DOUBLE-CLICK: the page object in the list area CHOOSE: File → Web Page Preview

Key Terms

This section specifies page references for the key terms identified in this chapter. For a complete list of definitions, refer to the Glossary at the end of this learning guide.

data access page, *p. IMO 104*

frame, *p. IMO 111*

Spreadsheet Office Web component, *p. IMO 114*

Web server, *p. IMO 120*

Web toolbar, *p. IMO 96*

Chapter
quiz

Short Answer

1. How do you edit a hyperlink that appears in a Word 2003 document?

2. What happens when you click the Back (⊚) and Forward (⊚) buttons on the Web toolbar?

3. Name three different types of targets for which you may use hyperlinks in a Word 2003 document.

4. If you want to make your Web pages accessible to others across the Internet, where must you store the pages?

5. In the Save As dialog box, why would you use the Change Title command button when saving a Word 2003 document as an HTML Web page?

6. What is a data access page?

7. What is a theme in Word 2003?

8. How can you tell if there is a hyperlink in a document?

9. In Microsoft Office 2003, for what is the Web toolbar used?

10. In Microsoft Office 2003, what activity does the Spreadsheet Office Web component enable?

True/False

1. _____ The File ➜ Web Page Preview command is available in Word 2003, Excel 2003, Access 2003, and PowerPoint 2003.

2. _____ When you save a PowerPoint 2003 presentation to HTML, PowerPoint 2003 automatically creates a frame for navigating the presentation.

3. _____ To create a hyperlink to an existing file name, type the file's name and path into your Word 2003 document and press (ENTER).

4. _____ A data access page is an Excel 2003 feature that allows you to import XML data into a worksheet.

5. _____ The Spreadsheet Office Web component enables you to edit a worksheet using the Internet Explorer Web browser.

6. _____ Once you add a frame to a Word 2003 document, it is also automatically converted to an HTML document.

7. _____ The PowerPoint Office Web component enables you to edit a presentation using the Internet Explorer Web browser.

8. _____ XML stands for Expandable Markup Language.

9. _____ After you have inserted a hyperlink, you cannot change its display text without deleting it and starting over again.

10. _____ Besides the necessary code, a data access page must store all of the data that existed in its original database.

Multiple Choice

1. To convert a Word 2003 document to HTML, do the following:
   a. CHOOSE: File ➜ Convert
   b. CHOOSE: File ➜ Export
   c. CHOOSE: File ➜ Format
   d. CHOOSE: File ➜ Save as Web Page

2. Which of the following procedures inserts a hyperlink to an existing file name?
   a. CHOOSE: Hyperlink ➜ Edit Hyperlink
   b. CHOOSE: Hyperlink ➜ Format Hyperlink
   c. CLICK: Insert Hyperlink button (🖳)
   d. All of the above

3. Which of the following is a feature that helps you navigate documents?
   a. Frames
   b. Hyperlinks
   c. Web toolbar
   d. All of the above

4. Which of the following enables you to view Access 2003 data using Internet Explorer?
   a. Data access page
   b. Frames
   c. Web toolbar
   d. Hyperlinks

5. The Spreadsheet Office Web component enables you to perform which of the following actions?
   a. Change a worksheet when viewing it in your browser
   b. Publish and display interactive worksheets
   c. Copy a worksheet into Word 2003
   d. Both a and b

6. Which of the following applications do you use to create a Web-enabled data access page?
   a. Word 2003
   b. Excel 2003
   c. Access 2003
   d. All of the above

Integrating

7. In Word 2003, which of the following features change the overall look of content in a document?

   a. Frame
   b. Theme
   c. Table of contents
   d. None of the above

8. Which of the following can you use to divide a Web page into areas or panes?

   a. Frame
   b. Theme
   c. Table of contents
   d. None of the above

9. By selecting which of the following in Excel 2003's Save As dialog box can you publish worksheets that use the Spreadsheet Office Web component?

   a. *Selection: Sheet* option button
   b. *Add interactivity* check box
   c. *Spreadsheet Office Web component* check box
   d. None of the above

10. When publishing PowerPoint 2003 presentations to HTML, you can specify which of the following option(s)?

   a. Whether a frames page displays
   b. What colors are used in the navigation frame
   c. Whether animated effects should be visible in the browser window
   d. All of the above

Hands-On
exercises

step by step

1. Inserting Hyperlinks

In this exercise, you are asked to create a new document using Word 2003 and will then insert and edit hyperlinks in the document.

1. Load Microsoft Office Word 2003 using the Start menu (**start**). A new document should appear in the application window.

2. Close the Getting Started task pane, if displayed, by clicking its Close button (**X**).

3. Save the document as "Toy Hyperlinks" to your personal storage location.

4. Create a heading for the document entitled "Web Pages of Toy Companies," and then insert a couple of blank lines.

5. Enter a title for **Fisher-Price Toys**, and then press **ENTER**.

6. Type the company's URL address **www.fisher-price.com.** (*Note:* Do not type the period at the end of the ".com" address.)

7. Press **ENTER** twice to insert two blank lines. Your screen should now appear similar to the one shown in Figure 3.33.

Figure 3.33

Inserting hyperlinks into the "Toy Hyperlinks" document

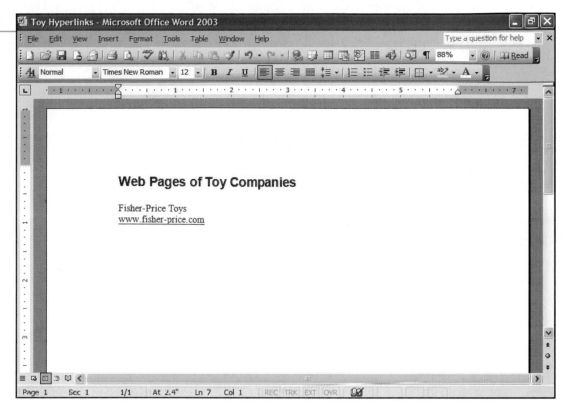

8. Enter a title for **Mattel, Inc.**, and then press (**ENTER**).

9. Using the Insert Hyperlink button ( ) on the Standard toolbar, create a hyperlink to Mattel with the URL address "www.mattel.com." (*Hint:* Make the *Text to display* and the *Address* the same.)

10. Insert two more blank lines.

11. Insert a hyperlink named "Career Opportunities" that will open the IM03HE01 document file, stored in the Advantage student data files folder. Your dialog box should appear similar to the one shown in Figure 3.34 before clicking the OK command button.

Figure 3.34

Insert Hyperlink dialog box

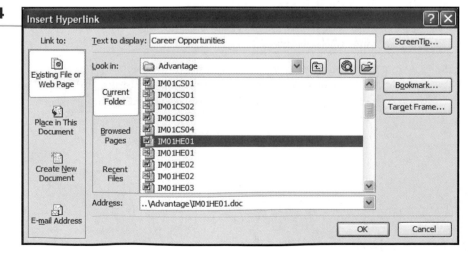

12. Save the document, and then exit Microsoft Office Word 2003.

2. Inserting Hyperlinks and Browsing

You will now practice preparing and testing an existing document that contains a hyperlink.

1. Load Microsoft Office Word 2003 using the Start menu (start).

2. Open the IMOHE02 document file, and save it as "Browsing Hyperlinks" to your personal storage location. Your screen should appear similar to the one shown in Figure 3.35.

Figure 3.35

"Browsing Hyperlinks" document

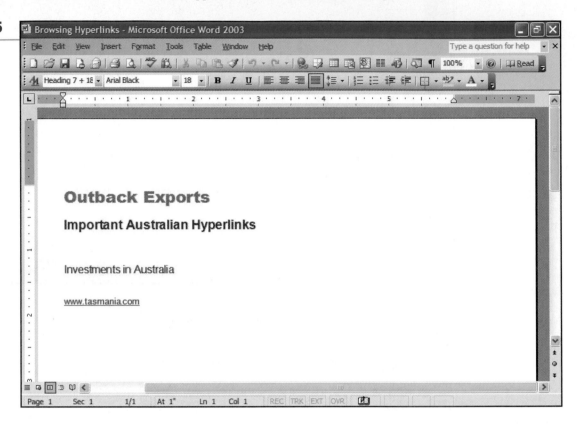

3. To begin, change the text "Investments in Australia" to a hyperlink that opens an Excel 2003 workbook named IMOHE02.

4. When you return to the document, position your mouse pointer over the hyperlink to view the ScreenTip. Rather than leave the file's name and path in the ScreenTip, edit the hyperlink to display "Open the Investments workbook."

5. Now test the hyperlink by pressing and holding down the CTRL key and then clicking the "Investments in Australia" hyperlink. After a few moments, the worksheet displayed in Figure 3.36 should appear. Notice that the Web toolbar is also displayed in the application window.

Figure 3.36

Viewing the IMOHE02 workbook

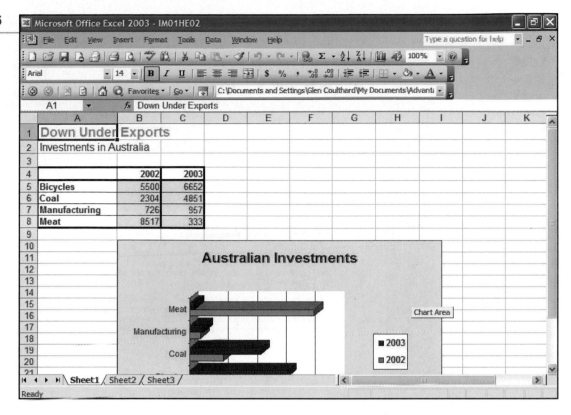

6. Return to the "Browsing Hyperlinks" document in Word 2003 using the Web toolbar.

7. Now visit the hyperlink for "www.tasmania.com" in the document.

8. After viewing the Web page, use your Web browser's Back button to return to "Browsing Hyperlinks" in Word 2003.

9. Save the revised document, and then exit Microsoft Office Word 2003.

10. Exit Microsoft Office Excel 2003.

3. Preparing a Word 2003 Document for the Web

In this exercise, you are asked to prepare an existing Word 2003 document for publishing to the Web.

1. Load Microsoft Office Word 2003 using the Start menu (**start**).

2. Open the IMOHE03 document file, and save it as "Bud's History" to your personal storage location. Your screen should appear similar to the one shown in Figure 3.37.

Integrating

Figure 3.37

"Bud's History" document

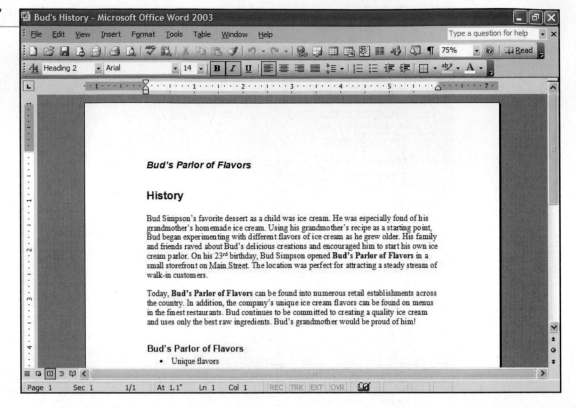

3. Preview how the document will appear in a Web browser using the File ➜ Web Page Preview command.

4. After viewing the document, close the Web browser's application window in order to return to Word 2003.

5. Enhance the document's appearance by applying a theme of your own choosing.

6. Save the document as a Web page entitled "**Bud's History**," but change the page's title to read "**How We Got Started**."

7. Preview the Web page once again to confirm the changes that you have made to the document.

Figure 3.38

Previewing "Bud's
History" using
Internet Explorer

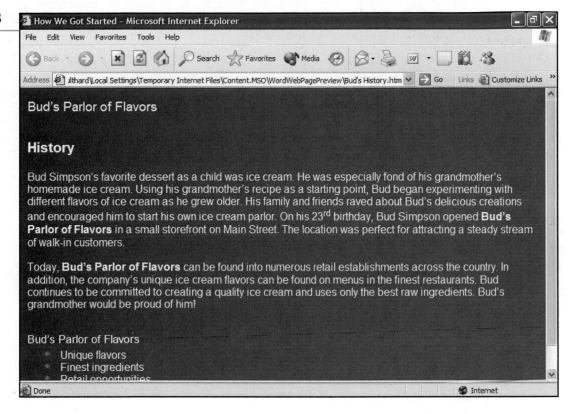

8. When you are ready to proceed, close the Web browser's application window in order to return to Word 2003.

9. Print and then save the revised document.

10. Exit Microsoft Office Word 2003.

 your own

4. Customizing a Web Presentation

As the Microsoft Office System 2003 guru for your office, you have been asked by your supervisor to prepare one of his PowerPoint 2003 presentations for display on the Web. Your supervisor tells you that the file is named IM03HE04 and that it is located in the Advantage student data files folder. After opening the presentation, you save it as "Orientation" to your personal storage location. You then preview how the presentation will appear when displayed using a Web browser; the result appears in Figure 3.39.

Figure 3.39

Previewing the "Orientation" presentation using Internet Explorer

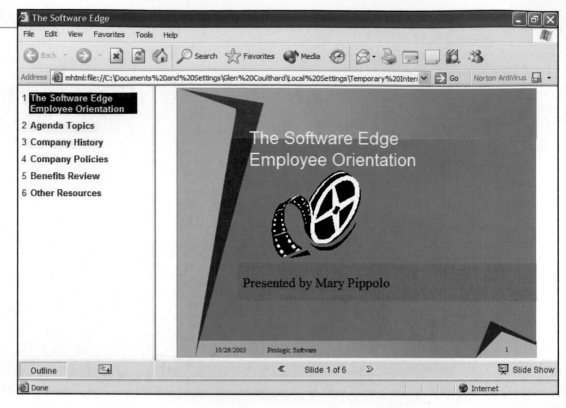

After closing your Web browser's application window and returning to PowerPoint 2003, you decide to save the presentation as a Web page. In order to customize some of the display options, you click the Publish command button to display the Publish as Web Page dialog box. You then click the Web Options command button and change the colors in the navigation area to the "Presentation colors (text color)" option. You then preview the results in your Web browser. Satisfied with the results, you exit the Web browser's application window. You then save the presentation and exit Microsoft Office PowerPoint 2003.

5. Publishing an Access Database to the Web

In this exercise, you are tasked with publishing an Access 2003 database to the Web using the Data Access Page Wizard. To begin, load Microsoft Office Access 2003, and then open the IM03HE05 database. Create a data access page for the "Used Cars" table using the wizard. Make sure that you include all fields in the page. Group the contents by Year and sort the contents by ID. On the last step of the wizard, name the page "Used Car Inventory" and open it for display. In your Web browser, the completed data access page should appear similar to the one shown in Figure 3.40.

Figure 3.40

Data access page with a grouping level on "Year"

Click here to expand the display of results.

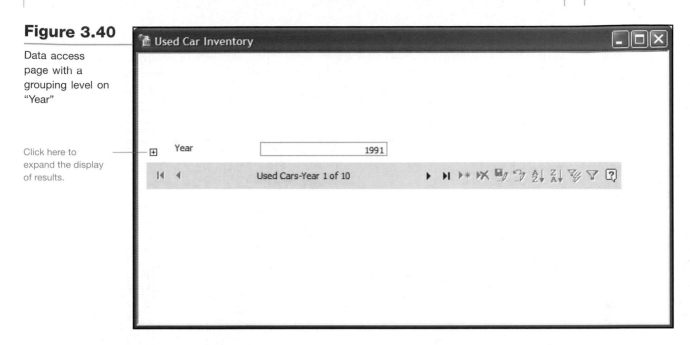

On your own, expand the results display by clicking on the plus sign beside the Year grouping level. Use the navigation bars shown in Figure 3.41 to move through the records in the database.

Figure 3.41

Displaying results with grouping levels

Use this navigation bar to move between vehicles within the selected model year.

Use this navigation bar to move between model years.

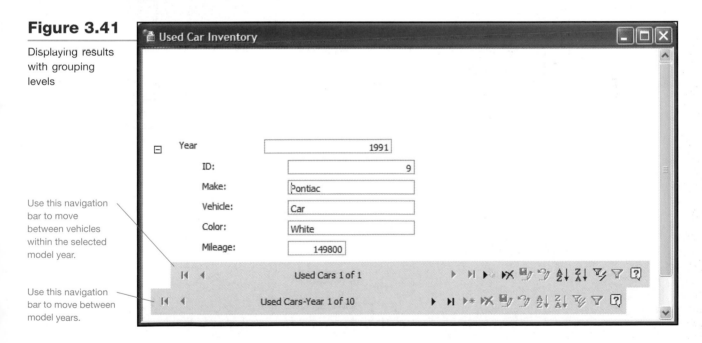

Display the one car that has a 2003 model year, and then print this page. When you are finished, close the data access page window and save the changes as "Used Car Inventory." Close the Database window, and then exit Microsoft Office Access 2003.

6. Creating an Online Resume

In this exercise, you will create an online resume using Word 2003. After loading Microsoft Office Word 2003, begin a new document by choosing the "On my computer" option under the *Templates* heading of the New Document task pane. Select the "Professional Resume" template from the *Other Documents* tab, as shown in Figure 3.42.

Figure 3.42

Accessing the Professional Resume template

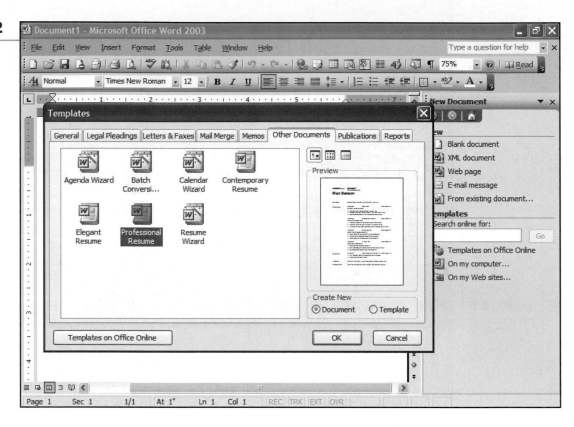

When the template appears, save the document as "My Resume" to your personal storage location. Edit the template to include your personal information. If you do not have any work experience, use fictitious data, such as your parent's place of employment. Then use what you know about embellishing Word 2003 documents to create an HTML Web-based resume. Preview and save the document as a Web page, with your name as the title of the page. When finished, close your Web browser's application window and exit Microsoft Office Word 2003.

CaseStudy   MANFRED'S GARDEN CENTER

Manfred Schickering is the owner of Manfred's Garden Center, a gardening supply store with franchise operations in Texas and Oklahoma. As an old-fashioned businessman, Manfred admits to being slow in adopting use of the Internet and the World Wide Web for his business. Finally having succumbed to its marketing potential for expanding his business, Manfred has asked Cynthia, his marketing director, to create an Internet presence for Manfred's Garden Center. Although Cynthia is comfortable using

Web browser software and Microsoft Office System 2003, she does not have any experience with dedicated Web development software. Fortunately, she has recently discovered how to extend the power of Office 2003 to the Web. She decides to begin with what she knows and to develop some prototype Web pages using Office 2003 for Manfred's review.

In the following case problems, assume the role of Cynthia and perform the same steps that she identifies.

1. Cynthia wants her marketing staff to have instant access to the department's Office 2003 documents and key Web sites. She decides to list the files and URL addresses in an interactive Word 2003 document. Her staff will be able to click on the hyperlinked items for display. To this end, she creates a new Word 2003 document named "Manfred's Links" in her personal storage location. At the top of the document, she types the heading "**Manfred's Favorite Links**," formats the heading, and then inserts three blank lines.

To prepare the target files for hyperlinking, Cynthia loads Microsoft Office Excel 2003 and then opens the IM03CS01 workbook. She saves the workbook as "Campaigns" to her personal storage location and then exits Excel 2003. Cynthia then loads Microsoft Office PowerPoint 2003. She opens the IM03CS01 presentation and saves it as "Marketing Plan" to the same folder. She then exits PowerPoint 2003. Word 2003 is now the active application window.

At the insertion point, Cynthia creates a hyperlink to the "Campaigns" workbook and inserts three blank lines. She then creates another hyperlink to display the "Marketing Plan" presentation. Finally, she types the URL "**www.gardening.com**" three lines below the last entry. Before continuing, Cynthia changes the "Campaigns" hyperlink to read "Marketing Campaigns," as shown in Figure 3.43. She then prints the document, saves the revisions, and exits Microsoft Office Word 2003.

Figure 3.43

"Manfred's Links" document

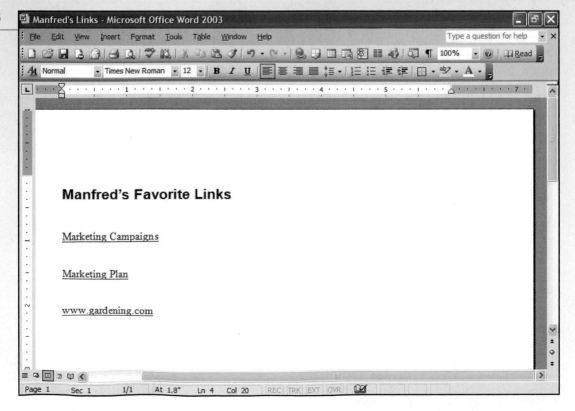

2. Cynthia is ready to publish an existing Word 2003 document to the Web. She opens the IM03CS02 document and saves it as "Plants" to her personal storage location. Cynthia applies a theme to the document that supports the company's image, as shown in Figure 3.44.

Figure 3.44

Applying a theme to "Plants"

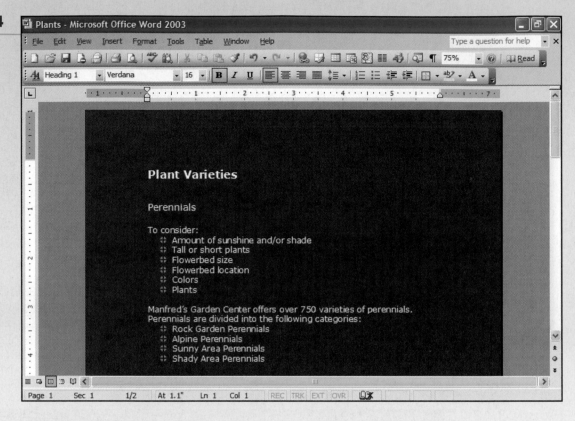

Cynthia uses the Save as Web Page command to save the file and to change the page's title from "Plants" to "Manfred's Plant Varieties." She proceeds to save the Web page and then previews it using Web Page Preview. After closing her Web browser, Cynthia returns to Word 2003 and prints the "Plants" documents. She leaves the document open for use in the next case problem.

3. With the "Plants" document displayed, Cynthia inserts a framed table of contents on the left side of the document. Because the headings in the document are formatted properly, the navigation frame provides active hyperlinks to each heading level. To make the table of contents easier to read, Cynthia adds blank lines between the topic headings. She selects the headings in the navigation frame and then applies a 16-point font size and applies boldface. The document now appears similar to the one shown in Figure 3.45.

Figure 3.45

Inserting and formatting a framed table of contents

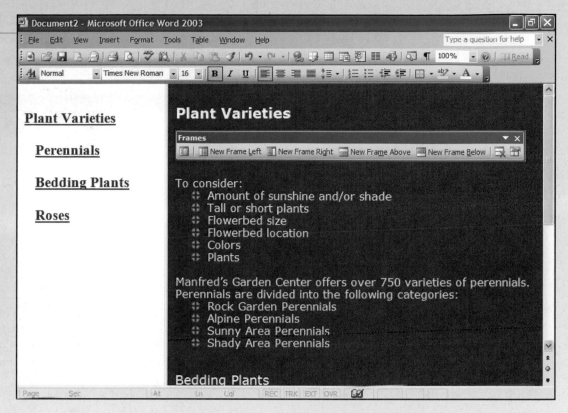

Cynthia tests the new table of contents by traveling to each of the hyperlinks in the left frame. Nearing the finish line, she prints and then saves the document as "Plants TOC." Finally, Cynthia exits Microsoft Office Word 2003.

4. Testing her mettle, Cynthia decides to create an interactive Excel 2003 worksheet page that can be accessed by all of Manfred's employees. She loads Microsoft Office Excel 2003 and then opens the IM03CS04 workbook. She saves the workbook as "Promotions" to her personal storage location.

To begin creating the interactive worksheet, Cynthia uses the Save as Web Page command. In the Save As dialog box, she selects the *Selection: Sheet* option button and the *Add interactivity* check box. She then clicks the Publish command button to display the dialog box shown in Figure 3.46.

Integrating

Figure 3.46

Saving a worksheet as an interactive Web page

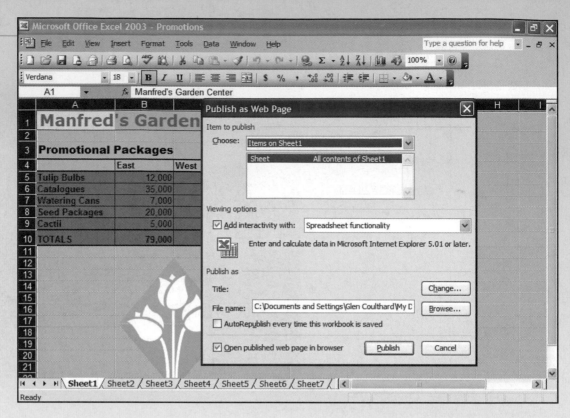

In the dialog box, Cynthia ensures that the worksheet will open in the Web browser after it has been published. She also confirms that the Spreadsheet Office Web component will be present. To start the conversion, she clicks the Publish button and then accepts any additional dialog boxes that appear. When completed, the worksheet appears in the Internet Explorer application window (Figure 3.47).

Figure 3.47

Displaying an interactive worksheet

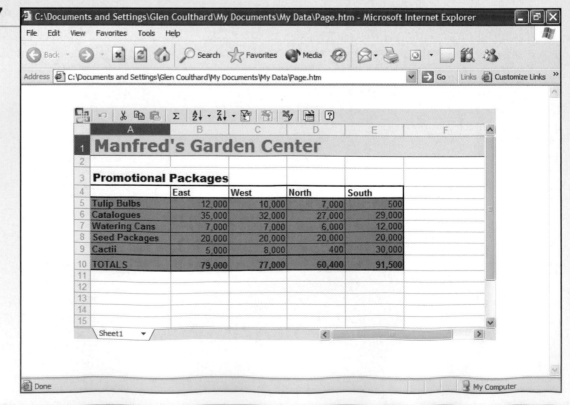

After testing the cells in the Spreadsheet Office Web component, Cynthia closes Internet Explorer. She then exits Microsoft Office Excel 2003 and saves any changes that have been made to the workbook.

Self-Check Answers

3.1 Provide an example of when you might use a hyperlink in an Office document to access information on the Web. If your document will be read onscreen, hyperlinks can enhance your readers' understanding of the current topic. For example, if your topic concerns travel in Asia, including a hyperlink to a Web site that specializes in Asian tours will help readers "drill down" for further information.

3.2 How do you convert a document, worksheet, or presentation to the HTML Web format? Choose the File → Save as Web Page command from the Menu bar in Word 2003, Excel 2003, or PowerPoint 2003.

3.3 Explain why you might want to use frames for a Web page. In this chapter, you learned to create navigation frames of shortcut hyperlinks to documents and slides. The bottom line, however, is that navigation frames let you work more efficiently and effectively.

Integrating

Notes

Answers
to self-check questions

1.1 How do you display standard and formatting toolbars on the different lines? To display the standard and formatting toolbars on different lines, click Tools, Customize, select the Options tab and check Show Standard and Formatting toolbars on two rows.

1.2 How do you insert the current date into a document? To insert the current date in a document choose Insert, Date and Time.

1.3 What are three ways to create a new document? Three ways to create a new document are start with a blank document, select a document template, or use a wizard.

1.4 How do you change the document's zoom setting? To change the document's zoom setting, click the Zoom drop-down arrow and choose a magnification. You can also choose View, Zoom and choose a setting.

2.1 How do you select a single sentence at one time? You select a single sentence by holding the key and left-clicking once anywhere within the sentence.

2.2 How does Word define a paragraph? Word defines a paragraph as any portion of text that is followed by a hard return.

2.3 What is the difference between Find and Replace? The difference between Find and Replace is that Find allows you to find specific text or formatting characteristics in a document; Replace allows you to quickly and easily make several changes at once.

2.4 What is the easiest method of moving text and graphics a short distance? The easiest method of moving text and graphics a short distance is using Drag and Drop.

2.5 What is the purpose of the Thesaurus tool? The purpose of the Thesaurus tool is to help you look up synonyms and antonyms for a word in your document.

3.1 What does *This point forward* mean in the margins dialog box? What does *This point forward* mean in the margins dialog box? When changing margins in a document, selecting *This Point Forward* means that the margin change will not take effect until the next page.

3.2 Describe how to easily display a list of styles available in the Normal template. By holding down the Shift key (**SHIFT**) as you click the drop-down arrow on the Style button (Regular + Arial ▾), you can display a list of all styles available in the template.

3.3 Describe how to change line spacing in a document. Click the drop-down arrow on the Line Spacing button (▾) on the Formatting toolbar. Select the desired spacing.

3.4 What happens when you insert an item between two existing items in an outline numbered list? The remaining items are automatically renumbered.

3.5 Describe how to set dot leaders. Choose the Format, Tabs dialog box and select the desired leader.

3.6 How do you apply a page border? Choose Format, Borders and Shading. Select the Page tab and choose the desired border.

4.1 What is the procedure for printing your work? Click the Print button (⊟) to send your work directly to the printer or choose File, Print to display the Print dialog box. Using the Print dialog box, you can specify what to print and how many copies to produce.

4.2 In inches, how wide are the left and right margins by default? By default, the left and right margins are 1.25 inches. In contrast, the top and bottom margins are 1 inch each.

4.3 How do you insert page numbers in a document? Choose Insert, Page Numbers. If the Header and Footer toolbar is displayed, click the Insert Page Number button (⊞).

4.4 For what purposes are sections used? Sections are useful for varying the formatting within a document.

4.5 Why might you want to convert a Word document to HTML? You must convert your documents to HTML before you can post them on a Web site or your company's intranet.

Glossary

Adaptive menus: The dynamic menu bars and toolbars that are personalized to the way you work. Office 2000 watches the tasks that you perform in an application and then displays only those commands and buttons that you use most often.

Application window: In Microsoft Windows, each running application program appears in its own application window. These windows can be sized and moved anywhere on the Windows desktop.

AutoCorrect feature: Software feature that corrects common typing and spelling mistakes automatically as you type. It also enables you to enter complex symbols quickly and easily.

AutoFormat feature: Software feature that enhances your text's appearance as you type, applying special formatting to headings, bulleted and numbered lists, borders, and numbers.

AutoText feature: Software features that make it easy to insert frequently used text, such as the current date.

Bullets: The symbols used to set apart points in a document. Bullets typically are round dots that appear in paragraphs with a hanging indent.

Drag and drop: A software feature that allows you to copy and move information by dragging information from one location to another using the mouse.

End of Document Marker: The black horizontal bar that appears at the end of a Word document. You cannot move the insertion point beyond this marker.

Font(s): All the characters of one size in a particular *typeface*; includes numbers, punctuation marks, and upper- and lowercase letters.

Footer(s): Descriptive information (such as page number and date) that appears at the bottom of each page of a document.

Format Painter: Software feature that enables you to copy only the formatting attributes and styles from one location to another.

Gutter: In Word, the gutter is where pages are joined together in a bound document.

Header(s): Descriptive information (such as page number and data) that appears at the top of each page of a document.

HTML: An acronym for Hypertext Markup Language, which is the standardized markup language used in creating documents for display on the World Wide Web.

Hyperlink(s): In terms of Internet technologies, a text string or graphics that when clicked take you to another location, either within the same document or to a separate document stored on your computer, an intranet resource, or onto the Internet.

Insertion point: The vertical flashing bar in Word that indicates your current position in the document. The insertion point shows where the next typed characters will appear.

Internet: A worldwide network of computer networks that are interconnected by standard telephone lines, fiber optics, and satellites.

Intranet: A private local or wide area network that uses Internet protocols and technologies to share information within an institution or corporation.

Justification: Refers to how a paragraph is aligned within the left and right indent markers (left, centered, right, or justified).

Landscape orientation: Describes how a page is printed. Letter-size paper with a landscape orientation measures 11 inches wide by 8.5 inches high. Legal-size paper with a landscape orientation measures 14 inches wide by 8.5 inches high.

Leaders: The symbols, lines, dots, or dashes that fill the gap between text and tab stops.

Normal view: In this display mode, your document displays without headers, footers, and columns.

Office Clipboard: A program in Office 2000 that allows you to copy and move information within or among Office 2000 applications. Unlike the Windows Clipboard, the Office Clipboard can store up to 12 items and then paste them all at once.

Orphan: Single sentence that appears at the bottom of a page, separated from the rest of its paragraph on the next page.

Outline view: In this display mode, you view the main headings of a document. This view mode also provides a convenient environment for organizing a document.

Paragraph mark: The symbol (¶) at the end of a paragraph that stores all of Word's paragraph formatting information.

Places bar: The strip of icon buttons appearing in the Open and Save As dialog boxes that allows you to display the most common areas for retrieving and storing files using a single mouse click.

Portrait orientation: Describes how a page is printed. Letter-size paper with a portrait orientation measures 8.5 inches wide by 11 inches high. Legal-size paper with a landscape orientation measures 8.5 inches wide by 14 inches high.

Print Layout view: In this display mode, you see how text and graphics will appear on the printed page.

Reading Layout view: In this view, the document is formatted (temporarily) to make it easier to read on the screen. This includes displaying larger text and smaller pages.

Repeat command: Repeats the last action you performed.

Research Tool: This tool allows you to quickly reference information online and on your computer without leaving your Office program. You can easily insert definitions, stock quotes, and other research information into your document, as well as customize settings to suit your research needs.

Section break: A nonprinting code that marks the beginning of a new document section.

Selection bar: The leftmost column of the document window. The Selection bar provides shortcut methods for selecting text in a document using the mouse.

Smart tag: Data that Word recognizes and marks with a purple dotted underline. Using an associated Smart Tag Actions menu, you can perform several different actions on the data.

Smart Tag Actions button: Button that appears when you move the mouse pointer over a smart tag.

Spelling and Grammar command: A proofing tool that analyzes your document all at once for spelling and grammar errors and reports the results.

Style: A collection of character and/or paragraph formatting commands.

Task Pane: Context-sensitive toolbar in Word that provides convenient access to relevant commands and procedures.

Template: A document that has been saved to a special file and location so that it may be used again and again as a model for creating new documents.

Thesaurus: A proofing tool that provides quick access to synonyms and antonyms for a given word or phrase. A synonym is a word that has the same meaning as another word. An antonym has the opposite meaning.

Undo command: A command that makes it possible to reverse up to the last 16 commands or actions performed.

Web Layout view: In this display mode, you see how your document will look in a Web browser.

Widow: Single sentence that appears at the top of a page, separated from the rest of its paragraph on the previous page.

Windows Clipboard: A program, in Windows, that allows you to copy and move information within an application or among applications. The Windows Clipboard temporarily stores the information in memory before you paste the data in a new location.

Wizard: A program or process whereby a series of dialog boxes lead you step by step through performing a procedure.

Word processing: Preparation of a document using a microcomputer.

Word wrap: When the insertion point reaches the right-hand margin of a line, it automatically wraps to the left margin of the next line; the user does not have to press at the end of each line.

World Wide Web: A visual interface to the Internet based on *hyperlinks*. Using Web browser software, you click on hyperlinks to navigate resources on the Internet.

Index

Word

Answers
to self-check questions

1.1 How do you turn the adaptive menus feature on or off? Choose the Tools, Customize command and then check the Always show full menus check box to turn the adaptive menus feature off. Remove the check to turn the feature back on.

1.2 Explain why a phone number is not considered a numeric value in an Excel worksheet. Although it contains numbers, a phone number is never used to perform mathematical calculations.

1.3 Why is worksheet editing such a valuable skill? Most worksheets in use today are revisions and updates of older worksheets. As a novice user, you often spend more time updating existing worksheets than constructing new ones.

1.4 In the Open and Save As dialog boxes, how do the List and Details views differ? Name two other views that are accessible from the Views button. The List view uses a multicolumn format. The Details view displays one file per row. Furthermore, the Details view displays other information, including the file size, type, and modification date. The other views that appear on the drop-down menu include: Thumbnails, Tiles, Icons, Properties, Preview, and WebView.

2.1 Which of the "Auto" features enables you to sum a range of values and display the result in the Status bar? AutoCalculate

2.2 Which method would you use to copy several nonadjacent (not beside one another) values for placement into a single worksheet column? The Office Clipboard would provide the fastest method. After displaying the Clipboard task pane, clear the Clipboard and then collect up to 24 items in the desired sequence. You would then move to the target range and paste these items into a single column using the Paste All button (Paste All).

2.3 Why must you be careful when deleting rows or columns? You must be careful because if you delete the entire row or column, you may inadvertently delete data that exists further down a column or further across a row. Ensure that a row or column is indeed empty before deleting it.

3.1 What is the basic difference between using the Underline button (**U**) and the Borders button ? When you apply an underline to a cell, only the words in the cell appear underlined. When you apply a border underline to a cell, the entire cell is underlined. Also, borders may be applied to each side of a cell, such as top, bottom, left, and right.

3.2 How might you ensure that related worksheets and workbooks are formatted consistently? Use the same predefined AutoFormat style to format data in all of the worksheets.

3.3 How does the Print Preview display mode differ from the Web Page Preview display mode? Print Preview appears in the Excel application window and displays the workbook as it will appear when printed. Web Page Preview uses the computer's default Web browser to display an HTML rendering of the current worksheet.

3.4 How would you create a custom footer that displayed your name against the left page border and your company's name against the right page border? In the Page Setup dialog box, click the Custom Footer command button on the *Header/Footer* tab. Then, enter your name into the left text box and your company's name into the right text box of the Footer dialog box.

4.1 Why is "AD2002" an unacceptable name for a cell range? You cannot name a cell range using an actual cell reference on the worksheet.

4.2 When might you use the Function Arguments dialog box or Insert Function dialog box to enter a function into the worksheet? If you need help entering the arguments in the correct order or if you cannot remember a function's name or proper syntax, you can use these tools to refresh your memory or to assist you in completing the task.

4.3 What must you do when selecting the print range for a worksheet that contains an embedded chart? Because charts do not appear in cells on a worksheet, you must be sure to select the print range to include these graphic objects. For example, select the cells that appear underneath the embedded chart that you want to print.

Glossary

Absolute cell address: Cell reference in a worksheet that does not adjust when copied to other cells. You make a cell address absolute by placing dollar signs ($) before the column letter and row number, such as $C$4.

Adaptive menus: The dynamic menu bars and toolbars that are personalized to the way you work. Office 2003 watches the tasks that you perform in an application and then displays only those commands and buttons that you use most often.

Application window: In Windows, each running application program appears in its own application window. These windows may be sized and moved anywhere on the Windows desktop.

Arguments: The parameters used in entering a function according to its *syntax*. Arguments may include text, numbers, formulas, functions, and cell references.

AutoCalculate: In Excel, a software feature that sums the selected range of cells and displays the result in the Status bar.

AutoComplete: In Excel, a software feature that assists you in entering data into a worksheet by filling in letters from existing entries in the column as you type.

AutoFill: In Excel, a software feature that enables you to copy and extend a formula or data series automatically in a worksheet.

AutoFit: In Excel, a software feature that calculates the optimal row height or column width based on existing data in the worksheet.

AutoFormat: A software feature that applies professionally designed formatting styles to your documents.

AutoSum: A software feature that automatically inserts a formula for adding values from a surrounding row or column of cells.

Bar chart: A chart that compares one data element to another data element using horizontal bars. Similar to a *column chart*.

Cell: The intersection of a column and a row.

Cell address: The location of a cell on a worksheet given by the intersection of a column and a row. Columns are labeled using letters. Rows are numbered. A cell address combines the column letter with the row number (for example, B9 or DF134.)

Cell alignment: The positioning of data entered into a worksheet cell in relation to the cell borders.

Cell pointer: The cursor on a worksheet that points to a cell. The cell pointer is moved using the arrow keys or the mouse.

Cell range: One or more cells in a worksheet that together form a rectangle.

Chart sheet: A sheet tab or page within a workbook file that is used to create, modify, and display a chart graphic.

Chart Wizard: A linear step progression of dialog boxes that leads you through creating a chart in Excel.

Column chart: A chart that compares one data element with another data element and can show variations over a period of time.

Comment: A special text box that is attached to a cell and used to display helpful information. You display a cell's comment by moving the mouse pointer over the cell containing a comment indicator, a small red triangle in the upper-right corner of the cell.

Document window: In Excel, each open *workbook* appears in its own document window. These windows may be sized and moved anywhere within the application window.

Drag and drop: A software feature that allows you to copy and move information by dragging information from one location to another using the mouse.

Embedded chart: A chart that is placed on the draw layer of a worksheet.

Fill handle: The small black square that is located in the bottom right-hand corner of a cell or cell range. You use the fill handle to create a series or to copy cell information.

Font(s): All the characters of one size in a particular *typeface*; includes numbers, punctuation marks, and upper- and lower-case letters.

Footer(s): Descriptive information (such as page number and date) that appears at the bottom of each page of a document.

Format Painter: A software feature that enables you to copy only the formatting attributes and styles from one location to another.

Formula: A mathematical expression that typically defines the relationships among various cells in a worksheet or table.

Functions: Built-in shortcuts that can be used in formulas to perform calculations.

Gridlines: The lines on a worksheet that assist the user in lining up the cell pointer with a particular column letter or row number.

Header(s): Descriptive information (such as page number and data) that appears at the top of each page of a document.

HTML: An acronym for Hypertext Markup Language, which is the standardized markup language used in creating documents for display on the World Wide Web.

Hyperlinks: In terms of Internet technologies, a text string or graphics that when clicked take you to another location, either within the same document or to a separate document stored on your computer, an intranet resource, or onto the Internet.

In-cell editing: In Excel, the feature that enables you to revise text labels, numbers, dates, and other entries directly within a cell. To activate in-cell editing, you double-click a cell.

Internet: A worldwide network of computer networks that are interconnected by standard telephone lines, fiber optics, and satellites.

Intranet: A private local or wide area network that uses Internet protocols and technologies to share information within an institution or corporation.

Line chart: A chart that plots trends or shows changes over a period of time.

Macro virus: A malicious program that attaches itself to a document or template and performs instructions that may damage files on your computer.

Margins: Space between the edge of the paper and the top, bottom, left, and right edges of the printed document.

Mixed cell address: Cell reference in a worksheet that includes both *relative* and *absolute cell references*. For example, the address C$4 provides a "relative" column letter and an "absolute" row number.

Name box: The text box appearing at the left-hand side of the Formula bar that displays the current cell address and that enables you to navigate quickly to any cell location in the worksheet.

Natural language formula: In Excel, a type of *formula* that allows you to use the column and row labels within a worksheet in building a mathematical expression.

Normal view: In Excel, the standard view mode used for creating a workbook. You can adjust a zoom factor for viewing more or less of a worksheet in this mode.

Office Clipboard: A program, in Office 2003, that allows you to copy and move information within or among Office 2003 applications. Unlike the Windows Clipboard, the Office Clipboard can store up to 24 items and then paste them all at once.

Page Break Preview: In Excel, the preview mode used prior to printing in order to adjust the print area and page breaks that occur in a workbook.

Pie chart: A chart that shows the proportions of individual components compared to the whole.

Places bar: The strip of icon buttons appearing in the Open and Save As dialog boxes that allow you to display the most common areas for retrieving and storing files using a single mouse click.

Print Preview: In Excel, the preview mode used to view a workbook in a full-page WYSIWYG display prior to printing. You can use Print Preview to move through pages, zoom in and out on areas of a worksheet, and adjust page margins and column widths.

Range Finder: An Excel feature that color-codes the cell or range references in a formula expression for easy reference and error-checking.

Range name: A name that is given to a range of cells in the worksheet. This name can then be used in formulas and functions to refer to the cell range.

Redo command: A command that makes it possible to reverse the effects of an Undo command.

Relative cell address: Default cell reference in a worksheet that automatically adjusts when copied to other cells.

Scatter plot chart: A chart that shows how one or more data elements relate to another data element. Also called *XY charts*.

Series: A sequence of numbers or dates that follows a mathematical or date pattern.

Syntax: The rules, structure, and order of *arguments* used in entering a formula or function.

Task Pane: A toolbar-like window providing quick access to frequently used commands. By default, the Task Pane appears docked to the right side of the application window, but it may be displayed and hidden using the View menu command.

Template: A workbook or document that has been saved to a special file and location so that it may be used again and again as a model for creating new documents.

Typeface(s): The shape and appearance of characters. There are two categories of typefaces: serif and sans serif. Serif type (for example, Times Roman) is more decorative and, some say, easier to read than sans serif type (for example, Arial).

Undo command: A command that makes it possible to reverse up to the last 16 commands or actions performed.

Windows Clipboard: A program, in Windows, that allows you to copy and move information within an application or among applications. The system or Windows Clipboard temporarily stores the information in memory before you paste the data in a new location.

Wizard: A program or process whereby a series of dialog boxes lead you step-by-step through performing a procedure.

Workbook: The disk file that contains the *worksheets* and *chart sheets* that you create in Excel.

Worksheet: A sheet tab or page within a workbook file that is used to create, modify, and display a worksheet grid of columns and rows.

World Wide Web: A visual interface to the Internet based on *hyperlinks*. Using Web browser software, you click on hyperlinks to navigate resources on the Internet.

XY charts: Charts that show how one or more data elements relate to another data element. Also called *scatter plot diagrams*.

Index

Answers

1.1 How do you remove a right-click menu from view? Click outside the right-click menu or press **ESC**.

1.2 How does starting a presentation with the AutoContent Wizard differ from starting a presentation using a design template? Whereas the AutoContent Wizard provides content suggestions, a design template provides design, not content, suggestions. The AutoContent Wizard asks you a series of questions and then builds your slides based on the responses you give.

1.3 What does it mean to demote or to promote text in a bulleted list? To demote text, you show decreased importance or emphasis. Move the text to the right one outline level to show a subpoint under the existing bullet. To promote text, you show increased importance or emphasis. Move a second-level bulleted item to the first level, or make a first-level bulleted item become a slide title.

1.4 Why would you want to save a file under a different filename? You may want to keep different versions of the same presentation on your disk. You may want to use one presentation as a template for future presentations that are similar in style and format. You may want to make a backup copy of your presentation.

2.1 How do you rearrange slide order? Use the Outline and Slides pane or Slide Sorter view to drag and drop slide icons or thumbnails.

2.2 What is the procedure for moving and resizing object placeholders? To move a placeholder, position the mouse pointer over the placeholder until a four-headed arrow appears. Then drag the placeholder to a new location. You resize placeholders by dragging the object's sizing handles.

2.3 How can you go to a specific slide in Slide Show view? Right-click anywhere on the slide and then choose Go, Slide Navigator from the right-click menu. Then, click the slide you want to display and click the Go To command button.

3.1 How can you search for photographs but not clip art images, movies, or sounds? At the time you activate the search, specify the media file type that you want to use instead of searching for all media types.

3.2 When is it helpful to use grids and guides? Grids and guides allow you to examine alignment of objects on the screen. They are especially useful in checking positioning between slides that have similar elements that should be positioned consistently.

3.3 When would it be better to use a text box instead of a bulleted list placeholder? Text boxes are commonly used for labeling AutoShapes and adding text in various locations on a slide. When compared to text placeholders, text boxes provide greater flexibility.

4.1 How can the width of a table column be changed? Drag the column edges to the left or right.

4.2 Which chart type is best suited for comparing two data series with four categories? The column (or bar) chart is well suited to make this type of comparison using a clustered arrangement.

4.3 What is the purpose of an organization chart? An organization chart is a drawing showing a hierarchy of relationships, such as the superior-subordinate or line-of-authority relationships among a company's employees.

Glossary

3-D effect: The illusion of depth.

Adaptive menus: A dynamic feature developed by Microsoft that displays only the most commonly used menu items; all menu features can be accessed by clicking on the chevron shape at the bottom of the menu list.

Adjustment handle: Tiny yellow diamond that lets you change the appearance, not the size, of most AutoShapes.

Alignment: Text alignment options include left, centered, right, and justified. Alignment also refers to how you arrange slide elements in relationship to other elements.

Application window: In Windows, each running program appears in its own application window, which contains the primary interface components for the program. These windows can be sized and moved anywhere on the Windows desktop.

AutoContent Wizard: A PowerPoint feature that assists you in beginning new presentations by providing content suggestions.

AutoCorrect feature: A feature that fixes spelling or capitalization errors as you type. This feature will also some punctuation marks used, too, to make them look more modern.

AutoFit feature: With this option enabled, PowerPoint automatically resizes text if you enter too much text to fit within a placeholder with the current font and size settings.

AutoShapes: Ready-made shapes that you can insert in your document and then move, resize, and otherwise format to meet your illustration needs.

Bar chart: A chart that compares one data element to another data element using horizontal bars. Similar to a *column chart.*

Chart types: Microsoft Graph, accessed from within PowerPoint, can produce more than 12 different chart types in a variety of layouts. These include column, bar, line, and pie charts.

Clip art: A graphic image that you can insert into your document to make it more interesting or entertaining.

Color scheme: A set of eight colors used in a slide design template. These colors appear in the background, text and lines, shadows, title text, fills, accents, and *hyperlinks.*

Column chart: A chart that compares one data element with another data element and can show variations over a period of time.

Crop: To remove unnecessary details around the edges of a picture by trimming the horizontal or vertical edges so attention is focused on a certain area of a picture.

Data labels: The words that identify data on a chart.

Datasheet: A table similar to an electronic spreadsheet where you type row and column labels and data to create a chart.

Design template: A PowerPoint feature that provides background graphics, color schemes, fonts, and other formatting options that can be applied to presentations.

Diagram: A schematic made up of shapes representing the parts of a process to help people understand or see a particular relationship. Connecting lines or arrows show the path or sequence needed.

Diagram Gallery: A PowerPoint feature that provides six business diagrams (organization chart and cycle, radial, pyramid, Venn, and target diagrams) for insertion on slides.

Fill colors: The colors used for AutoShapes, text boxes, or WordArt.

Font: All the characters of one size in a particular *typeface;* includes numbers, punctuation marks, and upper- and lowercase letters.

Footer: Descriptive information (such as page number and date) that appears at the bottom of each page of a document or each slide in a presentation.

Gradient: Gradually blended colors.

Grayscale: Shades of gray color.

Grid: A set of intersecting lines used to align objects that you can show or hide. For the grid you can choose from a range of preset measurements and can use a snap-to option to align on the grid.

Gridlines: The background lines on a chart that aid interpretation of data quantities. The lines extend from the tick marks across the plot area. For example, with column charts the gridlines appear horizontally behind the columns; for horizontal bars, the gridlines appear vertically behind the bars.

Hyperlinks: In terms of Internet technologies, a text string or graphics that when clicked take you to another location, either within the same document or to a separate document stored on your computer, an intranet resource, or onto the Internet.

Legend: A box containing the colors that identify each data series or categories in a chart.

Line chart: A chart that plots trends or shows changes over a period of time.

Microsoft Graph: An Office application that lets you create charts for insertion in the current presentation or document.

Navigating: Moving through your slide show.

Normal view: In this view mode, the Outline and Slides pane, Slide pane, and Notes pane appear. This view mode provides one place for viewing the different parts of your presentation.

Organization chart: Schematic drawing showing superior/subordinate or line-of-authority relationships.

Outline and Slides pane: In PowerPoint's Normal view, this is the pane displayed on the left that displays a text outline and slide thumbnails of a presentation.

Pie chart: A chart that shows the proportions of individual components compared to the whole.

Placeholders: Mark the location of a text objects with a dotted or hatch-marked border.

Places bar: The strip of icon buttons appearing in the Open and Save As dialog boxes that allow you to display the most common areas for retrieving and storing files with a single mouse click.

Print Preview: In PowerPoint, the preview mode used to view a presentation in a full-page WYSIWYG display prior to printing. You can use Print Preview to see individual slides, handouts, or notes pages.

Rotation handle: A green circle that appears on an object's border when it is selected so you can angle the object.

Rule of 49: A general guideline for the appropriate amount of text on a slide. You should have no more than seven words of text on each bulleted item, no more than seven lines of bulleted text on a slide; therefore, you should have no more than a total of 49 words on a text slide.

Sizing handles: Tiny circles on the border line that surrounds a selected object. You drag the sizing handles to resize an object.

Slide pane: In PowerPoint's Normal view, this is the large area where you develop slides.

Slide show: The PowerPoint view that enables you to display your slides sequentially in full-screen display. This view can display timings, movies, animated elements and transition effects.

Slide Sorter: The PowerPoint view that displays thumbnails of your slides, making it easy to reorder, add, delete, or duplicate slides and set transition effects.

Spell checker: This proofing feature can be used at any time during a presentation's development. However, PowerPoint does not check the spelling in embedded objects such as WordArt, charts, or other inserted documents.

Task pane: A toolbar-like window providing quick access to frequently used commands. By default, the Task pane appears docked to the right side of the application window, but it may be displayed and hidden using the View menu command.

Text boxes: Containers for text that you can position anywhere on a slide.

Thesaurus: An editing feature found in the Research task pane that enables you to look up synonyms (or antonyms) of words.

Thumbnails: Miniature images of slides shown in the Slide pane or Slide Sorter. Also miniature images of design templates and media files shown in the Task pane.

Typeface: A type design with a particular style for the shape and appearance of letters. There are two main categories of typefaces: serif and sans serif. Serif type (for example, Times Roman) is a very commonly used for paragraph text; sans serif type (for example, Arial) can be easier to read for presentation slides because of the simplicity of the letterforms.

Washout: A color adjustment that displays a picture in very faint colors.

WordArt: Text objects you create with special shape and color effects.

x-axis: The horizontal axis on a chart used as a frame of reference for measurement. It usually contains categories.

y-axis: The vertical axis on a chart used as a frame of reference for measurement. It usually contains data.

PowerPoint

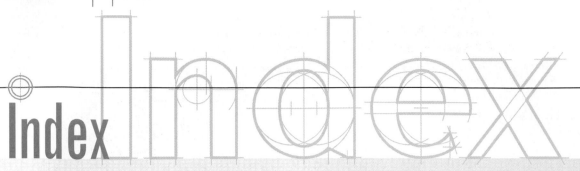

Index

PowerPoint

PowerPoint

Answers
to self-check questions

 SelfCheck

1.1 How do you close a window that appears in the Access work area? Click on its Close button (☒).

1.2 Describe two methods for moving the cursor to the last record in a large datasheet. Here are three methods. First, you can use the cursor movement keys CTRL + ↓ or CTRL + END to move the cursor to the last record. Second, you can use the mouse to click the Last Record button (▶|). Third, you can scroll the window by dragging the vertical scroll box and then click in a field of the last record. (*Note:* You must click in the record's row in order to move the cursor. Otherwise, you simply scroll the window.)

1.3 When does Access save the editing changes that you have made to a record? Editing changes to a record are saved permanently to disk when the cursor is moved to another record or when the user presses the SHIFT + ENTER combination.

2.1 What two objects are most closely associated with the output of a database application? Query objects (the questions you ask of a database) and Report objects (the structured printed output from a database).

2.2 How do you specify the name of a field when creating a table in Datasheet view? You double-click the column name in the field header area and then type the desired field name.

2.3 What is an AutoNumber field? Why is it useful as a primary key? An AutoNumber field is a data type that automatically increments a numeric value each time a new record is added to a table. It is useful as a primary key because it already supplies a unique field value for identifying each record in a table.

2.4 What happens to your table's data if you delete a field in table Design view? The table data that is stored in the field is removed along with the field definition in Design view.

3.1 Name two reasons for changing the field column order in a datasheet. Some reasons for changing the field order include customizing a datasheet's appearance for printing, displaying fields side by side in a datasheet, and arranging columns for performing multiple-field sort operations.

3.2 How do you perform a sort operation using more than one field column? You must first ensure that the columns are adjacent to one another. The leftmost column should contain the primary or first sort key. The next column(s) provides the secondary sort level(s). You must then select all of the columns involved in the sort operation and click the appropriate Sort button on the toolbar.

3.3 In a personnel table, how would you display a subset of those employees working in the Accounting department? Using Filter For Input, you enter "Accounting" as the criterion. Using Filter By Selection, you select "Accounting" from the datasheet. Using Filter By Form, you select "Accounting" from the drop-down list attached to the department field. You then apply and remove the filter by clicking on the Apply/Remove Filter button (▽) on the toolbar.

3.4 Name one way that a query's dynaset may differ from a table's datasheet. A query's dynaset may display results from two or more tables in the same Datasheet window.

4.1 Name the layout options for designing a form using the Form Wizard. Columnar, Tabular, Datasheet, Justified, PivotTable, and PivotChart.

4.2 What does the term "grouping data" refer to in a report? You can arrange data so that it appears combined into categories in a report. The categories are based on field values and appear sorted into ascending order, by default. Grouping data also enables you to prepare subtotal calculations.

4.3 How could you use table and report objects to print diskette labels? You store the diskette names, titles, and other information in a table and then use a mailing labels report to print the information using the Avery 5296 diskette label.

4.4 Name two operating system tools that you can use to back up a database. Windows Explorer and "My Computer"

Glossary

Application window: In Windows, each running application program appears in its own application window. These windows may be sized and moved anywhere on the Windows desktop.

AutoForm Wizard: An Access wizard that creates a form automatically, using all of the fields from the selected table object in the Database window. There are three types of AutoForm Wizards: Columnar, Tabular, and Datasheet.

AutoNumber: A field data type that provides a unique value for each record automatically. The three types of AutoNumber fields include sequential (incremented by 1), random, and replication. You cannot delete or modify the values generated for an AutoNumber field.

AutoReport Wizard: An Access wizard that creates a columnar or tabular report automatically, using all of the fields from the selected table or query object in the Database window. There are two types of AutoReport Wizards: Columnar and Tabular.

Cell: In a datasheet, the intersection of a column (field) and a row (record).

Database: A collection of related data. In Access, a database includes a collection of objects—tables, queries, reports, forms, and other objects.

Database management system (DBMS): A software tool that lets you create and maintain an information database. :

Database window: The control center for an Access database. Using the *Objects bar,* categorizes and lists the objects stored in a database.

Database Wizard: In Access, a software feature for creating a complete database application based on professionally designed database templates.

Datasheet: A window used for displaying multiple records from a table using an electronic spreadsheet layout of horizontal rows and vertical columns.

Datasheet view: The method or mode of displaying table data using a datasheet.

Design view: Each database object in Access may be opened in display mode or Design view mode. You use Design view to define table structures, construct queries, build forms, and design reports.

Documenter: In Access, a tool for documenting and printing the design characteristics of a database object.

Dynaset: In Access, the result of a query. A dynaset is displayed as a table in Datasheet view of the records matching the query parameters.

Field: A single item, or column, of information in a *record.*

Field Grid pane: In table Design view, the top portion of the window where you specify field names, data types, and descriptions.

Field header area: In an Access Datasheet window, the top frame or border area that contains the field names as column headings.

Field Properties pane: In table Design view, the bottom portion of the window where you specify field properties and characteristics.

Filter: The process or method of temporarily restricting the display of records in a table to those that match a particular search criterion or pattern.

Filter By Form: In Access, a command that returns a subset of records from a table matching a filter specification.

Filter By Selection: In Access, a command that returns a subset of records from a table matching the selected value in a datasheet.

Filter Excluding Selection: In Access, a command that returns a subset of records from a table not matching the selected value in a datasheet.

Filter For Input: In Access, a command that returns a subset of records from a table matching a filter specification that you enter in a right-click menu's text box.

Form: A database object used for displaying table data one record at a time.

Form window: In Access, a window that displays a form object.

Form wizards: Access tools that simplify the process of creating a form.

Groups bar: The icon buttons appearing in the Database window that allow you to create custom groups and organize object shortcuts for managing a database.

HTML: An acronym for Hypertext Markup Language, which is the standardized markup language used in creating documents for display on the *World Wide Web.*

Index: A feature of a table object that allows you to presort a table based on key values. Indexes speed up searching, sorting, and other database operations. (*Note:* The *primary key* is indexed automatically.)

Internet: A worldwide network of computer networks that are interconnected by standard telephone lines, fiber optics, and satellites.

Label Wizard: An Access wizard that creates a mailing labels report based on the size, shape, and formatting of standard mailing labels.

Null value: Nothing; an empty or zero-length string.

Objects bar: The strip of icon buttons appearing in the Database window that allows you to display a particular category of database objects.

Places bar: The strip of icon buttons appearing in the Open and Save As dialog boxes that allow you to display the most common areas for retrieving and storing files using a single mouse click.

Preview: The act of displaying on screen a document, worksheet, or report prior to sending it to the printer. An on-screen preview window displays a *soft copy* of a document, while the printer prepares the *hard copy*.

Primary key: A field whose values uniquely identify each record in a table. The primary key provides the default sort order for a table and is used to establish connections to and relationships with other tables.

Query: A database object that you use to ask a question of your data. The results from a query are typically displayed using a *datasheet*.

Record: An individual entry, or row, in a *table*. A record contains one or more *fields*.

Record selection area: The row frame area located to the left of the first column in a *datasheet*. Used for selecting records.

Report snapshot: A Windows graphic metafile that stores an accurate representation, including fonts, graphics, and colors, of each page in a report. You do not need Access installed on your computer to view a report snapshot. Instead, you can use the free Microsoft Snapshot Viewer to open, view, and print snapshots.

Report wizards: Access tools that simplify the process of creating a report.

Report(s): A database object used for viewing, compiling, summarizing, and printing information.

Select query: A type of query object that lets you ask questions of your database, retrieve data from multiple tables, sort the data, and display the results in a datasheet.

Simple Query Wizard: In Access, a software feature that simplifies the process of creating a query.

Sort key: The field or column used to sort the contents of a datasheet.

Subdatasheet: An extension of a datasheet that provides a picture-in-picture display of related or hierarchical data.

Table: A database object used to collect and store data relating to a particular subject or topic.

Table Wizard: In Access, a software feature that simplifies the process of creating a table.

Task Pane: A toolbar-like window providing quick access to frequently used commands. By default, the Task Pane appears docked to the right side of the application window, but it may be displayed and hidden using the View, Toolbars menu command.

Typeface: The shape and appearance of characters. There are two categories of typefaces: serif and sans serif. Serif type (for example, Times Roman) is more decorative and, some say, easier to read than sans serif type (for example, Arial).

Undo command: A command that makes it possible to reverse the last command or action performed.

Wildcard characters: Special symbols that are used to represent other alphanumeric characters in search, filter, and query operations. You can use the question mark (?) to represent any single character and the asterisk (*) to represent any group of characters.

World Wide Web: A visual interface to the Internet based on hyperlinks. Using Web browser software, you click on hyperlinks to navigate resources on the Internet.

Access

Index

Answers
to self-check questions

1.1 Name two methods for activating the Office Clipboard and displaying the Clipboard task pane. Copy two items successively to the Clipboard or choose the Edit . Office Clipboard command.

1.2 When you copy worksheet data from Excel 2003, what is the default data format for pasting that data into Word 2003? HTML format.

1.3 How do you proportionally resize a shared object? To resize an object proportionally, drag one of its corner sizing handles inward or outward.

1.4 How do you activate the visual editing feature for embedded objects? Double-click the embedded object to activate visual editing.

2.1 How does PowerPoint 2003 determine the number of slides to add to a presentation when converting a Word 2003 outline document? Power-Point 2003 creates a new slide for each topic heading that is formatted using the "Heading 1" style.

2.2 How would you edit a Microsoft Office Excel chart object that you had pasted onto a slide in PowerPoint 2003? To edit an embedded object using Microsoft Office System's Visual Editing feature, you simply double-click the object.

2.3 In what circumstances might you export a report created in Access 2003 to Word 2003? You may choose to export an Access 2003 report to Word 2003 in order to apply additional formatting or to more easily include it in a report document.

3.1 Provide an example of when you might use a hyperlink in an Office document to access information on the Web. If your document will be read onscreen, hyperlinks can enhance your readers' understanding of the current topic. For example, if your topic concerns travel in Asia, including a hyperlink to a Web site that specializes in Asian tours will help readers "drill down" for further information.

3.2 How do you convert a document, worksheet, or presentation to the HTML Web format? Choose the File ➜ Save as Web Page command from the Menu bar in Word 2003, Excel 2003, or PowerPoint 2003.

3.3 Explain why you might want to use frames for a Web page. In this chapter, you learned to create navigation frames of shortcut hyperlinks to documents and slides. The bottom line, however, is that navigation frames let you work more efficiently and effectively.

Glossary

Data access page: A special type of Web page that is connected to a database and allows you to work with data through the Microsoft Internet Explorer Web browser.

Destination document: An Office 2003 document that contains data that is copied from another application.

Embedding: A method for sharing data in Microsoft Office 2003 applications. Embedded data is fully editable within the destination document and does not retain a connection to its source document.

Frame: A separate area on a Web page that provides hyperlinks to a document's table of contents or other pages on a Web site.

HTML: An acronym for Hypertext Markup Language, which is the standardized markup language used in creating documents for display on the World Wide Web.

Linking: A method for sharing data in Microsoft Office 2003 applications. In linking, you not only paste the data, but you also establish a dynamic link between the source and destination documents.

Office Clipboard: An Office 2003 program that allows you to copy and move information within or among Office 2003 applications. Unlike the Windows Clipboard, the Office Clipboard can store up to 24 items and then paste them all at once.

Pasting: A method for sharing data in Microsoft Office 2003 applications. Pasting data involves inserting a static representation of the source data into the destination document.

Server application: For data shared among Office 2003 applications, this term refers to the application that was used to create the shared data.

Sizing handles: Small boxes or circles that appear on the perimeter of an object when it is selected; dragging the sizing handles will resize an object both vertically and horizontally.

Source document: Original document in which information is created for transfer to a destination document.

Spreadsheet Office Web component: A Microsoft Office Web component; an ActiveX object that provides basic interactive spreadsheet functionality using the Microsoft Internet Explorer Web browser.

Web server: A special type of host computer that runs Web server software and is directly connected to the Internet. A Web server responds to requests and serves *HTML* and *XML* documents to your Web browser software.

Web toolbar: A toolbar that provides buttons for accessing navigation and other Web browsing features for *HTML* and *XML* documents.

Windows Clipboard: A program in Windows that allows you to copy and move information within an application or among applications. The system or Windows Clipboard temporarily stores the information in memory before you paste the data into a new location.

XML: A standardized meta-markup language used to define, maintain, and exchange structured data using Web-based documents. Microsoft provides an XML Spreadsheet schema specification that defines a special XML file format for storing and manipulating workbook data.

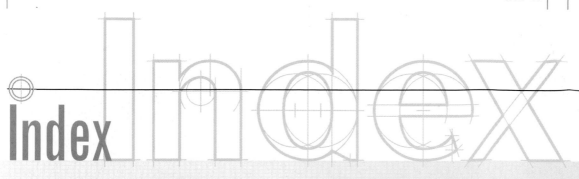

Index

Integrating

Appendix

Preparing to Use Microsoft Office

Getting Started with Windows

Microsoft Windows is an operating system intended for use on desktop and notebook computers. An *operating system* is a collection of software programs that manage, coordinate, and, in a sense, bring life to the computer hardware (the physical components of a computer). Every computer must have an operating system to control its basic input and output operations, such as receiving commands from the keyboard or mouse (input) and displaying information to the screen (output). An operating system is also responsible for managing the storage areas of the computer, namely, hard disks and diskettes, and for connecting to networks and the Internet. Without an operating system, you cannot communicate with your computer.

Starting Windows

→ ### Feature

Microsoft Windows provides a graphical environment for working in your application software, such as Microsoft Office. In Windows, you display your work in one or more *windows,* often called dialog boxes, on the desktop. You interact with content in these windows using the keyboard, mouse, voice command, or other input device.

→ ### Method

- Turn on your computer and monitor.

- If you are attached to a network, enter your assigned user name and password.

→ ### Practice

In this lesson, you will start your computer and load Windows.

1. Turn on your computer and monitor.

2. After a few seconds, a dialog box may appear asking you to enter your *User name* and *Password.* Enter this information now or ask your instructor for further instructions. (*Note:* If this dialog box does not display on your computer, proceed to the next step.)

3. The entire screen area is referred to as your *desktop.* If there are any windows open on your *desktop,* do the following:
CLICK: Close button (☒) in the top right-hand corner of each open window
Your Windows desktop should now appear similar, but not identical, to the one showbn in Figure 1. Think of the Windows desktop as a virtual desktop on which you view your work in progress. In addition, graphical *icons,* such as "My Computer," represent the tools on your desktop that you use most. Some icons allow you to launch applications. Other icons allow you to access and display the contents of storage areas. Because the Windows desktop represents your personal working area, it is likely that your desktop will look different from the one shown in Figure 1.

Figure 1

The Windows desktop

Desktop icon

Start button

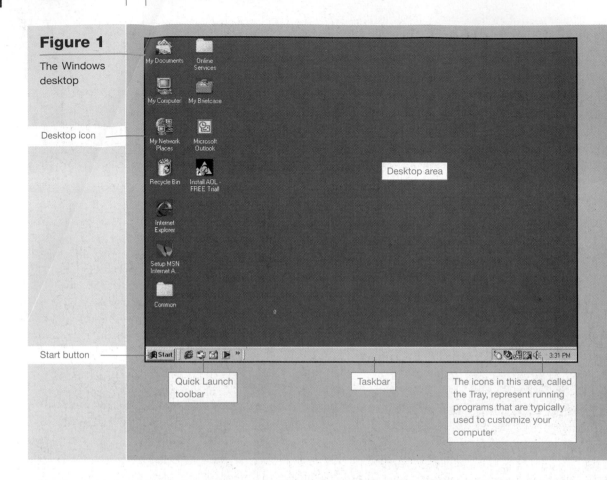

Quick Launch toolbar

Taskbar

The icons in this area, called the Tray, represent running programs that are typically used to customize your computer

---

Using the Mouse

→ **Feature**

A mouse is an input device that is rolled about on a desktop to direct a pointer on your computer's display screen. To work effectively in Windows, you must know how to use the mouse.

→ **Method**

The most common mouse actions in Windows are:

- **Point**   Slide the mouse on your desk to position the tip of the mouse pointer over the desired object on the screen.

- **Click**   Press down and release the left mouse button quickly. This action, often referred to as single-clicking, is typically used for selecting items.

- **Right-click**   Press down and release the right mouse button quickly. Right-clicking the mouse pointer on an object, such as an icon, displays a context-sensitive menu, if available.

- **Double-click**   Press down and release the left mouse button twice in rapid succession. This action is typically used for opening items or programs.

- **Drag**   Press down and hold the left mouse button as you move the mouse pointer across the screen. When the mouse pointer reaches the desired location, release the mouse button. Dragging is used to move objects or windows or to create shortcuts for objects.

→ **Practice**

In this lesson, you practice pointing, clicking, right clicking, and double-clicking with the mouse.

Setup: Having loaded Windows, ensure that your Windows desktop appears similar to the one shown in Figure 1.

1. The default shape for the mouse pointer looks like a left-pointing diagonal arrow. While you are working in Windows, the mouse pointer will change shape when you move it over different parts of the screen or when an application performs a certain task. Each mouse pointer shape has its own purpose and may provide you with important information. There are four primary mouse pointer shapes of which you should be aware:

▹	**left arrow**	Used to select objects, choose menu commands, and access buttons on the taskbar and application toolbars.
⧗	**hourglass**	Informs you that Windows is busy and requests that you wait.
I	**I-beam**	Used to edit text and to position the insertion point (also called a *cursor*).
⫸	**hand**	In the Help window, the hand is used to select topics and definitions. When browsing your computer or the Web, the hand is used to select a hyperlink that launches an application or takes you to a new document or bookmark.

2. To practice clicking with the mouse:
CLICK: "My Computer" icon (▣) on your desktop
The "My Computer" icon should now appear shaded. This shading indicates that the object is now selected.

3. To deselect the "My Computer" icon:
CLICK: on a blank area of the desktop

4. To practice right-clicking, do the following:
RIGHT-CLICK: on a blank area of the desktop
A context-sensitive menu is displayed, as shown here. In this learning guide, we refer to menus that you display by right clicking as *right-click menus*.

5. To remove the right-click menu:
CLICK: on a blank area of the desktop

6. To practice double-clicking, do the following:
DOUBLE-CLICK: "My Computer" icon (▣) on your desktop
A window should have opened, similar to the one shown in Figure 2.

7. Keep this window open for use in the next lesson.

Figure 2

The "My Computer" window

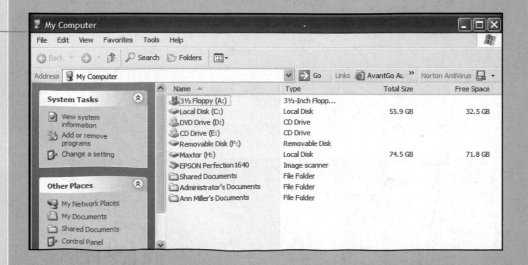

Using Dialog Boxes

→ **Feature**

In Windows applications, dialog boxes are also used to display messages or to ask for the confirmation of commands. In a dialog box, you indicate the options you want to use and then click the OK command button when you are finished. Dialog boxes are sometimes composed of multiple tabs that allow you to access additional pages within the dialog box by simply clicking on the named tab.

→ **Method**

A dialog box uses the following types of controls or components for collecting information:

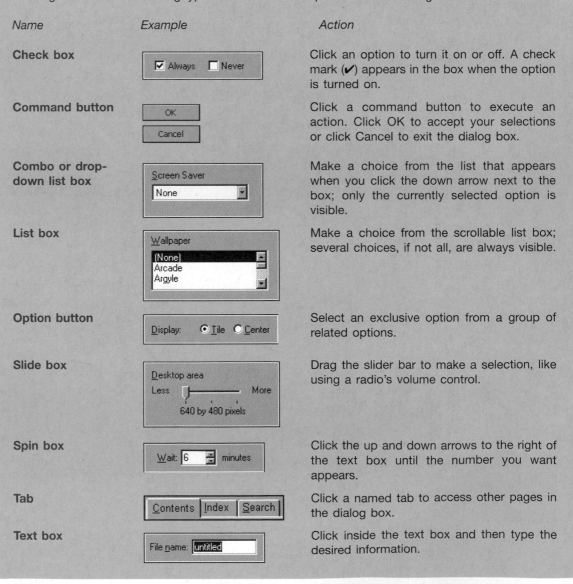

Name	Example	Action
Check box	☑ Always ☐ Never	Click an option to turn it on or off. A check mark (✔) appears in the box when the option is turned on.
Command button	OK / Cancel	Click a command button to execute an action. Click OK to accept your selections or click Cancel to exit the dialog box.
Combo or drop-down list box	Screen Saver: None	Make a choice from the list that appears when you click the down arrow next to the box; only the currently selected option is visible.
List box	Wallpaper: (None), Arcade, Argyle	Make a choice from the scrollable list box; several choices, if not all, are always visible.
Option button	Display: ⦿ Tile ○ Center	Select an exclusive option from a group of related options.
Slide box	Desktop area: Less — More / 640 by 480 pixels	Drag the slider bar to make a selection, like using a radio's volume control.
Spin box	Wait: 6 minutes	Click the up and down arrows to the right of the text box until the number you want appears.
Tab	Contents	Index	Search	Click a named tab to access other pages in the dialog box.
Text box	File name: untitled	Click inside the text box and then type the desired information.

→ **Practice**

In this lesson, you will practice using a dialog box.

Setup: Ensure that the "My Computer" window is open on the desktop.

1. To practice using a dialog box, let's open the Folder Options dialog box. In this step, you choose the Tools option by clicking it once in the Menu bar.
CHOOSE: Tools (as shown here)

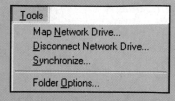

2. From the Tools menu, you will now choose the Folder Options by clicking it in the drop-down menu. Do the following:
CHOOSE: Folder Options from the Tools menu

Figure 3

Folder Options
dialog box:
General tab

The contents of
the *General* tab are
displaying.

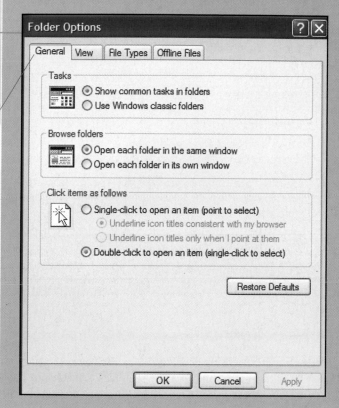

The Folder Options dialog box appears, as shown in Figure 3. Depending on the version of Windows you are using, this dialog box displays four tabs: *General, View, File Types,* and *Offline Files.*

3. To leave the dialog box without making a selection:
CLICK: Cancel command button

Shutting Down Windows

→ **Feature**

In Windows, the task of exiting Windows is referred to as "shutting down" the computer. You should always follow the suggested steps in this lesson before turning off the computer's power. Otherwise, you run the risk of losing your data.

→ **Method**

- CLICK: Start button (_start_)
- CLICK: Turn Off Computer from the bottom of the Start menu
- CLICK: Turn Off

→ **Practice**

In this lesson, you display the Shut Down Windows dialog box.

1. CLICK: _start_
CLICK: Turn Off Computer from the bottom of the Start menu

Figure 4

Turn off computer Windows dialog box

The Turn off computer dialog box should now display (Figure 4). Depending on your version of Windows, the dialog box may appear differently on your computer.

2. Three options are available; these are explained in Table 1.

3. To leave the dialog box without shutting down your computer:
   CLICK: Cancel command button

Table 1

Windows Shut Down Options

Command	When to Use
Stand By	Use this to conserve power. Your computer will appear to shut down, but it is actually still running, and all open documents and windows are restored when you press the power switch on your computer.
Turn Off	Use this option when you are done with the current work session and want to turn off your computer. After choosing this option, your computer will shut down.
Restart	Use this option when you want to continue working in Windows but want to "reboot" your computer. If your system locks up, you may find it necessary to restart your computer.

Getting Help in Microsoft Office

Microsoft Office provides several context-sensitive help features and a comprehensive library of online documentation. Like many developers trying to minimize the retail price of software and maximize profits, Microsoft has stopped shipping volumes of print-based documentation in favor of online and Web-based Help options. This module describes several methods for finding answers to your questions.

Using the Ask a Question Text Box

→ **Feature**

The Ask a Question text box is located on the right side of the Menu bar and provides quick access to your application's Help system. This text box is a convenient starting point for finding answers to your questions. Furthermore, it is available across all of the Microsoft Office applications.

→ **Method**

- CLICK: in the Ask a Question text box
- TYPE: **a question or topic**
- PRESS: **ENTER**

→ **Practice**

In this lesson, you will use the Ask a Question box to access an application's Help system.

1. Let's begin by loading an Office XP application. To load Microsoft Word, do the following:
   CLICK: Start button (**start**)

CHOOSE: Programs in the displayed menu
CHOOSE: Microsoft Word from the list of programs
The Microsoft Word application window should appear.

2. Locate the Ask a Question text box on the right side of the Menu bar (Figure 5).

3. To find out how to write a formal letter using Word, do the following:
CLICK: in the Ask a Question text box
TYPE: **create a letter**

Figure 5

Microsoft Word
application
window

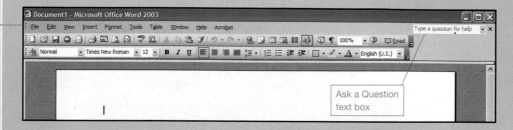

PRESS: (ENTER)
A list of choices should now appear in the Search Results Task Pane, as shown in Figure 6.

Figure 6

Search Results

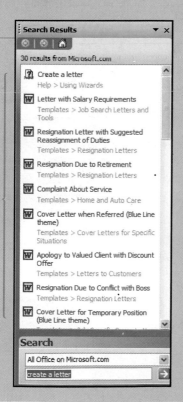

Each of these items
is formatted as a
hyperlink that you
can click to access
Word's Help system.

Figure 7

Create a letter
help

4. To display information for
a specific topic:
CLICK: "Create a letter"
topic. Your screen should
now appear similar to the
one shown in Figure 7.

5. Close the Help window.
CLICK: Close (☒) button

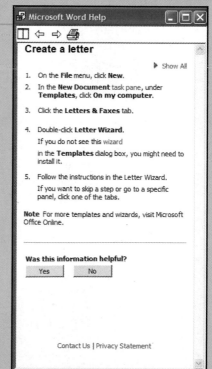

Using the Help Window

 Feature

You can think of the Help window as the front door to your application's vast help resources. The Help window provides various methods of searching for information easily and quickly. The *Table of Contents* task pane displays a list of help topics organized as a hierarchy of books and pages.

→ ## Method

To access the Help window:

- CHOOSE: Help, Microsoft Word Help from the Menu bar
  (*Note:* For this command to work, you must have previously deactivated the Office Assistant, a procedure we describe in the next lesson.)

→ ## Practice

In this lesson, you use the Help window.

Setup: Ensure that the Microsoft Word Help window is displaying. Your screen should appear similar to the one shown in Figure 8.

Figure 8

Help Task Pane

Figure 9

Help Task Pane

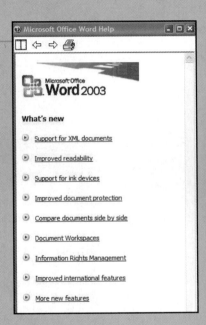

1. To display information about what's new in Microsoft Word:
   CLICK: "What's New" topic
   Your screen should now appear similar to the one shown in Figure 9.
   (*Note:* You may need to scroll down to see this option.)

2. Review the choices and then close the help window.

Figure 10

Help window

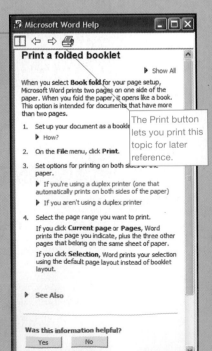

3. Now, let's practice using the *Table of Contents*.
   CLICK: *Table of Contents*

4. To retrieve help information on the Printing command:
   CLICK: **Printing**
   In this case, there are several print-related topics from which to choose.

5. To display information about the "Print a folded booklet" topic:
   CLICK: "Print a folded booklet" in the topics list
   The Help window should now appear similar to the one shown in Figure 10.

6. To close the Help window:
   CLICK: its Close button (☒)

Using the Office Assistant

→ **Feature**

The Office Assistant watches your keystrokes and mouse clicks as you work and offers suggestions and shortcuts to make you more productive and efficient. For example, in Word, if the Assistant sees that you are creating a letter, it will provide a list of Help topics and tips for creating the letter. You can choose to hide or turn off the Assistant, or otherwise customize it to meet your needs.

→ **Method**

To hide or show the Office Assistant:

• CHOOSE: Help, Hide the Office Assistant

or

• CHOOSE: Help, Show the Office Assistant

To obtain help from the Office Assistant:

• CLICK: the Office Assistant character to display the question window

• TYPE: **a description of what you would like to do**

• CLICK: Search

To deactivate the Office Assistant:

• RIGHT-CLICK: the Office Assistant character

• SELECT: Hide

→ **Practice**

In this lesson, you practice using the Office Assistant.

Setup: Ensure that Microsoft Word is loaded.

1. If the Office Assistant character is not displaying, do the following:
CHOOSE: Help, Show the Office Assistant
An Office Assistant character should be displaying, as shown to the right. Because you may choose Office Assistant characters, the character on your computer from among several may be different from ours.

2. To display a question window:
CLICK: the Office Assistant character
The Office Assistant and associated question window might now look like the one shown in Figure 11. As you did in the Ask a Question text box, described earlier, you type your question in the tip window and then press (ENTER) or click the Search button. A list of suggested topics will display.

Figure 11

Office Assistant and associated tip window

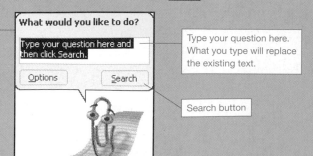

3. To remove the tip window:
CLICK: in your document
The insertion point is blinking at the very beginning of your document.

4. To close Microsoft Word:
CLICK: Close button (☒) appearing in the top right-hand corner

---

In Addition GETTING HELP ON THE WEB

You can obtain additional help from the Web by choosing Help, Microsoft Office Online from your application's Menu bar.

Notes

Notes

Notes

Notes

Notes